650 Best Selling HOME PLANS

Director
Stephen Culpepper

Managing Editor
Debra Cochran

Associate Editor
Gia Manalio

Cover Design
Andy Russell

Table of Contents:

Library of Congress No.: 00-136066
ISBN: 0-938708-96-1
cover photography from top to bottom:
20144 photography by John Ehrenclou pg.345
51019 photography supplied by Bloodgood Plan Service pg.419
60137 photography supplied by Frank Betz Associates pg.419
10334 photography by John Ehrenclou pg.339

the
Garlinghouse
company

Submit all Canadian plan orders to:
The Garlinghouse Company
102 Ellis Street
Penticton, BC V2A 4L5

Canadian Orders Only: 1-800-361-7526
Fax No. 1-250-493-7526

Photography by John Ehrenclou

Rear Elevation

Warm Welcome

PLAN NO.24245

Price Code: D

- This plan features:
  - — Three bedrooms
  - — Two full and one half baths
- A Living Room that includes a wonderful fireplace
- Direct access from the formal Dining Room to the Kitchen
- A U-shaped Kitchen including a Breakfast Bar, built-in Pantry and planning desk and a double sink
- A Mudroom Entry that will help keep the dirt from play or muddy shoes away from the rest of the home
- An expansive Family Room with direct access to the rear Deck
- A Master Suite highlighted by a walk-in closet and a private Master Bath
- This home is designed with basement, slab and crawlspace foundation options

First floor — 1,113 sq. ft.
Second floor — 970 sq. ft.
Garage — 480 sq. ft.
Basement — 1,113 sq. ft.

***TOTAL LIVING AREA:* 2,083 SQ. FT.**

FIRST FLOOR

WIDTH 74'-0"
DEPTH 41'-6"

Deck
Nook
Garage 21-5 x 21-5
Kitchen 12-0 x 12-5
Family 23-1 x 12-5
Mud Room
Dining 12-0 x 14-2
Living 13-1 x 14-2
Porch

SECOND FLOOR

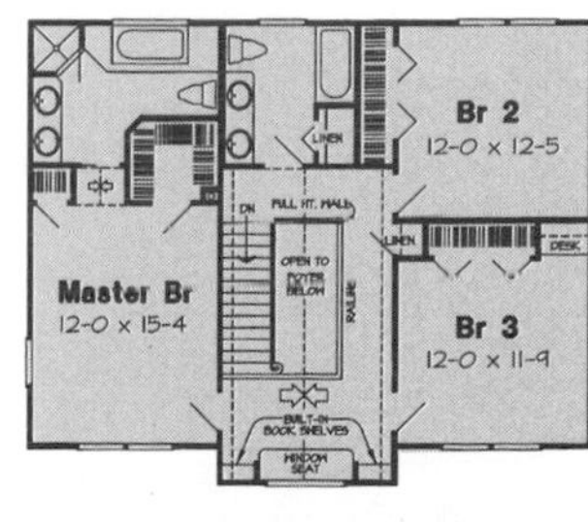
Br 2
12-0 x 12-5
Master Br
12-0 x 15-4
Br 3
12-0 x 11-9

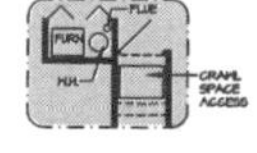

CRAWLSPACE/SLAB FOUNDATION OPTION

PLAN NO. 97412

Colonial Styling

Price Code: F

- This plan features:
- — Four bedrooms
- — Two full, one three-quarter, and one half baths
- The Dining Room has a built-in hutch and a wetbar
- The Parlor may be used for formal entertaining space or a quiet repose
- The Great Room has a rear wall fireplace with windows set to either side
- The Kitchen has a smart arrangement and shares a snack bar with the Nook
- The Breakfast Nook has a bay with windows and transoms above
- The Master Bedroom is located on the first floor for privacy
- This home is designed with a basement foundation

FIRST FLOOR — 1,865 SQ. FT.
SECOND FLOOR — 774 SQ. FT.

TOTAL LIVING AREA:
2,639 SQ. FT.

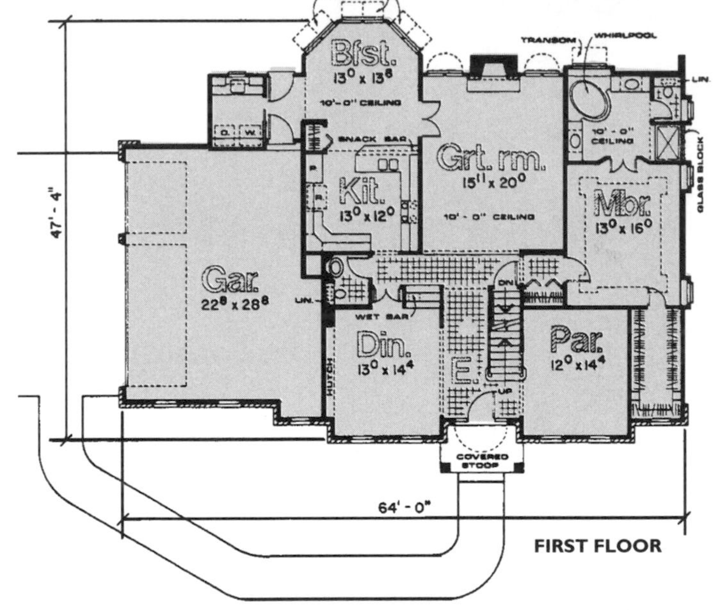
TRANSOMS
Bfst.
13^0 x 13^8
10'-0" CEILING
TRANSOM
WHIRLPOOL
LIN.
SNACK BAR
Grt. rm.
15^{11} x 20^0
Kit.
13^0 x 12^0
10'-0" CEILING
10'-0" CEILING
Mbr.
13^0 x 16^0
GLASS BLOCK
47'-4"
Gar.
22^8 x 28^8
LIN.
WET BAR
Din.
13^0 x 14^4
HUTCH
E.
DN
UP
Par.
12^0 x 14^4
COVERED STOOP
64'-0"
FIRST FLOOR

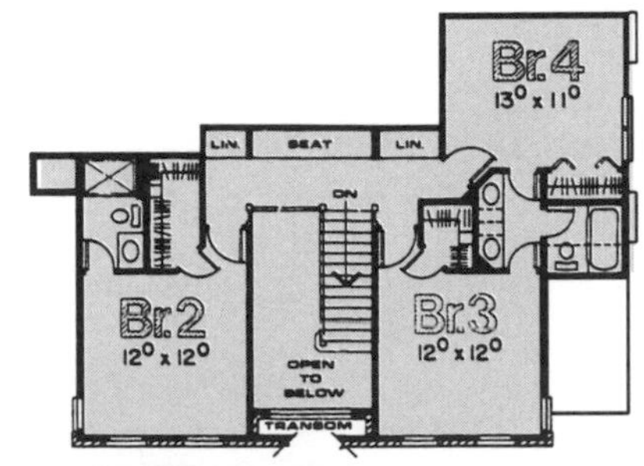
Br. 4
13^0 x 11^0
LIN.
SEAT
LIN.
DN
Br. 2
12^0 x 12^0
OPEN TO BELOW
Br. 3
12^0 x 12^0
TRANSOM
SECOND FLOOR

PLAN NO. 92671

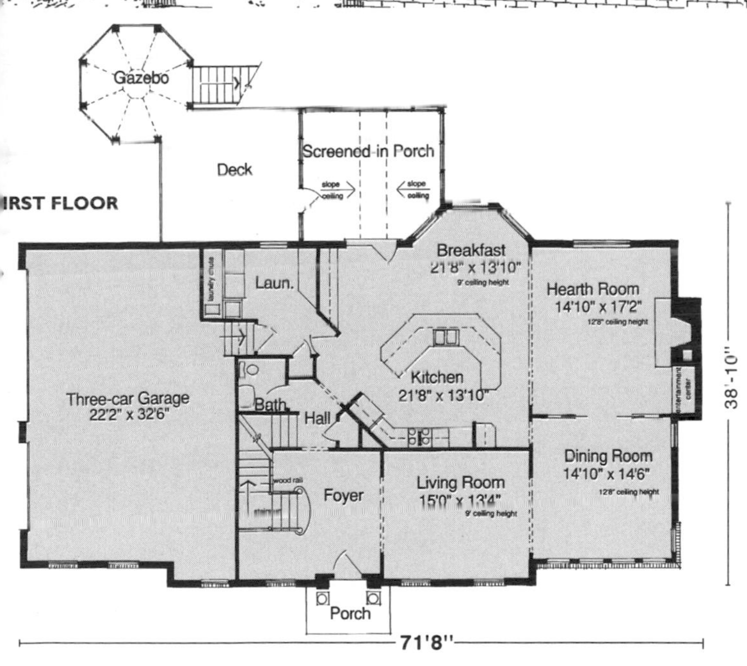

Gazebo
Deck
Screened-in Porch
slope ceiling
FIRST FLOOR
Breakfast
21'8" x 13'10"
Hearth Room
14'10" x 17'2"
Laun.
Three-car Garage
22'2" x 32'6"
Kitchen
21'8" x 13'10"
Bath
Hall
Foyer
Living Room
15'0" x 13'4"
Dining Room
14'10" x 14'6"
Porch
71'8"
38'-10"
SECOND FLOOR
Bedroom
13'7" x 17'1"
Dressing
Master Bedroom
16'11" x 20'8"
Hall
Bath
Bedroom
16'10" x 12'9"
Bedroom
15'10" x 12'0"
Balcony

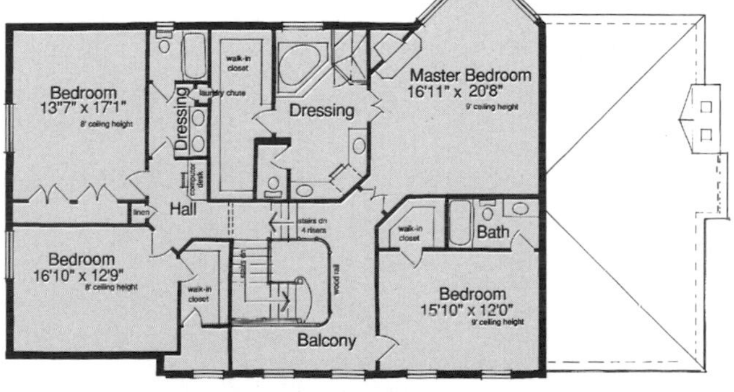

Two-Story Brick Colonial

Price Code: I

- This plan features:
  - Four bedrooms
  - Three full and one half baths
- A covered front Porch and Foyer with lovely staircase greet you
- The Living Room flows freely into the Dining Room for carefree entertaining
- The Hearth Room has a 12-foot ceiling, fireplace, and entertainment center
- The unique Kitchen design is a cook's delight and it adjoins the Breakfast Nook and a Screened Porch
- This home is designed with a basement foundation

First floor — 1,666 sq. ft.
Second floor — 1,036 sq. ft.
Lower Floor — 743 sq. ft.
Basement — 1,612 sq. ft.
Garage — 740 sq. ft.

Total Living Area:
3,445 sq. ft.

PLAN NO. 93219

Old-Fashioned Porch

Price Code: B

- This plan features:
- — Three bedrooms
- — Two full and one half baths
- Traditional front Porch, with matching dormers above and a Garage hidden below, leading into a open, contemporary layout
- A Living Area with a cozy fireplace visible from the Dining Room for warm entertaining
- A convenient half Bath/Laundry center on the first floor
- A spacious Master Suite with a lavish Master Bath including a double vanity, walk-in closet and an oval, corner window tub
- This home is designed with a basement foundation

FIRST FLOOR — 1,057 SQ. FT.
SECOND FLOOR — 611 SQ. FT.
BASEMENT — 511 SQ. FT.
GARAGE — 546 SQ. FT.

TOTAL LIVING AREA:
1,668 SQ. FT.

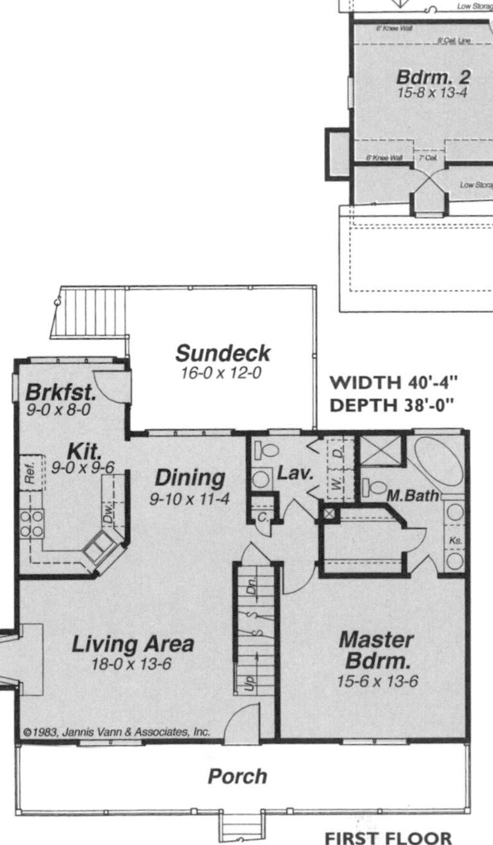
Bath 2
Low Storage
Bdrm. 2
15-8 x 13-4
Bdrm. 3
15-6 x 11-0
SECOND FLOOR
Sundeck
16-0 x 12-0
WIDTH 40'-4"
DEPTH 38'-0"
Brkfst.
9-0 x 8-0
Kit.
9-0 x 9-6
Dining
9-10 x 11-4
Lav.
M.Bath
Living Area
18-0 x 13-6
Master
Bdrm.
15-6 x 13-6
©1983, Jannis Vann & Associates, Inc.
Porch
FIRST FLOOR

PLAN NO. 97621

62'-0"
61'-8"
RAD. WDW.
Sitting Area
FRENCH DOOR
TRAY CEILING
Master Suite
16⁶ x 14⁰
ACTIVE DORMER W/ RAD. WDW.
Breakfast
11'-0" HIGH CLG.
FRENCH DOOR
VAULT
Vaulted Family Room
15⁸ x 20²
FPL.
DBL. OVEN
DW.
Kitchen
11'-0" HIGH CLG.
RANGE
ISLAND
REF.
PANTRY
Bedroom 2
11⁰ x 13⁰
W.i.c.
Bath
LINEN
SHWR.
Vaulted M.Bath
COATS
LINEN
DECORATIVE COLUMNS
ARCHED OPENINGS
PLANT SHELF
Pwdr.
W.H.
Bedroom 3
12¹⁰ x 11⁸
Foyer
14'-0" HIGH CLG.
Dining Room
12⁰ x 14⁰
14'-0" HIGH CLG.
Laund.
FRENCH DOORS
OPT. STAIR TO BSMT.
Living Room
13⁵ x 14⁰
COVERED ENTRY
Garage
20⁵ x 20⁹
MAIN FLOOR
copyright © 1995 frank betz associates, inc.
GARAGE LOCATION WITH BASEMENT

Outstanding Arched Window

Price Code: E

- This plan features:
- — Three bedrooms
- — Two full and one half baths
- An outstanding front window accents the formal Dining Room
- Expansive Family Room accented by a fireplace
- Luxurious Master Suite highlighted by a tray ceiling
- Formal Living Room entered through French doors
- Efficient Kitchen including double oven, work island and built-in Pantry
- This home is designed with basement, slab and crawlspace foundation options

MAIN FLOOR — 2,322 SQ. FT.
GARAGE — 453 SQ. FT.

TOTAL LIVING AREA:
2,322 SQ. FT.

PLAN NO. 92237

Opulent Luxury

Price Code: K

- This plan features:
- — Four bedrooms
- — Two full, one three-quarter, and one half baths
- Columns frame elegant two-story Entry with a graceful banister staircase
- A stone hearth fireplace and built-in bookshelves enhance the Living Room
- Comfortable Family Room with a huge fireplace, cathedral ceiling and access to covered Veranda
- Lavish Master Bedroom with a Sitting Area, private Patio and a huge Bath with two walk-in closets and a whirpool tub
- This home is designed with basement and slab foundation options

FIRST FLOOR — 2,804 SQ. FT.
SECOND FLOOR — 979 SQ. FT.
BASEMENT — 2,804 SQ. FT.
GARAGE — 802 SQ. FT.

TOTAL LIVING AREA:
3,783 SQ. FT.

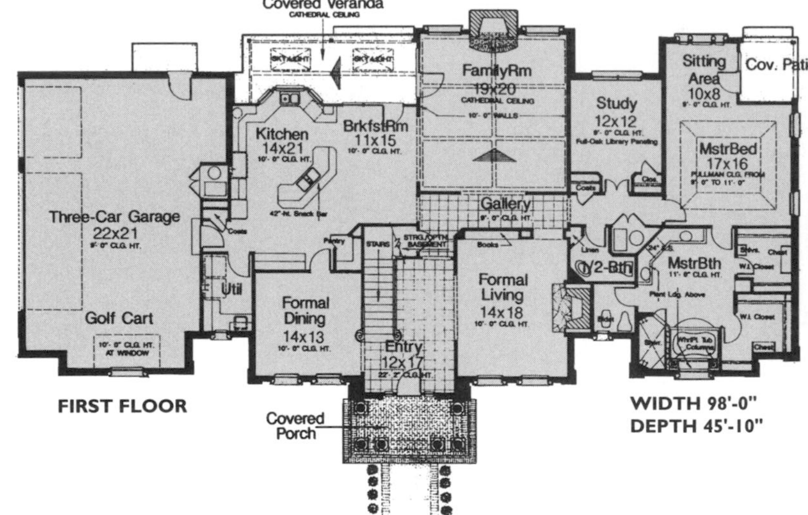
Covered Veranda
CATHEDRAL CEILING
FamilyRm
19x20
CATHEDRAL CEILING
Sitting Area
10x8
Cov. Patio
Study
12x12
Kitchen
14x21
BrkfstRm
11x15
MstrBed
17x16
Three-Car Garage
22x21
Gallery
Golf Cart
Util
Formal Dining
14x13
Formal Living
14x18
1/2-Bth
MstrBth
Entry
12x17
Covered Porch
FIRST FLOOR
WIDTH 98'-0"
DEPTH 45'-10"

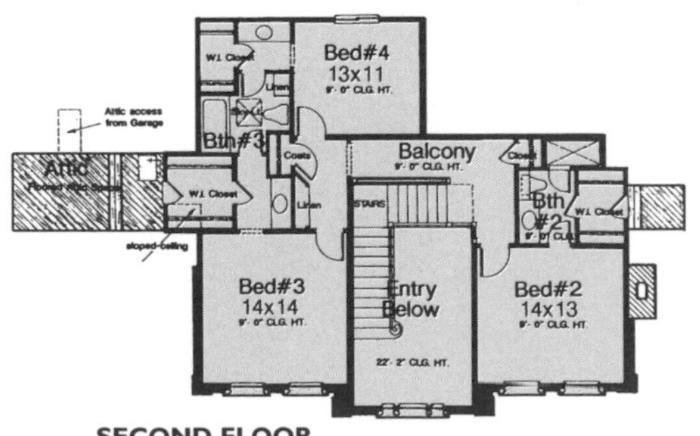
Bed#4
13x11
Attic
Bth#3
Balcony
Bth #2
Bed#3
14x14
Entry Below
Bed#2
14x13
SECOND FLOOR

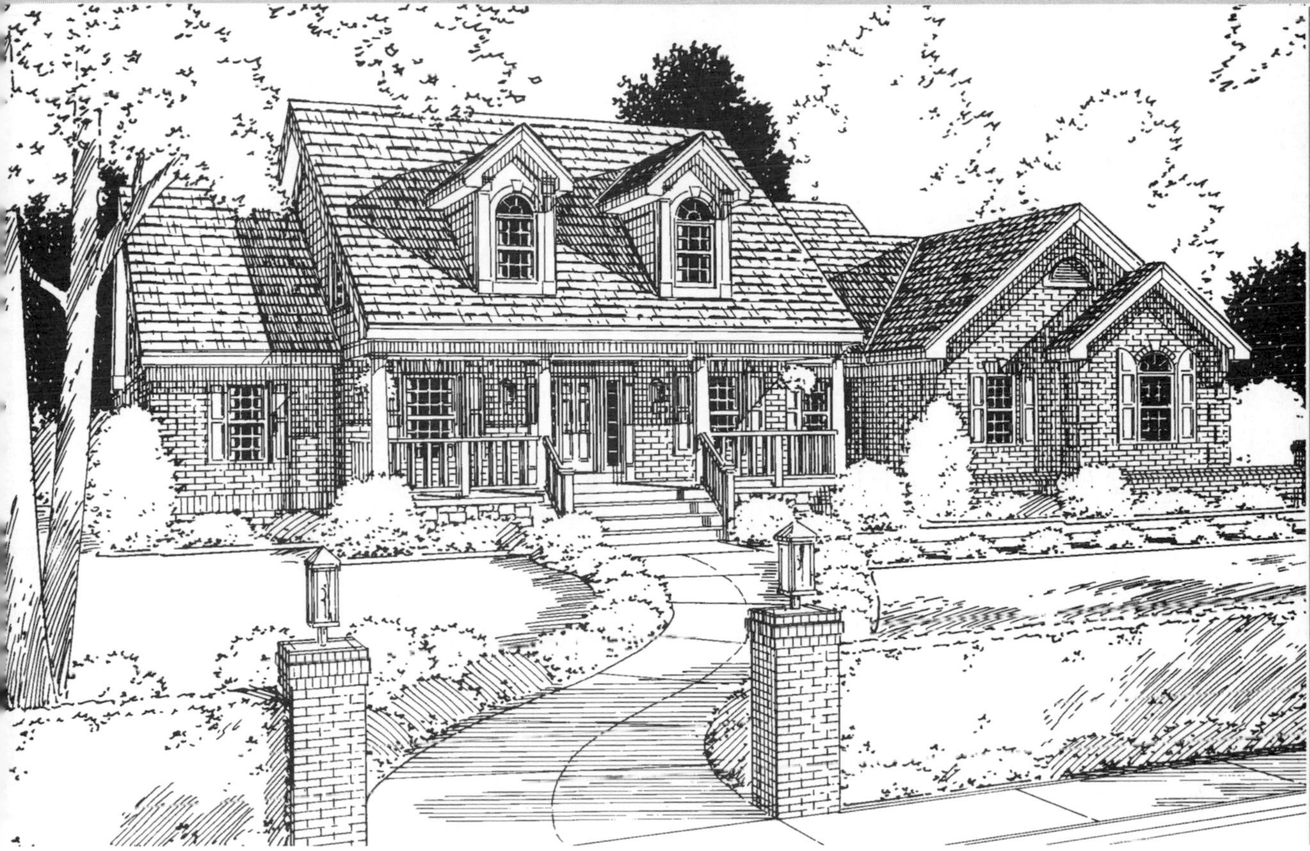

PLAN NO. 97709

FIRST FLOOR

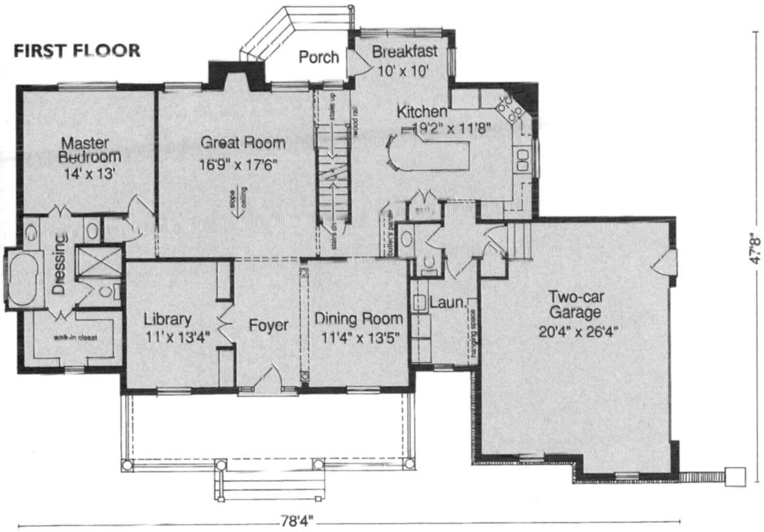

Porch
Breakfast 10' x 10'
Kitchen 19'2" x 11'8"
Master Bedroom 14' x 13'
Great Room 16'9" x 17'6"
Dressing
walk-in closet
Library 11' x 13'4"
Foyer
Dining Room 11'4" x 13'5"
Laun.
Two-car Garage 20'4" x 26'4"
47'8"
78'4"

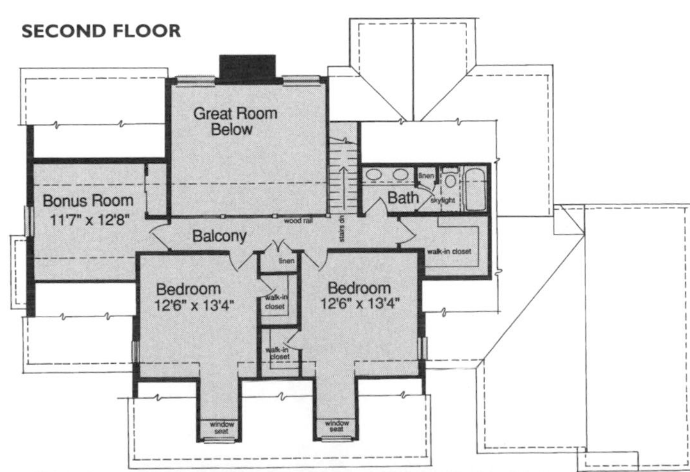

SECOND FLOOR
Great Room Below
Bonus Room 11'7" x 12'8"
Bath
Balcony
walk-in closet
Bedroom 12'6" x 13'4"
Bedroom 12'6" x 13'4"

Traditional Cape Cod

Price Code: E

- This plan features:
- — Three bedrooms
- — Two full and one half baths
- With easy access from the Foyer, there is a Library with built-in shelves
- The formal Dining Room has columns and a dramatic view through the Great Room to the fireplace and rear windows
- The spacious Kitchen offers an island with seating which opens into a roomy Breakfast Area surrounded by windows
- A Master Bedroom Suite with deluxe Bath and a spacious walk-in closet
- This home is designed with a basement foundation

FIRST FLOOR — 1,710 SQ. FT.
SECOND FLOOR — 733 SQ. FT.
BONUS ROOM — 181 SQ. FT.
BASEMENT — 1,710 SQ. FT.

TOTAL LIVING AREA:
2,443 SQ. FT.

PLAN NO. 60014

Convenient Laundry Location

Price Code: A

- This plan features:
- — Three bedrooms
- — Two full baths
- The designer has placed the Laundry in a location that is convenient to all the Bedrooms
- Luxurious features include special ceilings in the Master Suite
- Vaulted ceilings and special windows add dimension and style to the Dining and Great Rooms
- The Kitchen has a convenient Pantry closet for added storage option
- This home is designed with a basement foundation

MAIN FLOOR — 1,322 SQ. FT.
LOWER FLOOR — 60 SQ. FT.
BASEMENT — 1,254 SQ. FT.

TOTAL LIVING AREA
1,382 SQ. FT.

MAIN FLOOR

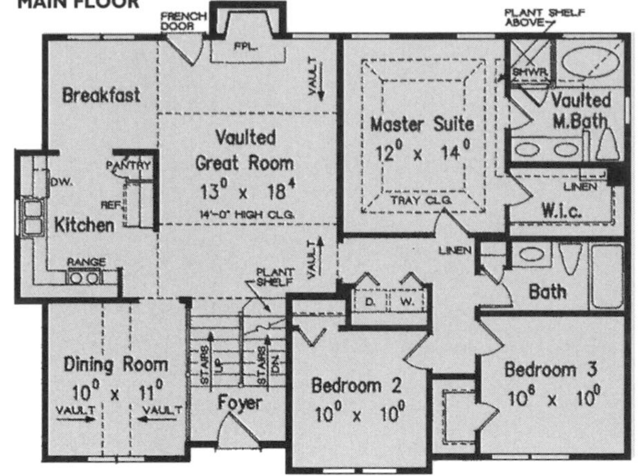

FRENCH DOOR
FPL.
PLANT SHELF ABOVE
Breakfast
VAULT
Vaulted Great Room
13^0 x 18^4
14'-0" HIGH CLG.
Master Suite
12^0 x 14^0
TRAY CLG.
SHWR.
Vaulted M.Bath
LINEN
W.i.c.
PANTRY
DW.
REF.
Kitchen
RANGE
PLANT SHELF
VAULT
LINEN
D.
W.
Bath
Dining Room
10^0 x 11^0
VAULT
VAULT
STAIRS UP
STAIRS DN
Foyer
Bedroom 2
10^0 x 10^0
Bedroom 3
10^6 x 10^0

WIDTH 44'-6"
DEPTH 33'-10"

LOWER FLOOR

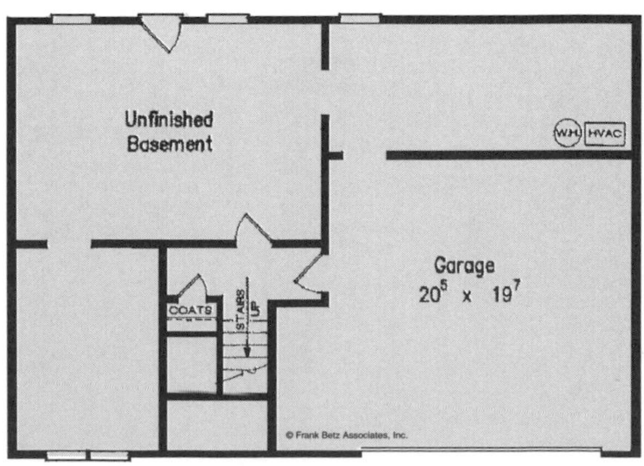

Unfinished Basement
W.H.
HVAC
Garage
20^5 x 19^7
COATS
STAIRS UP
© Frank Betz Associates, Inc.

PLAN NO. 98200

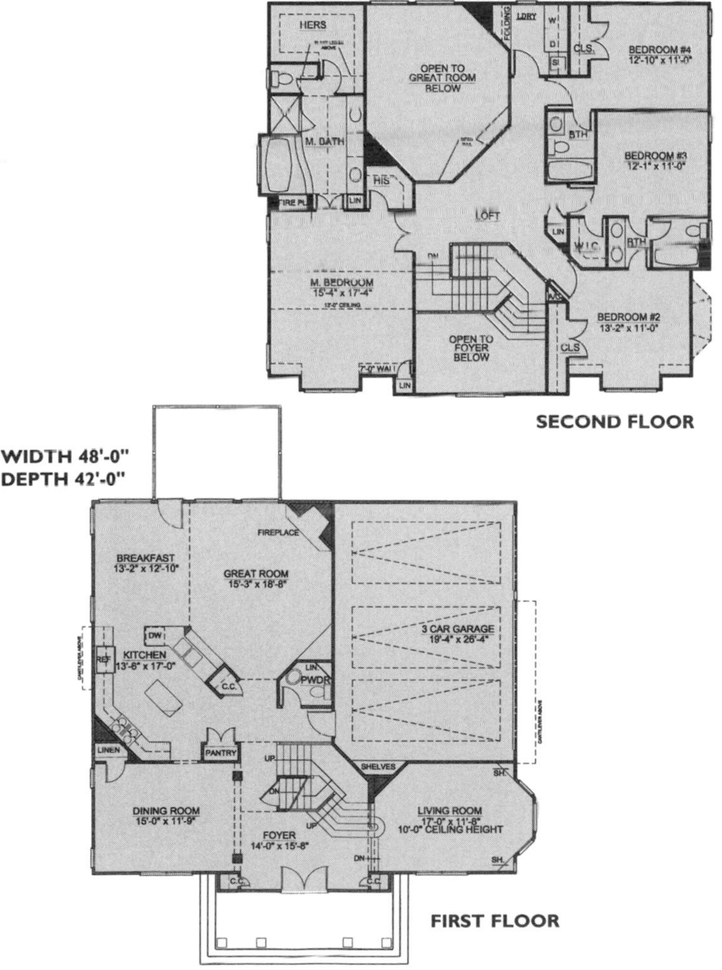
HERS
M. BATH
HIS
FIRE PL
LIN
OPEN TO GREAT ROOM BELOW
LOFT
LDRY
CLS.
BEDROOM #4 12'-10" x 11'-0"
BTH
BEDROOM #3 12'-1" x 11'-0"
W.I.C.
M. BEDROOM 15'-4" x 17'-4"
OPEN TO FOYER BELOW
BEDROOM #2 13'-2" x 11'-0"
SECOND FLOOR
WIDTH 48'-0"
DEPTH 42'-0"
FIREPLACE
BREAKFAST 13'-2" x 12'-10"
GREAT ROOM 15'-3" x 18'-8"
3 CAR GARAGE 19'-4" x 26'-4"
DW
REF
KITCHEN 13'-6" x 17'-0"
C.C.
PWDR
LINEN
PANTRY
SHELVES
DINING ROOM 15'-0" x 11'-9"
FOYER 14'-0" x 15'-8"
LIVING ROOM 17'-0" x 11'-8" 10'-0" CEILING HEIGHT
FIRST FLOOR

Stately Traditional

Price Code: F

- This plan features:
- — Four bedrooms
- — Three full and one half baths
- The spacious Foyer leads to an impressive staircase
- The formal Living Room is accented by a bay window
- The traditional Dining Room has direct access to the Kitchen
- The gourmet Kitchen includes an island, a pass-through to the Great Room, and a large Breakfast Area with access to a backyard Deck
- A cozy corner fireplace and a built-in entertainment center enhance the Great Room
- This home is designed with a basement foundation

FIRST FLOOR — 1,332 SQ. FT.
SECOND FLOOR — 1,331 SQ. FT.

TOTAL LIVING AREA:
2,663 SQ. FT.

PLAN NO. 93446

All On One Floor

Price Code: D

This home features:

— Three bedrooms

— Two full and one half baths

The Master Suite boasts a tray ceiling over the Bedroom, two walk-in closets, two sinks with vanities, a step-in shower, a whirlpool tub, and linen storage

The secondary Bedrooms have easy access to a full Bath in the hall

The Family Room offers access to the rear Porch, a fireplace with built-ins and easy access to the Dining Room and Kitchen

The Kitchen includes a peninsula counter and ample work and storage space

A bonus room is available, if expansion becomes an option

This home is designed with a slab foundation

MAIN FLOOR — 2,215 SQ. FT.
BONUS ROOM — 253 SQ. FT.
GARAGE — 491 SQ. FT.

TOTAL LIVING AREA
2,215 SQ. FT.

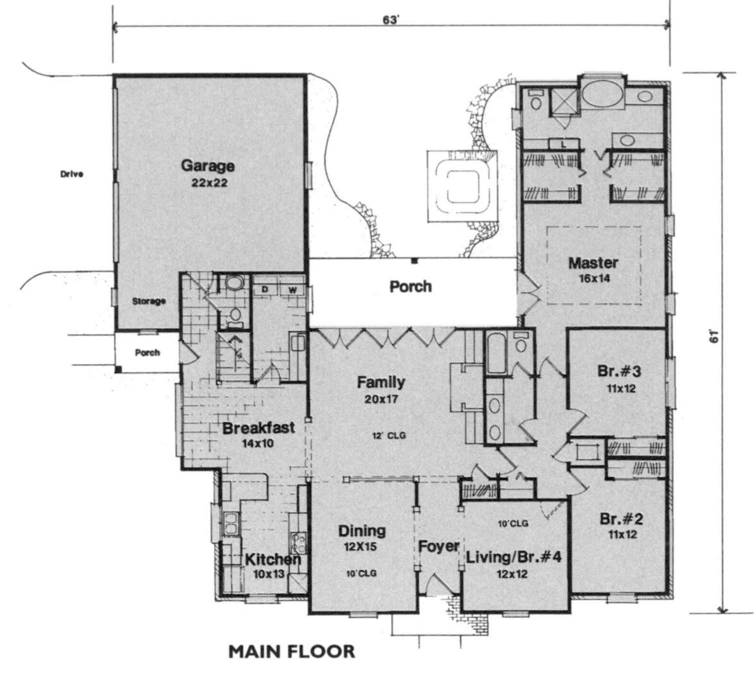

63'
61'
Drive
Garage
22x22
Storage
Porch
D W
Porch
Master
16x14
Family
20x17
12' CLG
Breakfast
14x10
Br.#3
11x12
Br.#2
11x12
10'CLG
Dining
12X15
10'CLG
Foyer
Living/Br.#4
12x12
Kitchen
10x13

MAIN FLOOR

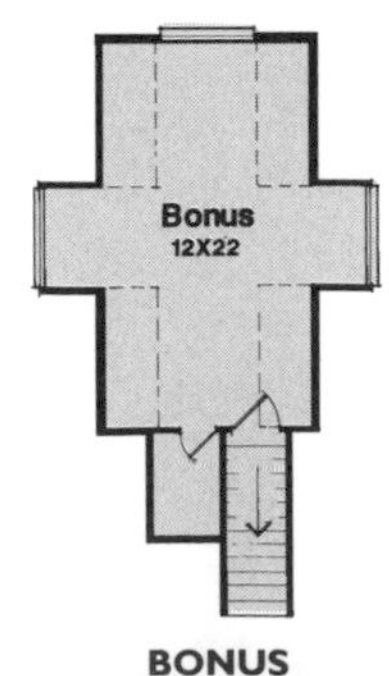

Bonus
12X22

BONUS

PLAN NO. 92613

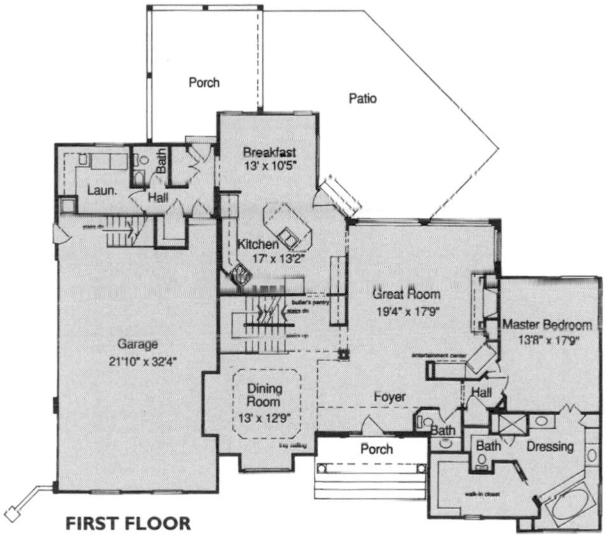

FIRST FLOOR

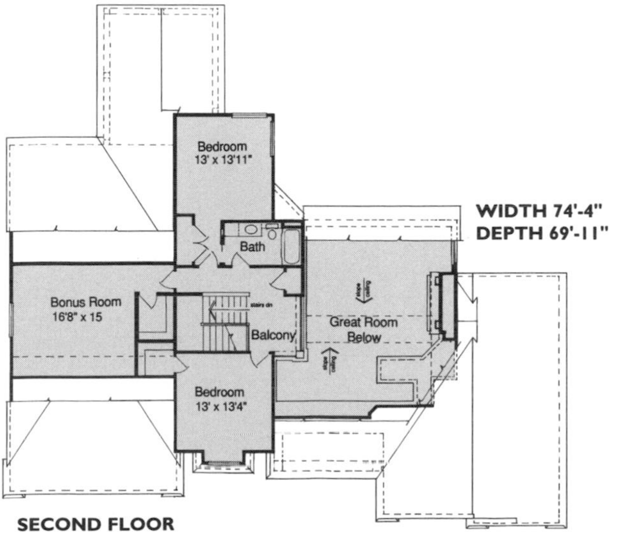
Bedroom
13' x 13'11"
Bath
Bonus Room
16'8" x 15
Balcony
Great Room
Below
Bedroom
13' x 13'4"
WIDTH 74'-4"
DEPTH 69'-11"

SECOND FLOOR

European Classic

Price Code: G

- This plan features:
  - Three bedrooms
  - Two full and two half baths
- A classic design with decorative stucco, keystone arches and boxed windows surrounding a broad, pillar entrance into a spacious Foyer and two-story Great Room beyond
- An efficient, island Kitchen opening to the Patio through Atrium doors and a spacious Breakfast Room
- A private wing, featuring the Master Bedroom Suite with a luxurious Bath, an over-sized walk-in closet, two vanities and a raised, corner window tub
- This home is designed with a basement foundation

FIRST FLOOR — 2,192 SQ. FT.
SECOND FLOOR — 654 SQ. FT.
BONUS ROOM — 325 SQ. FT.

TOTAL LIVING AREA:
2,846 SQ. FT.

PLAN NO. 99045

Convenient Country

Price Code: C

- This plan features:
  - — Three bedrooms
  - — Two full and one half baths
- Full front Porch provides a sheltered entrance
- Expansive Living Room with an inviting fireplace opens to bright Dining Room and Kitchen
- U-shaped Kitchen with peninsula serving counter, Dining Room and nearby Pantry, Laundry and Garage Entry
- Secluded Master Bedroom with two closets and a double vanity Bath
- Two second floor Bedrooms with ample closets, share a full Bath
- This home is designed with a basement foundation

FIRST FLOOR — 1,108 SQ. FT.
SECOND FLOOR — 659 SQ. FT.
BASEMENT — 875 SQ. FT.

TOTAL LIVING AREA:
1,767 SQ. FT.

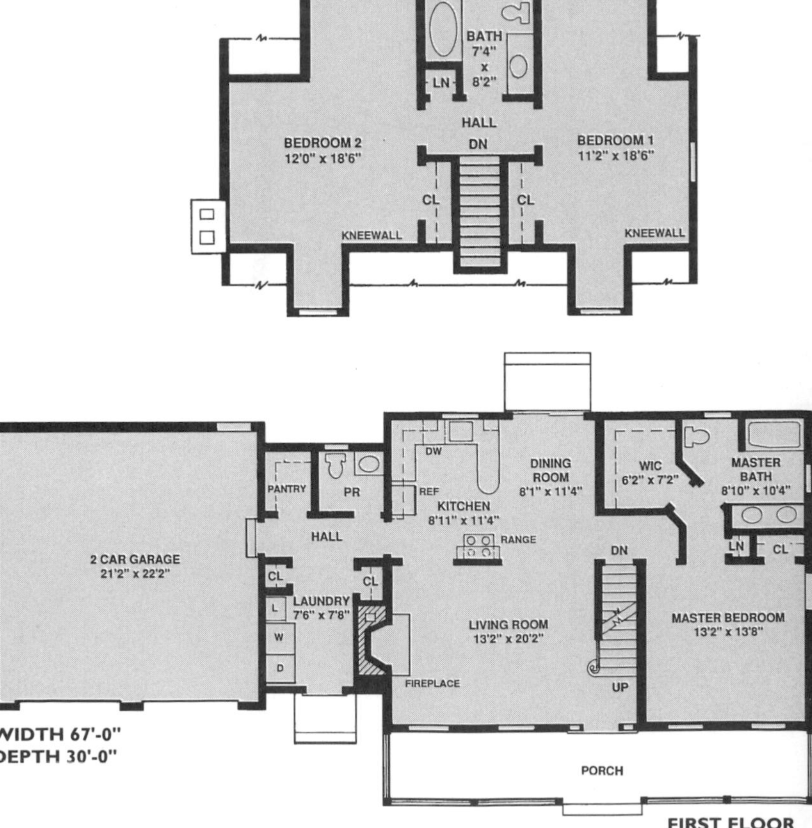
SECOND FLOOR
BATH
7'4" x 8'2"
LN
HALL
DN
BEDROOM 2
12'0" x 18'6"
BEDROOM 1
11'2" x 18'6"
CL
CL
KNEEWALL
KNEEWALL
DW
DINING ROOM
8'1" x 11'4"
WIC
6'2" x 7'2"
MASTER BATH
8'10" x 10'4"
PANTRY
PR
REF
KITCHEN
8'11" x 11'4"
RANGE
HALL
LN
CL
DN
2 CAR GARAGE
21'2" x 22'2"
CL
CL
LAUNDRY
7'6" x 7'8"
L
W
D
LIVING ROOM
13'2" x 20'2"
MASTER BEDROOM
13'2" x 13'8"
FIREPLACE
UP
WIDTH 67'-0"
DEPTH 30'-0"
PORCH
FIRST FLOOR

PLAN NO. 92552

European Styling with a Georgian Flair

Price Code: C

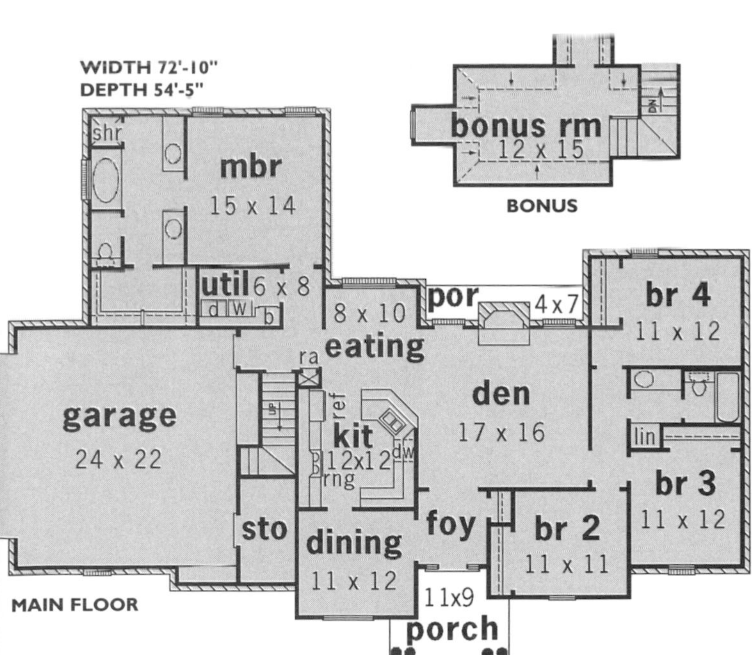
WIDTH 72'-10"
DEPTH 54'-5"
bonus rm
12 x 15
BONUS
shr
mbr
15 x 14
util 6 x 8
d w b
8 x 10
por
4 x 7
br 4
11 x 12
ra
eating
den
17 x 16
garage
24 x 22
ref
kit
12x12
dw
rng
lin
br 3
11 x 12
sto
dining
11 x 12
foy
br 2
11 x 11
11x9
porch
MAIN FLOOR

- This plan features:
  - — Four bedrooms
  - — Two full baths
- Arched windows, quoins and shutters create an eye-catching home
- Formal Foyer accesses the Dining Room and Den
- Kitchen flows into the informal Eating Area and is separated from the Den by an angled extended counter eating bar
- Split Bedroom plan, Master Suite is privately place to the rear
- Three additional Bedrooms share a full Bath in the hall
- This home is designed with crawlspace and slab foundation options

MAIN FLOOR — 1,873 SQ. FT.
BONUS ROOM — 145 SQ. FT.
GARAGE — 613 SQ. FT.

TOTAL LIVING AREA:
1,873 SQ. FT.

PLAN NO. 92277

Luxurious Elegance

Price Code: H

- This plan features:
- — Four bedrooms
- — Two full, one three-quarter, and one half baths
- Double doors leads into two-story Entry with an exquisite curved staircase
- Formal Living Room features a marble hearth fireplace, triple window and built-in bookshelves
- The Kitchen has a cooktop/work island and a Utility/Garage Entry
- Expansive Great Room with entertainment center and fieldstone fireplace
- Vaulted ceiling crowns Master Bedroom suite offering a plush Bath and two walk-in closets
- This home is designed with basement and slab foundation options

FIRST FLOOR — 2,190 SQ. FT.
SECOND FLOOR — 920 SQ. FT.
GARAGE — 624 SQ. FT.

TOTAL LIVING AREA:
3,110 SQ. FT.

WIDTH 69'-0"
DEPTH 53'-10"

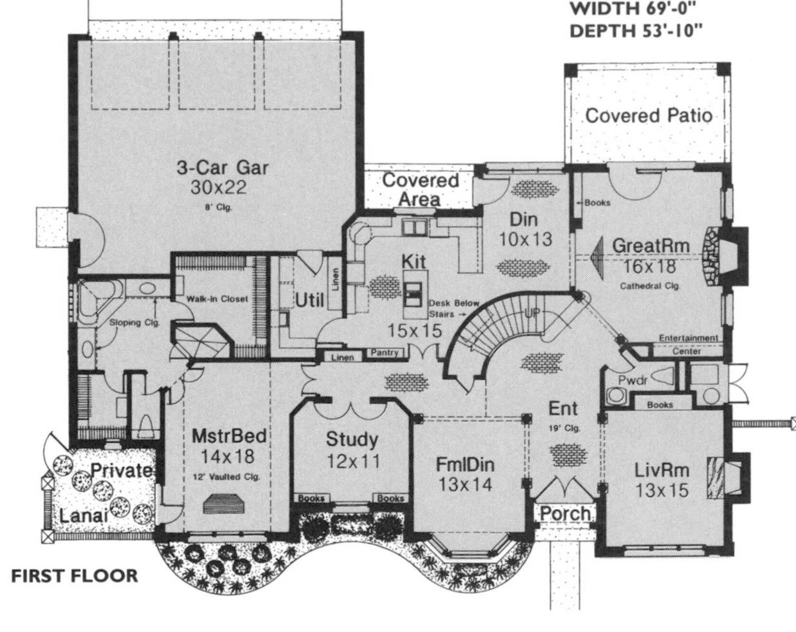

3-Car Gar
30x22
8' Clg.
Covered Area
Covered Patio
Din
10x13
GreatRm
16x18
Cathedral Clg.
Books
Kit
15x15
Desk Below Stairs
Util
Linen
Walk-in Closet
Sloping Clg.
Pantry
UP
Entertainment Center
Pwdr
Books
Ent
19' Clg.
MstrBed
14x18
12' Vaulted Clg.
Study
12x11
FmlDin
13x14
LivRm
13x15
Private
Lanai
Porch

FIRST FLOOR

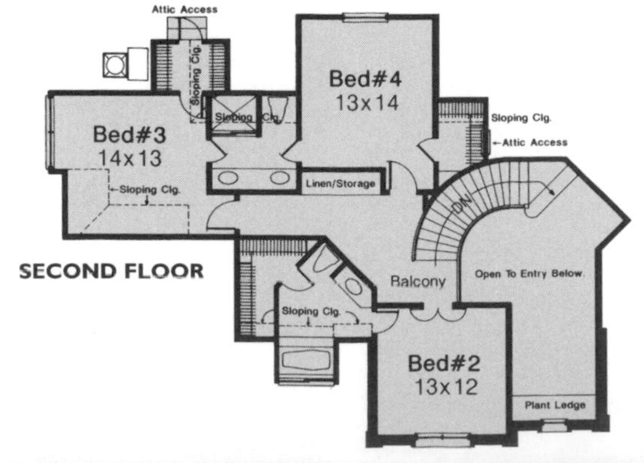

Attic Access
Sloping Clg.
Bed#4
13x14
Bed#3
14x13
Sloping Clg.
Attic Access
Linen/Storage
DN
Balcony
Open To Entry Below
Bed#2
13x12
Plant Ledge

SECOND FLOOR

PLAN NO. 92549

SECOND FLOOR

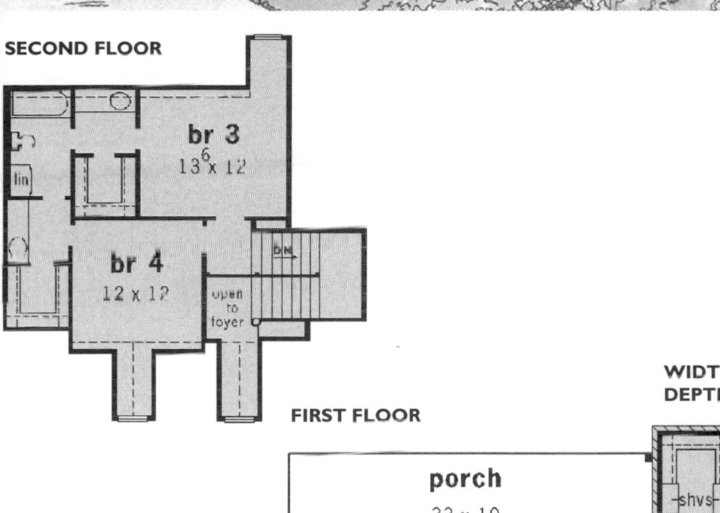

br 3
13⁶ x 12
lin
br 4
12 x 12
open to foyer
DN

WIDTH 57'-10"
DEPTH 56'-10"

FIRST FLOOR

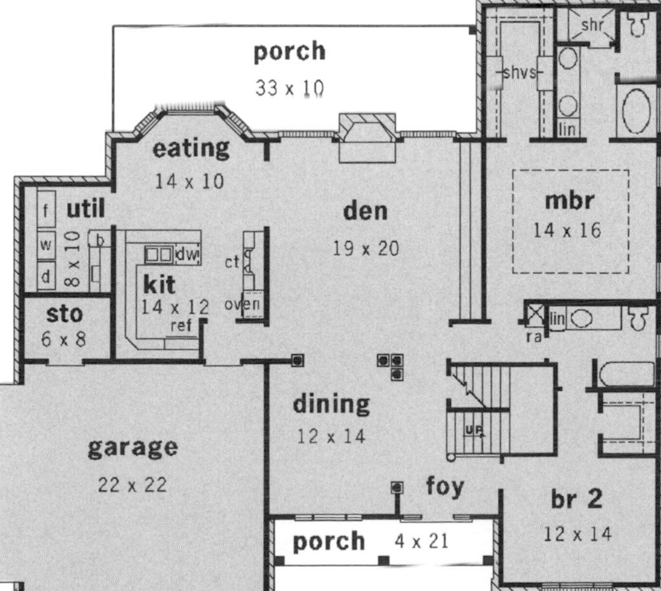

porch
33 x 10
eating
14 x 10
den
19 x 20
shr
shvs
lin
mbr
14 x 16
util
8 x 10
f
w
d
b
dw
kit
14 x 12
ref
ct
oven
sto
6 x 8
lin
ra
garage
22 x 22
dining
12 x 14
UP
foy
br 2
12 x 14
porch
4 x 21

French Flavor

Price Code: E

- This plan features:
  - — Four bedrooms
  - — Three full baths
- Porch Entry into open Foyer with a lovely, landing staircase
- Elegant columns define Dining and Den Area for gracious entertaining
- Efficient, U-shaped Kitchen with a serving counter, Eating Bay, and nearby Utility Area and Garage
- Decorative ceiling tops Master Bedroom offering a huge walk-in closet and plush Bath
- This home is designed with crawlspace and slab foundation options

FIRST FLOOR — 1,911 SQ. FT.
SECOND FLOOR — 579 SQ. FT.
GARAGE — 560 SQ. FT.

TOTAL LIVING AREA:
2,490 SQ. FT.

PLAN NO. 24742

Space for Quiet Time

Price Code: B

■ This plan features:

— Three bedrooms

— Two full and one half baths

■ The cozy Reading Room has a built-in window seat and bookshelves

■ The Great Room has a ceiling with exposed beams

■ The Dining Room has sliding glass doors that lead to the Screened Porch

■ This home is designed with a basement foundation

FIRST FLOOR — 946 SQ. FT.
SECOND FLOOR — 786 SQ. FT.
BASEMENT — 946 SQ. FT.

TOTAL LIVING AREA:
1,732 SQ. FT.

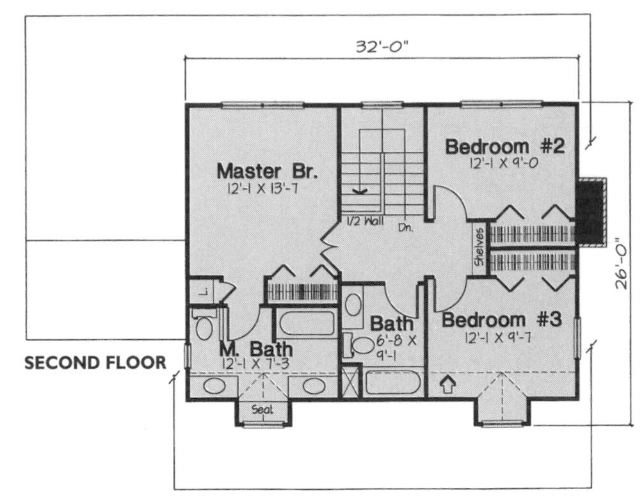

32'-0"
Master Br.
12'-1 X 13'-7
1/2 Wall
Dn.
Bedroom #2
12'-1 X 9'-0
Shelves
26'-0"
Bath
6'-8 X 9'-1
Bedroom #3
12'-1 X 9'-7
M. Bath
12'-1 X 7'-3
Seat
SECOND FLOOR

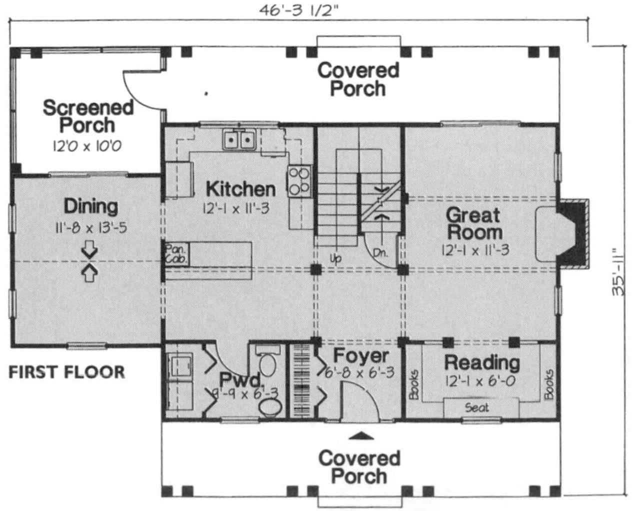

46'-3 1/2"
Covered Porch
Screened Porch
12'0 x 10'0
Dining
11'-8 x 13'-5
Kitchen
12'-1 x 11'-3
Pan. Cab.
Up
Dn.
Great Room
12'-1 x 11'-3
35'-11"
Pwd
9'-9 x 6'-3
Foyer
6'-8 x 6'-3
Reading
12'-1 x 6'-0
Books
Seat
Books
FIRST FLOOR
Covered Porch

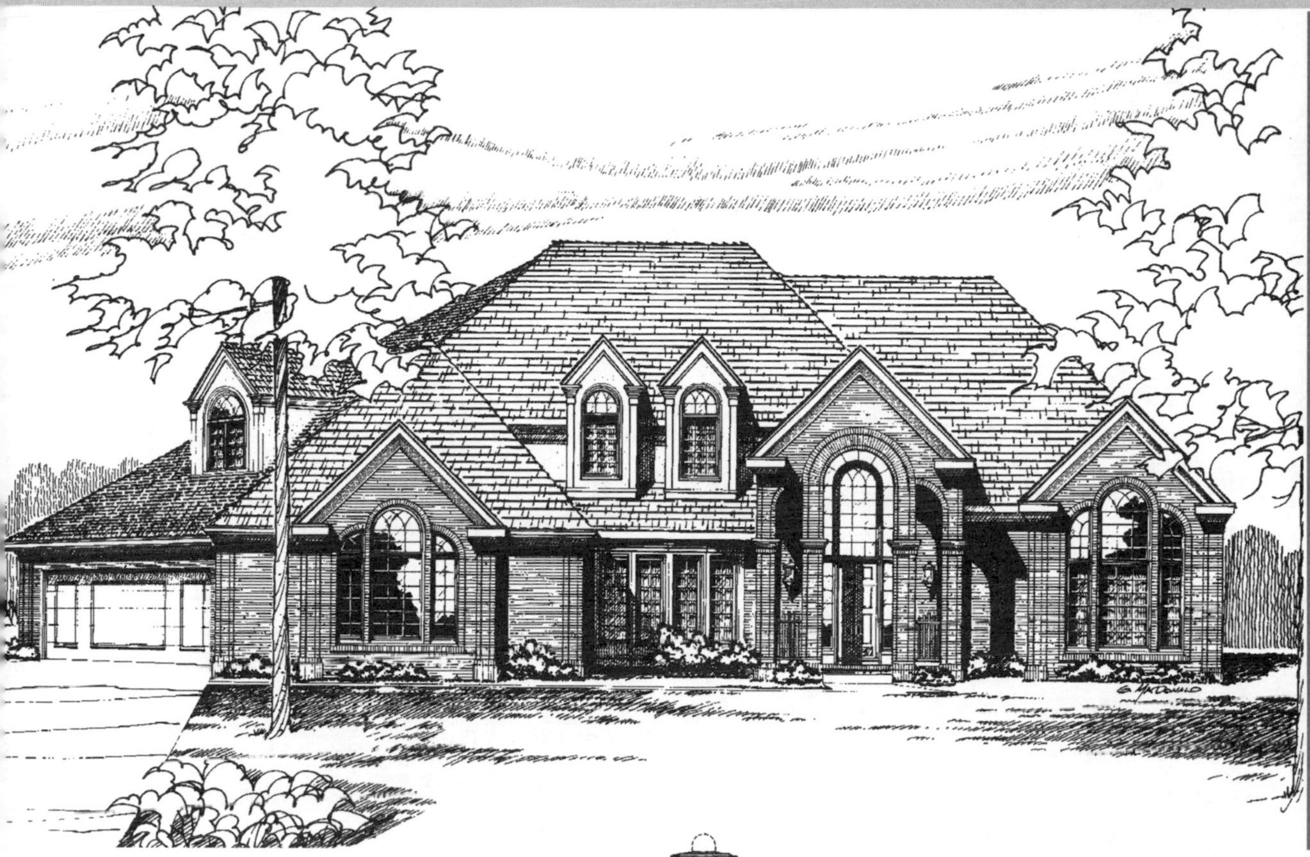

PLAN NO. 99464

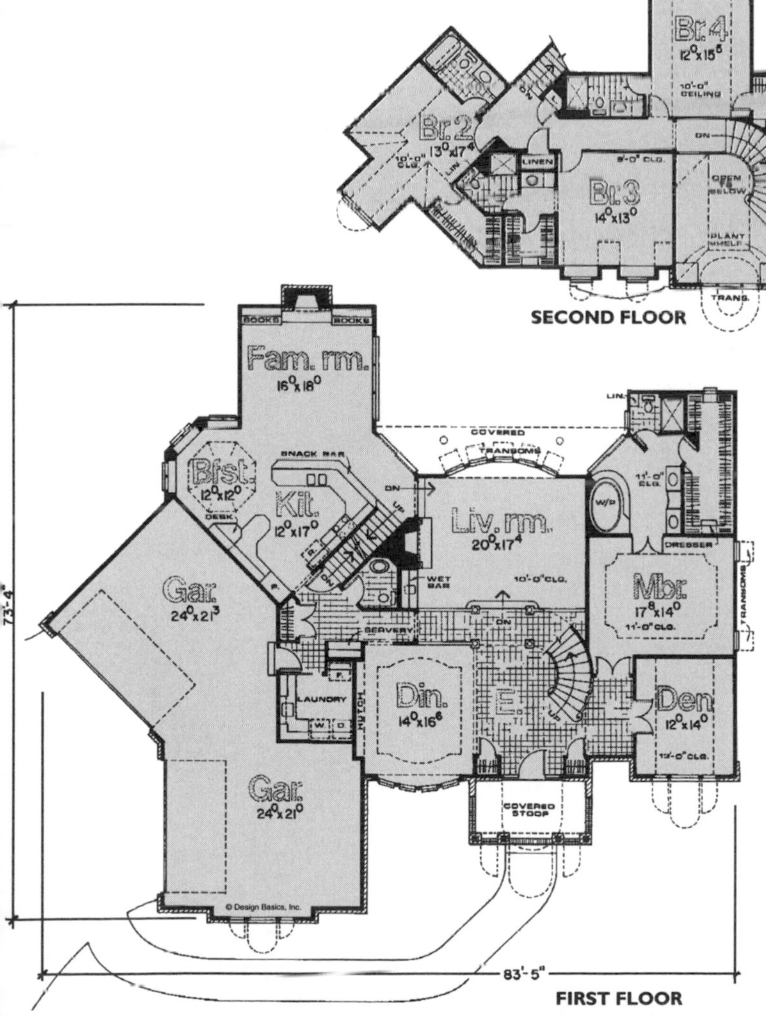

Br.4
12⁰x15⁸
Br.2
13⁰x17⁴
Br.3
14⁰x13⁰
SECOND FLOOR
Fam. rm.
16⁰x18⁰
Bfst.
12⁰x12⁰
Kit.
12⁰x17⁰
Liv. rm.
20⁰x17⁴
Mbr.
17⁸x14⁰
Gar.
24⁰x21³
Din.
14⁰x16⁶
E.
Den
12⁰x14⁰
Gar.
24⁰x21⁰
© Design Basics, Inc.
73'-4"
83'-5"
FIRST FLOOR

Spectacular Voluminous Entry

Price Code: J

- This plan features:
  - — Four bedrooms
  - — Two full, two three-quarter, one half baths
- Dramatic Kitchen is equipped with a large snack bar, Pantry and desk
- Double doors introduce the Master Suite with private back Patio door, oval whirlpool and large walk-in closet
- A beautiful arched window in each secondary Bedroom adds natural light and elegance
- This home is designed with a basement foundation
- Alternate foundation options available at an additional charge. Please call 1-800-235-5700 for more information.

FIRST FLOOR — 2,617 SQ. FT.
SECOND FLOOR — 1,072 SQ. FT.

TOTAL LIVING AREA:
3,689 SQ. FT.

PLAN NO. 94112

Distinguished Dwelling

Price Code: F

- This plan features:
- — Four bedrooms
- — Two full and one half baths
- Grand two-story Entry into Foyer
- Formal Living Room with a decorative window and a vaulted ceiling extending into Family Room with cozy fireplace
- Convenient Kitchen with cooktop work island, Pantry, octagon Dining Area, and nearby Study, Laundry and Garage Entry
- Luxurious Master Bedroom offers a glass alcove, walk-in closet and pampering Bath with a corner tub
- This home is designed with a basement foundation

FIRST FLOOR — 1,514 SQ. FT.
SECOND FLOOR — 1,219 SQ. FT.
BASEMENT — 1,465 SQ. FT.
GARAGE — 596 SQ. FT.

TOTAL LIVING AREA:
2,733 SQ. FT.

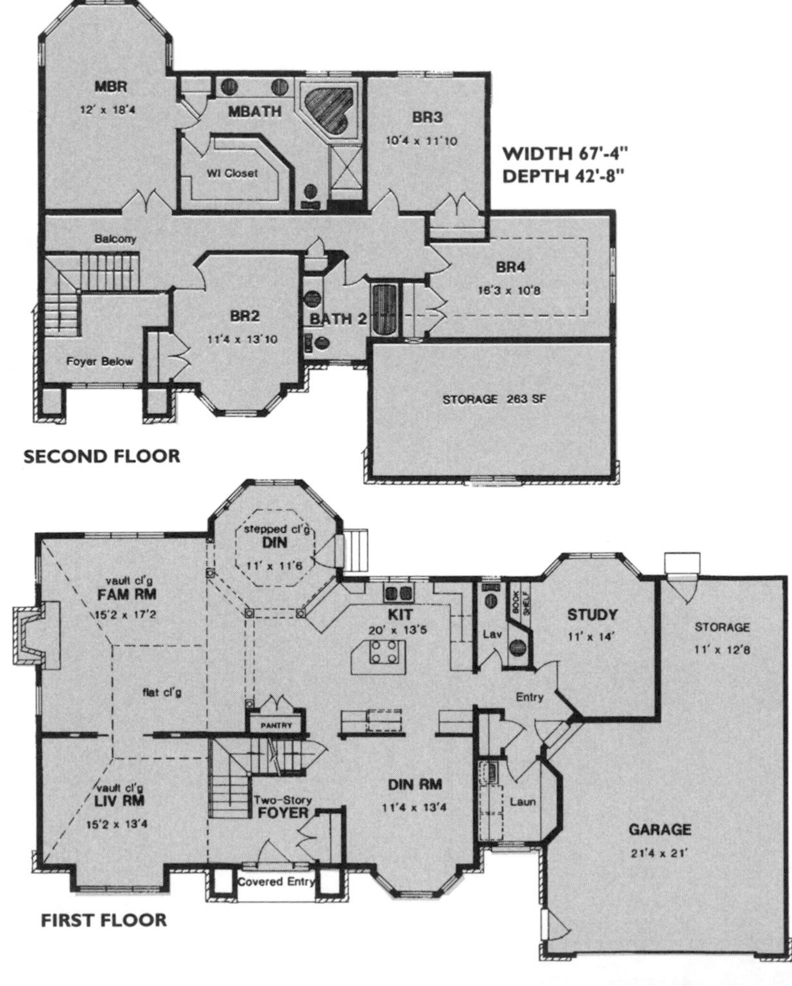

MBR
12' x 18'4
MBATH
WI Closet
BR3
10'4 x 11'10
WIDTH 67'-4"
DEPTH 42'-8"
Balcony
BR4
16'3 x 10'8
BR2
11'4 x 13'10
BATH 2
Foyer Below
STORAGE 263 SF
SECOND FLOOR
stepped cl'g
DIN
11' x 11'6
vault cl'g
FAM RM
15'2 x 17'2
KIT
20' x 13'5
Lav
BOOK SHELF
STUDY
11' x 14'
STORAGE
11' x 12'8
flat cl'g
Entry
PANTRY
vault cl'g
LIV RM
15'2 x 13'4
Two-Story
FOYER
DIN RM
11'4 x 13'4
Laun
GARAGE
21'4 x 21'
Covered Entry
FIRST FLOOR

PLAN NO.19422

Photography supplied by The Meredith Corporation

Master Retreat Crowns Spacious Home

Price Code: B

- This plan features:
  - — Two bedrooms
  - — Two full baths
- A unique four-sided fireplace separates the Living Room, Dining Area, and Kitchen
- A well-equipped Kitchen featuring a cooktop island and a walk-in Pantry
- A three-season Screened Porch and Deck beyond adjoining Dining Room, Living Room, and second Bedroom
- A private upper floor Master Suite offering a balcony, and relaxing window tub
- This home is designed with basement and crawlspace foundation options

MAIN FLOOR — 1,290 SQ. FT.
UPPER FLOOR — 405 SQ. FT.
PORCH — 152 SQ. FT.
GARAGE — 513 SQ. FT.

TOTAL LIVING AREA:
1,695 SQ. FT.

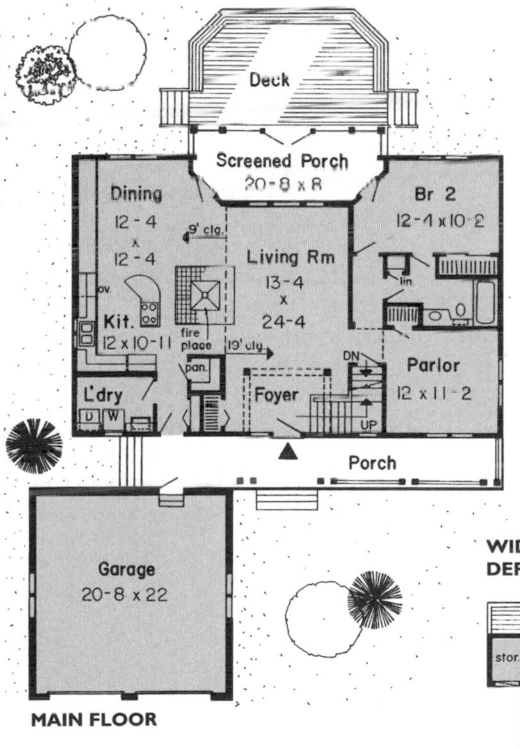
Deck
Screened Porch
20-8 x 8
Dining
12-4
x
12-4
9' clg.
Living Rm
13-4
x
24-4
Br 2
12-4 x 10-2
lin
Kit.
12 x 10-11
fire place
10' clg.
pan.
DN
Parlor
12 x 11-2
L'dry
D W
Foyer
UP
Porch
Garage
20-8 x 22
MAIN FLOOR

WIDTH 50'-8"
DEPTH 61'-8"

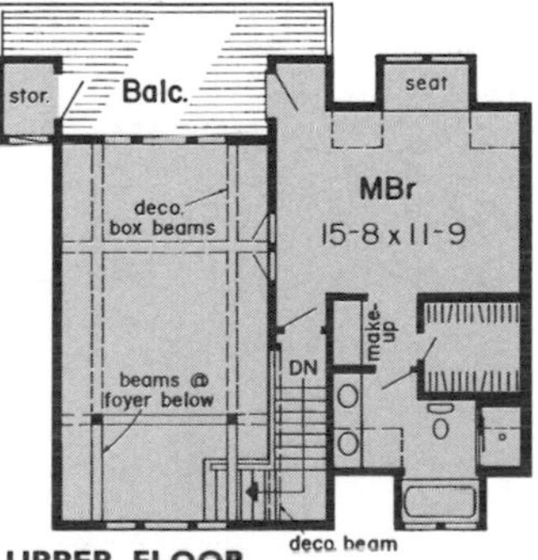
stor.
Balc.
seat
deco. box beams
MBr
15-8 x 11-9
make-up
beams @ foyer below
DN
deco. beam

UPPER FLOOR

PLAN NO. 91033

Neat and Tidy

Price Code: A

- This plan features:
  - — Two bedrooms
  - — Two full baths
- A two-story Living Room and Dining Room with a handsome stone fireplace
- A well-appointed Kitchen with a peninsula counter
- A Master Suite with a walk-in closet and private Master Bath
- A large Utility Room with Laundry facilities
- This home is designed with basement and crawlspace foundation options

FIRST FLOOR — 952 SQ. FT.
SECOND FLOOR — 297 SQ. FT.

TOTAL LIVING AREA:
1,249 SQ. FT.

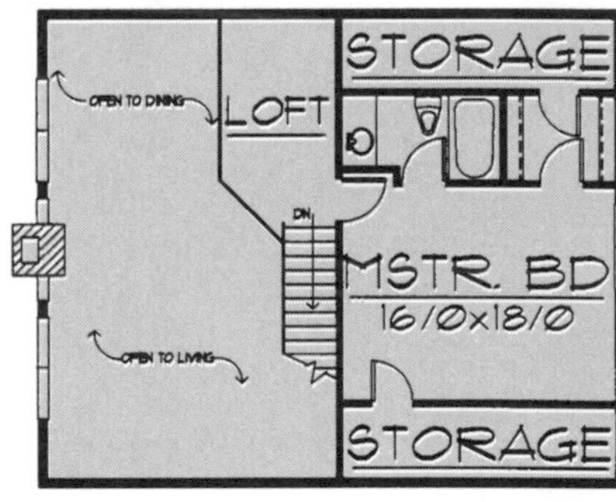
STORAGE
LOFT
MSTR. BD
16/0x18/0
STORAGE

SECOND FLOOR

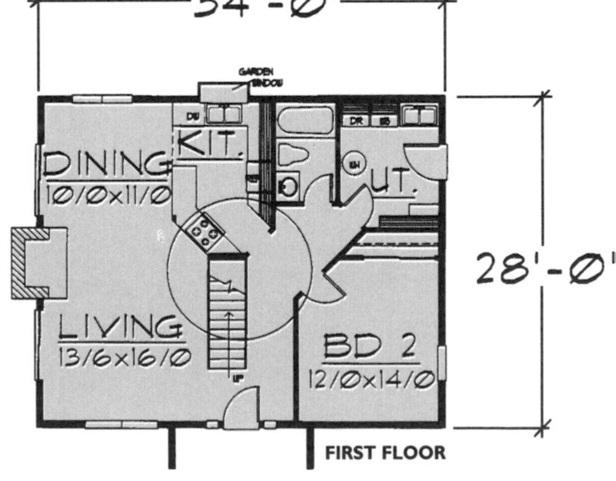
34'-0"
DINING
10/0x11/0
KIT.
UT.
LIVING
13/6x16/0
BD 2
12/0x14/0
28'-0"

FIRST FLOOR

CRAWLSPACE/SLAB FOUNDATION OPTION

PLAN NO.10534

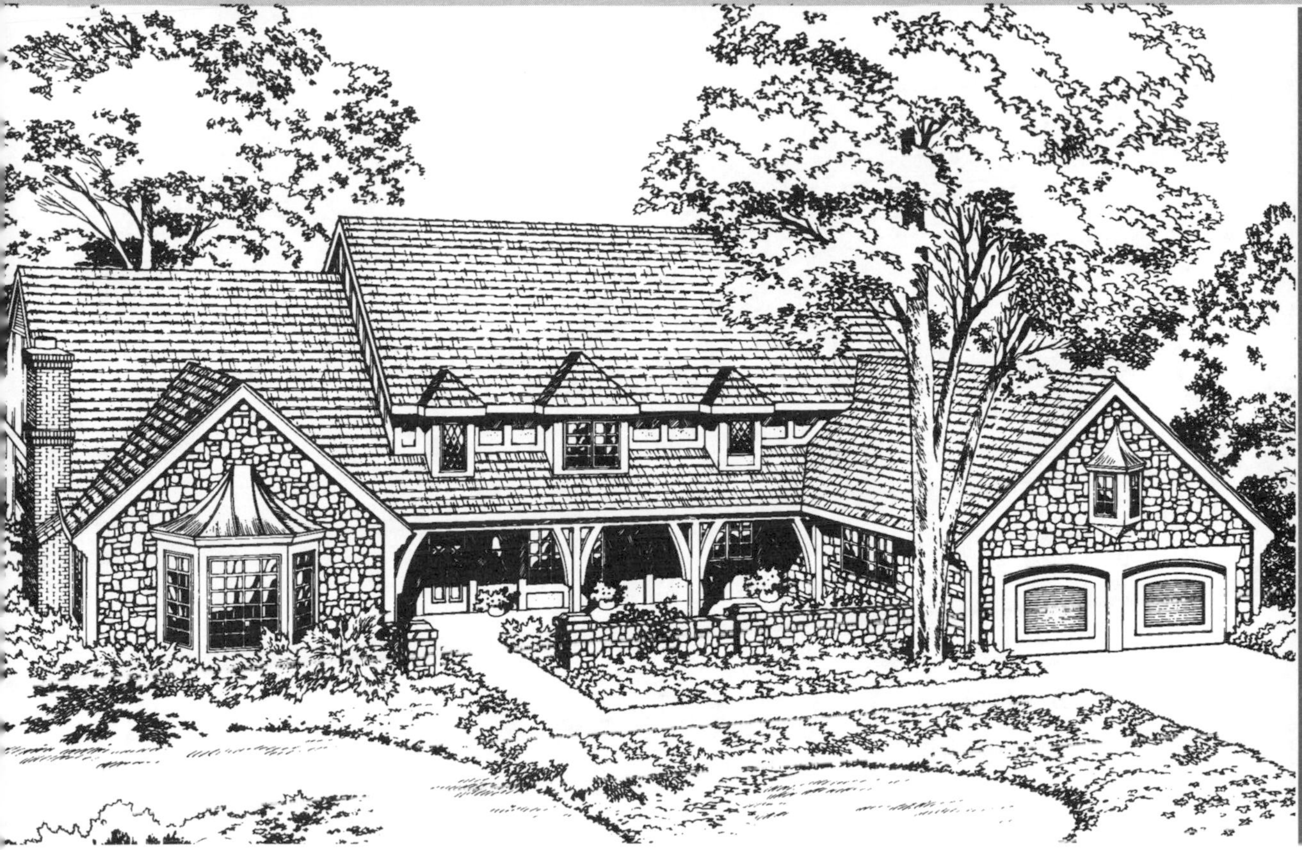

Private Court with Hot Tub

Price Code: I

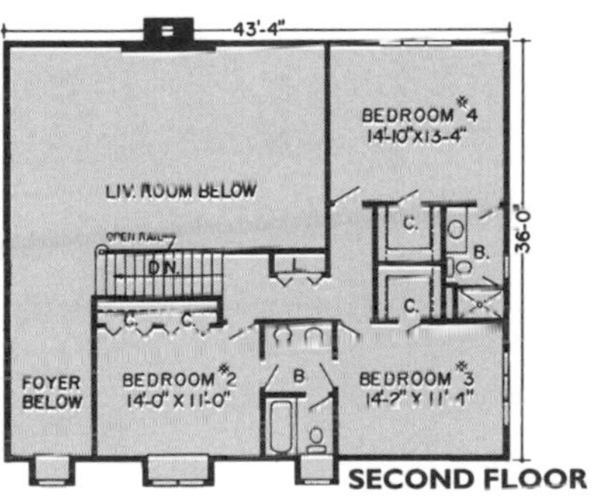

43'-4"
BEDROOM #4
14'-10"X13'-4"
LIV. ROOM BELOW
OPEN RAIL
DN
36'-0"
FOYER BELOW
BEDROOM #2
14'-0" X 11'-0"
BEDROOM #3
14'-2" X 11'-4"
SECOND FLOOR

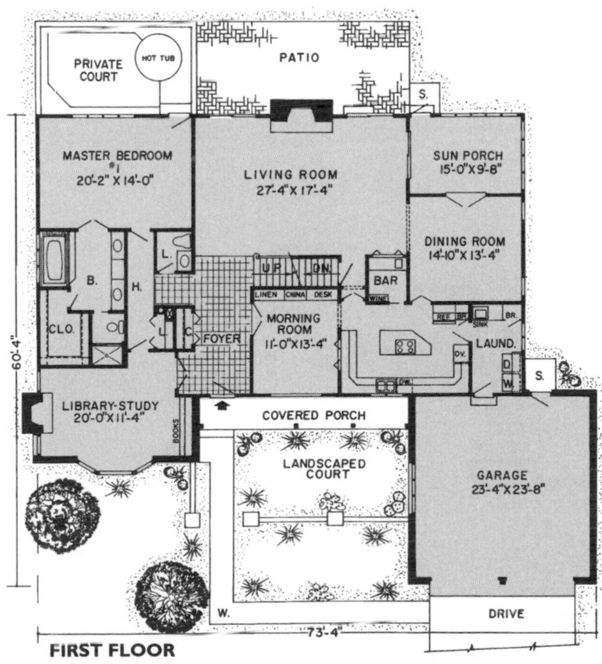

PRIVATE COURT
HOT TUB
PATIO
MASTER BEDROOM #1
20'-2" X 14'-0"
LIVING ROOM
27'-4"X17'-4"
SUN PORCH
15'-0"X9'-8"
DINING ROOM
14'-10"X13'-4"
BAR
MORNING ROOM
11'-0"X13'-4"
FOYER
LAUND.
LIBRARY-STUDY
20'-0"X11'-4"
COVERED PORCH
LANDSCAPED COURT
GARAGE
23'-4"X23'-8"
DRIVE
60'-4"
73'-4"
FIRST FLOOR

- This plan features:
  - — Four bedrooms
  - — Three full and one half baths
- A private Court adjoining the Master Suite which includes a hot tub
- A cozy Library which opens onto the two-story Foyer through French doors
- A Morning Room with built-ins, a bar with wine storage, and a Sun Porch
- This home is designed with basement, slab and crawlspace foundation options

FIRST FLOOR — 2,486 SQ. FT.
SECOND FLOOR — 954 SQ. FT.
BASEMENT — 2,486 SQ. FT.
GARAGE — 576 SQ. FT.

TOTAL LIVING AREA:
3,440 SQ. FT.

PLAN NO. 24594

Impressive Two-Story

Price Code: G

- This plan features:
- — Four bedrooms
- — Two full and one half baths
- Two-story Foyer highlighted by lovely, angled staircase and decorative window
- Bay windows enhance Dining and Living Rooms
- Efficient Kitchen with work island and an open Breakfast Area with backyard access
- Spacious, yet cozy Family Room with a fireplace and future Sunroom access
- Private Master Suite offers a walk-in closet and pampering Bath
- This home is designed with basement, slab and crawlspace foundation options

FIRST FLOOR — 1,497 SQ. FT.
SECOND FLOOR — 1,460 SQ. FT.
FUTURE SUNROOM — 210 SQ. FT.
GARAGE — 680 SQ. FT.

TOTAL LIVING AREA:
2,957 SQ. FT.

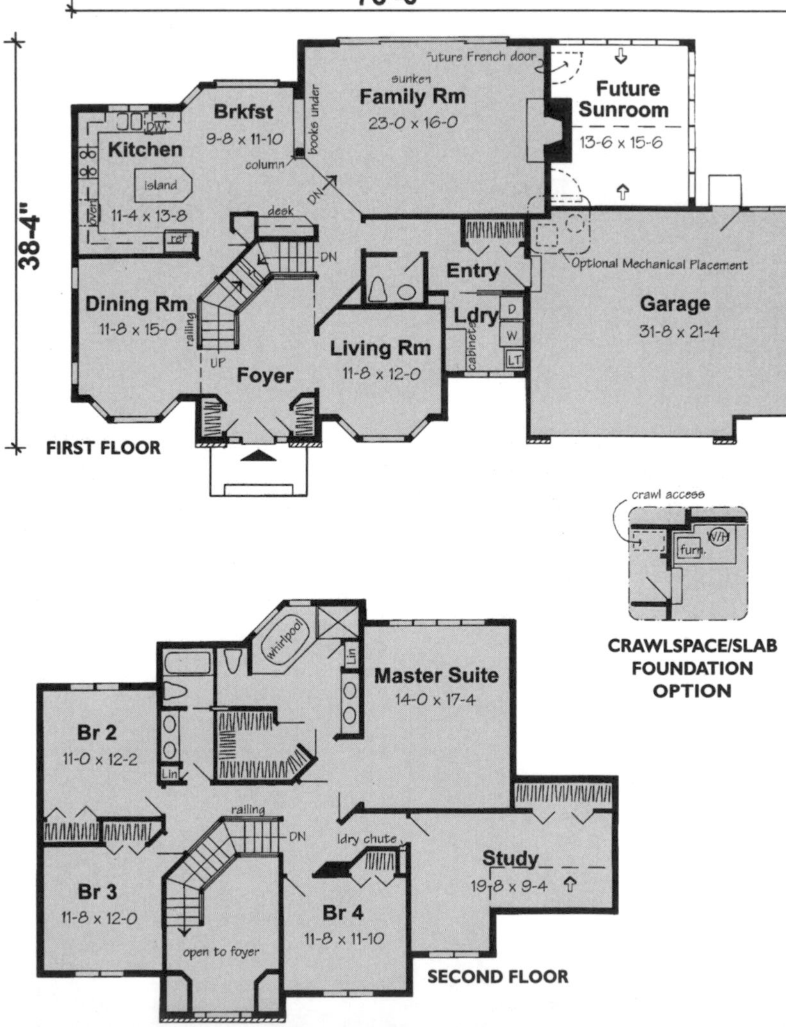
76'-0"
38'-4"
Future French door
sunken
Family Rm
23-0 x 16-0
books under
Future
Sunroom
13-6 x 15-6
Brkfst
9-8 x 11-10
Kitchen
island
11-4 x 13-8
column
desk
DN
ref
oven
DW
Dining Rm
11-8 x 15-0
railing
UP
Foyer
Entry
Ldry
cabinets
D
W
LT
Living Rm
11-8 x 12-0
Optional Mechanical Placement
Garage
31-8 x 21-4
FIRST FLOOR
crawl access
W/H
furn.
CRAWLSPACE/SLAB
FOUNDATION
OPTION
whirlpool
Lin
Master Suite
14-0 x 17-4
Br 2
11-0 x 12-2
Lin
railing
DN
ldry chute
Study
19-8 x 9-4
Br 3
11-8 x 12-0
Br 4
11-8 x 11-10
open to foyer
SECOND FLOOR

PLAN NO.91343

Customized for Sloping View Site

Price Code: D

SECOND FLOOR

FIRST FLOOR

LOWER FLOOR

WIDTH 67'-0"
DEPTH 41'-0"

- This plan features:
- — Three bedrooms
- — Two full and one half baths
- A stone-faced fireplace and vaulted ceiling in the Living Room
- An island food preparation center with a sink and a breakfast bar in the Kitchen
- Sliding glass doors leading from the Dining Room to the adjacent Deck
- A Master Suite with a vaulted ceiling, a Sitting Room, and a lavish Master Bath with a whirlpool tub, skylights, double vanity, and walk-in closet
- This home is designed with a combo basement/crawlspace foundation

FIRST FLOOR — 1,338 SQ. FT.
SECOND FLOOR — 763 SQ. FT.
LOWER FLOOR — 61 SQ. FT.
GARAGE — 779 SQ. FT.

TOTAL LIVING AREA:
2,162 SQ. FT.

PLAN NO. 98590

Magnificent Stature

Price Code: L

- This plan features:
- — Four bedrooms
- — Three full and one half baths
- A two-story cathedral ceiling crowns the Living Room of this manor-styled home
- The first floor Master Suite features a private, octagonal Study with a wetbar
- The second floor includes a Media Area and a bonus space
- The expansive Family Room opens on to the Covered Patio
- This home is designed with basement, slab and crawlspace foundation options

FIRST FLOOR — 3,168 SQ. FT.
SECOND FLOOR — 998 SQ. FT.
BONUS — 320 SQ. FT.
GARAGE — 810 SQ. FT.

TOTAL LIVING AREA:
4,166 SQ. FT.

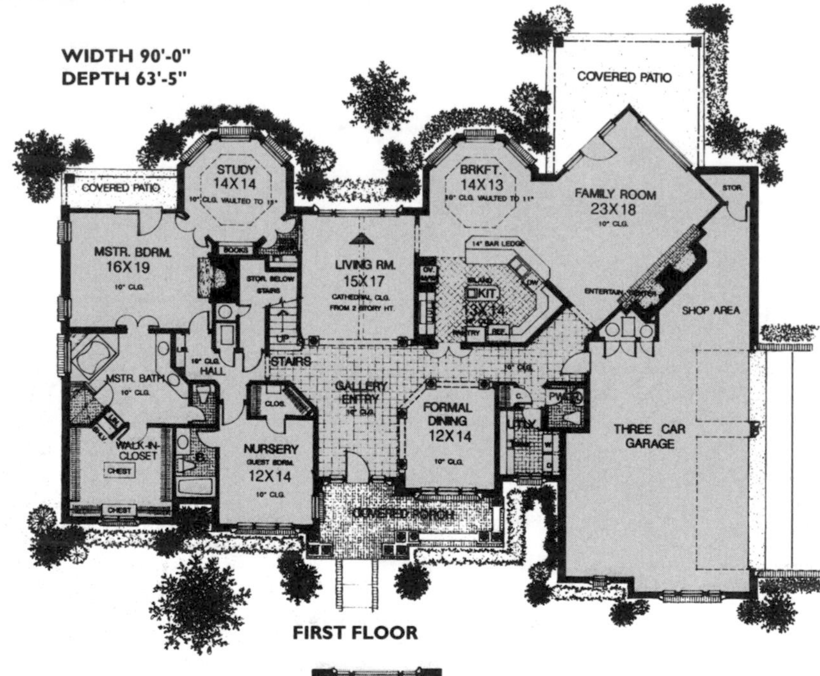
WIDTH 90'-0"
DEPTH 63'-5"
COVERED PATIO
COVERED PATIO
STUDY
14X14
BRKFT.
14X13
FAMILY ROOM
23X18
MSTR. BDRM.
16X19
LIVING RM.
15X17
SHOP AREA
STAIRS
HALL
MSTR. BATH
GALLERY ENTRY
FORMAL DINING
12X14
THREE CAR GARAGE
WALK-IN-CLOSET
NURSERY
12X14
COVERED PORCH
FIRST FLOOR

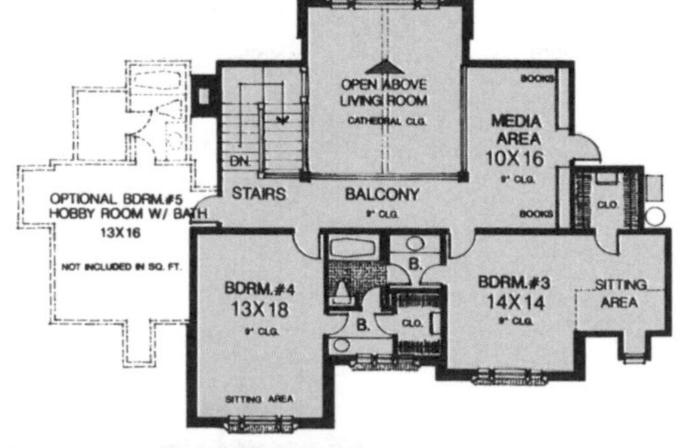
OPEN ABOVE LIVING ROOM
MEDIA AREA
10X16
DN
STAIRS
BALCONY
OPTIONAL BDRM.#5 HOBBY ROOM W/ BATH
13X16
BDRM.#4
13X18
BDRM.#3
14X14
SITTING AREA
SECOND FLOOR

PLAN NO. 92048

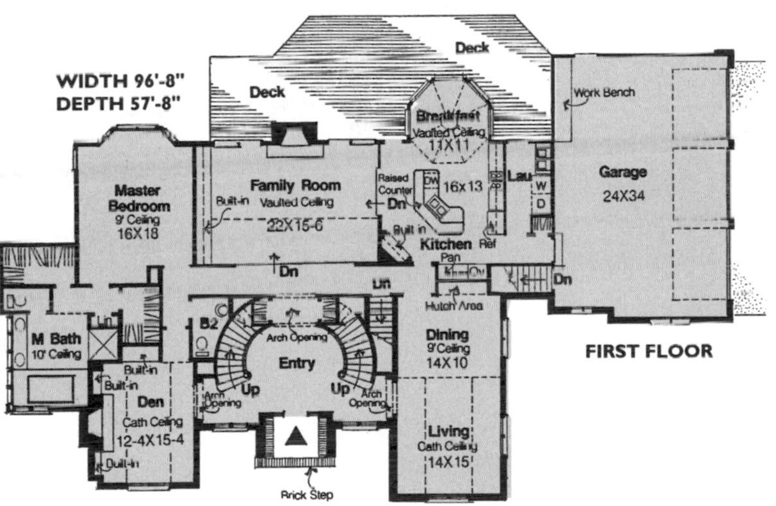

WIDTH 96'-8"
DEPTH 57'-8"
Deck
Deck
Breakfast
Vaulted Ceiling
11X11
Work Bench
Garage
24X34
Master
Bedroom
9' Ceiling
16X18
Family Room
Built-in
Vaulted Ceiling
22X15-6
Raised Counter
Dn
16x13
Lau
W
D
Kitchen
Ref
Pan
Dn
Dn
Dn
Hutch Area
M Bath
10' Ceiling
B2
Arch Opening
Entry
Dining
9' Ceiling
14X10
Built-in
Den
Cath Ceiling
12-4X15-4
Up
Up
Living
Cath Ceiling
14X15
Brick Step
FIRST FLOOR

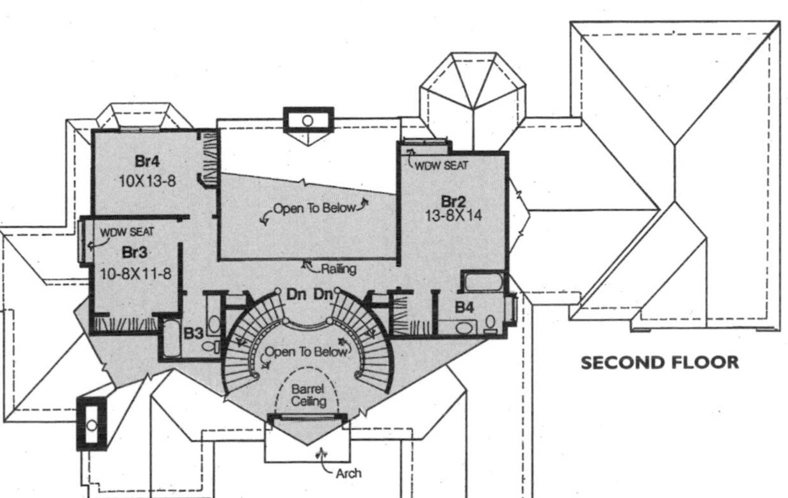

Br4
10X13-8
WDW SEAT
Open To Below
Br2
13-8X14
WDW SEAT
Br3
10-8X11-8
Railing
Dn Dn
B4
B3
Open To Below
Barrel Ceiling
Arch
SECOND FLOOR

Unusual and Dramatic

Price Code: I

- This plan features:
- — Four bedrooms
- — Three full and one half baths
- Elegant Entry with arched openings and a double curved staircase
- Cathedral ceilings crown arched windows in the Den and Living Room
- Spacious Family Room with a vaulted ceiling and a large fireplace
- Hub Kitchen with a work island/serving counter, Breakfast Alcove
- Secluded Master Suite with a lovely bay window, two walk-in closets and a plush Bath
- This home is designed with a basement foundation

First floor — 2,646 sq. ft.
Second floor — 854 sq. ft.
Basement — 2,656 sq. ft.

Total living area:
3,500 sq. ft.

PLAN NO. 93432

Country-Styled Home

Price Code: C

- This plan features:
- — Three bedrooms
- — Two full and one half baths
- A Country-styled front Porch provides a warm welcome
- The Family Room is highlighted by a fireplace and front windows
- The Dining Room is separated from the U-shaped Kitchen by only an extended counter
- The first floor Master Suite pampers it's owners with a walk-in closet and a five-piece Bath
- There are two additional Bedrooms with a convenient Bath in the hall
- This home is designed with crawlspace and slab foundation options

FIRST FLOOR — 1,288 SQ. FT.
SECOND FLOOR — 545 SQ. FT.
GARAGE — 540 SQ. FT.

TOTAL LIVING AREA:
1,833 SQ. FT.

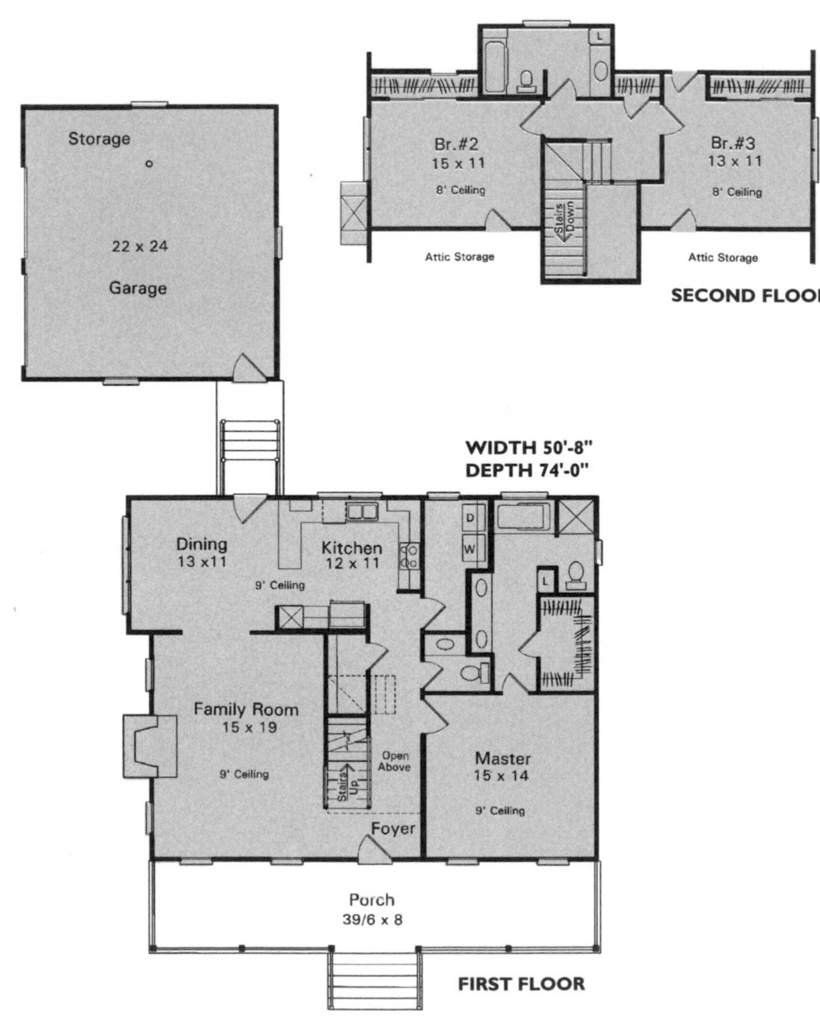
Storage
22 x 24
Garage
Br.#2
15 x 11
8' Ceiling
Br.#3
13 x 11
8' Ceiling
Stairs Down
Attic Storage
Attic Storage
SECOND FLOOR
WIDTH 50'-8"
DEPTH 74'-0"
Dining
13 x11
Kitchen
12 x 11
9' Ceiling
Family Room
15 x 19
9' Ceiling
Stairs Up
Open Above
Master
15 x 14
9' Ceiling
Foyer
Porch
39/6 x 8
FIRST FLOOR

PLAN NO. 92631

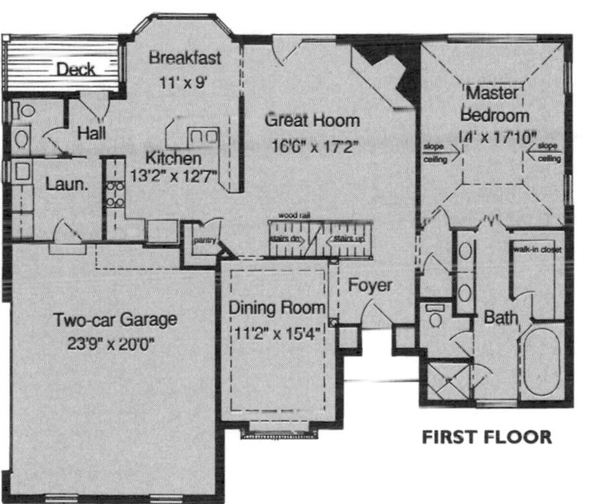

Deck
Breakfast
11' x 9'
Hall
Kitchen
13'2" x 12'7"
Great Room
16'6" x 17'2"
Master
Bedroom
14' x 17'10"
slope ceiling
slope ceiling
Laun.
pantry
wood rail
stairs dn
stairs up
walk-in closet
Foyer
Bath
Two-car Garage
23'9" x 20'0"
Dining Room
11'2" x 15'4"
FIRST FLOOR
46'8"
54'8"

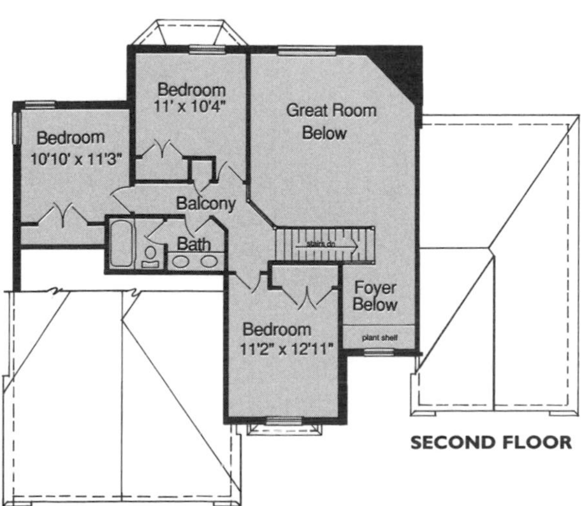

Bedroom
11' x 10'4"
Great Room
Below
Bedroom
10'10' x 11'3"
Balcony
Bath
stairs dn
Foyer
Below
Bedroom
11'2" x 12'11"
plant shelf
SECOND FLOOR

A Traditional Two-Story with Character

Price Code: D

- This plan features:
  - Four bedrooms
  - Two full and one half baths
- Front entrance into two-story Foyer with a plant shelf and lovely railing staircase
- Expansive Great Room with corner fireplace and access to rear yard topped by two-story ceiling
- Efficient Kitchen with peninsula counter, walk-in Pantry, Breakfast bay and access to Deck, Laundry and Garage Entry
- Secluded Master Bedroom offers a sloped ceiling and lavish Bath with walk-in closet
- This home is designed with a basement foundation

FIRST FLOOR — 1,511 SQ. FT.
SECOND FLOOR — 646 SQ. FT.
BASEMENT — 1,479 SQ. FT.
GARAGE — 475 SQ. FT.

TOTAL LIVING AREA:
2,157 SQ. FT.

PLAN NO. 32063

Photography supplied by The Meredith Corporatior

Forest Cottage

Price Code: L

- This plan features:
- — Four Bedrooms
- — Four full and one half baths
- The bow-shaped front Deck mirrors the eyebrow dormer and large arched window
- Kitchen with an island and a built-in Pantry
- The Great Room is highlighted by a fireplace and access to the Screen Porch
- The second floor Master Suite has two walk-in closets and is pampered by a five-piece Bath
- The lower floor contains a Media Room, a Playroom, and a Guest Suite
- This home is designed with a basement foundation

FIRST FLOOR — 1,642 SQ. FT.
SECOND FLOOR — 1411 SQ. FT.
LOWER FLOOR — 1,230 SQ. FT.
BASEMENT — 412 SQ. FT.

TOTAL LIVING AREA:
4,283 SQ. FT.

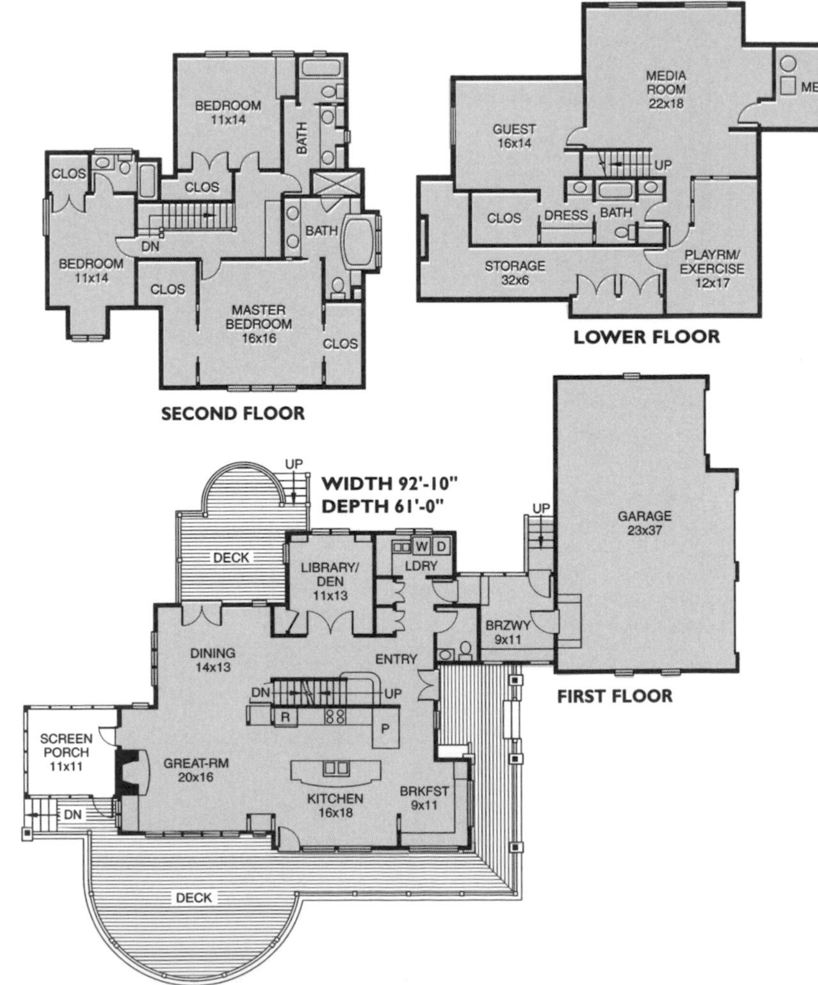

BEDROOM 11x14
BATH
CLOS
CLOS
DN
BATH
BEDROOM 11x14
CLOS
MASTER BEDROOM 16x16
CLOS
SECOND FLOOR
MEDIA ROOM 22x18
MECH
GUEST 16x14
UP
CLOS
DRESS
BATH
STORAGE 32x6
PLAYRM/ EXERCISE 12x17
LOWER FLOOR
UP
WIDTH 92'-10"
DEPTH 61'-0"
DECK
LIBRARY/ DEN 11x13
W
D
LDRY
UP
GARAGE 23x37
BRZWY 9x11
DINING 14x13
ENTRY
DN
UP
R
P
SCREEN PORCH 11x11
GREAT-RM 20x16
KITCHEN 16x18
BRKFST 9x11
DN
FIRST FLOOR
DECK

PLAN NO. 92643

Exciting Impact

Price Code: D

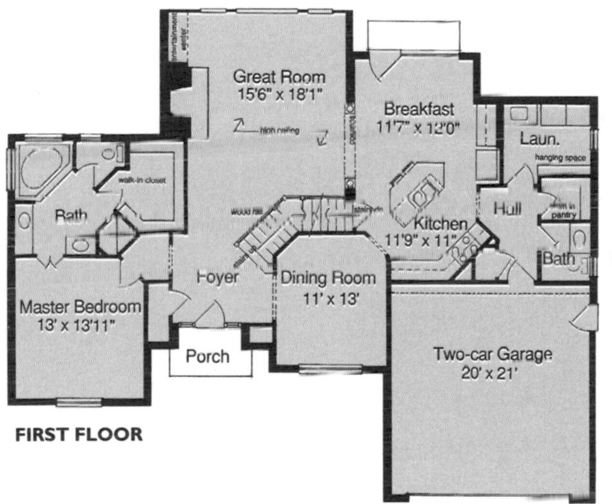

Great Room
15'6" x 18'1"
Breakfast
11'7" x 12'0"
Laun.
Bath
Kitchen
Hall
Bath
Foyer
Dining Room
11' x 13'
Master Bedroom
13' x 13'11"
Porch
Two-car Garage
20' x 21'
49'
58'6"

FIRST FLOOR

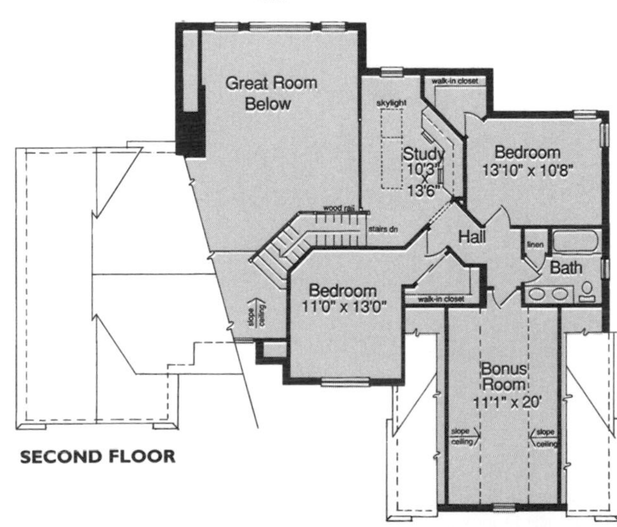

Great Room
Below
Study
10'3" x 13'6"
Bedroom
13'10" x 10'8"
Hall
Bath
Bedroom
11'0" x 13'0"
Bonus
Room
11'1" x 20'

SECOND FLOOR

- This plan features:
  - Three bedrooms
  - Two full and one half baths
- Keystone arch accents entrance into open Foyer with lovely angled staircase
- Great Room with entertainment center, hearth fireplace and a wall of windows
- The Kitchen offers work island/snack bar, Laundry, and Garage Entry
- Master Bedroom wing features a lavish Bath, large walk-in closet, and corner window tub
- This home is designed with a basement foundation

FIRST FLOOR — 1,542 SQ. FT.
SECOND FLOOR — 667 SQ. FT.
BONUS ROOM — 236 SQ. FT.
GARAGE — 420 SQ. FT.
BASEMENT — 1,470 SQ. FT.

TOTAL LIVING AREA:
2,209 SQ. FT.

PLAN NO. 98596

Stately Presence

Price Code: H

- This plan features:
- — Four bedrooms
- — Three full and one half baths
- The Patio and covered Patio expand living space to the outdoors
- The cathedral ceiling in the Living Room gives added volume to the room
- The future Playroom on the second floor has a perfect location for keeping peace and quiet on the first floor
- This home is designed with basement, slab and crawlspace foundation options

FIRST FLOOR — 2,115 SQ. FT.
SECOND FLOOR — 947 SQ. FT.
BONUS ROOM — 195 SQ. FT.
GARAGE — 635 SQ. FT.
DECK — 210 SQ. FT.

TOTAL LIVING AREA:
3,062 SQ. FT.

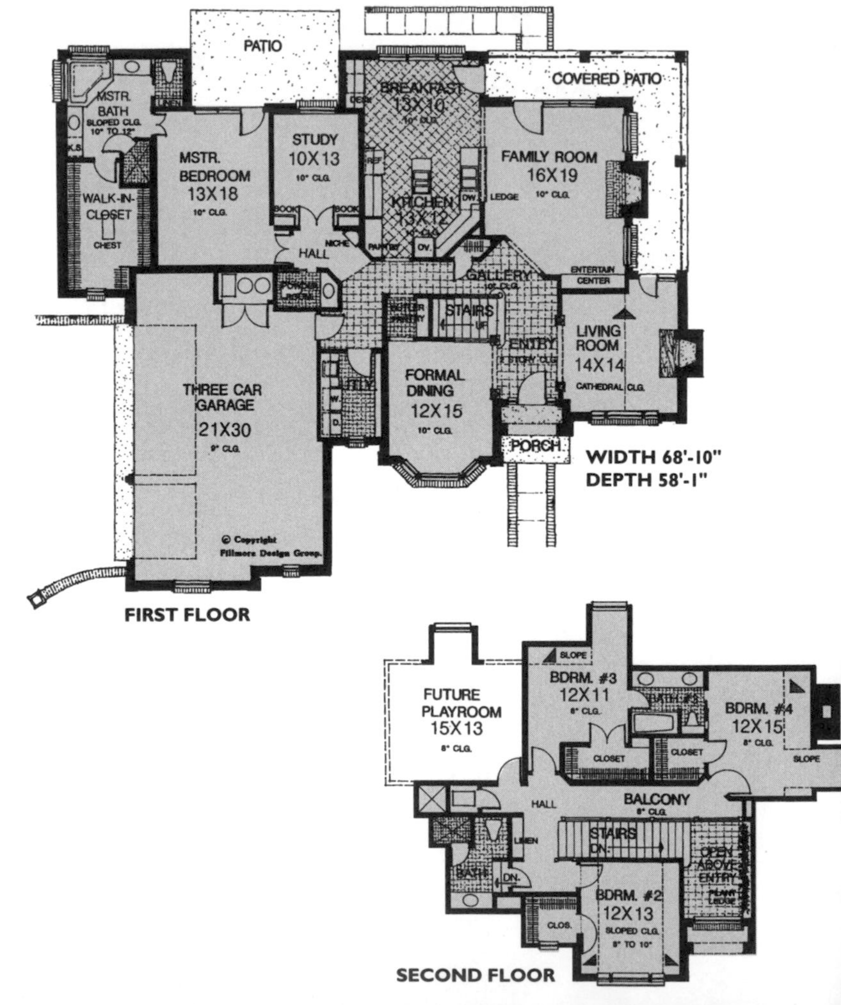
PATIO
COVERED PATIO
MSTR. BATH
BREAKFAST 13X10
MSTR. BEDROOM 13X18
STUDY 10X13
FAMILY ROOM 16X19
KITCHEN 13X12
WALK-IN-CLOSET
HALL
GALLERY
STAIRS
LIVING ROOM 14X14
THREE CAR GARAGE 21X30
FORMAL DINING 12X15
PORCH
WIDTH 68'-10"
DEPTH 58'-1"
FIRST FLOOR
FUTURE PLAYROOM 15X13
BDRM. #3 12X11
BDRM. #4 12X15
BALCONY
HALL
STAIRS
BATH
BDRM. #2 12X13
SECOND FLOOR

PLAN NO.92651

Dynamic Two-Story

Price Code: E

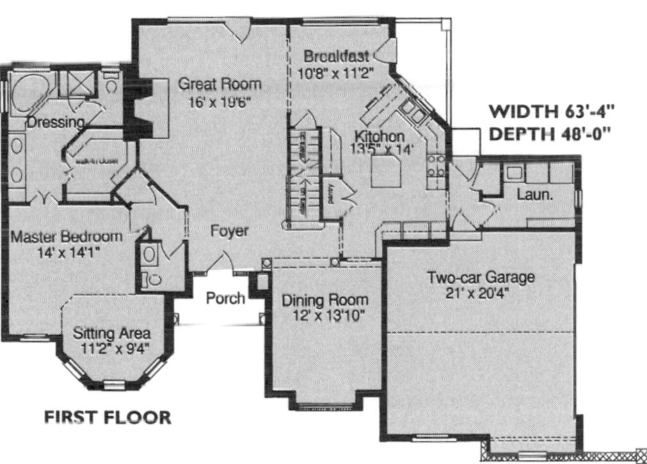
Breakfast
10'8" x 11'2"
Great Room
16' x 19'6"
Dressing
Kitchen
13'5" x 14'
WIDTH 63'-4"
DEPTH 48'-0"
Laun.
Master Bedroom
14' x 14'1"
Foyer
Porch
Dining Room
12' x 13'10"
Two-car Garage
21' x 20'4"
Sitting Area
11'2" x 9'4"

FIRST FLOOR

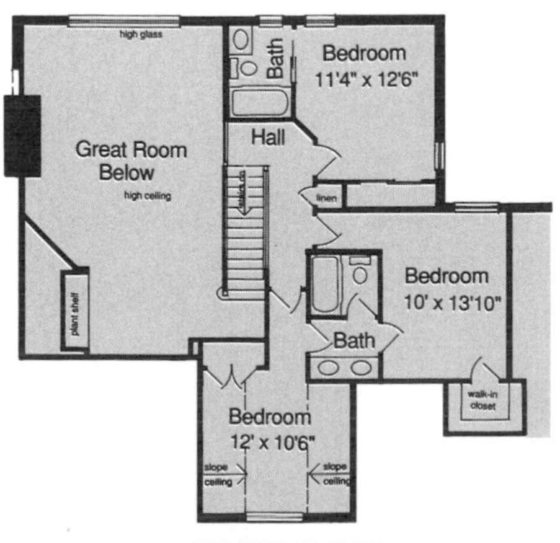
high glass
Bath
Bedroom
11'4" x 12'6"
Hall
Great Room
Below
high ceiling
linen
Bedroom
10' x 13'10"
plant shelf
Bath
walk-in closet
Bedroom
12' x 10'6"
slope ceiling
slope ceiling

SECOND FLOOR

- This plan features:
  - — Four bedrooms
  - — Three full and one half baths
- Sheltered Entry surrounded by glass leads into open Foyer and Great Room with high ceiling, hearth fireplace and Atrium door to backyard
- Columns frame entrance to conveniently located Dining Room
- Efficient Kitchen with built-in Pantry, work island and bright Breakfast Area accesses Laundry, backyard and Garage
- Master Bedroom wing with Sitting Area, private Bath with corner window tub
- This home is designed with basement and slab foundation options

FIRST FLOOR — 1,710 SQ. FT.
SECOND FLOOR — 693 SQ. FT.
BASEMENT — 1,620 SQ. FT.
GARAGE — 467 SQ. FT.

TOTAL LIVING AREA:
2,403 SQ. FT.

PLAN NO. 32101

Photography supplied by The Meredith Co

Traditional Exterior

Price Code: G

- This plan features:
  - — Three bedrooms
  - — Two full and one half baths
- The Master Bedroom includes a private balcony
- The two secondary Bedrooms are identical in size
- A see-through fireplace warms two rooms
- Relax with a cup of coffee in the Morning Room
- A Studio Apartment is located over the Garage
- This home is designed with a crawlspace foundation

FIRST FLOOR — 1,546 SQ. FT.
SECOND FLOOR — 1,218 SQ. FT.
BONUS — 403 SQ. FT.
GARAGE — 624 SQ. FT.

TOTAL LIVING AREA:
2,764 SQ. FT.

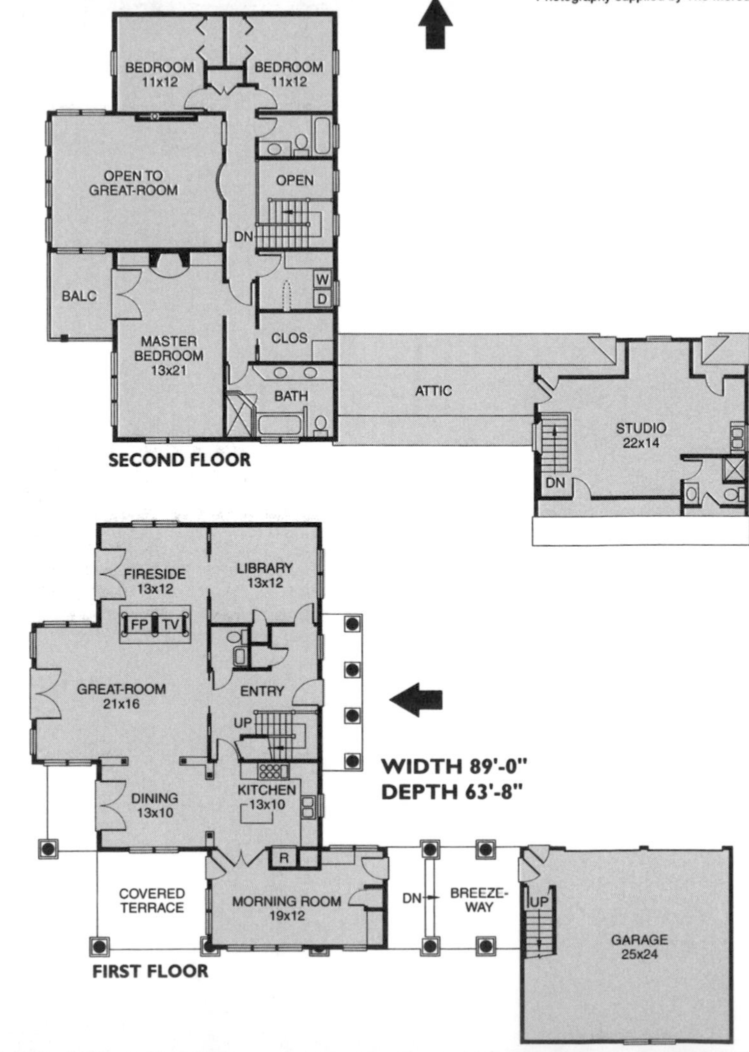
BEDROOM 11x12
BEDROOM 11x12
OPEN TO GREAT-ROOM
OPEN
DN
BALC
W
D
MASTER BEDROOM 13x21
CLOS
BATH
ATTIC
STUDIO 22x14
DN
SECOND FLOOR
FIRESIDE 13x12
LIBRARY 13x12
FP
TV
GREAT-ROOM 21x16
ENTRY
UP
WIDTH 89'-0"
DEPTH 63'-8"
DINING 13x10
KITCHEN 13x10
R
COVERED TERRACE
MORNING ROOM 19x12
DN
BREEZE-WAY
UP
GARAGE 25x24
FIRST FLOOR

PLAN NO. 92644

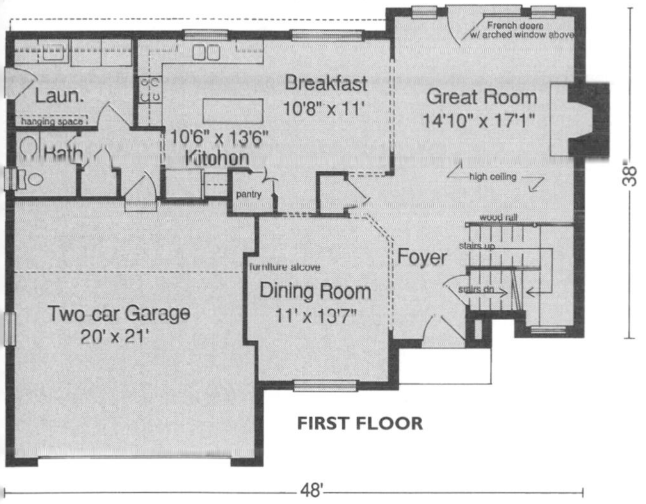

Two car Garage 20' x 21'
Laun.
hanging space
Bath
10'6" x 13'6" Kitchen
pantry
Breakfast 10'8" x 11'
Great Room 14'10" x 17'1"
French doors w/ arched window above
high ceiling
wood rail
stairs up
stairs dn
Foyer
furniture alcove
Dining Room 11' x 13'7"
38'
48'

FIRST FLOOR

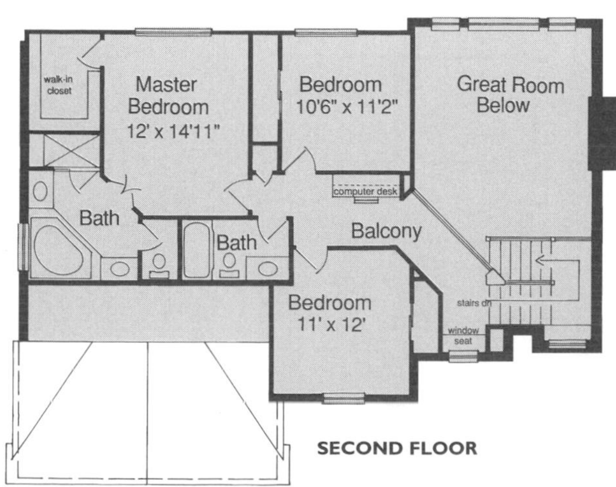

walk-in closet
Master Bedroom 12' x 14'11"
Bedroom 10'6" x 11'2"
Great Room Below
computer desk
Bath
Bath
Balcony
Bedroom 11' x 12'
stairs dn
window seat

SECOND FLOOR

Detail and Design

Price Code: C

- This plan features:
  - — Three bedrooms
  - — Two full and one half baths
- Impressive Entry into open Foyer with landing staircase highlighted by decorative windows
- Great Room accented by hearth fireplace and French doors with arched window above and topped by a high ceiling
- Efficient, L-shaped Kitchen with work island, walk-in Pantry, bright Breakfast Area, adjoining Laundry, half Bath and Garage Entry
- Quiet Master Bedroom offers a walk-in closet, and plush Bath with two vanities and whirlpool tub
- This home is designed with a basement foundation

FIRST FLOOR — 1,036 SQ. FT.
SECOND FLOOR — 861 SQ. FT.
GARAGE — 420 SQ. FT.

TOTAL LIVING AREA:
1,897 SQ. FT.

PLAN NO. 91133

Impressive Plan

Price Code: G

- This plan features:
- — Four bedrooms
- — Two full and one half baths
- A see-through fireplace straddles the Living and Hearth Rooms
- The U-shaped Kitchen has an island in its center
- A tray ceiling graces the Dining Room
- The Master Suite is in its own wing
- Three Bedrooms are on the second floor
- This home is designed with a slab foundation

FIRST FLOOR — 1,893 SQ. FT.
SECOND FLOOR — 893 SQ. FT.
GARAGE — 632 SQ. FT.

TOTAL LIVING AREA:
2,786 SQ. FT.

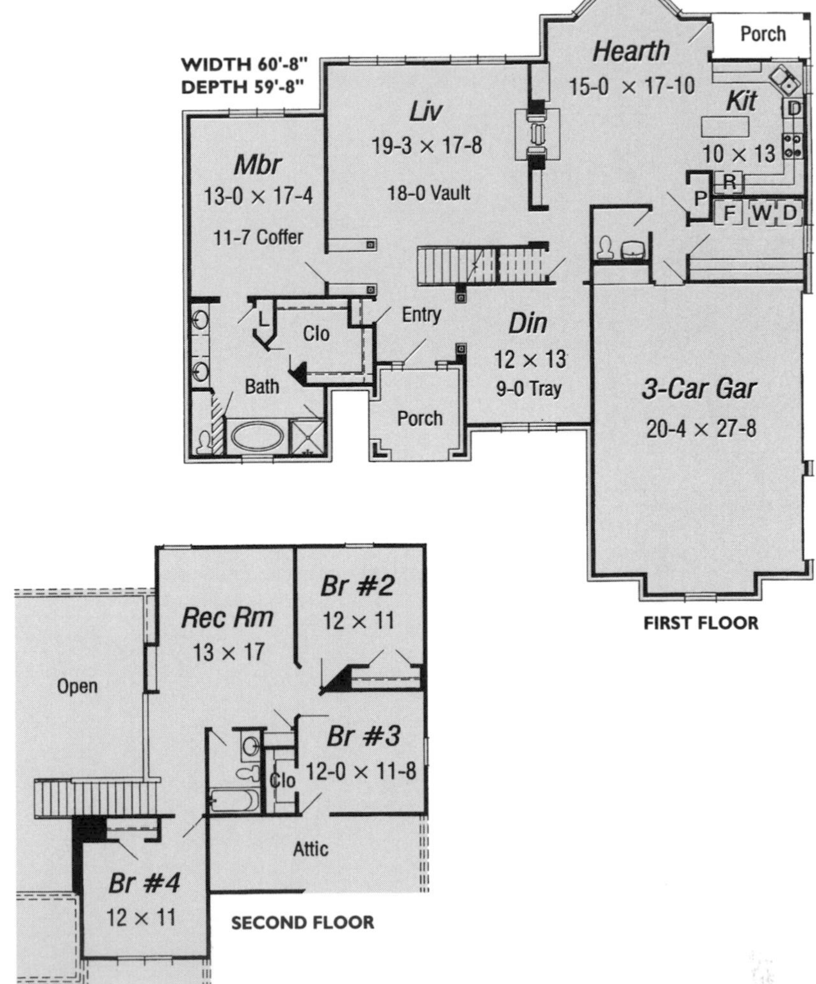

WIDTH 60'-8"
DEPTH 59'-8"
Porch
Hearth
15-0 × 17-10
Kit
10 × 13
Liv
19-3 × 17-8
18-0 Vault
Mbr
13-0 × 17-4
11-7 Coffer
Entry
Clo
Bath
Porch
Din
12 × 13
9-0 Tray
3-Car Gar
20-4 × 27-8
FIRST FLOOR
Rec Rm
13 × 17
Br #2
12 × 11
Open
Br #3
12-0 × 11-8
Clo
Attic
Br #4
12 × 11
SECOND FLOOR

PLAN NO. 24610

Second Floor Balcony Overlooks Great Room

Price Code: C

Rear Elevation

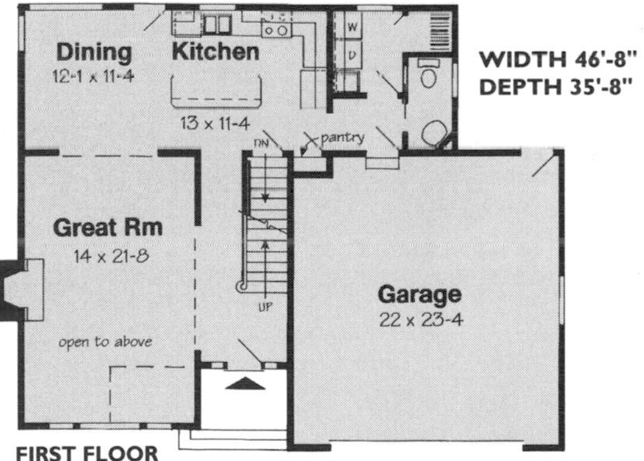

Dining
12-1 x 11-4
Kitchen
13 x 11-4
W
D
pantry
DN
Great Rm
14 x 21-8
open to above
UP
Garage
22 x 23-4
WIDTH 46'-8"
DEPTH 35'-8"
FIRST FLOOR

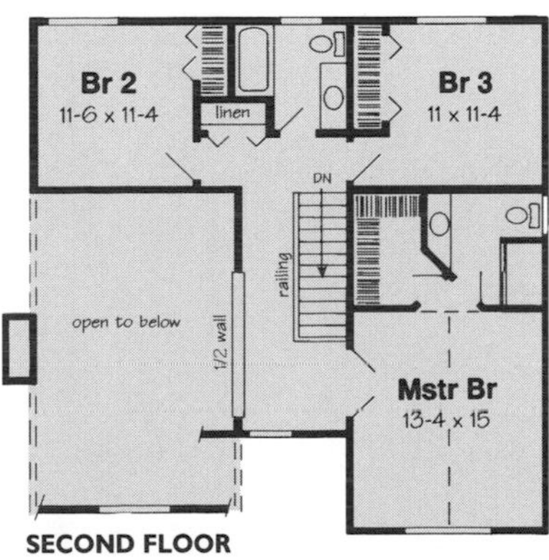

Br 2
11-6 x 11-4
linen
Br 3
11 x 11-4
DN
railing
open to below
1/2 wall
Mstr Br
13-4 x 15
SECOND FLOOR

- This plan features:
  - Three bedrooms
  - One full, and one three-quarter baths
- A Great Room with a focal point fireplace and a two-story ceiling
- An efficient Kitchen with an island, double sinks, built-in Pantry and ample storage and counter space
- A convenient first floor Laundry Room
- A Dining Room with easy access to both the Kitchen and the outside
- A Master Suite with a private Master Bath and a walk-in closet
- This home is designed with basement, slab and crawlspace foundation options

FIRST FLOOR — 891 SQ. FT.
SECOND FLOOR — 894 SQ. FT.
GARAGE — 534 SQ. FT.
BASEMENT — 891 SQ. FT.

TOTAL LIVING AREA:
1,785 SQ. FT.

PLAN NO.97409

A Home of Distinction

Price Code: F

- This plan features:
- — Four bedrooms
- — Three full and one half baths
- The Dining Room and the Study are to either side of the Entry
- The Study entrance is at an angle with a double door Entry
- The two-story Family Room includes a fireplace and a highly windowed rear wall
- The Breakfast Room is open to he Kitchen
- The first floor Master Suite includes a whirlpool tub
- This home is designed with a slab foundation
- Alternate foundation options available at an additional charge. Please call 1-800-235-5700 for more information.

FIRST FLOOR — 1,844 SQ. FT.
SECOND FLOOR — 794 SQ. FT.

TOTAL LIVING AREA:
2,638 SQ. FT.

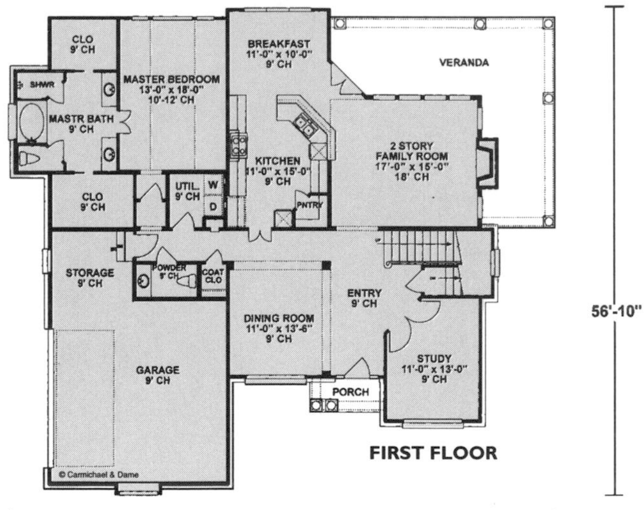
CLO
9' CH
MASTER BEDROOM
13'-0" x 18'-0"
10'-12' CH
BREAKFAST
11'-0" x 10'-0"
9' CH
VERANDA
SHWR
MASTR BATH
9' CH
KITCHEN
11'-0" x 15'-0"
9' CH
2 STORY
FAMILY ROOM
17'-0" x 15'-0"
18' CH
CLO
9' CH
UTIL.
9' CH
W
D
PNTRY
STORAGE
9' CH
POWDER
9' CH
COAT
CLO
ENTRY
9' CH
DINING ROOM
11'-0" x 13'-6"
9' CH
STUDY
11'-0" x 13'-0"
9' CH
GARAGE
9' CH
PORCH
© Carmichael & Dame
56'-10"
65'-6"
FIRST FLOOR

BEDROOM 4
11'-0" x 15'-0"
8'-10' CH
2 STORY
FAMILY ROOM
17'-0" x 15'-0"
18' CH
BATH 3
8' CH
324 sq. ft.
OPTIONAL ATTIC
BDRM 3
11'-0" x 12'-0"
8'-10' CH
BEDROOM 2
11'-0" x 13'-0"
8'-10' CH
SECOND FLOOR

PLAN NO. 93609

Ideal Family Home

Price Code: G

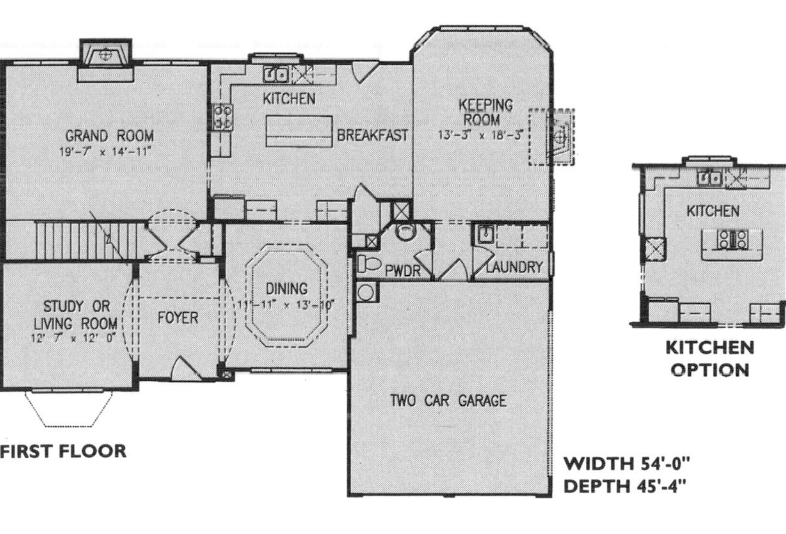

GRAND ROOM
19'-7" x 14'-11"
KITCHEN
BREAKFAST
KEEPING ROOM
13'-3" x 18'-3"
STUDY OR LIVING ROOM
12' 7" x 12' 0"
FOYER
DINING
11'-11" x 13'-10"
PWDR
LAUNDRY
TWO CAR GARAGE

FIRST FLOOR

WIDTH 54'-0"
DEPTH 45'-4"

KITCHEN

KITCHEN OPTION

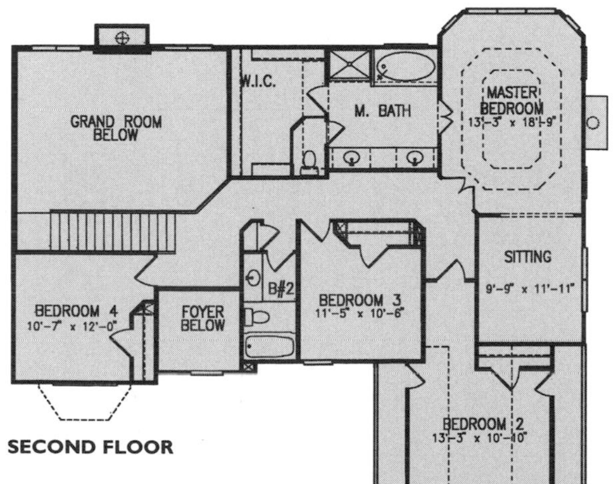

GRAND ROOM BELOW
W.I.C.
M. BATH
MASTER BEDROOM
13'-3" x 18'-9"
SITTING
9'-9" x 11'-11"
B#2
BEDROOM 3
11'-5" x 10'-6"
BEDROOM 4
10'-7" x 12'-0"
FOYER BELOW
BEDROOM 2
13'-3" x 10'-10"

SECOND FLOOR

- This plan features:
  - Four bedrooms
  - Two full and one half baths
- Inside, from the two-story Foyer enter either the Living Room or the Dining Room
- In the rear of the home there is the Grand Room and the Keeping Room both with fireplaces
- The L-shaped Kitchen has a center island and is open to the Breakfast Nook
- Upstairs the Master Bedroom has a decorative ceiling and a huge walk-in closet
- This home is designed with basement and slab foundation options

First floor — 1,535 sq. ft.
Second floor — 1,236 sq. ft.
Garage — 418 sq. ft.

Total Living Area:
2,771 sq. ft.

PLAN NO. 97735

Brick and Stone

Price Code: G

- This plan features:
  - — Four bedrooms
  - — Three full and one half baths
- Beautiful front Entry on this exciting two-story begins at the covered Porch
- Great Room with a gas fireplace and built-in bookcases
- First floor Master Suite with deluxe Dressing Area and spacious walk-in closet
- This home is designed with a basement foundation

FIRST FLOOR — 1,978 SQ. FT.
SECOND FLOOR — 958 SQ. FT.
GARAGE — 651 SQ. FT.
DECK — 181 SQ. FT.
PORCH — 72 SQ. FT.

TOTAL LIVING AREA:
2,936 SQ. FT.

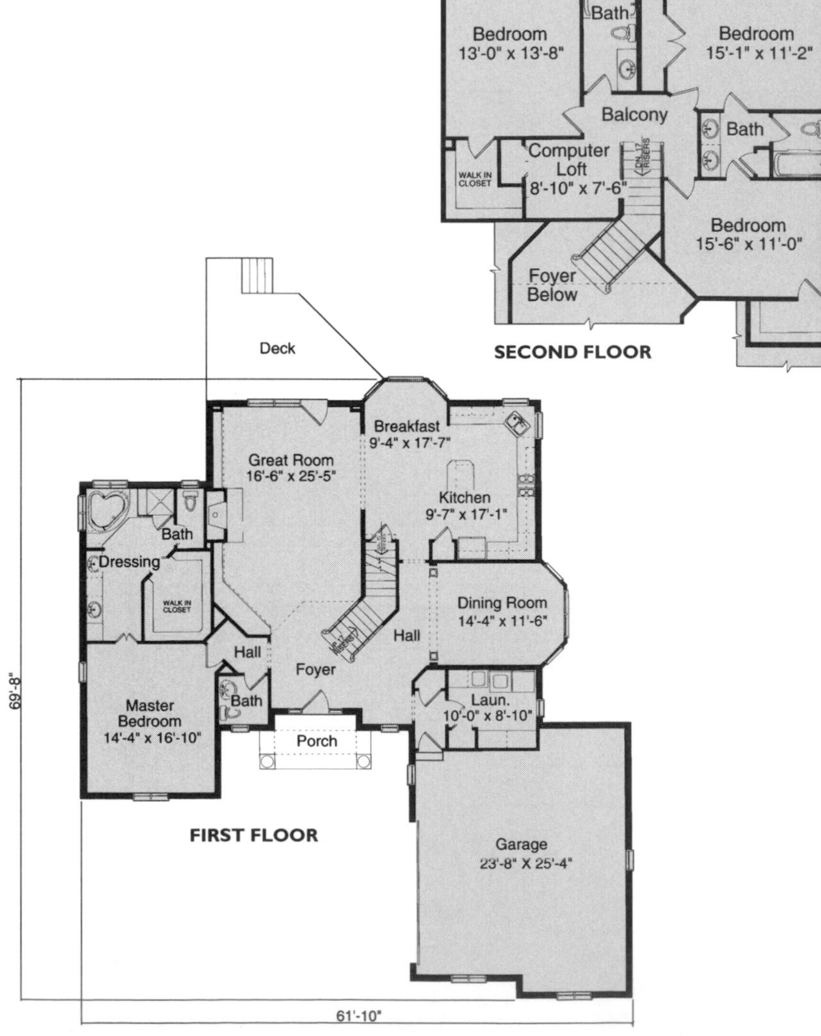
Bedroom
13'-0" x 13'-8"
Bath
Bedroom
15'-1" x 11'-2"
Balcony
Bath
Walk in closet
Computer Loft
8'-10" x 7'-6"
Bedroom
15'-6" x 11'-0"
Foyer Below
SECOND FLOOR
Deck
Breakfast
9'-4" x 17'-7"
Great Room
16'-6" x 25'-5"
Kitchen
9'-7" x 17'-1"
Bath
Dressing
Walk in closet
Dining Room
14'-4" x 11'-6"
Hall
Hall
Foyer
Master Bedroom
14'-4" x 16'-10"
Bath
Laun.
10'-0" x 8'-10"
Porch
69'-8"
FIRST FLOOR
Garage
23'-8" X 25'-4"
61'-10"

PLAN NO. 90443

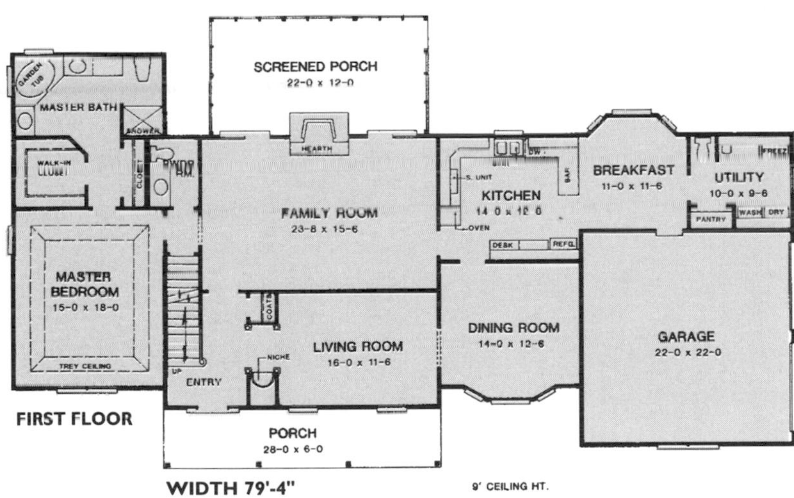

SCREENED PORCH
22-0 x 12-0
MASTER BATH
SHOWER
WALK-IN CLOSET
CLOSET
HEARTH
FAMILY ROOM
23-8 x 15-6
KITCHEN
14-0 x 12-6
S. UNIT
OVEN
DW
BAR
DESK
REFG.
BREAKFAST
11-0 x 11-6
UTILITY
10-0 x 9-6
PANTRY
WASH
DRY
FREEZ
MASTER
BEDROOM
15-0 x 18-0
TREY CEILING
COATS
NICHE
LIVING ROOM
16-0 x 11-6
UP
ENTRY
DINING ROOM
14-0 x 12-6
GARAGE
22-0 x 22-0
FIRST FLOOR
PORCH
28-0 x 6-0
WIDTH 79'-4"
DEPTH 46'-0"
9' CEILING HT.

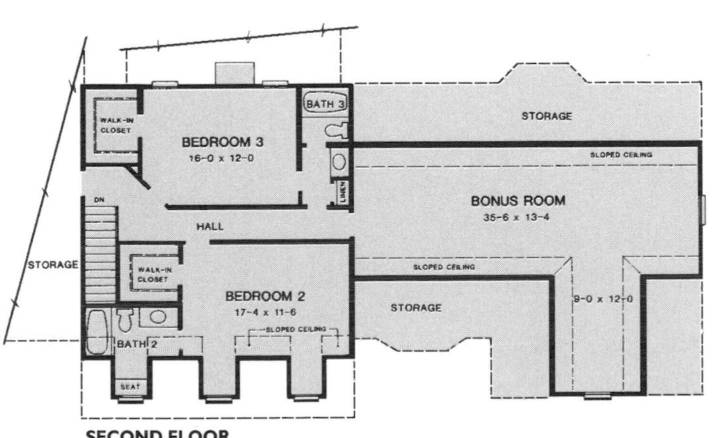

WALK-IN CLOSET
BEDROOM 3
16-0 x 12-0
BATH 3
STORAGE
SLOPED CEILING
LINEN
DN
HALL
BONUS ROOM
35-6 x 13-4
STORAGE
WALK-IN CLOSET
BEDROOM 2
17-4 x 11-6
SLOPED CEILING
STORAGE
9-0 x 12-0
BATH 2
SEAT
SECOND FLOOR

Traditional That has it All

Price Code: G

- This plan features:
- — Three bedrooms
- — Three full and two half baths
- A Master Suite with two closets and a private Bath with separate shower, corner tub and dual vanity
- A large Dining Room with a bay window, adjacent to the Kitchen
- A formal Living Room for entertaining and a cozy Family Room with fireplace for informal relaxation
- A bonus room to allow the house to grow with your needs
- This home is designed with basement, slab and crawlspace foundation options

FIRST FLOOR — 1,927 SQ. FT.
SECOND FLOOR — 832 SQ. FT.
BONUS ROOM — 624 SQ. FT.
BASEMENT — 1,674 SQ. FT.

TOTAL LIVING AREA:
2,759 SQ. FT.

PLAN NO. 98581

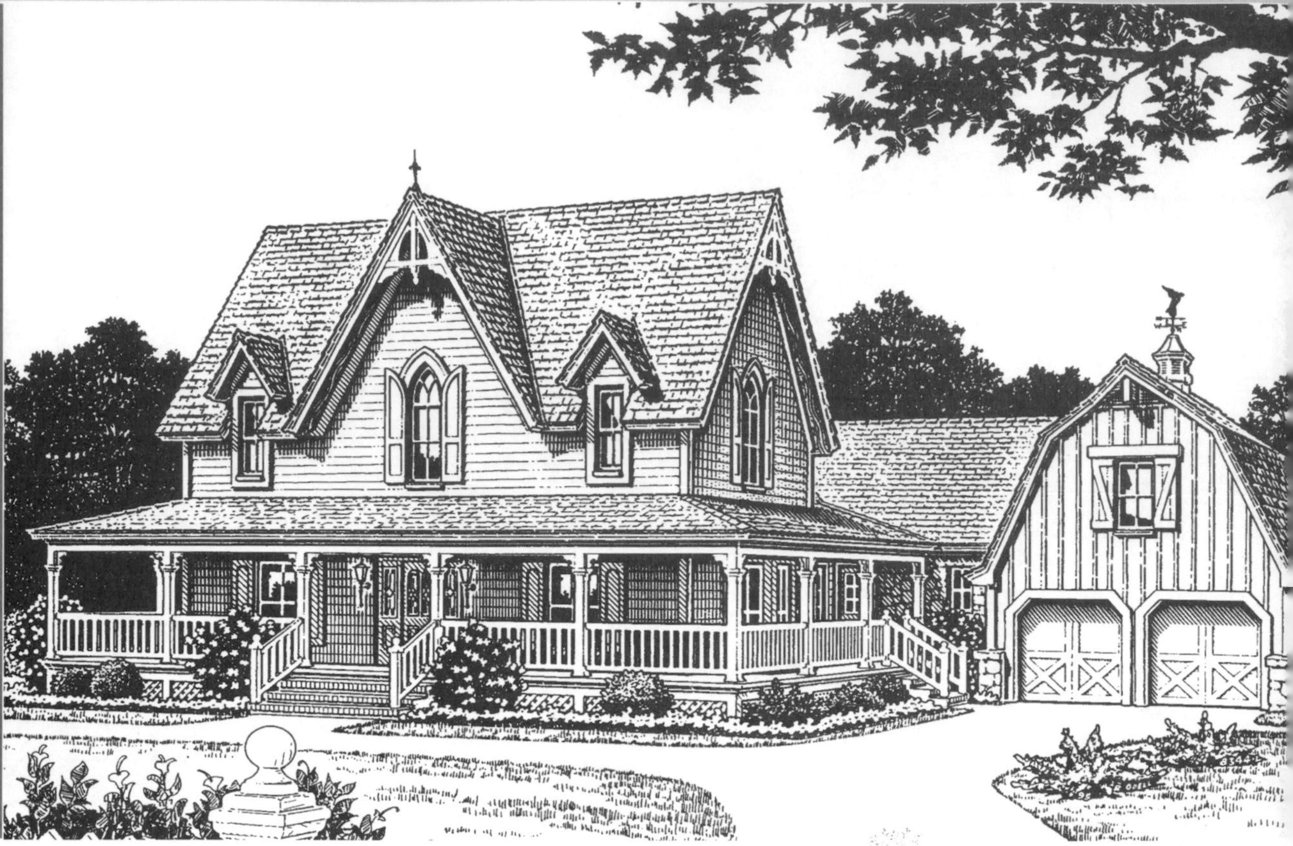

Sprawling Farmhouse

Price Code: G

- This plan features:
  - — Four bedrooms
  - — Three full and one half baths
- The Kitchen opens past a snack bar to the Family Room with a fireplace and access to the rear Deck and side Porch
- The Master Bedroom enjoys direct access to the rear Deck
- The front Music Room has a bayed windowed area
- This home is designed with basement and slab foundation options

FIRST FLOOR — 2,023 SQ. FT.
SECOND FLOOR — 749 SQ. FT.
BONUS — 256 SQ. FT.
GARAGE —546 SQ. FT.

TOTAL LIVING AREA:
2,772 SQ. FT.

77'-2"
A/C PAD
COVERED DECK
MSTR. BDRM. 19X13
MSTR. BATH
WALK-IN CLOSET
DOUBLE GARAGE 21X26
STAIRS
SERVICE ENTRY
T.V./ STEREO
FAMILY ROOM 22X17
FORMAL DINING 11X14
DECK
57'-11"
KIT./BRKFT. 16X15
ENT
PARLOR/ MUSIC RM. 16X15
COVERED WOOD DECK PORCH

FIRST FLOOR

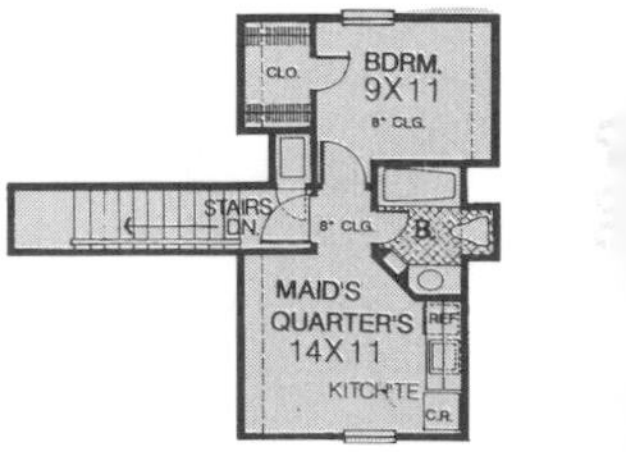

SECOND FLOOR

MAID'S QUARTER'S NOT INCLUDED IN SQ. FT. AREA

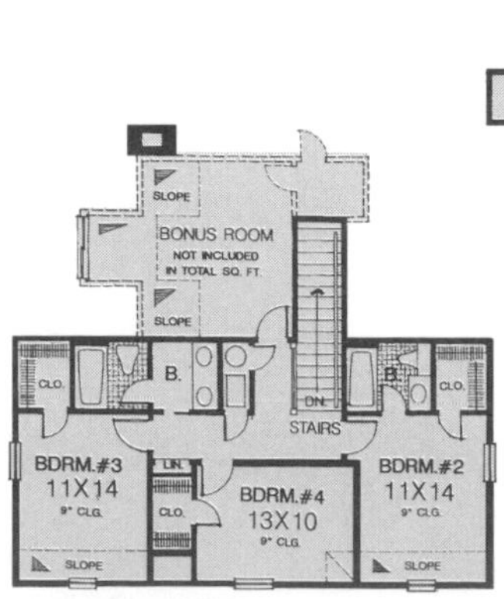

PLAN NO. 99436

SECOND FLOOR

FIRST FLOOR

Arched and Bayed Windows

Price Code: F

- This plan features:
- — Three bedrooms
- — Two full and one half baths
- The Entry is dominated by a T-shaped staircase and accented by tile flooring
- The casual Family Room boasts a wetbar, see-through fireplace and a view of the outdoors through the large rear window
- A skylight enhances the sloped ceiling over the whirlpool tub in the Master Bath
- This home is designed with a basement foundation
- Alternate foundation options available at an additional charge. Please call 1-800-235-5700 for more information.

First floor — 1,392 sq. ft.
Second floor — 1,335 sq. ft.
Basement — 1,392 sq. ft.
Garage — 738 sq. ft.
Bonus — 111 sq. ft.

Total living area:
2,727 sq. ft.

PLAN NO. 24653

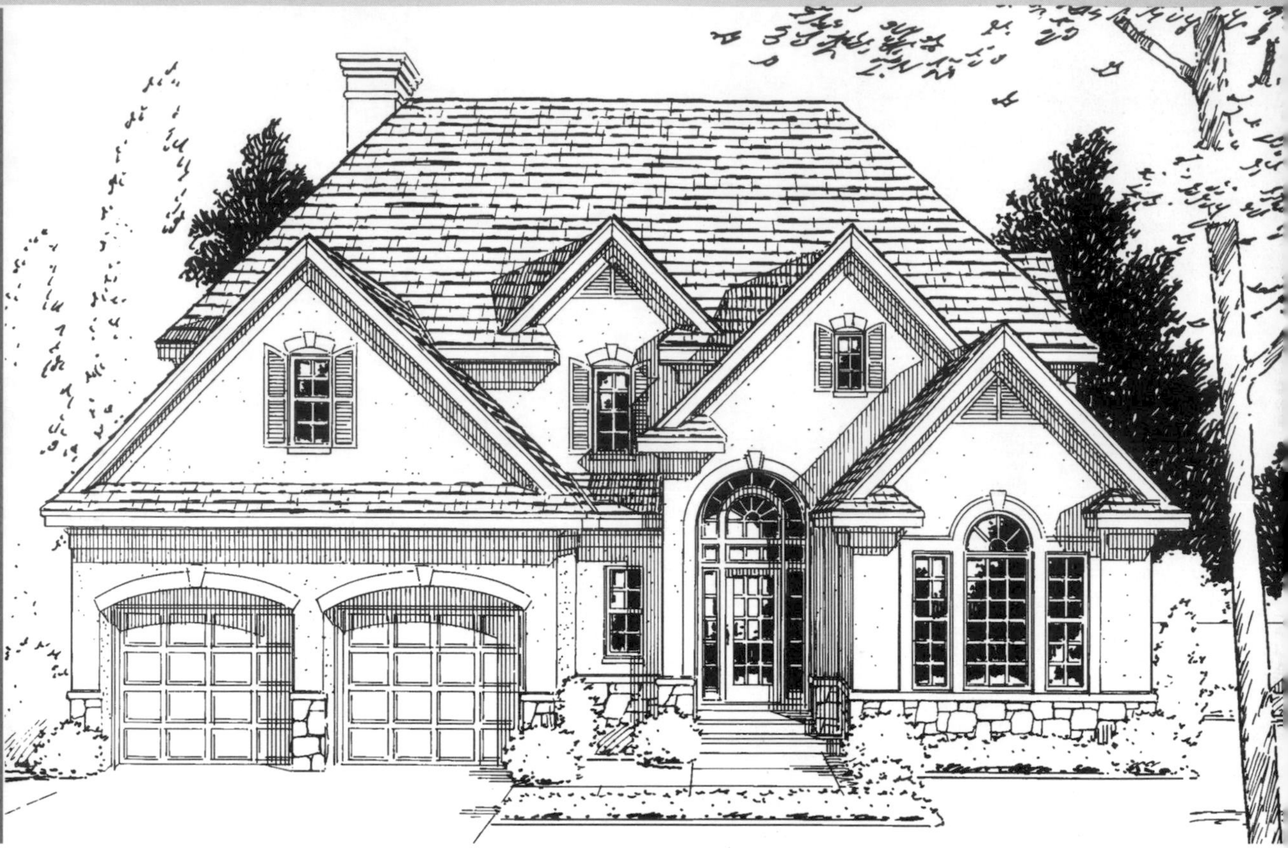

Dignified Family Home

Price Code: F

- This plan features:
  - — Three bedrooms
  - — Two full and one half baths
- The Living Room adjoins the formal Dining Room
- A U-shaped Kitchen equipped with a built-in Pantry
- A large Family Room flows from the Kitchen
- A second floor Master Suite topped by a decorative ceiling
- A bonus room for future needs
- This home is designed with basement, slab and crawlspace foundation options

First floor — 1,245 sq. ft.
Second floor — 1,333 sq. ft.
Bonus room — 192 sq. ft.
Garage — 614 sq. ft.

Total living area:
2,578 sq. ft.

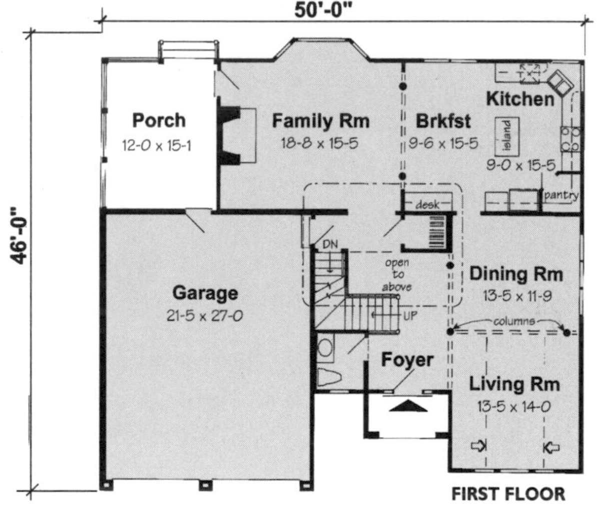

50'-0"
46'-0"
Porch
12-0 x 15-1
Family Rm
18-8 x 15-5
Brkfst
9-6 x 15-5
Kitchen
9-0 x 15-5
island
desk
pantry
Garage
21-5 x 27-0
DN
open to above
UP
Dining Rm
13-5 x 11-9
columns
Foyer
Living Rm
13-5 x 14-0

FIRST FLOOR

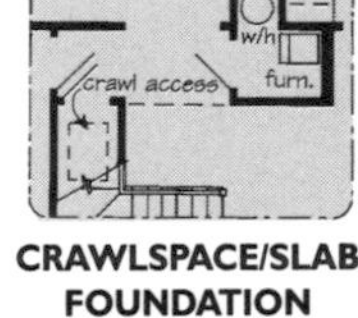

crawl access
w/h
furn.

CRAWLSPACE/SLAB FOUNDATION OPTION

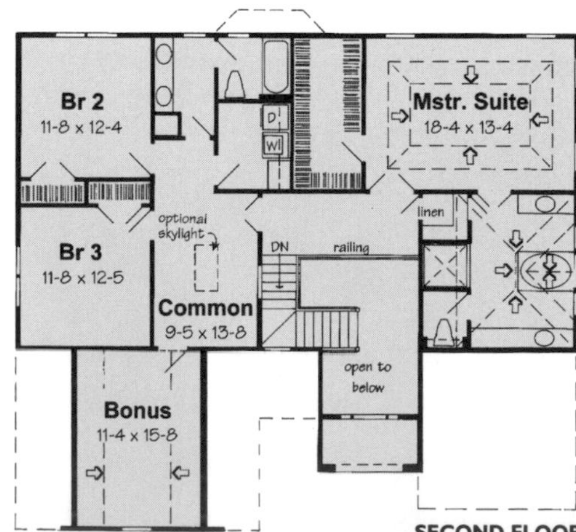

Br 2
11-8 x 12-4
Mstr. Suite
18-4 x 13-4
linen
Br 3
11-8 x 12-5
optional skylight
DN
railing
Common
9-5 x 13-8
open to below
Bonus
11-4 x 15-8

SECOND FLOOR

PLAN NO. 97255

Grand Styling

Price Code: E

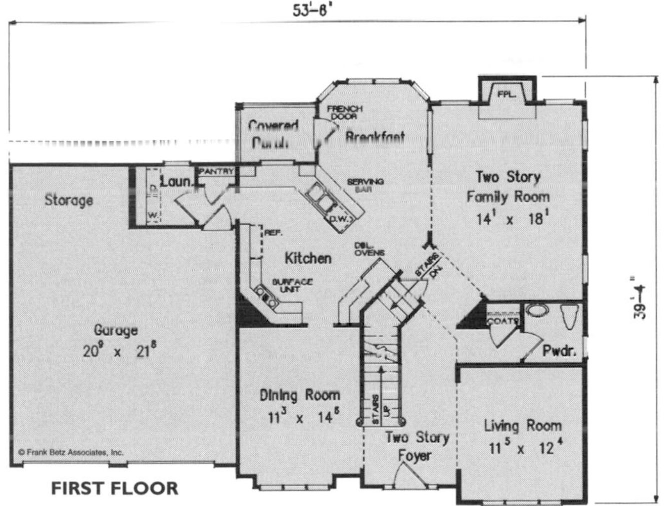

53'-8"
39'-4"
FPL.
FRENCH DOOR
Covered Porch
Breakfast
Two Story Family Room
14¹ x 18¹
Storage
Laun.
PANTRY
SERVING BAR
D.W.
REF.
Kitchen
DBL. OVENS
SURFACE UNIT
STAIRS DN.
COATS
Pwdr.
Garage
20⁹ x 21⁸
Dining Room
11³ x 14⁸
STAIRS UP
Two Story Foyer
Living Room
11⁵ x 12⁴
© Frank Betz Associates, Inc.

FIRST FLOOR

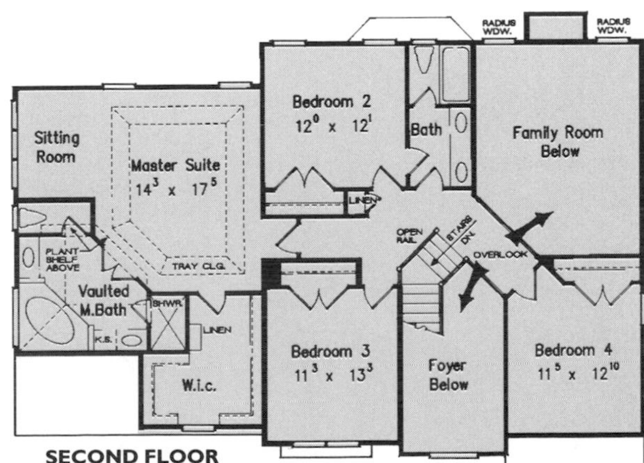

RADIUS WDW.
RADIUS WDW.
Bedroom 2
12⁰ x 12¹
Bath
Family Room Below
Sitting Room
Master Suite
14³ x 17⁵
LINEN
OPEN RAIL
STAIRS DN.
OVERLOOK
PLANT SHELF ABOVE
TRAY CLG.
Vaulted M.Bath
SHWR.
K.S.
LINEN
W.i.c.
Bedroom 3
11³ x 13³
Foyer Below
Bedroom 4
11⁵ x 12¹⁰

SECOND FLOOR

- This plan features:
- — Four bedrooms
- — Two full and one half baths
- The Family Room, Breakfast Room, and Kitchen are laid out so the open feeling prevails through-out
- There is a fireplace in the Family Room
- The Master Suite includes a walk-in closet and a cozy Sitting Room
- The Master Bedroom is topped by a tray ceiling
- This home is designed with basement and crawlspace foundation options

FIRST FLOOR — 1,205 SQ. FT.
SECOND FLOOR — 1,277 SQ. FT.
BASEMENT — 1,128 SQ. FT.
GARAGE — 528 SQ. FT.

TOTAL LIVING AREA:
2,482 SQ. FT.

PLAN NO.24743

Sunny and Bright

Price Code: C

- This plan features:
- — Three bedrooms
- — Two full baths
- The front Porch offers a great place to sit and watch the world pass by
- The Kitchen will get plenty of light, thanks to the adjoining turret-style Breakfast Area
- The Great Room features a sloped ceiling, a focal-point fireplace and access to the Deck
- A split-bedroom design is popular for those craving a private retreat
- The Master Bedroom Suite includes a large walk-in closet and a Bathroom with all the amenities
- This home is designed with a basement foundation

MAIN FLOOR — 1,990 SQ. FT.
BASEMENT — 1,338 SQ. FT.
GARAGE — 660 SQ. FT.

TOTAL LIVING AREA:
1,990 SQ. FT.

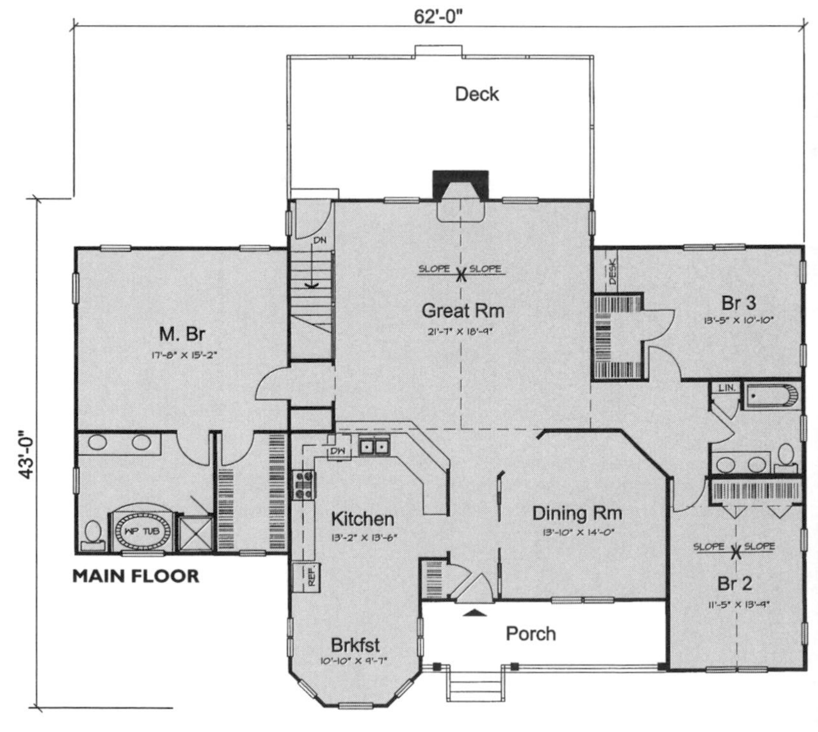
62'-0"
Deck
DN
SLOPE SLOPE
Great Rm
21'-7" X 18'-9"
M. Br
17'-8" X 15'-2"
DESK
Br 3
13'-5" X 10'-10"
LIN.
DW
WP TUB
43'-0"
Kitchen
13'-2" X 13'-6"
Dining Rm
13'-10" X 14'-0"
SLOPE SLOPE
Br 2
11'-5" X 13'-4"
REF.
MAIN FLOOR
Porch
Brkfst
10'-10" X 9'-7"

PLAN NO.24746

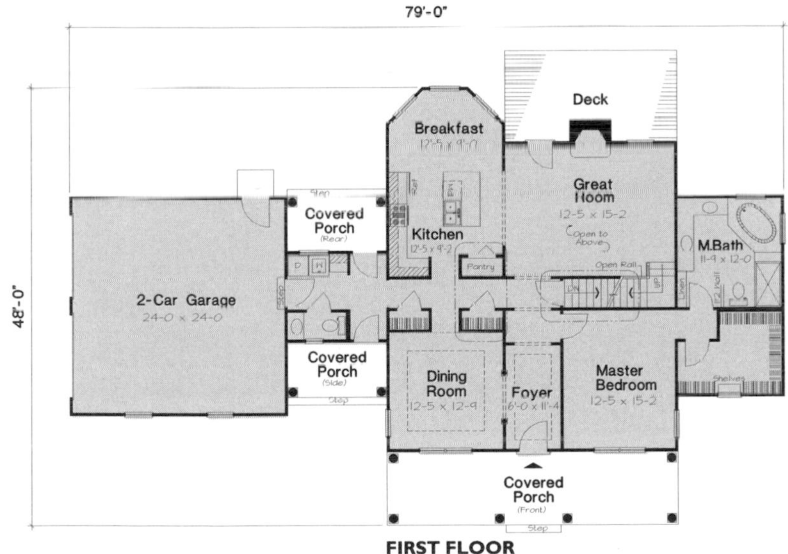

79'-0"
48'-0"
Deck
Breakfast
Great Room
12-5 x 15-2
Covered Porch
(Rear)
Kitchen
Pantry
Open Rail
M.Bath
11-4 x 12-0
2-Car Garage
24-0 x 24-0
Covered Porch
(Side)
Dining Room
12-5 x 12-4
Foyer
Master Bedroom
12-5 x 15-2
Shelves
Covered Porch
(Front)
Step

FIRST FLOOR

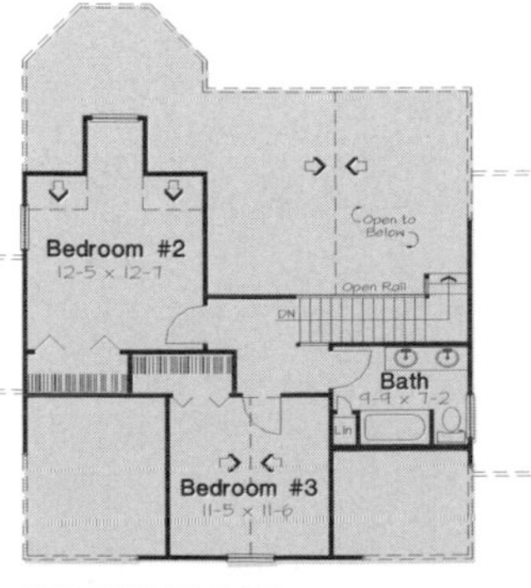

Bedroom #2
12-5 x 12-1
Open Rail
DN
Bath
Bedroom #3
11-5 x 11-6

SECOND FLOOR

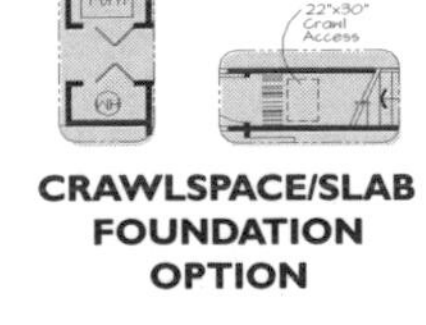

Furn

CRAWLSPACE/SLAB FOUNDATION OPTION

Country Details

Price Code: C

- This plan features:
- — Three bedrooms
- — Two full and one half baths
- Clapboard siding enhances the country appeal of this home
- The Dining Room with a tray ceiling is steps away from the Kitchen
- The Master Bedroom has a private Bath with a luxurious corner tub
- This home is designed with basement, slab, and crawlspace foundation options

FIRST FLOOR — 1,524 SQ. FT.
SECOND FLOOR — 506 SQ. FT.
BASEMENT — 1,403 SQ. FT.
GARAGE — 576 SQ. FT.

TOTAL LIVING AREA:
2,030 SQ. FT.

PLAN NO. 99142

Elegant Living

Price Code: F

- This plan features:
- — Three bedrooms
- — Two full and one half baths
- The spacious Great Room has a two-story ceiling, a fireplace and naturally illuminating rear windows
- The Den features built-in cabinetry located immediately off the Great Room
- The formal Dining Room located at the front of the house provides a quiet place for entertaining
- The first floor Laundry is located just off the three-car Garage
- The Master suite with generous windows to the rear, also has a private Bath
- This home is designed with a basement foundation

FIRST FLOOR — 1,408 SQ. FT.
SECOND FLOOR — 1,184 SQ. FT.
BASEMENT — 1,408 SQ. FT.

TOTAL LIVING AREA:
2,592 SQ. FT.

WIDTH 64'-0"
DEPTH 45'-0"

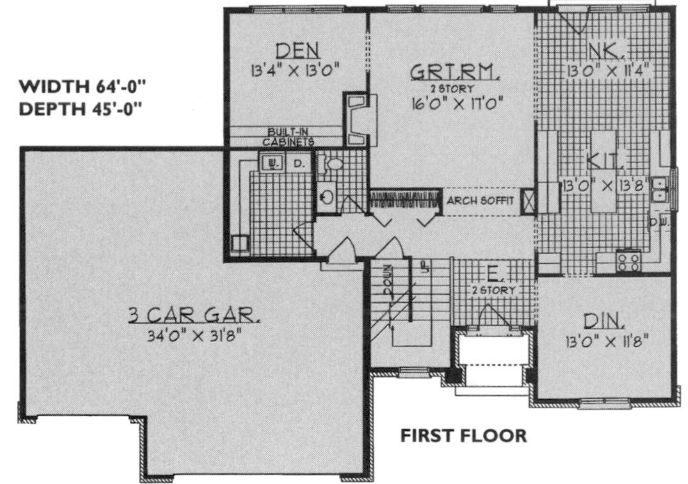
DEN
13'4" X 13'0"
GRT.RM.
2 STORY
16'0" X 17'0"
NK.
13'0" X 11'4"
BUILT-IN CABINETS
KIT.
13'0" X 13'8"
ARCH SOFFIT
3 CAR GAR.
34'0" X 31'8"
E.
2 STORY
DIN.
13'0" X 11'8"

FIRST FLOOR

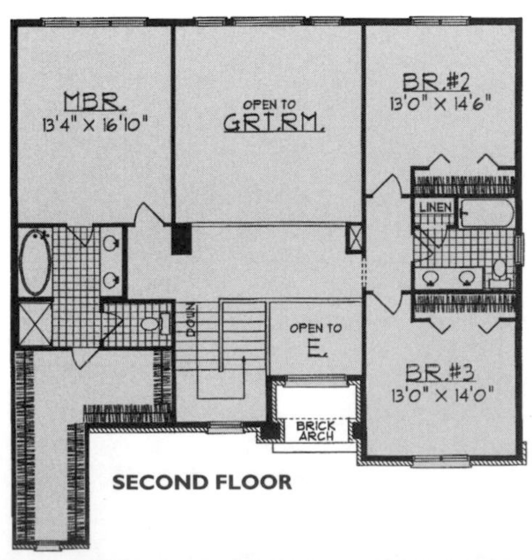
MBR.
13'4" X 16'10"
OPEN TO
GRT.RM.
BR.#2
13'0" X 14'6"
LINEN
OPEN TO
E.
BR.#3
13'0" X 14'0"
BRICK ARCH

SECOND FLOOR

PLAN NO. 32006

otography supplied by The Meredith Corporation

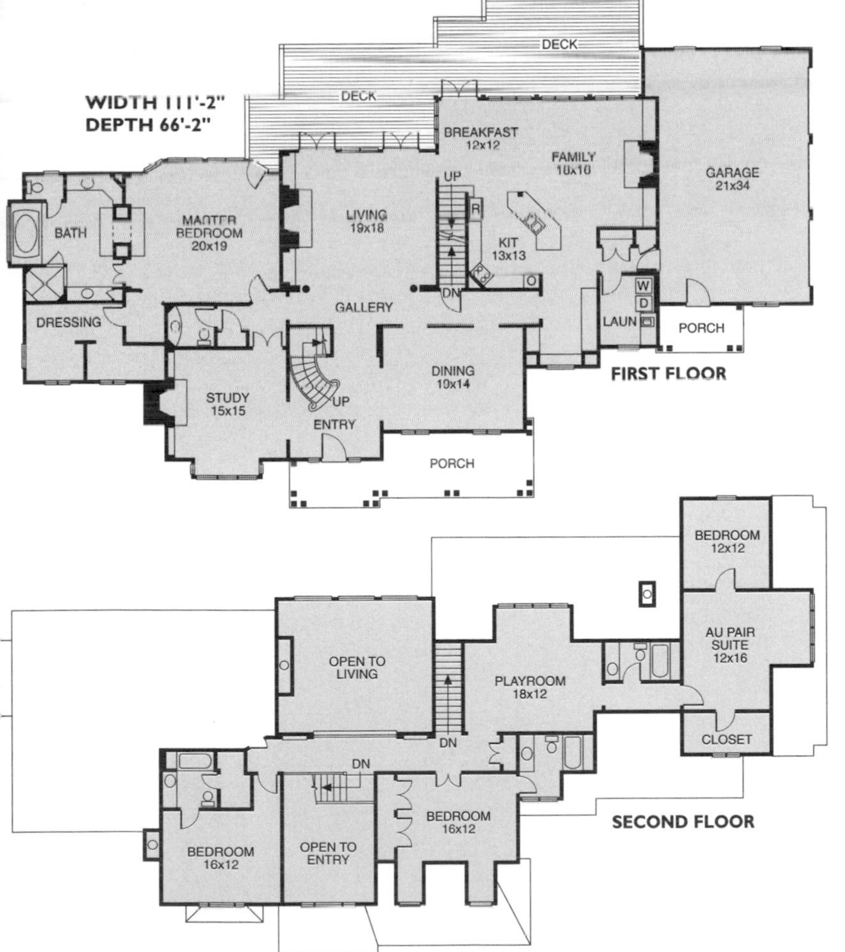

WIDTH 111'-2"
DEPTH 66'-2"
DECK
DECK
BREAKFAST 12x12
FAMILY 18x10
GARAGE 21x34
UP
MASTER BEDROOM 20x19
BATH
LIVING 19x18
R
KIT 13x13
DN
W
D
GALLERY
DRESSING
LAUN
PORCH
DINING 19x14
FIRST FLOOR
STUDY 15x15
UP
ENTRY
PORCH
BEDROOM 12x12
AU PAIR SUITE 12x16
OPEN TO LIVING
PLAYROOM 18x12
CLOSET
DN
DN
BEDROOM 16x12
SECOND FLOOR
BEDROOM 16x12
OPEN TO ENTRY

Country Manor

Price Code: L

- This plan features:
  - Four Bedrooms
  - Four full and one half baths
- Combined with the Study, Master Suite occupies entire wing of the first floor
- Living Room and Dining Room with adjacent locations for ease in entertaining
- Kitchen, Breakfast Nook and Family Room create large informal area
- Three Bedrooms, Au Pair Suite, three Baths and Playroom complete the second floor
- Second floor balcony connects the Bedroom wings and overlooks Living Room above Foyer
- This home is designed with a basement foundation

FIRST FLOOR — 3,322 SQ. FT.
SECOND FLOOR — 1,966 SQ. FT.

TOTAL LIVING AREA:
5,288 SQ. FT.

PLAN NO. 98458

Lasting Impression

Price Code: G

- This plan features:
- — Four bedrooms
- — Three full and one half baths
- The two-story Foyer is enhanced by a cascading staircase with an open rail
- The Living Room is topped by a 12-foot tray ceiling
- Double doors lead from the Dining Room to the covered Porch
- The Master Suite includes a Sitting Area and a five-piece Bath
- Three additional Bedrooms have access to a full Bath
- This home is designed with basement, slab and crawlspace foundation options

FIRST FLOOR — 2,044 SQ. FT.
SECOND FLOOR — 896 SQ. FT.

TOTAL LIVING AREA:
2,940 SQ. FT.

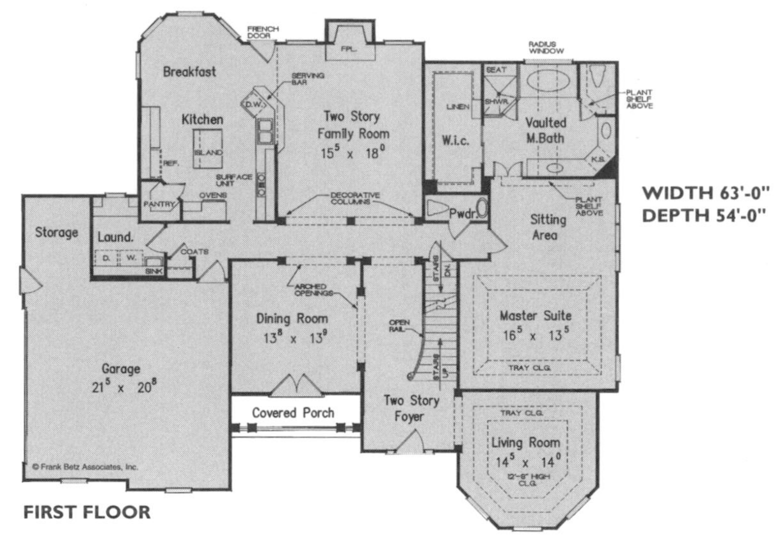

Breakfast
French Door
FPL.
Serving Bar
Kitchen
Island
Two Story Family Room
$15^{5} \times 18^{0}$
W.i.c.
Linen
Seat
Radius Window
Vaulted M.Bath
Plant Shelf Above
K.S.
Pantry
Ovens
Decorative Columns
Pwdr.
Sitting Area
Storage
Laund.
Coats
Dining Room
$13^{8} \times 13^{9}$
Arched Openings
Open Rail
Master Suite
$16^{5} \times 13^{5}$
Tray Clg.
Garage
$21^{5} \times 20^{8}$
Covered Porch
Two Story Foyer
Living Room
$14^{5} \times 14^{0}$
12'-8" High Clg.
© Frank Betz Associates, Inc.

WIDTH 63'-0"
DEPTH 54'-0"

FIRST FLOOR

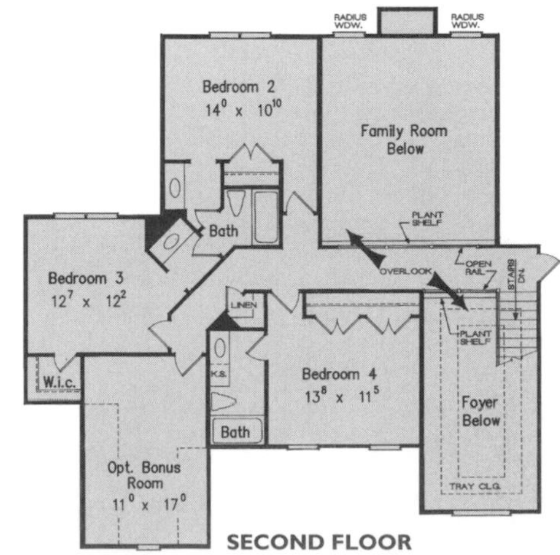

Radius Wdw.
Bedroom 2
$14^{0} \times 10^{10}$
Family Room Below
Plant Shelf
Bath
Bedroom 3
$12^{7} \times 12^{2}$
Overlook
Open Rail
Linen
Plant Shelf
Bedroom 4
$13^{8} \times 11^{5}$
W.i.c.
K.S.
Bath
Foyer Below
Opt. Bonus Room
$11^{0} \times 17^{0}$
Tray Clg.

SECOND FLOOR

PLAN NO. 92609

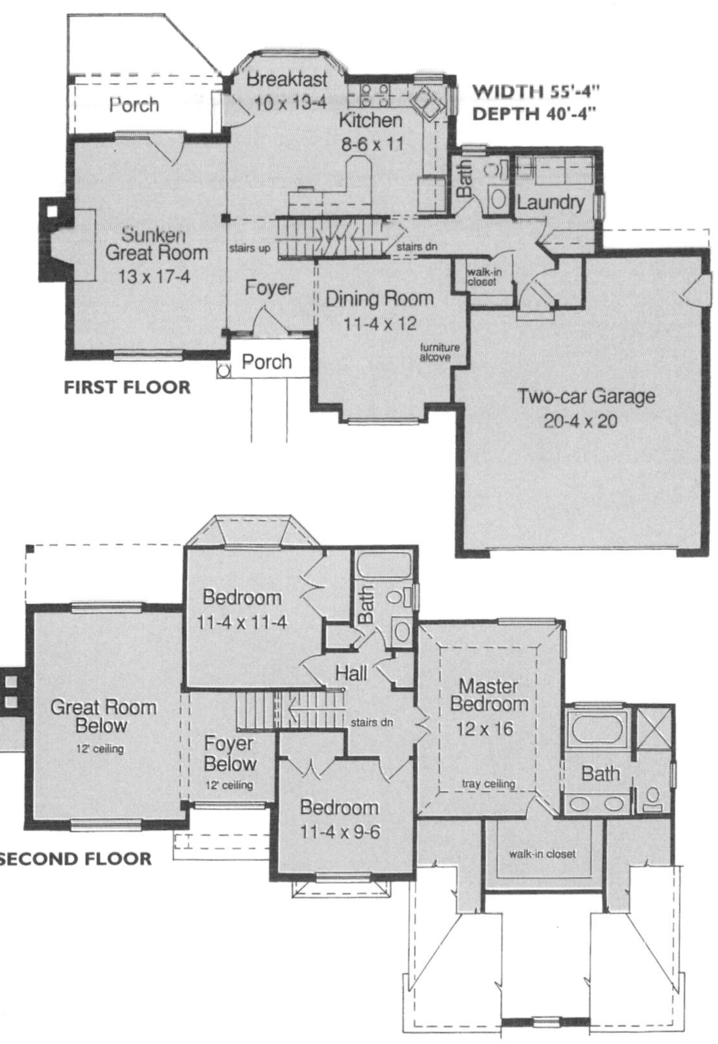

Porch
Breakfast
10 x 13-4
Kitchen
8-6 x 11
WIDTH 55'-4"
DEPTH 40'-4"
Bath
Laundry
Sunken
Great Room
13 x 17-4
stairs up
stairs dn
Foyer
walk-in closet
Dining Room
11-4 x 12
furniture alcove
Porch
FIRST FLOOR
Two-car Garage
20-4 x 20
Bedroom
11-4 x 11-4
Bath
Hall
Great Room
Below
12' ceiling
stairs dn
Master
Bedroom
12 x 16
Foyer
Below
12' ceiling
tray ceiling
Bath
Bedroom
11-4 x 9-6
walk-in closet
SECOND FLOOR

A Little Drama

Price Code: C

- This plan features:
  - — Three bedrooms
  - — Two full and one half baths
- A 12-foot-high Entry with transom and sidelights, multiple gables and a box window
- A sunken Great Room with a fireplace and access to a rear Porch
- A Breakfast Bay and Kitchen flowing into each other and a rear Porch
- A Master Bedroom with a tray ceiling, walk-in closet and a private Master Bath
- This home is designed with a basement foundation

FIRST FLOOR — 960 SQ. FT.
SECOND FLOOR — 808 SQ. FT.

TOTAL LIVING AREA:
1,768 SQ. FT.

PLAN NO. 24735

A Splendid Porch

Price Code: E

- This plan features:
- — Four bedrooms
- — Two full and one half baths
- A stylish front Porch enhances this attractive home
- Dual closets and an attractive staircase greet you upon entering
- There is a room devoted to a Home Office or a Media Center
- The Great Room is open to the Kitchen and they share a serving bar
- The Breakfast Nook overlooks the rear Deck
- This home is designed with basement, slab and crawlspace foundation options

FIRST FLOOR — 1,305 SQ. FT.
SECOND FLOOR — 1,121 SQ. FT.
BASEMENT — 1,194 SQ. FT.
GARAGE — 576 SQ. FT.

TOTAL LIVING AREA:
2,426 SQ. FT.

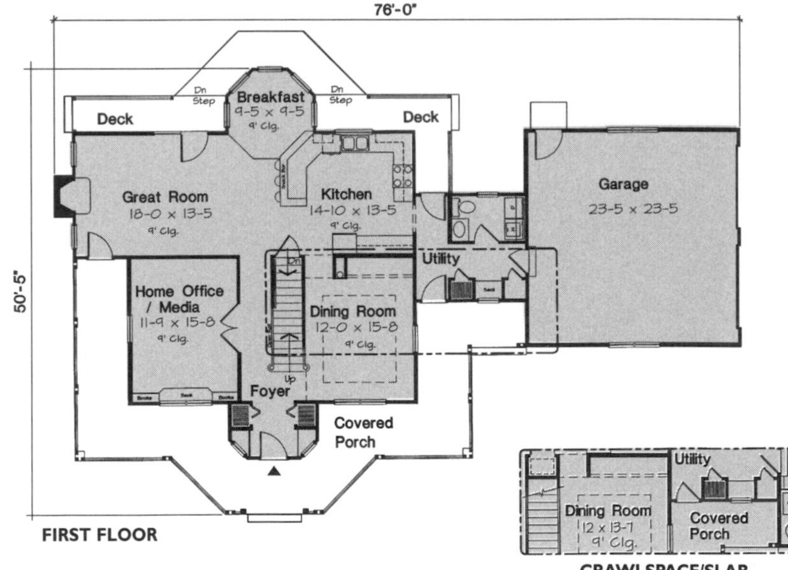

76'-0"
50'-5"
Deck
Dn Step
Breakfast
9-5 x 9-5
9' Clg.
Dn Step
Deck
Great Room
18-0 x 13-5
9' Clg.
Kitchen
14-10 x 13-5
9' Clg.
Garage
23-5 x 23-5
Utility
Home Office / Media
11-9 x 15-8
9' Clg.
Dining Room
12-0 x 15-8
9' Clg.
Foyer
Covered Porch
Utility
Dining Room
12 x 13-7
9' Clg.
Covered Porch

FIRST FLOOR

CRAWLSPACE/SLAB FOUNDATION OPTION

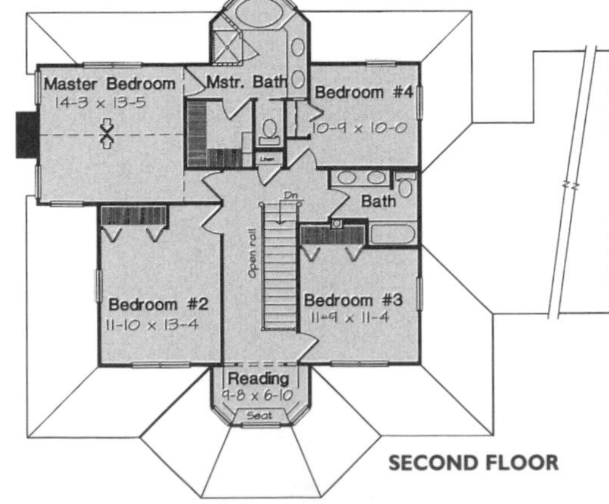

Master Bedroom
14-3 x 13-5
Mstr. Bath
Bedroom #4
10-9 x 10-0
Bath
Dn
Open rail
Bedroom #2
11-10 x 13-4
Bedroom #3
11-9 x 11-4
Reading
9-8 x 6-10
Seat

SECOND FLOOR

PLAN NO. 99062

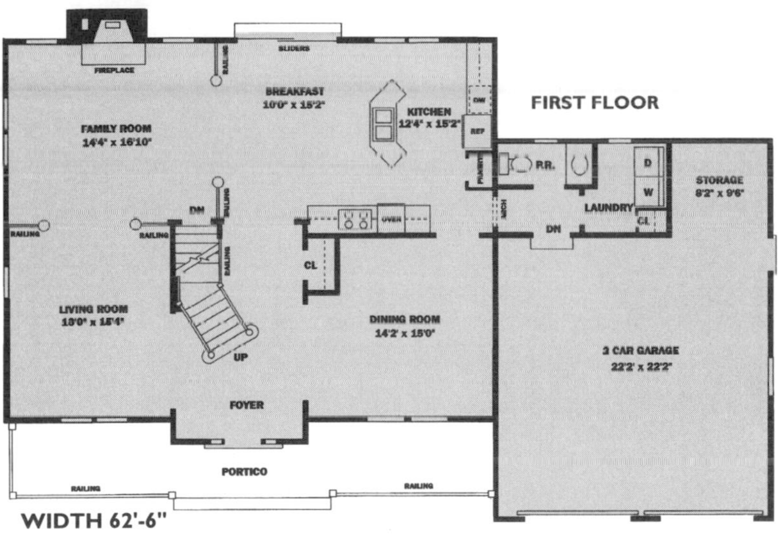
FIREPLACE
SLIDERS
BREAKFAST
10'0" x 15'2"
KITCHEN
12'4" x 15'2"
FAMILY ROOM
14'4" x 16'10"
FIRST FLOOR
STORAGE
8'2" x 9'6"
LAUNDRY
LIVING ROOM
13'0" x 15'4"
DINING ROOM
14'2" x 15'0"
2 CAR GARAGE
22'2" x 22'2"
FOYER
PORTICO
WIDTH 62'-6"
DEPTH 38'-6"

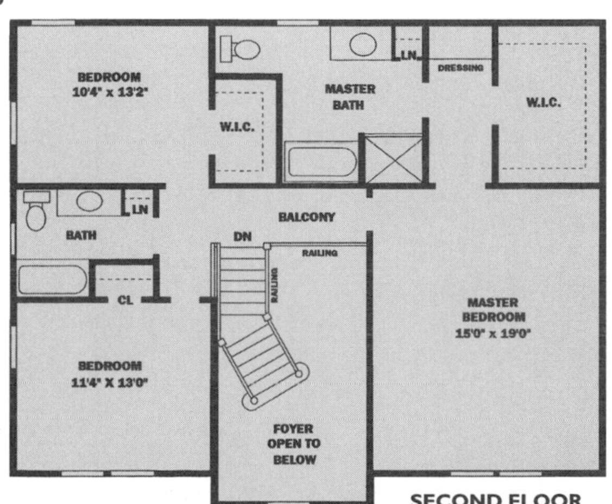
BEDROOM
10'4" x 13'2"
MASTER
BATH
DRESSING
W.I.C.
W.I.C.
BALCONY
BATH
MASTER
BEDROOM
15'0" x 19'0"
BEDROOM
11'4" X 13'0"
FOYER
OPEN TO
BELOW

SECOND FLOOR

Cascading Gable Roofs

Price Code: E

- This plan features:
- — Three bedrooms
- — Two full and one half baths
- A well designed exterior with clean lines, cascading gable roofs, covered Porch and clap board siding
- An open floor plan on the first floor for a feeling of more space
- Wood columns define the Living Room from the Family Room and the Family Room form the Breakfast Room
- The Kitchen has an angled island and abundant counter space
- This home is designed with a basement foundation

FIRST FLOOR — 1,354 SQ. FT.
SECOND FLOOR — 1,072 SQ. FT.
BASEMENT — 1,354 SQ. FT.

TOTAL LIVING AREA:

2,426 SQ. FT.

PLAN NO. 92535

Rewards of Success

Price Code: G

- This plan features:
- — Four bedrooms
- — Three full and one half baths
- An open Foyer flanked by formal areas, left to the Dining Room, right to the Living Room
- An expansive Den with a large fireplace with a flat tiled hearth warming the room
- Built-in cabinets and shelves providing an added convenience in the Den
- A well-appointed Kitchen serving the formal Dining Room and the informal Kitchen with equal ease and providing a snack bar for meals on the run
- A Master Bedroom with a lavish Bath and a walk-in closet
- This home is designed with crawlspace and slab foundation options

FIRST FLOOR — 2,019 SQ. FT.
SECOND FLOOR — 946 SQ. FT.
GARAGE — 577 SQ. FT.

TOTAL LIVING AREA:
2,965 SQ. FT.

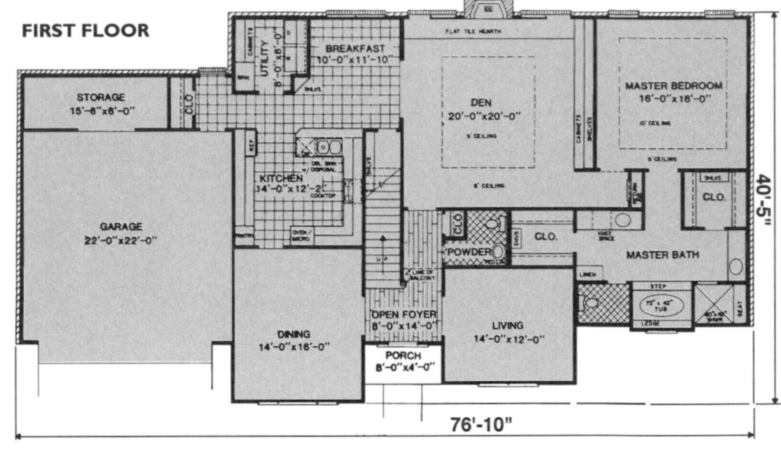
FIRST FLOOR
BREAKFAST 10'-0"x11'-10"
UTILITY 8'-0"x6'-0"
STORAGE 15'-6"x6'-0"
CLO.
DEN 20'-0"x20'-0"
MASTER BEDROOM 16'-0"x16'-0"
KITCHEN 14'-0"x12'-2"
GARAGE 22'-0"x22'-0"
CLO.
POWDER
MASTER BATH
OPEN FOYER 8'-0"x14'-0"
DINING 14'-0"x16'-0"
LIVING 14'-0"x12'-0"
PORCH 8'-0"x4'-0"
40'-5"
76'-10"

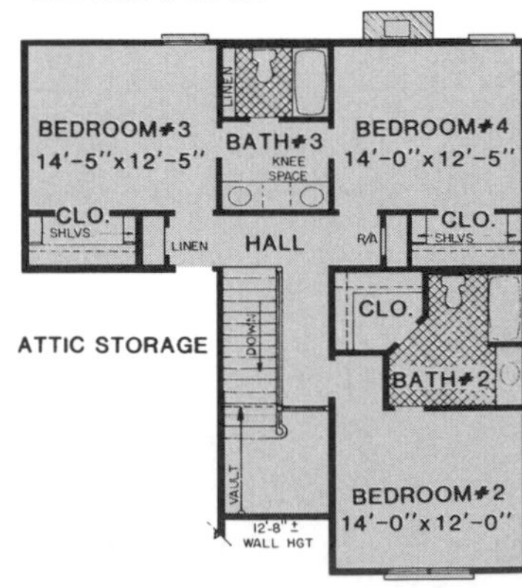
SECOND FLOOR
BEDROOM#3 14'-5"x12'-5"
BATH#3
BEDROOM#4 14'-0"x12'-5"
CLO.
HALL
CLO.
LINEN
ATTIC STORAGE
CLO.
BATH#2
BEDROOM#2 14'-0"x12'-0"
12'-8" ± WALL HGT

PLAN NO. 34601

Rear Elevation

Country Touch

Price Code: A

- This plan features:
  - — Three bedrooms
  - — Two full baths
- A Country-styled front Porch
- Vaulted ceiling in the Living Room which includes a fireplace
- An efficient Kitchen with double sinks and peninsula counter that may double as an eating bar
- Two first floor Bedrooms with ample closet space
- A second floor Master Suite with sloped ceiling, walk-in closet and private Master Bath
- This home is designed with basement, slab and crawlspace foundation options

FIRST FLOOR — 1,007 SQ. FT.
SECOND FLOOR — 408 SQ. FT.

TOTAL LIVING AREA:
1,415 SQ. FT.

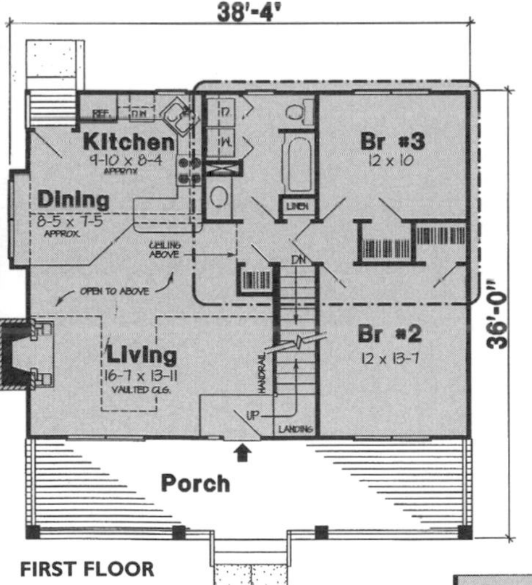

38'-4"
36'-0"
Kitchen
9-10 x 8-4
Dining
8-5 x 7-5
Br #3
12 x 10
Br #2
12 x 13-7
Living
16-7 x 13-11
VAULTED CLG.
Porch

FIRST FLOOR

CRAWLSPACE/SLAB FOUNDATION OPTION

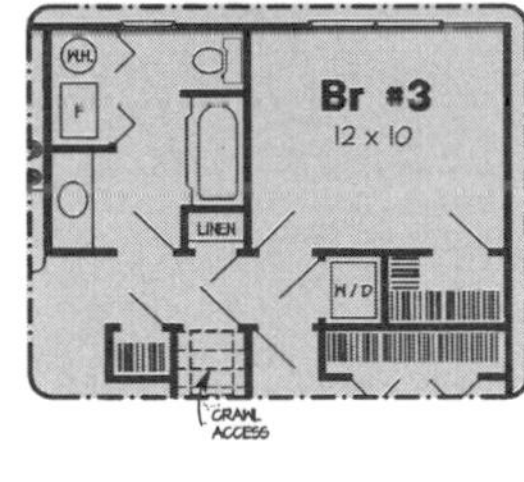

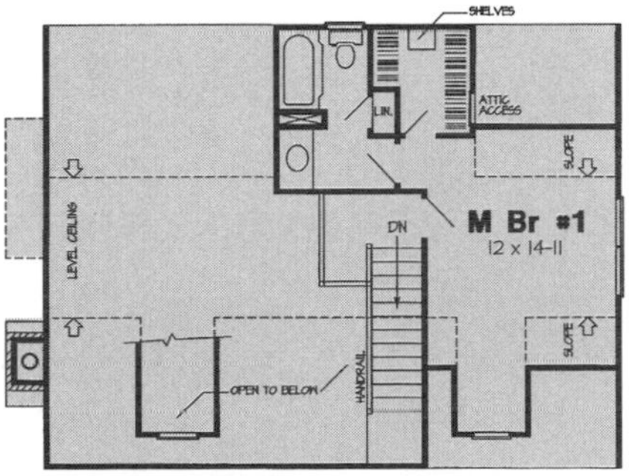

Br #3
12 x 10

M Br #1
12 x 14-11

SECOND FLOOR

PLAN NO. 24748

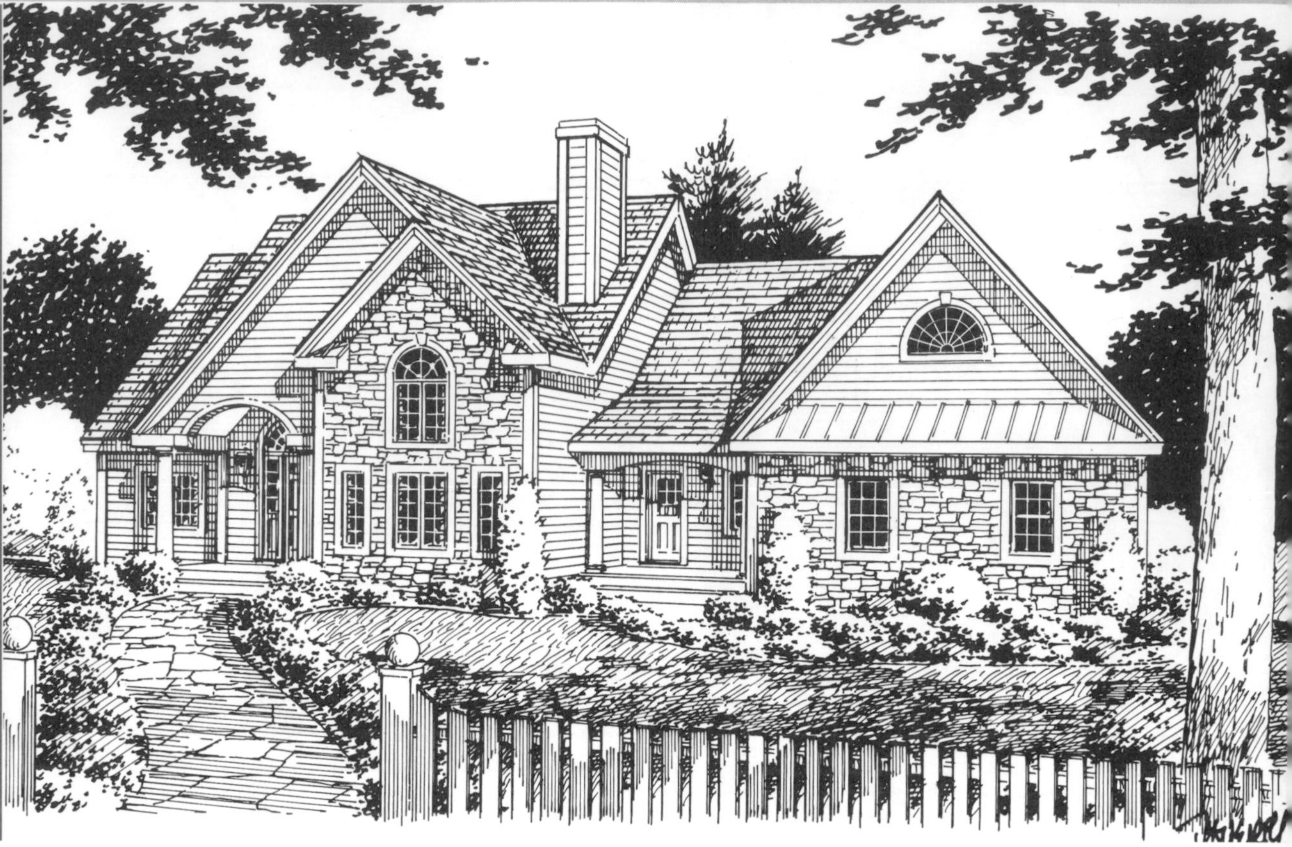

Awesome Artistry

Price Code: C

- This plan features:
- — Three bedrooms
- — Two full and one half baths
- Stone and wood, combined with decorative arched windows and multiple gables
- The Great Room features decorative windows letting in plenty of natural light, a focal point fireplace, and columns gracing each of its entrances
- Columns also adorn the entrance to the formal Dining Room, which has a wall of windows and a view of the rear Deck
- This home is designed with basement, slab and crawlspace foundation options

MAIN FLOOR — 2,161 SQ. FT.
BASEMENT — 2,161 SQ. FT.
GARAGE — 590 SQ. FT.

TOTAL LIVING AREA:
2,161 SQ. FT.

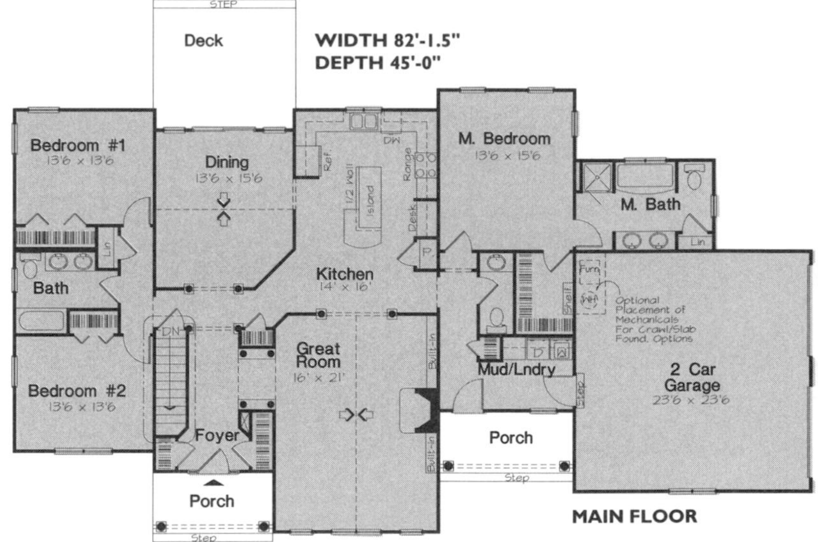

Step
Deck
WIDTH 82'-1.5"
DEPTH 45'-0"
Bedroom #1
13'6 x 13'6
Dining
13'6 x 15'6
Kitchen
14' x 16'
M. Bedroom
13'6 x 15'6
M. Bath
Bath
Great Room
16' x 21'
Bedroom #2
13'6 x 13'6
Foyer
Porch
Mud/Lndry
2 Car Garage
23'6 x 23'6
Porch
Step
MAIN FLOOR

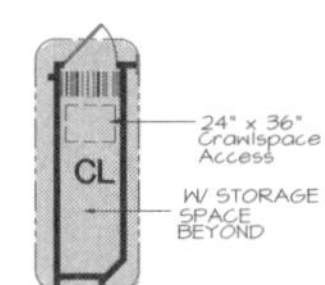

CL
24" x 36" Crawlspace Access
W/ STORAGE SPACE BEYOND

CRAWLSPACE/SLAB FOUNDATION OPTION

PLAN NO. 99443

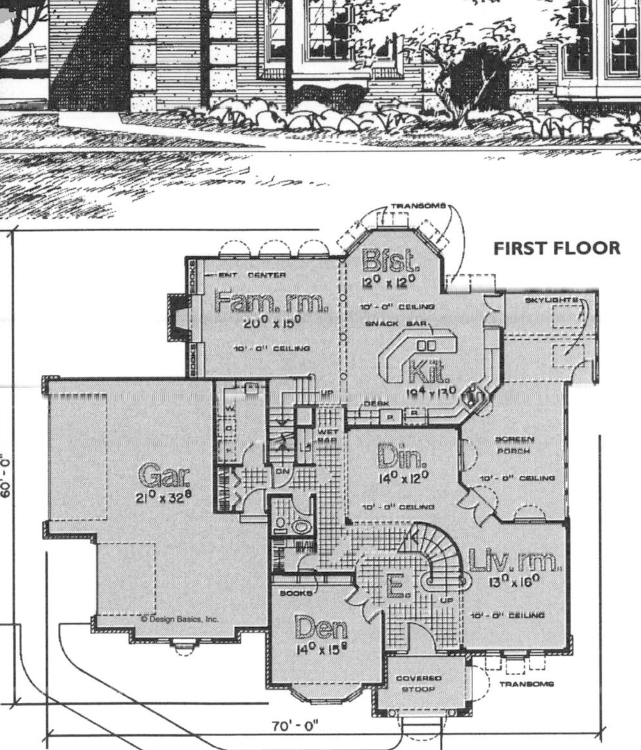
FIRST FLOOR
TRANSOMS
Bfst.
12^{0} x 12^{0}
ENT. CENTER
Fam. rm.
20^{0} x 15^{0}
10'-0" CEILING
10'-0" CEILING
SNACK BAR
SKYLIGHTS
Kit.
19^{4} x 13^{0}
DESK
WET BAR
UP
DN
Gar.
21^{0} x 32^{8}
Din.
14^{0} x 12^{0}
10'-0" CEILING
SCREEN PORCH
10'-0" CEILING
Liv. rm.
13^{0} x 16^{0}
10'-0" CEILING
E.
UP
BOOKS
Den
14^{0} x 15^{8}
COVERED STOOP
TRANSOMS
© Design Basics, Inc.
60'-0"
70'-0"

SECOND FLOOR

Grandeur Within

Price Code: K

- This plan features:
- — Four bedrooms
- — Two full, one three-quarter, and one half baths
- The Living and Dining Rooms both have 10-foot ceilings and access a Screen Porch
- The Family Room, Nook, and Kitchen contain all of the amenities that you expect
- The upstairs Master Suite has built-ins, a Sitting Area, and a wonderful Bath
- This home is designed with a basement foundation
- Alternate foundation options available at an additional charge. Please call 1-800-235-5700 for more information.

FIRST FLOOR — 1,923 SQ. FT.
SECOND FLOOR — 1,852 SQ. FT.
BASEMENT — 1,923 SQ. FT.
GARAGE — 726 SQ. FT.

TOTAL LIVING AREA:
3,775 SQ. FT.

PLAN NO. 24749

Volume Ceilings Add to Detail

Price Code: D

- This plan features:
  - — Three bedrooms
  - — Two full baths
- The Foyer welcomes family and friends directly into the formal Dining Room or the Great Room
- A tray ceiling, Bath with garden tub, and walk-in closet with shelves make an impressive Master Suite
- Windows line the Breakfast Area, offering a sunlit way to enjoy a meal
- A volume ceiling and window seat in a Secondary Bedroom make it a great retreat
- This home is designed with basement, slab, and crawlspace foundation options

MAIN FLOOR — 2,219 SQ. FT.
BASEMENT — 2,219 SQ. FT.
GARAGE — 671 SQ. FT.
PORCH — 120 SQ. FT.

TOTAL LIVING AREA:
2,219 SQ. FT.

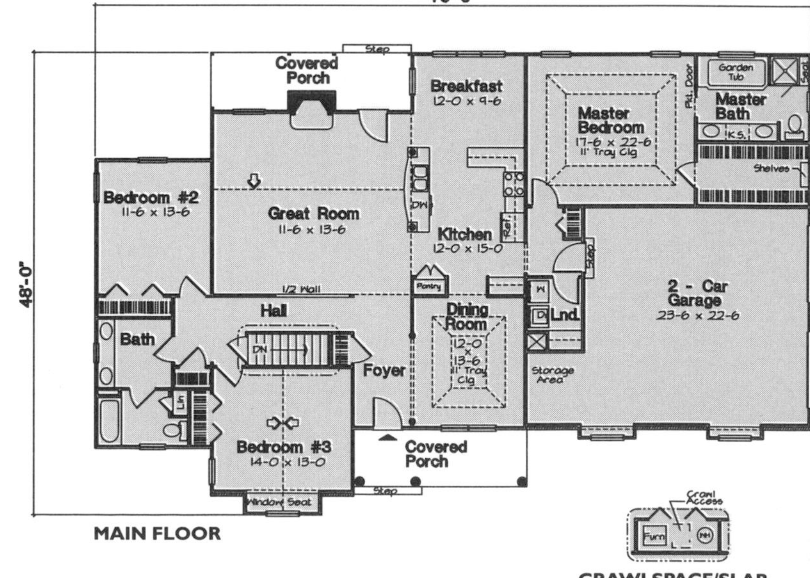

75'-0"
48'-0"
Covered Porch
Breakfast
12-0 x 9-6
Master Bedroom
17-6 x 22-6
11' Tray Clg
Garden Tub
Master Bath
Shelves
Bedroom #2
11-6 x 13-6
Great Room
11-6 x 13-6
Kitchen
12-0 x 15-0
Pantry
1/2 Wall
Hall
Dining Room
12-0 x 13-6
11' Tray Clg
Lnd.
2 - Car Garage
23-6 x 22-6
Bath
Foyer
Storage Area
Bedroom #3
14-0 x 13-0
Covered Porch
Window Seat
Step
MAIN FLOOR
Crawl Access
Furn
CRAWLSPACE/SLAB FOUNDATION OPTION

PLAN NO. 24654

Rear Elevation

Master Br
18-0 x 11-11
Br 2
11-8 x 10-8
Br 3
11-4 x 10-7
SECOND FLOOR

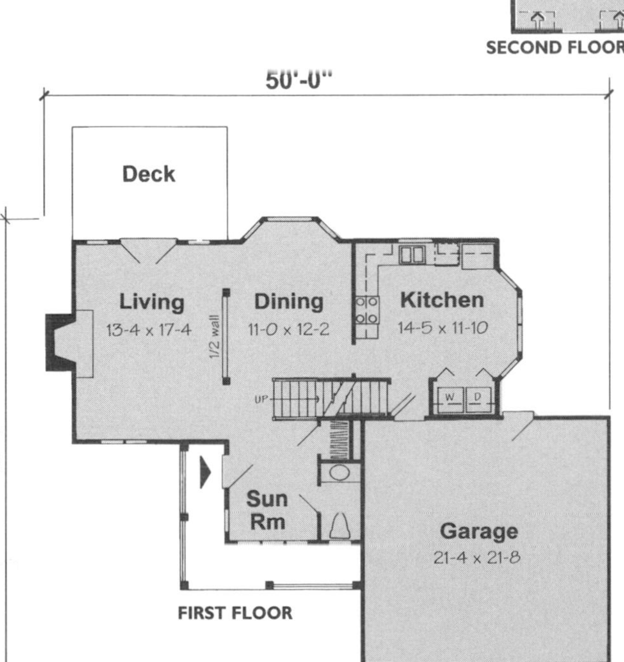
50'-0"
40'-0"
Deck
Living
13-4 x 17-4
1/2 wall
Dining
11-0 x 12-2
Kitchen
14-5 x 11-10
UP
W D
Sun
Rm
Garage
21-4 x 21-8
FIRST FLOOR

Country Influence

Price Code: B

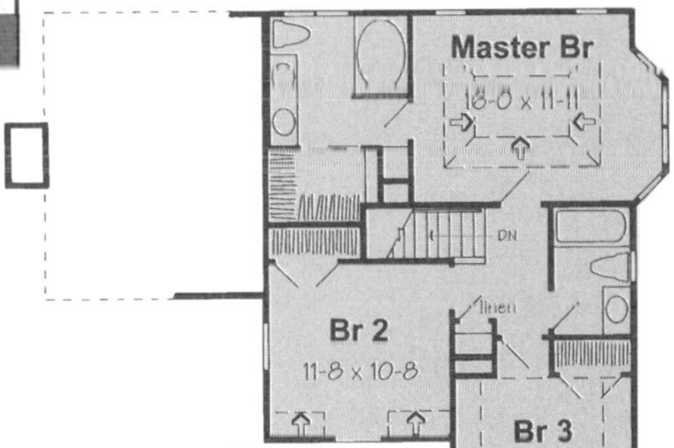

- This plan features:
  - Three bedrooms
  - Two full and one half baths
- Open Living Room enhanced by arch-top window, focal point fireplace and atrium door to Deck
- Bay window brightens formal Dining Room conveniently located between Living Room and Kitchen
- Efficient L-shaped Kitchen with bay window eating area, laundry closet and handy Garage entrance
- Plush Master Bedroom offers another bay window crowned by tray ceiling and private Bath with double vanity
- This home is designed with basement, slab, and crawlspace foundation options

FIRST FLOOR — 806 SQ. FT.
SECOND FLOOR — 748 SQ. FT.
GARAGE — 467 SQ. FT.

TOTAL LIVING AREA:
1,554 SQ. FT.

PLAN NO. 91514

Streaming Natural Light

Price Code: B

- This plan features:
- — Three bedrooms
- — Two full and one half baths
- An outstanding, two-story Great Room with an unusual floor-to-ceiling, corner front window and a cozy, hearth fireplace
- A formal Dining Room opening from the Great Room makes entertaining easy
- An efficient Kitchen, with a work island, Pantry, a corner double sink, opening to the Great Room, and a bright bay window Nook
- A quiet Master Suite with a vaulted ceiling and a plush Bath with double vanity, spa tub, and walk-in closet
- This home is designed with a crawlspace foundation

FIRST FLOOR — 1,230 SQ. FT.
SECOND FLOOR — 477 SQ. FT.
BONUS — 195 SQ. FT.

TOTAL LIVING AREA:
1,707 SQ. FT.

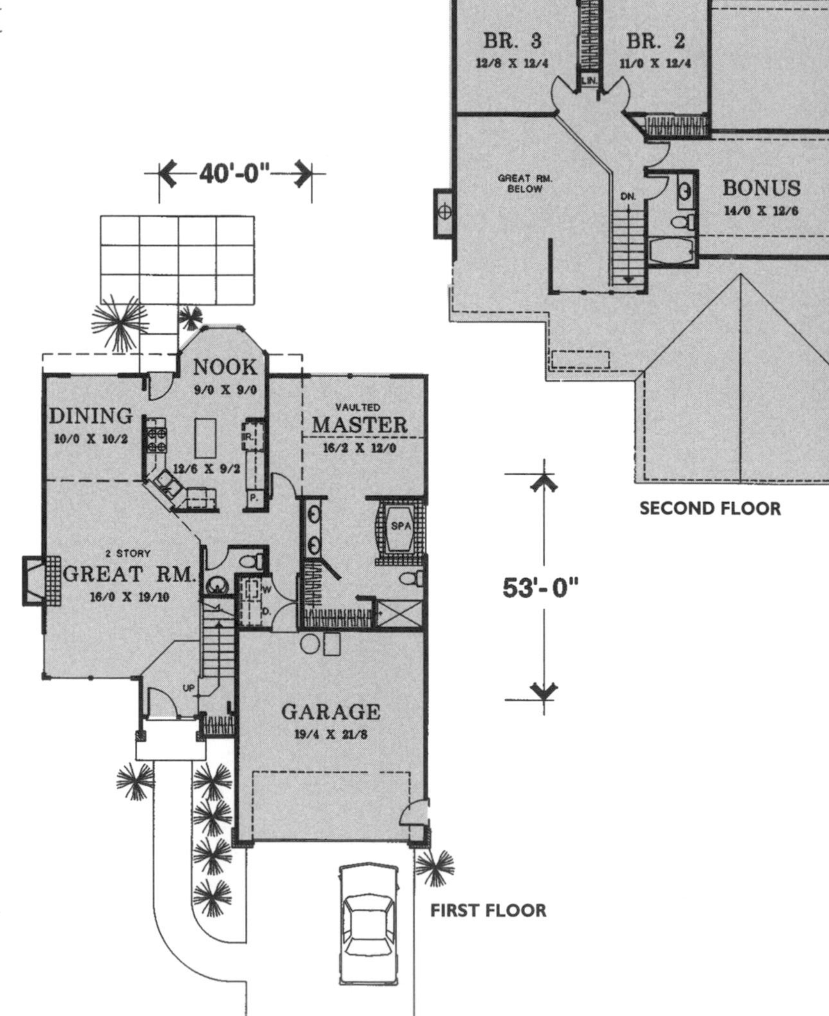

BR. 3
12/8 X 12/4
BR. 2
11/0 X 12/4
GREAT RM. BELOW
DN.
BONUS
14/0 X 12/6
SECOND FLOOR
40'-0"
NOOK
9/0 X 9/0
DINING
10/0 X 10/2
12/6 X 9/2
VAULTED
MASTER
16/2 X 12/0
SPA
2 STORY
GREAT RM.
16/0 X 19/10
UP
53'-0"
GARAGE
19/4 X 21/8
FIRST FLOOR

PLAN NO. 97403

Fam. rm.
18^8 x 15^0
Bfst.
11^0 x 13^0
Kit.
10^0 x 14^0
Din.
12^0 x 14^3
Liv. rm.
13^0 x 15^0
12'-0" CEILING
Gar.
32^0 x 23^4
Den
11^0 x 13^4
COVERED STOOP
TRANSOMS
FIRST FLOOR
WIDTH 65'-4"
DEPTH 50'-0"

Striking Brick Detailing

Price Code: H

- This plan features:
  - — Four bedrooms
  - — Two full, one three-quarter, and one half baths
- The formal Living Room has oak flooring and a 12-foot high ceiling
- There is a decorative ceiling and hutch space in the formal Dining Room
- The gourmet Kitchen includes a central island, a roomy Pantry and a lazy susan
- The comfortable Family Room is enhanced by a brick fireplace
- The Master Suite contains a vaulted ceiling and a built-in Kitchenette
- This home is designed with a basement foundation

FIRST FLOOR — 1,561 SQ. FT.
SECOND FLOOR — 1,458 SQ. FT.
BONUS ROOM — 160 SQ. FT.
BASEMENT — 1,561 SQ. FT.
GARAGE — 748 SQ. FT.

Mbr.
18^8 x 16^0
10'-0" CEILING
Br. 4
12^7 x 12^0
Br. 3
12^0 x 13^7
WHIRLPOOL
KITCHEN-ETTE
Br. 2
11^0 x 13^4
10'-0" CLG.
OPEN TO BELOW
UNFINISHED BONUS ROOM
8^4 x 15^0
SECOND FLOOR

TOTAL LIVING AREA:
3,019 SQ. FT.

PLAN NO. 24750

Future Space Included

Price Code: E

- This plan features:
- — Three bedrooms
- — Two full and one half baths
- A Bonus room over the Garage can be converted to an In-law Suite or Playroom
- The Dining Room with tray ceiling is open to the Foyer
- A Breakfast Area in the Kitchen faces the fireplace in the Great Room
- This home is designed with basement, slab, and crawlspace foundation options

MAIN FLOOR — 2,487 SQ. FT.
BONUS ROOM — 863 SQ. FT.
BASEMENT — 2,487 SQ. FT.
GARAGE — 582 SQ. FT.

TOTAL LIVING AREA:
2,487 SQ. FT.

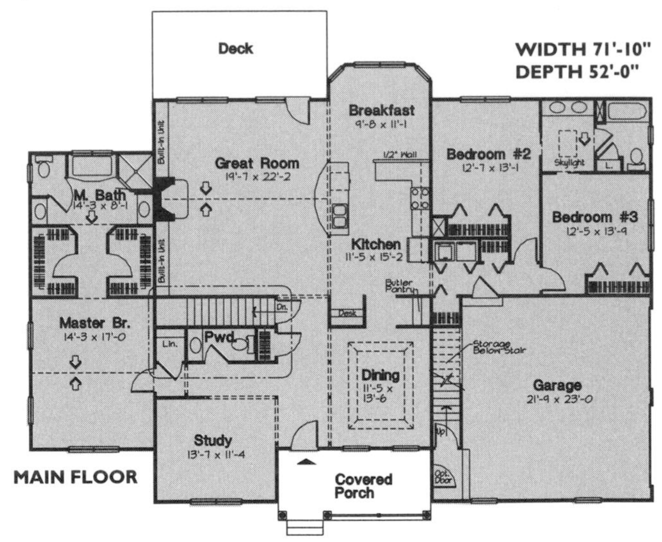

Deck
WIDTH 71'-10"
DEPTH 52'-0"
Breakfast 9'-8 x 11'-1
Great Room 14'-7 x 22'-2
Bedroom #2 12'-7 x 13'-1
M. Bath 14'-3 x 8'-1
Bedroom #3 12'-5 x 13'-9
Kitchen 11'-5 x 15'-2
Master Br. 14'-3 x 17'-0
Pwd.
Dining 11'-5 x 13'-6
Garage 21'-4 x 23'-0
Study 13'-7 x 11'-4
Covered Porch

MAIN FLOOR

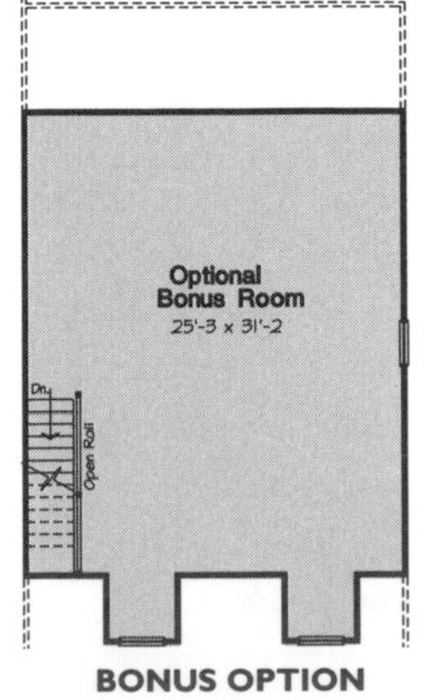

Optional Bonus Room 25'-3 x 31'-2

BONUS OPTION

Pwd.

CRAWLSPACE/SLAB FOUNDATION OPTION

PLAN NO. 99438

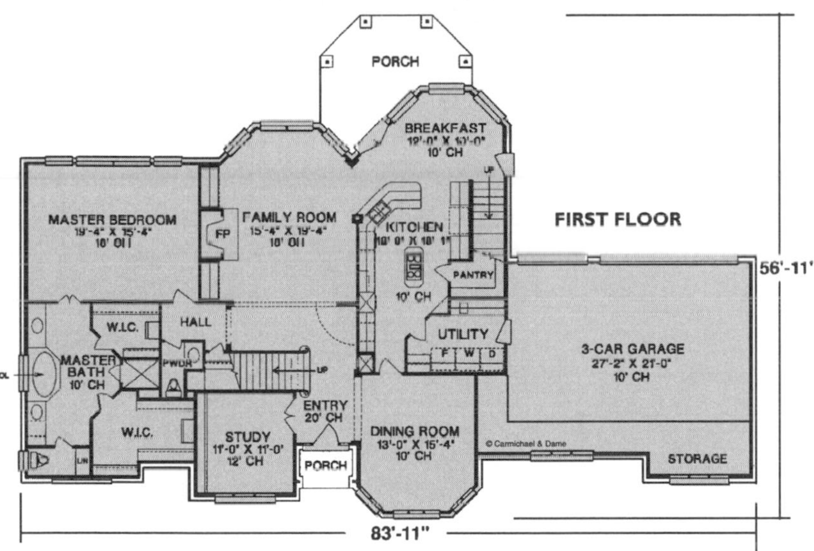

PORCH
BREAKFAST
10' CH
MASTER BEDROOM
FAMILY ROOM
18' CH
FP
KITCHEN
10' CH
PANTRY
FIRST FLOOR
56'-11"
HALL
W.I.C.
UTILITY
MASTER BATH
10' CH
PWDR
UP
3-CAR GARAGE
27'-2" X 21'-0"
10' CH
ENTRY
20' CH
W.I.C.
STUDY
11'-0" X 11'-0"
12' CH
PORCH
DINING ROOM
13'-0" X 15'-4"
10' CH
STORAGE
83'-11"

OPTIONAL BASEMENT ACCESS

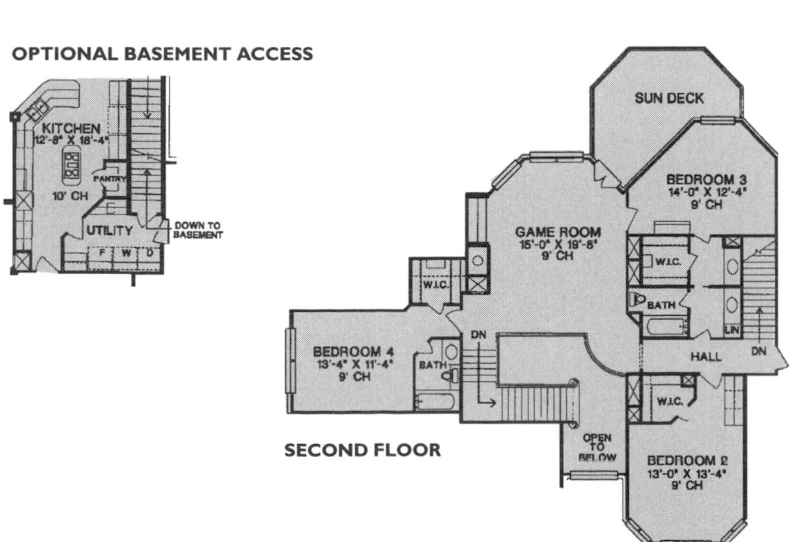

KITCHEN
10' CH
PANTRY
UTILITY
DOWN TO BASEMENT
SUN DECK
BEDROOM 3
14'-0" X 12'-4"
9' CH
GAME ROOM
15'-0" X 19'-8"
9' CH
W.I.C.
BATH
BEDROOM 4
13'-4" X 11'-4"
9' CH
DN
HALL
OPEN TO BELOW
BEDROOM 2
13'-0" X 13'-4"
9' CH
SECOND FLOOR

Eye Catching Tower

Price Code: I

- This plan features:
  - — Four bedrooms
  - — Three full and one half baths
- Study with high ceiling and windows
- Family Room with fireplace is open to the Breakfast Bay and gourmet Kitchen
- First floor Master Bedrooms spans the width of the home and contains every luxury imaginable
- This plan has a three-car Garage with Storage Space
- This home is designed with basement and slab foundation options
- Alternate foundation options available at an additional charge. Please call 1-800-235-5700 for more information.

FIRST FLOOR — 2,117 SQ. FT.
SECOND FLOOR — 1,206 SQ. FT.
GARAGE — 685 SQ. FT.

TOTAL LIVING AREA:
3,323 SQ. FT

PLAN NO. 24751

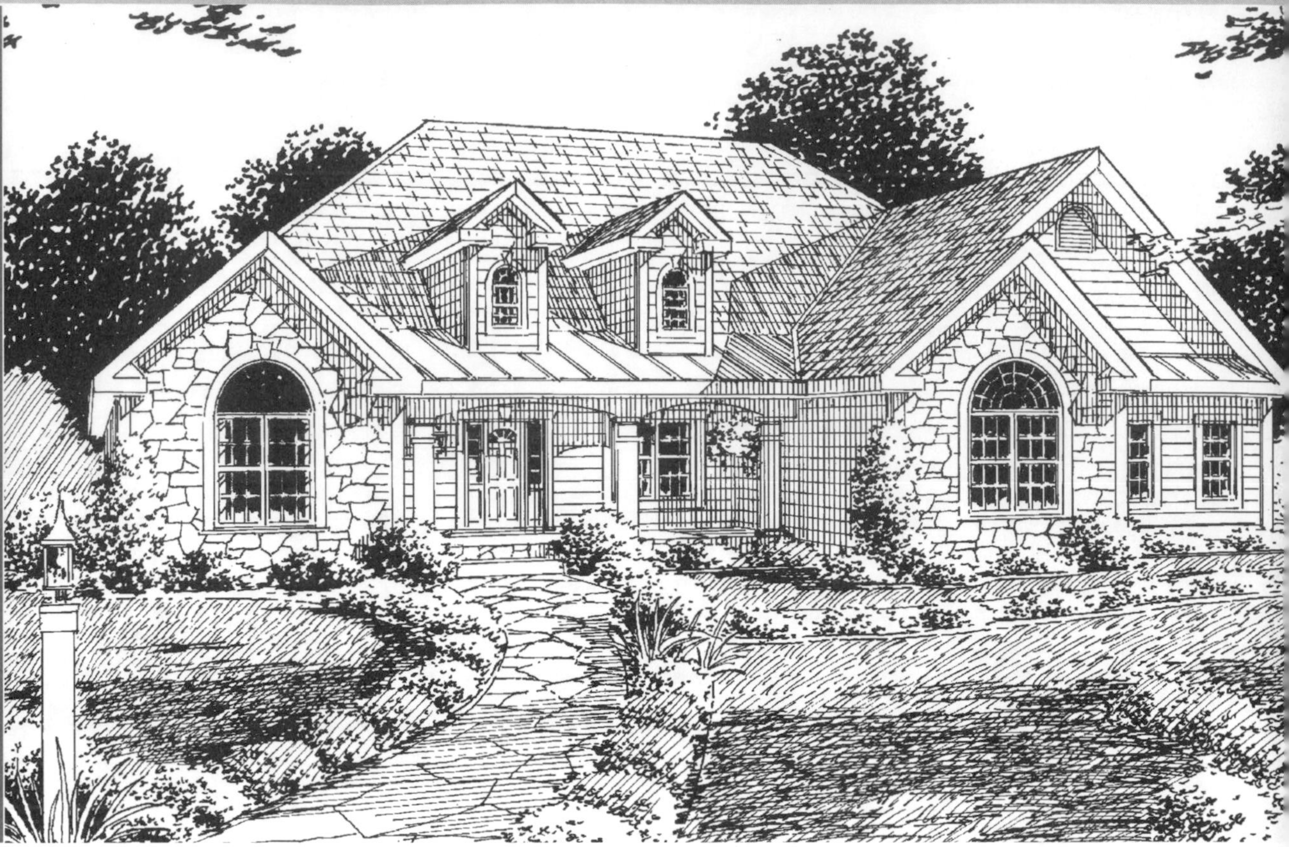

A Grand Plan

Price Code: D

- This plan features:
- — Three bedrooms
- — Two full baths
- The Kitchen includes ample storage and work space, and offers easy access to the Breakfast Nook and the formal Dining Room
- The Breakfast Nook has sliding doors leading to the rear yard
- The Master Suite is in one corner of the house, offering a private retreat when needed
- This home is designed with basement, slab, and crawlspace foundation options

MAIN FLOOR — 2,172 SQ. FT.
BASEMENT — 2,172 SQ. FT.
GARAGE — 623 SQ. FT.

TOTAL LIVING AREA:
2,172 SQ. FT.

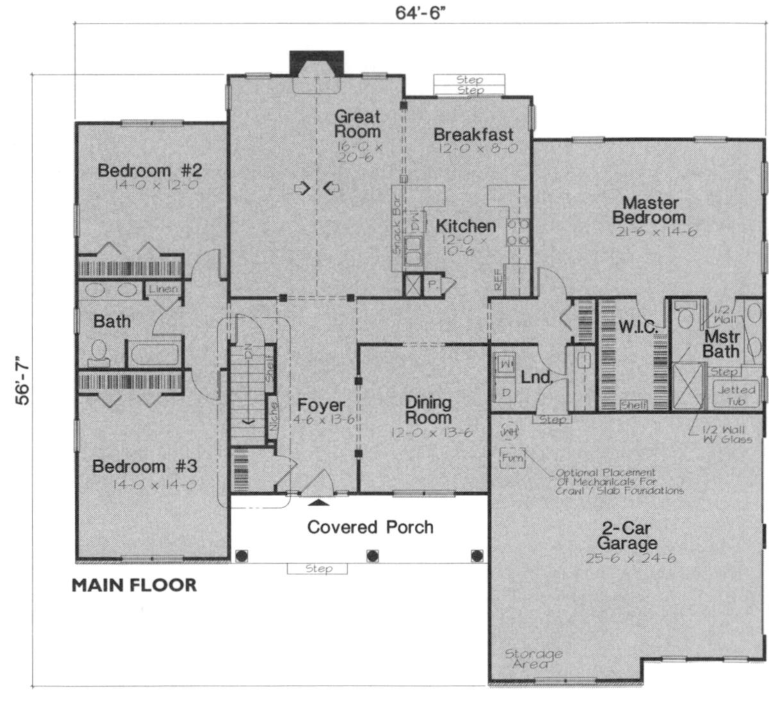
64'-6"
56'-7"
Great Room
16-0 x 20-6
Breakfast
12-0 x 8-0
Step
Bedroom #2
14-0 x 12-0
Kitchen
12-0 x 10-6
Master Bedroom
21-6 x 14-6
Linen
Bath
W.I.C.
Mstr Bath
Lnd.
Foyer
4-6 x 13-6
Dining Room
12-0 x 13-6
Jetted Tub
1/2 Wall W/ Glass
Bedroom #3
14-0 x 14-0
Optional Placement Of Mechanicals For Crawl / Slab Foundations
Covered Porch
2-Car Garage
25-6 x 24-6
MAIN FLOOR
Storage Area

OPTION

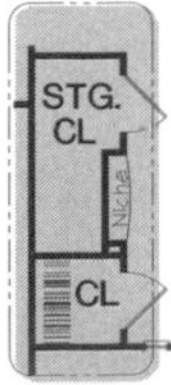
STG. CL
Niche
CL

PLAN NO. 32046

...aphy supplied by The Meredith Corporation

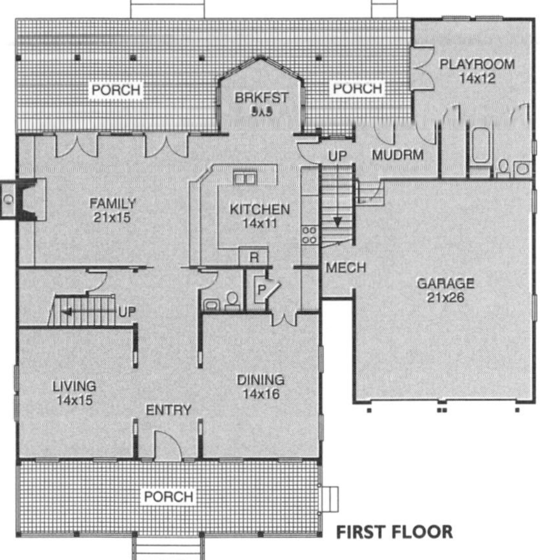

PORCH
BRKFST
PORCH
PLAYROOM
14x12
UP
MUDRM
FAMILY
21x15
KITCHEN
14x11
R
P
MECH
GARAGE
21x26
UP
LIVING
14x15
ENTRY
DINING
14x16
PORCH
FIRST FLOOR

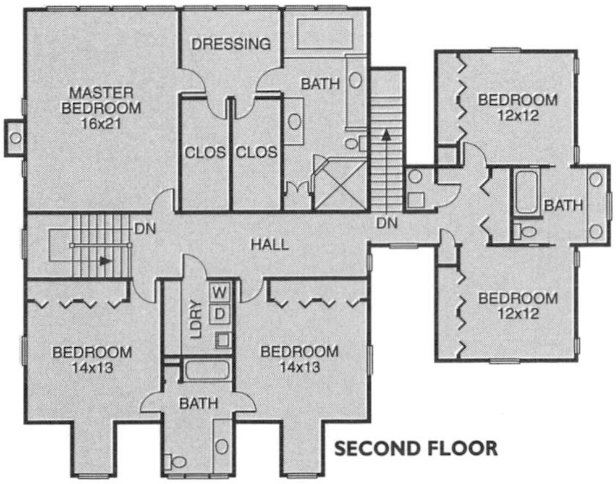

WIDTH 64'-0"
DEPTH 65'-0"

DRESSING
MASTER BEDROOM
16x21
BATH
CLOS
CLOS
BEDROOM
12x12
BATH
DN
HALL
DN
W
D
LDRY
BEDROOM
14x13
BEDROOM
14x13
BEDROOM
12x12
BATH
SECOND FLOOR

Luxurious Country

Price Code: L

- This plan features:
- — Five bedrooms
- — Four full and one half baths
- A welcoming front Porch adds style to this luxurious Country home
- The Living Room and the Dining Room are located in the front of the home
- The Family Room in the rear has a fireplace and doors to the rear Porch
- A Playroom is located behind the Garage for the kids
- The Kitchen is designed in a convenient U-shape
- Upstairs find the Master Bedroom which comprises half of the space
- This home is designed with a crawlspace foundation

FIRST FLOOR — 1,928 SQ. FT.
SECOND FLOOR — 2,364 SQ. FT.
GARAGE — 578 SQ. FT.

TOTAL LIVING AREA:
4,292 SQ. FT.

PLAN NO. 24403

Touch of Country

Price Code: F

- This plan features:
  - — Three bedrooms
  - — Two full and one three-quarter baths
- A Study/Guest Room with convenient access to a full, hall Bath
- An elegant Dining Room topped by a decorative ceiling treatment
- An expansive Family Room equipped with a massive fireplace with built-in bookshelves
- An informal Breakfast Room conveniently enhanced by a built-in planning desk
- A cathedral ceiling crowns the Master Suite
- This home is designed with basement, slab and crawlspace foundation options

FIRST FLOOR — 1,378 SQ. FT.
SECOND FLOOR — 1,269 SQ. FT.
BASEMENT — 1,378 SQ. FT.
GARAGE — 717 SQ. FT.

TOTAL LIVING AREA:
2,647 SQ. FT.

WIDTH 71'-0"
DEPTH 45'-0"

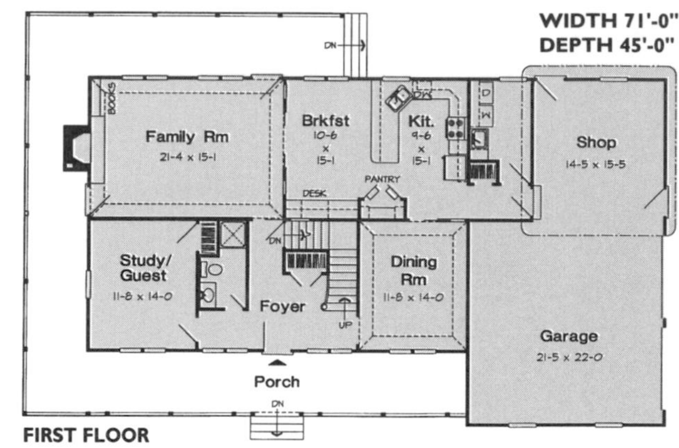
Family Rm
21-4 x 15-1
Brkfst
10-6 x 15-1
Kit.
9-6 x 15-1
Shop
14-5 x 15-5
DESK
PANTRY
Study/ Guest
11-8 x 14-0
Foyer
Dining Rm
11-8 x 14-0
Garage
21-5 x 22-0
Porch

FIRST FLOOR

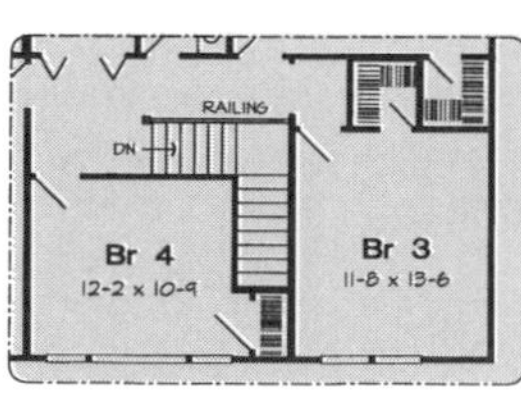
RAILING
Br 4
12-2 x 10-9
Br 3
11-8 x 13-6

OPTIONAL SECOND FLOOR

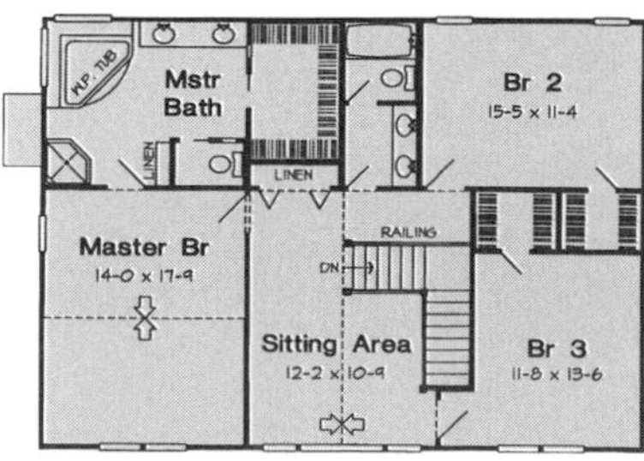
Mstr Bath
Br 2
15-5 x 11-4
LINEN
RAILING
Master Br
14-0 x 17-9
Sitting Area
12-2 x 10-9
Br 3
11-8 x 13-6

SECOND FLOOR

CRAWLSPACE/SLAB FOUNDATION OPTION

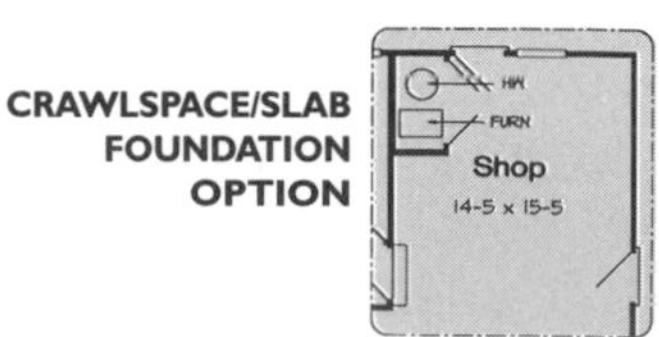
Shop
14-5 x 15-5

PLAN NO. 24319

Rear Elevation

28'-0"

Broom
Linen
Ref
Kitchen
11-1 X 7-7
DN
Flue
Brkfst Bar
Dining
11-11 X 8-7
DN
Br 1
12-0 X 11-3
Loft Above
Railing
Fireplace
UP
Living
15-1 X 14-10
DN
Deck

FIRST FLOOR

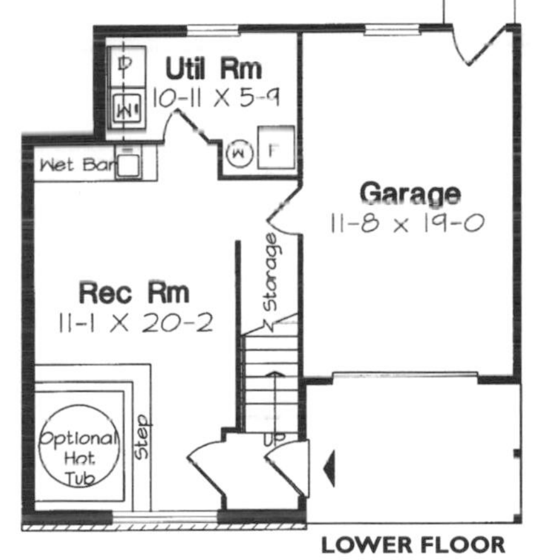

Util Rm
10-11 X 5-9
Wet Bar
Garage
11-8 x 19-0
Storage
Rec Rm
11-1 X 20-2
Optional Hot Tub
Step
UP
LOWER FLOOR

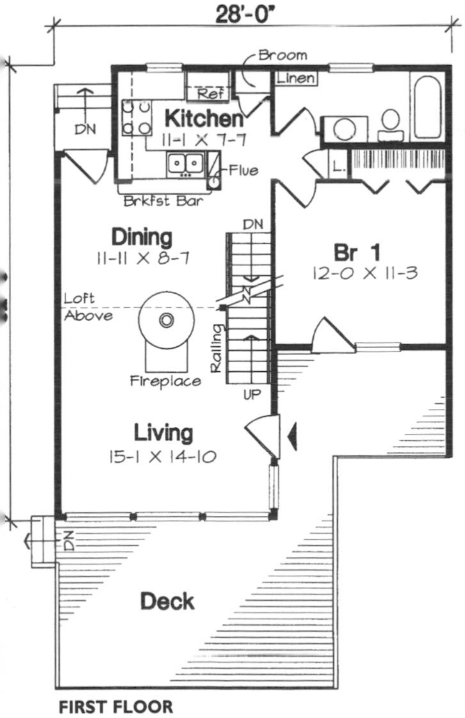

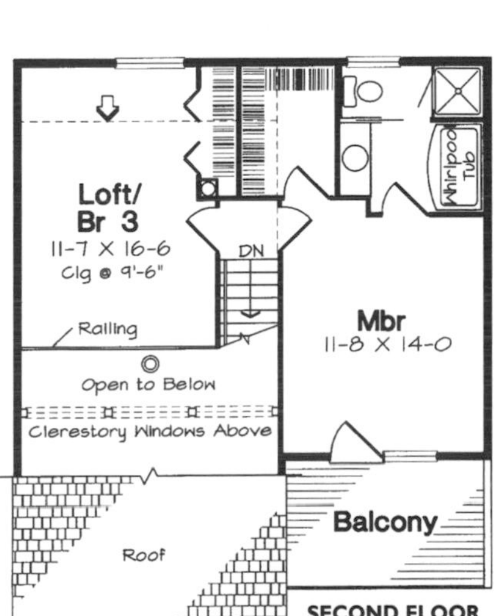

Loft/ Br 3
11-7 X 16-6
Clg @ 9'-6"
DN
Whirlpool Tub
Mbr
11-8 X 14-0
Railing
Open to Below
Clerestory Windows Above
Roof
Balcony
SECOND FLOOR

Home with Many Views

Price Code: B

- This plan features:
- — Three bedrooms
- — Two full baths
- Large Decks and windows taking full advantage of the view
- A fireplace that divides the Living Room from the Dining Room
- A Kitchen flowing into the Dining Room
- A Master Bedroom with a full Master Bath
- A Recreation Room sporting a whirlpool tub and a bar
- This home is designed with a basement foundation

MAIN FLOOR — 728 SQ. FT.
UPPER FLOOR — 573 SQ. FT.
LOWER FLOOR — 409 SQ. FT.
GARAGE — 244 SQ. FT.

TOTAL LIVING AREA:
1,710 SQ. FT.

PLAN NO.20209

Zoned for Harmony

PRICE CODE: E

- This plan features:
  - — Three bedrooms
  - — Two full and one half baths
- A lofty vaulted ceiling over the entire living level
- A spacious, efficient Kitchen with a peninsula counter separating it from the Breakfast Room
- A formal Living and Dining Room that efficiently flow into each other for ease in entertaining
- A Family Room with a fireplace and built-in bookshelves
- A Master Suite with a romantic window seat, a large walk-in closet and a lavish Master Bath
- Two additional Bedrooms, with walk-in closets, that share a full hall Bath
- This home is designed with a basement foundation

MAIN FLOOR — 1,861 SQ. FT.
LOWER FLOOR — 526 SQ. FT.
BASEMENT — 874 SQ. FT.
GARAGE — 574 SQ. FT.

TOTAL LIVING AREA:
2,387 SQ. FT.

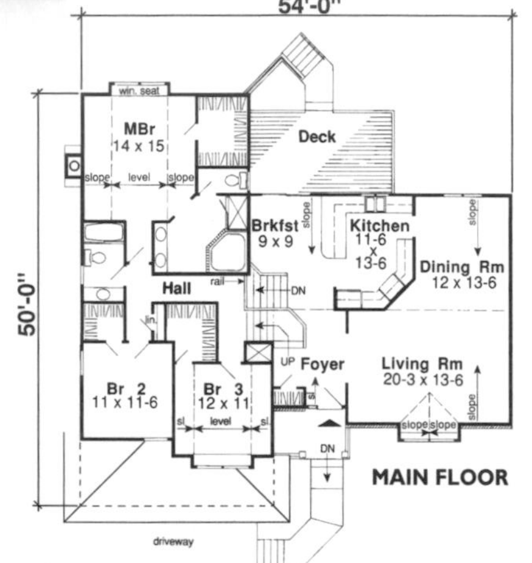
54'-0"
50'-0"
win. seat
MBr
14 x 15
Deck
Brkfst
9 x 9
Kitchen
11-6 x 13-6
Dining Rm
12 x 13-6
Hall
Foyer
Living Rm
20-3 x 13-6
Br 2
11 x 11-6
Br 3
12 x 11
driveway
MAIN FLOOR

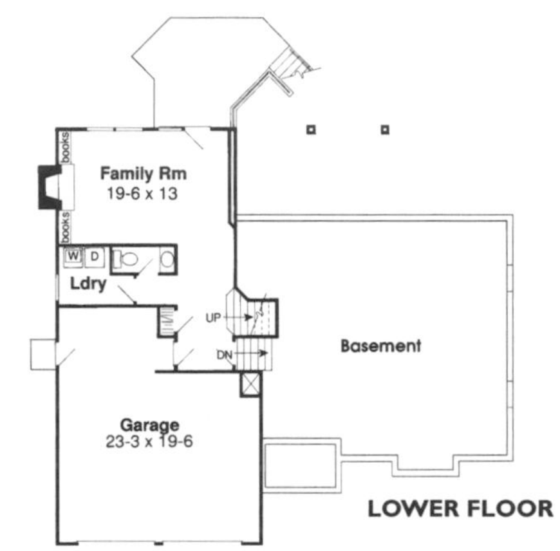
Family Rm
19-6 x 13
Ldry
Garage
23-3 x 19-6
Basement
LOWER FLOOR

PLAN NO.82043

Two Fireplaces Adding Warmth and Atmosphere

PRICE CODE: A

- This plan features:
  - — Three bedrooms
  - — Two full baths
- The Great Room has a 10-foot boxed ceiling and a gas fireplace
- The secondary Bedrooms share a full Bath located in close proximity
- The Master Suite enjoys a boxed ceiling and a luxurious private Bath
- The informal Hearth Room has an optional gas fireplace and access to the Grilling Porch
- This home is designed with basement, slab and crawlspace foundation options

MAIN FLOOR — 1,425 SQ. FT.
GARAGE — 353 SQ. FT.
PORCH — 137 SQ. FT.

TOTAL LIVING AREA:
1,425 SQ. FT.

GRILLING PORCH
HEARTH RM.
MASTER SUITE
GARAGE
KIT.
BEDROOM 2
GREAT RM.
BATH
COVERED PORCH
BEDROOM 3 / STUDY

MAIN FLOOR

WIDTH 45'-0"
DEPTH 64'-10"

Split-Bedroom Ranch

PRICE CODE: C

PLAN NO.90476

- This plan features:
  - — Three bedrooms
  - — Two full baths
- The formal Foyer opens into the Great Room which features a vaulted ceiling and a hearth fireplace
- The U-shaped Kitchen is located between the Dining Room and the Breakfast Nook
- The secluded Master Bedroom is spacious and includes amenities such as walk-in closets and a full Bath
- Two secondary Bedrooms have ample closet space and share a full Bath
- The covered front Porch and rear Deck provide additional space for entertaining
- This home is designed with basement, slab, and crawlspace foundation options

MAIN FLOOR — 1,804 SQ. FT.
BASEMENT — 1,804 SQ. FT.
GARAGE — 506 SQ. FT.

TOTAL LIVING AREA:
1,804 SQ. FT.

MASTER BEDROOM
15-4 x 13-8
WOOD DECK
22-0 x 10-0
BREAKFAST
12-6 x 8-0
HEARTH
BATH
LAUNDRY
KITCHEN
12-6 x 9-6
VAULTED CEILING
GREAT ROOM
14-8 x 19-0
BEDROOM
11-0 x 12-6
BATH
W.I. CLOSET
W.I. CLOSET
PANTRY
DOWN
DINING
11-0 x 11-6
FOYER
12-0 x 6-4
BEDROOM
13-4 x 12-0
GARAGE
21-4 x 21-4
PORCH
26-0 x 6-0
55'-8"
MAIN FLOOR
62'-0"

A Home for Today and Tomorrow

PRICE CODE: B

PLAN NO.34043

- This plan features:
  - — Three bedrooms
  - — Two full baths
- An intriguing Breakfast Nook off the Kitchen
- A wide open, Living Room with a fireplace and glass sliders to an optional Deck
- A step-saving Kitchen with a Pantry
- A handsome Master Bedroom with skylit compartmentalized Bath
- This home is designed with basement, slab, and crawlspace foundation options

MAIN FLOOR — 1,583 SQ. FT.
BASEMENT — 1,573 SQ. FT.
GARAGE — 484 SQ. FT.

TOTAL LIVING AREA:
1,583 SQ. FT.

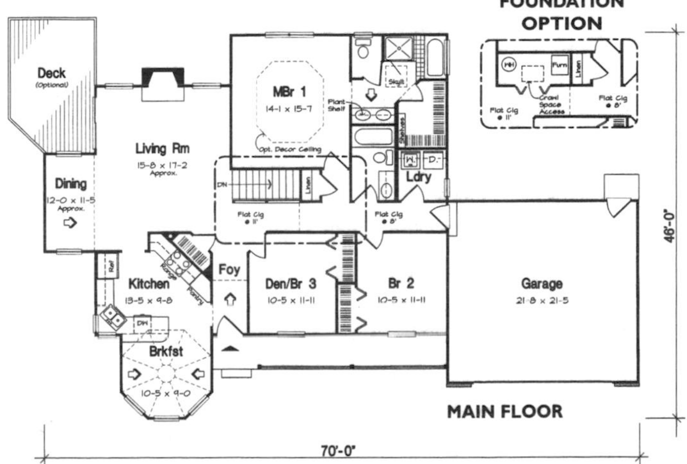

CRAWLSPACE/SLAB FOUNDATION OPTION
Deck
(Optional)
MBr 1
14-1 x 15-7
Living Rm
15-8 x 17-2
Approx.
Dining
12-0 x 11-5
Approx.
Ldry
Kitchen
13-5 x 9-8
Foy
Den/Br 3
10-5 x 11-11
Br 2
10-5 x 11-11
Garage
21-8 x 21-5
Brkfst
10-5 x 9-0
46'-0"
MAIN FLOOR
70'-0"

PLAN NO. 92697

Traditionally Styled

Price Code: D

- This plan features:
- — Three bedrooms
- — Two full and one half baths
- There are Porches both in the front and the rear
- The Kitchen is conveniently appointed and located
- A fireplace warms the Great Room
- The Master Bedroom is located on the first floor
- The secondary Bedrooms are located upstairs
- This home is designed with a basement foundation

FIRST FLOOR — 1,432 SQ. FT.
SECOND FLOOR — 585 SQ. FT.
BASEMENT — 1,432 SQ. FT.

TOTAL LIVING AREA:
2,017 SQ. FT.

Porch
Breakfast
12'1" x 11'7"
Great Room
20' x 15'4"
Laun
Kitchen
11'10" x 12'10"
Two-car Garage
21' x 20'
Bath
Dining Room
11'10" x 11'6"
Foyer
Master Bedroom
12' x 15'
FIRST FLOOR
Porch
58'
44'4"

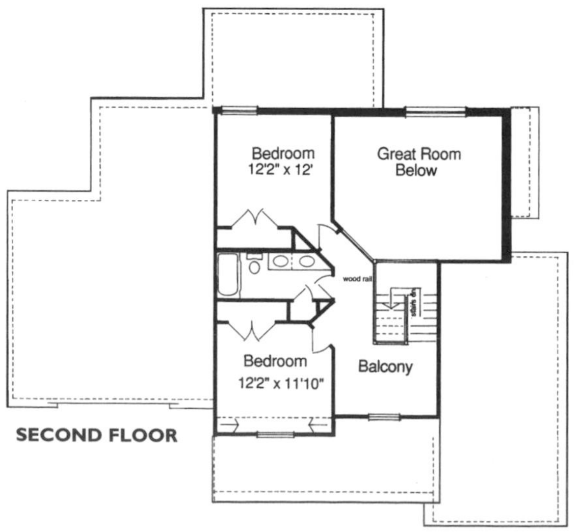

Bedroom
12'2" x 12'
Great Room Below
wood rail
Bedroom
12'2" x 11'10"
Balcony
SECOND FLOOR

PLAN NO. 24752

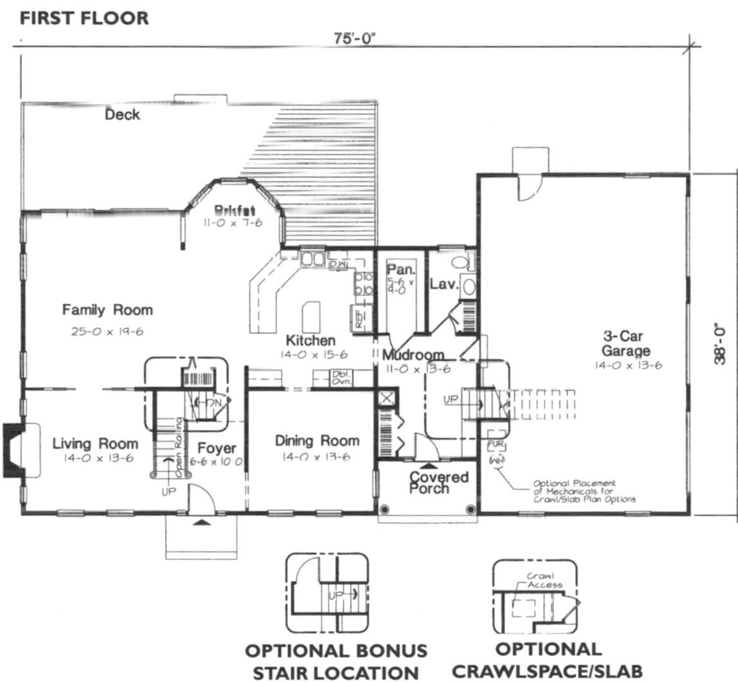

FIRST FLOOR
75'-0"
38'-0"
Deck
Brkfst
11-0 x 7-6
Family Room
25-0 x 19-6
Kitchen
14-0 x 15-6
Pan.
Lav.
Mudroom
11-0 x 13-6
3-Car Garage
14-0 x 13-6
Living Room
14-0 x 13-6
Foyer
6-6 x 10-0
Dining Room
14-0 x 13-6
Covered Porch
Dbl. Ovn.
UP
DN
Open Railing
Optional Placement of Mechanicals for Crawl/Slab Plan Options
OPTIONAL BONUS STAIR LOCATION
OPTIONAL CRAWLSPACE/SLAB
Crawl Access

Cozy Breakfast Nook

Price Code: H

- This plan features:
- — Three bedrooms
- — One full, one three-quarter, and one half baths
- Open design of first floor creates feeling of spaciousness
- Comfy Breakfast Nook looks out to large Deck
- Loft overlooks Kitchen and beyond into the Family Room
- Mudroom, Pantry, and Laundry Room offer plenty of space
- This home is designed with basement, slab and crawlspace foundation options

FIRST FLOOR — 1,674 SQ. FT.
SECOND FLOOR — 1,476 SQ. FT.
BONUS ROOM — 626 SQ. FT.
GARAGE — 912 SQ. FT.

TOTAL LIVING AREA:
3,150 SQ. FT.

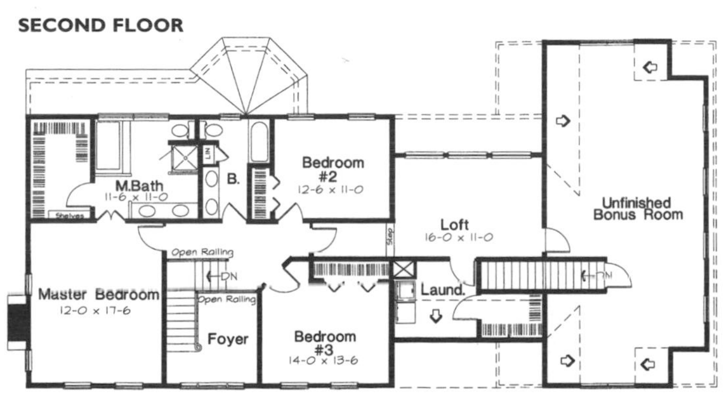

SECOND FLOOR
M.Bath
11-6 x 11-0
B.
Bedroom #2
12-6 x 11-0
Loft
16-0 x 11-0
Unfinished Bonus Room
Open Railing
DN
Master Bedroom
12-0 x 17-6
Foyer
Bedroom #3
14-0 x 13-6
Laund.

PLAN NO.82048

Covered Front Porch

PRICE CODE: B

- This plan features:
  - — Three bedrooms
  - — Two full and one half baths
- The Great Room has columns at its entrance, a fireplace and a media center
- There is a first floor Master Suite tucked into the rear fo privacy and topped by a boxed ceiling
- The Kitchen has easy access to the formal Dining Room the Garage, and the Grilling Porch
- There is storage space in the Attic, in the Garage and in the basement if you chooose that foundation option
- This home is designed with basement, slab and crawlspace foundation options

FIRST FLOOR — 1,112 SQ. FT.
SECOND FLOOR — 483 SQ. FT.
GARAGE — 342 SQ. FT.

TOTAL LIVING AREA:
1,595 SQ. FT.

WIDTH 44'-0"
DEPTH 59'-4"
M.BATH
MASTER SUITE
GRILLING PORCH
STORAGE
DINING
KITCHEN
GARAGE
GREAT RM.
FOYER
COVERED PORCH
FIRST FLOOR

ATTIC STORAGE
BED RM. 2
BED RM. 3
SECOND FLOOR

PLAN NO.24753

Balcony with Window Seat

PRICE CODE: D

- This plan features:
  - — Three bedrooms
  - — Two full and one half baths
- Two covered Porches are doubly classic and inviting
- Unique upstairs Hallway is open to Foyer below
- Kitchen, with Snack Bar, Pantry, and built-in desk opens to Nook and Family Room
- Master Bedroom, secondary Bedroom, and Hallway share access to Balcony with window seat
- This home is designed with basement, slab and crawlspace foundation options

FIRST FLOOR — 1,123 SQ. FT.
SECOND FLOOR — 1,036 SQ. FT.
GARAGE — 480 SQ. FT.
DECK — 330 SQ. FT.

TOTAL LIVING AREA:
2,159 SQ. FT.

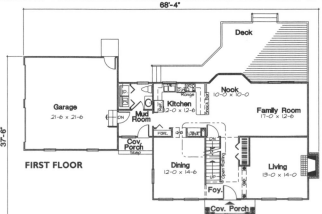

68'-4"
37'-6"
Deck
Garage 21-6 x 21-6
Kitchen 12-0 x 12-6
Nook 10-0 x 10-0
Family Room 17-0 x 12-6
Mud Room
Cov. Porch
Dining 12-0 x 14-6
Living 13-0 x 14-0
Foy.
Cov. Porch
FIRST FLOOR

M. Bath 12-0 x 9-0
Bedroom #2 12-0 x 12-6
Master Bedroom 12-0 x 15-6
Bedroom #3 12-0 x 12-0
Balcony
SECOND FLOOR

CRAWLSPACE/SLAB FOUNDATION OPTION

Secluded Master Suite

PRICE CODE: B

- This plan features:
  - Three bedrooms
  - Two full baths
- A convenient one-level design with an open floor plan between the Kitchen, Breakfast Area, and Great Room
- A vaulted ceiling and a cozy fireplace in the spacious Great Room
- A well-equipped Kitchen using a peninsula counter as an eating bar
- A Master Suite with a luxurious Master Bath
- Two additional Bedrooms having use of a full hall Bath
- This home is designed with slab and crawlspace foundation options

MAIN FLOOR — 1,680 SQ. FT.
GARAGE — 538 SQ. FT.

TOTAL LIVING AREA:
1,680 SQ. FT.

PLAN NO. 92527

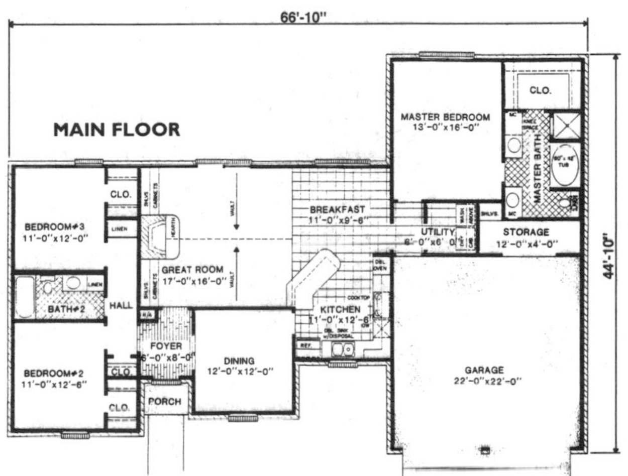

66'-10"
MAIN FLOOR
MASTER BEDROOM
13'-0"x16'-0"
CLO.
MASTER BATH
BEDROOM#3
11'-0"x12'-0"
CLO.
BREAKFAST
11'-0"x9'-6"
UTILITY
STORAGE
12'-0"x4'-0"
GREAT ROOM
17'-0"x16'-0"
BATH#2
HALL
KITCHEN
FOYER
DINING
12'-0"x12'-0"
BEDROOM#2
11'-0"x12'-6"
CLO.
PORCH
GARAGE
22'-0"x22'-0"
44'-10"

A Grand Entrance

PRICE CODE: F

- This plan features:
  - Five bedrooms
  - Three full baths
- The arched window above the front door provides a grand entrance
- Inside the two-story Foyer find the first of two open rail staircases in this home
- The formal Living and Dining rooms are only separated by a set of boxed columns
- The U-shaped Kitchen has a walk-in Pantry and a wall oven
- A serving bar services the Breakfast Nook
- The Family Room has a fireplace as well as a vaulted ceiling
- Rounding out the first floor is a Den/Bedroom with a Bath located off of it
- Upstairs find the family sleeping quarters and Baths
- This home is designed with basement and crawlspace foundation options

FIRST FLOOR — 1,424 SQ. FT.
SECOND FLOOR — 1,256 SQ. FT.
BASEMENT — 1,424 SQ. FT.
GARAGE — 494 SQ. FT.

TOTAL LIVING AREA:
2,680 SQ. FT.

PLAN NO. 98418

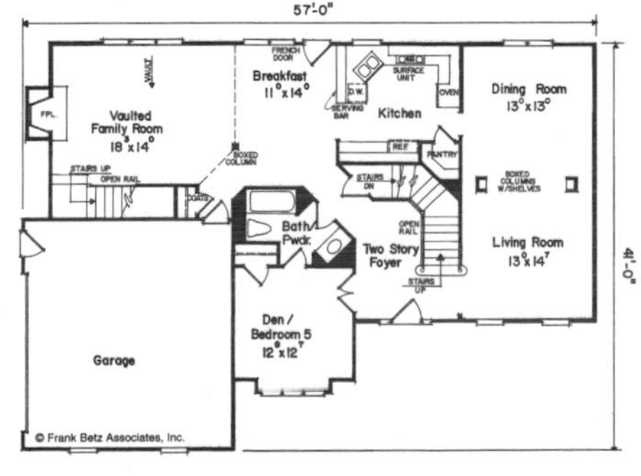

57'-0"
Vaulted Family Room
Breakfast
Kitchen
Dining Room
Two Story Foyer
Living Room
Den / Bedroom 5
Garage
© Frank Betz Associates, Inc.
41'-0"

FIRST FLOOR

Family Room Below
Bedroom 4
W.i.c.
Vaulted Master Bath
Master Suite
Bedroom 3
Bath
Laun.
Bedroom 2
Foyer Below

SECOND FLOOR

PLAN NO.90990

Comfort and Style

PRICE CODE: A

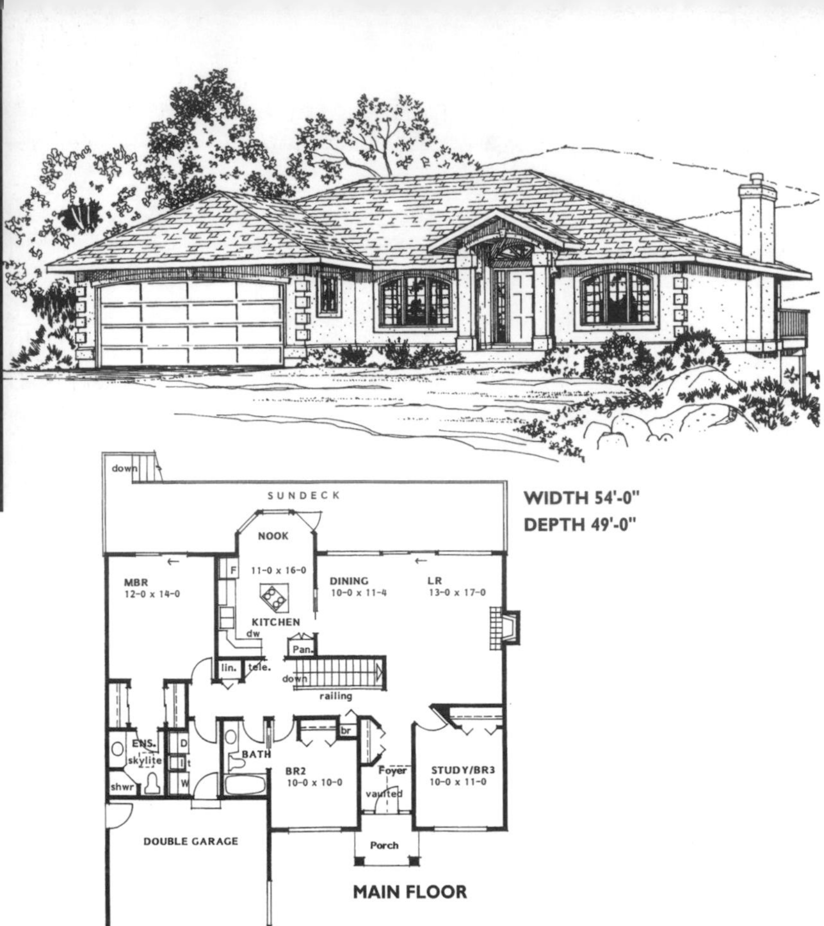

SUNDECK
NOOK 11-0 x 16-0
MBR 12-0 x 14-0
DINING 10-0 x 11-4
LR 13-0 x 17-0
KITCHEN
railing
BATH
BR2 10-0 x 10-0
Foyer
vaulted
STUDY/BR3 10-0 x 11-0
DOUBLE GARAGE
Porch
MAIN FLOOR
WIDTH 54'-0"
DEPTH 49'-0"

■ This plan features:
— Three bedrooms
— One full and one three-quarter baths
■ An unfinished daylight basement, providing possible space for family recreation
■ A Master Suite complete with private Bath and skylight
■ A large Kitchen including an Eating Nook
■ A Sun Deck that is easily accessible from the Master Suite, Nook, and the Living and Dining Areas
■ This home is designed with a basement foundation

MAIN FLOOR — 1,423 SQ. FT.
BASEMENT — 1,423 SQ. FT.
GARAGE — 399 SQ. FT.

TOTAL LIVING AREA:
1,423 SQ. FT.

PLAN NO.99208

Cozy Traditional with Style

PRICE CODE: C

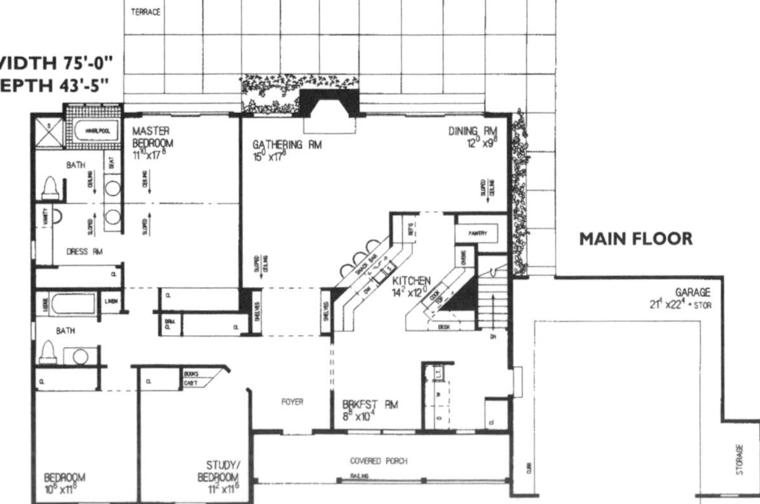

WIDTH 75'-0"
DEPTH 43'-5"
TERRACE
MASTER BEDROOM
GATHERING RM
DINING RM
DRESS RM
KITCHEN
GARAGE
FOYER
BRKFST RM
COVERED PORCH
BEDROOM
STUDY/ BEDROOM
MAIN FLOOR

■ This plan features:
— Three bedrooms
— Two full baths
■ A convenient one-level design
■ A galley-style Kitchen that shares a snack bar with the spacious Gathering Room
■ Inviting focal point fireplace in Gathering Room
■ An ample Master Suite with a luxury Bath which includes a whirlpool tub and separate Dressing Room
■ Two additional Bedrooms, one that could double as a Study, located at the front of the house
■ This home is designed with a basement foundation

MAIN FLOOR — 1,830 SQ. FT.
BASEMENT — 1,830 SQ. FT.

TOTAL LIVING AREA:
1,830 SQ. FT.

Roof Angles and Window Arches

PRICE CODE: A

PLAN NO.96924

- This plan features
  - Three bedrooms
  - Two full baths
- Positioned for privacy, the Master Suite has double doors leading to the Bath
- Dining Room conversation flows easily into the Great Room
- The Great Room includes a cozy fireplace
- Bedroom three can easily convert into a Home Office space
- This home is designed with basement, slab and crawlspace foundation options

MAIN FLOOR — 1,383 SQ. FT.
BASEMENT — 1,460 SQ. FT.
GARAGE — 416 SQ. FT.
DECK — 120 SQ. FT.
PORCH — 29 SQ.FT.

TOTAL LIVING AREA:
1,383 SQ. FT.

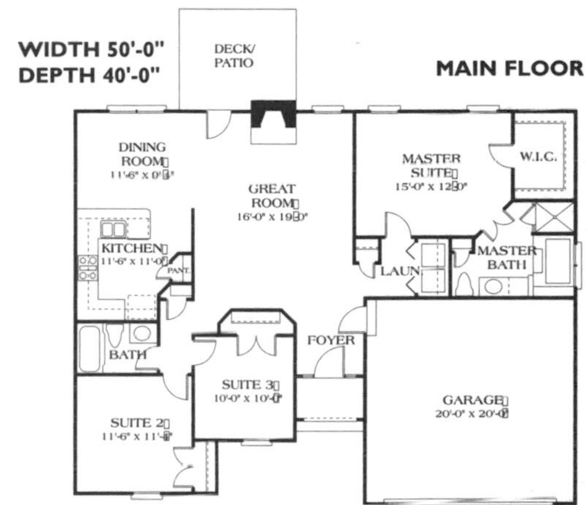

WIDTH 50'-0"
DEPTH 40'-0"
DECK/ PATIO
MAIN FLOOR
DINING ROOM 11'-6" x 9'-8"
GREAT ROOM 16'-0" x 19'-0"
MASTER SUITE 15'-0" x 12'-0"
W.I.C.
KITCHEN 11'-6" x 11'-0"
PANT
LAUN
MASTER BATH
BATH
FOYER
SUITE 3 10'-0" x 10'-0"
SUITE 2 11'-6" x 11'-6"
GARAGE 20'-0" x 20'-0"

Private Library

PRICE CODE: F

PLAN NO.24900

- This plan features:
  - Three bedrooms
  - Two full and one half baths
- Enjoy reading your favorite books in the secluded Library with wall-to-wall built-in shelves
- The Garage includes space for a workshop or extra storage
- This home is designed with basement, slab and crawlspace foundation options

FIRST FLOOR — 1,385 SQ. FT.
SECOND FLOOR — 1,214 SQ. FT.
BASEMENT — 1,385 SQ. FT.
GARAGE — 694 SQ. FT.

TOTAL LIVING AREA:
2,599 SQ. FT.

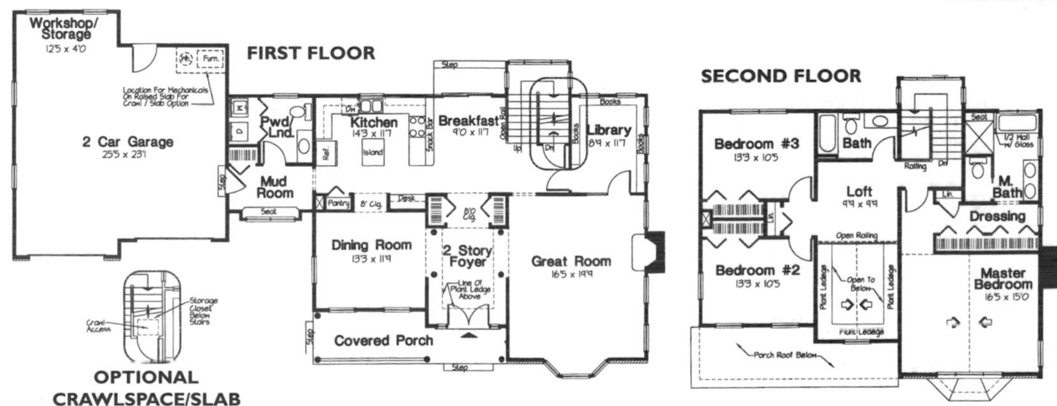

Workshop/ Storage 12'5 x 4'0
FIRST FLOOR
Location For Mechanicals On Raised Slab For Crawl / Slab Option
2 Car Garage 25'5 x 23'1
Pwd/ Lnd.
Kitchen 14'3 x 11'7
Breakfast 9'0 x 11'7
Library 8'9 x 11'7
Mud Room
Seat
Pantry
Desk
Dining Room 13'3 x 11'9
2 Story Foyer
Great Room 16'5 x 19'9
Covered Porch
OPTIONAL CRAWLSPACE/SLAB
SECOND FLOOR
Bedroom #3 13'3 x 10'5
Bath
Loft 9'9 x 9'9
M. Bath
Dressing
Bedroom #2 13'3 x 10'5
Open To Below
Master Bedroom 16'5 x 15'0
Porch Roof Below

PLAN NO. 92660

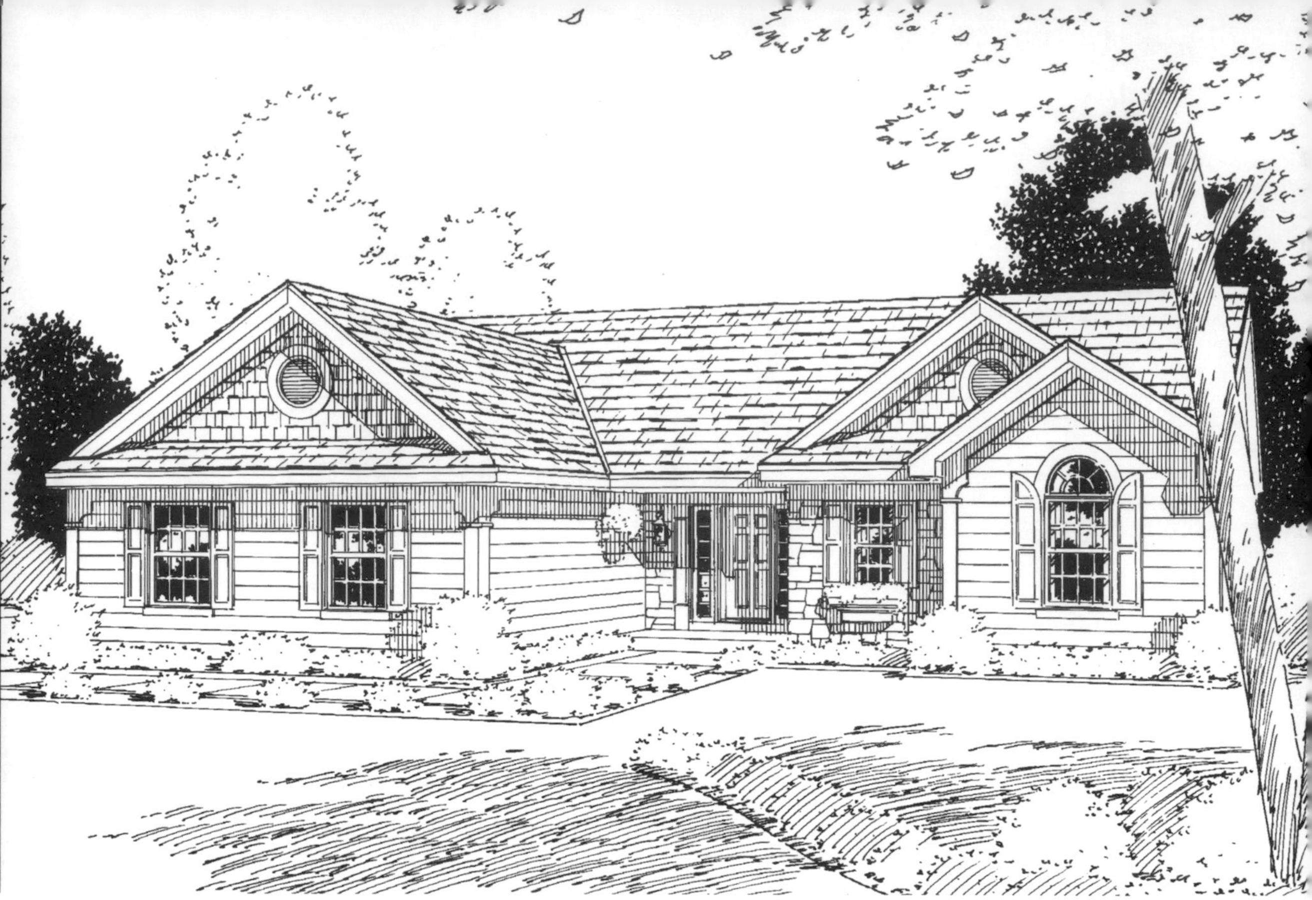

Comfortable and Charming

Price Code: C

- This plan features:
- — Three bedrooms
- — Two full baths
- Foyer flows into spacious Great Room with massive fireplace and lots of windows
- Formal Dining Room with sloped ceiling has expansive view of backyard
- Cooktop island and Pantry in Kitchen efficiently serves the Breakfast Area and Dining Room
- This home is designed with a basement foundation

MAIN FLOOR — 1,964 SQ. FT.
GARAGE — 447 SQ. FT.
BASEMENT — 1,809 SQ. FT.

TOTAL LIVING AREA:
***1,964** SQ. FT.*

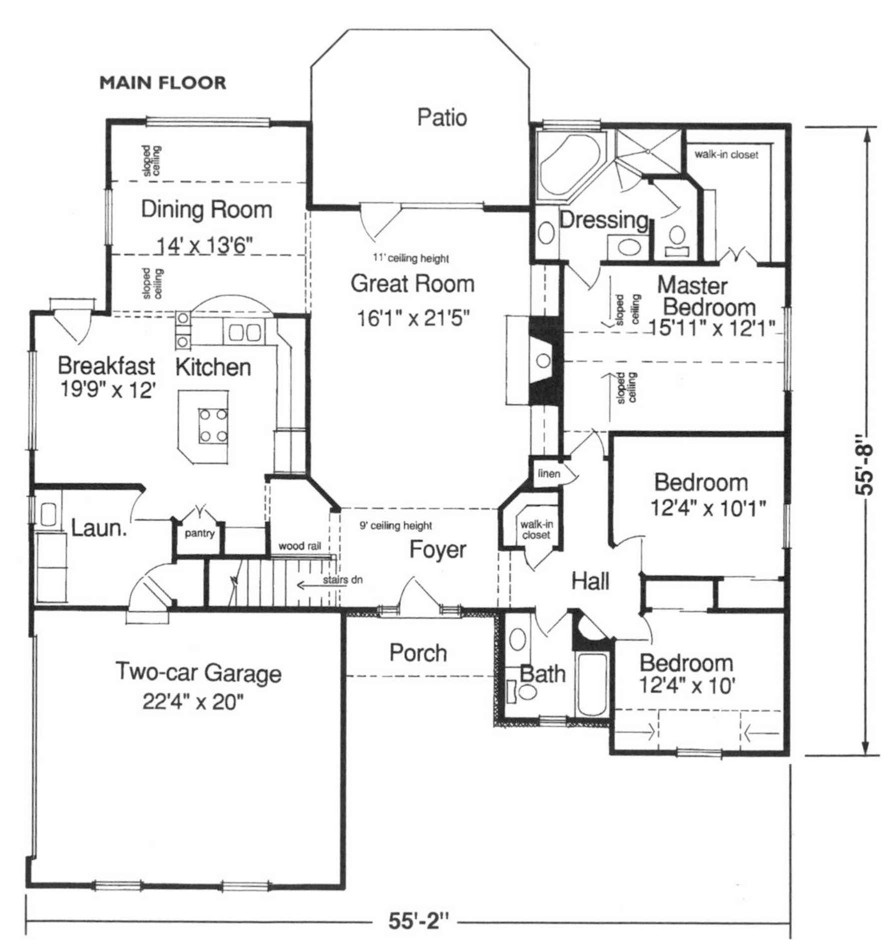
MAIN FLOOR
Patio
walk-in closet
sloped ceiling
Dining Room
14' x 13'6"
Dressing
11' ceiling height
Great Room
16'1" x 21'5"
Master Bedroom
15'11" x 12'1"
Breakfast
19'9" x 12'
Kitchen
linen
Bedroom
12'4" x 10'1"
55'-8"
Laun.
pantry
wood rail
9' ceiling height
Foyer
walk-in closet
Hall
stairs dn
Porch
Two-car Garage
22'4" x 20"
Bath
Bedroom
12'4" x 10'
55'-2"

Colonial Farmhouse

PRICE CODE: E

PLAN NO.24901

- This plan features:
  - Three bedrooms
  - Two full and one half baths
- The use of multiple exterior finishes, lends a vintage charm to this home
- The covered Porch with cozy Sitting Area provides an ideal space for outdoor enjoyment
- The Living and Dining Rooms share a two-sided fireplace
- This home is designed with basement, slab and crawlspace foundation options

FIRST FLOOR — 1,309 SQ. FT.
SECOND FLOOR — 1,023 SQ. FT.
BASEMENT — 1,385 SQ. FT.
GARAGE — 694 SQ. FT.

TOTAL LIVING AREA:
2,332 SQ. FT.

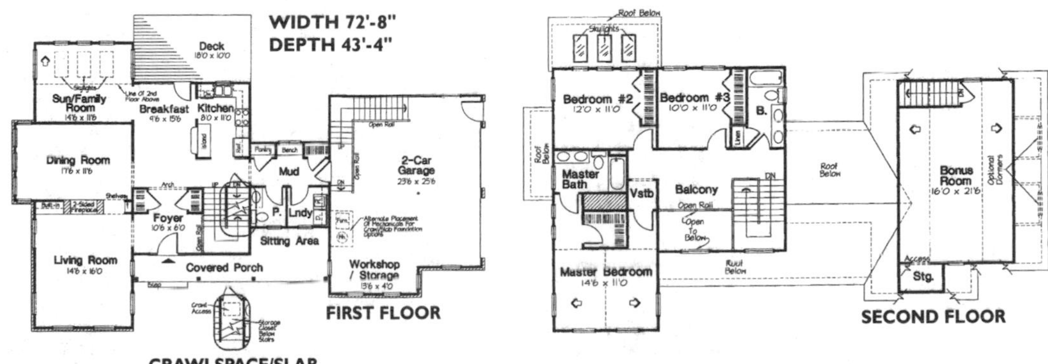
WIDTH 72'-8"
DEPTH 43'-4"
Deck
Sun/Family Room
Breakfast
Kitchen
Dining Room
Mud
Foyer
P.
Lndy
Sitting Area
Living Room
Covered Porch
2-Car Garage
Workshop / Storage
FIRST FLOOR
CRAWLSPACE/SLAB FOUNDATION OPTION
Roof Below
Skylights
Bedroom #2
Bedroom #3
B.
Master Bath
Vstb
Balcony
Open Rail
Open To Below
Master Bedroom
Bonus Room
Stg.
SECOND FLOOR

Cozy Front Porch

PRICE CODE: A

PLAN NO.82045

- This plan features:
  - Three bedrooms
  - Two full baths
- The Great Room, located in the center of the home, has a boxed ceiling and a gas fireplace
- The Kitchen includes a peninsula counter/snack bar perfect for meals on the go
- The Dining Area has direct access to the Grilling Porch
- Entrance from the Garage is into the Laundry Room, creating a Mud Room arrangement cutting down on tracked in dirt
- This home is designed with basement, slab and crawlspace foundation options

MAIN FLOOR — 1,289 SQ. FT.
GARAGE — 342 SQ. FT.
PORCH — 198 SQ. FT.

TOTAL LIVING AREA:
1,289 SQ. FT.

WIDTH 45'-6"
DEPTH 56'-10"
GARAGE
LAU.
DINING
GRILLING PORCH
KIT
BEDROOM 2
MAIN FLOOR
GREAT RM
GAS FIREPLACE
BATH
FOYER
BEDROOM 3 / OFFICE
MASTER SUITE
COVERED PORCH

PLAN NO.92523

Private Master Suite

PRICE CODE: A

- This plan features:
- — Three bedrooms
- — Two full baths
- A spacious Den enhanced by a vaulted ceiling and fireplace
- A well-equipped Kitchen with windowed double sink
- A secluded Master Suite with decorative ceiling, private Master Bath, and walk-in closet
- Two additional Bedrooms sharing hall Bath
- This home is designed with slab and crawlspace foundation options

MAIN FLOOR — 1,293 SQ. FT.
GARAGE — 433 SQ. FT.

TOTAL LIVING AREA:
1,293 SQ. FT.

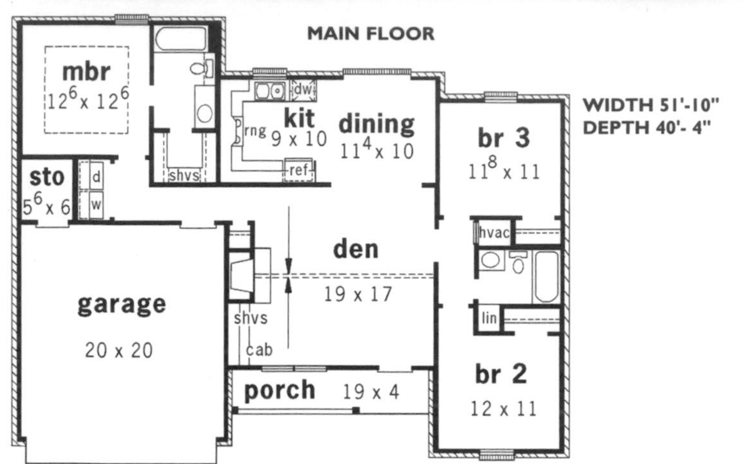

MAIN FLOOR
WIDTH 51'-10"
DEPTH 40'- 4"
mbr
12^6 x 12^6
dw
kit
9 x 10
rng
ref
dining
11^4 x 10
br 3
11^8 x 11
shvs
sto
5^6 x 6
d
w
hvac
den
19 x 17
garage
20 x 20
shvs
cab
lin
porch
19 x 4
br 2
12 x 11

PLAN NO.24951

Pleasingly Practical

PRICE CODE: G

- This plan features:
- — Three bedrooms
- — Two full, one three-quarter, and one half baths
- The second floor balcony features a ledge for displaying collectibles
- A vaulted ceiling enhances space in both the Kitchen and the Great Room
- There's direct access into the home from the Garage
- This home is designed with basement, crawlspace and slab foundation options

FIRST FLOOR — 1,762 SQ. FT.
SECOND FLOOR — 1,032 SQ. FT.
BONUS ROOM — 720 SQ. FT.
BASEMENT — 1,762 SQ. FT.
PORCH — 210 SQ. FT.
GARAGE — 941 SQ. FT.

TOTAL LIVING AREA:
2,794 SQ. FT.

WIDTH 71'-0"
DEPTH 50'-0"

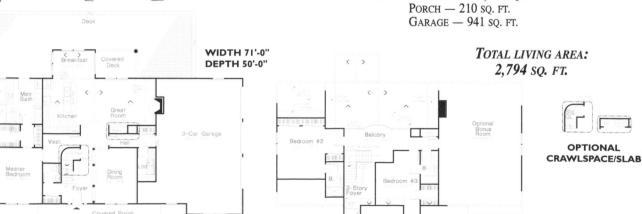

Deck
Breakfast
Covered Deck
Mstr Bath
Kitchen
Great Room
3-Car Garage
Vest.
Hall
Master Bedroom
Dining Room
Lnd
Foyer
Covered Porch

FIRST FLOOR

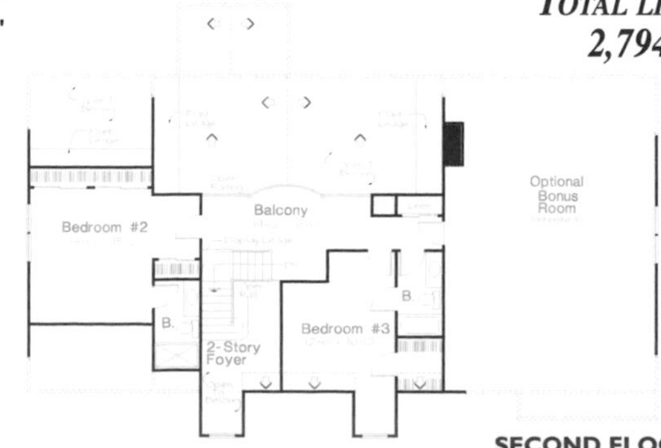

Bedroom #2
Balcony
Optional Bonus Room
B.
B
Bedroom #3
2-Story Foyer
SECOND FLOOR

Stg CL

OPTIONAL CRAWLSPACE/SLAB

PLAN NO. 24265

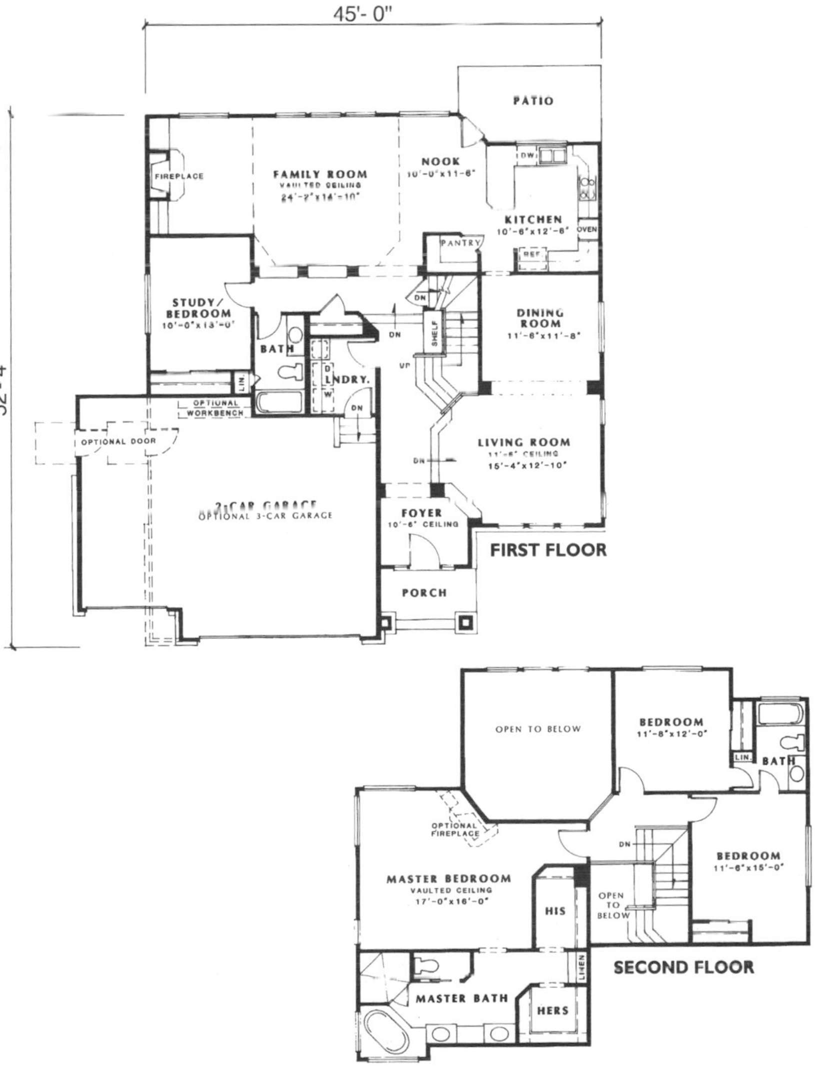

Comfortable Living

Price Code: F

- This plan features:
  - Three bedrooms
  - Three full baths
- Easy access between Living Room and Dining Room for ease in entertaining
- Modern Kitchen with double sink, built-in Pantry and peninsula counter
- Vaulted ceiling in the Family Room which also features a fireplace
- A Master Suite with vaulted ceiling, optional fireplace, his and her walk-in closets and lavish Master Bath
- This home is designed with basement, slab and crawlspace foundation options

FIRST FLOOR — 1,574 SQ. FT.
SECOND FLOOR — 1,098 SQ. FT.

TOTAL LIVING AREA:
2,672 SQ. FT.

OPEN TO BELOW
BEDROOM
11'-8"x12'-0"
LIN
BATH
OPTIONAL FIREPLACE
DN
BEDROOM
11'-6"x15'-0"
MASTER BEDROOM
VAULTED CEILING
17'-0"x16'-0"
HIS
OPEN TO BELOW
LINEN
MASTER BATH
HERS
SECOND FLOOR

To order your Blueprints, call 1-800-235-5700

PLAN NO. 92248

Opulence and Grandeur

Price Code: K

This plan features:

— Four bedrooms

— Three full and one half baths

Dramatic two-story glass Entry with a curved staircase

Both Living and Family Rooms offer high ceilings, decorative windows and large fireplaces

Large, but efficient Kitchen with a cooktop serving island, walk-in Pantry, bright Breakfast Area and Patio access

Lavish Master Bedroom with a cathedral ceiling, two walk-in closets, and Bath

This home is designed with basement and slab foundation options

FIRST FLOOR — 2,506 SQ. FT.
SECOND FLOOR — 1,415 SQ. FT.
GARAGE — 660 SQ. FT.

TOTAL LIVING AREA:
3,921 SQ. FT.

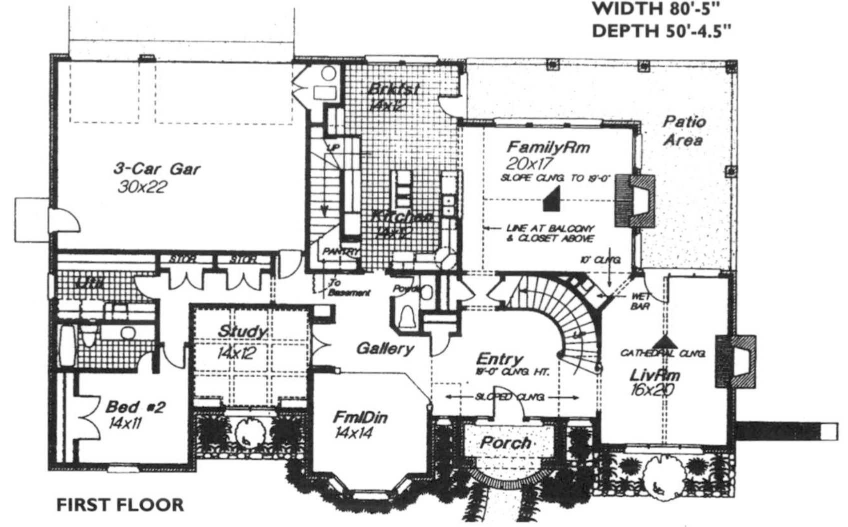
WIDTH 80'-5"
DEPTH 50'-4.5"
Brkfst
3-Car Gar
30x22
Patio
Area
FamilyRm
20x17
SLOPE CLNG. TO 18'-0"
Kitchen
PANTRY
LINE AT BALCONY & CLOSET ABOVE
10' CLNG.
STOR
STOR
To Basement
Powder
WET BAR
Study
14x12
Gallery
Entry
18'-0" CLNG. HT.
CATHEDRAL CLNG.
LivRm
16x20
SLOPED CLNG.
Bed #2
14x11
FmlDin
14x14
Porch
FIRST FLOOR

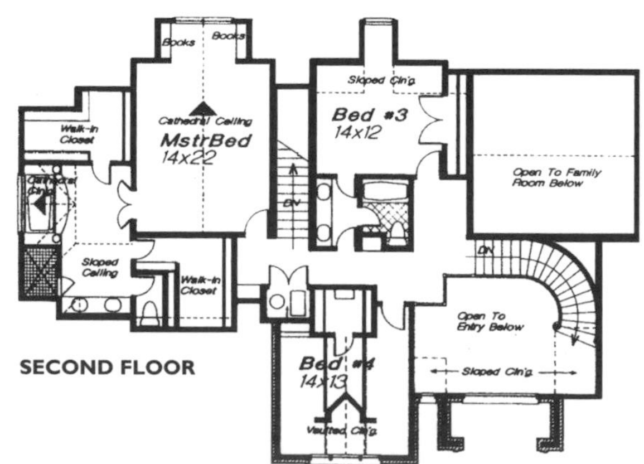
Books
Books
Sloped Clg.
Walk-in Closet
Cathedral Ceiling
MstrBed
14x22
Bed #3
14x12
Open To Family Room Below
Sloped Ceiling
Walk-in Closet
DN
Open To Entry Below
Bed #4
14x13
Sloped Clg.
Vaulted Clg.
SECOND FLOOR

A Compact Home

PRICE CODE: A

PLAN NO. 93018

- This plan features:
  - Three bedrooms
  - Two full baths
- Siding with brick wainscoting distinguishing the elevation
- A large Family Room with a corner fireplace and direct access to the outside
- An arched opening leading to the Breakfast Area
- A bay window illuminating the Breakfast Area with natural light
- An efficiently designed, U-shaped Kitchen with ample cabinet and counter space
- A Master Suite with a private Master Bath
- Two additional Bedrooms that share a full hall Bath
- This home is designed with crawlspace and slab foundation options

MAIN FLOOR — 1,142 SQ. FT.
GARAGE — 428 SQ. FT.

TOTAL LIVING AREA:
1,142 SQ. FT.

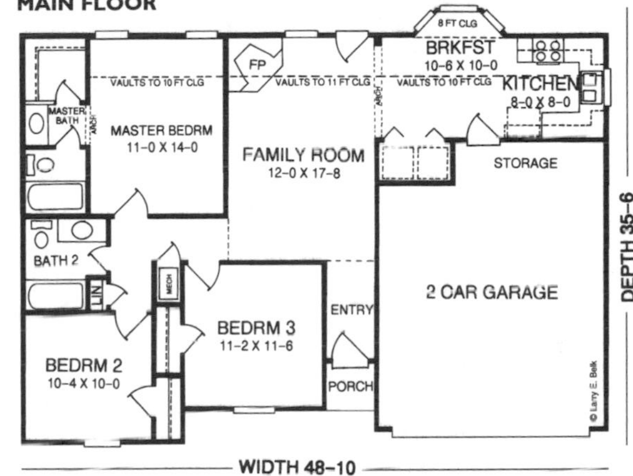
MAIN FLOOR
8 FT CLG
BRKFST
10-6 X 10-0
FP
VAULTS TO 10 FT CLG
VAULTS TO 11 FT CLG
VAULTS TO 10 FT CLG
KITCHEN
8-0 X 8-0
MASTER BATH
MASTER BEDRM
11-0 X 14-0
FAMILY ROOM
12-0 X 17-8
STORAGE
BATH 2
LIN
MECH
ENTRY
2 CAR GARAGE
DEPTH 35-6
BEDRM 3
11-2 X 11-6
BEDRM 2
10-4 X 10-0
PORCH
© Larry E. Belk
WIDTH 48-10

Studious Stucco

PRICE CODE: H

PLAN NO. 96946

- This plan features:
  - Four bedrooms
  - Three full baths
- Columns delineate the Dining Room
- There is a huge walk in closet in the Master Suite
- The Great Room has a fireplace flanked by built-ins
- A covered Porch is located off the Nook
- Storage and bonus space can be found upstairs
- This home is designed with a crawlspace foundation

FIRST FLOOR — 2,167 SQ. FT.
SECOND FLOOR — 891 SQ. FT.
BONUS ROOM — 252 SQ. FT.
GARAGE — 725 SQ. FT.

TOTAL LIVING AREA:
3,058 SQ. FT.

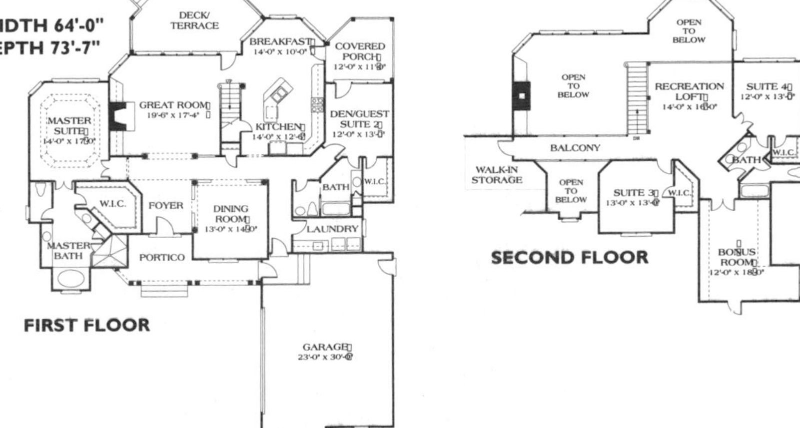
WIDTH 64'-0"
DEPTH 73'-7"
DECK/ TERRACE
BREAKFAST
14'-0" x 10'-0"
COVERED PORCH
GREAT ROOM
19'-6" x 17'-4"
MASTER SUITE
14'-0" x 17'-0"
KITCHEN
14'-0" x 12'-6"
DEN/GUEST SUITE 2
12'-0" x 13'-0"
BATH
W.I.C.
FOYER
DINING ROOM
13'-0" x 14'-0"
LAUNDRY
MASTER BATH
PORTICO
GARAGE
23'-0" x 30'-6"
FIRST FLOOR
OPEN TO BELOW
RECREATION LOFT
14'-0" x 16'-0"
SUITE 4
12'-0" x 13'-0"
BALCONY
WALK-IN STORAGE
SUITE 3
13'-0" x 13'-0"
BONUS ROOM
12'-0" x 18'-0"
SECOND FLOOR

PLAN NO.93095

Photography supplied by Larry E. Belk

Stately Elegance

PRICE CODE: E

- This plan features:
  - — Three bedrooms
  - — Two full and one half baths
- Elegant columns frame Entry into Foyer and expansive Great Room beyond
- Efficient Kitchen ideal for busy cook with walk-in Pantry, Breakfast Area and access to formal Dining Room, Laundry and Garage
- A private Master Suite boasts a plush Bath with two huge, walk-in closets, a double vanity and whirlpool tub
- Two secondary Bedrooms with large closets, share a double vanity Bath
- Staircase in Kitchen area leads to expandable second floor
- This home is designed with crawlspace and slab foundation options

MAIN FLOOR — 2,409 SQ. FT.
GARAGE — 644 SQ. FT.
BONUS — 709 SQ. FT.

TOTAL LIVING AREA:
2,409 SQ. FT.

WIDTH 85'-8"
DEPTH 68'-4"
STORAGE
DOUBLE GARAGE
MASTER BATH
MASTER BEDROOM
COVERED PORCH
BREAKFAST
PWDR
UTIL
GREAT ROOM
BEDROOM 2
KITCHEN
FOYER
DINING ROOM
BATH 2
BEDROOM 3
PORCH
© Larry E. Belk
FIRST FLOOR

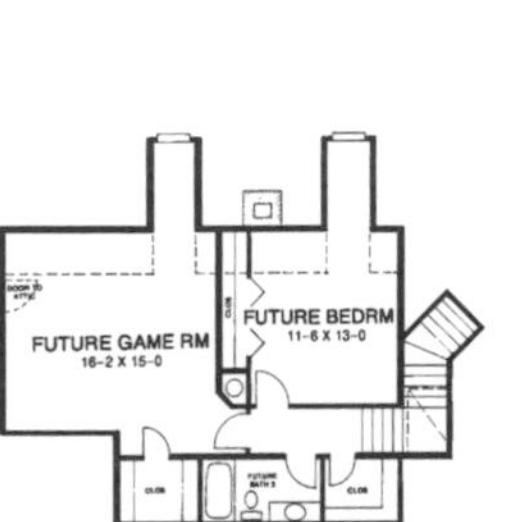
FUTURE GAME RM
FUTURE BEDRM
SECOND FLOOR

PLAN NO.98419

Stucco & Stone

PRICE CODE: E

- This plan features:
  - — Three bedrooms
  - — Two full and one half baths
- Vaulted Great Room unfolds directly in front of the Entry, this room is highlighted by a fireplace and French doors to the rear yard
- Decorative columns define the Dining Room adding elegance
- A built-in Pantry and a radius window above the double sink in the Kitchen add style
- The Breakfast Bay is crowned by a vaulted ceiling
- There is a tray ceiling over the Master Bedroom and Sitting Area, while a vaulted ceiling crowns the Master Bath
- Two additional Bedrooms, each with a walk-in closet, share the full, double vanity Bath in the hall
- This home is designed with basement, slab and crawlspace foundation options

FIRST FLOOR — 1,796 SQ. FT.
SECOND FLOOR — 629 SQ. FT.
BONUS ROOM — 208 SQ. FT.
BASEMENT — 1,796 SQ. FT.
GARAGE — 588 SQ. FT.

TOTAL LIVING AREA:
2,425 SQ. FT.

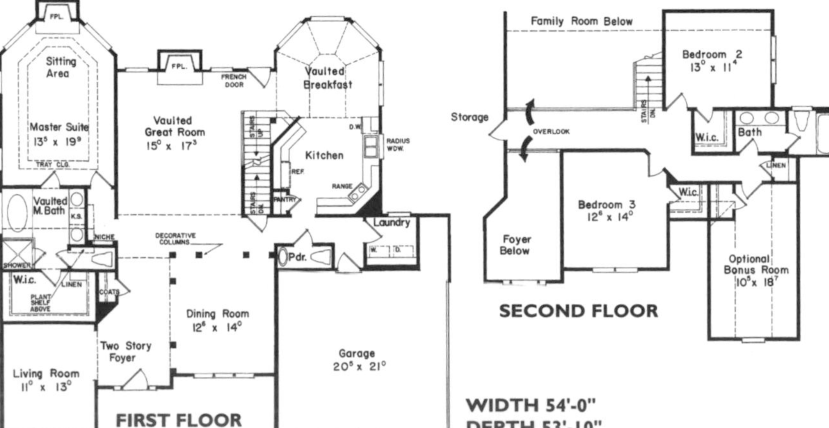
Sitting Area
Master Suite
Vaulted Great Room
Vaulted Breakfast
Kitchen
Vaulted M.Bath
Laundry
Pdr.
Dining Room
Two Story Foyer
Living Room
Garage
FIRST FLOOR
© Frank Betz Associates, Inc.
Family Room Below
Bedroom 2
Storage
OVERLOOK
Bath
Bedroom 3
Foyer Below
Optional Bonus Room
SECOND FLOOR
WIDTH 54'-0"
DEPTH 53'-10"

PLAN NO. 24952

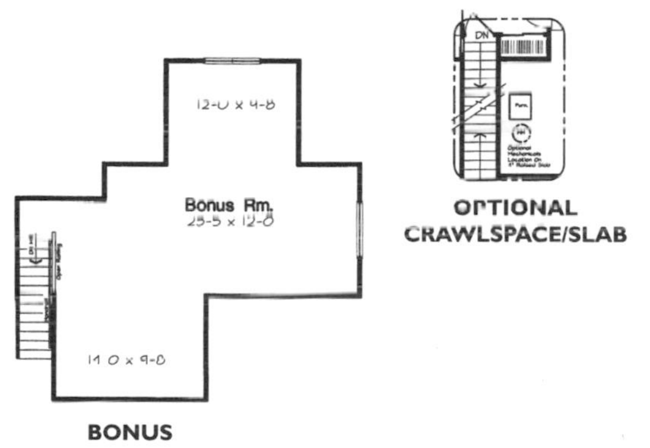
12-0 x 4-8
Bonus Rm.
23-5 x 12-0
14-0 x 9-0
BONUS
OPTIONAL
CRAWLSPACE/SLAB

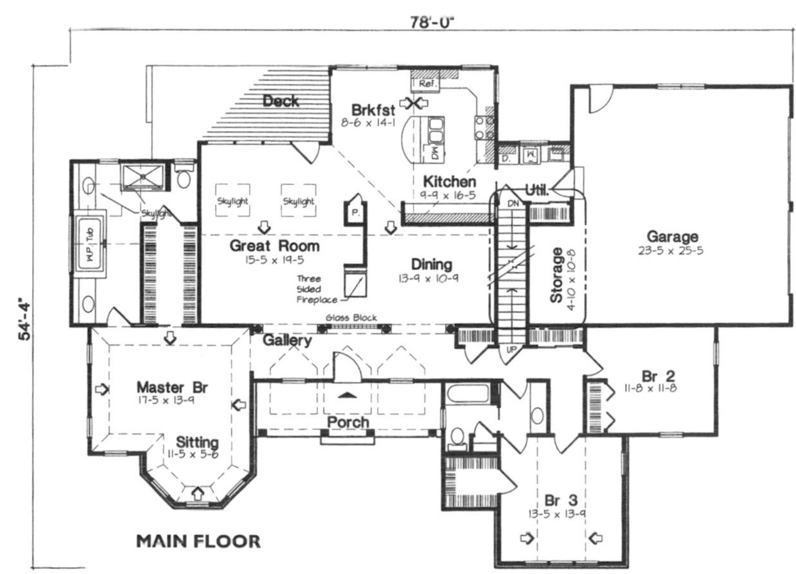
78'-0"
54'-4"
Deck
Brkfst
8-6 x 14-1
Ref.
Kitchen
9-9 x 16-5
Util.
Garage
23-5 x 25-5
Skylight
Skylight
Skylight
Great Room
15-5 x 19-5
Three Sided Fireplace
Dining
13-9 x 10-9
Storage
4-10 x 10-8
Glass Block
Gallery
Master Br
17-5 x 13-9
Sitting
11-5 x 5-6
Porch
Br 2
11-8 x 11-8
Br 3
13-5 x 13-9
MAIN FLOOR

Skylights Add Natural Light

Price Code: D

■ This plan features:

— Three bedrooms

— Two full baths

■ Master Bedroom features cozy octagonal Sitting Area

■ A skylight and whirlpool tub add light and luxury to the Master Bath

■ A glass block separating Gallery from Great Room and Dining Area adds artistic detail

■ This home is designed with basement, slab and crawlspace foundation options

MAIN FLOOR — 2,179 SQ. FT.
BONUS ROOM — 644 SQ. FT.
BASEMENT — 2,179 SQ. FT.
GARAGE — 671 SQ. FT.
PORCH — 120 SQ. FT.

TOTAL LIVING AREA:
2,179 SQ. FT.

PLAN NO. 92052

For a Small Lot

Price Code: A

This plan features:

— Three bedrooms

— Two full and one half baths

At 36-feet wide, this home still has a double Garage, a Great Room and a large Dining Area

The Great Room is topped by a cathedral ceiling and flows into the Dining Area

The Dining Area has direct access to the rear Patio

The Master Bedroom is highlighted by a cathedral ceiling and a wardrobe closet

This home is designed with a basement foundation

FIRST FLOOR — 615 SQ. FT.
SECOND FLOOR — 574 SQ. FT.
BASEMENT — 615 SQ. FT.

TOTAL LIVING AREA:
1,189 SQ. FT.

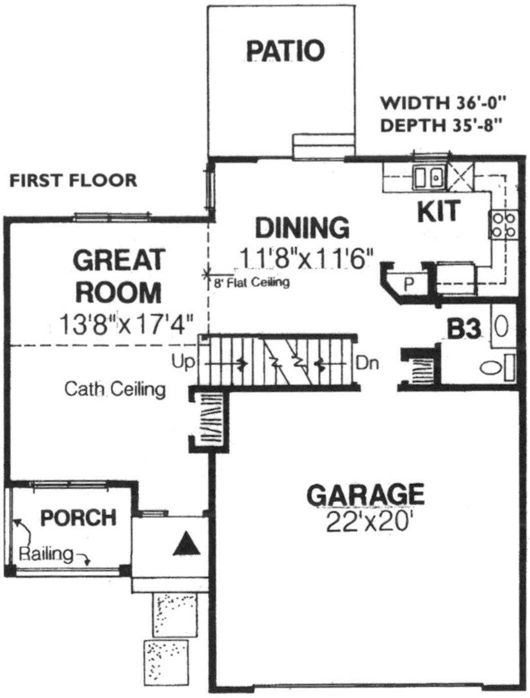

PATIO

WIDTH 36'-0"
DEPTH 35'-8"

FIRST FLOOR

DINING
11'8"x11'6"
8' Flat Ceiling

KIT

P

GREAT ROOM
13'8"x17'4"

B3

Up

Dn

Cath Ceiling

GARAGE
22'x20'

PORCH

Railing

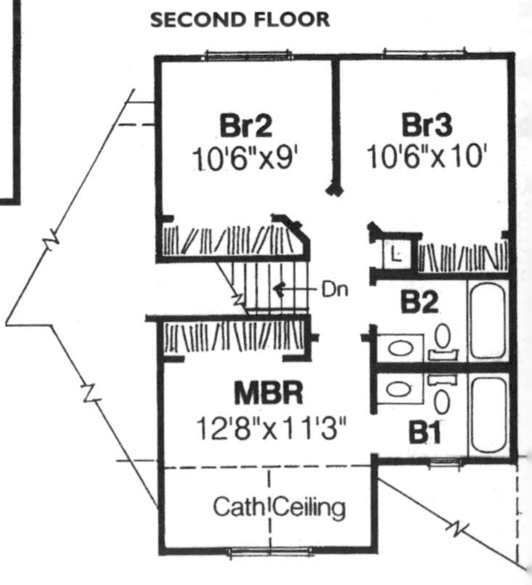

SECOND FLOOR

Br2
10'6"x9'

Br3
10'6"x10'

L

Dn

B2

MBR
12'8"x11'3"

B1

Cath Ceiling

Especially Unique

PRICE CODE: F

Cov. Area
Roof line
Patio
Brkfst
13x10
Family
Room
17x16
Bed#4
11x12
Walk-in Closet
Bth
#3
MstrBed
15x17
Marble Hearth
LivRm
13x16
13'-0" CLG. HT
Kit
13x13
Entertainment Center
Pwdr
Closet
Bed#3
13x11
Linen
Mstr
Bth
10" Wood Columns
Pantry
Gallery
Util
Bed#2
13x11
Bth#2
FmlDin
13x13
11'-0" CLG. HT
Entry
11'-0" CLG. HT
Coats
Walk-in Closet
3-Car Garage
22x30
Cov.
Porch
Study/
MediaRm
12x11
Full Oak Paneling
12" wing wall
8" brick planter
Books
MAIN FLOOR
WIDTH 75'-0"
DEPTH 64'-5"

PLAN NO.98528

- This plan features:
  - Four bedrooms
  - Three full and one half baths
- An arch covered Entry and arched windows add a unique flair to the home
- From the 11-foot Entry turn left in to the Study/Media Room
- The formal Dining Room is open to the Gallery, and the Living Room beyond
- The Family Room has a built-in entertainment center, fireplace and access to the rear Patio
- The Master Bedroom is isolated, and has a fireplace, a private Bath, and a walk-in closet
- Three additional Bedrooms on the opposite side of the home share two full Baths
- This home is designed with a slab foundation

MAIN FLOOR — 2,748 SQ. FT.
GARAGE — 660 SQ. FT.

TOTAL LIVING AREA:
2,748 SQ. FT.

Classic Facade, Artistic Interior

Price Code: E

PLAN NO.24954

- This plan features:
  - Three bedrooms
  - Two full and one half baths
- A Covered Porch and rear elevated Patio Deck are an outdoor lover's dream
- Arches and columns grace the entrances to the Dining and Great Rooms
- The L-shaped Kitchen, with island, has an abundance of counter space
- A jetted tub and glass block wall in the Master Bath is of artistic interest
- Secondary Bedrooms, each with walk-in closet, share a full Bath and the privacy of the left wing
- This home is designed with basement, slab, and crawlspace foundation options

MAIN FLOOR — 3,028 SQ. FT.
BASEMENT — 3,013 SQ. FT.
GARAGE — 674 SQ. FT.
PORCH — 238 SQ. FT.

TOTAL LIVING AREA:
3,028 SQ. FT.

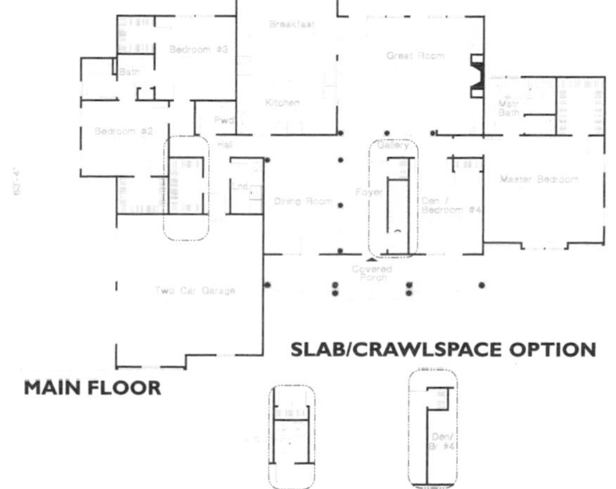

MAIN FLOOR
SLAB/CRAWLSPACE OPTION

PLAN NO.96945

Luxurious Living

PRICE CODE: H

- This plan features:
  - — Four bedrooms
  - — Three full and one half baths
- A covered Portico greets your Entry
- The bay shape of the Dining Room adds expanse
- The Kitchen has an island and a walk-in Pantry
- Access the rear Deck from the open living space
- The Master Suite is located for privacy
- A large Multi-purpose Room is located upstairs
- This home is designed with a crawlspace foundation

FIRST FLOOR — 1,725 SQ. FT.
SECOND FLOOR — 1,317 SQ. FT.
GARAGE — 435 SQ. FT.

TOTAL LIVING AREA: 3,042 SQ. FT.

WIDTH 45'-10"
DEPTH 59'-2"

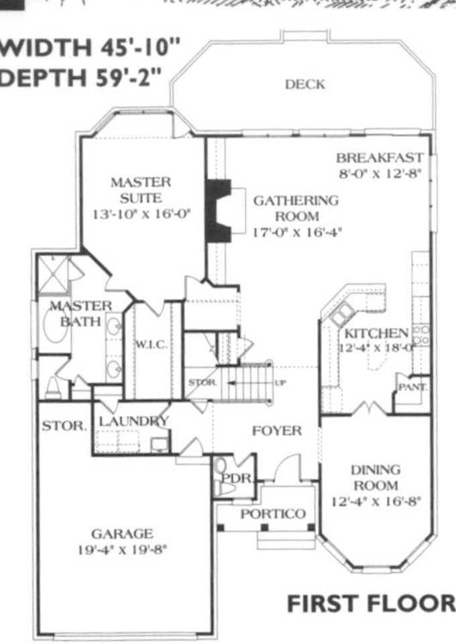
DECK
BREAKFAST
8'-0" x 12'-8"
MASTER
SUITE
13'-10" x 16'-0"
GATHERING
ROOM
17'-0" x 16'-4"
MASTER
BATH
W.I.C.
KITCHEN
12'-4" x 18'-0"
STOR.
UP
PANT.
STOR.
LAUNDRY
FOYER
PDR
DINING
ROOM
12'-4" x 16'-8"
PORTICO
GARAGE
19'-4" x 19'-8"

FIRST FLOOR

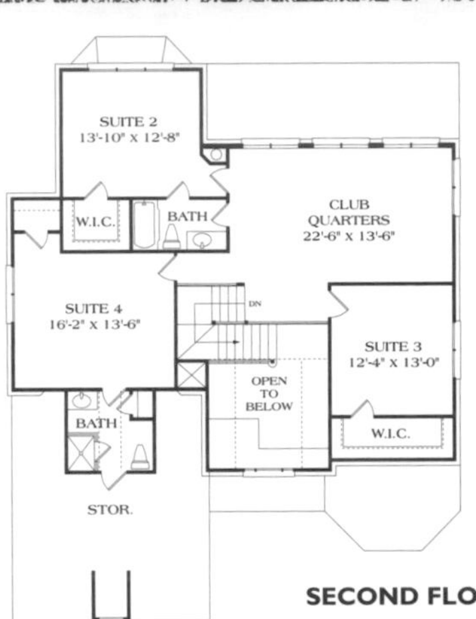
SUITE 2
13'-10" x 12'-8"
W.I.C.
BATH
CLUB
QUARTERS
22'-6" x 13'-6"
SUITE 4
16'-2" x 13'-6"
DN
SUITE 3
12'-4" x 13'-0"
OPEN
TO
BELOW
BATH
W.I.C.
STOR.

SECOND FLOOR

PLAN NO.93442

Character and Charm

PRICE CODE: D

- This plan features:
  - — Three bedrooms
  - — Two full and one half baths
- Dining Room with direct access to the Kitchen, yet can be made private by the pocket door
- Kitchen made efficient by a cooktop island, an abundance of counter space and a built-in Pantry
- Sun room adjoining Kitchen and the Family Room
- Fireplace and a 14-foot ceiling highlighting the Family Room
- Master Suite with a five-piece Bath and a walk-in closet
- This home is designed with a basement foundation

FIRST FLOOR — 1,626 SQ. FT.
SECOND FLOOR — 522 SQ. FT.
BONUS — 336 SQ. FT.
GARAGE — 522 SQ. FT.

TOTAL LIVING AREA: 2,148 SQ. FT.

WIDTH 54'-7"
DEPTH 62'-8"

Porch 7/6 x 9/10
Sunroom 12/10 x 12/7
Family Room 18 x 15
Master 14 x 15
Breakfast 11/7 x 10/3
Kitchen 10/9 x 14/2
Dining 11 x 12
Foyer 6/7 x 8/8
8 x 12
5/4 x 8/5
Garage 22 x 23/5

FIRST FLOOR

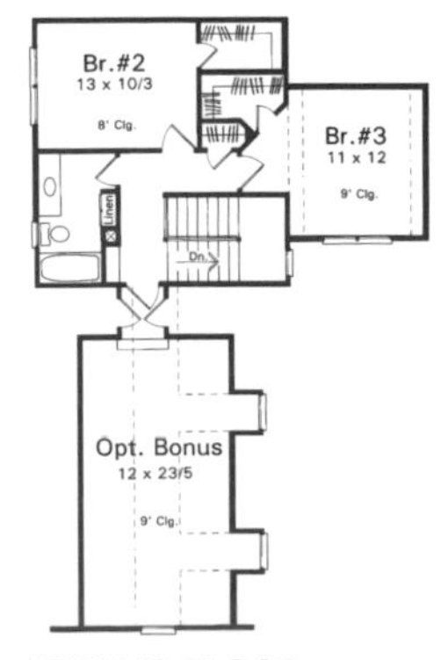
Br.#2
13 x 10/3
Br.#3
11 x 12
Opt. Bonus
12 x 23/5

SECOND FLOOR

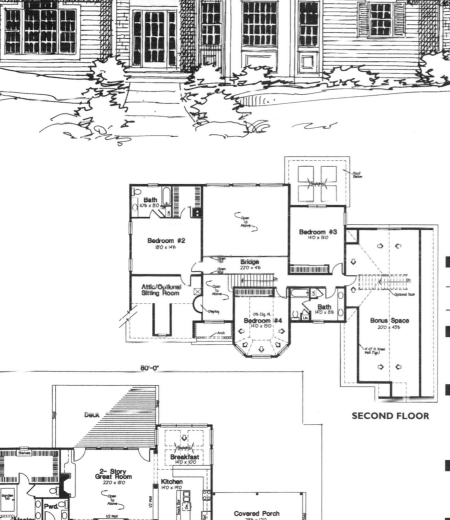

PLAN NO. 24955

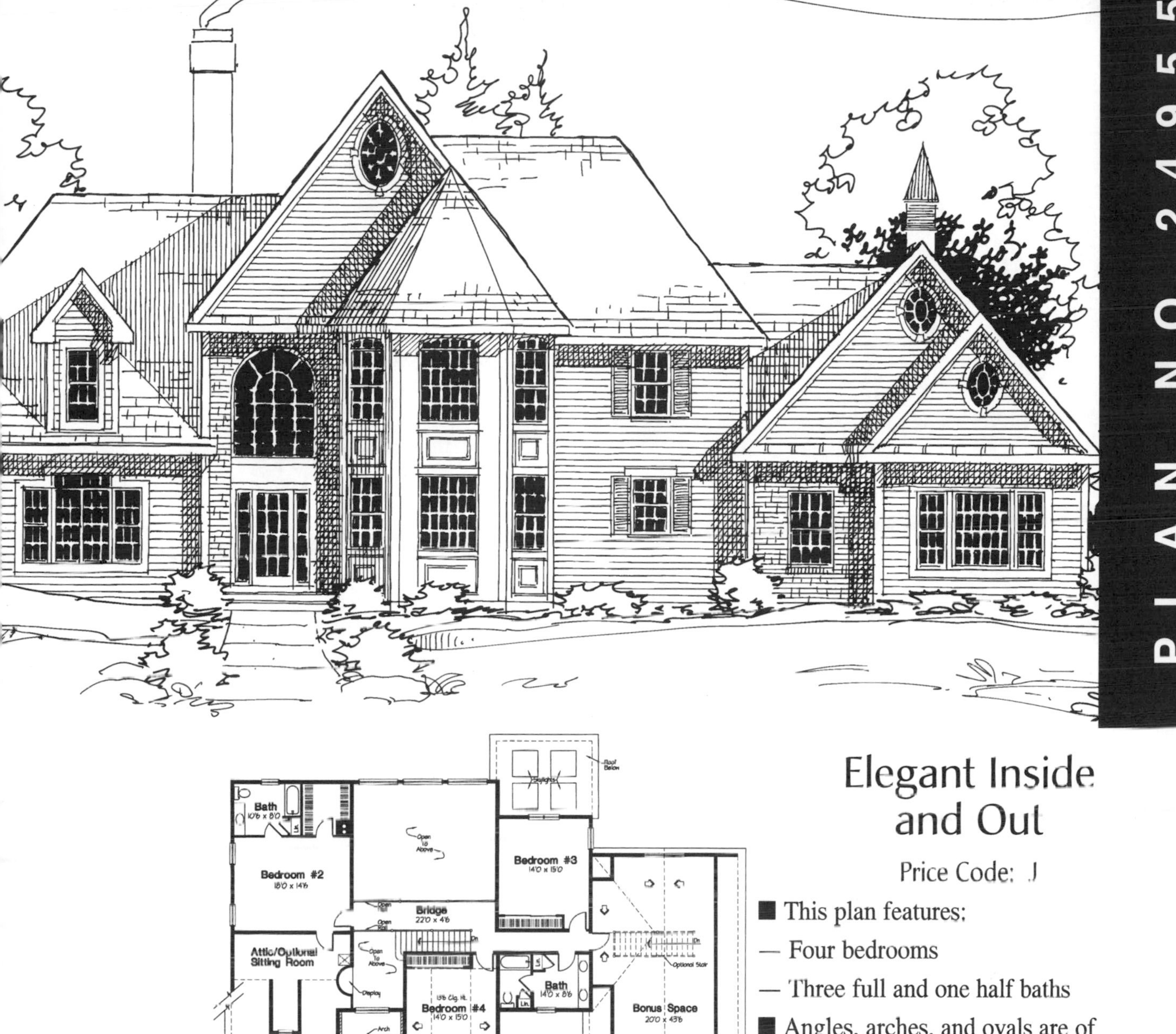

SECOND FLOOR

OPTIONAL CRAWLSPACE/SLAB

FIRST FLOOR

Elegant Inside and Out

Price Code: J

- This plan features:
- — Four bedrooms
- — Three full and one half baths
- Angles, arches, and ovals are of architectural interest on the facade of this home
- The Master Suite features a luxurious Bath with shower surrounded by glass blocks, garden tub, and a room-size walk-in closet with shelves
- Lined with windows and topped with skylights, the Breakfast Area offers sunlit and moonlit dining
- This home is designed with basement, slab, and crawlspace foundation options

FIRST FLOOR — 2,315 SQ. FT.
SECOND FLOOR — 1,278 SQ. FT.
BONUS ROOM — 780 SQ. FT.
BASEMENT — 2,315 SQ. FT.
GARAGE — 726 SQ. FT.

TOTAL LIVING AREA:
3,593 SQ. FT.

PLAN NO.10698

Vaulted Ceilings Make Every Room Special

PRICE CODE: L

- This plan features:
  - — Five bedrooms
  - — Four full and one three-quarter baths
- An enjoyable view from the island Kitchen which is separated from the Morning Room by only a counter
- Access to the Pool from the covered Patio or from the Living and Family Rooms
- The Living and Family Rooms with beamed 10-foot ceilings and massive fireplaces
- A Master Suite with a raised tub, built-in dressing tables and a fireplaced Sitting Room with vaulted ceiling
- This home is designed with a slab foundation

FIRST FLOOR — 4,014 SQ. FT.
SECOND FLOOR — 727 SQ. FT.
GARAGE — 657 SQ. FT.

TOTAL LIVING AREA: 4,741 SQ. FT.

90'-0"
Pool
Sitting Room
Patio
Family Rm
Master Br
Living Rm
Bar
Morning Rm
Br 2 / Study
Entry
Dining Rm
Kitchen
Porch
3-Car Garage
Br 3
FIRST FLOOR

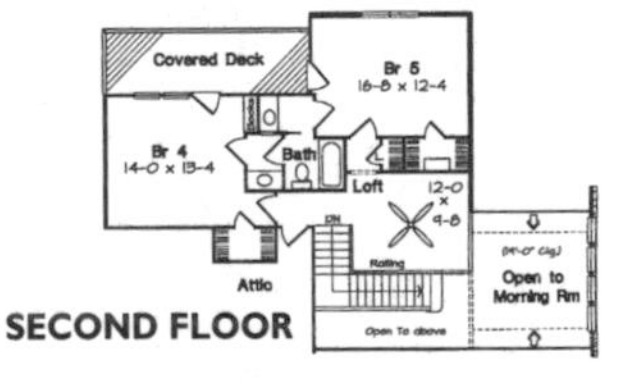
Covered Deck
Br 5
Br 4
Bath
Loft
Attic
Open to Morning Rm
SECOND FLOOR

PLAN NO.82047

Quaint and Cozy

PRICE CODE: C

- This plan features:
  - — Three bedrooms
  - — Two full and one half baths
- The Dining Room is defined at its corner by an elegant column
- The Kitchen includes a work island and a peninsula counter/snack bar separating it from the Breakfast Room
- The Breakfast Room has direct access to the rear covered Porch
- This home is designed with basement, slab and crawlspace foundation options

FIRST FLOOR — 1,334 SQ. FT.
SECOND FLOOR — 437 SQ. FT.
GARAGE — 342 SQ. FT.

TOTAL LIVING AREA: 1,771 SQ. FT.

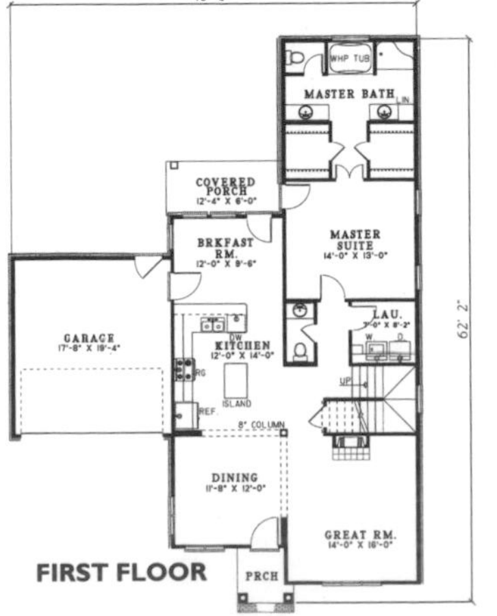
45' 0"
MASTER BATH
COVERED PORCH
BRKFAST RM.
MASTER SUITE
GARAGE
KITCHEN
LAU.
DINING
GREAT RM.
PRCH
FIRST FLOOR

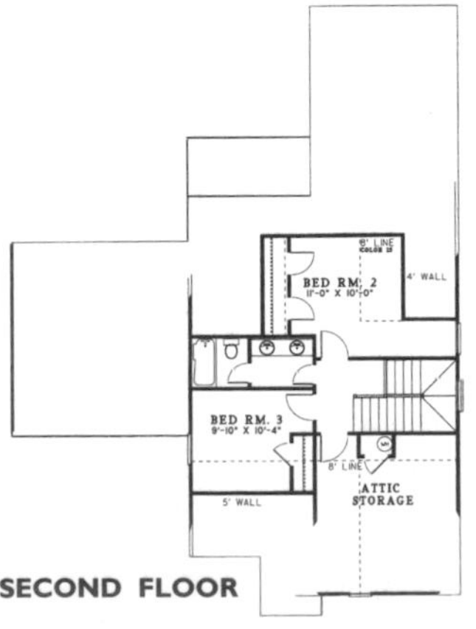
BED RM. 2
BED RM. 3
ATTIC STORAGE
SECOND FLOOR

Classical Style

PRICE CODE: C

- This plan features:
  - Three bedrooms
  - Two full baths
- There are 10-foot ceilings in many of the rooms
- This home has plenty of Storage Space
- The Dining Room is open to the Foyer and Living Room
- A fireplace is set between built in cabinets in the Living Room
- The Kitchen is well planned and executed
- This home is designed with crawlspace and slab foundation options

MAIN FLOOR — 1,890 SQ. FT.
GARAGE — 565 SQ. FT.

TOTAL LIVING AREA:
1,890 SQ. FT.

PLAN NO. 93080

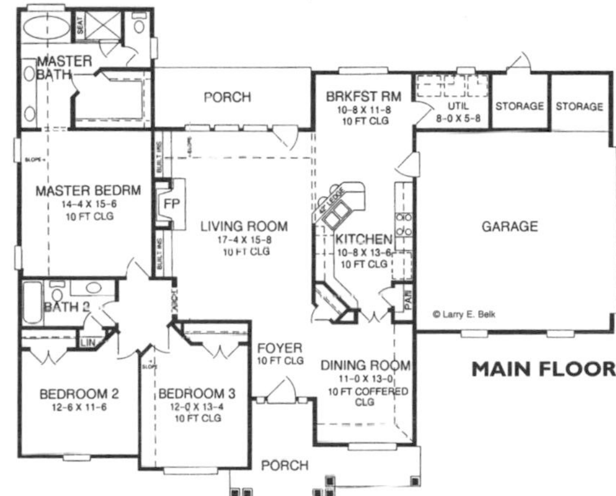

MASTER BATH
PORCH
BRKFST RM
10-8 X 11-8
10 FT CLG
UTIL
8-0 X 5-8
STORAGE
STORAGE
MASTER BEDRM
14-4 X 15-6
10 FT CLG
FP
LIVING ROOM
17-4 X 15-8
10 FT CLG
KITCHEN
10-8 X 13-6
10 FT CLG
GARAGE
BATH 2
© Larry E. Belk
FOYER
10 FT CLG
DINING ROOM
11-0 X 13-0
10 FT COFFERED CLG
BEDROOM 2
12-6 X 11-6
BEDROOM 3
12-0 X 13-4
10 FT CLG
PORCH
MAIN FLOOR

Spacious and Detailed

PRICE CODE: I

- This plan features:
  - Four bedrooms
  - Three full and two one half baths
- A Study, with private entrance and built-ins, is perfect for a private retreat
- Columns and half walls define the boundaries of the Great Room that houses a focal point fireplace
- On the second floor, secondary Bedrooms are connected by a bridge overlooking the Great Room
- A Screened Porch opens onto a covered Porch
- This home is designed with basement, slab, and crawlspace foundation options

FIRST FLOOR — 2,519 SQ. FT.
SECOND FLOOR — 956 SQ. FT.
BASEMENT — 2,534 SQ. FT.
GARAGE — 785 SQ. FT.
PORCH — 269 SQ. FT.

TOTAL LIVING AREA:
3,475 SQ. FT.

PLAN NO. 24956

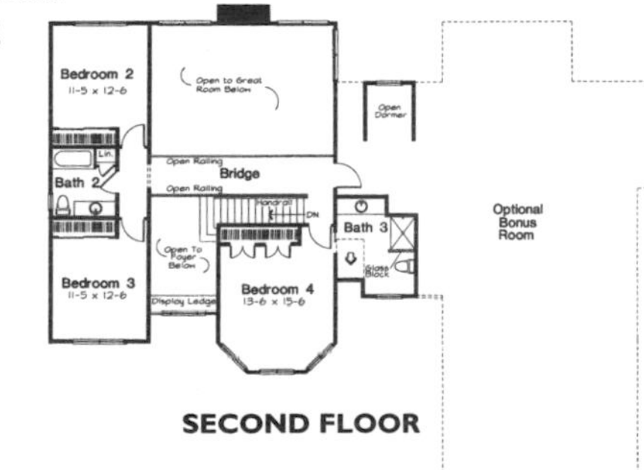

Bedroom 2
Bath 2
Bridge
Bath 3
Optional Bonus Room
Bedroom 3
Bedroom 4
SECOND FLOOR

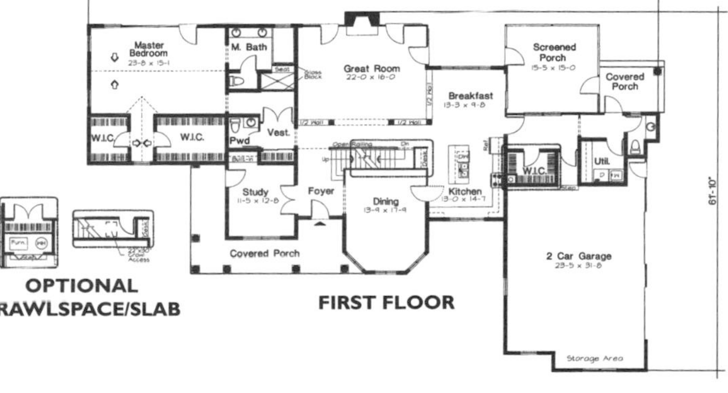

97'4"
Master Bedroom
M. Bath
Great Room
Screened Porch
Covered Porch
Breakfast
W.I.C.
W.I.C.
Pwd
Vest.
Study
Foyer
Dining
Kitchen
Util.
Covered Porch
2 Car Garage
Storage Area
OPTIONAL CRAWLSPACE/SLAB
FIRST FLOOR

To order your Blueprints, call 1-800-235-5700

PLAN NO.20507

Luxury and Style

PRICE CODE: G

- This plan features:
  - — Three bedrooms
  - — Two full and one half baths
- A two-story Foyer setting the tone for grandeur
- A two-story ceiling and two-way fireplace in the formal Living Room and the Family Room
- A terrific Living Area created by the Family Room, Breakfast Nook and Kitchen designed in an open layout
- A first floor Master Suite crowned by a tray ceiling and enhanced by a lavish Bath and walk-in closet
- Two additional Bedrooms, one with a sloped ceiling and built-in desk, on the second floor
- This home is designed with crawlspace and slab foundation options

FIRST FLOOR — 1,979 SQ. FT.
SECOND FLOOR — 948 SQ. FT.

TOTAL LIVING AREA: 2,927 SQ. FT.

65'-8"
46'-4"
glass block
Master Suite
15-8 x 15-0
9'-4" clg. ht.
Brkfst
10-0 x 8-4
Patio
Kitchen
13-0 x 14-8
pantry
snack bar
Family
18-0 x 15-0
2-story clg.
pass-thru cabinets
Garage
19-4 x 21-8
dry bar
UP
2-way fireplace
Living
14-6 x 16-6
2-story clg.
Foyer
Dining
14-4 x 13-4
10' clg. ht.
FIRST FLOOR

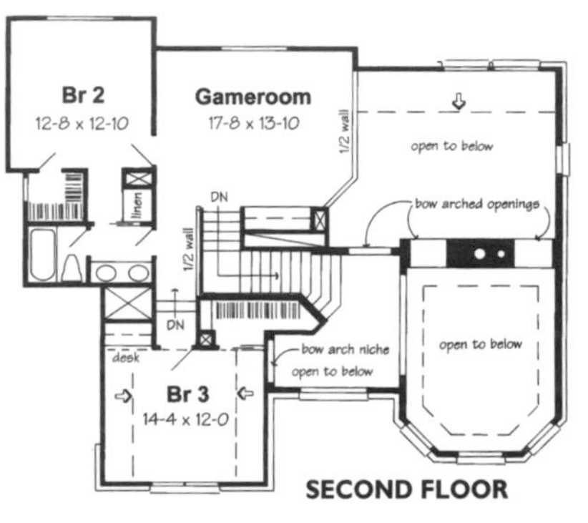

Br 2
12-8 x 12-10
Gameroom
17-8 x 13-10
1/2 wall
open to below
bow arched openings
DN
1/2 wall
desk
Br 3
14-4 x 12-0
bow arch niche open to below
open to below
SECOND FLOOR

PLAN NO.24958

Patio or Screened Porch

PRICE CODE: E

- This plan features:
  - — Three bedrooms
  - — Two full and one half baths
- The covered Patio with columns can also be built as a Screened Porch
- Access the Patio from the two-story Great Room which expands living space to the outdoors
- There's flexible space off the Foyer; this room can be turned into a Home Office
- This home is designed with basement, crawlspace and slab foundation options

FIRST FLOOR — 3,029 SQ. FT.
SECOND FLOOR — 1,647 SQ. FT.
BASEMENT — 1,647 SQ. FT.
GARAGE — 688 SQ. FT.

TOTAL LIVING AREA: 3,026 SQ. FT.

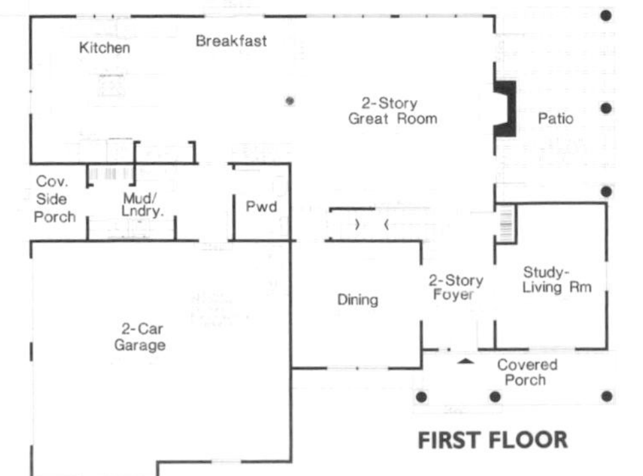

62'-0"
Kitchen
Breakfast
2-Story
Great Room
Patio
Cov. Side Porch
Mud/ Lndry.
Pwd
50'-0"
Dining
2-Story Foyer
Study-Living Rm
2-Car Garage
Covered Porch
FIRST FLOOR

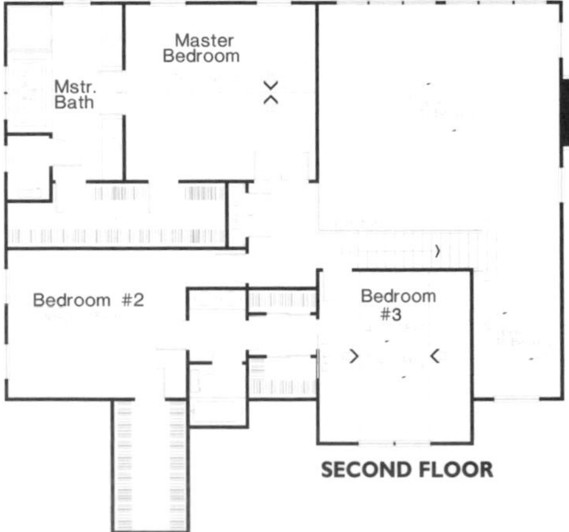

Master Bedroom
Mstr. Bath
Bedroom #2
Bedroom #3
SECOND FLOOR

Stg.

CRAWLSPACE/SLAB FOUNDATION OPTION

PLAN NO. 24960

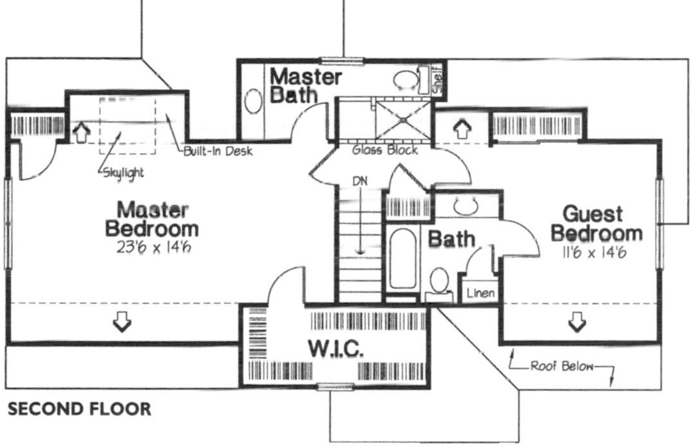

Master Bath
Shelf
Built-In Desk
Skylight
Glass Block
DN
Master Bedroom
23'6 x 14'6
Bath
Guest Bedroom
11'6 x 14'6
Linen
W.I.C.
Roof Below

SECOND FLOOR

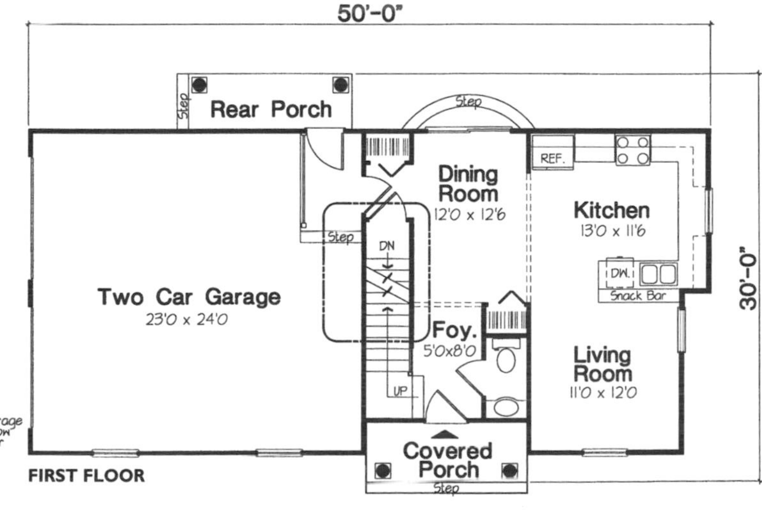

50'-0"
Rear Porch
Step
Dining Room
12'0 x 12'6
REF.
Kitchen
13'0 x 11'6
DW.
Snack Bar
Two Car Garage
23'0 x 24'0
DN
Foy.
5'0x8'0
UP
Living Room
11'0 x 12'0
Covered Porch
30'-0"

FIRST FLOOR

LSPACE/SLAB
UNDATION
OPTION

Crawl Access
Furn.
Wh.
Storage Below Stair

Fabulous Master Suite

Price Code: A

- This plan features:
- — Two bedrooms
- — Two full and one half baths
- The Master Suite features a skylit built-in desk, shower flanked with glass blocks, and a room-size walk-in closet
- The Guest Bedroom has its own Bath, making for a comfortable stay
- The U-shaped Kitchen boasts plenty of counter space, including an eating bar
- This home is designed with basement, slab, and crawlspace foundation options

FIRST FLOOR — 559 SQ. FT.
SECOND FLOOR — 906 SQ. FT.
BASEMENT — 559 SQ. FT.
GARAGE — 582 SQ. FT.
PORCH — 62 SQ. FT.

TOTAL LIVING AREA:
1,465 SQ. FT.

PLAN NO.82046

Covered Porch

PRICE CODE: B

- This plan features:
  - — Three bedrooms
  - — Two full baths
- A welcoming Covered Porch and dormer windows provide an old-fashioned appeal to this home
- The Great Room includes a fireplace to gather around colder evenings
- The Master Bedroom is located on the first floor with two walk-in closets and a whirlpool tub
- The Kitchen is efficiently arranged and includes a Pantry for easy storage
- The Breakfast Room has access to the rear Grilling Porch
- This home is designed with basement, slab, and crawlspace foundation options

FIRST FLOOR — 980 SQ. FT.
SECOND FLOOR — 561 SQ. FT.
GARAGE — 342 SQ. FT.

TOTAL LIVING AREA:
1,541 SQ. FT.

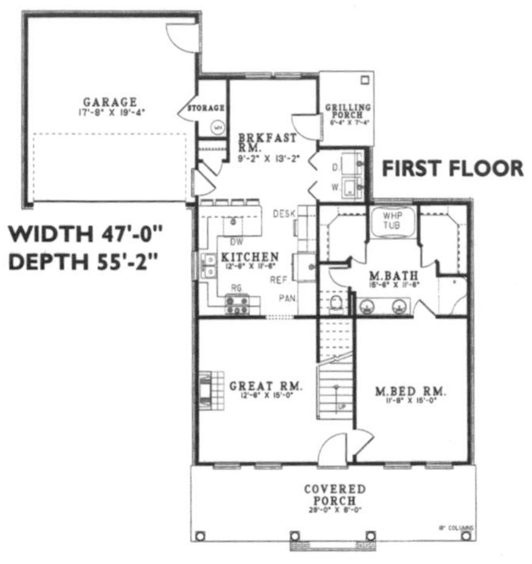
GARAGE
STORAGE
BRKFAST RM.
GRILLING PORCH
FIRST FLOOR
WIDTH 47'-0"
DEPTH 55'-2"
KITCHEN
M.BATH
GREAT RM.
M.BED RM.
COVERED PORCH

SECOND FLOOR

BED RM. 2

BED RM. 3

PLAN NO.24961

Family Friendly

PRICE CODE: C

- This plan features:
  - — Three bedrooms
  - — Two full and one half baths
- An arched Entry, flanked by columns and capped with a radius window, provides a warm and elegant welcome
- Plenty of counter space surrounds the Kitchen, making food preparation a snap
- The open design of the first floor creates a sense of community
- This home is designed with basement, slab, and crawlspace foundation options

FIRST FLOOR — 778 SQ. FT.
SECOND FLOOR — 1,339 SQ. FT.
BASEMENT — 778 SQ. FT.
GARAGE — 776 SQ. FT.
PORCH — 97 SQ. FT.

TOTAL LIVING AREA:
2,117 SQ. FT.

WIDTH 58'-0"
DEPTH 37'-0"

Rear Porch

Two Car Garage 27-6 x 27-6

Dining 10-0 x 13-6

Kitchen 15-6 x 15-0

Living Room 13-6 x 14-0

Pwd

Front Porch

FIRST FLOOR

Optional Placement Of Mechanicals For Crawl / Slab Foundations

Crawl Access

Storage Below Stair

CRAWLSPACE/SLAB FOUNDATION OPTION

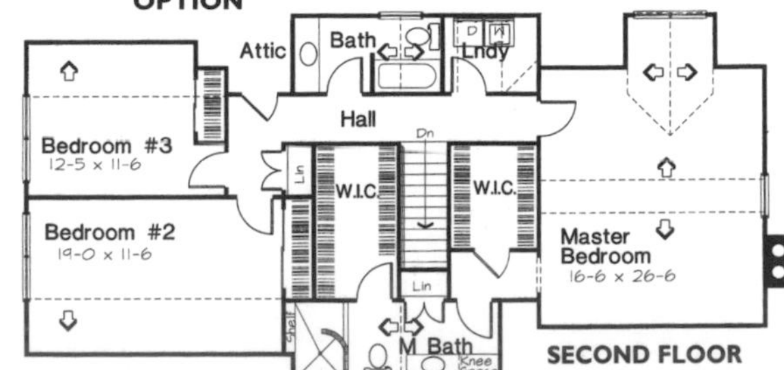
Attic
Bath
Lndy
Hall
Bedroom #3
12-5 x 11-6
Bedroom #2
19-0 x 11-6
W.I.C.
W.I.C.
Master Bedroom
16-6 x 26-6
M Bath
SECOND FLOOR

Fit for a Family

PRICE CODE: D

PLAN NO. 24964

This plan features:
- Three bedrooms
- Two full and one half bath
- A two-story Breakfast Area provides plenty of sunlight to begin your family's day
- An optional built-in entertainment center flanks the focal point fireplace in the Great Room
- The private Master Bedroom Suite features a Bathroom that includes a corner tub with glass-block windows
- The bonus room can be finished to suit your needs as your family grows
- This home is designed with basement, crawlspace and slab foundation options

IRST FLOOR — 1,195 SQ. FT.
ECOND FLOOR — 1,045 SQ. FT.
ONUS ROOM — 338 SQ. FT.
ASEMENT — 1,195 SQ. FT.
ARAGE — 635 SQ. FT.

TOTAL LIVING AREA:
2,240 SQ. FT.

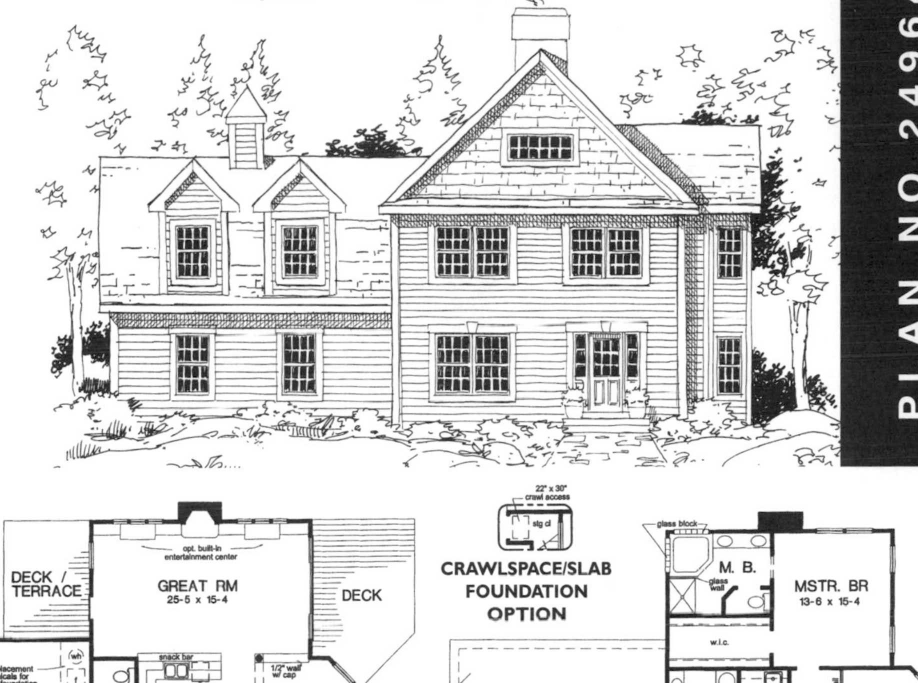

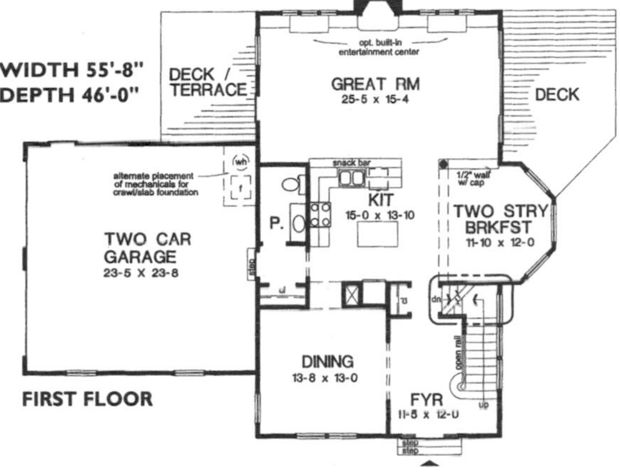
WIDTH 55'-8"
DEPTH 46'-0"
DECK / TERRACE
opt. built-in entertainment center
GREAT RM
25-5 x 15-4
DECK
snack bar
KIT
15-0 x 13-10
TWO STRY BRKFST
11-10 x 12-0
TWO CAR GARAGE
23-5 X 23-8
P.
DINING
13-8 x 13-0
FYR
11-5 x 12-0
open rail
FIRST FLOOR

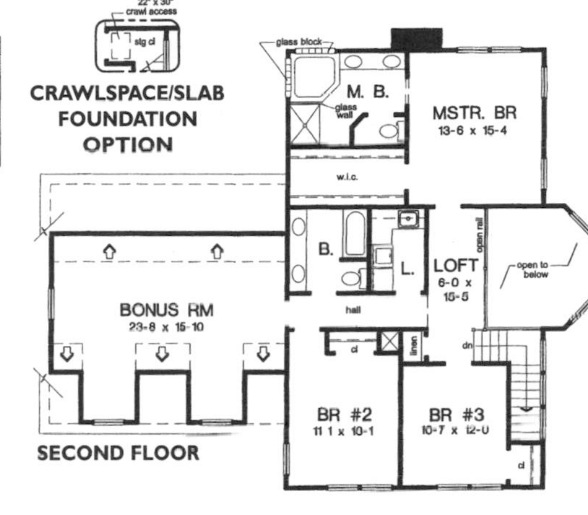
CRAWLSPACE/SLAB FOUNDATION OPTION
glass block
M. B.
MSTR. BR
13-6 x 15-4
w.i.c.
B.
L.
LOFT
6-0 x 15-5
BONUS RM
23-8 x 15-10
hall
BR #2
11 1 x 10-1
BR #3
10-7 x 12-0
SECOND FLOOR

Easy Living

PRICE CODE: A

PLAN NO. 93447

This plan features:
- Three bedrooms
- Two full baths
- A covered front Porch shelters the Entry to this home
- The Family Room is enlarged by a vaulted ceiling and also has a fireplace
- The Kitchen is L-shaped and includes a center island
- The Dining Room is open to the Kitchen for maximum convenience
- A covered walkway leads to the two-car Garage
- The Master Bedroom has a private Bath, which has two building options
- Both of the secondary Bedrooms have walk-in closets
- This home is designed with crawlspace and slab foundation options

AIN FLOOR — 1,474 SQ. FT.
ARAGE — 454 SQ. FT.

TOTAL LIVING AREA:
1,474 SQ. FT.

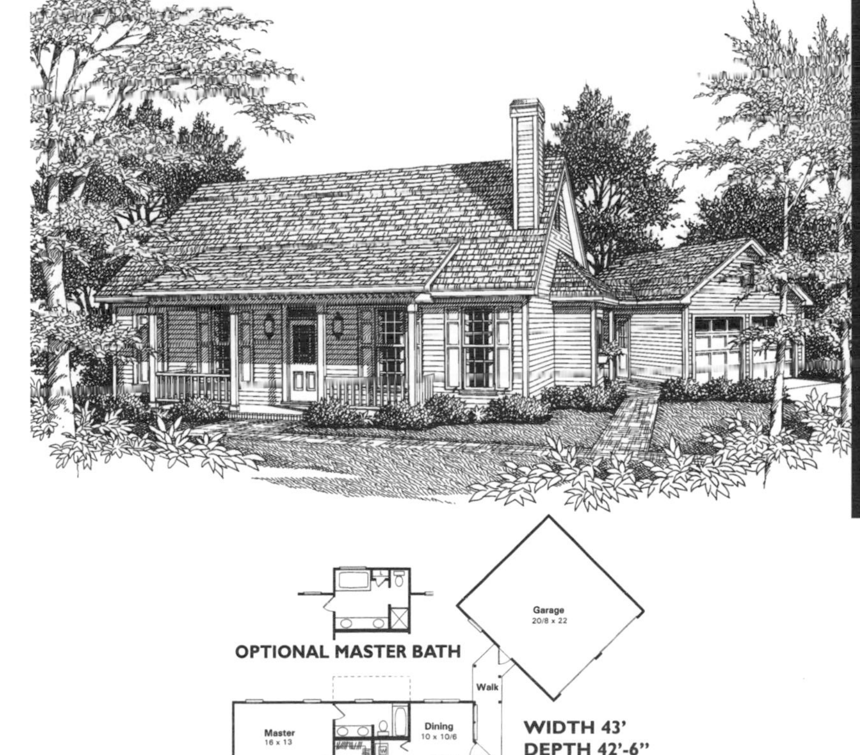

OPTIONAL MASTER BATH

Garage 20/8 x 22

Walk

WIDTH 43'
DEPTH 42'-6"

Master 16 x 13 · Dining 10 x 10/6 · Kitchen 14 x 10 · Br. #3 10 x 11 · Br. # 2 12/6 x 11/2 · Family Room 21/4 x 15 · Porch 23/6 x 6

MAIN FLOOR

PLAN NO.24965

A Place to Work and Play

PRICE CODE: F

- This plan features:
- — Three bedrooms
- — Two full and one half baths
- Windows, angles, and columns define the facade of this home
- The Kitchen has easy access to the Formal Dining Room, with a Butler's Panty in-between, making serving a snap
- The sunken Family Room, with built-in media center and focal point fireplace, offers a cozy place for family to gather
- It's some work and some admiring the view in the Computer Center which features a floor-to-ceiling window, flanked by built-in desks
- The first floor Living Room may be converted into a Library for private ventures
- This home is designed with basement, slab, and crawl-space foundation options

FIRST FLOOR — 1,483 SQ. FT.
SECOND FLOOR — 1,282 SQ. FT.
BONUS — 772 SQ. FT.
BASEMENT — 1,483 SQ. FT.
GARAGE — 854 SQ. FT.
PORCH — 59 SQ. FT.

TOTAL LIVING AREA:
2,765 SQ. FT.

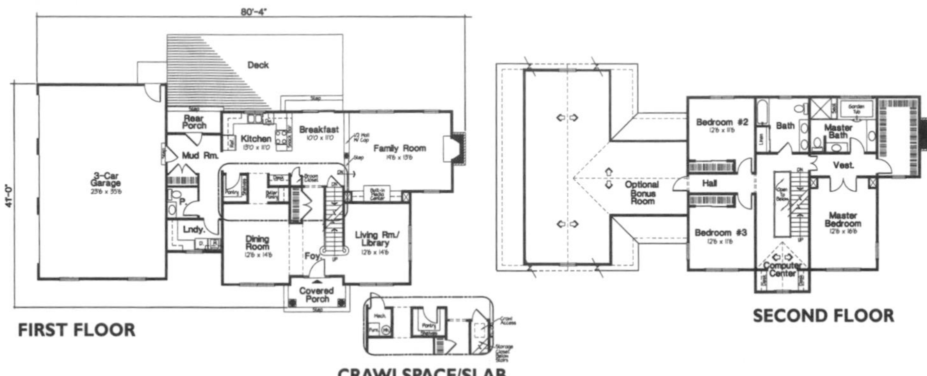
80'-4"
41'-0"
Deck
Rear Porch
Kitchen
Breakfast
Family Room
3-Car Garage
Mud Rm.
Lndy.
Dining Room
Foy
Living Rm./ Library
Covered Porch
Optional Bonus Room
Bedroom #2
Bath
Master Bath
Hall
Vest.
Bedroom #3
Master Bedroom
Computer Center
FIRST FLOOR
SECOND FLOOR

CRAWLSPACE/SLAB FOUNDATION OPTION

PLAN NO.99440

Classic Home

PRICE CODE: L

- This plan features:
- — Four bedrooms
- — Three full and one half baths
- Space and light connect the Entry, Gallery, Dining Room, and Living Room
- A Butler's Pantry connects the Kitchen to the Dining Room
- The Master Suite encompasses a whole wing on the first floor
- Up the curved staircase find three Bedrooms all with walk-in closets
- Also upstairs is a Game Room with built-in cabinets
- A three-car Garage completes this home
- This home is designed with basement and slab foundation options

FIRST FLOOR — 2,688 SQ. FT.
SECOND FLOOR — 1,540 SQ. FT.
BASEMENT — 2,688 SQ. FT.
GARAGE — 635 SQ. FT.

TOTAL LIVING AREA:
4,228 SQ. FT.

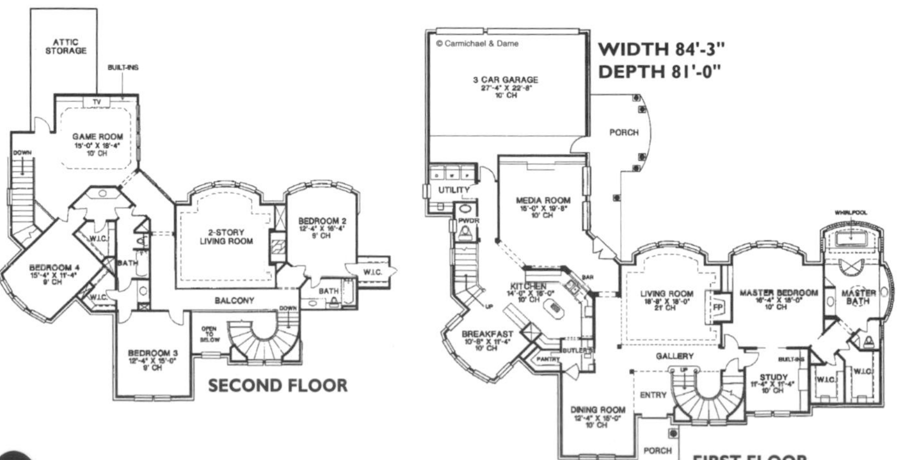
ATTIC STORAGE
GAME ROOM
2-STORY LIVING ROOM
BEDROOM 2
BEDROOM 4
BALCONY
BEDROOM 3
SECOND FLOOR
© Carmichael & Dame
3 CAR GARAGE
WIDTH 84'-3"
DEPTH 81'-0"
PORCH
UTILITY
MEDIA ROOM
KITCHEN
BREAKFAST
LIVING ROOM
MASTER BEDROOM
MASTER BATH
GALLERY
ENTRY
STUDY
DINING ROOM
PORCH
FIRST FLOOR

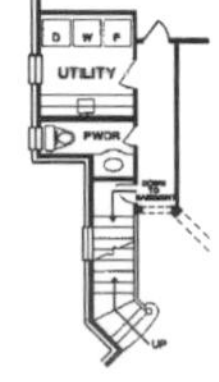

OPTIONAL BASEMENT STAIR LOCATION

Full Of Options

PRICE CODE: D

PLAN NO.24966

'his plan features:
- Three bedrooms
- Two full and one half baths
- 'he focal point fireplace casts its glow over the Family Room and beyond into the Breakfast Area and Kitchen
- A built-in desk in the Kitchen allows family members to tend to private tasks while remaining in the hub of activity
- 'he Bedrooms share the privacy of the second floor
- A generous bonus space can be used for anything you can imagine
- 'his home is designed with basement, slab, and crawlspace foundation options

ST FLOOR — 1,172 SQ. FT.
COND FLOOR — 966 SQ. FT.
NUS — 778 SQ. FT.
SEMENT — 1,172 SQ. FT.
RAGE — 857 SQ. FT.

TOTAL LIVING AREA:
2,138 SQ. FT.

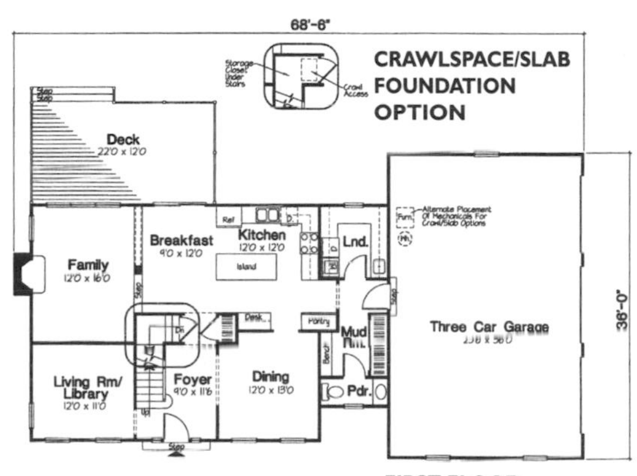
68'-6"
CRAWLSPACE/SLAB FOUNDATION OPTION
Deck
22'0 x 12'0
Family
12'0 x 16'0
Breakfast
9'0 x 12'0
Kitchen
12'0 x 12'0
Island
Lnd.
Mud Rm.
Pantry
Desk
Living Rm/ Library
12'0 x 11'0
Foyer
9'0 x 11'6
Dining
12'0 x 13'0
Pdr.
Three Car Garage
36'-0"
FIRST FLOOR

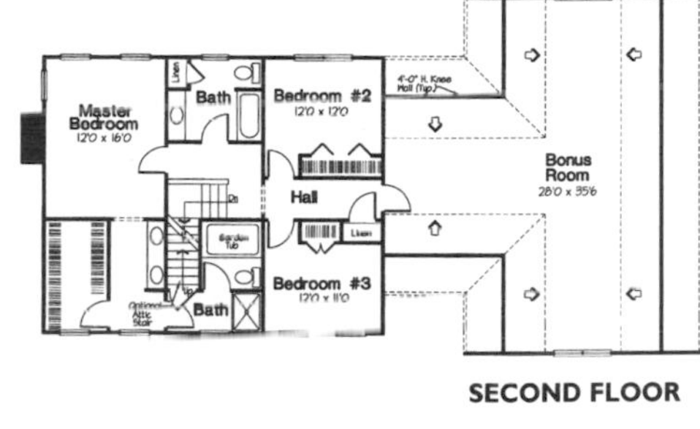
Master Bedroom
12'0 x 16'0
Bath
Bedroom #2
12'0 x 12'0
Hall
Bonus Room
28'0 x 35'6
Bedroom #3
Bath
Linen
SECOND FLOOR

Kitchen Island

PRICE CODE: C

PLAN NO.96925

This plan features:
- Three bedrooms
- Two full and one half baths
- This private Master Suite is entered through double doors, and boasts an oversized walk-in closet
- The Dining Room conversation easily flows to the open Great Room in this layout
- A huge bonus room is included with this plan
- This home is designed with crawlspace and slab foundation options

RST FLOOR — 1,251 SQ. FT.
COND FLOOR — 505 SQ. FT.
NUS — 447 SQ. FT.
ARAGE — 463 SQ. FT.
CK — 120 SQ. FT.

TOTAL LIVING AREA:
1,756 SQ. FT.

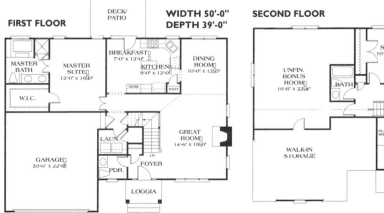

FIRST FLOOR
DECK/ PATIO
WIDTH 50'-0"
DEPTH 39'-0"
MASTER BATH
MASTER SUITE
12'-0" x 16'-0"
W.I.C.
BREAKFAST
7'-0" x 12'-0"
KITCHEN
9'-0" x 12'-0"
DINING ROOM
10'-0" x 12'-0"
DESK
PANT.
GREAT ROOM
14'-6" x 19'-0"
LAUN.
GARAGE
20'-0" x 22'-0"
PDR.
FOYER
LOGGIA

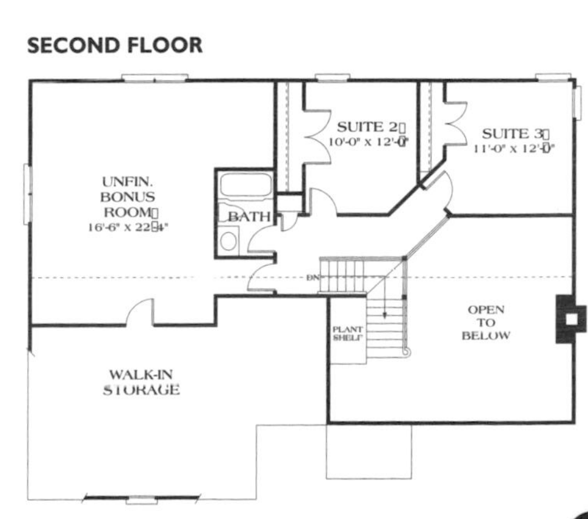
SECOND FLOOR
UNFIN. BONUS ROOM
16'-6" x 22'-4"
BATH
SUITE 2
10'-0" x 12'-0"
SUITE 3
11'-0" x 12'-0"
OPEN TO BELOW
PLANT SHELF
WALK-IN STORAGE

PLAN NO. 93075

Timeless Appeal

PRICE CODE: A

- This plan features:
  - — Three bedrooms
  - — Two full baths
- 10-foot ceilings giving the Living Room an open feel
- A cozy corner fireplace and access to the rear yard highlight the Living Room
- The Dining Area is enhanced by a sunny bay window and is open to the Kitchen
- Bedrooms are conveniently grouped and include room closets
- The Master Bedroom features a private Bath
- The Garage is located in the rear, leaving the curb appeal intact
- This home is designed with crawlspace and slab foundation options

MAIN FLOOR — 1,170 SQ. FT.
GARAGE — 478 SQ. FT.

TOTAL LIVING AREA:
1,170 SQ. FT.

WIDTH 51'-10"
DEPTH 53'-6"

MAIN FLOOR

GARAGE
STORAGE
MSTR BDRM 11-0x13-8 10 FT CLG
LIVING 13-0x17-8 10 FT CLG
DINING 11-0x 9-2
KITCH 11-6x 8-0
MSTR BATH
BATH 2
FOYER
BDRM 3 10-10x11-6
BDRM 2 10-4x10-2
COVERED PORCH
© Larry E. Belk

PLAN NO. 24967

Amenities Abound

PRICE CODE: D

- This plan features:
  - — Three bedrooms
  - — Two full and one half baths
- A grand Foyer presents a welcoming first impression
- Direct access to the Dining Room and the Breakfast Area make serving from the L-shaped Kitchen easy
- The Master Suite features a generous walk-in closet and a Bath with garden tub
- This home is designed with basement, slab, and crawl space foundation options

FIRST FLOOR — 1,201 SQ. FT.
SECOND FLOOR — 1,027 SQ. FT.
BONUS — 597 SQ. FT.
BASEMENT — 1,201 SQ. FT.
GARAGE — 854 SQ. FT.
PORCH — 32 SQ. FT.

TOTAL LIVING AREA:
2,228 SQ. FT.

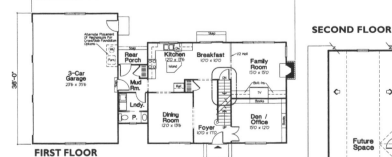

72'-4"
36'-0"

3-Car Garage 23'6 x 35'6
Rear Porch
Mud Rm.
Lndy.
Kitchen 12'0 x 13'6
Breakfast 10'0 x 10'0
Family Room 15'0 x 15'0
Dining Room 12'0 x 13'6
Foyer 10'0 x 17'0
Den / Office 15'0 x 12'0

FIRST FLOOR

SECOND FLOOR

Future Space
Bonus
Computer Alcove
Hall
Br #2 9'6 x 11'6
Br #3 9'6 x 11'6
M. Bath
Master Bedroom 15'0 x 15'6

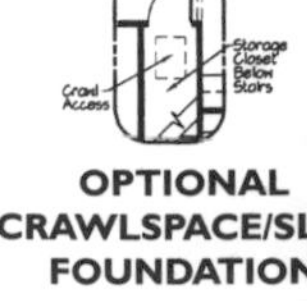

OPTIONAL CRAWLSPACE/SLAB FOUNDATION

Brick Home with Four Bedrooms

PRICE CODE: D

PLAN NO. 22004

This plan features:
- Four bedrooms
- Two full and one three-quarter baths
- Four roomy Bedrooms, including the Master Bedroom
- A centrally located Family Room including a fireplace, wetbar, and access to the Patio
- A large Dining Room at the front of the home for entertaining
- An interesting Kitchen and Nook with an adjoining Utility Room
- This home is designed with a slab foundation

AIN FLOOR — 2,070 SQ. FT.
ARAGE — 474 SQ. FT.

TOTAL LIVING AREA:
2,070 SQ. FT.

Rear Elevation
WIDTH 52'-0"
DEPTH 68'-6"
GARAGE
20'-6" X 21'-2"
UTILITY
NOOK
11'-0" X 10'-6"
PATIO
BATH
MASTER BEDROOM
14'-8" X 15'-8"
KITCHEN
FAMILY ROOM
23'-2" X 15'-4"
BATH
BATH
DINING
11'-0" X 12'-0"
ENTRY
BAR
BEDROOM
10'-6" X 12'-6"
PORCH
BEDROOM
11'-0" X 11'-6"
BEDROOM
12'-0" X 11'-0"
MAIN FLOOR

Easy One Floor Living

PRICE CODE: B

PLAN NO. 98423

This plan features:
- Three bedrooms
- Two full baths
- A spacious Family Room topped by a vaulted ceiling and highlighted by a large fireplace and a French door to the rear yard
- A serving bar open to the Family Room and the Dining Room, a Pantry and a peninsula counter adding more efficiency to the Kitchen
- A crowning tray ceiling over the Master Bedroom and a vaulted ceiling over the Master Bath
- A vaulted ceiling over the cozy Sitting Room in the Master Suite
- Two additional Bedrooms, roomy in size sharing the full Bath in the hall
- This home is designed with basement, slab and crawlspace foundation options

AIN FLOOR — 1,671 SQ. FT.
ASEMENT — 1,685 SQ. FT.
ARAGE — 400 SQ. FT.

TOTAL LIVING AREA:
1,671 SQ. FT.

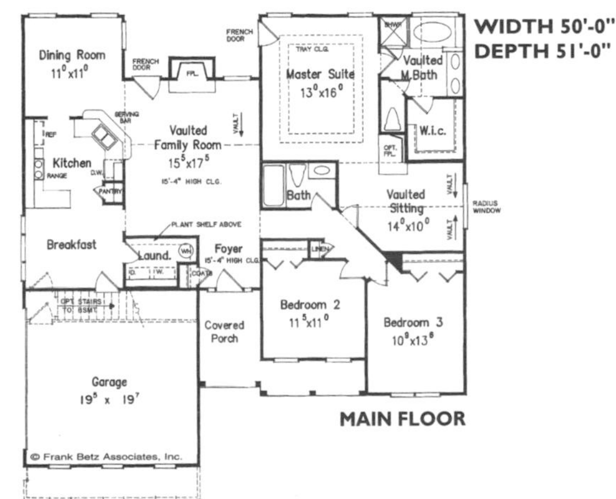

WIDTH 50'-0"
DEPTH 51'-0"
Dining Room
11⁰x11⁰
FRENCH DOOR
Master Suite
13⁰x16⁰
TRAY CLG.
Vaulted M.Bath
W.i.c.
Vaulted Family Room
15⁵x17⁵
Kitchen
Bath
Vaulted Sitting
14⁰x10⁰
RADIUS WINDOW
Breakfast
Laund.
Foyer
PLANT SHELF ABOVE
Bedroom 2
11⁵x11⁰
Bedroom 3
10⁶x13⁶
Covered Porch
Garage
19⁵ x 19⁷
© Frank Betz Associates, Inc.
MAIN FLOOR

PLAN NO.24405

Comfortable Country Ease

PRICE CODE: D

- This plan features:
  - — Three or four bedrooms
  - — Two full and two half baths
- A sprawling front Porch giving way to a traditional Foyer area with a half Bath and a graceful staircase
- A tray ceiling adding elegance to the Dining Room which directly accesses the Kitchen
- A large Country Kitchen with a center work island including plenty of storage and work space
- A tray ceiling accenting the Family Room, also highlighted by a fireplace
- A vaulted ceiling and a private Bath enhancing the Master Suite
- This home is designed with basement, slab and crawlspace foundation options

FIRST FLOOR — 1,104 SQ. FT.
SECOND FLOOR — 960 SQ. FT.

TOTAL LIVING AREA:* 2,064 *SQ. FT.

WIDTH 65'-8.5"
DEPTH 35'-3"

furn. w/h
CRAWLSPACE/SLAB
FOUNDATION
OPTION

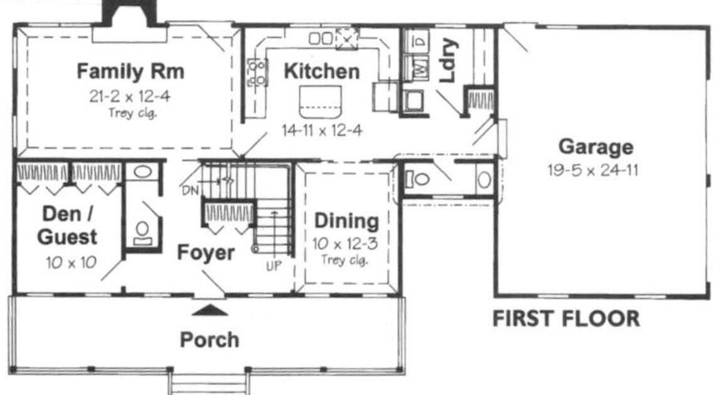

Family Rm
21-2 x 12-4
Trey clg.
Kitchen
14-11 x 12-4
Ldry
Garage
19-5 x 24-11
Den / Guest
10 x 10
Foyer
DN
UP
Dining
10 x 12-3
Trey clg.
Porch
FIRST FLOOR

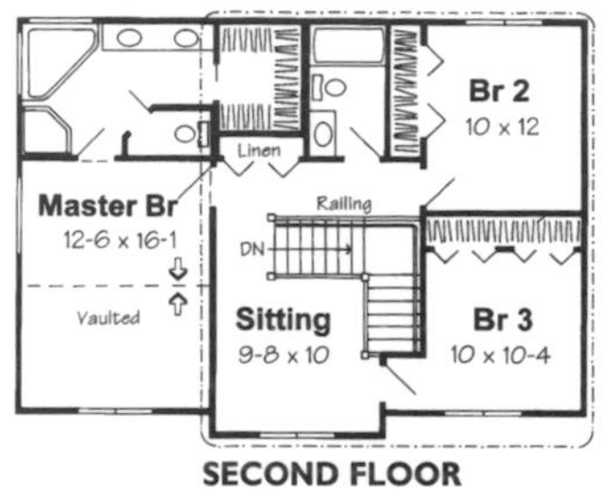

Br 2
10 x 12
Linen
Master Br
12-6 x 16-1
Railing
DN
Vaulted
Sitting
9-8 x 10
Br 3
10 x 10-4
SECOND FLOOR

PLAN NO.82049

Very Versatile

PRICE CODE: A

- This plan features:
  - — Three bedrooms
  - — Two full baths
- The Great Room has a boxed ceiling and a gas firepl
- An efficient U-shaped design in the Kitchen allows a the appliances to be convenient to each other
- The Breakfast Room has direct access to the Grilling Porch, as does the Master Suite
- The Master Suite includes a 10-foot boxed ceiling and a luxurious Master Bath
- The study could easily be converted into a third Bedroom
- This home is designed with crawlspace and slab foundation

MAIN FLOOR — 1,447 SQ. FT.
GARAGE — 342 SQ. FT.

TOTAL LIVING AREA* 1,447 *SQ. FT.

44' 0"
MASTER BATH
GRILLING PORCH
MASTER SUITE
STORAGE
BRKFAST RM.
GARAGE
BED RM. 2
KITCHEN
BATH
GREAT RM.
OFFICE / BED RM. 3
COVERED PORCH

MAIN FLOOR

PLAN NO. 93241

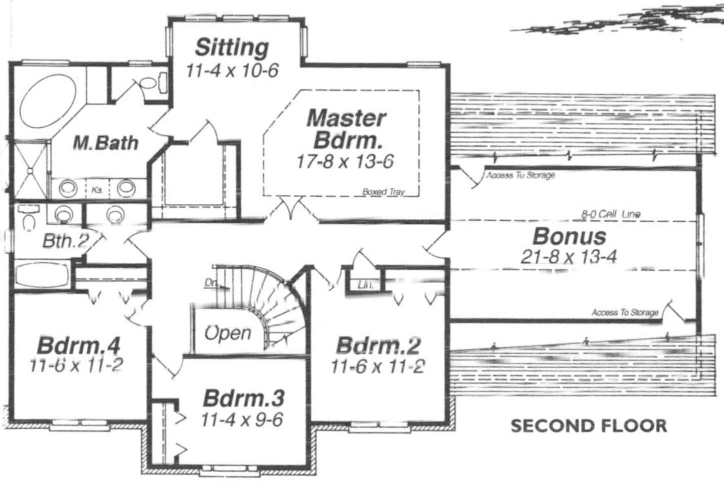

Sitting
11-4 x 10-6
Master Bdrm.
17-8 x 13-6
Boxed Tray
M.Bath
Bth.2
Access To Storage
8-0 Ceil. Line
Bonus
21-8 x 13-4
Access To Storage
Open
Bdrm.4
11-6 x 11-2
Bdrm.2
11-6 x 11-2
Bdrm.3
11-4 x 9-6

SECOND FLOOR

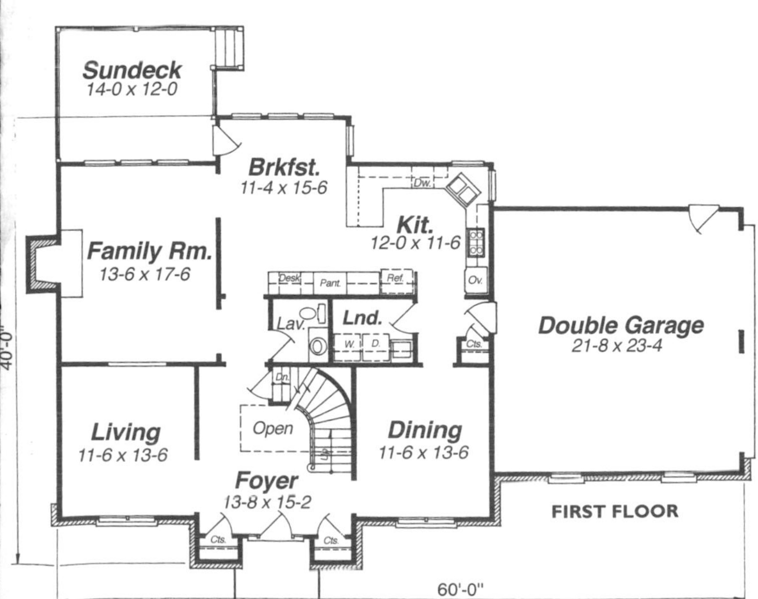

Sundeck
14-0 x 12-0
Brkfst.
11-4 x 15-6
Kit.
12-0 x 11-6
Family Rm.
13-6 x 17-6
Desk
Pant.
Ref.
Ov.
Lav.
Lnd.
Double Garage
21-8 x 23-4
Open
Living
11-6 x 13-6
Dining
11-6 x 13-6
Foyer
13-8 x 15-2
40'-0"
60'-0"
FIRST FLOOR

Elegant Master Suite

Price Code: F

- This plan features:
- — Four bedrooms
- — Two full and one half baths
- Comfortable Family Room with a fireplace
- Efficient Kitchen with built-in Pantry and serving counter
- Master Suite with decorative ceiling, Sitting Room and a plush Bath
- This home is designed with basement, slab and crawlspace foundation options

FIRST FLOOR — 1,307 SQ. FT.
SECOND FLOOR — 1,333 SQ. FT.
BONUS — 308 SQ. FT.
BASEMENT — 1,307 SQ. FT.
GARAGE — 528 SQ. FT.

TOTAL LIVING AREA:
2,640 SQ. FT.

PLAN NO.24268

Photography by Eastern Construction and Trading, Inc.

Stately Entrance Adds to Home's Exterior

PRICE CODE: D

- This plan features:
- — Three bedrooms
- — Two full and one half baths
- A vaulted ceiling in the Living Room adding to its spaciousness
- A formal Dining Room with easy access to both the Living Room and the Kitchen
- An efficient Kitchen with double sinks, and ample storage and counter space
- An informal Eating Nook with a built-in Pantry
- A large Family Room with a fireplace
- A plush Master Suite with a vaulted ceiling and luxurious Master Bath plus two walk-in closets
- Two additional Bedrooms share a full Bath with a convenient laundry chute
- This home is designed with basement, slab and crawlspace foundation options

FIRST FLOOR — 1,115 SQ. FT.
SECOND FLOOR — 1,129 SQ. FT.
BASEMENT — 1,096 SQ. FT.
GARAGE — 415 SQ. FT.

TOTAL LIVING AREA:
2,244 SQ. FT.

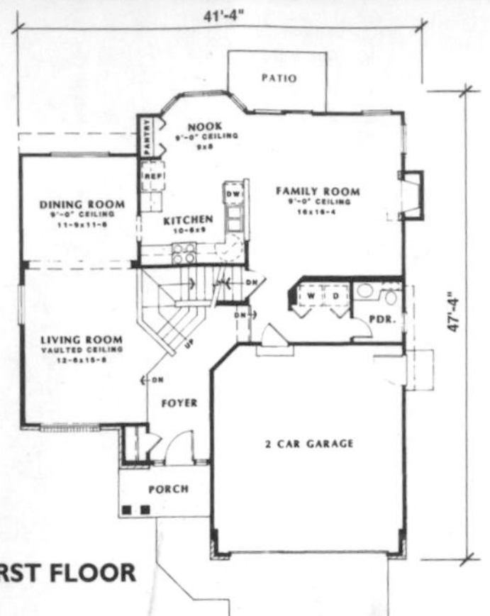
41'-4"
47'-4"
PATIO
NOOK
DINING ROOM
FAMILY ROOM
KITCHEN
LIVING ROOM
PDR.
FOYER
2 CAR GARAGE
PORCH

FIRST FLOOR

LOFT / BEDROOM
BEDROOM
BEDROOM
HALL
BATH
OPEN TO BELOW
MASTER BATH
MASTER SUITE

SECOND FLOOR

PLAN NO.24968

Front, Side, and Screened Porch

PRICE CODE: G

- This plan features:
- — Four bedrooms
- — Two full and one half baths
- Elegant columns define the boundaries of the Foyer, Dining Room, and Living Room
- The Master Suite features a vestibule entrance, a room walk-in closet with Dressing Area, and a luxurious Ba with garden tub and shower with built-in seat
- Counter space, including an island and snack bar, abounds in the efficient Kitchen
- Windows flank the focal point fireplace in the Great Room
- A bench in the side Hall offers private retreat
- This home is designed with a basement foundation

FIRST FLOOR — 1,527 SQ. FT.
SECOND FLOOR — 1,350 SQ. FT.
BASEMENT — 1,527 SQ. FT.
GARAGE — 576 SQ. FT.
PORCH — 304 SQ. FT.

TOTAL LIVING AREA:
2,877 SQ. FT.

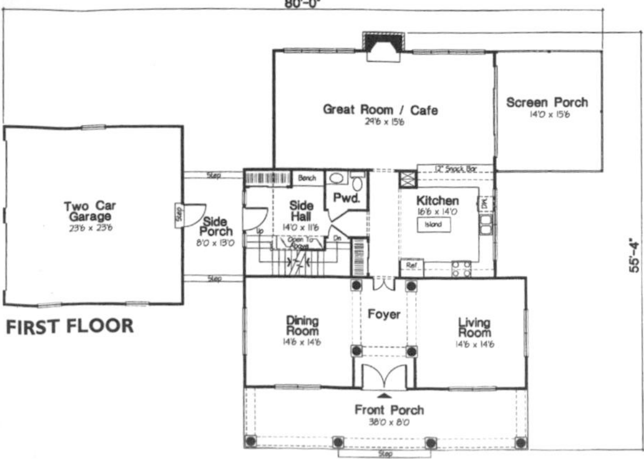
80'-0"
55'-4"
Great Room / Cafe
29'6 x 15'6
Screen Porch
14'0 x 15'6
Two Car Garage
23'6 x 23'6
Side Porch
8'0 x 13'0
Side Hall
14'0 x 11'6
Pwd.
Kitchen
16'6 x 14'0
Island
Foyer
Dining Room
14'6 x 14'6
Living Room
14'6 x 14'6
Front Porch
38'0 x 8'0

FIRST FLOOR

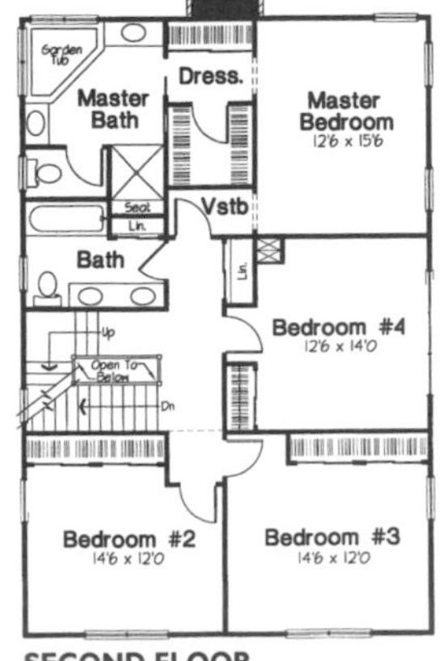
Master Bath
Dress.
Master Bedroom
12'6 x 15'6
Vstb
Bath
Bedroom #4
12'6 x 14'0
Bedroom #2
14'6 x 12'0
Bedroom #3
14'6 x 12'0

SECOND FLOOR

Charming Brick Home

PRICE CODE: C

This plan features:
- Three bedrooms
- Two full baths
- A covered entrance leading into a spacious Living Room with a fireplace and an airy Dining Room with access to the Patio
- An island Kitchen, open to the Dining Room, offering ample storage and easy access to the Laundry Area and the Garage
- A Master Bedroom with a walk-in closet, access to the Patio and a plush Bath offering a window tub, a step-in shower and a double vanity
- Two additional Bedrooms, with decorative windows, sharing a full hall Bath
- This home is designed with a basement foundation

AIN FLOOR — 1,868 SQ. FT.
ASEMENT — 1,868 SQ. FT.
ARAGE — 782 SQ. FT.

TOTAL LIVING AREA:
1,868 SQ. FT.

PLAN NO. 93107

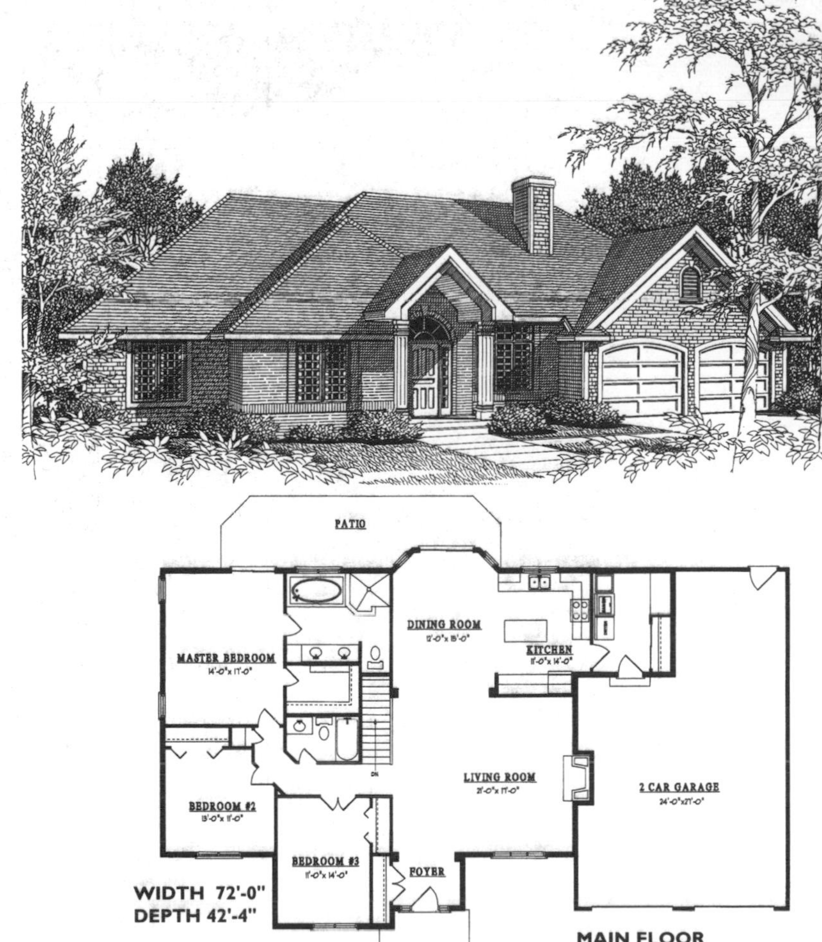

PATIO
DINING ROOM
MASTER BEDROOM
KITCHEN
LIVING ROOM
2 CAR GARAGE
BEDROOM #2
BEDROOM #3
FOYER
WIDTH 72'-0"
DEPTH 42'-4"
MAIN FLOOR

Eye-Catching Glass Turrets

PRICE CODE: F

This plan features:
- Three bedrooms
- Three full baths
- Two-story Foyer with a curved staircase, opens to a unique Living Room with an alcove of windows and inviting fireplace
- Alcove of glass and a vaulted ceiling in the open Dining Area
- Kitchen with built-in Pantry and desk, cooktop island/snack bar and a Nook with double door
- Comfortable Family Room highlighted by another fireplace and wonderful outdoor views
- Vaulted Master Suite offers a plush Dressing Area with walk-in closet and Spa tub
- Two additional Bedrooms, one with a glass alcove, share a double vanity Bath
- This home is designed with a crawlspace foundation

RST FLOOR — 1,592 SQ. FT.
COND FLOOR — 958 SQ. FT.
ONUS ROOM — 194 SQ. FT.
ARAGE — 956 SQ. FT.

TOTAL LIVING AREA:
2,550 SQ. FT.

PLAN NO. 91518

◀ 63' ▶

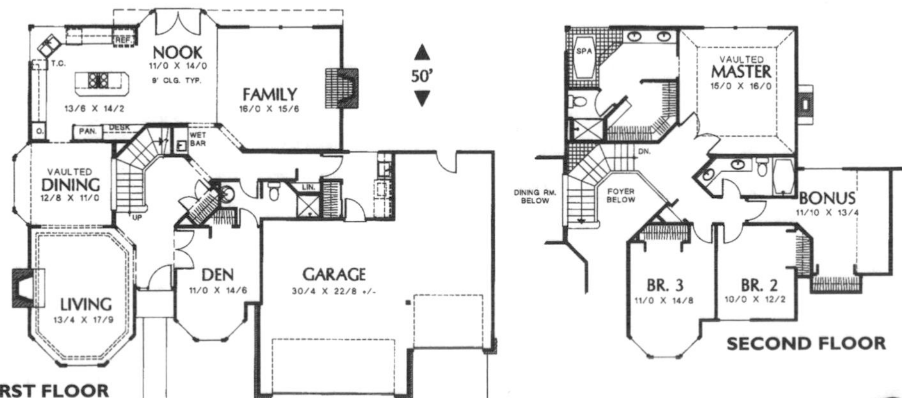

NOOK
11/0 X 14/0
9' CLG. TYP.
FAMILY
16/0 X 15/6
13/6 X 14/2
50'
VAULTED
DINING
12/8 X 11/0
LIVING
13/4 X 17/9
DEN
11/0 X 14/6
GARAGE
30/4 X 22/8 +/-
FIRST FLOOR
VAULTED
MASTER
15/0 X 16/0
BONUS
11/10 X 13/4
BR. 3
11/0 X 14/8
BR. 2
10/0 X 12/2
SECOND FLOOR

PLAN NO.93161

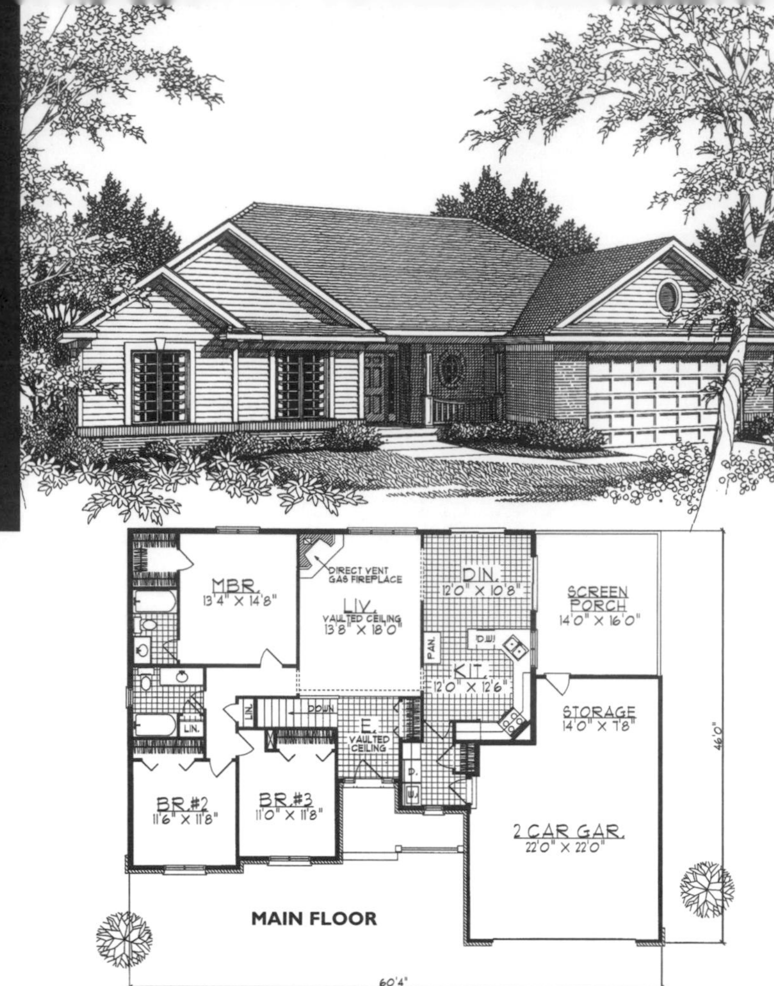

MBR.
13'4" X 14'8"
DIRECT VENT GAS FIREPLACE
LIV.
VAULTED CEILING
13'8" X 18'0"
DIN.
12'0" X 10'8"
SCREEN PORCH
14'0" X 16'0"
PAN.
D/W
KIT.
12'0" X 12'6"
LIN.
DOWN
E.
VAULTED CEILING
STORAGE
14'0" X 7'8"
46'0"
BR.#2
11'6" X 11'8"
BR.#3
11'0" X 11'8"
2 CAR GAR.
22'0" X 22'0"
MAIN FLOOR
60'4"

Hip Roof Ranch

PRICE CODE: B

- This plan features:
- — Three bedrooms
- — Two full baths
- Cozy front Porch leads into Entry with vaulted ceiling and sidelights
- Open Living Room enhanced by a cathedral ceiling, a wall of windows and corner fireplace
- Large and efficient Kitchen with an extended counter and a bright Dining Area with access to a Screened Porch
- Convenient Utility Area with access to Garage and Storage Area
- Spacious Master Bedroom with a walk-in closet and private Bath
- Two additional Bedrooms with ample closets, share a full Bath
- This home is designed with a basement foundation

MAIN FLOOR — 1,540 SQ. FT.
BASEMENT — 1,540 SQ. FT.

TOTAL LIVING AREA:
1,540 SQ. FT.

PLAN NO.98425

WIDTH 56'-0"
DEPTH 60'-0"

Master Suite 14⁰ x 17⁰ — Tray Ceiling; Breakfast; Kitchen; Vaulted Living Room 15⁶ x 20²; Bedroom 2 11² x 11⁰; Bath; Vaulted M.Bath; Pwdr.; Foyer; Dining Room 11³ x 12⁰; Covered Porch; Bedroom 3 11² x 11⁶; W.i.c.; Laund.; Stor.; Garage 23⁰ x 19⁵

© Frank Betz Associates, Inc.

MAIN FLOOR

Bath; W.i.c.; Optional Bonus Room 11⁰ x 19²

BONUS

Small, Yet Lavishly Appointed

PRICE CODE: C

- This plan features:
- — Three bedrooms
- — Two full and one half baths
- The Dining Room, Living Room, Foyer and Master B all topped by high ceilings
- Master Bedroom includes a decorative tray ceiling and a walk-in closet
- Kitchen open to the Breakfast Room enhanced by a serving bar and a Pantry
- Living Room with a large fireplace and a French door to the rear yard
- Master Suite located on opposite side from secondary Bedrooms, allowing for privacy
- This home is designed with basement and crawlspace foundation options

MAIN FLOOR — 1,845 SQ. FT.
BONUS — 409 SQ. FT.
BASEMENT — 1,845 SQ. FT.
GARAGE — 529 SQ. FT.

TOTAL LIVING AREA:
1,845 SQ. FT.

Delightful

PRICE CODE: C

This plan features:
- Three bedrooms
- Three full baths
- A bonus second floor has a Game Room and a full Bath
- The secondary Bedrooms each have a vanity, but share the rest of the Bath
- The Master Suite has a large walk- in closet and a Bath with a clawfoot tub
- The Living Room features a fireplace with a built-in media center to its left
- Porches and Decking wrap this home for outdoor options
- Another fireplace can be found in the Hearth/Dining Room
- This home is designed with basement, slab and crawlspace foundation options

AIN FLOOR — 1,921 SQ. FT.
ONUS — 812 SQ. FT.
ARAGE — 505 SQ. FT.

TOTAL LIVING AREA:* 1,921 *SQ. FT.

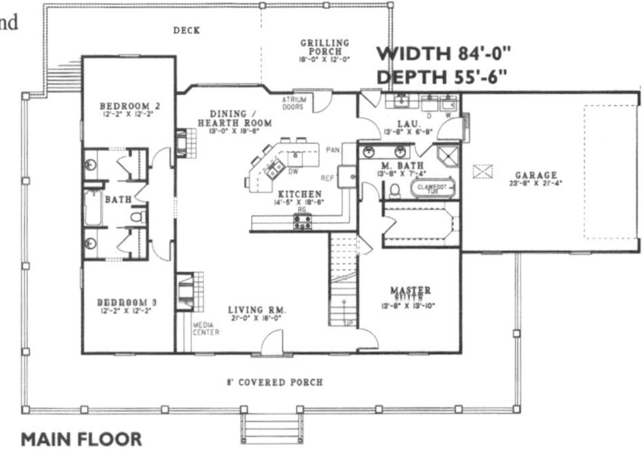

DECK
GRILLING PORCH 18'-0" X 12'-0"
WIDTH 84'-0"
DEPTH 55'-6"
BEDROOM 2 12'-2" X 12'-2"
DINING / HEARTH ROOM 13'-0" X 19'-6"
ATRIUM DOORS
LAU. 13'-8" X 6'-8"
M. BATH 13'-8" X 7'-4"
CLAWFOOT TUB
GARAGE 23'-8" X 27'-4"
BATH
KITCHEN 14'-5" X 18'-6"
BEDROOM 3 12'-2" X 12'-2"
LIVING RM. 21'-0" X 18'-0"
MEDIA CENTER
MASTER SUITE 13'-8" X 13'-10"
8' COVERED PORCH
MAIN FLOOR

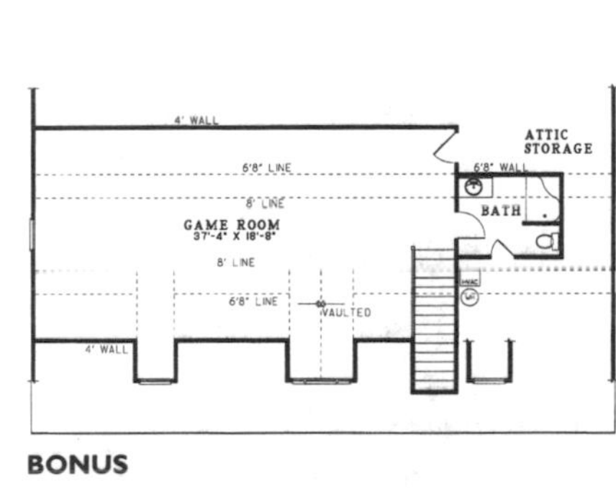

4' WALL
ATTIC STORAGE
6'8" WALL
6'8" LINE
8' LINE
GAME ROOM 37'-4" X 18'-8"
BATH
VAULTED
4' WALL
BONUS

Details, Details, Details

PRICE CODE: J

This plan features:
- Four bedrooms
- Two full and two one half baths
- Accent windows and brick define this home's facade
- The two-story Entry makes a grand first impression
- Elegant columns mark the boundaries to the formal Dining Room, with arch recess, and the two-story Gathering Room
- The impressive Master Suite features a volume ceiling, room-sized walk-in closet, and lush Bath with a garden tub and class blocks surrounding the shower
- On the second floor, three Secondary Bedrooms each have direct access to a full Bath
- A rear Deck and Patio extend living space outdoors
- This home is designed with basement, slab and crawlspace foundation options

RST FLOOR — 1,999 SQ. FT.
ECOND FLOOR — 1,677 SQ. FT.
ONUS — 371 SQ. FT.
ASEMENT — 1,999 SQ. FT.
ARAGE — 736 SQ. FT.
ORCH — 112 SQ. FT.

TOTAL LIVING AREA:* 3,676 *SQ. FT.

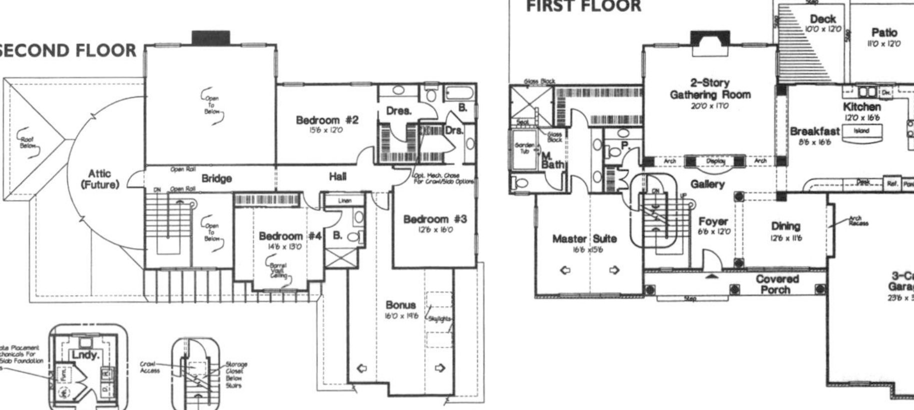

SECOND FLOOR
Attic (Future)
Bridge
Hall
Bedroom #2 15'6 x 12'0
Dres.
B.
Bedroom #3 12'6 x 16'0
Bedroom #4 14'6 x 13'0
Bonus 16'0 x 14'6
FIRST FLOOR
73'-0"
Deck 10'0 x 12'0
Patio 11'0 x 12'0
2-Story Gathering Room 20'0 x 17'0
Kitchen 12'0 x 16'6
Lndy.
Breakfast 8'6 x 16'6
M. Bath
Gallery
Foyer 6'6 x 12'0
Dining 12'6 x 11'6
Master Suite 16'6 x 15'6
Covered Porch
3-Car Garage 23'6 x 32'0
57'-0"

CRAWLSPACE/SLAB FOUNDATION OPTION

PLAN NO. 93098

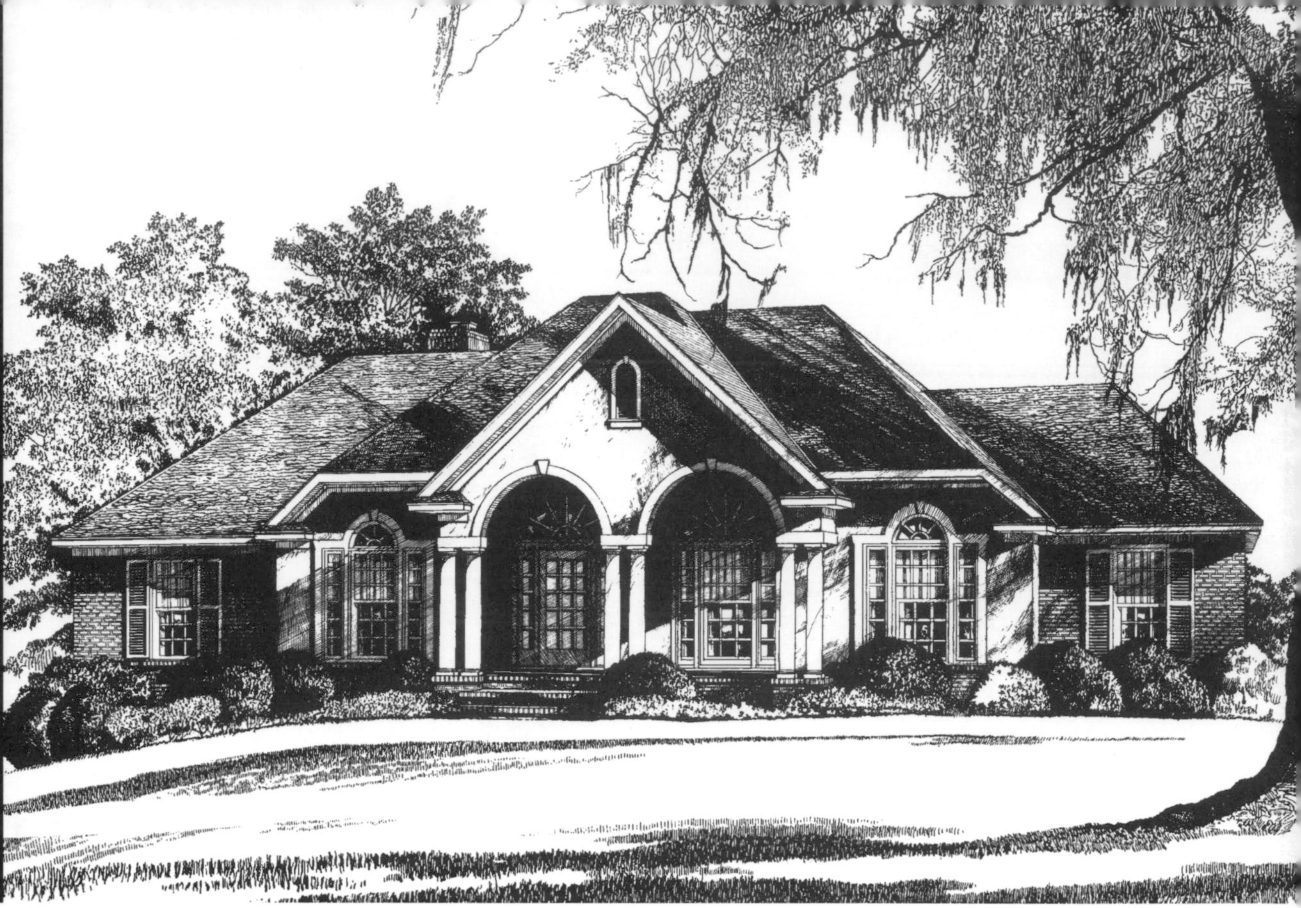

Double Arches Add Elegance

Price Code: C

- This plan features:
- — Three bedrooms
- — Two full baths
- Double arches form the entrance to this elegantly styled home
- Two palladian windows add distinction to the elevation
- 10-foot ceilings in all major living areas give the home an expansive feeling
- The Kitchen features an angled eating bar and opens to the Breakfast Room
- This home is designed with crawlspace and slab foundation options

MAIN FLOOR — 1,932 SQ. FT.
GARAGE — 552 SQ. FT.

TOTAL LIVING AREA:
1,932 SQ. FT.

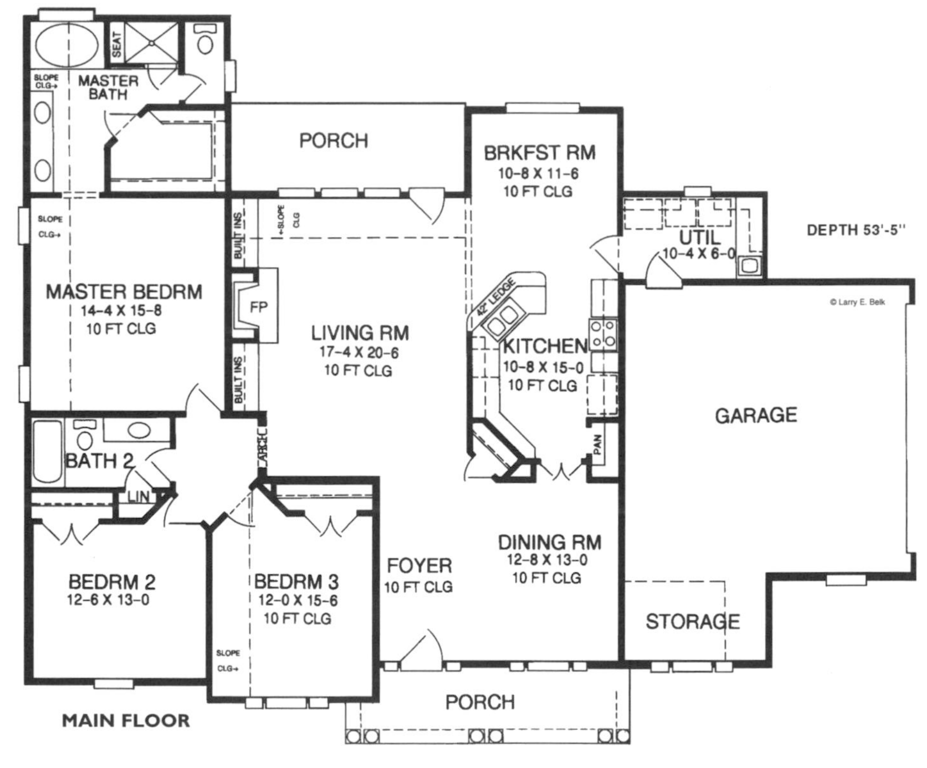

MASTER BATH
SEAT
SLOPE CLG
PORCH
BRKFST RM
10-8 X 11-6
10 FT CLG
UTIL
10-4 X 6-0
DEPTH 53'-5"
© Larry E. Belk
MASTER BEDRM
14-4 X 15-8
10 FT CLG
BUILT INS
FP
LIVING RM
17-4 X 20-6
10 FT CLG
42" LEDGE
KITCHEN
10-8 X 15-0
10 FT CLG
GARAGE
BATH 2
LIN
PAN
DINING RM
12-8 X 13-0
10 FT CLG
FOYER
10 FT CLG
BEDRM 2
12-6 X 13-0
BEDRM 3
12-0 X 15-6
10 FT CLG
STORAGE
PORCH
MAIN FLOOR
WIDTH 65'-10"

PLAN NO. 24970

A Classic Colonial

Price Code: F

- This plan features:
- — Four bedrooms
- — Two full and one half baths
- The Foyer provides access to the formal Living and Dining Rooms
- The Country Kitchen has plenty of room for the family to cook together
- The Breakfast Area offers adjoins the Kitchen and provides access to the rear Deck
- The Master Bedroom Suite is privately located on one side of the second floor
- This home is designed with basement, slab, and crawlspace foundation options

FIRST FLOOR — 1,283 SQ. FT.
SECOND FLOOR — 1,333 SQ. FT.
BASEMENT — 1,292 SQ. FT.
GARAGE — 695 SQ. FT.

TOTAL LIVING AREA:
2,616 SQ. FT.

storage closet below stair
22" x 30" crawl access
OPTIONAL CRAWLSPACE/SLAB

SECOND FLOOR
MB
B
BR #2
13-5 x 15-0
w.i.c.
optional fireplace
open railing
foyer
MSTR BR
13-6 x 19-0
BR #4
10-3 x 12-0
BR #3
13-5 x 12-0

WIDTH 66'-6"
DEPTH 32'-6"

DECK
20-0 x 14-0
concrete pad
storage area
alternate placement of mechanicals for crawl/slab foundations
mech chase
P
MD
KITCHEN
12-6 x 12-0
island
BRKF
7-6 x 12-0
masonry fireplace
FAMILY RM
13-6 x 19-6
TWO CAR GARAGE
24-0 x 28-0
optional fireplace
DINING RM
13-6 x 15-6
FOYER
12-0 x 11-6
LIVING RM/ LIBRARY
15-0 x 12-0
concrete stoop
FIRST FLOOR

PLAN NO. 97135

A Must See Design

Price Code: D

- This plan features:
  - — Three bedrooms
  - — Two full baths
- Attractive, arched entrance leads into Great Room with a wall of windows and expansive cathedral ceiling above a cozy fireplace
- Convenient Kitchen easily accesses Nook and Dining Areas, Laundry and Garage
- Corner Master Bedroom enhanced by two large, walk-in closets, cathedral ceiling and private, double vanity Bath
- Two secondary Bedrooms with large closets share a double vanity Bath
- This home is designed with a basement foundation

MAIN FLOOR — 2,229 SQ. FT.
BASEMENT — 2,229 SQ. FT.
GARAGE — 551 SQ. FT.

TOTAL LIVING AREA:
2,229 SQ. FT.

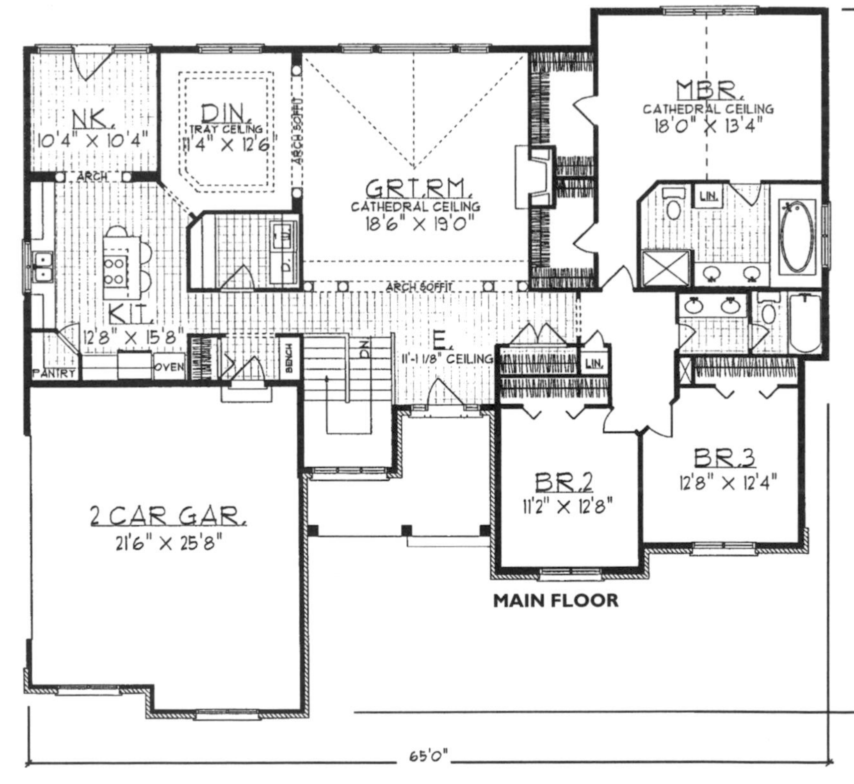

NK.
10'4" X 10'4"
DIN.
TRAY CEILING
11'4" X 12'6"
ARCH SOFFIT
GRT.RM.
CATHEDRAL CEILING
18'6" X 19'0"
MBR.
CATHEDRAL CEILING
18'0" X 13'4"
LIN.
ARCH
KIT.
12'8" X 15'8"
PANTRY
OVEN
BENCH
DN
ARCH SOFFIT
E.
11'-1 1/8" CEILING
LIN.
BR.2
11'2" X 12'8"
BR.3
12'8" X 12'4"
2 CAR GAR.
21'6" X 25'8"
65'0"

MAIN FLOOR

Cater to Comfort

PRICE CODE: H

PLAN NO. 24971

This plan features:
- Four bedrooms
- Two full and two half baths
- A curved open-rail staircase adds elegance to the two-story Foyer
- All Bedrooms are on the second floor with a balcony overlooking the Foyer
- This home is designed with basement, slab, and crawlspace foundation options

RST FLOOR — 1,644 SQ. FT.
COND FLOOR — 1,440 SQ. FT.
ONUS ROOM — 775 SQ. FT.
ASEMENT — 1,644 SQ. FT.
ARAGE — 858 SQ. FT.

TOTAL LIVING AREA:
3,084 SQ. FT.

WIDTH 76'-4"
DEPTH 44'-0"

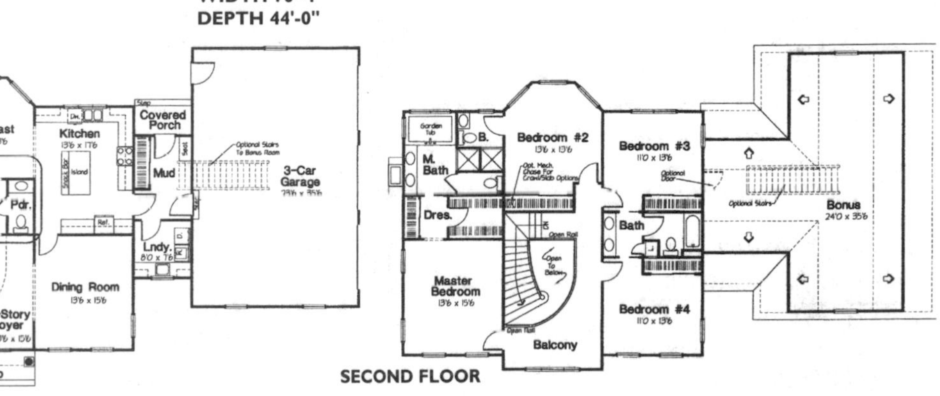
Family Room
Breakfast
Kitchen
Covered Porch
Mud
3-Car Garage
Pdr.
Lndy.
Living Room
Dining Room
2-Story Foyer
Stoop
FIRST FLOOR
M. Bath
B.
Bedroom #2
Bedroom #3
Dres.
Bath
Bonus
Master Bedroom
Bedroom #4
Balcony
SECOND FLOOR

Large Living in a Small Space

PRICE CODE: A

PLAN NO. 24304

This plan features:
- Three bedrooms
- Two full baths
- A sheltered entrance leads into an open Living Room with a corner fireplace and a wall of windows
- A well-equipped Kitchen features a peninsula counter with a Nook, a Laundry and clothes closet, and a built-in Pantry
- A Master Bedroom with a private Bath
- Two additional Bedrooms that share full hall Bath
- This home is designed with basement and crawlspace foundation options

AIN FLOOR — 993 SQ. FT.
ASEMENT — 987 SQ. FT.
ARAGE — 390 SQ. FT.

TOTAL LIVING AREA:
993 SQ. FT.

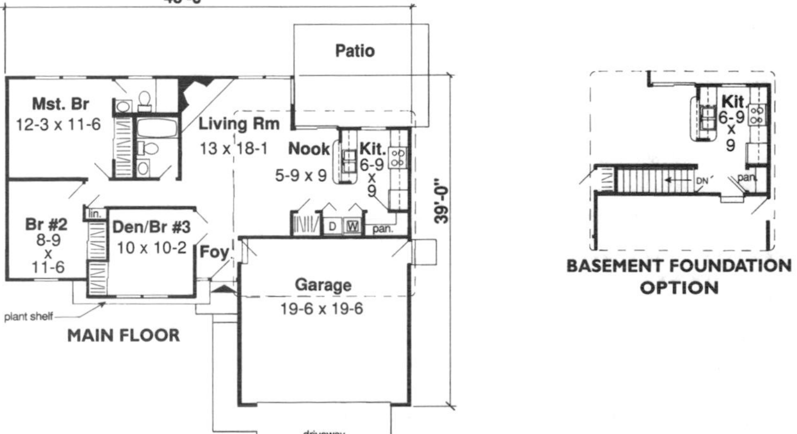
48'-0"
Patio
Mst. Br
12-3 x 11-6
Living Rm
13 x 18-1
Nook
5-9 x 9
Kit.
6-9 x 9
39'-0"
Br #2
8-9 x 11-6
Den/Br #3
10 x 10-2
Foy
Garage
19-6 x 19-6
plant shelf
MAIN FLOOR
driveway
BASEMENT FOUNDATION OPTION

PLAN NO. 93165

Brick Details Add Class

PRICE CODE: A

- This plan features:
- — Three bedrooms
- — Two full baths
- Keystone entrance leads into easy care, tile Entry with plant ledge and convenient closet
- Expansive Great Room with cathedral ceiling over triple window and a corner gas fireplace
- Hub Kitchen accented by arches and columns serving Great Room and Dining Area, near Laundry Area and Garage
- Adjoining Dining Area with large windows, access to rear yard and Screen Porch
- Private Master Suite with a walk-in closet and plush Bath with corner whirlpool tub
- Two additional Bedrooms share a full Bath
- This home is designed with a basement foundation
- This plan is not to be built within a 20 mile radius of Iowa City, IA

MAIN FLOOR — 1,472 SQ. FT.
BASEMENT — 1,472 SQ. FT.
GARAGE — 424 SQ. FT.

TOTAL LIVING AREA:
1,472 SQ. FT.

WIDTH 48'-0"
DEPTH 56'-4"

BR.#3 10'4" X 10'4"
DIRECT VENT GAS FIREPLACE
GRT.RM. CATHEDRAL CEILING 12'8" X 16'4"
DIN. CATHEDRAL CEILING 12'4" X 10'0"
SCREEN PORCH 10'4" X 10'0"
KIT. 10'0" X 10'8"
MBR. 13'0" X 14'0"
PLANT LEDGE
PAN.
E.
BR.#2 CATHEDRAL CEILING 10'4" X 11'8"
2 CAR GAR. 20'0" X 20'0"

MAIN FLOOR

PLAN NO. 92166

Medieval Elegance

PRICE CODE: K

- This plan features:
- — Three bedrooms
- — Two full baths
- The Great Room and Den connected by a built-in bar that opens up to the terrace makes entertaining easy
- A large private Studio fills the right wing of the second floor
- Light pours into the Master Bedroom from its own private balcony
- The Kitchen, with island and Pantry, opens to a cozy, well-lit nook and Great Room
- A carport connects the living quarters with a three-car Garage
- This home is designed with combination basement/crawlspace foundation options

FIRST FLOOR — 1,668 SQ. FT.
SECOND FLOOR — 2,116 SQ. FT.
BASEMENT — 911 SQ. FT.

TOTAL LIVING AREA:
3,784 SQ. FT.

WIDTH 107'-0"
DEPTH 45'-0"

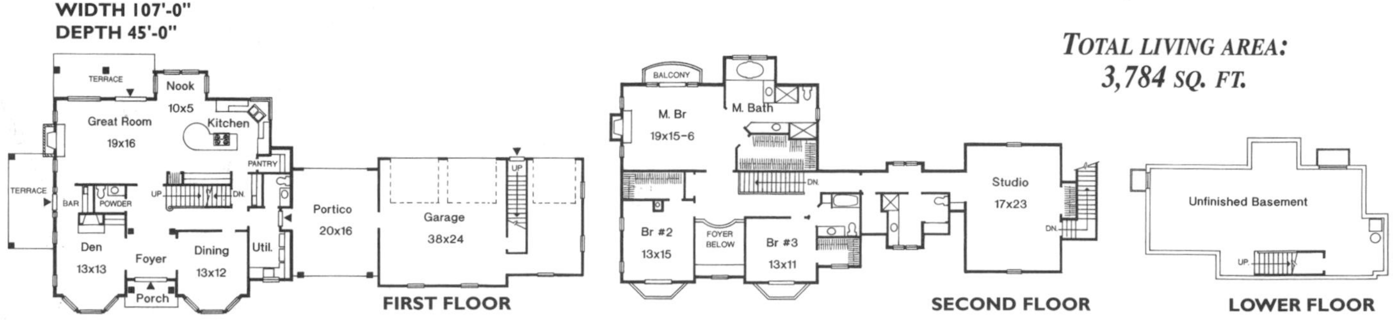

TERRACE
Nook 10x5
Great Room 19x16
Kitchen
PANTRY
TERRACE
BAR
POWDER
UP
DN.
Den 13x13
Foyer
Dining 13x12
Util.
Porch
Portico 20x16
Garage 38x24
UP
FIRST FLOOR
BALCONY
M. Br 19x15-6
M. Bath
DN.
Br #2 13x15
FOYER BELOW
Br #3 13x11
Studio 17x23
DN.
SECOND FLOOR
Unfinished Basement
UP
LOWER FLOOR

Full of Amenities

PRICE CODE: I

PLAN NO.24972

This plan features:
- Three bedrooms
- Two full and one half baths
- Different styles of siding set off the symmetry of this home
- The Y-shaped Foyer leads to the Bedrooms in the left wing, straight into the Living Room, or to the right wing common areas
- A snack bar for casual dining and more joins the Great Room and Kitchen, creating a hub for family activity
- The Master Suite features a window-lined Sitting Area, two walk-in closets and a lush Bath, filled with detail
- A Covered Terrace opens on to an Open Terrace, offering outdoor living no matter the weather
- A skylit Bonus Room leaves expansion possibilities up to the imagination
- This home is designed with a basement foundation

RST FLOOR — 3,370 SQ. FT.
:COND FLOOR — 675 SQ. FT.
ASEMENT — 3,370 SQ. FT.
ARAGE — 978 SQ. FT.
)RCH — 535 SQ. FT.

TOTAL LIVING AREA:
3,370 SQ. FT.

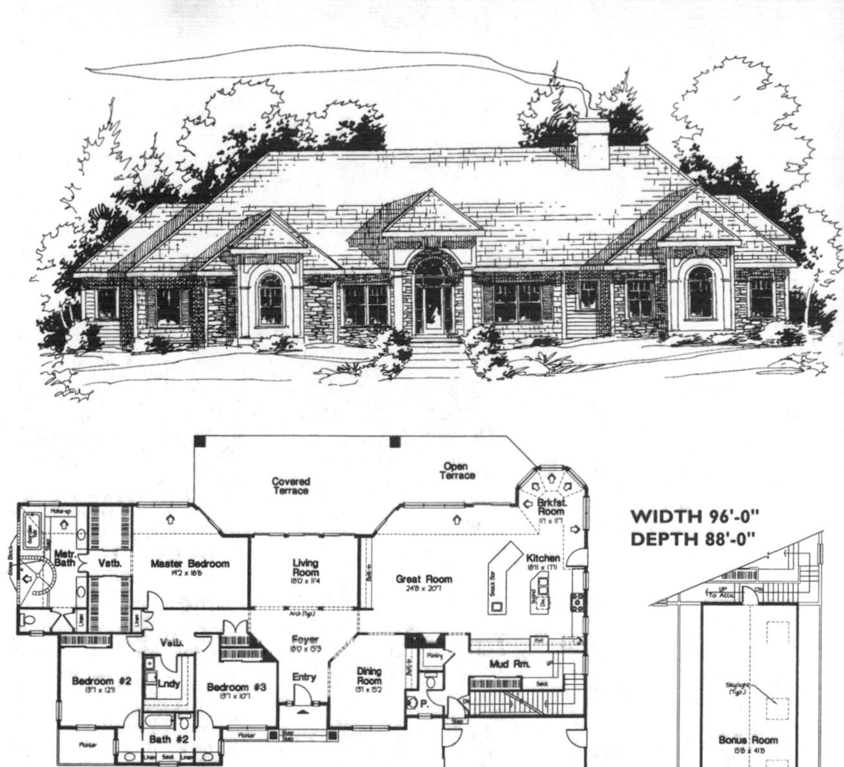

Covered Terrace
Open Terrace
Brkfst. Room
Mstr. Bath
Vstb.
Master Bedroom
Living Room
Great Room
Kitchen
Foyer
Vstb.
Bedroom #2
Lndy
Bedroom #3
Entry
Dining Room
Mud Rm.
Bath #2
3-Car Garage
MAIN FLOOR
WIDTH 96'-0"
DEPTH 88'-0"
Bonus Room
BONUS

Stately Colonial Home

PRICE CODE: G

PLAN NO.98534

This plan features:
- Four bedrooms
- Three full and one half baths
- Stately columns and arched windows project luxury and quality that is evident throughout this home
- The Entry is highlighted by a palladian window, a plant shelf and an angled staircase
- The formal Living and Dining Rooms located off the Entry for ease in entertaining
- The comfortable Great Room has an inviting fireplace and opens to Kitchen/Breakfast Area and the Patio
- The Master Bedroom wing offers Patio access, a luxurious Bath and a walk-in closet
- This home is designed with crawlspace, slab and combination basement/crawlspace foundation options

RST FLOOR — 1,848 SQ. FT.
:COND FLOOR — 1,111 SQ. FT.
ARAGE & SHOP — 722 SQ. FT.

TOTAL LIVING AREA:
2,959 SQ. FT.

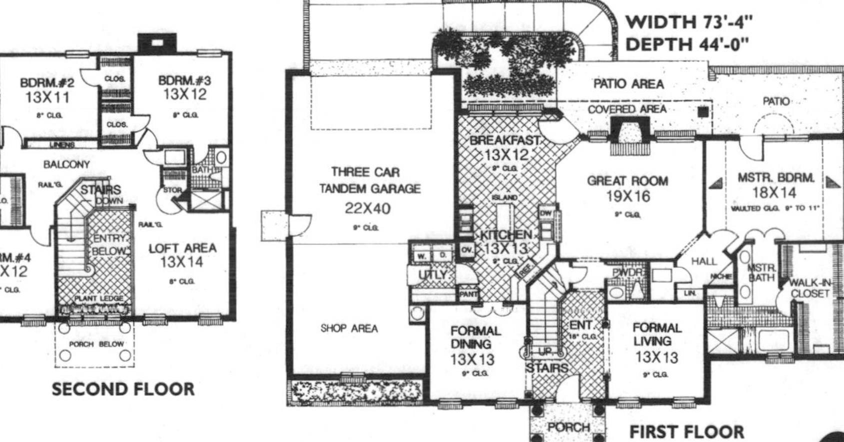

WIDTH 73'-4"
DEPTH 44'-0"
BDRM.#2 13X11
BDRM.#3 13X12
BALCONY
STAIRS DOWN
BDRM.#4 13X12
ENTRY BELOW
LOFT AREA 13X14
PLANT LEDGE
PORCH BELOW
SECOND FLOOR
PATIO AREA
COVERED AREA
PATIO
THREE CAR TANDEM GARAGE 22X40
BREAKFAST 13X12
GREAT ROOM 19X16
MSTR. BDRM. 18X14
KITCHEN 13X13
UTLY
PWDR
HALL
MSTR. BATH
WALK-IN CLOSET
SHOP AREA
FORMAL DINING 13X13
ENT.
STAIRS
FORMAL LIVING 13X13
PORCH
FIRST FLOOR

PLAN NO.98427

Split Bedroom Plan

PRICE CODE: D

- This plan features:
- — Three bedrooms
- — Two full baths
- Dining Room is crowned by a tray ceiling
- Living Room/Den privatized by double doors at its entrance, and is enhanced by a bay window
- The Kitchen includes a walk-in Pantry and a corner double sink
- The vaulted Breakfast Room flows naturally from the Kitchen
- The Master Suite is topped by a tray ceiling, and contains a compartmental Bath plus two walk-in closet
- Two roomy additional Bedrooms share a full Bath in the hall
- This home is designed with basement, slab and crawlspace foundation options

MAIN FLOOR — 2,051 SQ. FT.
BASEMENT — 2,051 SQ. FT.
GARAGE — 441 SQ. FT.

TOTAL LIVING AREA:
2,051 SQ. FT.

WIDTH 56'-0"
DEPTH 60'-6"

Bath
Vaulted Breakfast
Bedroom 2
11° x 11°
Bedroom 3
11° x 12¹⁰
Kitchen
Family Room
16° x 22°
Vaulted Master Bath
W.i.c.
Master Suite
13¹ x 17°
W.i.c.
Laund.
Stor.
Foyer
Dining Room
12° x 13°
Living Room/Den
13¹ x 13°
Garage

MAIN FLOOR

© Frank Betz Associates, Inc.

PLAN NO.24973

Angled Rooms Make an Impression

PRICE CODE: J

- This plan features:
- — Four bedrooms
- — Three full and one half baths
- Dormers and a Portico present a friendly facade
- With its snack bar and island with work bar, the Kitche will please the cooks of the house
- An angled fireplace casts its glow over the window-lined, sunken octagonal Family Room
- The Bedrooms share the second floor, creating a retreat from the hub of activity
- Outside aficionados will love the Sunroom and brick Patio
- This home is designed with basement, slab, and crawlspace foundation options

FIRST FLOOR — 2,242 SQ. FT.
SECOND FLOOR — 1,483 SQ. FT.
BASEMENT — 2,242 SQ. FT.
GARAGE — 858 SQ. FT.
PORCH — 60 SQ. FT.

TOTAL LIVING AREA:
3,725 SQ. FT.

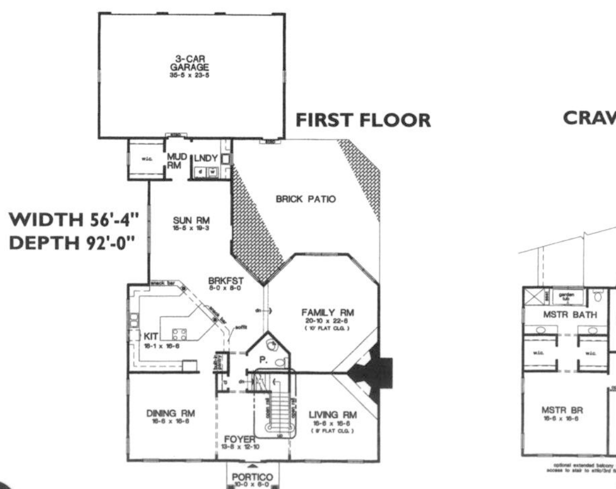
3-CAR GARAGE
FIRST FLOOR
MUD RM
LNDY
BRICK PATIO
WIDTH 56'-4"
DEPTH 92'-0"
SUN RM
BRKFST
FAMILY RM
KIT
DINING RM
FOYER
LIVING RM
PORTICO

CRAWLSPACE/SLAB OPTION

SECOND FLOOR

MSTR BATH
BR #3
BR #4
MSTR BR
BR #2

PLAN NO.93099

Out of the English Countryside

Price Code: F

- This plan features:
  - — Four bedrooms
  - — Three full baths
- From the Foyer, arched entrances lead into the Dining Room and the Great Room
- The Great Room is complimented by a 10-foot tray ceiling
- The Master Suite is located in a secluded part of the first floor
- The Breakfast Room shares a see-through fireplace with the Great Room
- This home is designed with basement, slab and crawlspace foundation options

FIRST FLOOR — 2,050 SQ. FT.
SECOND FLOOR — 561 SQ. FT.
BONUS — 272 SQ. FT.
GARAGE — 599 SQ. FT.

TOTAL LIVING AREA:
2,611 SQ. FT.

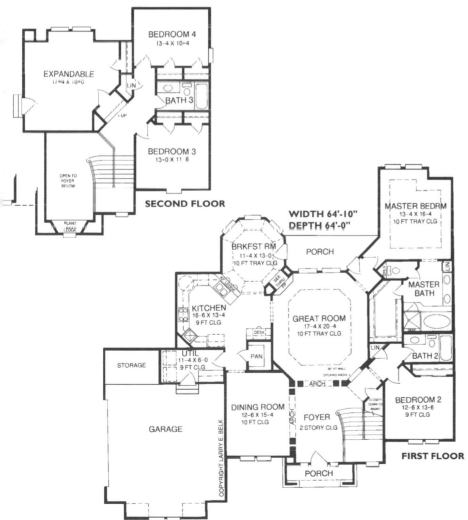

BEDROOM 4
13-4 X 10-4
EXPANDABLE
LIN
BATH 3
UP
BEDROOM 3
13-0 X 11-6
OPEN TO FOYER BELOW
PLANT LEDGE
SECOND FLOOR
WIDTH 64'-10"
DEPTH 64'-0"
MASTER BEDRM
13-4 X 16-4
10 FT TRAY CLG
BRKFST RM
11-4 X 13-0
10 FT TRAY CLG
PORCH
SEE THRU FP
MASTER BATH
LIN
KITCHEN
16-6 X 13-4
9 FT CLG
GREAT ROOM
17-4 X 20-4
10 FT TRAY CLG
DESK
PAN
LIN
BATH 2
STORAGE
UTIL
11-4 X 6-0
9 FT CLG
ARCH
DINING ROOM
12-6 X 15-4
10 FT CLG
ARCH
FOYER
2 STORY CLG
BEDROOM 2
12-6 X 13-6
9 FT CLG
GARAGE
COPYRIGHT LARRY E. BELK
PORCH
FIRST FLOOR

PLAN NO.93341

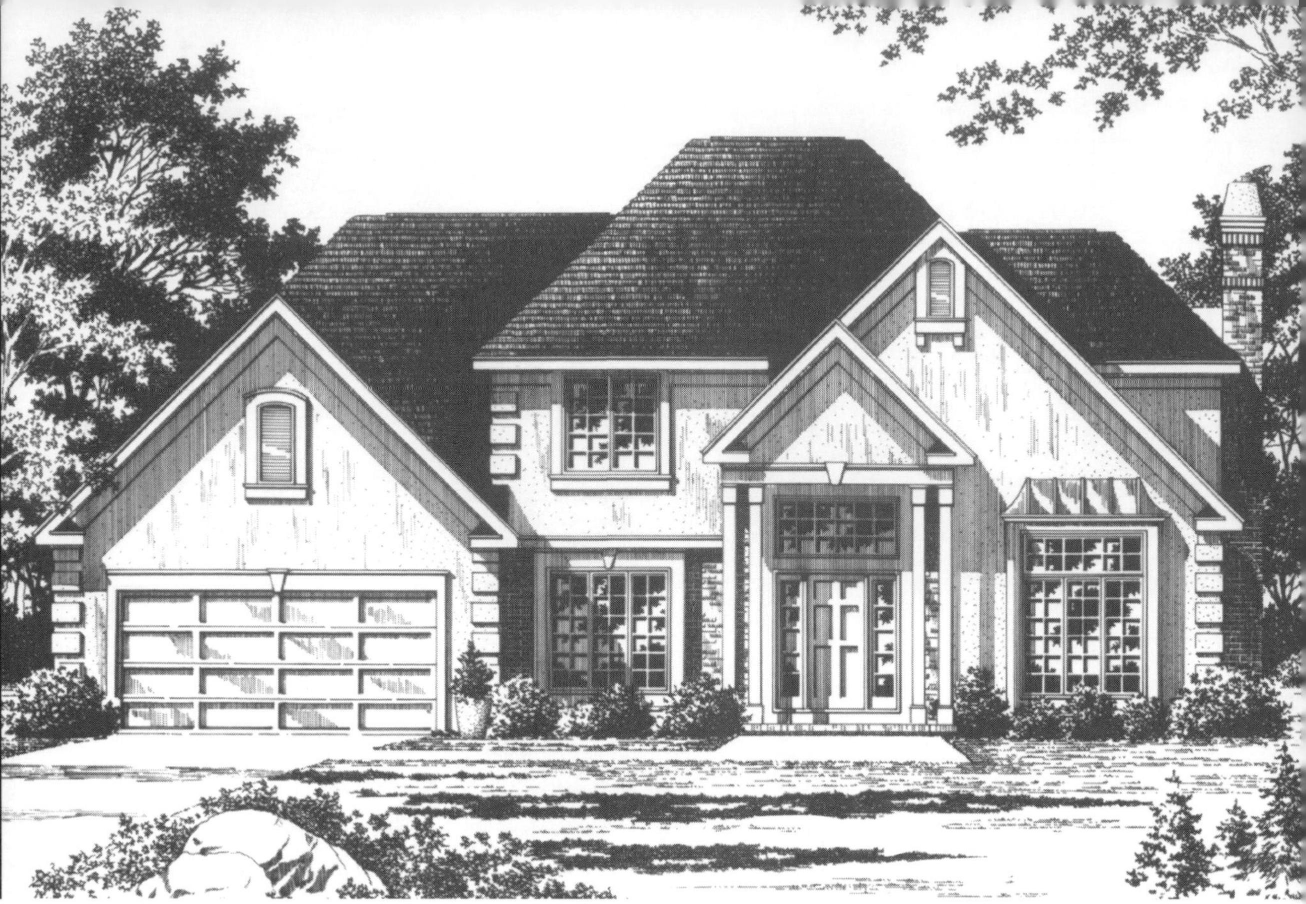

Multiple Roof Lines and Siding

Price Code: E

- This plan features:
- — Three bedrooms
- — Two full and one half baths
- High ceiling in Foyer
- Living Room accented by tray ceiling, boxed window and pocket doors to Family Room
- Comfortable Family Room with a cozy fireplace and wood Deck access
- Open Kitchen with a cooktop island, peninsula counter/snack bar and glass Dinette Area
- This home is designed with a basement foundation

FIRST FLOOR — 1,430 SQ. FT.
SECOND FLOOR — 1,027 SQ. FT.
GARAGE — 528 SQ. FT.
BASEMENT — 1,430 SQ. FT.

TOTAL LIVING AREA:
2,457 SQ. FT.

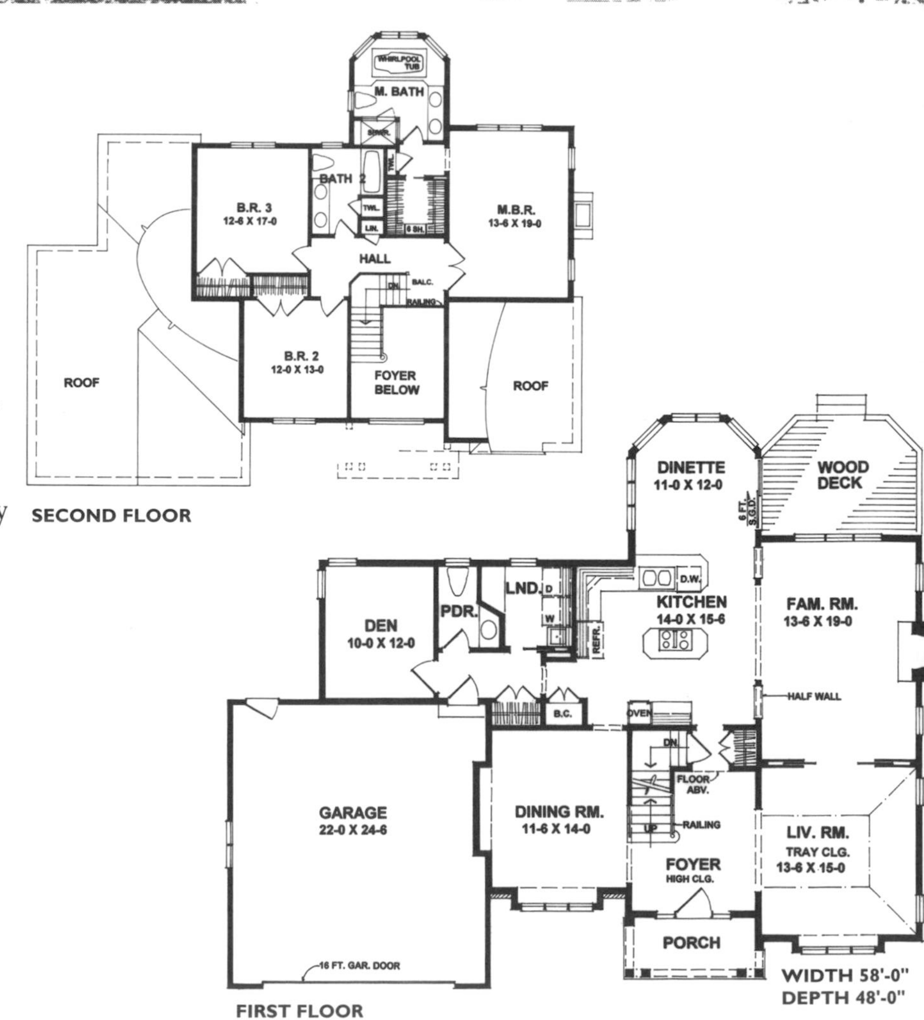
WHIRLPOOL TUB
M. BATH
BATH 2
B.R. 3
12-6 X 17-0
M.B.R.
13-6 X 19-0
HALL
BALC.
RAILING
B.R. 2
12-0 X 13-0
FOYER BELOW
ROOF
ROOF
SECOND FLOOR
DINETTE
11-0 X 12-0
WOOD DECK
KITCHEN
14-0 X 15-6
FAM. RM.
13-6 X 19-0
HALF WALL
DEN
10-0 X 12-0
PDR.
LND.
REFR.
B.C.
OVEN
GARAGE
22-0 X 24-6
DINING RM.
11-6 X 14-0
FLOOR ABV.
RAILING
FOYER
HIGH CLG.
LIV. RM.
TRAY CLG.
13-6 X 15-0
PORCH
16 FT. GAR. DOOR
FIRST FLOOR
WIDTH 58'-0"
DEPTH 48'-0"

Fashionable Country-Style

PRICE CODE: F

PLAN NO. 99450

This plan features:

- Four bedrooms
- Two full, one three-quarter and one half baths
- The large Covered Porch adds old-fashioned appeal to this modern floor plan
- The Dining Room features a decorative ceiling and a built-in hutch
- The Kitchen has a center island and is adjacent to the Gazebo-shaped Nook
- The Great Room is accented by transom windows and a fireplace with bookcases on either side of it
- The Master Bedroom has a cathedral ceiling, a door to the front Porch, and a large Bath with a whirlpool tub
- Upstairs are three additional Bedrooms and two full Baths
- This home is designed with basement and slab foundation options
- Alternate foundation options available at an additional charge. Please call 1-800-235-5700 for more information.

RST FLOOR — 1,881 SQ. FT.
COND FLOOR — 814 SQ. FT.
ARAGE — 534 SQ. FT.

TOTAL LIVING AREA: 2,695 SQ. FT.

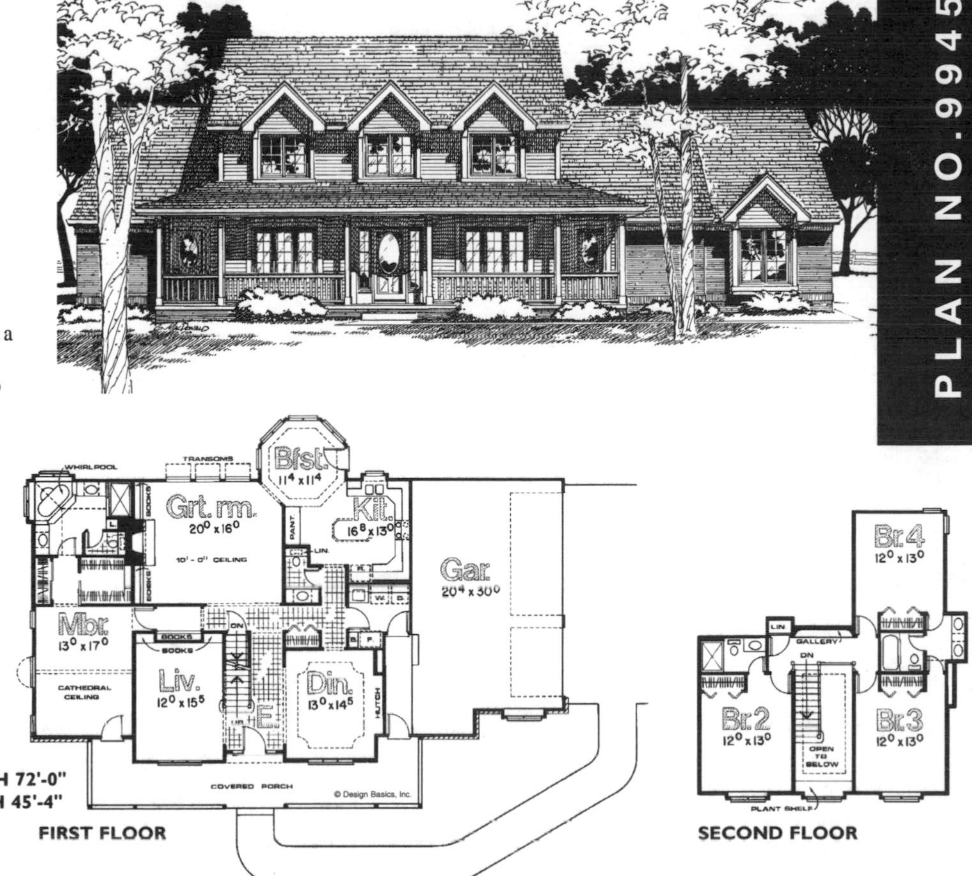

Bfst.
11⁴ x 11⁴
TRANSOMS
WHIRLPOOL
Grt. rm.
20⁰ x 16⁰
10'-0" CEILING
Kit.
16⁸ x 13⁰
Gar.
20⁴ x 30⁰
Mbr.
13⁰ x 17⁰
CATHEDRAL CEILING
BOOKS
Liv.
12⁰ x 15⁵
E
Din.
13⁰ x 14⁵
HUTCH
COVERED PORCH
© Design Basics, Inc.
WIDTH 72'-0"
DEPTH 45'-4"
FIRST FLOOR
Br. 4
12⁰ x 13⁰
LIN
GALLERY
DN
Br. 2
12⁰ x 13⁰
Br. 3
12⁰ x 13⁰
OPEN TO BELOW
PLANT SHELF
SECOND FLOOR

Country Flair

PRICE CODE: A

PLAN NO. 97137

This plan features:

- Three bedrooms
- Two full baths
- An inviting front Porch leads into a tiled Entry and Great Room with focal point fireplace
- Open layout of Great Room, Dining Area, wood Deck and Kitchen easily accommodates a busy family
- Master Bedroom set in a quiet corner, offers a huge walk-in closet and double vanity Bath
- Two additional Bedrooms, one an optional Den, share a full hall Bath
- This home is designed with a basement foundation

AIN FLOOR — 1,461 SQ. FT.
ASEMENT — 1,461 SQ. FT.
ARAGE — 458 SQ. FT.

TOTAL LIVING AREA: 1,461 SQ. FT.

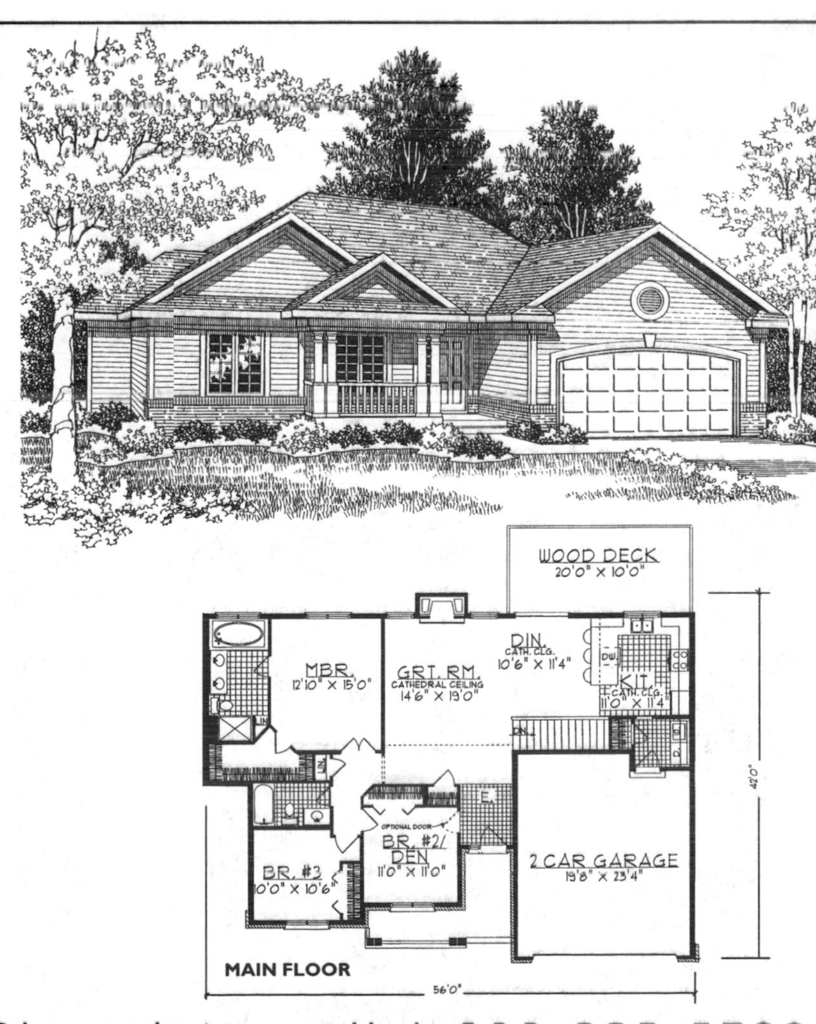

WOOD DECK
20'0" X 10'0"
MBR.
12'10" X 15'0"
GRT. RM.
CATHEDRAL CEILING
14'6" X 19'0"
DIN.
CATH. CLG.
10'6" X 11'4"
KIT.
CATH. CLG.
11'0" X 11'4"
DW
E
OPTIONAL DOOR
BR. #2/
DEN
11'0" X 11'0"
BR. #3
10'0" X 10'6"
2 CAR GARAGE
19'8" X 23'4"
42'0"
56'0"
MAIN FLOOR

PLAN NO.24974

THIRD FLOOR
Bedroom #4
Bedroom #5
Landing
Sitting
SECOND FLOOR
Bedroom #2
Bedroom #3
Master Bedroom
Optional Bonus Room
Computer Center
FIRST FLOOR
3-Car Garage
Deck
Kitchen
Breakfast
Family Room
Dining Room
Living Rm./ Library
Covered Porch
80'-4"
41'-0"
CRAWLSPACE/SLAB FOUNDATION OPTION

Bedrooms Fit for Royalty

PRICE CODE: J

- This plan features:
- — Five bedrooms
- — Four full and one half baths
- The Master Suite encompasses its own Vestibule, room size walk-in closet, and Bath with garden tub and show with built-in seat
- Two secondary Bedrooms feature Sitting Areas, walk-i and pull-out closets, Dressing Area, full Bath, and Stud Area with desk
- The Dining Room is easy accessed by the Kitchen via Hall with Butler's Pantry
- The three-car Garage is discreetly located on the side o the home
- This home is designed with basement, slab, and crawlspace foundation options

FIRST FLOOR — 1,483 SQ. FT.
SECOND FLOOR — 1,282 SQ. FT.
THIRD FLOOR — 952 SQ. FT.
BONUS — 772 SQ. FT.
BASEMENT — 1,483 SQ. FT.
GARAGE — 854 SQ. FT.
PORCH — 59 SQ. FT.

TOTAL LIVING AREA:
3,717 SQ. FT.

PLAN NO.98535

Tremendous Appeal

PRICE CODE: J

- This plan features:
- — Four bedrooms
- — Three full and one half baths
- A European country exterior with a modern American interior
- The circular stairway highlights the Entry
- The formal Dining Room has a bay window and easy access to the Kitchen
- A private Study with a double door Entry
- Formal Living Room has a fireplace and elegant columns
- The large Family Room boasts a large brick fireplace and a built-in TV cabinet
- An angled Kitchen contains all the conveniences that tl cook demands, including a built-in Pantry and ovens
- A large informal Dining Area that is adjacent to the Kitchen
- The Master Suite occupies one wing of the house with Bath and a huge walk-in closet
- This home is designed with a slab foundation

FIRST FLOOR — 2,658 SQ. FT.
SECOND FLOOR — 854 SQ. FT.
GARAGE — 660 SQ. FT.

TOTAL LIVING AREA:
3,512 SQ. FT.

SECOND FLOOR

FIRST FLOOR

WIDTH 86'-0"
DEPTH 58'-1"

PLAN NO. 93342

Home for Today and Tomorrow

Price Code: C

- This plan features:
  - Three bedrooms
  - Two full and one half baths
- The Foyer is flanked by the Dining and Living rooms
- A cozy fireplace in the Family Room adds warmth
- The Master Suite includes a walk-in closet, whirlpool tub, separate shower and double vanity
- This home is designed with a basement foundation

FIRST FLOOR — 1,004 SQ. FT.
SECOND FLOOR — 946 SQ. FT.
BONUS — 200 SQ. FT.
BASEMENT — 1,004 SQ. FT.
GARAGE — 450 SQ. FT.

TOTAL LIVING AREA:
1,950 SQ. FT.

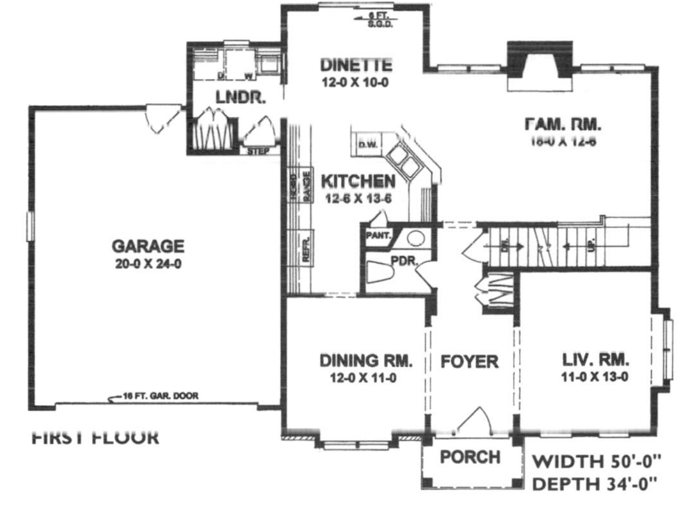

6 FT. S.G.D.
DINETTE
12-0 X 10-0
LNDR.
FAM. RM.
18-0 X 12-6
D.W.
KITCHEN
12-6 X 13-6
STEP
GARAGE
20-0 X 24-0
REFR.
PANT.
PDR.
DINING RM.
12-0 X 11-0
FOYER
LIV. RM.
11-0 X 13-0
16 FT. GAR. DOOR
FIRST FLOOR
PORCH
WIDTH 50'-0"
DEPTH 34'-0"

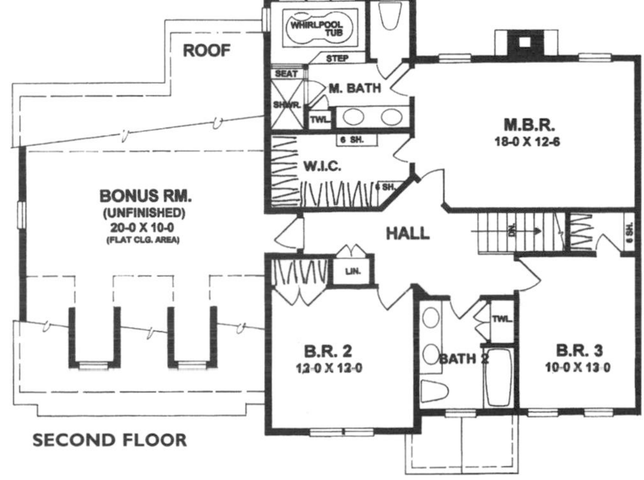

ROOF
WHIRLPOOL TUB
STEP
SEAT
M. BATH
SHWR.
TWL.
6 SH.
M.B.R.
18-0 X 12-6
W.I.C.
BONUS RM.
(UNFINISHED)
20-0 X 10-0
(FLAT CLG. AREA)
HALL
LIN.
TWL.
B.R. 2
12-0 X 12-0
BATH 2
B.R. 3
10-0 X 13-0
SECOND FLOOR

PLAN NO.24700

Fan-lights Highlight Facade

PRICE CODE: A

- This plan features:
  - — Three bedrooms
  - — Two full baths
- Front Porch Entry leads into an open Living Room, accented by a hearth fireplace below a sloped ceiling
- Efficient Kitchen with a peninsula counter convenient to the Laundry, Garage, Dining Area and Deck
- Master Bedroom accented by a decorative ceiling, a double closet and a private Bath
- Two additional Bedrooms with decorative windows and ample closets share a full Bath
- This home is designed with basement, slab and crawlspace foundation options

MAIN FLOOR — 1,312 SQ. FT.
BASEMENT — 1,293 SQ. FT.
GARAGE — 459 SQ. FT.

TOTAL LIVING AREA:
1,312 SQ. FT.

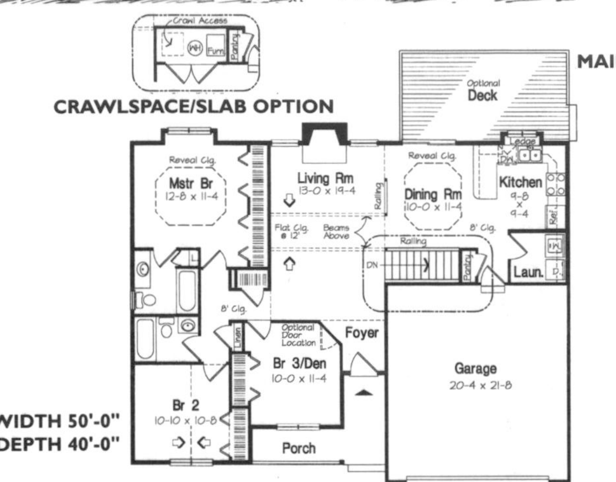
CRAWLSPACE/SLAB OPTION
MAIN FLOOR
Optional Deck
Reveal Clg.
Mstr Br
12-8 x 11-4
Living Rm
13-0 x 19-4
Dining Rm
10-0 x 11-4
Kitchen
9-8 x 9-4
Laun.
Foyer
Br 3/Den
10-0 x 11-4
Br 2
10-10 x 10-8
Garage
20-4 x 21-8
Porch
WIDTH 50'-0"
DEPTH 40'-0"

PLAN NO.97141

Traditional Stucco and Stone

PRICE CODE: L

- This plan features:
  - — Four bedrooms
  - — Three full and one half baths
- There is a Study, complete with fireplace and cathedral ceiling
- The terrific bonus room could become a fifth Bedroom
- The Master Suite has an expansive walk-in closet, tray ceiling and private Bath containing a whirlpool tub, double sinks, and a dressing table
- The Great Room is complimented by soffits upon Entry and a central fireplace flanked on both side by built-in cabinets
- This home is designed with a basement foundation

FIRST FLOOR — 2,639 SQ. FT.
SECOND FLOOR — 1,570 SQ. FT.

TOTAL LIVING AREA:
4,209 SQ. FT.

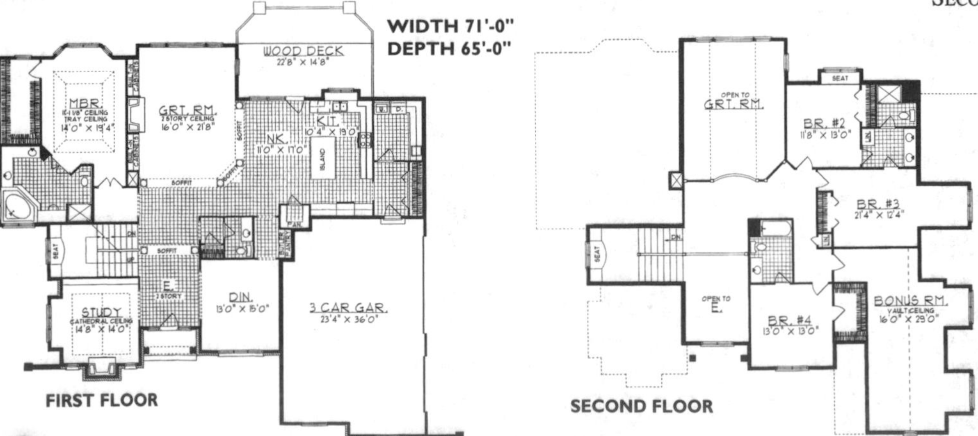
WIDTH 71'-0"
DEPTH 65'-0"
WOOD DECK
MBR.
GRT. RM.
NK.
KIT.
STUDY
DIN.
3 CAR GAR.
FIRST FLOOR
GRT. RM.
BR. #2
BR. #3
BR. #4
BONUS RM.
SECOND FLOOR

A Country Estate

PRICE CODE: L

PLAN NO. 93200

This plan features:
- Four bedrooms
- Four full and one half baths
- A formal Living Room and Dining Room located at opposite sides of the Foyer
- A Library tucked into a corner of the house for quiet study
- A sunken Family Room highlighted by a fireplace and built-in shelves
- A gourmet Kitchen with two built-in Pantries, generous counter and storage space and an island with a vegetable sink
- This home is designed with a basement foundation

RST FLOOR — 3,199 SQ. FT.
ECOND FLOOR — 2,531 SQ. FT.
ASEMENT — 3,199 SQ. FT.
ARAGE — 748 SQ. FT.
ONUS — 440 SQ. FT.

TOTAL LIVING AREA:
5,730 SQ. FT.

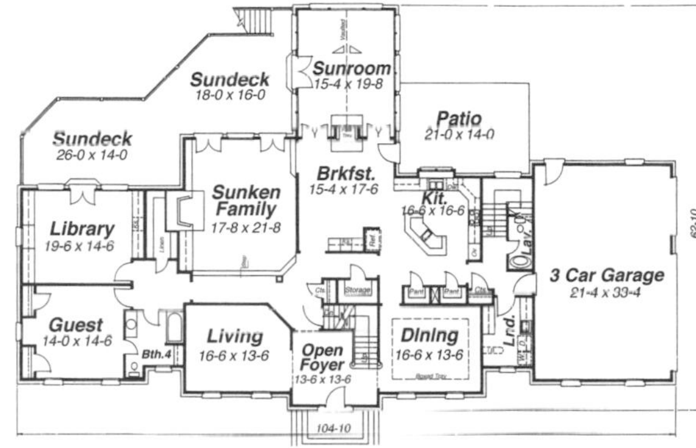
Sundeck
18-0 x 16-0
Sunroom
15-4 x 19-8
Sundeck
26-0 x 14-0
Patio
21-0 x 14-0
Library
19-6 x 14-6
Sunken Family
17-8 x 21-8
Brkfst.
15-4 x 17-6
Kit.
16-6 x 16-6
3 Car Garage
21-4 x 33-4
Guest
14-0 x 14-6
Bth.4
Living
16-6 x 13-6
Open Foyer
13-6 x 13-6
Dining
16-6 x 13-6
Lnd.
104-10
62-10

SECOND FLOOR

FIRST FLOOR

Sense of Community and Privacy

PRICE CODE: C

PLAN NO. 24975

- This plan features:
- Three bedrooms
- Two and one half full baths
- Radius windows, a cupola, and framed Entry add detail to this home's facade
- A focal point fireplace casts its glow over the Family Room and into the Breakfast Area and beyond
- Windows line the front and rear of the home, filtering natural light through the rooms
- An isolated Den creates an ideal space for quieter family activities
- This home is designed with basement, slab, and crawlspace foundation options

IRST FLOOR — 1,016 SQ. FT.
ECOND FLOOR — 860 SQ. FT.
ASEMENT — 1,016 SQ. FT.
ARAGE — 478 SQ. FT.

TOTAL LIVING AREA:
1,876 SQ. FT.

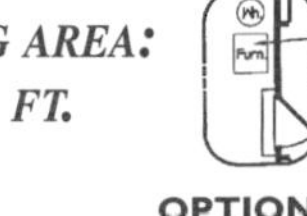

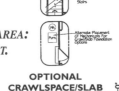

OPTIONAL CRAWLSPACE/SLAB FOUNDATION

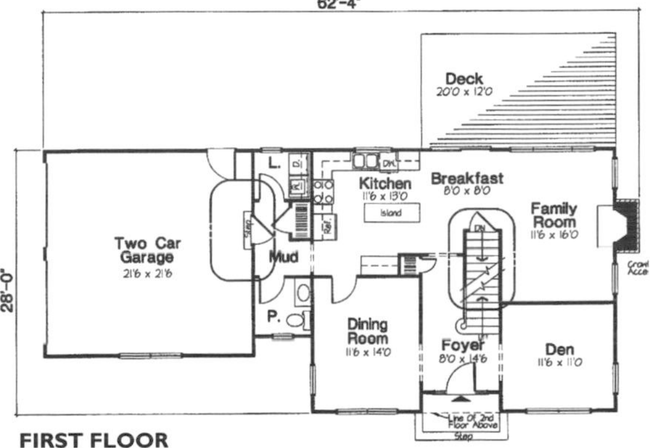
62'-4"
Deck
20'0 x 12'0
Kitchen
11'6 x 13'0
Breakfast
8'0 x 8'0
Family Room
11'6 x 16'0
Two Car Garage
21'6 x 21'6
Mud
Dining Room
11'6 x 14'0
Foyer
8'0 x 14'6
Den
11'6 x 11'0
28'-0"

FIRST FLOOR

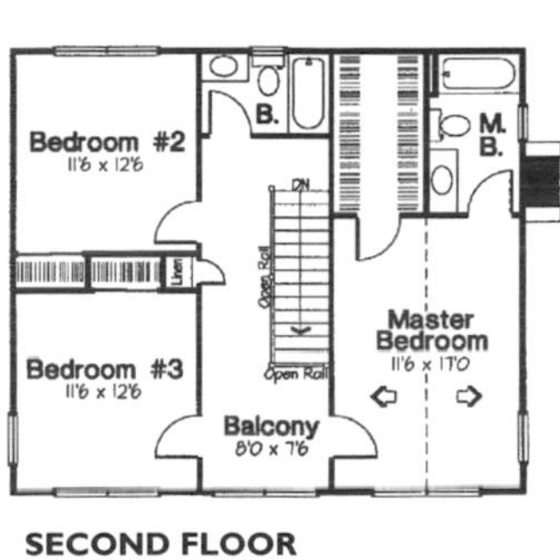
Bedroom #2
11'6 x 12'6
B.
M. B.
Bedroom #3
11'6 x 12'6
Master Bedroom
11'6 x 17'0
Balcony
8'0 x 7'6

SECOND FLOOR

PLAN NO.24976

Lots of Light

PRICE CODE: C

- This plan features:
  - Three bedrooms
  - One full, one three-quarter, and one half full baths
- Windows line the front and rear of this home, filtering light throughout the rooms
- Ample counter space, including an island, surrounds the Kitchen
- The focal point fireplace, flanked by built-ins, sparks a cozy atmosphere in the Family Room
- This home is designed with basement, slab, and crawlspace foundation options

FIRST FLOOR — 1,006 SQ. FT.
SECOND FLOOR — 903 SQ. FT.
BONUS — 402 SQ. FT.
BASEMENT — 1,006 SQ. FT.
GARAGE — 479 SQ. FT.

TOTAL LIVING AREA:
1,909 SQ. FT.

FIRST FLOOR

SECOND FLOOR

CRAWLSPACE/SLAB FOUNDATION OPTION

PLAN NO.94124

Open Family Living Area

PRICE CODE: E

- This plan features:
  - Four bedrooms
  - Two full and one half baths
- An immediate spacious feeling created by a two-story Foyer
- Formal Living Room topped by a vaulted ceiling
- Pocket doors between the Family Room and the Living Room
- Open layout between the Family Room, Dinette and Kitchen
- Efficient Kitchen with an island, Pantry and snack bar
- A bayed window enhancing elegant formal Dining Roo
- Secluded Master Suite with a double door Entry and plush Master Bath
- This home is designed with a basement foundation

FIRST FLOOR — 1,861 SQ. FT.
SECOND FLOOR — 598 SQ. FT.
BASEMENT — 1,802 SQ. FT.
GARAGE — 523 SQ. FT.

TOTAL LIVING AREA:
2,459 SQ. FT.

FIRST FLOOR

SECOND FLOOR

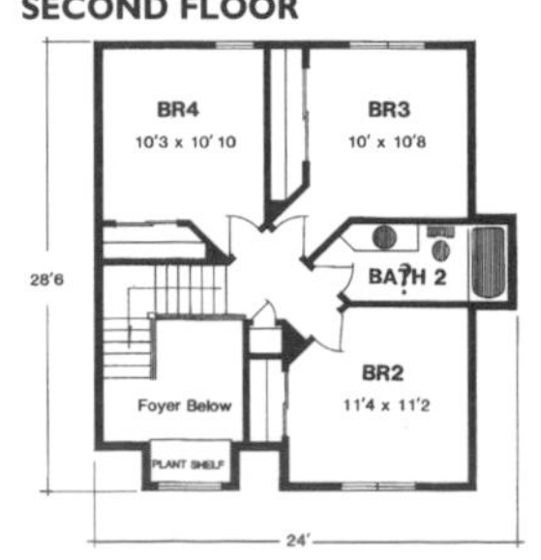
BR4
10'3 x 10'10
BR3
10' x 10'8
BATH 2
BR2
11'4 x 11'2
Foyer Below
PLANT SHELF
28'6
24'

PLAN NO. 93333

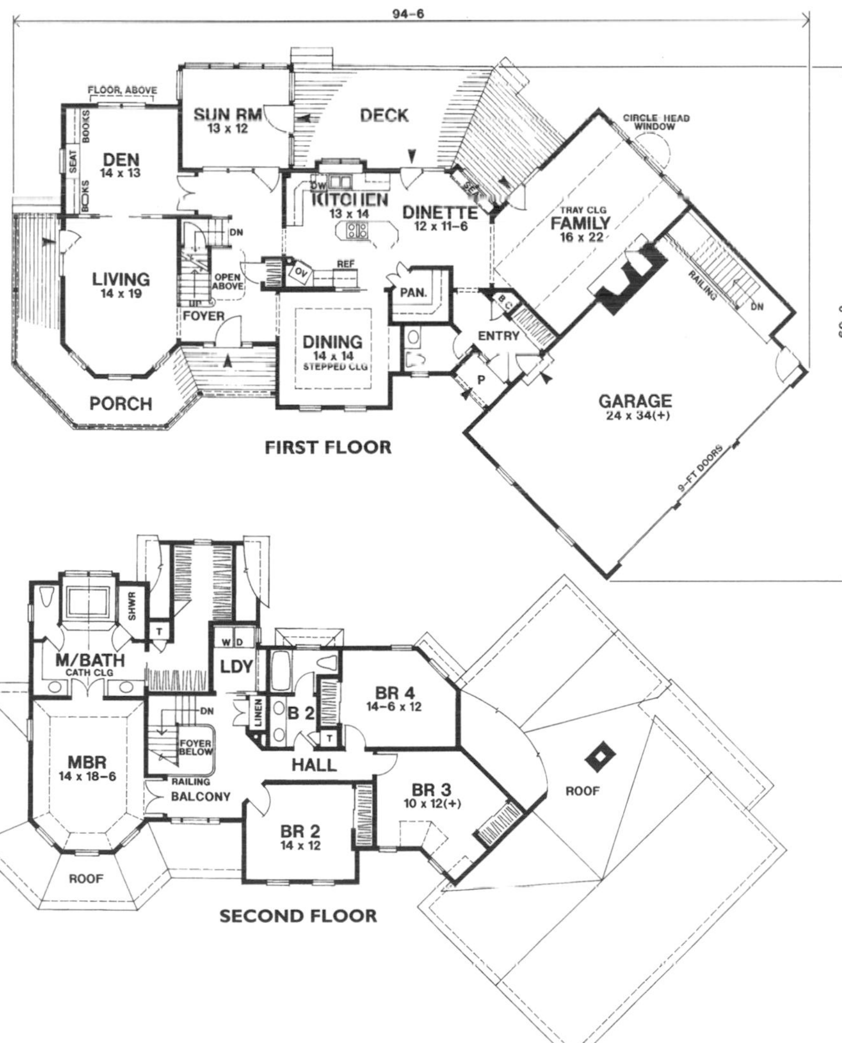

94-6
FLOOR ABOVE
SUN RM
13 x 12
DECK
CIRCLE HEAD WINDOW
BOOKS
SEAT
DEN
14 x 13
KITCHEN
13 x 14
DINETTE
12 x 11-6
TRAY CLG
FAMILY
16 x 22
LIVING
14 x 19
DN
OPEN ABOVE
FOYER
REF
PAN.
DINING
14 x 14
STEPPED CLG
ENTRY
RAILING
GARAGE
24 x 34(+)
9-FT DOORS
PORCH
FIRST FLOOR
60-2
SHWR
M/BATH
CATH CLG
LDY
LINEN
B 2
BR 4
14-6 x 12
MBR
14 x 18-6
FOYER BELOW
RAILING
BALCONY
HALL
BR 3
10 x 12(+)
ROOF
BR 2
14 x 12
ROOF
SECOND FLOOR

A Whisper of Victorian

Price Code: H

- This plan features:
- — Four bedrooms
- — Two full and one half baths
- A formal Living Room with wraparound windows and access to the cozy Den
- An elegant, formal Dining Room accented by a stepped ceiling
- An efficient Kitchen equipped with a cooktop island/eating bar, a huge walk-in Pantry and a Dinette with a window seat and a Deck access
- A fireplaced Family Room, with a tray ceiling topping a circle-head window
- A Master Suite with a decorative ceiling and a Bath with a raised, Atrium tub, and two vanities
- This home is designed with a basement foundation

First floor — 1,743 sq. ft.
Second floor — 1,455 sq. ft.

Total Living Area:
3,198 sq. ft.

PLAN NO.51007

Angular Beauty

PRICE CODE: F

- This plan features:
  - — Three bedrooms
  - — Two full and one half baths
- The two-story foyer leads into an open Dining Area, Living Room, Kitchen, and Breakfast Nook
- Bay windows radiate light through the Dining Area, a secondary Bedroom, Breakfast Nook, and Master Bath
- A wall of windows, fireplace, luxurious Bath, and two walk-in closets make an impressive Master Suite
- This home is designed with a basement foundation

FIRST FLOOR — 1,444 SQ. FT.
SECOND FLOOR — 1,238 SQ. FT.
BASEMENT — 1,444 SQ. FT.
GARAGE — 528 SQ. FT.

TOTAL LIVING AREA:
2,682 SQ. FT.

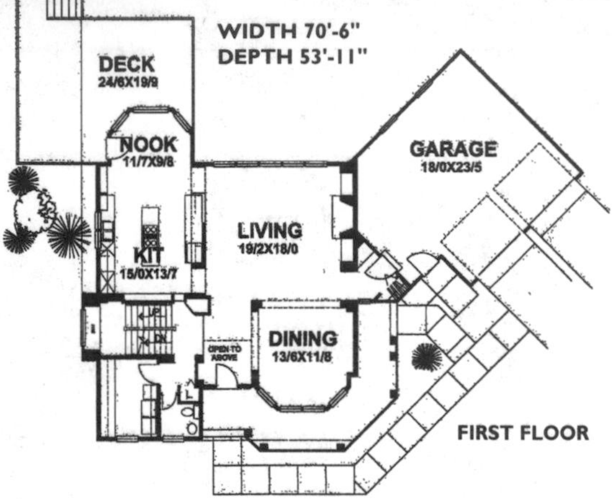
WIDTH 70'-6"
DEPTH 53'-11"
DECK
24/6X19/9
NOOK
11/7X9/8
GARAGE
18/0X23/5
LIVING
19/2X18/0
KIT
15/0X13/7
DINING
13/6X11/8
OPEN TO ABOVE
FIRST FLOOR

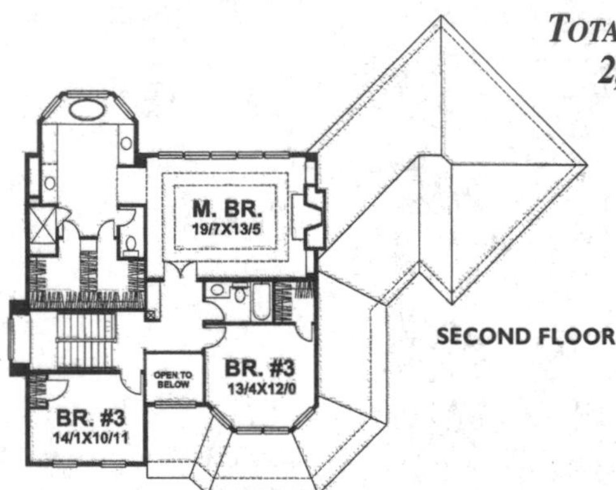
M. BR.
19/7X13/5
OPEN TO BELOW
BR. #3
13/4X12/0
BR. #3
14/1X10/11
SECOND FLOOR

PLAN NO.24307

Contemporary Simplicity

PRICE CODE: A

- This plan features:
  - — Two bedrooms
  - — One full and one three-quarter baths
- A tile entrance leading into a two-story, beamed Living Room with a circular, center fireplace
- An efficient, U-shaped Kitchen, with plenty of counter and cabinet space opens into the Dining Area, with sliding glass doors to an optional Deck
- Two Bedrooms, one with a private shower, both with ample closet space
- A second floor Loft overlooking the Living Area
- This home is designed with a crawlspace foundation

MAIN FLOOR — 866 SQ. FT.
LOFT — 172 SQ. FT.

TOTAL LIVING AREA:
1,038 SQ. FT.

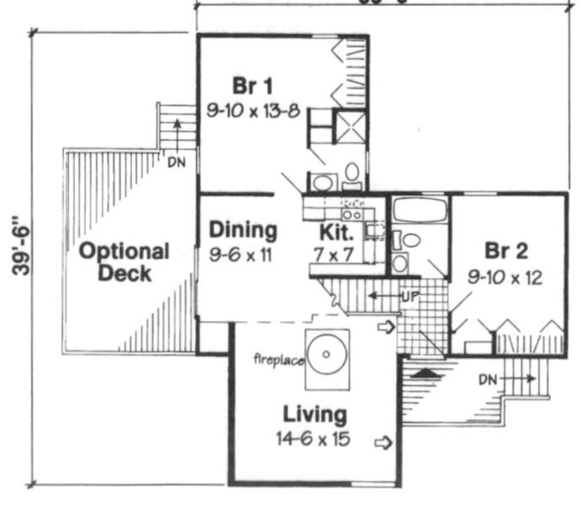
33'-0"
39'-6"
Br 1
9-10 x 13-8
DN
Optional Deck
Dining
9-6 x 11
Kit.
7 x 7
Br 2
9-10 x 12
UP
fireplace
Living
14-6 x 15
DN
MAIN FLOOR
Loft
14-6 x 10
DN
railing
beam above
open to below
LOFT

Sunlit, Octagonal Breakfast Nook

PRICE CODE: E

PLAN NO.24977

This plan features:
- Three bedrooms
- Two full and one half baths
- Radius windows and stone are just some of the features that add artistic detail to this home's facade
- The open design of the Kitchen, Breakfast Area, and Family Room creates the hub of family activity
- Closets align the Foyer, providing plenty of storage room
- The Master Suite features a roomy walk-in closet and plush Bath with garden tub and shower with built-in seat
- This home is designed with basement, slab, and crawlspace foundation options

RST FLOOR — 1,247 SQ. FT.
ECOND FLOOR — 1,058 SQ. FT.
ONUS — 443 SQ. FT.
ASEMENT — 1,247 SQ. FT.
ARAGE — 604 SQ. FT.

TOTAL LIVING AREA:
2,305 SQ. FT.

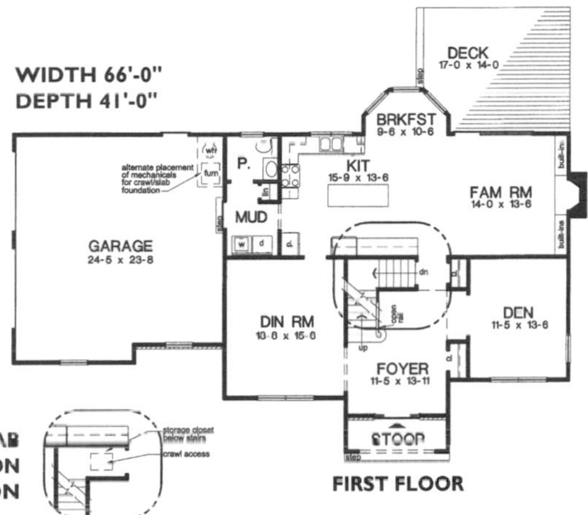

WIDTH 66'-0"
DEPTH 41'-0"
DECK 17-0 x 14-0
BRKFST 9-6 x 10-6
KIT 15-9 x 13-6
FAM RM 14-0 x 13-6
GARAGE 24-5 x 23-8
MUD
P.
DIN RM 10-8 x 15-0
DEN 11-5 x 13-6
FOYER 11-5 x 13-11
STOOP
FIRST FLOOR
CRAWLSPACE/SLAB FOUNDATION OPTION

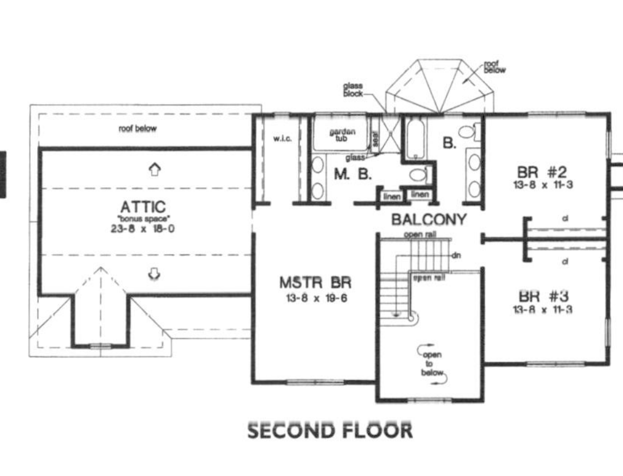

roof below
ATTIC "bonus space" 23-8 x 18-0
M. B.
B.
BR #2 13-8 x 11-3
BALCONY
MSTR BR 13-8 x 19-6
BR #3 13-8 x 11-3
SECOND FLOOR

Country Cottage Charm

PRICE CODE: I

PLAN NO.98536

This plan features:
- Four bedrooms
- Two full and one half baths
- Vaulted Master Bedroom has a private skylight Bath and large walk-in closet with a built-in chest of drawers
- Three more Bedrooms (one possibly a Study) have walk-in closets and share a full Bath
- A Loft and bonus room above the Living Room
- Family Room has built-in bookshelves, a fireplace, and overlooks the covered Veranda in the backyard
- The huge three-car Garage has a separate Shop Area
- This home is designed with crawlspace and slab foundation options

RST FLOOR — 2,787 SQ. FT.
ECOND FLOOR — 636 SQ. FT.
ARAGE — 832 SQ. FT.

TOTAL LIVING AREA:
3,423 SQ. FT.

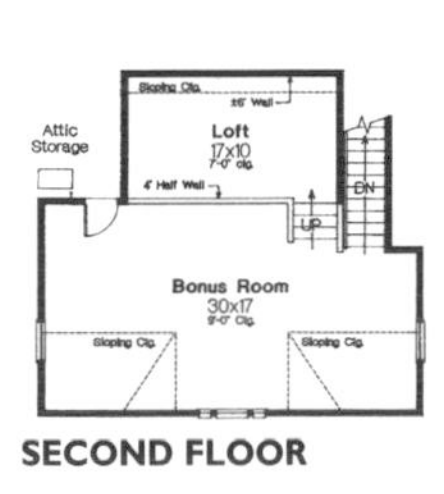

Attic Storage
Loft 17x10
Bonus Room 30x17
SECOND FLOOR

WIDTH 101'-0"
DEPTH 58'-8"

Covered Patio
Covered Veranda
FamilyRm 16x20
MstrBed 18x14
LivRm 17x16
Brkfst 12x10
3-Car Gar 24x32
Bed#2 13x11
Gallery
Kit 17x14
Shop Area
Bed#3 14x11
Utl
Bed#4/ Study 12x13
Ent
FmlDin 12x13
Covered Porch
FIRST FLOOR

PLAN NO. 98430

With All the Amenities

PRICE CODE: C

- This plan features:
  - — Three bedrooms
  - — Two full and one half baths
- A 16-foot high ceiling over the Foyer
- Arched openings highlight the hallway accessing the Great Room which is further enhanced by a fireplace
- A French door to the rear yard and decorative columns at its arched entrance
- Another vaulted ceiling topping the Dining Room, convenient to both the living room and the Kitchen
- An expansive Kitchen features a center work island, a built-in Pantry and a Breakfast Area defined by a tray ceiling
- A Master Suite also has a tray ceiling treatment and includes a lavish private Bath and a huge walk-in close
- Secondary Bedrooms have private access to a full Bath
- This home is designed with basement, slab and crawlspace foundation options

MAIN FLOOR — 1,884 SQ. FT.
BASEMENT — 1,908 SQ. FT.
GARAGE — 495 SQ. FT.

TOTAL LIVING AREA:
1,884 SQ. FT.

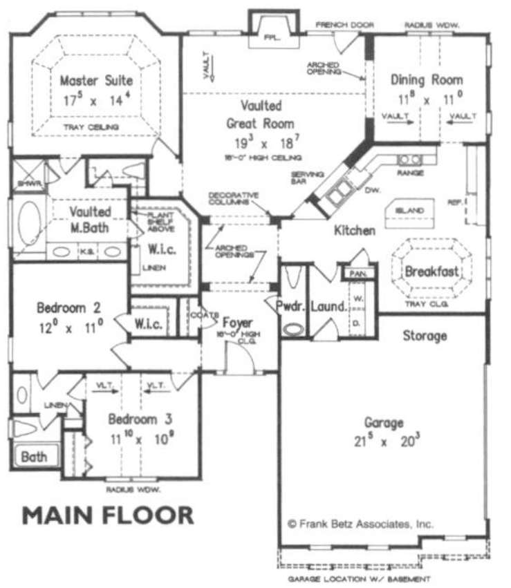
Master Suite
Vaulted Great Room
Dining Room
Vaulted M.Bath
Kitchen
Breakfast
Bedroom 2
Foyer
Pwdr.
Laund.
Storage
Bedroom 3
Bath
Garage
MAIN FLOOR
© Frank Betz Associates, Inc.

WIDTH 50'-0"
DEPTH 55'-4"

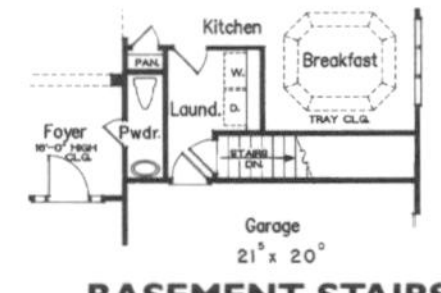
Kitchen
Breakfast
Foyer
Pwdr.
Laund.
Garage

BASEMENT STAIRS LOCATION OPTION

PLAN NO. 99454

Captivating Colonial

PRICE CODE: F

- This plan features:
  - — Four bedrooms
  - — Two full and one half baths
- Decorative windows and brick detailing
- Dining Room highlighted by decorative ceiling, French doors, and hutch space
- The Family Room has a fireplace and a bow window
- The Breakfast Nook and Kitchen are perfectly set up for meals on the run
- Upstairs find the Master Bedroom and Bath fully complemented
- Three more Bedrooms and a Bath completed the second floor plan
- This home is designed with basement and slab foundation options
- Alternate foundation options available at an additional charge. Please call 1-800-235-5700 for more information

FIRST FLOOR — 1,362 SQ. FT.
SECOND FLOOR — 1,223 SQ. FT.
GARAGE — 734 SQ. FT.

TOTAL LIVING AREA:
2,585 SQ. FT.

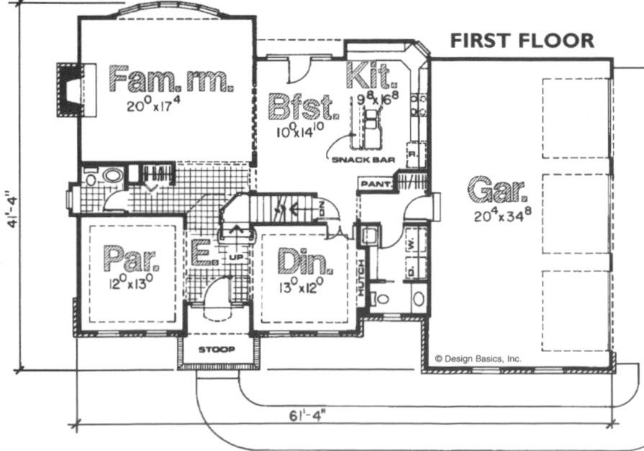
FIRST FLOOR
Fam. rm.
Bfst.
Kit.
Gar.
Par.
Din.
STOOP
61'-4"
41'-4"
© Design Basics, Inc.

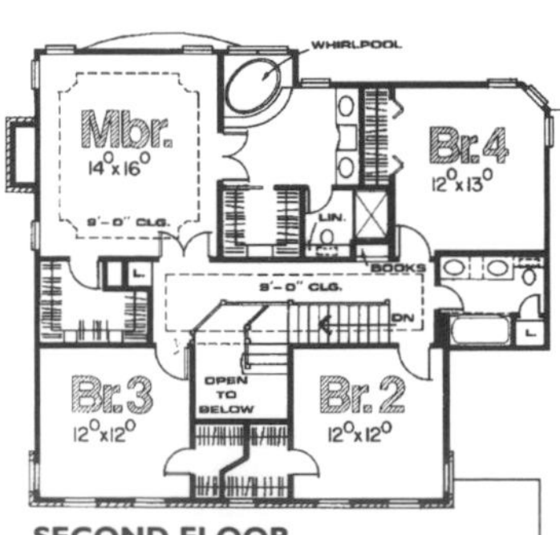
Mbr.
Br. 4
Br. 3
Br. 2
WHIRLPOOL
OPEN TO BELOW
SECOND FLOOR

Adding Ease to Busy Lifestyles

PRICE CODE: G

PLAN NO.97130

This plan features:

- Four bedrooms
- Two full and one half baths
- An elegant two-story Foyer leads the way to the spacious Family Room
- The Family Room has built-in cabinets surrounding the comforting fireplace
- A Den with a built-in desk off the Family Room
- An open Kitchen with ample counter space, a walk-in Pantry, an island Breakfast Bar, and a sunny Nook for family meals
- A formal Dining Room and a Living Room provide an elegant atmosphere for entertaining
- The second floor Master Suite has a private Bath with a garden spa tub, and a large walk-in closet
- This home is designed with a basement foundation

RST FLOOR — 1,533 SQ. FT.
COND FLOOR — 1,255 SQ. FT.
ASEMENT — 1,533 SQ. FT.

TOTAL LIVING AREA:
2,788 SQ. FT.

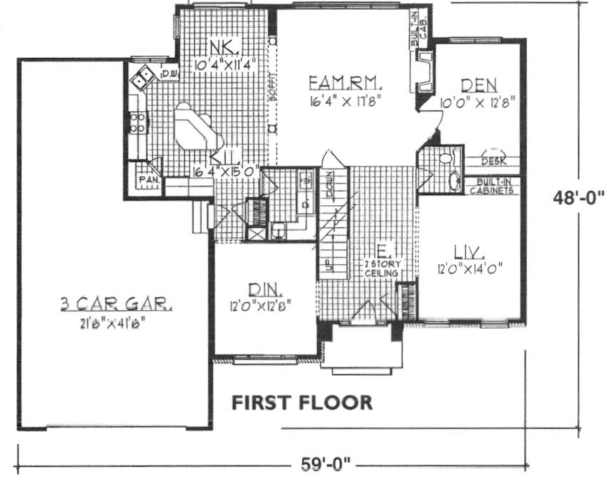

NK.
10'4"X11'4"
FAM.RM.
16'4" X 17'8"
DEN
10'0" X 12'8"
DESK
BUILT-IN CABINETS
KIT.
16'4"X15'0"
PAN
E.
2 STORY CEILING
LIV.
12'0"X14'0"
3 CAR GAR.
21'8"X41'8"
DIN.
12'0"X12'8"
48'-0"
FIRST FLOOR
59'-0"

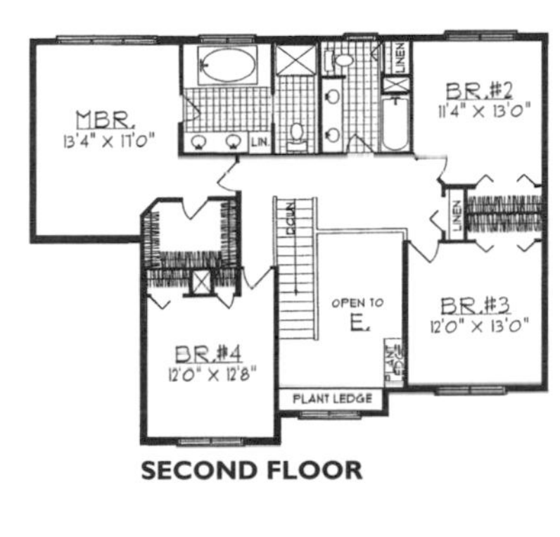

MBR.
13'4" X 17'0"
BR.#2
11'4" X 13'0"
LIN
LINEN
OPEN TO
E.
BR.#4
12'0" X 12'8"
BR.#3
12'0" X 13'0"
PLANT LEDGE
SECOND FLOOR

Distinctive Ranch

PRICE CODE: C

PLAN NO.93143

- This plan features:
- Three bedrooms
- Two full baths
- This hip roof ranch has an exterior that mixes brick and siding
- The cozy front Porch leads into a recessed Entry with sidelights and transoms
- The Great Room has a cathedral ceiling, and a rear wall fireplace
- The Kitchen has a center island and opens into the Nook
- The Dining Room features a high ceiling and a bright front window
- The Bedroom wing has three large Bedrooms and two full Baths
- The two-car Garage could easily be expanded to three with a door placed in the rear Storage Area
- This home is designed with a basement foundation

AIN FLOOR — 1,802 SQ. FT.
ASEMENT — 1,802 SQ. FT.

TOTAL LIVING AREA:
1,802 SQ. FT.

MBR.
13'x15'
GRT.RM.
CATHEDRAL CEILING
17'x16'
NK.
9'6"x11'0"
KIT.
10'x13'
STOR.
9'6"X20'
E.
10'-1 1/8" CEILING
DIN.
10'-1 1/8" CEILING
11'6"x11'
BR.3
12'x11'9"
BR.2
CATHEDRAL CEILING
11'x12'
2 CAR GAR.
24'x24'6"
51'-4"
69'-0"
MAIN FLOOR

PLAN NO. 93196

Turn Of The Century Charm

Price Code: I

- This plan features:
- — Four bedrooms
- — Three full and two half baths
- Old fashioned turn of the century exterior
- Gourmet Kitchen is open to the Sunroom and the Breakfast Nook
- Large Family Room features a cozy fireplace
- Master Suite has a luxurious Bath and large Sitting Area
- Three additional Bedrooms on the second floor share two full Baths
- This home is designed with a basement foundation

FIRST FLOOR — 2,470 SQ. FT.
SECOND FLOOR — 1,000 SQ. FT.
BASEMENT — 2,470 SQ. FT.

TOTAL LIVING AREA:
3,470 SQ. FT.

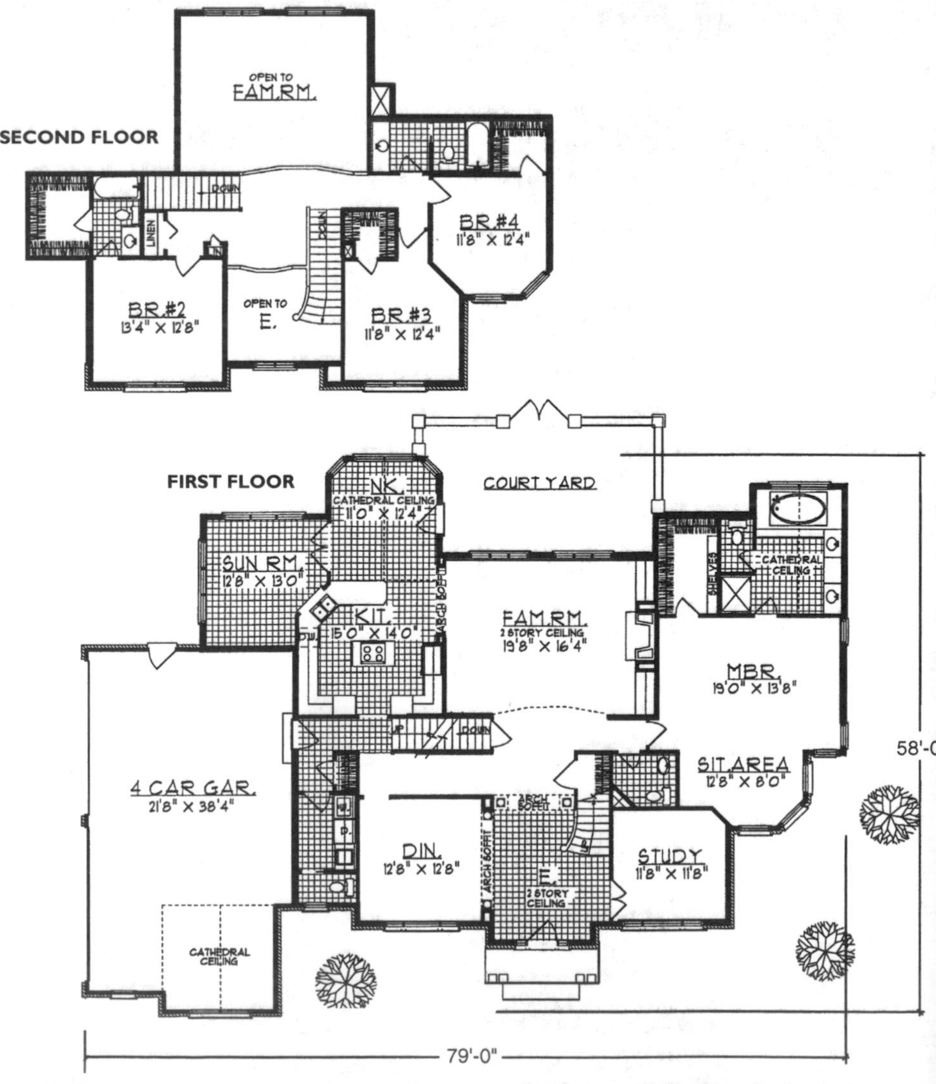

SECOND FLOOR
OPEN TO FAM.RM.
DOWN
LINEN
BR.#4 11'8" x 12'4"
BR.#2 13'4" x 12'8"
OPEN TO E.
BR.#3 11'8" x 12'4"
FIRST FLOOR
NK. CATHEDRAL CEILING 11'0" x 12'4"
COURT YARD
SUN RM. 12'8" x 13'0"
KIT. 15'0" x 14'0"
FAM.RM. 2 STORY CEILING 19'8" x 16'4"
CATHEDRAL CEILING
MBR. 19'0" x 13'8"
SIT AREA 12'8" x 8'0"
4 CAR GAR. 21'8" x 38'4"
DIN. 12'8" x 12'8"
E. 2 STORY CEILING
STUDY 11'8" x 11'8"
CATHEDRAL CEILING
79'-0"

PLAN NO. 90671

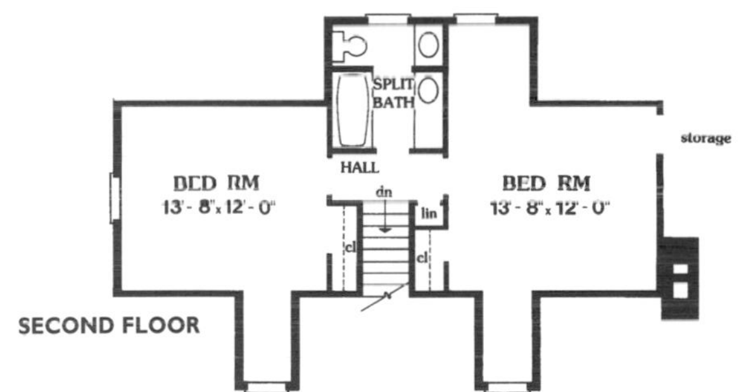

SPLIT BATH
HALL
BED RM
13'-8"x12'-0"
dn
lin
cl
cl
BED RM
13'-8"x12'-0"
storage
SECOND FLOOR

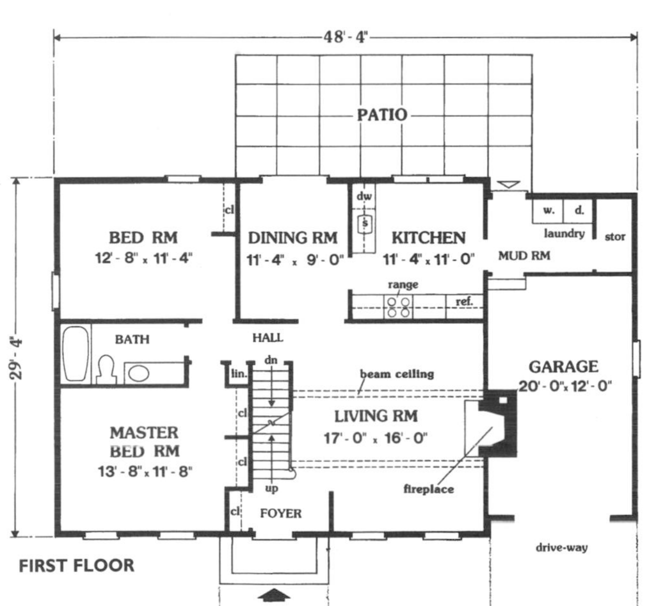

48'-4"
PATIO
29'-4"
BED RM
12'-8" x 11'-4"
cl
DINING RM
11'-4" x 9'-0"
dw
s
KITCHEN
11'-4" x 11'-0"
w.
d.
laundry
stor
MUD RM
range
ref.
BATH
HALL
dn
lin.
beam ceiling
GARAGE
20'-0"x12'-0"
cl
LIVING RM
17'-0" x 16'-0"
MASTER
BED RM
13'-8"x11'-8"
cl
up
fireplace
cl
FOYER
drive-way
FIRST FLOOR

Adapt this Colonial to Your Lifestyle

Price Code: B

- This plan features:
  - — Four bedrooms
  - — Two full baths
- A Living Room with a beam ceiling and a fireplace
- An eat-in Kitchen efficiently serving the formal Dining Room
- A Master Bedroom with his and her closets
- Two upstairs Bedrooms sharing a split Bath
- This home is designed with a basement foundation

FIRST FLOOR — 1,056 SQ. FT.
SECOND FLOOR — 531 SQ. FT.

TOTAL LIVING AREA:
1,587 SQ. FT.

PLAN NO. 93190

Luxury on One Level

Price Code: D

This plan features:

— Three bedrooms

— Two full and one half baths

Covered front Porch leads into Entry and Great Room with vaulted ceilings

Huge Great Room perfect for entertaining or family gatherings with cozy fireplace

Country-size Kitchen with a Pantry, work island, bright, Eating Nook with Screened Porch beyond, and nearby Laundry/Garage Entry

Corner Master Bedroom offers a large walk-in closet and a luxurious Bath with a double vanity and spa tub

This home is designed with a basement foundation

MAIN FLOOR — 2,196 SQ. FT.
BASEMENT — 2,196 SQ. FT.

TOTAL LIVING AREA:
2,196 SQ. FT.

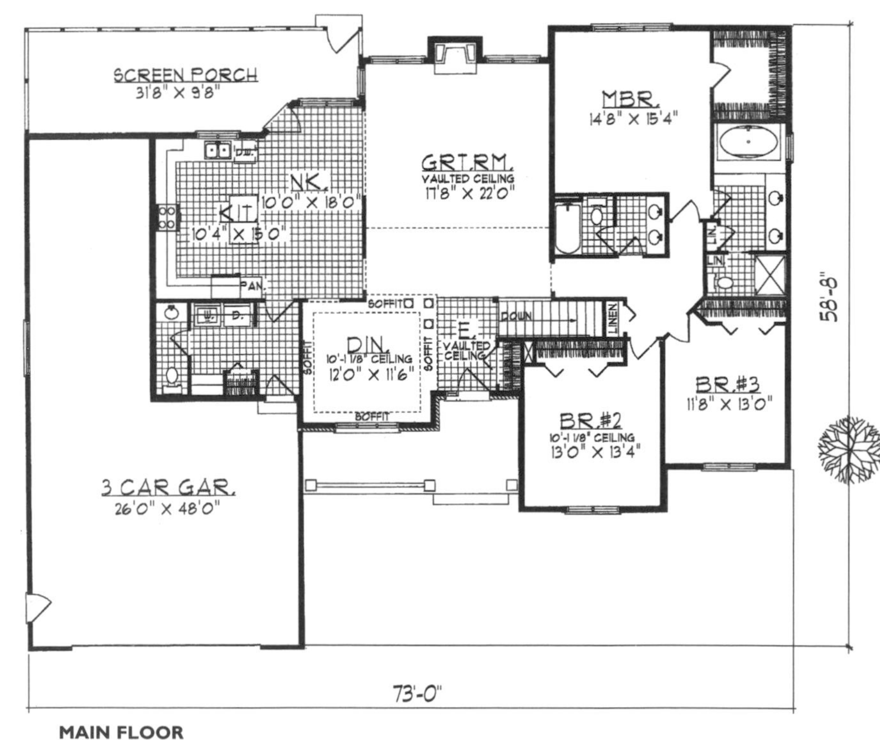

SCREEN PORCH
31'8" X 9'8"
MBR.
14'8" X 15'4"
GRT.RM.
VAULTED CEILING
17'8" X 22'0"
NK.
10'0" X 18'0"
KIT.
10'4" X 15'0"
PAN.
DIN.
10'-1 1/8" CEILING
12'0" X 11'6"
E.
VAULTED CEILING
SOFFIT
DOWN
LINEN
LIN
BR.#2
10'-1 1/8" CEILING
13'0" X 13'4"
BR.#3
11'8" X 13'0"
3 CAR GAR.
26'0" X 48'0"
58'-8"
73'-0"

MAIN FLOOR

Stucco Accents

PRICE CODE: H

PLAN NO.99456

This plan features:

- Four bedrooms
- Two full, one three-quarter and one half baths
- Stucco accents and graceful window treatments enhance the front of this home
- Double doors open to the private Den which features brilliant bayed windows
- French doors open to a large Screened Veranda ideal for outdoor entertaining
- The open Living Room and handsome curved staircase add drama to the Entry Area
- The gourmet Kitchen, Dinette Bay and Family Room flow together for easy living
- The elegant Master Bedroom has a 10-foot vaulted ceiling
- Two walk-in closets, his and her vanities and a whirlpool tub highlight the Master Bath
- Three additional Bedrooms have private access to full Baths
- This home is designed with a basement foundation
- Alternate foundation options available at an additional charge. Please call 1-800-235-5700 for more information.

RST FLOOR — 1,631 SQ. FT.
ECOND FLOOR — 1,426 SQ. FT.
ASEMENT — 1,631 SQ. FT.
ARAGE — 681 SQ. FT.

TOTAL LIVING AREA:
3,057 SQ. FT.

WIDTH 60'-0"
DEPTH 58'-0"

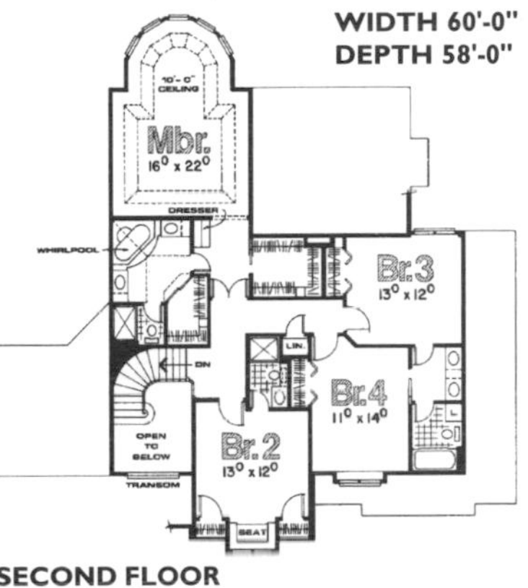

Mbr.
16⁰ x 22⁰
Br.3
13⁰ x 12⁰
Br.4
11⁰ x 14⁰
Br.2
13⁰ x 12⁰

SECOND FLOOR

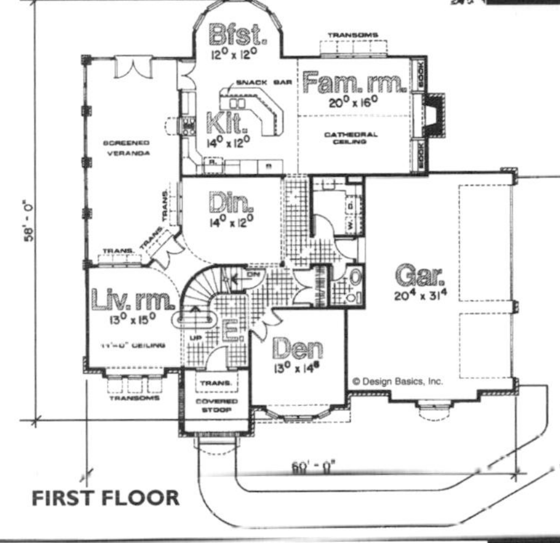

Bfst.
12⁰ x 12⁰
Fam. rm.
20⁰ x 16⁰
Kit.
14⁰ x 12⁰
Din.
14⁰ x 12⁰
Liv. rm.
13⁰ x 15⁰
Den
13⁰ x 14⁸
Gar.
20⁴ x 31⁴
© Design Basics, Inc.

FIRST FLOOR

Exceptional Family Living

PRICE CODE: L

PLAN NO.98538

This plan features:

- Four bedrooms
- Three full and one half baths
- Decorative dormers, a bay window and an eyebrow arched window provide for a pleasing country farmhouse facade
- The cozy Study has its own fireplace and a bay window
- The large formal Living Room has a fireplace and built-in bookcases
- The huge island Kitchen is open to the Breakfast Bay and the Family Room
- The Master Suite includes a large Bath with a unique closet
- Three more Bedrooms located at the other end of the home each have private access to a full Bath
- This home is designed with a slab foundation

AIN FLOOR — 4,082 SQ. FT.
ARAGE — 720 SQ. FT.

TOTAL LIVING AREA:
4,082 SQ. FT.

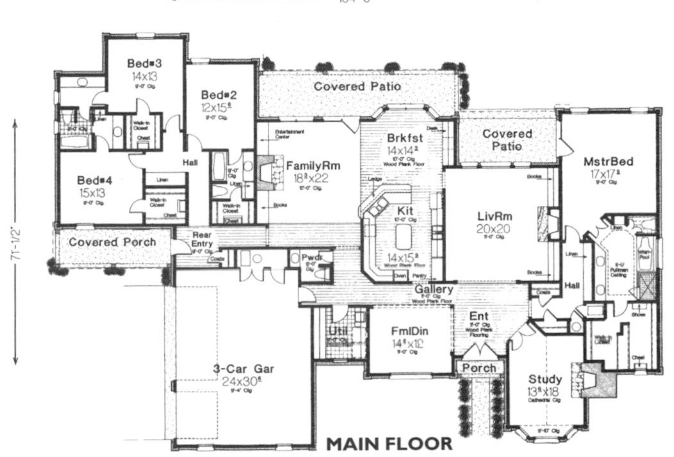

104'-0"
Bed#3
14x13
Bed#2
12x15
Covered Patio
Brkfst
14x14
Covered Patio
MstrBed
17x17
Bed#4
15x13
FamilyRm
18x22
Kit
LivRm
20x20
Covered Porch
Gallery
FmlDin
14x12
Ent
Util
3-Car Gar
24x30
Porch
Study
13x18
71'-1/2"

MAIN FLOOR

PLAN NO. 98431

With Room to Expand

PRICE CODE: B

- This plan features:
  - — Three bedrooms
  - — Two full and one half baths
- An impressive two-story Foyer
- The Kitchen is equipped with ample cabinet and counter space
- Spacious Family Room flows from the Breakfast Bay and is highlighted by a fireplace and a French door to the rear yard
- The Master Suite is topped by a tray ceiling and is enhanced by a vaulted, five-piece Master Bath
- This home is designed with basement, slab and crawlspace foundation options

FIRST FLOOR — 882 SQ. FT.
SECOND FLOOR — 793 SQ. FT.
BONUS ROOM — 416 SQ. FT.
BASEMENT — 882 SQ. FT.
GARAGE — 510 SQ. FT.

TOTAL LIVING AREA: 1,675 SQ. FT.

WIDTH 49'-6"
DEPTH 35'-4"

Breakfast
Pantry
French Door
FPL.
Family Room 17^4 x 12^0
Garage 19^9 x 25^0
Range
DW.
Kitchen
Ref.
Coats
Pwdr.
Stairs Up
Niche
Stairs Dn.
Dining Room 11^4 x 10^0
Two Story Foyer
Living Room 12^5 x 11^4
Covered Porch
© Frank Betz Associates, Inc.

FIRST FLOOR

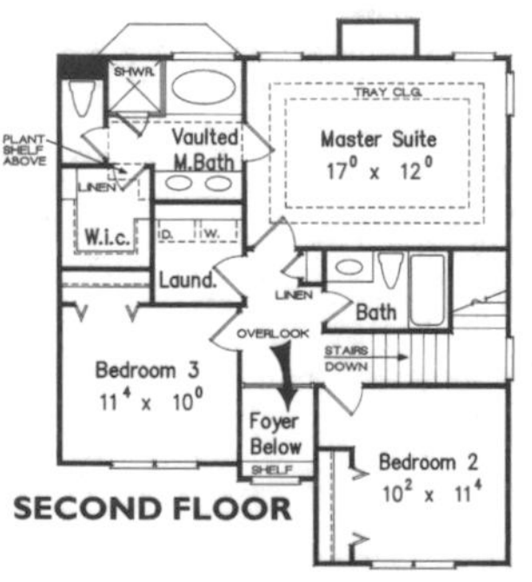

Shwr.
Plant Shelf Above
Vaulted M.Bath
Tray Clg.
Master Suite 17^0 x 12^0
Linen
W.i.c.
D.
W.
Laund.
Linen
Bath
Overlook
Stairs Down
Bedroom 3 11^4 x 10^0
Foyer Below
Shelf
Bedroom 2 10^2 x 11^4

SECOND FLOOR

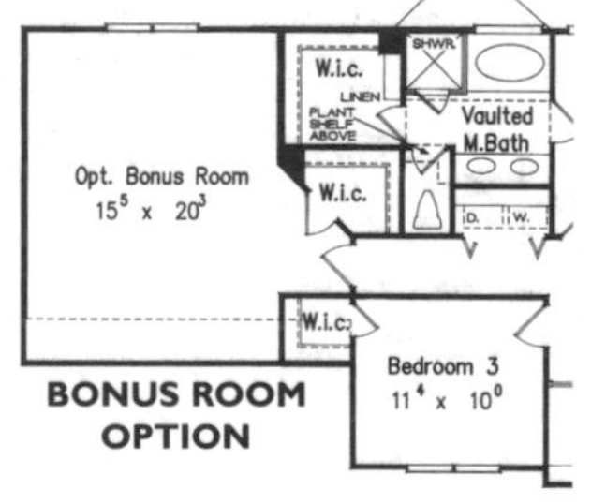

W.i.c.
Shwr.
Linen
Plant Shelf Above
Vaulted M.Bath
Opt. Bonus Room 15^5 x 20^3
W.i.c.
D.
W.
W.i.c.
Bedroom 3 11^4 x 10^0

BONUS ROOM OPTION

PLAN NO. 82050

Secluded Master Suite

PRICE CODE: B

- This plan features:
  - — Three bedrooms
  - — Two full baths
- The centrally located Great Room is crowned in an 11-foot box ceiling and includes a fireplace
- The Kitchen and Breakfast Room flow into each other with a center island doubling as a snack bar
- The formal Dining Room has direct access to the Kitchen and a 10-foot boxed ceiling
- This home has a split-Bedroom set up affording more privacy to the Master Suite
- This home is designed with basement, slab and crawlspace foundation options

MAIN FLOOR — 1,746 SQ. FT.
GARAGE — 491 SQ. FT.

TOTAL LIVING AREA: 1,746 SQ. FT.

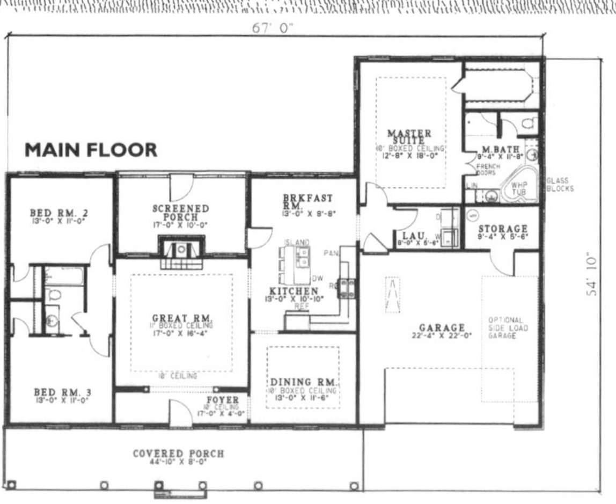

67' 0"
MAIN FLOOR
MASTER SUITE
M.BATH
BED RM. 2
SCREENED PORCH
BRKFAST RM.
LAU.
STORAGE
ISLAND
KITCHEN
GREAT RM.
GARAGE
54' 10"
BED RM. 3
FOYER
DINING RM.
COVERED PORCH

PLAN NO. 93118

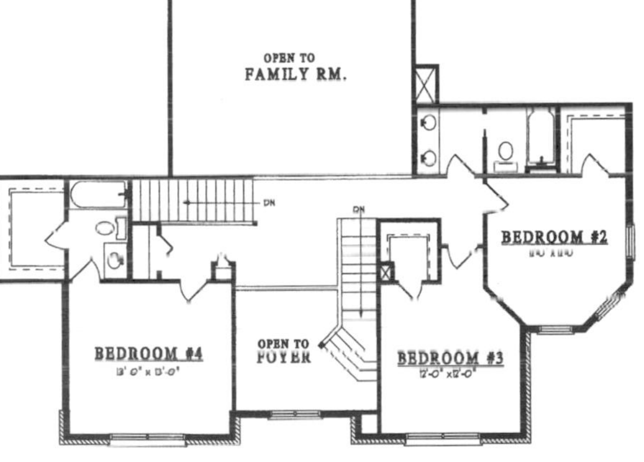

OPEN TO FAMILY RM.
BEDROOM #2
BEDROOM #4
OPEN TO FOYER
BEDROOM #3

FIRST FLOOR

WIDTH 79'-0"
DEPTH 55'-0"
EATING AREA
SUNROOM
KITCHEN
FAMILY ROOM
MASTER BEDROOM
SITTING AREA
4 CAR GARAGE
DINING ROOM
STUDY
FOYER

SECOND FLOOR

Contemporary Plan with an Old-Fashioned Look

Price Code: I

- This plan features:
  - — Four bedrooms
  - — Three full and one half baths
- Gracious Entry with arched window, sidelights and two-story Foyer
- Formal Dining Room and quiet Study have decorative windows
- Convenient Kitchen with cooktop island, opens to Eating Area
- This home is designed with a basement foundation
- This plan cannot be built within a 25 mile radius of Cedar Rapids, IA.

FIRST FLOOR — 2,385 SQ. FT.
SECOND FLOOR — 1,012 SQ. FT.
GARAGE — 846 SQ. FT.
BASEMENT — 2,385 SQ. FT.

TOTAL LIVING AREA:
3,397 SQ. FT.

PLAN NO. 94950

Notable Windows

Price Code: D

- This plan features:
  - — Four bedrooms
  - — Two full and one half baths
- Comfortable Family Room offers a fireplace, wetbar, and a wall of windows
- Kitchen includes an island counter and adjoins the Breakfast Bay
- This home is designed with basement and slab foundation options
- Alternate foundation options available at an additional charge. Please call 1-800-235-5700 for more information

FIRST FLOOR — 1,179 SQ. FT.
SECOND FLOOR — 1,019 SQ. FT.
BASEMENT — 1,179 SQ. FT.
GARAGE — 466 SQ. FT.

TOTAL LIVING AREA:
2,198 SQ. FT.

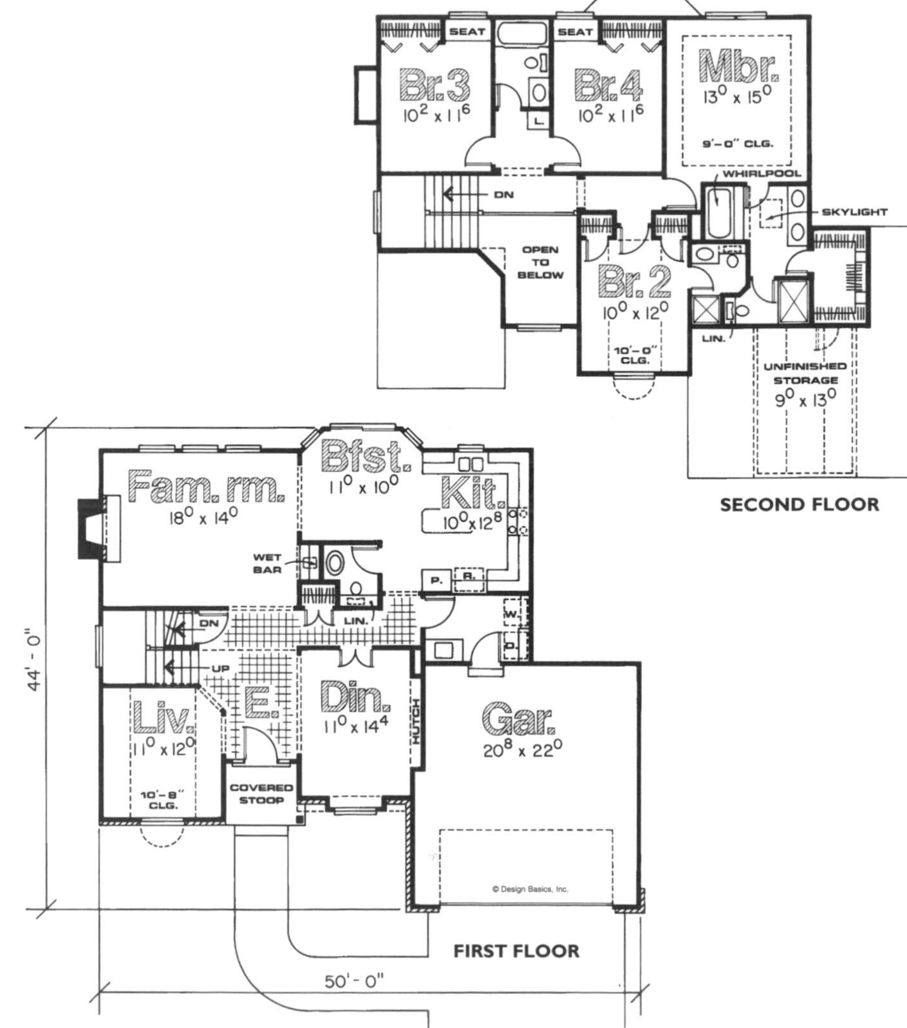

SEAT
SEAT
Br.3
10² x 11⁶
Br.4
10² x 11⁶
Mbr.
13⁰ x 15⁰
9'-0" CLG.
WHIRLPOOL
SKYLIGHT
DN
OPEN TO BELOW
Br.2
10⁰ x 12⁰
10'-0" CLG.
LIN.
UNFINISHED STORAGE
9⁰ x 13⁰
SECOND FLOOR
Bfst.
11⁰ x 10⁰
Fam. rm.
18⁰ x 14⁰
Kit.
10⁰ x 12⁸
WET BAR
P.
R.
LIN.
W.
D.
DN
UP
44'-0"
Liv.
11⁰ x 12⁰
10'-8" CLG.
E.
Din.
11⁰ x 14⁴
HUTCH
Gar.
20⁸ x 22⁰
COVERED STOOP
© Design Basics, Inc.
FIRST FLOOR
50'-0"

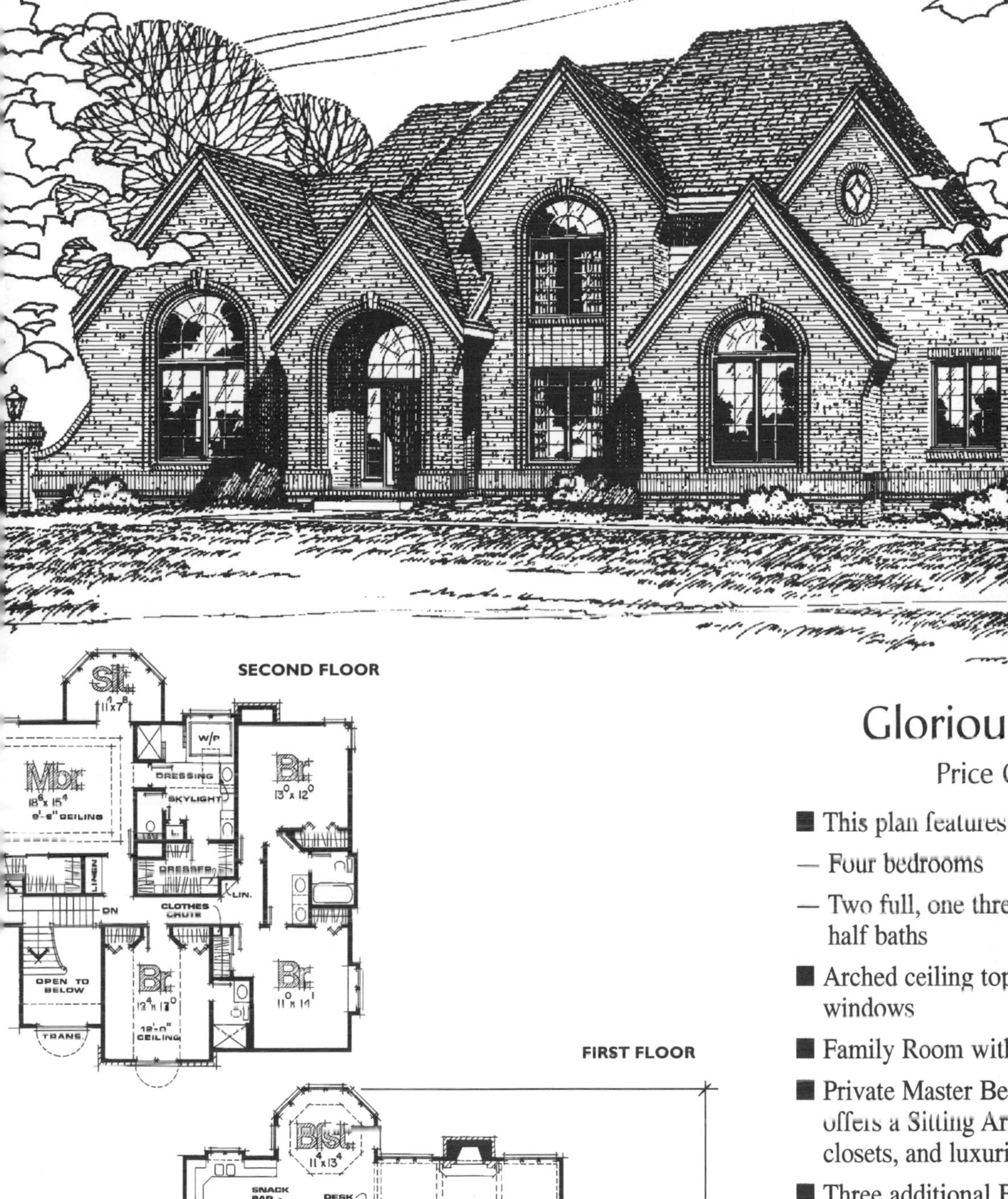
SECOND FLOOR
FIRST FLOOR
© Design Basics, Inc.

Glorious Gables

Price Code: 1

- This plan features:
- — Four bedrooms
- — Two full, one three-quarter and one half baths
- Arched ceiling topping decorative windows
- Family Room with hearth fireplace
- Private Master Bedroom Suite offers a Sitting Area, two walk-in closets, and luxurious Bath
- Three additional Bedrooms with ample closets and private access to a full Bath
- This home is designed with a basement foundation
- Alternate foundation options available at an additional charge. Please call 1-800-235-5700 for more information.

FIRST FLOOR — 1,709 SQ. FT.
SECOND FLOOR — 1,597 SQ. FT.
GARAGE — 721 SQ. FT.
BASEMENT — 1,709 SQ. FT.

TOTAL LIVING AREA:
3,306 SQ. FT.

PLAN NO. 94904

Distinctive Design

Price Code: C

This plan features:

— Three bedrooms

— Two full and one half baths

Living Room is distinguished by a bay window and French doors leading to Family Room

Well-appointed Kitchen with island cooktop, Breakfast Area, adjoining Laundry and Garage Entry

Spacious Master Bedroom Suite with vaulted ceiling and plush Dressing Area

This home is designed with a basement foundation

Alternate foundation options available at an additional charge. Please call 1-800-235-5700 for more information.

FIRST FLOOR — 1,093 SQ. FT.
SECOND FLOOR — 905 SQ. FT.
GARAGE — 527 SQ. FT.
BASEMENT — 1,093 SQ. FT.

TOTAL LIVING AREA:
1,998 SQ. FT.

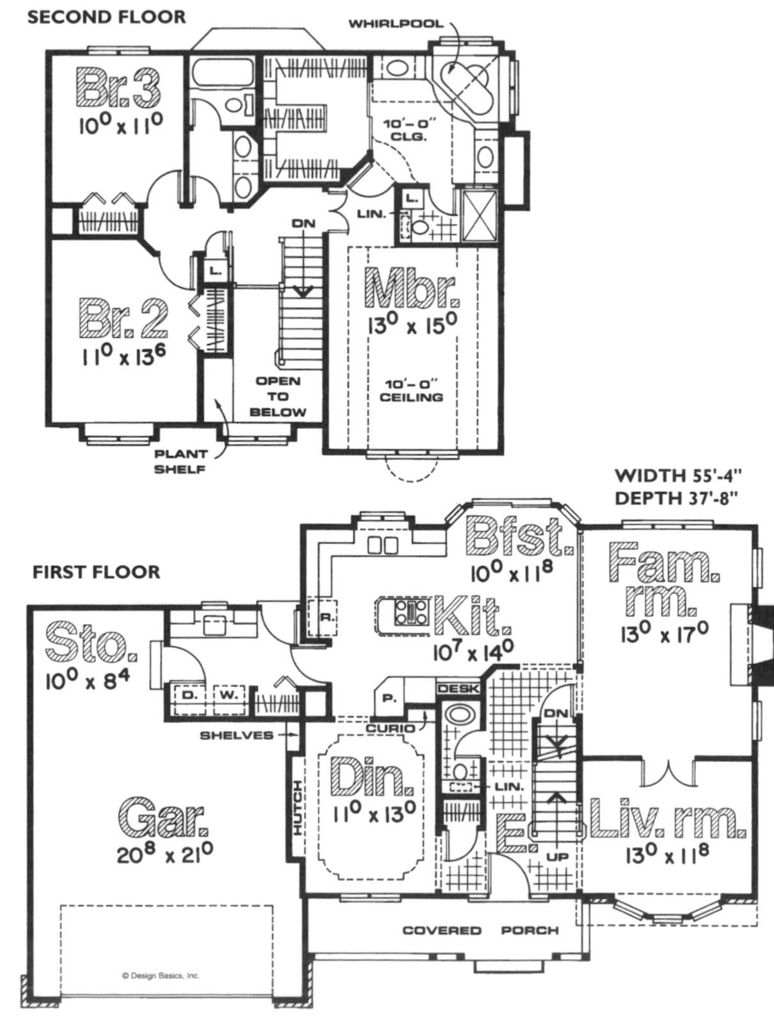

SECOND FLOOR
WHIRLPOOL
Br.3
10⁰ x 11⁰
10'-0" CLG.
LIN.
L.
DN
Br.2
11⁰ x 13⁶
L.
Mbr.
13⁰ x 15⁰
OPEN TO BELOW
10'-0" CEILING
PLANT SHELF
WIDTH 55'-4"
DEPTH 37'-8"
FIRST FLOOR
Bfst.
10⁰ x 11⁸
Fam. rm.
13⁰ x 17⁰
Sto.
10⁰ x 8⁴
R.
Kit.
10⁷ x 14⁰
D.
W.
P.
DESK
SHELVES
CURIO
DN
HUTCH
Din.
11⁰ x 13⁰
LIN.
Gar.
20⁸ x 21⁰
E.
UP
Liv. rm.
13⁰ x 11⁸
COVERED PORCH
© Design Basics, Inc.

n Estate of Epic Proportion

PRICE CODE: K

his plan features
- our bedrooms
- hree full and one half baths
- ront door opening into a grand Entry with a 20-foot iling and a spiral staircase
- anking the Entry on the right is the Living Room with thedral ceiling and fireplace, and on the left is the yed formal Dining Room
- alk down the Gallery to the Study with a full wall ilt-in bookcase
- e enormous Master Bedroom has a walk-in closet, mptuous Bath and a bayed Sitting Area
- amily Room has a wetbar, a fireplace, and a door hich leads outside to the covered Veranda
- his home is designed with basement and slab undation options

ST FLOOR — 2,751 SQ. FT.
OND FLOOR — 1,185 SQ. FT.
NUS — 343 SQ. FT.
RAGE — 790 SQ. FT.

TOTAL LIVING AREA:
3,936 SQ. FT.

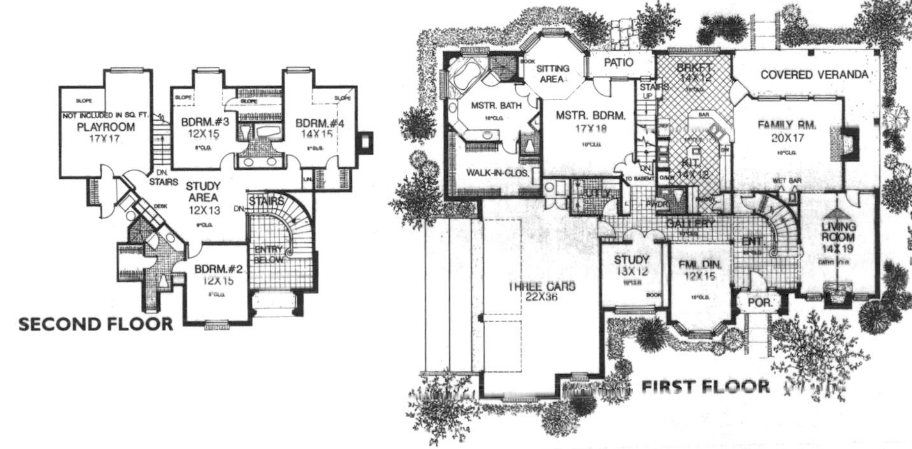

79'-0"
PLAYROOM 17X17
NOT INCLUDED IN SQ. FT.
BDRM.#3 12X15
BDRM.#4 14X15
STUDY AREA 12X13
STAIRS
ENTRY BELOW
BDRM.#2 12X15
SECOND FLOOR
SITTING AREA
PATIO
BRKFT. 14X12
COVERED VERANDA
MSTR. BATH
MSTR. BDRM. 17X18
FAMILY RM. 20X17
WALK-IN-CLOS.
GALLERY
LIVING ROOM 14X19
STUDY 13X12
FML.DIN. 12X15
THREE CARS 22X36
POR.
FIRST FLOOR

PLAN NO. 98539

Open Spaces

PRICE CODE: A

his plan features:
- Three bedrooms
- Two full baths
- Family Room, Kitchen and Breakfast Area that all onnects to form a great space
- central, double fireplace adding warmth and tmosphere to the Family Room, Kitchen and the Breakfast Area
- n efficient Kitchen that is highlighted by a peninsula ounter and doubles as a snack bar
- Master Suite that includes a walk-in closet, a double anity, separate shower and tub Bath
- wo additional Bedrooms sharing a full hall Bath
- wooden Deck that can be accessed from the Breakfast Area
- his home is designed with slab and crawlspace oundation options

AIN FLOOR — 1,388 SQ. FT.
RAGE — 400 SQ. FT.

TOTAL LIVING AREA:
1,388 SQ. FT.

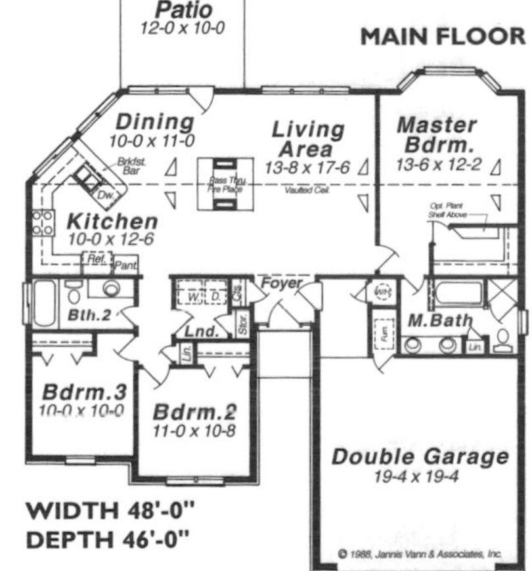

Patio
12-0 x 10-0
MAIN FLOOR
Dining
10-0 x 11-0
Living Area
13-8 x 17-6
Master Bdrm.
13-6 x 12-2
Kitchen
10-0 x 12-6
Foyer
Bth.2
Lnd.
M.Bath
Bdrm.3
10-0 x 10-0
Bdrm.2
11-0 x 10-8
Double Garage
19-4 x 19-4
WIDTH 48'-0"
DEPTH 46'-0"

PLAN NO. 93279

PLAN NO.10274

Fireplace Center of Circula Living Area

PRICE CODE: C

- This plan features:
  - — Three bedrooms
  - — One full and one three-quarter baths
- A dramatically positioned fireplace as a focal point f the main Living Area
- The Kitchen, Dining and Living Rooms form a circle that allows work areas to flow into living areas
- Sliding glass doors accessible to Deck
- A convenient Laundry Room located off the Kitchen
- A double Garage providing excellent storage
- This home is designed with a slab foundation

MAIN FLOOR— 1,783 SQ. FT.
GARAGE — 576 SQ. FT.

TOTAL LIVING AREA: 1,783 SQ. FT.

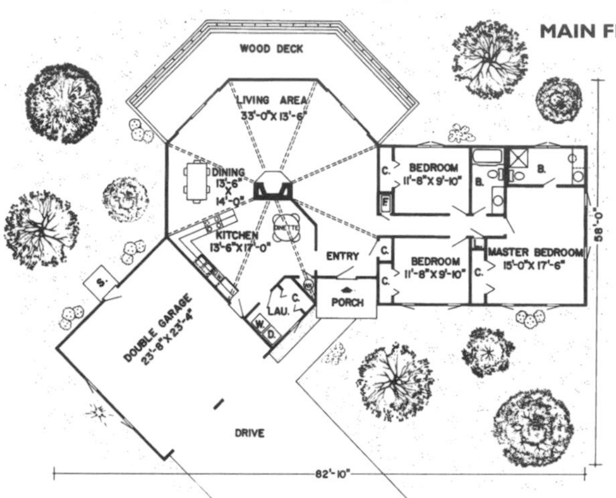
WOOD DECK
LIVING AREA 33'-0"X13'-6"
DINING 13'-6" X 14'-0"
KITCHEN 13'-6"X17'-0"
BEDROOM 11'-8"X9'-10"
BEDROOM 11'-8"X9'-10"
MASTER BEDROOM 15'-0"X17'-6"
ENTRY
PORCH
LAU.
DOUBLE GARAGE 23'-8"X23'-4"
DRIVE
82'-10"
58'-0"

MAIN FLOOR

PLAN NO.94202

Coastal Delight

PRICE CODE: H

- This plan features:
  - — Three bedrooms
  - — Two full baths
- Living Area above the Garage and Storage/Bonus are offering a "piling" design for coastal, waterfront or low-lying terrain
- Double-door Entry into an open Foyer with landing staircase leads into the Great Room
- Three sets of double doors below a vaulted ceiling in Great Room offer lots of air, light and easy access to both the Sun Deck and Veranda
- A Dining Room convenient to the Great Room and Kitchen featuring vaulted ceilings and decorative windows
- A glassed-in Nook adjacent to the efficient Kitchen w an island work center
- A second floor Master Suite with a vaulted ceiling, double door to a private Deck, his and her closets an a plush Bath
- This home is designed with pier and post foundation options
- Alternate foundation options available at an additional charge. Please call 1-800-235-5700 for more information.

FIRST FLOOR — 1,736 SQ. FT.
SECOND FLOOR — 640 SQ. FT.
BONUS ROOM — 253 SQ. FT.
CARPORT — 840 SQ. FT.

TOTAL LIVING AREA: 2,376 SQ. FT.

deck
storage
bonus
carport
bonus
up

CARPORT

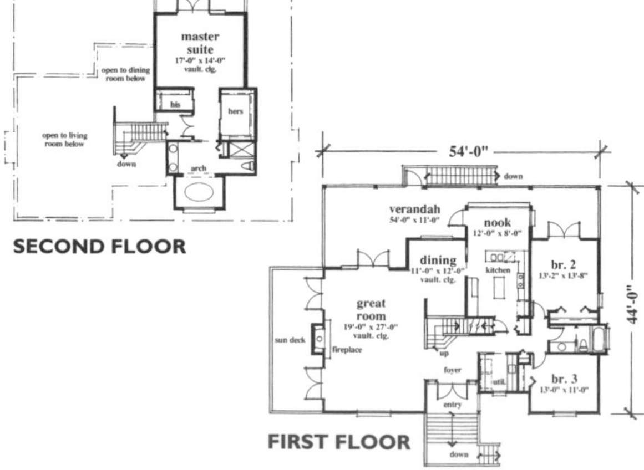
deck
master suite
his
hers
down
arch
54'-0"
verandah
nook
dining
kitchen
br. 2
great room
sun deck
fireplace
foyer
entry
up
down
br. 3
44'-0"

SECOND FLOOR

FIRST FLOOR

For The Young Family

PRICE CODE: E

PLAN NO.97142

'his plan features:
- 'our bedrooms
- Two full and one half baths
- Built-in cabinets surrounding a beautiful fireplace add oziness for large family get-togethers
- 'he Den has a unique window seat providing a retreat rom the commotion of everyday life
- large island, centered in the Kitchen, supplies the erfect resting place for a quick snack or a convenient pace to prepare special meals
- 'his home is designed with a basement foundation

ST FLOOR — 1,339 SQ. FT.
COND FLOOR — 1,081 SQ. FT.

TOTAL LIVING AREA: 2,420 SQ. FT.

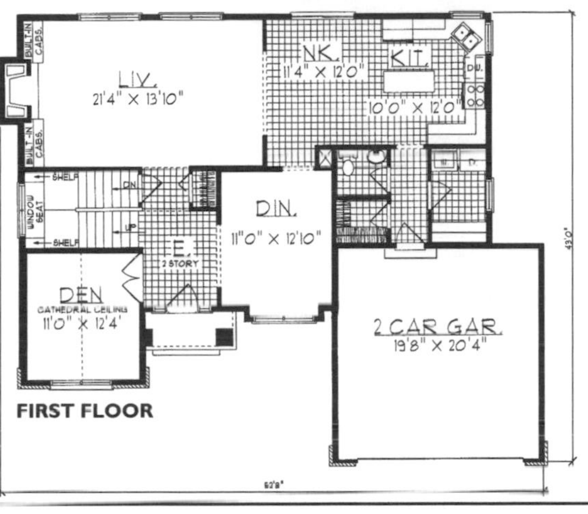

LIV.
21'4" X 13'10"
NK.
11'4" X 12'0"
KIT.
10'0" X 12'0"
DIN.
11'0" X 12'10"
DEN
CATHEDRAL CEILING
11'0" X 12'4'
2 CAR GAR.
19'8" X 20'4"
WINDOW SEAT
SHELF
BUILT-IN CABS.

FIRST FLOOR

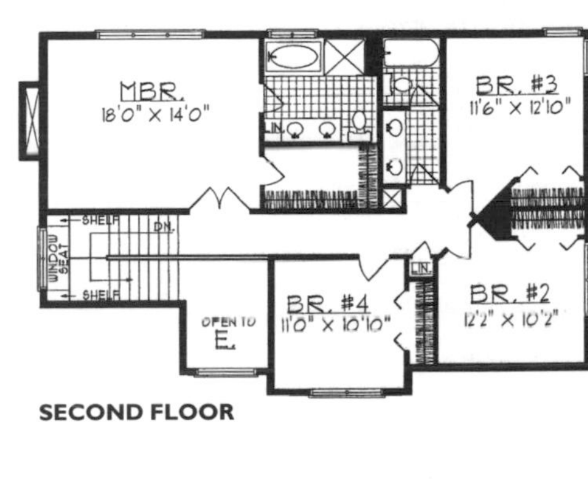

MBR.
18'0" X 14'0"
BR. #3
11'6" X 12'10"
BR. #4
11'0" X 10'10"
BR. #2
12'2" X 10'2"
OPEN TO E.
WINDOW SEAT
SHELF

SECOND FLOOR

Impressive Manor

PRICE CODE: E

PLAN NO.98221

This plan features:
- Four bedrooms
- Two full and one half baths
- The Foyer leads to the Dining Room and Parlor with windows overlooking the front yard
- The Family Room has a fireplace and leads into the sunny Breakfast Bay
- Upstairs find the Master Bedroom with a see-through fireplace and a Sitting Room
- The Master Bath is spacious and includes a walk-in closet and a skylight
- This home is designed with a basement foundation

RST FLOOR — 1,113 SQ. FT.
COND FLOOR — 1,148 SQ. FT.
ASEMENT — 1,113 SQ. FT.
ARAGE — 529 SQ. FT.

TOTAL LIVING AREA: 2,261 SQ. FT.

WIDTH 66'-0"
DEPTH 31'-0"

BREAKFAST
KITCHEN
LNDRY
FAMILY ROOM
PARLOR
FOYER
DINING ROOM
3 CAR GARAGE
P.R.
PANTRY

FIRST FLOOR

BEDROOM #2
BATH
SITTING ROOM
MASTER BEDROOM
HALL
W.I.C.
BEDROOM #3
FOYER BELOW
BEDROOM #4
MSTR BATH
CLO.
SKYLIGHT

SECOND FLOOR

PLAN NO. 94902

Inviting Covered Porch

Price Code: C

- This plan features:
- — Four bedrooms
- — Two full and one half baths
- Interesting staircase with landing in volume Entry
- 10-foot ceiling above transom windows and hearth fireplace accent the Great Room
- Master Bedroom Suite features decorative ceiling to walk-in closets and double vanity Bath with a whirlpool tub
- This home is designed with a basement foundation
- Alternate foundation options available at an additional charge. Please call 1-800-235-5700 for more information.

FIRST FLOOR — 944 SQ. FT.
SECOND FLOOR — 987 SQ. FT.
BASEMENT — 944 SQ. FT.
GARAGE — 557 SQ. FT.

TOTAL LIVING AREA:
1,931 SQ. FT.

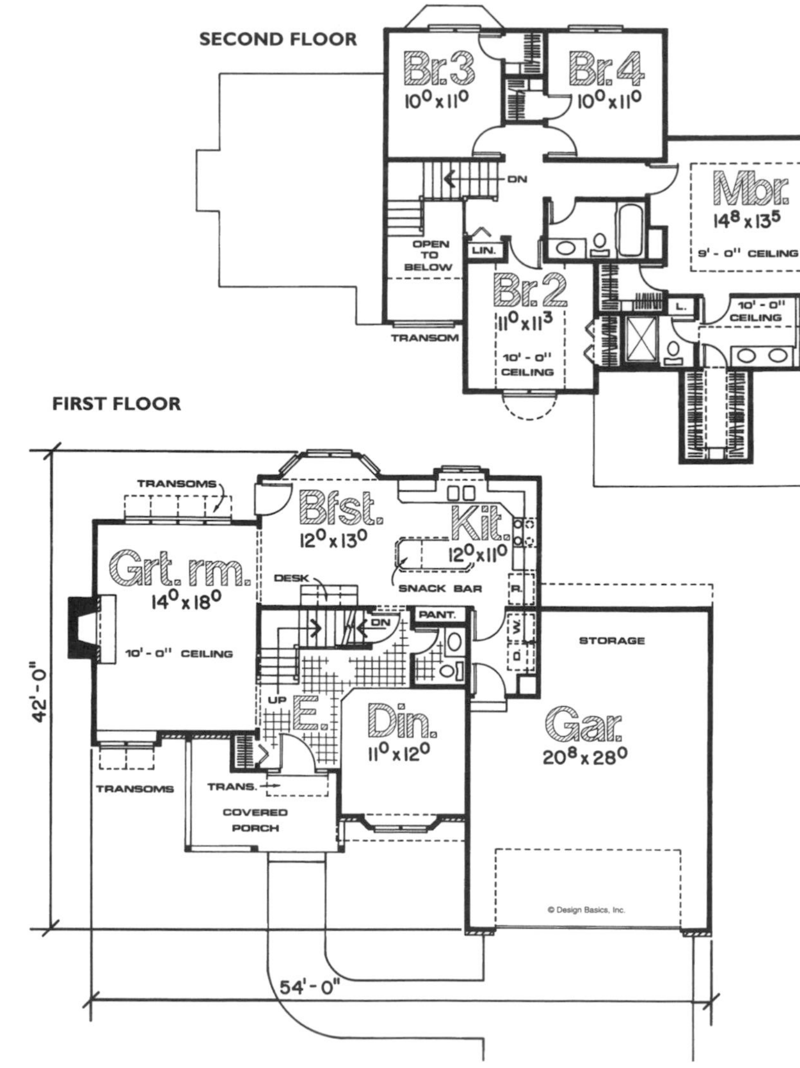

SECOND FLOOR
Br.3
$10^0 x 11^0$
Br.4
$10^0 x 11^0$
DN
Mbr.
$14^8 x 13^5$
9'-0" CEILING
OPEN TO BELOW
LIN.
Br.2
$11^0 x 11^3$
10'-0" CEILING
10'-0" CEILING
L.
W/P
TRANSOM
FIRST FLOOR
TRANSOMS
Bfst.
$12^0 x 13^0$
Kit.
$12^0 x 11^0$
Grt. rm.
$14^0 x 18^0$
10'-0" CEILING
DESK
SNACK BAR
R.
PANT.
DN
W.
D.
STORAGE
UP
E.
Din.
$11^0 x 12^0$
Gar.
$20^8 x 28^0$
42'-0"
TRANSOMS
TRANS.
COVERED PORCH
© Design Basics, Inc.
54'-0"

Convenient Floor Plan

PRICE CODE: B

PLAN NO.24701

'his plan features:
- Three bedrooms
- Two full baths
- Central Foyer leads to Den/Guest Room with arched window below vaulted ceiling and Living Room accented by two-sided fireplace
- Efficient, U-shaped Kitchen with peninsula counter/Breakfast Bar serving Dining Room and adjacent Utility/Pantry
- Master Suite features large walk-in closet and private Bath with double vanity and whirlpool tub
- Two additional Bedrooms with ample closet space share full Bath
- This home is designed with a basement foundation

AIN FLOOR — 1,625 SQ. FT.
SEMENT — 1,625 SQ. FT.
RAGE — 455 SQ. FT.

TOTAL LIVING AREA: 1,625 SQ. FT.

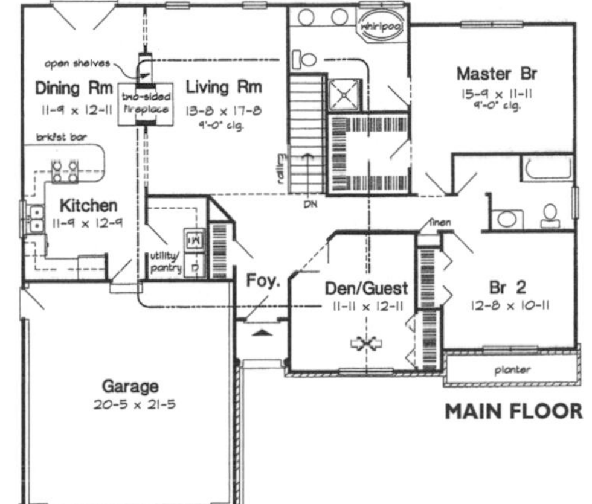
Dining Rm
11-9 x 12-11
open shelves
two-sided fireplace
Living Rm
13-8 x 17-8
9'-0" clg.
whirlpool
Master Br
15-9 x 11-11
9'-0" clg.
brkfst bar
Kitchen
11-9 x 12-9
DN
linen
utility/pantry
Foy.
Den/Guest
11-11 x 12-11
Br 2
12-8 x 10-11
planter
Garage
20-5 x 21-5
MAIN FLOOR

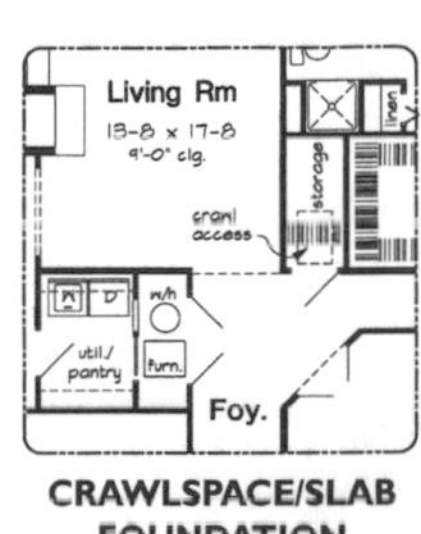
Living Rm
13-8 x 17-8
9'-0" clg.
storage
crawl access
util./pantry
furn.
Foy.

CRAWLSPACE/SLAB FOUNDATION OPTION

WIDTH 54'-0"
DEPTH 48'-4"

Compact and Comfortable

PRICE CODE: A

PLAN NO.93202

This plan features:
- Three bedrooms
- Two full baths
- Arched window highlights front entrance, Foyer and staircase
- Spacious Living Area with focal point fireplace and Deck access
- Efficient, U-shaped Kitchen easily serves bright Dining Room and Deck
- Private Master Bedroom with walk-in closet and double vanity Bath with a raised tub
- Two additional Bedrooms with ample closets, share a full Bath
- Lower level with Garage, Storage and future Playroom
- This home is designed with a basement foundation

AIN FLOOR — 1,407 SQ. FT.
)NUS — 224 SQ. FT.
ASEMENT — 732 SQ. FT.
AIRS — 40 SQ. FT.
ARAGE — 400 SQ. FT.

TOTAL LIVING AREA: 1,447 SQ. FT.

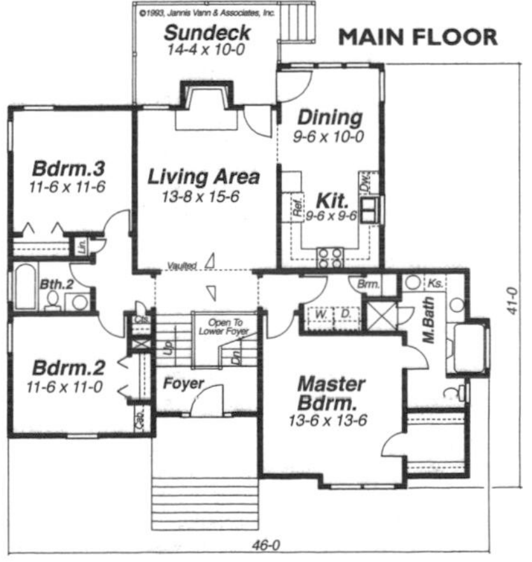
Sundeck
14-4 x 10-0
Bdrm.3
11-6 x 11-6
Living Area
13-8 x 15-6
Dining
9-6 x 10-0
Kit.
9-6 x 9-6
Vaulted
Bth.2
Brm.
M.Bath
Open To Lower Foyer
Bdrm.2
11-6 x 11-0
Foyer
Master Bdrm.
13-6 x 13-6
41-0
46-0

MAIN FLOOR

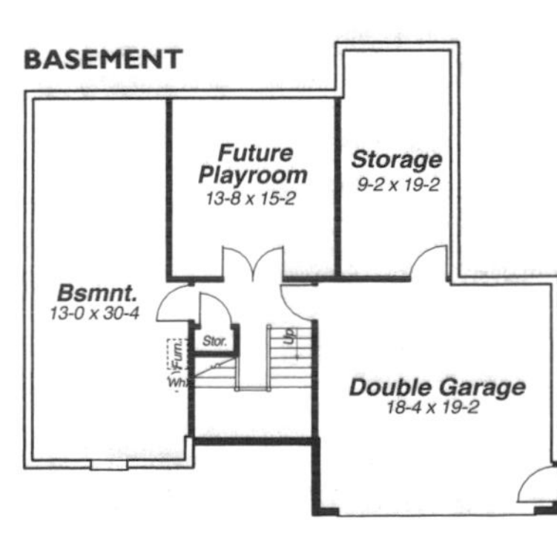
Future Playroom
13-8 x 15-2
Storage
9-2 x 19-2
Bsmnt.
13-0 x 30-4
Stor.
Double Garage
18-4 x 19-2

BASEMENT

PLAN NO. 86012

Country Classic

PRICE CODE: E

- This plan features:
  - Four bedrooms
  - Two full and one half baths
- All of the Bedrooms are located upstairs for privacy
- A family Entry in the rear will cut down on tracked-in dirt
- A vaulted ceiling and fireplace complete the Family Room
- Columns separate the Living and Dining Rooms
- The L-shaped Kitchen includes an island with a cook
- This home is designed with a combo basement/slab foundation

FIRST FLOOR — 1,412 SQ. FT.
SECOND FLOOR — 1,003 SQ. FT.
BASEMENT — 992 SQ. FT.
GARAGE — 576 SQ. FT.

TOTAL LIVING AREA:
2,415 SQ. FT.

PORCH
FAMILY ROOM
18'-0"x19'-6"
VAULTED CEILING
FAMILY ENTRY
FP
MORNING ROOM
8'-0"x11'-6"
KITCHEN
10'-0"x11'-6"
DINING ROOM
13'-9"x14'-4"
PANTRY
LAUNDRY
W
D
LAV.
ENTRY FOYER
LIVING ROOM
13'-9"x18'-6"
DN
UP
PORCH
TWO-CAR GARAGE
23'-4"x23'-2"
FIRST FLOOR

WIDTH 58'-0"
DEPTH 44'-0"

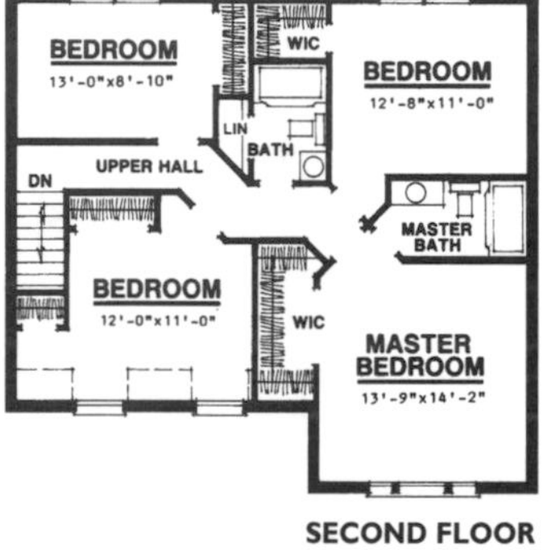
BEDROOM
13'-0"x8'-10"
WIC
BEDROOM
12'-8"x11'-0"
LIN
BATH
UPPER HALL
DN
MASTER BATH
BEDROOM
12'-0"x11'-0"
WIC
MASTER BEDROOM
13'-9"x14'-2"

SECOND FLOOR

PLAN NO. 98414

Three Bedroom Ranch

PRICE CODE: B

- This plan features:
  - Three bedrooms
  - Two full baths
- Formal Dining Room enhanced by a plant shelf and a side window
- Wetbar located between the Kitchen and the Dining Room
- Built-in Pantry, a double sink, and a snack bar highlig the Kitchen
- Breakfast Room containing a radius window and a French door to the rear yard
- Large cozy fireplace framed by windows in the Great Room
- Master Suite with a vaulted ceiling over the Sitting Area, a Master Bath, and a walk-in closet
- Two additional Bedrooms sharing the full Bath in the Hall
- This home is designed with basement and crawlspace foundation options

MAIN FLOOR — 1,575 SQ. FT.
BASEMENT — 1,658 SQ. FT.
GARAGE — 459 SQ. FT.

TOTAL LIVING AREA:
1,575 SQ. FT.

WIDTH 50'-0"
DEPTH 52'-6"

OPTIONAL BASEMENT STAIR LOCATION

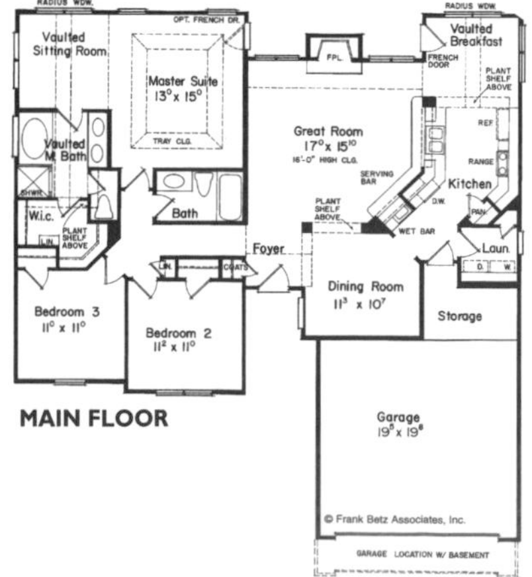
Vaulted Sitting Room
Master Suite
Vaulted M. Bath
Great Room
Vaulted Breakfast
Kitchen
Bath
Foyer
Dining Room
Bedroom 3
Bedroom 2
Storage
Garage
© Frank Betz Associates, Inc.

MAIN FLOOR

Keystones, Arches and Gables

PRICE CODE: B

PLAN NO.93171

This plan features:

- Three bedrooms
- Two full and one half baths
- Tiled Entry opens to Living Room with focal point fireplace
- U-shaped Kitchen with a built-in Pantry, eating bar and nearby Laundry/Garage Entry
- Comfortable Dining Room with bay window and French doors to Screened Porch expanding living area outdoors
- Corner Master Bedroom offers a great walk-in closet and private Bath
- Two additional Bedrooms with ample closets and double windows, share a full Bath
- This home is designed with a basement foundation

AIN FLOOR — 1,642 SQ. FT.
SEMENT — 1,642 SQ. FT.

TOTAL LIVING AREA:
1,642 SQ. FT.

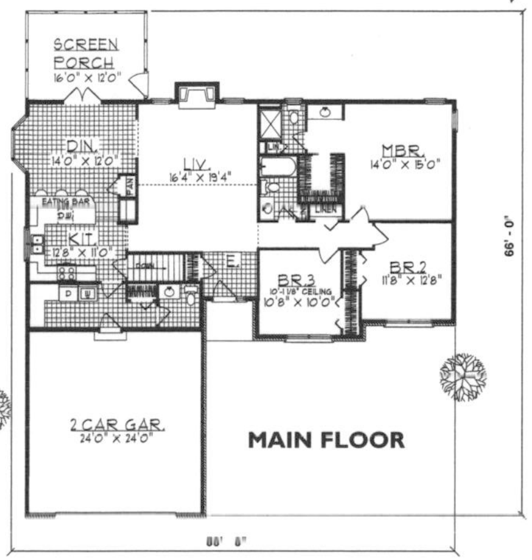

SCREEN PORCH
16'0" X 12'0"
DIN.
14'0" X 12'0"
LIV.
16'4" X 19'4"
MBR.
14'0" X 15'0"
EATING BAR
KIT.
12'8" X 11'0"
BR.3
10'8" X 10'0"
BR.2
11'8" X 12'8"
2 CAR GAR.
24'0" X 24'0"
MAIN FLOOR
66'-0"

Keystones and Arched Windows

PRICE CODE: B

PLAN NO.98432

This plan features:

- Three bedrooms
- Two full baths
- A large arched window in the Dining Room offers eye-catching appeal
- A decorative column helps to define the Dining Room from the Great Room
- A fireplace and French door to the rear yard can be found in the Great Room
- An efficient Kitchen includes a serving bar, Pantry and pass through to the Great Room
- A vaulted ceiling over the Breakfast Room
- A plush Master Suite includes a private Bath and a walk-in closet
- Two additional Bedrooms share a full Bath in the hall
- This home is designed with basement, slab and crawlspace foundation options

AIN FLOOR — 1,670 SQ. FT.
ARAGE — 240 SQ. FT.

TOTAL LIVING AREA:
1,670 SQ. FT.

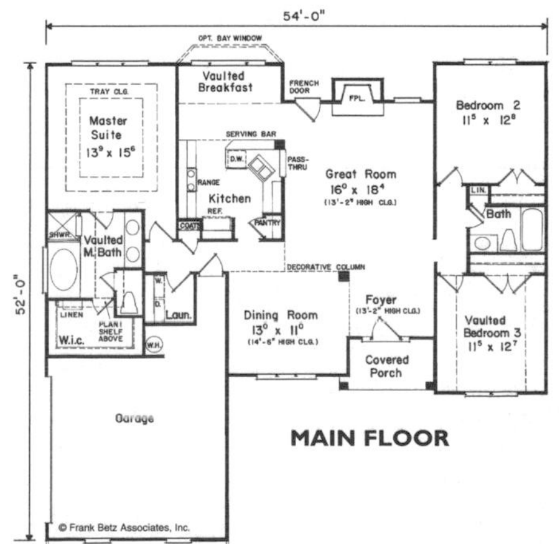

54'-0"
OPT. BAY WINDOW
Vaulted Breakfast
FRENCH DOOR
FPL.
Master Suite
13^{0} x 15^{6}
TRAY CLG.
SERVING BAR
Great Room
16^{0} x 18^{4}
(13'-2" HIGH CLG.)
Kitchen
Bedroom 2
11^{5} x 12^{8}
Bath
Vaulted M.Bath
W.i.c.
Laun.
DECORATIVE COLUMN
Dining Room
13^{0} x 11^{0}
(14'-6" HIGH CLG.)
Foyer
(13'-2" HIGH CLG.)
Covered Porch
Vaulted Bedroom 3
11^{5} x 12^{7}
52'-0"
Garage
MAIN FLOOR
© Frank Betz Associates, Inc.
GARAGE LOCATION WITH BASEMENT

PLAN NO.24978

Details, Details, Details

PRICE CODE: L

- This plan features:
- — Five bedrooms
- — Five full and two half baths
- The symmetrical design of this home is of architectural interest
- In the Foyer, an elegant, spiral staircase leads to the second floor
- A private Vestibule leads to the impressive Master Suit
- Secondary Bedrooms, each with skylit full Bath, fill th second floor
- Fireplaces in the Living, Dining, and Family Rooms pr vide a sense of coziness to the casual and formal areas
- This home is designed with basement, slab, and crawlspace foundation options

FIRST FLOOR — 2,764 SQ. FT.
SECOND FLOOR — 1,443 SQ. FT.
BASEMENT — 2,764 SQ. FT.
GARAGE — 663 SQ. FT.

TOTAL LIVING AREA:
4,207 SQ. FT.

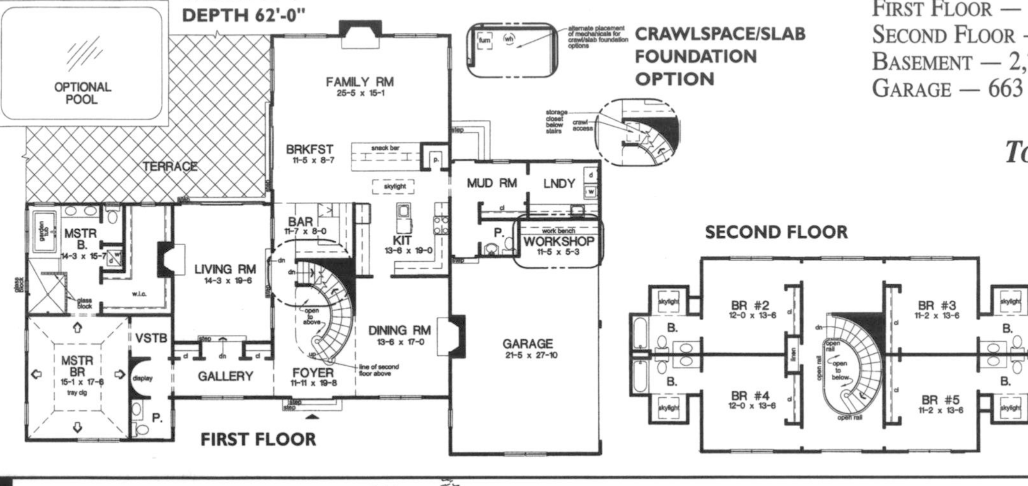
WIDTH 84'-0"
DEPTH 62'-0"
OPTIONAL POOL
TERRACE
FAMILY RM 25-5 x 15-1
BRKFST 11-5 x 8-7
MUD RM
LNDY
BAR 11-7 x 8-0
KIT 13-6 x 19-0
WORKSHOP 11-5 x 5-3
MSTR B. 14-3 x 15-7
LIVING RM 14-3 x 19-6
VSTB
MSTR BR 15-1 x 17-6
GALLERY
FOYER 11-11 x 19-8
DINING RM 13-6 x 17-0
GARAGE 21-5 x 27-10
FIRST FLOOR
CRAWLSPACE/SLAB FOUNDATION OPTION
SECOND FLOOR
BR #2 12-0 x 13-6
BR #3 11-2 x 13-6
BR #4 12-0 x 13-6
BR #5 11-2 x 13-6

PLAN NO.24708

Cozy Country Ranch

PRICE CODE: B

- This plan features:
- — Three bedrooms
- — Two full baths
- Front Porch shelters outdoor visiting and entrance into Living Room
- Expansive Living Room highlighted by a boxed windo and hearth fireplace between built-ins
- Columns frame entrance to Dining Room with access to the backyard
- Efficient, U-shaped Kitchen with direct access to the Screened Porch and the Dining Room
- Master Bedroom wing enhanced by a large walk-in closet and a double vanity Bath with a whirlpool tub
- Two additional Bedrooms with large closets share a double vanity Bath with Laundry Center
- This home is designed with basement, slab, and crawlspace foundation options

MAIN FLOOR — 1,576 SQ. FT.
BASEMENT — 1,454 SQ. FT.
GARAGE — 576 SQ. FT.

TOTAL LIVING AREA:
1,576 SQ. FT.

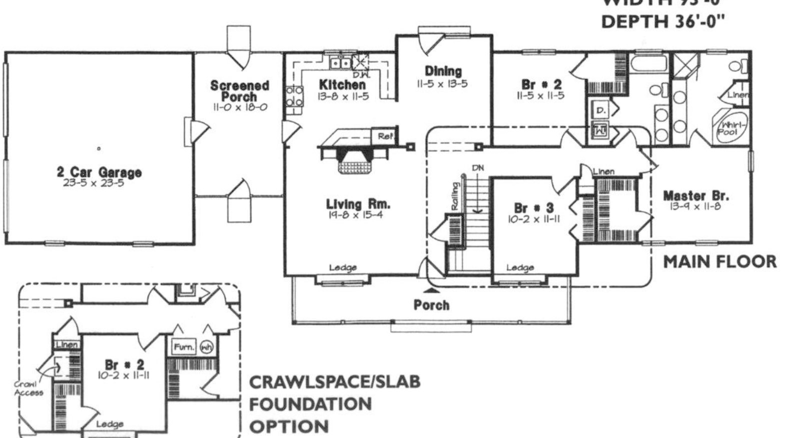
WIDTH 93'-0"
DEPTH 36'-0"
2 Car Garage 23-5 x 23-5
Screened Porch 11-0 x 18-0
Kitchen 13-8 x 11-5
Dining 11-5 x 13-5
Br # 2 11-5 x 11-5
Living Rm. 19-8 x 15-4
Br # 3 10-2 x 11-11
Master Br. 13-4 x 11-8
Porch
MAIN FLOOR
Br # 2 10-2 x 11-11
CRAWLSPACE/SLAB FOUNDATION OPTION

PLAN NO. 94944

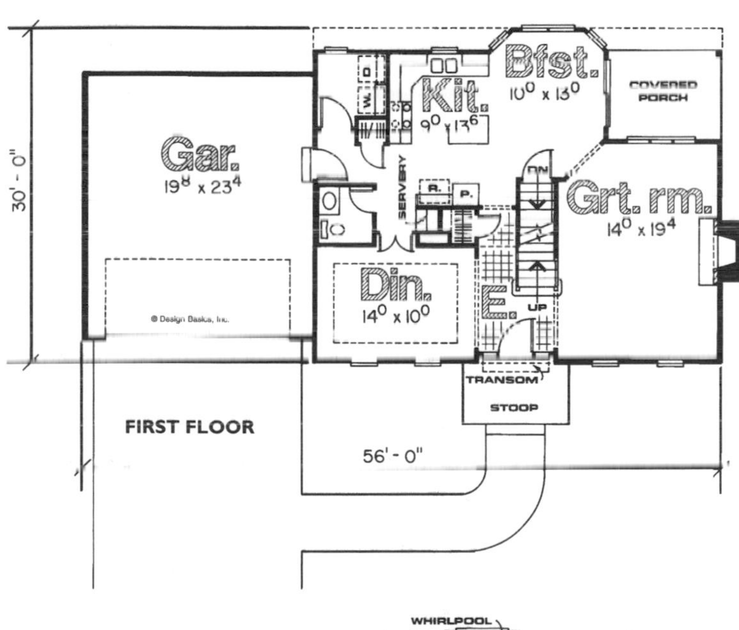

Bfst.
10⁰ x 13⁰
Kit.
9⁰ x 13⁶
COVERED PORCH
Gar.
19⁸ x 23⁴
30' - 0"
SERVERY
Grt. rm.
14⁰ x 19⁴
Din.
14⁰ x 10⁰
UP
DN
TRANSOM
STOOP
FIRST FLOOR 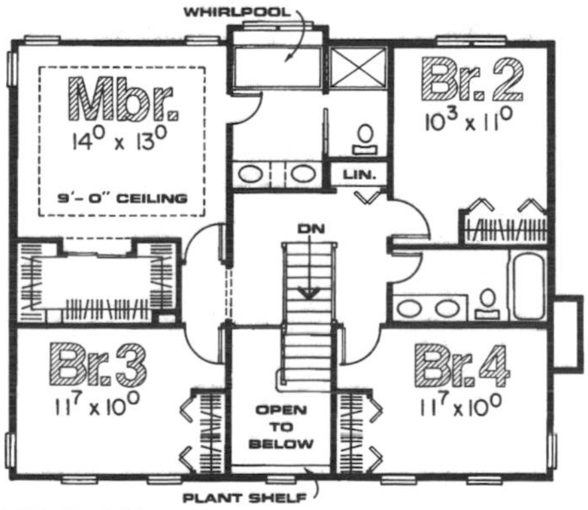
56' - 0"

WHIRLPOOL
Mbr.
14⁰ x 13⁰
9'- 0" CEILING
Br. 2
10³ x 11⁰
LIN.
DN
Br. 3
11⁷ x 10⁰
OPEN TO BELOW
Br. 4
11⁷ x 10⁰
PLANT SHELF
SECOND FLOOR

Spectacular Sophistication

Price Code: C

- This plan features:
  - — Four bedrooms
  - — Two full and one half baths
- Open Foyer with circular window and a plant shelf leads into the Dining Room
- Great Room with an inviting fireplace and windows front and back
- Master Bedroom features a nine-foot boxed ceiling, a walk-in closet and whirlpool Bath
- This home is designed with basement and slab foundation options
- Alternate foundation options available at an additional charge. Please call 1-800-235-5700 for more information.

FIRST FLOOR — 941 SQ. FT.
SECOND FLOOR — 992 SQ. FT.
BASEMENT — 941 SQ. FT.
GARAGE — 480 SQ. FT.

TOTAL LIVING AREA:
1,933 SQ. FT.

PLAN NO.94247

Designed for Entertaining

Price Code: J

- This plan features:
- — Three bedrooms
- — Three full and one half baths
- Large, open floor plan with an array of amenities
- Grand Room and Dining Area separated by 3-sided fireplace
- Secluded Master Suite enhanced by a private Spa Deck
- This home is designed with pier and post foundation options
- Alternate foundation options available at an additional charge. Please call 1-800-235-5700 for more information.

MAIN FLOOR — 2,066 SQ. FT.
UPPER FLOOR — 809 SQ. FT.
BONUS — 1,260 SQ. FT.
GARAGE — 798 SQ. FT.

TOTAL LIVING AREA:
2,875 SQ. FT.

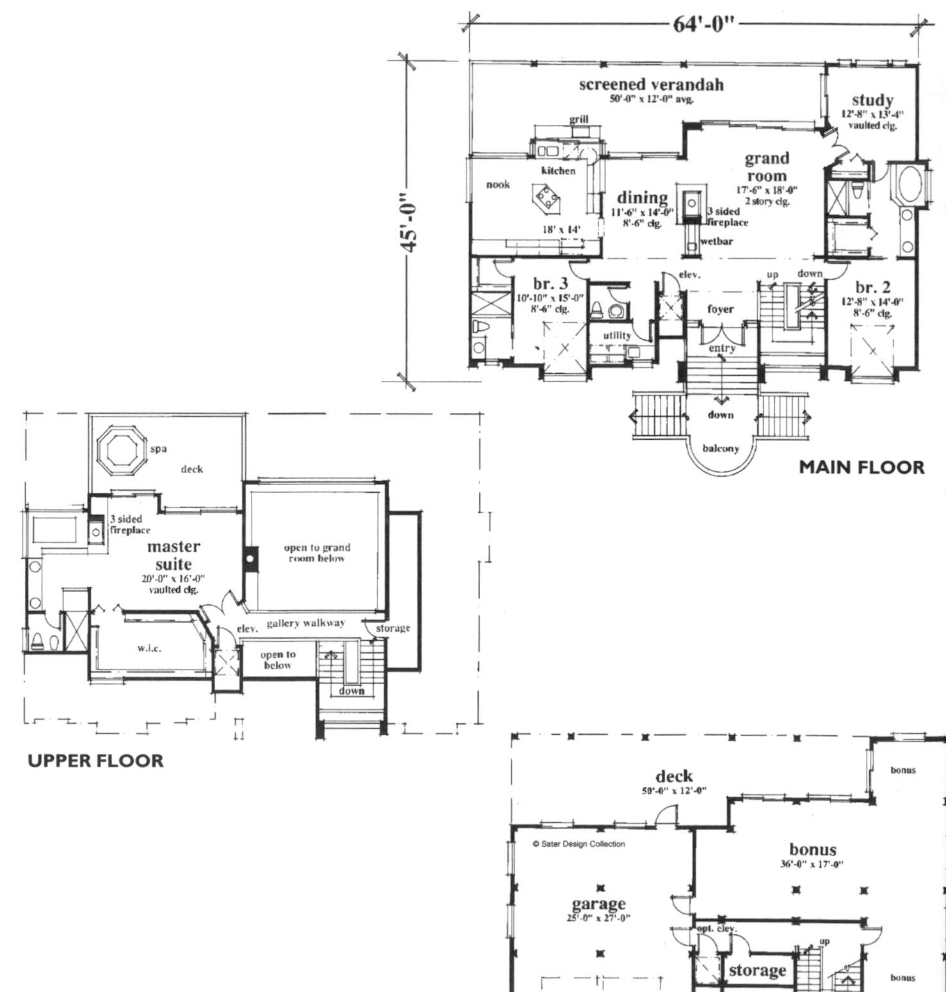
64'-0"
45'-0"
screened verandah
50'-0" x 12'-0" avg.
study
12'-8" x 13'-4"
vaulted clg.
grill
kitchen
nook
18' x 14'
dining
11'-6" x 14'-0"
8'-6" clg.
grand
room
17'-6" x 18'-0"
2 story clg.
3 sided
fireplace
wetbar
br. 3
10'-10" x 15'-0"
8'-6" clg.
utility
elev.
foyer
entry
up
down
br. 2
12'-8" x 14'-0"
8'-6" clg.
down
balcony
MAIN FLOOR
spa
deck
3 sided
fireplace
master
suite
20'-0" x 16'-0"
vaulted clg.
open to grand
room below
w.i.c.
elev.
gallery walkway
storage
open to
below
down
UPPER FLOOR
deck
50'-0" x 12'-0"
bonus
bonus
36'-0" x 17'-0"
© Sater Design Collection
garage
25'-0" x 27'-0"
opt. elev.
storage
up
bonus
LOWER FLOOR

PLAN NO. 98204

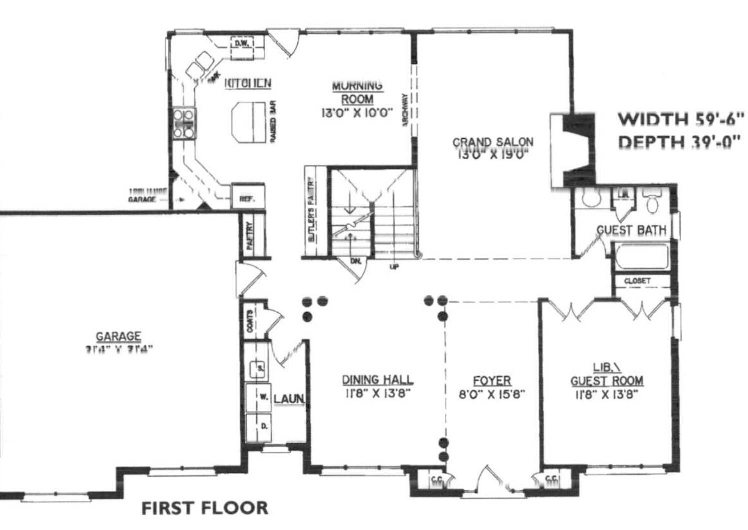
KITCHEN
MORNING ROOM
13'0" X 10'0"
GRAND SALON
13'0" X 19'0"
WIDTH 59'-6"
DEPTH 39'-0"
GUEST BATH
CLOSET
GARAGE
DINING HALL
11'8" X 13'8"
FOYER
8'0" X 15'8"
LIB.\
GUEST ROOM
11'8" X 13'8"
LAUN.
FIRST FLOOR

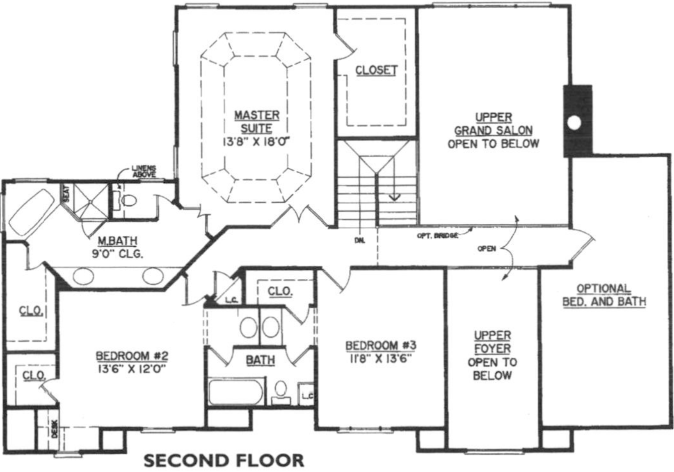
MASTER SUITE
13'8" X 18'0"
CLOSET
UPPER GRAND SALON
OPEN TO BELOW
M.BATH
9'0" CLG.
CLO.
CLO.
BEDROOM #2
13'6" X 12'0"
CLO.
BATH
BEDROOM #3
11'8" X 13'6"
UPPER FOYER
OPEN TO BELOW
OPTIONAL
BED. AND BATH
SECOND FLOOR

Windows Abound

Price Code: E

- This plan features:
  - Four bedrooms
  - Three full baths
- The Foyer opens to the Dining Room and the Grand Salon, which is highlighted by a fireplace
- The Kitchen enjoys all amenities including a center island and a Morning Room
- The Library could easily become a Guest Bedroom with a Bath just steps away
- The plush Master Suite enjoys an abundance of storage space having two-walk in closets, and a lavish Master Bath
- This home is designed with basement and slab foundation options

First Floor — 1,375 sq. ft.
Second Floor — 1,087 sq. ft.

Total Living Area:
2,462 sq. ft.

PLAN NO. 94261

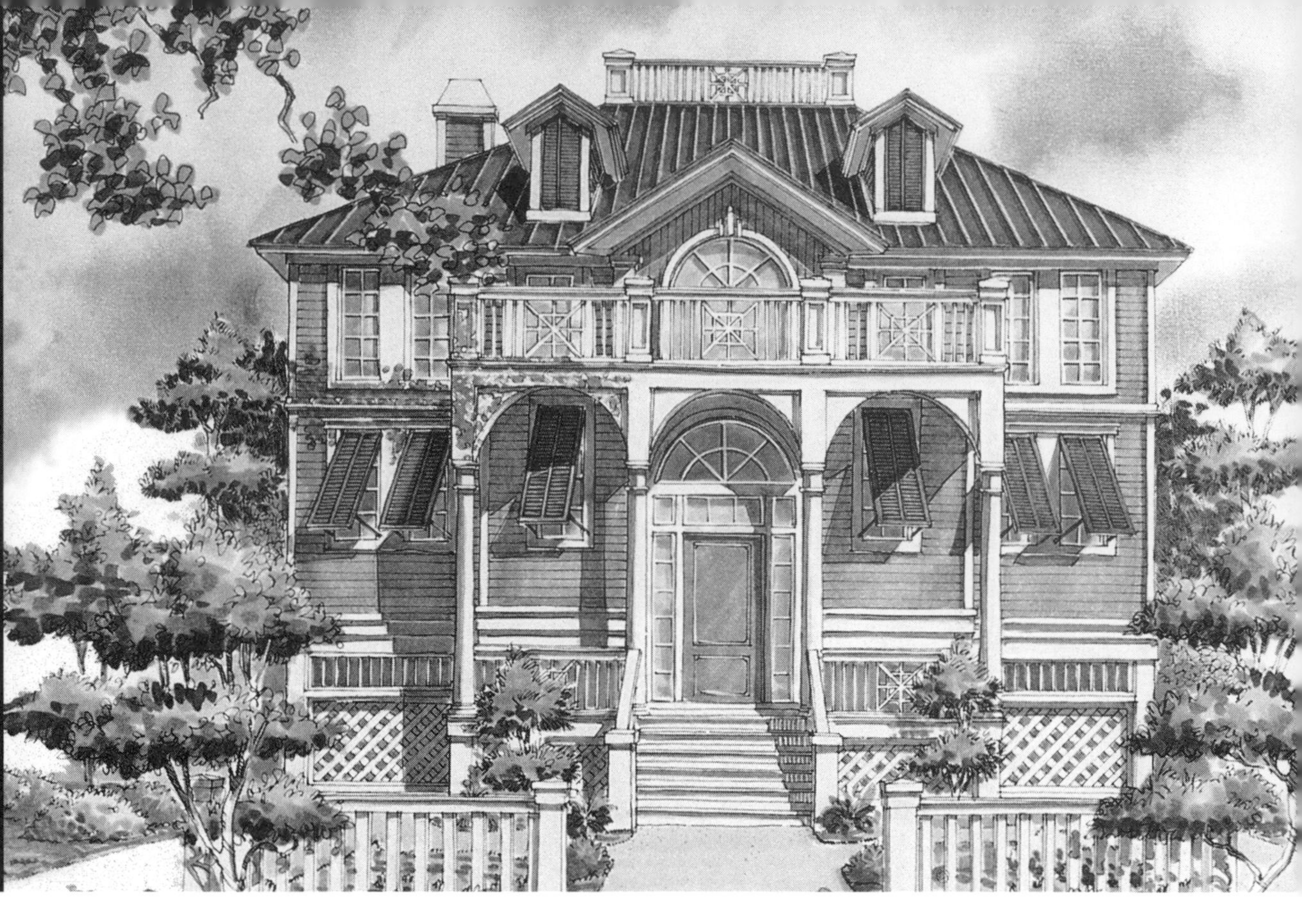

Poetic Symmetry

Price Code: G

- This plan features:
- — Three bedrooms
- — Three full and one half baths
- The open Living and Dining Areas are defined by French doors with windows above
- The Master Suite is located on the main floor for maximum in privacy
- Also upstairs is a Gallery Loft and a Computer Loft, which overlooks the Grand Room
- The ground level features a two-car Garage and plenty of storage space
- This home is designed with pier and post foundation options
- Alternate foundation options available at an additional charge. Please call 1-800-235-5700 for more information.

MAIN FLOOR — 1,642 SQ. FT.
UPPER FLOOR — 1,165 SQ. FT.
LOWER FLOOR — 150 SQ. FT.

TOTAL LIVING AREA:
2,957 SQ. FT.

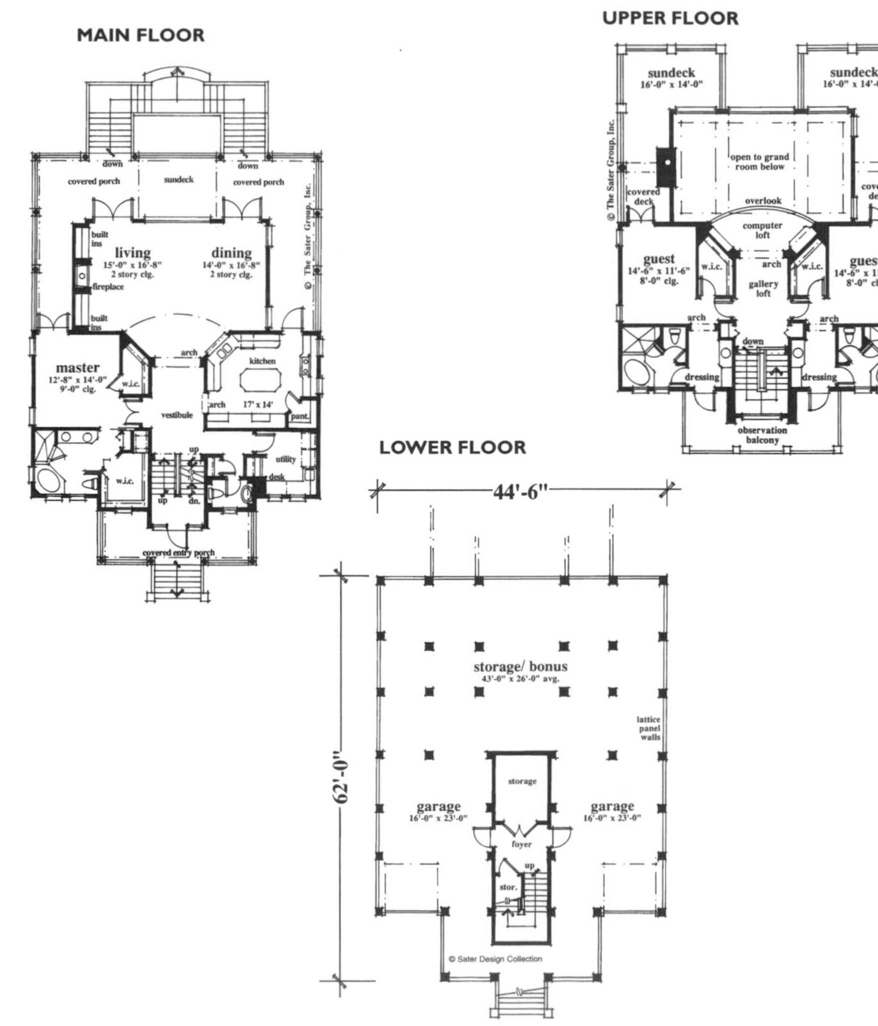
MAIN FLOOR
covered porch
sundeck
covered porch
living
15'-0" x 16'-8"
2 story clg.
dining
14'-0" x 16'-8"
2 story clg.
master
12'-8" x 14'-0"
9'-0" clg.
kitchen
17' x 14'
vestibule
utility
covered entry porch
© The Sater Group, Inc.
UPPER FLOOR
sundeck
16'-0" x 14'-0"
sundeck
16'-0" x 14'-0"
open to grand room below
overlook
computer loft
guest
14'-6" x 11'-6"
8'-0" clg.
gallery loft
guest
14'-6" x 11'-6"
8'-0" clg.
observation balcony
LOWER FLOOR
44'-6"
62'-0"
storage/ bonus
43'-0" x 26'-0" avg.
lattice panel walls
garage
16'-0" x 23'-0"
garage
16'-0" x 23'-0"
storage
foyer
© Sater Design Collection

English Tudor Styling

PRICE CODE: G

This plan features:
- Four bedrooms
- Three full and one half baths
- This Tudor-styled gem has a unique mix of exterior materials
- Inside the Entry either turn left to the Living Room or right into the Dining Room
- At the end of the Gallery is the Master Bedroom, which has dual walk-in closets
- The Family Room has a sloped ceiling and a rear wall fireplace
- The Kitchen has a center island and opens to the Breakfast Area
- A skylight brightens the staircase to the second floor
- Upstairs find three large Bedrooms and two full Baths
- Also upstairs access the future bonus room that is located over the Garage
- This home is designed with basement, slab and crawlspace foundation options

RST FLOOR — 2,082 SQ. FT.
ECOND FLOOR — 904 SQ. FT.
ONUS — 408 SQ. FT.
ARAGE — 605 SQ. FT.

TOTAL LIVING AREA:
2,986 SQ. FT.

PLAN NO.98546

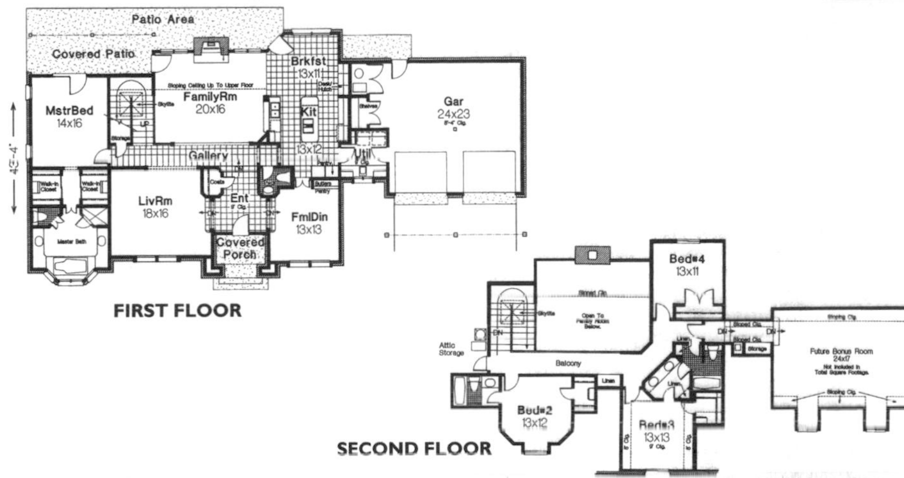

88'-1"
43'-4"
Patio Area
Covered Patio
Brkfst
13x11
MstrBed
14x16
FamilyRm
20x16
Kit
13x12
Gar
24x23
Gallery
LivRm
18x16
Ent
FmlDin
13x13
Covered Porch
FIRST FLOOR
Bed#4
13x11
Attic Storage
Balcony
Future Bonus Room
Bed#2
13x12
Bed#3
13x13
SECOND FLOOR

Arches are Appealing

PRICE CODE: B

This plan features:
- Three bedrooms
- Two full baths
- Welcoming front Porch enhanced by graceful columns and curved windows
- Parlor and Dining Room frame Entry hall
- Expansive Great Room accented by a corner fireplace and outdoor access
- Open and convenient Kitchen with a work island, angled, peninsula counter/eating bar, and nearby Laundry and Garage Entry
- Secluded Master Bedroom with a large walk-in closet and luxurious Bath with a dressing table
- Two additional Bedrooms with ample closets, share a double vanity Bath
- This home is designed with basement, slab and crawlspace foundation options

IAIN FLOOR — 1,642 SQ. FT.
ASEMENT — 1,642 SQ. FT.
ARAGE — 430 SQ. FT.

TOTAL LIVING AREA:
1,642 SQ. FT.

PLAN NO.24717

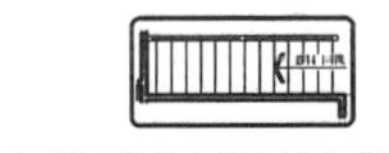

BASEMENT STAIRS OPTION

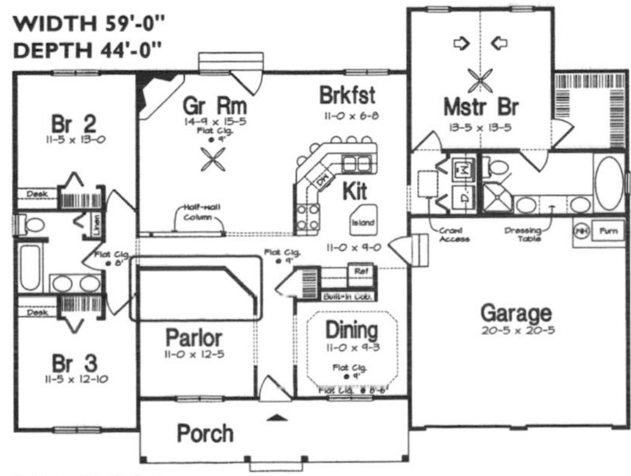

WIDTH 59'-0"
DEPTH 44'-0"
Br 2
11-5 x 13-0
Gr Rm
14-9 x 15-5
Brkfst
11-0 x 6-8
Mstr Br
13-5 x 13-5
Kit
11-0 x 9-0
Garage
20-5 x 20-5
Parlor
11-0 x 12-5
Dining
11-0 x 9-3
Br 3
11-5 x 12-10
Porch

MAIN FLOOR

PLAN NO.24714

Energy Efficient Air-Lock Entry

PRICE CODE: C

- This plan features:
- — Two bedrooms
- — Two full baths
- The attractive covered Porch highlights the curb appea of this charming home
- A cozy window seat and a vaulted ceiling enhance the private Den
- The sunken Great Room is accented by a fireplace that nestled between windows
- A Screened Porch, accessed from the Dining Room, extends the living space to the outdoors
- The Master Bath features a garden tub, separate showe his and her walk-in closets and a skylight
- This home is designed with crawlspace and slab and combo basement/crawlspace foundation options

MAIN FLOOR — 1,771 SQ. FT.
BASEMENT — 1,194 SQ. FT.
GARAGE — 517 SQ. FT.

TOTAL LIVING AREA:
1,771 SQ. FT.

WIDTH 54'-0"
DEPTH 50'-0"

MAIN FLOOR

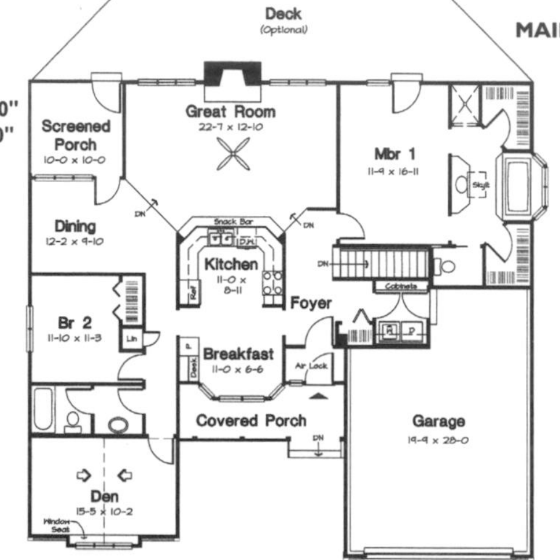
Deck
(Optional)
Screened Porch
10-0 x 10-0
Great Room
22-7 x 12-10
Mbr 1
11-9 x 16-11
Dining
12-2 x 9-10
Kitchen
11-0 x 8-11
Foyer
Br 2
11-10 x 11-3
Breakfast
11-0 x 6-6
Air Lock
Covered Porch
Garage
19-9 x 28-0
Den
15-5 x 10-2
Window Seat

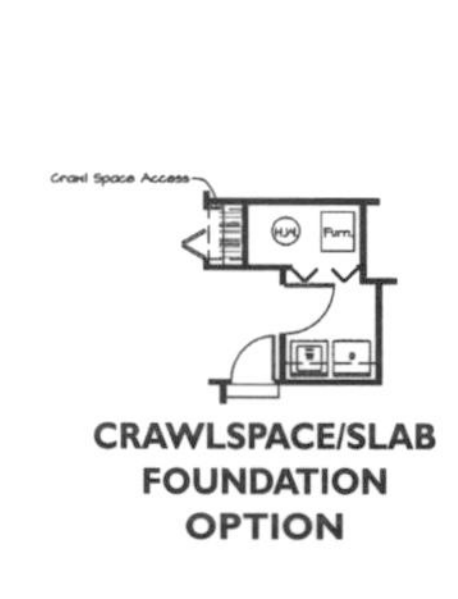

CRAWLSPACE/SLAB FOUNDATION OPTION

PLAN NO.86014

Victorian Inspired

PRICE CODE: B

- This plan features:
- — Three bedrooms
- — Two full baths
- A quaint exterior harkens back to time gone by
- A bay extends the space in the Dining Room
- The Kitchen is well planned and placed within the hon
- A fireplace warms the open living space
- A Screened Porch in the rear is perfect for pest free entertaining
- The Master Bedroom has a large walk-in closet
- This home is designed with a crawlspace foundation

FIRST FLOOR — 949 SQ. FT.
SECOND FLOOR — 633 SQ. FT.
PORCH — 415 SQ. FT.

TOTAL LIVING AREA:
1,582 SQ.FT.

40'-3"
SCREENED PORCH 9'-10"x9'-8"
PORCH
INFORMAL DINING 8'-0"x8'-0"
LIVING ROOM 13'-8"x14'-4"
BEDROOM 12'-1"x11'-0"
KITCHEN 14'-0"x8'-4"
ENTRY
BATH
DINING 10'-4"x10'-9"
PORCH
40'-6"

FIRST FLOOR

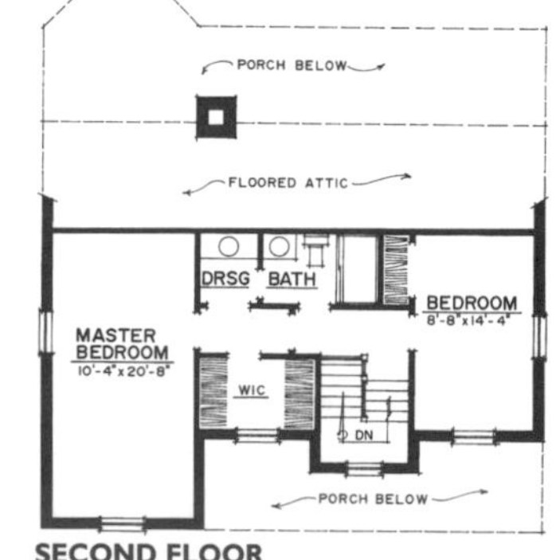
PORCH BELOW
FLOORED ATTIC
DRSG
BATH
BEDROOM
8'-8"x14'-4"
MASTER BEDROOM
10'-4"x20'-8"
WIC
DN
PORCH BELOW

SECOND FLOOR

High Windows

PRICE CODE: D

PLAN NO.97219

This plan features:

- Four bedrooms
- Three full and one half baths
- The Dining Room enjoys the natural illumination from the large window to the left of the front door
- The Living Room has decorative columns defining the entrance into the room and over looks the Porch
- The second floor Master Suite is crowned in a tray ceiling and includes French doors to the lavish Master Bath
- This home is designed with basement and crawlspace foundation options

IRST FLOOR — 1,257 SQ. FT.
ECOND FLOOR — 871 SQ. FT.
ONUS ROOM — 444 SQ. FT.
ASEMENT — 1,275 SQ. FT.

TOTAL LIVING AREA:
2,128 SQ. FT.

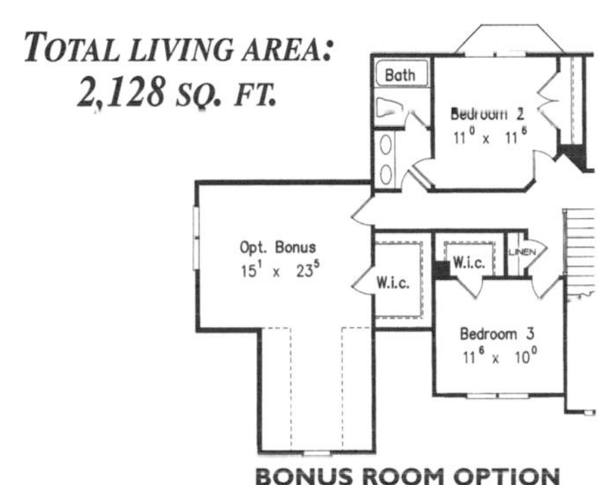
Bath
Bedroom 2
11⁰ x 11⁶
Opt. Bonus
15¹ x 23⁵
W.i.c.
W.i.c.
Linen
Bedroom 3
11⁶ x 10⁰

BONUS ROOM OPTION

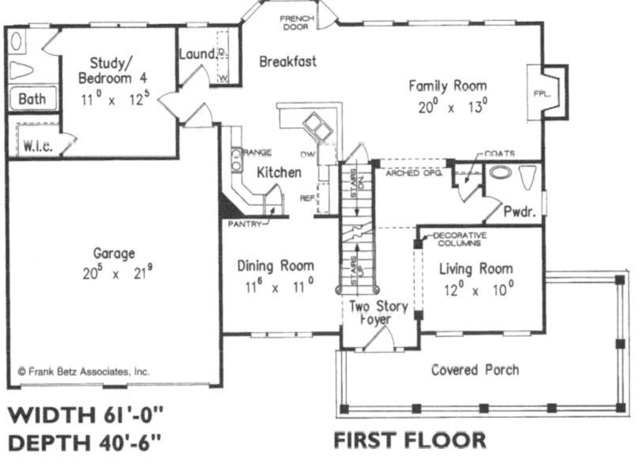
Study/
Bedroom 4
11⁰ x 12⁵
Bath
W.i.c.
Laund.
Breakfast
French Door
Family Room
20⁰ x 13⁰
Kitchen
Pantry
Arched Opg.
Coats
Pwdr.
Garage
20⁵ x 21⁹
Dining Room
11⁶ x 11⁰
Decorative Columns
Living Room
12⁰ x 10⁰
Two Story Foyer
Covered Porch
© Frank Betz Associates, Inc.

WIDTH 61'-0"
DEPTH 40'-6"

FIRST FLOOR

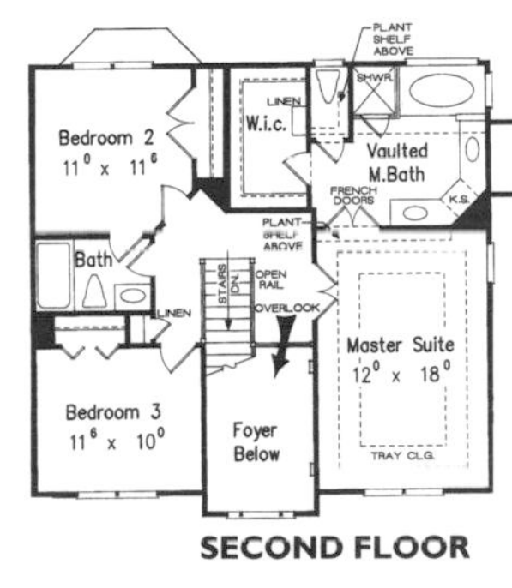
Plant Shelf Above
Bedroom 2
11⁰ x 11⁶
W.i.c.
Linen
Vaulted
M.Bath
French Doors
Bath
Linen
Open Rail
Overlook
Master Suite
12⁰ x 18⁰
Bedroom 3
11⁶ x 10⁰
Foyer
Below
Tray Clg.

SECOND FLOOR

Elegantly Adorned

PRICE CODE: B

PLAN NO.98337

- This plan features:
  - Three bedrooms
  - Two full baths
- Only 1,633 square feet of living space, yet the designer never skimped on style and convenience.
- The Living Room has a dramatic appeal having a fireplace and a vaulted ceiling.
- Columns accent the entrance into the formal Dining Room.
- A Laundry is conveniently located off the Kitchen
- The Master Suite is designed with an intimate Sitting Area and a private Bath and walk-in closet
- This home is designed with a basement foundation

IAIN FLOOR — 1,633 SQ. FT.
ASEMENT — 1,633 SQ. FT.
ARAGE — 450 SQ. FT.

TOTAL LIVING AREA:
1,633 SQ. FT.

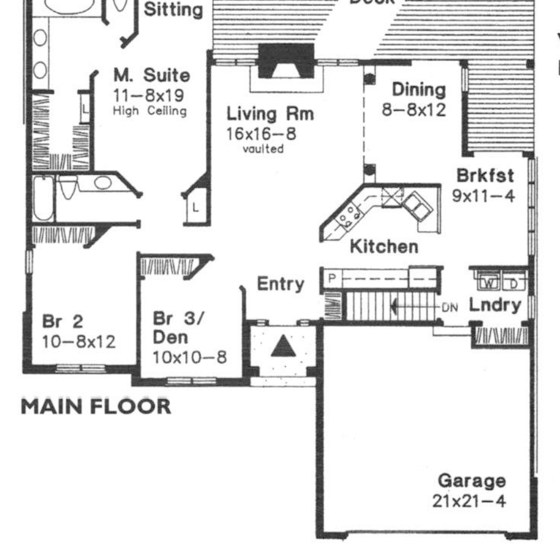
Sitting
Deck
M. Suite
11–8x19
High Ceiling
Living Rm
16x16–8
vaulted
Dining
8–8x12
Brkfst
9x11–4
Kitchen
Entry
Lndry
Br 2
10–8x12
Br 3/
Den
10x10–8
Garage
21x21–4

WIDTH 52'-4"
DEPTH 57'-4"

MAIN FLOOR

PLAN NO.93269

Cozy Front Porch

PRICE CODE: B

- This plan features:
  - — Three bedrooms
  - — Two full and one half baths
- A Living Area enhanced by a large fireplace
- A formal Dining Room that is open to the Living Area, giving a more spacious feel to the rooms
- An efficient Kitchen that includes ample counter and cabinet space as well as double sinks and pass-thru window to living area
- A sunny Breakfast Area with vaulted ceiling and a door to the Sun Deck
- A first floor Master Suite with separate tub and shower stall and walk-in closet
- A first floor Powder Room with a hide-away Laundry Center
- This home is designed with a basement foundation

FIRST FLOOR — 1,045 SQ. FT.
SECOND FLOOR — 690 SQ. FT.
BASEMENT — 465 SQ. FT.
GARAGE — 580 SQ. FT.

TOTAL LIVING AREA:
1,735 SQ. FT.

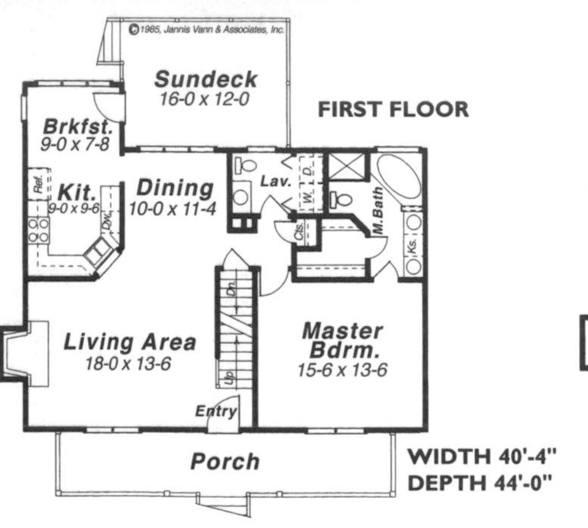

©1985, Jannis Vann & Associates, Inc.
Sundeck
16-0 x 12-0
FIRST FLOOR
Brkfst.
9-0 x 7-8
Kit.
9-0 x 9-6
Dining
10-0 x 11-4
Lav.
M.Bath
Living Area
18-0 x 13-6
Master
Bdrm.
15-6 x 13-6
Entry
Porch
WIDTH 40'-4"
DEPTH 44'-0"

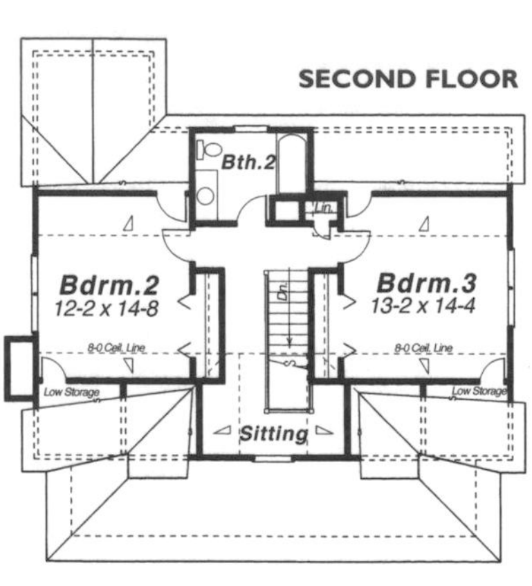

SECOND FLOOR
Bth.2
Bdrm.2
12-2 x 14-8
Bdrm.3
13-2 x 14-4
Low Storage
Sitting

PLAN NO.24718

Gazebo Porch Creates Old-Fashioned Feel

PRICE CODE: A

- This plan features:
  - — Three bedrooms
  - — Two full baths
- An old-fashioned welcome is created by the covered Porch
- The Breakfast Area overlooks the Porch and is separated from the Kitchen by an extended counter
- The Dining Room and the Great Room are highlighted by a two-sided fireplace, enhancing the temperature as well as the atmosphere
- The roomy Master Suite is enhanced by a whirlpool Bath with double vanity and a walk-in closet
- Each of the two secondary Bedrooms feature a walk-in closet
- This home is designed with crawlspace and slab foundation

MAIN FLOOR — 1,452 SQ. FT.
GARAGE — 584 SQ. FT.

TOTAL LIVING AREA:
1,452 SQ. FT.

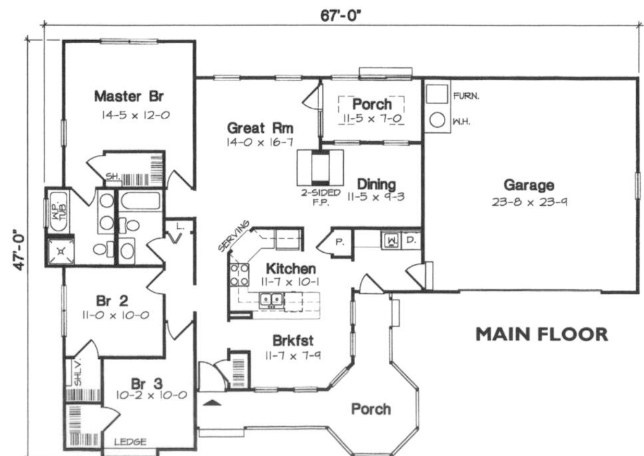

67'-0"
47'-0"
Master Br
14-5 x 12-0
Great Rm
14-0 x 16-7
Porch
11-5 x 7-0
FURN.
W.H.
Garage
23-8 x 23-9
2-SIDED F.P.
Dining
11-5 x 9-3
Kitchen
11-7 x 10-1
Br 2
11-0 x 10-0
Brkfst
11-7 x 7-9
MAIN FLOOR
Br 3
10-2 x 10-0
Porch
LEDGE

PLAN NO. 99457

Expansive Covered Porch

Price Code: E

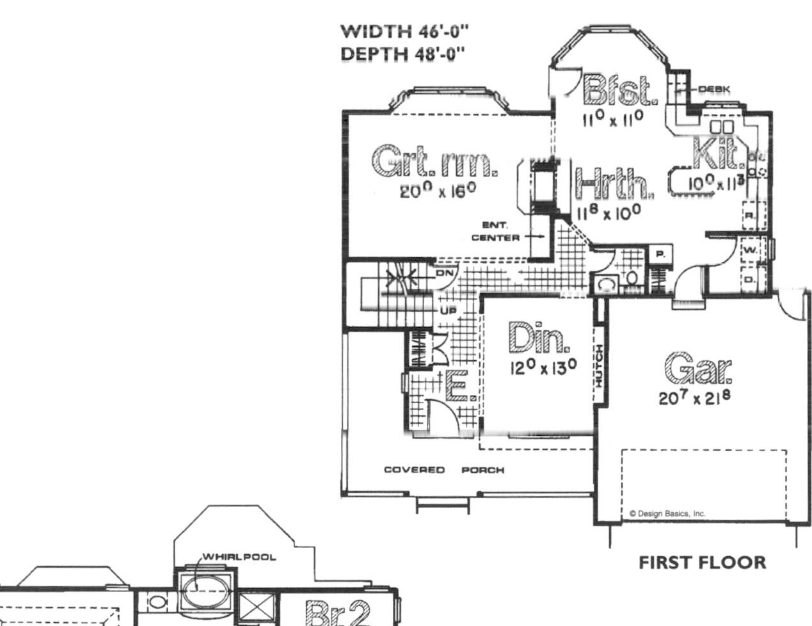
WIDTH 46'-0"
DEPTH 48'-0"
Bfst.
11⁰ x 11⁰
DESK
Grt. rm.
20⁰ x 16⁰
Hrth.
11⁸ x 10⁰
Kit.
10⁰ x 11³
ENT. CENTER
DN
UP
Din.
12⁰ x 13⁰
HUTCH
Gar.
20⁷ x 21⁸
E.
COVERED PORCH
© Design Basics, Inc.
FIRST FLOOR 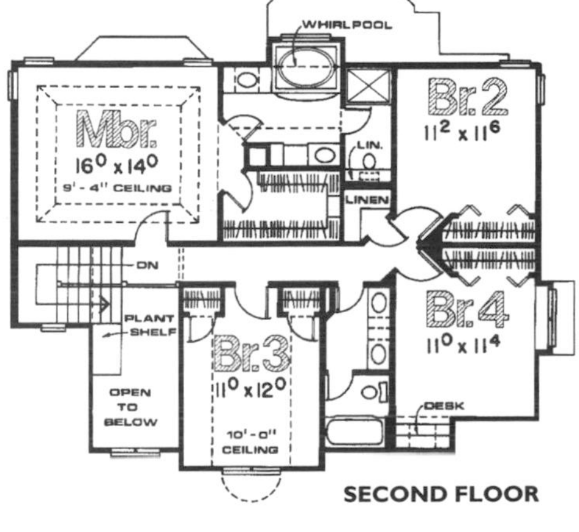
WHIRLPOOL
Mbr.
16⁰ x 14⁰
9'-4" CEILING
LIN.
LINEN
Br. 2
11² x 11⁶
DN
PLANT SHELF
OPEN TO BELOW
Br. 3
11⁰ x 12⁰
10'-0" CEILING
Br. 4
11⁰ x 11⁴
DESK
SECOND FLOOR

- This plan features:
  - — Four bedrooms
  - — Two full and one half baths
- The Kitchen/Breakfast/Hearth Room with gazebo, wrapping counters and an open layout add an open airy feeling to the home
- The luxurious Master Suite is topped by a decorative ceiling and has a lavish bath featuring a whirlpool tub and his and her vanities
- This home is designed with a basement foundation
- Alternate foundation options available at an additional charge. Please call 1-800-235-5700 for more information.

First floor — 1,150 sq. ft.
Second floor — 1,120 sq. ft.
Basement — 1,150 sq. ft.
Garage — 457 sq. ft.

Total Living Area:
2,270 sq. ft.

PLAN NO. 98416

Bathed in Natural Light

PRICE CODE: B

- This plan features:
- — Three bedrooms
- — Two full and one half baths
- A high arched window illuminates the Foyer and adds style to the exterior of the home
- Vaulted ceilings in the formal Dining Room, Breakfast Room and Great Room create volume
- The Master Suite is crowned with a decorative tray ceiling
- The Master Bath has a double vanity, oval tub, separate shower and a walk-in closet
- The Loft, with the option of becoming a fourth Bedroom, highlights the second floor
- This home is designed with basement and crawlspace foundation options

FIRST FLOOR — 1,133 SQ. FT.
SECOND FLOOR — 486 SQ. FT.
BASEMENT — 1,133 SQ. FT.
BONUS — 134 SQ. FT.
GARAGE — 406 SQ. FT.

TOTAL LIVING AREA:
1,619 SQ. FT.

WIDTH 41'-0"
DEPTH 46'-4"

French Door
FPL.
Vault
Vaulted Breakfast
Vaulted Great Room 14° x 16⁹
Tray Clg.
Master Suite 16° x 11°
Serving Bar
Range
D.W.
Kitchen
Pan.
Ref.
Pwdr.
Coats
Stairs Dn.
Linen
Master Bath
Laun.
W.i.c.
Shwr.
Vaulted Dining Room 10° x 12°
Vault
Vault
Two Story Foyer
Stairs Up
Garage 19⁵ x 19⁹
© Frank Betz Associates, Inc.

FIRST FLOOR

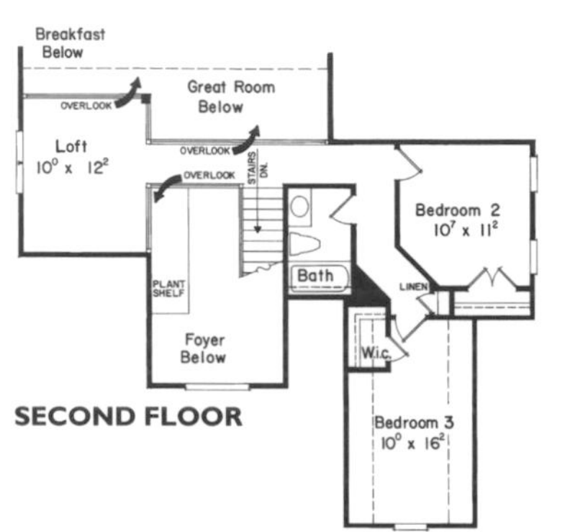

Breakfast Below
Overlook
Great Room Below
Loft 10° x 12²
Overlook
Overlook
Stairs Dn.
Plant Shelf
Foyer Below
Bath
Bedroom 2 10⁷ x 11²
Linen
W.i.c.
Bedroom 3 10° x 16²

SECOND FLOOR

Opt. Bedroom 4 10° x 10°

BONUS OPTION

PLAN NO. 24979

Windows, Windows Everywhere

PRICE CODE: E

- This plan features:
- — Three bedrooms
- — Two full and one half baths
- Dormers highlight the facade of this home
- The octagonal Breakfast Nook is lined with windows that spill natural light into the Kitchen and Family Roo
- An isolated Den offers space for quieter family activiti
- The Master Suite features a lavish Bath with a glass-enclosed shower, garden tub, and double vanity
- The secondary Bedrooms each have a roomy closet
- This home is designed with basement, slab, and crawlspace foundation options

FIRST FLOOR — 1,176 SQ. FT.
SECOND FLOOR — 1,120 SQ. FT.
BONUS — 435 SQ. FT.
BASEMENT — 1,176 SQ. FT.
GARAGE — 576 SQ. FT.

TOTAL LIVING AREA:
2,296 SQ. FT.

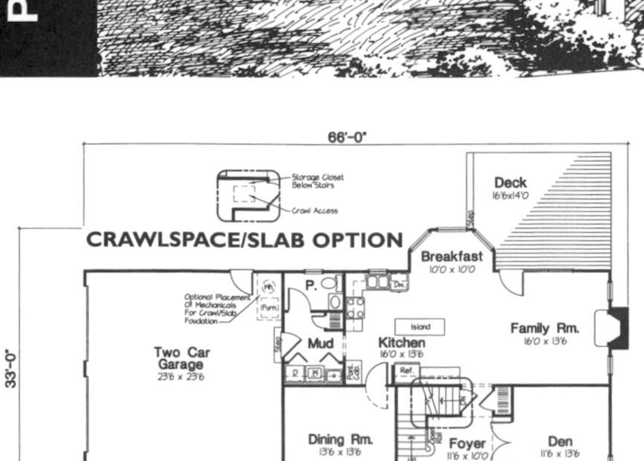

66'-0"
CRAWLSPACE/SLAB OPTION
Deck 16'6x14'0
Breakfast 10'0 x 10'0
Two Car Garage 23'6 x 23'6
P.
Mud
Island
Kitchen 16'0 x 13'6
Family Rm. 16'0 x 13'6
33'-0"
Dining Rm. 13'6 x 13'6
Foyer 11'6 x 10'0
Den 11'6 x 13'6
Stoop

FIRST FLOOR

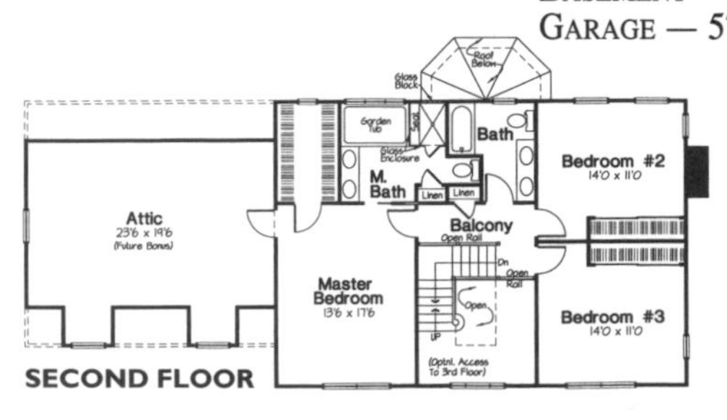

Attic 23'6 x 14'6 (Future Bonus)
Bath
Bedroom #2 14'0 x 11'0
M. Bath
Balcony
Master Bedroom 13'6 x 17'6
Bedroom #3 14'0 x 11'0

SECOND FLOOR

PLAN NO. 94116

Small, But Not Lacking

Price Code: B

- This plan features:
  - — Three bedrooms
  - — One full and one three-quarter baths
- Great Room adjoining the Dining Room for ease in entertaining
- Kitchen highlighted by a peninsula counter/snack bar extending work space and offering convenience in serving informal meals or snacks
- Split-Bedroom plan allowing for privacy for the Master Bedroom with a private Bath and a walk-in closet
- Two additional Bedrooms share the full family Bath in the hall
- Garage Entry convenient to the Kitchen
- This home is designed with a basement foundation

MAIN FLOOR — 1,546 SQ. FT.
BASEMENT — 1,530 SQ. FT.
GARAGE — 440 SQ. FT.

TOTAL LIVING AREA:
1,546 SQ. FT.

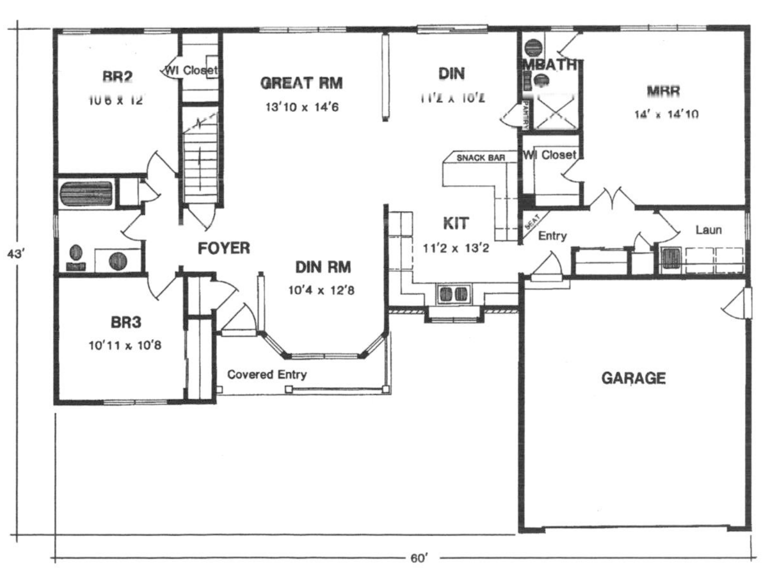
MAIN FLOOR
BR2
WI Closet
GREAT RM
13'10 x 14'6
DIN
MBATH
MBR
14' x 14'10
SNACK BAR
WI Closet
KIT
11'2 x 13'2
Entry
Laun
FOYER
DIN RM
10'4 x 12'8
BR3
10'11 x 10'8
Covered Entry
GARAGE
43'
60'

PLAN NO. 98415

Split Bedroom Plan

PRICE CODE: A

- This plan features:
- —Three bedrooms
- —Two full baths
- A tray ceiling giving a decorative touch to the Master Bedroom and a vaulted ceiling topping the five-piece Master Bath
- A full Bath located between the secondary Bedrooms
- A corner fireplace and a vaulted ceiling highlighting th heart of the home, the Family Room
- A wetbar, serving bar to the Family Room and a built-i Pantry adding to the convenience of the Kitchen
- A formal Dining Room crowned in an elegant high ceiling
- This home is designed with basement, slab and crawlspace foundation options

MAIN FLOOR — 1,429 SQ. FT.
BASEMENT — 1,472 SQ. FT.
GARAGE — 438 SQ. FT.

TOTAL LIVING AREA:
1,429 SQ. FT.

WIDTH 49'-0"
DEPTH 53'-0"

MAIN FLOOR

© Frank Betz Associates, Inc.

PLAN NO. 93261

Bay Windows and a Terrific Front Porch

PRICE CODE: C

- This plan features:
- — Three bedrooms
- — Two full baths
- An expansive Living Area that includes a fireplace
- A Master Suite with a private Master Bath and a walk-in closet, as well as a bay window view of the front yard
- An efficient Kitchen that serves the sunny Breakfast Area and the Dining Room with equal ease
- A built-in Pantry and a desk add to the conveniences in the Breakfast Area
- Two additional Bedrooms that share the full hall Bath
- A convenient main floor Laundry Room
- This home is designed with a basement foundation

MAIN FLOOR — 1,778 SQ. FT.
BASEMENT — 1,008 SQ. FT.
GARAGE — 728 SQ. FT.

TOTAL LIVING AREA:
1,778 SQ. FT.

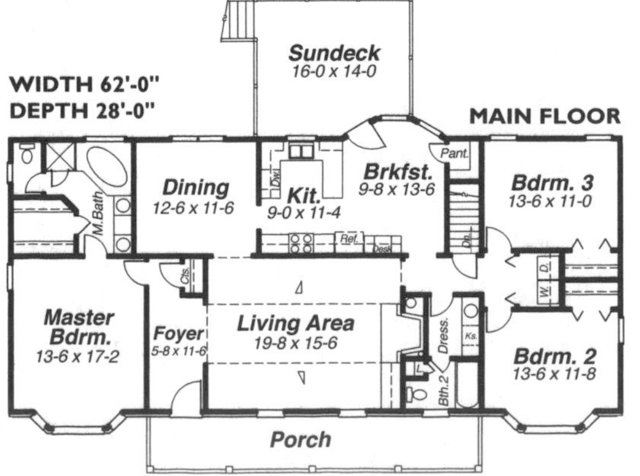

WIDTH 62'-0"
DEPTH 28'-0"
MAIN FLOOR
Sundeck
16-0 x 14-0
Dining
12-6 x 11-6
Kit.
9-0 x 11-4
Brkfst.
9-8 x 13-6
Pant.
Bdrm. 3
13-6 x 11-0
M.Bath
Master
Bdrm.
13-6 x 17-2
Foyer
5-8 x 11-6
Living Area
19-8 x 15-6
Dress.
Bdrm. 2
13-6 x 11-8
Bth.2
Porch

PLAN NO. 99490

Arched Front Porch

Price Code: A

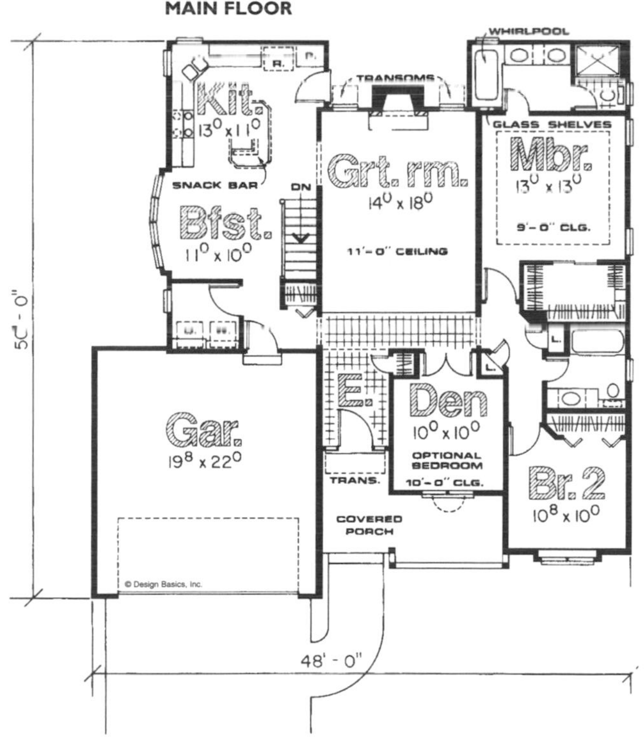

MAIN FLOOR
WHIRLPOOL
TRANSOMS
GLASS SHELVES
Kit. 13⁰ x 11⁰
SNACK BAR
DN
Grt. rm. 14⁰ x 18⁰
11'-0" CEILING
Mbr. 13⁰ x 13⁰
9'-0" CLG.
Bfst. 11⁰ x 10⁰
E.
Den 10⁰ x 10⁰
OPTIONAL BEDROOM
10'-0" CLG.
TRANS.
Gar. 19⁸ x 22⁰
COVERED PORCH
Br. 2 10⁸ x 10⁰
50'-0"
48'-0"
© Design Basics, Inc.

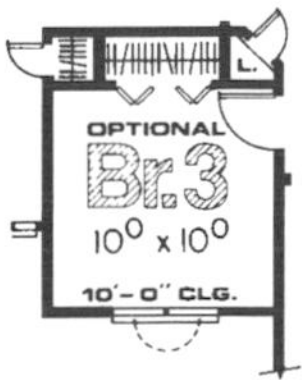

OPTIONAL Br. 3 10⁰ x 10⁰ 10'-0" CLG.

OPTION

- This plan features:
  - Three bedrooms
  - Two full baths
- The cozy front Porch of this home gives an attractive Country appearance
- The tiled Foyer leads into the Great Room, which is accented by a fireplace with transom windows to either side
- The Kitchen includes a snack bar/island and a Pantry, and is open to the Breakfast Room
- The Master Suite includes a whirlpool Bath and a walk-in closet
- This home is designed with basement and slab foundation options
- Alternate foundation options available at an additional charge. Please call 1-800-235-5700 for more information

MAIN FLOOR — 1,479 SQ. FT.

TOTAL LIVING AREA:
1,479 SQ. FT.

PLAN NO. 97152

Cute Starter Home

PRICE CODE: B

- This plan features:
  - — Three bedrooms
  - — Two full baths
- Simple design with quality details provides charm inside and out
- Spacious Living/Dining Room allows comfortable gatherings with multiple windows and outdoor access
- Open Kitchen/Nook easily accesses Dining Area, Laundry closet and Garage
- Corner Master Bedroom boasts full view of rear yard, walk-in closet and private Bath
- Two additional Bedrooms with ample closets, share a full Bath
- This home is designed with a basement foundation

MAIN FLOOR — 1,557 SQ. FT.
BASEMENT — 1,557 SQ. FT.
GARAGE — 400 SQ. FT.

TOTAL LIVING AREA:
1,557 SQ. FT.

MBR. 15'8" x 13'0"
LIV. 10'-1 1/8" CLG. HGT. 17'8" x 13'4"
BR. #3 12'2" x 11'0"
DIN. 10'-1 1/8" CLG. HGT. 17'8" x 10'2"
BR. #2 12'2" x 11'0"
KIT. 11'4" x 16'4"
NK. 10'-1 1/8" CLG. HGT.
E.
2 CAR GAR. 19'10" x 21'8"
40'0"
61'0"

MAIN FLOOR

PLAN NO. 86013

Country Character

PRICE CODE: E

- This plan features:
  - — Three bedrooms
  - — Two full and one half baths
- The wraparound Porch adds style and living space
- Bays enhance the formal Living and Dining Rooms
- A see-through fireplace warms the Living and Family Rooms
- The gallery upstairs is a quiet retreat
- The Master Bedroom has space saving built-in dresser
- This home is designed with a combination basement/crawlspace foundation

FIRST FLOOR — 1,308 SQ. FT.
SECOND FLOOR — 992 SQ. FT.
BASEMENT — 1,087 SQ. FT.
GARAGE — 455 SQ. FT.

TOTAL LIVING AREA:
2,300 SQ. FT.

70'-8"
TERRACE
GARAGE 20'-9"x20'-9"
1/2B
KITCHEN 12'-6"x11'-6"
MORNING ROOM 8'-8"x8'-10"
FAMILY ROOM 19'-2"x13'-9"
FP
DINING ROOM 12'-6"x14'-0"
FOYER
LIVING ROOM 13'-4"x15'-2"
BROOM CLOSET
WRAP-AROUND-PORCH
42'-8"

FIRST FLOOR

BEDROOM 12'-6"x10'-7"
B.
W/C
MASTER BATHROOM
LINEN
BUILT-IN DRESSERS
MASTER BEDROOM 12'-6"x16'-0"
BEDROOM 12'-6"x11'-0"
GALLERY 13'-3"x6'-2"
SLOPED CEILING

SECOND FLOOR

PLAN NO. 24980

SECOND FLOOR

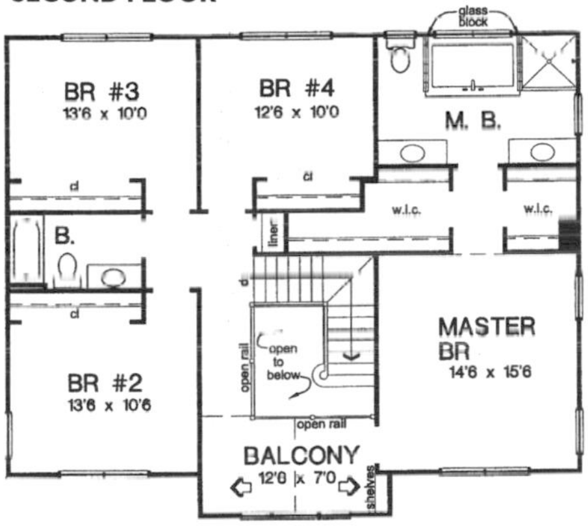

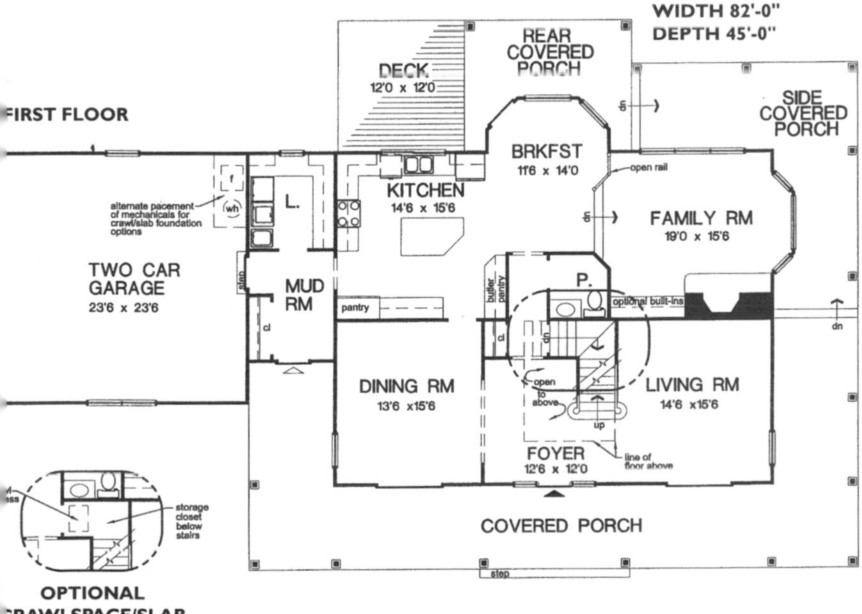
WIDTH 82'-0"
DEPTH 45'-0"
FIRST FLOOR
REAR COVERED PORCH
DECK
12'0 x 12'0
SIDE COVERED PORCH
BRKFST
11'6 x 14'0
KITCHEN
14'6 x 15'6
FAMILY RM
19'0 x 15'6
TWO CAR GARAGE
23'6 x 23'6
MUD RM
L.
P.
pantry
DINING RM
13'6 x15'6
LIVING RM
14'6 x15'6
FOYER
12'6 x 12'0
COVERED PORCH
OPTIONAL CRAWLSPACE/SLAB

A True Wraparound Porch

Price Code: G

- This plan features:
- — Four bedrooms
- — Two full and one half baths
- The Covered Porch wraps around to the rear of the home and opens onto a Deck
- A center island, Pantry, and Butler's Pantry provide plenty of room for food preparation in the Kitchen
- Roomy walk-in closets flank the Entry from the Master Bedroom into the Master Bath
- This home is designed with basement, slab, and crawlspace foundation options

FIRST FLOOR — 1,706 SQ. FT.
SECOND FLOOR — 1,319 SQ. FT.
BASEMENT — 1,706 SQ. FT.
GARAGE — 569 SQ. FT.
PORCH — 688 SQ. FT.

TOTAL LIVING AREA:
3,025 SQ. FT.

PLAN NO. 93420

Family Room with Skylights

Price Code: C

This plan features:

— Three bedrooms

— Two full and one half baths

In the center of the home is the Family Room with skylights

The Dining Room is separated from the Foyer by columns

The first floor Master Bedroom spans the width of the home

Upstairs, a balcony overlooks the Family Room below

This home is designed with a basement foundation

FIRST FLOOR — 1,299 SQ. FT.
SECOND FLOOR — 557 SQ. FT.
BONUS — 272 SQ. FT.
BASEMENT — 1,299 SQ. FT.
GARAGE — 494 SQ. FT.

TOTAL LIVING AREA: 1,856 SQ. FT.

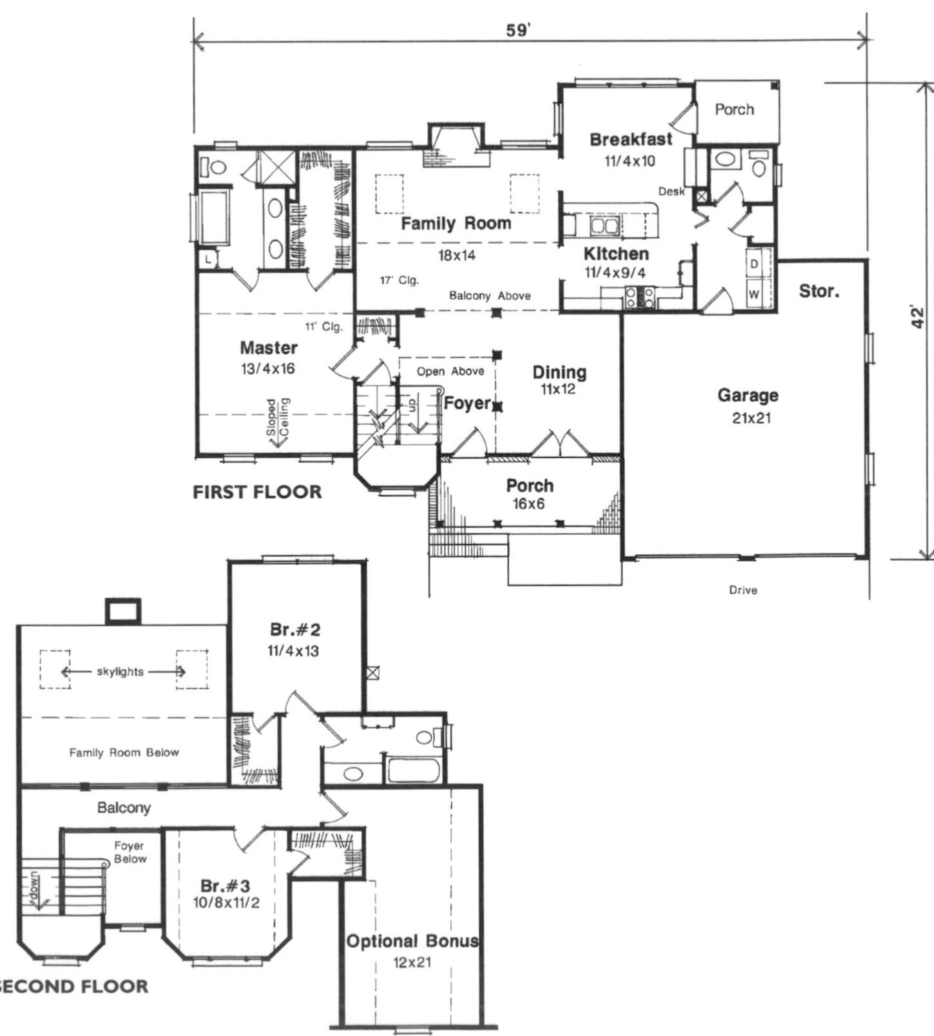

59'
42'
Porch
Breakfast
11/4x10
Desk
Family Room
18x14
17' Clg.
Balcony Above
Kitchen
11/4x9/4
D
W
Stor.
11' Clg.
Master
13/4x16
Sloped Ceiling
Open Above
Dining
11x12
Foyer
up
Garage
21x21
Porch
16x6
FIRST FLOOR
Drive
Br.#2
11/4x13
skylights
Family Room Below
Balcony
Foyer Below
down
Br.#3
10/8x11/2
Optional Bonus
12x21
SECOND FLOOR

For Outdoor Lovers: Deck and Brick Terrace

PRICE CODE: G

PLAN NO.24981

This plan features:
- Five bedrooms
- Three full and one half baths
- A half wall between the Breakfast Area and two-story Great Room creates a family friendly atmosphere
- A Vestibule, flanked by a half Bath and closet, separates the first floor Master Suite from the community area
- The Butler's Pantry between the Kitchen and Dining Area make serving convenient
- The secondary Bedrooms share the privacy of the second floor
- A bonus room offers plenty of options for future expansion
- A third port in the Garage offers extra space for storage or even a workshop
- This home is designed with basement, slab, and crawl-space foundation options

RST FLOOR — 1,868 SQ. FT.
COND FLOOR — 1,105 SQ. FT.
)NUS — 767 SQ. FT.
SEMENT — 1,868 SQ. FT.
ARAGE — 856 SQ. FT.
RCH — 240 SQ. FT.

TOTAL LIVING AREA:* 2,973 *SQ. FT.

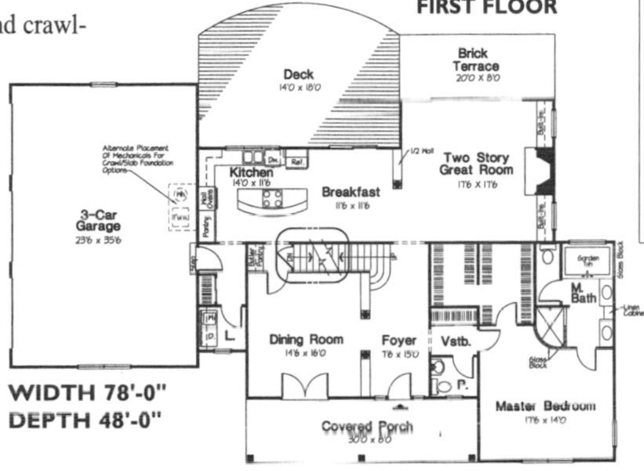
FIRST FLOOR
Deck
Brick Terrace
Kitchen
Breakfast
Two Story Great Room
3-Car Garage
Dining Room
Foyer
Vstb.
M. Bath
Master Bedroom
Covered Porch
WIDTH 78'-0"
DEPTH 48'-0"

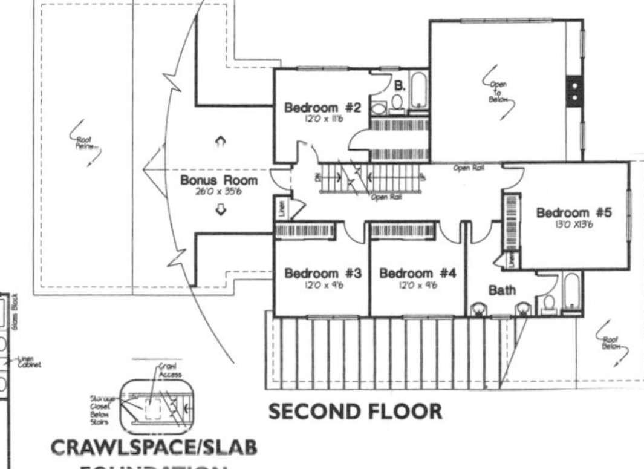
Bedroom #2
B.
Bonus Room
Bedroom #5
Bedroom #3
Bedroom #4
Bath
SECOND FLOOR

CRAWLSPACE/SLAB FOUNDATION OPTION

Champagne Style on a Soda-Pop Budget

PRICE CODE: A

PLAN NO.24302

This plan features:
- Three bedrooms
- One full and one three-quarter baths
- Multiple gables, circle-top windows, and a unique exterior setting this delightful Ranch apart in any neighborhood
- Living and Dining Rooms flowing together to create a very roomy feeling
- Sliding doors leading from the Dining Room to a covered Patio
- A Master Bedroom with a private Bath
- This home is designed with basement and crawlspace foundation options

AIN FLOOR — 988 SQ. FT.
SEMENT — 988 SQ. FT.
ARAGE — 280 SQ. FT
PTIONAL 2-CAR GARAGE — 384 SQ. FT.

TOTAL LIVING AREA:* 988 *SQ. FT.

Kitchen
8-6 x 8-3
Ref.
DN
Flue

BASEMENT FOUNDATION OPTION

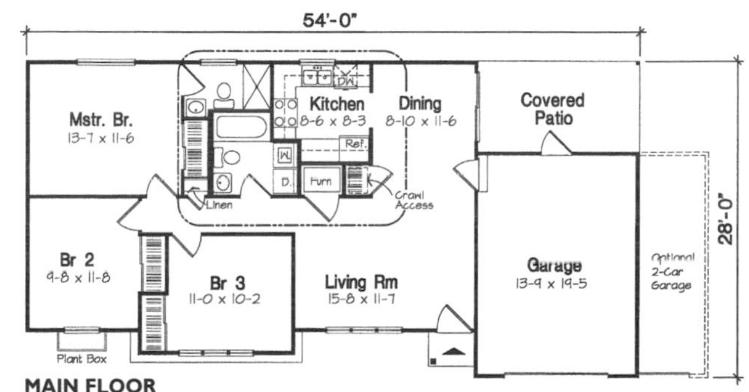
54'-0"
Mstr. Br.
13-7 x 11-6
Kitchen
8-6 x 8-3
Dining
8-10 x 11-6
Covered Patio
Crawl Access
Linen
Br 2
9-8 x 11-8
Br 3
11-0 x 10-2
Living Rm
15-8 x 11-7
Garage
13-9 x 19-5
Optional 2-Car Garage
28'-0"
Plant Box
MAIN FLOOR

PLAN NO.94231

Impressive Elevation

PRICE CODE: H

- This plan features:
- — Three bedrooms
- — Two full and one three-quarter baths
- Glass arch entrance into Foyer and Grand Room accented by fireplace between built-ins and multiple french doors leading to Veranda
- Decorative windows highlight Study and formal Dining Room
- Spacious Kitchen with walk-in Pantry and peninsula serving counter easily serves Nook, Veranda and Dining Room
- Luxurious Master Suite with step ceiling, Sitting Area his and her closets and pampering Bath
- Two additional Bedrooms, one with a private Deck, have bay windows and walk-in closets
- This home is designed with basement and slab foundation options
- Alternate foundation options available at an additional charge. Please call 1-800-235-5700 for more information.

FIRST FLOOR — 2,181 SQ. FT.
SECOND FLOOR — 710 SQ. FT.
GARAGE —658 SQ. FT.

TOTAL LIVING AREA:
2,891 SQ. FT.

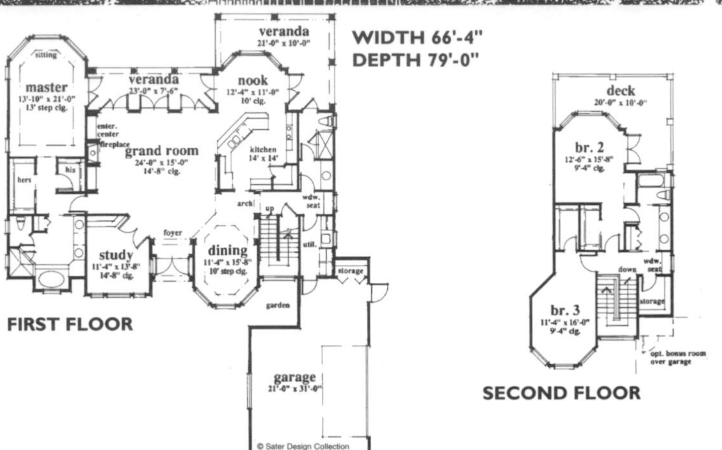

WIDTH 66'-4"
DEPTH 79'-0"
veranda
master
veranda
nook
grand room
kitchen
study
dining
garden
garage
storage
FIRST FLOOR
deck
br. 2
br. 3
storage
SECOND FLOOR
© Sater Design Collection

PLAN NO.24982

Columns, Volume Ceilings, Built-Ins

PRICE CODE: D

- This plan features:
- — Three bedrooms
- — Two full baths
- An arch, lined with columns, creates a warm welcome for family and friends
- Inside, columns mark the boundaries of the formal Dining Room and the Great Room
- A private Vestibule separates the Master Suite from th rest of the home
- The efficient Kitchen features an abundance of counte space, island, eating bar, and direct access to the Dini Room and Breakfast Nook
- Second floor bonus space leaves plenty up to the imagination for expansion
- This home is designed with basement, slab, and crawlspace foundation options

MAIN FLOOR — 2,078 SQ. FT.
BONUS — 510 SQ. FT.
BASEMENT — 2,078 SQ. FT.
GARAGE — 763 SQ. FT.
PORCH — 60 SQ. FT.

TOTAL LIVING AREA:
2,078 SQ. FT.

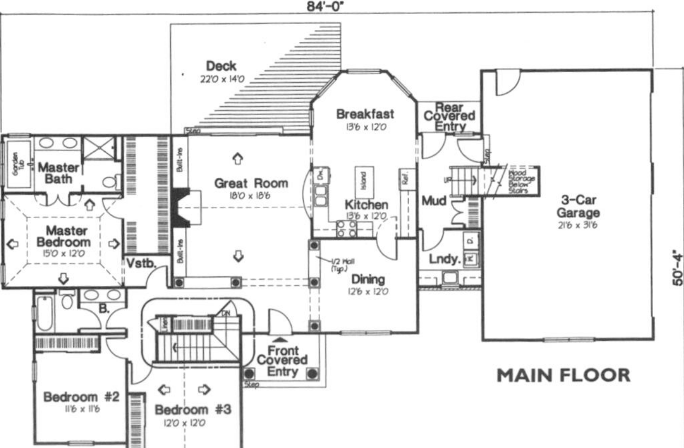

84'-0"
Deck
Breakfast
Rear Covered Entry
Master Bath
Great Room
Kitchen
Mud
3-Car Garage
Master Bedroom
Vstb.
Dining
Lndy.
50'-4"
Front Covered Entry
Bedroom #2
Bedroom #3
MAIN FLOOR

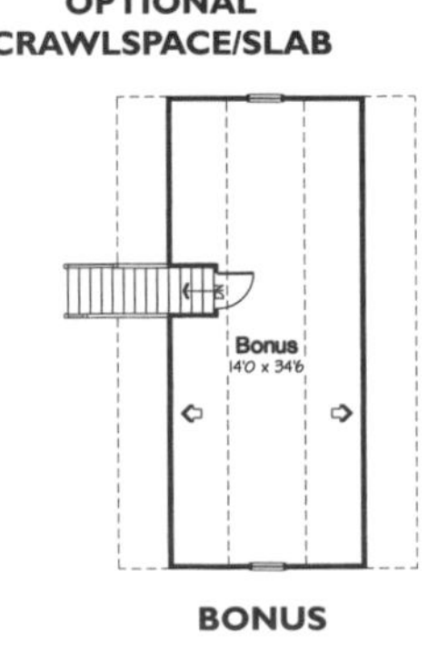

OPTIONAL CRAWLSPACE/SLAB
Bonus
BONUS

PLAN NO. 94239

Spectacular Stucco and Stone

Price Code: L

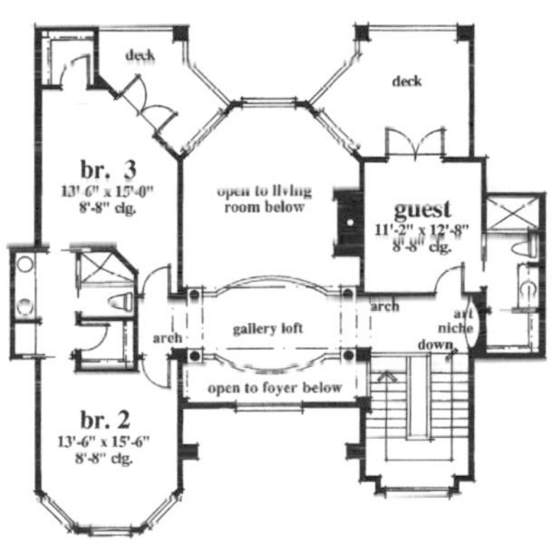
deck
deck
br. 3
13'-6" x 15'-0"
8'-8" clg.
open to living room below
guest
11'-2" x 12'-8"
8'-8" clg.
arch
art niche
gallery loft
down
open to foyer below
br. 2
13'-6" x 15'-6"
8'-8" clg.

SECOND FLOOR

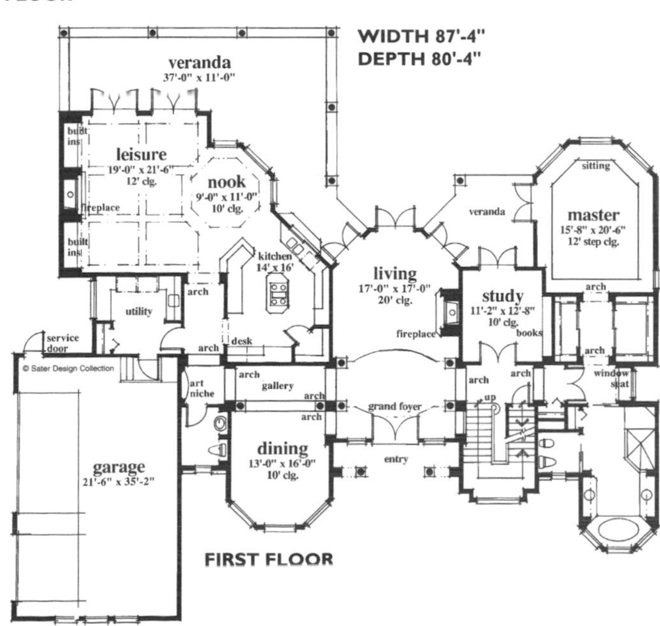
WIDTH 87'-4"
DEPTH 80'-4"
veranda
37'-0" x 11'-0"
built ins
leisure
19'-0" x 21'-6"
12' clg.
fireplace
nook
9'-0" x 11'-0"
10' clg.
kitchen
14' x 16'
veranda
sitting
master
15'-8" x 20'-6"
12' step clg.
living
17'-0" x 17'-0"
20' clg.
fireplace
study
11'-2" x 12'-8"
10' clg.
books
utility
arch
desk
service door
© Sater Design Collection
art niche
gallery
grand foyer
entry
window seat
up
dining
13'-0" x 16'-0"
10' clg.
garage
21'-6" x 35'-2"

FIRST FLOOR

- This plan features:
- — Four bedrooms
- — One full, two three-quarter and one half baths
- Open Living Room with fireplace and multiple doors to rear grounds
- Formal Dining Room has a bay window conveniently located
- Master wing offers a step ceiling, two walk-in closets and a lavish Bath
- This home is designed with basement, slab and combo basement/slab foundation options
- Alternate foundation options available at an additional charge. Please call 1-800-235-5700 for more information.

First floor — 3,027 sq. ft.
Second floor — 1,079 sq. ft.
Basement — 3,027 sq. ft.
Garage — 802 sq. ft.

Total Living Area:
4,106 sq. ft.

PLAN NO. 94139

Appealing Gables

Price Code: C

- This plan features:
- — Three or four bedrooms
- — Two full and one half baths
- The Foyer is highlighted by sidelights and a banister staircase
- Formal Living Room is accented by a lovely bay window
- Expansive Family Room has a cozy fireplace between windows
- The efficient Kitchen has a work island and a Pantry
- Master Bedroom offers a walk-in closet and private Bath
- This home is designed with a basement foundation

FIRST FLOOR — 1,009 SQ. FT.
SECOND FLOOR — 862 SQ. FT.
BASEMENT — 994 SQ. FT.
GARAGE — 506 SQ. FT.

TOTAL LIVING AREA: 1,871 SQ. FT.

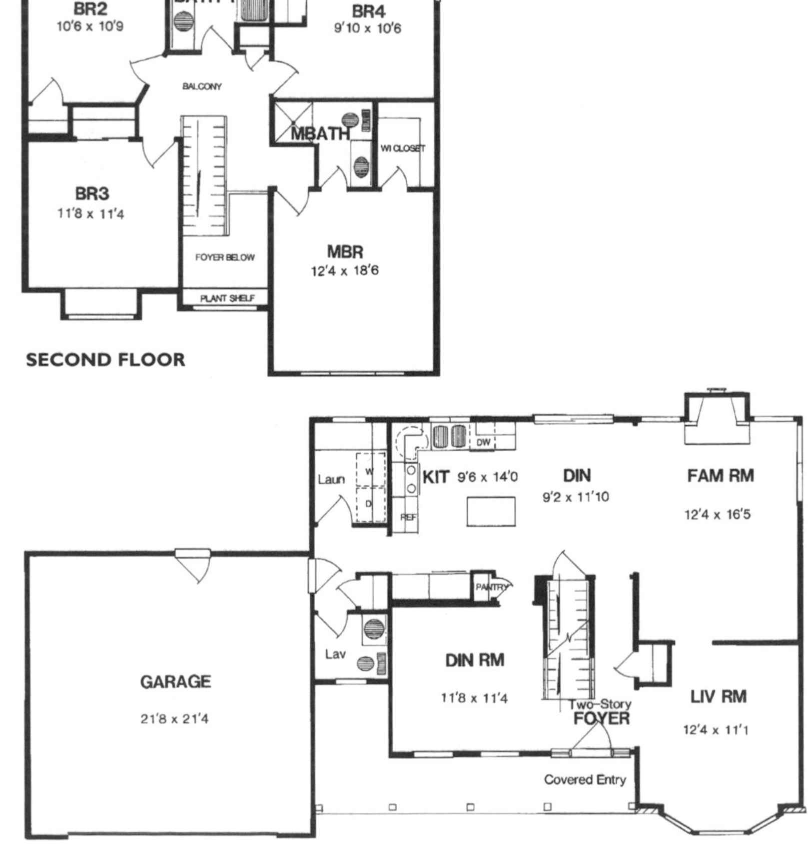

WIDTH 60'-0"
DEPTH 33'-8"
BR2
10'6 x 10'9
BATH 1
BR4
9'10 x 10'6
BALCONY
MBATH
WI CLOSET
BR3
11'8 x 11'4
FOYER BELOW
PLANT SHELF
MBR
12'4 x 18'6
SECOND FLOOR
DW
Laun
W
D
KIT 9'6 x 14'0
REF
DIN
9'2 x 11'10
FAM RM
12'4 x 16'5
PANTRY
GARAGE
21'8 x 21'4
Lav
DIN RM
11'8 x 11'4
Two-Story
FOYER
LIV RM
12'4 x 11'1
Covered Entry
FIRST FLOOR

Charming Country Home

PRICE CODE: A

PLAN NO. 24711

Chis plan features:
- Chree bedrooms
- Cwo full baths
- A welcoming front Porch invites visiting ınd shelters entrance
- Cozy fireplace below a vaulted ceiling and lormer window in Living Room
- Cwo first floor Bedrooms share a full Bath and Laundry
- Private second floor Master Suite offers a dormer window, walk-in closet and private Bath
- 'his home is designed with basement, slab and rawlspace foundation options

ST FLOOR — 1,018 SQ. FT.
COND FLOOR — 416 SQ. FT.
RAGE — 624 SQ. FT.

TOTAL LIVING AREA:
1,434 SQ. FT.

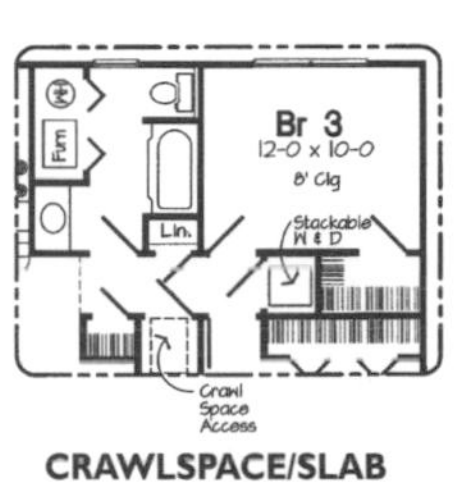

Br 3
12-0 x 10-0
8' Clg
Lin.
Stackable W & D
Crawl Space Access

CRAWLSPACE/SLAB FOUNDATION OPTION

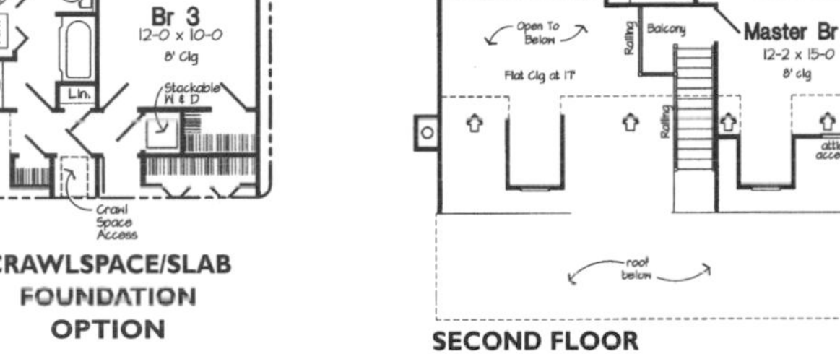

Shelves
Attic Access
Open To Below
Flat Clg at 17'
Balcony
Railing
Master Br
12-2 x 15-0
8' clg
attic access
roof below

SECOND FLOOR

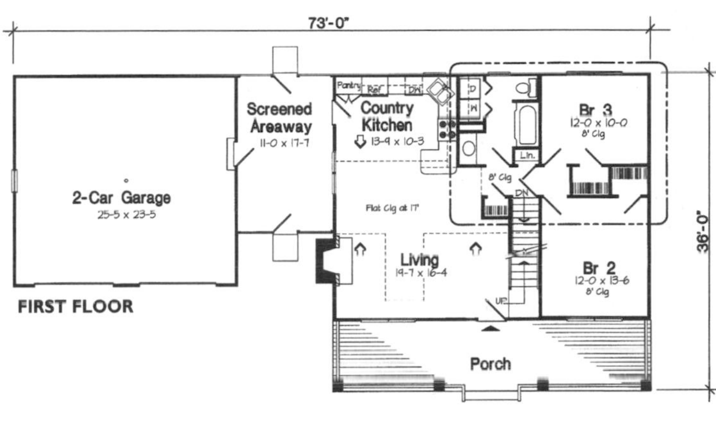

73'-0"
36'-0"
Screened Areaway
11-0 x 17-7
2-Car Garage
25-5 x 23-5
Pantry
Ref
DW
Country Kitchen
13-9 x 10-3
Flat Clg at 17'
Br 3
12-0 x 10-0
8' Clg
Lin.
Living
14-7 x 16-4
Br 2
12-0 x 13-6
8' Clg
DN
UP
Porch

FIRST FLOOR

xpansive Family Living Area

PRICE CODE: E

PLAN NO. 93340

This plan features:
- Four bedrooms
- Two full and one half baths
- A vaulted ceiling tops the Foyer, achieving a feeling of volume
- The Living Room showcases a tray ceiling, ınd is enhanced by a boxed bay window
- The Dining Room adjoins the Living Room ınd has direct access to the Kitchen
- The Kitchen features a cooktop island ınd flows into the Dinette
- The Family Room includes a fireplace framed by windows and adjoins the Dinette
- Double doors add privacy to the Den
- A tray ceiling tops the Master Bedroom which also ıncludes a walk-in closet and a full Bath
- The secondary Bedrooms are in close proximity to a full Bath
- This home is designed with a basement foundation

RST FLOOR — 1,378 SQ. FT.
COND FLOOR — 1,084 SQ. FT.
SEMENT — 1,378 SQ. FT.
RAGE — 448 SQ. FT.

TOTAL LIVING AREA:
2,462 SQ. FT.

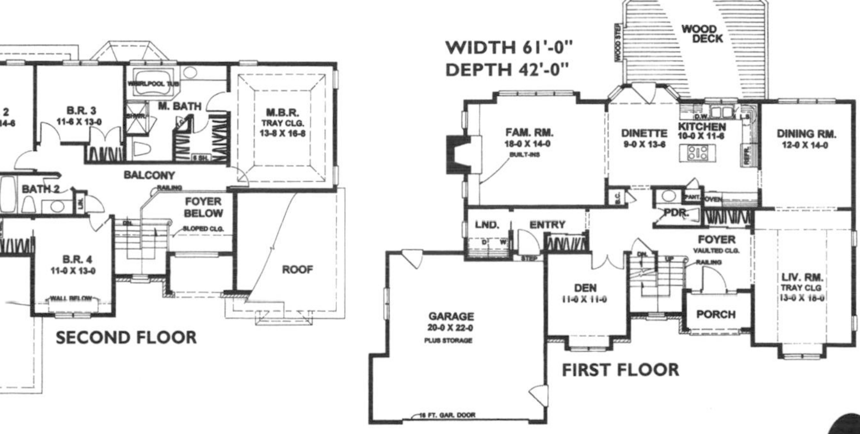

B.R. 2
10-6 X 14-6
B.R. 3
11-6 X 13-0
M. BATH
M.B.R.
TRAY CLG.
13-6 X 16-8
BALCONY
BATH 2
FOYER BELOW
B.R. 4
11-0 X 13-0
ROOF
ROOF
WIDTH 61'-0"
DEPTH 42'-0"
WOOD DECK
FAM. RM.
18-0 X 14-0
DINETTE
9-0 X 13-6
KITCHEN
10-0 X 11-6
DINING RM.
12-0 X 14-0
LND.
ENTRY
PDR.
FOYER
VAULTED CLG.
DEN
11-0 X 11-0
GARAGE
20-0 X 22-0
PLUS STORAGE
PORCH
LIV. RM.
TRAY CLG
13-0 X 18-0
16 FT. GAR. DOOR

SECOND FLOOR

FIRST FLOOR

PLAN NO. 90454

Traditional Ranch Plan

Price Code: D

This plan features:

— Three bedrooms

— Two full baths

Spacious Great Room adjacent to the open Kitchen/Breakfast Area

Secluded Master Bedroom highlighted by the Master Bath with a Spa tub, separate shower, and his and her vanities

Bay window allows bountiful natural light into the Breakfast Area

Two additional Bedrooms sharing a full Bath

This home is designed with basement and crawlspace foundation options

MAIN FLOOR — 2,218 SQ. FT.
BASEMENT — 1,658 SQ. FT.
GARAGE — 528 SQ. FT.

TOTAL LIVING AREA:
2,218 SQ. FT.

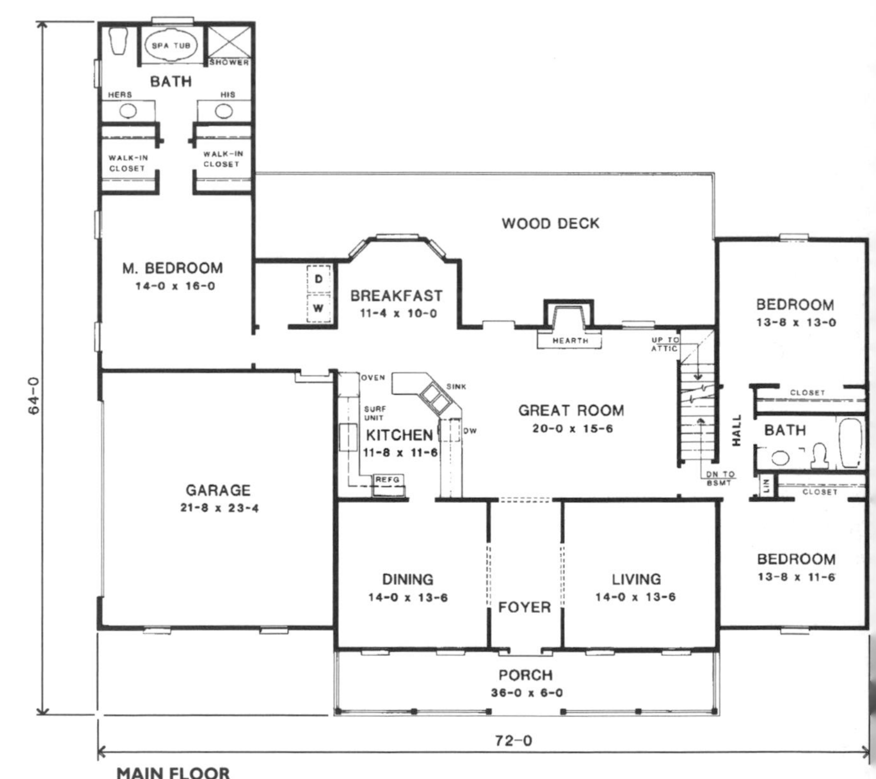
SPA TUB
SHOWER
BATH
HERS
HIS
WALK-IN CLOSET
WALK-IN CLOSET
WOOD DECK
M. BEDROOM
14-0 x 16-0
D
W
BREAKFAST
11-4 x 10-0
HEARTH
UP TO ATTIC
BEDROOM
13-8 x 13-0
CLOSET
OVEN
SINK
SURF UNIT
KITCHEN
11-8 x 11-6
DW
REFG
GREAT ROOM
20-0 x 15-6
HALL
BATH
LIN
CLOSET
DN TO BSMT
GARAGE
21-8 x 23-4
DINING
14-0 x 13-6
FOYER
LIVING
14-0 x 13-6
BEDROOM
13-8 x 11-6
PORCH
36-0 x 6-0
64-0
72-0
MAIN FLOOR

Expansive Living Room

PRICE CODE: A

PLAN NO.98434

his plan features:
- 'hree bedrooms
- 'wo full baths
- 'aulted ceiling crowns spacious Living Room ighlighted by a fireplace
- uilt-in Pantry and direct access from the Garage adding) the conveniences of the Kitchen
- Valk-in closet and a private five-piece Bath topped by vaulted ceiling in the Master Bedroom Suite
- roximity to the full Bath in the hall from the econdary Bedrooms
- his home is designed with basement, slab or rawlspace foundation options

IN FLOOR — 1,346 SQ. FT.
SEMENT — 1,358 SQ. FT.
RAGE — 395 SQ. FT.

TOTAL LIVING AREA:
1,346 SQ. FT.

39'-0"
51'-0"
Vaulted M. Bath
W.i.c.
Dining Room
FPL
Vaulted Living Room 14° x 17°
Master Suite 14° x 12²
Kitchen
Bath
Bedroom 2 10° x 11°
Laundry
Storage
Foyer
Vaulted Bedroom 3 10² x 13³
Garage
© Frank Betz Associates, Inc.
MAIN FLOOR

A Comfortable Informal Design

PRICE CODE: B

PLAN NO.94801

This plan features:
- Three bedrooms
- Two full baths
- Warm, Country front Porch with wood details
- Spacious Activity Room enhanced by a pre-fab fireplace
- Open and efficient Kitchen/Dining Area highlighted by bay window, adjacent to Laundry and Garage Entry
- Corner Master Bedroom offers a pampering Bath with a garden tub and double vanity topped by a vaulted ceiling
- Two additional Bedrooms with ample closets, share a full Bath
- This home is designed with slab and crawlspace foundation options

AIN FLOOR — 1,300 SQ. FT.
ARAGE — 576 SQ. FT.

TOTAL LIVING AREA:
1,300 SQ. FT.

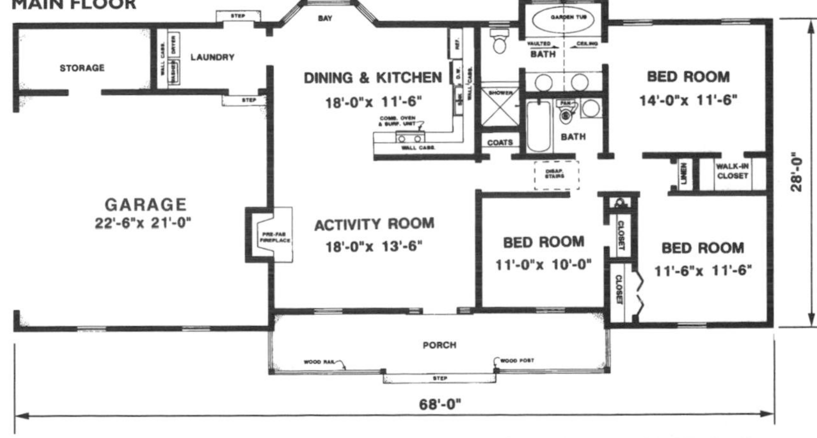
MAIN FLOOR
STORAGE
LAUNDRY
BAY
DINING & KITCHEN
18'-0"x 11'-6"
BATH
BED ROOM
14'-0"x 11'-6"
COATS
BATH
WALK-IN CLOSET
28'-0"
GARAGE
22'-6"x 21'-0"
ACTIVITY ROOM
18'-0"x 13'-6"
BED ROOM
11'-0"x 10'-0"
BED ROOM
11'-6"x 11'-6"
PORCH
68'-0"

PLAN NO. 24984

Built-in Amenities

PRICE CODE: J

- This plan features:
- — Four bedrooms
- — Two full, one three-quarter, and one half baths
- Accent windows give this home a warm and welcoming facade
- The Foyer opens to the Vestibule, which opens to the Hallway, keeping the interior rooms out of the public eye
- Lined with windows, the Breakfast Area provides a sunlit or moonlit dining atmosphere
- The Bedrooms are isolated on the second floor for privacy
- Each secondary Bedroom has direct access to a full B
- A three-car Garage, with bump-out Storage Area, provides ample space
- Generous counter space in the Kitchen will please the cooks of the house
- This home is designed with basement, slab, and crawlspace foundation options

FIRST FLOOR — 1,799 SQ. FT.
SECOND FLOOR — 1,679 SQ. FT.
BASEMENT — 1,799 SQ. FT.
GARAGE — 828 SQ. FT.

TOTAL LIVING AREA:
3,478 SQ. FT.

63'-8"
LOWER DECK 12-0 x 18-0
UPPER DECK 16-0 x 18-0
FAMILY RM 19-5 x 18-0
BRKFST 9-3 x 16-0
3-CAR GARAGE 23-1 x 36-5
KIT 11-5 x 13-5
MUD RM
STAIR/HALL 19-1 x 10-8
DINING 12-5 x 16-1
LNDY
VST
PWD
FOYER 7-8 x 9-8
LIV RM/ LIBRARY 16'-10 x 17-5
57'-2"
FIRST FLOOR
CRAWLSPACE/SLAB FOUNDATION OPTION
ATTIC
MSTR BR 19-1 x 14-0
M.B. 11-5 x 14-8
B.
BR #2 12-6 x 14-2
BR #4 12-9 x 12-5
B.
BR #3 15-8 x 14-7
SECOND FLOOR

PLAN NO. 93344

Elegant Dining Room

PRICE CODE: E

- This plan features:
- — Four Bedrooms
- — Two full and one half baths
- Grand two-story Foyer with graceful staircase and acc to Living and Dining rooms
- Double door Entry into Dining Room with a boxed ba window, stepped ceiling and buffet recess
- Work island/snack bar, corner Pantry and a bright Dinette bay with Deck access highlight Kitchen
- Pocket doors lead into the expansive Family Room with cozy fireplace
- A tray ceiling, whirlpool tub with a separate shower, double vanity and a walk-in closet enhance the Master Suite
- This home is designed with a basement foundation

FIRST FLOOR — 1,194 SQ. FT.
SECOND FLOOR — 1,065 SQ. FT.

TOTAL LIVING AREA:
2,259 SQ. FT.

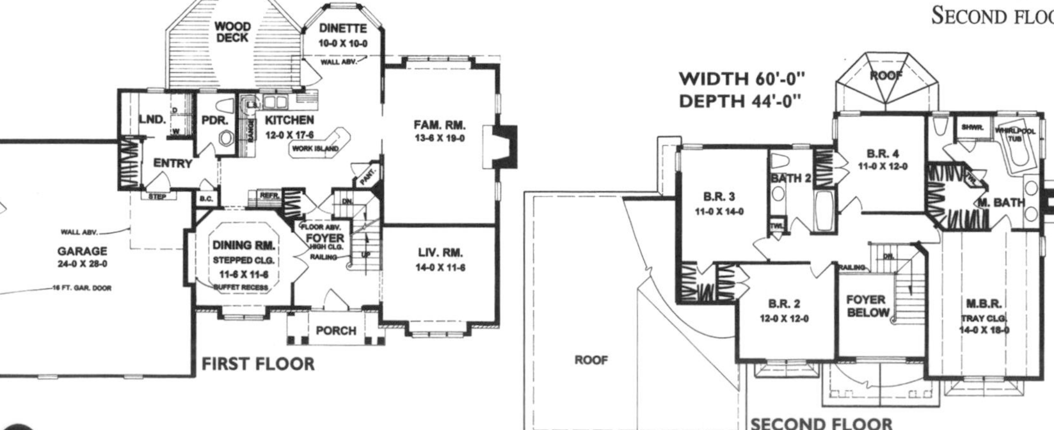

WOOD DECK
DINETTE 10-0 X 10-0
LND.
PDR.
KITCHEN 12-0 X 17-6
WORK ISLAND
FAM. RM. 13-6 X 19-0
ENTRY
GARAGE 24-0 X 28-0
16 FT. GAR. DOOR
DINING RM. STEPPED CLG. 11-6 X 11-6 BUFFET RECESS
FOYER HIGH CLG.
LIV. RM. 14-0 X 11-6
PORCH
FIRST FLOOR
WIDTH 60'-0"
DEPTH 44'-0"
ROOF
B.R. 3 11-0 X 14-0
BATH 2
B.R. 4 11-0 X 12-0
M. BATH
B.R. 2 12-0 X 12-0
FOYER BELOW
M.B.R. TRAY CLG. 14-0 X 18-0
SECOND FLOOR

To order your Blueprints, call 1-800-235-5700

PLAN NO. 24985

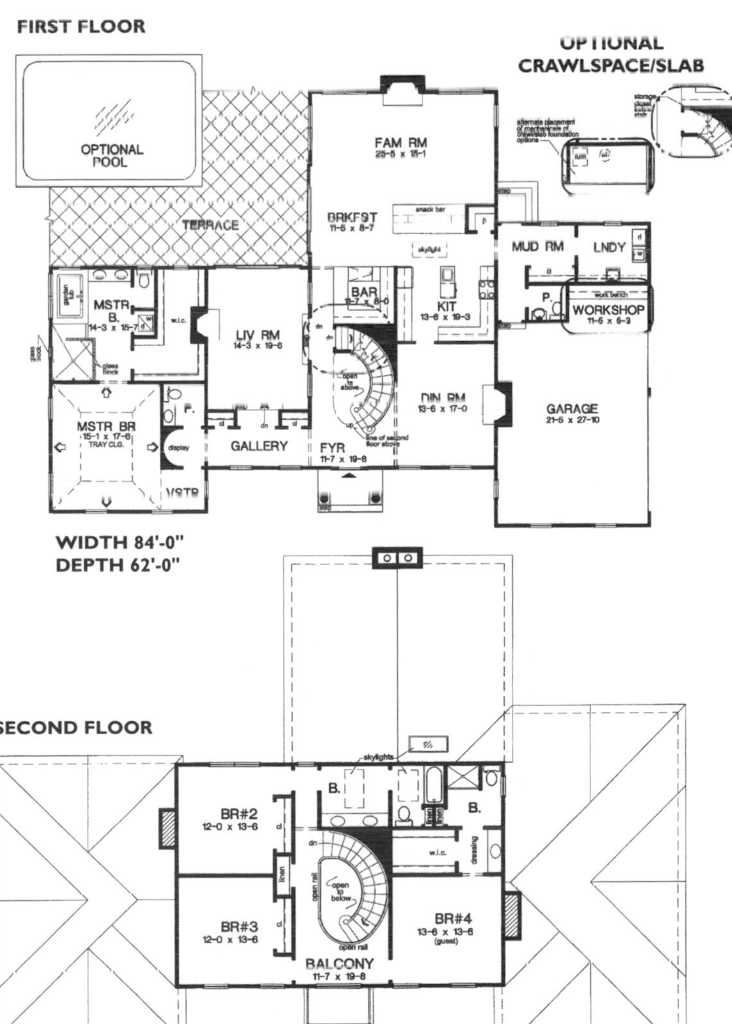
FIRST FLOOR
OPTIONAL CRAWLSPACE/SLAB
OPTIONAL POOL
TERRACE
FAM RM
25-5 x 15-1
BRKFST
11-5 x 8-7
snack bar
MUD RM
LNDY
BAR
KIT
13-6 x 19-3
WORKSHOP
11-5 x 6-3
MSTR. B.
14-3 x 15-7
LIV RM
14-3 x 19-6
DIN RM
13-6 x 17-0
GARAGE
21-5 x 27-10
MSTR BR
15-1 x 17-6
TRAY CLG.
GALLERY
FYR
11-7 x 19-8
WIDTH 84'-0"
DEPTH 62'-0"
SECOND FLOOR
skylights
BR#2
12-0 x 13-6
BR#3
12-0 x 13-6
BR#4
13-6 x 13-6
(guest)
BALCONY
11-7 x 19-8
open to below
open rail

Elegance in Symmetry

Price Code: K

- This plan features:
- — Four bedrooms
- — Two full, one three-quarter, and two half baths
- In the Foyer, a spiral staircase leads up to a Balcony
- Fireplaces cast their glow over the Dining, Family, and Living Rooms
- The skylit Kitchen is a chef's dream with its ample counter space, island, Pantry, and snack bar
- Lined with windows and topped with skylights, the rooms of this home receive plenty of natural light
- This home is designed with basement, slab, and crawlspace foundation options

First floor — 2,764 sq. ft.
Second floor — 1,443 sq. ft.
Basement — 2,764 sq. ft.
Garage — 663 sq. ft.

Total living area:
4,207 sq. ft.

PLAN NO.97224

Spacious Feelings

PRICE CODE: A

- This plan features:
- — Three bedrooms
- — Two full baths
- Open layout with vaulted ceilings in Foyer, Great Roo and Breakfast Area
- Kitchen with pass-thru and Pantry, efficiently serves bright Breakfast Area, Great Room and formal Dining Room
- Luxurious Master Suite offers a tray ceiling, two walk closets and a double vanity Bath with vaulted ceiling
- Two secondary Bedrooms share a full Bath, and Launc and closets
- This home is designed with a basement foundation

MAIN FLOOR — 1,363 SQ. FT.
BASEMENT — 715 SQ. FT.
GARAGE — 677 SQ. FT

TOTAL LIVING AREA:
1,363 SQ. FT.

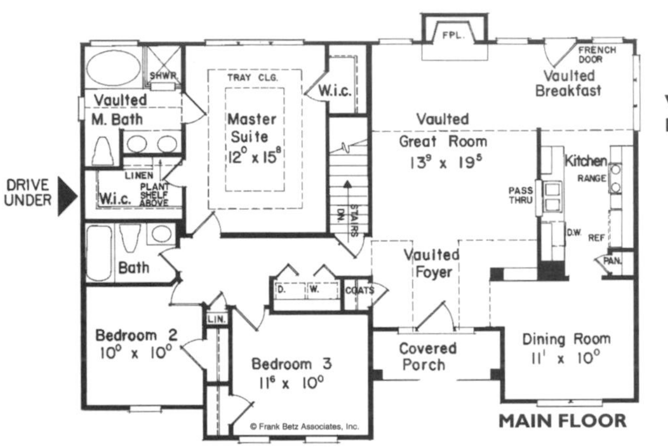

FPL.
FRENCH DOOR
Vaulted Breakfast
SHWR
TRAY CLG.
W.i.c.
Vaulted M. Bath
Master Suite 12° x 15⁸
Vaulted Great Room 13⁹ x 19⁵
Kitchen
RANGE
LINEN
PLANT SHELF ABOVE
W.i.c.
DRIVE UNDER
PASS THRU
D.W
REF
PAN.
Bath
Vaulted Foyer
D.
W.
COATS
LIN.
Bedroom 2 10° x 10°
Bedroom 3 11⁶ x 10°
Covered Porch
Dining Room 11' x 10°
© Frank Betz Associates, Inc.
MAIN FLOOR

WIDTH 47'-0"
DEPTH 35'-4"

PLAN NO.90007

Truly Western Approach to the Ranch House

PRICE CODE: C

- This plan features:
- — Four bedrooms
- — Three full baths
- Authentic Ranch styling with long Loggia, posts and braces, hand-split shake roof and cross-buck doors
- A Texas-sized hexagonal, sunken Living Room with tw solid walls, one with a fireplace, and two 10' walls of sliding glass doors
- A Porch surrounding the Living Room on three sides
- A Master Suite with a private Master Bath
- An efficient well-equipped Kitchen flowing into the Family Room
- This home is designed with a basement foundation

MAIN FLOOR — 1,830 SQ. FT.
BASEMENT — 1,830 SQ. FT.
GARAGE — 540 SQ. FT.

TOTAL LIVING AREA:
1,830 SQ. FT.

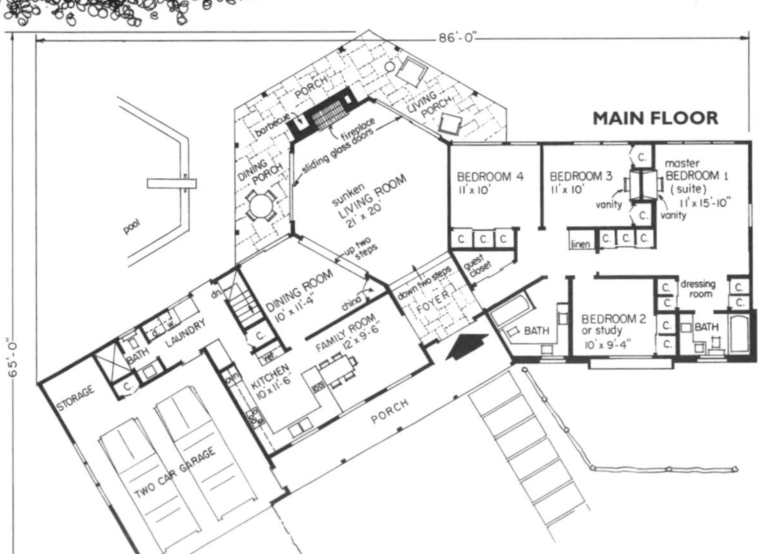

86'-0"
65'-0"
MAIN FLOOR
PORCH
LIVING PORCH
barbecue
fireplace
sliding glass doors
DINING PORCH
pool
sunken LIVING ROOM 21' x 20'
BEDROOM 4 11' x 10'
BEDROOM 3 11' x 10'
master BEDROOM 1 (suite) 11' x 15'-10"
vanity
linen
up two steps
guest closet
down two steps
dressing room
DINING ROOM 10' x 11'-4"
china
FOYER
BATH
BEDROOM 2 or study 10' x 9'-4"
BATH
LAUNDRY
BATH
FAMILY ROOM 12' x 9'-6"
KITCHEN 10' x 11'-6"
STORAGE
PORCH
TWO CAR GARAGE

PLAN NO. 24986

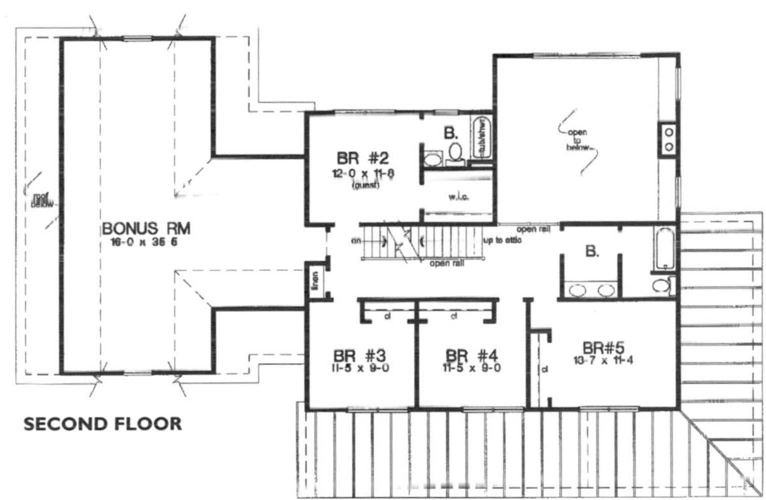

BONUS RM
16-0 x 35-6
BR #2
12-0 x 11-8
(guest)
B.
w.i.c.
open to below
open rail
up to attic
dn
B.
linen
BR #3
11-5 x 9-0
BR #4
11-5 x 9-0
BR#5
10-7 x 11-4
cl

SECOND FLOOR

OPTIONAL CRAWLSPACE/SLAB

WIDTH 78'-0"
DEPTH 48'-0"

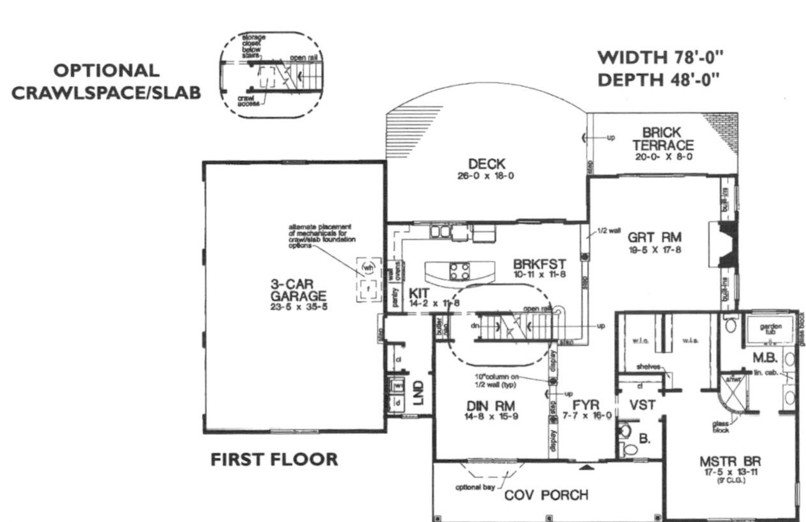

DECK
26-0 x 18-0
BRICK TERRACE
20-0 x 8-0
3-CAR GARAGE
23-5 x 35-5
KIT
14-2 x 11-8
BRKFST
10-11 x 11-8
GRT RM
19-5 X 17-8
DIN RM
14-8 x 15-9
FYR
7-7 x 16-0
VST
B.
M.B.
MSTR BR
17-5 x 13-11
LND
COV PORCH
optional bay

FIRST FLOOR

Private and Open Rooms

Price Code: F

- This plan features:
- — Five bedrooms
- — Three full and one half baths
- A bay window option lets you decide the design of your home's facade
- A half wall separates the Great Room from the Breakfast Area, creating a community atmosphere
- The Master Bath is of artistic interest with its shower stall and garden tub adorned with glass blocks
- This home is designed with basement, slab, and crawlspace foundation options

FIRST FLOOR — 1,868 SQ. FT.
SECOND FLOOR — 1,035 SQ. FT.
BONUS ROOM — 767 SQ. FT.
BASEMENT — 1,868 SQ. FT.
GARAGE — 856 SQ. FT.
PORCH — 240 SQ. FT.

TOTAL LIVING AREA:
2,903 SQ. FT.

PLAN NO. 98462

Grace with an Elegant Front Porch

PRICE CODE: B

- This plan features:
  - Three bedrooms
  - Two full and one half baths
- The two-story Foyer accesses the Dining Room, Living Room and Family Room with ease
- The Kitchen opens to the Breakfast Area and in turn the Breakfast Area is open to the Family Room
- The Family Room is enhanced by a fireplace
- A work island adds counter space to the Kitchen
- The Master Suite with a private Bath is topped by a vaulted ceiling
- The front secondary Bedroom is highlighted by a window seat
- This home is designed with basement, slab and crawlspace foundation options

FIRST FLOOR — 926 SQ. FT.
SECOND FLOOR — 824 SQ. FT.
BONUS ROOM — 282 SQ. FT.
BASEMENT — 926 SQ. FT.
GARAGE — 440 SQ. FT.

TOTAL LIVING AREA:* 1,750 *SQ. FT.

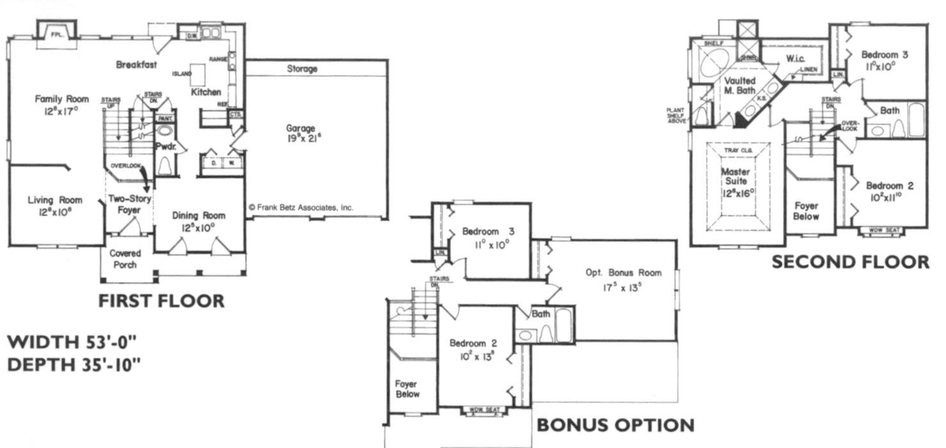

FPL.
Breakfast
Family Room
12⁸ x 17⁰
Kitchen
Storage
Garage
19⁵ x 21⁴
Pwdr.
Living Room
12⁸ x 10⁸
Two-Story Foyer
Dining Room
12⁵ x 10⁰
Covered Porch
© Frank Betz Associates, Inc.
FIRST FLOOR
WIDTH 53'-0"
DEPTH 35'-10"
Bedroom 3
11⁰ x 10⁰
Opt. Bonus Room
17⁵ x 13⁵
Bath
Bedroom 2
10² x 13⁸
Foyer Below
WDW. SEAT
BONUS OPTION
W.i.c.
Vaulted M. Bath
Bedroom 3
11⁰ x 10⁰
Bath
TRAY CLG.
Master Suite
12⁸ x 16⁰
Foyer Below
Bedroom 2
10² x 11¹⁰
SECOND FLOOR

PLAN NO. 98422

Covered Porch Shelters Entry

PRICE CODE: A

- This plan features:
  - Three bedrooms
  - Two full and one half baths
- There is a convenient pass-thru from the Kitchen into the Family Room
- An easy flow into the Dining Room enhances the interaction of the living spaces on the first floor
- A fireplace highlights the spacious Family Room
- The Kitchen opens to the Breakfast Room which has a French door that accesses the rear yard
- Decorative ceiling treatment highlights the Master Bedroom while a vaulted ceiling tops the Master Bath
- Two additional Bedrooms share the use of the full Bat in the hall
- This home is designed with basement and crawlspace foundation options

FIRST FLOOR — 719 SQ. FT.
SECOND FLOOR — 717 SQ. FT.
BASEMENT — 719 SQ. FT.
GARAGE — 480 SQ. FT.
BONUS — 290 SQ. FT.

TOTAL LIVING AREA:* 1,436 *SQ. FT.

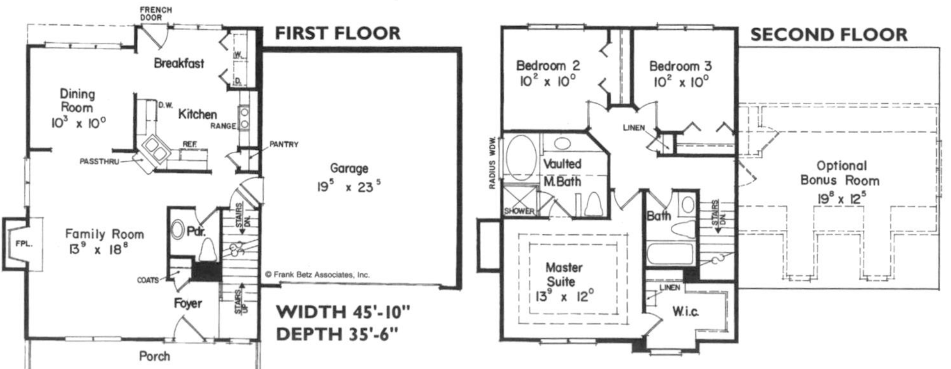

FRENCH DOOR
FIRST FLOOR
Breakfast
Dining Room
10³ x 10⁰
Kitchen
RANGE
REF.
PANTRY
PASSTHRU
Garage
19⁵ x 23⁵
Family Room
13⁹ x 18⁸
FPL.
Pdr.
COATS
Foyer
© Frank Betz Associates, Inc.
Porch
WIDTH 45'-10"
DEPTH 35'-6"
SECOND FLOOR
Bedroom 2
10² x 10⁰
Bedroom 3
10² x 10⁰
LINEN
RADIUS WDW.
Vaulted M.Bath
SHOWER
Bath
Optional Bonus Room
19⁸ x 12⁵
Master Suite
13⁹ x 12⁰
LINEN
W.i.c.

Packed with Options

PRICE CODE: D

PLAN NO.98559

This plan features:
- Three bedrooms
- Two full and one three quarter baths
- This home has a tiled Entry and Gallery that connects the living space
- The Great Room has a rear wall fireplace that is set between windows
- Both Dining Areas are located steps away from the Kitchen
- The Study has a sloped ceiling and a front bay of windows
- The Master Bedroom has a private Bath and a galley-like walk-in closet
- Two secondary Bedrooms are on the opposite side of the home
- This home is designed with a slab foundation

AIN FLOOR — 2,081 SQ. FT.
ARAGE — 422 SQ. FT.

TOTAL LIVING AREA:
2,081 SQ. FT.

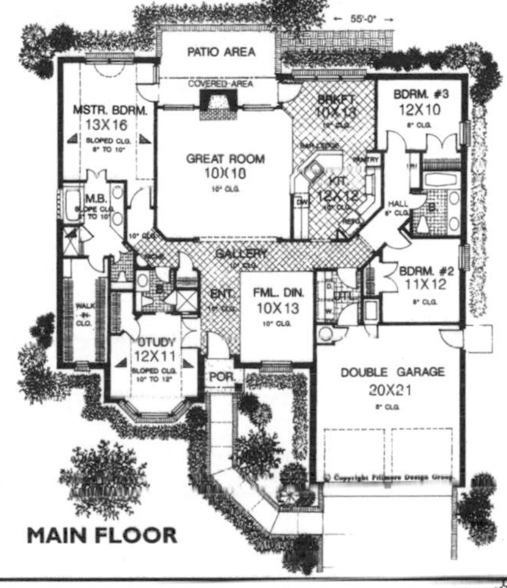
PATIO AREA
MSTR. BDRM. 13X16
GREAT ROOM 10X10
BRKFT.
BDRM. #3 12X10
KIT. 12X12
GALLERY
ENT.
FML. DIN. 10X13
BDRM. #2 11X12
STUDY 12X11
POR.
DOUBLE GARAGE 20X21
MAIN FLOOR

WIDTH 55'-0"
DEPTH 57'-10"

Great Open Spaces

PRICE CODE: C

PLAN NO.98484

This plan features:
- Three bedrooms
- Two full and one half baths
- The terrific covered front Porch of this home leads into an impressive two-story Foyer
- The expansive Family Room flows into the Breakfast Room and the Breakfast Room into the Kitchen for an easy open traffic pattern
- The formal areas, the Living Room and the Dining Room are located to the front of the home on either side of the Foyer
- The Master Suite includes a tray ceiling over the Bedroom, a French door to the Master Bath, a vaulted ceiling over the Master Bath and walk-in closet
- An optional bonus room awaits future expansion
- This home is designed with basement and crawlspace foundation options

IRST FLOOR — 1,071 SQ. FT.
ECOND FLOOR — 924 SQ. FT.
ONUS ROOM — 280 SQ. FT.
ASEMENT — 1,071 SQ. FT.
ARAGE — 480 SQ. FT.

TOTAL LIVING AREA:
1,995 SQ. FT.

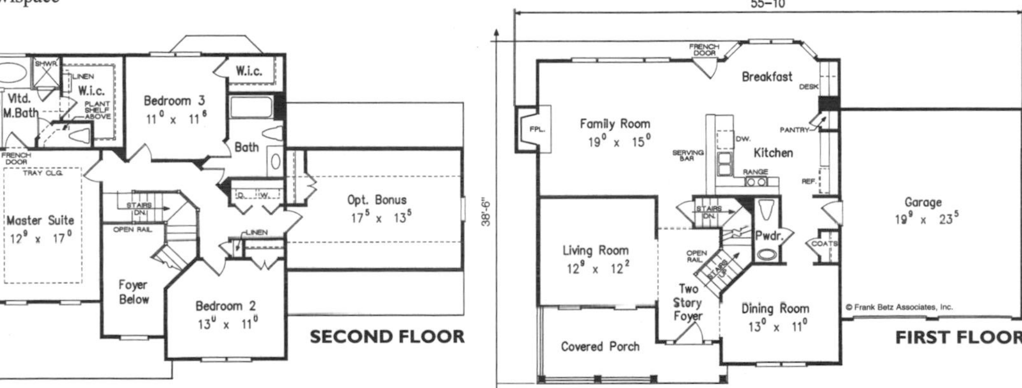
Vltd. M.Bath
W.i.c.
Bedroom 3 $11^0 \times 11^6$
Bath
Master Suite $12^9 \times 17^0$
Opt. Bonus $17^5 \times 13^5$
Foyer Below
Bedroom 2 $13^0 \times 11^0$
SECOND FLOOR
55'-10"
Breakfast
Family Room $19^0 \times 15^0$
Kitchen
Garage $19^9 \times 23^5$
Living Room $12^9 \times 12^2$
Pwdr.
Two Story Foyer
Dining Room $13^0 \times 11^0$
Covered Porch
FIRST FLOOR
© Frank Betz Associates, Inc.

PLAN NO.90689

Formal Balance

PRICE CODE: A

- This plan features:
- — Three bedrooms
- — Two full baths
- A cathedral ceiling in the Living Room with a heat-circulating fireplace as the focal point
- A bow window in the Dining Room that adds elegance as well as natural light
- A well-equipped Kitchen that serves both the Dinette and the formal Dining Room efficiently
- A Master Bedroom with three closets and a private Master Bath with sliding glass doors to the Master Deck with a hot tub
- This home is designed with basement and slab foundation options

MAIN FLOOR — 1,476 SQ. FT.
BASEMENT — 1,361 SQ. FT.
GARAGE — 548 SQ. FT.

TOTAL LIVING AREA:
1,476 SQ. FT.

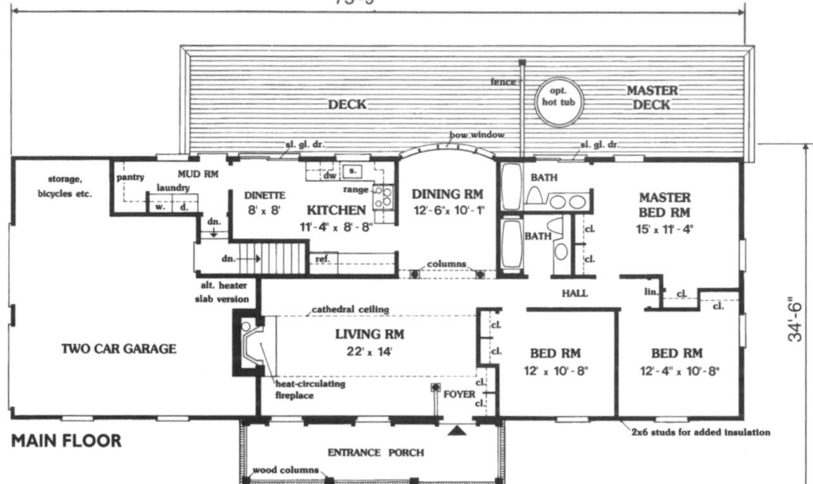

75'-9"
34'-6"
DECK
fence
opt. hot tub
MASTER DECK
sl. gl. dr.
bow window
storage, bicycles etc.
pantry
MUD RM
laundry
w. d.
dn.
DINETTE 8' x 8'
dw
range
KITCHEN 11'-4" x 8'-8"
ref.
DINING RM 12'-6"x 10'-1"
columns
BATH
MASTER BED RM 15' x 11'-4"
cl.
HALL
lin.
alt. heater slab version
cathedral ceiling
LIVING RM 22' x 14'
TWO CAR GARAGE
heat-circulating fireplace
FOYER
BED RM 12' x 10'-8"
BED RM 12'-4" x 10'-8"
2x6 studs for added insulation
ENTRANCE PORCH
wood columns
MAIN FLOOR

PLAN NO.98449

Elegantly Styled

PRICE CODE: B

- This plan features:
- — Three bedrooms
- — Two full and one half baths
- Architectural details create eye-catching appeal to this home's facade
- The two-story Foyer is flanked by the formal Living and Dining Rooms
- Open and comfortable, the Family Room is highlighted by a fireplace and windows
- The Master Suite is enhanced by a tray ceiling and a plush Bath with a vaulted ceiling
- Second floor offers an optional bonus room for future expansion
- This home is designed with basement and crawlspace foundation options

FIRST FLOOR — 922 SQ. FT.
SECOND FLOOR — 778 SQ. FT.
BONUS ROOM — 369 SQ. FT.
BASEMENT — 922 SQ. FT.
GARAGE & STORAGE — 530 SQ. FT.

TOTAL LIVING AREA:
1,700 SQ. FT.

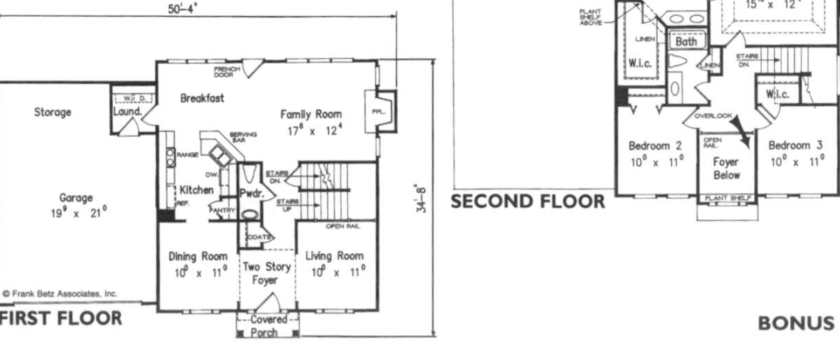

50'-4"
34'-8"
Storage
Laund.
Breakfast
Family Room 17⁶ x 12⁴
Garage 19⁹ x 21⁰
Kitchen
Pwdr.
Dining Room 10⁰ x 11⁰
Two Story Foyer
Living Room 10⁰ x 11⁰
Covered Porch
© Frank Betz Associates, Inc.
FIRST FLOOR
Vaulted M.Bath
Master Suite 15¹⁰ x 12⁴
Bath
W.i.c.
Bedroom 2 10⁰ x 11⁰
Foyer Below
Bedroom 3 10⁰ x 11⁰
SECOND FLOOR
Opt. Bonus Room 15⁵ x 16⁰
Bedroom 2 10⁰ x 12⁰
BONUS

Small and Stylish

PRICE CODE: B

PLAN NO.97235

This plan features:
- Three bedrooms
- Two full baths
- The Kitchen includes a built-in Pantry and a peninsula counter/serving bar
- The Great Room includes a fireplace and a French door to a covered Porch
- The Master Suite has a lavish Bath and a huge walk-in closet
- This home is designed with a basement foundation

PER LEVEL — 1,509 SQ. FT.
WER LEVEL — 100 SQ. FT.
SEMENT — 954 SQ. FT.
RAGE — 484 SQ. FT.

TOTAL LIVING AREA:
1,609 SQ. FT.

WIDTH 49'-0"
DEPTH 34'-4"

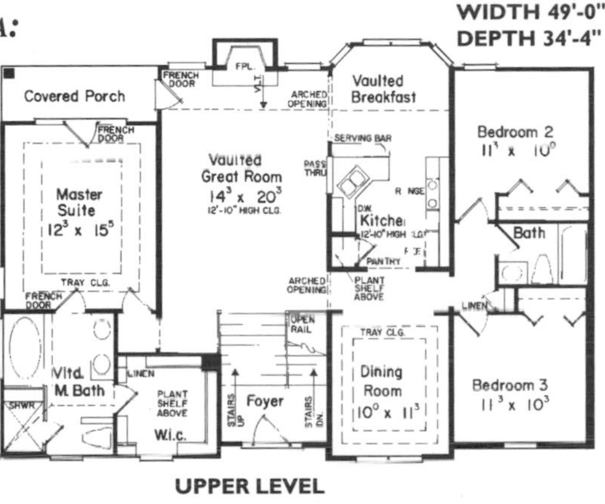

Covered Porch
French Door
FPL
Arched Opening
Vaulted Breakfast
Bedroom 2
11^1 x 10^0
Serving Bar
Master Suite
12^3 x 15^5
Vaulted Great Room
14^3 x 20^3
12'-10" High Clg.
Kitchen
Pantry
Bath
Tray Clg.
Arched Opening
Plant Shelf Above
Linen
Open Rail
Vltd. M.Bath
Shwr
Plant Shelf Above
W.i.c.
Foyer
Stairs Up
Stairs Dn
Dining Room
10^0 x 11^3
Bedroom 3
11^3 x 10^3

UPPER LEVEL

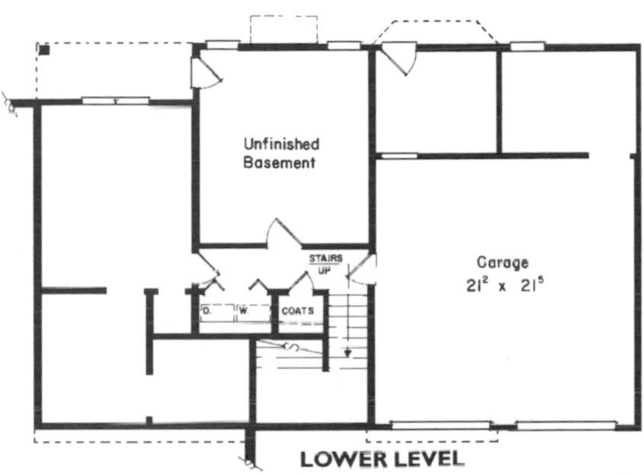

Unfinished Basement
Stairs Up
Coats
Garage
21^2 x 21^5

LOWER LEVEL

Unique A-Frame

PRICE CODE: A

PLAN NO.90025

This plan features:
- Three bedrooms
- Two full baths
- Exterior highlighted by fieldstone chimney, red cedar roof, vertical siding and a redwood Sun Deck
- Open Living Room, Dining and Kitchen layout provides a spacious feeling
- Efficient, U-shaped Kitchen with built-in Pantry and serving bar
- Spacious first floor Bedroom convenient to full Bath and Laundry
- Two second floor Bedrooms with ample closet space share a full Bath
- This home is designed with a crawlspace foundation

RST FLOOR — 867 SQ. FT.
COND FLOOR — 442 SQ. FT.

TOTAL LIVING AREA:
1,309 SQ. FT.

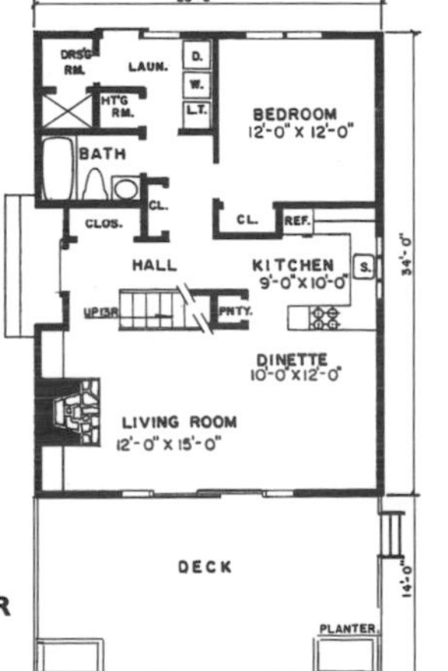

26'-0"
DRSG. RM.
LAUN.
HT'G RM.
BEDROOM
12'-0" x 12'-0"
BATH
CL.
CLOS.
REF.
HALL
KITCHEN
9'-0" x 10'-0"
PNTY.
DINETTE
10'-0" x 12'-0"
LIVING ROOM
12'-0" x 15'-0"
34'-0"
DECK
14'-0"
PLANTER

FIRST FLOOR

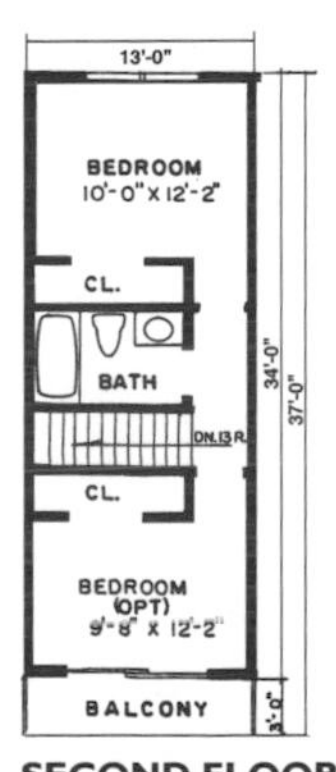

13'-0"
BEDROOM
10'-0" x 12'-2"
CL.
BATH
CL.
BEDROOM (OPT)
9'-8" x 12'-2"
BALCONY
34'-0"
37'-0"

SECOND FLOOR

PLAN NO.10686

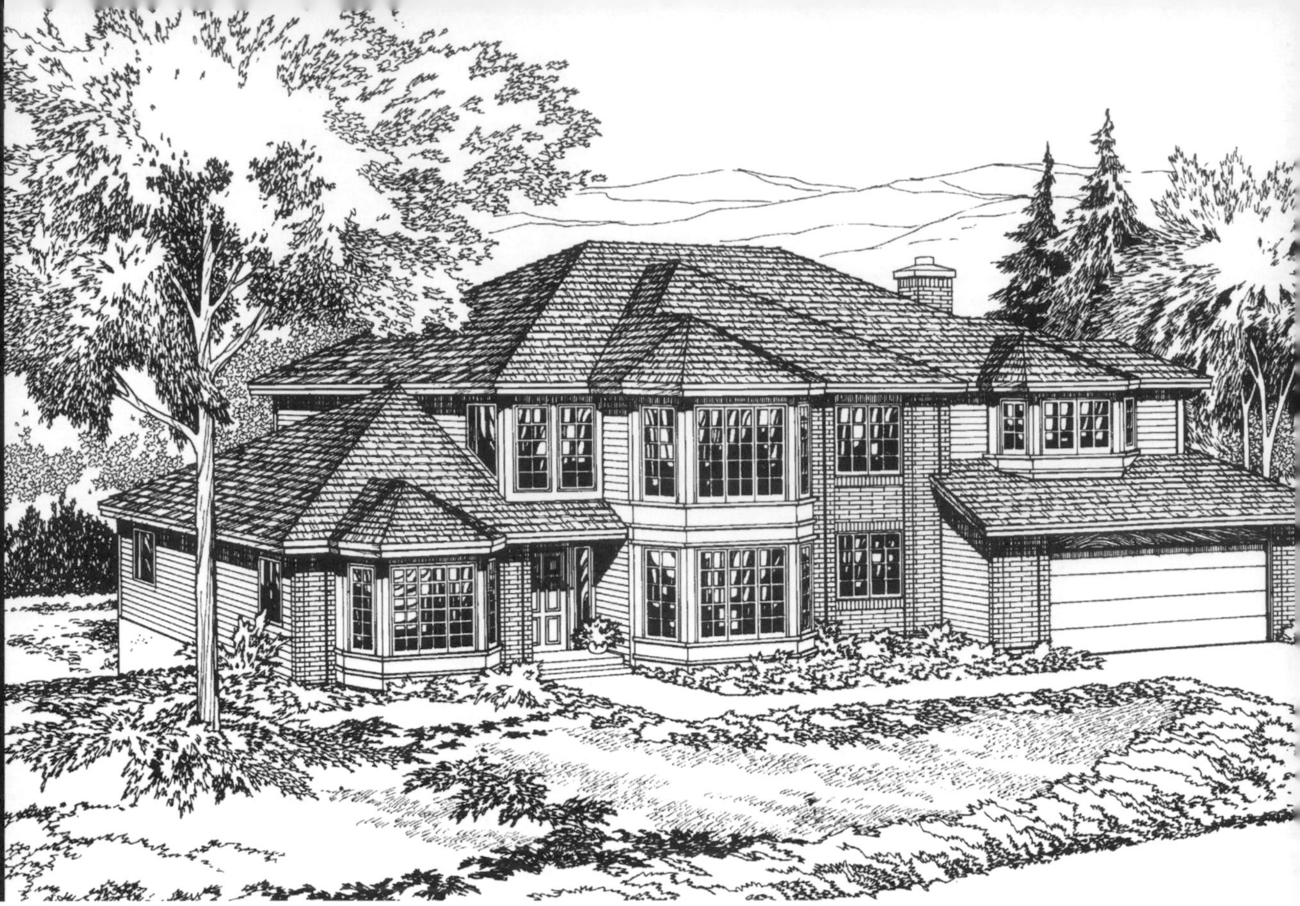

Every Luxurious Feature One Could Want

Price Code: I

- This plan features:
- — Four bedrooms
- — Two full and one half baths
- An open staircase leading to the Bedrooms and dividing the space between the vaulted Living and Dining Rooms
- A wide family area including the Kitchen, Dinette and Family Room
- A Master Bedroom with a vaulted ceiling, spacious closets and Jacuzzi
- This home is designed with a basement foundation

FIRST FLOOR — 1,786 SQ. FT.
SECOND FLOOR — 1,490 SQ. FT.
BASEMENT — 1,773 SQ. FT.
GARAGE — 579 SQ. FT.

TOTAL LIVING AREA:
3,276 SQ. FT.

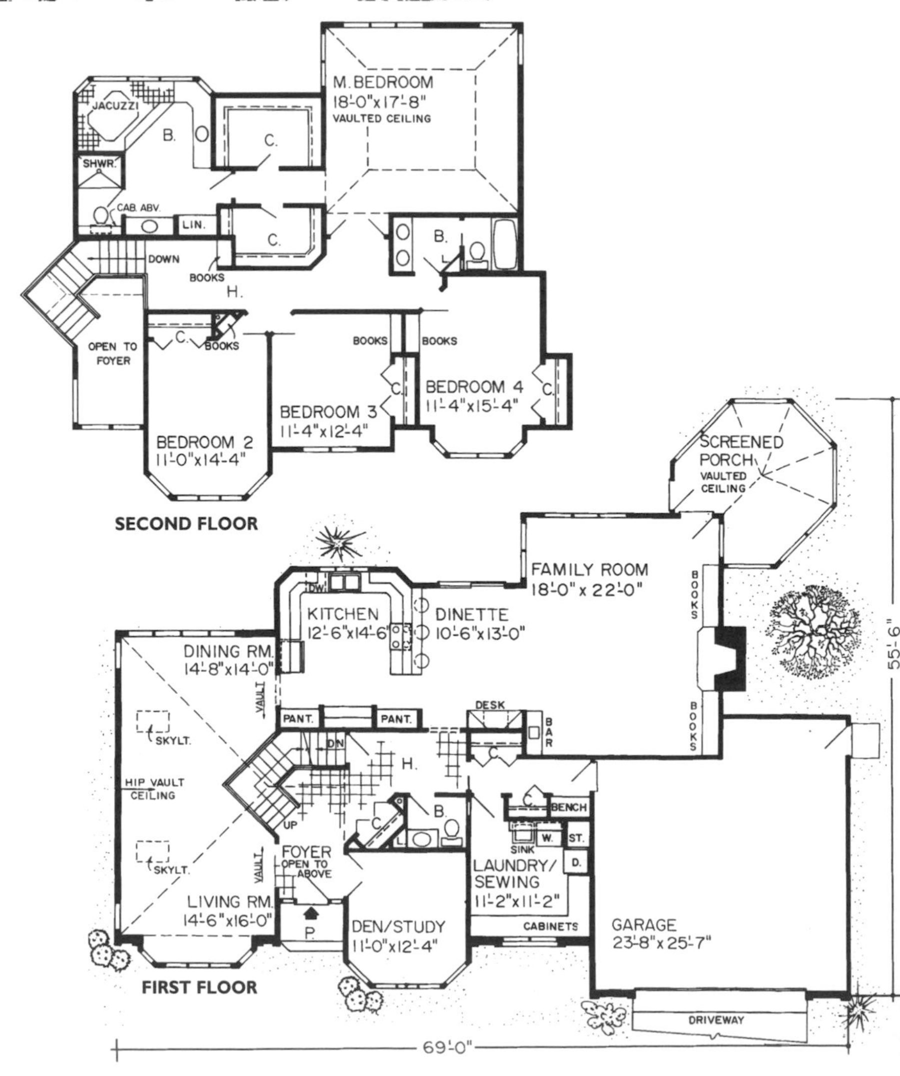
M. BEDROOM
18'-0"x17'-8"
VAULTED CEILING
JACUZZI
SHWR.
CAB. ABV.
LIN.
DOWN
BOOKS
OPEN TO FOYER
BEDROOM 2
11'-0"x14'-4"
BEDROOM 3
11'-4"x12'-4"
BEDROOM 4
11'-4"x15'-4"
SECOND FLOOR
SCREENED PORCH
VAULTED CEILING
FAMILY ROOM
18'-0" x 22'-0"
KITCHEN
12'-6"x14'-6"
DINETTE
10'-6"x13'-0"
DINING RM.
14'-8"x14'-0"
PANT.
DESK
BAR
SKYLT.
HIP VAULT CEILING
FOYER
OPEN TO ABOVE
LIVING RM.
14'-6"x16'-0"
DEN/STUDY
11'-0"x12'-4"
LAUNDRY/ SEWING
11'-2"x11'-2"
CABINETS
BENCH
SINK
GARAGE
23'-8"x25'-7"
DRIVEWAY
FIRST FLOOR
69'-0"
55'-6"

PLAN NO.10690

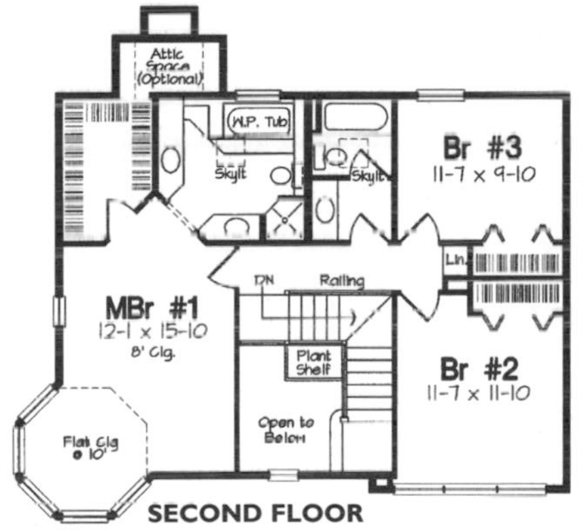
Attic Space (Optional)
W.P. Tub
Skylt
Skylt
Br #3
11-7 x 9-10
Lin.
DN
Railing
MBr #1
12-1 x 15-10
8' Clg.
Plant Shelf
Open to Below
Br #2
11-7 x 11-10
Flat Clg @ 10'
SECOND FLOOR

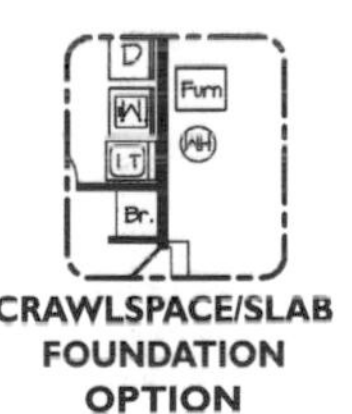
D
W
LT
Br.
Furn
WH
CRAWLSPACE/SLAB FOUNDATION OPTION

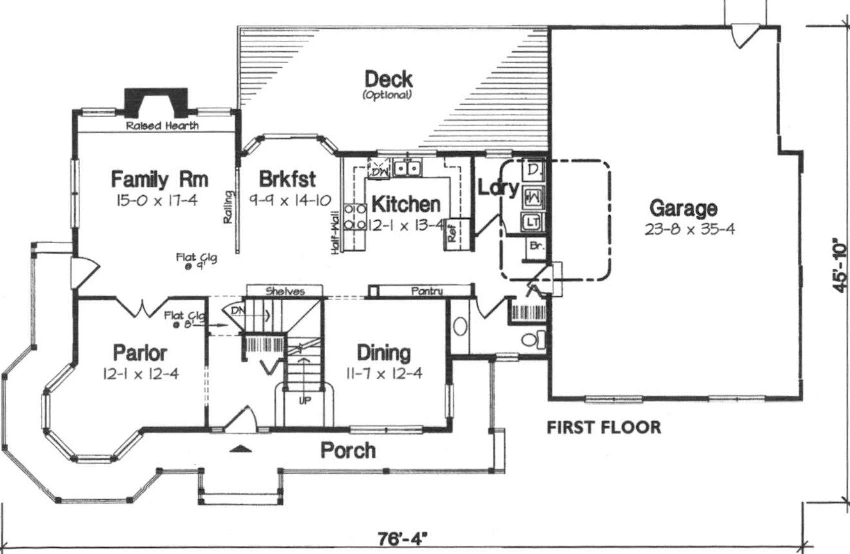
Deck (Optional)
Raised Hearth
Family Rm
15-0 x 17-4
Railing
Brkfst
9-9 x 14-10
Kitchen
12-1 x 13-4
Half-Wall
Ref
Ldry
D
W
LT
Br.
Garage
23-8 x 35-4
45'-10"
Flat Clg @ 9'
Shelves
Pantry
Flat Clg @ 8'
DN
Parlor
12-1 x 12-4
Dining
11-7 x 12-4
UP
Porch
FIRST FLOOR
76'-4"

Gingerbread Charm

Price Code: F

- This plan features:
  - — Three bedrooms
  - — Two full and one half baths
- A wrap around Porch and rear Deck adding lots of outdoor living space
- A formal Parlor and Dining Room just off the central Entry
- A Family Room with a fireplace
- A Master Suite complete with a five-sided Sitting Nook, walk-in closets and a sunken tub
- This home is designed with basement, slab and crawlspace foundation options

FIRST FLOOR — 1,260 SQ. FT.
SECOND FLOOR — 1,021 SQ. FT.
BASEMENT — 1,186 SQ. FT.
GARAGE — 851 SQ. FT.

TOTAL LIVING AREA:
2,281 SQ. FT.

PLAN NO.97246

Those Fabulous Details

PRICE CODE: E

- This plan features:
- — Four bedrooms
- — Two full and one half baths
- Unique style created by keystone, arched windows and entrance outside continue inside with arched openings
- Hub of home is vaulted Family Room with French door arched window, cozy fireplace and pass-thru to Kitchen
- Vaulted Breakfast Area expands efficient Kitchen for a busy household
- Spacious Master Suite boasts a Sitting Area with fireplace, tray ceiling, his and her walk-in closets, and a vaulted Master Bath
- Three or four additional Bedrooms with large closets, share a full Bath
- Plan offers optional expansion to second floor bonus room and Bath
- This home is designed with basement and crawlspace foundation options

MAIN FLOOR — 2,311 SQ. FT.
BONUS — 425 SQ. FT.
BASEMENT — 2,311 SQ. FT.
GARAGE — 500 SQ. FT.

TOTAL LIVING AREA:
2,311 SQ. FT.

Sitting Area
Master Suite
17^{9} x 20^{0}
Vaulted Breakfast
Kitchen
Vaulted Family Room
16^{0} x 22^{6}
Bedroom 2
12^{2} x 11^{6}
Bath
Bedroom 3
11^{0} x 11^{0}
Vaulted M.Bath
Hers
His
Pwdr.
Laund.
Dining Room
12^{6} x 12^{8}
Foyer
Vaulted Living Room/ Opt. Bedroom 4
12^{5} x 12^{9}
Garage
22^{5} x 21^{0}
© Frank Betz Associates, Inc.
MAIN FLOOR

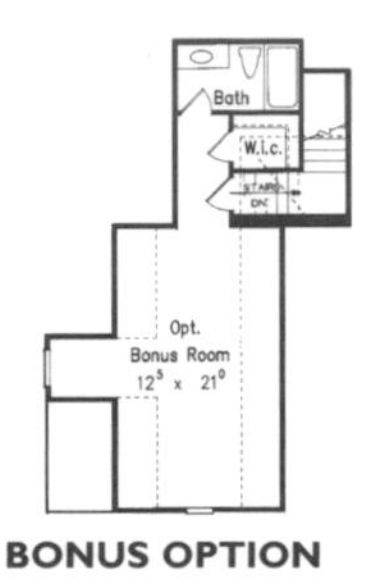
Bath
W.I.c.
Opt. Bonus Room
12^{5} x 21^{0}

BONUS OPTION

WIDTH 61'-0"
DEPTH 65'-4"

PLAN NO.32291

Photography supplied by the Meredith Corporation

Comfortable Cape

PRICE CODE: C

- This plan features:
- — Three bedrooms
- — Three full baths
- This home has plenty of space for outdoor entertaining
- The living room has a fireplace set between doors
- The Kitchen has plenty of counter space
- The Dining Room is brightened by a wall of windows
- This home is designed with a crawlspace and pier/post foundation options

FIRST FLOOR — 936 SQ. FT.
SECOND FLOOR — 916 SQ. FT.
GARAGE — 576 SQ. FT.

TOTAL LIVING AREA:
1,852 SQ. FT.

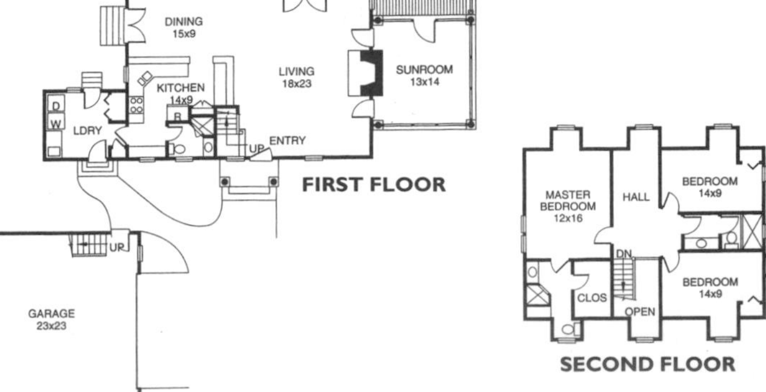
WIDTH 70'-0"
DEPTH 68'-0"
VERANDA
DECK
DINING
15x9
LIVING
18x23
SUNROOM
13x14
KITCHEN
14x9
LDRY
ENTRY
FIRST FLOOR
GARAGE
23x23
MASTER BEDROOM
12x16
HALL
BEDROOM
14x9
BEDROOM
14x9
CLOS
OPEN
SECOND FLOOR

Outstanding Four Bedroom

PRICE CODE: C

PLAN NO. 98435

This plan features:

- Four bedrooms
- Two full baths
- Radius window highlighting the exterior and the formal Dining Room
- High ceiling topping the Foyer for a grand first impression
- Vaulted ceiling enhances the Great Room accented by a fireplace framed by windows to either side
- Arched opening to the Kitchen from the Great Room
- Breakfast Room topped by a vaulted ceiling and enhanced by elegant French door to the rear yard
- Tray ceiling and a five-piece Bath gives luxurious presence to the Master Suite
- Three additional Bedrooms share a full, double vanity Bath in the hall
- This home is designed with basement and crawlspace foundation options

MAIN FLOOR — 1,945 SQ. FT.

TOTAL LIVING AREA:
1,945 SQ. FT.

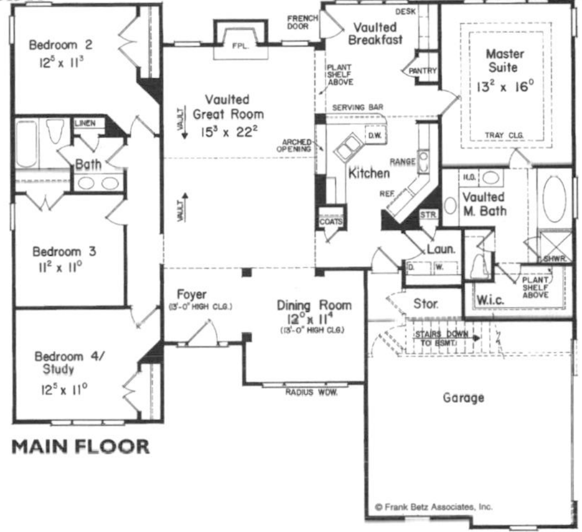
Bedroom 2
12^5 x 11^3
FPL.
Vaulted
Great Room
15^3 x 22^2
FRENCH DOOR
Vaulted
Breakfast
DESK
PLANT SHELF ABOVE
PANTRY
Master
Suite
13^2 x 16^0
TRAY CLG.
SERVING BAR
LINEN
Bath
ARCHED OPENING
D.W.
RANGE
Kitchen
REF.
Vaulted
M. Bath
STR.
COATS
Laun.
Bedroom 3
11^2 x 11^0
Foyer
Dining Room
12^0 x 11^4
Stor.
W.i.c.
PLANT SHELF ABOVE
STAIRS DOWN TO BSMT.
Bedroom 4/
Study
12^5 x 11^0
RADIUS WDW.
Garage
MAIN FLOOR
© Frank Betz Associates, Inc.

WIDTH 56'-6"
DEPTH 52'-6"

Second Floor Laundry

PRICE CODE: F

PLAN NO. 24988

This plan features:

- Four bedrooms
- Two full and one half baths
- Convenience counts, with the Laundry room on the second floor with all four Bedrooms
- The Great Room is flanked by wooden decks, increasing your entertainment options
- This home is designed with basement, slab, and crawlspace foundation options

FIRST FLOOR — 1,388 SQ. FT.
SECOND FLOOR — 1,241 SQ. FT.
BONUS ROOM — 474 SQ. FT.
BASEMENT — 1,388 SQ. FT.
GARAGE — 569 SQ. FT.

TOTAL LIVING AREA:
2,629 SQ. FT.

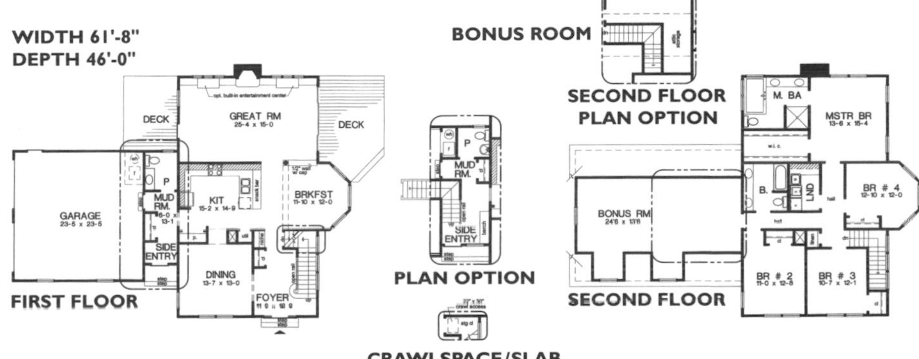
WIDTH 61'-8"
DEPTH 46'-0"
BONUS ROOM
SECOND FLOOR
PLAN OPTION
DECK
GREAT RM
DECK
MUD RM.
KIT
BRKFST
GARAGE
SIDE ENTRY
DINING
FOYER
FIRST FLOOR
PLAN OPTION
CRAWLSPACE/SLAB
OPTION
M. BA
MSTR BR
BR # 4
BONUS RM
BR # 2
BR # 3
SECOND FLOOR

PLAN NO.24989

Sightly Simplicity

PRICE CODE: F

- This plan features:
- — Three bedrooms
- — Two full and one half baths
- The covered Porch opens into a two-story Foyer, which adds dramatic scale to the entrance of this home
- Skylights in the vaulted ceiling flood the Great Room with light
- Conveniently-located Mud and Laundry Rooms separate the Garage from the Living Areas
- Secondary Bedrooms share the privacy of the second floor
- This home is designed with basement, slab, crawlspace, and combo basement/crawlspace foundation options

FIRST FLOOR — 1,782 SQ. FT.
SECOND FLOOR — 810 SQ. FT.
BASEMENT — 1,644 SQ. FT.
GARAGE — 569 SQ. FT.

TOTAL LIVING AREA:
2,562 SQ. FT.

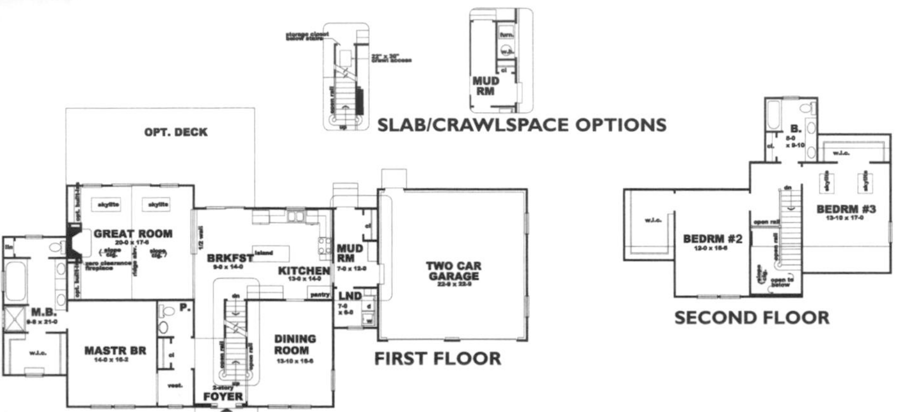

SLAB/CRAWLSPACE OPTIONS
MUD RM
OPT. DECK
GREAT ROOM
BRKFST
KITCHEN
MUD RM
LND
TWO CAR GARAGE
M.B.
MASTR BR
DINING ROOM
FOYER
COV PORCH
FIRST FLOOR
B.
BEDRM #2
BEDRM #3
SECOND FLOOR

PLAN NO.98498

Open Spaces

PRICE CODE: A

- This plan features:
- — Three bedrooms
- — Two full baths
- Open floor plan between the Family Room and the Dining Room
- Vaulted ceilings adding volume and a fireplace in the Family Room
- Three Bedrooms, the Master Suite with a five-piece private Bath
- Convenient laundry center located outside the Bedrooms
- This home is designed with a crawlspace foundation

MAIN FLOOR — 1,135 SQ. FT.

TOTAL LIVING AREA:
1,135 SQ. FT.

60'-0"
Opt. Breakfast
Storage
Kitchen
Vaulted Dining Room 10⁰x10³
Master Suite 11¹x14⁰
M.Bath
W.i.c.
Garage
Vaulted Family Room 18⁵x13²
Bath
Bedroom 2 10¹x10³
Bedroom 3 10³x10⁰
33'-6"
© Frank Betz Associates, Inc.

MAIN FLOOR

Isolated Master Suite

PRICE CODE: E

PLAN NO. 90420

This plan features:

- Three bedrooms
- Two full and one half baths
- A spacious, sunken Living Room with a cathedral ceiling
- An isolated Master Suite with a private Bath and walk-in closet
- Two additional Bedrooms with a unique Bath-and-a-half and ample closet space
- An efficient U-shaped Kitchen with a double sink, ample cabinets, counter space, and a Breakfast Area
- A second floor Studio overlooking the Living Room
- This home is designed with basement, slab, and crawlspace foundation options

RST FLOOR — 2,213 SQ. FT.
COND FLOOR — 260 SQ. FT.
ASEMENT — 2,213 SQ. FT.
ARAGE — 422 SQ. FT.

TOTAL LIVING AREA:
2,473 SQ. FT.

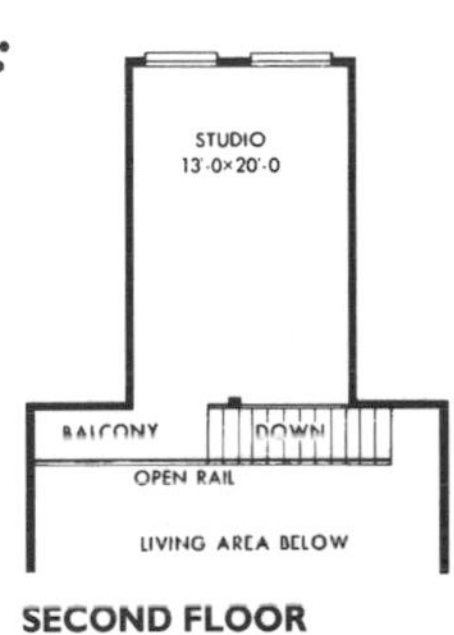
STUDIO
13-0×20-0
BALCONY
DOWN
OPEN RAIL
LIVING AREA BELOW
SECOND FLOOR

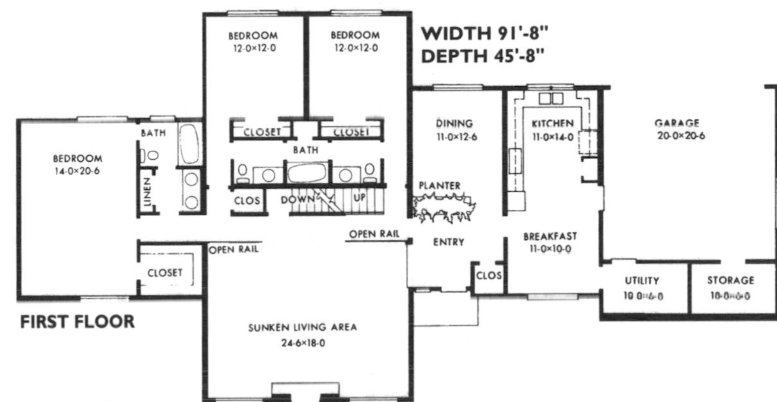
WIDTH 91'-8"
DEPTH 45'-8"
BEDROOM
12-0×12-0
BEDROOM
12-0×12-0
BEDROOM
14-0×20-6
BATH
LINEN
CLOSET
CLOSET
BATH
CLOS
DOWN
UP
CLOSET
OPEN RAIL
OPEN RAIL
DINING
11-0×12-6
PLANTER
KITCHEN
11-0×14-0
ENTRY
BREAKFAST
11-0×10-0
CLOS
GARAGE
20-0×20-6
UTILITY
STORAGE
SUNKEN LIVING AREA
24-6×18-0
FIRST FLOOR

Delightful Detailing

PRICE CODE: F

PLAN NO. 98426

- This plan features:
- Three bedrooms
- Two full and one half baths
- The vaulted ceiling extends from the Foyer into the Living Room
- The Dining Room is delineated by columns with a plant shelf above
- Family Room has a vaulted ceiling and a wall of radius windows
- The Kitchen is equipped with an island serving bar, a desk, a wall oven, a Pantry, and a Breakfast Bay
- The Master Suite is highlighted by a Sitting Room, a walk-in closet, and a private Bath with a vaulted ceiling
- Two additional large Bedrooms share a Bath in the Hall
- There is an optional bonus room located over the Garage
- This home is designed with basement and crawlspace foundation options

AIN FLOOR — 2,622 SQ. FT.
ONUS ROOM — 478 SQ. FT.
ASEMENT — 2,622 SQ. FT.
ARAGE — 506 SQ. FT.

TOTAL LIVING AREA:
2,622 SQ. FT.

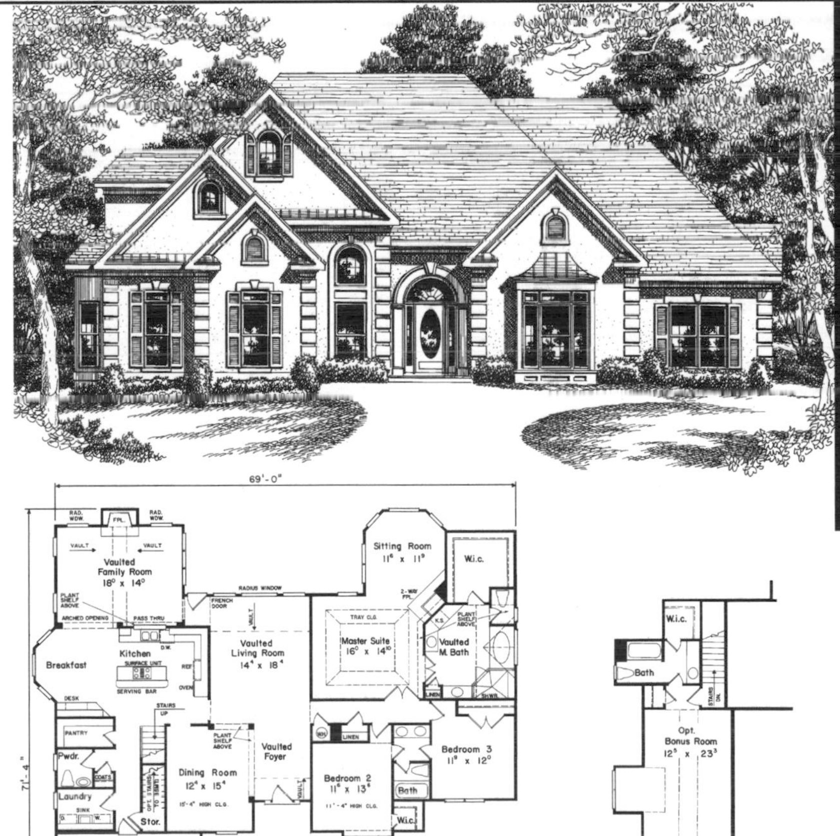
69'-0"
71'-4"
Vaulted
Family Room
18° x 14°
Breakfast
Kitchen
SERVING BAR
Vaulted
Living Room
14⁴ x 18⁴
Sitting Room
11⁶ x 11⁹
W.i.c.
Master Suite
16° x 14°
Vaulted
M. Bath
Vaulted
Foyer
Dining Room
12° x 15⁴
Bedroom 2
11⁶ x 13⁶
Bedroom 3
11⁹ x 12°
Bath
W.i.c.
PANTRY
Pwdr.
Laundry
Stor.
Garage
20⁵ x 23⁵
© Frank Betz Associates, Inc.
MAIN FLOOR
W.i.c.
Bath
Opt.
Bonus Room
12⁵ x 23⁵
BONUS

PLAN NO. 96503

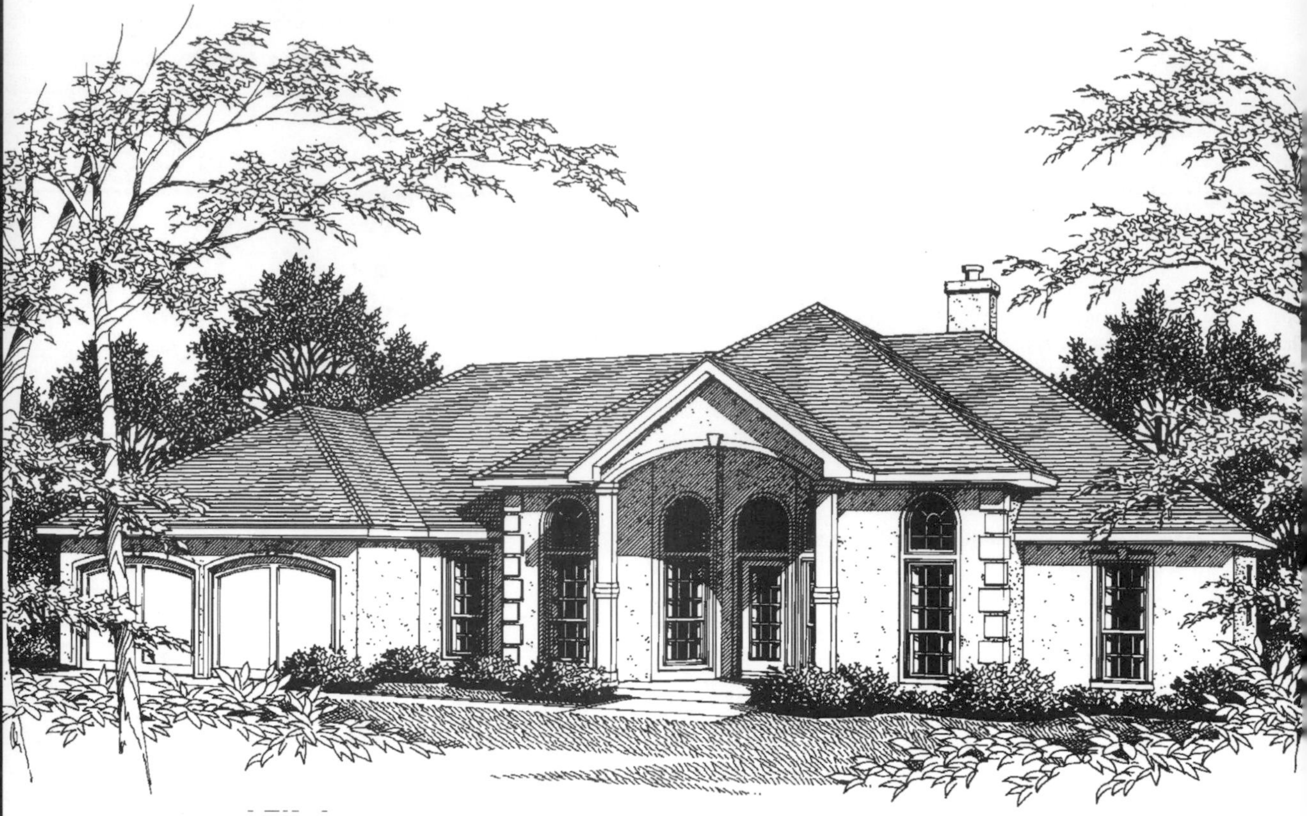

Columned Keystone Arched Entry

Price Code: E

This plan features:

- Three bedrooms
- Two full baths

Keystone arches and arched transoms above the windows

Formal Dining Room and Study flank the Foyer

Fireplace in the Great Room

Efficient Kitchen with a peninsula counter and bayed Nook

A step ceiling in the Master Suite and interesting Master Bath with a triangular area for the oval bath tub

This home is designed with crawlspace and slab foundation options

MAIN FLOOR — 2,256 SQ. FT.
GARAGE — 514 SQ. FT.

TOTAL LIVING AREA:
2,256 SQ. FT.

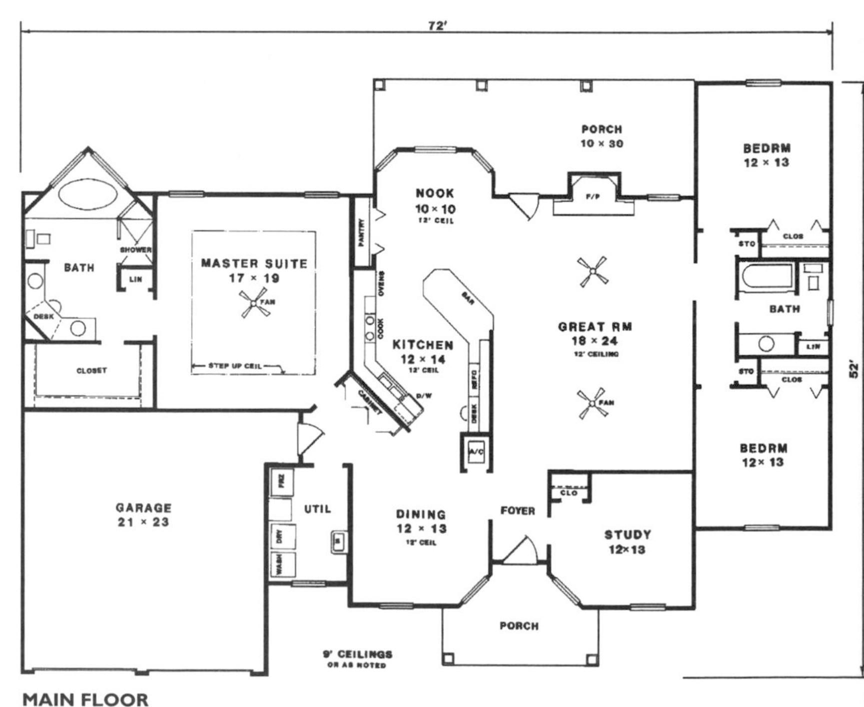
72'
PORCH 10 × 30
BEDRM 12 × 13
NOOK 10 × 10 12' CEIL
MASTER SUITE 17 × 19
BATH
SHOWER
LIN
DESK
CLOSET
STEP UP CEIL
KITCHEN 12 × 14 12' CEIL
GREAT RM 18 × 24 12' CEILING
BATH
BEDRM 12 × 13
52'
GARAGE 21 × 23
UTIL
DINING 12 × 13 12' CEIL
FOYER
STUDY 12×13
PORCH
9' CEILINGS OR AS NOTED

MAIN FLOOR

Vaulted Ceilings

PRICE CODE: E

PLAN NO.98428

'his plan features:
- ·our bedrooms
- Two full and one half baths
- vaulted ceiling crowns the Foyer and flows on into ıe Family Room
- fireplace adds a warm an cozy atmosphere to the ntire home
- nee-walls with built-in shelves and a plant shelf above eparate the Family Room from the Breakfast Room
- 'his home is designed with basement and crawlspace oundation options

ST FLOOR — 1,637 SQ. FT.
:OND FLOOR — 671 SQ. FT.
SEMENT — 1,637 SQ. FT.
RAGE — 466 SQ. FT.

TOTAL LIVING AREA:
2,308 SQ. FT.

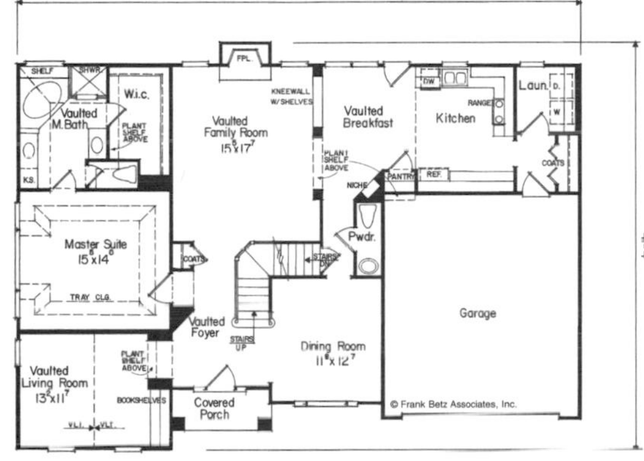

58'-0"
41'-4"
Vaulted M.Bath
W.i.c.
Vaulted Family Room 15⁵x17⁷
Vaulted Breakfast
Kitchen
Laun.
Master Suite 15x14
Pwdr.
Vaulted Foyer
Dining Room 11⁶x12⁷
Garage
Vaulted Living Room 13⁵x11⁷
Covered Porch
© Frank Betz Associates, Inc.

FIRST FLOOR

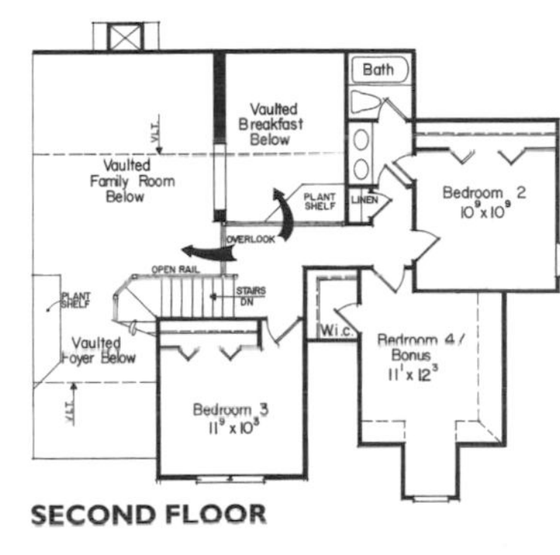

Bath
Vaulted Breakfast Below
Vaulted Family Room Below
Bedroom 2 10⁹x10⁹
Vaulted Foyer Below
Bedroom 3 11⁹x10⁸
W.i.c.
Bedroom 4/ Bonus 11¹x12³

SECOND FLOOR

Massive Curb Appeal

PRICE CODE: D

PLAN NO.98517

This plan features:
- Four bedrooms
- Two full and one half baths
- An arched two story entrances sets the luxurious stage of this fine home
- The expansive Great Room boasts a large fireplace flanked by windows
- The angled Kitchen has a large pass-thru to the Great Room
- The first floor Master Suite includes sloped ceilings and a luxurious private Bath
- This home is designed with a slab foundation

RST FLOOR — 1,472 SQ. FT.
:OND FLOOR — 703 SQ. FT.
ARAGE — 540 SQ. FT.

TOTAL LIVING AREA:
2,175 SQ. FT.

PATIO
PATIO
MSTR. BDRM. 13 X 17
GREAT ROOM 16 X 21
BRKFT. 11 X 12
STOR.
KIT. 12 X 12
GARAGE 20 X 24
M.B.
STAIRS
PANTRY
ENT.
FML. DINE 12 X 12
UTLY.
W-I-CLO.
POR.
BDRM. #2 11 X 12
BDRM. #3 10 X 10
STAIRS
BDRM. #4 12 X 12

WIDTH 58'-0"
DEPTH 39'-10"

FIRST FLOOR

SECOND FLOOR

PLAN NO. 97259

Charming Three Bedroom

PRICE CODE: A

- This plan features:
  - Three bedrooms
  - Two full baths
- Covered Porch leads into Foyer with plant shelves and Vaulted Family Room beyond
- Efficient Kitchen with Pantry, Laundry and pass-thru opens to bright Breakfast Area
- Private Master Suite offers a vaulted ceiling, walk-in closet and vaulted Master Bath
- Two secondary Bedrooms, with spacious closets, share full Bath in the hall
- This home is designed with basement and crawlspace foundation options

MAIN FLOOR — 1,222 SQ. FT.
BASEMENT — 1,218 SQ. FT.
GARAGE — 410 SQ. FT.

TOTAL LIVING AREA:
1,222 SQ. FT.

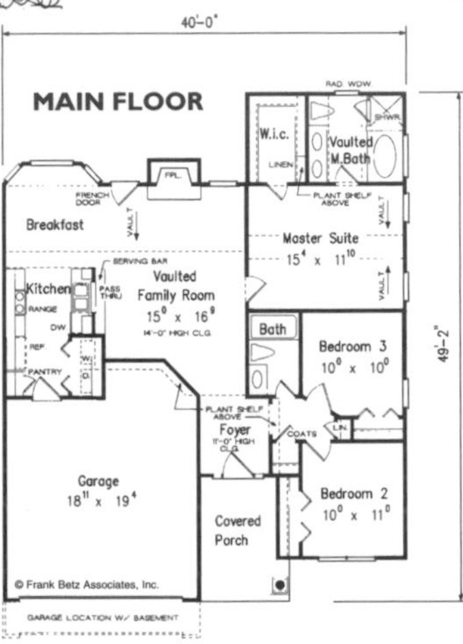
40'-0"
MAIN FLOOR
W.i.c.
Vaulted M.Bath
Breakfast
Master Suite
15⁴ x 11¹⁰
Kitchen
Vaulted Family Room
15⁰ x 16⁹
Bath
Bedroom 3
10⁰ x 10⁰
Foyer
Garage
18¹¹ x 19⁴
Covered Porch
Bedroom 2
10⁰ x 11⁰
49'-2"
© Frank Betz Associates, Inc.

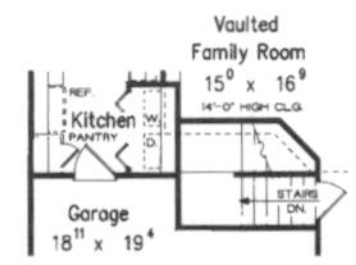
Vaulted Family Room
15⁰ x 16⁹
Kitchen
Garage
18¹¹ x 19⁴

BASEMENT STAIR LOCATION OPTION

PLAN NO. 93716

Italian Styled Exterior

PRICE CODE: F

- This plan features:
  - Four bedrooms
  - Three full and one half baths
- Ten-foot ceilings which add to the open feeling of the first floor design
- Interior columns and French doors add drama on entering the Foyer from the front Porch
- The large covered Porch at the rear extends the Living Area outdoors and also has an optional Kitchen for outdoor entertaining.
- This home is designed with a crawlspace foundation

FIRST FLOOR — 1,814 SQ. FT.
SECOND FLOOR — 884 SQ. FT.

TOTAL LIVING AREA:
2,698 SQ. FT.

54'-10"

FIRST FLOOR

optional summer kitchen
Porch
M. Bdrm.
16'6" x 13'8"
Brkfst.
11'8" x 10'0"
clos.
Family Room
19'6" x 17'6"
Util.
Ktchn.
Garage
21'6" x 21'6"
Dng. Rm.
13'6" x 11'2"
Foyer
Lvng. Rm.
11'6" x 11'6"
Porch
51'-2"

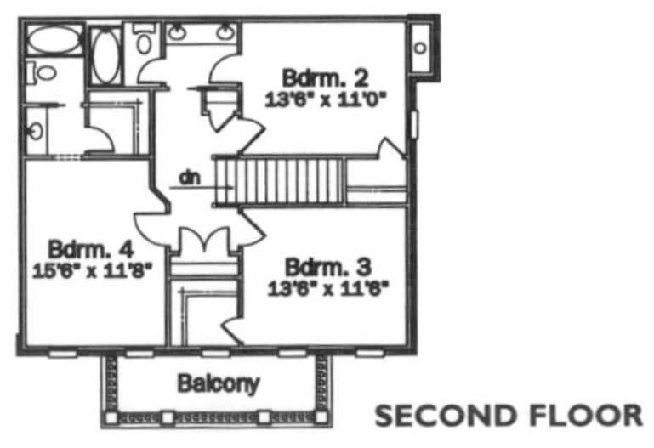
Bdrm. 2
13'6" x 11'0"
dn
Bdrm. 4
15'6" x 11'8"
Bdrm. 3
13'6" x 11'6"
Balcony

SECOND FLOOR

Country Exterior with Formal Interior

PRICE CODE: D

PLAN NO. 90451

This plan features:

- Three bedrooms
- Two full and one half baths
- Wraparound Porch leads into central Foyer and formal Living and Dining Rooms
- Large Family Room with a cozy fireplace and Deck access
- Convenient Kitchen opens to Breakfast Area, with a bay window and built-in Pantry
- Corner Master Bedroom with walk-in closet and appealing Bath
- Two additional Bedrooms plus a bonus room share a full Bath and Laundry
- This home is designed with basement and crawlspace foundation options

IST FLOOR — 1,046 SQ. FT.
COND FLOOR — 1,022 SQ. FT.
NUS — 232 SQ. FT.
SEMENT — 1,046 SQ. FT.

TOTAL LIVING AREA: 2,068 SQ. FT.

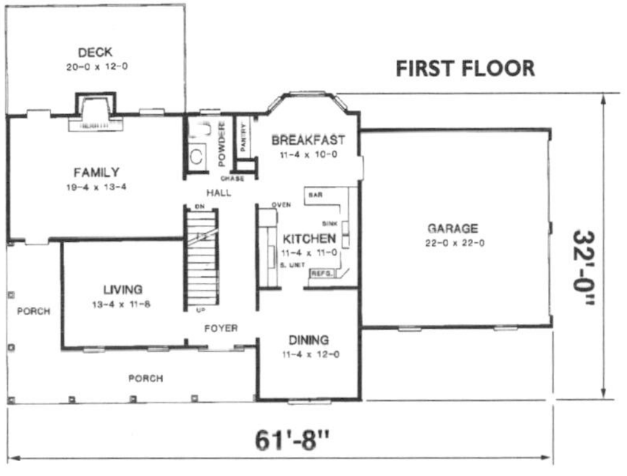
FIRST FLOOR
DECK
20-0 x 12-0
FAMILY
19-4 x 13-4
BREAKFAST
11-4 x 10-0
POWDER
PANTRY
HALL
KITCHEN
11-4 x 11-0
GARAGE
22-0 x 22-0
LIVING
13-4 x 11-8
FOYER
PORCH
DINING
11-4 x 12-0
PORCH
32'-0"
61'-8"

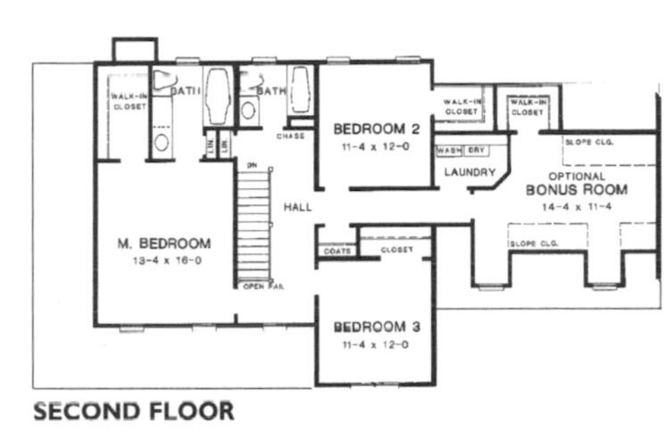
WALK-IN CLOSET
BATH
BATH
BEDROOM 2
11-4 x 12-0
WALK-IN CLOSET
WALK-IN CLOSET
LAUNDRY
OPTIONAL BONUS ROOM
14-4 x 11-4
M. BEDROOM
13-4 x 16-0
HALL
COATS
CLOSET
BEDROOM 3
11-4 x 12-0
SECOND FLOOR

Decorative Ceilings Inside

PRICE CODE: A

PLAN NO. 98468

This plan features:

- Three bedrooms
- Two full baths
- The Family Room has a vaulted ceiling, a corner fireplace, and a French door to the rear yard
- The Breakfast Nook is brightened by windows on two of its walls
- The galley Kitchen has a Pantry, and a serving bar into the Family Room
- The Master Suite has a tray ceiling, a walk-in closet, and a private Bath
- Two secondary Bedrooms have ample closet space, bright front wall windows, and one has a vaulted ceiling
- This home has a two-car Garage with Storage Space
- This home is designed with basement, slab, and crawlspace foundation options

AIN FLOOR — 1,104 SQ. FT.
ASEMENT — 1,104 SQ. FT.
ARAGE — 400 SQ. FT.

TOTAL LIVING AREA: 1,104 SQ. FT.

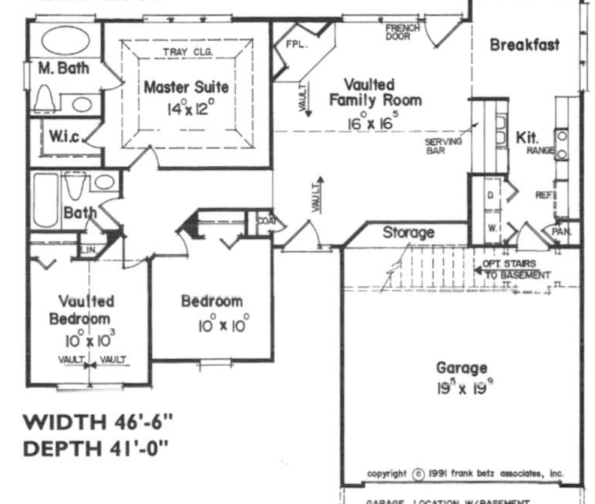
MAIN FLOOR
M. Bath
TRAY CLG.
Master Suite
14⁰x12⁰
FPL.
FRENCH DOOR
Vaulted Family Room
16⁰x16⁵
Breakfast
W.i.c
SERVING BAR
Kit.
RANGE
Bath
Storage
OPT STAIRS TO BASEMENT
Vaulted Bedroom
10⁰x10³
Bedroom
10⁰x10⁰
Garage
19⁵x19⁹
WIDTH 46'-6"
DEPTH 41'-0"
copyright © 1991 frank betz associates, inc.
GARAGE LOCATION W/BASEMENT

PLAN NO. 96505

Private Master Suite

PRICE CODE: D

- This plan features:
  - — Three bedrooms
  - — Two full and one half baths
- Secluded Master Bedroom Suite tucked into the rear left corner of the home with a five-piece Bath and two walk-in closets
- Two additional Bedrooms at the opposite side of the home sharing the full Bath in the hall
- Expansive Living Room highlighted by a corner fireplace and access to the rear Porch
- Kitchen is located between the bright, bayed Nook and the formal Dining Room providing ease in serving
- This home is designed with crawlspace and slab foundation options

MAIN FLOOR — 2,069 SQ. FT.
GARAGE — 481 SQ. FT.

TOTAL LIVING AREA:
2,069 SQ. FT.

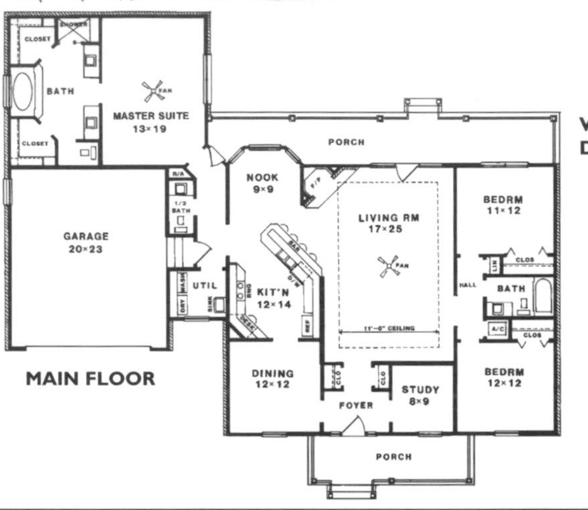
CLOSET
SHOWER
BATH
FAN
MASTER SUITE
13×19
CLOSET
PORCH
NOOK
9×9
LIVING RM
17×25
BEDRM
11×12
GARAGE
20×23
1/2 BATH
UTIL
KIT'N
12×14
HALL
BATH
CLOS
11'-0" CEILING
DINING
12×12
FOYER
STUDY
8×9
BEDRM
12×12
PORCH
MAIN FLOOR

WIDTH 70'-0"
DEPTH 58'-0"

PLAN NO. 98486

Sunken Family Room

PRICE CODE: E

- This plan features:
  - — Four bedrooms
  - — Two full and one half baths
- A grand two-story Foyer creates an impressive Entry
- The see-through fireplace in the Family Room is shared with the Keeping Room
- A terrific informal Living Area is created by the open floor plan between the Kitchen, Breakfast Room and Keeping Room
- The Master Suite has a tray ceiling above the Bedroom, an optional Sitting Room, a vaulted ceiling above the Master Bath and a walk-in closet
- This home is designed with basement and crawlspace foundation options

FIRST FLOOR — 1,223 SQ. FT.
SECOND FLOOR — 1,163 SQ. FT.
BASEMENT — 1,223 SQ. FT.
GARAGE — 400 SQ. FT.
BONUS — 204 SQ. FT.

TOTAL LIVING AREA:
2,386 SQ. FT.

50'- 0"
Breakfast
Keeping Room 12^{10} x 20^{0}
Family Room 19^{0} x 14^{9}
Kitchen
Dining Room 11^{0} x 12^{2}
Two Story Foyer
Laundry
Garage 19^{5} x 21^{9}
Covered Porch
48'- 0"

FIRST FLOOR

Bedroom 4
12^{10} x 11^{0}
W.i.c.
Bedroom 3
11^{0} x 12^{0}
Bath
Vaulted
M. Bath
Master Suite
17^{0} x 13^{9}
Bedroom 2
11^{0} x 12^{0}
Foyer Below
Opt.
Sitting Room
11^{5} x 16^{9}
SECOND FLOOR

To order your Blueprints, call 1-800-235-5700

PLAN NO. 24990

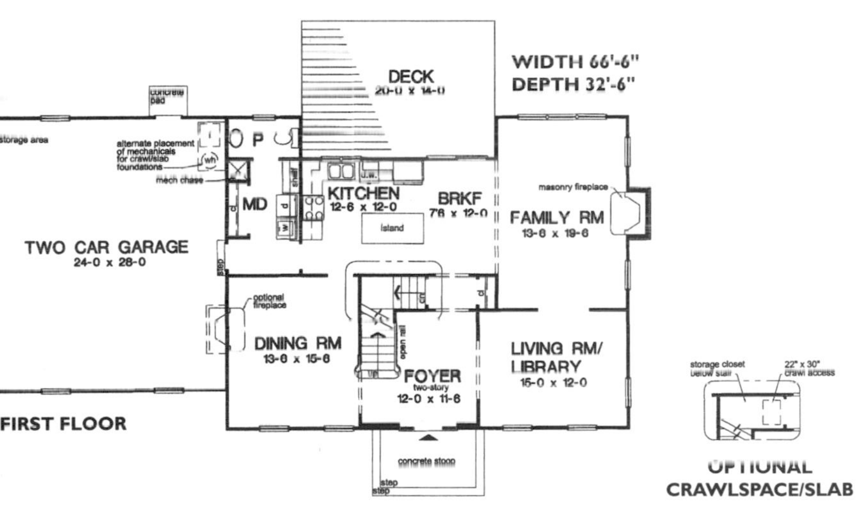

DECK
20-0 x 14-0
WIDTH 66'-6"
DEPTH 32'-6"
concrete pad
storage area
alternate placement of mechanicals for crawl/slab foundations
mech chase
P
MD
KITCHEN
12-6 x 12-0
island
BRKF
7'6 x 12-0
masonry fireplace
FAMILY RM
13-6 x 19-6
TWO CAR GARAGE
24-0 x 28-0
optional fireplace
DINING RM
13-6 x 15-6
open rail
FOYER
two-story
12-0 x 11-6
LIVING RM/
LIBRARY
15-0 x 12-0
concrete stoop
step
FIRST FLOOR
storage closet below stair
22" x 30" crawl access
OPTIONAL
CRAWLSPACE/SLAB

shwr
glass
MB
w/p tub
lin
tub/shwr
B
BR #2
13-5 x 15-0
w.i.c.
open railing
balc
cl
optional fireplace
open railing
open rail
open to below
MSTR BR
13-6 x 19-0
BR #3
15-4 x 12-0
SECOND FLOOR

Optional Fireplaces

Price Code: E

- This plan features:
- — Three bedrooms
- — Two full and one half baths
- The traditional design of this home's facade is welcoming, like an old friend
- A masonry fireplace in the Family Room provides a warm atmosphere in which family can gather
- An optional fireplace would embellish the already impressive Master Suite and formal Dining Room
- A convenient Storage Area is located in the two-car Garage
- This home is designed with a basement foundation

FIRST FLOOR — 1,280 SQ. FT.
SECOND FLOOR — 1,210 SQ. FT.
BASEMENT — 1,270 SQ. FT.
GARAGE — 698 SQ. FT.

TOTAL LIVING AREA:
2,490 SQ. FT.

PLAN NO. 65000

Lakeside Look

Price Code: A

- This plan features:
- — Three bedrooms
- — Two full baths
- The combined Kitchen/Dining/Family Area is the heart of this cozy cottage
- Twin sliders lead to elevated screened and open Porches
- The first floor Bedroom is tucked behind the staircase with easy access to the Bathroom
- This home is designed with a basement foundation

FIRST FLOOR — 895 SQ. FT.
SECOND FLOOR — 576 SQ. FT.
BASEMENT — 895 SQ. FT.

TOTAL LIVING AREA:
1,471 SQ. FT.

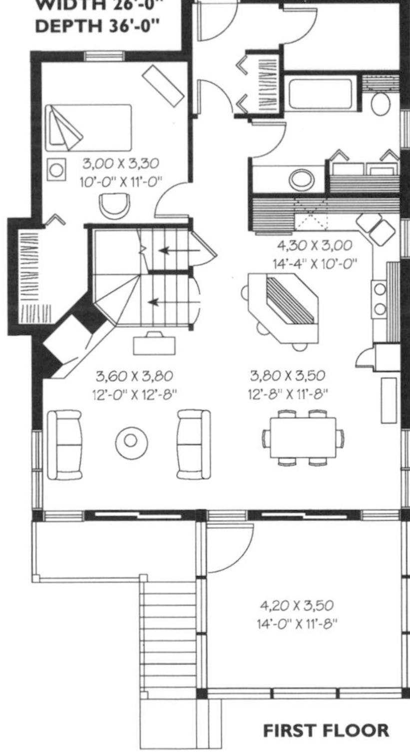
WIDTH 26'-0"
DEPTH 36'-0"
3,00 X 3,30
10'-0" X 11'-0"
4,30 X 3,00
14'-4" X 10'-0"
3,60 X 3,80
12'-0" X 12'-8"
3,80 X 3,50
12'-8" X 11'-8"
4,20 X 3,50
14'-0" X 11'-8"
FIRST FLOOR

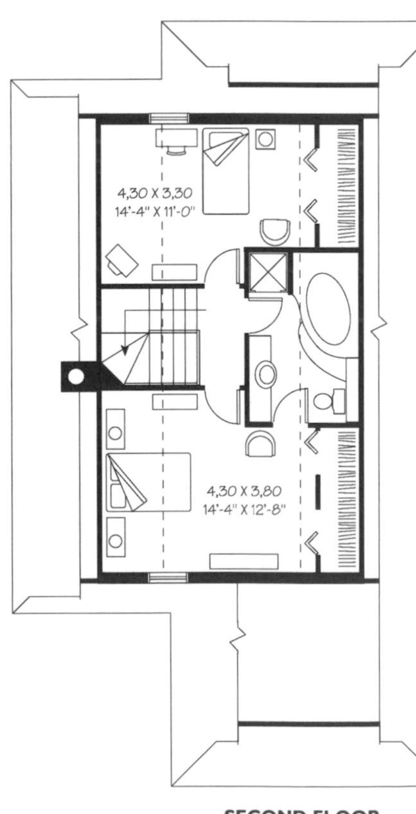
4,30 X 3,30
14'-4" X 11'-0"
4,30 X 3,80
14'-4" X 12'-8"
SECOND FLOOR

PLAN NO. 93212

An Old-Fashioned Country Feeling

Price Code: D

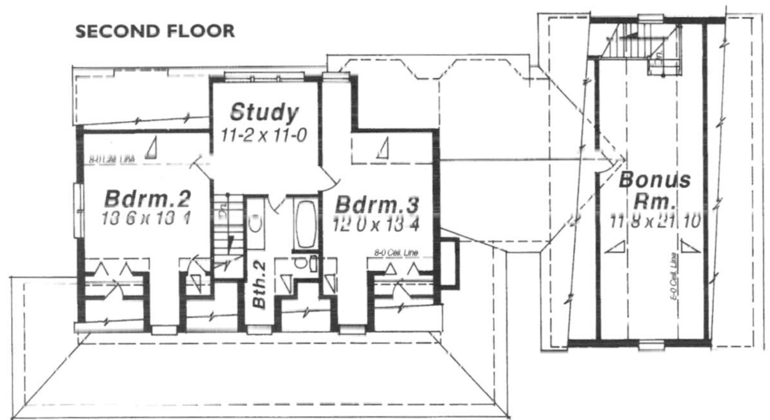

SECOND FLOOR
Study
11-2 x 11-0
Bdrm.2
13-6 x 13-1
Bdrm.3
12-0 x 13-4
Bth.2
8-0 Ceil. Line
Bonus Rm.
11-8 x 21-10

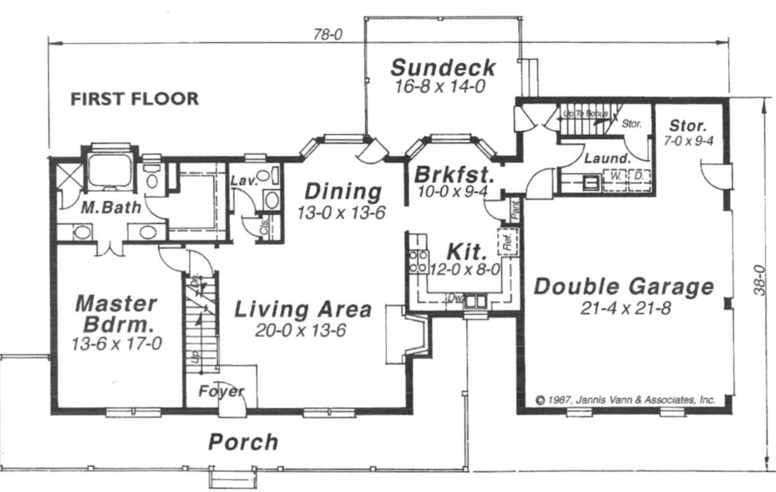

FIRST FLOOR
78-0
Sundeck
16-8 x 14-0
Stor.
7-0 x 9-4
Laund.
Brkfst.
10-0 x 9-4
Dining
13-0 x 13-6
Lav.
M.Bath
Kit.
12-0 x 8-0
Double Garage
21-4 x 21-8
Master Bdrm.
13-6 x 17-0
Living Area
20-0 x 13-6
Foyer
Porch
38-0
© 1987, Jannis Vann & Associates, Inc.

- This plan features:
  - Three bedrooms
  - Two full and one half baths
- A large Living Room with a cozy fireplace opens to the Dining Room for easy entertaining
- A formal Dining Room with a bay window and direct access to the Sun Deck
- A U-shaped Kitchen, efficiently arranged with ample work space and a Pantry
- A first floor Master Bedroom with an elegant Bath complete with jacuzzi, two vanities and a walk-in closet
- This home is designed with basement, slab and crawlspace foundation options

First floor — 1,362 sq. ft.
Second floor — 729 sq. ft.
Bonus room — 384 sq. ft.
Garage — 559 sq. ft.

Total Living Area:
2,091 sq. ft.

One Floor Living

Price Code: A

- This plan features:
- — Three bedrooms
- — Two full baths
- A covered front Porch is supported by columns and accented by balusters
- The Living Room features a cozy fireplace and a ceiling fan
- The Kitchen is distinguished by an angled serving bar
- The Dining Room is convenient to the Kitchen and accessed the rear Porch
- The Master Bedroom has a walk-in closet and a private Bath
- A two-car Garage with storage space is located in the rear of the home
- This home is designed with crawlspace and slab foundation options

MAIN FLOOR — 1,247 SQ. FT.
GARAGE — 512 SQ. FT.

TOTAL LIVING AREA:
1,247 SQ. FT.

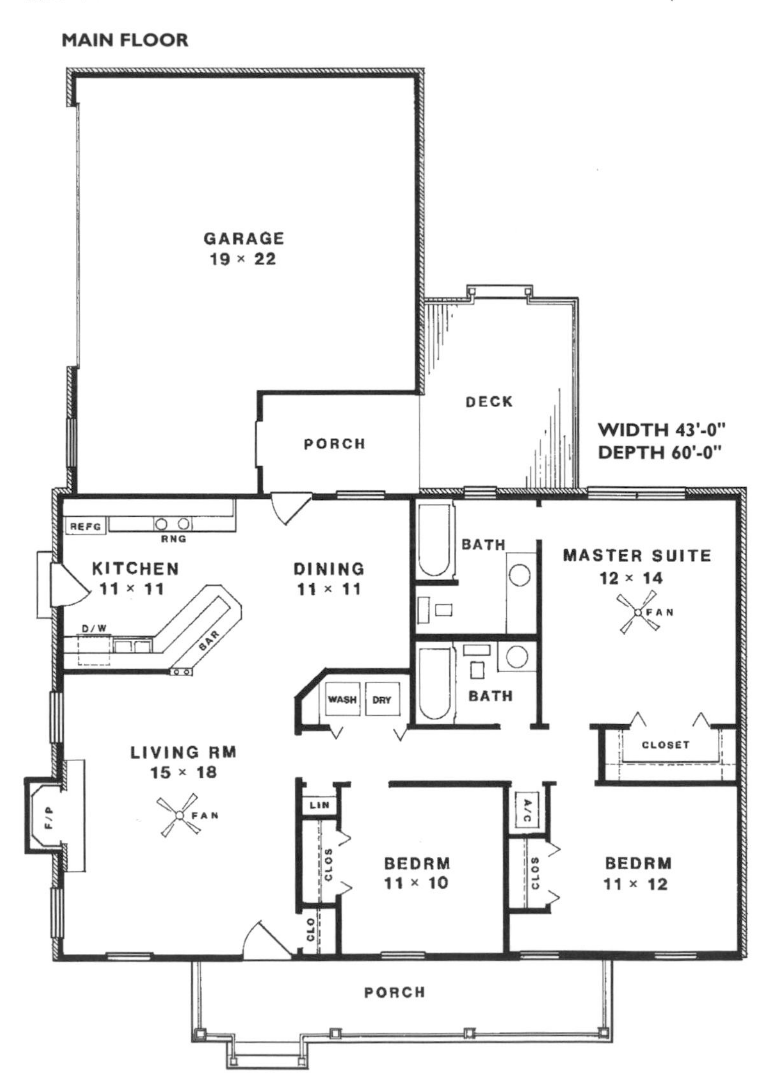
MAIN FLOOR
GARAGE
19 × 22
DECK
PORCH
WIDTH 43'-0"
DEPTH 60'-0"
REFG
RNG
KITCHEN
11 × 11
DINING
11 × 11
D/W
BAR
BATH
MASTER SUITE
12 × 14
FAN
WASH
DRY
BATH
CLOSET
LIVING RM
15 × 18
F/P
FAN
LIN
CLOS
BEDRM
11 × 10
A/C
CLOS
BEDRM
11 × 12
CLO
PORCH

To order your Blueprints, call 1-800-235-5700

Varied Roof Heights Create Interesting Lines

PRICE CODE: B

PLAN NO.90601

his plan features:
- hree bedrooms
- wo full and one half baths
- spacious Family Room with a heat-circulating replace, which is visible from the Foyer
- large Kitchen with a cooktop island opening into e Dinette
- Master Suite with his and her closets and a private laster Bath
- wo additional Bedrooms which share a full hall Bath
- ormal Dining and Living Rooms, flowing into each her for easy entertaining
- his home is designed with basement and slab oundation options

IN FLOOR — 1,613 SQ. FT.
EMENT — 1,060 SQ. FT.
RAGE — 461 SQ. FT.

TOTAL LIVING AREA:
1,613 SQ. FT.

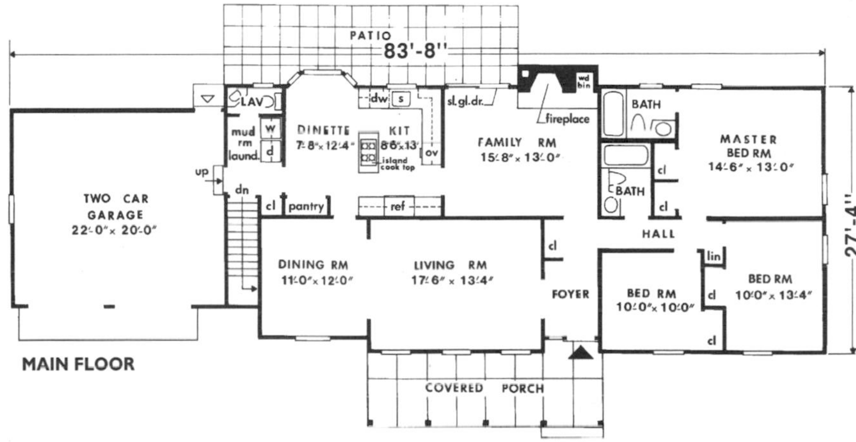
PATIO
83'-8"
27'-4"
LAV
mud rm laund.
DINETTE 7'-8"x 12'-4"
KIT 8'-6"x 13'
island cook top
sl.gl.dr.
fireplace
FAMILY RM 15'-8" x 13'-0"
BATH
MASTER BED RM 14'-6" x 13'-0"
TWO CAR GARAGE 22'-0"x 20'-0"
pantry
ref
HALL
DINING RM 11'-0"x 12'-0"
LIVING RM 17'-6" x 13'-4"
FOYER
BED RM 10'-0"x 10'-0"
BED RM 10'-0" x 13'-4"
MAIN FLOOR
COVERED PORCH

Windows Distinguish Design

PRICE CODE: J

PLAN NO.98438

his plan features:
- ive bedrooms
- our full and one half baths
- ight shines into the Dining and Living Room through eir respective elegant windows
- Hall through the Butler's Pantry leads the way into the reakfast Nook
- he two-story Family Room has a fireplace with built-in ookcases on either side
- he upstairs Master Suite has a Sitting Room and a rench door that leads into the Master Bath
- here are three additional Bedrooms upstairs
- his home is designed with basement and crawlspace oundation options

ST FLOOR — 1,786 SQ. FT.
OND FLOOR — 1,739 SQ. FT.
EMENT — 1,786 SQ. FT.
RAGE — 704 SQ. FT.

TOTAL LIVING AREA:
3,525 SQ. FT.

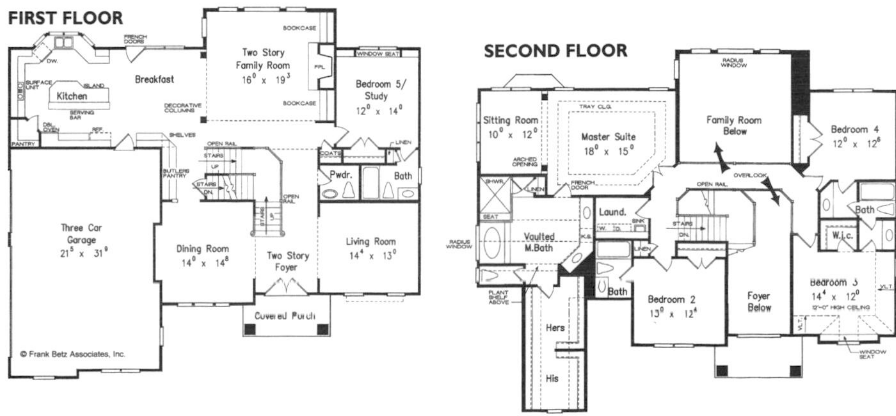
FIRST FLOOR
Breakfast
Kitchen
Two Story Family Room 16⁰ x 19³
Bedroom 5/ Study 12⁰ x 14⁰
Pwdr.
Bath
Three Car Garage 21⁵ x 31⁹
Dining Room 14⁰ x 14⁸
Two Story Foyer
Living Room 14⁴ x 13⁰
Covered Porch
© Frank Betz Associates, Inc.
SECOND FLOOR
Sitting Room 10⁰ x 12⁰
Master Suite 18⁰ x 15⁰
Family Room Below
Bedroom 4 12⁰ x 12⁶
Laund.
Vaulted M.Bath
Bath
Bedroom 2 13⁰ x 12⁴
Foyer Below
Bedroom 3 14⁴ x 12⁰
Hers
His

PLAN NO. 96506

Attractive Ceiling Treatmen and Open Layout

PRICE CODE: B

- This plan features:
  - — Three bedrooms
  - — Two full and one half baths
- Great Room and Master Suite with step-up ceiling treatments
- A cozy fireplace providing warm focal point in the Great Room
- Open layout between Kitchen, Dining and Great Roo lending a more spacious feeling
- Five-piece, private Bath and walk-in closet pamperin Master Suite
- Two additional Bedrooms located at opposite end of home from the Master Suite
- Master Suite sharing the full Bath in the hall
- This home is designed with crawlspace and slab foundation

MAIN FLOOR — 1,654 SQ. FT.
GARAGE — 480 SQ. FT.

TOTAL LIVING AREA:
1,654 SQ. FT.

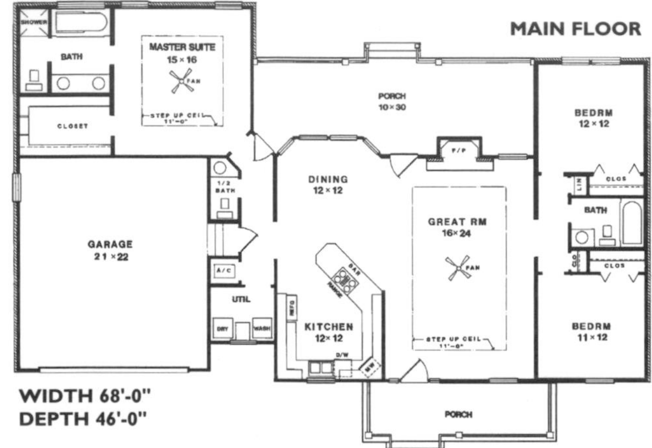
MAIN FLOOR
MASTER SUITE
15×16
BATH
CLOSET
PORCH
10×30
BEDRM
12×12
DINING
12×12
GREAT RM
16×24
GARAGE
21×22
BATH
KITCHEN
12×12
BEDRM
11×12
PORCH
WIDTH 68'-0"
DEPTH 46'-0"

PLAN NO. 97239

Impressive Presence

PRICE CODE: G

- This plan features:
  - — Four bedrooms
  - — Three full and one half baths
- The angled Garage combines with varied rooflines tc create an impressive presence
- The Living Room has a vaulted ceiling and a beautif window
- The Dining Room features a boxed bay window
- Enter the Family Room through and arched opening from the Foyer
- The Kitchen is open to the Nook and has a center isl
- The Master Suite is secluded behind the Garage on t first floor
- Upstairs find three Bedrooms all with walk in closets
- An optional Bonus Room is located over the Garage
- This home is designed with basement and crawlspac foundation options

FIRST FLOOR — 1,904 SQ. FT.
SECOND FLOOR — 860 SQ. FT.
BONUS — 388 SQ. FT.
BASEMENT — 1,904 SQ. FT.
GARAGE — 575 SQ. FT.

TOTAL LIVING AREA:
2,764 SQ. FT.

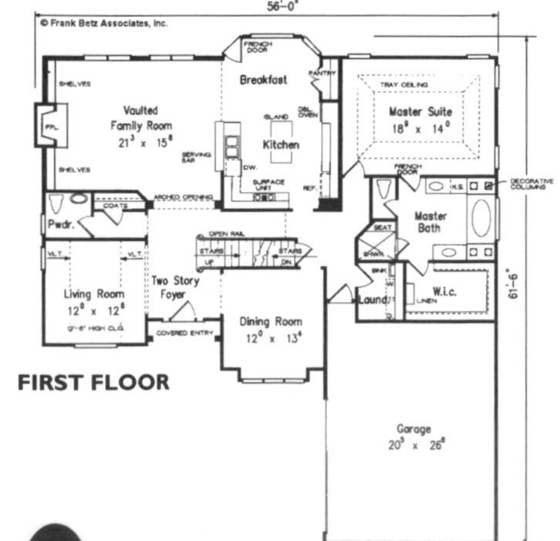
© Frank Betz Associates, Inc.
56'-0"
Breakfast
Vaulted
Family Room
Kitchen
Master Suite
Master
Bath
Pwdr.
Living Room
Two Story
Foyer
Dining Room
W.i.c.
Laund.
Garage
61'-6"
FIRST FLOOR

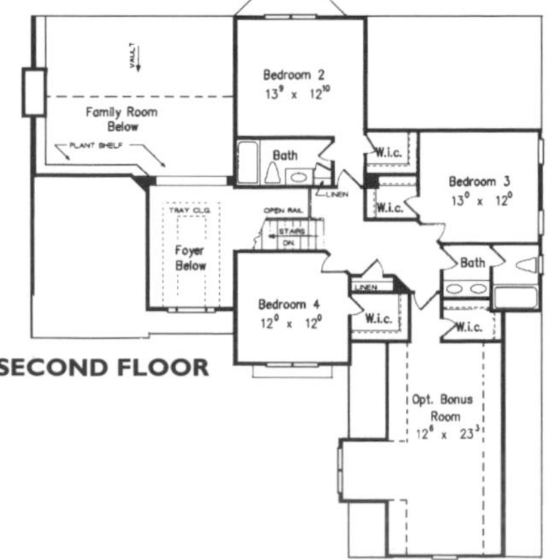
Family Room
Below
Bedroom 2
Bath
W.i.c.
Bedroom 3
Foyer
Below
Bedroom 4
Bath
W.i.c.
Opt. Bonus
Room
SECOND FLOOR

PLAN NO. 91323

Duplex for a Sloping Lot

Price Code: G

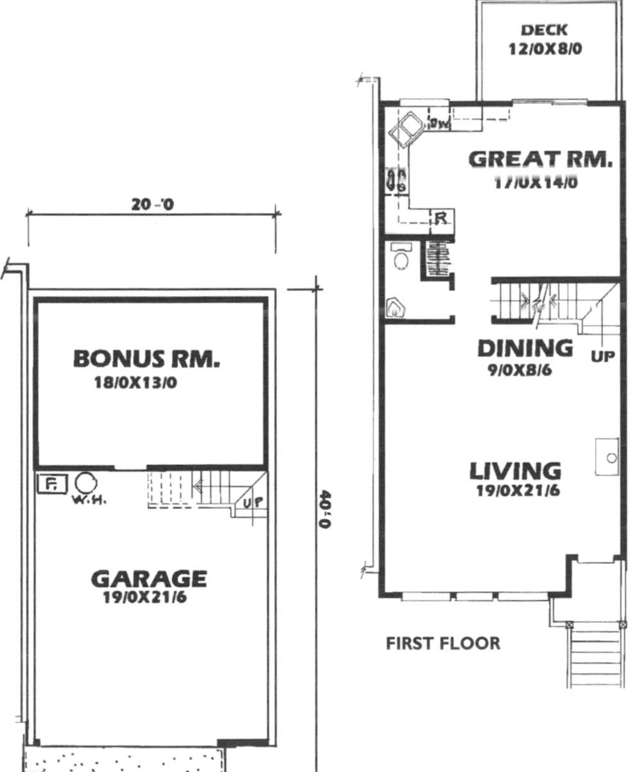
WIDTH 20'-0"
DEPTH 40'-0"
DECK
12/0X8/0
GREAT RM.
17/0X14/0
DINING
9/0X8/6
UP
LIVING
19/0X21/6
FIRST FLOOR
20'-0
BONUS RM.
18/0X13/0
W.H.
UP
GARAGE
19/0X21/6
40'-0
LOWER FLOOR

BEDRM
9/6X10/6
BEDRM
9/6X11/6
MASTER DR.
13/6X19/0
SECOND FLOOR

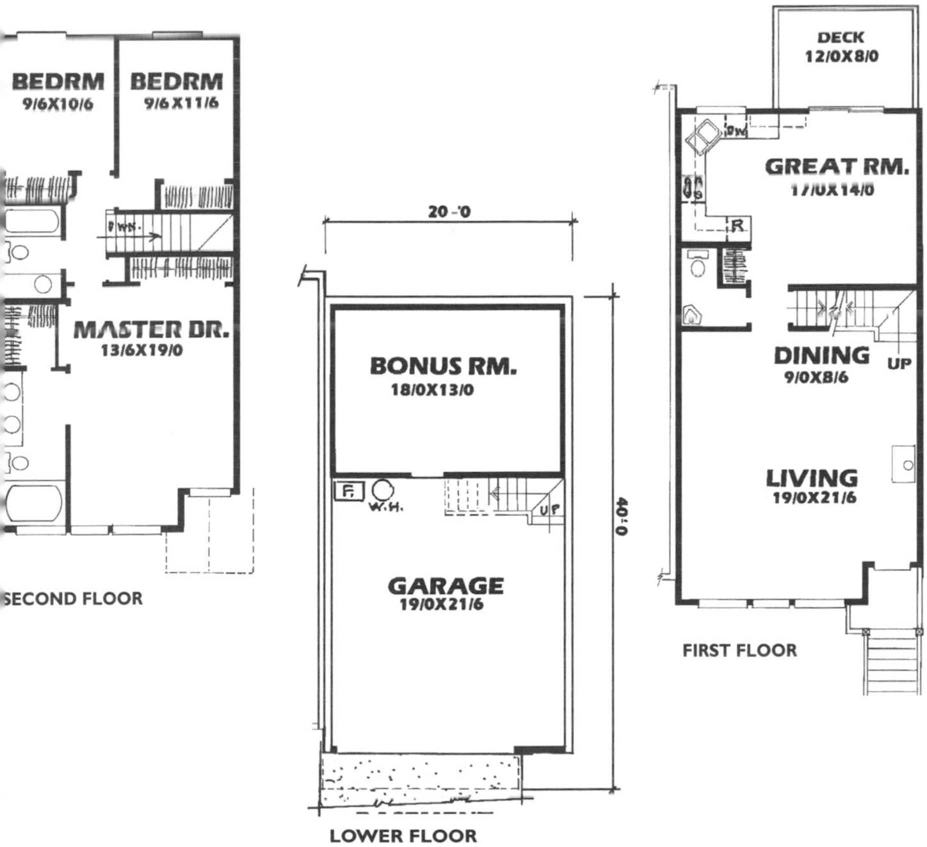

- This plan features:
  - Three bedrooms
  - Two full and one half baths
- Multiple windows front and back provide lots of natural light
- Expansive Living/Dining Area with cozy fireplace for easy entertaining
- U-shaped Kitchen opens to Great Room and Deck beyond for expanded living space
- Two additional Bedrooms with ample closets, share a full Bath
- Bonus room behind Garage available for many uses
- This home is designed with a basement foundation

FIRST FLOOR — 788 SQ. FT.
SECOND FLOOR — 733 SQ. FT.

TOTAL LIVING AREA:
1,521 SQ. FT.

PLAN NO. 92501

European Style

Price Code: F

- This plan features:
- — Four bedrooms
- — Three full and one half baths
- Central Foyer between spacious Living and Dining Rooms with arched windows
- Hub Kitchen with extended counter and nearby Utility/Garage Entry, easily serves Breakfast Area and Dining Room
- Spacious Den with a hearth fireplace between built-ins and sliding glass doors to Porch
- Master Bedroom wing with decorative ceiling, plush Bath with two walk-in closets
- This home is designed with crawlspace and slab foundation options

MAIN FLOOR — 2,727 SQ. FT.
GARAGE — 569 SQ. FT.

TOTAL LIVING AREA:
2,727 SQ. FT.

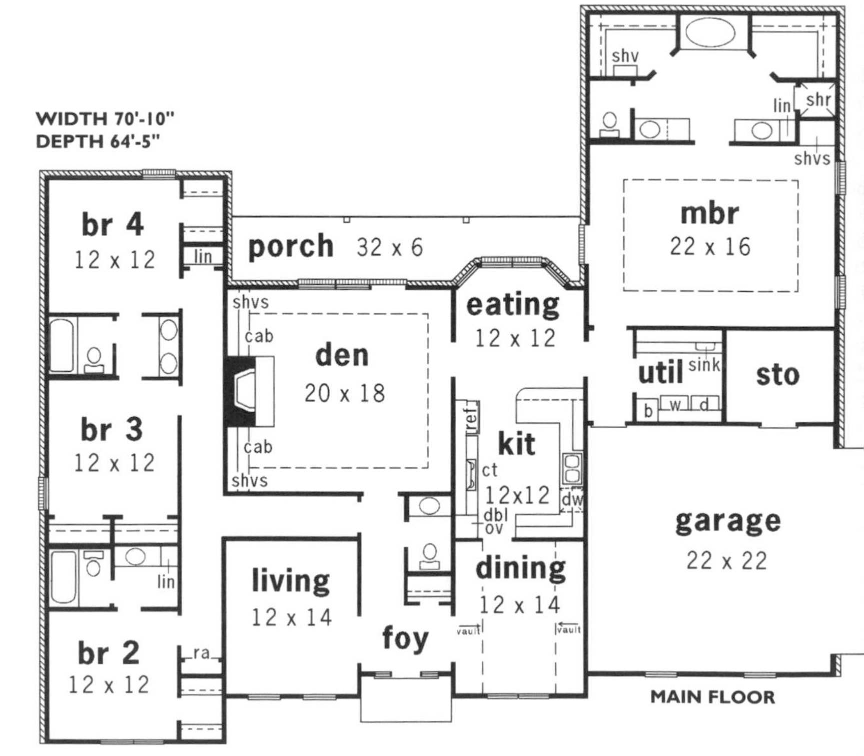

WIDTH 70'-10"
DEPTH 64'-5"
br 4
12 x 12
lin
porch 32 x 6
shv
lin
shr
shvs
mbr
22 x 16
shvs
cab
den
20 x 18
cab
shvs
eating
12 x 12
util
sink
sto
b
w
d
br 3
12 x 12
ref
kit
ct
12x12
dw
dbl
ov
garage
22 x 22
lin
living
12 x 14
dining
12 x 14
vault
vault
br 2
12 x 12
ra
foy
MAIN FLOOR

Moderate Ranch

PRICE CODE: C

PLAN NO.90441

is plan features:
- ree bedrooms
- vo full baths
- large Great Room with a vaulted ceiling and a stone eplace with bookshelves on either side
- spacious Kitchen, with ample cabinet space, nveniently located next to the large Dining Room
- Master Suite with a large Bath with a garden tub, uble vanity, and a walk-in closet
- vo other large Bedrooms, each with a walk-in closet d access to the full Bath
- is home is designed with basement, slab, and crawl- ace foundation options

N FLOOR — 1,811 SQ. FT.
EMENT — 1,811 SQ. FT.
AGE — 484 SQ. FT.

TOTAL LIVING AREA:
1,811 SQ. FT.

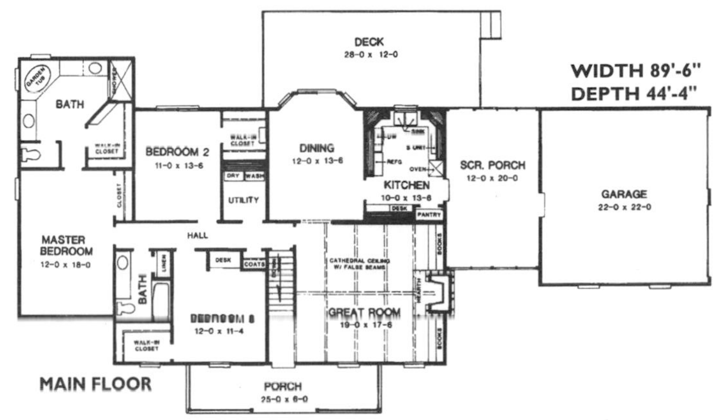
WIDTH 89'-6"
DEPTH 44'-4"
DECK 28-0 x 12-0
BATH
BEDROOM 2 11-0 x 13-6
DINING 12-0 x 13-6
KITCHEN 10-0 x 13-6
SCR. PORCH 12-0 x 20-0
GARAGE 22-0 x 22-0
MASTER BEDROOM 12-0 x 18-0
UTILITY
HALL
BATH
BEDROOM 3 12-0 x 11-4
GREAT ROOM 19-0 x 17-6
MAIN FLOOR
PORCH 25-0 x 6-0

Cozy Yet Roomy

PRICE CODE: A

PLAN NO.98444

his plan features:
- hree bedrooms
- wo full and one half baths
- warm and cozy fireplace highlights the Great Room
- he Dining Room and the Kitchen are adjoined, giving e living area a larger feel
- he Master Bedroom has a tray ceiling and a vaulted iling tops the Master Bath
- his home is designed with basement, slab, and awlspace foundation options

ST FLOOR — 628 SQ. FT.
OND FLOOR — 660 SQ. FT.
EMENT — 628 SQ. FT.
AGE — 424 SQ. FT.

TOTAL LIVING AREA:
1,288 SQ. FT.

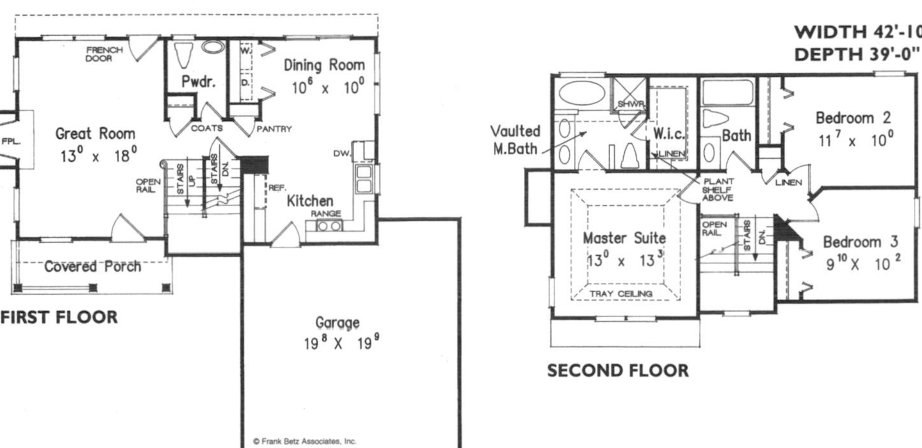
WIDTH 42'-10"
DEPTH 39'-0"
Great Room 13° x 18°
Pwdr.
Dining Room 10⁶ x 10°
Kitchen
Covered Porch
FIRST FLOOR
Garage 19⁸ X 19⁹
Vaulted M.Bath
W.i.c.
Bath
Bedroom 2 11⁷ x 10°
Master Suite 13° x 13³
TRAY CEILING
Bedroom 3 9¹⁰ X 10²
SECOND FLOOR
© Frank Betz Associates, Inc.

PLAN NO.96513

A Modern Slant On A Country Theme

Price Code: B

- This plan features:
- —Three bedrooms
- —Two full and one half baths
- Country-styled front Porch highlighting exterior enhanced by dormer windows
- Great Room accented by a quaint, corner fireplace and a ceiling fan
- Dining Room flowing from the Great Room for easy entertaining
- Kitchen graced by natural light from attractive bay window and a convenient snack bar for meals on the go
- Master Suite secluded in separate wing for total privacy
- This home is designed with crawlspace and slab foundation options

MAIN FLOOR — 1,648 SQ. FT.
GARAGE — 479 SQ. FT.

TOTAL LIVING AREA:
1,648 SQ. FT.

MAIN FLOOR

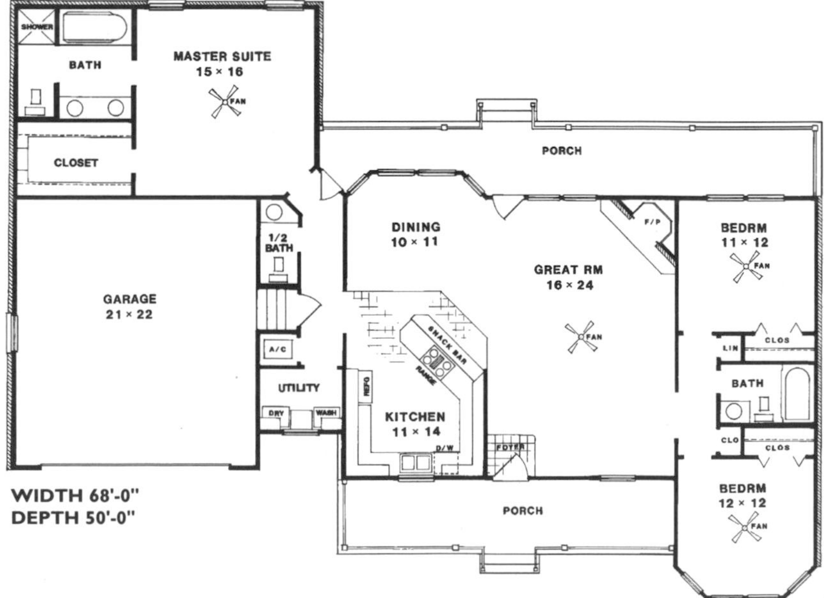
SHOWER
BATH
MASTER SUITE
15 × 16
FAN
CLOSET
PORCH
DINING
10 × 11
GREAT RM
16 × 24
F/P
BEDRM
11 × 12
1/2 BATH
GARAGE
21 × 22
SNACK BAR
RANGE
A/C
UTILITY
DRY
WASH
REFG
KITCHEN
11 × 14
D/W
FOYER
LIN
CLOS
BATH
CLO
CLOS
BEDRM
12 × 12
PORCH
WIDTH 68'-0"
DEPTH 50'-0"

Easy Everyday Living and Entertaining

PRICE CODE: B

ıis plan features:
- hree bedrooms
- wo full baths
- ʼont entrance accented by segmented arches, ꞁdelight and transom windows
- pen Living Room with focal point fireplace, et bar and access to Patio
- ining Area open to both the Living Room ıd the Kitchen
- ficient Kitchen with a cooktop island, alk-in Pantry and Utility Area with a Garage Entry
- ırge walk-in closet, double vanity Bath and access to ıtio featured in the Master Bedroom Suite
- wo additional Bedrooms share a double vanity Bath
- ıis home is designed with basement, slab and awlspace foundation options
- N FLOOR — 1,664 SQ. FT.
- EMENT — 1,600 SQ. FT.
- ꝚAGE — 440 SQ. FT

TOTAL LIVING AREA:
1,664 SQ. FT.

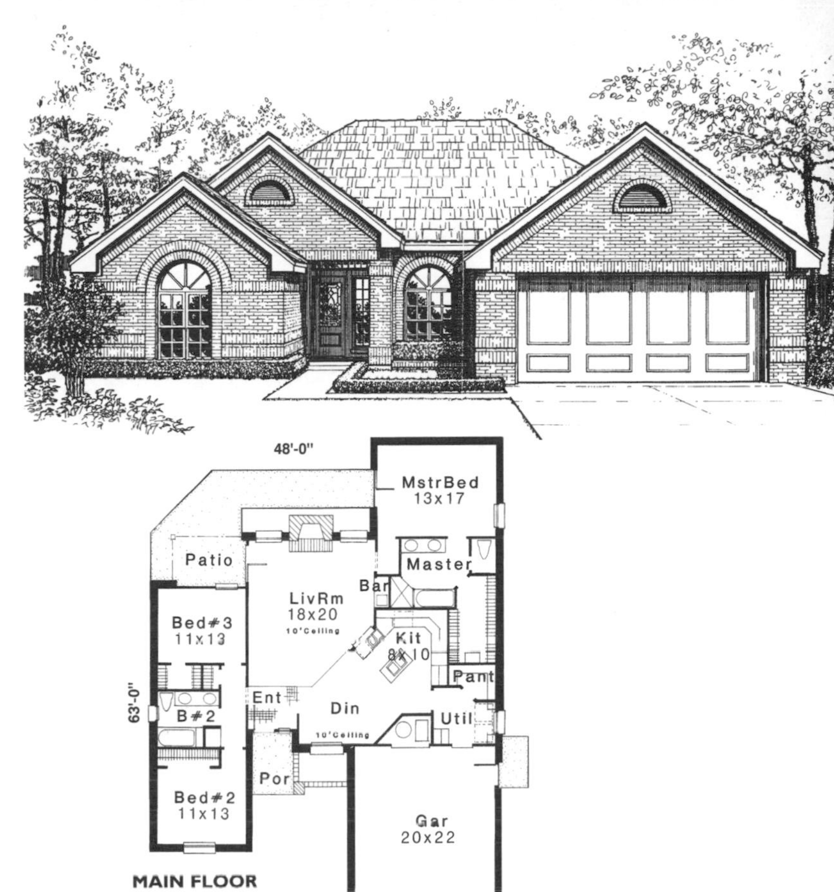

48'-0"
MstrBed
13x17
Patio
Master
Bar
LivRm
18x20
10'Ceiling
Bed#3
11x13
Kit
8x10
Pant
63'-0"
Ent
B#2
Din
Util
10'Ceiling
Por
Bed#2
11x13
Gar
20x22
MAIN FLOOR

PLAN NO.92238

Easy Living

PRICE CODE: A

his plan features:
- Three bedrooms
- Two full baths
- he front Porch spans the width of the home
- fireplace warms the Family Room
- he U-shaped Kitchen has an island in the center
- ll of the Bedrooms have ample closet space
- he Carport has a connected Storage Space
- his home is designed with crawlspace and slab oundation
- IN FLOOR — 1,333 SQ. FT.

TOTAL LIVING AREA:
1,333 SQ. FT

PLAN NO.93453

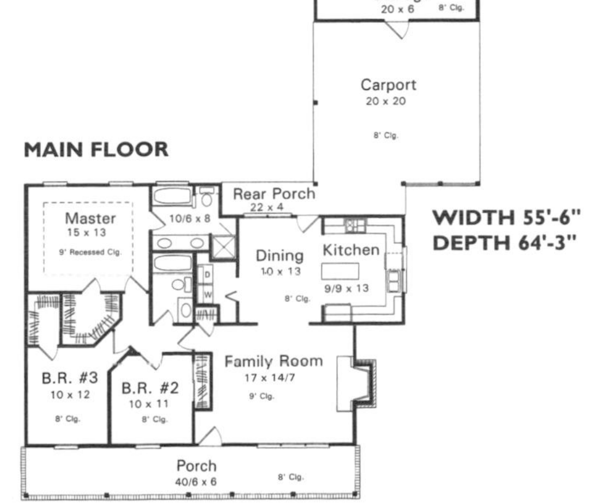

Storage
20 x 6
8' Clg.
Carport
20 x 20
8' Clg.
MAIN FLOOR
Rear Porch
22 x 4
Master
15 x 13
9' Recessed Clg.
10/6 x 8
Dining
10 x 13
8' Clg.
Kitchen
9/9 x 13
WIDTH 55'-6"
DEPTH 64'-3"
B.R. #3
10 x 12
8' Clg.
B.R. #2
10 x 11
8' Clg.
Family Room
17 x 14/7
9' Clg.
Porch
40/6 x 6
8' Clg.

PLAN NO. 90458

Two-Story Farmhouse

Price Code: E

- This plan features:
- — Three bedrooms
- — Two full and one half baths
- The wraparound Porch gives a nostalgic appeal to this home
- The Great Room with fireplace is accessed directly from the Foyer
- The formal Dining Room has direct access to the efficient Kitchen
- An island, double sink, plenty of counter and cabinet space, and a built-in Pantry complete the Kitchen
- The second floor Master Suite has a five-piece, private Bath
- This home is designed with basement and crawlspace foundation options

FIRST FLOOR — 1,125 SQ. FT.
SECOND FLOOR — 1,138 SQ. FT.
BASEMENT — 1,125 SQ. FT.

TOTAL LIVING AREA:
2,263 SQ. FT.

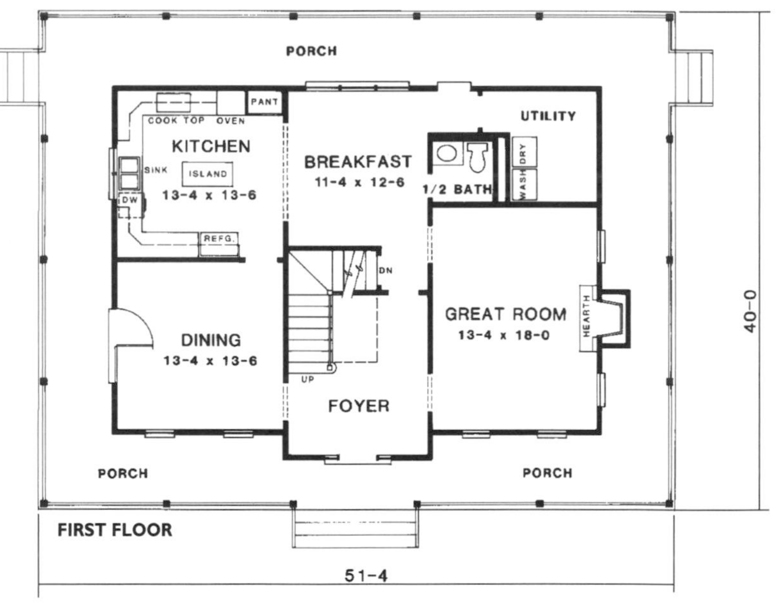
PORCH
PANT
COOK TOP OVEN
KITCHEN
SINK
ISLAND
13-4 x 13-6
DW
REFG.
BREAKFAST
11-4 x 12-6
UTILITY
1/2 BATH
DRY
WASH
DN
GREAT ROOM
13-4 x 18-0
HEARTH
DINING
13-4 x 13-6
UP
FOYER
PORCH
PORCH
40-0
FIRST FLOOR
51-4

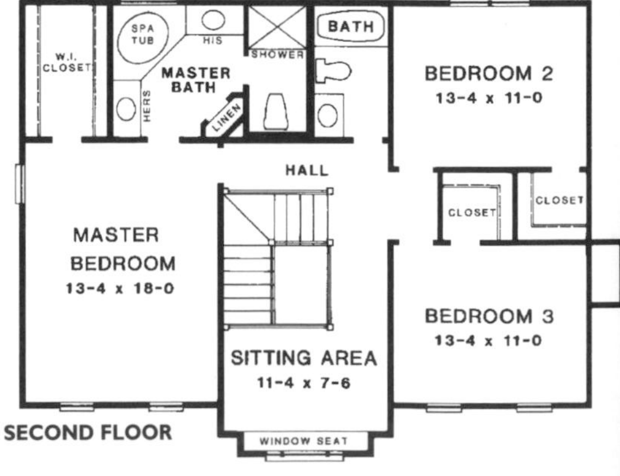
W.I. CLOSET
SPA TUB
HIS
SHOWER
BATH
MASTER BATH
HERS
LINEN
BEDROOM 2
13-4 x 11-0
HALL
CLOSET
CLOSET
MASTER BEDROOM
13-4 x 18-0
BEDROOM 3
13-4 x 11-0
SITTING AREA
11-4 x 7-6
WINDOW SEAT
SECOND FLOOR

Striking Style

PRICE CODE: A

PLAN NO.97274

his plan features:
- hree bedrooms
- wo full baths
- 'indows and exterior detailing create a riking elevation
- he Dining Room has a front window wall and ched openings
- he secondary Bedrooms are in their own wing and are a Bath
- he Great Room has a vaulted ceiling and a fireplace ith a French door beside it
- he Breakfast Bay is open to the galley Kitchen
- he Master Suite features a tray ceiling, a walk-in closet d a private Bath
- his home is designed with basement and crawlspace undation options

N FLOOR — 1,432 SQ. FT.
EMENT — 1,454 SQ. FT.
AGE — 440 SQ. FT.

TOTAL LIVING AREA:
1,432 SQ. FT.

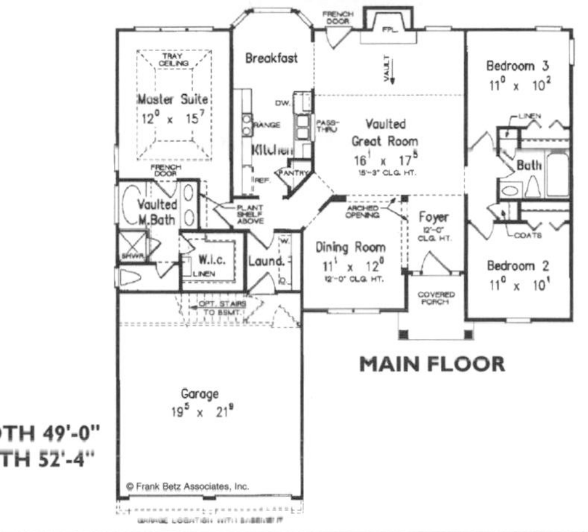

French Door
FPL.
Tray Ceiling
Breakfast
Bedroom 3
11⁰ x 10²
Master Suite
12⁰ x 15⁷
DW.
Range
Kitchen
Pantry
Vaulted Great Room
16¹ x 17⁵
Linen
Bath
French Door
Plant Shelf Above
Arched Opening
Vaulted M.Bath
Foyer
12'-0" CLG. HT.
Coats
W.I.c.
Linen
Laund.
Dining Room
11¹ x 12⁶
12'-0" CLG. HT.
Bedroom 2
11⁰ x 10¹
Covered Porch
Opt. Stairs to Bsmt.
Garage
19⁵ x 21⁹
© Frank Betz Associates, Inc.

MAIN FLOOR

WIDTH 49'-0"
DEPTH 52'-4"

Year Round Leisure

PRICE CODE: A

PLAN NO.90630

'his plan features:
- Three bedrooms
- One full and one three-quarter baths
- cathedral ceiling with exposed beams and a stone wall ith heat-circulating fireplace in the Living Room
- hree sliding glass doors leading from the Living Room a large Deck
- built-in Dining Area that separates the Kitchen from e far end of the Living Room
- Master Suite with his and her closets and private Bath
- wo additional Bedrooms, one double sized, sharing a ll hall Bath
- his home is designed with a crawlspace foundation

IN FLOOR — 1,207 SQ. FT.

TOTAL LIVING AREA:
1,207 SQ. FT.

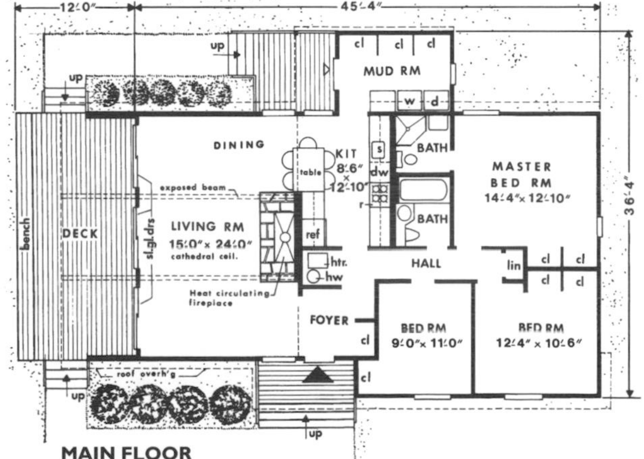

12'-0"
45'-4"
up
cl
cl
cl
MUD RM
w
d
DINING
KIT
8'6" x 12'-10"
table
dw
BATH
MASTER BED RM
14'4" x 12'10"
exposed beam
BATH
36'4"
bench
DECK
sl.gl.drs
LIVING RM
15'0" x 24'0"
cathedral ceil.
ref
htr.
hw
HALL
lin
cl
cl
cl
cl
Heat circulating fireplace
FOYER
cl
BED RM
9'0" x 11'0"
BED RM
12'4" x 10'6"
roof overh'g
up
cl
up

MAIN FLOOR

PLAN NO. 65001

At Home on Sloping Lot

Price Code: A

- This plan features:
- — Two bedrooms
- — Two full baths
- Covered front Porch welcomes guests and offers you with extra living space
- Combination Living/Dining Room features a focal point fireplace and plenty of windows for light
- The L-shaped Kitchen offers a cooktop island
- A back Entry has a large closet to store coats and gear, plus a door to separate it from the rest of the house
- This home is designed with a basement foundation

FIRST FLOOR — 1,024 SQ. FT.
SECOND FLOOR — 456 SQ. FT.
BASEMENT — 1,024 SQ. FT.

TOTAL LIVING AREA:
1,480 SQ. FT.

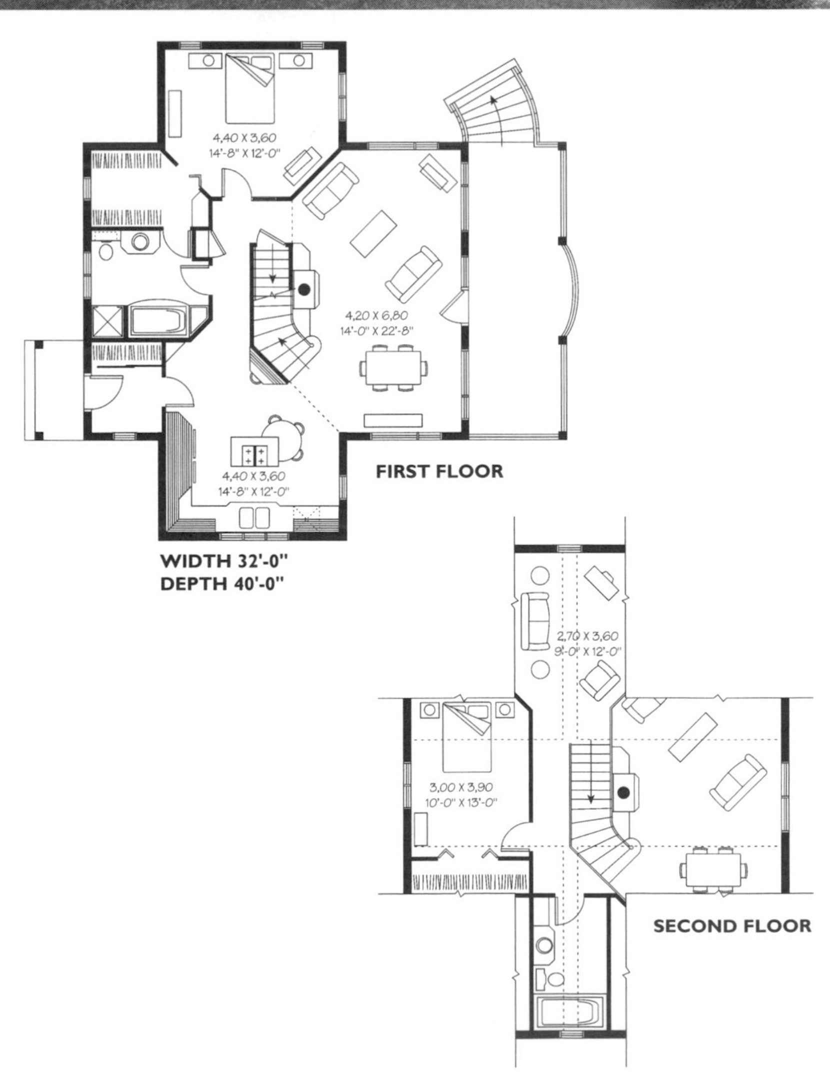
4,40 X 3,60
14'-8" X 12'-0"
4,20 X 6,80
14'-0" X 22'-8"
4,40 X 3,60
14'-8" X 12'-0"
FIRST FLOOR
WIDTH 32'-0"
DEPTH 40'-0"
2,70 X 3,60
9'-0" X 12'-0"
3,00 X 3,90
10'-0" X 13'-0"
SECOND FLOOR

urret Study Creates Impact

PRICE CODE: I

PLAN NO.94220

is plan features:
- hree bedrooms
- wo full, and one three-quarter, and one half baths
- try doors opening into the formal Living Room cusing to the Lanai through sliding glass doors and nitered glass corner
- ouble sided fireplace in the Living Room shared the Master Suite
- etbar easily serves the Living Room, Dining Room d Lanai
- and Kitchen easily serves all informal family areas
- tagon Nook with windows spanning to all views
- isure Room with fireplace wall having built-ins along back wall
- acious Master Suite including a fireplace, morning tchen bar, and Lanai access
- is home is designed with a slab foundation
- ternate foundation options available at an ditional charge. Please call 1-800-235-5700 more information.

N FLOOR — 3,477 SQ. FT.
AGE — 771 SQ. FT.

***TOTAL LIVING AREA:* 3,477 SQ. FT.**

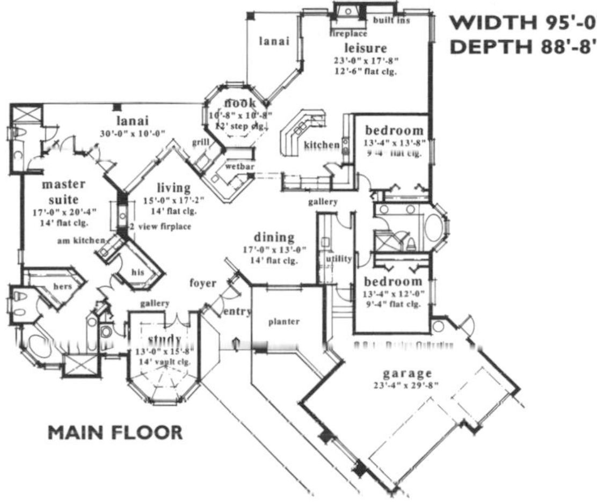
WIDTH 95'-0"
DEPTH 88'-8"
lanai
leisure
23'-0" x 17'-8"
12'-6" flat clg.
fireplace
built ins
nook
lanai
30'-0" x 10'-0"
kitchen
bedroom
13'-4" x 13'-8"
master suite
17'-0" x 20'-4"
14' flat clg.
living
15'-0" x 17'-2"
14' flat clg.
wetbar
grill
gallery
dining
17'-0" x 13'-0"
14' flat clg.
utility
bedroom
13'-4" x 12'-0"
9'-4" flat clg.
foyer
entry
planter
study
garage
23'-4" x 29'-8"
MAIN FLOOR

For The Busy Family

PRICE CODE: D

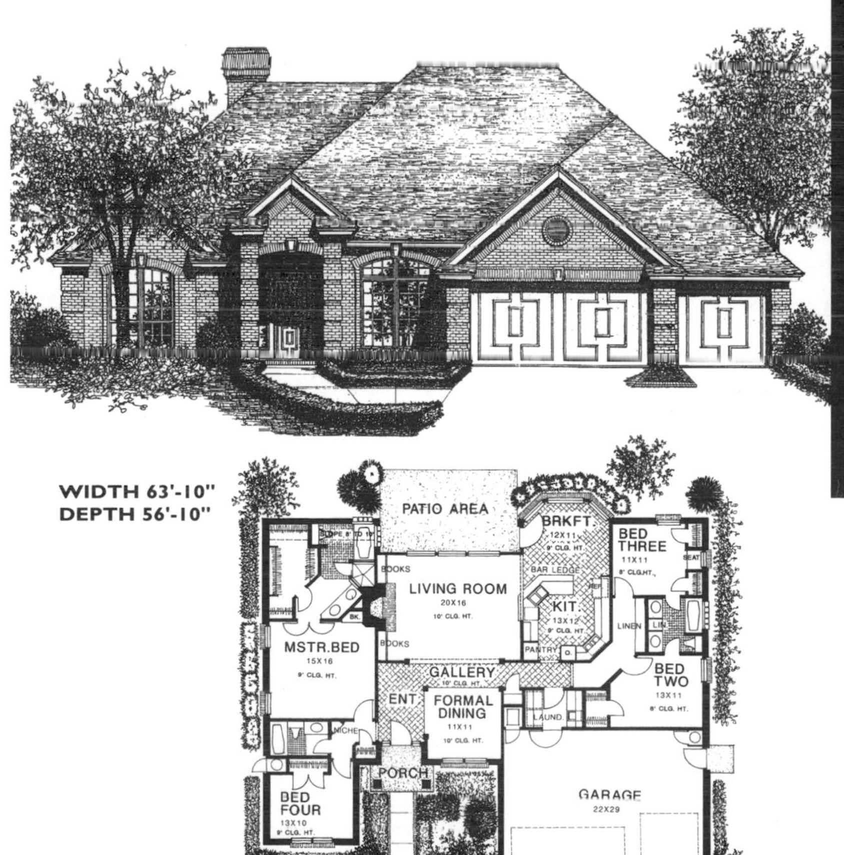
WIDTH 63'-10"
DEPTH 56'-10"
PATIO AREA
BRKFT.
BED THREE
11X11
LIVING ROOM
20X16
10' CLG. HT.
KIT.
13X12
MSTR.BED
15X16
9' CLG. HT.
GALLERY
BED TWO
13X11
ENT.
FORMAL DINING
11X11
10' CLG. HT.
LAUND.
PORCH
GARAGE
22X29
BED FOUR
13X10
9' CLG. HT.
MAIN FLOOR

PLAN NO.98521

his plan features:
- our Bedrooms
- hree full baths
- esigned for a busy family that likes their privacy too
- orch shelters Entry into Gallery, Formal Dining Area, d Living Room with cozy fireplace between bookelves and a wall of windows
- pen and efficient Kitchen easily serves Breakfast lcove, Patio and Dining Area
- orner Master Bedroom provides a huge walk-in closet d lavish Bath
- wo Bedrooms, one with two closets and a window seat, are a full Bath, while fourth Bedroom has parate Bath
- his home is designed with a slab foundation

IN FLOOR — 2,233 SQ. FT.
RAGE — 635 SQ. FT.

***TOTAL LIVING AREA:* 2,233 SQ. FT.**

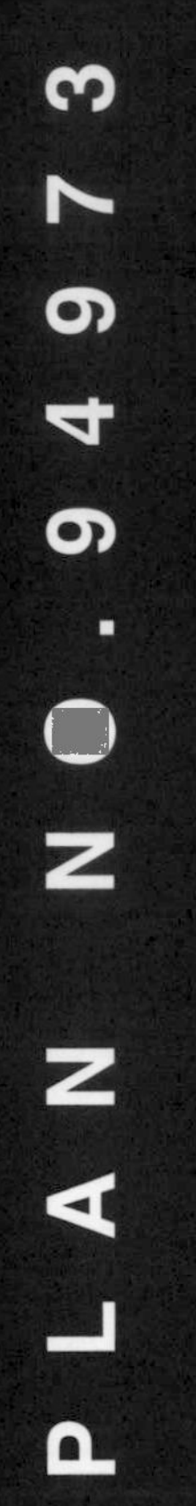
PLAN NO. 94973

Bricks and Arches Detail this Ranch

Price Code: F

This plan features:

— Two bedrooms

— Two full and one half baths

A Master Bedroom with a vaulted ceiling, luxurious Bath, complimented by a skylit walk-in closet

Columns and arched windows define the elegant Dining Room

A Great Room shares a see-through fireplace with the Hearth Room, which also has a built-in entertainment center

This home is designed with a basement foundation

Alternate foundation options available at an additional charge. Please call 1-800-235-5700 for more information.

MAIN FLOOR — 2,512 SQ. FT.
GARAGE — 783 SQ. FT.

TOTAL LIVING AREA:
2,512 SQ. FT.

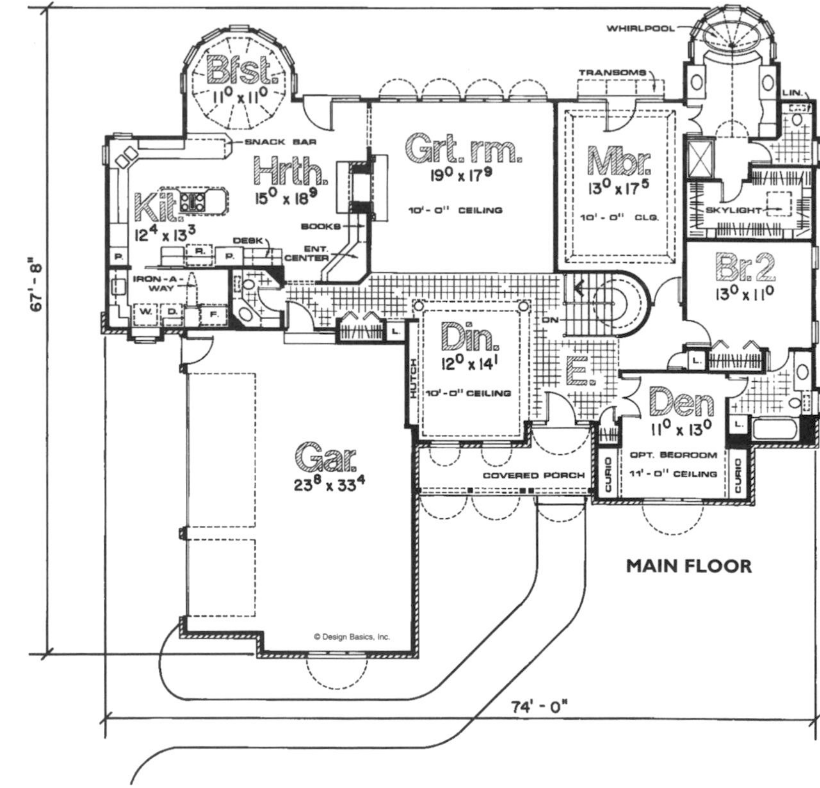
WHIRLPOOL
Bfst.
11⁰ x 11⁰
TRANSOMS
LIN.
SNACK BAR
Hrth.
15⁰ x 18⁹
Grt. rm.
19⁰ x 17⁹
10'-0" CEILING
Mbr.
13⁰ x 17⁵
10'-0" CLG.
Kit.
12⁴ x 13³
BOOKS
DESK
ENT. CENTER
SKYLIGHT
IRON-A-WAY
Br.2
13⁰ x 11⁰
67'-8"
Din.
12⁰ x 14¹
10'-0" CEILING
HUTCH
E.
Den
11⁰ x 13⁰
OPT. BEDROOM
11'-0" CEILING
CURIO
Gar.
23⁸ x 33⁴
COVERED PORCH
MAIN FLOOR
© Design Basics, Inc.
74'-0"

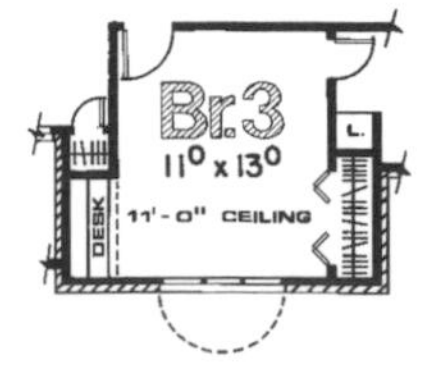
Br.3
11⁰ x 13⁰
11'-0" CEILING
DESK

BEDROOM OPTION

Country Charmer

PRICE CODE: A

PLAN NO. 96509

Ṭhis plan features:
- Three bedrooms
- Two full baths
- Quaint front Porch is perfect for sitting and relaxing
- Great Room opening into Dining Area and Kitchen
- Corner Deck in rear of home accessed from Kitchen and Master Suite
- Master Suite with a private Bath, walk-in closet and built-in shelves
- Two large secondary Bedrooms in the front of the home share a hall Bath
- Two-car Garage located in the rear of the home
- This home is designed with crawlspace and slab foundation

MAIN FLOOR — 1,438 SQ. FT.
GARAGE — 486 SQ. FT.

TOTAL LIVING AREA:
1,438 SQ. FT.

GARAGE
22 × 22
DECK
WIDTH 54'-0"
DEPTH 57'-0"
DINING
12 × 11
KITCHEN
12 × 10
BATH
MASTER SUITE
13 × 15
BATH
GREAT RM
17 × 18
BEDRM
14 × 11
BEDRM
11 × 13
PORCH
MAIN FLOOR

Delightful Home

PRICE CODE: D

PLAN NO. 94248

This plan features:
- Three bedrooms
- Two full baths
- Grand Room with a fireplace, vaulted ceiling and double French doors to the rear Deck
- Kitchen and Dining Room open to continue the overall feel of spaciousness
- Kitchen has a large walk-in Pantry, island with a sink and dishwasher creating a perfect triangular workspace
- Dining Room with doors to both Decks, has expanses of glass looking out to the rear yard
- Master Bedroom features a double door Entry, private Bath, and a morning Kitchen
- This home is designed with pier and post foundation options
- Alternate foundation options available at an additional charge. Please call 1-800-235-5700 for more information.

FIRST FLOOR — 1,342 SQ. FT.
SECOND FLOOR — 511 SQ. FT.

TOTAL LIVING AREA:
1,853 SQ. FT.

WIDTH 44'-0"
DEPTH 40'-0"

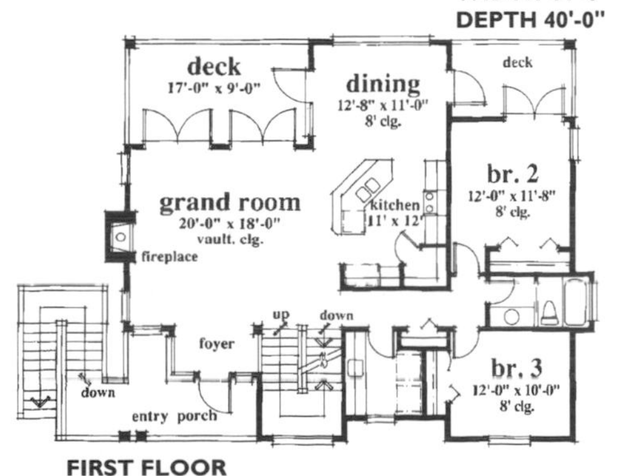
deck
17'-0" x 9'-0"
dining
12'-8" x 11'-0"
8' clg.
deck
grand room
20'-0" x 18'-0"
vault. clg.
fireplace
kitchen
11' x 12'
br. 2
12'-0" x 11'-8"
8' clg.
up
down
foyer
down
entry porch
br. 3
12'-0" x 10'-0"
8' clg.
FIRST FLOOR

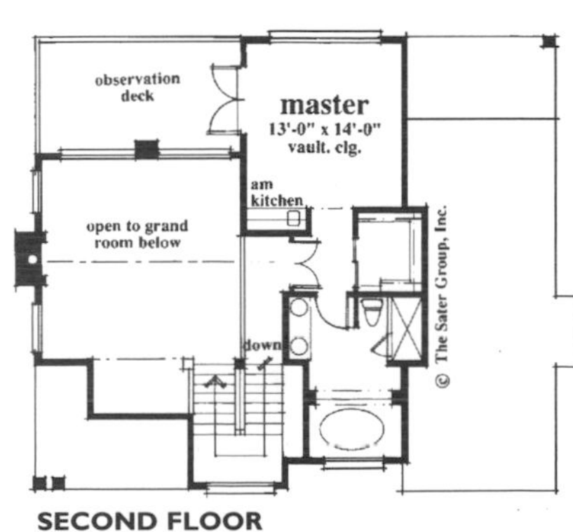
observation
deck
master
13'-0" x 14'-0"
vault. clg.
am
kitchen
open to grand
room below
down
© The Sater Group, Inc.
SECOND FLOOR

PLAN NO.98441

High Ceilings and Arched Windows

PRICE CODE: B

- This plan features:
  - — Three bedrooms
  - — Two full baths
- Natural illumination streaming into the Dining Room and Sitting Area of the Master Suite through large arched windows
- Kitchen with convenient pass through to the Great Rc and a serving bar for the Breakfast Room
- Great Room topped by a vaulted ceiling accented by fireplace and a French door
- Decorative columns accenting the entrance of the Dining Room
- Tray ceiling over the Master Suite and a vaulted ceili over the sitting room and the Master Bath
- This home is designed with basement and crawlspace foundation options

MAIN FLOOR — 1,502 SQ. FT.
GARAGE — 448 SQ. FT.

TOTAL LIVING AREA:
1,502 SQ. FT.

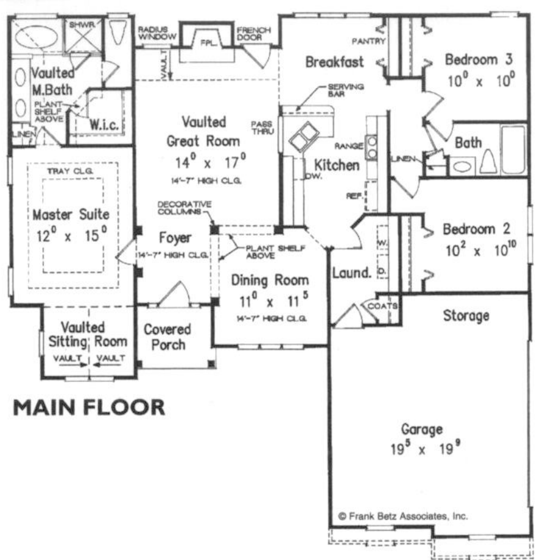
Vaulted M.Bath
W.i.c.
Vaulted Great Room
14^0 x 17^0
Breakfast
Bedroom 3
10^0 x 10^0
Kitchen
Bath
Master Suite
12^0 x 15^0
Foyer
Dining Room
11^0 x 11^5
Laund.
Bedroom 2
10^2 x 10^{10}
Storage
Vaulted Sitting Room
Covered Porch
Garage
19^5 x 19^9
© Frank Betz Associates, Inc.
GARAGE LOCATION W/ BASEMENT
MAIN FLOOR

WIDTH 51'-0"
DEPTH 50'-6"

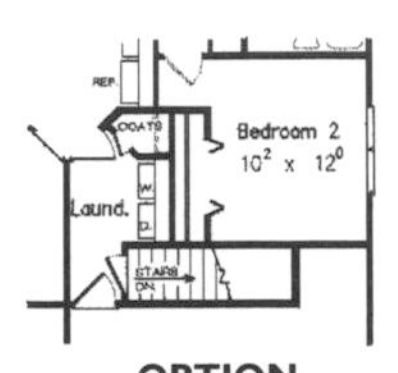
Bedroom 2
10^2 x 12^0
Laund.
OPTION

PLAN NO.97293

Cozy Yet Spacious

PRICE CODE: E

- This plan features:
  - — Four bedrooms
  - — Two full and one half baths
- The Living Room has an elegant arched opening fron the Foyer and from the Dining Room
- The sunken Family Room has a fireplace and French doors to the rear yard
- The Breakfast Room is enhanced by decorative colun and a serving bar from the Kitchen adds to the room' convenience
- The Master Suite features a tray ceiling in the Bedroc and a vaulted ceiling over the Master Bath
- The home is designed with basement, slab and crawlspace foundation options

FIRST FLOOR — 1,186 SQ. FT.
SECOND FLOOR — 1,084 SQ. FT.
GARAGE — 440 SQ. FT.

TOTAL LIVING AREA:
2,270 SQ. FT.

61'-10"
37'-6"

Family Room 16^9 x 14^0
Breakfast
Kitchen
Garage
Pwdr.
Laundry
2 Story Foyer
Living Room 13^0 x 14^{10}
Dining Room 12^3x 12^0
Porch
Covered Porch

FIRST FLOOR

Master Suite 16^9x 14^0
Vaulted M.Bath
W.i.c.
Bedroom 2 12^3x 11^0
Foyer Below
Bath
Bedroom 3 11^0 x 12^1
Bedroom 4 13^0 x 10^0

SECOND FLOOR

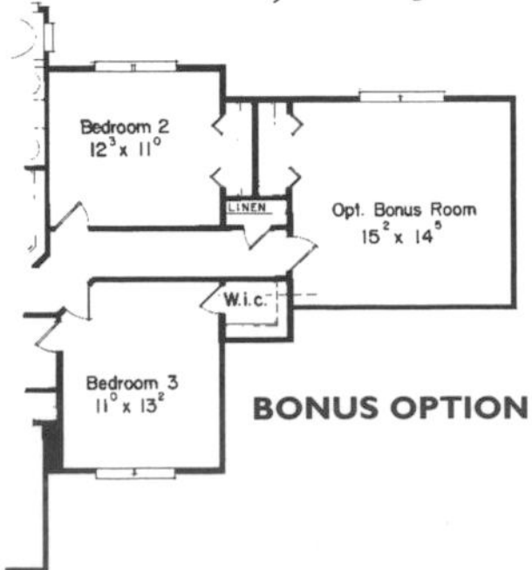
Bedroom 2
12^3x 11^0
Opt. Bonus Room
15^2x 14^5
W.i.c.
Bedroom 3
11^0x 13^2
BONUS OPTION

To order your Blueprints, call 1-800-235-5700

PLAN NO. 65002

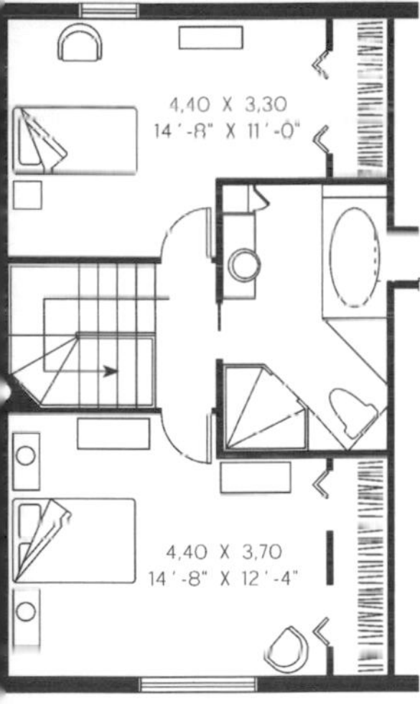

4,40 X 3,30
14'-8" X 11'-0"
4,40 X 3,70
14'-8" X 12'-4"

ECOND FLOOR

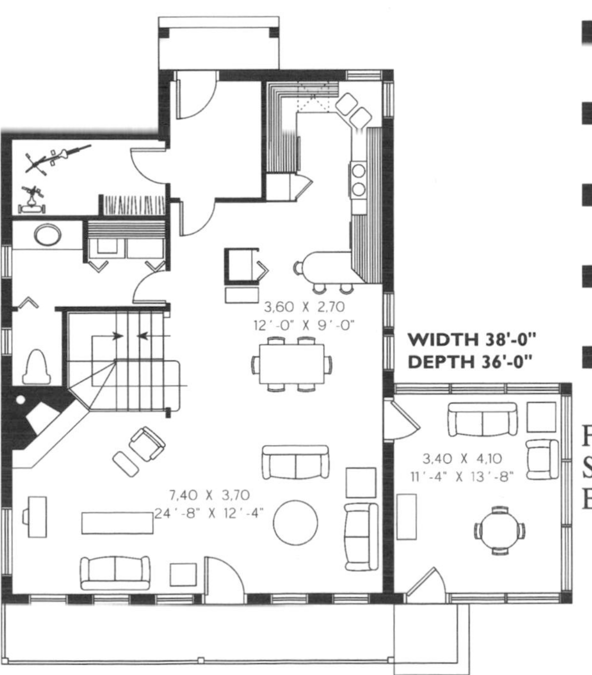

3,60 X 2,70
12'-0" X 9'-0"
7,40 X 3,70
24'-8" X 12'-4"
3,40 X 4,10
11'-4" X 13'-8"
WIDTH 38'-0"
DEPTH 36'-0"

FIRST FLOOR

Let the Sun Shine In

Price Code: B

- This plan features:
  - — Two bedrooms
  - — One full and one half baths
- Large windows will bring lots of natural light into virtually every room
- The Sun Porch expands entertaining options and living space
- The U-shaped Kitchen is designed for convenience and efficiency
- An eating bar in the Kitchen can double a serving area for the Dining Room
- The Living Room features a corner fireplace
- This home is designed with a basement foundation

FIRST FLOOR — 895 SQ. FT.
SECOND FLOOR — 565 SQ. FT.
BASEMENT — 1,074 SQ. FT.

TOTAL LIVING AREA:
1,460 SQ. FT.

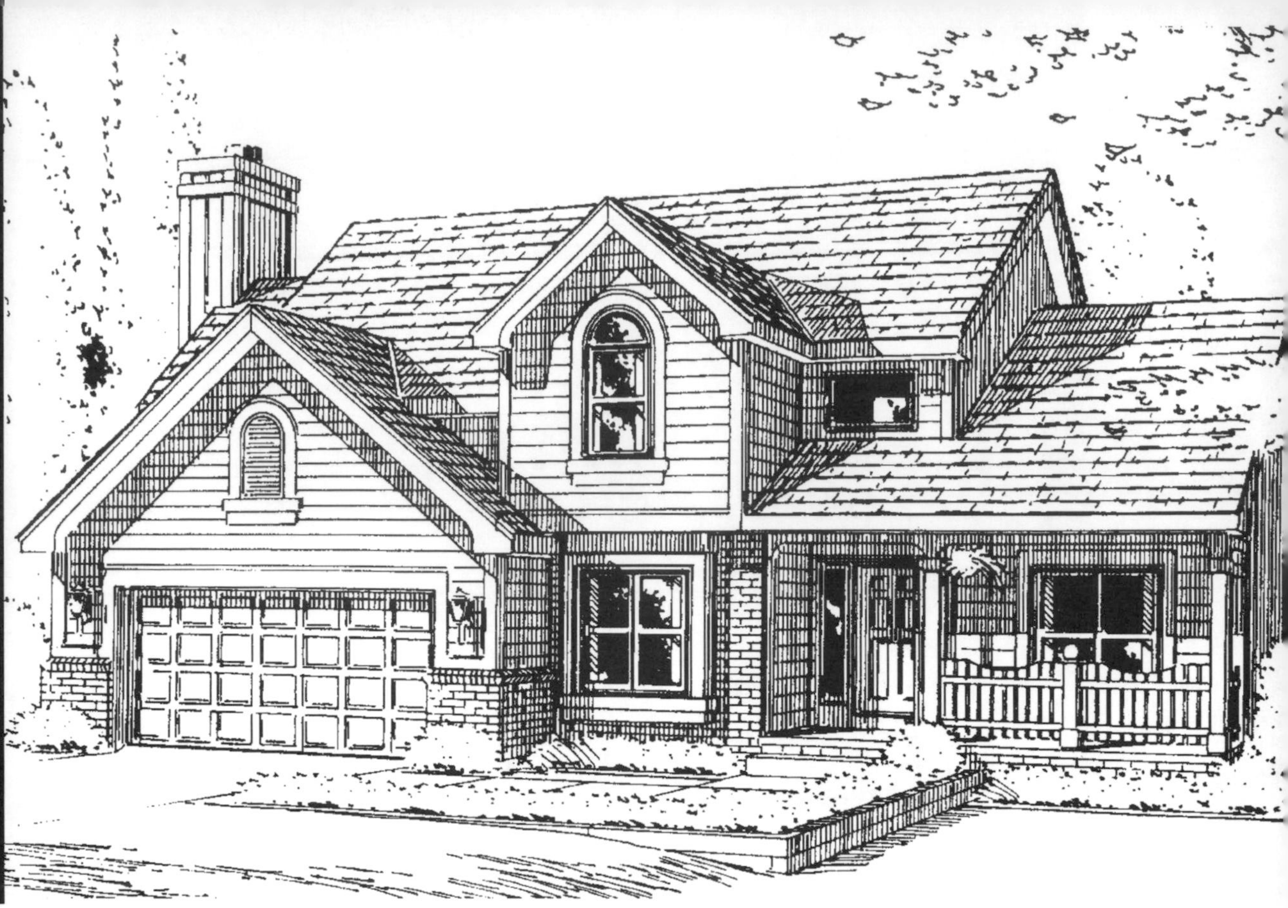

Spacious Family Living

Price Code: E

- This plan features:
- — Four bedrooms
- — Two full and one half baths
- Front Porch welcomes friends and family home
- Entry opens to spacious Living Room with a tiered ceiling and Dining Room beyond
- Hub Kitchen easily serves the Dining Room, the Breakfast Bay and the Family Room
- This home is designed with basement and slab foundation options
- Alternate foundation options available at an additional charge. Please call 1-800-235-5700 for more information.

FIRST FLOOR — 1,269 SQ. FT.
SECOND FLOOR — 1,034 SQ. FT.
BASEMENT — 1,269 SQ. FT.
GARAGE — 485 SQ. FT.

TOTAL LIVING AREA:
2,303 SQ. FT.

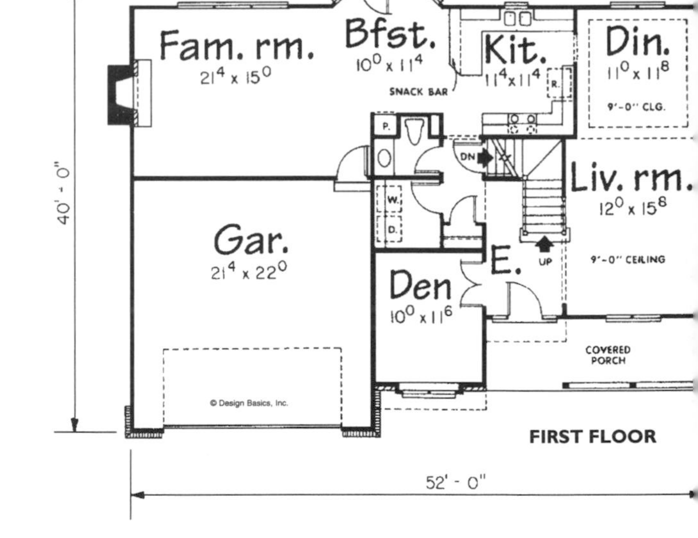
Fam. rm.
21^{4} x 15^{0}
Bfst.
10^{0} x 11^{4}
SNACK BAR
Kit.
11^{4}x11^{4}
Din.
11^{0} x 11^{8}
9'-0" CLG.
Liv. rm.
12^{0} x 15^{8}
9'-0" CEILING
Gar.
21^{4} x 22^{0}
Den
10^{0} x 11^{6}
E.
UP
DN
COVERED PORCH
© Design Basics, Inc.
40' - 0"
52' - 0"
FIRST FLOOR

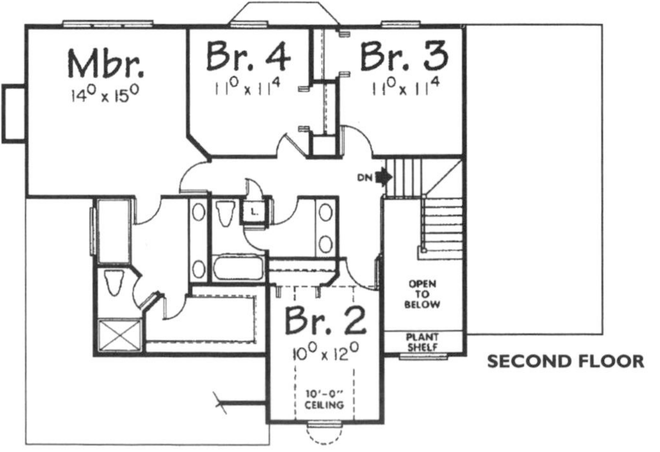
Mbr.
14^{0} x 15^{0}
Br. 4
11^{0} x 11^{4}
Br. 3
11^{0} x 11^{4}
DN
OPEN TO BELOW
PLANT SHELF
Br. 2
10^{0} x 12^{0}
10'-0" CEILING
SECOND FLOOR

PLAN NO. 24262

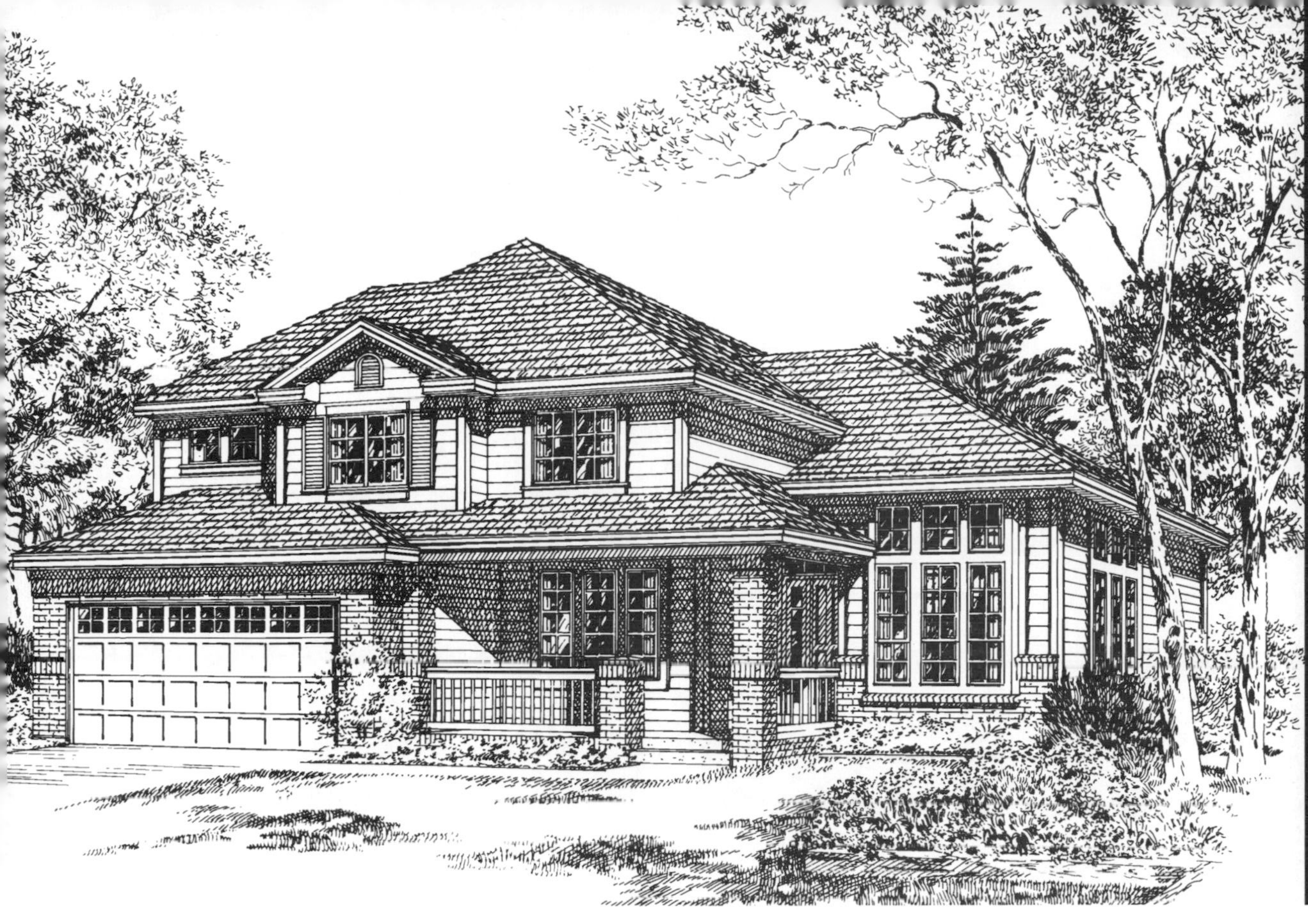

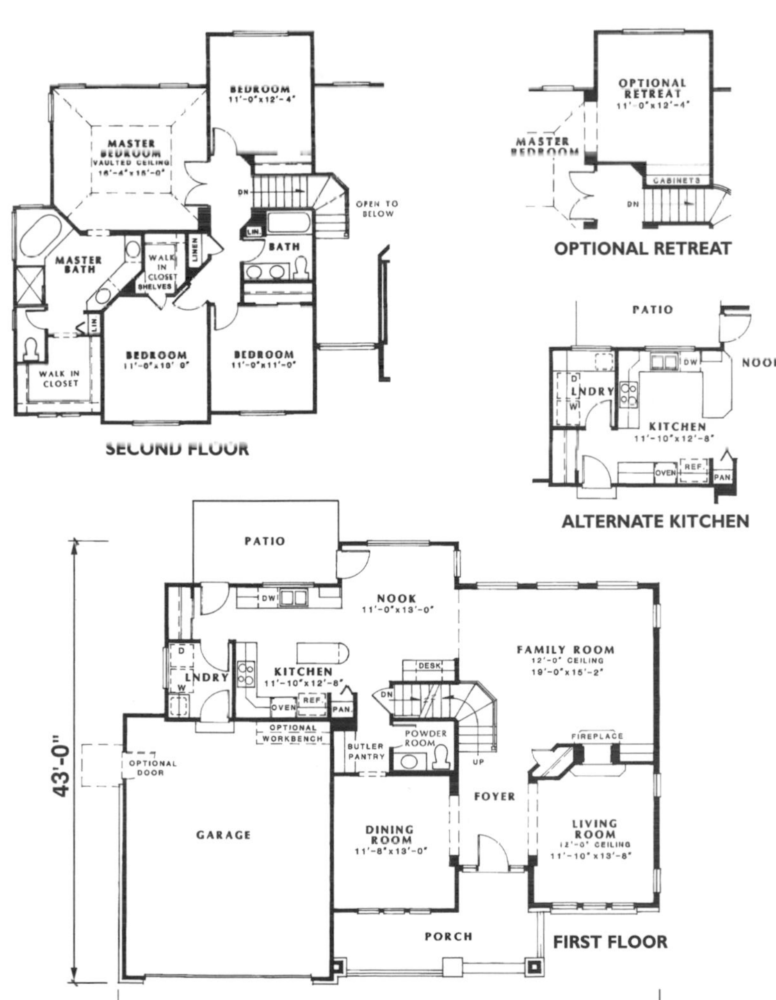

BEDROOM
11'-0"x12'-4"
MASTER BEDROOM
VAULTED CEILING
16'-4"x15'-0"
OPEN TO BELOW
MASTER BATH
WALK IN CLOSET
SHELVES
LINEN
BATH
BEDROOM
BEDROOM
11'-0"x11'-0"
WALK IN CLOSET
SECOND FLOOR
OPTIONAL RETREAT
11'-0"x12'-4"
MASTER BEDROOM
CABINETS
OPTIONAL RETREAT
PATIO
NOOK
LNDRY
KITCHEN
11'-10"x12'-8"
OVEN
REF.
PAN
ALTERNATE KITCHEN
PATIO
NOOK
11'-0"x13'-0"
FAMILY ROOM
12'-0" CEILING
19'-0"x15'-2"
DESK
LNDRY
KITCHEN
11'-10"x12'-8"
OVEN
REF.
PAN
OPTIONAL WORKBENCH
BUTLER PANTRY
POWDER ROOM
FIREPLACE
OPTIONAL DOOR
FOYER
GARAGE
DINING ROOM
11'-8"x13'-0"
LIVING ROOM
12'-0" CEILING
11'-10"x13'-8"
PORCH
FIRST FLOOR
43'-0"
52'-0"

Attractive Hip and Valley-Style Roof

Price Code: E

- This plan features:
- — Four bedrooms
- — Two full and one half baths
- A see-through fireplace between the Living Room and the Family Room
- A gourmet Kitchen with an extended serving counter, built-in Pantry, and nearby Laundry
- A Master Bedroom with a vaulted ceiling, double vanity Bath, and walk-in closet
- Three additional Bedrooms, one with walk-in closet, share a full hall Bath
- This home is designed with basement, slab, and crawlspace foundation options

FIRST FLOOR — 1,241 SQ. FT.
SECOND FLOOR — 1,170 SQ. FT.
GARAGE — 500 SQ. FT.

TOTAL LIVING AREA:
2,411 SQ. FT.

PLAN NO. 94994

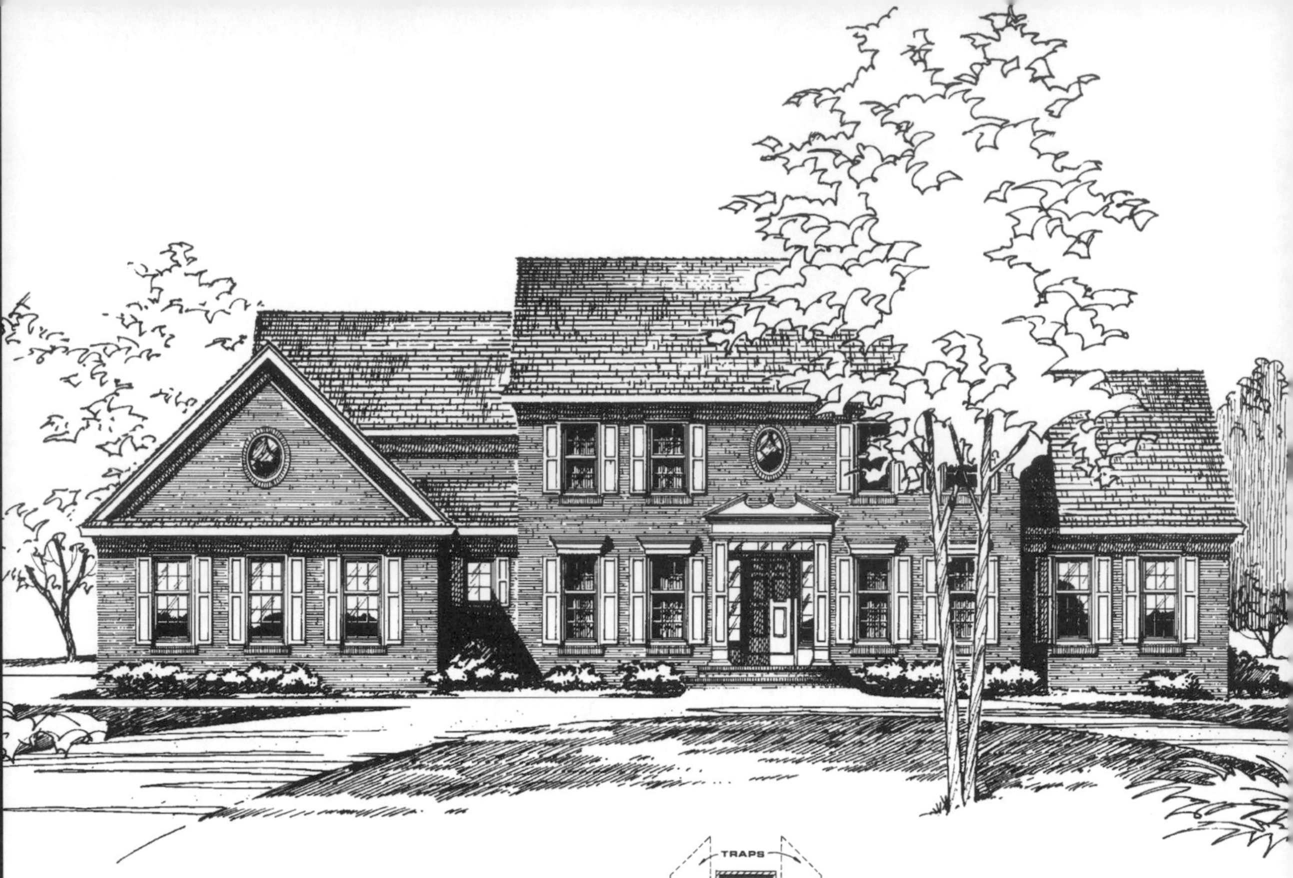

Timeless Beauty

Price Code: G

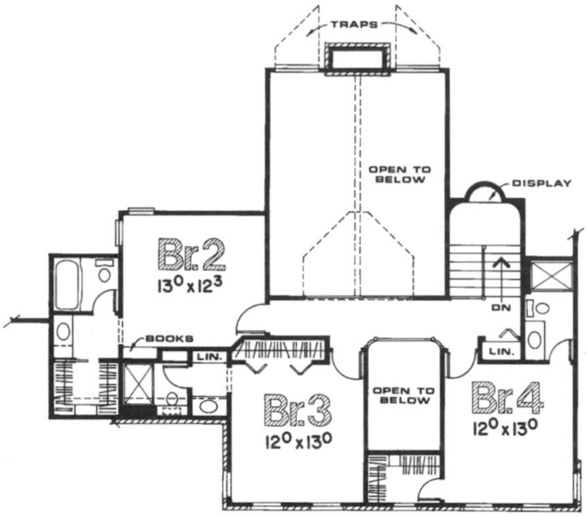

This plan features:
- Four bedrooms
- Two full, two three-quarter and one half baths

Two-story Entry hall accesses formal Dining and Living Room

Spacious Great Room with cathedral ceiling and fireplace

Ideal Kitchen with Pantry

Master Bedroom wing offers a decorative ceiling, and luxurious Dressing/Bath Area

This home is designed with a basement foundation

Alternate foundation options available at an additional charge. Please call 1-800-235-5700 for more information.

FIRST FLOOR — 2,063 SQ. FT.
SECOND FLOOR — 894 SQ. FT.
GARAGE — 666 SQ. FT.
BASEMENT — 2,063 SQ. FT.

TOTAL LIVING AREA:
2,957 SQ. FT.

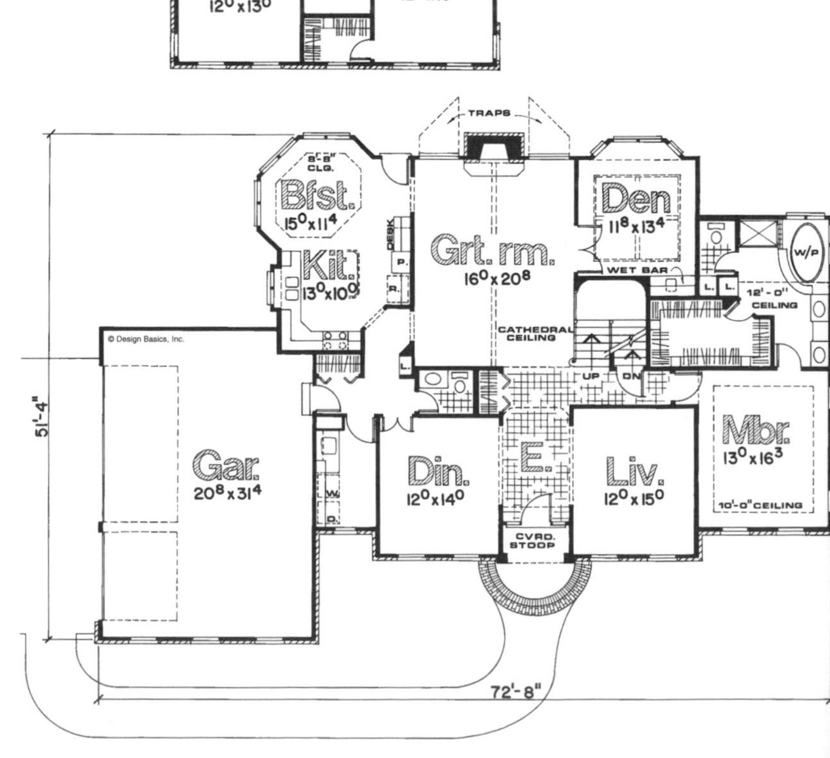
TRAPS
8'-2" CLG.
Bfst. 15⁰x11⁴
DESK
P.
Kit. 13⁰x10⁰
Grt. rm. 16⁰x20⁸
CATHEDRAL CEILING
Den 11⁸x13⁴
WET BAR
W/P
12'-0" CEILING
L.
UP
DN
© Design Basics, Inc.
Gar. 20⁸x31⁴
Din. 12⁰x14⁰
E.
Liv. 12⁰x15⁰
Mbr. 13⁰x16³
10'-0" CEILING
CVRD. STOOP
51'-4"
72'-8"

Elegant Row House

PRICE CODE: F

PLAN NO.94259

'his plan features:
- Three bedrooms
- Two full and one half baths
- Arched columns define the formal and casual spaces
- Wraparound porticos on two levels provide views o the living areas
- 'our sets of French doors let the outside in to the Great Room
- 'he Master Suite features a private Bath designed or two people
- Generous bonus space awaits your ideas for completion
- 'he Guest Bedroom leads to a gallery hallway with Deck access
- 'his home is designed with slab and pier/post oundation options
- Alternate foundation options available at an dditional charge. Please call 1-800-235-5700 or more information.

AIN FLOOR — 1,305 SQ. FT.
PER FLOOR — 1,215 SQ. FT.
WER FLOOR — 935 SQ. FT.
RAGE — 480 SQ. FT.

TOTAL LIVING AREA:
2,520 SQ. FT.

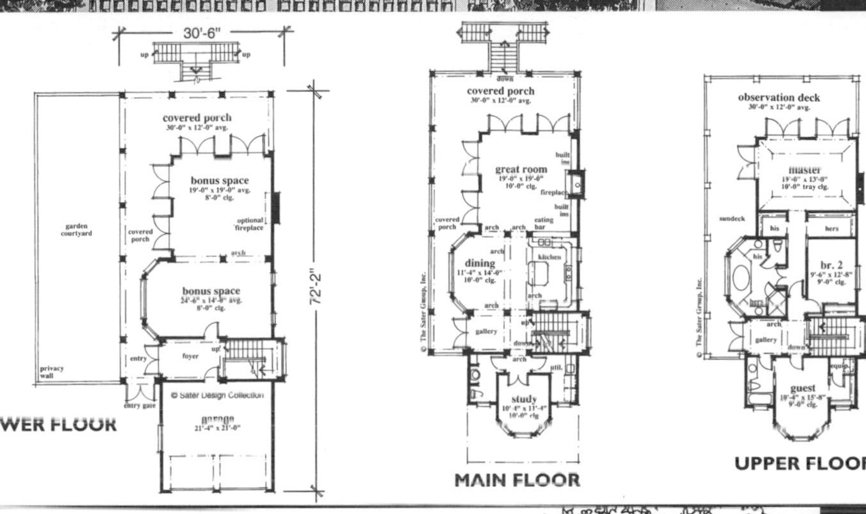

30'-6"
72'-2"
covered porch
bonus space
garden courtyard
covered porch
optional fireplace
bonus space
entry
foyer
privacy wall
entry gate
© Sater Design Collection
garage
LOWER FLOOR
covered porch
great room
fireplace
eating bar
dining
kitchen
gallery
study
MAIN FLOOR
observation deck
master
sundeck
his
hers
br. 2
gallery
guest
UPPER FLOOR

L-Shaped Front Porch

PRICE CODE: A

PLAN NO.98747

'his plan features:
- Three bedrooms
- Two full baths
- Attractive wood siding and a large L-shaped overed Porch
- 'ront Entry leading to generous Living Room with a aulted ceiling
- Large two-car Garage with access through Utility Room
- Roomy secondary Bedrooms share the full Bath n the hall
- Kitchen highlighted by a built-in Pantry and garden window
- 'aulted ceiling adds volume to the Dining Room
- Master Suite in an isolated location enhanced by bundant closet space, separate vanity, and linen storage
- 'his home is designed with a crawlspace foundation

AIN FLOOR — 1,280 SQ. FT.

TOTAL LIVING AREA:
1,280 SQ. FT.

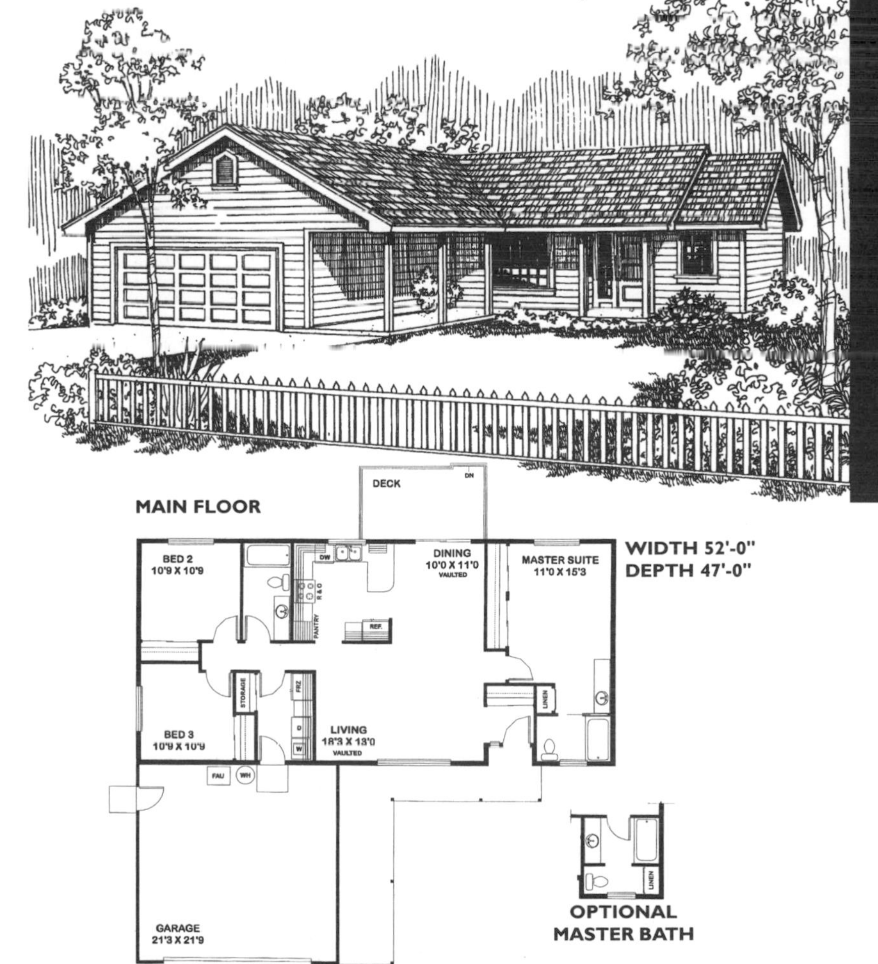

MAIN FLOOR
DECK
BED 2
10'9 X 10'9
DINING
10'0 X 11'0
VAULTED
MASTER SUITE
11'0 X 15'3
PANTRY
REF.
LINEN
STORAGE
BED 3
10'9 X 10'9
LIVING
18'3 X 13'0
VAULTED
FAU
WH
GARAGE
21'3 X 21'9
OPTIONAL
MASTER BATH

WIDTH 52'-0"
DEPTH 47'-0"

PLAN NO.98443

One Floor Convenience

PRICE CODE: A

- This plan features:
- — Three bedrooms
- — Two full baths
- Vaulted Foyer blending with the vaulted Great Room giving a larger feeling to the home
- Formal Dining Room opening into the Great Room, allowing for a terrific living area in which to entertai
- Kitchen including a serving bar and easy flow into th Breakfast Room
- Master Suite topped by a decorative tray ceiling and a vaulted ceiling in the Master Bath
- Two additional Bedrooms sharing the full Bath in the hall
- This home is designed with slab and crawlspace foundation options

MAIN FLOOR — 1,359 SQ. FT.
GARAGE — 439 SQ. FT.

TOTAL LIVING AREA:
1,359 SQ. FT.

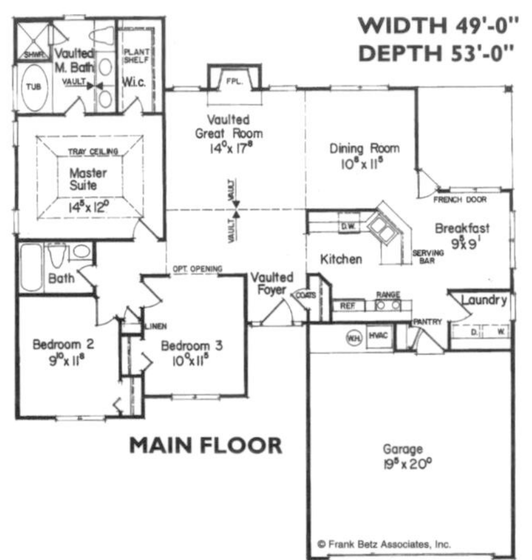
WIDTH 49'-0"
DEPTH 53'-0"
Vaulted M. Bath
PLANT SHELF
W.i.c.
TUB
VAULT
TRAY CEILING
Master Suite
FPL
Vaulted Great Room
Dining Room
FRENCH DOOR
Breakfast
Kitchen
SERVING BAR
Bath
OPT OPENING
Vaulted Foyer
COATS
REF
RANGE
Laundry
PANTRY
HVAC
LINEN
Bedroom 2
Bedroom 3
MAIN FLOOR
Garage
© Frank Betz Associates, Inc.

PLAN NO.65003

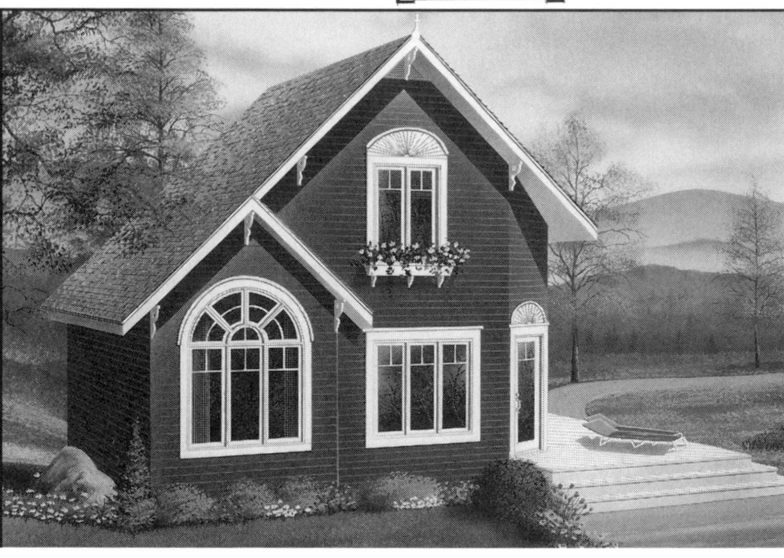

Compact Cottage

PRICE CODE: A

- This plan features:
- — Two bedrooms
- — Two full baths
- Efficient use of space packs a lot of living into this cozy design
- Although compact, this home offers space amplifying features like ample storage and volume ceilings
- A second floor Loft with open-rail balcony creates a private Sitting Area
- This home is designed with a crawlspace foundation

FIRST FLOOR — 593 SQ. FT.
SECOND FLOOR — 383 SQ. FT.
BASEMENT — 593 SQ. FT.

TOTAL LIVING AREA:
976 SQ. FT.

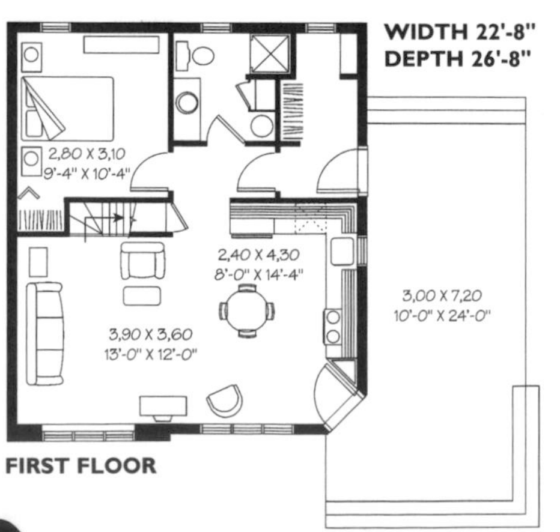
WIDTH 22'-8"
DEPTH 26'-8"
2,80 X 3,10
9'-4" X 10'-4"
2,40 X 4,30
8'-0" X 14'-4"
3,00 X 7,20
10'-0" X 24'-0"
3,90 X 3,60
13'-0" X 12'-0"
FIRST FLOOR

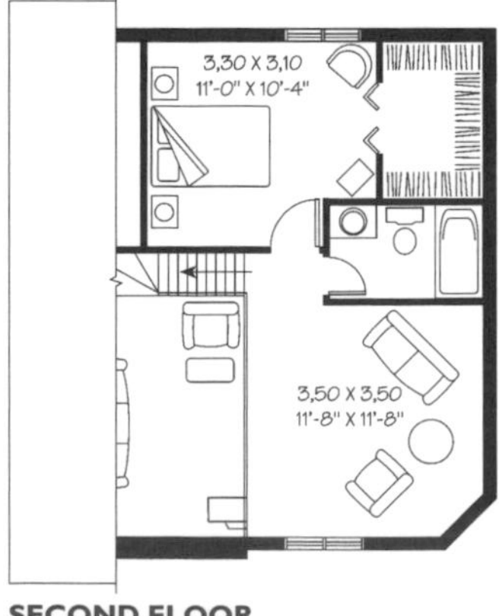
3,30 X 3,10
11'-0" X 10'-4"
3,50 X 3,50
11'-8" X 11'-8"
SECOND FLOOR

Jp and Down Living Areas

PRICE CODE: E

PLAN NO.65004

'his plan features:
- Three bedrooms
- Two full and one half baths
- A huge, angled front Porch provides a unique, outdoor Foyer with access to the Living Room and Dining Room
- Freestanding and angled workspaces make it convenient to enjoy the Kitchen
- Luxurious appointments in the Master Suite include a fireplace, and a private Bath featuring a columned whirlpool tub
- The home is designed with a basement foundation

RST FLOOR — 1,067 SQ. FT.
COND FLOOR — 1,233 SQ. FT.
SEMENT — 593 SQ. FT.

TOTAL LIVING AREA:
2,300 SQ. FT.

FIRST FLOOR

6,60 X 4,20
22'-0" X 14'-0"
6,00 X 6,00
20'-0" X 20'-0"
3,90 X 5,10
13'-0" X 17'-0"
3,00 X 3,60
10'-0" X 12'-0"
3,00 X 1,80
10'-0" X 6'-0"
6,00 X 6,00
20'-0" X 20'-0"

SECOND FLOOR
5,40 X 4,30
18'-0" X 14'-4"
4,50 X 4,50
15'-0" X 15'-0"
3,80 X 4,80
12' 8" X 16'-0"
3,00 X 4,20
10'-0" X 14'-0"
3,00 X 3,60
10'-0" X 12'-0"

WIDTH 58'-0"
DEPTH 34'-0"

A Traditional Approach

PRICE CODE: D

PLAN NO.94109

This plan features:
- Four bedrooms
- Two full and one half baths
- A Covered Entry leading to a two-story Foyer
- A well-appointed Kitchen with direct access to the Garage
- A bright and sunny Dinette for informal eating
- An expansive Family Room highlighted by a large fireplace
- A roomy Master Suite including a private Bath and a walk-in closet
- Three additional Bedrooms sharing use of a full hall Bath
- This home is designed with a basement foundation

RST FLOOR — 1,025 SQ. FT.
COND FLOOR — 988 SQ. FT.

TOTAL LIVING AREA:
2,013 SQ. FT.

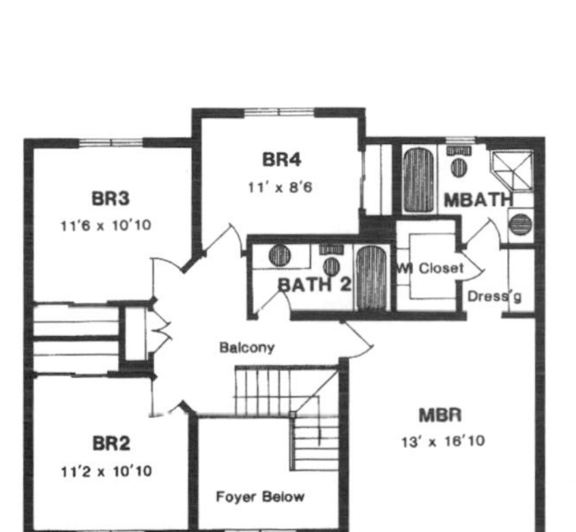

BR4
11' x 8'6
BR3
11'6 x 10'10
MBATH
BATH 2
W Closet
Dress'g
Balcony
BR2
11'2 x 10'10
Foyer Below
MBR
13' x 16'10
SECOND FLOOR

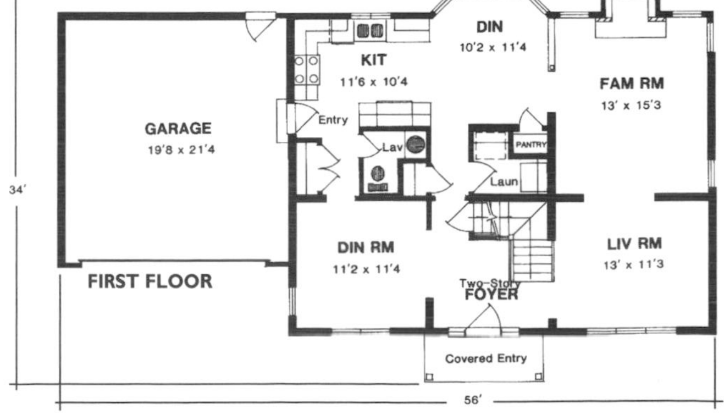

DIN
10'2 x 11'4
KIT
11'6 x 10'4
FAM RM
13' x 15'3
GARAGE
19'8 x 21'4
Entry
Lav
PANTRY
Laun
34'
DIN RM
11'2 x 11'4
LIV RM
13' x 11'3
Two-Story
FOYER
FIRST FLOOR
Covered Entry
56'

PLAN NO. 9850

Rear Elevation

Home Recalls the South

Price Code: E

This plan features:

— Three bedrooms

— Two full and one half baths

- A Master Bedroom Suite with a private Study
- Fireplaces enhancing the formal Living Room and Family Room
- A lovely, Screened Porch/Patio skirting the Family Room and the Kitchen
- A Utility Room with access into the storage and Garage areas
- This home is designed with a basement foundation

MAIN FLOOR — 2,466 SQ. FT.
BASEMENT — 1,447 SQ. FT.
GARAGE — 664 SQ. FT.

TOTAL LIVING AREA:
2,466 SQ. FT.

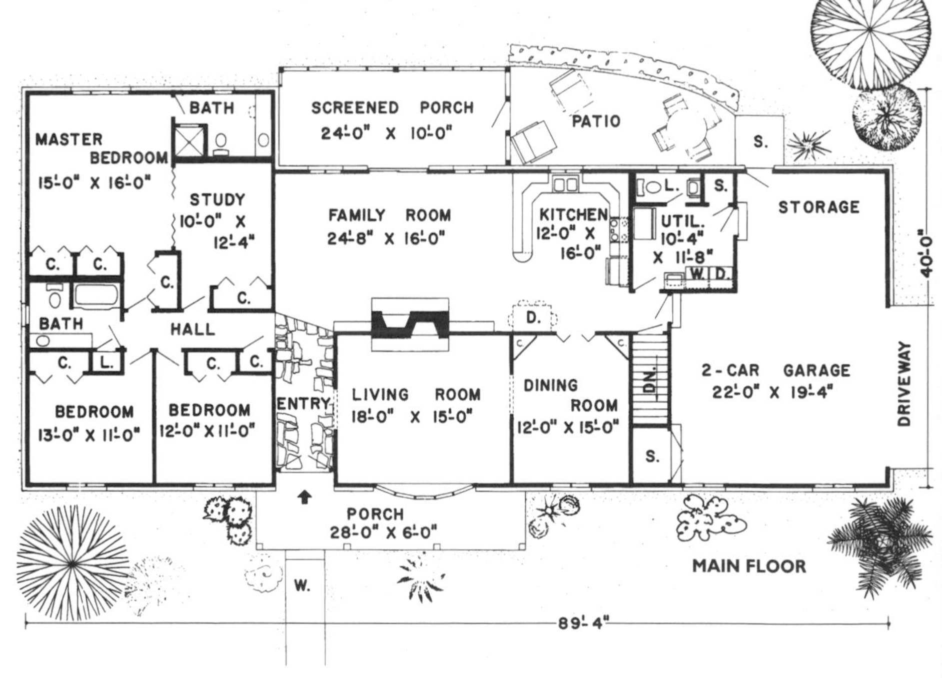

BATH
MASTER BEDROOM
15'-0" X 16'-0"
SCREENED PORCH
24'-0" X 10'-0"
PATIO
S.
STUDY
10'-0" X 12'-4"
FAMILY ROOM
24'-8" X 16'-0"
KITCHEN
12'-0" X 16'-0"
L.
S.
UTIL.
10'-4" X 11'-8"
W. D.
STORAGE
40'-0"
C.
BATH
HALL
D.
L.
ENTRY
LIVING ROOM
18'-0" X 15'-0"
DINING ROOM
12'-0" X 15'-0"
DN.
2-CAR GARAGE
22'-0" X 19'-4"
DRIVEWAY
BEDROOM
13'-0" X 11'-0"
BEDROOM
12'-0" X 11'-0"
PORCH
28'-0" X 6'-0"
W.
MAIN FLOOR
89'-4"

PLAN NO. 20230

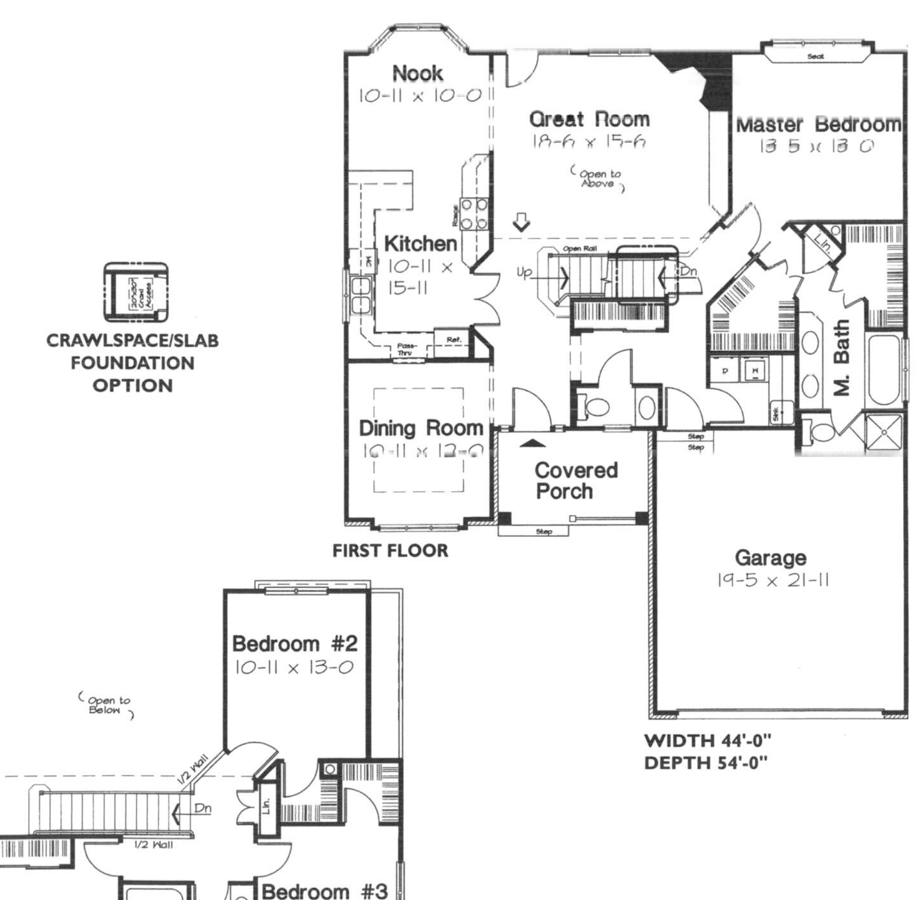

Nook
10-11 x 10-0
Great Room
18-6 x 15-6
Open to Above
Master Bedroom
13-5 x 13-0
Kitchen
10-11 x 15-11
M. Bath
Dining Room
10-11 x 12-0
Covered Porch
Garage
19-5 x 21-11
FIRST FLOOR
CRAWLSPACE/SLAB FOUNDATION OPTION
WIDTH 44'-0"
DEPTH 54'-0"
Bedroom #2
10-11 x 13-0
Open to Below
Bedroom #3
11-0 x 10-8
Bedroom #4
10-5 x 11-4
SECOND FLOOR

Stupendous Design

Price Code: C

- This plan features:
  - Four bedrooms
  - Two full and one half baths
- A covered Porch Entry opens to the formal Dining Room and Great Room beyond
- A bright Kitchen,with lot of counter space, easily serves the eating Nook, Great Room, and Dining Room
- The Master Bedroom Suite privately pampers its owners with two walk-in closets and a plush Bath
- This home is designed with basement, slab, and crawlspace foundation options

FIRST FLOOR — 1,365 SQ. FT.
SECOND FLOOR — 630 SQ. FT.
BASEMENT — 1,419 SQ. FT.
GARAGE — 426 SQ. FT.

TOTAL LIVING AREA:
1,995 SQ. FT.

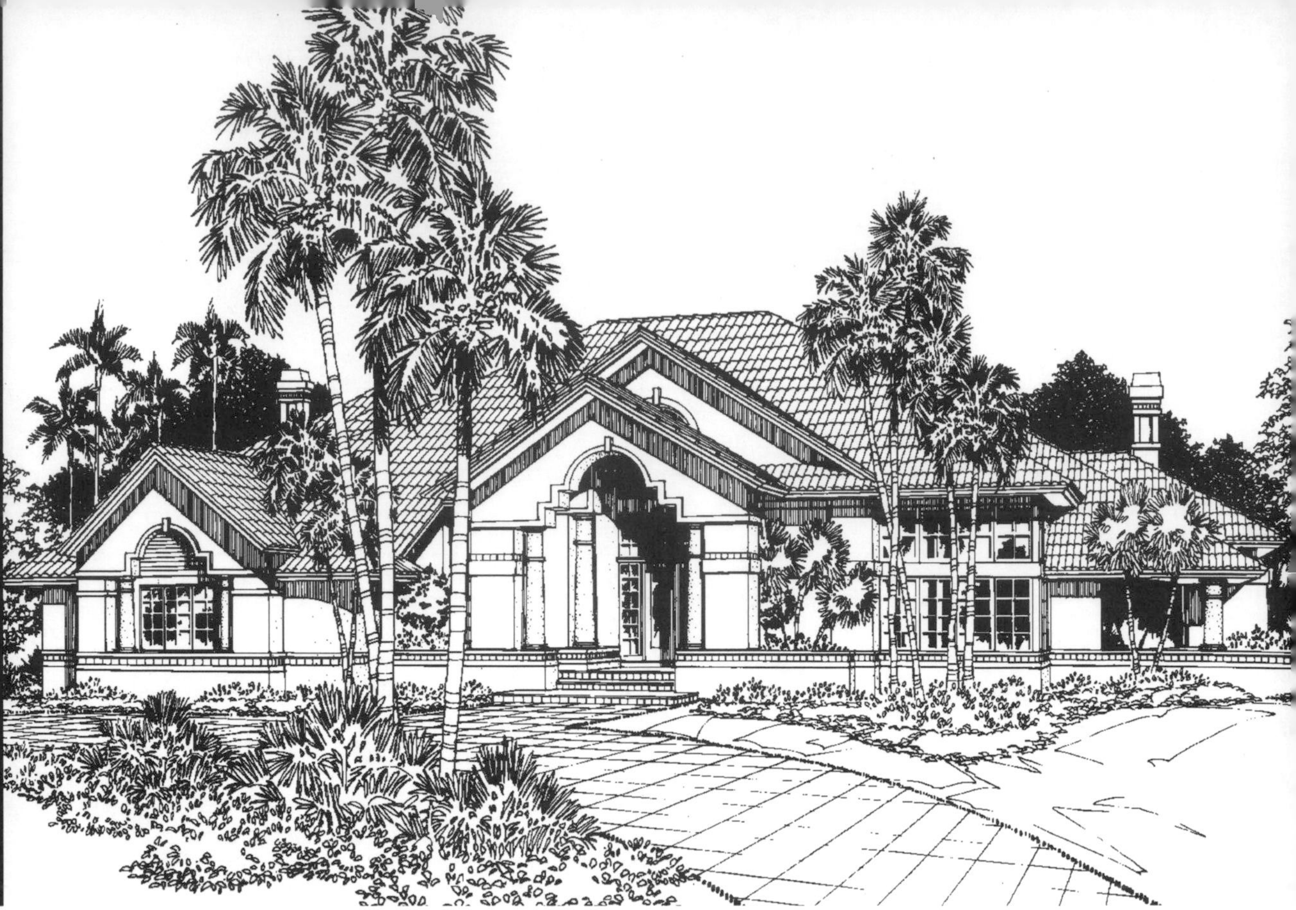

Luxurious Residence

Price Code: L

- This plan features:
- — Three bedrooms
- — Three full and one half baths
- High ceilings in the formal Living and Dining Areas
- Kitchen with cooking island opens to the round Nook and the Leisure Room
- Spacious Master's wing includes a Study, Exercise Room, captivating Bath and pampering Suite
- This home is designed with basement and slab foundation
- Alternate foundation options available at an additional charge. Please call 1-800-235-5700 for more information.

MAIN FLOOR — 4,565 SQ. FT.
GARAGE — 757 SQ. FT.

TOTAL LIVING AREA:
4,565 SQ. FT.

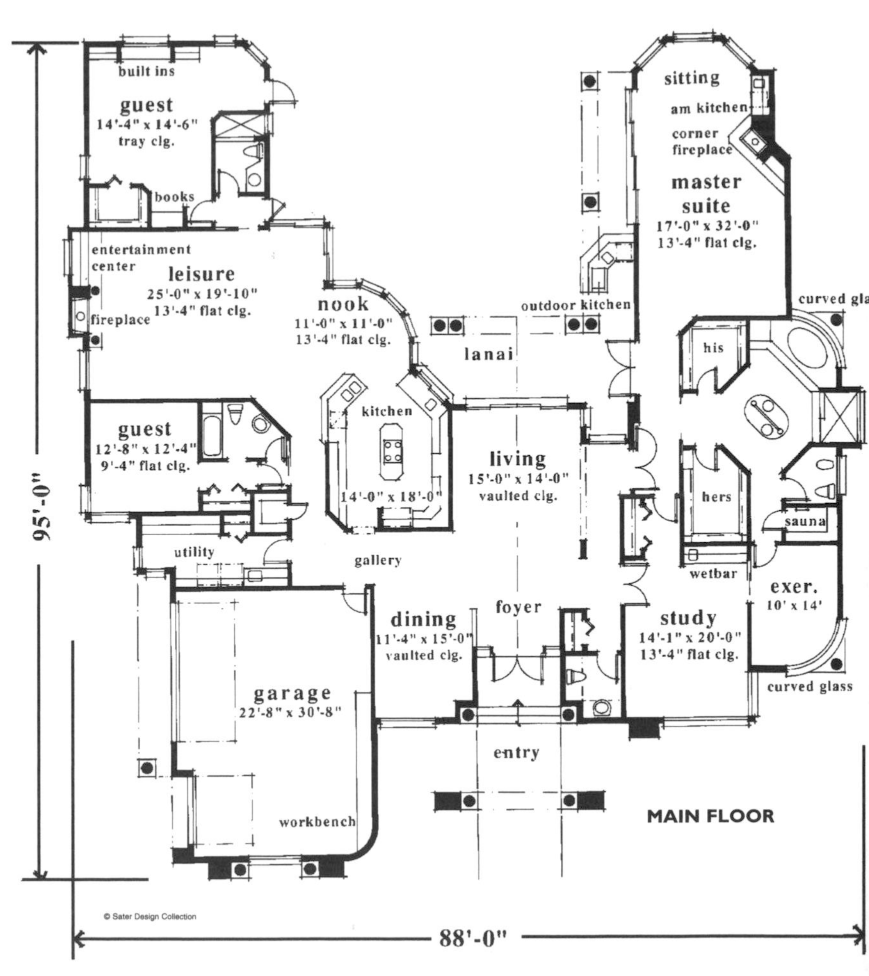
built ins
guest
14'-4" x 14'-6"
tray clg.
books
entertainment center
leisure
25'-0" x 19'-10"
13'-4" flat clg.
fireplace
nook
11'-0" x 11'-0"
13'-4" flat clg.
kitchen
14'-0" x 18'-0"
guest
12'-8" x 12'-4"
9'-4" flat clg.
utility
gallery
lanai
outdoor kitchen
living
15'-0" x 14'-0"
vaulted clg.
sitting
am kitchen
corner fireplace
master suite
17'-0" x 32'-0"
13'-4" flat clg.
curved glass
his
hers
sauna
wetbar
exer.
10' x 14'
study
14'-1" x 20'-0"
13'-4" flat clg.
curved glass
dining
11'-4" x 15'-0"
vaulted clg.
foyer
garage
22'-8" x 30'-8"
workbench
entry
MAIN FLOOR
95'-0"
88'-0"
© Sater Design Collection

Impressive Entry

PRICE CODE: D

This plan features:
- Three bedrooms
- Two full and one half baths
- High arched Entry as a prelude to impressive floor plan
- Living Room topped by a vaulted ceiling and enhanced by a gas fireplace
- Dining Room topped by a vaulted ceiling adjoins the Living Room to create a large living space
- Pocket doors opening to the Kitchen/Nook Area from the Dining Room
- A work island and a walk-in Pantry add to the convenience and efficiency of the Kitchen
- An attractive French door accesses the covered patio from Nook Area
- Family Room contains another gas fireplace
- Master Suite includes a whirlpool bath and a separate shower
- This home is designed with a basement foundation

IRST FLOOR — 1,212 SQ. FT.
ECOND FLOOR — 922 SQ. FT.
ASEMENT — 1,199 SQ. FT.
ARAGE — 464 SQ. FT.

TOTAL LIVING AREA:
2,134 SQ. FT.

PLAN NO.98812
40'0"
50'4"
COVERED PATIO
NOOK
french door
work island
KITCHEN
16'8 x 15'6
pantry
DINING ROOM
10'10 x 11'8
vaulted ceiling
FAMILY ROOM
11'8 x 14'6
gas fireplace
LAUNDRY ROOM
railing
up
dn
line of floor above
guest
storage
gas fireplace
LIVING ROOM
13'2 x 15'4
vaulted ceiling
FOYER
covered entry
TWO-CAR GARAGE
21' x 21'
FIRST FLOOR
jetted tub
ENSUITE
sh
walk-in closet
MASTER SUITE
14'8 x 15'
dn
railing
open to below
BEDROOM
10' x 11'
shelves
desk
BEDROOM
13'6 x 10'
SECOND FLOOR

Distinctive Design

PRICE CODE: A

This plan features:
- Two bedrooms
- One full bath
- The architectural details in this home will attract plenty of curb appeal
- The Entry includes a coat closet for added convenience
- A turret-style alcove off the Living Room provides a quiet spot to read or reflect
- The angled Kitchen has plenty of work space, yet it maintains flow from the living areas
- A Laundry closet is conveniently located by the Bedrooms and the Kitchen
- This home is designed with a basement foundation

AIN FLOOR — 972 SQ. FT.
ASEMENT — 972 SQ. FT.

TOTAL LIVING AREA:
972 SQ. FT.

PLAN NO.65005

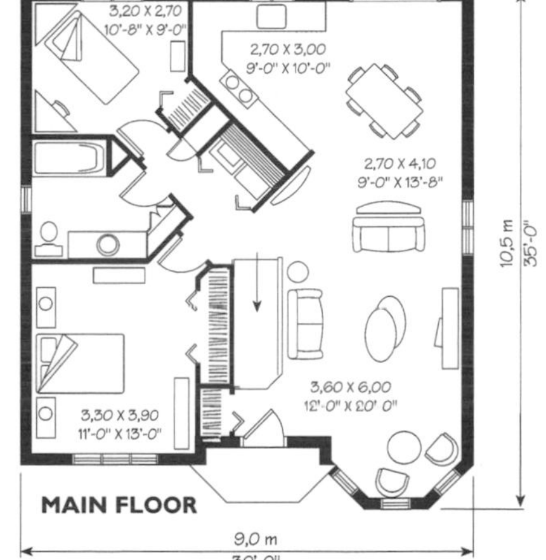
3,20 X 2,70
10'-8" X 9'-0"
2,70 X 3,00
9'-0" X 10'-0"
2,70 X 4,10
9'-0" X 13'-8"
3,60 X 6,00
12'-0" X 20' 0"
3,30 X 3,90
11'-0" X 13'-0"
10,5 m
35'-0"
9,0 m
30'-0"
MAIN FLOOR

PLAN NO.98445

Beautiful Stucco & Stone

PRICE CODE: C

- This plan features:
- — Three bedrooms
- — Two full and one half baths
- This home is accented by keystone arches and a turret-styled roof
- The two-story Foyer includes a half Bath
- The vaulted Family Room is highlighted by a fireplace and French doors to the rear yard
- The Dining Room adjoins the Family Room which has access to the covered Porch and the Kitchen
- The Master Bedroom is crowned by a tray ceiling, whil Master Bath has a vaulted ceiling
- Two additional Bedrooms share a full double vanity Ba
- A Balcony overlooks the Family Room and Foyer belov
- This home is designed with basement and crawlspace foundation options

FIRST FLOOR — 1,398 SQ. FT.
SECOND FLOOR — 515 SQ. FT.
BASEMENT — 1,398 SQ. FT.
GARAGE — 421 SQ. FT.

TOTAL LIVING AREA: 1,913 SQ. FT.

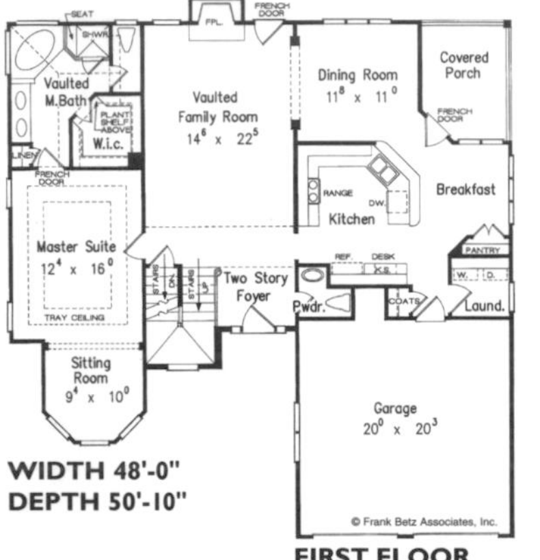
Vaulted M.Bath
W.i.c.
Vaulted Family Room 14⁶ x 22⁵
Dining Room 11⁶ x 11⁰
Covered Porch
Kitchen
Breakfast
Master Suite 12⁴ x 16⁰
TRAY CEILING
Two Story Foyer
Pwdr.
Laund.
Sitting Room 9⁴ x 10⁰
Garage 20⁰ x 20³
© Frank Betz Associates, Inc.

WIDTH 48'-0"
DEPTH 50'-10"

FIRST FLOOR

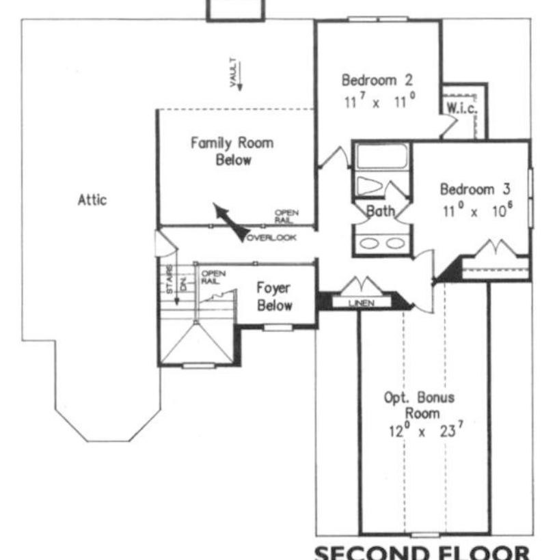
Attic
Family Room Below
Bedroom 2 11⁷ x 11⁰
W.i.c.
Bedroom 3 11⁰ x 10⁶
Bath
Foyer Below
Opt. Bonus Room 12⁰ x 23⁷

SECOND FLOOR

PLAN NO.92557

Elegant Brick Exterior

PRICE CODE: A

- This plan features:
- — Three bedrooms
- — Two full baths
- Detailing and accenting columns highlighting the covered front Porch
- Den is enhanced by a corner fireplace and adjoining wi Dining Room
- Efficient Kitchen well-appointed and with easy access t the Utility/Laundry Room
- Master Bedroom topped by a vaulted ceiling and pampered by a private Bath and a walk-in closet
- Two secondary Bedrooms are located at the opposite end of the home sharing a full Bath located between the two rooms
- This home is designed with slab and crawlspace foundation options

MAIN FLOOR — 1,390 SQ. FT.
GARAGE — 590 SQ. FT.

TOTAL LIVING AREA: 1,390 SQ. FT.

sto 4 x 8⁶ sto 4 x 8⁶
garage 22 x 22
util 7 x 7
kit 10 x 11⁶
dining 12 x 11
br 2 12 x 11
den 16 x 17
mbr 13 x 15
ledge
br 3 12 x 11
porch 4 x 16

WIDTH 67'-4"
DEPTH 32'-10"

MAIN FLOOR

Small Yet Stylish

PRICE CODE: A

PLAN NO.98549

This plan features:
- Three bedrooms
- Two full baths
- The Living Room is topped by a 10-foot ceiling and highlighted by a fireplace and a built-in entertainment center
- A walk-in closet and a five-piece Bath further enhance the Master Suite
- The Kitchen and the Dining Room are open to each other and topped by a cathedral ceiling
- A walk-in Pantry is located in the Utility Room
- This home is designed with a slab foundation

AIN FLOOR — 1,431 SQ. FT.
RAGE — 410 SQ. FT.

TOTAL LIVING AREA:
1,431 SQ. FT.

WIDTH 44'-0"
DEPTH 57'-1"
MstrBed
12x15
Patio
Din
11x10
Kit
11x10
LivRm
19x17
Bed#3
11x11
Util
Bed#2
12x11
Por
Gar
19x21
MAIN FLOOR

Window Boxes Add Romantic Charm

PRICE CODE: B

PLAN NO.90684

This plan features:
- Three bedrooms
- Two full and one half baths
- A spacious Living Room and formal Dining Room combination that is perfect for entertaining
- A Family Room with a large fireplace and an expansive glass wall that overlooks the Patio
- An informal Dining bay, convenient to both the Kitchen and the Family Room
- An efficient and well-equipped Kitchen with a peninsula counter dividing it from the Family Room
- A Master Bedroom with his and her closets and a private Master Bath
- This home is designed with basement and slab foundation options

AIN FLOOR — 1590 SQ. FT.
ASEMENT — 900 SQ. FT.

TOTAL LIVING AREA:
1,590 SQ. FT.

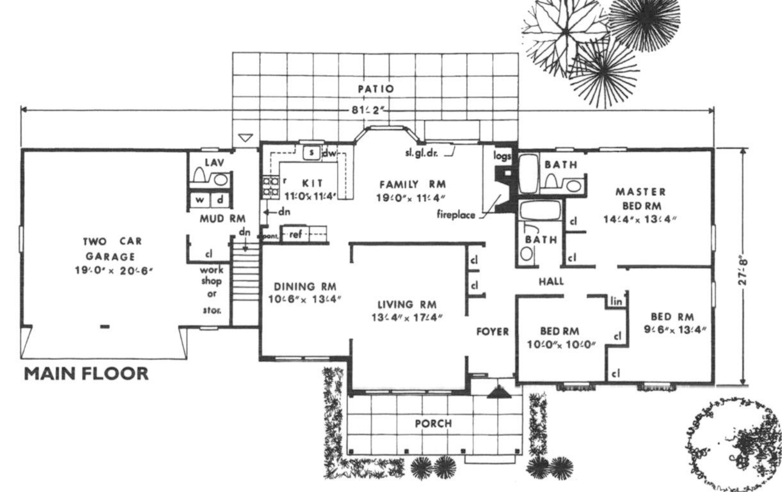
PATIO
81'-2"
LAV
MUD RM
KIT
11'-0"x 11'-4"
FAMILY RM
19'-0"x 11'-4"
sl.gl.dr.
fireplace
BATH
MASTER
BED RM
14'-4"x 13'-4"
TWO CAR
GARAGE
19'-0"x 20'-6"
work
shop
or
stor.
DINING RM
10'-6"x 13'-4"
LIVING RM
13'-4"x 17'-4"
FOYER
HALL
BED RM
10'-0"x 10'-0"
BED RM
9'-6"x 13'-4"
27'-8"
PORCH
MAIN FLOOR

PLAN NO. 94975

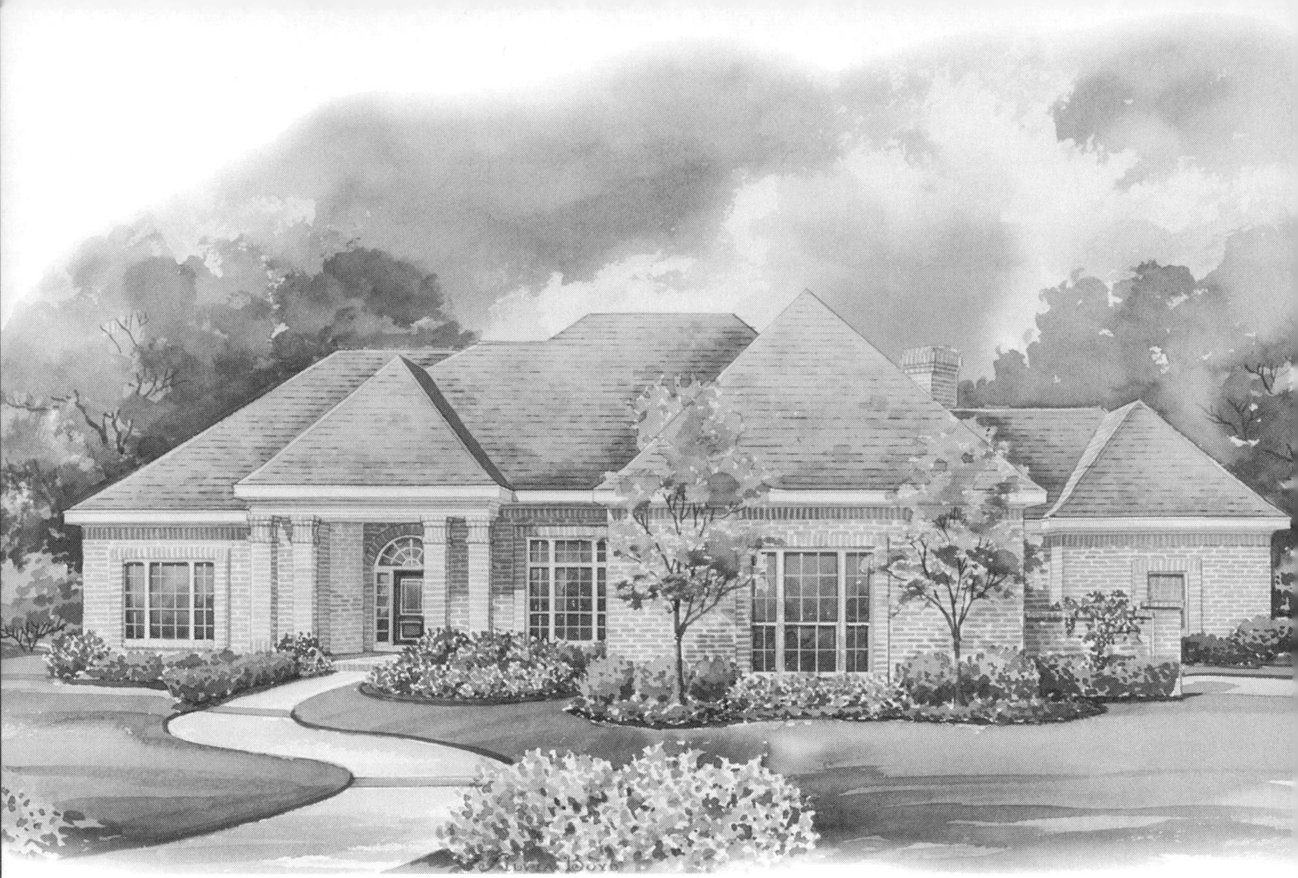

A Streamlined Design

Price Code: I

- This plan features:
- — Three bedrooms
- — One full, one three-quarter and two half baths
- Recessed, glass arched entrance leads into unique Entry and Living Room with alcove access to Covered Porch
- Dining Room with triple arch window, adjoins Living Room
- Master Bedroom wing offers an alcove of windows, two walk-in closets and a luxurious Bath
- This home is designed with basement and slab foundation options
- Alternate foundation options available at an additional charge. Please call 1-800-235-5700 for more information.

MAIN FLOOR — 3,312 SQ. FT.
GARAGE — 752 SQ. FT.

TOTAL LIVING AREA:
3,312 SQ. FT.

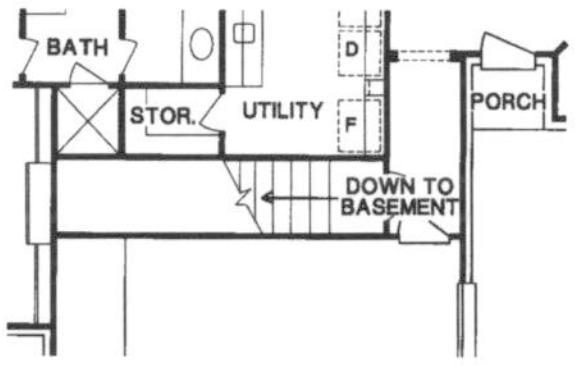

BATH
STOR.
UTILITY
PORCH
DOWN TO BASEMENT

OPTIONAL BASEMENT STAIR LOCATION

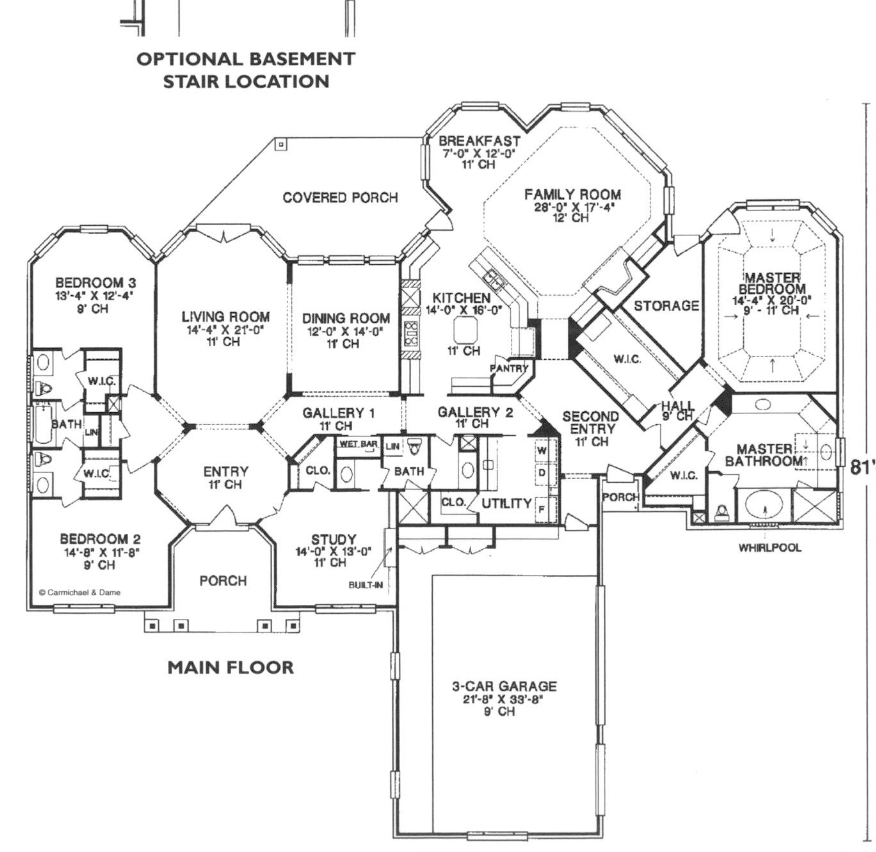
BREAKFAST
7'-0" X 12'-0"
11' CH
COVERED PORCH
FAMILY ROOM
28'-0" X 17'-4"
12' CH
BEDROOM 3
13'-4" X 12'-4"
9' CH
LIVING ROOM
14'-4" X 21'-0"
11' CH
DINING ROOM
12'-0" X 14'-0"
11' CH
KITCHEN
14'-0" X 16'-0"
11' CH
PANTRY
STORAGE
MASTER BEDROOM
14'-4" X 20'-0"
9' - 11' CH
W.I.C.
HALL
9' CH
GALLERY 1
11' CH
GALLERY 2
11' CH
SECOND ENTRY
11' CH
WET BAR
LIN
BATH
CLO.
ENTRY
11' CH
UTILITY
MASTER BATHROOM
PORCH
WHIRLPOOL
BEDROOM 2
14'-8" X 11'-8"
9' CH
STUDY
14'-0" X 13'-0"
11' CH
BUILT-IN
PORCH
3-CAR GARAGE
21'-8" X 33'-8"
9' CH
90'-11"
81'-

MAIN FLOOR

European Styling

PRICE CODE: E

'his plan features:
- Three bedrooms
- Two full and one half baths
- 'he large Foyer leads to the open Great and Dining Rooms
- A large informal area includes the Kitchen, Gathering, ınd Breakfast Rooms
- 'he Kitchen features an island bar, double sink, Pantry, lesk, and wall oven
- 'he home has two fireplaces, one in the Great Room, the ›ther in the Gathering Room
- Decorative ceiling can be found in the Dining Room, the Master Suite, and Breakfast Nook
- 'he Master Suite features dual walk-in closets and a five-piece Bath
- This home is designed with basement and crawlspace foundation options

AIN FLOOR — 2,290 SQ. FT.
ONUS ROOM — 304 SQ. FT.
SEMENT — 2,290 SQ. FT.
RAGE — 544 SQ. FT.

TOTAL LIVING AREA:
2,290 SQ. FT.

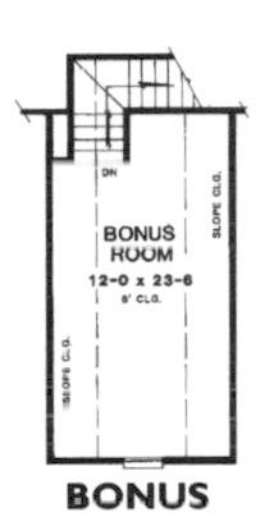
BONUS ROOM
12-0 x 23-6
BONUS

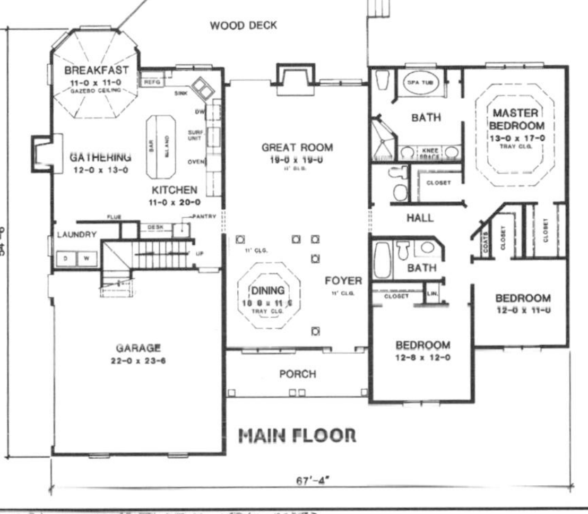
WOOD DECK
BREAKFAST
11-0 x 11-0
GATHERING
12-0 x 13-0
KITCHEN
11-0 x 20-0
LAUNDRY
GREAT ROOM
19-6 x 19-0
MASTER BEDROOM
13-0 x 17-0
BATH
CLOSET
HALL
BATH
BEDROOM
12-0 x 11-0
BEDROOM
12-8 x 12-0
DINING
10-8 x 11-6
FOYER
PORCH
GARAGE
22-0 x 23-6
54'-6"
67'-4"
MAIN FLOOR

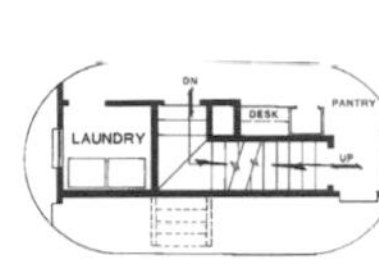
LAUNDRY
DESK

CRAWLSPACE/SLAB FOUNDATION OPTION

Essence of Style and Grace

PRICE CODE: G

This plan features:
- Four bedrooms
- Three full and one half baths
- French doors introduce the Study and columns define the Gallery and formal areas
- The expansive Family Room with an inviting fireplace and a cathedral ceiling opens to the Kitchen
- The Kitchen features a cooktop island, Butler's Pantry, Breakfast Area, and Patio access
- The first floor Master Bedroom offers a private Patio, vaulted ceiling, twin vanities, and walk-in closet
- Three second floor Bedrooms each access a full Bath
- This home is designed with basement and slab foundation options

RST FLOOR — 2,036 SQ. FT.
COND FLOOR — 866 SQ. FT.
ARAGE — 720 SQ. FT.

TOTAL LIVING AREA:
2,902 SQ. FT.

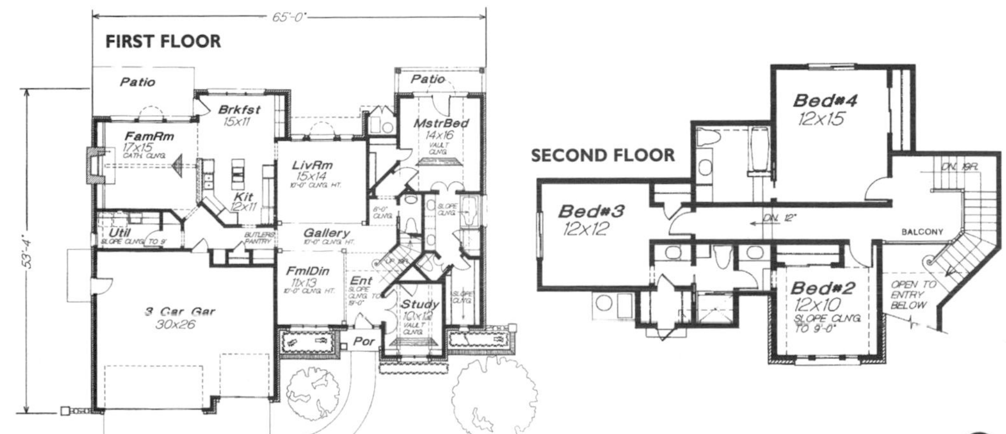
65'-0"
FIRST FLOOR
Patio
Brkfst
15x11
FamRm
17x15
LivRm
15x14
Patio
MstrBed
14x16
Kit
12x11
Util
Gallery
FmlDin
11x13
Ent
Study
10x12
3 Car Gar
30x26
Por
53'-4"
SECOND FLOOR
Bed#4
12x15
Bed#3
12x12
Bed#2
12x10
BALCONY
OPEN TO ENTRY BELOW

PLAN NO. 97280

Easy Street

PRICE CODE: C

- This plan features:
- — Three bedrooms
- — Two full and one half baths
- A two-story Foyer is a grand introduction to this home
- The Living Room and the Dining Room connect throu an arched opening
- The Kitchen opens to the Breakfast Room and the Kitchen directly accesses the Dining Room
- The Family Room offers a vaulted ceiling, a fireplace with built-in bookcases and a plant shelf
- The Master Suite includes a tray ceiling and a French door into the Master Bathroom
- This home is designed with basement and crawlspace foundation options

FIRST FLOOR — 1,073 SQ. FT.
SECOND FLOOR — 742 SQ. FT.
BONUS — 336 SQ. FT.
BASEMENT — 1,073 SQ. FT.
GARAGE — 495 SQ. FT.

TOTAL LIVING AREA:
1,815 SQ. FT.

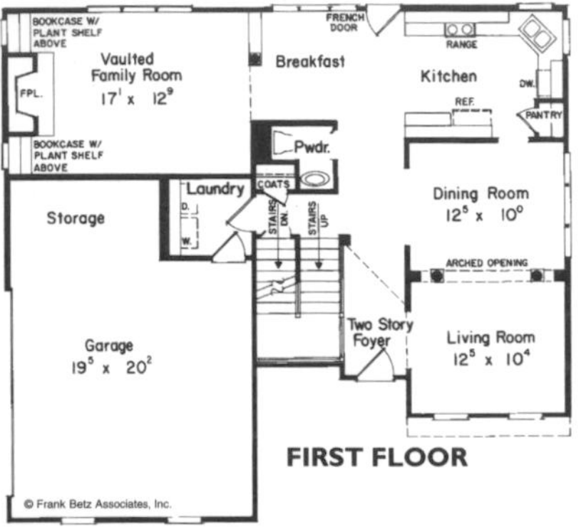

BOOKCASE W/ PLANT SHELF ABOVE
Vaulted Family Room 17¹ x 12⁹
FPL.
BOOKCASE W/ PLANT SHELF ABOVE
Breakfast
FRENCH DOOR
Kitchen
RANGE
REF.
DW
PANTRY
Pwdr.
Laundry
COATS
Storage
STAIRS DN
STAIRS UP
Dining Room 12⁵ x 10⁰
ARCHED OPENING
Two Story Foyer
Living Room 12⁵ x 10⁴
Garage 19⁵ x 20²
FIRST FLOOR
© Frank Betz Associates, Inc.

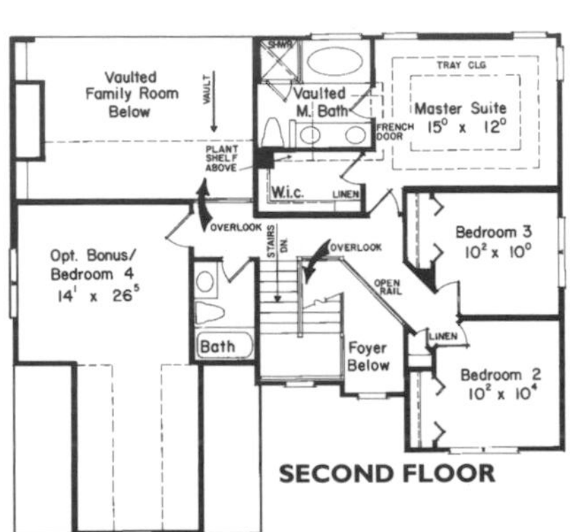

Vaulted Family Room Below
VAULT
PLANT SHELF ABOVE
Vaulted M. Bath
TRAY CLG
Master Suite 15⁰ x 12⁰
FRENCH DOOR
W.i.c.
LINEN
OVERLOOK
Opt. Bonus/ Bedroom 4 14¹ x 26⁵
STAIRS
OVERLOOK
OPEN RAIL
Bedroom 3 10² x 10⁰
Bath
Foyer Below
LINEN
Bedroom 2 10² x 10⁴
SECOND FLOOR

WIDTH 45'-0"
DEPTH 40'-0"

PLAN NO. 94242

A Custom Look

PRICE CODE: H

- This plan features:
- — Three bedrooms
- — Three full and one half baths
- Wonderfully balanced exterior highlighted by triple arched glass in Entry Porch, leading into the Gallery Foyer
- Triple arches lead into Formal Living and Dining Roo Veranda and beyond
- Kitchen, Nook, and Leisure Room area easily flow together
- Owners' wing has a Master Suite with glass alcove to rear yard, a lavish Bath and a Study offering many use
- Two additional Bedrooms with corner windows and over-sized closets access a full Bath
- This home is designed with a slab foundation
- Alternate foundation options available at an additional charge. Please call 1-800-235-5700 for more information.

MAIN FLOOR — 2,978 SQ. FT
GARAGE — 702 SQ. FT.

TOTAL LIVING AREA:
2,978 SQ. FT.

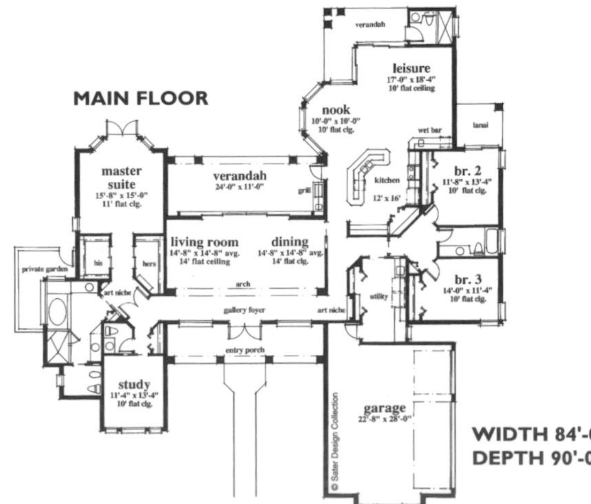

MAIN FLOOR
verandah
leisure 17'-0" x 18'-4" 10' flat ceiling
nook 10'-0" x 10'-0" 10' flat clg.
wet bar
lanai
master suite 15'-8" x 15'-0" 11' flat clg.
verandah 24'-0" x 11'-0"
grill
kitchen 12' x 16'
br. 2 11'-8" x 13'-4" 10' flat clg.
living room 14'-8" x 14'-8" avg. 14' flat ceiling
dining 14'-8" x 14'-8" avg. 14' flat clg.
his
hers
private garden
art niche
arch
gallery foyer
art niche
utility
br. 3 14'-0" x 11'-4" 10' flat clg.
entry porch
study 11'-4" x 13'-4" 10' flat clg.
garage 22'-8" x 28'-0"
© Sater Design Collection

WIDTH 84'-0"
DEPTH 90'-0"

To order your Blueprints, call 1-800-235-5700

PLAN NO. 98552

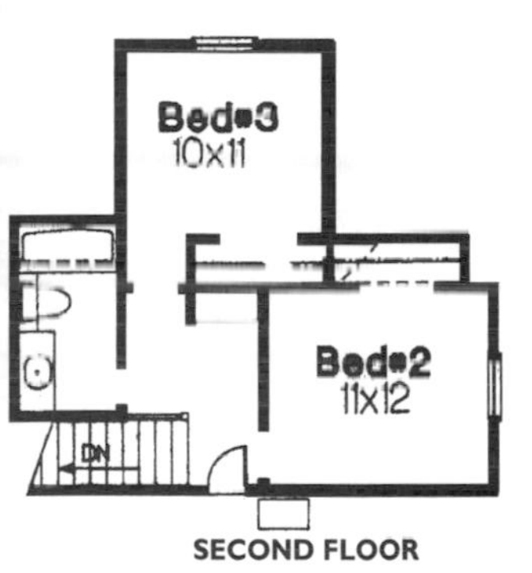

Bed#3
10x11
Bed#2
11x12
DN

SECOND FLOOR

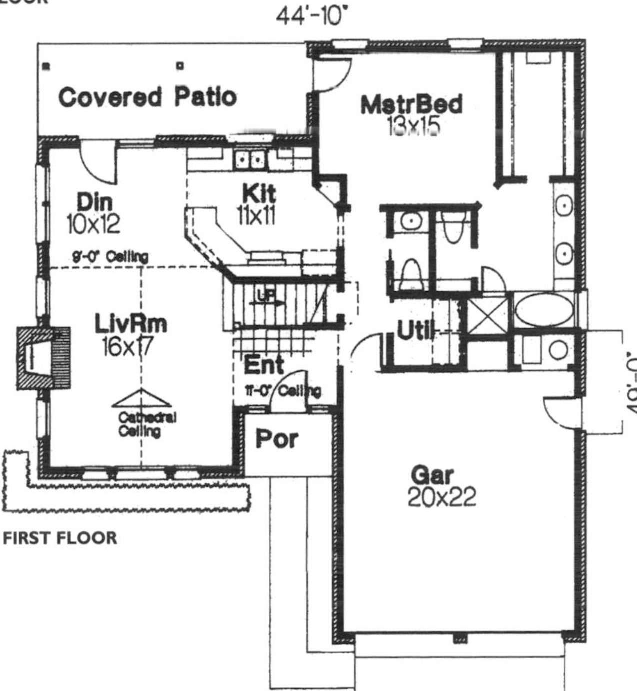

44'-10"
Covered Patio
MstrBed
13x15
Din
10x12
Kit
11x11
9'-0" Ceiling
UP
LivRm
16x17
Util
Ent
11'-0" Ceiling
Cathedral Ceiling
Por
Gar
20x22
49'-0"

FIRST FLOOR

Grand Front Window

PRICE CODE: B

- This plan features:
- — Three bedrooms
- — Two full and one half baths
- The high, arched front window gives this home curb appeal and natural illumination to the Living Room
- The Living Room is topped by a cathedral ceiling and enhanced by a fireplace
- The Master Suite has its own private corner of the home and includes a five-piece Bath and a walk-in closet
- The secondary Bedrooms are on the second floor with a full Bath easily accessible
- This home is designed with a slab foundation

FIRST FLOOR — 1,177 SQ. FT.
SECOND FLOOR — 406 SQ. FT.
GARAGE — 440 SQ. FT.

TOTAL LIVING AREA:
1,583 SQ. FT.

PLAN NO.98447

Details, Details, Details

PRICE CODE: D

- This plan features:
  - — Three bedrooms
  - — Two full and one half baths
- This elevation is highlighted by stucco, stone and detailing around the arched windows
- The two-story Foyer allows access to the Dining Roo and the Great Room
- A vaulted ceiling and a fireplace can be found in the Great Room
- The Breakfast Room has a vaulted ceiling and flows into the Kitchen and the Keeping Room
- Two secondary Bedrooms, each with a walk-in closet, share a full hall Bath
- The Master Suite has a tray ceiling, a huge walk-in cl and a compartmental Bath
- This home is designed with basement and crawlspace foundation options

FIRST FLOOR — 1,628 SQ. FT.
SECOND FLOOR — 527 SQ. FT.
BONUS ROOM — 207 SQ. FT.
BASEMENT — 1,628 SQ. FT.
GARAGE — 440 SQ. FT.

TOTAL LIVING AREA:
2,155 SQ. FT.

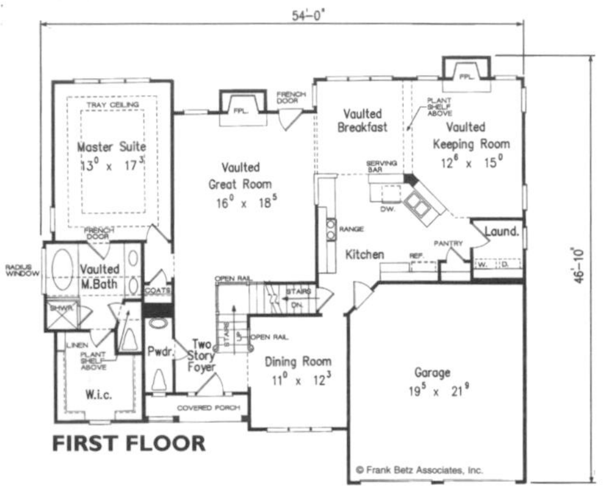
54'-0"
46'-10"
Master Suite
13⁰ x 17⁰
Vaulted
Great Room
16⁰ x 18⁵
Vaulted
Breakfast
Vaulted
Keeping Room
12⁶ x 15⁰
Kitchen
Laund.
Vaulted
M.Bath
W.i.c.
Pwdr.
Two
Story
Foyer
Dining Room
11⁰ x 12³
Garage
19⁵ x 21⁹
© Frank Betz Associates, Inc.

FIRST FLOOR

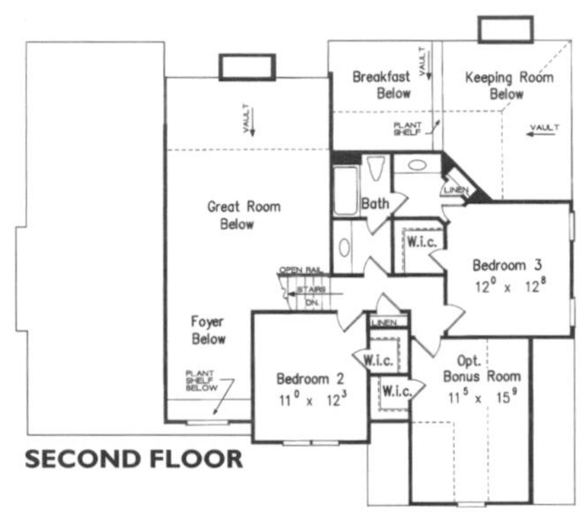
Breakfast
Below
Keeping Room
Below
Great Room
Below
Bath
Bedroom 3
12⁰ x 12⁸
Foyer
Below
Bedroom 2
11⁰ x 12³
W.i.c.
Opt.
Bonus Room
11⁵ x 15⁹

SECOND FLOOR

PLAN NO.98540

Stunning First Impression

PRICE CODE: E

- This plan features:
  - — Four bedrooms
  - — Two full and one half baths
- Dormer windows on the second floor, arched window and entrance, brick quoin corners come together for a stunning first impression
- Large Living Room with a fireplace and an open form Dining Area
- Family Room at the rear of home containing a bar
- Huge island Kitchen with a Breakfast Area and plenty of work and storage space
- Luxurious Master Suite occupying an entire wing of t home and providing a quiet retreat
- Three additional Bedrooms on the second floor sharin a large Bath
- This home is designed with basement, slab and crawlspace foundation options

MAIN FLOOR — 1,805 SQ. FT.
UPPER FLOOR — 659 SQ. FT.
BASEMENT — 1,800 SQ. FT.
GARAGE — 440 SQ. FT.

TOTAL LIVING AREA:
2,464 SQ. FT.

58' - 0"
57' - 10"
Patio
FamilyRm 14x17
Breakfast 10x10
Bar
Kit 10x14
LivRm 17x17
MstrBed 14x17
Master
Gallery
Ent
Util
FmlDin 12x13
Por
Gar 20x23

MAIN FLOOR

Bed#4 10x12
Bed#3 11x13
B#2
Bed#2 11x12

UPPER FLOOR

Fabulous Family Living

PRICE CODE: D

'his plan features:
- 'our bedrooms
- Two full and one half baths
- 'he covered Porch leads to an Entry with a athedral ceiling
- 'he formal Dining Room adjoins the Great Room or an easy transition when entertaining
- cathedral ceiling adds volume to the Master Suite
- 'his home is designed with slab and crawlspace oundation options

ST FLOOR — 1,359 SQ. FT.
OND FLOOR — 697 SQ. FT.
RAGE — 440 SQ. FT.

TOTAL LIVING AREA:
2,056 SQ. FT.

PLAN NO. 98551

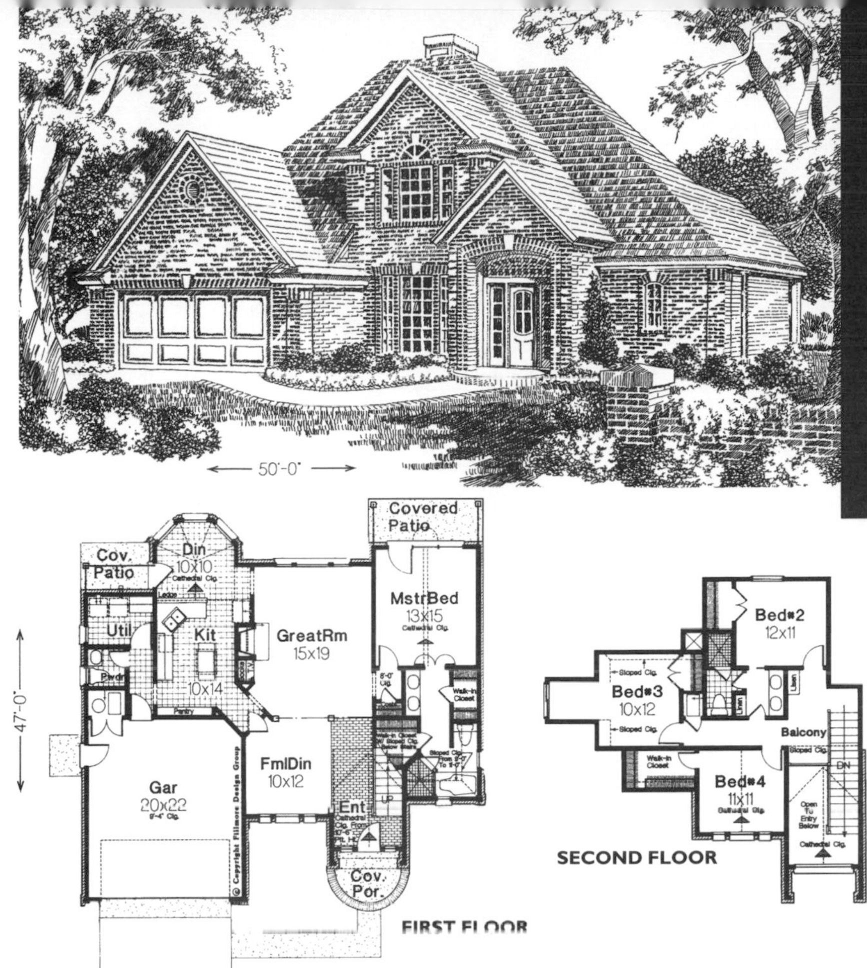

50'-0"
47'-0"
Covered Patio
Cov. Patio
Din 10x10
Util
Kit 10x14
Pwdr
Pantry
GreatRm 15x19
MstrBed 13x15
FmlDin 10x12
Gar 20x22
Ent
Cov. Por.
FIRST FLOOR
Bed#2 12x11
Bed#3 10x12
Balcony
Bed#4 11x11
DN
SECOND FLOOR

Easy to Build

PRICE CODE: A

This plan features:
- Two bedrooms
- One bathroom
- Affordable ranch with all the amenities
- Covered Entry leads into Foyer and Living and Dining Rooms
- Focal-point fireplace and bay window enhance the Living Room
- Country-style Kitchen opens to Dining Room, Nook, Utility Room and Garage
- Master Bedroom features an oversized closet and private access to full Bath with whirlpool tub
- Second Bedroom has an oversized closet and access to full bath
- This home is designed with a crawlspace foundation

AIN FLOOR — 1,313 SQ. FT.
ARAGE — 385 SQ. FT.

TOTAL LIVING AREA:
1,313 SQ. FT.

PLAN NO. 90865

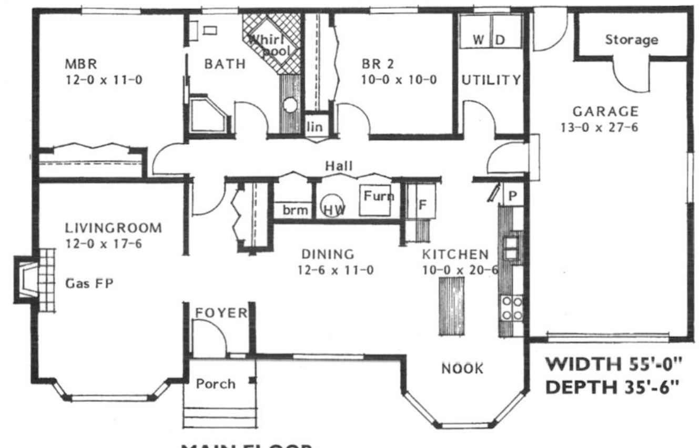

MBR 12-0 x 11-0
BATH
Whirlpool
BR 2 10-0 x 10-0
W D
UTILITY
Storage
GARAGE 13-0 x 27-6
lin
Hall
brm
HW
Furn
F
P
LIVINGROOM 12-0 x 17-6
Gas FP
DINING 12-6 x 11-0
KITCHEN 10-0 x 20-6
FOYER
Porch
NOOK
WIDTH 55'-0"
DEPTH 35'-6"
MAIN FLOOR

PLAN NO.98522

Brick Abounds

PRICE CODE: B

- ■ This plan features:
- — Three bedrooms
- — Two full baths
- ■ The covered front Porch opens into the Entry that has a 10-foot ceiling and a coat closet
- ■ The large Living Room is distinguished by a fireplace and a front window wall
- ■ The Dining Room features a 10-foot ceiling and access to the rear covered Patio
- ■ The Kitchen is angled and has a Pantry, and a cooktop island
- ■ The Master Bedroom is located in the rear for privacy and boasts a triangular walk-in closet, plus a private B
- ■ Two more Bedrooms each have large closets and share a hallway Bath
- ■ This home has a two-car Garage that is accessed throu the Utility Room
- ■ This home is designed with a slab foundation

MAIN FLOOR — 1,528 SQ. FT.
GARAGE — 440 SQ. FT.

TOTAL LIVING AREA:* 1,528 *SQ. FT.

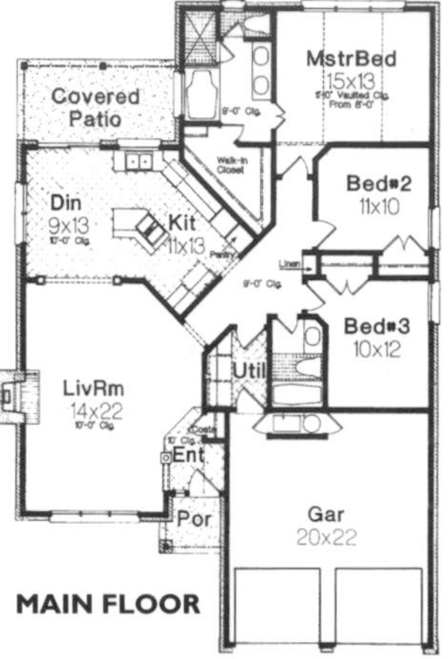

MstrBed
15x13
Covered Patio
Din
9x13
Kit
11x13
Bed#2
11x10
Bed#3
10x12
Util
LivRm
14x22
Ent
Por
Gar
20x22

WIDTH 40'-0"
DEPTH 60'-8"

MAIN FLOOR

PLAN NO.94260

Southampton Style Cottage

PRICE CODE: F

- ■ This plan features:
- — Three bedrooms
- — Two full baths
- ■ Stairs lead up to the covered Entry Porch and into the Foyer
- ■ An arched opening leads into the Grand Room, which has a fireplace
- ■ Five French doors in various rooms open out onto the rear Lanai
- ■ Access the Dining Room from the Kitchen through an arched opening
- ■ The Kitchen has a walk-in Pantry located next to the Nook
- ■ The secondary Bedrooms share a Bath in their own wi of the home
- ■ On the opposite side of the home are a Study and the Master Suite
- ■ The space on the ground level can be finished into a Recreation Room
- ■ This home is designed with a pier/post foundation
- ■ Alternate foundation options available at an additional charge. Please call 1-800-235-5700 for more informati

MAIN FLOOR — 2,068 SQ. FT.
BONUS — 1,402 SQ. FT.
GARAGE — 560 SQ. FT.

TOTAL LIVING AREA:* 2,068 *SQ. FT.

© Sater Design Collection

lanai 58'-0" x 10'-8"
master suite 13'-0" x 15'-0" 9'-4" stepped clg.
grand room 20'-0" x 18'-0" avg. tray ceiling
nook 11'-0" x 9'-4"
br. 2 12'-0" x 11'-4" 9'-4" flat clg.
kitchen 11' x 11'
study 11'-0" x 11'-0" 9'-4" flat clg.
dining 10'-10" x 15'-0" 9'-4" flat clg.
br. 3 12'-0" x 11'-0" 9'-4" flat clg.
foyer
entry porch
planter

MAIN FLOOR

54'-0"
58'-0"
verandah 58'-0" x 12'-0"
recreation 25'-0" x 35'-0"
storage
garage 23'-4" x 24'-0"

LOWER FLOOR

Great Starter Home

PRICE CODE: B

PLAN NO. 65245

his plan features:

- 'hree bedrooms
-)ne full bath
- he Foyer offers easy access to the Living Room, e Kitchen and Dining Area, the Bedrooms and e basement
- lenty of natural light enters the Living Room, anks to the tall arch-topped window
- he L-shaped Kitchen is open to the other ving areas, with a pentagon-shaped island leneating the space
- he three Bedrooms share a full Bath with corner b and separte shower
- his home is designed with a asement foundation

IN FLOOR — 1,504 SQ. FT.
RAGE — 424 SQ. FT.

TOTAL LIVING AREA:
1,504 SQ. FT.

MAIN FLOOR
4,70 X 3,30
15'-8" X 11'-0"
3,20 X 3,70
10'-8" X 12'-4"
3,00 X 3,00
10'-0" X 10'-0"
3,60 X 4,80
12'-0" X 16'-0"
6,20 X 6,10
20'-8" X 20'-4"
3,30 X 3,70
10'-0" X 12'-4"
3,90 X 5,20
13'-0" X 17'-4"
WIDTH 59' 8"
DEPTH 44'-4"

Three-Sided Fireplace

PRICE CODE: E

PLAN NO. 65255

'his plan features:

- Three bedrooms
- Three full and one half baths
- 'he angled fireplace is shared y the Living Room, Dining Room, nd Kitchen
- n second floor Media Room rovides privacy in this open plan
- 'his home is designed with a asement foundation

ST FLOOR — 1,437 SQ. FT.
COND FLOOR — 1,060 SQ. FT.
SEMENT — 1,437 SQ. FT.
RAGE — 438 SQ. FT.

TOTAL LIVING AREA:
2,497 SQ. FT.

FIRST FLOOR
SECOND FLOOR

PLAN NO. 90502

Stucco Captures Shade

Price Code: B

- This plan features:
- — Three bedrooms
- — Two full baths
- Sheltered Entry opens to airy Living/Dining Room with an inviting fireplace
- Central Family Room with another fireplace opens to glass Nook with access to Covered Patio
- Open Kitchen easily serves nearby Dining Area, Nook, and Patio beyond
- French doors open to Master Suite with Patio access and a private Bath
- Two additional Bedrooms, with ample closets, share a full Bath and Laundry
- This home is designed with crawlspace and slab foundation options

MAIN FLOOR — 1,642 SQ. FT.

TOTAL LIVING AREA:
1,642 SQ. FT.

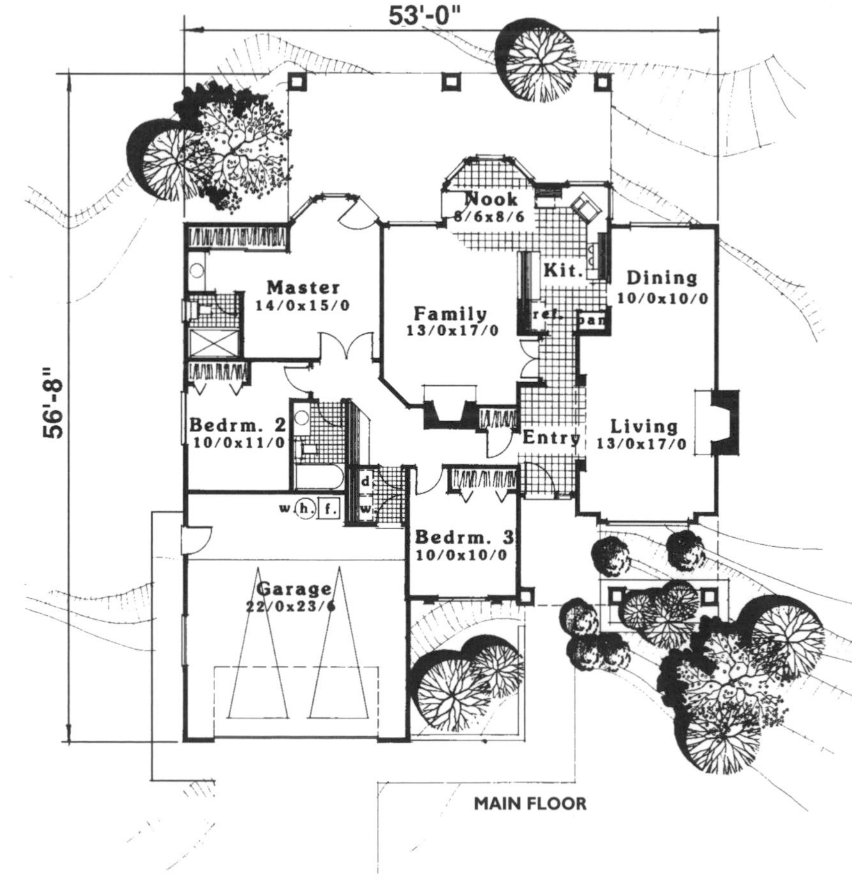
53'-0"
56'-8"
Nook
8/6x8/6
Kit.
Dining
10/0x10/0
Master
14/0x15/0
Family
13/0x17/0
ref.
pan
Bedrm. 2
10/0x11/0
Entry
Living
13/0x17/0
w
h.
f.
d
w
Bedrm. 3
10/0x10/0
Garage
22/0x23/6
MAIN FLOOR

Cozy Comfort

PRICE CODE: A

This plan features:
- Two bedrooms
- One full bath
- With two front Porches, you can choose a favorite spot to watch the world pass by
- The U-shaped Kitchen includes an eating bar that is also a divider to the Dining Room
- The Laundry closet is tucked away in the full Bathroom
- This home is designed with a basement foundation

MAIN FLOOR — 970 SQ. FT.
PORCH — 152 SQ. FT.

TOTAL LIVING AREA:
920 SQ. FT.

PLAN NO.65006

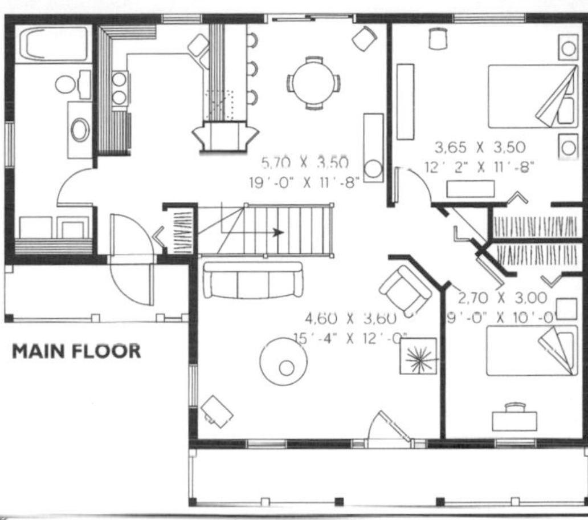

5.70 X 3.50
19'-0" X 11'-8"
3.65 X 3.50
12' 2" X 11'-8"
2.70 X 3.00
9'-0" X 10'-0
4.60 X 3.60
15'-4" X 12'-0"
MAIN FLOOR

WIDTH 38'-0"
DEPTH 28'-0"

Split Bedroom Floor Plan

PRICE CODE: A

This plan features:
- Three bedrooms
- Two full baths
- A split-Bedroom floor plan gives the Master Bedroom ultimate privacy
- The Great Room is highlighted by a fireplace and a vaulted 10-foot ceiling
- A snack bar peninsula counter is one of the many conveniences of the Kitchen
- The Patio is accessed from the Dining Room and expands dining to the outdoors
- Two additional Bedrooms share the full Bath in the hall
- This home is designed with crawlspace and slab foundation options

MAIN FLOOR — 1,243 SQ. FT.
GARAGE — 523 SQ. FT.

TOTAL LIVING AREA:
1,243 SQ. FT.

PLAN NO.96519

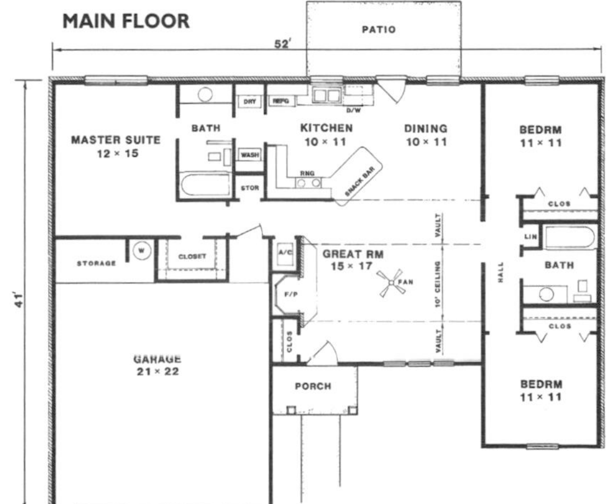

MAIN FLOOR
PATIO
52'
41'
MASTER SUITE
12 × 15
BATH
KITCHEN
10 × 11
DINING
10 × 11
BEDRM
11 × 11
GREAT RM
15 × 17
FAN
10' CEILING
VAULT
HALL
BATH
GARAGE
21 × 22
PORCH
BEDRM
11 × 11
STORAGE
CLOSET
SNACK BAR

PLAN NO.97288

On A Grand Scale

PRICE CODE: H

- This plan features:
- — Four bedrooms
- — Four full baths
- The Dining Room's entrance is defined by columns and the Living Room is to the right of the Foyer
- The Family Room has a two-story ceiling and a cozy fireplace
- The Kitchen includes a cooktop island, Pantry, and generous counter space
- The Master Suite is on the second floor and includes a tray ceiling over the Bedrooms and lavish Bath
- This home is designed with basement and crawlspace foundation options

FIRST FLOOR — 1,595 SQ. FT.
SECOND FLOOR — 1,518 SQ. FT.
BASEMENT — 1,595 SQ. FT.
GARAGE — 475 SQ. FT.

TOTAL LIVING AREA:
3,113 SQ. FT.

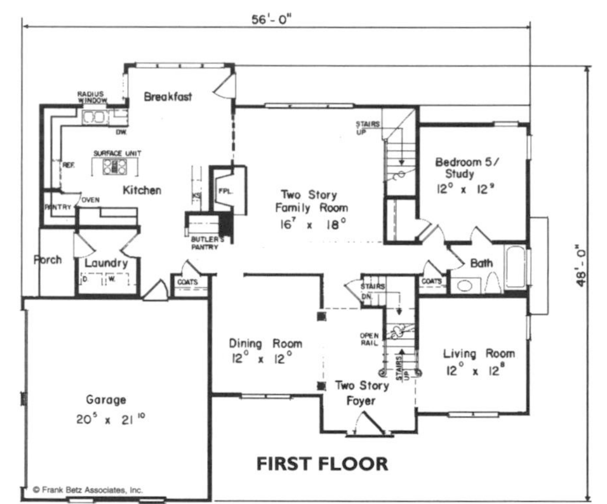

56'-0"
48'-0"
Breakfast
Kitchen
Porch
Laundry
Two Story Family Room 16⁷ x 18⁰
Bedroom 5/ Study 12⁰ x 12⁹
Bath
Dining Room 12⁰ x 12⁰
Two Story Foyer
Living Room 12⁰ x 12⁸
Garage 20⁵ x 21¹⁰
FIRST FLOOR
© Frank Betz Associates, Inc.

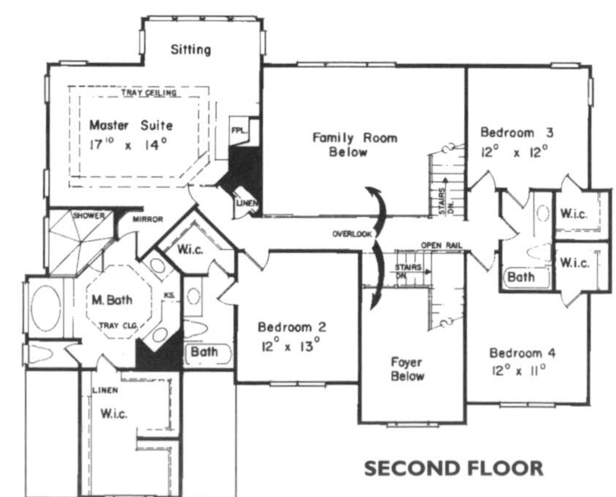

Sitting
Master Suite 17¹⁰ x 14⁰
Family Room Below
Bedroom 3 12⁰ x 12⁰
M.Bath
W.i.c.
Bath
Bedroom 2 12⁰ x 13⁰
Foyer Below
Bedroom 4 12⁰ x 11⁰
SECOND FLOOR

Old World Style

PRICE CODE: H

PLAN NO. 98532

'his plan features:
- 'our bedrooms
- Three full and one half baths
- 'he stone and brick veneer combines with eyebrow windows, a dormer window, and a bay window creating haracter for this elevation
- :legance is created by the curved staircase in the Gallery, nd the columns and arched window in the Dining Room
- 'he angled Kitchen with brick accents and a large Pantry re open to the large informal Dining Area and the 'amily Room
- 'his home is designed with slab and crawlspace oundation options

ST FLOOR — 2,263 SQ. FT.
:OND FLOOR — 849 SQ. FT.
NUS — 430 SQ. FT.
RAGE — 630 SQ. FT.

TOTAL LIVING AREA:
3,112 SQ. FT.

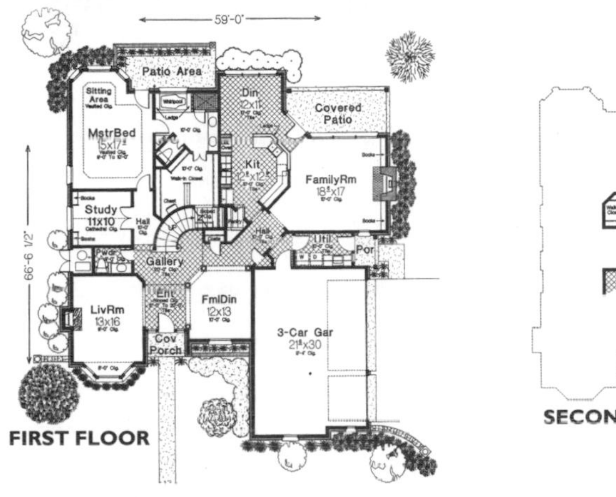
59'-0"
66'-6 1/2"
Patio Area
Sitting Area
MstrBed
15x17
Study
11x10
Hall
Din
Kit
Covered Patio
FamilyRm
18x17
Gallery
Ent
LivRm
13x16
FmlDin
12x13
Cov Porch
3-Car Gar
21x30
Por
FIRST FLOOR

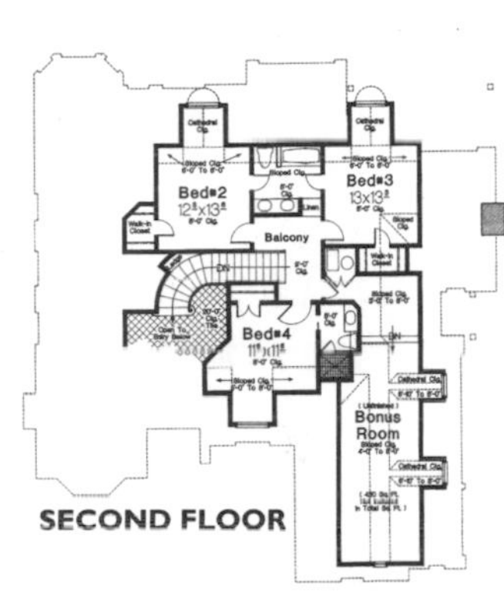
Bed#2
Bed#3
Balcony
Bed#4
Bonus Room
SECOND FLOOR

Secluded Suite

PRICE CODE: A

PLAN NO. 94135

his plan features:
- 'hree bedrooms
- 'wo full and one half baths
- here are high ceilings in both the Great and ining Rooms
- 'olumns support a plant shelf at the Entry to the ining Room
- he L-shaped Kitchen has an adjacent snack bar
- he Master Bedroom is located for privacy on e first floor
- balcony and plant shelf overlook the first floor
- he secondary Bedrooms upstairs share a Bath
- his home is designed with a basement foundation

IN FLOOR — 973 SQ. FT.
'ER FLOOR — 520 SQ. FT.
SEMENT — 973 SQ. FT.
RAGE — 462 SQ. FT.

TOTAL LIVING AREA:
1,493 SQ. FT.

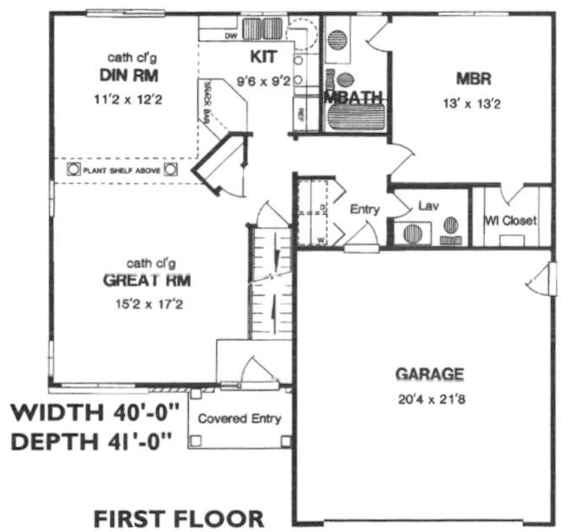
cath c/g
DIN RM
11'2 x 12'2
KIT
9'6 x 9'2
MBATH
MBR
13' x 13'2
PLANT SHELF ABOVE
Entry
Lav
WI Closet
cath c/g
GREAT RM
15'2 x 17'2
GARAGE
20'4 x 21'8
Covered Entry
WIDTH 40'-0"
DEPTH 41'-0"
FIRST FLOOR

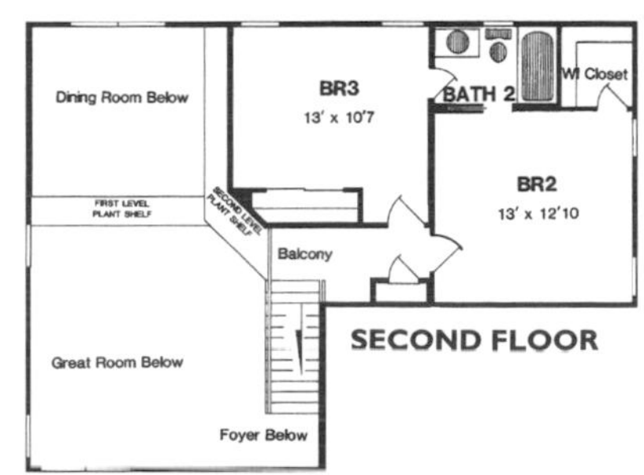
Dining Room Below
BR3
13' x 10'7
BATH 2
WI Closet
BR2
13' x 12'10
Balcony
Great Room Below
Foyer Below
SECOND FLOOR

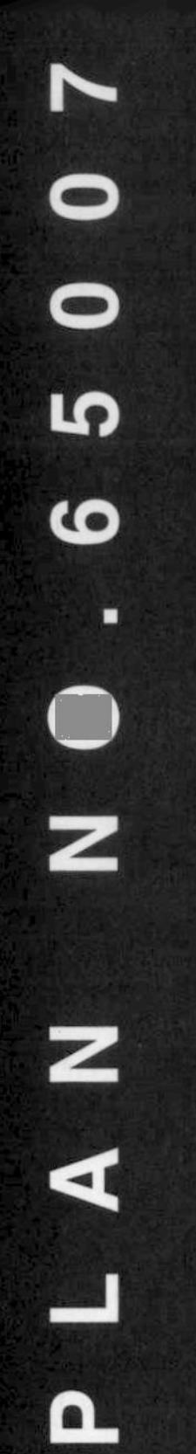
PLAN NO.65007

Windows to the World

Price Code: B

- This plan features:
- — Three bedrooms
- — Two full baths
- Walls of windows flood both floors of this home with natural light
- The L-shaped Kitchen includes all the amenities and provides easy access to the Living and the Dining Room, and the Patio beyond the sliding glass doors
- A wood-burning stove keeps this home warm and cozy when the sun isn't shining
- Two Bedrooms on the second floor share a full Bath and a Sitting Room that accesses the wraparound Porch
- This home is designed with a basement foundation

FIRST FLOOR — 787 SQ. FT.
SECOND FLOOR — 787 SQ. FT.
BASEMENT — 787 SQ. FT.

TOTAL LIVING AREA:
1,574 SQ. FT.

FIRST FLOOR

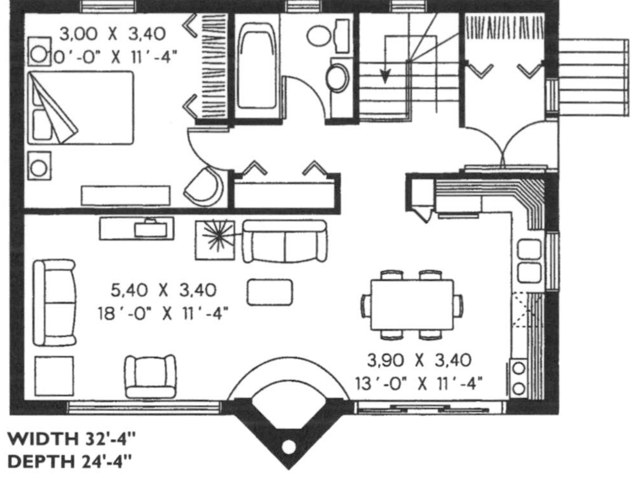
3,00 X 3,40
0'-0" X 11'-4"
5,40 X 3,40
18'-0" X 11'-4"
3,90 X 3,40
13'-0" X 11'-4"

WIDTH 32'-4"
DEPTH 24'-4"

SECOND FLOOR

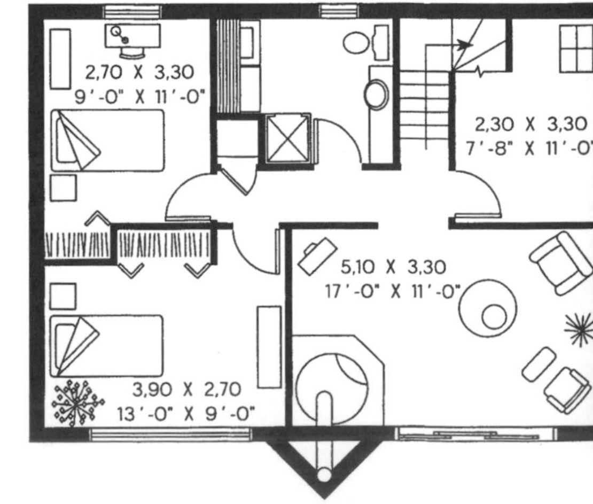
2,70 X 3,30
9'-0" X 11'-0"
2,30 X 3,30
7'-8" X 11'-0"
5,10 X 3,30
17'-0" X 11'-0"
3,90 X 2,70
13'-0" X 9'-0"

PLAN NO. 34901

Photography by Laurie Solomon

Rear Elevation

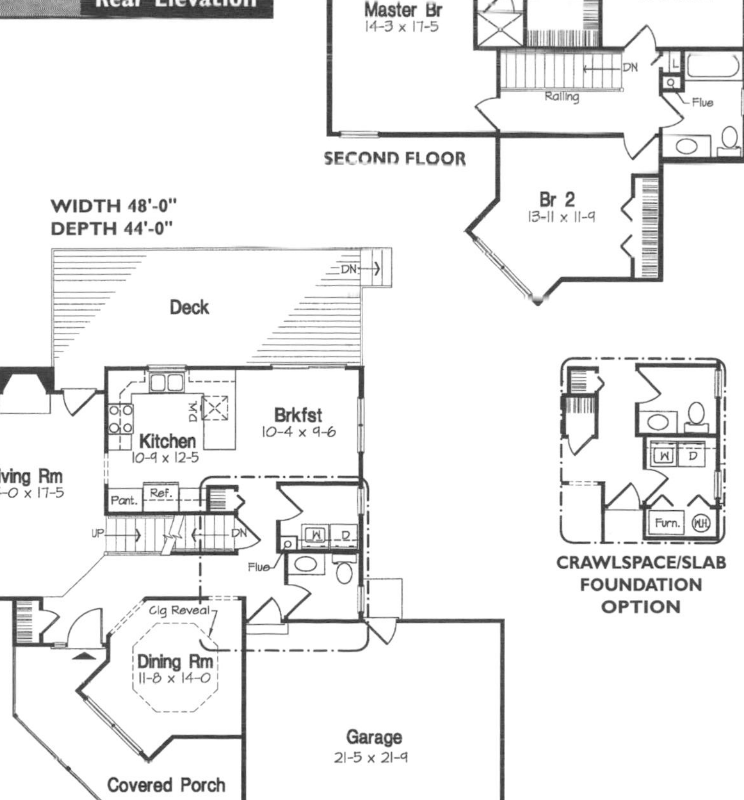
Line of Floor Below
Master Br
14-3 x 17-5
Br 3
12-2 x 10-1
DN
Railing
Flue
SECOND FLOOR
Br 2
13-11 x 11-9
WIDTH 48'-0"
DEPTH 44'-0"
Deck
DN
Brkfst
10-4 x 9-6
Kitchen
10-9 x 12-5
DW
Living Rm
14-0 x 17-5
Pant.
Ref.
UP
DN
W
D
Flue
Clg Reveal
Dining Rm
11-8 x 14-0
Garage
21-5 x 21-9
Covered Porch
FIRST FLOOR
Furn.
WH
CRAWLSPACE/SLAB
FOUNDATION
OPTION

Covered Porch on Farm-Style Traditional

Price Code: C

- This plan features:
  - — Three bedrooms
  - — Two full and one half baths
- A Dining Room with bay window and elevated ceiling
- A Living Room complete with gas light fireplace
- A two-car Garage
- Ample storage space throughout the home
- This home is designed with basement, slab, and crawlspace foundation options

FIRST FLOOR — 909 SQ. FT
SECOND FLOOR — 854 SQ. FT.
BASEMENT — 899 SQ. FT.
GARAGE — 491 SQ. FT.

TOTAL LIVING AREA:
1,763 SQ. FT.

PLAN NO.91091

Narrow Lot

PRICE CODE: A

- This plan features:
  - — Three bedrooms
  - — Two full baths
- This home will easily accommodate a narrow lot
- A covered Porch and a trellis highlight the front
- A vaulted ceiling and a wood stove complement the Living Room
- The Kitchen flows into the Dining Room
- The Garage is in the rear and has an optional door location
- The secondary Bedrooms are on the second floor
- The Master Bedroom Suite is tucked in the rear of th home
- This home is designed with a crawlspace foundation

FIRST FLOOR — 842 SQ. FT.
SECOND FLOOR — 408 SQ. FT.

TOTAL LIVING AREA: 1,250 SQ. FT.

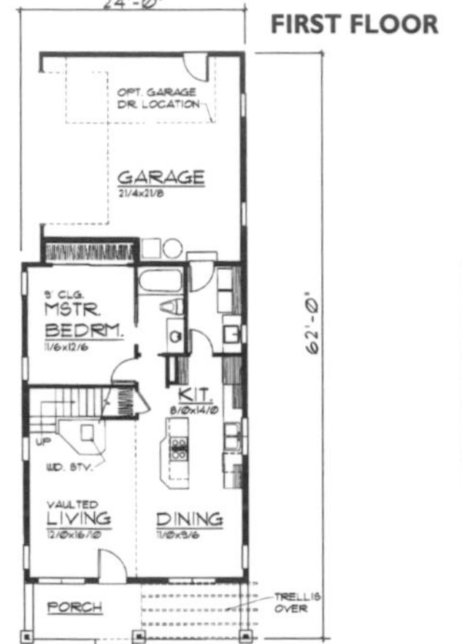

24'-0"
FIRST FLOOR
OPT. GARAGE DR. LOCATION
GARAGE
MSTR. BEDRM.
KIT.
UP
VAULTED LIVING
DINING
PORCH
TRELLIS OVER
62'-0"

BED-2
DN
OPEN TO BELOW
BED-3
SECOND FLOOR

PLAN NO.97294

Vaulted Breakfast
Bedrm.3/In-Law Suite/Study
Kitchen
Vaulted Family Room
Vaulted M.Bath
W.i.c.
Master Suite
Bath
Laund.
Dining Room
Foyer
Bedrm.4/ Living Rm.
Bedroom 2
Covered Porch
Garage
MAIN FLOOR
WIDTH 63'-0"
DEPTH 63'-6"
OPTIONAL BASEMENT STAIR LOCATION

Convenience and Style

PRICE CODE: D

- This plan features:
  - — Four bedrooms
  - — Three full baths
- The Dining Room has decorative columns at its entrance in addition to a plant shelf above
- The Family Room has a vaulted ceiling and a focal point fireplace
- The Master Suite is topped by a tray ceiling in the sleeping area and a vaulted ceiling over the private I
- There is a Private Suite at the other end of the house includes a private Bath
- This home is designed with basement and crawlspac foundation options

MAIN FLOOR — 2,158 SQ. FT.
BASEMENT — 2,190 SQ. FT.
GARAGE — 485 SQ. FT.

TOTAL LIVING AREA: 2,158 SQ. FT.

Cozy Three Bedroom

PRICE CODE: B

his plan features:
- hree bedrooms
- 'wo full baths
- he triple arched front Porch adds to the curb ›peal of the home
- he expansive Great Room is accented by a ›zy gas fireplace
- he efficient Kitchen includes an eating bar that ›parates it from the Great Room
- he Master Bedroom is highlighted by a walk-in oset and a whirlpool Bath
- vo secondary Bedrooms share use of the full hall Bath
- he rear Porch extends dining to the outdoors
- his home is designed with crawlspace and slab undation

:N FLOOR — 1,515 SQ. FT.
:AGE — 528 SQ. FT.

TOTAL LIVING AREA:
1,515 SQ. FT.

PLAN NO. 96522

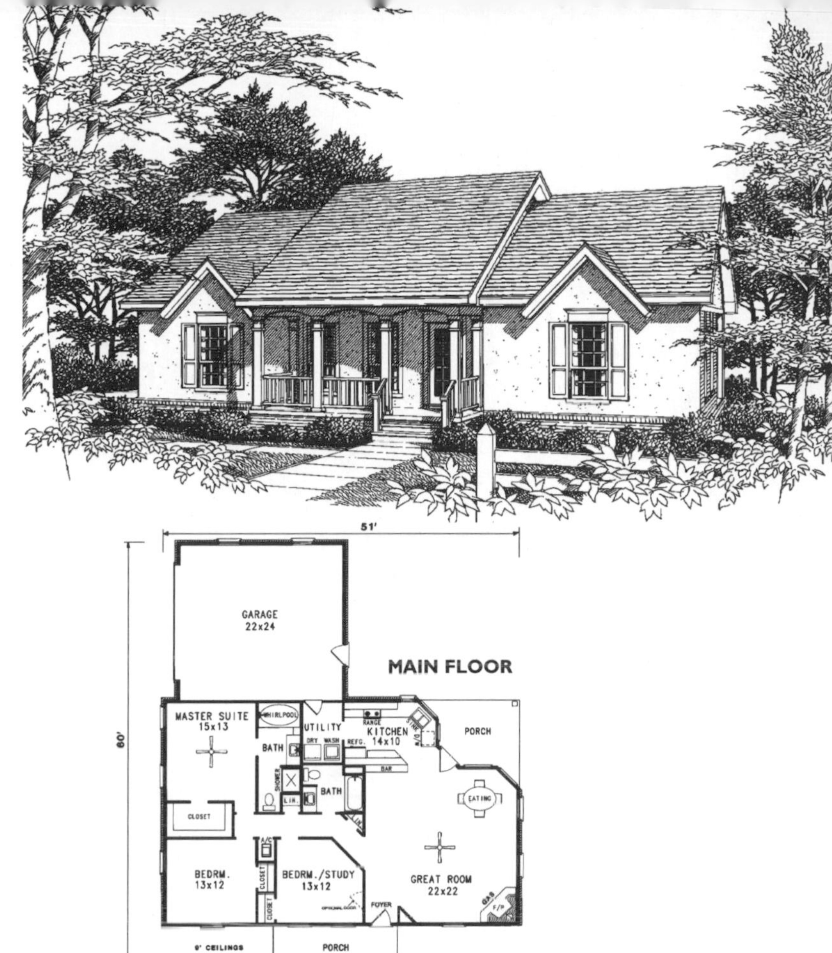

51'
60'
GARAGE
22x24
MAIN FLOOR
MASTER SUITE
15x13
WHIRLPOOL
BATH
UTILITY
DRY WASH
RANGE
REFG.
KITCHEN
14x10
BAR
PORCH
BATH
EATING
CLOSET
BEDRM.
13x12
CLOSET
BEDRM./STUDY
13x12
GREAT ROOM
22x22
FOYER
9' CEILINGS
PORCH

Sophisticated Southern Styling

PRICE CODE: G

his plan features:
- ive bedrooms
- hree full and one half baths
- overed front and rear Porches expanding the living ›ace to the outdoors
- Den with a large fireplace and built-in cabinets ›d shelves
- cooktop island, built-in desk, and eating bar ›mplete the Kitchen
- he Master Suite has two walk-in closets and a xurious Bath
- ›ur additional Bedrooms, two on the first floor ›d two on the second floor, all have easy access to full Bath
- his home is designed with crawlspace and slab undation

›T FLOOR — 2,256 SQ. FT.
OND FLOOR — 602 SQ. FT.
IUS — 264 SQ. FT.
:AGE — 484 SQ. FT.

TOTAL LIVING AREA:
2,858 SQ. FT.

PLAN NO. 92576

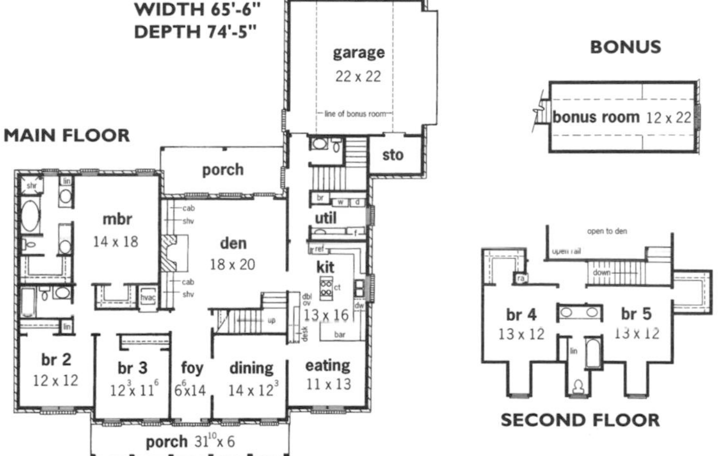

WIDTH 65'-6"
DEPTH 74'-5"
MAIN FLOOR
garage
22 x 22
line of bonus room
sto
porch
util
mbr
14 x 18
den
18 x 20
kit
13 x 16
bar
br 2
12 x 12
br 3
foy
dining
eating
11 x 13
porch
BONUS
bonus room 12 x 22
open to den
br 4
13 x 12
br 5
13 x 12
SECOND FLOOR

PLAN NO. 99087

Full-Length Covered Porch

PRICE CODE: K

- This plan features:
- — Five bedrooms
- — Three full and one half baths
- Natural light floods the entrance Foyer through the dramatic palladium-style window
- A grand Family Room with a fireplace and a full length, covered entrance Porch
- The first floor Master Suite features a large walk-in closet and a Bath with a separate bath tub and stall shower
- This home is designed with a basement foundation

FIRST FLOOR — 2,538 SQ. FT.
SECOND FLOOR — 1,295 SQ. FT.
GARAGE — 900 SQ. FT.

TOTAL LIVING AREA:
3,833 SQ. FT.

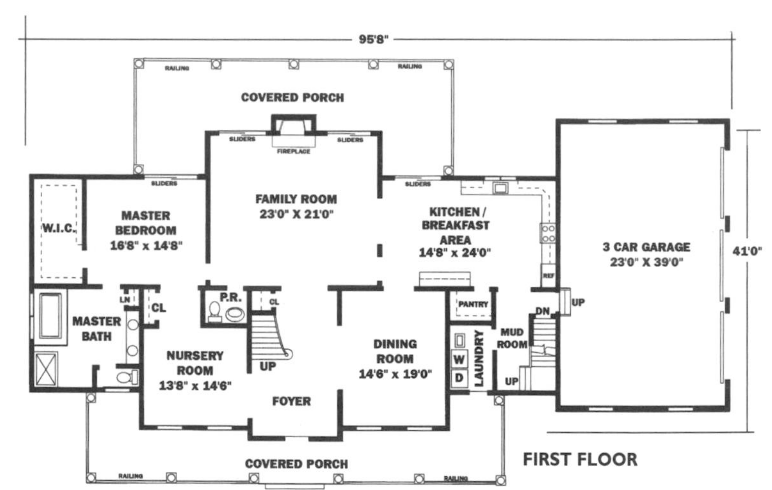
95'8"
COVERED PORCH
FAMILY ROOM 23'0" X 21'0"
MASTER BEDROOM 16'8" x 14'8"
W.I.C.
KITCHEN / BREAKFAST AREA 14'8" x 24'0"
3 CAR GARAGE 23'0" X 39'0"
41'0"
MASTER BATH
CL
P.R.
NURSERY ROOM 13'8" x 14'6"
UP
DINING ROOM 14'6" x 19'0"
PANTRY
LAUNDRY
W
D
MUD ROOM
DN
UP
FOYER
COVERED PORCH
FIRST FLOOR

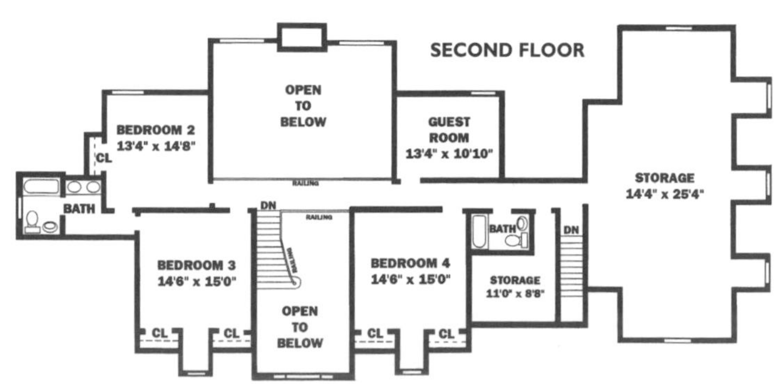
SECOND FLOOR
OPEN TO BELOW
BEDROOM 2 13'4" x 14'8"
GUEST ROOM 13'4" x 10'10"
STORAGE 14'4" x 25'4"
CL
BATH
DN
BEDROOM 3 14'6" x 15'0"
BEDROOM 4 14'6" x 15'0"
BATH
STORAGE 11'0" x 8'8"
OPEN TO BELOW
CL

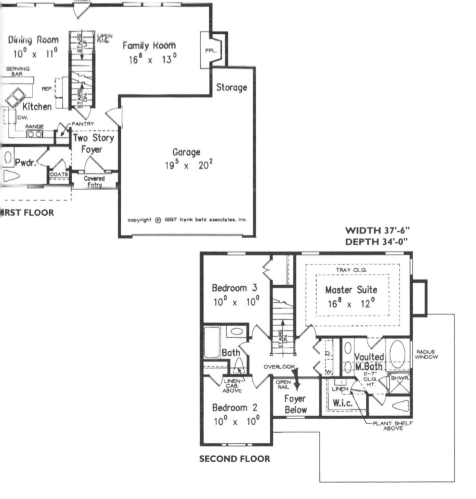

Two-Story Foyer

Price Code: A

- This plan features:
  - — Three bedrooms
  - — Two full and one half baths
- An upstairs balcony overlooks the Foyer below
- Space is reserved in the rear of the Garage for storage
- A serving bar between the Kitchen and the Dining Room is great for buffets
- The Master Suite has a beautiful tray ceiling overhead
- This home is designed with basement and crawlspace foundation options

FIRST FLOOR — 637 SQ. FT.
SECOND FLOOR — 730 SQ. FT.
BASEMENT — 587 SQ. FT.
GARAGE — 392 SQ. FT.

TOTAL LIVING AREA:
1,367 SQ. FT.

FRENCH DOOR
Dining Room 10^0 x 11^0
OPEN RAIL
STAIRS UP
Family Room 16^8 x 13^0
FPL.
SERVING BAR
REF.
STAIRS DN
Storage
Kitchen
DW.
RANGE
PANTRY
Two Story Foyer
Garage 19^5 x 20^2
Pwdr.
COATS
Covered Entry
FIRST FLOOR

WIDTH 37'-6"
DEPTH 34'-0"

Bedroom 3 10^0 x 10^0
TRAY CLG.
Master Suite 16^8 x 12^0
STAIRS DN
Bath
OVERLOOK
Vaulted M.Bath
11'-7" CLG. HT.
RADIUS WINDOW
SHWR.
LINEN CAB. ABOVE
OPEN RAIL
LINEN
Foyer Below
W.i.c.
Bedroom 2 10^0 x 10^0
PLANT SHELF ABOVE
SECOND FLOOR

PLAN NO.90871

Fabulous Four

PRICE CODE: D

- This plan features:
- — Four bedrooms
- — Two full and one half baths
- A Veranda wraps the front and side of the home
- The formal Living Room opens to the Dining Room
- A space for your china is reserved in the Dining Roo
- The Kitchen is open to the Nook and has a center isla
- A gas fireplace is located in the Family Room
- Upstairs find four Bedrooms with ample closet space
- This home is designed with a basement foundation

FIRST FLOOR — 1,155 SQ. FT.
SECOND FLOOR — 1,027 SQ. FT.
BASEMENT — 1,136 SQ. FT.
GARAGE — 507 SQ. FT.

TOTAL LIVING AREA:
2,182 SQ. FT.

Patio
Dining Rm
11-0 x 12-0
China
Kitchen
10-6 x 12-0
Nook
8-0 x 13-6
Family Room
21-6 x 12-0
Gas fp
Pan
desk
dn
Pwdr Rm
frzr
Utility
Open over
Living Rm
13-0 x 16-6
up
Foyer
Double Garage
20-6 x 21-0
Verandah
FIRST FLOOR

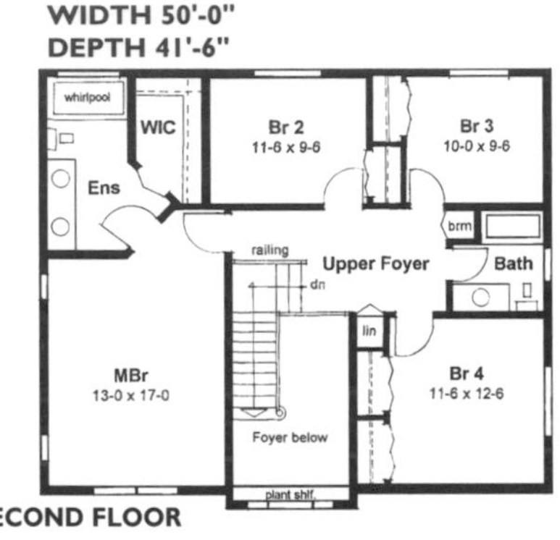

WIDTH 50'-0"
DEPTH 41'-6"
whirlpool
WIC
Ens
Br 2
11-6 x 9-6
Br 3
10-0 x 9-6
brm
Bath
railing
Upper Foyer
dn
lin
MBr
13-0 x 17-0
Foyer below
Br 4
11-6 x 12-6
plant shlf
SECOND FLOOR

PLAN NO.98580

Brilliance in Brick and Fieldstone

PRICE CODE: B

- This plan features:
- — Three bedrooms
- — Two full baths
- Stately appearance of entrance and arched windows gives style to modest plan
- Hub of home is Great Room opening to Study/Forma Dining Area, Covered Patio and Dining/Kitchen
- An efficient Kitchen features a Pantry, serving ledge, bright Dining Area
- Master Bedroom wing offers access to Covered Patio huge walk-in closet, and a whirlpool Bath
- Two additional Bedrooms with large closets, share a Bath, linen closet, and Laundry utilities
- This home is designed with a slab foundation

MAIN FLOOR — 1,640 SQ. FT.
GARAGE — 408 SQ. FT.

TOTAL LIVING AREA:
1,640 SQ. FT.

50'-0"
Bed#2 11x11
Din 11x11
Covered Patio
MstrBed 13x18
Kit
GreatRm 15x19
Hall
Bed#3 10x11
Util
Study/ FmlDin 10x10
Ent
Cov Por
56'-4"
Gar 19x21
MAIN FLOOR

Key West Island Style

PRICE CODE: G

PLAN NO. 94265

ıis plan features:
- hree bedrooms
- hree full baths
- lass doors open the great room to a Deck, hile arch-top clerestory windows enhance the sual atmosphere with natural light
- ıe gourmet Kitchen has a center island/eating bar r easy meals, plus a window wrapped counter
- winding staircase leads to a luxurious upper floor aster Suite that opens to a private balcony
- ıis home is designed with pier and post foundation tions
- lternate foundation options available at an additional ıarge. Please call 1-800-235-5700 for more formation.

N FLOOR — 1,684 SQ. FT.
ER FLOOR — 1,195 SQ. FT.
ER FLOOR — 1,433 SQ. FT.

TOTAL LIVING AREA:
2,879 SQ. FT.

Rear Elevation

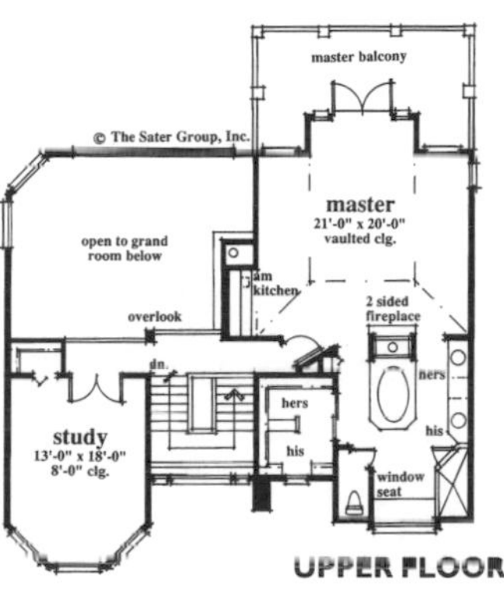
© The Sater Group, Inc.
master balcony
master
21'-0" x 20'-0"
vaulted clg.
open to grand room below
overlook
kitchen
2 sided fireplace
hers
his
study
13'-0" x 18'-0"
8'-0" clg.
window seat
UPPER FLOOR

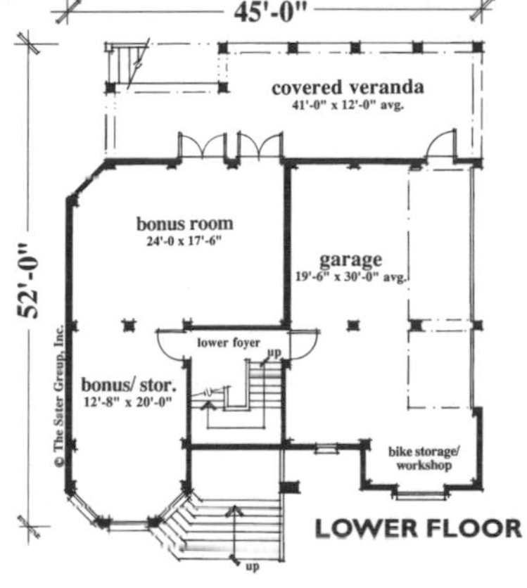
45'-0"
52'-0"
covered veranda
41'-0" x 12'-0" avg.
bonus room
24'-0 x 17'-6"
garage
19'-6" x 30'-0" avg.
lower foyer
bonus/ stor.
12'-8" x 20'-0"
bike storage/ workshop
© The Sater Group, Inc.
LOWER FLOOR

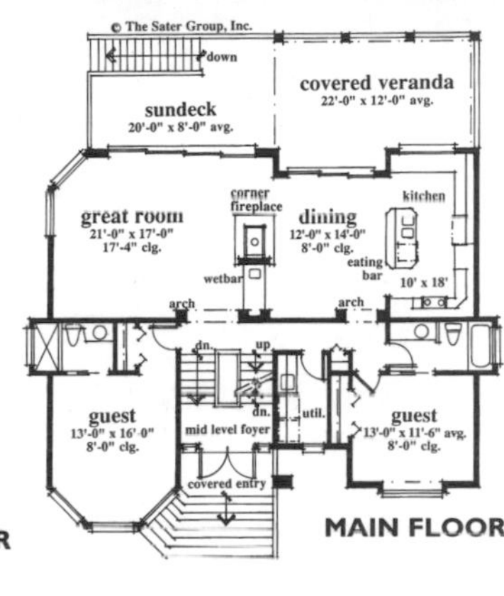
© The Sater Group, Inc.
sundeck
20'-0" x 8'-0" avg.
covered veranda
22'-0" x 12'-0" avg.
great room
21'-0" x 17'-0"
17'-4" clg.
corner fireplace
wetbar
dining
12'-0" x 14'-0"
8'-0" clg.
kitchen
eating bar
10' x 18'
arch
guest
13'-0" x 16'-0"
8'-0" clg.
mid level foyer
util.
guest
13'-0" x 11'-6" avg.
8'-0" clg.
covered entry
MAIN FLOOR

Eye Catching Style

PRICE CODE: E

PLAN NO. 99138

'his plan features:
- Three bedrooms
- Two full and one half baths
- Covered front Porch shelters from inclement weather nd opens into tiled Entry hall
- Dining Room has a cathedral ceiling and distinctive ront windows
- he Master Bedrooms has a bay at one end and includes Bath with a cathedral ceiling
- Enter the Great Room through an arched soffit to view ıe rear wall fireplace
- ın L-shaped Kitchen with adjacent Nook also includes a urved snack bar
- 'wo Bedrooms and a full Bath are located on the econd floor
- 'his home is designed with a basement foundation

ST FLOOR — 1,944 SQ. FT.
COND FLOOR — 495 SQ. FT.
SEMENT — 1,944 SQ. FT.

TOTAL LIVING AREA:
2,439 SQ. FT.

GRT.RM.
11'0" X 18'8"
KIT.
NK.
10'8" X 14'8"
12'0" X 14'8"
MBR.
19'0" X 13'8"
DIN.
14'0" X 12'0"
CATHEDRAL CEILING
3 CAR GAR.
26'4" X 36'0"
CATHEDRAL CEILING
FIRST FLOOR

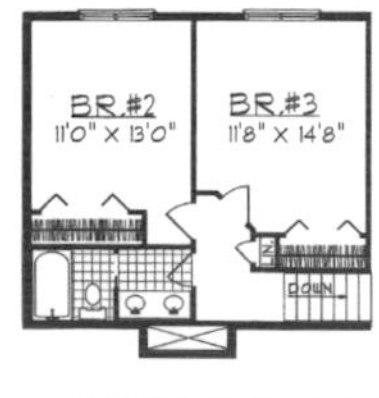
BR.#2
11'0" X 13'0"
BR.#3
11'8" X 14'8"

SECOND FLOOR

PLAN NO. 65008

Windows Illuminate Living Areas

Price Code: H

- This plan features:
- — Four bedrooms
- — Two full and one half baths
- A bay-shaped front Deck adds living space to this home
- An angled, three-sided fireplace is open to the Living Area, Dining Room, and Kitchen
- The secondary Bedrooms share the second floor Sitting Room
- This home is designed with a slab foundation

FIRST FLOOR — 1,437 SQ. FT.
SECOND FLOOR — 1,635 SQ. FT.
GARAGE — 474 SQ. FT.

TOTAL LIVING AREA:
3,072 SQ. FT.

MAIN FLOOR

WIDTH 36'-0"
DEPTH 62'-0"

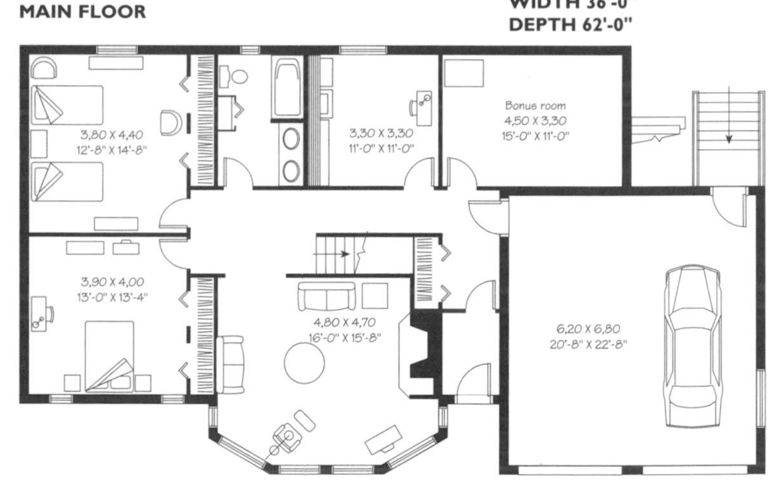
3,80 X 4,40
12'-8" X 14'-8"
3,30 X 3,30
11'-0" X 11'-0"
Bonus room
4,50 X 3,30
15'-0" X 11'-0"
3,90 X 4,00
13'-0" X 13'-4"
4,80 X 4,70
16'-0" X 15'-8"
6,20 X 6,80
20'-8" X 22'-8"

UPPER FLOOR

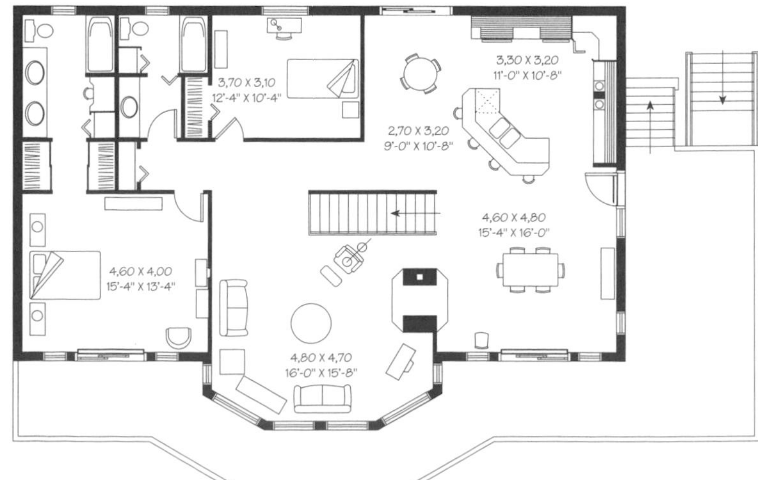
3,70 X 3,10
12'-4" X 10'-4"
3,30 X 3,20
11'-0" X 10'-8"
2,70 X 3,20
9'-0" X 10'-8"
4,60 X 4,80
15'-4" X 16'-0"
4,60 X 4,00
15'-4" X 13'-4"
4,80 X 4,70
16'-0" X 15'-8"

Executive Two-Story

PRICE CODE: D

PLAN NO.98800

This plan features:
- Three bedrooms
- Two full and one half baths
- ɜracefully curving staircase dominating the Foyer and eading to the Bedrooms
- Kitchen and Breakfast Nook separated from the Family Room by only a railing and a step down
- Built-in entertainment center and a warming fireplace highlighting the sunken Family Room
- Formal Living Room and Dining Room that adjoin and nclude a fireplace in the Living Room and a built-in china cabinet area in the Dining Room
- Lavish Master Suite boasts a Sitting Room and a deluxe five-piece Bath
- Bonus room to be finished for future needs
- This home is designed with a basement foundation

RST FLOOR — 1,258 SQ. FT.
COND FLOOR — 858 SQ. FT.
ARAGE — 441 SQ. FT.
NUS — 263 SQ. FT.

TOTAL LIVING AREA:
2,116 SQ. FT.

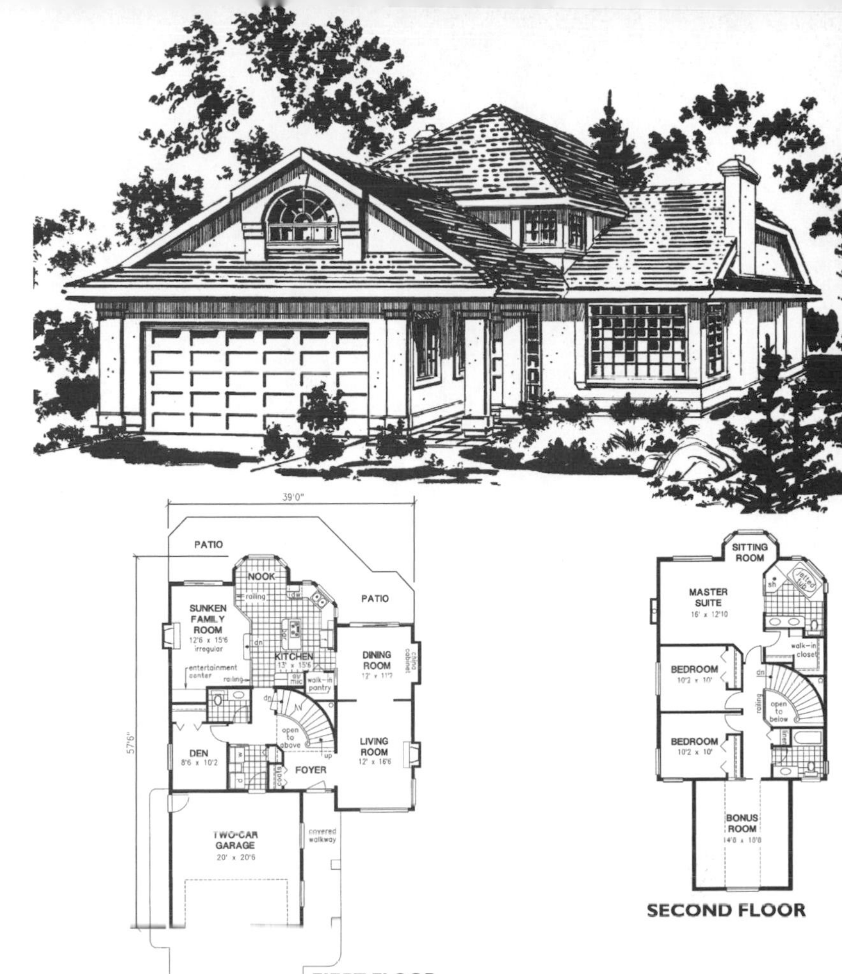

39'0"
PATIO
NOOK
PATIO
SUNKEN FAMILY ROOM
12'6 x 15'6 irregular
KITCHEN
13' x 15'6
DINING ROOM
12' x 11'0
entertainment center
walk-in pantry
open to above
LIVING ROOM
12' x 16'6
DEN
8'6 x 10'2
FOYER
57'6"
TWO-CAR GARAGE
20' x 20'6
covered walkway
FIRST FLOOR
SITTING ROOM
MASTER SUITE
16' x 12'10
walk-in closet
BEDROOM
10'2 x 10'
open to below
BEDROOM
10'2 x 10'
BONUS ROOM
14'8 x 18'8
SECOND FLOOR

Spacious Elegance

PRICE CODE: E

PLAN NO.98455

This plan features:
- Four bedrooms
- Three full baths
- Gables, a hip roof and keystone window accents
- The two-story Foyer with palladian window illuminates a lovely staircase and the Dining Room entry way
- The Family Room has a vaulted ceiling and an inviting fireplace
- Vaulted ceiling and a radius window highlight the Breakfast Area and the efficient Kitchen
- The Master Bedroom Suite boasts a tray ceiling, luxurious Bath and a walk-in closet
- This home is designed with basement and crawlspace foundation options

RST FLOOR — 1,761 SQ. FT.
COND FLOOR — 588 SQ. FT.
NUS ROOM — 267 SQ. FT.
ARAGE — 435 SQ. FT.

TOTAL LIVING AREA:
2,349 SQ. FT.

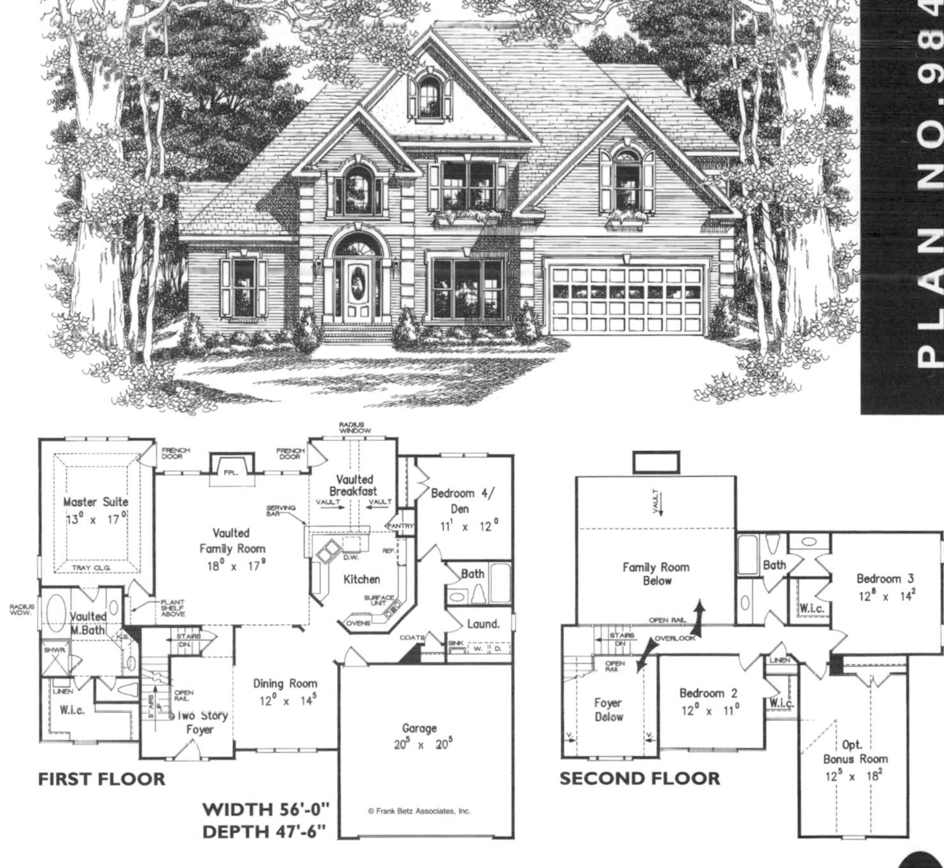

Master Suite
13^0 x 17^0
TRAY CLG.
Vaulted Family Room
18^0 x 17^9
Vaulted Breakfast
Bedroom 4/ Den
11^1 x 12^0
Kitchen
Bath
Laund.
Vaulted M.Bath
W.i.c.
Two Story Foyer
Dining Room
12^0 x 14^5
Garage
20^5 x 20^5
FIRST FLOOR
WIDTH 56'-0"
DEPTH 47'-6"
© Frank Betz Associates, Inc.
Family Room Below
Bath
Bedroom 3
12^8 x 14^2
W.i.c.
Foyer Below
Bedroom 2
12^0 x 11^0
W.i.c.
Opt. Bonus Room
12^5 x 18^2
SECOND FLOOR

PLAN NO.65009

Warm and Cozy

PRICE CODE: A

- This plan features:
  - — Two bedrooms
  - — One full bath
- A covered Porch and arched Entry offer a quaint welcome
- The Kitchen features generous counter space, includir an eating bar
- The open design of the community areas allow family always be nearby
- The Bedrooms are isolated in the right wing of the ho
- A Carport provides shelter from the elements
- This home is designed with a basement foundation

MAIN FLOOR — 947 SQ. FT.
BASEMENT — 947 SQ. FT.

TOTAL LIVING AREA:
947 SQ. FT.

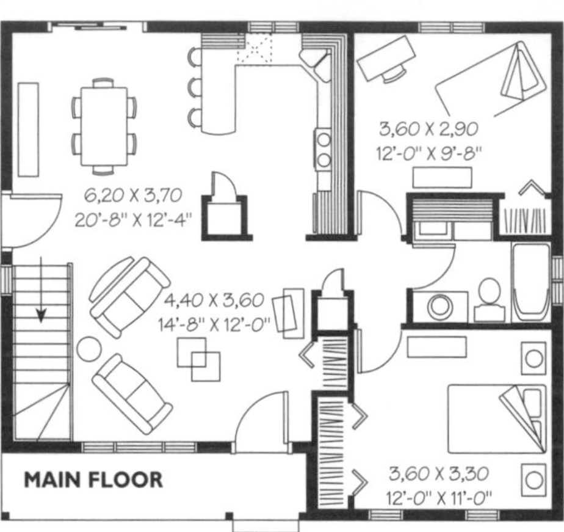
3,60 X 2,90
12'-0" X 9'-8"
6,20 X 3,70
20'-8" X 12'-4"
4,40 X 3,60
14'-8" X 12'-0"
3,60 X 3,30
12'-0" X 11'-0"
MAIN FLOOR

WIDTH 34'-0"
DEPTH 30'-0"

PLAN NO.94804

European Flair in Tune with Today

PRICE CODE: C

- This plan features:
  - — Three bedrooms
  - — Two full baths
- European flavor with decorative windows, gable roof lines and a stucco finish
- Formal Dining Room with floor to ceiling window treatment
- Expansive Activity Room with decorative ceiling, hearth fireplace and Deck access
- Open, efficient Kitchen with snack bar, Laundry, Breakfast Area and Screened Porch beyond
- Private Master Bedroom suite with a decorative ceilin large walk-in closet and luxurious Bath
- Two additional Bedrooms, one with a bay window sha a full Bath
- This home is designed with a basement foundation

MAIN FLOOR — 1,855 SQ. FT.
GARAGE — 439 SQ. FT.

TOTAL LIVING AREA:
1,855 SQ. FT.

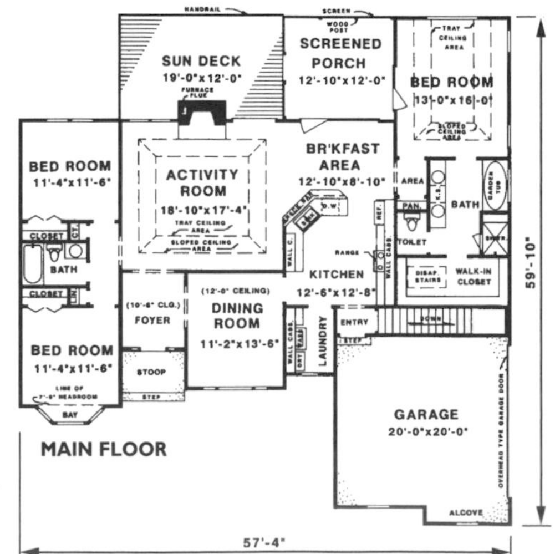
SUN DECK
19'-0"x12'-0"
SCREENED
PORCH
12'-10"x12'-0"
BED ROOM
13'-0"x16'-0"
BED ROOM
11'-4"x11'-6"
ACTIVITY
ROOM
18'-10"x17'-4"
BR'KFAST
AREA
12'-10"x8'-10"
BATH
KITCHEN
12'-6"x12'-8"
WALK-IN
CLOSET
FOYER
DINING
ROOM
11'-2"x13'-6"
LAUNDRY
ENTRY
BED ROOM
11'-4"x11'-6"
STOOP
GARAGE
20'-0"x20'-0"
MAIN FLOOR
59'-10"
57'-4"

PLAN NO. 60017

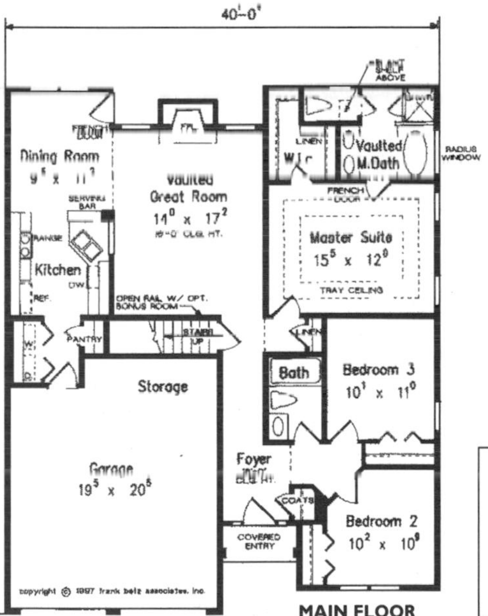

Big on Style

Price Code: A

MAIN FLOOR

OPT. STAIRS TO BSMT
STAIRS UP
PANTRY

OPTIONAL BASEMENT STAIR LOCATION

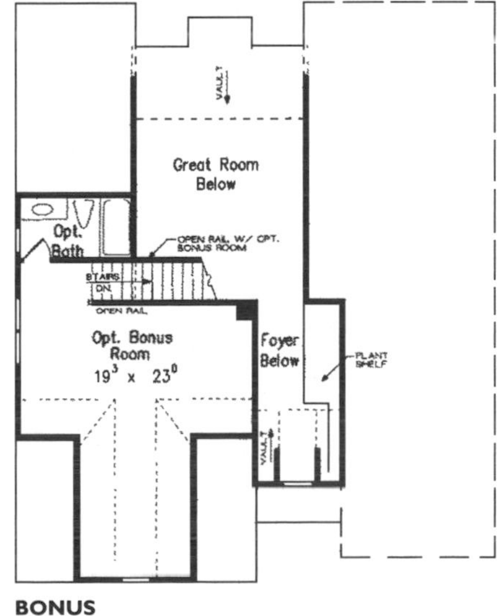
Great Room
Below
Opt.
Bath
OPEN RAIL W/ OPT. BONUS ROOM
STAIRS DN.
OPEN RAIL
Opt. Bonus
Room
19³ x 23⁰
Foyer
Below
PLANT SHELF

BONUS

- This plan features:
  - Three bedrooms
  - Two full baths
- An optional bonus room on the second floor would make a great Guest Room
- A vaulted ceiling adds dimension to the Great Room
- A radius window allows sunlight into the Master Bath
- A Pantry closet adds storage options in the Kitchen
- This home is designed with basement and crawlspace foundation options

MAIN FLOOR — 1,347 SQ. FT.
BONUS — 428 SQ. FT.
BASEMENT — 1,353 SQ. FT.
GARAGE — 441 SQ. FT.

TOTAL LIVING AREA:
1,347 SQ. FT.

Single-Level Living

Price Code: B

- This plan features:
- — Three bedrooms
- — Two full baths
- A fireplace forms the focus of the Living Room
- The angled Kitchen has a sunny Breakfast Room, built-in Pantry and ample storage and counter space
- A vaulted ceiling in the Master Suite plus a sky lit Bath and walk-in closet
- Two additional Bedrooms are served by a full hall Bath
- This home is designed with a basement foundation

MAIN FLOOR — 1,642 SQ. FT.
BASEMENT — 1,642 SQ. FT.
GARAGE — 448 SQ. FT.

TOTAL LIVING AREA:
1,642 SQ. FT.

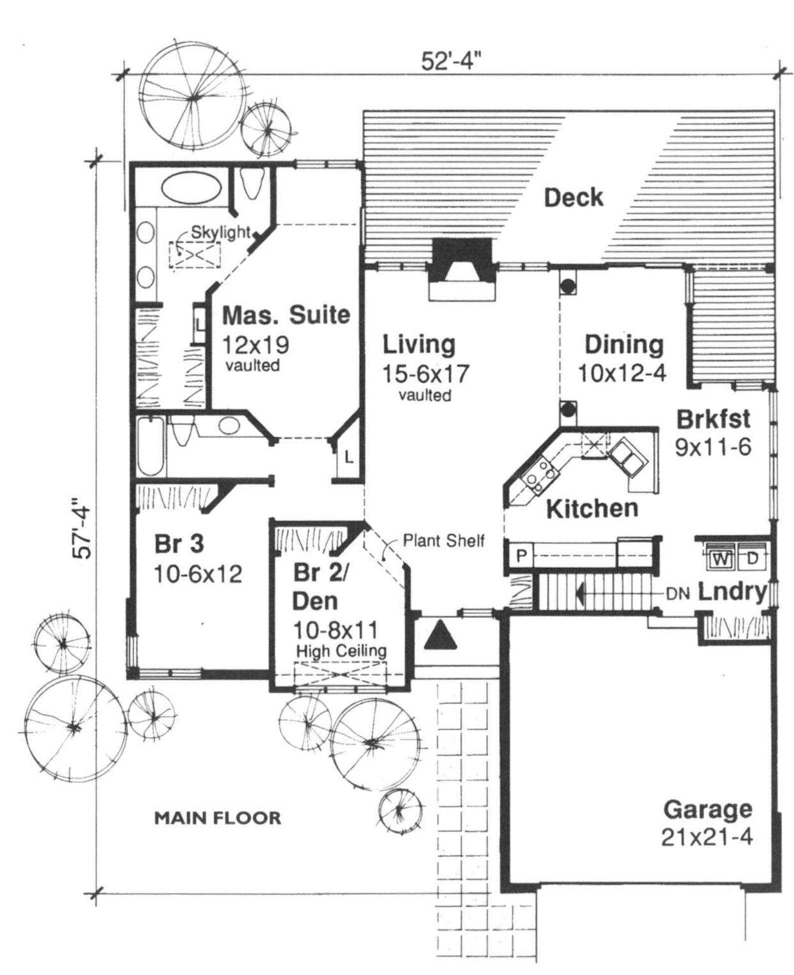
52'-4"
57'-4"
Deck
Skylight
Mas. Suite
12x19
vaulted
Living
15-6x17
vaulted
Dining
10x12-4
Brkfst
9x11-6
Kitchen
L
Plant Shelf
P
W
D
DN
Lndry
Br 3
10-6x12
Br 2/
Den
10-8x11
High Ceiling
MAIN FLOOR
Garage
21x21-4

PLAN NO.90986

Surrounded with Sunshine

PRICE CODE: B

This plan features:
- Three bedrooms
- Two full and one half baths
- An Italianette style, featuring columns and tile originally designed to sit on the edge of a golf course
- An open design with pananoramic vistas in every direction
- Tile adorns the Foyer, into the Kitchen and Nook, as well as in the Utility Room
- A whirlpool tub in the elaborate and spacious Master Bedroom suite
- A Great Room with a corner gas fireplace
- A turreted Breakfast Nook and an efficient Kitchen with peninsula counter
- Two family Bedrooms that share a full hall Bath
- This home is designed with basement and crawlspace foundation options

MAIN FLOOR — 1,731 SQ. FT.
BASEMENT — 1,715 SQ. FT.
GARAGE — 888 SQ. FT.

TOTAL LIVING AREA: 1,731 SQ. FT.

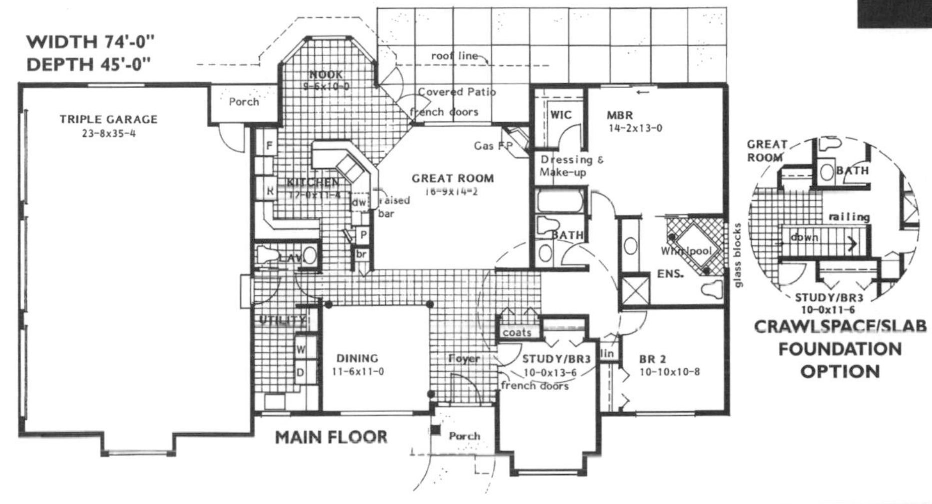

WIDTH 74'-0"
DEPTH 45'-0"
TRIPLE GARAGE
23-8x35-4
Porch
NOOK
9-6x10-0
roof line
Covered Patio
french doors
WIC
MBR
14-2x13-0
Gas FP
GREAT ROOM
16-9x14-2
KITCHEN
raised bar
Dressing & Make-up
BATH
Whirlpool
ENS.
glass blocks
LAV
UTILITY
DINING
11-6x11-0
Foyer
coats
STUDY/BR3
10-0x13-6
french doors
BR 2
10-10x10-8
MAIN FLOOR
Porch
GREAT ROOM
BATH
railing
down
STUDY/BR3
10-0x11-6
CRAWLSPACE/SLAB FOUNDATION OPTION

PLAN NO.98587

Grand Plan

PRICE CODE: L

This plan features:
- Five bedrooms
- Five full and two half baths
- Separate Garages form a Parking Court alongside this regal home
- A Guest Suite, complete with a full Bath and a large closet, is located on the first floor
- The Master Suite is on the opposite side of the first floor, where it is enhanced by a Sitting Bay and a luxurious Bath
- Fireplaces warm the formal Living Room at the front of the home and the Family Room in the rear
- This home is designed with a slab foundation

FIRST FLOOR — 3,188 SQ. FT.
SECOND FLOOR — 1,426 SQ. FT.
GARAGE — 740 SQ. FT.

TOTAL LIVING AREA: 4,614 SQ. FT.

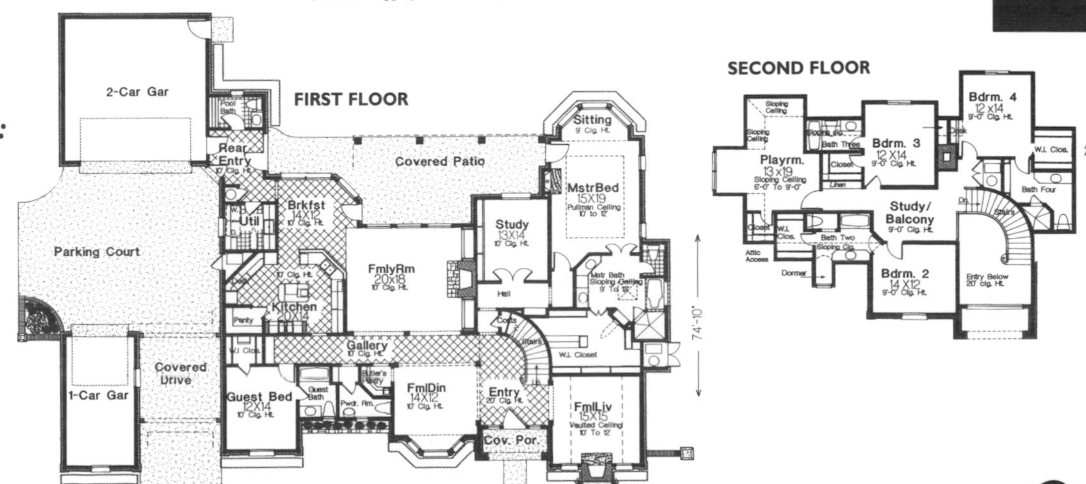

99'-10"
2-Car Gar
FIRST FLOOR
Rear Entry
Covered Patio
Sitting
Brkfst
14X12
Util
Parking Court
Study
13X14
MstrBed
15X19
FmlyRm
20X18
Kitchen
Gallery
Covered Drive
1-Car Gar
Guest Bed
12X14
FmlDin
14X12
Entry
FmlLiv
15X15
Cov. Por.
74'-10"
SECOND FLOOR
Playrm.
13X19
Bdrm. 3
12X14
Bdrm. 4
12x14
Study/ Balcony
Bdrm. 2
14X12

PLAN NO.91053

Updated Victorian

PRICE CODE: D

- ■ This plan features:
- — Three bedrooms
- — Two full and one half baths
- ■ A classic Victorian exterior design accented by a wonderful Turret Room and second floor covered Porch above a sweeping Veranda
- ■ A spacious formal Living Room leading into a formal Dining Room for ease in entertaining
- ■ An efficient, U-shaped Kitchen with plenty of counter space and a peninsula snackbar, opens to an eating No and Family Room for informal gatherings and activiti
- ■ An elegant Master Suite with a unique, octagon Sitting Area, private Porch, oversized, walk-in closet, and private Bath with a double vanity and a window tub
- ■ Two additional Bedrooms, with ample closets, sharing full hall Bath
- ■ This home is designed with a crawlspace foundation

FIRST FLOOR — 1,150 SQ. FT.
SECOND FLOOR — 949 SQ. FT.
GARAGE — 484 SQ. FT.

TOTAL LIVING AREA:
2,099 SQ. FT.

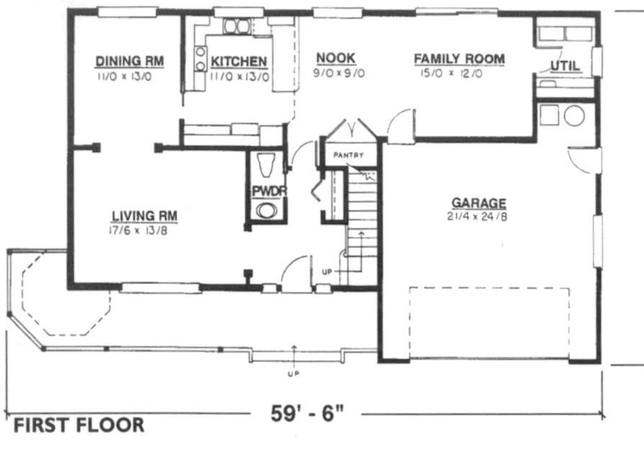
DINING RM
11/0 x 13/0
KITCHEN
11/0 x 13/0
NOOK
9/0 x 9/0
FAMILY ROOM
15/0 x 12/0
UTIL
PANTRY
PWDR
LIVING RM
17/6 x 13/8
GARAGE
21/4 x 24/8
UP
35' - 0"
59' - 6"
FIRST FLOOR

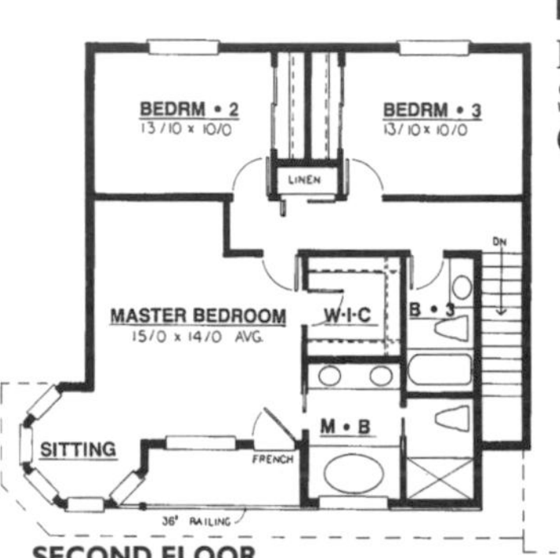
BEDRM • 2
13/10 x 10/0
BEDRM • 3
13/10 x 10/0
LINEN
MASTER BEDROOM
15/0 x 14/0 AVG.
W-I-C
B • 3
M • B
SITTING
FRENCH
36" RAILING
DN
SECOND FLOOR

PLAN NO.97410

Expand Your Options

PRICE CODE: H

- ■ This plan features:
- — Three bedroom
- — Two full and one half baths
- ■ On the main floor, the Dining Room has a towering front wall window
- ■ The Great Room has a rear bow window
- ■ The Kitchen is brightened by a window with a transom over the sink
- ■ The Gathering Room shares a fireplace with the window-lined gazebo-shaped Breakfast Nook
- ■ The Master Bedroom has a French door to the backya
- ■ The large walk-in closet in the Master Bedroom conta a built-in cedar chest
- ■ This home is designed with a basement foundation
- ■ Alternate foundation options available at an additional charge. Please call 1-800-235-5700 for more information.

MAIN FLOOR — 1,887 SQ. FT.
LOWER FLOOR — 1,338 SQ. FT.
BASEMENT — 549 SQ. FT.
GARAGE — 738 SQ. FT.

TOTAL LIVING AREA:
3,225 SQ. FT.

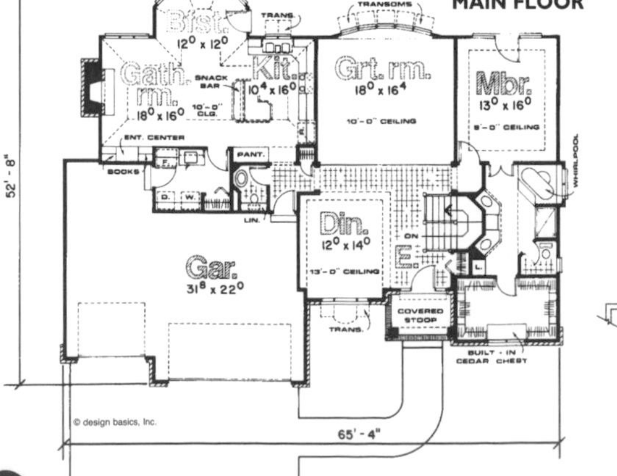
MAIN FLOOR
Bfst.
TRANSOMS
Gath. rm.
Kit.
Grt. rm.
Mbr.
SNACK BAR
10'-0" CEILING
9'-0" CEILING
ENT. CENTER
BOOKS
PANT.
WHIRLPOOL
Din.
13'-0" CEILING
Gar.
COVERED STOOP
BUILT - IN CEDAR CHEST
© design basics, inc.
52' - 8"
65' - 4"

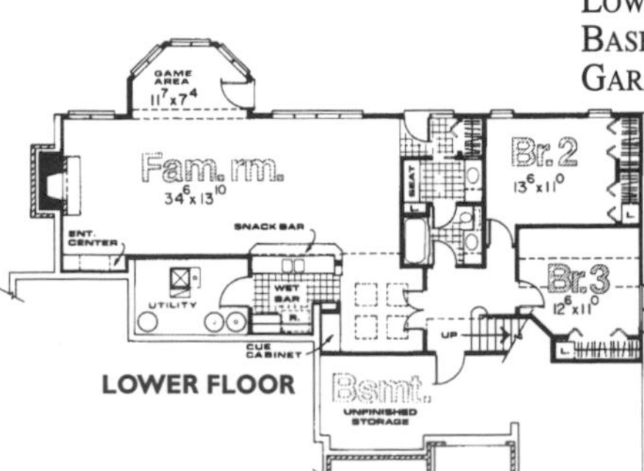
GAME AREA
Fam. rm.
SNACK BAR
ENT. CENTER
UTILITY
WET BAR
CUE CABINET
Br. 2
Br. 3
UP
LOWER FLOOR
Bsmt.
UNFINISHED STORAGE

raditional Three Bedroom

PRICE CODE: C

PLAN NO.99154

his plan features:
- hree bedrooms
- wo full and one half baths
- vaulted Entry and Great Room provide this home ith a wonderful first impression
- he large three-stall Garage includes ample storage ace for hobby materials and yard equipment
- covered Porch accessed from the Dining Room xpands living space to the outdoors.
- his home is designed with a basement foundation

IN FLOOR — 1,907 SQ. FT.
SEMENT — 1,907 SQ. FT.
RAGE — 678 SQ. FT.

TOTAL LIVING AREA :
1,907 SQ. FT.

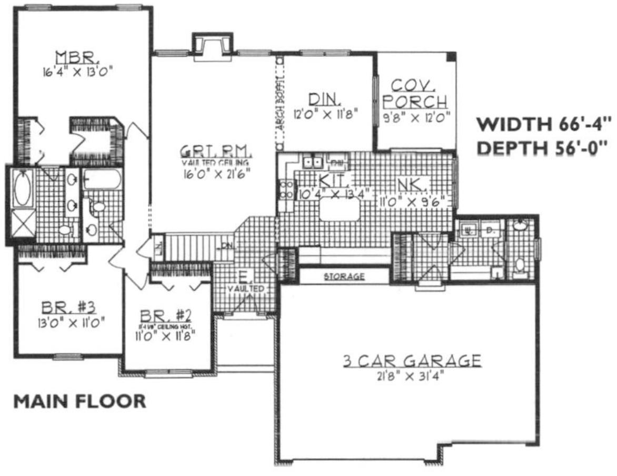
MBR.
16'4" X 13'0"
GRT. RM.
VAULTED CEILING
16'0" X 21'6"
DIN.
12'0" X 11'8"
COV. PORCH
9'8" X 12'0"
KIT.
10'4" X 13'4"
NK.
11'0" X 9'6"
STORAGE
E.
VAULTED
BR. #3
13'0" X 11'0"
BR. #2
11'0" X 11'8"
3 CAR GARAGE
21'8" X 31'4"
WIDTH 66'-4"
DEPTH 56'-0"

MAIN FLOOR

Symmetrical Southern Beauty

PRICE CODE: E

PLAN NO.94611

his plan features:
- our bedrooms
- hree full and one half baths
- nviting front Porch shades arched windows n warm climate
- pacious Family Room with cozy fireplace and access o covered Porch and Patio
- pen Dining Room accented by columns onveniently located
- eninsula counter/eating bar and adjoining Breakfast rea, Garage Entry and Utility Room in efficient Kitchen
- orner Master Bedroom with large walk-in closet and ouble vanity Bath
- irst floor Bedroom with a walk-in closet and rivate Bath
- wo additional Bedrooms on second floor with walk-in losets, share a full Bath and Balcony
- his home is designed with slab and crawlspace oundation options

RST FLOOR — 1,796 SQ. FT.
COND FLOOR — 610 SQ. FT.
RAGE — 570 SQ. FT.

TOTAL LIVING AREA:
2,406 SQ. FT.

WIDTH 65'-8.5"
DEPTH 64'-8.5"

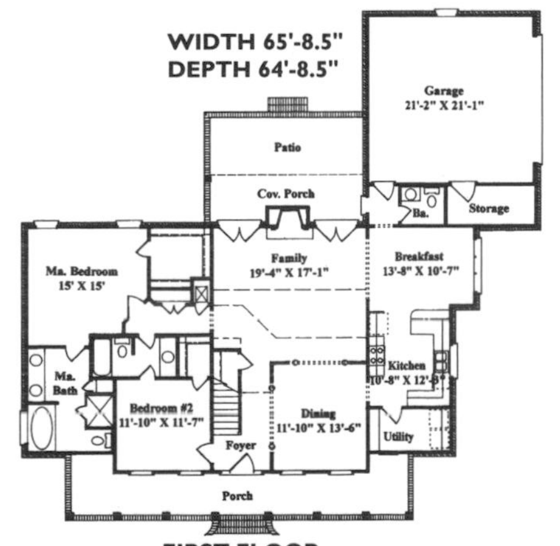
Garage
21'-2" X 21'-1"
Patio
Cov. Porch
Ba.
Storage
Ma. Bedroom
15' X 15'
Family
19'-4" X 17'-1"
Breakfast
13'-8" X 10'-7"
Ma. Bath
Kitchen
Bedroom #2
11'-10" X 11'-7"
Dining
11'-10" X 13'-6"
Foyer
Utility
Porch

FIRST FLOOR

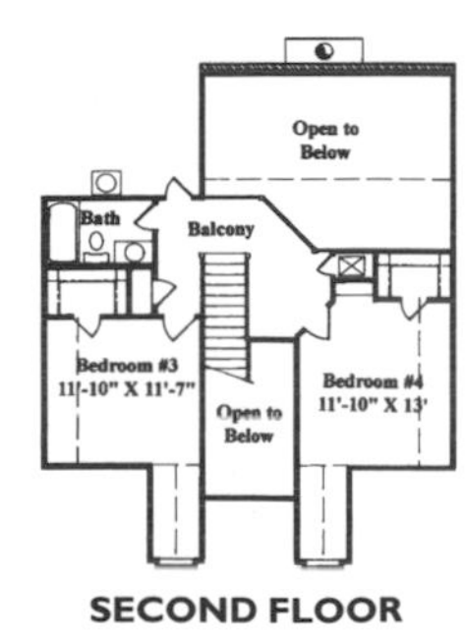
Open to Below
Bath
Balcony
Bedroom #3
11'-10" X 11'-7"
Open to Below
Bedroom #4
11'-10" X 13'

SECOND FLOOR

PLAN NO. 98456

High Ceilings Add Volume

PRICE CODE: B

- This plan features:
  - — Three bedrooms
  - — Two full baths
- A covered Entry gives way to a 14-foot high ceiling in the Foyer
- An arched opening greets you in the Great Room that also has a vaulted ceiling and a fireplace
- The Dining Room is brightened by triple windows wi transoms above
- The Kitchen is a gourmet's delight and is open to the Breakfast Nook
- The Master Suite is sweet with a tray ceiling, vaulted Sitting Area and private Bath
- Two Bedrooms on the opposite side of the home share a Bath in the hall
- This home is designed with basement, slab and crawlspace foundation options

MAIN FLOOR — 1,715 SQ. FT.
BASEMENT — 1,715 SQ. FT.
GARAGE — 450 SQ. FT.

TOTAL LIVING AREA:
1,715 SQ. FT.

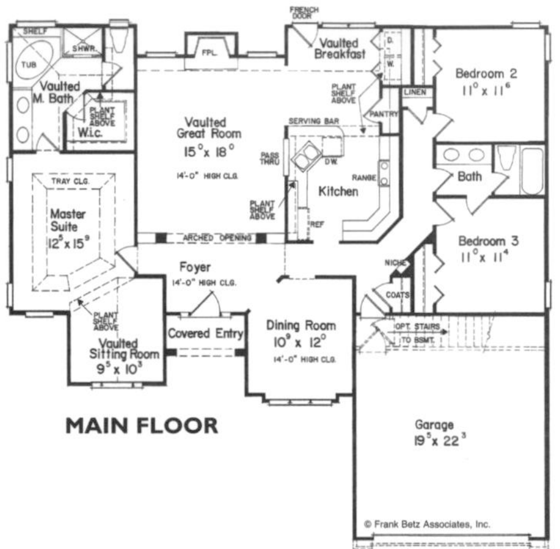

Vaulted Breakfast
Vaulted M. Bath
W.I.c.
Vaulted Great Room 15° x 18°
14'-0" HIGH CLG.
Kitchen
Bedroom 2 11° x 11⁶
Bath
Bedroom 3 11° x 11⁴
Master Suite 12⁵ x 15⁹
TRAY CLG.
Foyer 14'-0" HIGH CLG.
ARCHED OPENING
Covered Entry
Dining Room 10⁹ x 12°
14'-0" HIGH CLG.
Vaulted Sitting Room 9⁵ x 10³
Garage 19⁵ x 22³
MAIN FLOOR
© Frank Betz Associates, Inc.

WIDTH 55'-0"
DEPTH 51'-6"

PLAN NO. 94917

Enticing Design

PRICE CODE: C

- This plan features:
  - — Three bedrooms
  - — Two full baths
- The all brick facade offers the homeowner low exterior maintenance
- A three-sided fireplace which warms both the angled Great Room and the Hearth Room
- The Kitchen incorporates a peninsula snack bar that opens to the Great Room and the Hearth Room
- The private Master Suite has a nine-foot boxed ceilin a large walk-in closet, double vanity and a whirlpool
- This home is designed with basement and slab foundation options
- Alternate foundation options available at an additional charge. Please call 1-800-235-5700 for more information.

MAIN FLOOR — 1,782 SQ. FT.
GARAGE — 466 SQ. FT

TOTAL LIVING AREA:
1,782 SQ. FT.

Hrth. 10° x 11°
Bfst. 9° x 10°
SNACK BAR
Mbr. 13° x 15°
9'-0" CLG.
Kit. 10⁴ x 12°
Grt. rm. 15° x 20°
10'-0" CEILING
Br. 2 12° x 10°
WHIRLPOOL
Din. 11° x 13°
10'-0" CEILING
E.
Br. 3 12° x 10°
Gar. 22° x 22⁴

COVERED STOOP

WIDTH 52'-0"
DEPTH 59'-4"

MAIN FLOOR

© Design Basics, Inc.

PLAN NO. 65011

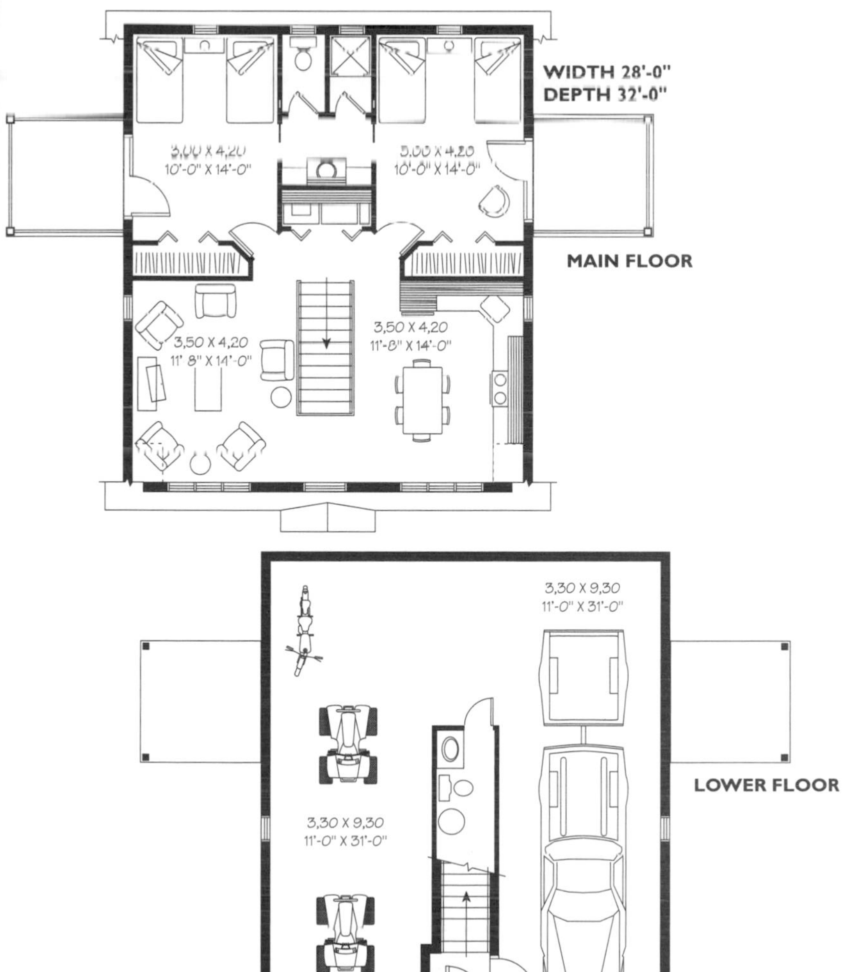

WIDTH 28'-0"
DEPTH 32'-0"
10'-0" X 14'-0"
10'-0" X 14'-0"
MAIN FLOOR
3,50 X 4,20
11' 8" X 14'-0"
3,50 X 4,20
11'-8" X 14'-0"
3,30 X 9,30
11'-0" X 31'-0"
LOWER FLOOR
3,30 X 9,30
11'-0" X 31'-0"

Welcoming Symmetry

Price Code: A

- This plan features:
  - — Two bedrooms
  - — One full and one half baths
- Windows in the front of the home filter light throughout
- The Bedrooms are located in the rear of the home for privacy
- Each Bedroom has generous closet space and access to its own private Deck
- A Bath on the lower floor is close by and convenient when working in the Garage or outdoors
- This home is designed with a slab foundation

MAIN FLOOR — 896 SQ. FT.
LOWER FLOOR — 100 SQ. FT.
GARAGE — 796 SQ. FT.

TOTAL LIVING AREA:
996 SQ. FT.

PLAN NO. 97600

Secluded Suite

Price Code: A

- This plan features:
  - — Three bedrooms
  - — Two full baths
- This plan has a low maintenance stucco exterior
- A French door is set beside the fireplace in the Family Room
- All of the Bedrooms have walk-in closets
- This home is designed with basement and crawlspace foundation options

MAIN FLOOR — 1,361 SQ. FT.
BASEMENT — 1,359 SQ. FT.
GARAGE — 530 SQ. FT.

TOTAL LIVING AREA:
1,361 SQ. FT.

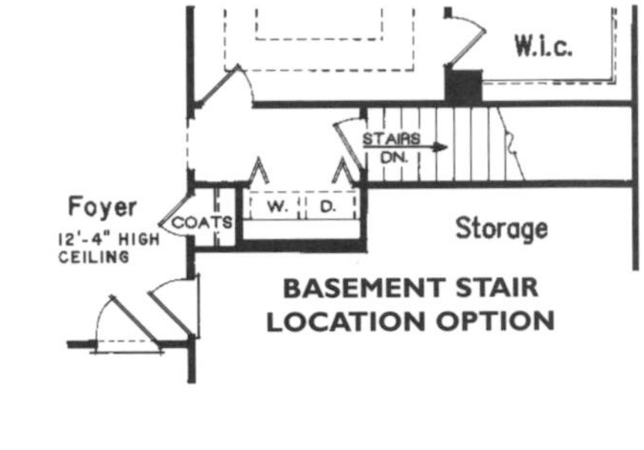
W.i.c.
STAIRS DN.
Foyer
12'-4" HIGH CEILING
COATS
W.
D.
Storage
BASEMENT STAIR LOCATION OPTION

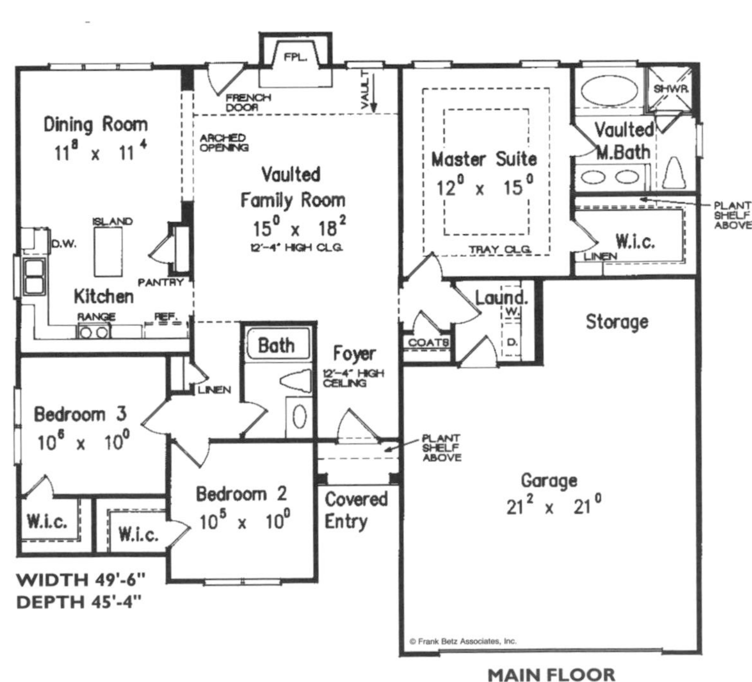
FPL.
FRENCH DOOR
VAULT
ARCHED OPENING
Dining Room
11⁸ x 11⁴
Vaulted Family Room
15⁰ x 18²
12'-4" HIGH CLG.
Master Suite
12⁰ x 15⁰
TRAY CLG.
SHWR.
Vaulted M.Bath
PLANT SHELF ABOVE
W.i.c.
LINEN
ISLAND
D.W.
PANTRY
Kitchen
RANGE
REF.
Laund.
W.
D.
COATS
Storage
Bath
Foyer
12'-4" HIGH CEILING
LINEN
Bedroom 3
10⁶ x 10⁰
PLANT SHELF ABOVE
Bedroom 2
10⁵ x 10⁰
Covered Entry
Garage
21² x 21⁰
W.i.c.
W.i.c.
WIDTH 49'-6"
DEPTH 45'-4"
© Frank Betz Associates, Inc.
MAIN FLOOR

PLAN NO. 94614

WIDTH 66'-0"
DEPTH 66'-0"
Garage
21'-4"x 23'-4"
Wd. Deck
33' x 9'
Cov. Porch
33' x 6'
Util.
Great Room
19'-4"x 18'
Ma. Suite
14' x 18'
Brkfst.
14'x 9'
Hall
Ma. Ba.
Ba. 3
Kit.
12'x 12'
Dining
14'-10"x 11'-3"
Stdy./Gst.Bdrm.
11'-4"x 11'-4"
Foyer
Porch
32'x 6'
FIRST FLOOR
Ba. 2
Dr.
Dr.
Bdrm. 2
11'-6"x 12'
open to below
Bdrm. 3
11'-6"x 12'
SECOND FLOOR

Cottage Influence

Price Code: F

- This plan features:
  - — Four bedrooms
  - — Three full and one half baths
- Expansive Great Room with focal point fireplace and access to Covered Porch and Deck
- Cooktop island in Kitchen easily serves Breakfast Bay and formal Dining Room
- Large Master Suite with access to Covered Porch, walk-in closet, and double-vanity Bath
- This home is designed with crawlspace and slab foundation options

FIRST FLOOR — 1,916 SQ. FT.
SECOND FLOOR — 617 SQ. FT.
GARAGE — 516 SQ. FT.

TOTAL LIVING AREA:
2,533 SQ. FT.

PLAN NO.97413

Enticing Elevation with Spacious Porch

Price Code: E

- This plan features:
  - Four bedrooms
  - Two full and one half baths
- The Parlor is enhanced by bright Gazebo windows
- A bright window wall and a cozy fireplace highlight the Gathering Room
- There are Gazebo windows in the third Bedroom and a walk-in closet in the fourth Bedroom
- This home is designed with a basement foundation
- Alternate foundation options available at an additional charge. Please call 1-800-235-5700 for more information.

FIRST FLOOR — 1,183 SQ. FT.
SECOND FLOOR — 1,209 SQ. FT.

TOTAL LIVING AREA:
2,392 SQ. FT.

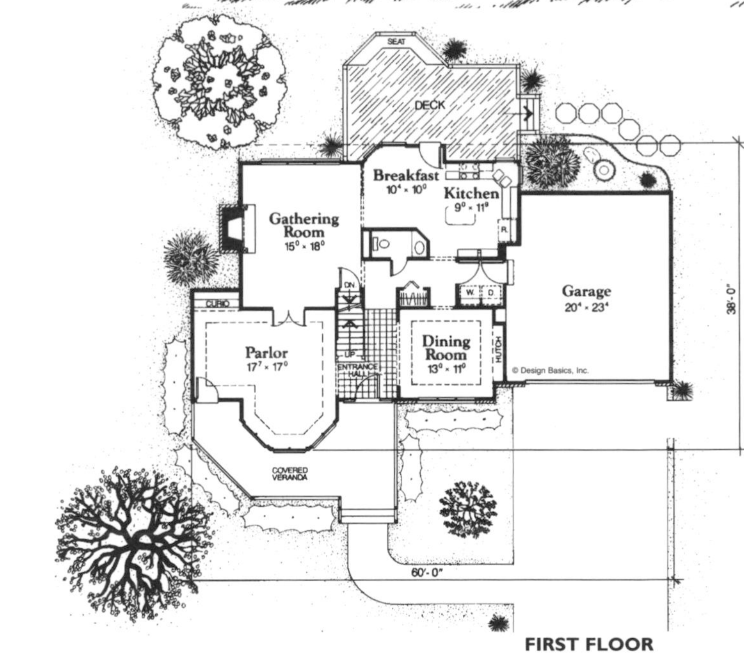

SEAT
DECK
Breakfast
$10^4 \times 10^0$
Kitchen
$9^0 \times 11^9$
Gathering Room
$15^0 \times 18^0$
Garage
$20^4 \times 23^4$
38'-0"
Parlor
$17^7 \times 17^0$
ENTRANCE HALL
Dining Room
$13^0 \times 11^0$
HUTCH
© Design Basics, Inc.
COVERED VERANDA
60'-0"

FIRST FLOOR

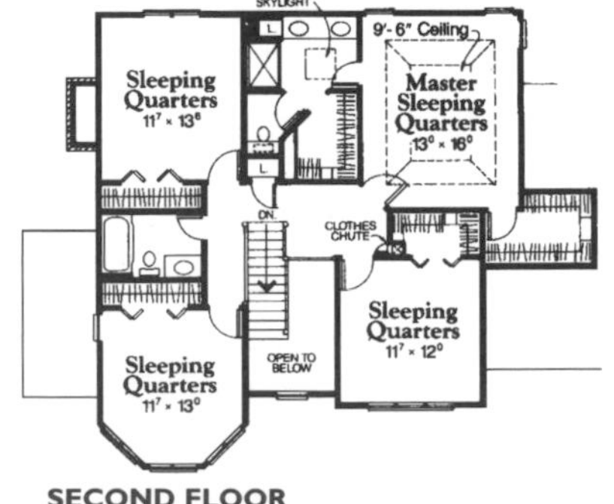

SKYLIGHT
9'-6" Ceiling
Sleeping Quarters
$11^7 \times 13^8$
Master Sleeping Quarters
$13^0 \times 16^0$
CLOTHES CHUTE
Sleeping Quarters
$11^7 \times 12^0$
OPEN TO BELOW
Sleeping Quarters
$11^7 \times 13^0$

SECOND FLOOR

SKYLIGHT

BASEMENT PLAN OPTION

Captivating Views

PRICE CODE: B

PLAN NO. 98801

This plan features:
- Three bedrooms
- One full and one three-quarter baths
- Appealing grade-level entry home is designed to capture a front view
- Combined formal Living and Dining Rooms create a feeling of space
- A dream Kitchen with a peninsula counter, corner window and a Nook
- The Master Bedroom suite boasts a walk-in closet and a private Bath
- The lower floor offers future expansion ideas
- This home is designed with basement and slab foundation options

AIN FLOOR — 1,388 SQ. FT.
WER FLOOR — 169 SQ. FT.
SEMENT — 930 SQ. FT.
RAGE — 453 SQ. FT.

TOTAL LIVING AREA:
1,557 SQ. FT.

BEDROOM
10' x 10'4
walk-in closet
BEDROOM
10'8 x 10'2
MASTER BEDROOM
12' x 14'
french door
dn
railing
KITCHEN
14'8 x 11'8
NOOK
8' x 7'8
LIVING ROOM
12' x 17'10
DINING ROOM
9' x 9'8
french door
COVERED DECK
railing
MAIN FLOOR

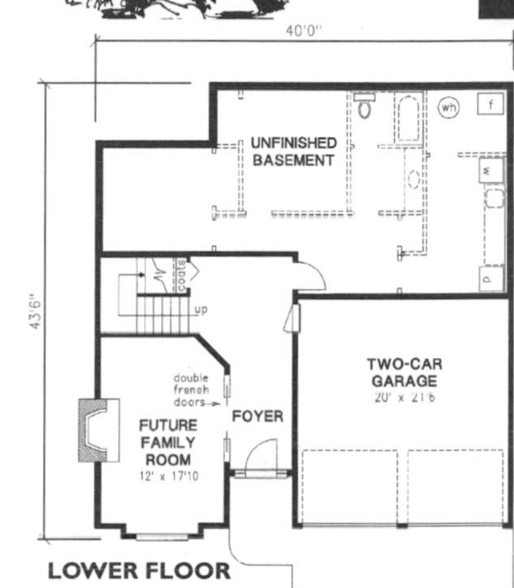
40'0"
43'6"
UNFINISHED BASEMENT
up
double french doors
FOYER
TWO-CAR GARAGE
20' x 21'6
FUTURE FAMILY ROOM
12' x 17'10
LOWER FLOOR

Wonderful Windows

PRICE CODE: C

PLAN NO. 90870

This plan features:
- Three bedrooms
- Two full baths
- Walls of windows let in plenty of sunshine
- A fireplace warms the Living Room
- The Dining Room is conveniently located near the Kitchen
- There is a convenient work triangle in the Kitchen
- The Master Bedroom has a private Deck
- The upstairs Loft is a great place for the kids to camp out
- Finish off the Basement as your needs require
- This home is designed with a basement foundation

RST FLOOR — 1,208 SQ. FT.
COND FLOOR — 547 SQ. FT.
SEMENT — 1,208 SQ. FT.

TOTAL LIVING AREA:
1,755 SQ. FT.

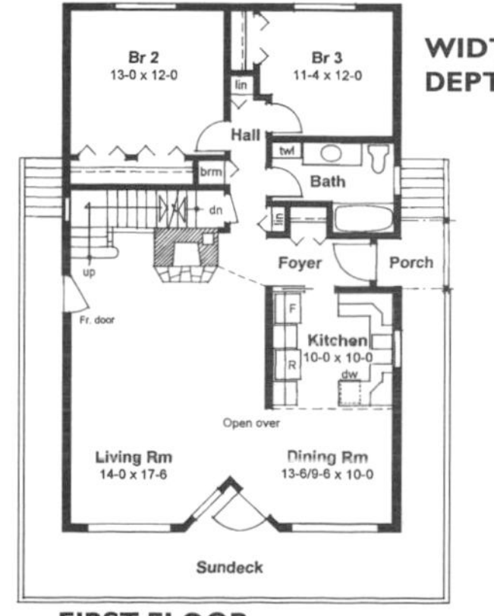
WIDTH 36'-0"
DEPTH 50'-0"
Br 2
13-0 x 12-0
Br 3
11-4 x 12-0
lin
Hall
brm
twl
Bath
dn
up
Foyer
Porch
Fr. door
Kitchen
10-0 x 10-0
dw
Open over
Living Rm
14-0 x 17-6
Dining Rm
13-6/9-6 x 10-0
Sundeck
FIRST FLOOR

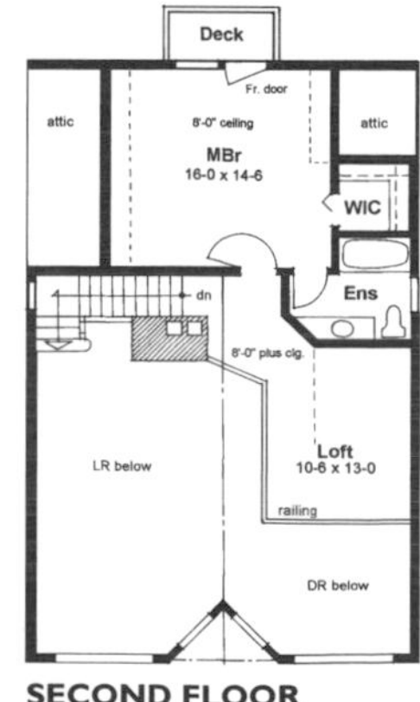
Deck
Fr. door
attic
8'-0" ceiling
MBr
16-0 x 14-6
attic
WIC
dn
Ens
8'-0" plus clg.
LR below
Loft
10-6 x 13-0
railing
DR below
SECOND FLOOR

PLAN NO.98591

Hints of English Tudor

PRICE CODE: L

- This plan features:
  - — Four Bedrooms
  - — Three full and one half baths
- Built-in entertainment centers enhance the Living Roo and the Master Suite
- The Family Room has a fireplace and a door to one of the two covered rear Patios
- A Recreation Room on the second floor keeps noisy pl away from formal areas
- The Kitchen, Breakfast Room and Family Room flow easily into each other forming a terrific informal Living Space
- This home is designed with basement and slab foundation options

FIRST FLOOR — 2,755 SQ. FT.
SECOND FLOOR — 1,412 SQ. FT.

TOTAL LIVING AREA:
4,167 SQ. FT.

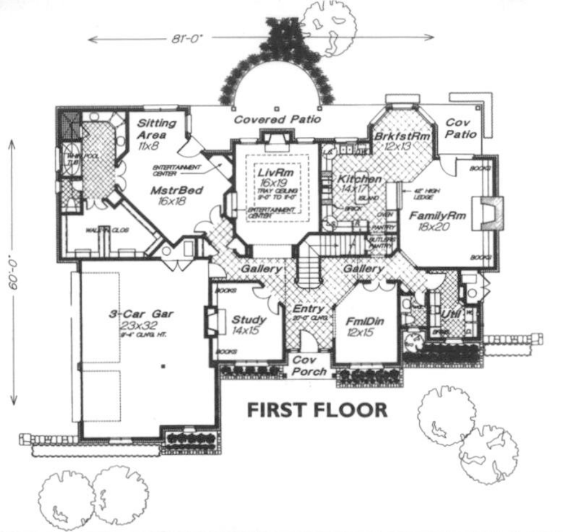

81'-0"
60'-0"
Covered Patio
Sitting Area 11x8
MstrBed 16x16
LivRm 16x19
Kitchen
BrkfstRm 12x13
Cov Patio
FamilyRm 18x20
Gallery
Gallery
3-Car Gar 23x32
Study 14x15
Entry
FmlDin 12x15
Cov Porch
FIRST FLOOR

Bed#4 14x12
Bed#3 15x12
RecRm 20x13
Bed#2 13x15
SECOND FLOOR

PLAN NO.94613

First Floor Master Suite

PRICE CODE: E

- This plan features:
  - — Four bedrooms
  - — Three full and one half baths
- Welcoming Country Porch adds to appeal and living space
- Central Foyer provides ventilation and access to all areas of home
- Spacious Living Room enhanced by fireplace and acce to covered Porch
- Efficient Kitchen with work island, built-in Pantry, Utility Room, Garage Entry and Breakfast Area
- Spacious Master Bedroom Suite with a pampering, private Bath
- Three second floor Bedrooms with walk-in closets, share two full Baths and a Game Room
- This home is designed with slab and crawlspace foundation options

FIRST FLOOR — 1,492 SQ. FT.
SECOND FLOOR — 865 SQ. FT.
UNFINISHED GAME ROOM — 303 SQ. FT.
GARAGE — 574 SQ. FT.

TOTAL LIVING AREA:
2,357 SQ. FT.

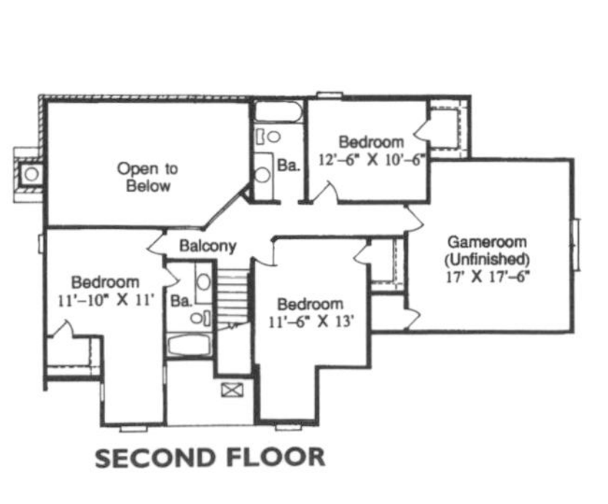

Open to Below
Bedroom 12'-6" X 10'-6"
Ba.
Balcony
Gameroom (Unfinished) 17' X 17'-6"
Bedroom 11'-10" X 11'
Ba.
Bedroom 11'-6" X 13'
SECOND FLOOR

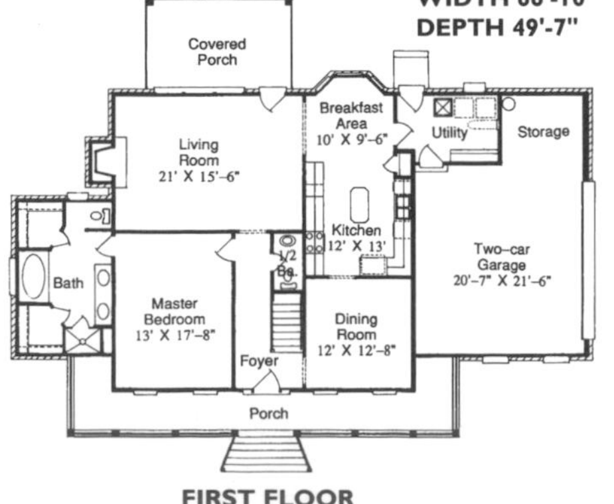

WIDTH 66'-10"
DEPTH 49'-7"
Covered Porch
Living Room 21' X 15'-6"
Breakfast Area 10' X 9'-6"
Utility
Storage
Kitchen 12' X 13'
Two-car Garage 20'-7" X 21'-6"
Bath
1/2 Ba.
Master Bedroom 13' X 17'-8"
Dining Room 12' X 12'-8"
Foyer
Porch
FIRST FLOOR

PLAN NO. 91109

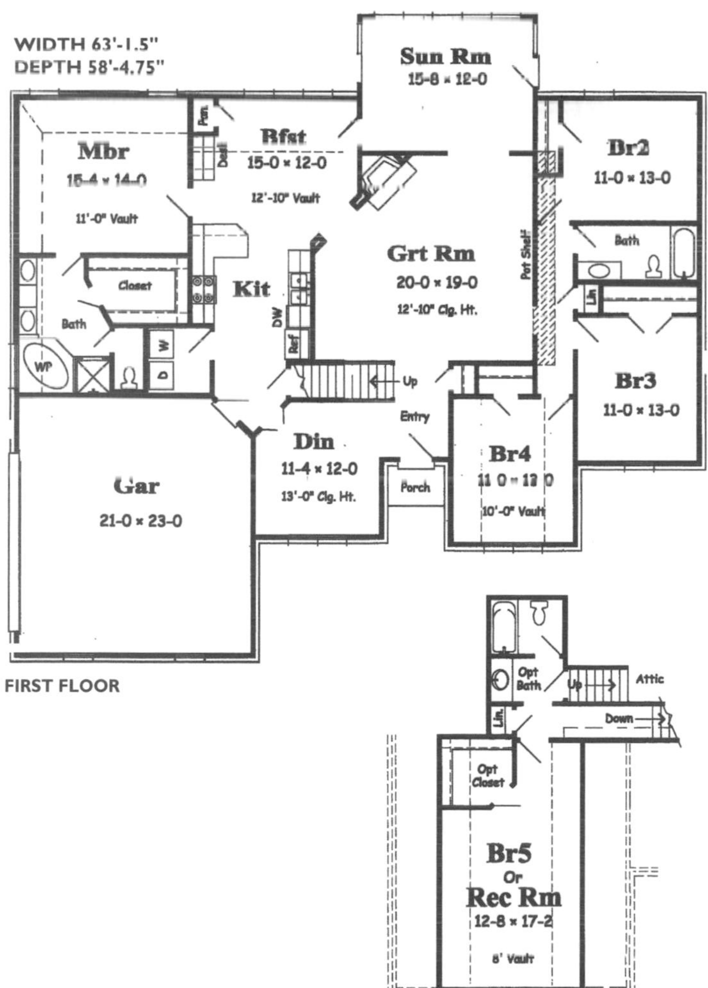

WIDTH 63'-1.5"
DEPTH 58'-4.75"
Sun Rm
15-8 × 12-0
Bfst
15-0 × 12-0
12'-10" Vault
Mbr
15-4 × 14-0
11'-0" Vault
Br2
11-0 × 13-0
Grt Rm
20-0 × 19-0
12'-10" Clg. Ht.
Pot Shelf
Kit
Closet
Bath
WP
DW
Ref
Up
Entry
Br3
11-0 × 13-0
Din
11-4 × 12-0
13'-0" Clg. Ht.
Br4
10'-0" Vault
Porch
Gar
21-0 × 23-0
FIRST FLOOR
Opt Bath
Attic
Down
Opt Closet
Br5
Or
Rec Rm
12-8 × 17-2
8' Vault
SECOND FLOOR

Family Matters

Price Code: F

- This plan features:
- — Five bedrooms
- — Three full baths
- A beautiful brick exterior is accentuated by double transoms over double windows
- Big Bedrooms and an oversized Great Room, desirable for a large family
- Volume ceilings in the Master Suite, Great Room, Dining Room, Breakfast Nook, and Bedroom 4
- Three Bathrooms, including a plush Master Bath, with a double vanity
- This home is designed with a slab foundation

FIRST FLOOR
SECOND FLOO
GARAGE — 5

To

248
To ord

PLAN NO.99113

Ranch of Distinction

PRICE CODE: C

- This plan features:
- — Three bedrooms
- — Two full and one half baths
- The recessed Entrance has an arched transom window over the door and a sidelight windows beside it
- Once inside the Living Room boasts a high ceiling and a warm fireplace
- The large Kitchen area includes the open Dining Area with a rear bay that accessed the backyard
- There is a large Utility Room, Garage Access, and a half Bath located off of the Kitchen
- The Master and third Bedrooms both have bay windows
- All of the Bedrooms have ample closet space and they are serviced by two full Baths
- This home has a three-car Garage
- This home is designed with a basement foundation

MAIN FLOOR — 1,906 SQ. FT.
BASEMENT — 1,906 SQ. FT.

TOTAL LIVING AREA:
1,906 SQ. FT.

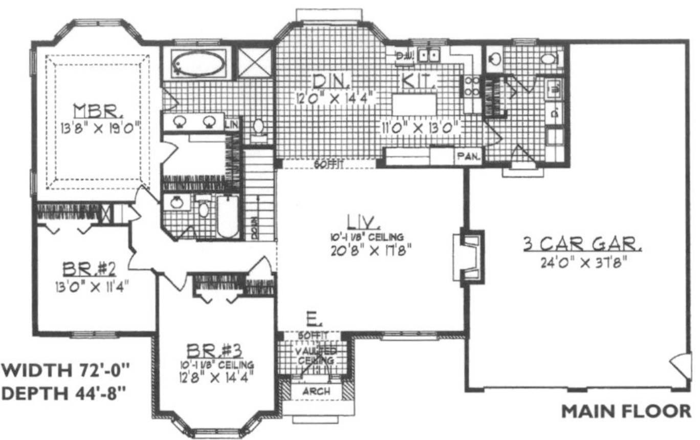
MBR.
13'8" X 19'0"
DIN.
12'0" X 14'4"
KIT.
11'0" X 13'0"
PAN.
LIV.
10'-1 1/8" CEILING
20'8" X 17'8"
3 CAR GAR.
24'0" X 37'8"
BR.#2
13'0" X 11'4"
BR.#3
10'-1 1/8" CEILING
12'8" X 14'4"
E.
ARCH
WIDTH 72'-0"
DEPTH 44'-8"
MAIN FLOOR

PLAN NO.97299

Details! Details!

PRICE CODE: E

- This plan features:
- — Three bedrooms
- — Two full and one half baths
- Decorative columns define the Dining Room entrance and a tray ceiling bringing elegance to the room
- The Living Room has a high ceiling and radius window at the far end
- The Kitchen includes a cooktop island/serving bar, a walk-in Pantry and ample work and storage space
- The Breakfast Room and the Family Room flow into the Kitchen for a feeling of spaciousness
- This home is designed with basement and crawlspace foundation options

MAIN FLOOR — 2,491 SQ. FT.
BONUS ROOM — 588 SQ. FT.
BASEMENT — 2,491 SQ. FT.
GARAGE — 522 SQ. FT.

TOTAL LIVING AREA:
2,491 SQ. FT.

WIDTH 64'-0"
DEPTH 72'-4"

MAIN FLOOR

BEDROOM OPTION

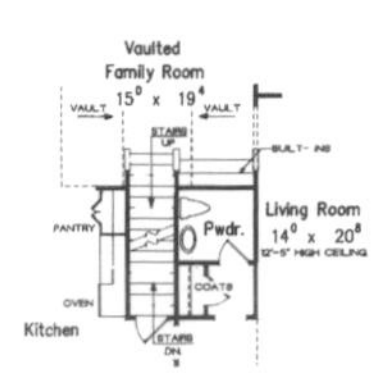
Vaulted
Family Room
15^0 x 19^4
Pwdr.
Living Room
14^0 x 20^8
Kitchen

BASEMENT OPTION

PLAN NO. 32109

tography supplied by The Meredith Corporation

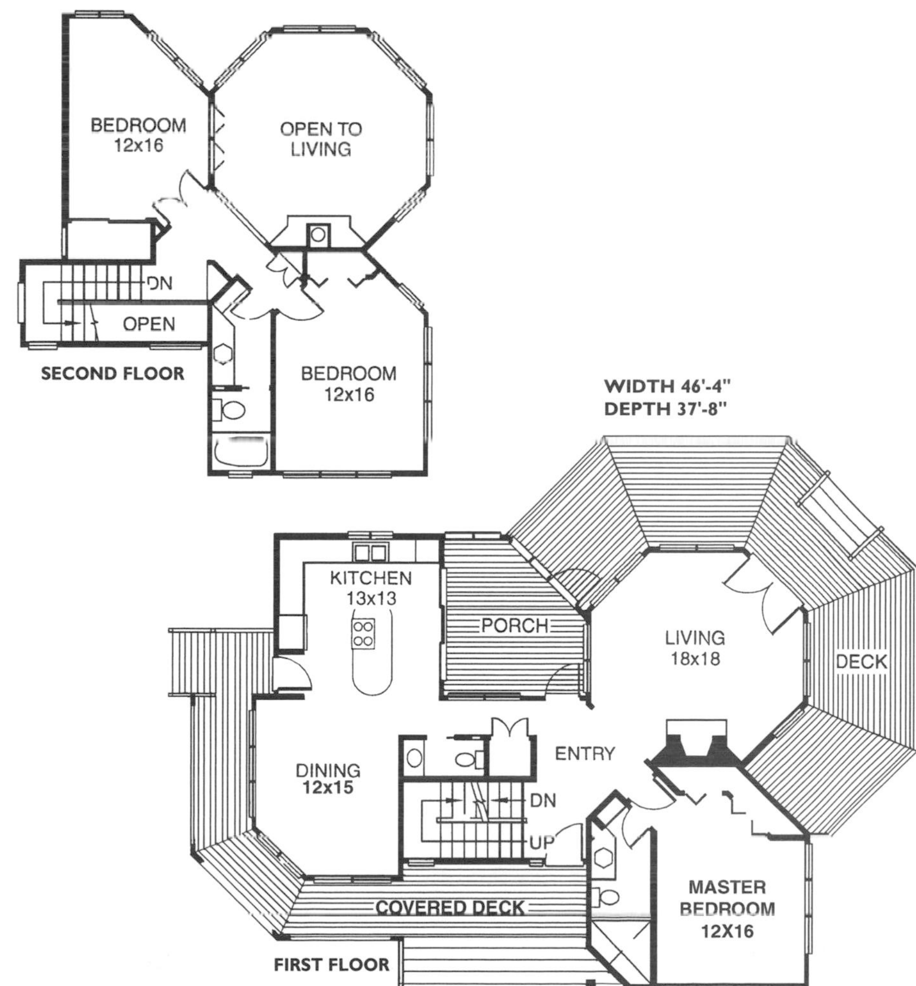
BEDROOM
12x16
OPEN TO
LIVING
DN
OPEN
SECOND FLOOR
BEDROOM
12x16
WIDTH 46'-4"
DEPTH 37'-8"
KITCHEN
13x13
PORCH
LIVING
18x18
DECK
DINING
12x15
ENTRY
DN
UP
COVERED DECK
MASTER
BEDROOM
12X16
FIRST FLOOR

Prairie-Style Retreat

Price Code: D

- This plan features:
  - — Three bedrooms
  - — Two full and one half baths
- Shingle siding, tall expanses of glass, and wrapping Decks accent the exterior
- The octagonal-shaped Living Room has a two story ceiling and French doors
- The Kitchen is enhanced by a cooktop island
- The first floor Master Suite offers a private Bath
- This home is designed with a basement foundation

FIRST FLOOR — 1,213 SQ. FT.
SECOND FLOOR — 825 SQ. FT.
BASEMENT — 1,213 SQ. FT.

TOTAL LIVING AREA:
2,038 SQ. FT.

PLAN NO. 32146

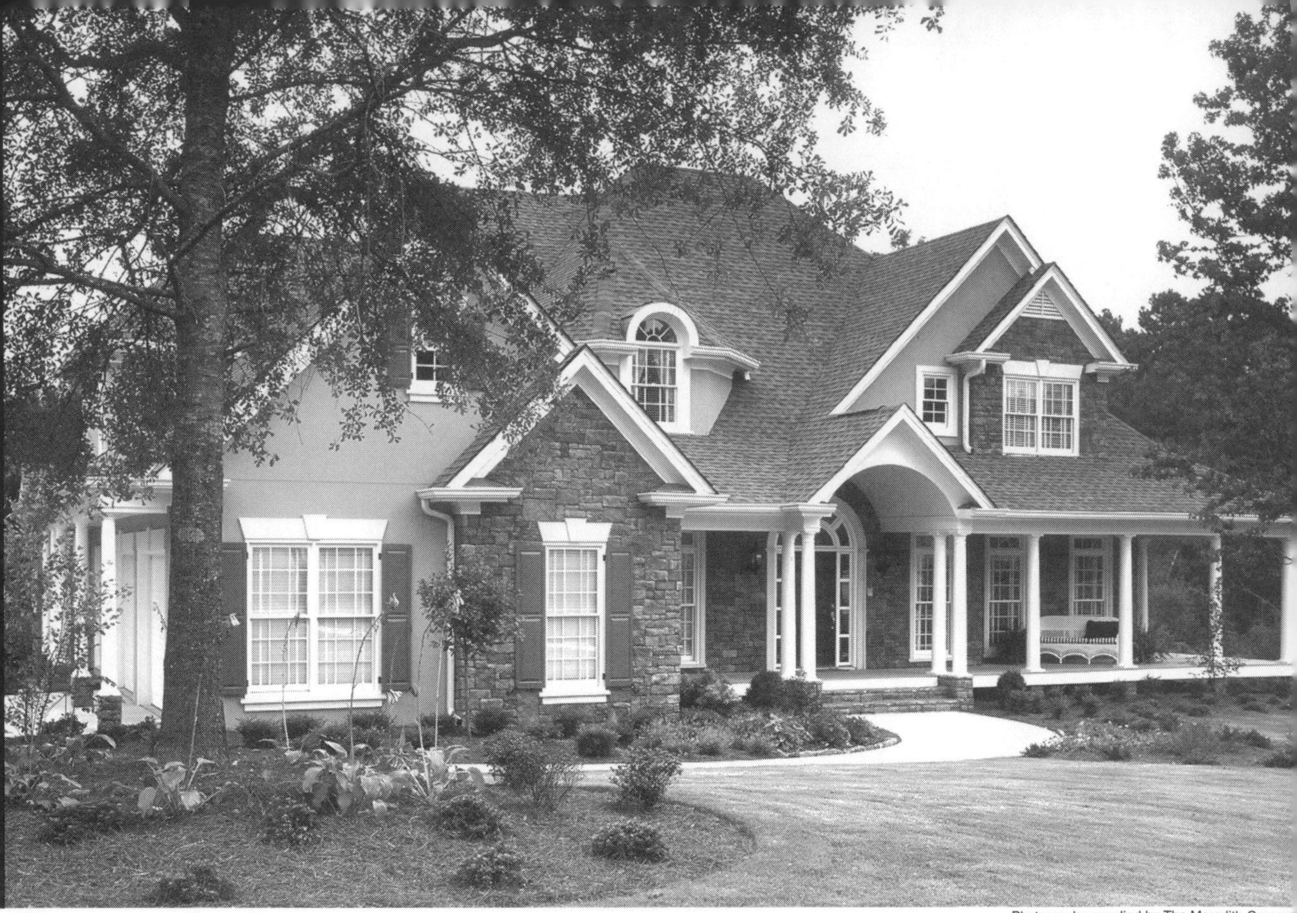

Photography supplied by The Meredith Corpora

Mansion Mystique

Price Code: K

- This plan features:
- — Four bedrooms
- — Four full and one half baths
- A beautiful exterior includes multiple rooflines and a covered Porch
- The Entry includes a curved staircase
- Multi-purpose rooms include a Guest Room/Study and an upstairs Office
- Both the Family Room and the Great Room have fireplaces
- The L-shaped Kitchen opens to the Breakfast Nook
- Upstairs find multiple Bedrooms, Baths, and a bonus space
- This home is designed with a basement foundation

FIRST FLOOR — 2,727 SQ. FT.
SECOND FLOOR — 1,168 SQ. FT.
BONUS — 213 SQ. FT.
BASEMENT — 2,250 SQ. FT.
GARAGE — 984 SQ. FT.

TOTAL LIVING AREA:

3,895 SQ. FT.

PATIO
FAMILY 15x19
DECK
PORCH
BRKFST 12x10
MASTER BEDROOM 15x18
CLOS
UP
GREAT-ROOM 18x16
KIT 18x14
BATH
CLOS
O R
DN
W D
P
LDRY
DINING 12x17
ENTRY
GUEST/ STUDY 14x11
UP
GARAGE 20x14
PORCH
FIRST FLOOR
OPEN TO FAMILY
WIDTH 73'-8"
DEPTH 72'-2"
OFFICE 10x13
OPEN TO GREAT-ROOM
DN
BRIDGE
DN
BEDROOM 12x12
BEDROOM 12x18
BEDROOM 12x14
OPEN TO ENTRY
CLOS
BONUS ROOM 10x19
SECOND FLOOR

Luxurious Styling

PRICE CODE: K

PLAN NO. 98586

'his plan features:
- 'our bedrooms
- Three full and one half baths
- 'legance prevails in the Master Suite, which occupies quiet corner of the first floor
- 'he Master Bedroom has a door to a covered rear Patio nd shares a two sided fireplace with a Study
- 'he Living Room has a cathedral ceiling a fireplace, nd a wetbar
- 'he Kitchen includes a Pantry, a snack bar, and work island
- 'his home is designed with basement, slab and rawlspace foundation options

ST FLOOR — 2,860 SQ. FT.
'OND FLOOR — 1,140 SQ. FT.

TOTAL LIVING AREA:* 4,000 *SQ. FT.

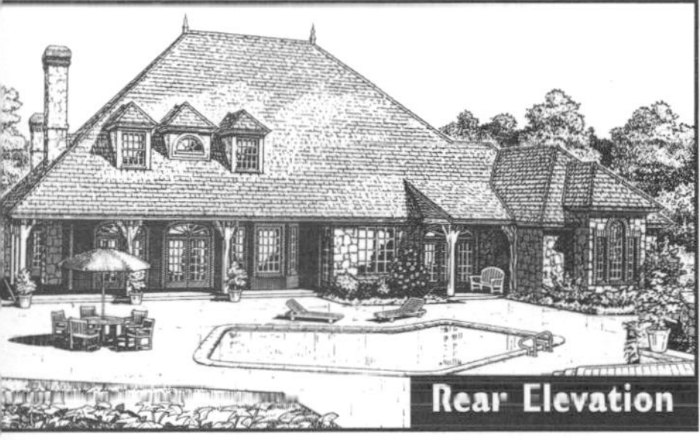
Rear Elevation

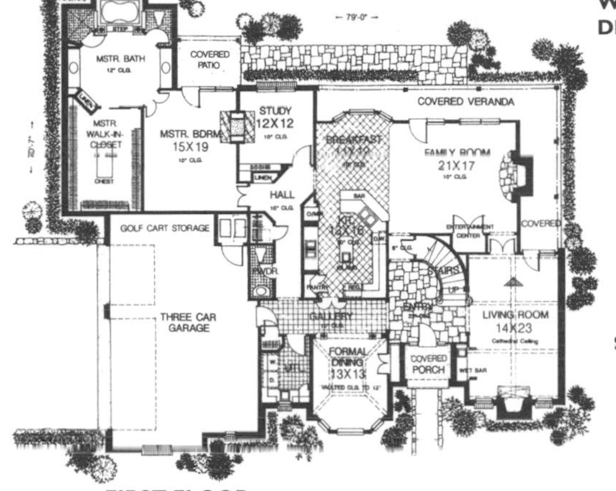
79'-0"
MSTR. BATH
COVERED PATIO
MSTR. WALK-IN CLOSET
MSTR. BDRM 15X19
STUDY 12X12
BREAKFAST
COVERED VERANDA
FAMILY ROOM 21X17
HALL
GOLF CART STORAGE
THREE CAR GARAGE
GALLERY
ENTRY
STAIRS
LIVING ROOM 14X23
FORMAL DINING 13X13
COVERED PORCH
WET BAR

FIRST FLOOR

WIDTH 79'-0"
DEPTH 70'-7"

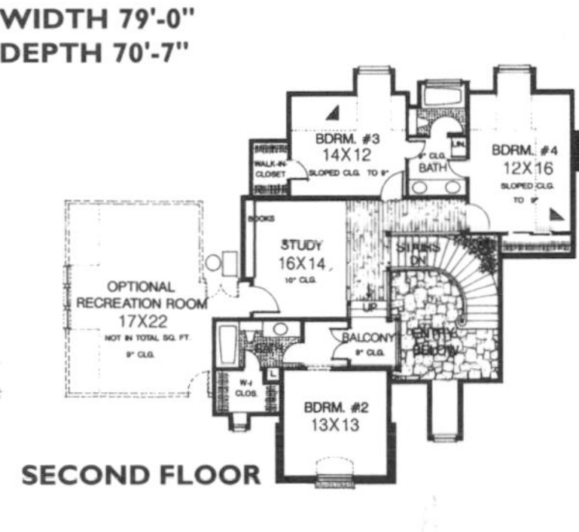
BDRM. #3 14X12
BDRM. #4 12X16
BATH
STUDY 16X14
OPTIONAL RECREATION ROOM 17X22
BALCONY
BDRM. #2 13X13

SECOND FLOOR

Double Gables and Exciting Entry

PRICE CODE: E

PLAN NO. 92692

'his plan features:
- 'our bedrooms
- Two full and one half baths
- mpressive exterior features double gables and arched vindow
- 'pacious Foyer separates the formal Dining Room and Living Room
- Roomy Kitchen and Breakfast Bay are adjacent to the arge Family Room which has a fireplace and accesses he rear Deck
- 'pacious Master Bedroom features private Bath with ual vanity, shower stall and whirlpool tub
- 'hree additional Bedrooms share a full hall Bath
- 'his home is designed with a basement foundation

ST FLOOR — 1,207 SQ. FT.
'OND FLOOR — 1,181 SQ. FT.
SEMENT — 1,207 SQ. FT.

TOTAL LIVING AREA:* 2,388 *SQ. FT.

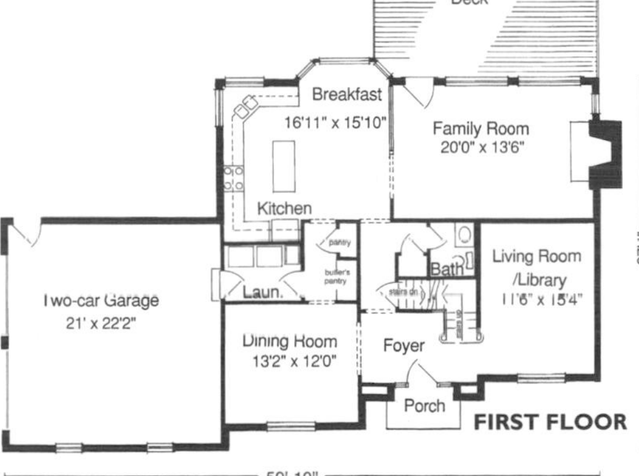
Deck
Breakfast
16'11" x 15'10"
Family Room
20'0" x 13'6"
Kitchen
Bath
Living Room /Library
11'6" x 15'4"
Two-car Garage
21' x 22'2"
Laun.
Dining Room
13'2" x 12'0"
Foyer
Porch
37'4"
59'-10"

FIRST FLOOR

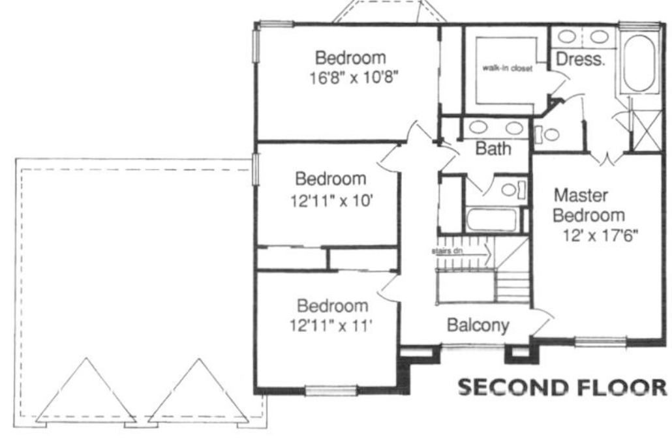
Bedroom
16'8" x 10'8"
Dress.
Bath
Bedroom
12'11" x 10'
Master Bedroom
12' x 17'6"
Bedroom
12'11" x 11'
Balcony

SECOND FLOOR

PLAN NO.91129

Splendid Space

PRICE CODE: C

- This plan features:
  - — Three bedrooms
  - — Two full baths
- Split-Bedroom plan allows for privacy
- Arched entries lead into the Living and Dining Room
- A Sunroom is located in the rear
- The Nook has a built-in desk
- Plant ledges are a nice touch
- This home is designed with a slab foundation

MAIN FLOOR — 1,983 SQ. FT.
GARAGE — 492 SQ. FT.

TOTAL LIVING AREA:
1,983 SQ. FT.

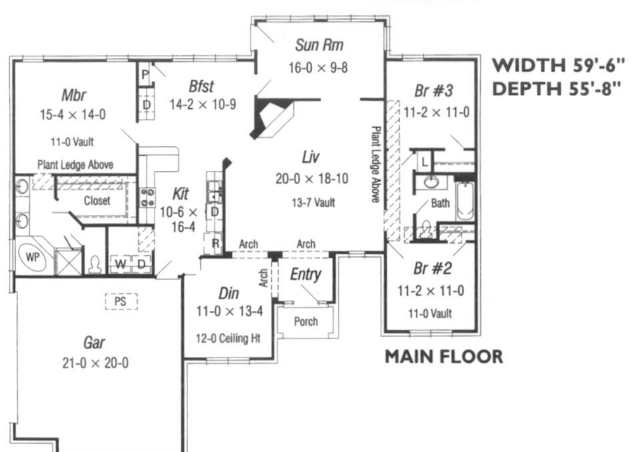
Sun Rm
16-0 × 9-8
Mbr
15-4 × 14-0
11-0 Vault
Plant Ledge Above
Closet
Bfst
14-2 × 10-9
P
D
Kit
10-6 × 16-4
R
D
WP
W D
Liv
20-0 × 18-10
13-7 Vault
Plant Ledge Above
Arch
Arch
Arch
Entry
Porch
Br #3
11-2 × 11-0
L
Bath
Br #2
11-2 × 11-0
11-0 Vault
Din
11-0 × 13-4
12-0 Ceiling Ht
PS
Gar
21-0 × 20-0
WIDTH 59'-6"
DEPTH 55'-8"
MAIN FLOOR

PLAN NO.94307

Easy Maintenance

PRICE CODE: A

- This plan features:
  - — Two bedrooms
  - — Two full and one three-quarter baths
- Abundant glass and a wraparound Deck to enjoy the outdoors
- A tiled Entry into a large Great Room, with a fieldst fireplace and dining area below a sloped ceiling
- A compact tiled Kitchen opens to a Great Room and adjacent to the Utility Area
- Two Bedrooms, one with a private Bath, offer ample closet space
- This home is designed with a crawlspace foundation

MAIN FLOOR — 786 SQ. FT.

TOTAL LIVING AREA:
786 SQ. FT.

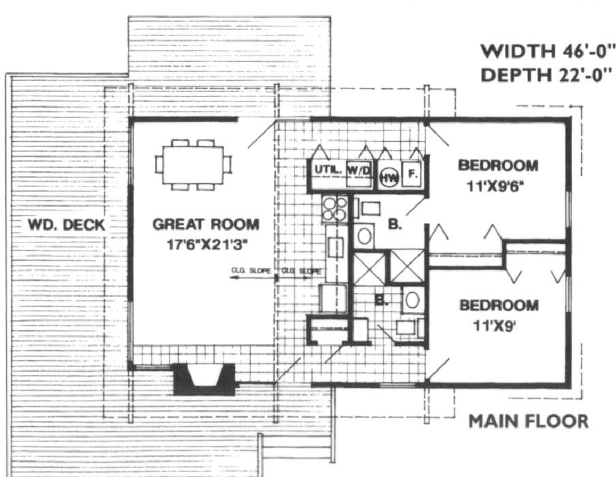
WIDTH 46'-0"
DEPTH 22'-0"
WD. DECK
GREAT ROOM
17'6"X21'3"
CLG. SLOPE
CLG. SLOPE
UTIL.
W/D
HW
F.
B.
B.
BEDROOM
11'X9'6"
BEDROOM
11'X9'
MAIN FLOOR

To order your Blueprints, call 1-800-235-5700

Columns Accentuate with Flair

PRICE CODE: E

PLAN NO.94641

'his plan features:
- Four bedrooms
- Two full baths
- 'our columns accentuate the front Porch
- 'he Foyer leads to the Living Room or the Dining Room
- 'he Kitchen includes a peninsula counter, plenty of torage space and an easy flow into the Breakfast Room
- 'he Master Bedroom is topped by a decorative ceiling reatment and has a compartmental Bath with a vhirlpool tub
- 'wo additional Bedrooms with walk-in closets share a ouble vanity Bath in the hall
- 'his home is designed with a slab foundation

IN FLOOR — 2,400 SQ. FT.
RAGE — 534 SQ. FT.

TOTAL LIVING AREA:
2,400 SQ. FT.

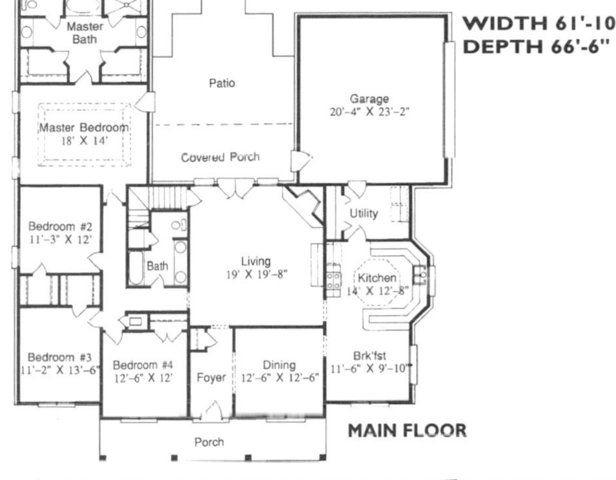
Master Bath
Patio
Garage
20'-4" X 23'-2"
Master Bedroom
18' X 14'
Covered Porch
Bedroom #2
11'-3" X 12'
Utility
Bath
Living
19' X 19'-8"
Kitchen
14' X 12'-8"
Bedroom #3
11'-2" X 13'-6"
Bedroom #4
12'-6" X 12'
Foyer
Dining
12'-6" X 12'-6"
Brk'fst
11'-6" X 9'-10"
Porch

WIDTH 61'-10"
DEPTH 66'-6"

MAIN FLOOR

Room for a Large Family

PRICE CODE: C

PLAN NO.99129

This plan features:
- Four bedrooms
- Two full and one half baths
- Front Porch leads into a two-story Foyer with an open L-shaped staircase
- Gracious Living Room archway leads into the formal Dining Room
- Relax by the fire in the Family Room
- The L-shaped Kitchen opens into the Nook and has a built-in planning desk
- The Master Bedroom is located on the second floor and has a private Bath
- Three more Bedrooms and a full Bath serve the rest of the family
- This home is designed with a basement foundation

RST FLOOR — 1,000 SQ. FT.
COND FLOOR — 960 SQ. FT.
SEMENT — 1,000 SQ. FT.

TOTAL LIVING AREA:
1,960 SQ. FT.

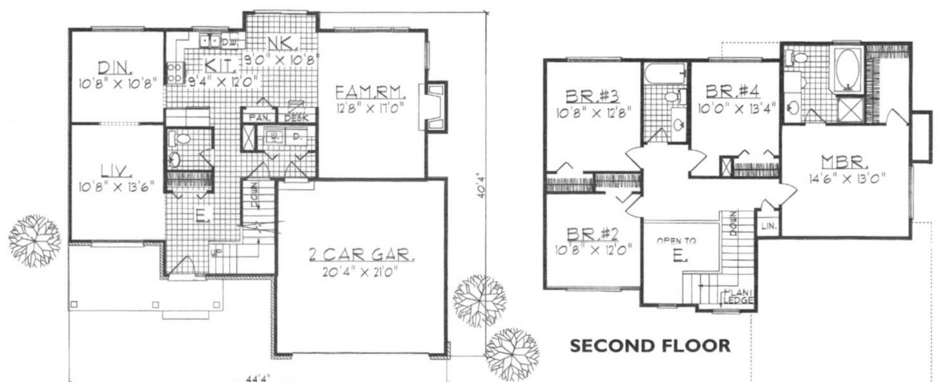
DIN.
10'8" X 10'8"
KIT.
9'4" X 12'0"
NK.
9'0" X 10'8"
FAM.RM.
12'8" X 17'0"
PAN.
DESK
LIV.
10'8" X 13'6"
E.
2 CAR GAR.
20'4" X 21'0"
40'4"
44'4"
BR.#3
10'8" X 12'8"
BR.#4
10'0" X 13'4"
MBR.
14'6" X 13'0"
BR.#2
10'8" X 12'0"
OPEN TO
E.
LIN.
PLANT LEDGE
SECOND FLOOR

FIRST FLOOR

PLAN NO. 90450

Elegant Brick Two-Story

Price Code: E

This plan features:

— Four bedrooms

— Two full and one half baths

A large two-story Great Room with a fireplace and access to the Deck

A secluded Master Suite with two walk-in closets and a private, lavish Master Bath

A large island Kitchen which can serve the formal Dining Room and the sunny Breakfast Nook with ease

Three additional Bedrooms, two with walk-in closets, sharing a full hall Bath

This home is designed with basement and crawlspace foundation options

FIRST FLOOR — 1,637 SQ. FT.
SECOND FLOOR — 761 SQ. FT.
BONUS — 453 SQ. FT.

TOTAL LIVING AREA:
2,398 SQ. FT.

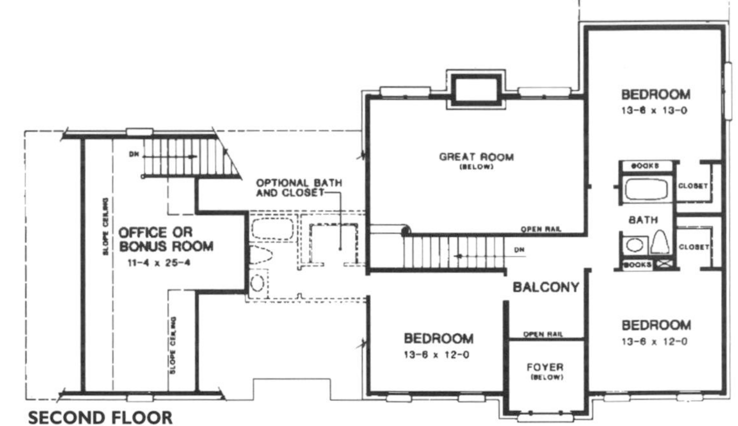
BEDROOM
13-6 x 13-0
GREAT ROOM
(BELOW)
OPTIONAL BATH
AND CLOSET
OFFICE OR
BONUS ROOM
11-4 x 25-4
SLOPE CEILING
BOOKS
CLOSET
BATH
OPEN RAIL
DN
BALCONY
BEDROOM
13-6 x 12-0
FOYER
(BELOW)
BEDROOM
13-6 x 12-0
SECOND FLOOR

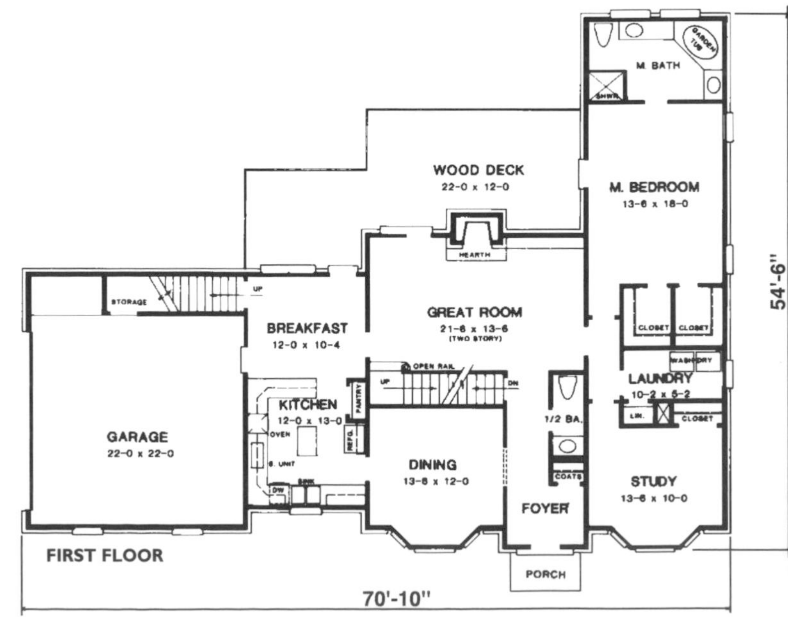
M. BATH
WOOD DECK
22-0 x 12-0
M. BEDROOM
13-6 x 18-0
HEARTH
STORAGE
UP
BREAKFAST
12-0 x 10-4
GREAT ROOM
21-6 x 13-6
(TWO STORY)
CLOSET
CLOSET
LAUNDRY
10-2 x 5-2
OPEN RAIL
KITCHEN
12-0 x 13-0
PANTRY
1/2 BA.
GARAGE
22-0 x 22-0
DINING
13-6 x 12-0
COATS
STUDY
13-6 x 10-0
FOYER
FIRST FLOOR
PORCH
70'-10"
54'-6"

Narrow Lot

PRICE CODE: B

PLAN NO.91102

ıis plan features:
- hree bedrooms
- wo full and one half baths
- : almost 38 feet wide, this home is suited r a narrow lot
- ıe Dining Room has a tray ceiling
- ıe vaulted Living Rroom has a corner fireplace
- ıe Galley Kitchen is adjacent to the Nook
- ıe Master Suite has a large walk-in closet
- dditional Bedrooms and bonus space are upstairs
- ıis home is designed with a basement foundation

ST FLOOR — 1,188 SQ. FT.
OND FLOOR — 513 SQ. FT.
AGE — 411 SQ. FT.

TOTAL LIVING AREA:
1,701 SQ. FT.

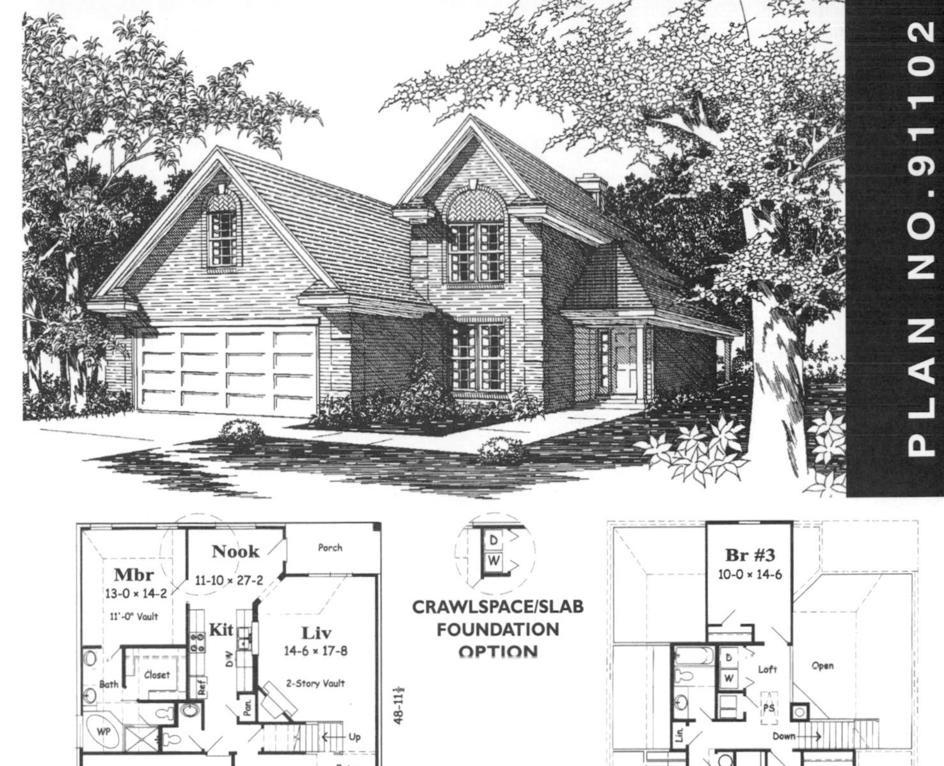

Mbr
13-0 × 14-2
11'-0" Vault
Nook
11-10 × 27-2
Porch
Kit
Liv
14-6 × 17-8
2-Story Vault
Bath
Closet
Ref
D/W
Pan
WP
Up
48-11½
Entry
Gar
18-8 × 20-0
Din
10-4 × 12-8
Tray Ceiling
Porch
FIRST FLOOR
37-11½
D
W
CRAWLSPACE/SLAB FOUNDATION OPTION
Br #3
10-0 × 14-6
Loft
Open
Lin.
PS
Down
Future
10-4 × 20-0
8'-0" Vault
Br #2
10-4 × 12-4
SECOND FLOOR

Cottage Appeal

PRICE CODE: H

PLAN NO.98588

his plan features:
- 'our bedrooms
- 'hree full and one half baths
- . curving staircase accents the formal Entry 'ith gracious elegance
- nhanced by a fireplace and a bay window, ıe Living Room is a welcoming spot
- he Great Room has a fireplace and access) the rear Patio
- 'ach Bedroom has private access to a full Bath
- hree-car Garage offers additional Storage Space and an asy Entry into the home
- his home is designed with basement and slab ›undation options

ST FLOOR — 2,337 SQ. FT.
:OND FLOOR — 882 SQ. FT.
NUS ROOM — 357 SQ. FT.
RAGE — 640 SQ. FT.

TOTAL LIVING AREA:
3,219 SQ. FT.

WIDTH 70'-0"
DEPTH 63'-2"
COVERED PATIO
MSTR. BATH
PATIO AREA
COVERED AREA
BRKFT.
MSTR. BDRM.
14X18
WALK-IN CLOSET
GREAT ROOM
20X18
KITCHEN
STUDY
11X11
HALL
GALLERY
STAIRS
ENTRY
FML. DIN.
12X12
FML. LIV.
14X14
POR.
THREE CAR GARAGE
22X30
SERV. POR.
FIRST FLOOR
BDRM.#3
12X14
BDRM.#2
12X12
HALL
STAIRS DN.
BDRM.#4
12X12
OPEN ABOVE ENTRY
FUTURE BONUS ROOM
SECOND FLOOR

PLAN NO. 97126

Charming Two-Story

Price Code: G

- This plan features:
- — Three bedrooms
- — Two full and one half baths
- The Kitchen has ample counter space and an island
- The sunny Nook provides access to the Screen Porch
- The Master Bedroom has two closets and a large Bath
- An optional room upstairs can serve as a fourth Bedroom or a Game Room
- This home is designed with a basement foundation

FIRST FLOOR — 2,172 SQ. FT.
SECOND FLOOR — 690 SQ. FT.
BONUS — 450 SQ. FT.

TOTAL LIVING AREA:
2,862 SQ. FT.

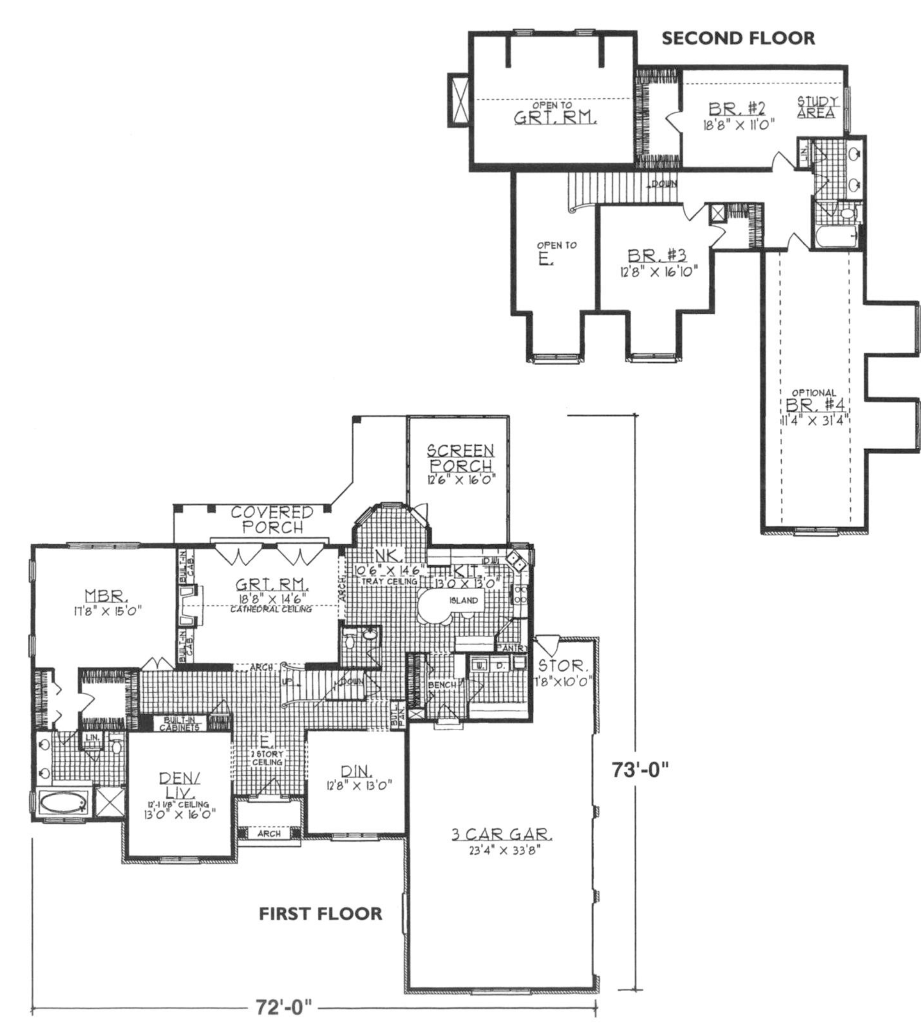
SECOND FLOOR
OPEN TO GRT. RM.
BR. #2
18'8" X 11'0"
STUDY AREA
DOWN
OPEN TO E.
BR. #3
12'8" X 16'10"
OPTIONAL BR. #4
11'4" X 31'4"
SCREEN PORCH
12'6" X 16'0"
COVERED PORCH
MBR.
17'8" X 15'0"
GRT. RM.
18'8" X 14'6"
CATHEDRAL CEILING
NK.
10'6" X 14'6"
TRAY CEILING
KIT.
13'0 X 13'0"
ISLAND
PANTRY
STOR.
7'8" X 10'0"
ARCH
BENCH
BUILT-IN CABINETS
E.
2 STORY CEILING
DEN/ LIV.
13'0" X 16'0"
DIN.
12'8" X 13'0"
ARCH
3 CAR GAR.
23'4" X 33'8"
73'-0"
FIRST FLOOR
72'-0"

PLAN NO. 91163

Made to Order

Price Code: B

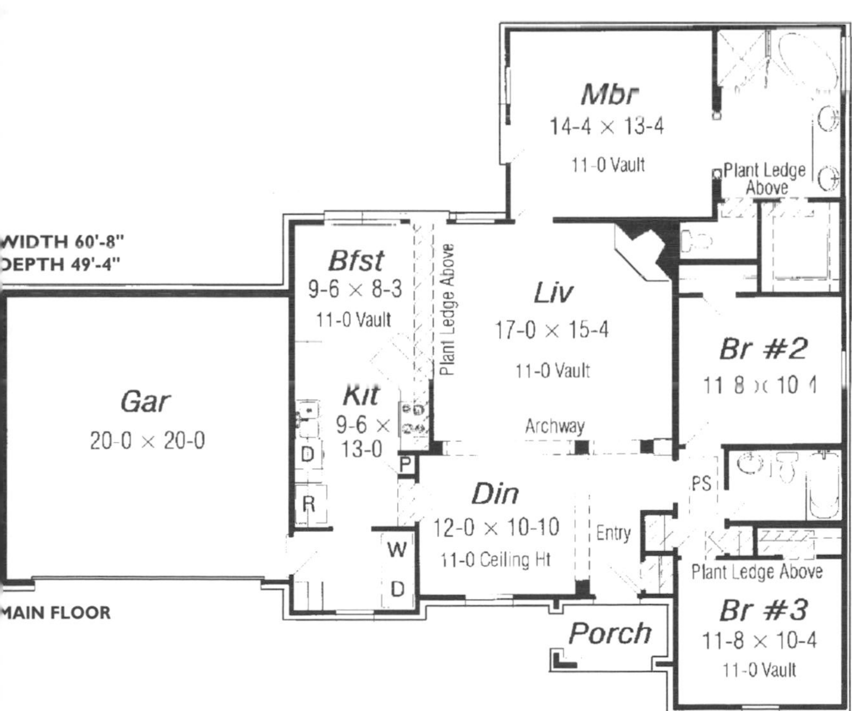

WIDTH 60'-8"
DEPTH 49'-4"
Mbr
14-4 × 13-4
11-0 Vault
Plant Ledge Above
Bfst
9-6 × 8-3
11-0 Vault
Plant Ledge Above
Liv
17-0 × 15-4
11-0 Vault
Br #2
Gar
20-0 × 20-0
Kit
9-6 ×
13-0
Archway
D
P
PS
R
Din
12-0 × 10-10
11-0 Ceiling Ht
Entry
W
D
Plant Ledge Above
Br #3
11-8 × 10-4
11-0 Vault
Porch
MAIN FLOOR

- This plan features:
  - Three bedrooms
  - Two full baths
- The Master Suite has a vaulted ceiling, private access to the backyard, and columns lining the entrance to the Bath
- There is a corner fireplace and a vaulted ceiling in the Living Room
- The Dining Room is topped by an 11-foot ceiling and has easy access to the Kitchen
- The Entry from the Garage opens to the Laundry Room, creating a Mudroom effect
- This home is designed with a crawlspace foundation

MAIN FLOOR — 1,561 SQ. FT.
GARAGE — 445 SQ. FT.

TOTAL LIVING AREA:
1,561 SQ. FT.

PLAN NO.94622

Multiple Porches Provid
Added Interest

PRICE CODE: H

- This plan features:
- — Four bedrooms
- — Three full and one half baths
- Two-story central Foyer flanked by Living and Dining Rooms
- Spacious Great Room with large fireplace between french doors to Porch and Deck
- Country-size Kitchen with cooktop work island, walk-in Pantry and Breakfast Area with Porch acce
- Pampering Master Bedroom offers a decorative cei Sitting Area, Porch and Deck access, a huge walk-i closet and lavish Bath
- Three second floor Bedrooms with walk-in closets, have private access to a full Bath
- This home is designed with slab and pier/post foundation options

FIRST FLOOR — 2,033 SQ. FT.
SECOND FLOOR — 1,116 SQ. FT.

TOTAL LIVING AREA:
3,149 SQ. FT.

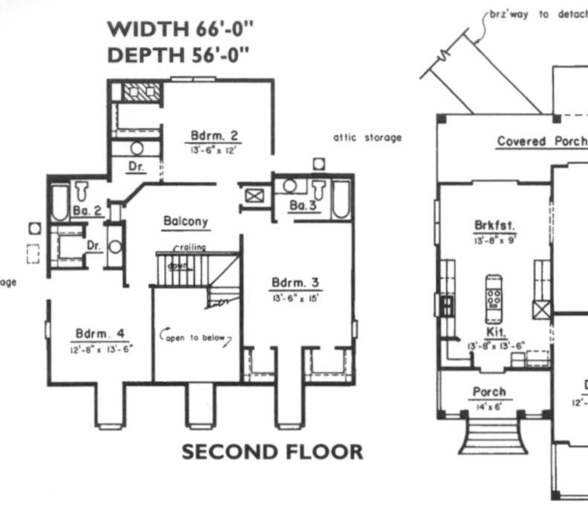
WIDTH 66'-0"
DEPTH 56'-0"
Bdrm. 2
13'-6" x 12'
attic storage
Dr.
Ba. 2
Dr.
Balcony
railing
Ba. 3
attic storage
Bdrm. 3
13'-6" x 15'
Bdrm. 4
12'-8" x 13'-6"
open to below
SECOND FLOOR

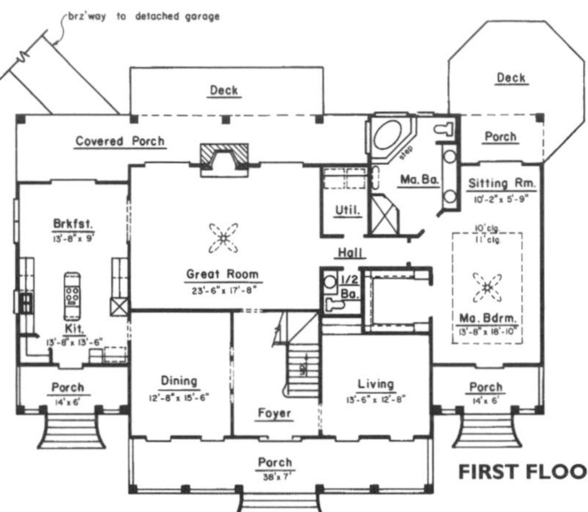
brz'way to detached garage
Deck
Deck
Covered Porch
Porch
Ma. Ba.
Sitting Rm.
10'-2" x 5'-9"
Util.
Brkfst.
13'-8" x 9'
Hall
Great Room
23'-6" x 17'-8"
1/2 Ba.
Kit.
13'-8" x 13'-6"
Ma. Bdrm.
13'-8" x 18'-10"
Porch
14' x 6'
Dining
12'-8" x 15'-6"
Living
13'-6" x 12'-8"
Porch
14' x 6'
Foyer
Porch
38' x 7'
FIRST FLOOR

PLAN NO.99162

Modern Comfort

PRICE CODE: F

- This plan features:
- — Three bedrooms
- — Two full and one half baths
- This home is a traditional ranch with country trimm
- Highly windowed Great Room is illuminated by na light creating an airy atmosphere
- Split-bedroom layout for a private Master Suite
- There is a see-through fireplace from the Master Bedroom to the Master Bath
- Formal Dining and a casual Nook, you can entertai for any occasion
- This home is designed with a basement foundation

MAIN FLOOR — 2,730 SQ. FT.
BASEMENT — 2,730 SQ. FT.
GARAGE — 707 SQ. FT.

TOTAL LIVING AREA:
2,730 SQ. FT.

MBR.
14'8" X 20'0"
NK.
14'0" X 10'2"
KIT.
14'0" X 14'8"
GRT. RM.
21'8" X 17'8"
BR. #2
13'0" X 12'10"
DIN.
14'8" X 13'0"
DEN/ BR. #3
12'8" X 12'8"
3 CAR GAR.
21'0" X 33'8"
MAIN FLOOR

Home Sweet Home

PRICE CODE: A

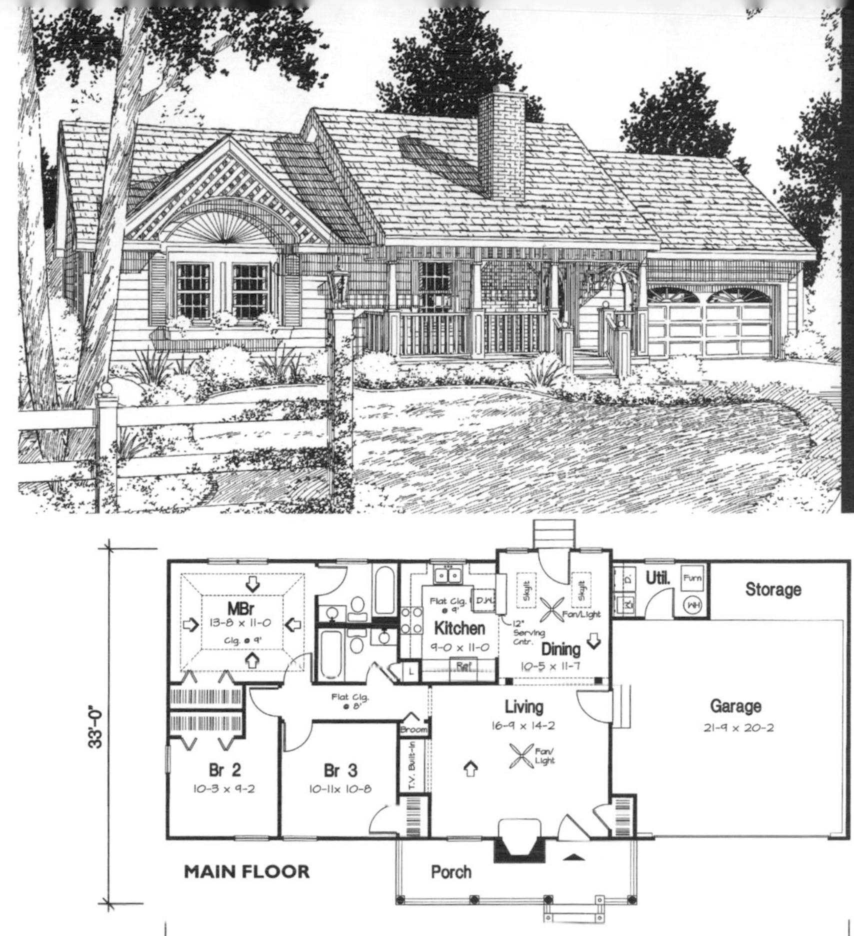

PLAN NO.24723
MBr
13-8 x 11-0
Clg. @ 9'
Flat Clg. @ 9'
D.W.
Kitchen
9-0 x 11-0
Ref
Skylt
Skylt
Fan/Light
12" Serving Cntr.
Dining
10-5 x 11-7
Util.
Furn
WH
Storage
Flat Clg. @ 8'
Living
16-9 x 14-2
Fan/Light
Garage
21-9 x 20-2
Broom
T.V. Built-in
Br 2
10-3 x 9-2
Br 3
10-11x 10-8
33'-0"
MAIN FLOOR
Porch
64'-0"

his plan features:

- 'hree bedrooms
- 'wo full baths
- ingle level format allows for step-saving convenience
- arge Living Room, highlighted by a fireplace and built- entertainment center, adjoins the Dining Room
- kylights, a ceiling fan and room defining columns ccent the Dining Room
- serving bar to the Dining Room, and ample counter nd cabinet space in the Kitchen
- ecorative ceiling treatment over the Master Bedroom nd a private Master Bath
- wo secondary Bedrooms with easy access to the full ath in the hall
- his home is designed with crawlspace and ab foundation

IN FLOOR — 1,112 SQ. FT.
RAGE — 563 SQ. FT.

TOTAL LIVING AREA:
1,112 SQ. FT.

Outdoor Circular Stair

PRICE CODE: C

PLAN NO.65012

'his plan features:

- Three bedrooms
- Two full and one half baths
- 'he spacious Kitchen offers ample cabinet space and as a built-in desk
- turreted, two-story plant area has spiral stair access nto the basement
- 'his home is designed with a basement foundation

ST FLOOR — 1,293 SQ. FT.
COND FLOOR — 629 SQ. FT.
SEMENT — 1,293 SQ. FT.
RAGE — 606 SQ. FT.

TOTAL LIVING AREA:
1,922 SQ. FT.

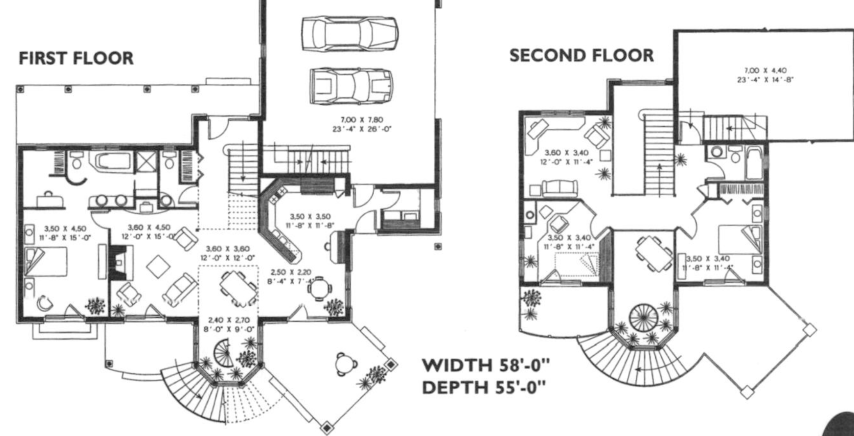

FIRST FLOOR
SECOND FLOOR
WIDTH 58'-0"
DEPTH 55'-0"

PLAN NO.91149

Stupendous Plan

PRICE CODE: A

- This plan features:
  - — Four bedrooms
  - — Two full baths
- The spacious Living Room has an optional fireplace and a vaulted ceiling
- The L-shaped Kitchen and Nook have a great bay window naturally illuminating the room and giving a view of the rear yard
- The Master Bedroom is split from the others and ha vaulted ceiling, walk-in closet, and private Master B
- This home is designed with a slab foundation

MAIN FLOOR — 1,370 SQ. FT.
PORCH — 78 SQ. FT.

TOTAL LIVING AREA:
1,370 SQ. FT.

WIDTH 38'-6"
DEPTH 45'-8"

Nook 15-0 × 13-4
Storage
Br #3 10-0 × 12-4
Br #2 10-2 × 11-0
Kit
D W
Clo
Pan
Bath
Hall
Hall
Br #4 10-0 × 11-8
Bath
Living 14-2 × 17-8 10-0 Ceiling Ht
Entry
Master 12-4 × 14-0 10-0 Ceiling Ht
Porch

MAIN FLOOR

PLAN NO.97506

European Flavor

PRICE CODE: F

- This plan features:
  - — Three bedrooms
  - — Two full and one half baths
- The exterior is stucco with ornate iron railings
- The Family Room is enhanced by a fireplace and is to the Dining Room
- There are pocket doors separating the Study from th Family Room
- The Kitchen includes a cooktop island with a snack and is open to the Breakfast Area
- The Master Bedroom Suite is lavishly appointed anc includes two walk-in closets
- This home is designed with a slab foundation

FIRST FLOOR — 2,005 SQ. FT.
SECOND FLOOR — 639 SQ. FT.
GARAGE — 443 SQ. FT.

TOTAL LIVING AREA:
2,644 SQ. FT.

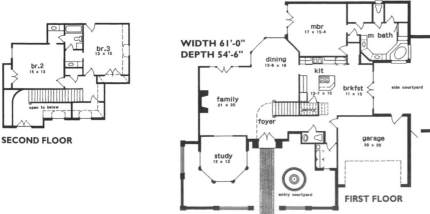

br.2 15 x 13
br.3 13 x 15
open to below

SECOND FLOOR

WIDTH 61'-0"
DEPTH 54'-6"

mbr 17 x 15-4
m bath
dining 13-6 x 18
kit 13-7 x 13
brkfst 11 x 15
side courtyard
family 21 x 20
pantry
foyer
garage 20 x 20
study 13 x 13
entry courtyard

FIRST FLOOR

PLAN NO. 65014

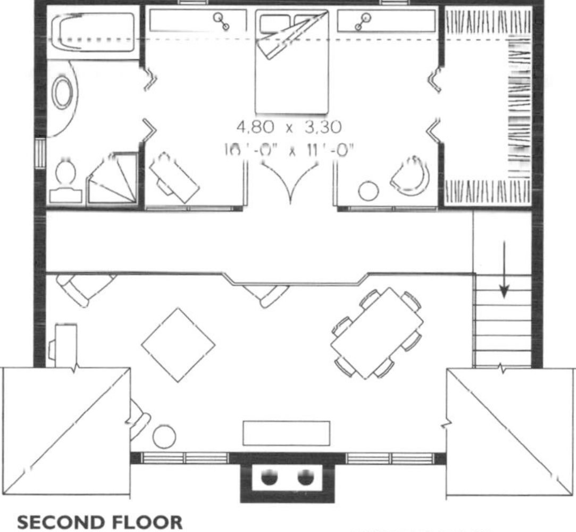
4,80 x 3,30
16'-0" x 11'-0"

SECOND FLOOR

WIDTH 28'-0"
DEPTH 26'-0"

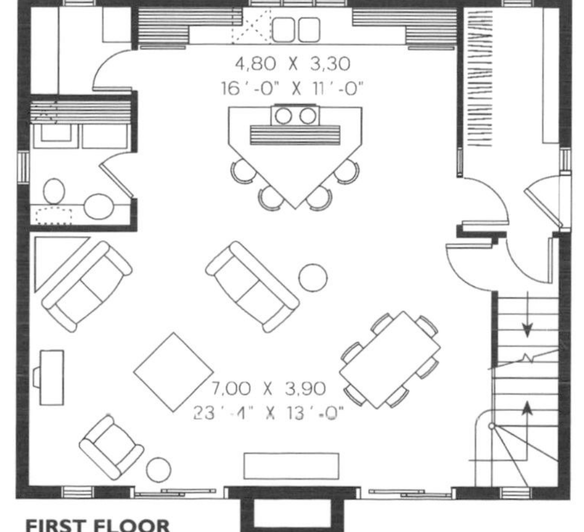
4,80 X 3,30
16'-0" X 11'-0"
7,00 X 3,90
23'-4" X 13'-0"

FIRST FLOOR

Isolated Bedroom

Price Code: A

- This plan features:
- — One bedroom
- — One full and one half baths
- Windows define the facade of this home, casting natural light through the interior
- The Living Room opens directly into the Kitchen, creating a sense of community
- The Bedroom is located on the second floor and has a full Bath and roomy walk-in closet
- The focal point fireplace warms the Living Room and beyond
- This home is designed with a basement foundation

First floor —728 sq. ft.
Second floor — 420 sq. ft.
Basement — 728 sq. ft.

Total living area:
1,148 sq. ft.

PLAN NO.97628

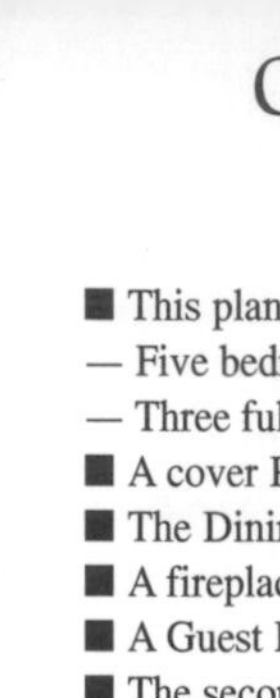

Open Rail Staircase

PRICE CODE: G

- This plan features:
  - — Five bedrooms
  - — Three full baths
- A cover Porch and two-story Foyer greet you
- The Dining Room has a Room expanding bay wind
- A fireplace warms the vaulted Family Room
- A Guest Room or Study is tucked in the rear
- The second floor contains the balance of the sleeping quarters
- This home is designed with basement and crawlspace foundation

FIRST FLOOR — 1,438 SQ. FT.
SECOND FLOOR — 1,395 SQ. FT.
BASEMENT — 1,438 SQ. FT.
GARAGE — 498 SQ. FT.

TOTAL LIVING AREA:
2,833 SQ. FT.

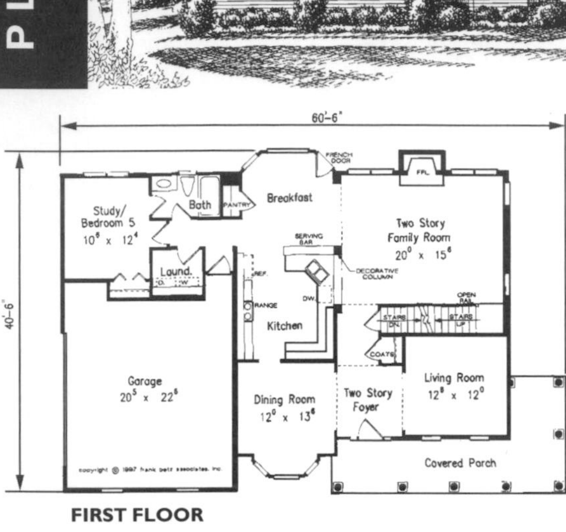
60'-6"
40'-6"
Study/
Bedroom 5
10⁶ x 12⁴
Bath
Pantry
Breakfast
French Door
FPL
Two Story
Family Room
20⁰ x 15⁶
Laund.
Kitchen
Garage
20⁵ x 22⁶
Dining Room
12⁰ x 13⁶
Two Story
Foyer
Living Room
12⁸ x 12⁰
Covered Porch

FIRST FLOOR

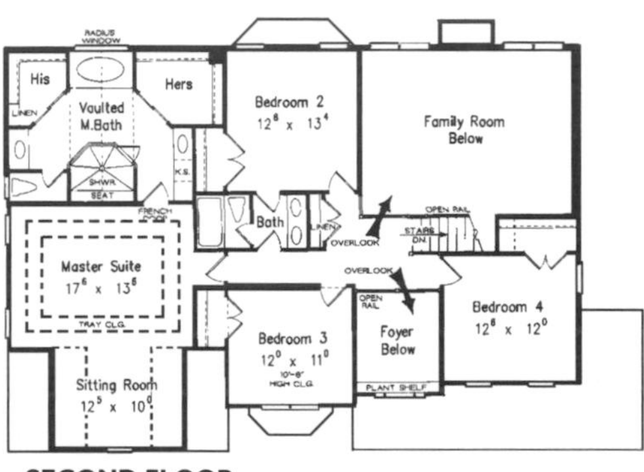
His
Vaulted
M.Bath
Hers
Bedroom 2
12⁸ x 13⁴
Family Room
Below
Bath
Master Suite
17⁶ x 13⁶
Sitting Room
12⁵ x 10⁰
Bedroom 3
12⁰ x 11⁰
Foyer
Below
Bedroom 4
12⁸ x 12⁰

SECOND FLOOR

PLAN NO.94923

Keystone Arches and Decorative Windows

PRICE CODE: B

- This plan features:
  - — Three bedrooms
  - — Two full baths
- Brick and stucco enhance the dramatic front elevation and volume entrance
- Inviting Entry leads into expansive Great Room with hearth fireplace framed by transom window
- Bay window Dining Room topped by decorative ceiling convenient to the Great Room and the Kitchen/Breakfast Area
- Corner Master Suite enjoys a tray ceiling, roomy walk-in closet and a plush Bath with a double vanity and whirlpool window tub
- Two additional Bedrooms with large closets, share a full Bath
- This home is designed with a basement foundation
- Alternate foundation options available at an additional charge. Please call 1-800-235-5700 for more information.

MAIN FLOOR — 1,666 SQ. FT.
BASEMENT — 1,666 SQ. FT.
GARAGE — 496 SQ. FT.

TOTAL LIVING AREA:
1,666 SQ. FT.

WIDTH 55'-4"
DEPTH 48'-0"

MAIN FLOOR

Three Season Porch

PRICE CODE: A

This plan features:
- Three bedrooms
- Two full baths
- A Three-Season Porch offers expanded living space during the mild weather months
- A cozy fireplace in the Living Room creates a warm atmosphere
- The first floor Bedroom has a full Bath with both shower and tub in close proximity
- The two secondary Bedrooms are located on the second floor
- The home is designed with a basement foundation
- FIRST FLOOR — 858 SQ. FT.
- SECOND FLOOR — 502 SQ. FT.

TOTAL LIVING AREA:
1,360 SQ. FT.

PLAN NO. 65015

WIDTH 35'-0"
DEPTH 29'-8"

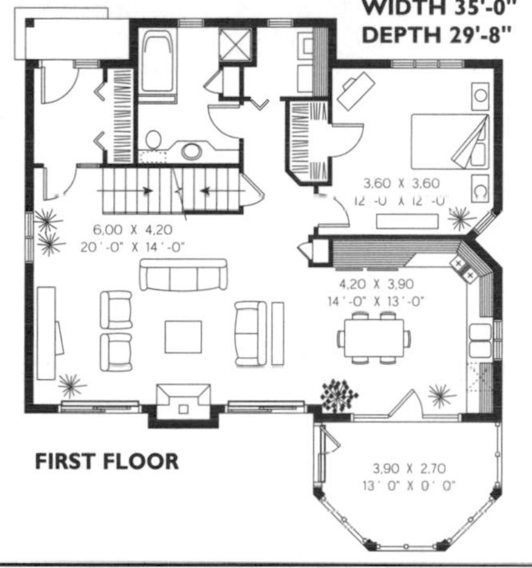

3,60 X 3,60
12'-0" X 12'-0"
6,00 X 4,20
20'-0" X 14'-0"
4,20 X 3,90
14'-0" X 13'-0"
3,90 X 2,70
13'-0" X 0'-0"

FIRST FLOOR

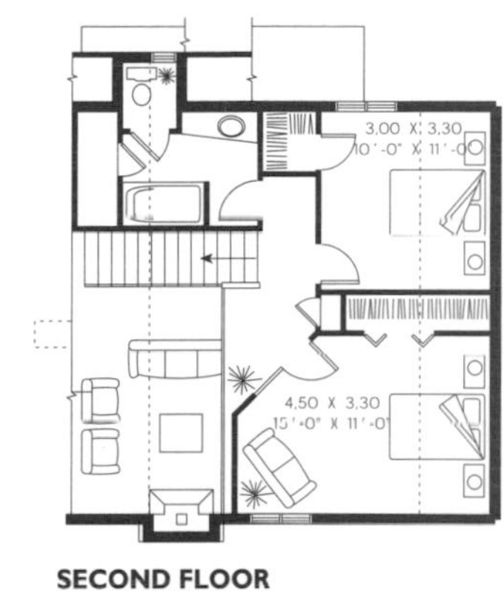

3,00 X 3,30
10'-0" X 11'-0"
4,50 X 3,30
15'-0" X 11'-0"

SECOND FLOOR

Central Courtyard Features Pool

PRICE CODE: D

This plan features:
- Three bedrooms
- One full and one three-quarter baths
- A central Courtyard complete with a Pool
- A secluded Master Bedroom accented by a skylight, a spacious walk-in closet, and a private Bath
- A convenient Kitchen easily serving the Patio for comfortable outdoor entertaining
- A detached two-car Garage
- This home is designed with a crawlspace foundation
- MAIN FLOOR — 2,194 SQ. FT.
- GARAGE — 576 SQ. FT.

TOTAL LIVING AREA:
2,194 SQ. FT.

PLAN NO. 10507

DINING
10'-6" X 10'-2"
LIVING ROOM
14'-6" X 25'-0"
PATIO
KITCHEN
10'-6" X 14'-6"
MASTER BEDROOM
23'-0" X 16'-0"
POOL
PATIO
FAMILY ROOM
13'-11" X 13'-8"
BEDROOM 3
11'-5" X 11'-0"
BEDROOM 2
10'-9" X 14'-6"
GARAGE
23'-4" X 23'-4"
75'-0"
76'-0"

MAIN FLOOR

PLAN NO.99439

Touch of French Styling

PRICE CODE: J

- This plan features:
- — Four bedrooms
- — Three full and one half baths
- A grand stair case dominating the Foyer and providir an elegant impression
- A fireplace and an abundance of windows accent the Great Room
- The first floor Master Suite includes a whirlpool Batl and a large walk-in closet
- Three secondary Bedrooms, two Baths and a Game Room make the second floor a private retreat
- This home is designed with basement and slab foundation options
- Alternate foundation options available at an additional charge. Please call 1-800-235-5700 for more information.

FIRST FLOOR — 2,274 SQ. FT.
SECOND FLOOR — 1,476 SQ. FT.
GARAGE — 744 SQ. FT.

TOTAL LIVING AREA:* 3,750 *SQ. FT.

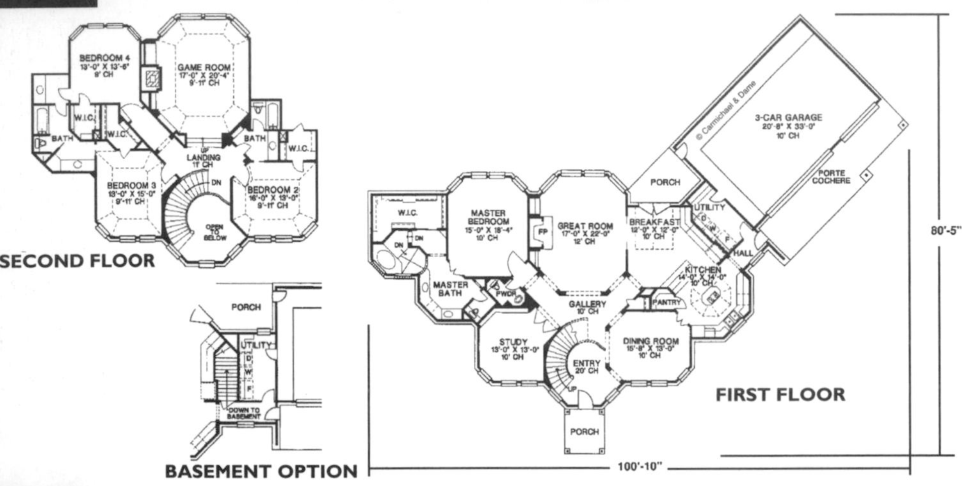

BEDROOM 4
GAME ROOM
BATH
W.I.C.
LANDING
BEDROOM 3
BEDROOM 2
SECOND FLOOR
PORCH
UTILITY
BASEMENT OPTION
MASTER BEDROOM
GREAT ROOM
BREAKFAST
3-CAR GARAGE
PORTE COCHERE
KITCHEN
MASTER BATH
GALLERY
STUDY
ENTRY
DINING ROOM
FIRST FLOOR
80'-5"
100'-10"

PLAN NO.94640

Family Room at the Heart of the Home

PRICE CODE: F

- This plan features:
- — Four bedrooms
- — Three full baths
- The Living Room and Dining Room are to the right left of the Foyer
- The Dining Room with French doors opens to the Kitchen
- An extended counter maximizes the work space in th Kitchen
- The Breakfast Room includes access to the Utility R and to the secondary Bedroom wing
- The Master Bedroom is equipped with a double vani Bath, two walk-in closets and a linear closet
- A cozy fireplace and a decorative ceiling highlight th Family Room
- Secondary Bedrooms have easy access to two full Ba
- This home is designed with slab and crawlspace foundation options

MAIN FLOOR — 2,558 SQ. FT.
GARAGE — 549 SQ. FT.

TOTAL LIVING AREA:* 2,558 *SQ. FT.

WIDTH 63'-6"
DEPTH 71'-6"

Two-car Garage 21'-4" X 22'-2"
Storage
Utility
Bath
Master Bedroom 17'-10" X 14'
Covered Porch
Breakfast 12'-4" X 12'
Bedroom 11' X 12'-6"
Family Room 20' X 17'-6"
Kitchen 12'-4" X 12'-6"
Ba.
Ba.
Bedroom 12'-2" X 13'
Bedroom 12'-1" X 12'
Living Room 13'-4" X 14'-6"
Foyer
Dining Room 13'-4" X 12'
Porch
MAIN FLOOR

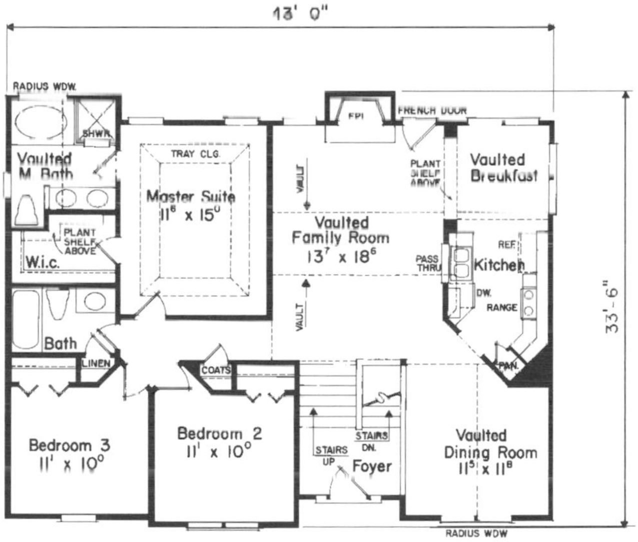

PLAN NO. 98487

Voluminous Vaulted Ceilings

Price Code: A

- This plan features:
- — Three bedrooms
- — Two full baths
- The Dining Room, Family Room and Breakfast Nook have vaulted ceilings
- The Family Room has a rear wall fireplace with a French door to one side
- There is a plant shelf above the entrance to the Nook
- With an angle at one end a new twist is placed on this galley-style Kitchen
- The Master Suite has a tray ceiling as well as a private Bath
- This home is designed with a basement foundation

UPPER LEVEL — 1,349 SQ. FT.
LOWER LEVEL — 871 SQ. FT.
FINISHED STAIRCASE — 52 SQ. FT.
GARAGE — 478 SQ. FT.

TOTAL LIVING AREA:
1,401 SQ. FT.

43' 0"
33'-6"
RADIUS WDW.
SHWR.
Vaulted M. Bath
TRAY CLG.
Master Suite 11⁶ x 15⁰
FP.
FRENCH DOOR
PLANT SHELF ABOVE
Vaulted Breakfast
VAULT
Vaulted Family Room 13⁷ x 18⁶
PASS THRU
REF.
Kitchen
DW.
RANGE
PAN.
PLANT SHELF ABOVE
W.i.c.
Bath
LINEN
COATS
Bedroom 3 11¹ x 10⁰
Bedroom 2 11¹ x 10⁰
STAIRS UP
STAIRS DN.
Foyer
Vaulted Dining Room 11⁵ x 11⁸
RADIUS WDW

UPPER LEVEL

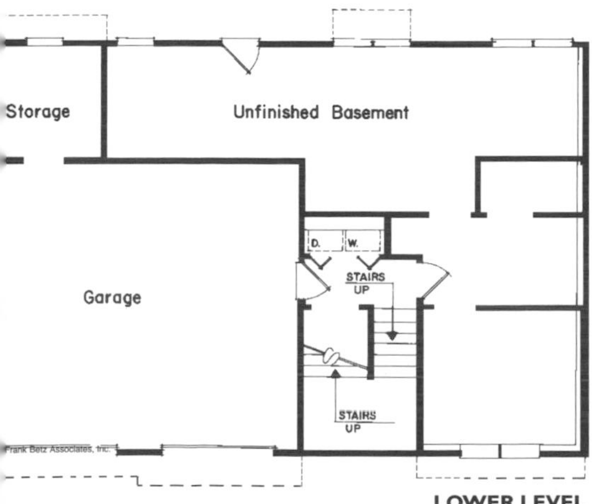

Storage
Unfinished Basement
Garage
D.
W.
STAIRS UP
STAIRS UP
Frank Betz Associates, Inc.

LOWER LEVEL

PLAN NO.26112

Contemporary Design

PRICE CODE: A

- This plan features:
  - — Three bedrooms
  - — One full and one half baths
- A solar design with southern glass doors, windows, a an air-lock Entry
- R-26 insulation used for floors and sloping ceilings
- A Deck rimming the front of the home
- A Dining Room separated from the Living Room by half wall
- An efficient Kitchen with an eating bar
- This home is designed with a basement foundation

FIRST FLOOR — 911 SQ. FT.
SECOND FLOOR — 576 SQ. FT.
BASEMENT — 911 SQ. FT.

TOTAL LIVING AREA:
1,487 SQ. FT.

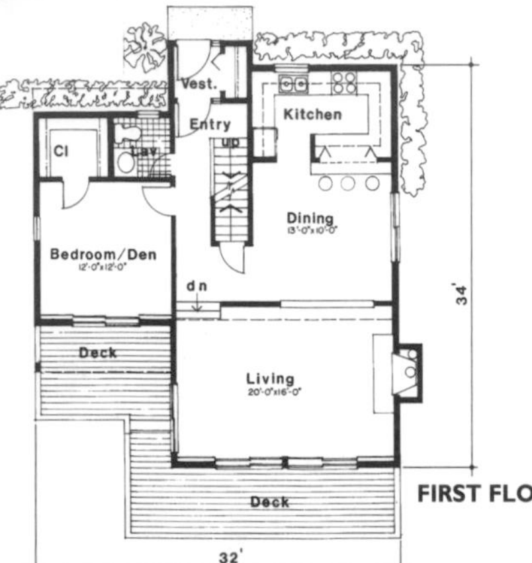
Vest.
Entry
Kitchen
Cl
Lav.
up
Dining
Bedroom/Den
dn
Deck
Living
Deck
34'
32'
FIRST FLOOR

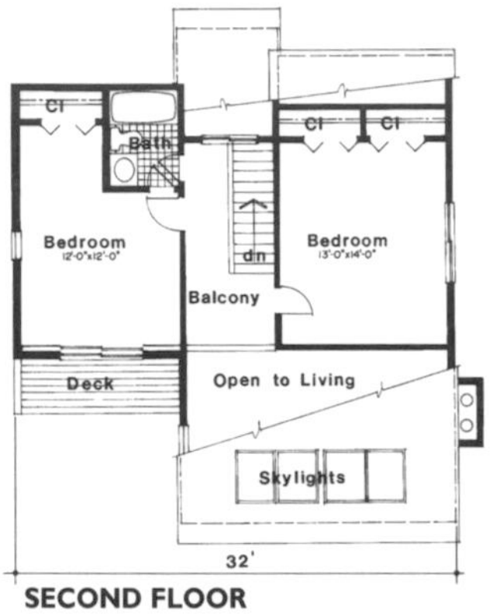
Cl
Bath
Cl
Cl
Bedroom
dn
Bedroom
Balcony
Deck
Open to Living
Skylights
32'
SECOND FLOOR

PLAN NO.97612

Those Special Touches

PRICE CODE: B

- This plan features:
  - — Three bedrooms
  - — Two full and one half baths
- The two-story Foyer adds volume to the Entry area
- The Dining Room and Family Room are crowned in vaulted ceilings
- The Master Suite has a tray ceiling and a five-piece Master Bath
- An optional bonus room over the Garage is available future expansion
- This home is designed with basement and crawlspac foundation options

FIRST FLOOR — 1,067 SQ. FT.
SECOND FLOOR — 464 SQ. FT.
BONUS ROOM — 207 SQ. FT.
BASEMENT — 1,067 SQ. FT.
GARAGE — 398 SQ. FT.

TOTAL LIVING AREA
1,531 SQ. FT.

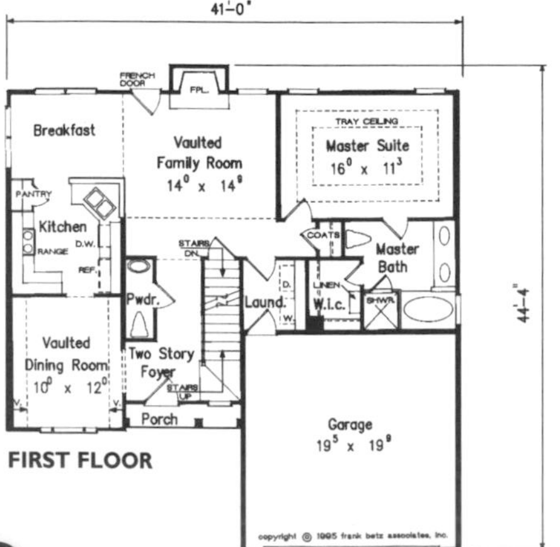
41'-0"
FRENCH DOOR
FPL.
Breakfast
Vaulted Family Room 14⁰ x 14⁹
TRAY CEILING
Master Suite 16⁰ x 11³
PANTRY
Kitchen
D.W.
RANGE
REF.
STAIRS DN.
COATS
Master Bath
Pwdr.
Laund.
W.I.c.
SHWR.
Vaulted Dining Room 10⁰ x 12⁰
Two Story Foyer
STAIRS UP
Porch
Garage 19⁵ x 19⁹
44'-4"
FIRST FLOOR

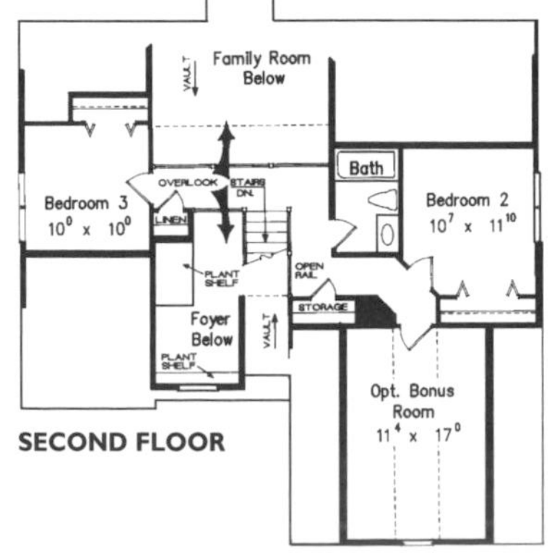
Family Room Below
VAULT
Bedroom 3 10⁰ x 10⁰
OVERLOOK
STAIRS DN.
LINEN
Bath
Bedroom 2 10⁷ x 11¹⁰
PLANT SHELF
OPEN RAIL
Foyer Below
STORAGE
Opt. Bonus Room 11⁴ x 17⁰
SECOND FLOOR

Down Home Goodness

PRICE CODE: B

PLAN NO. 91165

his plan features:
- Three bedrooms
- Two full baths
- his home has a split-bedroom floor plan allowing nore privacy for the Master Suite
- he Master Suite includes a full-size Bath with eparate shower
- he Dining Room is crowned in a tray ceiling and ıas an unusual shape to enhance its formal aspect
- he half wall separating the Living Room and Breakfast Nook adds to the open feel to the plan
- his home is designed with a crawlspace foundation

AIN FLOOR — 1,589 SQ. FT.
RAGE & STORAGE — 481 SQ. FT.

TOTAL LIVING AREA:
1,589 SQ. FT.

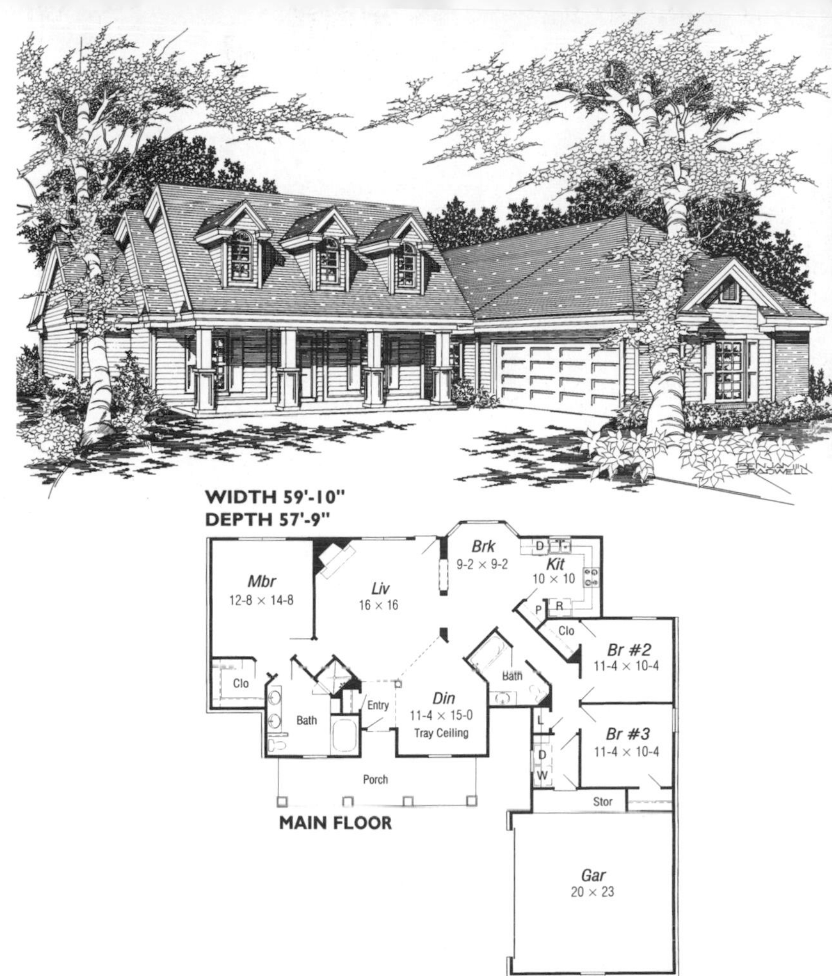
WIDTH 59'-10"
DEPTH 57'-9"
Mbr
12-8 × 14-8
Liv
16 × 16
Brk
9-2 × 9-2
Kit
10 × 10
D
R
P
Clo
Br #2
11-4 × 10-4
Clo
Bath
Entry
Din
11-4 × 15-0
Tray Ceiling
Bath
L
D
W
Br #3
11-4 × 10-4
Porch
Stor
MAIN FLOOR
Gar
20 × 23

Built to Please

PRICE CODE: C

PLAN NO. 91153

This plan features:
- Three bedrooms
- Two full and one half baths
- The Living Room has a vaulted ceiling and a corner fireplace
- There is both an informal Nook and a formal Dining Room located to either side of the Kitchen, for easy access
- The optional bay windows will add character and light with a touch of class
- A balcony overlooks the Entry and also the Living Room below
- There is a bonus room over the Garage for room to grow
- This home is designed with a slab foundation

RST FLOOR — 1,405 SQ. FT.
COND FLOOR — 554 SQ. FT.
ARAGE & STORAGE — 457 SQ. FT.

TOTAL LIVING AREA:
1,959 SQ. FT.

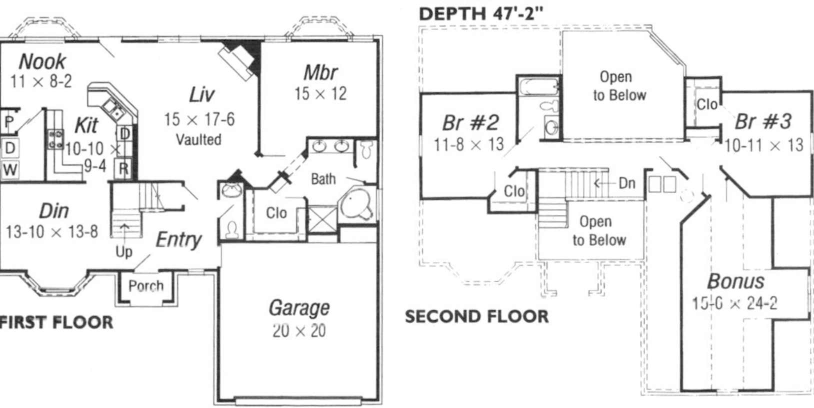
WIDTH 49'-0"
DEPTH 47'-2"
Nook
11 × 8-2
Liv
15 × 17-6
Vaulted
Mbr
15 × 12
P
D
W
Kit
10-10 × 9-4
D
R
Din
13-10 × 13-8
Up
Entry
Bath
Clo
Porch
FIRST FLOOR
Garage
20 × 20
Open
to Below
Br #2
11-8 × 13
Clo
Clo
Br #3
10-11 × 13
Dn
Open
to Below
Bonus
15-0 × 24-2
SECOND FLOOR

PLAN NO.94967

One Level Beauty

PRICE CODE: E

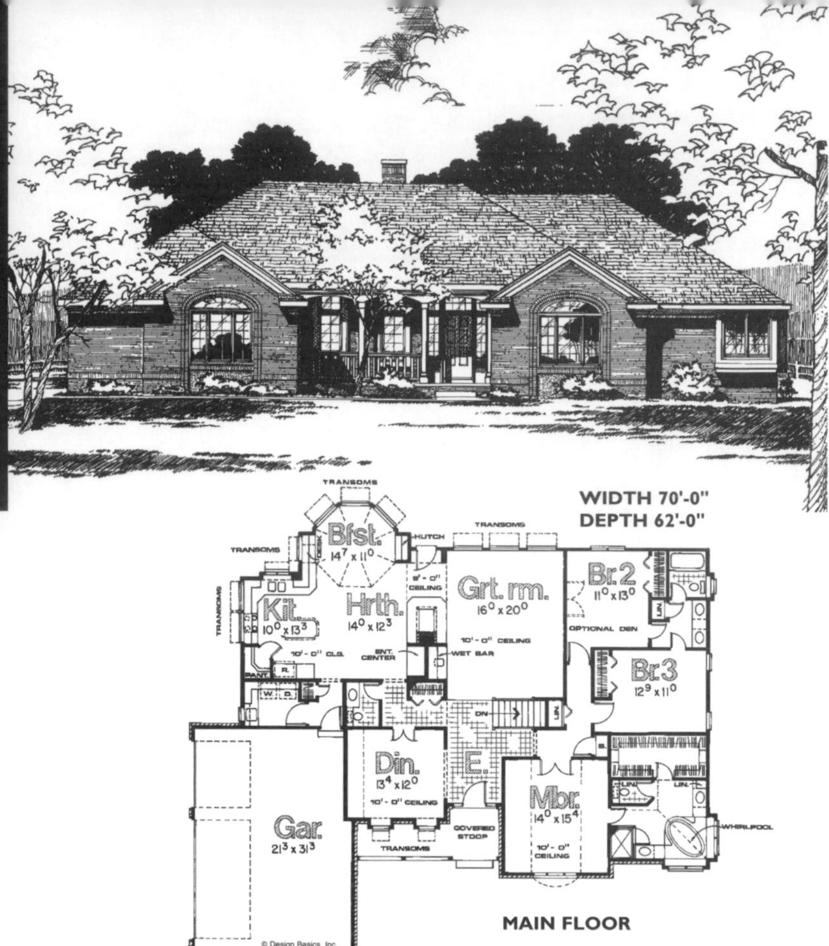

WIDTH 70'-0"
DEPTH 62'-0"
TRANSOMS
Bfst.
14^7 x 11^0
HUTCH
9'-0" CEILING
Grt. rm.
16^0 x 20^0
10'-0" CEILING
Br. 2
11^0 x 13^0
OPTIONAL DEN
Kit.
10^0 x 13^3
Hrth.
14^0 x 12^3
10'-0" CLG.
ENT. CENTER
WET BAR
Br. 3
12^9 x 11^0
PANT.
W. D.
DN
Din.
13^4 x 12^0
10'-0" CEILING
E.
Mbr.
14^0 x 15^4
10'-0" CEILING
WHIRLPOOL
COVERED STOOP
Gar.
21^3 x 31^3
© Design Basics, Inc.
MAIN FLOOR

- This plan features:
- — Three bedrooms
- — Two full and one half baths
- From the tiled Entry one can view the terrific Great Room
- Highlights of the Great Room include a built-in wetbar and a three-sided fireplace that is shared with the Hearth Room
- The Hearth Room, which is open to the Kitchen and the Breakfast Room has a built-in entertainment cent
- A sloped Gazebo-style ceiling and a built-in hutch ac the Breakfast Room
- The Master Bedroom is impressive with a luxurious l and a walk-in closet
- Secondary Bedrooms have private access to a full Ba
- This home is designed with a basement foundation
- Alternate foundation options available at an additional charge. Please call 1-800-235-5700 for more information.

MAIN FLOOR — 2,355 SQ. FT.
GARAGE — 673 SQ. FT.

TOTAL LIVING AREA:
2,355 SQ. FT.

PLAN NO.99373

High Impact Two-Story

PRICE CODE: L

- This plan features:
- — Four bedrooms
- — Three full and one half baths
- A high impact two-story, double door transom Entry
- A two-story Family Room with a wall consisting of a fireplace and windows
- A spacious Master Suite with unique curved glass blo behind the tub in the Master Bath and a semi-circular window wall with see-through fireplace in Sitting Are
- A gourmet Kitchen and Breakfast Area opening to the Lanai
- A Guest Suite with private Deck and walk-in closet
- This home is designed with a slab foundation

FIRST FLOOR — 3,158 SQ. FT.
SECOND FLOOR — 1,374 SQ. FT.
GARAGE — 758 SQ. FT.

TOTAL LIVING AREA:
4,532 SQ. FT.

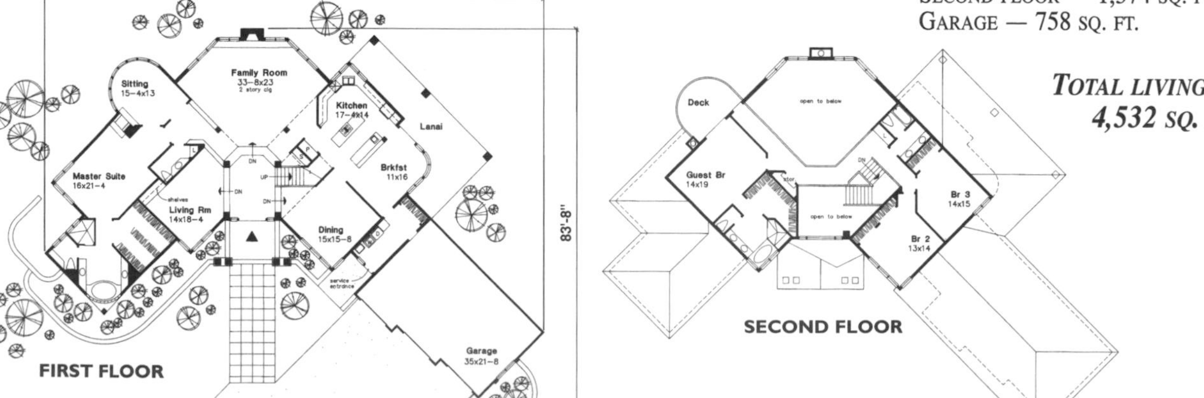

112'-0"
83'-8"
Sitting
15–4x13
Family Room
33–8x23
2 story clg
Kitchen
17–4x14
Lanai
Master Suite
16x21–4
Living Rm
14x18–4
Brkfst
11x16
Dining
15x15–8
Garage
35x21–8
FIRST FLOOR
Deck
open to below
Guest Br
14x19
Br 3
14x15
Br 2
13x14
SECOND FLOOR

Notable Master Suite

PRICE CODE: F

PLAN NO. 99156

This plan features:
- Three bedrooms
- Two full and one half baths
- The open Entry and Great Room gives the feeling of roominess and grandeur
- A large Kitchen with an island and an adjacent Nook provides ample space for creating both casual and formal meals
- Master Suite with his and her walk-in closets, double sinks, a private shower and a corner whirlpool Bath
- Loft at the top of the stairs could be converted into a Sitting Area or Study
- This home is designed with a basement foundation

ST FLOOR — 2,018 SQ. FT.
COND FLOOR — 655 SQ. FT.
SEMENT — 2,018 SQ. FT.

TOATL LIVING AREA: 2,673 SQ. FT.

BR.#2
12'0" X 14'4"
LOFT
8'0" X 14'4"
OPEN TO GRT.RM.
BR.#3
12'4" X 14'4"
OPEN TO E.
BRICK ARCH
SECOND FLOOR

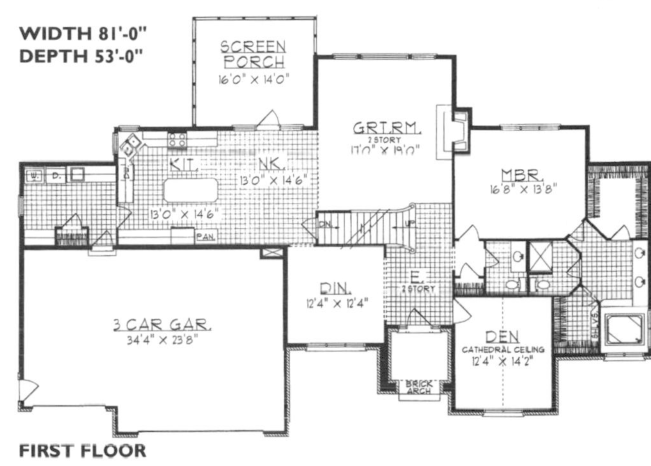

WIDTH 81'-0"
DEPTH 53'-0"
SCREEN PORCH
16'0" X 14'0"
KIT.
13'0" X 14'6"
NK.
13'0" X 14'6"
GRT.RM.
2 STORY
17'0" X 19'0"
MBR.
16'8" X 13'8"
DIN.
12'4" X 12'4"
E.
2 STORY
3 CAR GAR.
34'4" X 23'8"
DEN
CATHEDRAL CEILING
12'4" X 14'2"
BRICK ARCH
FIRST FLOOR

Superb Southern Styling

PRICE CODE: G

PLAN NO. 94644

This plan features:
- Five bedrooms
- Three full baths
- Terrific front Porch and dormers create a homey Southern-style
- A corner fireplace enhancing the Family Room
- A cooktop island and a peninsula counter adding to the efficiency of the Kitchen
- Convenient peninsula counter separates the Kitchen from the Breakfast Room
- Lavish Master Suite includes a whirlpool tub and a walk-in closet
- Secondary Bedrooms located in close proximity to a full Bath
- This home is designed with a crawlspace foundation

RST FLOOR — 2,135 SQ. FT.
COND FLOOR — 538 SQ. FT.
NUS — 225 SQ. FT.
RAGE — 436 SQ. FT.

TOTAL LIVING AREA: 2,898 SQ. FT.

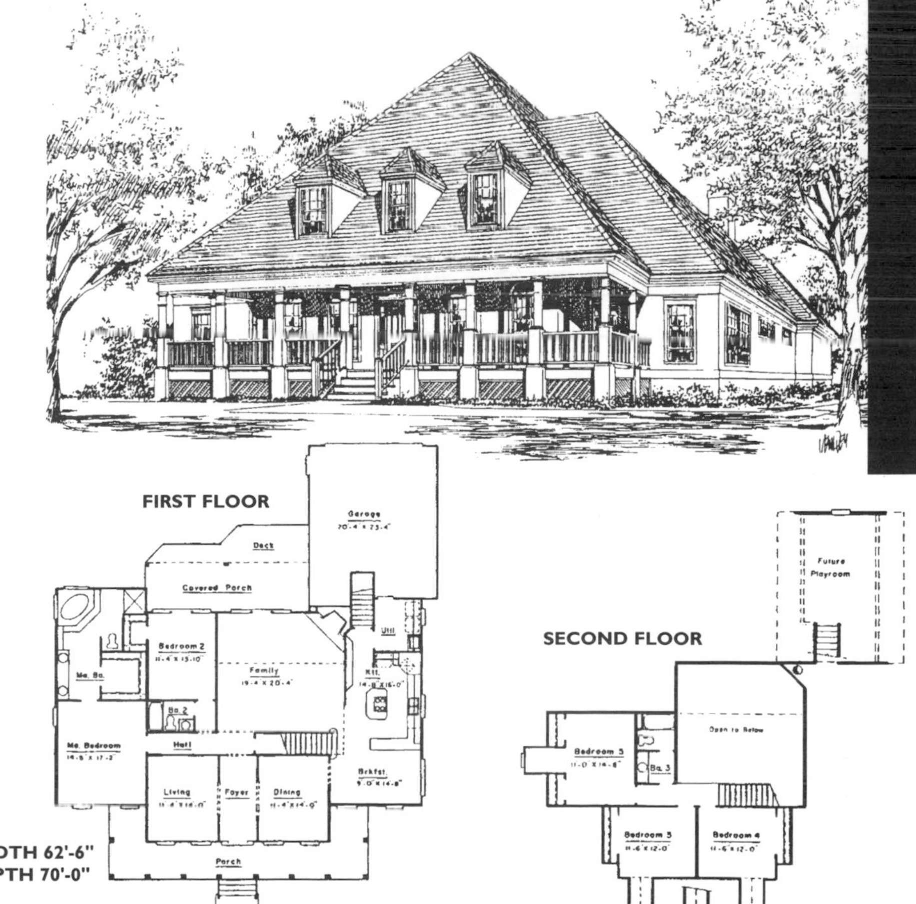

FIRST FLOOR
SECOND FLOOR
WIDTH 62'-6"
DEPTH 70'-0"

PLAN NO.93017

Quoin Accents Distinguish this Plan

PRICE CODE: A

- This plan features:
  - — Three bedrooms
  - — Two full baths
- A traditional brick elevation with quoin accents
- A large Family Room with a corner fireplace and dire access to the outside
- An arched opening leading to the Breakfast Area
- A bay window illuminating the Breakfast Area with natural light
- An efficiently designed, U-shaped Kitchen with ampl cabinet and counter space
- A Master Suite with a private Master Bath
- Two additional Bedrooms that share a full hall Bath
- This home is designed with crawlspace and slab foundation options

MAIN FLOOR — 1,142 SQ. FT.
GARAGE — 428 SQ. FT.

TOTAL LIVING AREA:
1,142 SQ. FT.

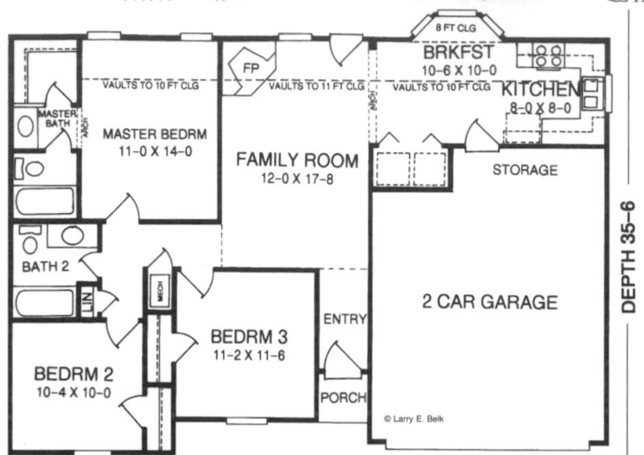

8 FT CLG
BRKFST
10-6 X 10-0
FP
VAULTS TO 10 FT CLG
VAULTS TO 11 FT CLG
VAULTS TO 10 FT CLG
KITCHEN
8-0 X 8-0
MASTER BATH
MASTER BEDRM
11-0 X 14-0
FAMILY ROOM
12-0 X 17-8
STORAGE
BATH 2
LIN
MECH
BEDRM 3
11-2 X 11-6
ENTRY
2 CAR GARAGE
BEDRM 2
10-4 X 10-0
PORCH
© Larry E. Belk
DEPTH 35-6
WIDTH 48-10

MAIN FLOOR

PLAN NO.98460

European Flair

PRICE CODE: B

- This plan features:
  - — Three bedrooms
  - — Two full baths
- Large fireplace serving as an attractive focal point fo the vaulted Family Room
- Decorative column defining the elegant Dining Roon
- Kitchen including a serving bar for the Family Room and a Breakfast Area
- Master Suite topped by a tray ceiling over the Bedro and a vaulted ceiling over the five-piece Master Bat
- Optional bonus room for future expansion
- This home is designed with basement, slab, and crawlspace foundation options

MAIN FLOOR — 1,544 SQ. FT.
BONUS ROOM — 284 SQ. FT.
GARAGE — 440 SQ. FT.

TOTAL LIVING AREA:
1,544 SQ. FT.

Bedroom 2 10° x 11° · Bath · French Door · Breakfast · FPL. · Vault · Master Suite 13° x 15° · Tray Clg. · Serving Bar · Range · Kitchen · Vaulted Family Room 15° x 18⁸ · 13'-0" High Clg. · Ref. · Bedroom 3 10° x 11° · Laund. · Pantry · Decorative Column · Foyer · Coats · Vaulted Master Bath · Dining Room 11² x 11⁹ · Linen · Plant Shelf Above · Shwr. · Covered Porch · W.I.c. · Garage 21⁵ x 19⁸ · © Frank Betz Associates, Inc.

WIDTH 54'-0"
DEPTH 47'-6"

MAIN FLOOR

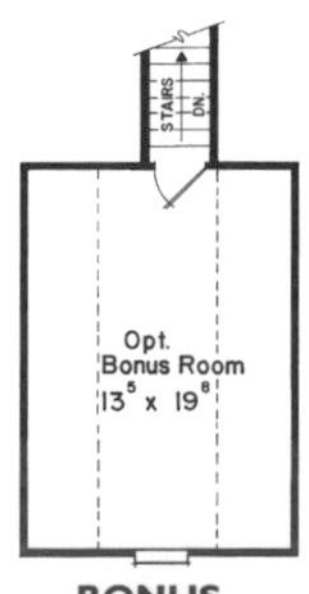

OPTIONAL BASEMENT STAIR LOCATION

Opt. Bonus Room 13⁵ x 19⁸

BONUS

PLAN NO. 99914

Rustic Styling

Price Code: B

■ This plan features:

— Two bedrooms

— Two full baths

■ A large Sun Deck wraps around this rustic home

■ The Living Room and Dining Room are combined

■ The Living Room has a gas fireplace and sliders to the Deck

■ There is a Bedroom, Bath and an ample Utility Room on the first floor

■ Upstairs the Master Bedroom has two closets and a private Deck

■ Relax in the whirlpool tub in the Master Bath

■ This home is designed with basement and crawlspace foundation options

FIRST FLOOR — 1,064 SQ. FT.
SECOND FLOOR — 613 SQ. FT.

TOTAL LIVING AREA:
1,677 SQ. FT.

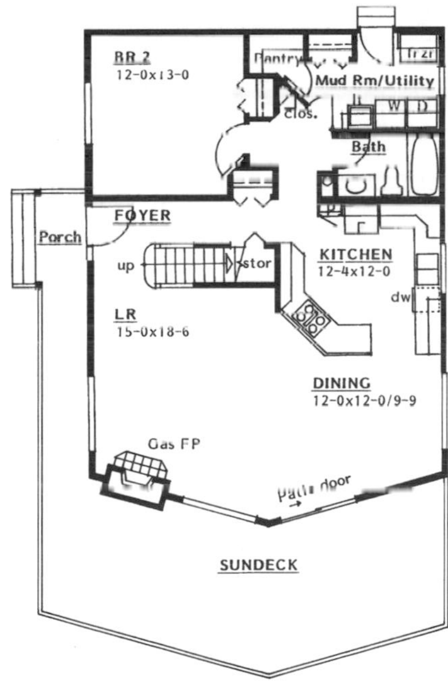

BR 2
12-0x13-0
Pantry
Mud Rm/Utility
frzr
W D
clos.
Bath
FOYER
Porch
up
stor
KITCHEN
12-4x12-0
dw
LR
15-0x18-6
DINING
12-0x12-0/9-9
Gas FP
patio door
SUNDECK

FIRST FLOOR

WIDTH 28'-0"
DEPTH 40'-0"

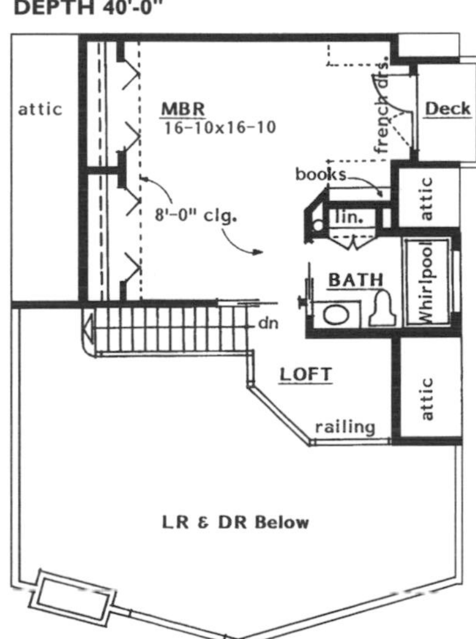

attic
MBR
16-10x16-10
french drs.
Deck
books
8'-0" clg.
lin.
attic
BATH
Whirlpool
dn
LOFT
railing
attic
LR & DR Below

SECOND FLOOR

PLAN NO. 97627

Special Sitting Room

Price Code: F

- This plan features:
- — Three bedrooms
- — Two full and one half baths
- Dual walk-in closets are featured in the Master Suite
- A walk-in Pantry and double ovens add convenience to the Kitchen
- A radius window and fireplace add warmth to the Keeping Room
- This home is designed with basement and crawlspace foundation options

FIRST FLOOR — 1,972 SQ. FT.
SECOND FLOOR — 579 SQ. FT.
BONUS ROOM — 256 SQ. FT.
BASEMENT — 1,972 SQ. FT.
GARAGE — 505 SQ. FT.

TOTAL LIVING AREA:
2,551 SQ. FT.

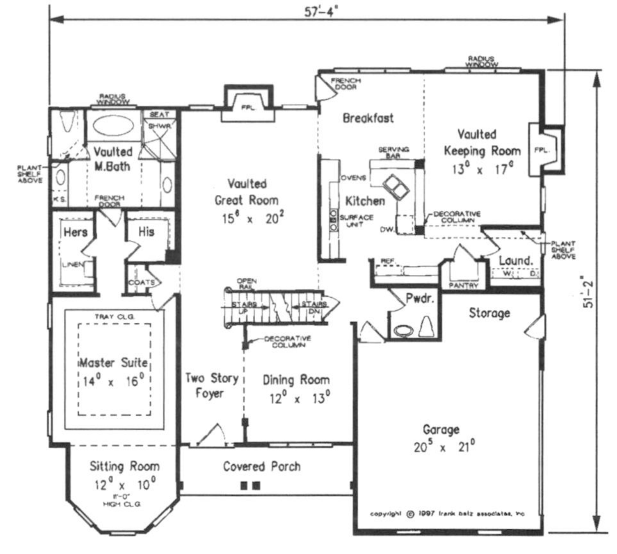
57'-4"
51'-2"
Breakfast
Vaulted
Keeping Room
13⁰ x 17⁰
Vaulted
M.Bath
Vaulted
Great Room
15⁶ x 20²
Kitchen
Hers
His
Laund.
Pwdr.
Storage
Master Suite
14⁰ x 16⁰
Two Story
Foyer
Dining Room
12⁰ x 13⁰
Garage
20⁵ x 21⁰
Sitting Room
12⁰ x 10⁰
Covered Porch

FIRST FLOOR

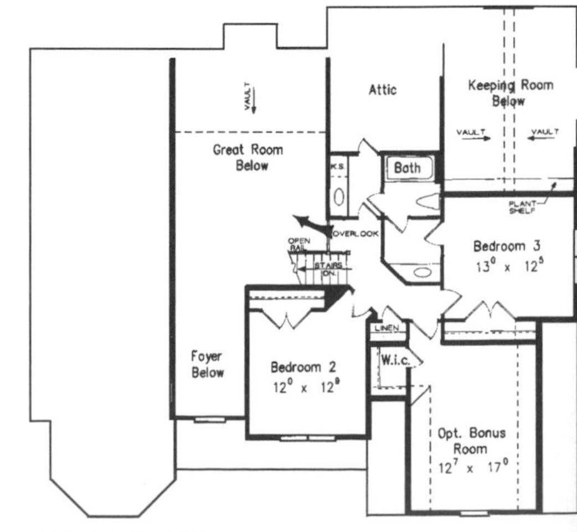
Attic
Keeping Room
Below
Great Room
Below
Bath
Bedroom 3
13⁰ x 12⁵
Foyer
Below
Bedroom 2
12⁰ x 12⁸
W.i.c.
Opt. Bonus
Room
12⁷ x 17⁰

SECOND FLOOR

PLAN NO. 65019

Great Things Come in Small Packages

Price Code: A

- This plan features:
  - — Two bedrooms
  - — One full bath
- Two covered Porches will please the outdoor lover
- The U-shaped Kitchen features plenty of counter space, including an eating bar
- The full Bath is completely private
- The Entry leads directly into the Family Room, instantly welcoming friends and family
- This home is designed with a basement foundation

MAIN FLOOR — 920 SQ. FT.

TOTAL LIVING AREA:
920 SQ. FT.

MAIN FLOOR

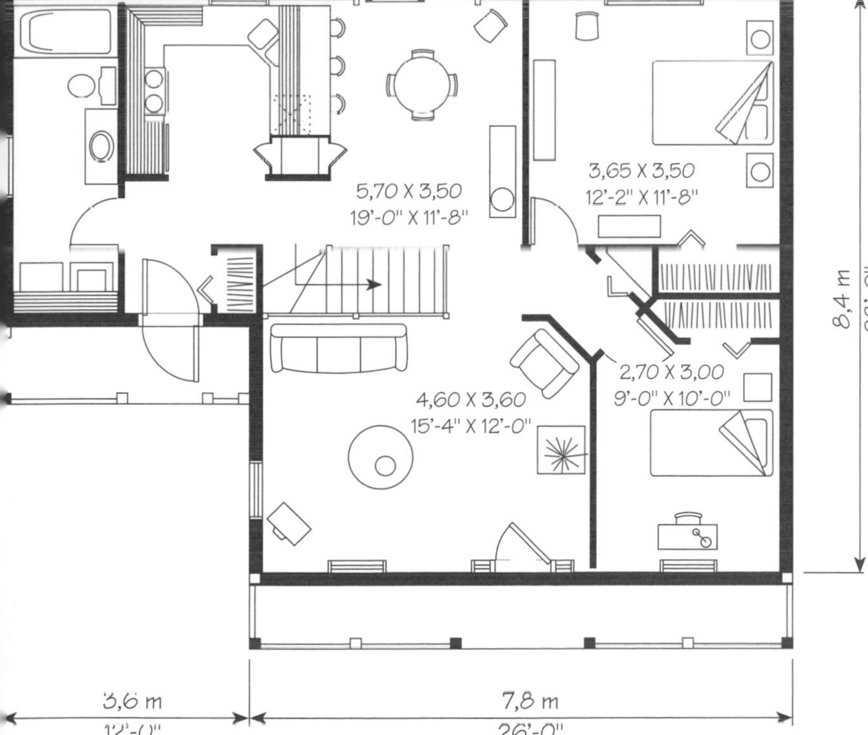
5,70 X 3,50
19'-0" X 11'-8"
3,65 X 3,50
12'-2" X 11'-8"
4,60 X 3,60
15'-4" X 12'-0"
2,70 X 3,00
9'-0" X 10'-0"
8,4 m
28'-0"
3,6 m
12'-0"
7,8 m
26'-0"

PLAN NO. 34011

Rear Elevatio

Bathed in Sunlight

Price Code: B

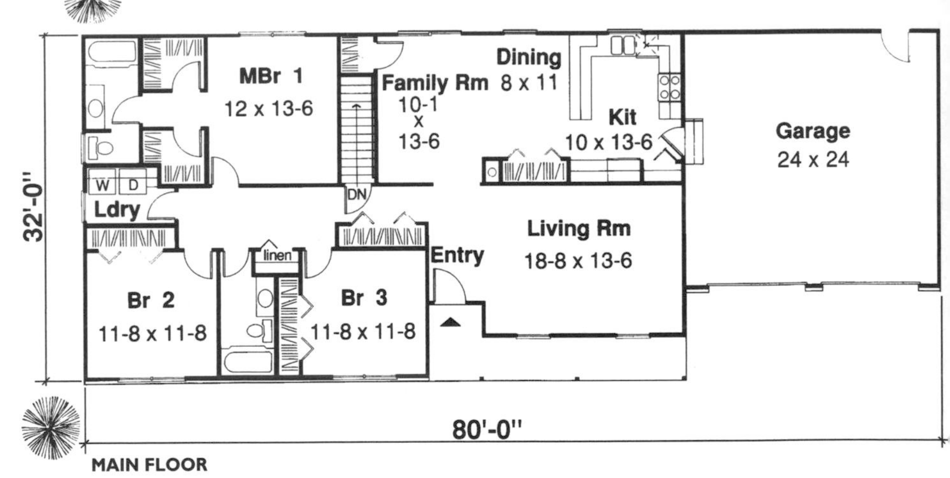

MBr 1
12 x 13-6
Family Rm
10-1
x
13-6
Dining
8 x 11
Kit
10 x 13-6
Garage
24 x 24
W
D
Ldry
DN
linen
Living Rm
18-8 x 13-6
Entry
Br 2
11-8 x 11-8
Br 3
11-8 x 11-8
32'-0"
80'-0"
MAIN FLOOR

- This plan features:
- — Three bedrooms
- — Two full baths
- A Master Suite with huge his and her walk-in closets and private Bath
- A Kitchen equipped with an island counter, and flowing easily into the Dining and Family Rooms
- A Laundry Room conveniently located near all three Bedrooms
- An optional Garage
- This home is designed with basement, slab and crawlspace foundation options

MAIN FLOOR — 1,672 SQ. FT.
GARAGE — 566 SQ. FT.

TOTAL LIVING AREA:
1,672 SQ. FT.

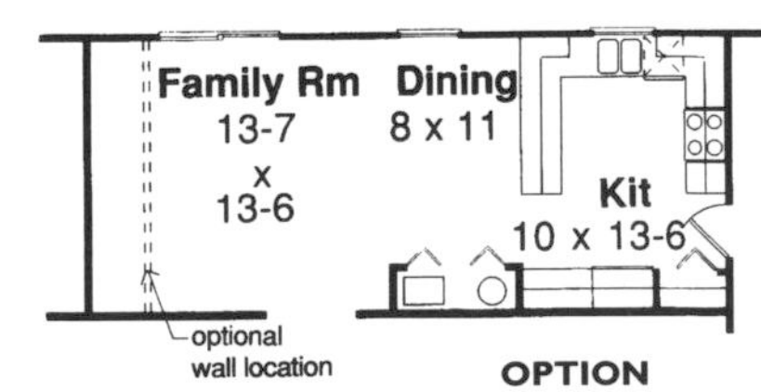

Family Rm
13-7
x
13-6
Dining
8 x 11
Kit
10 x 13-6
optional wall location
OPTION

Window Box Adds Warmth to Exterior

PRICE CODE: D

PLAN NO.97630

This plan features:

- Four bedrooms
- Two full and one half baths
- The luxurious Master Suite includes a tray ceiling and a built-in plant shelf
- The Master Bath has a vaulted ceiling, and a large walk-in closet with a second built-in plant shelf
- The stairway includes an open rail and leads to a balcony overlook
- This home is designed with basement and crawlspace foundation options

RST FLOOR — 1,209 SQ. FT.
ECOND FLOOR — 931 SQ. FT.
ONUS — 175 SQ. FT.
ASEMENT — 1,216 SQ. FT.
ARAGE — 410 SQ. FT.

TOTAL LIVING AREA:
2,140 SQ. FT.

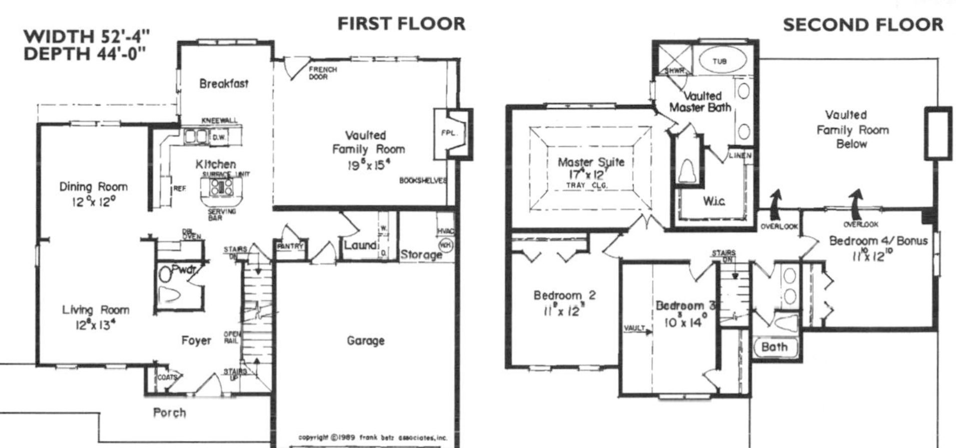
WIDTH 52'-4"
DEPTH 44'-0"
FIRST FLOOR
SECOND FLOOR
Breakfast
FRENCH DOOR
Vaulted Family Room
FPL
KNEEWALL
Kitchen
Dining Room
Living Room
Foyer
Laund
Storage
Garage
Pwdr
Porch
BOOKSHELVES
PANTRY
STAIRS DN
COATS
Vaulted Master Bath
TUB
Master Suite
TRAY CLG.
W.i.c.
LINEN
Vaulted Family Room Below
OVERLOOK
Bedroom 4/ Bonus
Bedroom 2
Bedroom 3
VAULT
Bath
copyright ©1989 frank betz associates, inc.

Porches Expands Living Space

PRICE CODE: D

PLAN NO.96529

This plan features:

- Three bedrooms
- Two full and one half baths
- Porches on the front and the rear of this home expand the living space to the outdoors
- The rear Porch is accessed directly from the Great Room
- The spacious Great Room is enhanced by a 12-foot ceiling and a fireplace
- The well-appointed Kitchen has an extended counter/ eating bar and easy access to the Dining Room
- Secondary Bedrooms have a full Bath located between the rooms
- The Master Suite is enhanced by his and her walk-in closets, a whirlpool tub and a separate shower
- There is a bonus room for the future expansion
- This home is designed with crawlspace and slab foundation options

AIN FLOOR — 2,089 SQ. FT.
ONUS ROOM — 497 SQ. FT.
ARAGE — 541 SQ. FT.

TOTAL LIVING AREA:
2,089 SQ. FT.

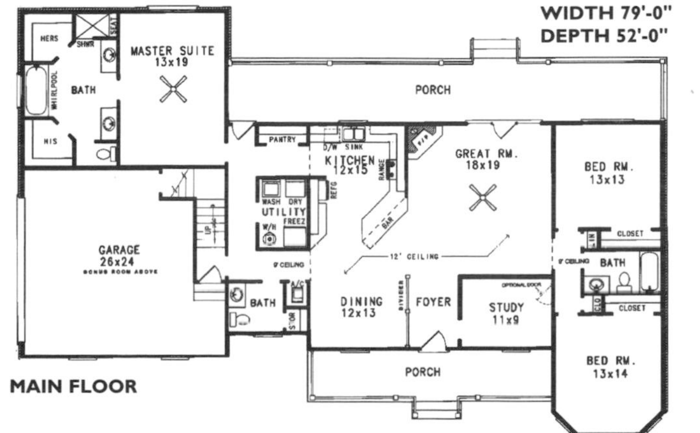
WIDTH 79'-0"
DEPTH 52'-0"
MASTER SUITE 13x19
BATH
WHIRLPOOL
HERS
HIS
PORCH
PANTRY
KITCHEN 12x15
GREAT RM. 18x19
BED RM. 13x13
CLOSET
BATH
BED RM. 13x14
GARAGE 26x24
UTILITY
12' CEILING
DINING 12x13
FOYER
STUDY 11x9
PORCH
MAIN FLOOR

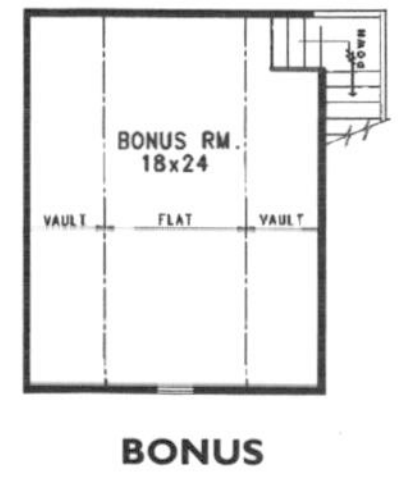
BONUS RM. 18x24
VAULT
FLAT
VAULT

BONUS

PLAN NO.94810

Stone and Siding

PRICE CODE: F

- This plan features:
  - — Four bedrooms
  - — Three full and one half baths
- Attractive styling using a combination of stone and siding and a covered Porch add to the curb appeal
- Formal Foyer giving access to the bedroom wing, Library or Activity Room
- Activity Room showcasing a focal point fireplace and including direct access to the rear Deck and the Breakfast Room
- Breakfast Room is topped by a vaulted ceiling and flows into the Kitchen
- A snack bar/peninsula counter highlights the Kitchen which also includes a built-in Pantry
- A secluded guest Bedroom suite is located off the Kitchen Area
- Master Suite topped by a tray ceiling and pampered by five-piece Bath
- This home is designed with a basement foundation

MAIN FLOOR — 2,690 SQ. FT.
BASEMENT — 2,690 SQ. FT.
GARAGE — 660 SQ. FT.

TOTAL LIVING AREA:
2,690 SQ. FT.

WHEELCHAIR BATH

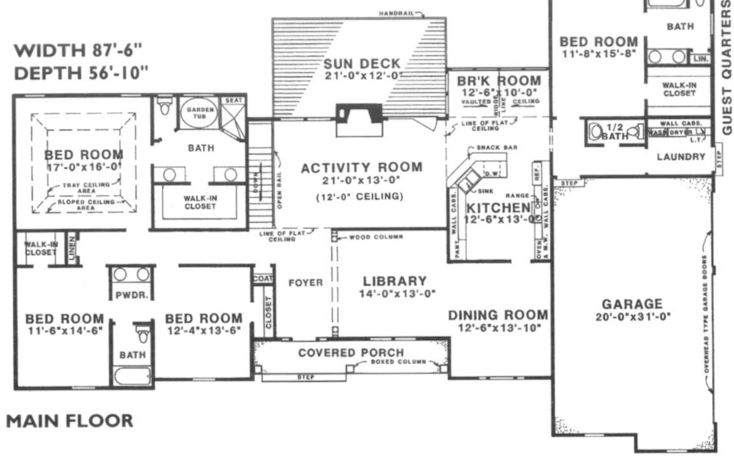

WIDTH 87'-6"
DEPTH 56'-10"
SUN DECK 21'-0"x12'-0"
BR'K ROOM 12'-6"x10'-0"
BED ROOM 11'-8"x15'-8"
BATH
WALK-IN CLOSET
GUEST QUARTERS
BED ROOM 17'-0"x16'-0"
BATH
WALK-IN CLOSET
ACTIVITY ROOM 21'-0"x13'-0" (12'-0" CEILING)
KITCHEN 12'-6"x13'-0"
1/2 BATH
LAUNDRY
FOYER
LIBRARY 14'-0"x13'-0"
PWDR.
BED ROOM 11'-6"x14'-6"
BED ROOM 12'-4"x13'-6"
BATH
DINING ROOM 12'-6"x13'-10"
GARAGE 20'-0"x31'-0"
COVERED PORCH
MAIN FLOOR

PLAN NO.99238

Economical Vacation Home

PRICE CODE: A

- This plan features:
  - — Three bedrooms
  - — Two full baths
- A large rectangular Living Room with a fireplace at one end and plenty of room for separate activities at the other end
- A galley-style Kitchen with adjoining Dining Area
- A second floor Master Bedroom with a Children's Dormitory across the hall
- A second floor Deck outside the Master Bedroom
- This home is designed with a basement foundation

FIRST FLOOR — 784 SQ. FT.
SECOND FLOOR — 504 SQ. FT.

TOTAL LIVING AREA:
1,288 SQ. FT.

FIRST FLOOR

WIDTH 28'-0"
DEPTH 28'-0"

SECOND FLOOR

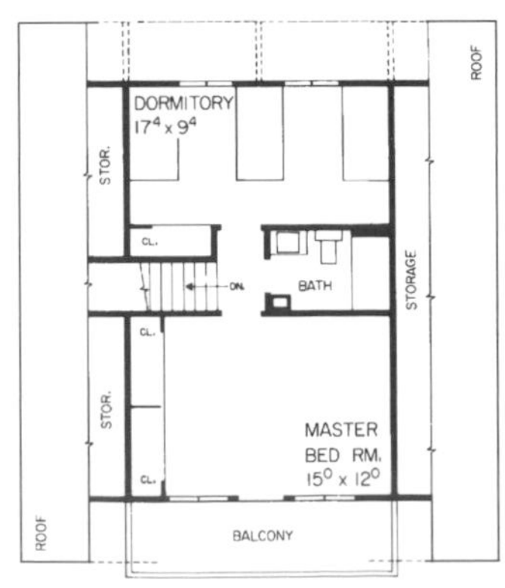

DORMITORY 17⁴ x 9⁴
STOR.
BATH
STORAGE
MASTER BED RM. 15⁰ x 12⁰
ROOF
BALCONY

PLAN NO. 96902

Step-Saving Floor Plan

Price Code: C

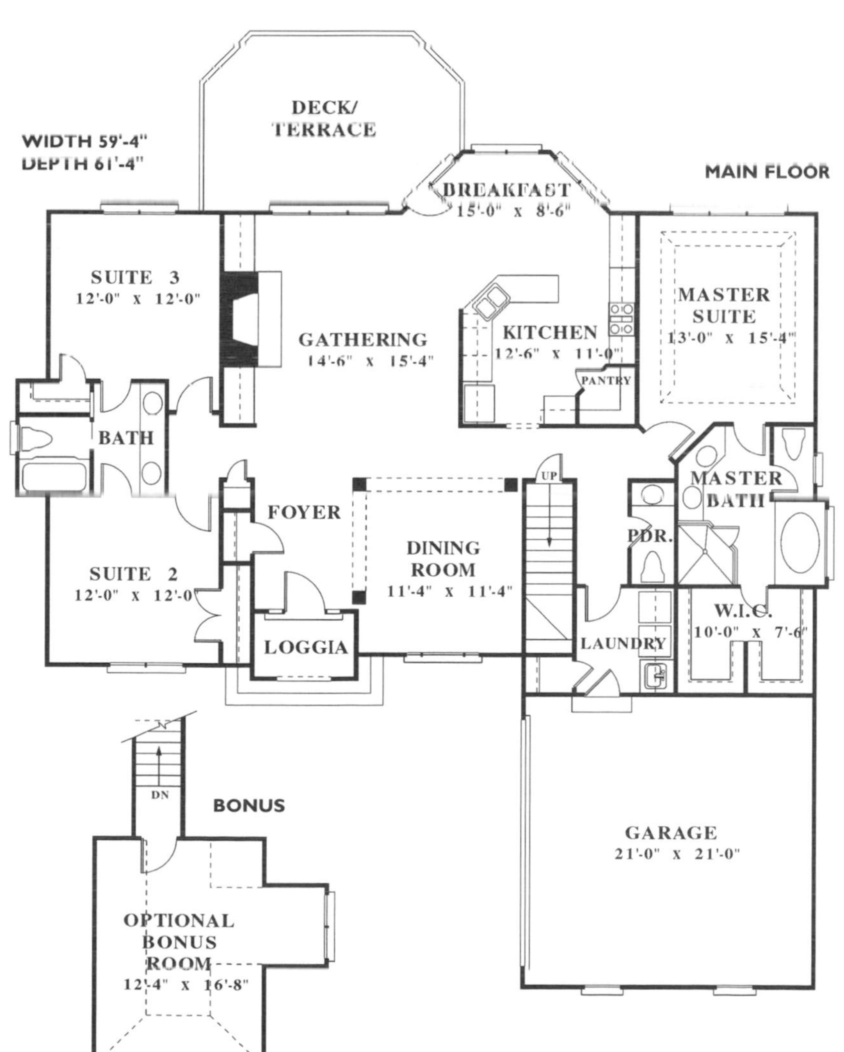

WIDTH 59'-4"
DEPTH 61'-4"
MAIN FLOOR
DECK/ TERRACE
BREAKFAST 15'-0" x 8'-6"
SUITE 3 12'-0" x 12'-0"
GATHERING 14'-6" x 15'-4"
KITCHEN 12'-6" x 11'-0"
PANTRY
MASTER SUITE 13'-0" x 15'-4"
BATH
MASTER BATH
FOYER
UP
DINING ROOM 11'-4" x 11'-4"
PDR.
SUITE 2 12'-0" x 12'-0"
LOGGIA
LAUNDRY
W.I.C. 10'-0" x 7'-6"
DN
BONUS
GARAGE 21'-0" x 21'-0"
OPTIONAL BONUS ROOM 12'-4" x 16'-8"

- This plan features:
  - — Three bedrooms
  - — Two full and one half baths
- Recessed entrance leads into Foyer and the Dining Room defined by columns
- Expansive Gathering Room with an inviting fireplace, opens to Deck/Terrace and Breakfast/ Kitchen Area
- Corner Master Suite offers a decorative ceiling, wall of windows, plush Bath and double, walk-in closet
- This home is designed with basement and crawlspace foundation options

MAIN FLOOR — 1,950 SQ. FT.
BONUS — 255 SQ. FT.
BASEMENT — 1,287 SQ. FT.
GARAGE — 466 SQ. FT.

TOTAL LIVING AREA:
1,950 SQ. FT.

PLAN NO.91157

One Great Choice

PRICE CODE: C

- This plan features:
  - Three bedrooms
  - Two full baths
- The Great Room has a fireplace and built-in shelves with a ledge above for display
- The back Porch integrates outdoor activities with the comfort of being close to the indoors
- Informal and formal eating space efficiently flanks the Kitchen
- Garage enters into the Kitchen for ease in unloading packages
- This home is designed with a crawlspace foundation

MAIN FLOOR — 1,862 SQ. FT.
GARAGE — 481 SQ. FT.

TOTAL LIVING AREA:
1,862 SQ. FT.

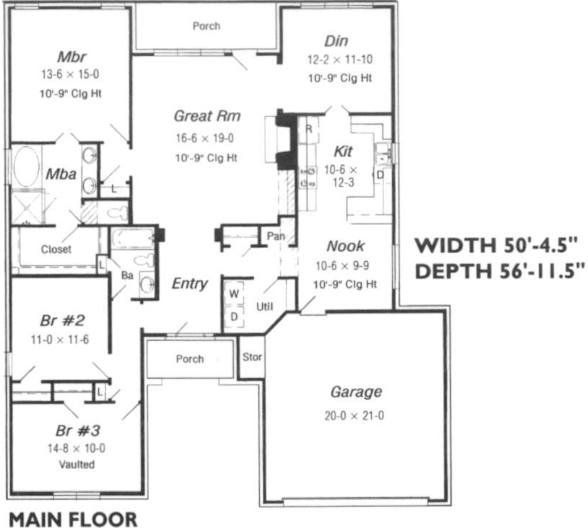

Porch
Mbr
13-6 × 15-0
10'-9" Clg Ht
Din
12-2 × 11-10
10'-9" Clg Ht
Great Rm
16-6 × 19-0
10'-9" Clg Ht
Kit
10-6 × 12-3
Mba
Closet
Ba
Entry
Pan
Nook
10-6 × 9-9
10'-9" Clg Ht
Util
Br #2
11-0 × 11-6
Porch
Stor
Garage
20-0 × 21-0
Br #3
14-8 × 10-0
Vaulted

WIDTH 50'-4.5"
DEPTH 56'-11.5"

MAIN FLOOR

PLAN NO.94971

Appealing Brick Elevation

PRICE CODE: D

- This plan features:
  - Three bedrooms
  - Three full baths
- Formal Living and Dining Room flanking the Entry
- Impressive Great Room topped by an 11-foot ceiling and enhanced by picture awning windows framing th raised hearth fireplace
- Attractive Kitchen/Breakfast Area includes an island, desk, wrapping counters, a walk-in Pantry, and acces to the covered Patio
- Pampering Master Suite with a skylight Dressing Are a walk-in closet, double vanity, whirlpool tub and decorative plant shelf
- This home is designed with a basement foundation
- Alternate foundation options available at an additional charge. Please call 1-800-235-5700 for more information.

MAIN FLOOR — 2,172 SQ. FT.
GARAGE — 680 SQ. FT.

TOTAL LIVING AREA:
2,172 SQ. FT.

© Design Basics, Inc.
Pto.
PARTIALLY COVERED
TRANSOMS
TRANSOMS
Kit.
9^0 x 14^0
Bfst.
10^0 x 14^0
Grt. rm.
16^0 x 20^0
Mbr.
13^0 x 16^4
10' - 0" CEILING
Gar.
20^4 x 28^7
DESK
11' - 0" CEILING
SKYLIGHT
PANT
SERVERY
BOOKS
WHIRL-POOL
DN
STORAGE
Br. 3
11^0 x 12^0
OPTIONAL DEN
Din.
12^0 x 15^4
E.
Liv.
12^0 x 13^4
OPT. BEDROOM
Br. 2
11^0 x 12^0
11' - 0" CEILING
COVERED STOOP
11' - 0" CEILING

WIDTH 76'-0"
DEPTH 46'-0"

MAIN FLOOR

PLAN NO. 34031

Rear Elevation

Exclusive Master Suite

Price Code: C

- This plan features:
  - — Three bedrooms
  - — Two full and one half baths
- Front Porch entry into Foyer and open Living and Dining Room
- Huge fireplace and double window highlight Living Room
- Convenient Kitchen with cooktop island/snackbar, Pantry, and bright Breakfast Area with backyard access
- Corner Master Bedroom offers a decorative ceiling, walk-in closets and a double vanity Bath
- This home is designed with basement, slab and crawlspace foundation options

MAIN FLOOR — 1,831 SQ. FT.
GARAGE — 484 SQ. FT.

TOTAL LIVING AREA:
1,831 SQ. FT.

CRAWLSPACE/SLAB FOUNDATION OPTION

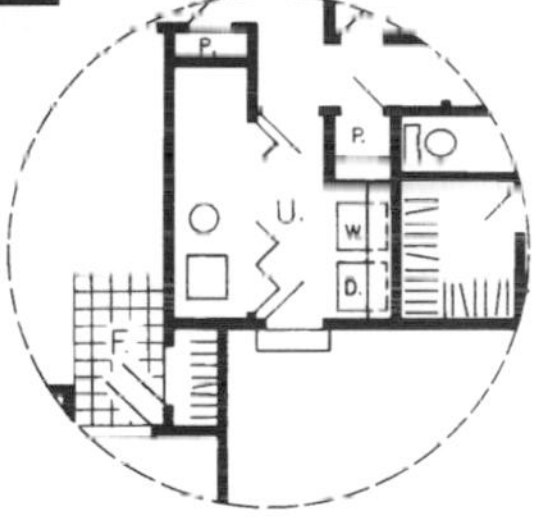

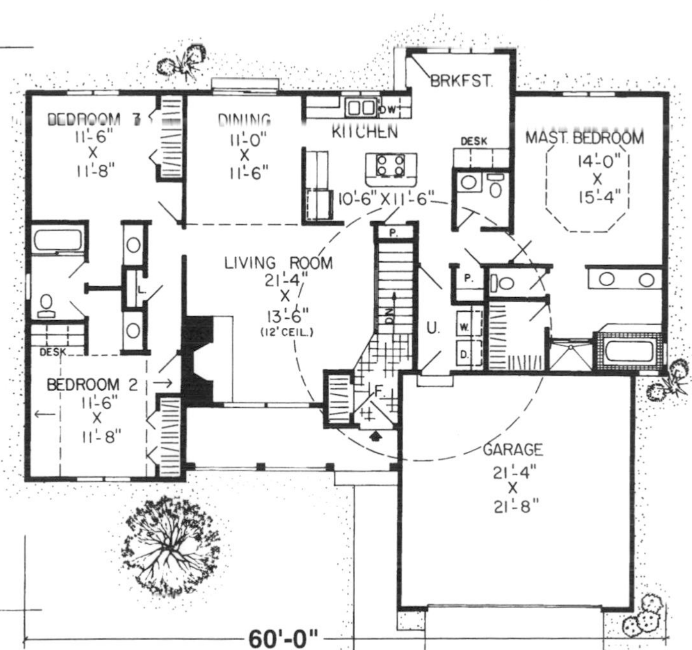
BRKFST.
BEDROOM 3
11'-6" X 11'-8"
DINING
11'-0" X 11'-6"
KITCHEN
10'-6" X 11'-6"
DESK
MAST. BEDROOM
14'-0" X 15'-4"
LIVING ROOM
21'-4" X 13'-6"
(12' CEIL.)
DESK
BEDROOM 2
11'-6" X 11'-8"
GARAGE
21'-4" X 21'-8"
60'-0"
MAIN FLOOR

PLAN NO. 32032

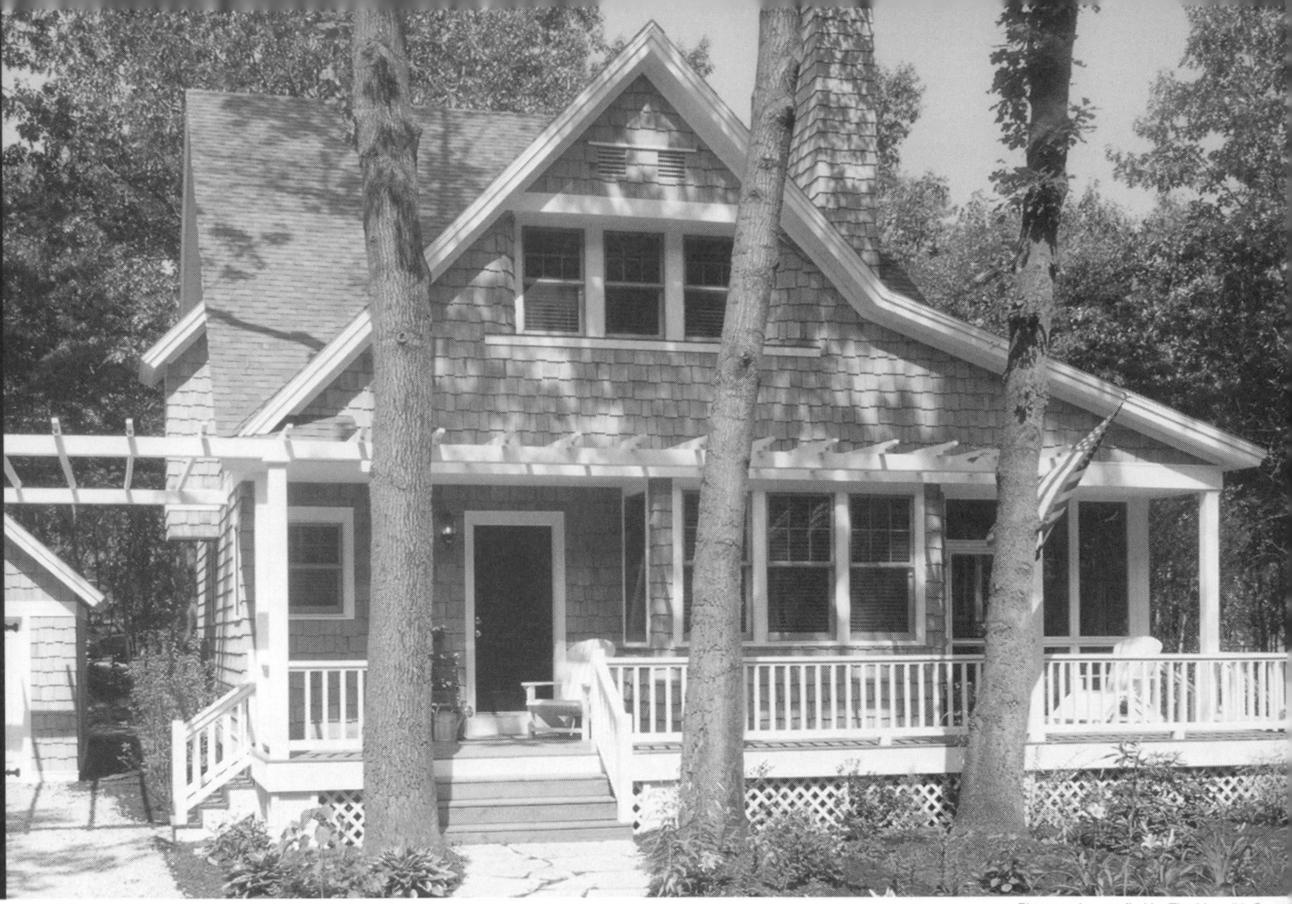

Photography supplied by The Meredith Corpo

New England Cottage

Price Code: C

- The plan features:
- — Three bedrooms
- — Three full baths
- A Porch and a Screened Porch add options for outdoors entertaining
- A fireplace warms the Living Room
- The U-shaped Kitchen is open to the Dining Room
- A full Bath is located next to the Den/Bedroom
- The Master Bedroom has a private Bath
- This home is designed with a crawlspace foundation

FIRST FLOOR — 1,109 SQ. FT.
SECOND FLOOR — 772 SQ. FT.

TOTAL LIVING AREA:
1,881 SQ. FT.

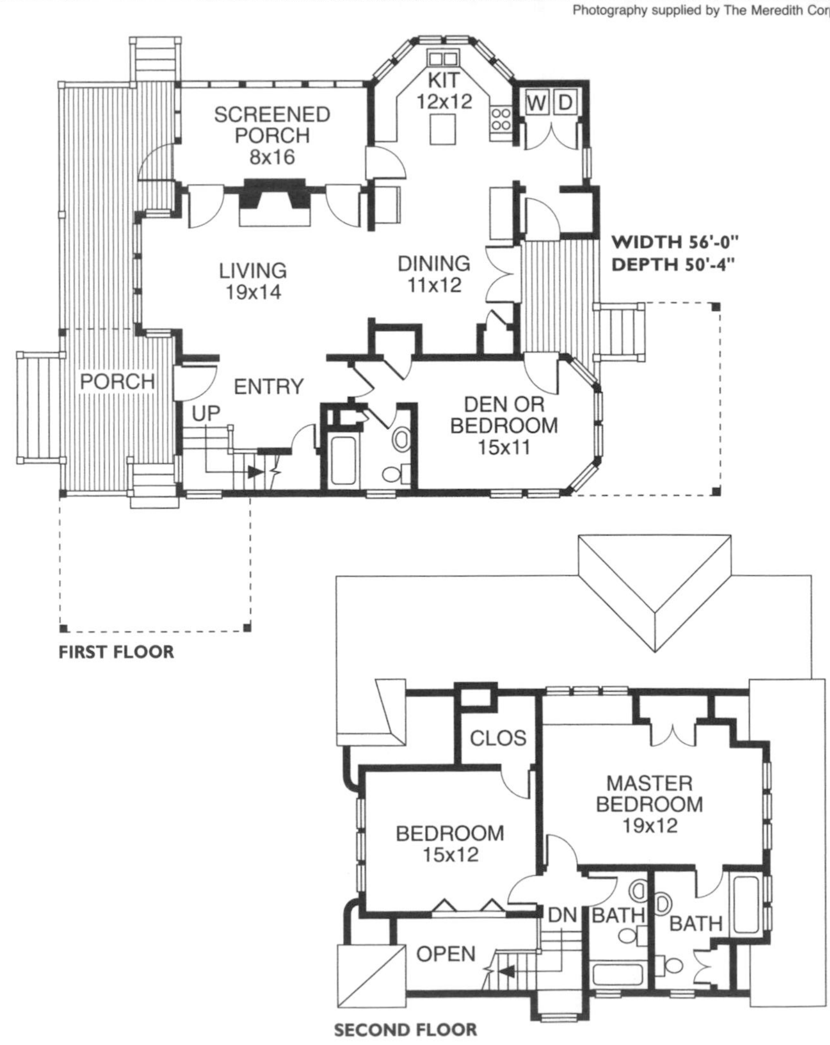

SCREENED PORCH 8x16
KIT 12x12
W D
LIVING 19x14
DINING 11x12
WIDTH 56'-0"
DEPTH 50'-4"
PORCH
ENTRY
UP
DEN OR BEDROOM 15x11
FIRST FLOOR
CLOS
MASTER BEDROOM 19x12
BEDROOM 15x12
DN
BATH
BATH
OPEN
SECOND FLOOR

Captivating Sun-Catcher

PRICE CODE: A

This plan features:
- Two bedrooms
- Two full baths
- A glass-walled Breakfast Room adjoining the vaulted-ceiling Kitchen
- A fireplaced, vaulted ceiling Living Room that flows from the Dining Room
- A greenhouse window over the tub in the luxurious Master Bath
- Two walk-in closets and glass sliders in the Master Bedroom
- This home is designed with a basement foundation

AIN FLOOR — 1,421 SQ. FT.
RAGE — 400 SQ. FT.

TOTAL LIVING AREA:
1,421 SQ. FT.

PLAN NO. 99303

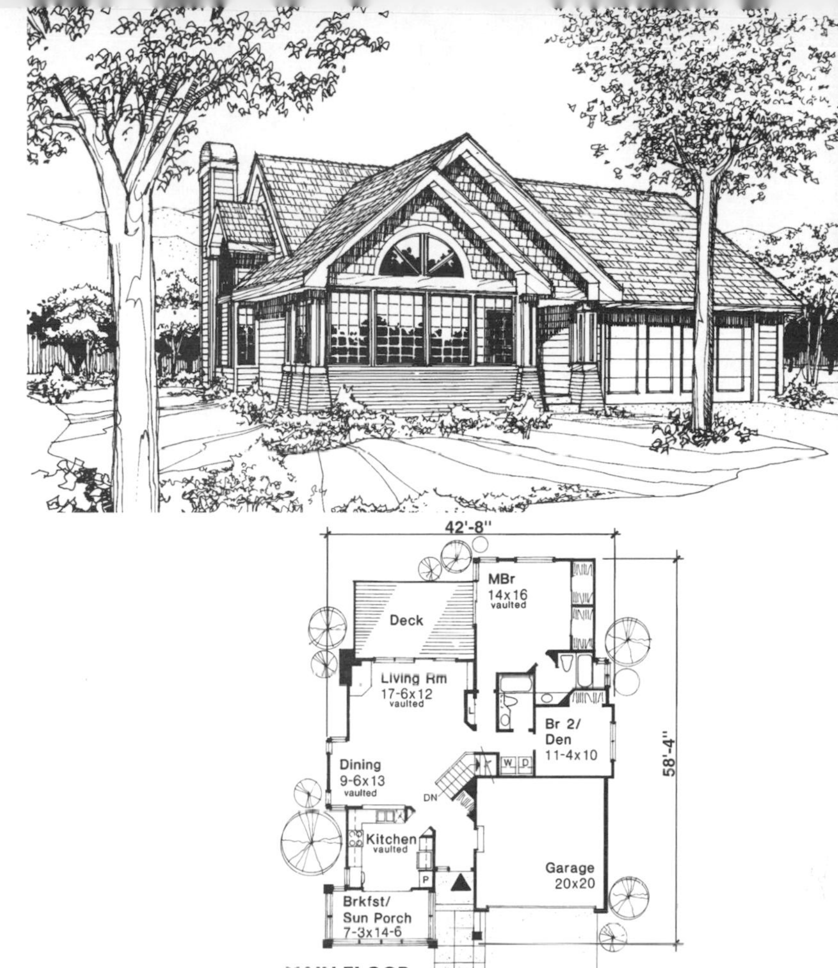

42'-8"
MBr
14x16
vaulted
Deck
Living Rm
17-6x12
vaulted
Br 2/
Den
11-4x10
58'-4"
Dining
9-6x13
vaulted
DN
Kitchen
vaulted
Garage
20x20
Brkfst/
Sun Porch
7-3x14-6
MAIN FLOOR

Exterior Shows Attention to Detail

PRICE CODE: D

This plan features:
- Three bedrooms
- Two full and one half baths
- Privately located Master Suite is complimented by a luxurious Bath with two walk-in closets
- Two additional Bedrooms have ample closet space and share a full Bath
- The Activity Room has a sloped ceiling, large fireplace and is accented with columns
- Access to Sun Deck from the Dining Room
- The island Kitchen and Breakfast Area have access to Garage for ease when bringing in groceries
- This home is designed with a basement foundation

AIN FLOOR — 2,165 SQ. FT.
RAGE — 484 SQ. FT.

TOTAL LIVING AREA:
2,165 SQ. FT.

PLAN NO. 94811

WIDTH 65'-6"
DEPTH 57'-0"

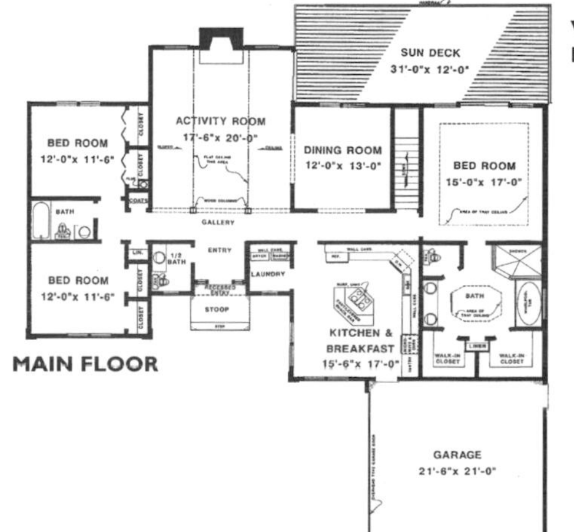

SUN DECK
31'-0"x 12'-0"
BED ROOM
12'-0"x 11'-6"
ACTIVITY ROOM
17'-6"x 20'-0"
DINING ROOM
12'-0"x 13'-0"
BED ROOM
15'-0"x 17'-0"
GALLERY
BATH
ENTRY
LAUNDRY
BED ROOM
12'-0"x 11'-6"
STOOP
KITCHEN &
BREAKFAST
15'-6"x 17'-0"
BATH
WALK-IN CLOSET
WALK-IN CLOSET
GARAGE
21'-6"x 21'-0"

MAIN FLOOR

PLAN NO.97602

Central Staircase

PRICE CODE: H

- This plan features:
- — Five bedrooms
- — Four full and one half baths
- The Family Room is open to the Kitchen Area
- The Dining Room has a bay window
- A formal Living Room is included
- The Laundry is conveniently placed on the second fl
- A huge walk-in closet is a part of the Master Bedroo
- This home is designed with basement and crawlspac foundation

FIRST FLOOR — 1,575 SQ. FT.
SECOND FLOOR — 1,480 SQ. FT.
BASEMENT — 1,575 SQ. FT.
GARAGE — 492 SQ. FT.

TOTAL LIVING AREA:
3,055 SQ. FT.

FIRST FLOOR

65'-4"

Two Story Family Room 20² x 14¹⁰
Breakfast
Kitchen
Bedroom 5/ Study 12⁰ x 12⁰
Bath
Pwdr.
Garage 20⁸ x 23²
Dining Room 13³ x 15¹⁰
Two Story Foyer
Living Room 13³ x 12⁶
Covered Porch
41'-0"
copyright © 1996 frank betz associates, inc.

SECOND FLOOR

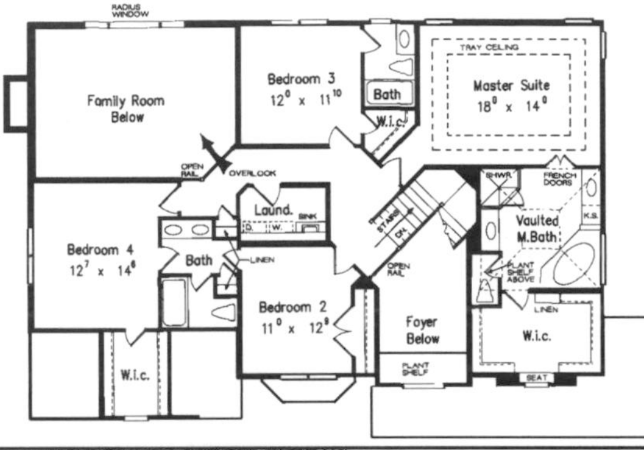

RADIUS WINDOW
Family Room Below
Bedroom 3
12⁰ x 11¹⁰
Bath
W.i.c.
TRAY CEILING
Master Suite
18⁰ x 14⁸
OVERLOOK
Laund.
Bedroom 4
12⁷ x 14⁸
Bath
Bedroom 2
11⁰ x 12⁸
Foyer Below
Vaulted M.Bath
W.i.c.
W.i.c.

PLAN NO.98463

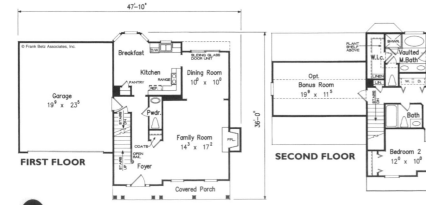

Open Plan is Full of Air & Light

PRICE CODE: B

- This plan features:
- — Three bedrooms
- — Two full and one half baths
- Foyer open to the Family Room and highlighted by a fireplace
- Dining Room with a sliding glass door to rear yard adjoins Family Room
- Kitchen and Nook in an efficient open layout
- Second floor Master Suite topped by tray ceiling ove the Bedroom and a vaulted ceiling over the lavish Ba
- Two additional Bedrooms sharing a full Bath in the h
- This home is designed with basement and crawlspac foundation options

FIRST FLOOR — 767 SQ. FT.
SECOND FLOOR — 738 SQ. FT.
BONUS ROOM — 240 SQ. FT.
BASEMENT — 767 SQ. FT.
GARAGE — 480 SQ. FT.

TOTAL LIVING AREA:
1,505 SQ. FT.

47'-10"
© Frank Betz Associates, Inc.
Breakfast
Kitchen
Dining Room
10⁰ x 10⁰
Garage
19⁹ x 23⁵
Pwdr.
Family Room
14³ x 17²
Foyer
Covered Porch
36'-0"
FIRST FLOOR

SECOND FLOOR

Opt. Bonus Room 19⁹ x 11⁵
W.i.c.
Vaulted M.Bath
Master Suite 12⁰ x 16¹⁰
Bath
Bedroom 2 12⁰ x 10⁰
Bedroom 3 10⁵ x 10⁰

PLAN NO. 99400

Stucco, Brick and Elegant Details

Price Code: G

- This plan features:
  - — Four bedrooms
  - — Three full and one half baths
- Majestic Entry opens to Den and Dining Room
- Expansive Great Room shares a see-thru fireplace with the Hearth Room
- Lovely Hearth Room enhanced by three skylights above triple arched windows
- Sumptuous Master Bedroom Suite with corner windows and two closets
- This home is designed with basement and slab foundation options
- Alternate foundation options available at an additional charge. Please call 1-800-235-5700 for more information.

FIRST FLOOR — 2,084 SQ. FT.
SECOND FLOOR — 848 SQ. FT.
BASEMENT — 2,084 SQ. FT.
GARAGE — 682 SQ. FT.

TOTAL LIVING AREA:
2,932 SQ. FT.

SECOND FLOOR

FIRST FLOOR

68' - 8"

COVERED VERANDA

COVERED STOOP

PLAN NO.91160

Practical Living Spaces

PRICE CODE: A

- This plan features:
  - — Three bedrooms
  - — Two full and one half baths
- The Living Room has a vaulted ceiling and a fireplac
- The Kitchen has a large snack bar for busy times and meals on-the-go
- The U-shaped Kitchen offers easy access to all the appliances
- The Master Suite has two window seats, a large walk-in closet, and a private Bath
- This home is designed with a slab foundation

FIRST FLOOR — 625 SQ. FT.
SECOND FLOOR — 848 SQ. FT.
GARAGE — 409 SQ. FT.

TOTAL LIVING AREA:
1,473 SQ. FT.

Kit 9-6 × 10-6
Din 7-10 × 10-6
Gar 18-4 × 20-0
Mec
Liv 14-2 × 15-8 Vaulted
Porch
FIRST FLOOR

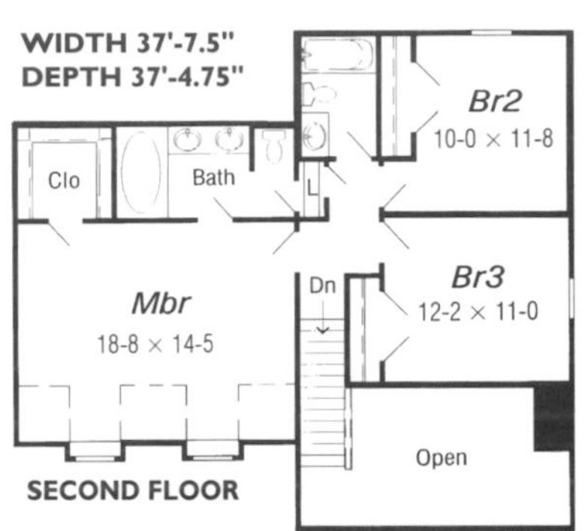
WIDTH 37'-7.5"
DEPTH 37'-4.75"
Clo
Bath
Br2 10-0 × 11-8
Mbr 18-8 × 14-5
Dn
Br3 12-2 × 11-0
Open
SECOND FLOOR

PLAN NO.94972

Impressive Two-Sided Fireplace

PRICE CODE: B

- This plan features:
  - — Three bedrooms
  - — Two full baths
- Foyer directs traffic flow into the Great Room, enhar by an impressive two-sided fireplace
- Formal Dining Area is open to the Great Room, offe a view of the fireplace
- French doors off Entry access Kitchen with a large Pantry, a desk, and a snack bar
- Dinette accesses a large comfortable Screened Porch
- Laundry Room is strategically located off the Kitche providing direct access from the Garage
- French doors provide access to the Master Suite whi topped by an elegant, decorative ceiling and highligh by a pampering Bath
- This home is designed with a basement foundation
- Alternate foundation options available at an additional charge. Please call 1-800-235-5700 for more information.

MAIN FLOOR — 1,580 SQ. FT.
GARAGE — 456 SQ. FT.

TOTAL LIVING AREA:
1,580 SQ. FT.

Mbr. 13⁰ x 13⁰
Grt. rm. 14⁴ x 20¹⁰
Din. 10⁴ x 11⁰
Bfst. 10⁰ x 14³
Kit. 9⁴ x 13⁰
Br. 3 10⁰ x 11⁰
Br. 2 10⁴ x 11⁰
Gar. 19³ x 22⁴
OPTIONAL DEN
Den 10⁴ x 13⁴
60'-0"
48'-0"
MAIN FLOOR
© Design Basics, Inc.

PLAN NO. 65022

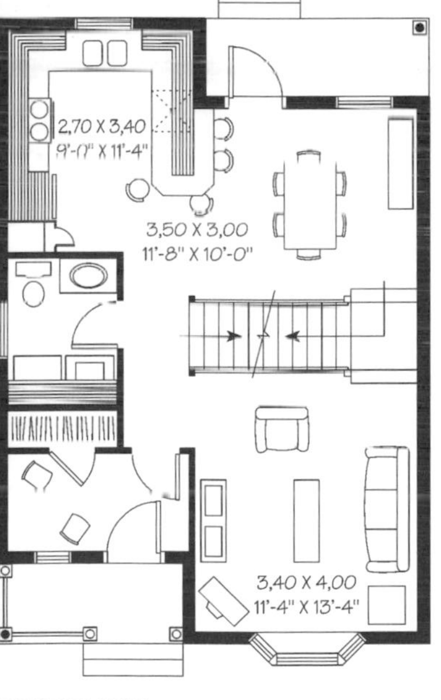

2,70 X 3,40
9'-0" X 11'-4"
3,50 X 3,00
11'-8" X 10'-0"
3,40 X 4,00
11'-4" X 13'-4"

WIDTH 22'-0"
DEPTH 32'-0"

FIRST FLOOR

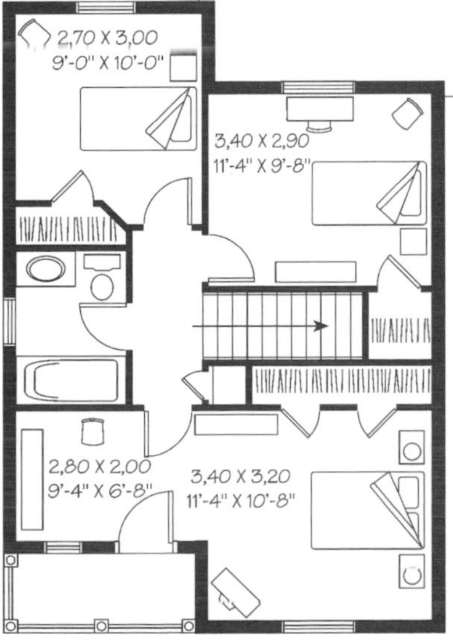

2,70 X 3,00
9'-0" X 10'-0"
3,40 X 2,90
11'-4" X 9'-8"
2,80 X 2,00
9'-4" X 6'-8"
3,40 X 3,20
11'-4" X 10'-8"

SECOND FLOOR

Standing Tall

Price Code: A

- This plan features:
  - — Three bedrooms
  - — One full and one half baths
- The U-shaped Kitchen has plenty of cupboard space and a double sink overlooking the rear yard
- The Dining Room adjoins the Kitchen and has access to the back Deck
- The Master Bedroom features a large closet, space to use as a Sitting or Dressing Area, and a door leading to a private Balcony
- This home is designed with a basement foundation

FIRST FLOOR — 620 SQ. FT.
SECOND FLOOR — 620 SQ. FT.

TOTAL LIVING AREA:
1,240 SQ. FT.

PLAN NO.97629

Multiple Gables

PRICE CODE: F

- This plan features:
  - — Five bedrooms
  - — Four full baths
- Multiple gables highlight the exterior
- The Dining Room and living room flank the Foyer
- A Den or guest Bedroom is on the first floor
- The Family Room has a rear wall fireplace
- A tray ceiling is above the Master Suite
- This home is designed with a basement foundation

FIRST FLOOR — 1,409 SQ. FT.
SECOND FLOOR — 1,300 SQ. FT.
BASEMENT — 1,409 SQ. FT.
GARAGE — 528 SQ. FT.

TOTAL LIVING AREA: 2,709 SQ. FT.

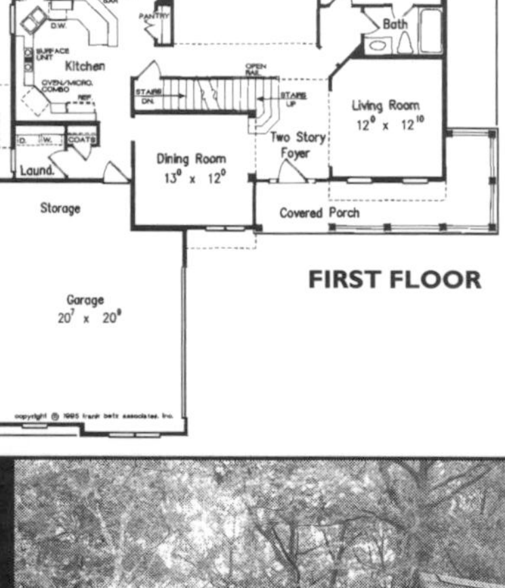
54'-6"
59'-4"
Covered Porch
Breakfast
Two Story Family Room 15⁶ x 18⁸
Den/ Bedroom 5 11⁰ x 11⁰
Bath
Kitchen
Living Room 12⁰ x 12¹⁰
Two Story Foyer
Dining Room 13⁰ x 12⁰
Laund.
Storage
Covered Porch
Garage 20⁷ x 20⁸
FIRST FLOOR

Vaulted M.Bath
W.i.c.
Attic

Master Suite 17¹ x 15²
Family Room Below
Bedroom 4 11⁰ x 11⁶
Bath
Foyer Below
Bedroom 3 12⁰ x 12⁰
Bedroom 2 12⁰ x 11⁸
Bath
SECOND FLOOR

PLAN NO.32122

Photography supplied by The Meredith Corporation

With Cottage Ambiance

PRICE CODE: A

- This plan features:
  - — Two bedrooms
  - — One full bath
- Covered Entry mimicks twin gables of activity and sleeping areas of home
- High ceilings and gable windows keep interior light and airy
- Spacious Living Area with window alcove opens to Screen Porch, and Kitchen with washer/dryer and Pantry
- Two Bedrooms share a full Bath and easy access to courtyard and Deck beyond
- This home is designed with basement and crawlspace foundation

MAIN FLOOR — 1,112 SQ. FT.
BASEMENT — 484 SQ. FT.

TOTAL LIVING AREA: 1,112 SQ. FT.

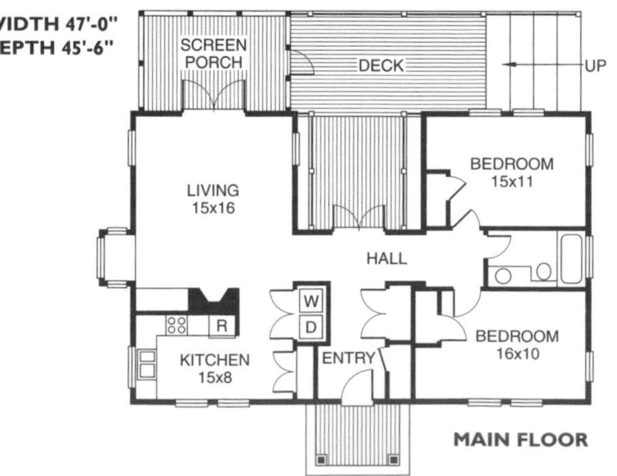
WIDTH 47'-0"
DEPTH 45'-6"
SCREEN PORCH
DECK
UP
LIVING 15x16
BEDROOM 15x11
HALL
W
D
R
KITCHEN 15x8
ENTRY
BEDROOM 16x10
MAIN FLOOR

Quaint Front Porch and Lovely Details

PRICE CODE: C

PLAN NO. 94900

'his plan features:
- Four bedrooms
- Two full and one half baths
- A Covered Porch and Victorian touches create unique elevation
- A one and a half story Entry hall leads into formal Dining Room
- A volume ceiling above abundant windows and a see-through fireplace highlight the Great Room
- Kitchen/Breakfast Area shares the fireplace and has a snack bar, desk, walk-in Pantry and abundant counter space
- Secluded Master Suite crowned by a vaulted ceiling and luxurious Bath
- Three additional Bedrooms on the second floor share a full Bath
- This home is designed with a basement foundation
- Alternate foundation options available at an additional charge. Please call 1-800-235-5700 for more information.

ST FLOOR — 1,421 SQ. FT.
COND FLOOR — 578 SQ. FT.
SEMENT — 1,421 SQ. FT.
RAGE — 480 SQ. FT.

***TOTAL LIVING AREA:* 1,999 SQ. FT.**

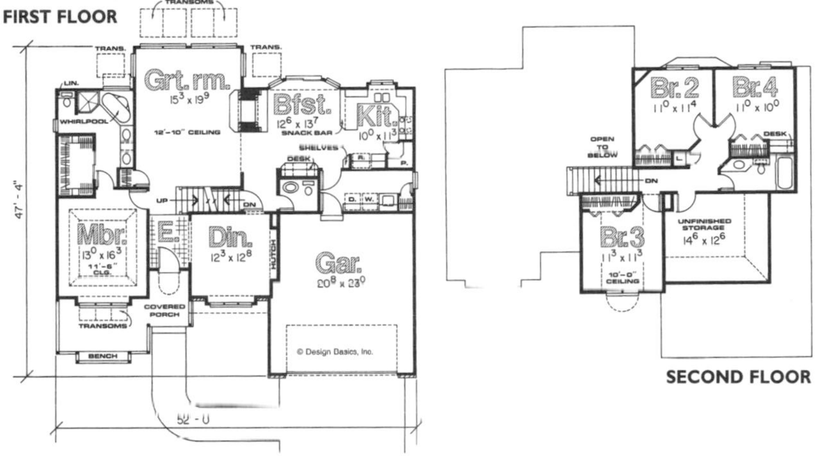
FIRST FLOOR
TRANSOMS
TRANS.
TRANS.
LIN.
WHIRLPOOL
Grt. rm.
$15^3 \times 19^9$
12'-10" CEILING
Bfst.
$12^6 \times 13^7$
SNACK BAR
Kit.
$10^0 \times 11^3$
SHELVES
DESK
D. W.
UP
DN
Mbr.
$13^0 \times 16^3$
11'-6" CLG.
E.
Din.
$12^3 \times 12^8$
HUTCH
Gar.
$20^8 \times 23^0$
TRANSOMS
COVERED PORCH
BENCH
© Design Basics, Inc.
47'-4"
52'-0"
Br. 2
$11^0 \times 11^4$
Br. 4
$11^0 \times 10^0$
DESK
OPEN TO BELOW
DN
Br. 3
$11^3 \times 11^3$
10'-0" CEILING
UNFINISHED STORAGE
$14^6 \times 12^6$
SECOND FLOOR

Timeless Two-Story

PRICE CODE: B

PLAN NO. 99155

FREILING

This plan features:
- Three bedrooms
- Two full and one half baths
- This plan has functionality with out sacrificing style
- The Dining Room runs the width of the home with a corner fireplace for added coziness
- The Kitchen/Dining Area is arranged for convenience and efficiency
- The Bedrooms are all located on the second floor
- This home is designed with a basement foundation

ST FLOOR — 786 SQ. FT.
COND FLOOR — 723 SQ. FT.
SEMENT — 786 SQ. FT.
RAGE — 406 SQ. FT.

***TOTAL LIVING AREA:* 1,509 SQ. FT.**

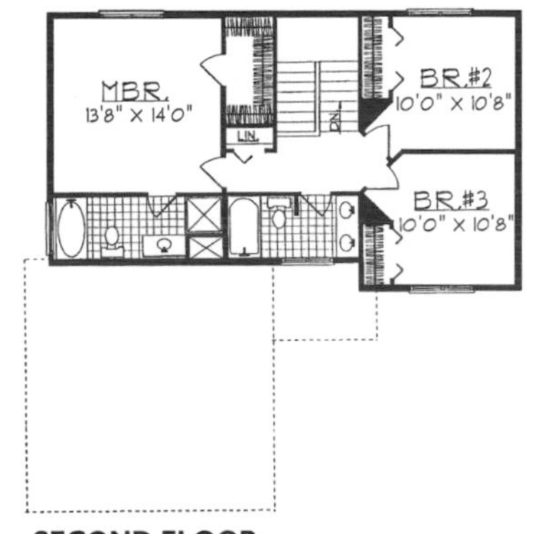
MBR.
13'8" X 14'0"
LIN.
BR.#2
10'0" X 10'8"
BR.#3
10'0" X 10'8"
SECOND FLOOR

DW
DIN.
9'4" X 13'0"
KIT.
8'4" X 11'4"
PANTRY
GRT.RM.
12'4" X 21'0"
E.
2 CAR GAR.
20'0" X 20'4"
40'0"
FIRST FLOOR
40'0"

PLAN NO. 65035

Petite Sophisticate

PRICE CODE: A

- ■ This plan features:
- — Two bedrooms
- — One full bath
- ■ The stylized turret creates a pleasing facade, unexpe interior angles, and adds space and light to this two b room charmer
- ■ Note the large Palladian window in the Master Bedr
- ■ This home is designed with a basement foundation

MAIN FLOOR — 972 SQ. FT.
BASEMENT — 972 SQ. FT.

TOTAL LIVING AREA:
972 SQ. FT.

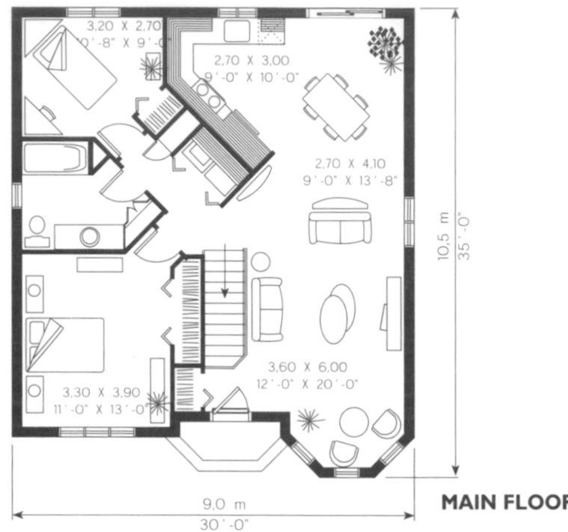
3.20 X 2.70
2.70 X 3.00
9'-0" X 10'-0"
2.70 X 4.10
9'-0" X 13'-8"
3.60 X 6.00
12'-0" X 20'-0"
3.30 X 3.90
11'-0" X 13'-0"
10,5 m
35'-0"
9.0 m
30'-0"
MAIN FLOOR

PLAN NO. 98211

Executive Features

PRICE CODE: H

- ■ This plan features:
- — Four bedrooms
- — Three full and one half baths
- ■ High volume ceilings
- ■ An extended staircase highlights the Foyer as colum define the Dining Room and the Grand Room
- ■ A massive glass exterior rear wall and high ceiling i Master Bedroom
- ■ His and her walk-in closets and a lavish five-piece B highlight the Master Bedroom
- ■ The island Kitchen, Keeping Room and Breakfast R create an open living space
- ■ A fireplace accents both the Keeping Room and the two-story Grand Room
- ■ Three additional Bedrooms with private Bathroom access and ample closet space
- ■ This home is designed with basement and crawlspac foundation options

FIRST FLOOR — 2,035 SQ. FT.
SECOND FLOOR — 1,028 SQ. FT.
BASEMENT — 2,035 SQ. FT.
GARAGE — 530 SQ. FT.

TOTAL LIVING AREA:
3,063 SQ. FT.

WIDTH 56'-0"
DEPTH 62'-6"
KEEPING RM.
BREAKFAST
KITCHEN
GRAND ROOM
MASTER BR.
3 CAR GARAGE
DINING ROOM
FOYER
M. BATH
PORCH
HERS
HIS
BEDROOM #4
BATH
UPPER GRAND ROOM
STORAGE
GALLERY
BEDROOM #3
OPEN TO BELOW
BEDROOM #2
FIRST FLOOR
SECOND FLOOR

PLAN NO. 91346

Four Bedroom Charmer

Price Code: D

WIDTH 58'-0"
DEPTH 60'-0"

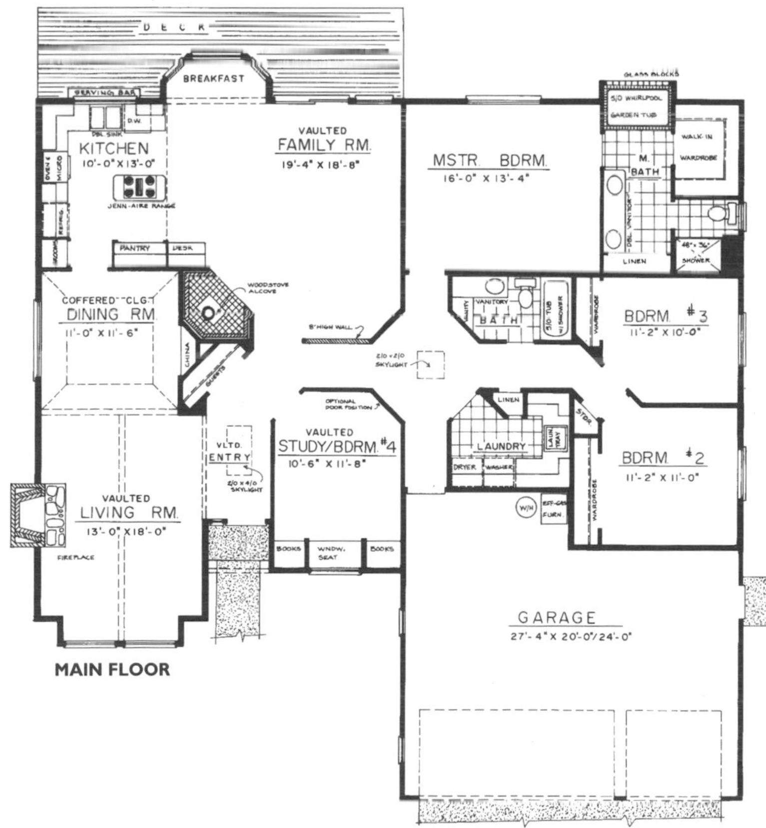
DECK
BREAKFAST
SERVING BAR
KITCHEN
10'-0" X 13'-0"
JENN-AIRE RANGE
PANTRY
DESK
VAULTED
FAMILY RM.
19'-4" X 18'-8"
MSTR. BDRM.
16'-0" X 13'-4"
GLASS BLOCKS
GARDEN TUB
WALK IN WARDROBE
M. BATH
LINEN
SHOWER
COFFERED CLG.
DINING RM
11'-0" X 11'-6"
WOODSTOVE ALCOVE
BATH
BDRM. #3
11'-2" X 10'-0"
LINEN
LAUNDRY
DRYER
WASHER
VAULTED
STUDY/BDRM. #4
10'-6" X 11'-8"
VLTD.
ENTRY
BDRM. #2
11'-2" X 11'-0"
VAULTED
LIVING RM.
13'-0" X 18'-0"
FIREPLACE
BOOKS
WNDW. SEAT
BOOKS
GARAGE
27'-4" X 20'-0"/24'-0"
MAIN FLOOR

- This plan features:
- — Four bedrooms
- — Two full baths
- A vaulted ceiling in the naturally lighted Entry
- A Living Room with a masonry fireplace, large windowed bay and vaulted ceiling
- A large Family Room with a wood stove alcove
- An island cooktop, built-in Pantry, and a desk in the efficient Kitchen
- A Study with a window seat and built-in bookshelves
- This home is designed with a crawlspace foundation

MAIN FLOOR — 2,185 SQ. FT.

TOTAL LIVING AREA:
2,185 SQ. FT.

PLAN NO.99424

Stately Exterior with an Open Interior

Price Code: F

- ■ This plan features:
- — Four bedrooms
- — Two full and one half baths
- ■ Central Family Room with an inviting fireplace and a cathedral ceiling extending into Kitchen
- ■ Spacious Kitchen offers a work island/snackbar, built-in Pantry, glass Breakfast Area and nearby Porch, Utilities and Garage Entry
- ■ This home is designed with basement and slab foundation options
- ■ Alternate foundation options available at an additional charge. Please call 1-800-235-5700 for more information.

FIRST FLOOR — 1,906 SQ. FT.
SECOND FLOOR — 749 SQ. FT.
BASEMENT — 1,906 SQ. FT.
GARAGE — 682 SQ. FT.

TOTAL LIVING AREA:
2,655 SQ. FT.

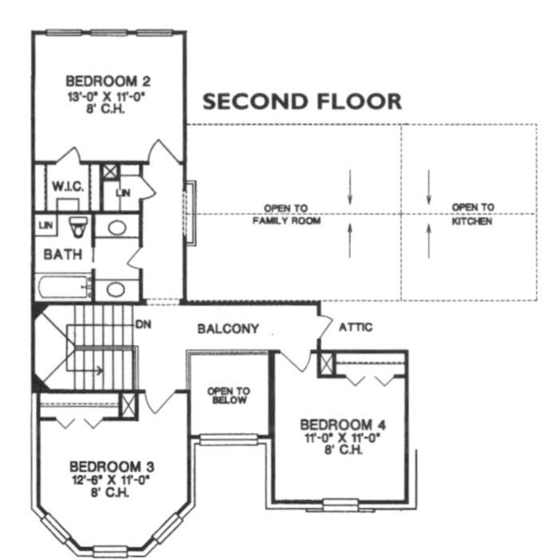

SECOND FLOOR
BEDROOM 2
13'-0" X 11'-0"
8' C.H.
W.I.C.
LIN
BATH
OPEN TO FAMILY ROOM
OPEN TO KITCHEN
DN
BALCONY
ATTIC
OPEN TO BELOW
BEDROOM 4
11'-0" X 11'-0"
8' C.H.
BEDROOM 3
12'-6" X 11'-0"
8' C.H.

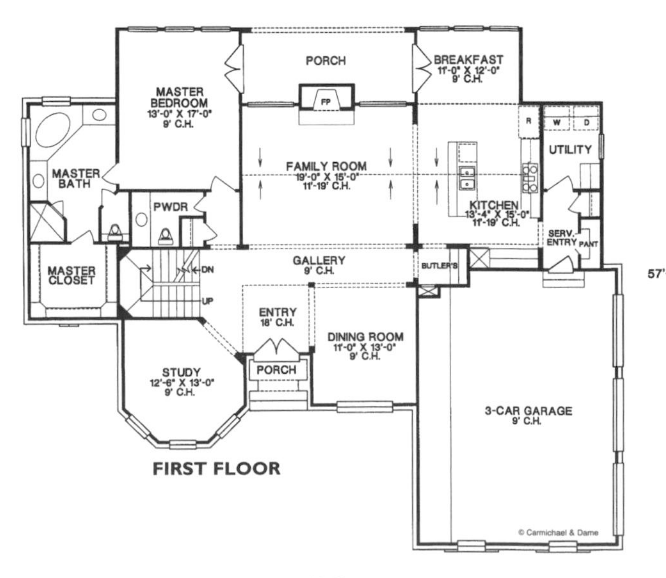

PORCH
BREAKFAST
11'-0" X 12'-0"
9' C.H.
MASTER BEDROOM
13'-0" X 17'-0"
9' C.H.
FP
UTILITY
MASTER BATH
FAMILY ROOM
19'-0" X 15'-0"
11'-19' C.H.
PWDR
KITCHEN
13'-4" X 15'-0"
11'-19' C.H.
SERV. ENTRY
PANT
GALLERY
9' C.H.
BUTLER'S
MASTER CLOSET
DN
UP
ENTRY
18' C.H.
DINING ROOM
11'-0" X 13'-0"
9' C.H.
STUDY
12'-6" X 13'-0"
9' C.H.
PORCH
3-CAR GARAGE
9' C.H.
FIRST FLOOR
© Carmichael & Dame
65'-3"

PLAN NO.10839

Photography by John Ehrenclou

Rear Elevation

Perfect Compact Ranch

Price Code: B

- This plan features:
  - — Two bedrooms
  - — Two full baths
- A large, sunken Great Room, centralized with a cozy fireplace
- A Master Bedroom with an unforgettable Bathroom including a skylight
- A huge three-car Garage, including a work area for the family carpenter
- A Kitchen, including a Breakfast Nook for family gatherings
- This home is designed with basement, slab and crawlspace foundation options

MAIN FLOOR — 1,738 SQ. FT.
BASEMENT — 1,083 SQ. FT.
GARAGE — 796 SQ. FT.

TOTAL LIVING AREA:
1,738 SQ. FT.

WLSPACE/SLAB
UNDATION
OPTION

MAIN FLOOR

WIDTH 66'-0"
DEPTH 52'-0"

PLAN NO. 98563

Lavish Appointments

Price Code: L

- This plan features:
- — Four bedrooms
- — Four full and one half baths
- Glassed two-story Entry
- The staircase to the second floor accents the marble Entry hall
- A sloped ceiling and a fireplace enhance the Living Room
- The Dining Room has a rear wall of windows
- The Kitchen has a center island with a cooktop
- The Study has a fireplace
- This home is designed with a slab foundation

FIRST FLOOR — 3,145 SQ. FT.
SECOND FLOOR — 1,181 SQ. FT.
GARAGE — 792 SQ. FT.

TOTAL LIVING AREA:
4,326 SQ. FT.

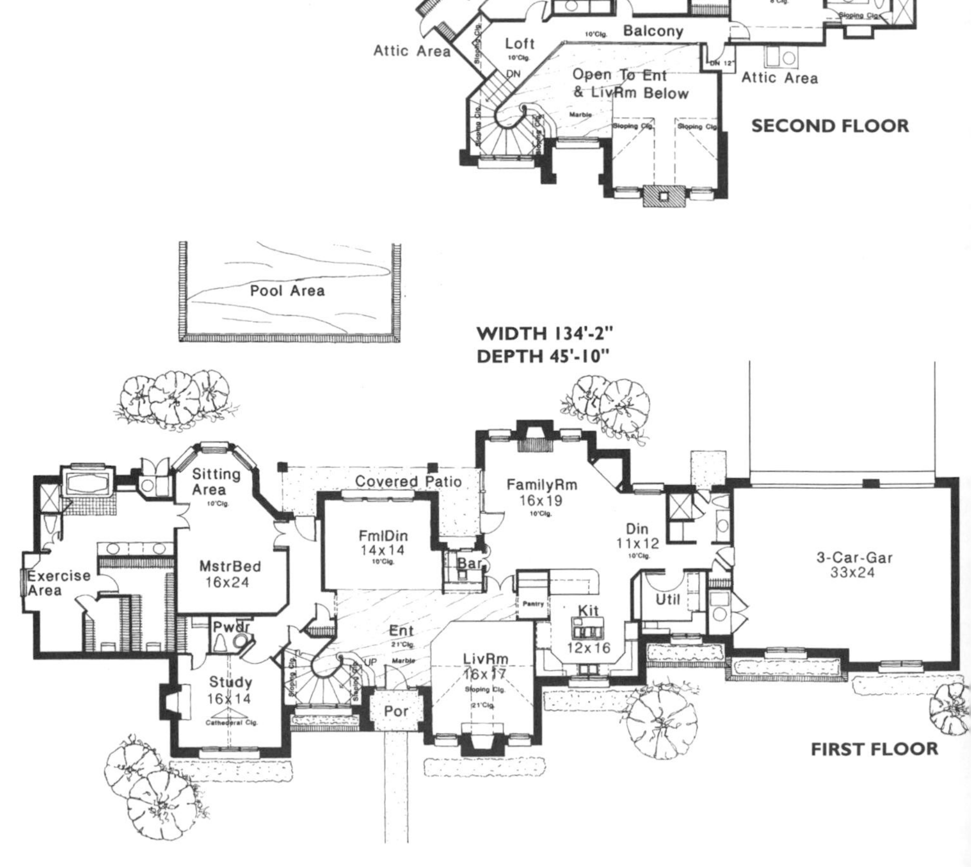

Bed#2
13x15
Bed#4
11x14
Bed#3
14x18
Balcony
Loft
Attic Area
Open To Ent & LivRm Below
Attic Area
SECOND FLOOR
Pool Area
WIDTH 134'-2"
DEPTH 45'-10"
Sitting Area
Covered Patio
FamilyRm
16x19
FmlDin
14x14
Din
11x12
3-Car-Gar
33x24
Exercise Area
MstrBed
16x24
Bar
Util
Pwdr
Ent
Kit
12x16
LivRm
16x17
Study
16x14
Por
FIRST FLOOR

PLAN NO. 35002

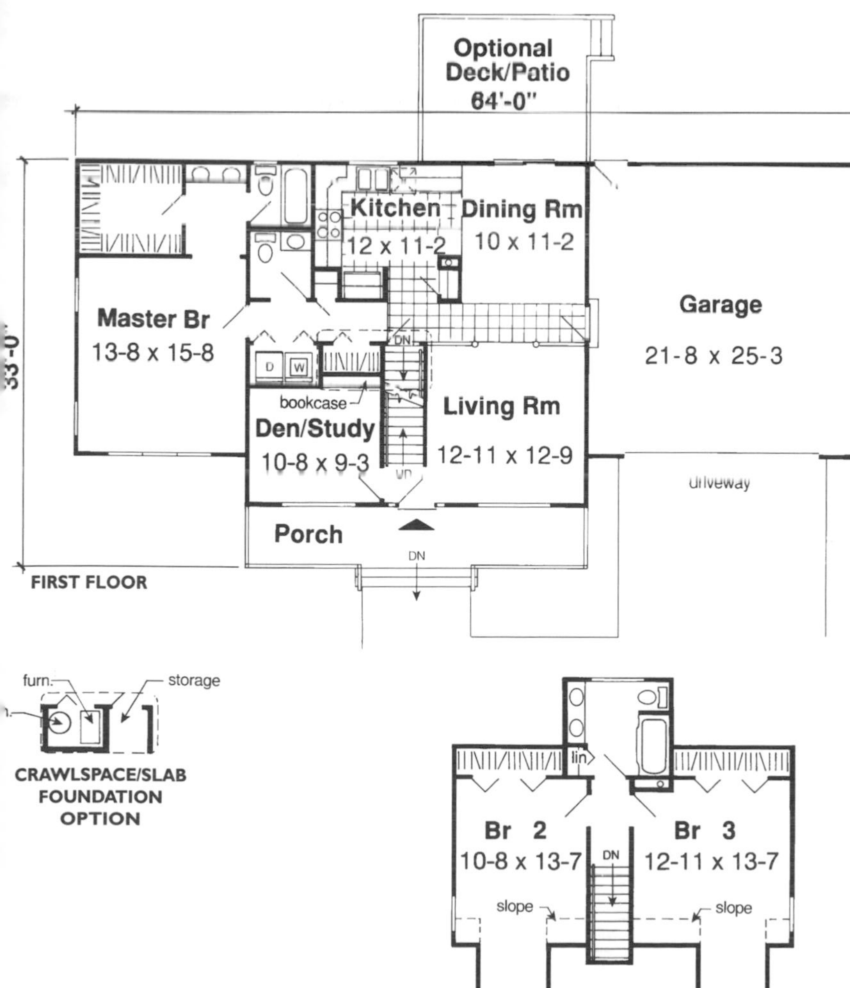

Optional
Deck/Patio
64'-0"
Kitchen
12 x 11-2
Dining Rm
10 x 11-2
Master Br
13-8 x 15-8
Garage
21-8 x 25-3
bookcase
Den/Study
10-8 x 9-3
Living Rm
12-11 x 12-9
driveway
Porch
DN
FIRST FLOOR
furn.
storage
CRAWLSPACE/SLAB
FOUNDATION
OPTION
lin
Br 2
10-8 x 13-7
Br 3
12-11 x 13-7
slope
slope
SECOND FLOOR

Roomy Three Bedroom Cape

Price Code: B

- This plan features:
  - Three bedrooms
  - Two full and one half baths
- Large front Porch with Country appeal
- Den includes picture window and built-in bookcase
- Dining Room flows into Living Room for easy entertaining
- L-shaped Kitchen has a double sink and ample counter space
- First floor Master Bedroom has bright front windows and a private Bath
- This home is designed with basement, slab and crawlspace foundation options

First floor — 1,120 sq. ft.
Second floor — 592 sq. ft.
Garage — 528 sq. ft.

Total Living Area:
1,712 sq. ft.

PLAN NO.98464

European Flavor

PRICE CODE: C

- This plan features:
  — Three bedrooms
  — Two full baths
- A covered Entry reveals a Foyer inside with a 14-foot ceiling
- The Family Room has a vaulted ceiling, a fireplace, and a French door to the rear yard
- The Breakfast Area has a tray ceiling and a bay of windows that overlooks the backyard
- The Kitchen has every imaginable convenience including a walk-in Pantry
- The Dining Room is delineated by columns and has plant shelf above it
- The privately located Master Suite has a tray ceiling, walk-in closet and a private Bath
- Two other Bedrooms share a full Bath on the opposi side of the home
- This home is designed with basement and crawlspac foundation options

MAIN FLOOR — 1,779 SQ. FT.
BASEMENT — 1,818 SQ. FT.
GARAGE — 499 SQ. FT.

TOTAL LIVING AREA:
1,779 SQ. FT.

WIDTH 57'-0"
DEPTH 56'-4"

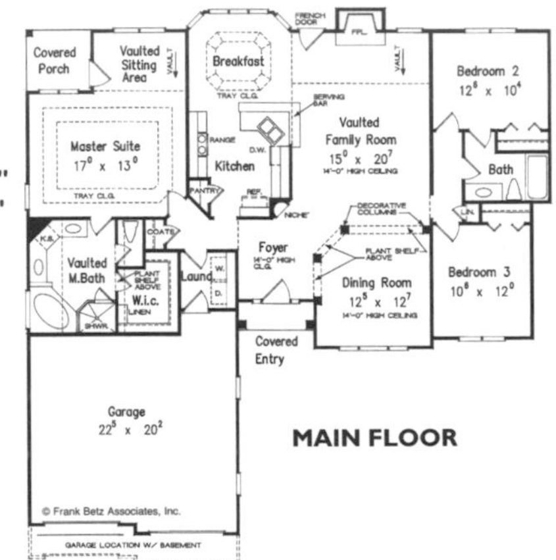

Covered Porch
Vaulted Sitting Area
Breakfast
Bedroom 2
12⁸ x 10⁴
Master Suite
17⁰ x 13⁰
Kitchen
Vaulted Family Room
15⁰ x 20⁷
Bath
Vaulted M.Bath
Laund.
Foyer
Dining Room
12⁵ x 12⁷
Bedroom 3
10⁶ x 12⁰
Covered Entry
Garage
22⁵ x 20²
© Frank Betz Associates, Inc.

MAIN FLOOR

Vaulted M.Bath
W.i.c.
Laund.
Garage
22⁵ x 20²

BASEMENT STAIR LOCATION OPTION

Master Retreat Welcome You Home

PRICE CODE: A

- This plan features:
  — Three bedrooms
  — Two full baths
- Foyer opens into an huge Living Room with a fireplace below a sloped ceiling and Deck access
- Efficient Kitchen with a Pantry, serving counter, Dining Area, Laundry closet and Garage Entry
- Corner Master Bedroom offers a walk-in closet and pampering Bath with a raised tub
- Two more Bedrooms, one with a Den option, share a full Bath
- This home is designed with basement, slab and crawlspace foundation options

MAIN FLOOR — 1,486 SQ. FT.
GARAGE — 462 SQ. FT.

TOTAL LIVING AREA:
1,486 SQ. FT.

SLAB/CRAWLSPACE OPTION

Rear Elevation

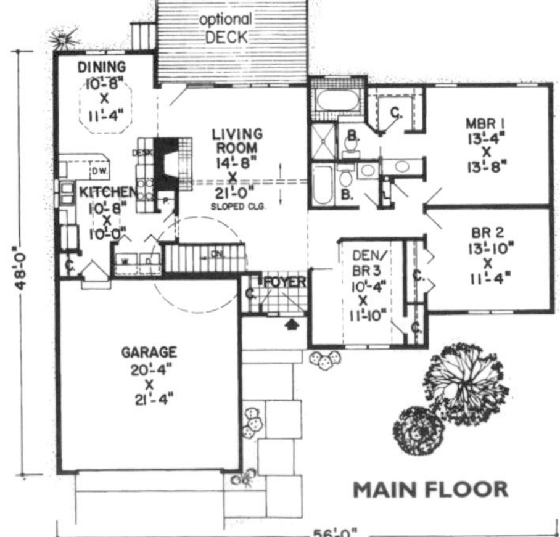

optional DECK
DINING
10'-8" x 11'-4"
LIVING ROOM
14'-8" x 21'-0"
SLOPED CLG.
MBR I
13'-4" x 13'-8"
KITCHEN
10'-8" x 10'-0"
BR 2
13'-10" x 11'-4"
DEN/ BR 3
10'-4" x 11'-10"
FOYER
GARAGE
20'-4" x 21'-4"
48'-0"
56'-0"

MAIN FLOOR

PLAN NO. 99425

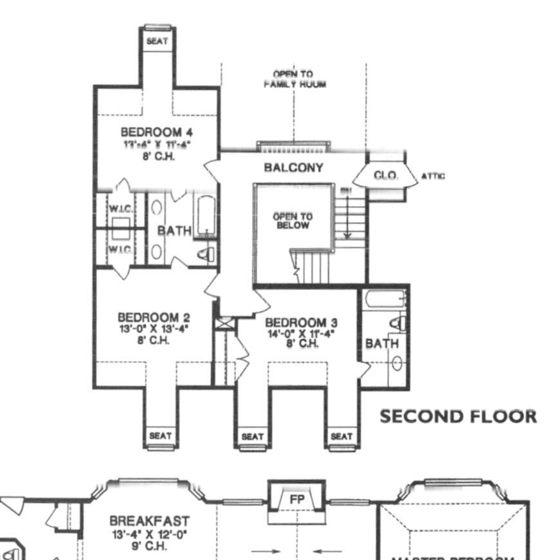

SEAT
OPEN TO FAMILY ROOM
BEDROOM 4
8' C.H.
BALCONY
CLO.
ATTIC
OPEN TO BELOW
W.I.C.
BATH
W.I.C.
BEDROOM 2
13'-0" X 13'-4"
8' C.H.
BEDROOM 3
14'-0" X 11'-4"
8' C.H.
BATH
SEAT
SEAT
SEAT
SECOND FLOOR

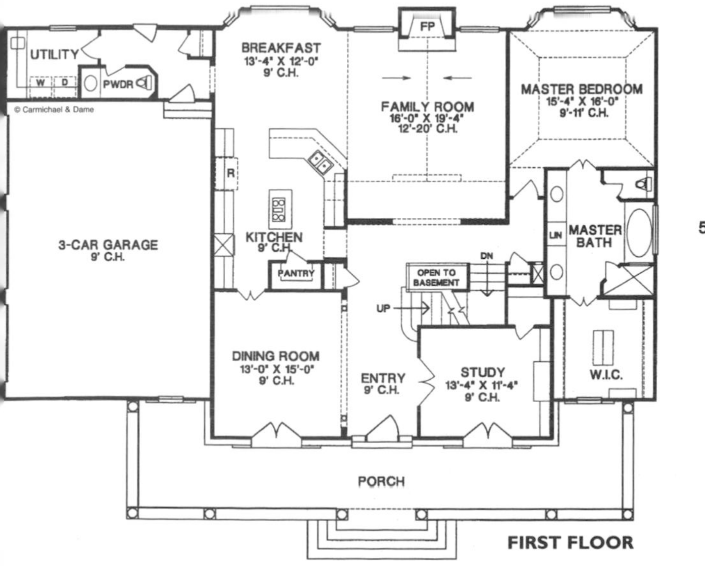

UTILITY
W D
PWDR
© Carmichael & Dame
BREAKFAST
13'-4" X 12'-0"
9' C.H.
FP
FAMILY ROOM
16'-0" X 19'-4"
12'-20' C.H.
MASTER BEDROOM
15'-4" X 16'-0"
9'-11' C.H.
3-CAR GARAGE
9' C.H.
R
KITCHEN
9' C.H.
PANTRY
OPEN TO BASEMENT
DN
UP
LIN
MASTER BATH
53'-0"
DINING ROOM
13'-0" X 15'-0"
9' C.H.
ENTRY
9' C.H.
STUDY
13'-4" X 11'-4"
9' C.H.
W.I.C.
PORCH
FIRST FLOOR
67'-8"

Dormers and Porch Create Country Atmosphere

Price Code: H

- This plan features:
- — Four bedrooms
- — Three full and one half baths
- French doors lead from both the Dining Room and the Study onto the front Porch
- This home is designed with a basement and slab foundation options
- Alternate foundation options available at an additional charge. Please call 1-800-235-5700 for more information.

FIRST FLOOR — 2,116 SQ. FT.
SECOND FLOOR — 956 SQ. FT.
BASEMENT — 2,116 SQ. FT.
GARAGE — 675 SQ. FT.

TOTAL LIVING AREA:
3,072 SQ. FT.

PLAN NO. 97151

Rear Elevati

Beautiful and Functional

Price Code: D

- This plan features:
  - — Three bedrooms
  - — Two full baths
- Gracious, keystone arch entry opens to formal Dining Room and Great Room beyond
- Spacious Great Room features fireplace surrounded by windows topped by a cathedral ceiling
- Kitchen/Nook layout ideal for busy household with easy access to Deck, Dining Room, Laundry and Garage
- This home is designed with a basement foundation

MAIN FLOOR — 2,007 SQ. FT.
GARAGE — 748 SQ. FT.

TOTAL LIVING AREA: 2,007 SQ. FT.

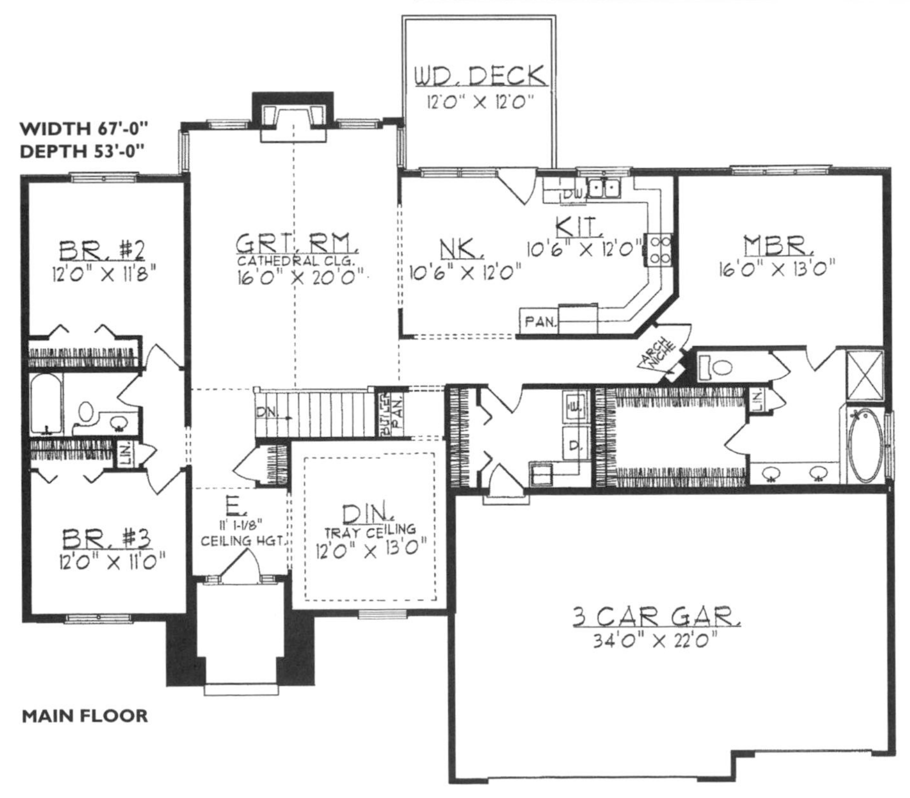

WIDTH 67'-0"
DEPTH 53'-0"
WD. DECK
12'0" X 12'0"
BR. #2
12'0" X 11'8"
GRT. RM.
CATHEDRAL CLG.
16'0" X 20'0"
NK.
10'6" X 12'0"
KIT.
10'6" X 12'0"
MBR.
16'0" X 13'0"
PAN.
ARCH NICHE
DN.
BUTLER PAN.
LIN.
BR. #3
12'0" X 11'0"
E.
11' 1-1/8" CEILING HGT.
DIN.
TRAY CEILING
12'0" X 13'0"
3 CAR GAR.
34'0" X 22'0"

MAIN FLOOR

Foyer Isolates Bedroom Wing

PRICE CODE: B

PLAN NO.20087

his plan features:
- hree bedrooms
- wo full baths
- Living Room complete with a window wall, anking a massive fireplace
- Dining Room with recessed ceilings and a ıss-through for convenience
- Master Suite tucked behind the two-car arage for maximum noise protection
- spacious Kitchen with built-ins and access the two-car Garage
- his home is designed with a basement foundation

IN FLOOR—1,568 SQ. FT.
EMENT — 1,568 SQ. FT.
RAGE — 484 SQ. FT.

TOTAL LIVING AREA:
1,568 SQ. FT.

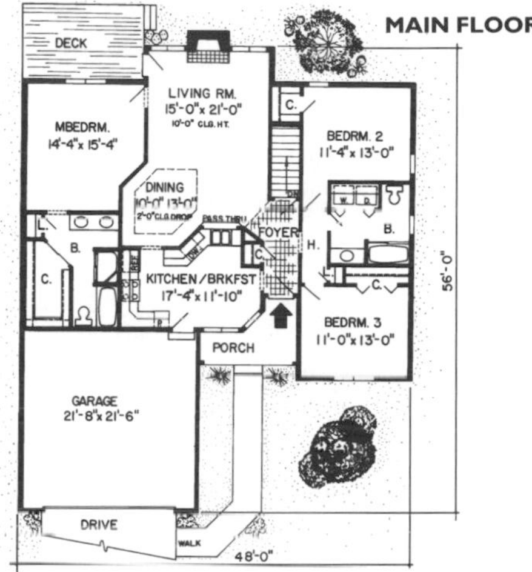

MAIN FLOOR
DECK
LIVING RM.
15'-0"x 21'-0"
10'-0" CLG.HT.
MBEDRM.
14'-4"x 15'-4"
DINING
10'-0" 13'-0"
BEDRM. 2
11'-4"x 13'-0"
FOYER
KITCHEN/BRKFST
17'-4"x 11'-10"
BEDRM. 3
11'-0"x 13'-0"
PORCH
GARAGE
21'-8"x 21'-6"
DRIVE
WALK
48'-0"
56'-0"

One-Story Country Home

PRICE CODE: A

PLAN NO.99639

his plan features:
- Three bedrooms
- Two full baths
- Living Room with an imposing, high ceiling that lopes down to a normal height of eight feet, focusing on ıe decorative heat-circulating fireplace at the rear wall
- n efficient Kitchen that adjoins the Dining Room that iews the front Porch
- Dinette Area for informal eating in the Kitchen that an comfortably seat six people
- Master Suite arranged with a large Dressing Area ıat has a walk-in closet plus two linear closets and pace for a vanity
- wo family Bedrooms that share a full hall Bath
- his home is designed with basement and lab foundation options

IN FLOOR — 1,367 SQ. FT.
EMENT — 1,267 SQ. FT.
RAGE — 431 SQ. FT.

TOTAL LIVING AREA:
1,367 SQ. FT.

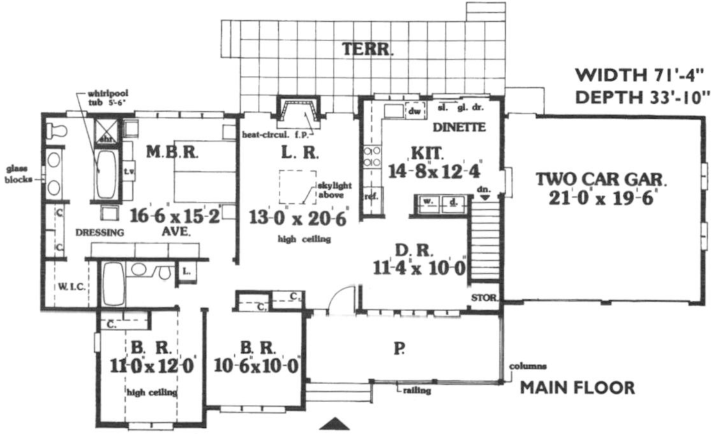

TERR.
WIDTH 71'-4"
DEPTH 33'-10"
whirlpool tub 5'-6"
glass blocks
M.B.R.
16-6 x 15-2
DRESSING
AVE.
W.I.C.
heat-circul. f.p.
L. R.
skylight above
13-0 x 20-6
high ceiling
DINETTE
KIT.
14-8x12-4
D. R.
11-4 x 10-0
STOR.
TWO CAR GAR.
21-0 x 19-6
B. R.
11-0x12-0
high ceiling
B. R.
10-6x10-0
P.
railing
columns
MAIN FLOOR

PLAN NO. 98494

It's All in the Details

Price Code: G

- This plan features:
- — Five bedrooms
- — Four full baths
- The exterior is appointed with keystones, arches and shutters
- The Living Room and Dining Room meet through an arched opening
- The Kitchen, Breakfast and Family Room are open to each other
- Master Suite has a tray ceiling in the Bedroom and a vaulted ceiling in the Master Bath
- This home is designed with basement and crawlspace foundation options

FIRST FLOOR — 1,447 SQ. FT.
SECOND FLOOR — 1,325 SQ. FT.
BONUS — 301 SQ. FT.
BASEMENT — 1,447 SQ. FT.
GARAGE — 393 SQ. FT.

TOTAL LIVING AREA:
2,772 SQ. FT.

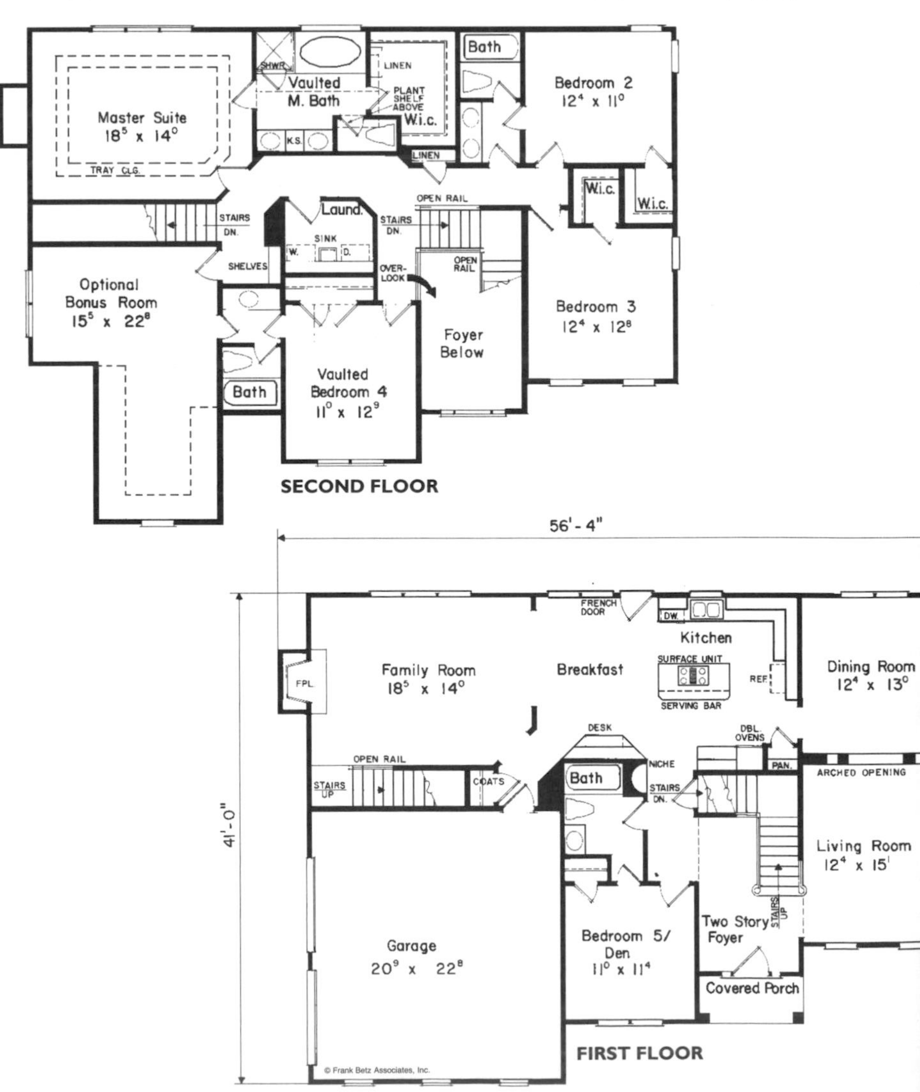

Master Suite
18⁵ x 14⁰
TRAY CLG.
SHWR.
Vaulted
M. Bath
K.S.
LINEN
PLANT SHELF ABOVE
W.i.c.
Bath
LINEN
Bedroom 2
12⁴ x 11⁰
W.i.c.
W.i.c.
STAIRS DN.
Laund.
SINK
W.
D.
STAIRS DN.
OPEN RAIL
SHELVES
OVER-LOOK
OPEN RAIL
Optional
Bonus Room
15⁵ x 22⁸
Foyer
Below
Bedroom 3
12⁴ x 12⁸
Bath
Vaulted
Bedroom 4
11⁰ x 12⁹
SECOND FLOOR
56'- 4"
41'-0"
FRENCH DOOR
DW.
Kitchen
FPL.
Family Room
18⁵ x 14⁰
Breakfast
SURFACE UNIT
REF.
SERVING BAR
Dining Room
12⁴ x 13⁰
DESK
DBL OVENS
OPEN RAIL
NICHE
PAN.
ARCHED OPENING
STAIRS UP
COATS
Bath
STAIRS DN.
Living Room
12⁴ x 15¹
STAIRS UP
Two Story
Foyer
Garage
20⁹ x 22⁸
Bedroom 5/
Den
11⁰ x 11⁴
Covered Porch
FIRST FLOOR
© Frank Betz Associates, Inc.

Fieldstone Facade and Arched Windows

PRICE CODE: C

'his plan features:
- Three bedrooms
- Two full and one half baths
- nviting Covered Porch shelters entrance
- Expansive Great Room enhanced by warm fireplace nd three transom windows
- Breakfast Area adjoins Great Room giving a feeling f more space
- An efficient Kitchen with counter snack bar and nearby aundry and Garage Entry
- A first floor Master Bedroom Suite with an arched vindow below a sloped ceiling and a double vanity Bath
- A bonus area for future expansion on the second floor
- 'his home is designed with a basement foundation
- Alternate foundation options available at an dditional charge. Please call 1-800-235-5700 for nore information.

ST FLOOR — 1,405 SQ. FT.
COND FLOOR — 453 SQ. FT.
NUS ROOM — 300 SQ. FT.
SEMENT — 1,405 SQ. FT.
RAGE — 490 SQ. FT.

TOTAL LIVING AREA:
1,858 SQ. FT.

PLAN NO.94911

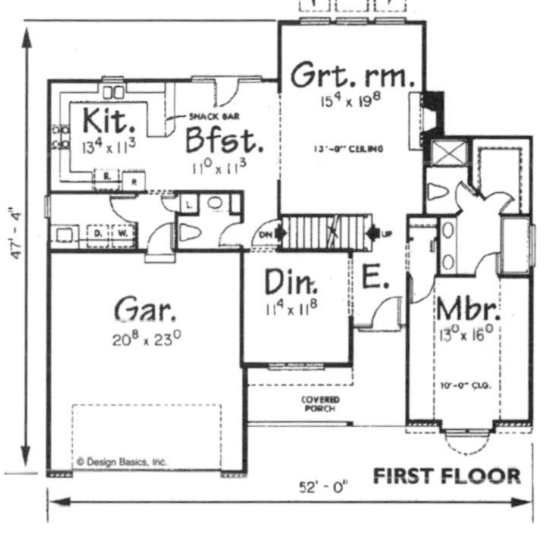
TRANSOMS
Grt. rm.
15⁴ x 19⁸
13'-0" CEILING
Kit.
13⁴ x 11³
SNACK BAR
Bfst.
11⁰ x 11³
Din.
11⁴ x 11⁸
E.
Mbr.
13⁰ x 16⁰
10'-0" CLG.
Gar.
20⁸ x 23⁰
COVERED PORCH
47' - 4"
52' - 0"
© Design Basics, Inc.
FIRST FLOOR

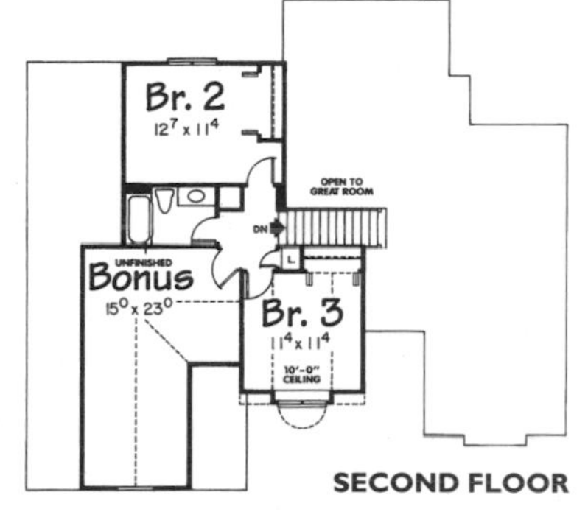
Br. 2
12⁷ x 11⁴
OPEN TO GREAT ROOM
UNFINISHED
Bonus
15⁰ x 23⁰
Br. 3
11⁴ x 11⁴
10'-0" CEILING
SECOND FLOOR

Glorious Arches

PRICE CODE: G

'his plan features:
- Four bedrooms
- Three full and one half baths
- Glorious arched openings distinguish the Family Room
- From the two-story Foyer you may enter either the Living Room or the Dining Room
- A three-car Garage completes this home design
- 'his home is designed with crawlspace and basement oundation options

ST FLOOR — 1,347 SQ. FT.
COND FLOOR — 1,493 SQ. FT.
NUS — 243 SQ. FT.
SEMENT — 1,347 SQ. FT.
RAGE — 778 SQ. FT.

TOTAL LIVING AREA:
2,840 SQ. FT.

PLAN NO.97208

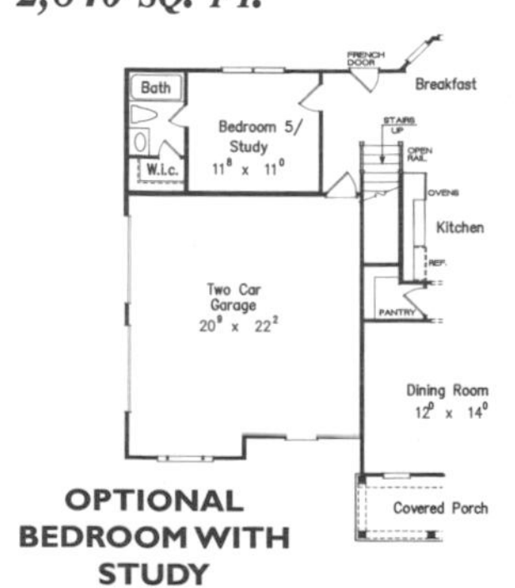
Bath
Bedroom 5/ Study
11⁶ x 11⁰
W.i.c.
Breakfast
Kitchen
Two Car Garage
20⁹ x 22²
PANTRY
Dining Room
12⁰ x 14⁰
Covered Porch

OPTIONAL BEDROOM WITH STUDY

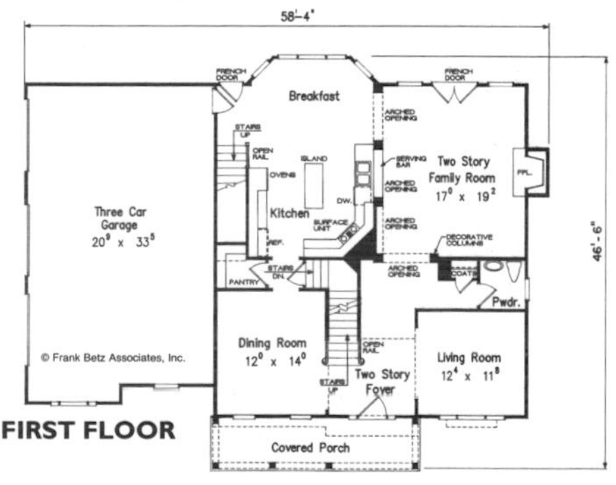
58'-4"
Breakfast
Three Car Garage
20⁹ x 33⁵
Kitchen
Two Story Family Room
17⁶ x 19²
Dining Room
12⁰ x 14⁰
Two Story Foyer
Living Room
12⁴ x 11⁸
Pwdr.
Covered Porch
46'-6"
© Frank Betz Associates, Inc.

FIRST FLOOR

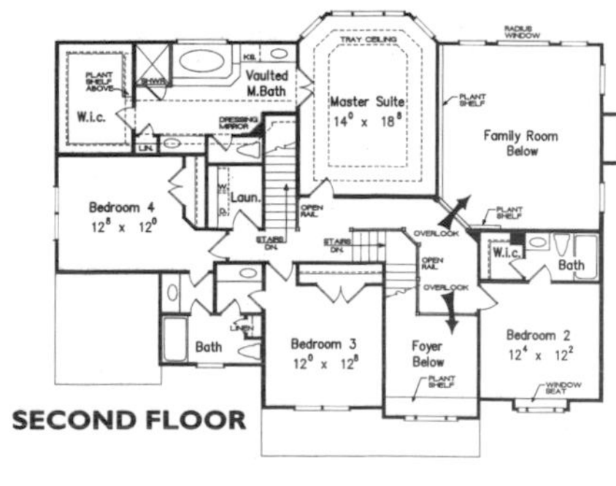
W.i.c.
Vaulted M.Bath
Master Suite
14⁰ x 18⁶
Family Room Below
Bedroom 4
12⁶ x 12⁰
Laun.
W.i.c.
Bath
Bath
Bedroom 3
12⁰ x 12⁶
Foyer Below
Bedroom 2
12⁴ x 12²

SECOND FLOOR

PLAN NO.91436

Accent on Privacy

PRICE CODE: F

- This plan features:
  - Three bedrooms
  - Two full and one half baths
- Stucco exterior and arched windows create a feeling of grandeur
- Sunken Living Room has a fireplace and elegant decorative ceiling
- Sweeping views of the backyard and direct access to the rear Deck from the Den, Kitchen and Breakfast N
- Gourmet Kitchen with two Pantries, full-height shelvi and a large island snack bar
- Master Bedroom enjoys its privacy on the opposite si of the home from the other Bedrooms
- Fabulous Master Bath with recessed tub and corner shower
- Continental Bath connecting the two secondary Bedrooms
- This home is designed with basement, slab, and crawlspace foundation options

MAIN FLOOR — 2,591 SQ. FT.
BASEMENT — 2,591 SQ. FT.

TOTAL LIVING AREA:
2,591 SQ. FT.

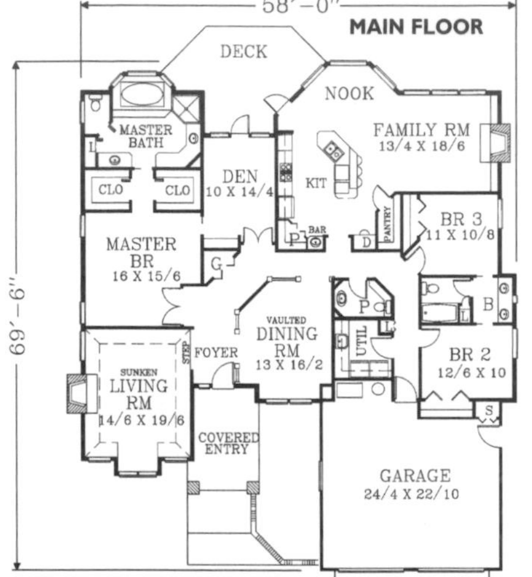
58′–0″
MAIN FLOOR
DECK
NOOK
MASTER BATH
FAMILY RM
13/4 X 18/6
DEN
10 X 14/4
KIT
CLO
CLO
BAR
PANTRY
BR 3
11 X 10/8
MASTER BR
16 X 15/6
VAULTED DINING RM
13 X 16/2
UTIL
FOYER
SUNKEN LIVING RM
14/6 X 19/6
BR 2
12/6 X 10
COVERED ENTRY
GARAGE
24/4 X 22/10
69′–6″

DINING RM
PDR
UTIL
DN

BASEMENT FOUNDATION OPTION

PLAN NO.97631

Kitchen Island Includes a Serving Bar

PRICE CODE: D

- This plan features:
  - Four bedrooms
  - Two full and one half baths
- This home includes two floor plans for the second flo one incorporates a bonus room for expanding needs
- The Bedrooms are all found upstairs, helping your children to sleep undisturbed
- This home is designed with basement and crawlspace foundation options

FIRST FLOOR — 1,032 SQ. FT.
SECOND FLOOR — 988 SQ. FT.
BONUS ROOM — 337 SQ. FT.
BASEMENT — 1,032 SQ. FT.
GARAGE — 500 SQ. FT.

TOTAL LIVING AREA:
2,020 SQ. FT.

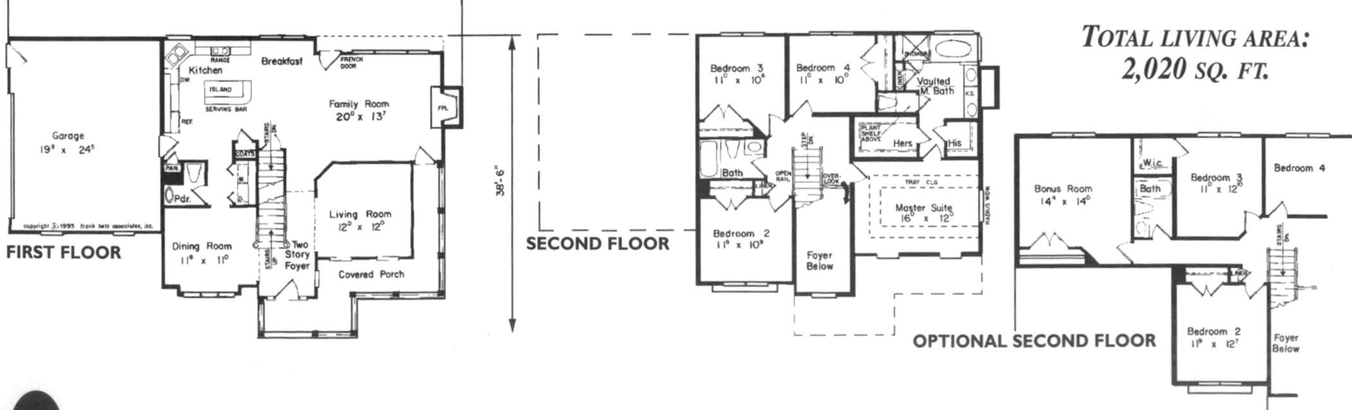
58′-4″
Kitchen
Breakfast
ISLAND
SERVING BAR
Family Room
20⁰ x 13⁷
Garage
19⁹ x 24⁵
Living Room
12⁰ x 12⁰
Dining Room
11⁶ x 11⁰
Two Story Foyer
Covered Porch
Pdr.
FIRST FLOOR
38′-6″
SECOND FLOOR
Bedroom 3
Bedroom 4
Vaulted M. Bath
Hers
His
Bath
Master Suite
Bedroom 2
Foyer Below
OPTIONAL SECOND FLOOR
Bonus Room
14⁴ x 14⁰
W.i.c.
Bath
Bedroom 3
Bedroom 4
Bedroom 2
Foyer Below

PLAN NO. 98508

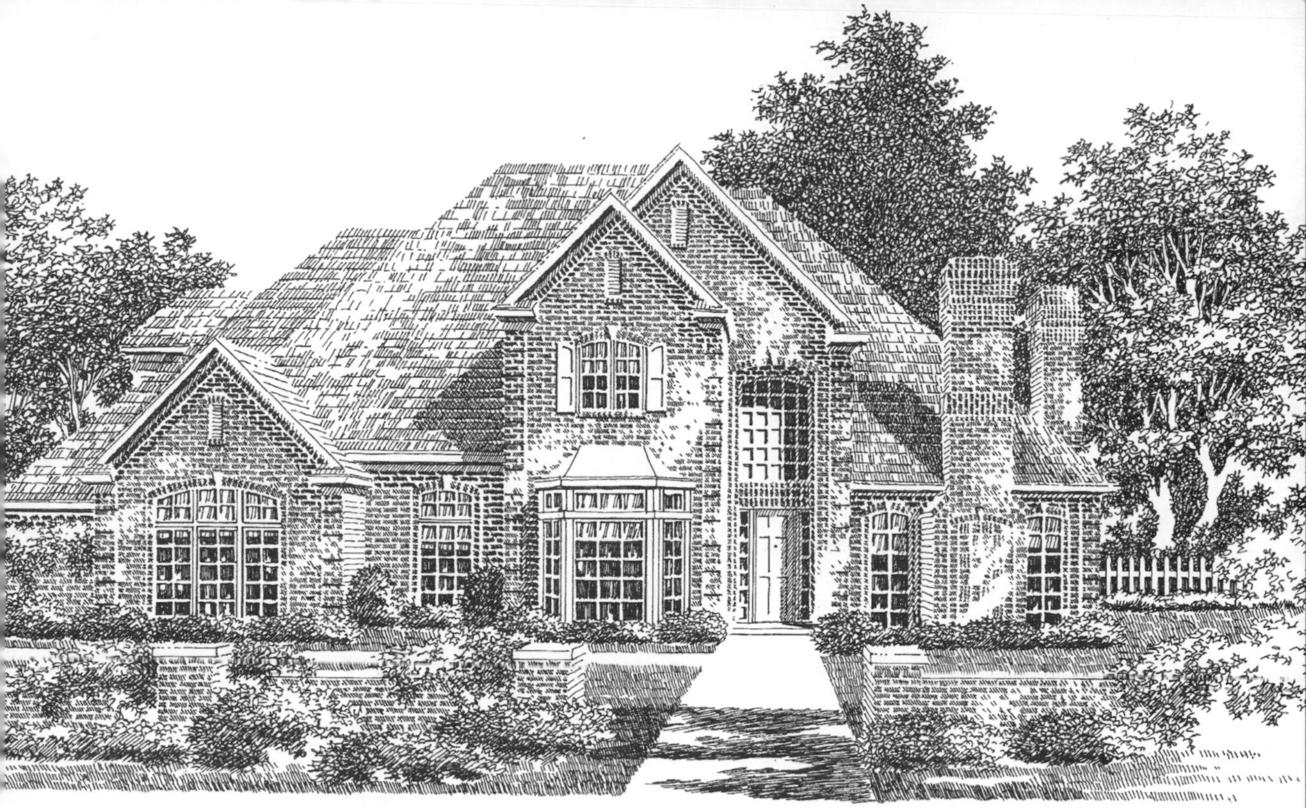

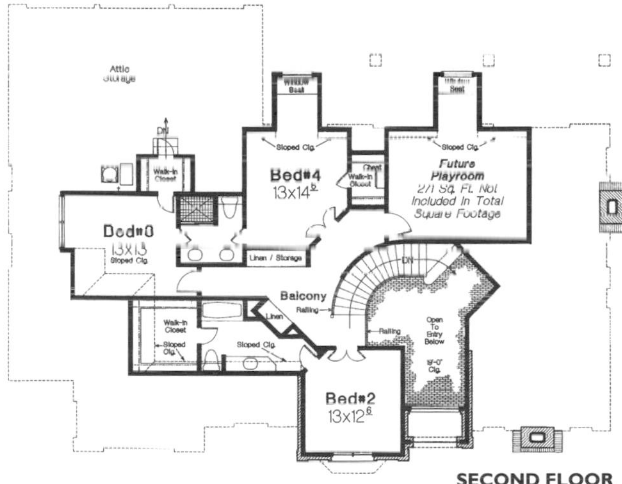

Bed#4
13x14
Future Playroom
271 Sq. Ft. Not Included In Total Square Footage
Balcony
Bed#2
13x12

SECOND FLOOR

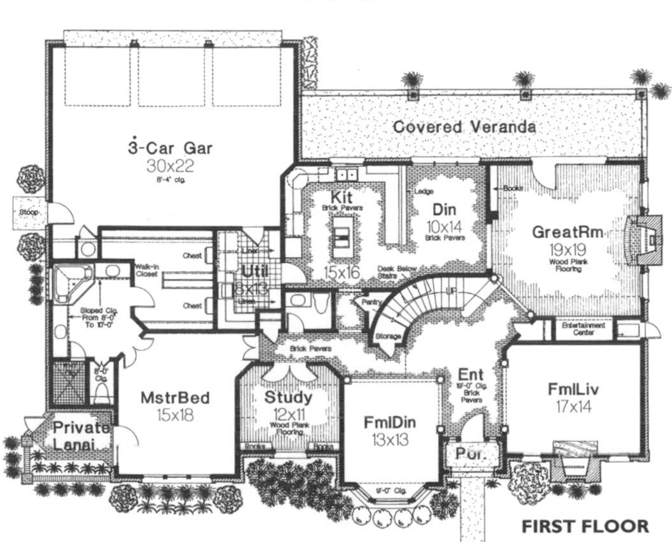

73'-0"
56'-6 1/2"
3-Car Gar
30x22
Covered Veranda
Kit
Din
10x14
GreatRm
19x19
15x16
Util
MstrBed
15x18
Study
12x11
FmlDin
13x13
Ent
FmlLiv
17x14
Por.
Private Lanai

FIRST FLOOR

Country Estate Home

Price Code: I

- This plan features:
  Four bedrooms
  — Three full and one half baths
- Impressive two-story Entry with a lovely curved staircase
- Formal Living and Dining rooms have columns and decorative windows
- Wood plank flooring, a large fireplace and Veranda access accent Great Room
- Hub Kitchen with brick pavers, extended serving counter, bright Breakfast Area, and nearby Utility/Garage Entry
- Private Master Bedroom suite offers a Private Lanai and plush Dressing Area
- Future Playroom offers many options
- This home is designed with a slab foundation

FIRST FLOOR — 2,441 SQ. FT.
SECOND FLOOR — 1,039 SQ. FT.
BONUS — 271 SQ. FT.
GARAGE — 660 SQ. FT.

TOTAL LIVING AREA:
3,480 SQ. FT.

PLAN NO.20161

Delightful Doll House

PRICE CODE: A

- This plan features:
  - — Three bedrooms
  - — Two full baths
- A sloped ceiling in the Living Room which also has a focal point fireplace
- An efficient Kitchen with a peninsula counter and a built-in Pantry
- A decorative ceiling and sliding glass doors to the Deck in the Dining Room
- A Master Suite with a decorative ceiling, ample closet space and a private full Bath
- Two additional Bedrooms that share a full hall Bath
- This home is designed with basement, slab and crawl space foundation options

MAIN FLOOR — 1,307 SQ. FT.
BASEMENT — 1,298 SQ. FT.
GARAGE — 462 SQ. FT.

TOTAL LIVING AREA:
1,307 SQ. FT.

Rear Elevation

MAIN FLOOR

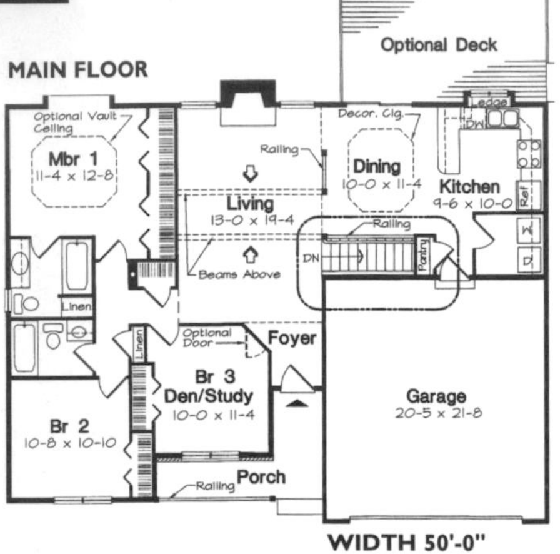
Optional Deck
Optional Vault Ceiling
Mbr 1
11-4 x 12-8
Decor. Clg.
Railing
Dining
10-0 x 11-4
Kitchen
9-6 x 10-0
Living
13-0 x 19-4
Beams Above
Optional Door
Foyer
Br 3
Den/Study
10-0 x 11-4
Br 2
10-8 x 10-10
Garage
20-5 x 21-8
Porch

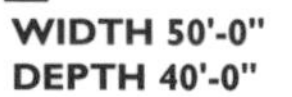
WIDTH 50'-0"
DEPTH 40'-0"

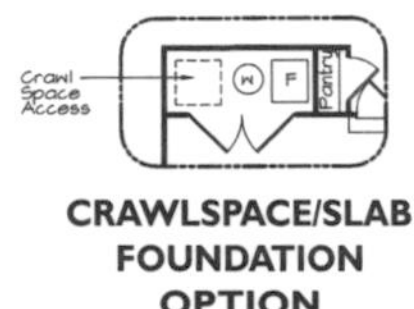
Crawl Space Access
CRAWLSPACE/SLAB FOUNDATION OPTION

PLAN NO.99449

Beautiful See-Through Fireplace

PRICE CODE: E

- This plan features:
  - — Four bedrooms
  - — Two full and one half baths
- Large repeating windows to the rear of the Great Room illuminate naturally
- The Great Room and the cozy Hearth Room share a beautiful see-through fireplace
- The bayed Breakfast Area is a bright and cheery way start your day
- The gourmet Kitchen includes a Pantry, work island, ample corner space and a corner sink
- Secluded Master Suite has a skylight in the Dressing Area and a large walk-in closet
- The secondary Bedrooms share a generous, compartmented Bathroom
- This home is designed with a basement foundation
- Alternate foundation options available at an additional charge. Please call 1-800-235-5700 for more information.

FIRST FLOOR — 1,733 SQ. FT.
SECOND FLOOR — 672 SQ. FT.
BASEMENT — 1,733 SQ. FT.
GARAGE — 613 SQ. FT.

TOTAL LIVING AREA:
2,405 SQ. FT.

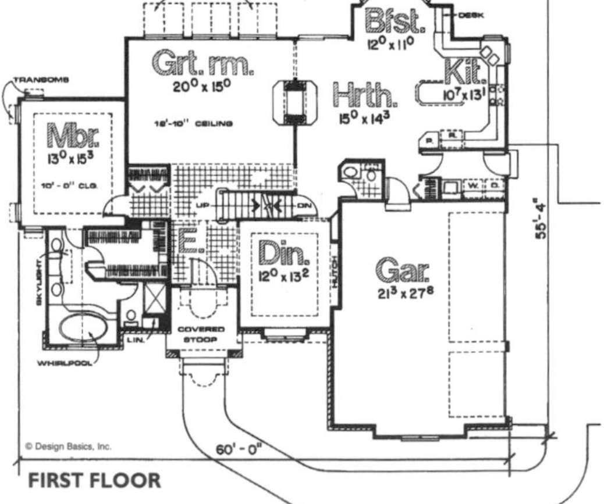
TRANSOMS
Bfst.
Grt. rm.
Hrth.
Kit.
Mbr.
Din.
Gar.
55'-4"
60'-0"
COVERED STOOP
WHIRLPOOL
© Design Basics, Inc.
FIRST FLOOR

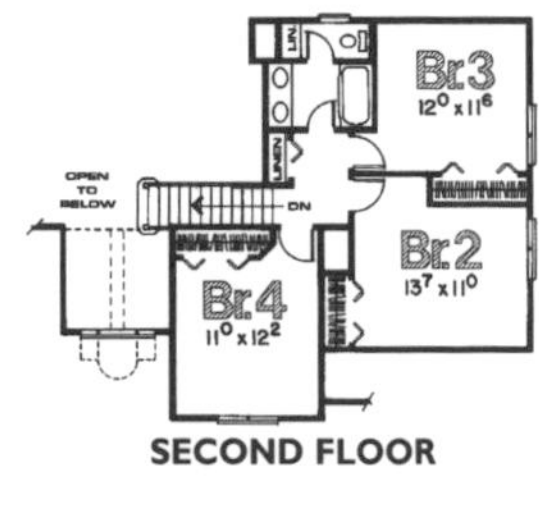
Br.3
Br.2
Br.4
OPEN TO BELOW
SECOND FLOOR

PLAN NO. 99452

FIRST FLOOR

SECOND FLOOR

Traditional Home

Price Code: G

- This plan features:
  - — Four bedrooms
  - — Two full, one three-quarter and one half baths
- Dining Room has a built-in hutch and a bay window
- Cozy Den and Great Room have high ceilings and transom windows
- The warm Gathering Room features a fireplace and a cathedral ceiling
- This home is designed with a basement foundation
- Alternate foundation options available at an additional charge. Please call 1-800-235-5700 for more information.

FIRST FLOOR — 2,158 SQ. FT.
SECOND FLOOR — 821 SQ. FT.
BASEMENT — 2,158 SQ. FT.
GARAGE — 692 SQ. FT.

TOTAL LIVING AREA:
2,979 SQ. FT.

PLAN NO. 20164

Photography supplied by Gauthier Roofing and Siding

Rear Elevation

Easy Living

Price Code: A

- This plan features:
- — Three bedrooms
- — Two full baths
- A dramatic sloped ceiling and a massive fireplace in the Living Room
- A Dining Room crowned by a sloping ceiling and a plant shelf also has sliding doors to the Deck
- A U-shaped Kitchen with abundant cabinets, a window over the sink and a walk-in Pantry
- A Master Suite with a private full Bath, decorative ceiling and walk-in closet
- This home is designed with basement, slab and crawlspace foundation options

MAIN FLOOR — 1,456 SQ. FT.
BASEMENT — 1,448 SQ. FT.
GARAGE — 452 SQ. FT.

TOTAL LIVING AREA:
1,456 SQ. FT.

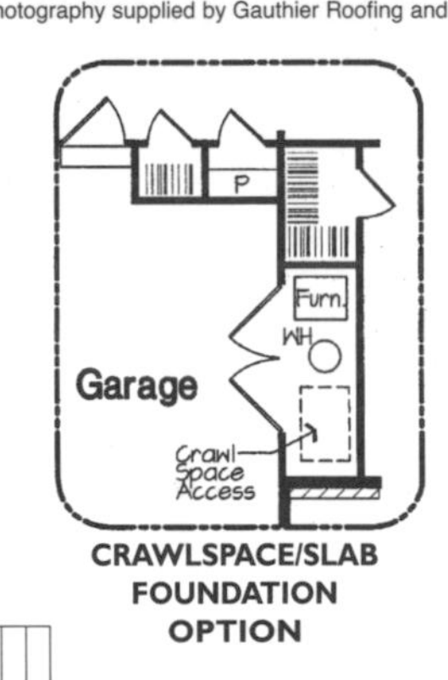
P
Furn.
WH
Garage
Crawl Space Access

CRAWLSPACE/SLAB FOUNDATION OPTION

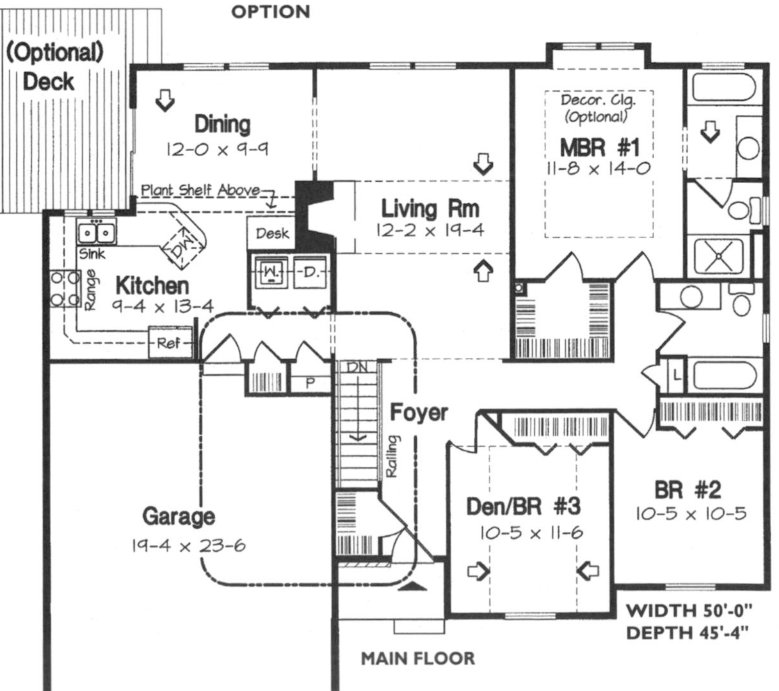
(Optional) Deck
Dining
12-0 x 9-9
Plant Shelf Above
Decor. Clg. (Optional)
MBR #1
11-8 x 14-0
Living Rm
12-2 x 19-4
Desk
Sink
DW
Range
Kitchen
9-4 x 13-4
W. D.
Ref
P
DN
Foyer
Railing
Garage
19-4 x 23-6
Den/BR #3
10-5 x 11-6
BR #2
10-5 x 10-5
L
WIDTH 50'-0"
DEPTH 45'-4"

MAIN FLOOR

To order your Blueprints, call 1-800-235-5700

Family Friendly

PRICE CODE: B

PLAN NO.65077

This plan features:
- Three bedrooms
- One full bath
- Angles and arches define this home's facade
- The open design of the community areas creates a hub for family activity
- The Bedrooms are isolated in the left wing of the home and share a luxurious full Bath
- Counter space, including a centralized island, abounds in the Kitchen
- This home is designed with a basement foundation

AIN FLOOR — 1,504 SQ. FT.
ASEMENT — 1,504 SQ. FT.
ARAGE — 424 SQ. FT.
RCH — 60 SQ. FT.

TOTAL LIVING AREA:
1,504 SQ. FT.

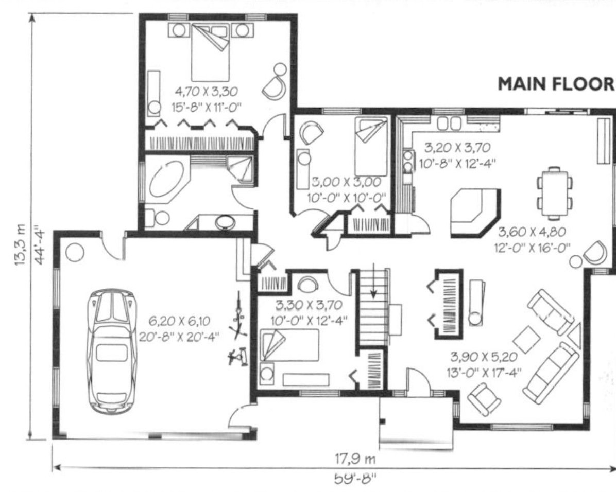

MAIN FLOOR
4,70 X 3,30
15'-8" X 11'-0"
3,00 X 3,00
10'-0" X 10'-0"
3,20 X 3,70
10'-8" X 12'-4"
3,60 X 4,80
12'-0" X 16'-0"
6,20 X 6,10
20'-8" X 20'-4"
3,30 X 3,70
10'-0" X 12'-4"
3,90 X 5,20
13'-0" X 17'-4"
13,3 m
44'-4"
17,9 m
59'-8"

Friendly Front Porch

PRICE CODE: B

PLAN NO.94138

This plan features:
- Three bedrooms
- One full and one half baths
- Country, homey feeling with wraparound Porch
- Adjoining Living Room and Dining Room creates spacious feeling
- Efficient Kitchen easily serves Dining Area with extended counter and a built-in Pantry
- Spacious Family Room with optional fireplace and access to Laundry/Garage Entry
- Large Master Bedroom with a walk-in closet and access to a full Bath, offers a private Bath option
- Two additional Bedrooms with ample closets and full Bath access
- This home is designed with a basement foundation

RST FLOOR — 900 SQ. FT.
COND FLOOR — 676 SQ. FT.
ASEMENT — 900 SQ. FT.
ARAGE — 448 SQ. FT.

TOTAL LIVING AREA:
1,576 SQ. FT.

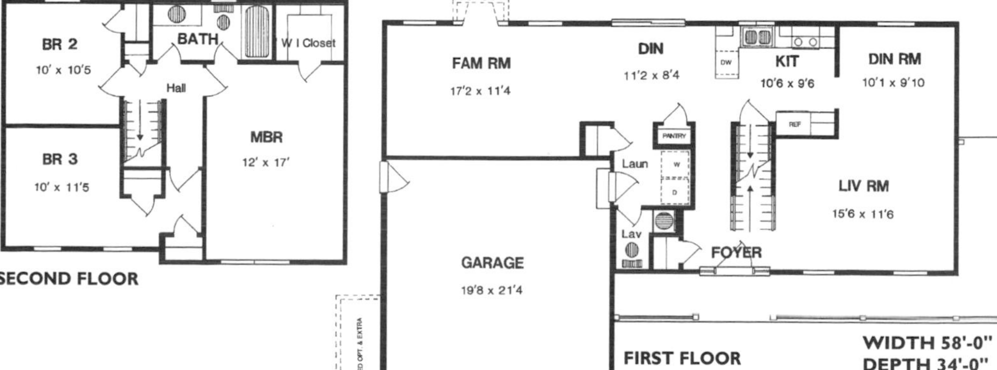

BR 2
10' x 10'5
BATH
W I Closet
Hall
BR 3
10' x 11'5
MBR
12' x 17'
SECOND FLOOR
FAM RM
17'2 x 11'4
DIN
11'2 x 8'4
KIT
10'6 x 9'6
DIN RM
10'1 x 9'10
PANTRY
REF
Laun
LIV RM
15'6 x 11'6
Lav
FOYER
GARAGE
19'8 x 21'4
FIRST FLOOR
WIDTH 58'-0"
DEPTH 34'-0"

PLAN NO.97108

Classic Ranch

PRICE CODE: C

■ This plan features:
- Three bedrooms
- Two full baths

■ A fabulous Great Room with a step ceiling and a cozy fireplace

■ An elegant arched soffit connects the Great Room to the Dining Room

■ The Kitchen has wraparound counters, a center island and a Nook

■ The Master Bedroom is completed with a walk-in close and a private Bath

■ Two additional Bedrooms with ample closet space shar a full Bath

■ This home is designed with a basement foundation

MAIN FLOOR — 1,794 SQ. FT.
BASEMENT — 1,794 SQ. FT.

TOTAL LIVING AREA:
1,794 SQ. FT.

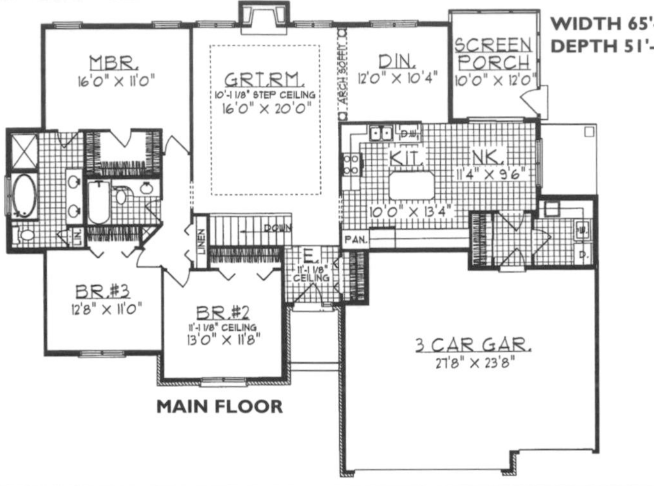
MBR.
16'0" X 11'0"
GRT.RM.
10'-1 1/8" STEP CEILING
16'0" X 20'0"
ARCH SOFFIT
DIN.
12'0" X 10'4"
SCREEN PORCH
10'0" X 12'0"
KIT.
10'0" X 13'4"
NK.
11'4" X 9'6"
PAN.
LINEN
DOWN
E.
11'-1 1/8" CEILING
BR.#3
12'8" X 11'0"
BR.#2
11'-1 1/8" CEILING
13'0" X 11'8"
3 CAR GAR.
27'8" X 23'8"
MAIN FLOOR

WIDTH 65'-4"
DEPTH 51'-4"

PLAN NO.93265

Plan for the Future

PRICE CODE: A

■ This plan features:
- Three bedrooms
- Two full baths

■ Entry leads up to Living Area accented by a vaulted ceiling and arched window

■ Compact, efficient Kitchen with serving counter/snack bar, serves Dining Area and Deck beyon

■ Comfortable Master Bedroom with a walk-in closet and double vanity Bath with a window tub

■ Two additional Bedrooms with large closets, share a full Bath

■ Entry leads down to Laundry, Garage and future Playroom

■ This home is designed with a basement foundation

MAIN FLOOR — 1,269 SQ. FT.
BASEMENT — 382 SQ. FT.
GARAGE — 598 SQ. FT.

TOTAL LIVING AREA:
1,325 SQ. FT.

WIDTH 45'-0"
DEPTH 36'-0"

Sundeck
14-0 x 10-0
Dining
10-0 x 9-6
M.Bath
Master Bdrm.
14-0 x 14-0
Kit.
8-0 x 9-6
Bth.2
Living Area
14-8 x 15-6
Entry
Bdrm.3
9-4 x 11-6
Bdrm.2
10-4 x 9-6
FIRST FLOOR

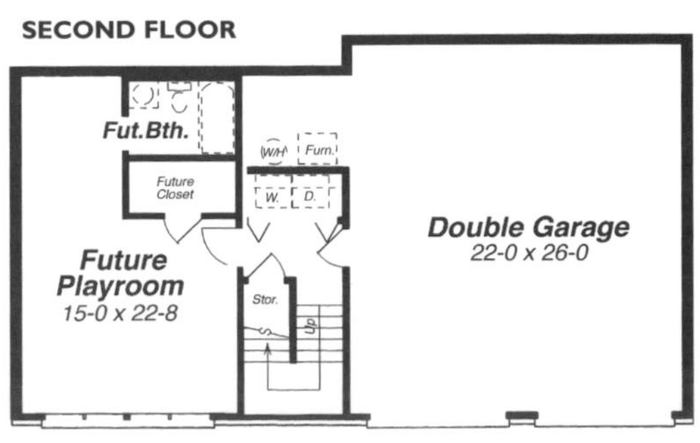
SECOND FLOOR
Fut.Bth.
Future Closet
W/H
Furn.
W.
D.
Future Playroom
15-0 x 22-8
Stor.
Up
Double Garage
22-0 x 26-0

Family Living Made Easy

PRICE CODE: B

PLAN NO. 35001

Γhis plan features:
- Three bedrooms
- Two full and one half baths
- A welcoming Country Porch sheltering the entrance
- A large Living Room that flows into the Dining Room :reating a great area for entertaining
- An efficient U-shaped Kitchen that includes an informal 3reakfast area and a Laundry Center
- A convenient entrance from the Garage into the Kitchen
- A private Master Suite with a full Bath and two closets
- A Den/Office with ample closet space, enabling it to louble as a Guest Room
- An optional Deck/Patio that will increase your living space in the warmer weather
- Γhis home is designed with basement, slab and :rawlspace foundation options

ɛST FLOOR — 1,081 SQ. FT.
ɔOND FLOOR — 528 SQ. FT.

TOTAL LIVING AREA:* 1,609 *SQ. FT.

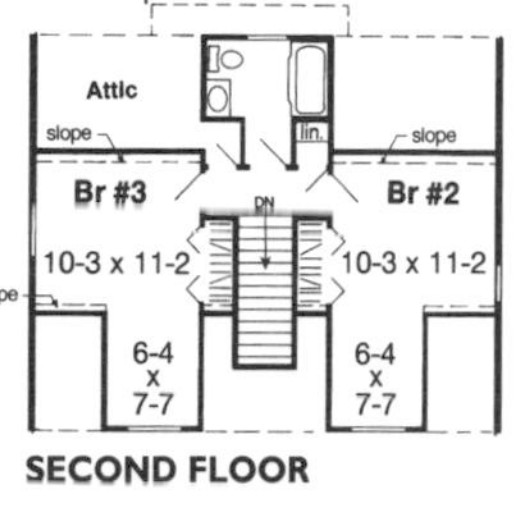

Attic
slope
lin.
slope
Br #3
DN
Br #2
10-3 x 11-2
10-3 x 11-2
slope
6-4
x
7-7
6-4
x
7-7

SECOND FLOOR

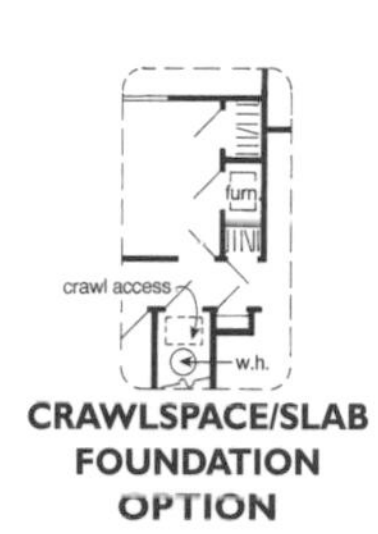

furn.
crawl access
w.h.

CRAWLSPACE/SLAB FOUNDATION OPTION

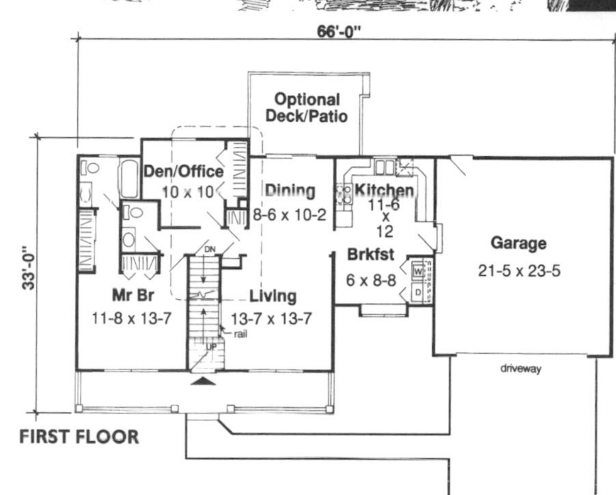

66'-0"
Optional
Deck/Patio
Den/Office
10 x 10
Dining
8-6 x 10-2
Kitchen
11-6
x
12
Brkfst
6 x 8-8
Garage
21-5 x 23-5
33'-0"
DN
Mr Br
11-8 x 13-7
Living
13-7 x 13-7
rail
UP
driveway

FIRST FLOOR

Secluded Vacation Retreat

PRICE CODE: C

PLAN NO. 91704

Γhis plan features:
- Two bedrooms
- One full and two three-quarter baths
- A high vaulted ceiling in the Living Area with a large masonry fireplace and circular stairway
- A wall of windows along the full cathedral height of the Living Area
- A Kitchen with ample storage and counter space including a sink with a chopping block
- Private Baths for each of the bedrooms with 10-foot closets
- A Loft with windowed doors opening to a Deck
- Γhis home is designed with a crawlspace foundation

AIN FLOOR — 1,448 SQ. FT.
ɒFT — 389 SQ. FT.
ʌRPORT — 312 SQ. FT.

TOTAL LIVING AREA:* 1,837 *SQ. FT.

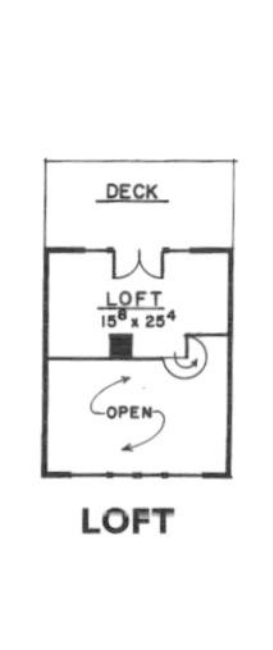

DECK
LOFT
OPEN

LOFT

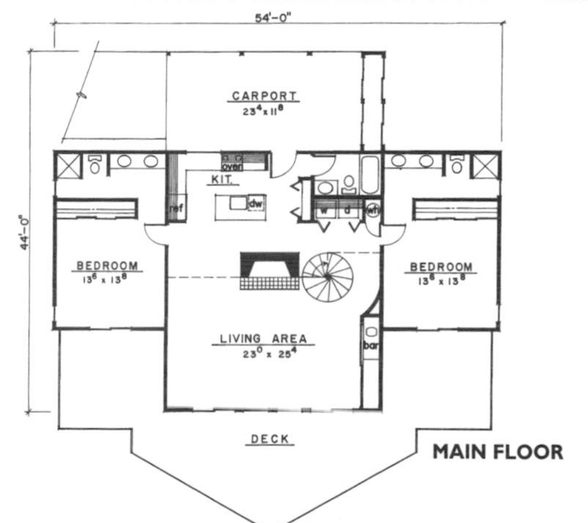

54'-0"
CARPORT
oven
KIT.
dw
ref
44'-0"
BEDROOM
BEDROOM
LIVING AREA
bar
DECK

MAIN FLOOR

PLAN NO. 97712

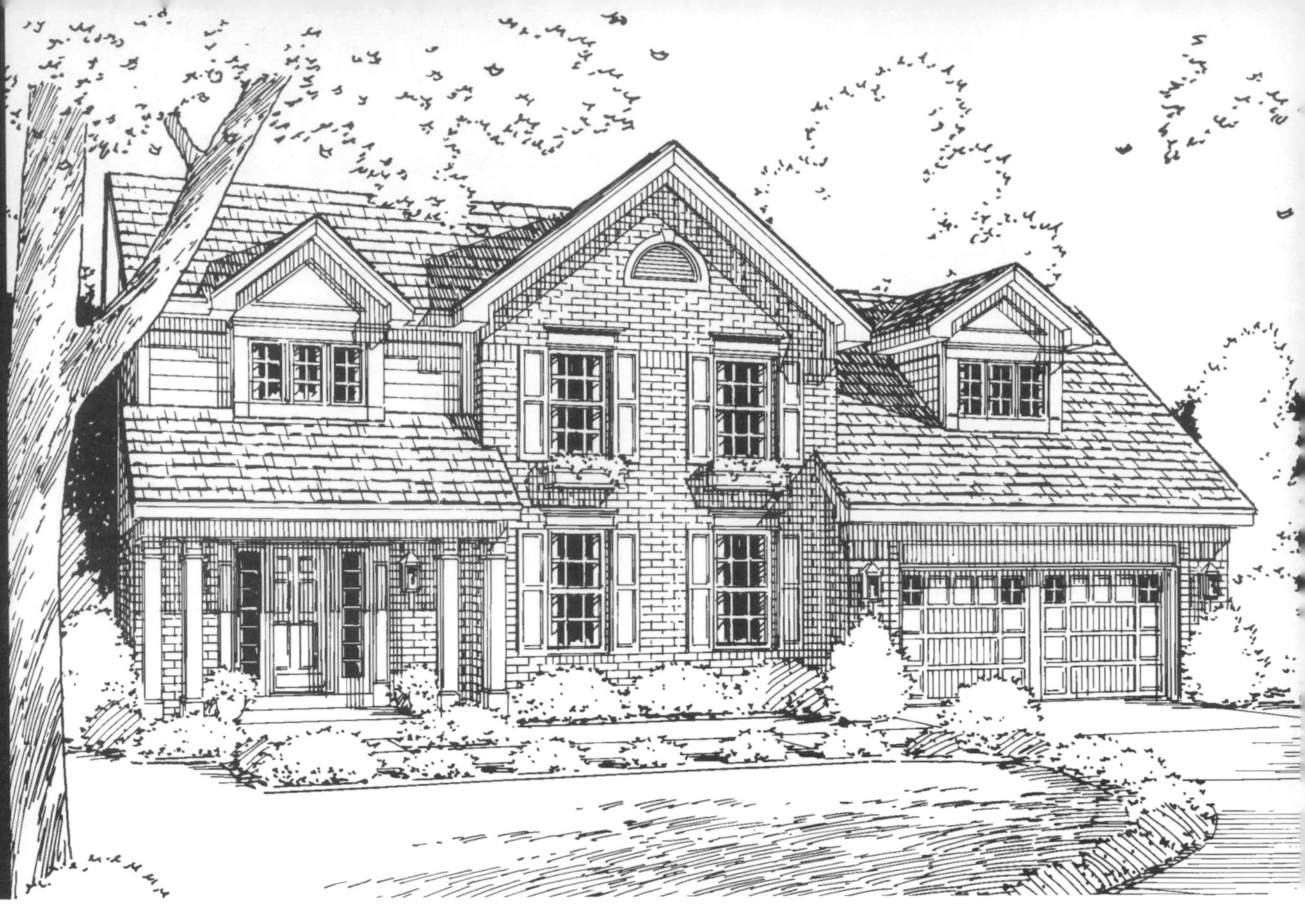

Designed for a Narrow Lot

Price Code: B

- This plan features:
- — Three bedrooms
- — Two full and one half baths
- Enter the home through the front door with transom and sidelights
- The Great Room with its corner fireplace is just steps beyond the Foyer
- The Dining Room accesses the rear Patio
- The Bedrooms are all on the second floor and have ample closets
- A bonus room is accessed from the second floor
- This home is designed with a basement foundation

FIRST FLOOR — 798 SQ. FT.
SECOND FLOOR — 777 SQ. FT.
BONUS ROOM — 242 SQ. FT.
BASEMENT — 798 SQ. FT.

TOTAL LIVING AREA:
1,575 SQ. FT.

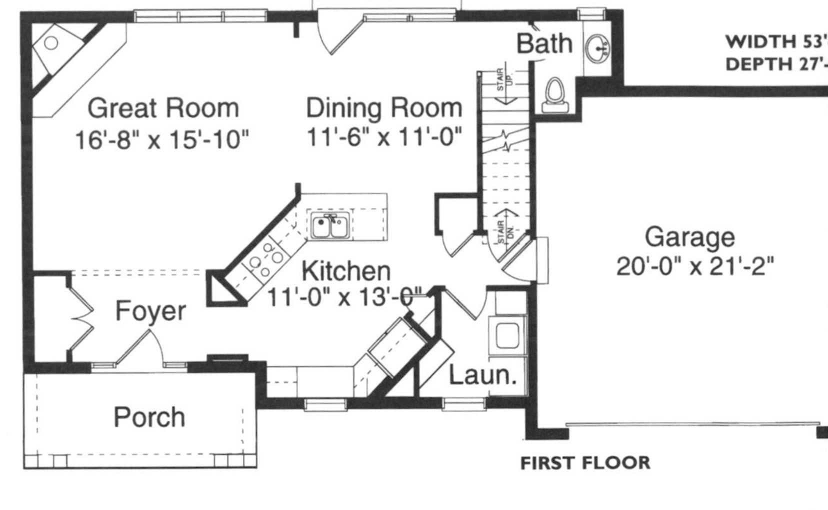

Bath
WIDTH 53'
DEPTH 27'
Great Room
16'-8" x 15'-10"
Dining Room
11'-6" x 11'-0"
Garage
20'-0" x 21'-2"
Kitchen
11'-0" x 13'-0"
Foyer
Laun.
Porch

FIRST FLOOR

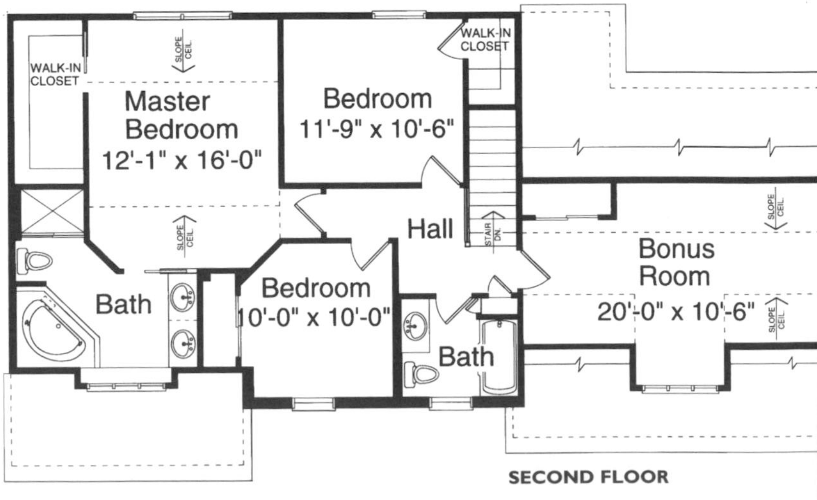

WALK-IN CLOSET
Master Bedroom
12'-1" x 16'-0"
Bedroom
11'-9" x 10'-6"
Hall
Bath
Bedroom
10'-0" x 10'-0"
Bath
Bonus Room
20'-0" x 10'-6"

SECOND FLOOR

Exquisite Master Suite

Price Code: C

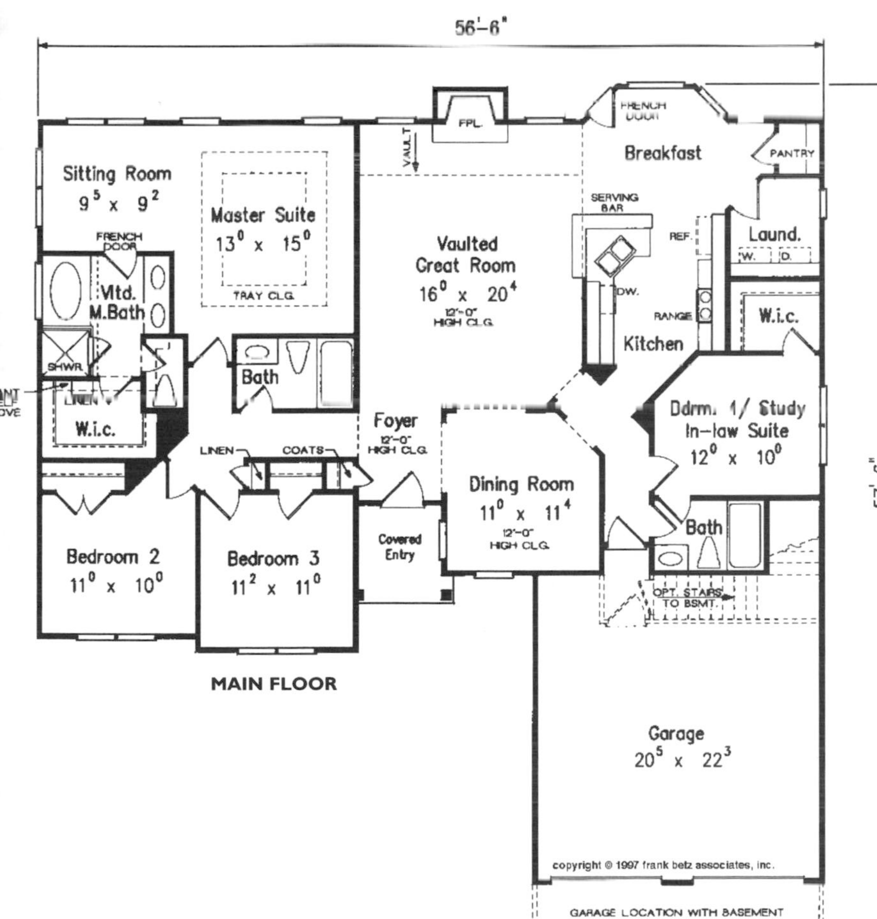
56'-6"
57'-6"
Sitting Room
9⁵ x 9²
Master Suite
13⁰ x 15⁰
TRAY CLG.
FRENCH DOOR
Mstr. M.Bath
SHWR.
LINEN
W.i.c.
Bath
FPL.
VAULT
Vaulted Great Room
16⁰ x 20⁴
12'-0" HIGH CLG.
FRENCH DOOR
Breakfast
PANTRY
SERVING BAR
REF.
DW.
RANGE
Kitchen
Laund.
W. D.
W.i.c.
Bdrm. 4/ Study In-law Suite
12⁰ x 10⁰
Foyer
12'-0" HIGH CLG.
LINEN
COATS
Dining Room
11⁰ x 11⁴
12'-0" HIGH CLG.
Bath
OPT. STAIRS TO BSMT.
Bedroom 2
11⁰ x 10⁰
Bedroom 3
11² x 11⁰
Covered Entry
MAIN FLOOR
Garage
20⁵ x 22³
copyright © 1997 frank betz associates, inc.
GARAGE LOCATION WITH BASEMENT

- This plan features:
  - — Four Bedrooms
  - — Three full baths
- Formal Foyer with a convenient coat closet
- Vaulted ceiling over the Great Room highlighted by a fireplace flanked by windows
- Cozy Breakfast Bay with French door to rear yard
- Master Suite pampered by private Sitting Room and luxurious Master Bath
- This home is designed with basement and crawlspace foundation options

MAIN FLOOR — 1,915 SQ. FT.
GARAGE — 489 SQ. FT.
BASEMENT — 1,932 SQ. FT.

TOTAL LIVING AREA:
1,915 SQ. FT.

PLAN NO.97633

Three Car Garage

PRICE CODE: I

- This plan features:
  - — Five bedrooms
  - — Four full and one half baths
- The Living and Dining Rooms are located off the Foy
- Columns separate the Family Room from the Kitchen
- A Study/Bedroom is tucked away on the first floor
- The Laundry Room is located upstairs
- The Master Suite is warmed by a fireplace in its Sitting Room
- This home is designed with basement and crawlspace foundation options

FIRST FLOOR — 1,577 SQ. FT.
SECOND FLOOR — 1,689 SQ. FT.
BASEMENT — 1,577 SQ. FT.
GARAGE — 694 SQ. FT.

TOTAL LIVING AREA:
3,266 SQ. FT.

WIDTH 59'-4"
DEPTH 49'-0"

Two Story Family Room 20² x 14¹⁰ · Breakfast · Kitchen · Study/Bedroom 5 12⁰ x 12⁰ · Pwdr. · Bath · Three Car Garage 20⁵ x 32² · Dining Room 13² x 13⁴ · Two Story Foyer · Living Room 13⁰ x 13⁸ · Covered Porch

FIRST FLOOR

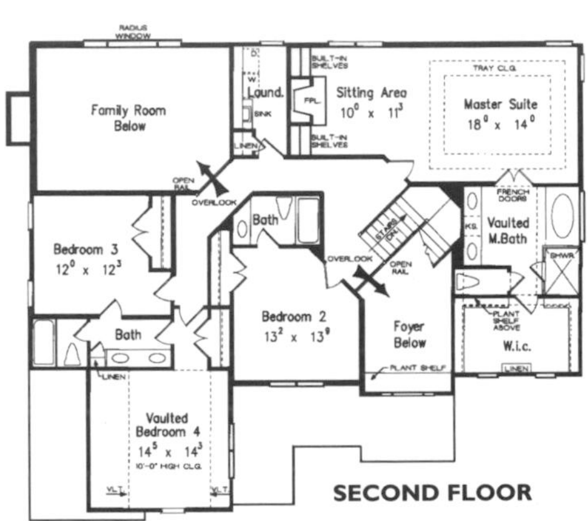

Family Room Below
Laund.
Sitting Area 10⁰ x 11³
Master Suite 18⁰ x 14⁰
Bedroom 3 12⁰ x 12³
Bath
Vaulted M.Bath
Bath
Bedroom 2 13² x 13⁸
Foyer Below
W.i.c.
Vaulted Bedroom 4 14⁵ x 14³
SECOND FLOOR

PLAN NO.91746

Economy at It's Best

PRICE CODE: B

- This plan features:
  - — Three bedrooms
  - — Two full and one three-quarter baths
- Attractive Porch adds to the curb appeal of this economical to build home
- A vaulted ceiling topping the Entry, Living and Dining Rooms
- A lovely bay window, adding sophistication to the Liv Room, which includes direct access to a side Deck
- A Master Suite with a walk-in closet, and a private compartment Bath with an oversized shower
- Two additional Bedrooms share a full hall Bath toppe by a skylight
- A vaulted ceiling topping the Dining Area which flow from the efficient island Kitchen
- A walk-in Pantry adds to the storage space of the cook island Kitchen, which is equipped with a double sink with a window above
- Garage offers direct entrance to the house
- This home is designed with a slab foundation

MAIN FLOOR — 1,717 SQ. FT.
GARAGE — 782 SQ. FT.

TOTAL LIVING AREA:
1,717 SQ. FT.

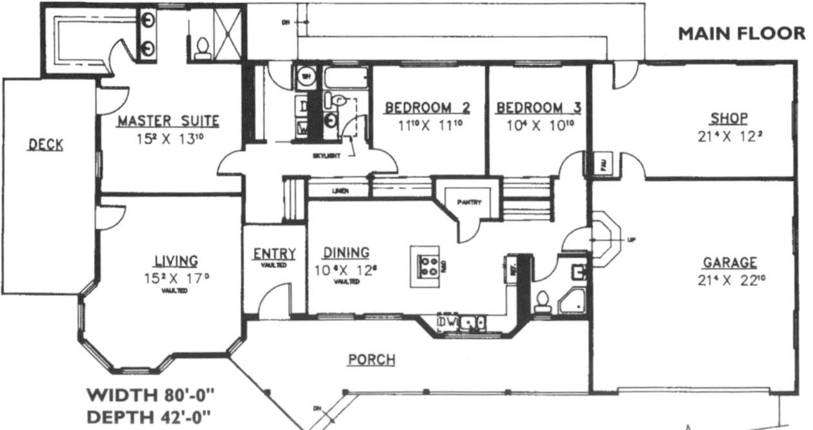

MAIN FLOOR
DECK
MASTER SUITE 15² X 13¹⁰
BEDROOM 2 11¹⁰ X 11¹⁰
BEDROOM 3 10⁴ X 10¹⁰
SHOP 21⁴ X 12²
LIVING 15² X 17⁰
ENTRY
DINING 10⁴ X 12⁸
GARAGE 21⁴ X 22¹⁰
PORCH
WIDTH 80'-0"
DEPTH 42'-0"

Enchanting Entry

PRICE CODE: C

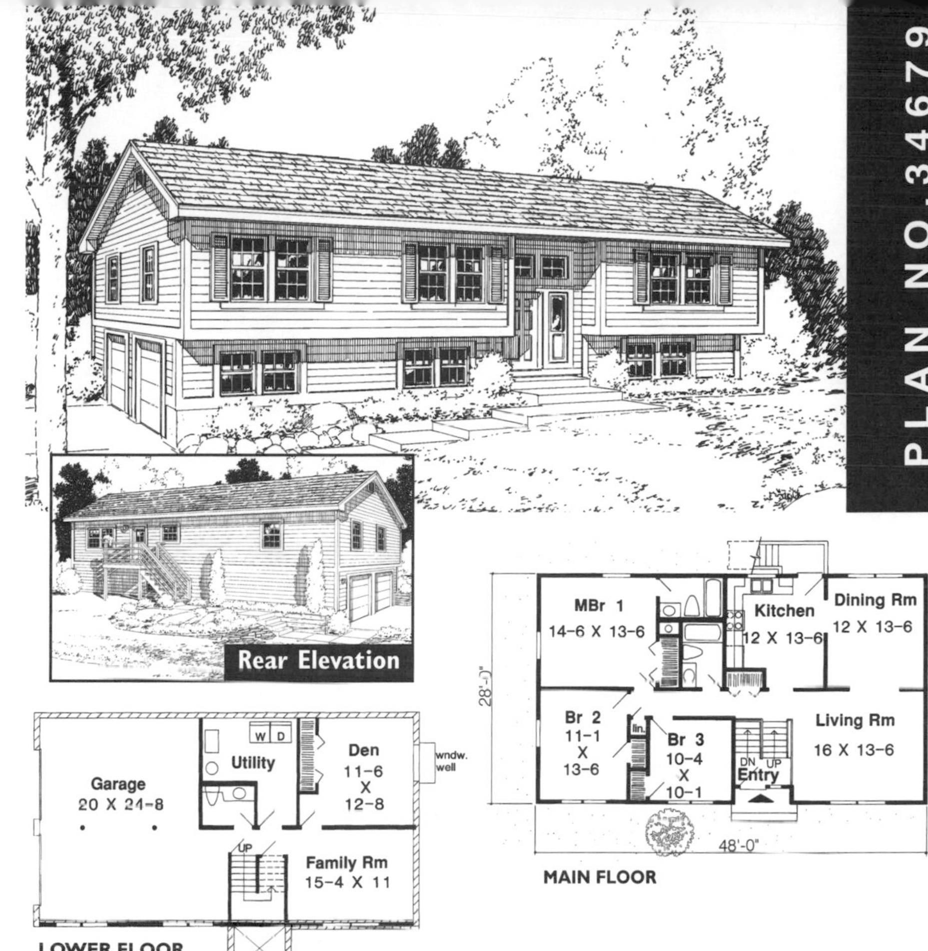

PLAN NO.34679
Rear Elevation
MBr 1
14-6 X 13-6
Kitchen
12 X 13-6
Dining Rm
12 X 13-6
Br 2
11-1
X
13-6
lin.
Br 3
10-4
X
10-1
DN UP
Entry
Living Rm
16 X 13-6
28'-0"
48'-0"
MAIN FLOOR
Garage
20 X 24-8
W D
Utility
Den
11-6
X
12-8
wndw. well
UP
Family Rm
15-4 X 11
LOWER FLOOR

Ihis plan features:
- Three bedrooms
- Two full and one half baths
- Split Entry leads down to Family Room, Utility Room, Den, half bath and two-car Garage
- Up a half-flight of stairs leads to the large Living Room highlighted by a double window
- Dining Room convenient to Living Room and Kitchen
- Efficient Kitchen with rear yard access and room for eating
- Corner Master Bedroom offers an over-sized closet and private Bath
- Two additional Bedrooms with double windows, share a full Bath
- This home is designed with a basement foundation

AIN FLOOR — 1,331 SQ. FT.
WER FLOOR — 663 SQ. FT.
RAGE — 584 SQ. FT.

TOTAL LIVING AREA:
1,994 SQ. FT.

For the Growing Family

PRICE CODE: C

PLAN NO.98473

his plan features:
- Three bedrooms
- Three full baths
- Formal areas are located to either side of the impressive two-story Foyer
- An open rail staircase adorning the Living Room while the Dining Room features easy access to the Kitchen
- Kitchen equipped with a corner double sink and a wrap-around snack bar is open to the Family Room and Breakfast Area
- Fireplace in the Family Room giving warmth and atmosphere to living space
- Secondary Bedroom or Study privately located in the left rear corner of the home with direct access to a full Bath
- Master Suite decorated by a tray ceiling in the Bedroom and a vaulted ceiling in the Master Bath
- This home is designed with basement and crawlspace foundation options

ST FLOOR — 1,103 SQ. FT.
COND FLOOR — 759 SQ. FT.
SEMENT — 1,103 SQ. FT.
RAGE — 420 SQ. FT.

TOTAL LIVING AREA:
1,862 SQ. FT.

50'-4"
35'-0"
Bedroom 4/ Study 10^0 x 11^7
Bath
Pantry
French Door
Breakfast
Family Room 17^2 x 13^2
FPL.
D. W.
Range
Kitchen
DW.
REF.
Coats
Stairs DN.
Stairs UP
Open Rail
Garage 19^8 x 20^4
Dining Room 10^0 x 11^0
Two Story Foyer
Living Room 10^6 x 10^0
Covered Porch
© Frank Betz Associates, Inc.

FIRST FLOOR

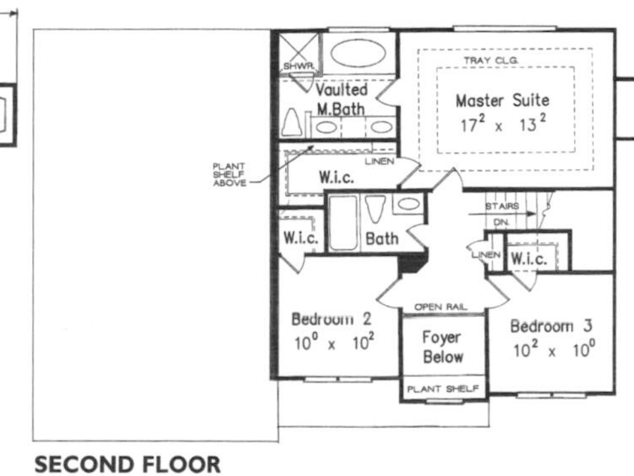

SHWR.
Vaulted M.Bath
Tray Clg.
Master Suite
17^2 x 13^2
Plant Shelf Above
W.i.c.
Linen
Stairs DN.
W.i.c.
Bath
Linen
W.i.c.
Open Rail
Bedroom 2
10^0 x 10^2
Foyer Below
Bedroom 3
10^2 x 10^0
Plant Shelf

SECOND FLOOR

PLAN NO.99081

Easy Living Ranch

PRICE CODE: B

- This plan features:
- — Three bedrooms
- — Two full baths
- Distinct exterior features, including vinyl siding, a ser of gables, an arched window in the Dining Room and protected front door with sidelights
- Dining Room with a 14-foot ceiling
- Directly behind the Dining Room is the Kitchen with serving bar
- Breakfast Area with easy access to the Great Room
- Master Bedroom crowned in a tray ceiling
- Master Bath including a large walk-in closet and separate shower and garden tub
- This home is designed with a basement foundation

MAIN FLOOR — 1,590 SQ. FT.
BASEMENT — 1,590 SQ. FT.
GARAGE — 560 SQ. FT.

TOTAL LIVING AREA:
1,590 SQ. FT.

DINETTE
11' x 8'
WALK-IN
CLOSET
MASTER
BATH
BEDROOM
11' x 10'-8"
GREAT
ROOM
15' x 18'
KITCHEN
11' x 10'
MASTER
BEDROOM
15' 8 x 13' 4
CLOSET
BATH
FOYER
DINING ROOM
11' x 10'
BEDROOM
11' x 10'-8"
2-CAR GARAGE
22' x 23'
MAIN FLOOR
80'-8"
53'-8"

PLAN NO.65078

Contemporary Living

PRICE CODE: A

- This plan features:
- — Two bedrooms
- — One full bath
- First-time buyers or empty-nesters who are looking to downsize will love this home
- A focal-point fireplace in the Living Room is flanked by tall arched windows
- The Kitchen provides ample space and adjoins the Dining Room
- The two Bedrooms have large closets and share the double vanity Bath
- This home is designed with a basement foundation

MAIN FLOOR — 1,059 SQ. FT.
GARAGE — 300 SQ. FT.

TOTAL LIVING AREA:
1,059 SQ. FT.

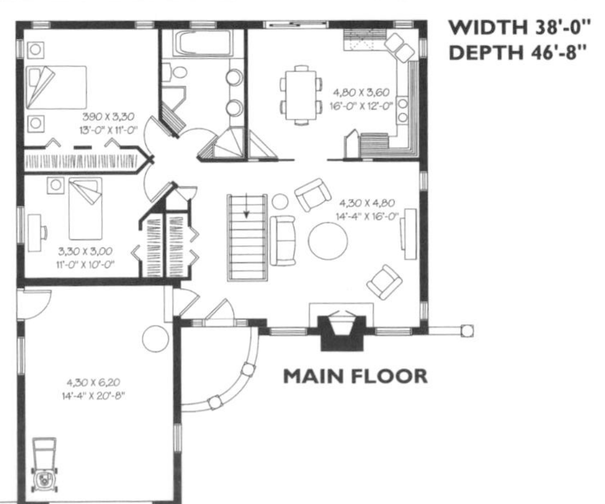
WIDTH 38'-0"
DEPTH 46'-8"
3,90 X 3,30
13'-0" X 11'-0"
4,80 X 3,60
16'-0" X 12'-0"
4,30 X 4,80
14'-4" X 16'-0"
3,30 X 3,00
11'-0" X 10'-0"
4,30 X 6,20
14'-4" X 20'-8"
MAIN FLOOR

PLAN NO. 92642

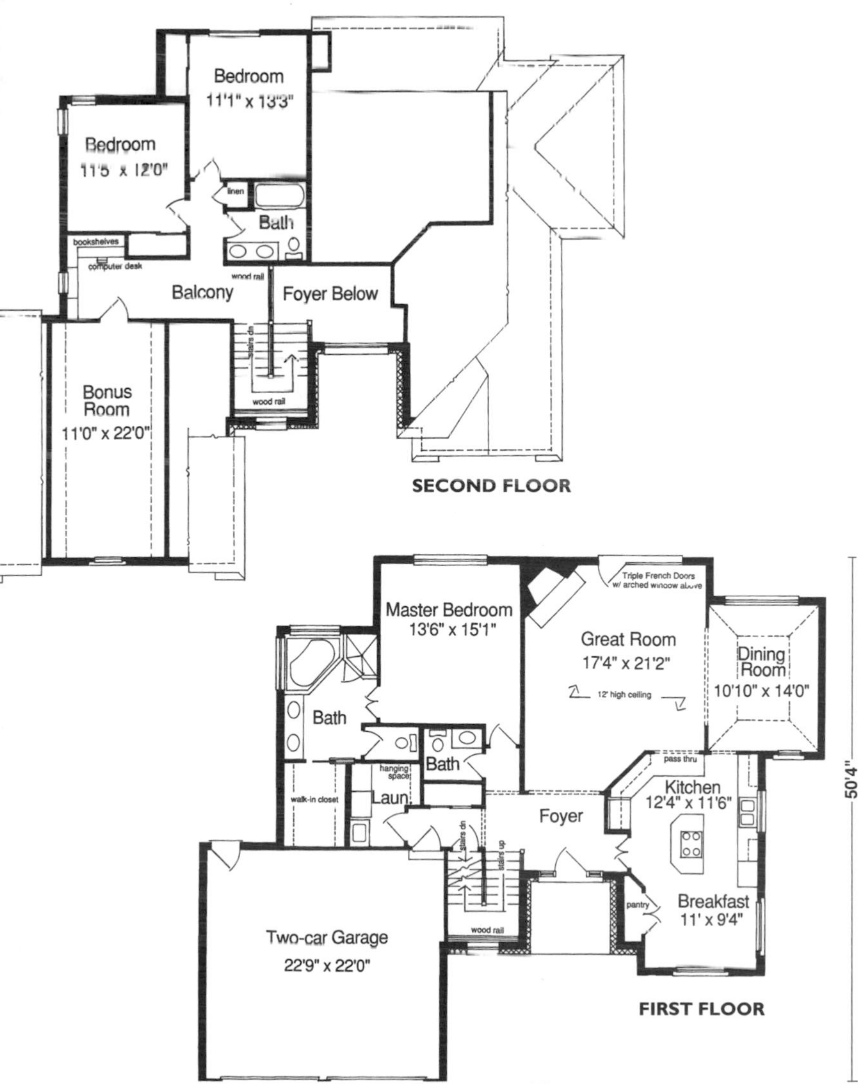
Bedroom
11'1" x 13'3"
Bedroom
11'5" x 12'0"
linen
Bath
bookshelves
computer desk
wood rail
Balcony
Foyer Below
stairs dn
Bonus
Room
11'0" x 22'0"
wood rail
SECOND FLOOR
Master Bedroom
13'6" x 15'1"
Triple French Doors
w/ arched window above
Great Room
17'4" x 21'2"
12' high ceiling
Dining
Room
10'10" x 14'0"
Bath
Bath
hanging space
pass thru
Kitchen
12'4" x 11'6"
walk-in closet
Laun
Foyer
stairs dn
stairs up
pantry
Breakfast
11' x 9'4"
Two-car Garage
22'9" x 22'0"
wood rail
50'4"
FIRST FLOOR
60'

An Elegant, Stylish Manner

Price Code: D

- This plan features:
  - — Three bedrooms
  - — Two full and one half baths
- A high ceiling through the Foyer and Great Room
- A cozy fireplace and a built-in entertainment center in the Great Room
- Kitchen serving the formal Dining Room and the Breakfast Area
- A whirlpool tub, shower stall, his and her vanities and a spacious walk-in closet in the Master Suite
- This home is designed with a basement foundation

FIRST FLOOR — 1,524 SQ. FT.
SECOND FLOOR — 558 SQ. FT.
BONUS ROOM — 267 SQ. FT.
BASEMENT — 1,460 SQ. FT.

TOTAL LIVING AREA:
2,082 SQ. FT.

PLAN NO.20093

Rear Elevation

Porch Adorns Elegant Bay

PRICE CODE: D

■ This plan features:
— Three bedrooms
— Two full and one half baths
■ A Master Suite with a romantic bay window and full Bath
■ Bedrooms with huge closets and use of the full hall B
■ A roomy island Kitchen with a modern, efficient layo
■ A Formal Dining Room with a recessed decorative ceiling
■ Sloping skylit ceilings illuminating the fireplaced Living Room
■ A rear Deck accessible from both the Kitchen and the Living Room
■ This home is designed with a basement foundation

FIRST FLOOR — 1,027 SQ. FT.
SECOND FLOOR — 974 SQ. FT.
GARAGE — 476 SQ. FT.
BASEMENT — 978 SQ. FT.

TOTAL LIVING AREA:
2,001 SQ. FT.

WIDTH 43'-0"
DEPTH 56'-0"

FIRST FLOOR
DECK
LIVING ROOM 14'-0"x19'-4"
DINING 10'-6"x13'-4"
K. 11'-0"x12'-0"
FOYER
BREAKFAST 11'-0"x 9'-6"
PORCH
GARAGE 21'-4"x21'-8"

SECOND FLOOR
BEDROOM 10'-6"x11'-4"
BEDROOM 10'-8"x11'-6"
MASTER BEDROOM 11'-0"x 21'-2"
HALL
BATH

PLAN NO.34603

Rear Elevation

Beckoning Country Porch

PRICE CODE: B

■ This plan features:
— Three bedrooms
— Two full and one half baths
■ Country-styled exterior with dormer windows above friendly front Porch
■ Vaulted ceiling and central fireplace accent the spacic Great Room
■ L-shaped Kitchen/Dining Room with work island anc atrium door to back yard
■ First floor Master Suite with vaulted ceiling, walk-in closet, private bath and optional private Deck with hot tub
■ This home is designed with basement, slab and crawlspace foundation options

FIRST FLOOR — 1,061 SQ. FT.
SECOND FLOOR — 499 SQ. FT.
BASEMENT — 1,061 SQ. FT.

TOTAL LIVING AREA:
1,560 SQ. FT.

FIRST FLOOR
Kitchen 8-1 x 12-7
Dining 9-8 x 12-7 8' clg
Master Br 12 x 14-6 vault clg
Great Room 14-7 x 14-10 vault clg
Porch
Optional Deck w/ Hot Tub
34'-0"
40'-0"

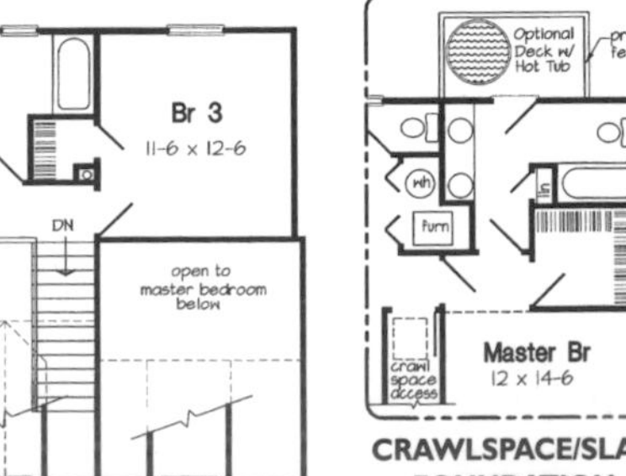

Br 2
10-10 x 12-6
Br 3
11-6 x 12-6
open to great room below
open to master bedroom below

SECOND FLOOR

Master Br 12 x 14-6
CRAWLSPACE/SLAB FOUNDATION OPTION

PLAN NO. 65084

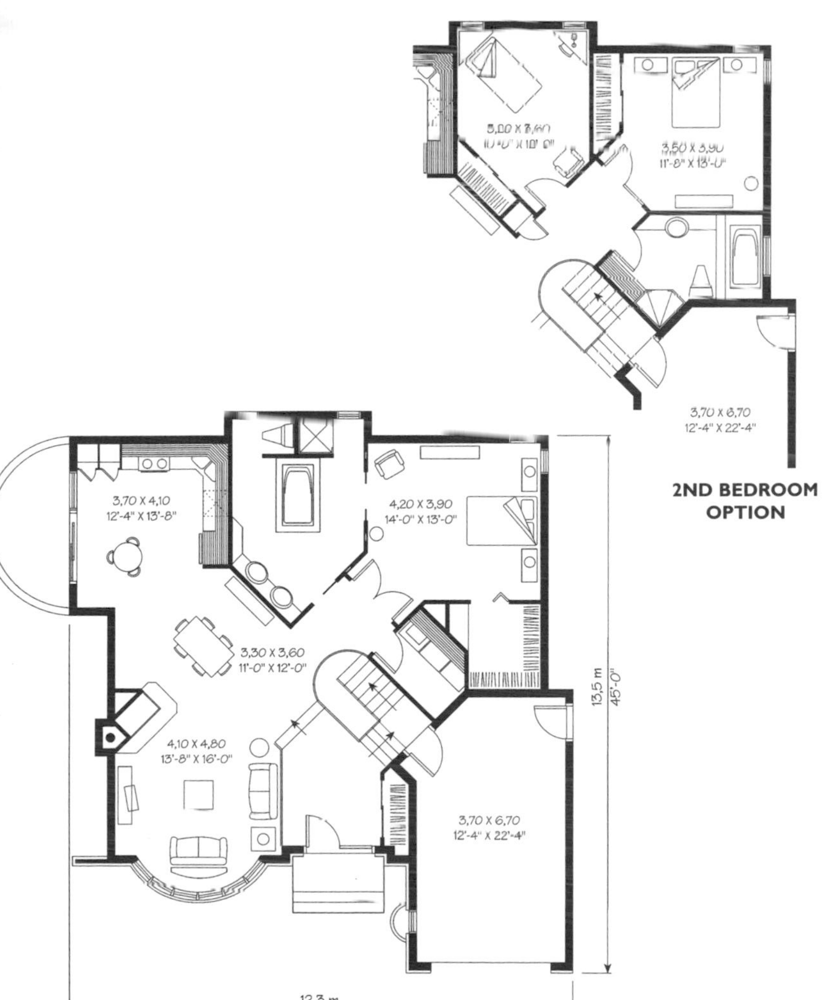

3,50 X 3,90
11'-8" X 13'-0"
3,70 X 6,70
12'-4" X 22'-4"
2ND BEDROOM OPTION
3,70 X 4,10
12'-4" X 13'-8"
4,20 X 3,90
14'-0" X 13'-0"
3,30 X 3,60
11'-0" X 12'-0"
4,10 X 4,80
13'-8" X 16'-0"
3,70 X 6,70
12'-4" X 22'-4"
13,5 m
45'-0"
12,3 m
41'-0"

MAIN FLOOR

Sunlit Simplicity

Price Code: A

- This plan features:
  - — One bedroom
  - — One full bath
- A combination of unique shapes defines this home's design
- Storage space abounds with closets, counters, and cabinets
- A large main floor Bath is centrally located for convenience
- The turreted Living Room provides a sunlit and cozy place for family to gather
- Double doors, topped with a transom, offer an elegant welcome
- This home is designed with a basement foundation

MAIN FLOOR — 1,208 SQ. FT.
GARAGE — 278 SQ. FT.

TOTAL LIVING AREA:
1,208 SQ. FT.

PLAN NO. 97713

Warm and Charming Showplace

Price Code: 1

- This plan features:
  - Four bedrooms
  - Three full and one half baths
- An imposing stone and brick exterior hides a warm and charming interior
- The Great Room has a fireplace and a rear wall of illuminating windows
- A three-car Garage with extra storage space finishes off the plan
- This home is designed with a basement foundation

FIRST FLOOR — 2,479 SQ. FT.
SECOND FLOOR — 956 SQ. FT.
BASEMENT — 2,479 SQ. FT.

TOTAL LIVING AREA:
3,435 SQ. FT.

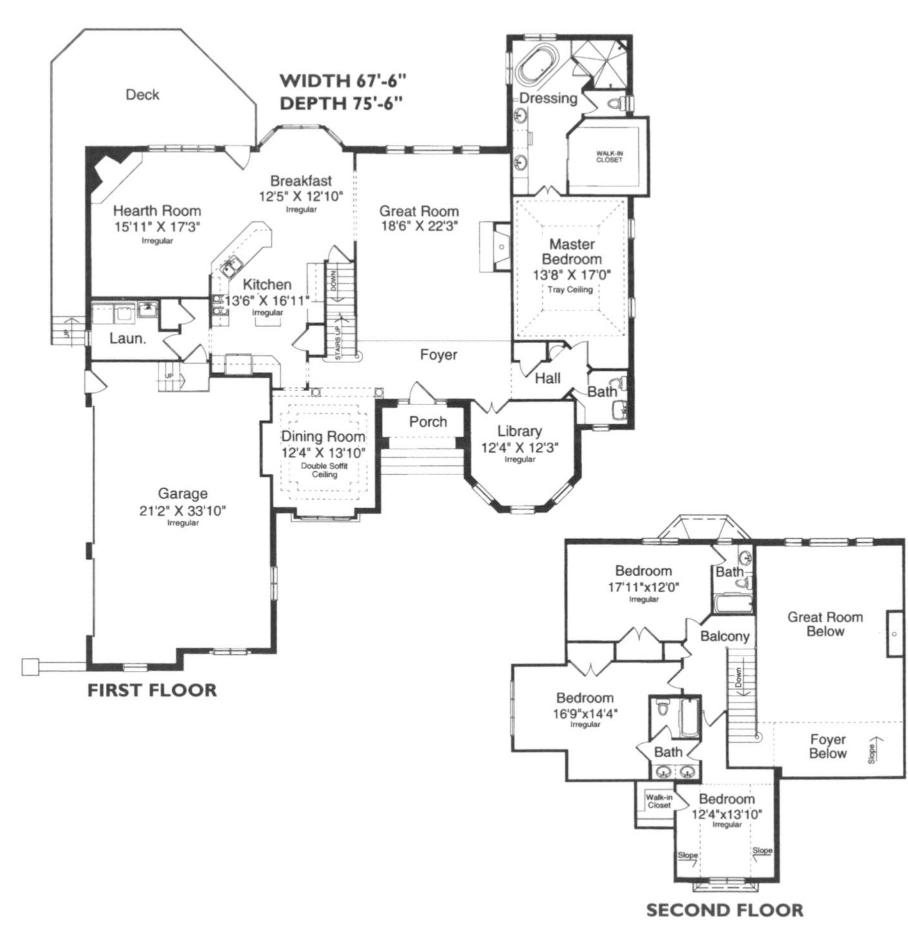

WIDTH 67'-6"
DEPTH 75'-6"
Deck
Breakfast
12'5" X 12'10"
Irregular
Hearth Room
15'11" X 17'3"
Irregular
Great Room
18'6" X 22'3"
Dressing
WALK-IN CLOSET
Master Bedroom
13'8" X 17'0"
Tray Ceiling
Kitchen
13'6" X 16'11"
Irregular
DOWN
STAIRS UP
Laun.
UP
Foyer
Hall
Bath
Porch
Library
12'4" X 12'3"
Irregular
Dining Room
12'4" X 13'10"
Double Soffit Ceiling
Garage
21'2" X 33'10"
Irregular
FIRST FLOOR
Bedroom
17'11"x12'0"
Irregular
Bath
Great Room Below
Balcony
Bedroom
16'9"x14'4"
Irregular
Down
Foyer Below
Slope
Bath
Walk-in Closet
Bedroom
12'4"x13'10"
Irregular
Slope
Slope
SECOND FLOOR

Triple Arched Porch

PLAN NO.98474

PRICE CODE: B

'his plan features:
- 'our bedrooms
- Three full baths
- A triple arched front Porch, segmented arched window eystones and shutters accent the exterior
- An impressive two-story Foyer adjoins the elegant)ining Room
- 'he Family Room, Breakfast Room and Kitchen have n open layout
- 'he Study/Bedroom is topped by a vaulted ceiling and s located close to a full Bath
- 'he Master Suite is topped by a tray ceiling while there s a vaulted ceiling over the Bath
- An optional bonus room offers expansion for uture needs
- 'his home is designed with basement and crawlspace oundation options

ST FLOOR — 972 SQ. FT.
:OND FLOOR — 772 SQ. FT.
NUS ROOM — 358 SQ. FT.
SEMENT — 972 SQ. FT.
RAGE — 520 SQ. FT.

TOTAL LIVING AREA:* 1,744 *SQ. FT.

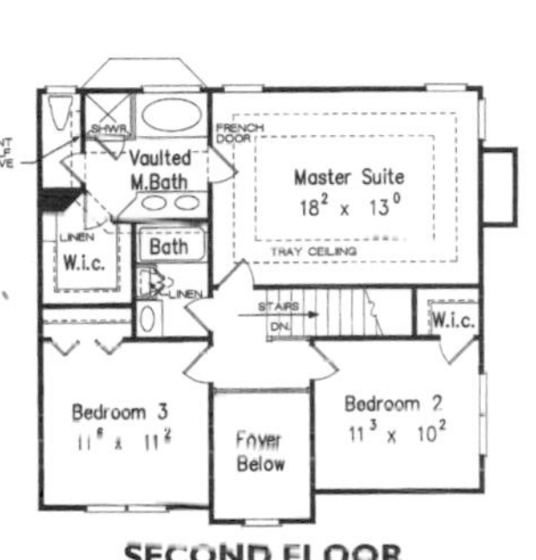

Vaulted M.Bath
Master Suite 18² x 13⁰
TRAY CEILING
W.i.c.
Bath
Bedroom 3 11⁶ x 11²
Foyer Below
Bedroom 2 11³ x 10²

SECOND FLOOR

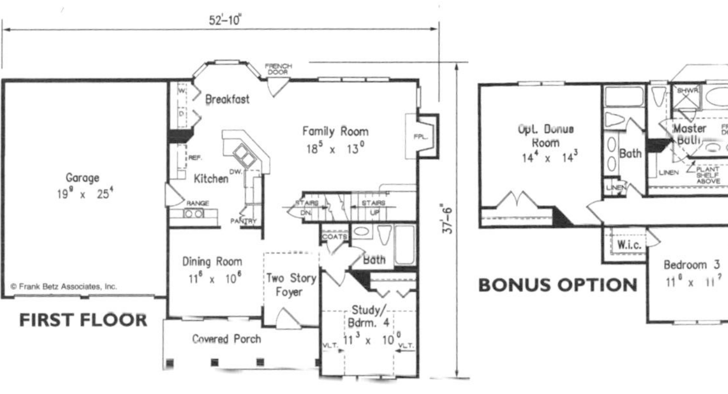

52'-10"
37'-6"
Breakfast
Family Room 18⁵ x 13⁰
Garage 19⁹ x 25⁴
Kitchen
Dining Room 11⁶ x 10⁶
Two Story Foyer
Bath
Study/ Bdrm. 4 11³ x 10⁰
Covered Porch
© Frank Betz Associates, Inc.
Opt. Bonus Room 14⁴ x 14³
Master Bath
Bath
W.i.c.
Bedroom 3 11⁶ x 11⁷

FIRST FLOOR

BONUS OPTION

Rewards of Success

PLAN NO.93254

PRICE CODE: F

'his plan features:
- 'hree bedrooms
- 'hree full and one half baths
- ormal areas, the Living Room and Dining Room, ›cated in the front of the house, each enhanced by bay window
- n expansive Family Room, including a fireplace anked by windows, at the rear of the house
- n open layout between the Family Room, reakfast Bay and the Kitchen
- lavish Master Suite crowned by a decorative ceiling ıd pampered by a private Master Bath
- wo additional Bedrooms, one has use of a full hall Bath ıe other has a private Bath
- 'his home is designed with basement, slab and rawlspace foundation options

ST FLOOR — 1,282 SQ. FT.
'OND FLOOR — 1,227 SQ. FT.
NUS ROOM — 314 SQ. FT.
RAGE — 528 SQ. FT.
SEMENT — 1,154 SQ. FT.

TOTAL LIVING AREA:* 2,509 *SQ. FT.

Photography by John Ehrenclou

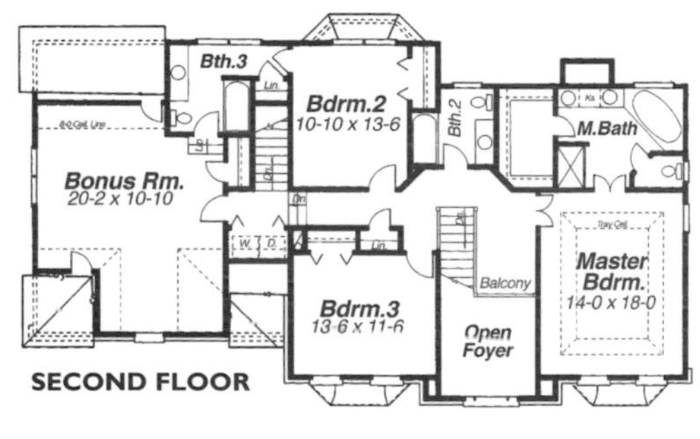

Bth.3
Bdrm.2 10-10 x 13-6
M.Bath
Bonus Rm. 20-2 x 10-10
Master Bdrm. 14-0 x 18-0
Balcony
Bdrm.3 13-6 x 11-6
Open Foyer

SECOND FLOOR

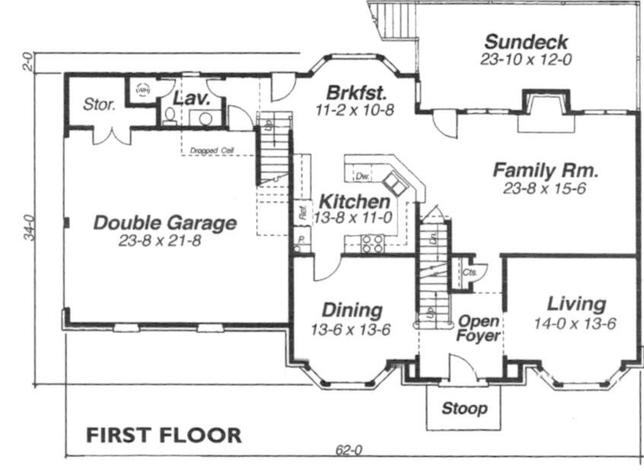

Sundeck 23-10 x 12-0
Stor.
Lav.
Brkfst. 11-2 x 10-8
Family Rm. 23-8 x 15-6
Double Garage 23-8 x 21-8
Kitchen 13-8 x 11-0
Dining 13-6 x 13-6
Open Foyer
Living 14-0 x 13-6
Stoop
62-0
34-0

FIRST FLOOR

PLAN NO.65135

Appealing Farmhouse

PRICE CODE: D

- ■ This plan features:
- — Three bedrooms
- — Two full and one half baths
- ■ Interior doors provide privacy options in the Study and Living Rooms
- ■ Luxurious amenities in the Master Suite include a fireplace, large walk-in closet and Bath with separate tub and shower
- ■ This home is designed with a basement foundation

FIRST FLOOR — 1,146 SQ. FT.
SECOND FLOOR — 943 SQ. FT.
BONUS ROOM — 313 SQ. FT.
BASEMENT — 483 SQ. FT.

TOTAL LIVING AREA:
2,089 SQ. FT.

5,60 X 3,90
18'-8" X 13'-0"
4,00 X 3,30
13'-4" X 11'-0"
6,40 X 6,80
21'-4" X 22'-8"
4,00 X 4,20
13'-4" X 14'-0"
3,60 X 4,00
12'-0" X 13'-4"

FIRST FLOOR

WIDTH 56'-0"
DEPTH 38'-0"

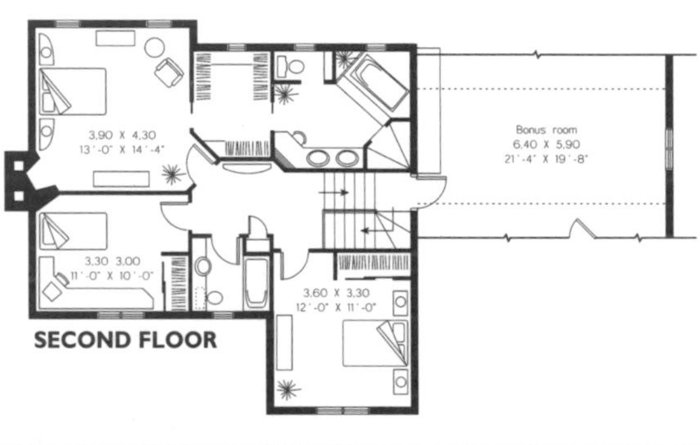

3,90 X 4,30
13'-0" X 14'-4"
Bonus room
6,40 X 5,90
21'-4" X 19'-8"
3,30 X 3,00
11'-0" X 10'-0"
3,60 X 3,30
12'-0" X 11'-0"

SECOND FLOOR

PLAN NO.97632

Vaulted Family Room

PRICE CODE: B

- ■ This plan features:
- — Three bedrooms
- — Two full and one half baths
- ■ A fireplace and vaulted ceiling highlight the Family Room
- ■ The Dining Room and Nook are set between the Kit
- ■ Upstairs the Master Suite has a tray ceiling
- ■ Two additional Bedrooms share a full Bath
- ■ A front Covered Porch adds character
- ■ This home is designed with basement and crawlspac foundation options

FIRST FLOOR — 760 SQ. FT.
SECOND FLOOR — 854 SQ. FT.
BASEMENT — 760 SQ. FT.
GARAGE — 399 SQ. FT.

TOTAL LIVING AREA:
1,614 SQ. FT.

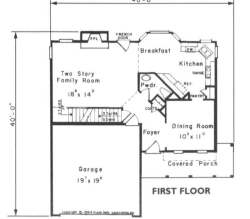

40'-0"
FPL
FRENCH DOOR
Breakfast
Kitchen
Two Story Family Room
18⁸x 14⁰
Pwdr.
Foyer
Dining Room
10³x 11⁰
Covered Porch
Garage
19⁷x 19⁸
40'-0"
copyright © 1994 frank betz associates, inc

FIRST FLOOR

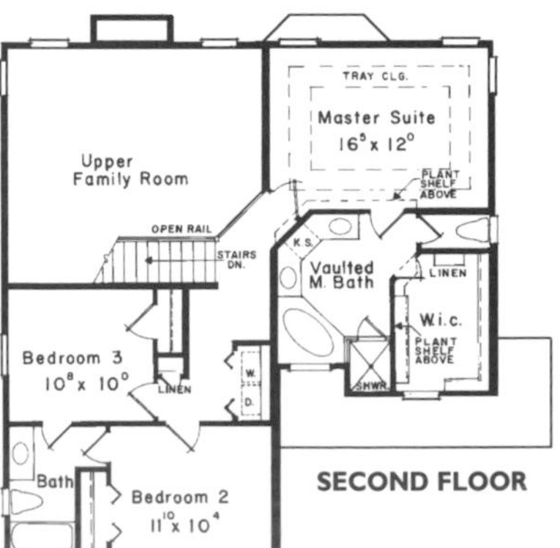

TRAY CLG.
Master Suite
16⁵x 12⁰
Upper Family Room
OPEN RAIL
STAIRS DN.
Vaulted M. Bath
LINEN
W.i.c.
Bedroom 3
10⁸x 10⁰
Bath
Bedroom 2
11¹⁰x 10⁴

SECOND FLOOR

PLAN NO. 99444

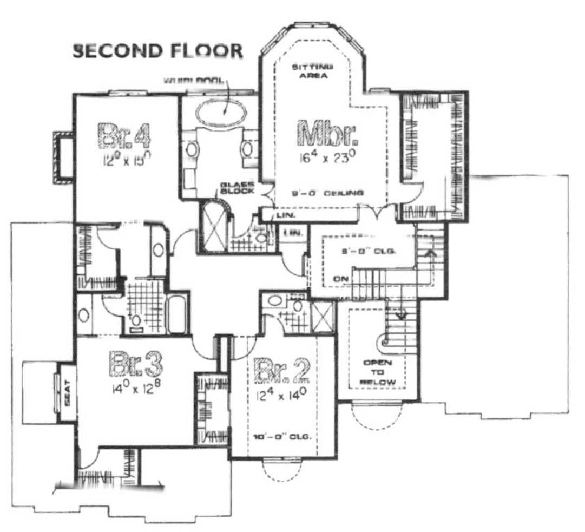

SECOND FLOOR
WHIRLPOOL
SITTING AREA
Br.4
Mbr.
GLASS BLOCK
9'-0" CEILING
LIN.
9'-0" CLG.
DN
OPEN TO BELOW
Br.3
SEAT
Br.2
10'-0" CLG.

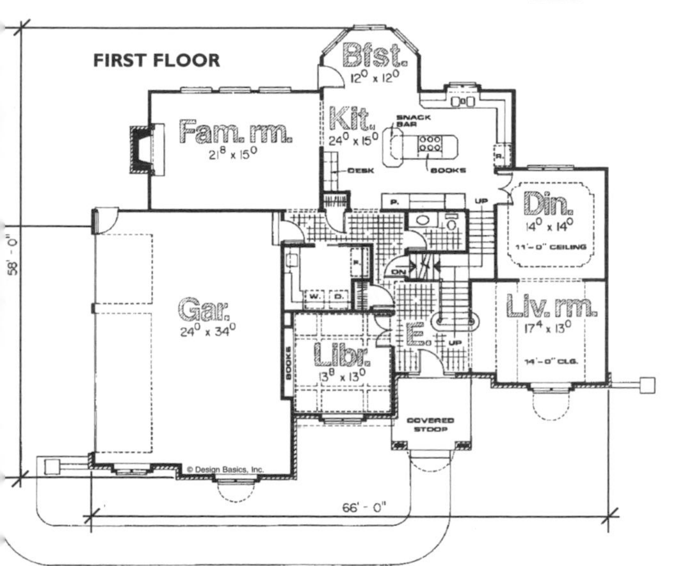

FIRST FLOOR
Bfst.
Fam. rm.
Kit.
SNACK BAR
DESK
BOOKS
P.
UP
Din.
11'-0" CEILING
Gar.
W.
D.
DN
Liv. rm.
E.
UP
Libr.
BOOKS
14'-0" CLG.
COVERED STOOP
© Design Basics, Inc.
58'-0"
66'-0"

Stone, Stucco & Band Boards

Price Code: J

- This plan features:
  - — Four bedrooms
  - — Two full, one three-quarter and one half baths
- The two-story Entry reveals French doors to the Library and the formal Living Room
- The gourmet Kitchen presents an expansive island with a triple cooktop
- This home is built with a basement foundation
- Alternate foundation options available at an additional charge. Please call 1-800-235-5700 for more information.

FIRST FLOOR — 1,857 SQ. FT.
SECOND FLOOR — 1,754 SQ. FT.
BASEMENT — 1,857 SQ. FT.
GARAGE — 633 SQ. FT.

TOTAL LIVING AREA: 3,611 SQ. FT.

PLAN NO. 65138

Farmhouse with Flair

Price Code: D

- This plan features:
- — Three bedrooms
- — Two full and one half baths
- Architectural elements and window treatments combine to create an inviting front elevation
- A room adjoining off the Entry could be a Home Office or a Study
- The Master Bedroom Suite features a walk-in closet and a Master Bath with separate tub and shower
- This home is designed with a basement foundation

FIRST FLOOR — 1,274 SQ. FT.
SECOND FLOOR — 983 SQ. FT.
GARAGE — 437 SQ. FT.
PORCH — 183 SQ. FT

TOTAL LIVING AREA:
2,257 SQ. FT.

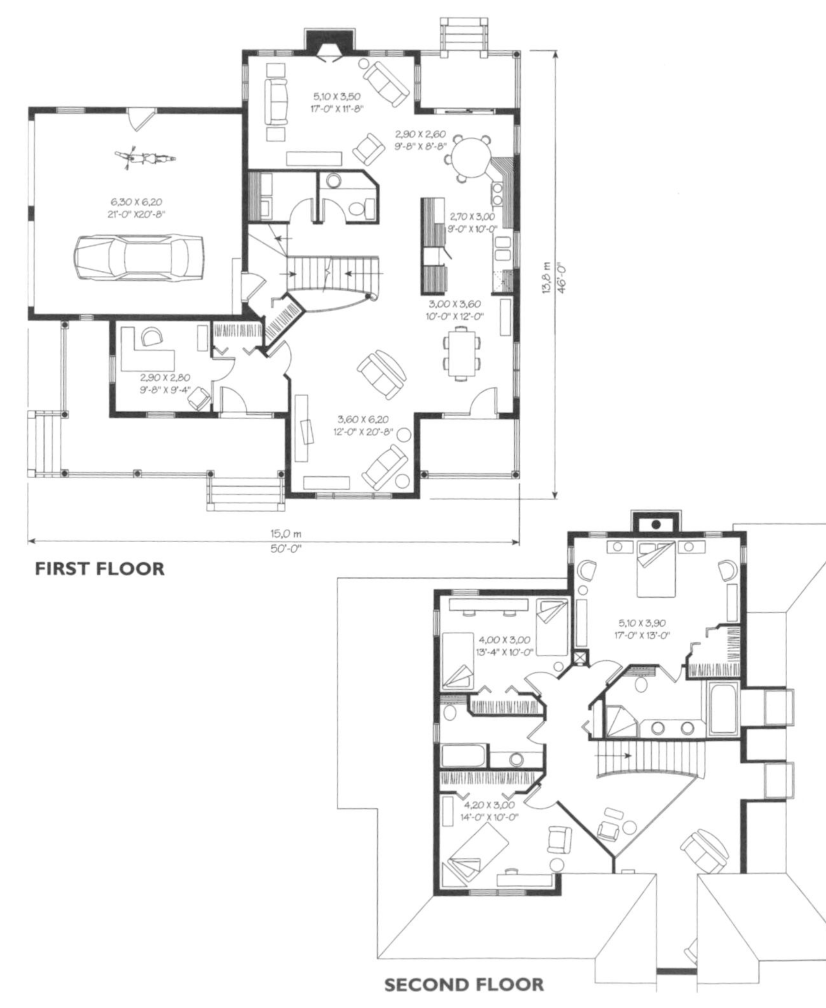
5,10 X 3,50
17'-0" X 11'-8"
2,90 X 2,60
9'-8" X 8'-8"
6,30 X 6,20
21'-0" X 20'-8"
2,70 X 3,00
9'-0" X 10'-0"
3,00 X 3,60
10'-0" X 12'-0"
2,90 X 2,80
9'-8" X 9'-4"
3,60 X 6,20
12'-0" X 20'-8"
13,8 m
46'-0"
15,0 m
50'-0"
FIRST FLOOR
5,10 X 3,90
17'-0" X 13'-0"
4,00 X 3,00
13'-4" X 10'-0"
4,20 X 3,00
14'-0" X 10'-0"
SECOND FLOOR

PLAN NO. 65140

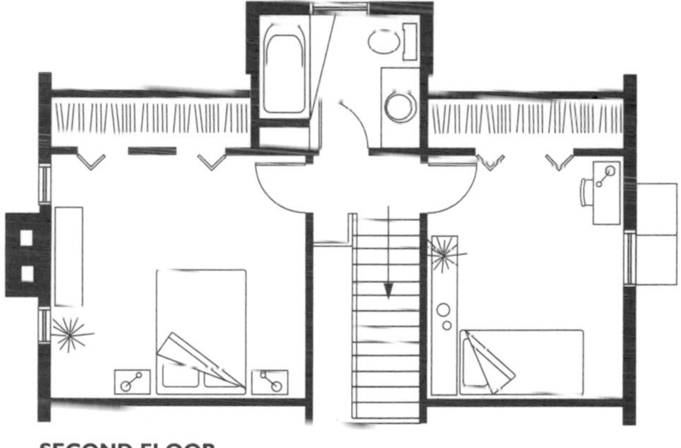

SECOND FLOOR

WIDTH 30'-0"
DEPTH 28'-0"

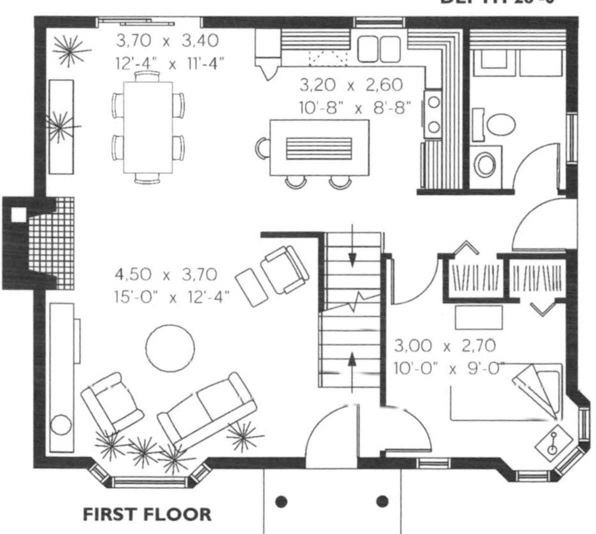

3,70 x 3,40
12'-4" x 11'-4"
3,20 x 2,60
10'-8" x 8'-8"
4,50 x 3,70
15'-0" x 12'-4"
3,00 x 2,70
10'-0" x 9'-0"
FIRST FLOOR

Quaint and Cozy

Price Code: A

- This plan features:
  - Three bedrooms
  - One full and one half baths
- A front Porch with two stately columns
- The fireplace is centrally located between the open Living and Dining Areas
- The Kitchen has ample cupboard space and a center island adds extra work space or serves as a snack bar
- The first floor Bedroom features a lovely bay window
- Two Bedrooms on the second floor each have large closets and share a full Bath
- This home is designed with a basement foundation

FIRST FLOOR — 753 SQ. FT.
SECOND FLOOR — 505 SQ. FT.
BASEMENT — 753 SQ. FT.

TOTAL LIVING AREA:
1,258 SQ. FT.

PLAN NO. 65141

Let the Sun Shine In

Price Code: B

- This plan features:
  - — Three bedrooms
  - — Two full baths
- The Living Room and Dining Room share a large open space, as well as a focal point fireplace to use on rainy days and cold nights
- The U-shaped Kitchen has a double sink that overlooks the backyard, and access to the rear Deck
- The first floor Bathroom includes the Laundry closet
- On the second floor, two Bedrooms share a full Bath and a Sitting Area that overlooks the Living Room
- This home is designed with a basement foundation

FIRST FLOOR — 946 SQ. FT.
SECOND FLOOR — 604 SQ. FT.

TOTAL LIVING AREA:
1,550 SQ. FT.

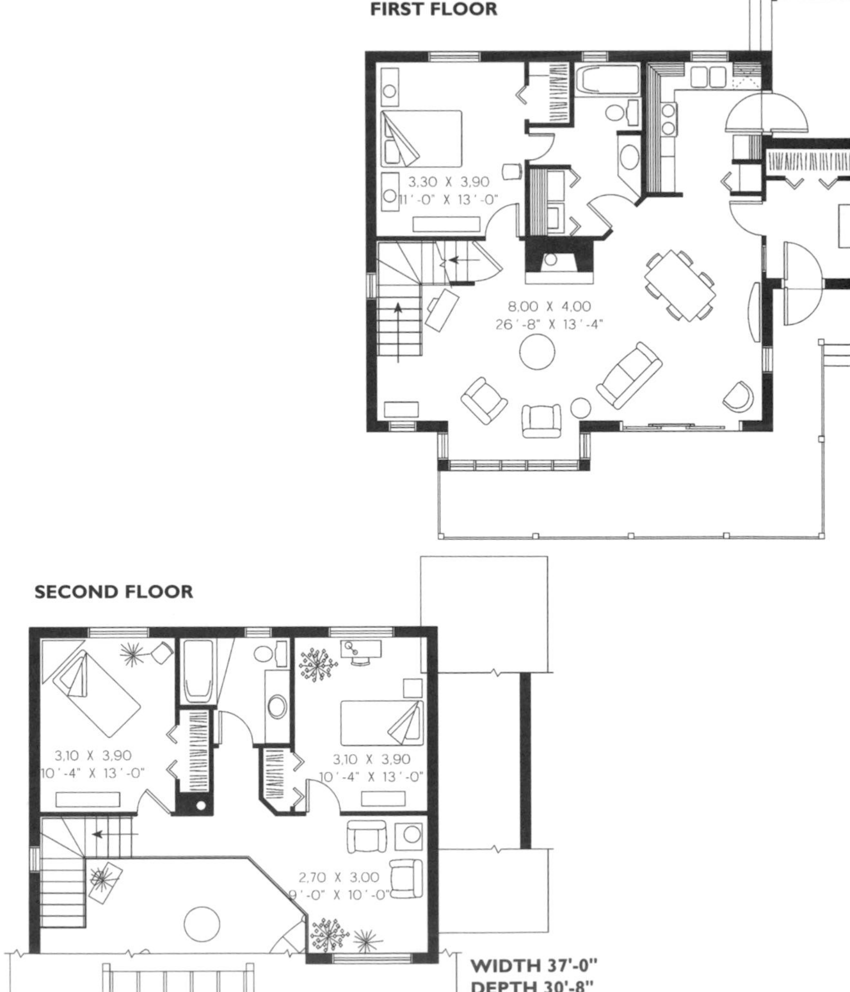
FIRST FLOOR
3,30 X 3,90
11'-0" X 13'-0"
8,00 X 4,00
26'-8" X 13'-4"
SECOND FLOOR
3,10 X 3,90
10'-4" X 13'-0"
3,10 X 3,90
10'-4" X 13'-0"
2,70 X 3,00
9'-0" X 10'-0"
WIDTH 37'-0"
DEPTH 30'-8"

Family Get-Away

PRICE CODE: B

PLAN NO.34602

is plan features:

- ıree bedrooms
- vo full and one half baths
- wraparound Porch for views and visiting provides cess into the Great Room and Dining Area
- spacious Great Room with a two-story ceiling and rmer window above a massive fireplace
- combination Dining/Kitchen with an island work area d breakfast bar opening to a Great Room and adjacent the Laundry/Storage and half Bath area
- private two-story Master Bedroom with a dormer ndow, walk-in closet, double vanity Bath and optional ck with hot tub
- vo additional Bedrooms on the second floor sharing ull Bath
- is home is designed with basement, slab, and awlspace foundation options

T FLOOR — 1,061 SQ. FT.
ND FLOOR — 499 SQ. FT.
EMENT — 1,061 SQ. FT.

TOTAL LIVING AREA:
1,560 SQ. FT.

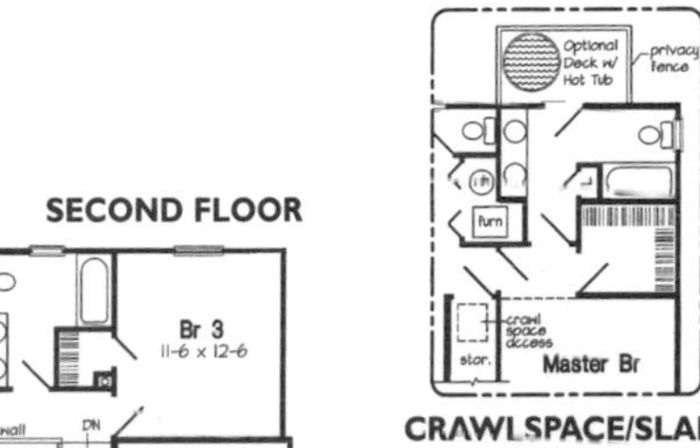

Optional Deck w/ Hot Tub
privacy fence
Master Br
CRAWLSPACE/SLAB FOUNDATION OPTION

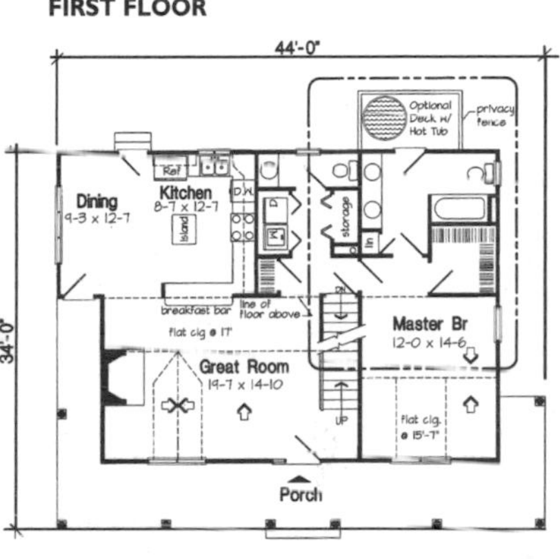

FIRST FLOOR
44'-0"
34'-0"
Dining 9-3 x 12-7
Kitchen 8-7 x 12-7
Optional Deck w/ Hot Tub
privacy fence
Master Br 12-0 x 14-6
Great Room 14-7 x 14-10
breakfast bar
Porch

SECOND FLOOR

Br 2 10-10 x 12-6
Br 3 11-6 x 12-6
1/2 wall
open to great room below
master bedroom below

Balcony Overlooks Living Room Below

PRICE CODE: A

PLAN NO.90356

his plan features:

- hree bedrooms
- wo full and one half baths
- vaulted ceiling Living Room with a balcony above d a fireplace
- n efficient, well-equipped Kitchen with stovetop island d easy flow of traffic into the Dining Room
- deck accessible from the Dining Room
- luxurious Master Suite with a bay window seat, walk- closet, Dressing Area, and a private shower
- vo additional Bedrooms that share a full hall Bath
- is home is designed with a basement foundation

T FLOOR — 674 SQ. FT.
OND FLOOR — 677 SQ. FT.
EMENT — 674 SQ. FT.

TOTAL LIVING AREA:
1,351 SQ. FT.

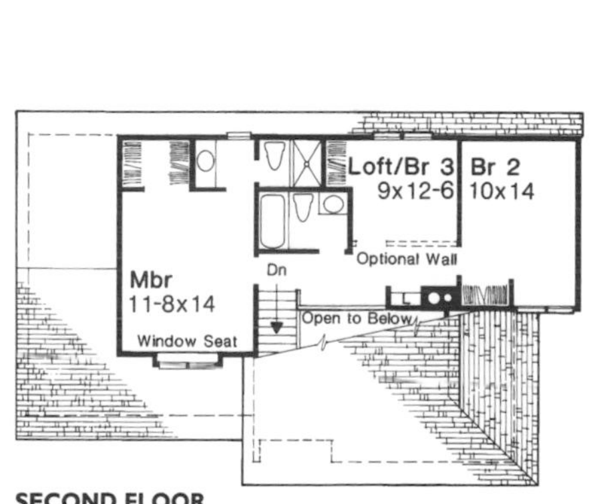

Loft/Br 3 9x12-6
Br 2 10x14
Optional Wall
Mbr 11-8x14
Dn
Open to Below
Window Seat
SECOND FLOOR

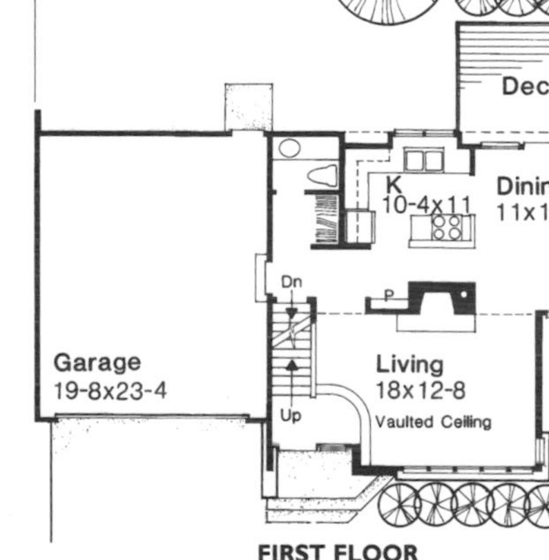

48'-0"
Deck
K 10-4x11
Dining 11x13-4
30'-2"
Dn
Garage 19-8x23-4
Living 18x12-8
Vaulted Ceiling
Up
FIRST FLOOR

PLAN NO.97206

Refinement with Brilliancy

PRICE CODE: F

- This plan features:
  - — Four bedrooms
  - — Three full baths
- Two-story foyer dominated by an open rail staircase
- Two-story Family Room enhanced by a fireplace
- Walk-in Pantry and ample counter space highlighting the Breakfast Room
- Secluded Study easily becoming an additional Bedro with a private Bath
- Second floor Master Suite with tray ceiling, bayed Sitting Area and a vaulted ceiling over the private Ba
- This home is designed with basement, slab, and crawlspace foundation options

FIRST FLOOR — 1,548 SQ. FT.
SECOND FLOOR — 1,164 SQ. FT.
BONUS — 198 SQ. FT.
BASEMENT — 1,548 SQ. FT.
GARAGE — 542 SQ. FT.

TOTAL LIVING AREA:* 2,712 *SQ. FT.

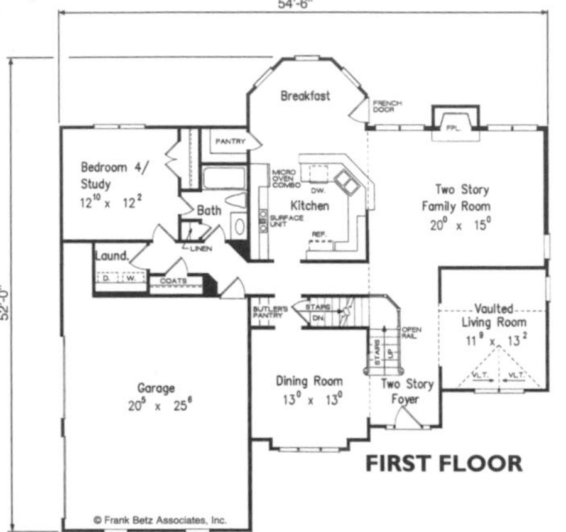

54'-6"
52'-0"
Breakfast
Bedroom 4/ Study
Bath
Kitchen
Two Story Family Room
Laund.
Vaulted Living Room
Garage
Dining Room
Two Story Foyer
© Frank Betz Associates, Inc.

FIRST FLOOR

Sitting Area
Master Suite
Vaulted M.Bath
W.i.c.
Family Room Below
Bedroom 2
Bedroom 3
Bath
Foyer Below
Opt. Bonus

SECOND FLOOR

PLAN NO.24706

Country Porch Topped by Dormer

PRICE CODE: A

- This plan features:
  - — Three bedrooms
  - — Two full baths
- Front Porch offers outdoor living and leads into tiled Entry and spacious Living Room with focal point fireplace
- Side entrance leads into Utility Room and central Fo with a landing staircase
- Country-size Kitchen with cooktop island, bright Breakfast Area and access to Deck
- Second floor Master Bedroom offers lovely dormer window, vaulted ceiling, walk-in closet and double vanity Bath
- Two additional Bedrooms with ample closets, share a full Bath
- This home is designed with basement, slab, and crawlspace foundation options

FIRST FLOOR — 1,035 SQ. FT.
SECOND FLOOR — 435 SQ. FT.
BASEMENT — 1,018 SQ. FT.

TOTAL LIVING AREA:* 1,470 *SQ. FT.

FIRST FLOOR

WIDTH 35'-0"
DEPTH 42'-0"

Deck
Brkfst 9-0 x 6-0
Kit. 11-6 x 9-8
Br #2 12-2 x 9-11
Foyer
Utility
Living Rm 18-11 x 12-11
Br #3 12-2 x 9-3
Porch

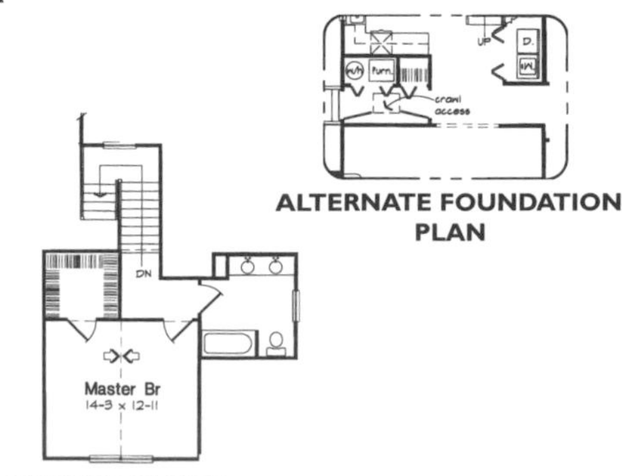

Master Br 14-3 x 12-11

SECOND FLOOR

ALTERNATE FOUNDATION PLAN

PLAN NO. 35003

Charming Bow Window

Price Code. A

- This plan features:
  - — Three bedrooms
  - — Two full baths
- An inviting Porch leads into Foyer and Living Room with a bow window and sloping ceiling
- Open Kitchen provides easy access to Dining Room, Deck/Patio, Laundry and Garage
- Private Master Bedroom offers two walk-in closets and a full Bath
- This home is designed with basement, slab and crawlspace foundation options

MAIN FLOOR — 1,373 SQ. FT.
GARAGE — 400 SQ. FT.

TOTAL LIVING AREA:
1,373 SQ. FT.

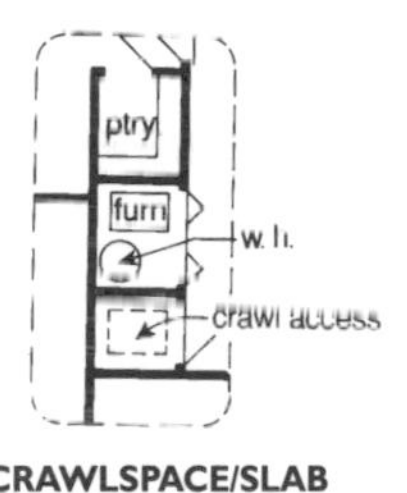
ptry
furn
w.h.
crawl access

CRAWLSPACE/SLAB FOUNDATION OPTION

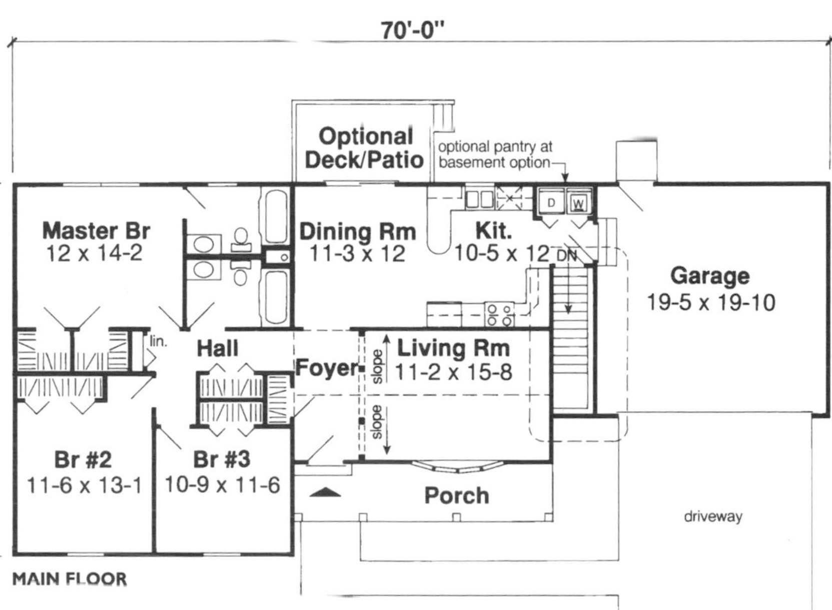
70'-0"
Optional Deck/Patio
optional pantry at basement option
Master Br
12 x 14-2
Dining Rm
11-3 x 12
Kit.
10-5 x 12
DN
D
W
Garage
19-5 x 19-10
lin.
Hall
Foyer
slope
Living Rm
11-2 x 15-8
slope
Br #2
11-6 x 13-1
Br #3
10-9 x 11-6
Porch
driveway

MAIN FLOOR

PLAN NO. 96600

A Classic Design

Price Code: F

- This plan features:
- — Four bedrooms
- — Two full and one half baths
- An elegant arched opening graces the Entrance of this classic design
- The dramatic arch detail is repeated at the Dining Room entrance
- The Kitchen, Breakfast Room and Family Room are open to one another
- The Kitchen has amenities including a walk-in Pantry, double ovens and an eating bar
- The Master Suite is designed apart from the other Bedrooms for privacy
- Two Bedrooms share a Bath and have walk-in closets
- This home is designed with crawlspace and slab foundation options

MAIN FLOOR — 2,678 SQ. FT
GARAGE — 474 SQ. FT.

TOTAL LIVING AREA:
2,678 SQ. FT.

HERS
HIS
MASTER BATH
11 FT TRAY CLG
SEAT
FP
PORCH
9 FT CLG
FAMILY ROOM
13-6 X 16-6
FIRST FLOOR
BRKFST RM
10-8 X 11-6
9 FT CLG
MASTER BEDRM
15-0 X 17-4
11 FT TRAY CLG
COVERED PORCH
9 FT CLG
BEDRM 4
14-8 X 12-8
9 FT CLG
ARCH
42" LEDGE
PWDR
ARCH
LIVING ROOM
18-4 X 18-6
11 FT CLG
KITCHEN
13-6 X 11-4
9 FT CLG
UTIL
12-6 X 5-8
9 FT CLG
BATH 2
PAN
GARAGE
DINING ROOM
14-0 X 13-6
11 FT CLG
BEDRM 3
11-0 X 13-4
9 FT CLG
BEDRM 2/ STUDY
11-6 X 13-0
11 FT TRAY CLG
FOYER
11 FT CLG
ARCH
COPYRIGHT LARRY E. BELK
PORCH
9 FT CLG
MAIN FLOOR
WIDTH 70-2

DEPTH 67-9

PLAN NO. 65145

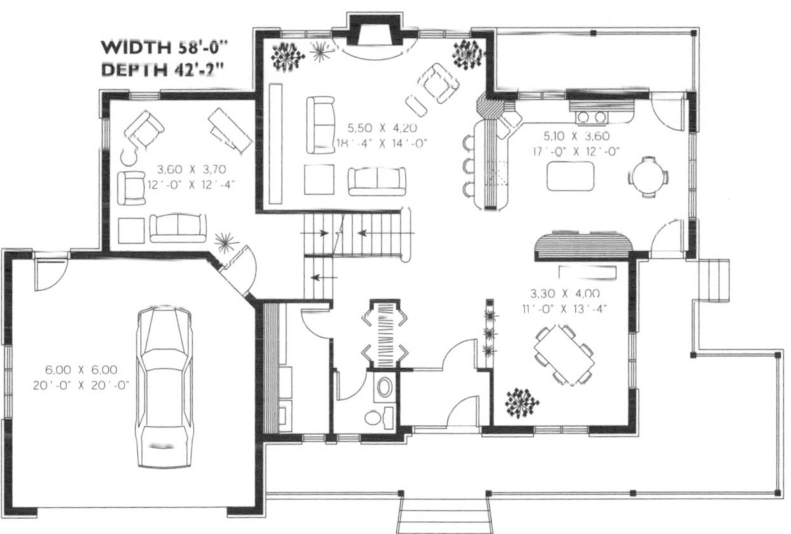
WIDTH 58'-0"
DEPTH 42'-2"
5,50 X 4,20
18'-4" X 14'-0"
3,60 X 3,70
12'-0" X 12'-4"
5,10 X 3,60
17'-0" X 12'-0"
3,30 X 4,00
11'-0" X 13'-4"
6,00 X 6,00
20'-0" X 20'-0"

FIRST FLOOR

5,10 X 4,20
17'-0" X 14'-0"

3,30 X 3,20
11'-0" X 10'-8"

3,30 X 4,00
11'-0" X 13'-4

SECOND FLOOR

Hidden Den

Price Code: E

- This plan features:
  - Three bedrooms
  - Two full and one half baths
- An open design allows the Kitchen and Dining Room to enjoy view of the fireplace in the Great Room
- The Master Suite features a fireplace, walk-in closet, and a spa tub in the Bath
- This home is designed with a basement foundation

FIRST FLOOR — 1,246 SQ. FT.
SECOND FLOOR — 1,046 SQ. FT.
BASEMENT — 1,246 SQ. FT.
GARAGE — 392 SQ. FT.

TOTAL LIVING AREA:
2,292 SQ. FT.

PLAN NO. 99475

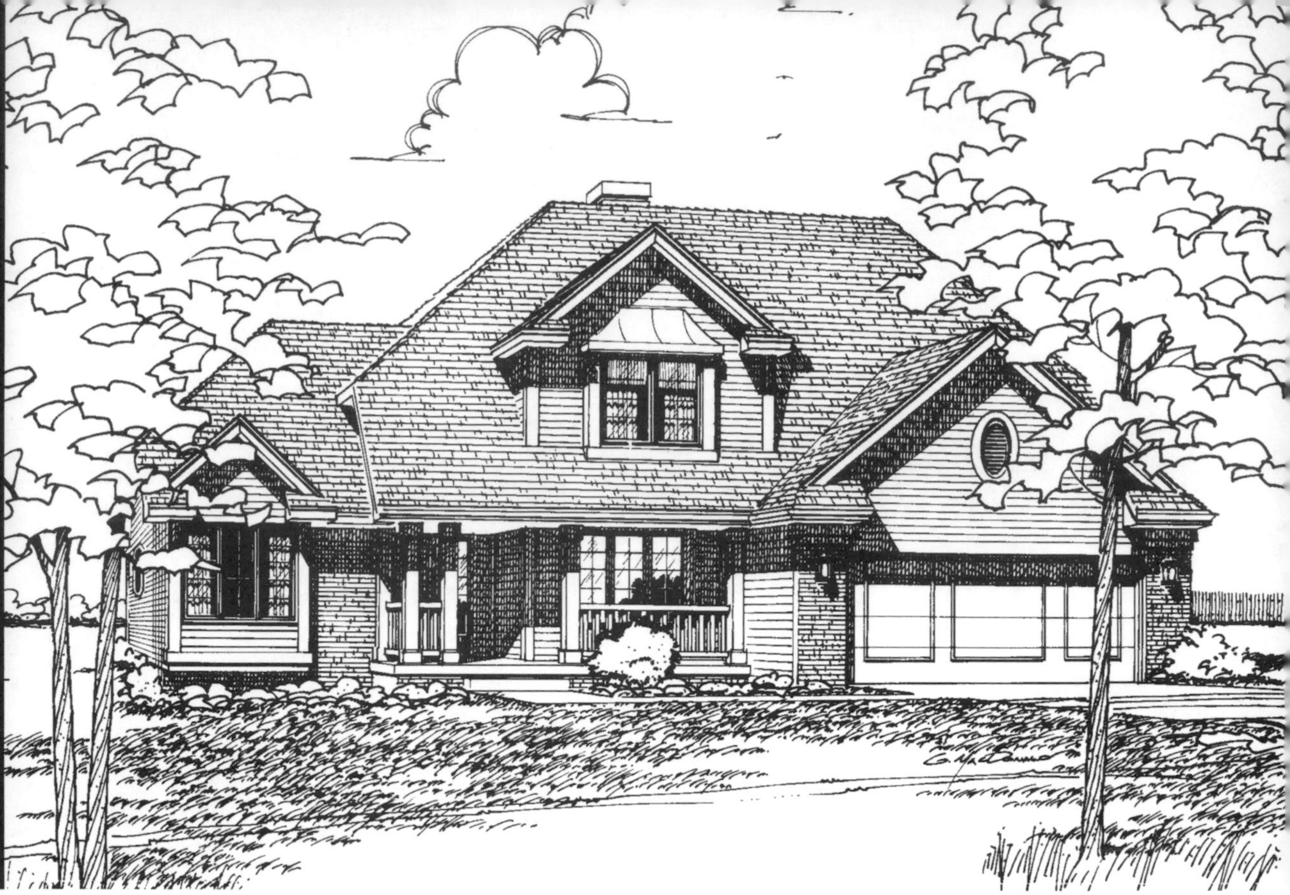

Just Perfect

Price Code: C

- This plan features:
  - — Four bedrooms
  - — Two full and one half baths
- The Dining Room has a built-in hutch and a front window wall overlooking the Porch
- The Great Room features a see-through fireplace and transom rear windows
- The Master Suite has a private Bath with a whirlpool tub
- This home is designed with a basement foundation
- Alternate foundation options available at an additional charge. Please call 1-800-235-5700 for more information.

FIRST FLOOR — 1,421 SQ. FT.
SECOND FLOOR — 578 SQ. FT.

TOTAL LIVING AREA:
1,999 SQ. FT.

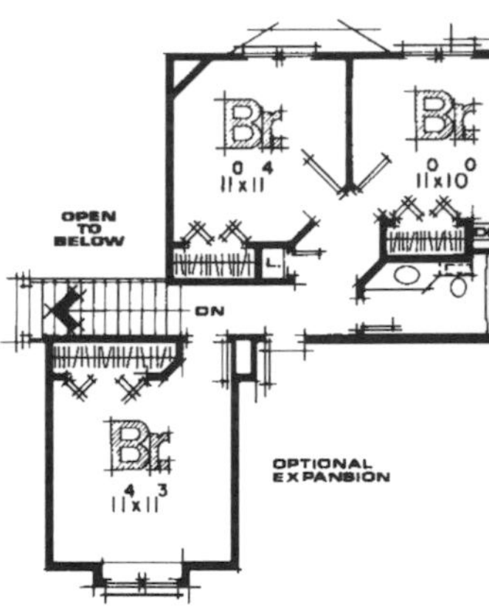
Br
11x11
Br
11x10
OPEN TO BELOW
DN
Br
11x11
OPTIONAL EXPANSION

SECOND FLOOR

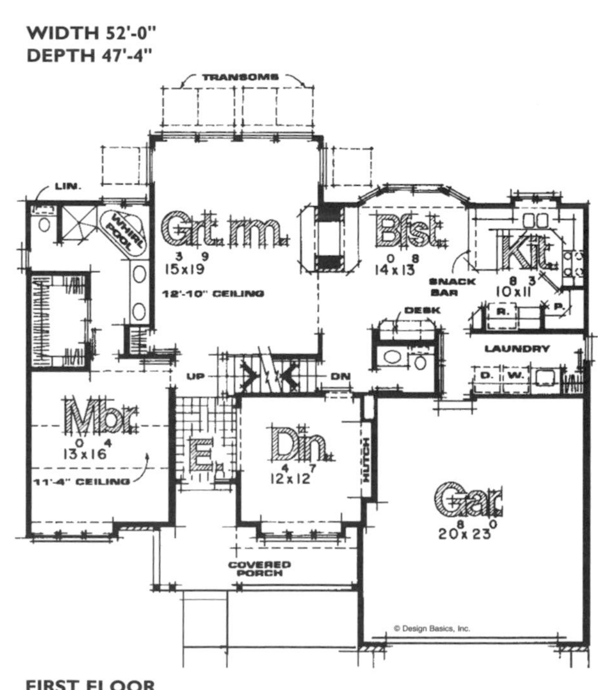
WIDTH 52'-0"
DEPTH 47'-4"
TRANSOMS
LIN.
WHIRLPOOL
Grt. rm.
15x19
12'-10" CEILING
Bfst.
14x13
SNACK BAR
Kit.
10x11
DESK
LAUNDRY
UP
DN
Mbr.
13x16
11'-4" CEILING
E.
Din.
12x12
HUTCH
Gar.
20x23
COVERED PORCH
© Design Basics, Inc.
FIRST FLOOR

Inviting Front Porch

PRICE CODE: B

PLAN NO.93298

'his plan features:
- Three bedrooms
- Two full and one half baths
-)etailed gables and inviting front Porch create a warm velcoming facade
-)pen Foyer features an angled staircase, a half Bath and coat closet
- 'he expansive, informal Living Area at the rear of the ome features a fireplace and opens onto the Sun Deck
- 'he efficient Kitchen has easy access to both the ormal and informal Dining Areas
- Aaster Bedroom includes a walk-in closet and ompartmented private Bath
- 'wo secondary Bedrooms share a Bath with a ouble vanity
- 'his home is designed with basement, slab and rawlspace foundation options

ST FLOOR — 797 SQ. FT.
:OND FLOOR — 886 SQ. FT.
SEMENT — 797 SQ. FT.
RAGE — 414 SQ. FT.

TOTAL LIVING AREA:
1,683 SQ. FT.

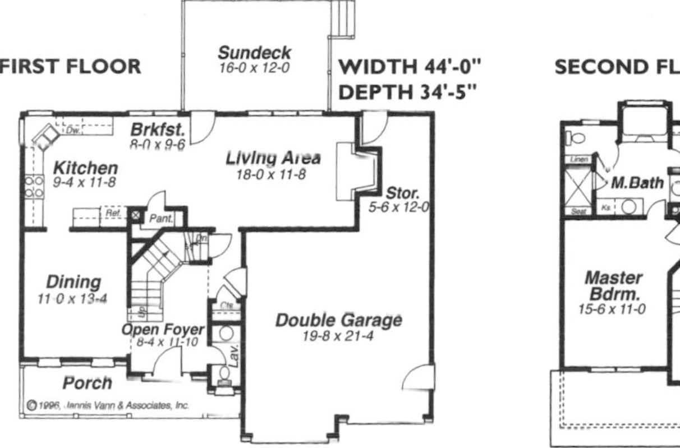

FIRST FLOOR
Sundeck
16-0 x 12-0
WIDTH 44'-0"
DEPTH 34'-5"
Brkfst.
8-0 x 9-6
Living Area
18-0 x 11-8
Kitchen
9-4 x 11-8
Stor.
5-6 x 12-0
Pant.
Dining
11-0 x 13-4
Open Foyer
8-4 x 11-10
Lav.
Double Garage
19-8 x 21-4
Porch
©1996 Jannis Vann & Associates, Inc.

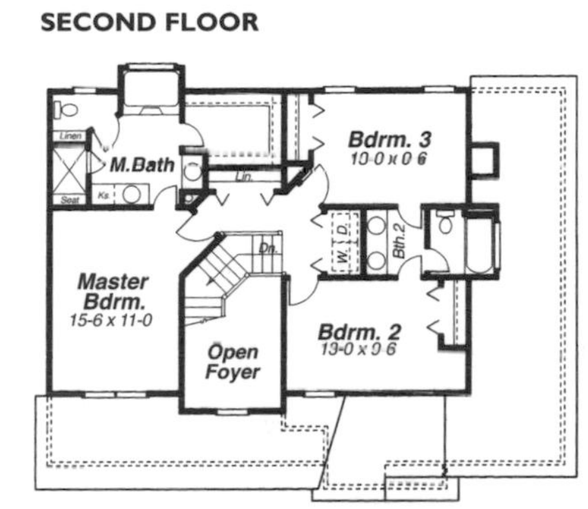

SECOND FLOOR
M.Bath
Bdrm. 3
10-0 x 0 6
Bth.2
Master
Bdrm.
15-6 x 11-0
Open
Foyer
Bdrm. 2
13-0 x 9 6

A-Frame for Year Round Living

PRICE CODE: B

PLAN NO.90930

'his plan features:
- Three bedrooms
- One full and one three-quarter baths
- A vaulted ceiling in the Living Room with a massive 'ireplace
- A wraparound Sun Deck that gives you a lot of outdoor iving space
- A luxurious Master Suite complete with a walk-in closet, 'ull Bath and private Deck
- Two additional Bedrooms that share a full hall Bath
- This home is designed with a basement foundation

AIN FLOOR — 1,238 SQ. FT.
FT — 464 SQ. FT.
SEMENT — 1,175 SQ. FT.

TOTAL LIVING AREA:
1,702 SQ. FT.

WIDTH 34'-0"
DEPTH 56'-0"

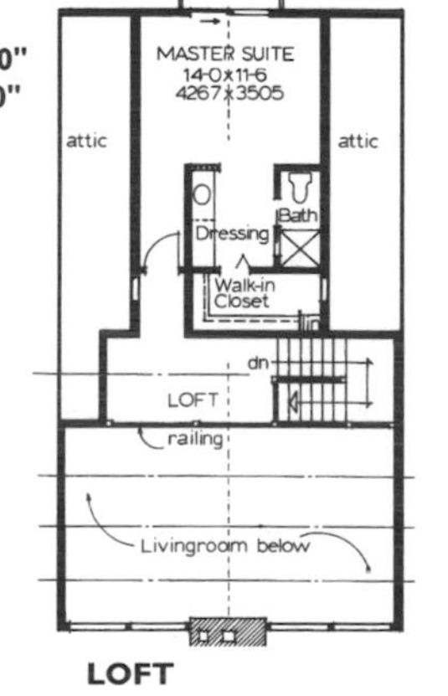

DECK
MASTER SUITE
14-0x11-6
4267x3505
attic
attic
Dressing
Bath
Walk-in
Closet
dn
LOFT
railing
Livingroom below
LOFT

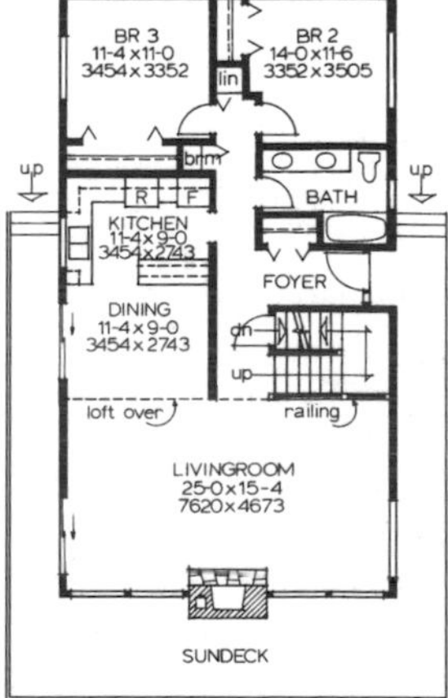

Full Basement under
BR 3
11-4x11-0
3454x3352
BR 2
14-0x11-6
3352x3505
BATH
KITCHEN
11-4x9-0
3454x2743
FOYER
DINING
11-4x9-0
3454x2743
loft over
railing
LIVINGROOM
25-0x15-4
7620x4673
SUNDECK
MAIN FLOOR

PLAN NO.90844

Open Space Living

PRICE CODE: B

- This plan features:
  - — Three bedrooms
  - — Two full and one half baths
- A wraparound Deck providing outdoor living space, ideal for a sloping lot
- Two and a half-story glass wall and two separate atriu doors providing natural light for the Living/Dining Room Area
- An efficient galley Kitchen with easy access to the Dining Area
- A Master Bedroom Suite with it's own Bath and ampl closet space
- A second floor Bedroom/Studio, with a private Deck, adjacent to a full hall Bath and a Loft Area
- This home is designed with a basement foundation

FIRST FLOOR — 1,086 SQ. FT.
SECOND FLOOR — 466 SQ. FT.
BASEMENT — 1,080 SQ. FT.

TOTAL LIVING AREA:
1,552 SQ. FT.

WIDTH 36'-0"
DEPTH 50'-0"

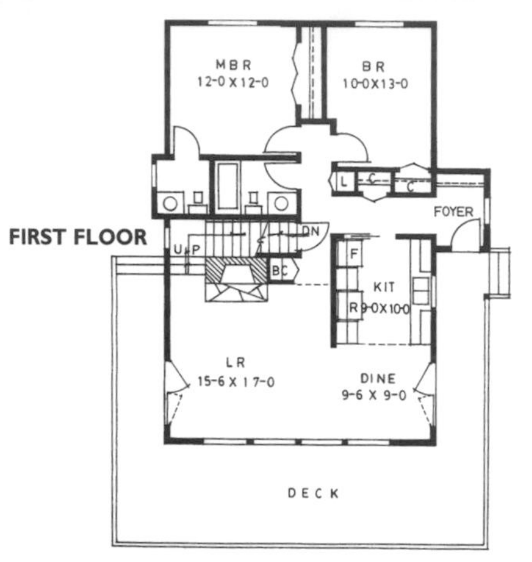
FIRST FLOOR
MBR
12-0 X 12-0
BR
10-0X13-0
FOYER
DN
UP
KIT
9-0X10-0
LR
15-6 X 17-0
DINE
9-6 X 9-0
DECK

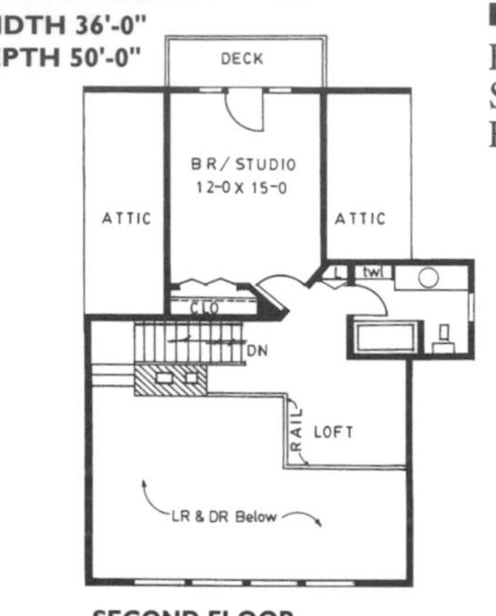
DECK
BR/STUDIO
12-0 X 15-0
ATTIC
ATTIC
CLO
DN
RAIL
LOFT
LR & DR Below
SECOND FLOOR

PLAN NO.94965

Enjoyable Living

PRICE CODE: F

- This plan features:
  - — Four bedrooms
  - — Two full, one three-quarter and one half baths
- The Master Bedroom is complete with a tray ceiling, walk-in closets, and a large Bath
- The Family Room has a beamed ceiling and a fireplac
- This home is designed with basement and slab foundation options
- Alternate foundation options available at an additional charge. Please call 1-800-235-5700 for more information.

FIRST FLOOR — 1,400 SQ. FT.
SECOND FLOOR — 1,315 SQ. FT.
BASEMENT — 1,400 SQ. FT.
GARAGE — 631 SQ. FT.

TOTAL LIVING AREA:
2,715 SQ. FT.

FIRST FLOOR

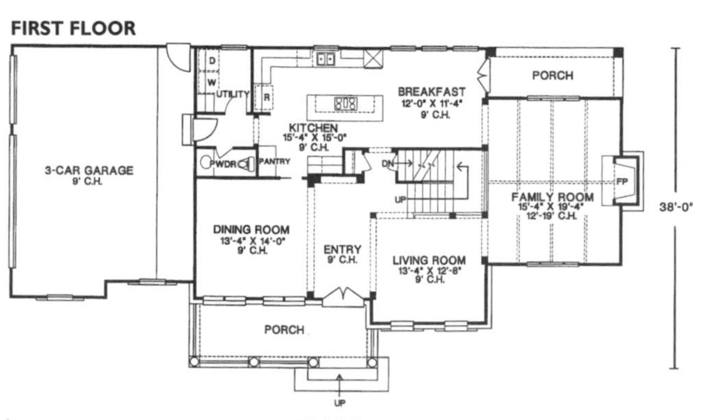
PORCH
BREAKFAST
12'-0" X 11'-4"
9' C.H.
UTILITY
KITCHEN
15'-4" X 15'-0"
9' C.H.
PANTRY
PWDR
3-CAR GARAGE
9' C.H.
FAMILY ROOM
15'-4" X 19'-4"
12'-19' C.H.
38'-0"
DINING ROOM
13'-4" X 14'-0"
9' C.H.
ENTRY
9' C.H.
LIVING ROOM
13'-4" X 12'-8"
9' C.H.
PORCH
UP
75'- 1 1/2"

© Carmichael & Dame

MASTER BEDROOM 13'-4" X 17'-4" 8'-10' C.H.
MASTER BATH
W.I.C.
BATH
BEDROOM 2 15'-4" X 11'-4" 8' C.H.
OPEN TO FAMILY ROOM
BATH
BEDROOM 4 11'-0" X 12'-8" 8'-10' C.H.
BEDROOM 3 11'-4" X 12'-4" 8'-10' C.H.

SECOND FLOOR

PLAN NO. 65177

Shapes and Textures Add Appeal

Price Code: C

- This plan features:
  - — Three bedrooms
  - — Two full and one half baths
- A curved, covered Porch offers a warm welcome to family and guests
- The Living Room and Dining Room share a see-through fireplace that also helps divide the areas
- The L-shaped Kitchen offers room to move and space for helpers, too
- The Master Bedroom Suite features a walk-through closet to the spacious Master Bath
- This home is designed with a basement foundation

FIRST FLOOR — 1,044 SQ. FT.
SECOND FLOOR — 894 SQ. FT.
GARAGE — 487 SQ. FT.

TOTAL LIVING AREA:

1,938 SQ. FT.

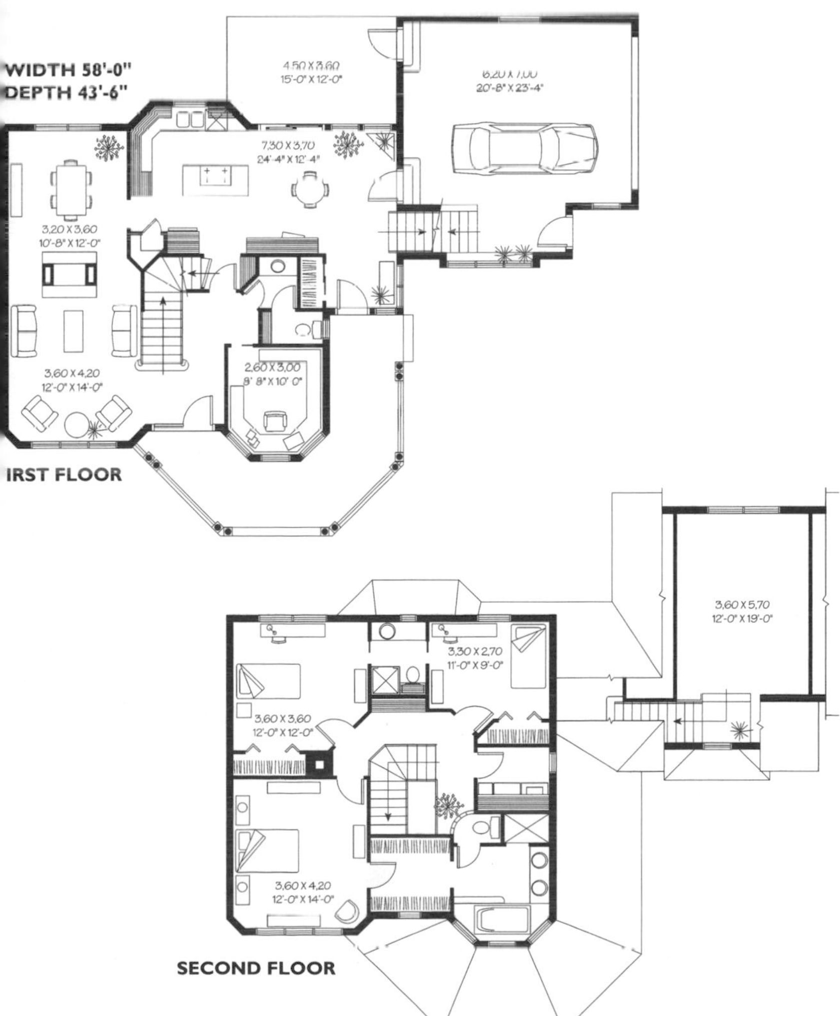

WIDTH 58'-0"
DEPTH 43'-6"
4,50 X 3,60
15'-0" X 12'-0"
7,30 X 3,70
24'-4" X 12'-4"
3,20 X 3,60
10'-8" X 12'-0"
3,60 X 4,20
12'-0" X 14'-0"
2,60 X 3,00
8'-8" X 10'-0"
IRST FLOOR
3,60 X 5,70
12'-0" X 19'-0"
3,30 X 2,70
11'-0" X 9'-0"
3,60 X 3,60
12'-0" X 12'-0"
3,60 X 4,20
12'-0" X 14'-0"
SECOND FLOOR

PLAN NO. 99485

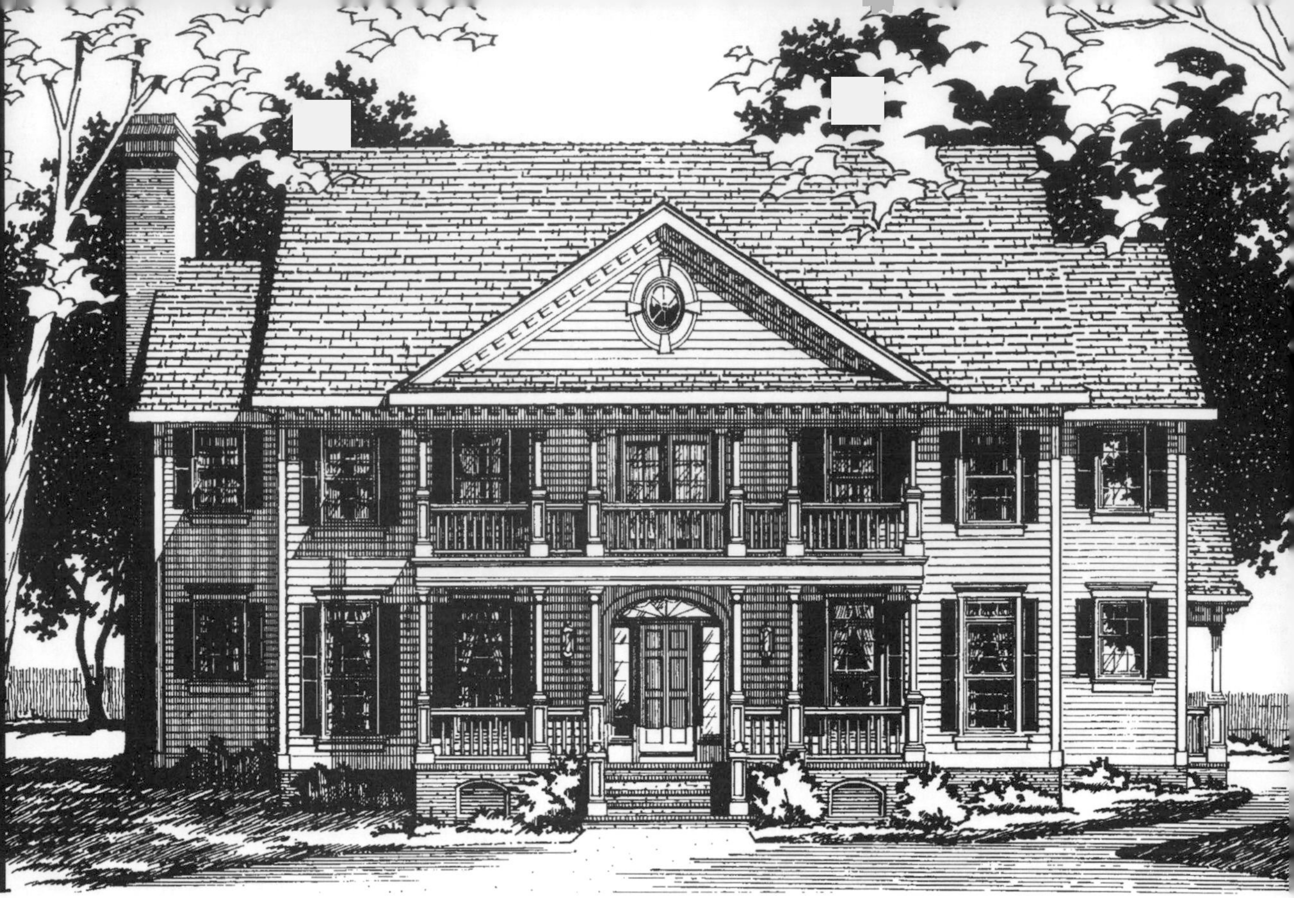

Southern Mansion

Price Code: I

- This plan features:
- — Four bedrooms
- — Three full and one half baths
- Covered Porches, intricate detailing and illuminating transom windows enhance this home
- The prominent Entry opens to the formal Dining and Living Rooms
- French doors open to the Master Suite, which includes his and her walk-in closets, a large dressing area, two vanities, and an oval whirlpool bath
- This home is designed with a basement foundation
- Alternate foundation options available at an additional charge. Please call 1-800-235-5700 for more information.

FIRST FLOOR — 1,598 SQ. FT.
SECOND FLOOR — 1,675 SQ. FT.

TOTAL LIVING AREA:
3,273 SQ. FT.

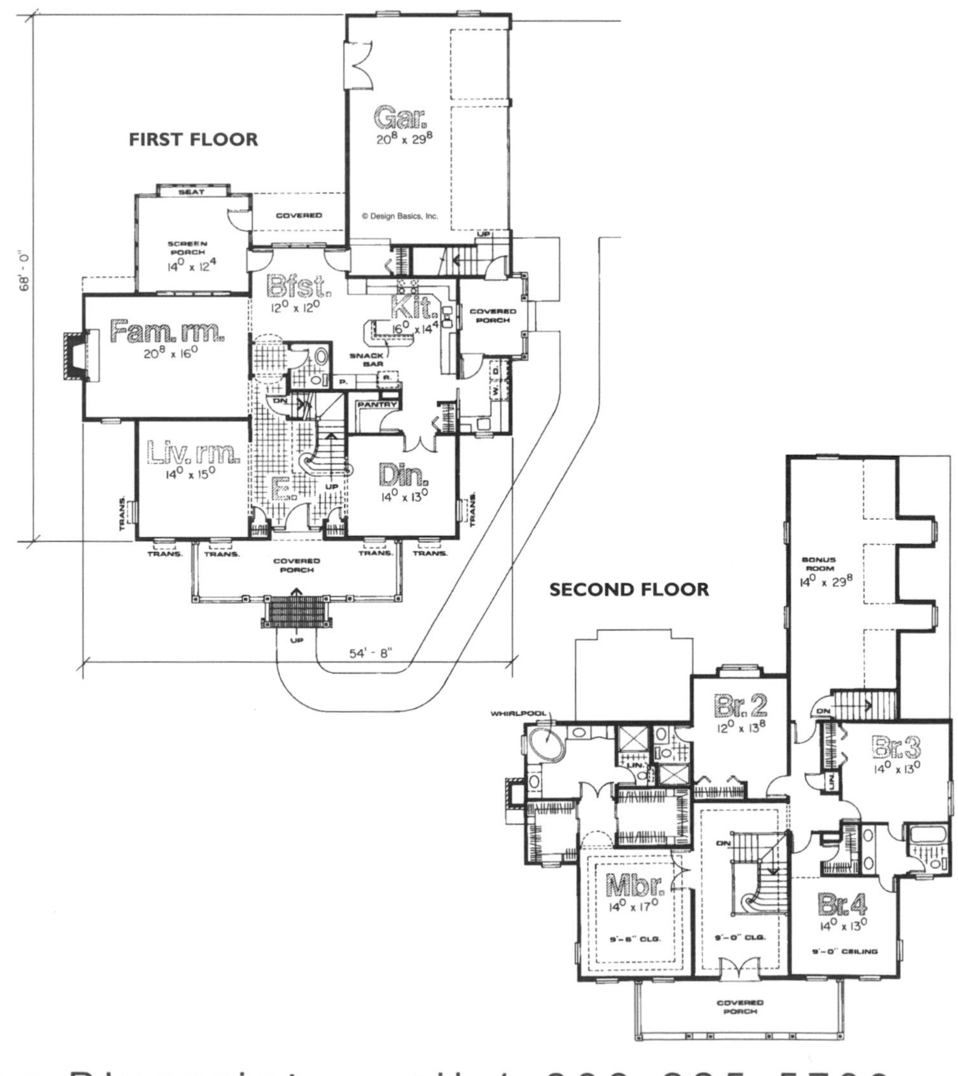

FIRST FLOOR
Gar.
20⁸ x 29⁸
© Design Basics, Inc.
SEAT
SCREEN PORCH
14⁰ x 12⁴
COVERED
Bfst.
12⁰ x 12⁰
Kit.
16⁰ x 14⁴
COVERED PORCH
Fam. rm.
20⁸ x 16⁰
SNACK BAR
PANTRY
Liv. rm.
14⁰ x 15⁰
Din.
14⁰ x 13⁰
TRANS.
COVERED PORCH
UP
68' - 0"
54' - 8"
SECOND FLOOR
BONUS ROOM
14⁰ x 29⁸
WHIRLPOOL
Br. 2
12⁰ x 13⁸
Br. 3
14⁰ x 13⁰
Mbr.
14⁰ x 17⁰
9'-8" CLG.
9'-0" CLG.
Br. 4
14⁰ x 13⁰
9'-0" CEILING
COVERED PORCH

PLAN NO. 97210

Notable Exterior

Price Code: F

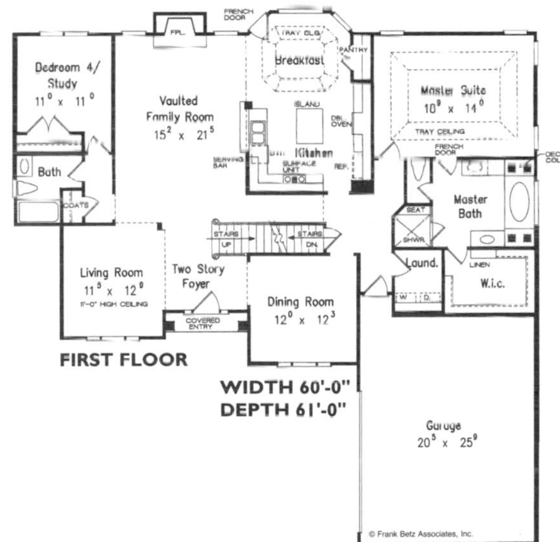

FRENCH DOOR
FPL.
TRAY CLG.
Breakfast
PANTRY
Bedroom 4/ Study
$11^0 \times 11^0$
Vaulted Family Room
$15^2 \times 21^5$
ISLAND
DBL OVEN
Master Suite
$16^9 \times 14^0$
TRAY CEILING
Kitchen
SERVING BAR
REF.
FRENCH DOOR
DECORATIVE COLUMNS
Bath
COATS
Master Bath
SEAT
STAIRS UP
STAIRS DN.
SHWR.
Laund.
LINEN
Living Room
$11^5 \times 12^0$
11'-0" HIGH CEILING
Two Story Foyer
W.i.c.
Dining Room
$12^0 \times 12^3$
COVERED ENTRY
FIRST FLOOR
WIDTH 60'-0"
DEPTH 61'-0"
Garage
$20^5 \times 25^9$
© Frank Betz Associates, Inc.

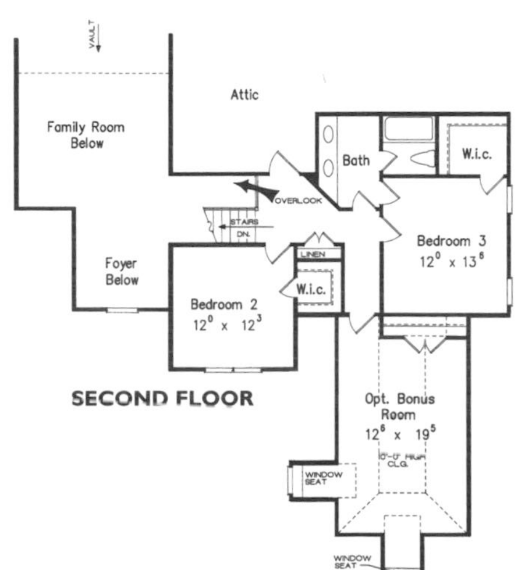

VAULT
Attic
Family Room Below
Bath
W.i.c.
OVERLOOK
STAIRS DN.
Bedroom 3
$12^0 \times 13^8$
Foyer Below
LINEN
W.i.c.
Bedroom 2
$12^0 \times 12^3$
SECOND FLOOR
Opt. Bonus Room
$12^6 \times 19^5$
WINDOW SEAT
WINDOW SEAT

- This plan features:
- — Four bedrooms
- — Three full baths
- Two-story Foyer adds a feeling of volume
- Family Room topped by vaulted ceiling and accented by a fireplace
- Formal Living Room with an eleven-foot ceiling
- Private Master Suite with a five-piece Bath and a large walk-in closet
- Rear Bedroom/Study located close to a full Bath
- This home is designed with basement, slab and crawlspace foundation options

FIRST FLOOR — 2,003 SQ. FT.
SECOND FLOOR — 598 SQ. FT.
BONUS — 321 SQ. FT.
BASEMENT — 2,003 SQ. FT.
GARAGE — 546 SQ. FT.

TOTAL LIVING AREA:
2,601 SQ. FT.

PLAN NO. 92156

Spectacular Views

PRICE CODE: F

- This plan features:
- — Four Bedrooms
- — Two full and one three-quarter baths
- Creates an indoor/outdoor relationship with terrific dec and large glass expanses
- Family Room and Living Room enjoy glassed walls taking in the vistas
- Living Room enhanced by a cathedral ceiling and a warm fireplace
- Dining Room and Kitchen are in an open layout and highlighted by a center cooktop island/snack bar in the Kitchen and large window in the Dining Room
- Master Bedroom enhanced by floor to ceiling window area allowing natural light to filter in
- Two additional downstairs Bedrooms, a three-quarter Bath and a Family Room complete the lower level
- This home is designed with a basement foundation

MAIN FLOOR — 1,707 SQ. FT.
LOWER FLOOR — 901 SQ. FT.

TOTAL LIVING AREA:
2,608 SQ. FT.

61'-0"
34'-6"
Util. 13-6 x 7-2
P.
Br #2 14 x 9-6
M.Bath
L.
DN.
Dining 11-6 x 15
CATH. CLG.
Kit.
Living 18 x 20
Entry
M. Br 12-6 x 14-6
Deck
Deck
DN.
MAIN FLOOR

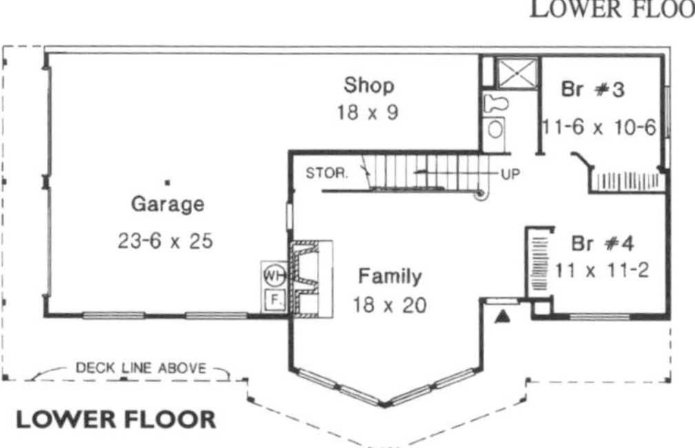

Shop
18 x 9
Br #3
11-6 x 10-6
STOR.
UP
Garage
23-6 x 25
WH
F.
Family
18 x 20
Br #4
11 x 11-2
DECK LINE ABOVE

LOWER FLOOR

PLAN NO. 65210

Your Own Castle

PRICE CODE: C

- This plan features:
- — Three bedrooms
- — Two full and one half baths
- The look of a castle, but the comforts and convenience of today
- The Kitchen is designed for maximum efficiency
- A half Bath, Laundry closet and coat closet complete the first floor
- The Master Bedroom Suite spans one side of the second floor
- This home is designed with a basement foundation

FIRST FLOOR — 924 SQ. FT.
SECOND FLOOR — 1,052 SQ. FT.
BASEMENT — 1,067 SQ. FT.
GARAGE — 388 SQ. FT.

TOTAL LIVING AREA:
1,976 SQ. FT.

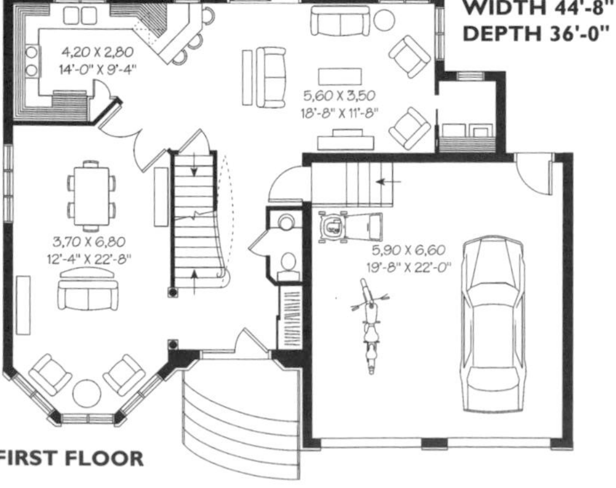

WIDTH 44'-8"
DEPTH 36'-0"
4,20 X 2,80
14'-0" X 9'-4"
5,60 X 3,50
18'-8" X 11'-8"
3,70 X 6,80
12'-4" X 22'-8"
5,90 X 6,60
19'-8" X 22'-0"

FIRST FLOOR

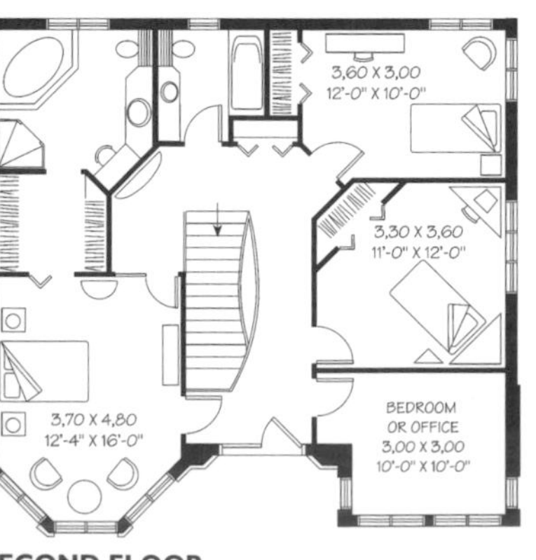

3,60 X 3,00
12'-0" X 10'-0"
3,30 X 3,60
11'-0" X 12'-0"
3,70 X 4,80
12'-4" X 16'-0"
BEDROOM
OR OFFICE
3,00 X 3,00
10'-0" X 10'-0"

SECOND FLOOR

European Influence

PRICE CODE: B

This plan features:
- Three bedrooms
- Two full baths
- Vaulted ceilings and columns give interest to the Breakfast, Dining and Family Rooms
- The floor layout is efficient yet elegant
- The Kitchen/ Breakfast Nook offer easy access to the Family Room
- Master Bedroom and Bath has a vaulted ceiling
- This home is designed with basement and crawlspace foundation options
- AIN FLOOR — 1,575 SQ. FT.
- RAGE — 456 SQ. FT.

TOTAL LIVING AREA:
1,575 SQ. FT.

PLAN NO.98479

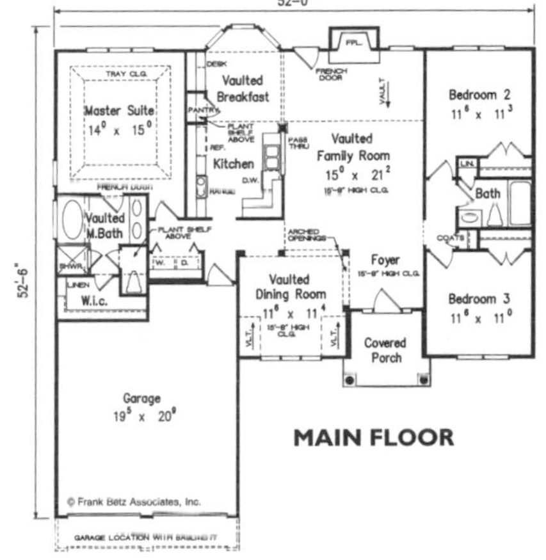
52'-0"
Master Suite 14⁰ x 15⁰
Vaulted Breakfast
Kitchen
Vaulted Family Room 15⁰ x 21²
Bedroom 2 11⁶ x 11³
Bath
Vaulted M.Bath
W.I.c.
Vaulted Dining Room 11⁶ x 11⁴
Foyer
Bedroom 3 11⁶ x 11⁰
Covered Porch
Garage 19⁵ x 20⁸
52'-6"
© Frank Betz Associates, Inc.
MAIN FLOOR

W.I.c.
Laun.
Garage 19⁵ x 20⁸

BASEMENT STAIR LOCATION OPTION

Beautiful Arched Window

PRICE CODE: C

This plan features:
- Three bedrooms
- Two full baths
- 0-foot ceilings topping the Entry and the Great Room
- A see-through fireplace is shared between the Great Room and the Hearth Room
- Built-in entertainment center and a bayed window highlighting the Hearth Room
- Breakfast Room and Hearth Room in an open layout separated by only a snack bar in the Kitchen
- Built-in Pantry and corner sinks enhancing efficiency in the Kitchen
- Split Bedroom plan assuring homeowner's privacy in the Master Suite which includes a decorative ceiling, private Bath and a large walk-in closet
- Two additional Bedrooms at the opposite side of the home sharing a full, skylit Bath in the hall
- This home is designed with a basement foundation
- Alternate foundation options available at an additional charge. Please call 1-800-235-5700 for more information.
- IN FLOOR — 1,911 SQ. FT.
- RAGE — 481 SQ. FT.

TOTAL LIVING AREA:
1,911 SQ. FT.

PLAN NO.94966

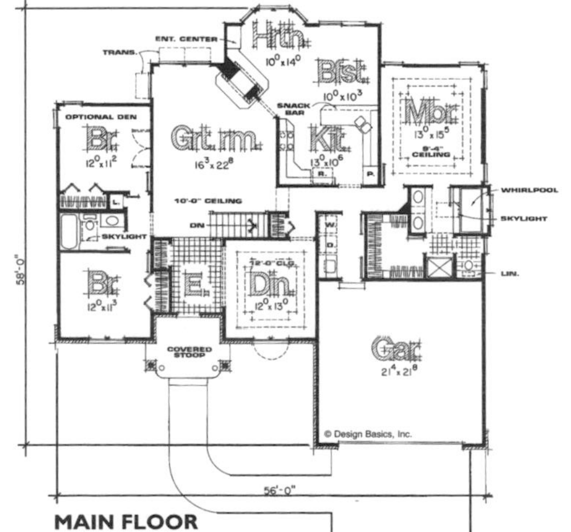
Hth. 10⁰x14⁰
Bfst. 10⁰x10³
Mbr. 13⁰x15⁸
Br. 12⁰x11²
Grt. rm. 16³x22⁸
Kit. 13⁰x10⁶
Br. 12⁰x11³
E.
Din. 12⁰x13⁰
Gar. 21⁴x21⁸
COVERED STOOP
56'-0"
© Design Basics, Inc.

MAIN FLOOR

PLAN NO.99115

A Very Distinctive Ranch

PRICE CODE: C

- This plan features:
- — Three bedrooms
- — Two full and one half baths
- This hip roofed ranch has an exterior mixing brick and siding
- The recessed entrance has sidelights which work to create a formal Entry
- The formal Dining Room has a Butler's Pantry for added convenience
- The Great Room features a vaulted ceiling and a fireplace for added atmosphere
- The large open Kitchen has ample cupboard space and spacious Breakfast Area
- The Master Suite includes a walk-in closet, private Ba and an elegant bay window
- A Laundry Room is on the main floor between the three-car Garage and the Kitchen
- This home is designed with a basement foundation

MAIN FLOOR — 1,947 SQ. FT.
BASEMENT — 1,947 SQ. FT.

TOTAL LIVING AREA:
1,947 SQ. FT.

WIDTH 69'-8"
DEPTH 46'-0"

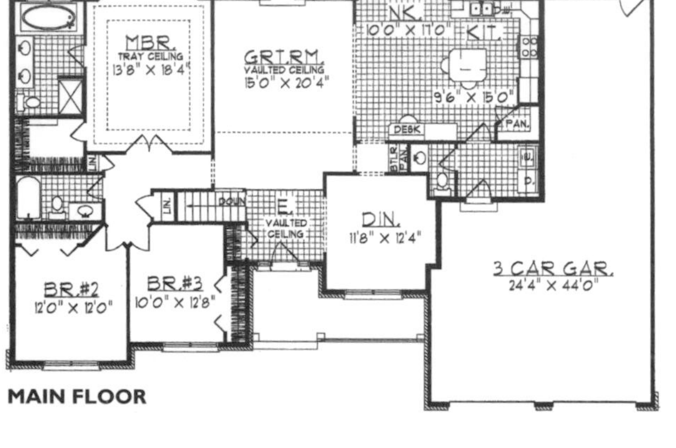

MBR.
TRAY CEILING
13'8" X 18'4"
GRT.RM.
VAULTED CEILING
15'0" X 20'4"
NK.
10'0" X 11'0"
KIT.
9'6" X 15'0"
DESK
PAN.
DIN.
11'8" X 12'4"
E.
VAULTED CEILING
BR.#2
12'0" X 12'0"
BR.#3
10'0" X 12'8"
3 CAR GAR.
24'4" X 44'0"

MAIN FLOOR

PLAN NO.65241

Envy of the Cul-de-Sac

PRICE CODE: A

- This plan features:
- — Two bedrooms
- — One full bath
- A closet just inside the front door is handy for coats, as well as dirty shoes
- The Living Room, Dining Room and Kitchen flow together
- The Kitchen gets plenty of light, thanks to a window over the double sink and sliding glass doors to the rear yard
- The Bedrooms share a full Bath with separate shower
- This home is designed with a basement foundation

MAIN FLOOR — 1,068 SQ. FT.
BASEMENT — 1,068 SQ. FT.
GARAGE — 245 SQ. FT.

TOTAL LIVING AREA:
1,068 SQ. FT.

WIDTH 30'-8"
DEPTH 48'-0"

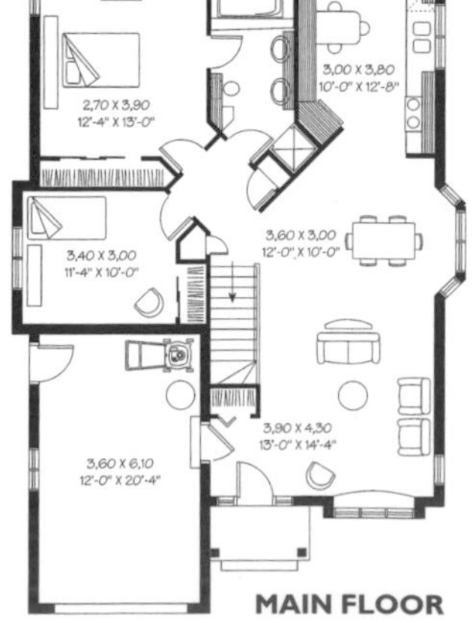

2,70 X 3,90
12'-4" X 13'-0"
3,00 X 3,80
10'-0" X 12'-8"
3,40 X 3,00
11'-4" X 10'-0"
3,60 X 3,00
12'-0" X 10'-0"
3,60 X 6,10
12'-0" X 20'-4"
3,90 X 4,30
13'-0" X 14'-4"

MAIN FLOOR

Traditional With a Twist

PRICE CODE: A

PLAN NO.65242

'his plan features:
- Three bedrooms
- One full and one half baths
- A closet just inside the front door is handy for coats
- The Living Room, Dining Room and Kitchen all flow together, providing a open space on the first floor
- The triple windows in the Living Room and in the second floor Master Bedroom provide plenty of light
- A Laundry Room and half Bath share a corner of the first floor, out of the flow of traffic
- This home is designed with a basement foundation

1ST FLOOR — 576 SQ. FT.
SECOND FLOOR — 576 SQ. FT.

TOTAL LIVING AREA:
1,152 SQ. FT.

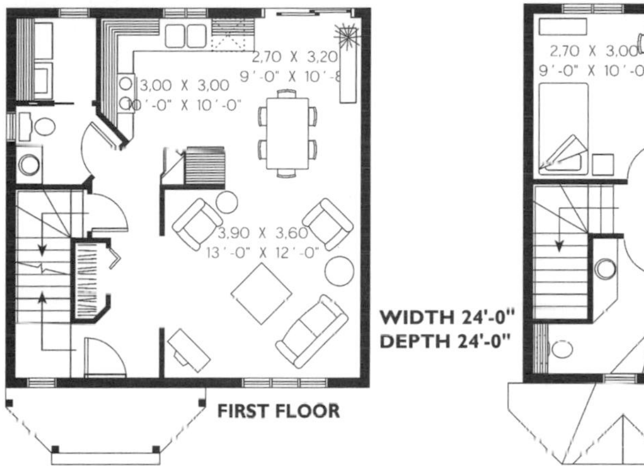
2,70 X 3,20
9'-0" X 10'-8
3,00 X 3,00
10'-0" X 10'-0"
3,90 X 3,60
13'-0" X 12'-0"
WIDTH 24'-0"
DEPTH 24'-0"
FIRST FLOOR
2,70 X 3,00
9'-0" X 10'-0
3,30 X 2,70
11'-0" X 9'-0"
3,30 X 3,30
11'-0" X 11'-0
SECOND FLOOR

Brick Magnificence

PRICE CODE: G

PLAN NO.92243

This plan features:
- Four bedrooms
- Three full baths
- Large windows and attractive brick detailing using segmented arches give fantastic curb appeal
- Convenient Ranch layout allows for step-saving one floor ease
- A fireplace in the Living Room adds a warm ambience
- The Family Room sports a second fireplace and built-in shelving
- Two additional Bedrooms include private access to a full double vanity Bath
- This home is designed with a basement foundation

MAIN FLOOR — 2,858 SQ. FT.
GARAGE — 768 SQ. FT.

TOTAL LIVING AREA:
2,858 SQ. FT.

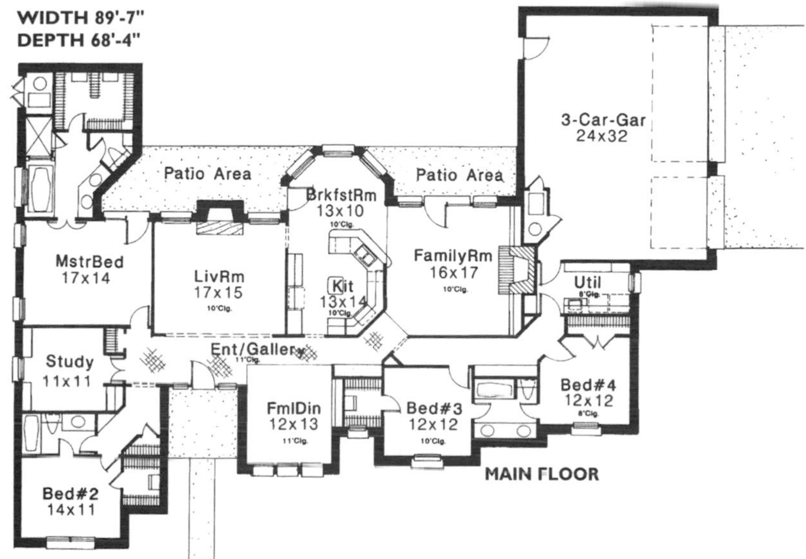
WIDTH 89'-7"
DEPTH 68'-4"
3-Car-Gar
24x32
Patio Area
Patio Area
BrkfstRm
13x10
MstrBed
17x14
LivRm
17x15
Kit
13x14
FamilyRm
16x17
Util
Study
11x11
Ent/Gallery
FmlDin
12x13
Bed#3
12x12
Bed#4
12x12
Bed#2
14x11
MAIN FLOOR

PLAN NO.35007

Perfect for a Woodland Setting

PRICE CODE: A

- This plan features:
- — Two bedrooms
- — One full bath
- A Living Room and Dining Room/Kitchen located to t front of the house
- A sloped ceiling adding to the cozy feeling of the hom
- A built-in entertainment center in the Living Room adding convenience
- An L-shaped Kitchen that includes a double sink and Dining area
- A full hall Bath easily accessible from either Bedroom
- A Loft and Balcony that overlooks the Living Room a the Dining area
- Storage on either side of the Loft
- This home is designed with basement, slab, and crawlspace foundation options

FIRST FLOOR — 763 SQ. FT.
SECOND FLOOR — 264 SQ. FT.

TOTAL LIVING AREA:
1,027 SQ. FT.

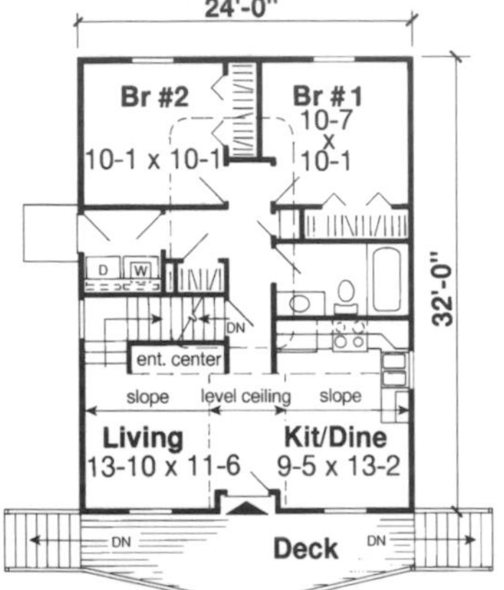

24'-0"
Br #2
10-1 x 10-1
Br #1
10-7 x 10-1
32'-0"
ent. center
DN
slope
level ceiling
slope
Living
13-10 x 11-6
Kit/Dine
9-5 x 13-2
Deck
DN
DN

FIRST FLOOR

Loft
11-4 x 22
Attic
Attic
optional wall
Balcony
flue
DN
ledge
railing
open to below
slope
level ceiling
slope
plant shelf

SECOND FLOOR

PLAN NO.97716

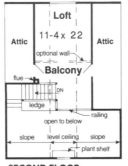

Photography supplied by Studer Residential Design, Inc.

European Richness

PRICE CODE: L

- This plan features:
- — Four bedrooms
- — Three full and two half baths
- The exterior of this home is graced by dual box bay windows and curved stairs
- A grand Foyer leading to the Gallery greets your guest
- The Dining Room and the Library each take advantage of light from their front windows
- The immense Master Suite includes a huge walk in closet and Bath
- Informal gathering can be held in the warm Hearth Room or the Breakfast Nook
- A rear Terrace is perfect for entertaining in warm weather
- A three-car Garage completes this luxurious home
- This home is designed with a basement foundation

FIRST FLOOR — 3,392 SQ. FT.
SECOND FLOOR — 1,197 SQ. FT.
BASEMENT — 3,392 SQ. FT.

TOTAL LIVING AREA:
4,589 SQ. FT.

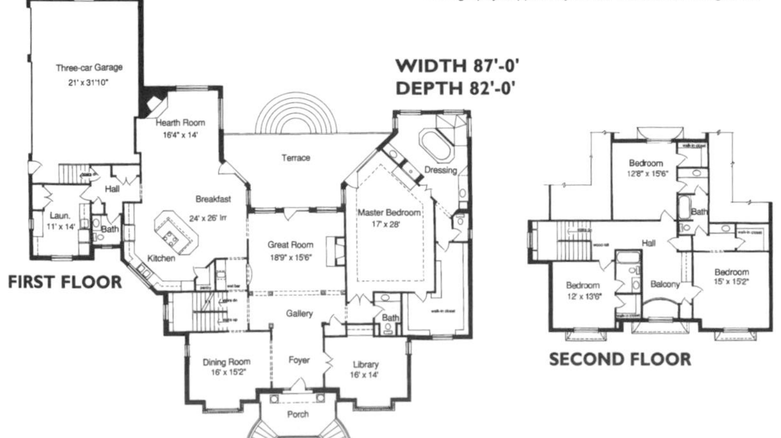

Three-car Garage
WIDTH 87'-0'
DEPTH 82'-0'
Hearth Room
Terrace
Dressing
Hall
Breakfast
Laun.
Bath
Master Bedroom
Great Room
Kitchen
FIRST FLOOR
Gallery
Bath
Dining Room
Foyer
Library
Porch
Bedroom
Bath
Hall
Bedroom
Balcony
Bedroom
SECOND FLOOR

A Nod to Yesteryear

PRICE CODE: A

is plan features:
- hree bedrooms
- ne full and one half baths
- touch of gingerbread and window boxes gives this me the look of a simpler time
- e Entry has a large closet to store coats and other gear
- nlike the homes of old, this first floor has an open yout, with columns delineating the living spaces
- is home is designed with a basement foundation
- T FLOOR — 759 SQ. FT.
- OND FLOOR — 735 SQ. FT.

TOTAL LIVING AREA:* 1,494 *SQ. FT.

PLAN NO.65244

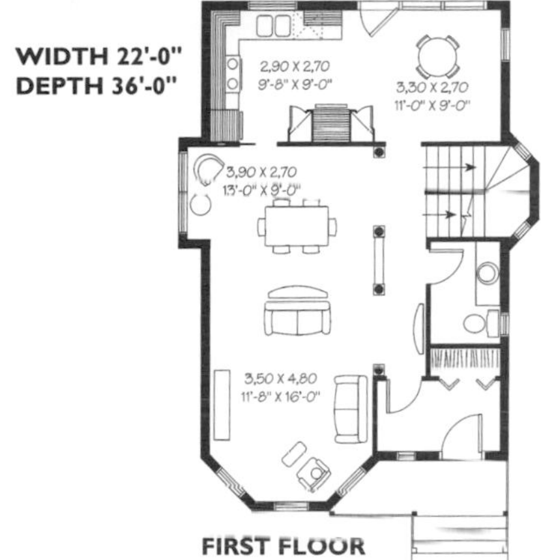

WIDTH 22'-0"
DEPTH 36'-0"
2,90 X 2,70
9'-8" X 9'-0"
3,30 X 2,70
11'-0" X 9'-0"
3,90 X 2,70
13'-0" X 9'-0"
3,50 X 4,80
11'-8" X 16'-0"
FIRST FLOOR

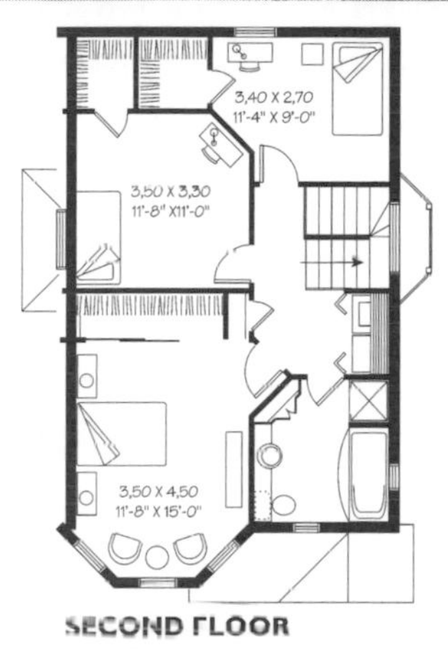

3,40 X 2,70
11'-4" X 9'-0"
3,50 X 3,30
11'-8" X11'-0"
3,50 X 4,50
11'-8" X 15'-0"
SECOND FLOOR

Master Suite Crowns Outstanding Plan

PRICE CODE: G

his plan features:
- our bedrooms
- hree full and one half baths
- Master Suite with a Study, a walk-in closet, and lavish hirlpool bath
- lower floor includes a Family Room with access to the atio via sliding doors
- spacious Great Room with a massive fireplace and ow windows
- his home is designed with a basement foundation
- T FLOOR — 1,742 SQ. FT.
- OND FLOOR — 809 SQ. FT.
- WER FLOOR — 443 SQ. FT.
- EMENT — 1,270 SQ. FT.
- RAGE — 558 SQ. FT.

TOTAL LIVING AREA:* 2,994 *SQ. FT.

Photography by John Ehrenclou

PLAN NO.10344

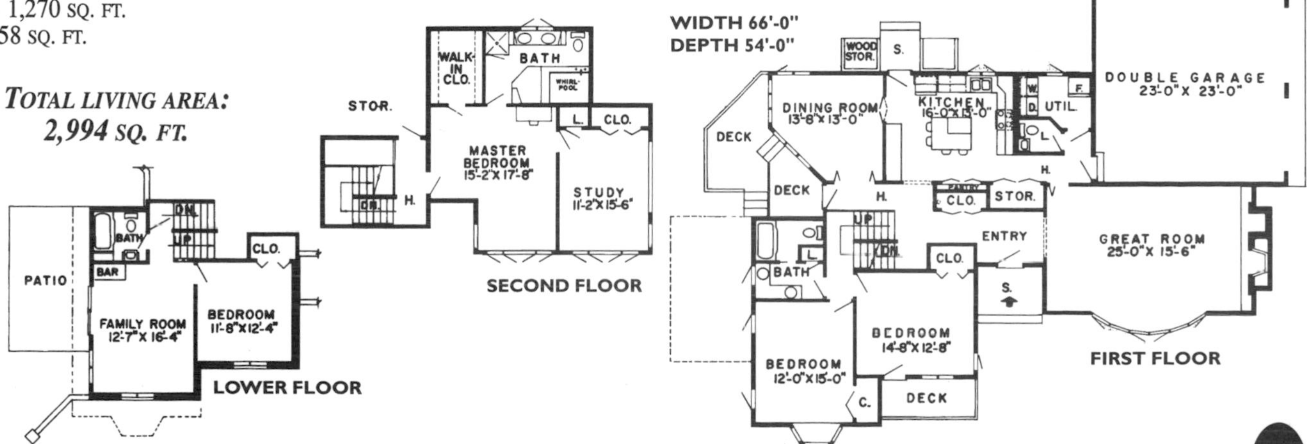

WIDTH 66'-0"
DEPTH 54'-0"
PATIO
BATH
BAR
DN
UP
CLO.
FAMILY ROOM
12'-7" X 16'-4"
BEDROOM
11'-8" X 12'-4"
LOWER FLOOR
STOR.
WALK-IN CLO.
BATH
WHIRL-POOL
L.
CLO.
MASTER BEDROOM
15'-2" X 17'-8"
STUDY
11'-2" X 15'-6"
H.
DN
SECOND FLOOR
WOOD STOR.
S.
DINING ROOM
13'-8" X 13'-0"
KITCHEN
16'-0" X 15'-0"
W
D
UTIL.
F.
L.
DOUBLE GARAGE
23'-0" X 23'-0"
DECK
DECK
H.
CLO.
STOR.
ENTRY
GREAT ROOM
25'-0" X 15'-6"
BATH
L
UP
DN
CLO.
S.
BEDROOM
14'-8" X 12'-8"
BEDROOM
12'-0" X 15'-0"
C.
DECK
FIRST FLOOR

PLAN NO. 99757

The Ultimate Kitchen

Price Code: C

- This plan features:
- — Three bedrooms
- — Two full and one half baths
- Front Porch invites visiting and leads into an open Entry with an angled staircase
- Living Room with a wall of windows and an island fireplace, opens to Dining Room with a bright, bay window
- Large and efficient Kitchen with a work island, walk-in Pantry, garden window over sink, skylit Nook and nearby Deck
- Corner Master Suite enhanced by Deck access, vaulted ceiling, a large walk-in closet and Spa Bath
- This home is designed with a crawlspace foundation

FIRST FLOOR — 1,472 SQ. FT.
SECOND FLOOR — 478 SQ. FT.
GARAGE — 558 SQ. FT.

TOTAL LIVING AREA:
1,950 SQ. FT.

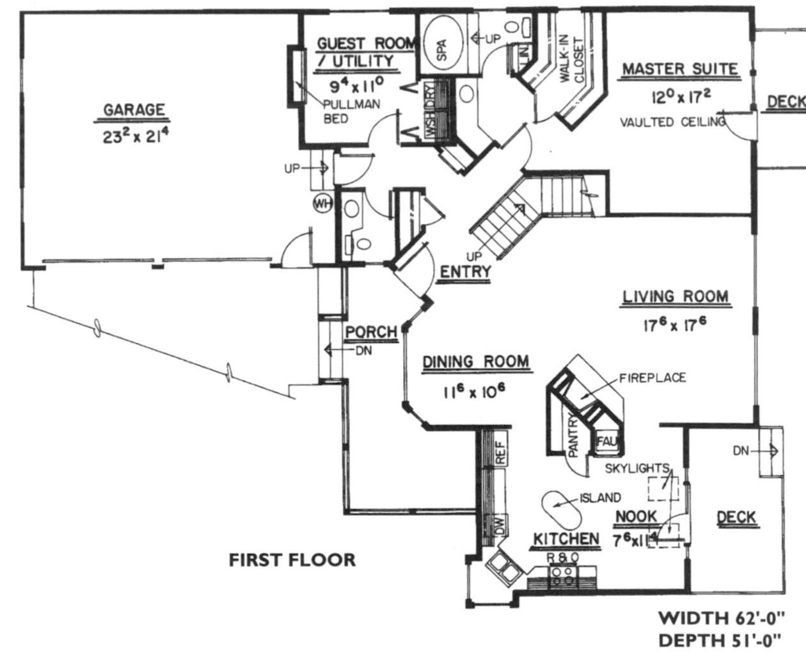

GARAGE
$23^{2} \times 21^{4}$
GUEST ROOM / UTILITY
$9^{4} \times 11^{0}$
PULLMAN BED
SPA
UP
WALK-IN CLOSET
MASTER SUITE
$12^{0} \times 17^{2}$
VAULTED CEILING
DECK
WH
ENTRY
UP
LIVING ROOM
$17^{6} \times 17^{6}$
PORCH
DN
DINING ROOM
$11^{6} \times 10^{6}$
FIREPLACE
PANTRY
REF
SKYLIGHTS
ISLAND
NOOK
$7^{6} \times 11^{4}$
KITCHEN
DW
DN
DECK
FIRST FLOOR
WIDTH 62'-0"
DEPTH 51'-0"

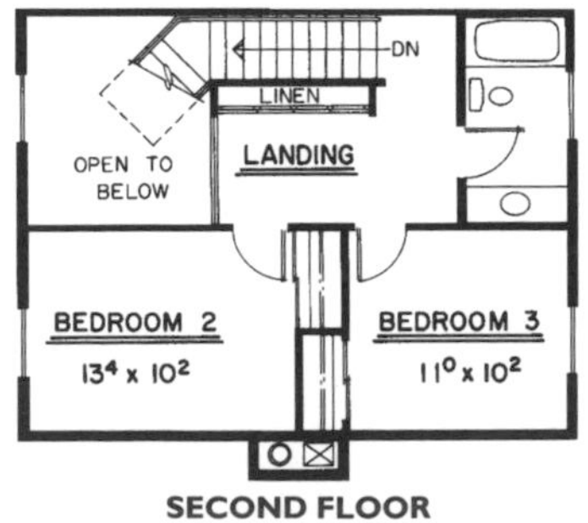

DN
LINEN
OPEN TO BELOW
LANDING
BEDROOM 2
$13^{4} \times 10^{2}$
BEDROOM 3
$11^{0} \times 10^{2}$
SECOND FLOOR

Luxurious Appointments

PRICE CODE: H

This plan features:
- Five bedrooms
- Four full and one half baths
- Formal areas located conveniently to promote elegant entertaining and family interaction
- Arched openings from the Foyer into the formal Dining Room and the Living Room
- Decorative columns highlighting the entrance to the Breakfast Room
- Two-Story ceiling topping the Family Room, highlighted by a fireplace
- Efficiency emphasized in the island Kitchen with a walk-in Pantry and abundant counter space
- Master Suite with lavish Bath topped by a vaulted ceiling
- This home is designed with basement and crawlspace foundation options

ST FLOOR — 1,527 SQ. FT.
COND FLOOR — 1,495 SQ. FT.
SEMENT — 1,527 SQ. FT.
RAGE — 440 SQ. FT.

TOTAL LIVING AREA:
3,022 SQ. FT.

PLAN NO.97213

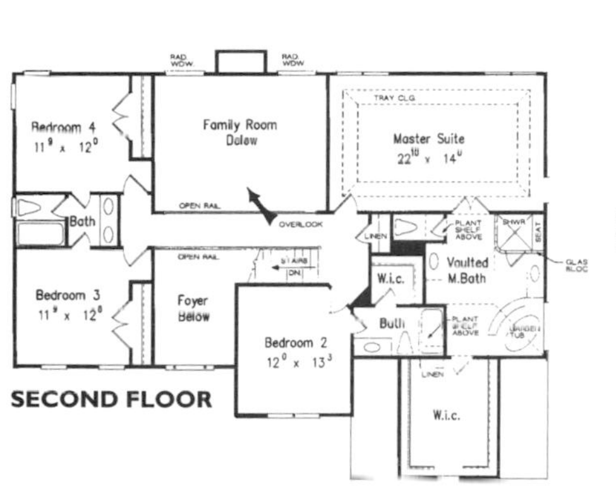

Bedroom 4
11⁹ x 12⁰
Family Room Below
Master Suite
22¹⁰ x 14⁰
TRAY CLG
OPEN RAIL
OVERLOOK
Bath
Bedroom 3
11⁹ x 12⁰
Foyer Below
W.i.c.
Vaulted M.Bath
Bath
Bedroom 2
12⁰ x 13³
W.i.c.
SECOND FLOOR

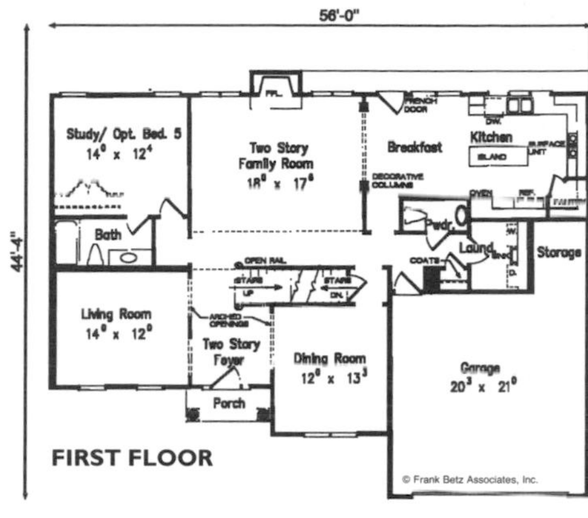

56'-0"
44'-4"
Study/ Opt. Bed. 5
14⁰ x 12⁴
Two Story Family Room
18⁸ x 17⁶
Breakfast
Kitchen
ISLAND
Bath
Pwdr.
Laund.
Storage
Living Room
14⁰ x 12⁶
Two Story Foyer
Porch
Dining Room
12⁰ x 13³
Garage
20³ x 21⁰
FIRST FLOOR
© Frank Betz Associates, Inc.

Compact and Convenient Colonial

PRICE CODE: A

This plan features:
- Three bedrooms
- Two full and one half baths
- Traditional Entry with landing staircase, closet and powder room
- Living Room with focal point fireplace opens to formal Dining Room for ease in entertaining
- Efficient, L-shaped Kitchen with built-in Pantry, eating Nook and Garage entry
- Corner Master Bedroom with private Bath and attic access
- Two additional Bedrooms with ample closets share a double vanity Bath
- This home is designed with a basement foundation

ST FLOOR — 700 SQ. FT.
COND FLOOR — 700 SQ. FT.
RAGE — 510 SQ. FT.

TOTAL LIVING AREA:
1,400 SQ. FT.

PLAN NO.99255

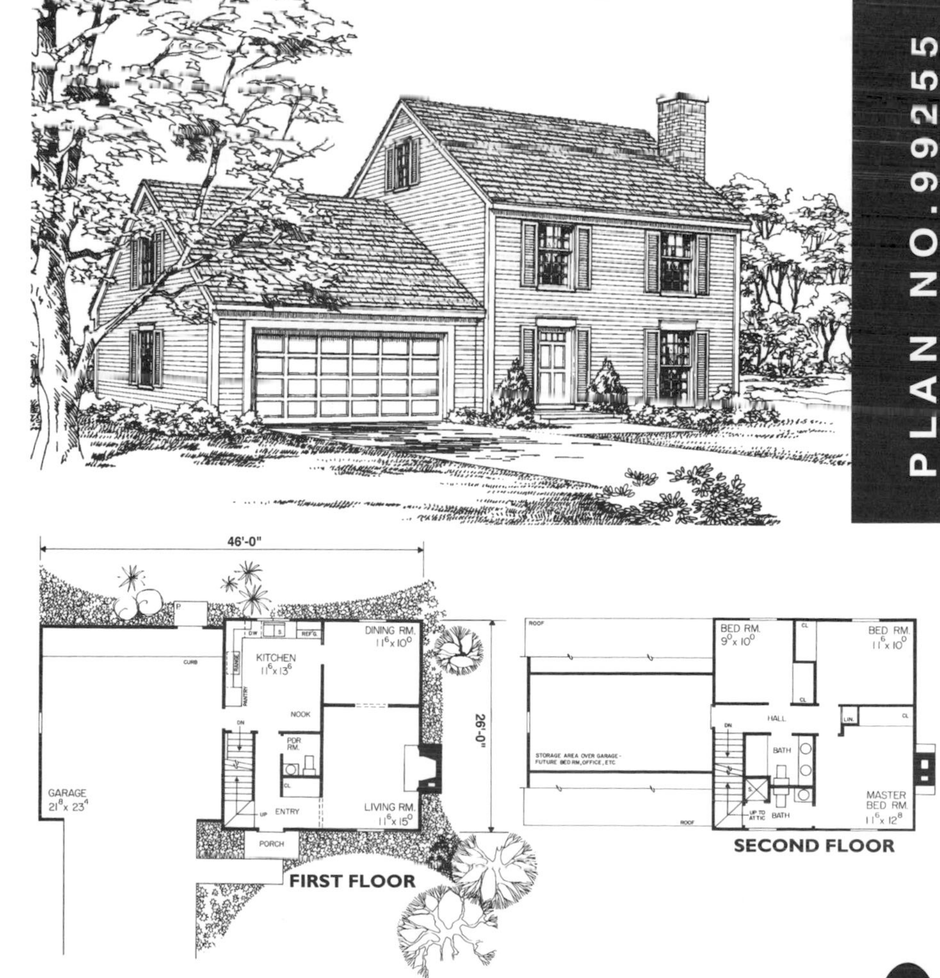

46'-0"
26'-0"
DINING RM.
11⁶x10⁰
KITCHEN
11⁶x13⁶
NOOK
PDR. RM.
ENTRY
PORCH
LIVING RM.
11⁶x15⁰
GARAGE
21⁸x 23⁴
FIRST FLOOR
BED RM.
9⁰x 10⁰
BED RM.
11⁶x 10⁰
HALL
BATH
MASTER BED RM.
11⁶x 12⁸
STORAGE AREA OVER GARAGE - FUTURE BEDRM, OFFICE, ETC
SECOND FLOOR

PLAN NO. 92265

Luxurious Masterpiece

PRICE CODE: K

- This plan features:
  - — Four bedrooms
  - — Three full and one half baths
- An elegant and distinguished exterior
- An expansive formal Living Room with a 14-foot ceil and a raised hearth fireplace
- Informal Family Room offers another fireplace, wetbar, cathedral ceiling and access to the covered Pa
- A hub Kitchen with a cooktop island, peninsula counter/snack bar, and a bright Breakfast Area
- French doors lead into a quiet Study offering many us
- Private Master Bedroom enhanced by a pullman ceilir lavish his and her Baths, and a garden window tub in one of them
- Three additional Bedrooms with walk-in closets and private access to a full Bath
- This home is designed with basement and slab foundation options

MAIN FLOOR — 3,818 SQ. FT.
GARAGE — 816 SQ. FT.

TOTAL LIVING AREA:
3,818 SQ. FT.

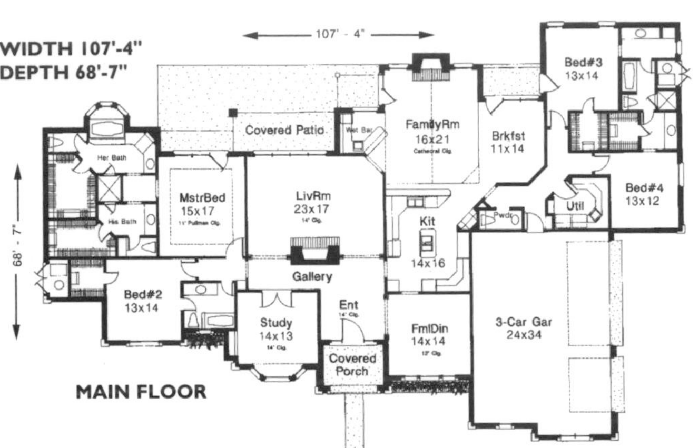
WIDTH 107'-4"
DEPTH 68'-7"
107' - 4"
68' - 7"
Covered Patio
Wet Bar
FamilyRm
16x21
Brkfst
11x14
Bed#3
13x14
Her Bath
His Bath
MstrBed
15x17
LivRm
23x17
Kit
14x16
Util
Bed#4
13x12
Gallery
Bed#2
13x14
Study
14x13
Ent
FmlDin
14x14
3-Car Gar
24x34
Covered
Porch
MAIN FLOOR

PLAN NO. 65246

Glass and Stone

PRICE CODE: B

- This plan features:
  - — Three bedrooms
  - — Two full baths
- The Kitchen wraps around the Dining Area
- A focal point fireplace highlights the Living Room
- This home is designed with a basement foundation

FIRST FLOOR — 1,109 SQ. FT.
SECOND FLOOR — 550 SQ. FT.
BASEMENT — 1,659 SQ. FT.

TOTAL LIVING AREA:
1,659 SQ. FT.

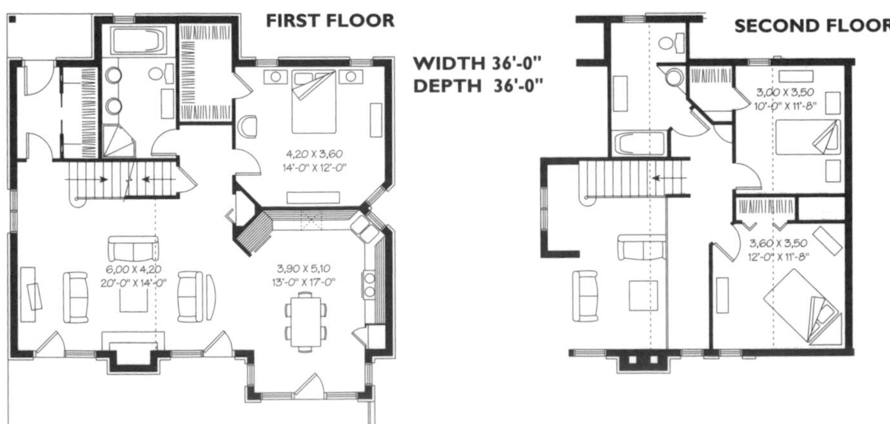
FIRST FLOOR
WIDTH 36'-0"
DEPTH 36'-0"
4,20 X 3,60
14'-0" X 12'-0"
6,00 X 4,20
20'-0" X 14'-0"
3,90 X 5,10
13'-0" X 17'-0"
SECOND FLOOR
3,00 X 3,50
10'-0" X 11'-8"
3,60 X 3,50
12'-0" X 11'-8"

PLAN NO. 65248

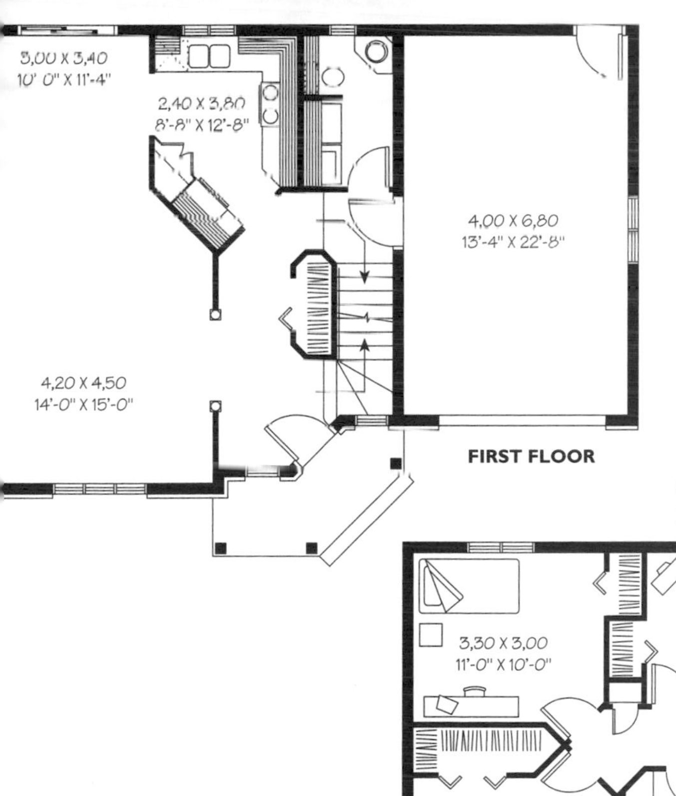
3,00 X 3,40
10' 0" X 11'-4"
2,40 X 3,80
8'-8" X 12'-8"
4,00 X 6,80
13'-4" X 22'-8"
4,20 X 4,50
14'-0" X 15'-0"
FIRST FLOOR

WIDTH 40'-0"
DEPTH 28'-0"

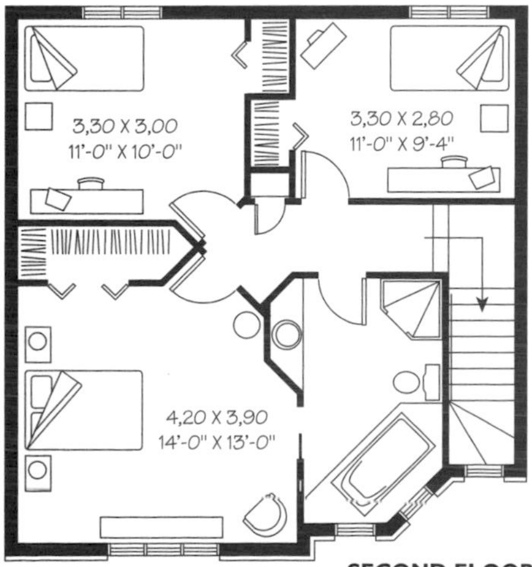

3,30 X 3,00
11'-0" X 10'-0"

3,30 X 2,80
11'-0" X 9'-4"

4,20 X 3,90
14'-0" X 13'-0"

SECOND FLOOR

Angled Design Adds Artistic Interest

Price Code: A

- This plan features:
  - — Three bedrooms
  - — One full and one half baths
- The open design of the first floor adds grand scale to the plan
- The Bedrooms share the privacy of the second floor and a lush Bath with window-lined, angled tub
- The Kitchen, with generous counter and cabinet space, is sure to please the cooks of the house
- This home is designed with a basement foundation

FIRST FLOOR — 702 SQ. FT.
SECOND FLOOR — 702 SQ. FT.
GARAGE — 306 SQ. FT.

TOTAL LIVING AREA:
1,404 SQ. FT.

PLAN NO. 92220

Southern Hospitality

PRICE CODE: C

- ■ This plan features:
  - — Three bedrooms
  - — Two full baths
- ■ Welcoming covered Veranda catches breezes
- ■ Easy-care, tiled Entry leads into Great Room with fieldstone fireplace and Atrium door to another covered Veranda topped by a cathedral ceiling
- ■ A bright Kitchen/Dining Room includes a stovetop island/snack bar, built-in Pantry and desk and access to covered Veranda
- ■ Vaulted ceiling crowns Master Bedroom that offers a plush Bath and huge walk-in closet
- ■ Two additional Bedrooms with ample closets share a double vanity Bath
- ■ This home is designed with basement, slab, and crawlspace foundation options

MAIN FLOOR — 1,830 SQ. FT.
GARAGE — 759 SQ. FT.

TOTAL LIVING AREA:
1,830 SQ. FT.

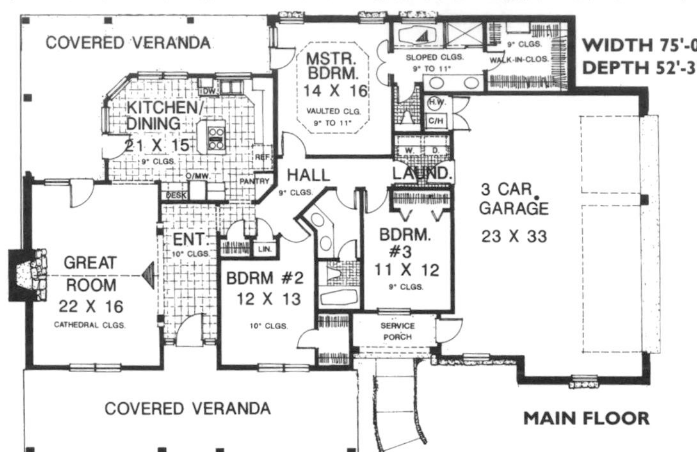
COVERED VERANDA
MSTR. BDRM. 14 X 16
VAULTED CLG. 9" TO 11"
SLOPED CLGS. 9" TO 11"
9" CLGS.
WALK-IN-CLOS.
WIDTH 75'-0"
DEPTH 52'-3"
KITCHEN/DINING 21 X 15
9" CLGS.
DW
O/MW.
REF.
PANTRY
DESK
HALL
9" CLGS.
H.W.
C/H
W. D.
LAUND.
3 CAR GARAGE 23 X 33
ENT.
10" CLGS.
LIN.
BDRM. #3 11 X 12
9" CLGS.
GREAT ROOM 22 X 16
CATHEDRAL CLGS.
BDRM #2 12 X 13
10" CLGS.
SERVICE PORCH
COVERED VERANDA
MAIN FLOOR

PLAN NO. 35009

Simple Yet Practical

PRICE CODE: A

- ■ This plan features:
  - — One bedroom
  - — One full bath
- ■ Simple yet practical cabin designed for weekend retr
- ■ A large Bedroom downstairs and a Loft upstairs prov plenty of sleeping room
- ■ Interesting sloped ceiling in the first floor living spac
- ■ Efficient U-shaped Kitchen opens into Dining Area
- ■ Spacious front Deck
- ■ This home is designed with basement, slab, and crawlspace foundation options

FIRST FLOOR — 763 SQ. FT.
SECOND FLOOR — 240 SQ. FT.

TOTAL LIVING AREA:
1,003 SQ. FT.

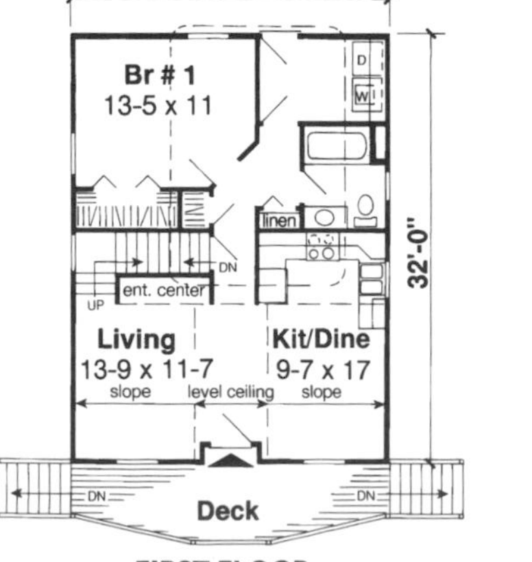
24'-0"
Br # 1
13-5 x 11
D
W
linen
DN
UP
ent. center
32'-0"
Living
13-9 x 11-7
slope
level ceiling
Kit/Dine
9-7 x 17
slope
DN
Deck
DN
FIRST FLOOR

Loft
11-4 x 20
flue at crawl/slab option
Attic
optional wall
Attic
Balcony
DN
ledge
railing
open to below
slope
level ceiling
slope
plant shelf
SECOND FLOOR

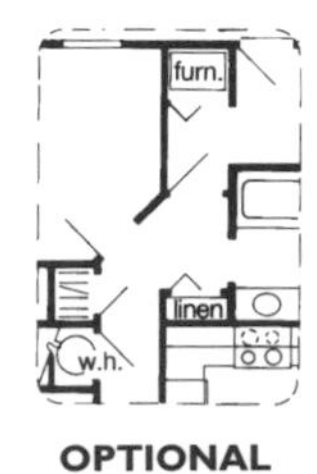
furn.
linen
w.h.

OPTIONAL CRAWLSPACE/SLAB

U-Shaped Staircase

PRICE CODE: D

ıis plan features:
- our bedrooms
- wo full and one half baths
- ıe Laundry Room is conveniently located on the second ɔor, no traveling up and down the stairs with loaded ıundry baskets
- Butler's Pantry connects that Kitchen and the Dining ɔom will be helpful when entertaining
- ıis home is designed with a crawlspace foundation

ST FLOOR — 1,070 SQ. FT.
OND FLOOR — 1,050 SQ. FT.

TOTAL LIVING AREA:
2,120 SQ. FT.

PLAN NO.81006

◀ 56' ▶

MASTER
14/0 X 12/6
LINEN
BR. 2
10/0 X 12/4
DN.
BR. 3
11/0 X 11/0
BR. 4
10/0 X 11/2
SECOND FLOOR

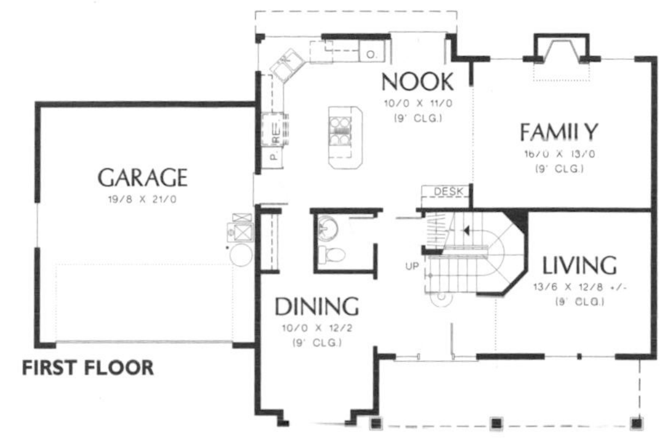

NOOK
10/0 X 11/0
(9' CLG.)
FAMILY
16/0 X 13/0
(9' CLG.)
GARAGE
19/8 X 21/0
DESK
UP
LIVING
13/6 X 12/8 +/-
(9' CLG.)
DINING
10/0 X 12/2
(9' CLG.)
FIRST FLOOR

▲ 37' ▼

Country Comforts

PRICE CODE: F

his plan features:
- 'our bedrooms
- Three full and one half bath
- sprawling front Porch
- two-way fireplace warming the Hearth Room and the iving Room
- formal, bayed Dining Room with decorative ceiling
- n efficient, well-appointed Kitchen with peninsula ɔunter and double sinks
- vaulted ceiling in the Master Suite which is equipped ith a private Master Bath
- hree additional Bedrooms each with adjoining ıll Baths
- his home is designed with a asement foundation

ST FLOOR — 1,737 SQ. FT.
OND FLOOR — 826 SQ. FT.
SEMENT — 1,728 SQ. FT.

TOTAL LIVING AREA:
2,563 SQ. FT.

PLAN NO.20144

Photography by Glenn Graves

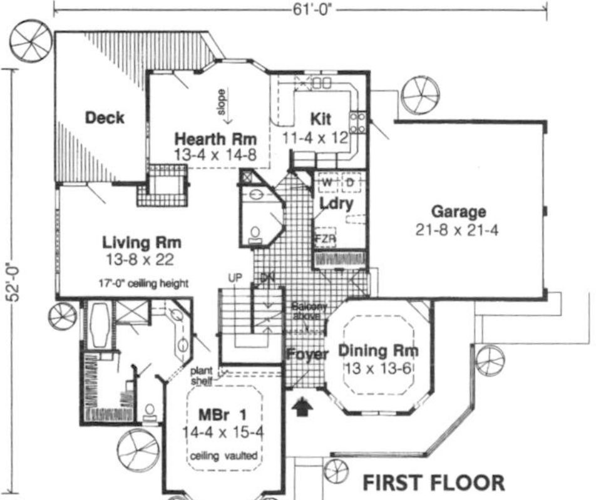

61'-0"
52'-0"
Deck
slope
Hearth Rm
13-4 x 14-8
Kit
11-4 x 12
W D
Ldry
FZR
Garage
21-8 x 21-4
Living Rm
13-8 x 22
17'-0" ceiling height
UP
DN
Balcony
Foyer
Dining Rm
13 x 13-6
plant shelf
MBr 1
14-4 x 15-4
ceiling vaulted
FIRST FLOOR

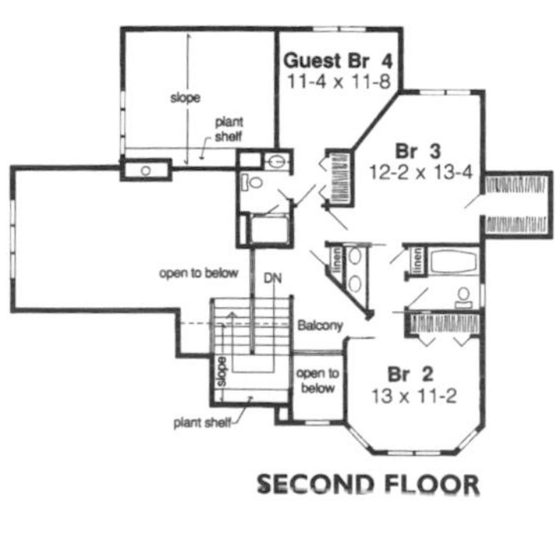

Guest Br 4
11-4 x 11-8
slope
plant shelf
Br 3
12-2 x 13-4
open to below
DN
Balcony
open to below
slope
Br 2
13 x 11-2
plant shelf
SECOND FLOOR

PLAN NO.65250

Graced by a Gazebo

PRICE CODE: B

■ This plan features:
— Three bedrooms
— Three full baths

■ The Entry to this home is unparalleled, with a curved stair leading to a Gazebo

■ The Living Room shares a two-sided fireplace with th Master Bedroom

■ The L-shaped Kitchen has plenty of cabinet space and a generous eating area

■ The Master Bedroom has double closets and a private balcony

■ This home is designed with a basement foundation

FIRST FLOOR — 840 SQ. FT.
SECOND FLOOR — 757 SQ. FT.

TOTAL LIVING AREA:
1,597 SQ. FT.

WIDTH 26'-0"
DEPTH 32'-0"

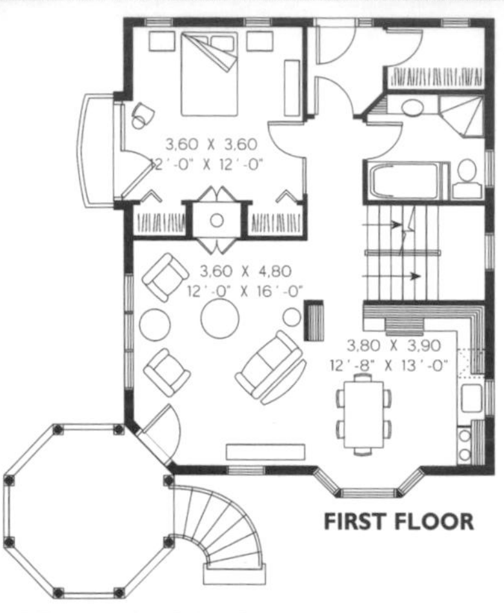

3,60 X 3,60
12'-0" X 12'-0"
3,60 X 4,80
12'-0" X 16'-0"
3,80 X 3,90
12'-8" X 13'-0"

FIRST FLOOR

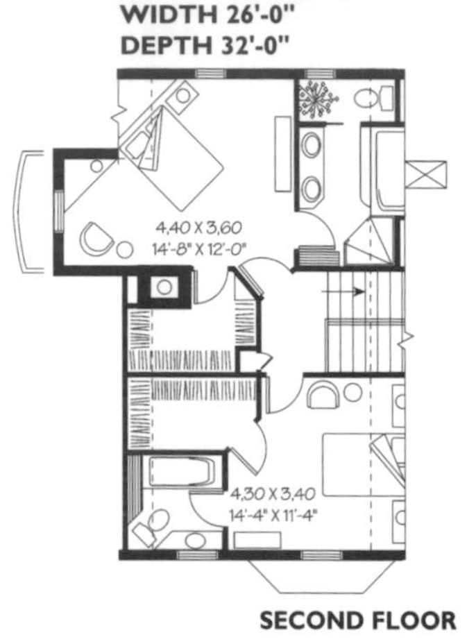

4,40 X 3,60
14'-8" X 12'-0"
4,30 X 3,40
14'-4" X 11'-4"

SECOND FLOOR

PLAN NO.97714

Multiple Gables

PRICE CODE: J

■ This plan features:
— Three bedrooms
— Three full and one half baths

■ Impressive Foyer offers dramatic view past the Dining Room and open stairs through the Great Room to the rear yard

■ Exquisite columns, 13-foot ceiling heights and detaile ceiling treatments decorating the Dining Room and Great Room

■ Gourmet Kitchen with island and snack bar combines with the spacious Breakfast Room and the Hearth Roo to create a warm atmosphere

■ The Master Suite has a fireplace complemented by a deluxe Dressing Room with whirlpool tub, shower an dual vanity

■ This home is designed with a basement foundation

MAIN FLOOR — 3,570 SQ. FT.
LOWER FLOOR — 1,203 SQ. FT.
BONUS — 2,367 SQ. FT.

TOTAL LIVING AREA:
3,570 SQ. FT.

WIDTH 84'-6"
DEPTH 69'-4"

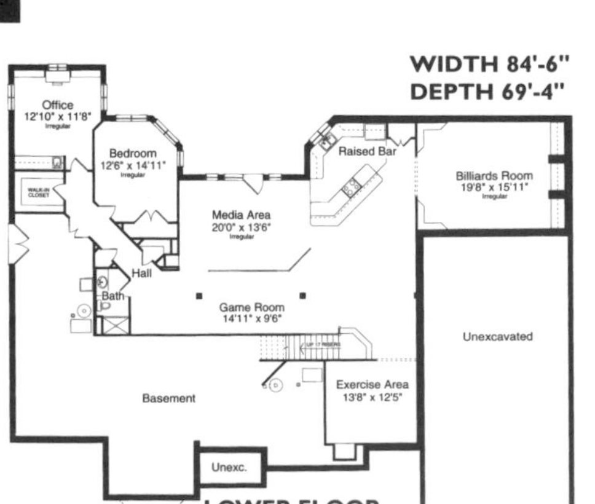

Office
12'10" x 11'8"
Bedroom
12'6" x 14'11"
Raised Bar
Billiards Room
19'8" x 15'11"
Media Area
20'0" x 13'6"
Hall
Bath
Game Room
14'11" x 9'6"
Unexcavated
Basement
Exercise Area
13'8" x 12'5"
Unexc.

LOWER FLOOR

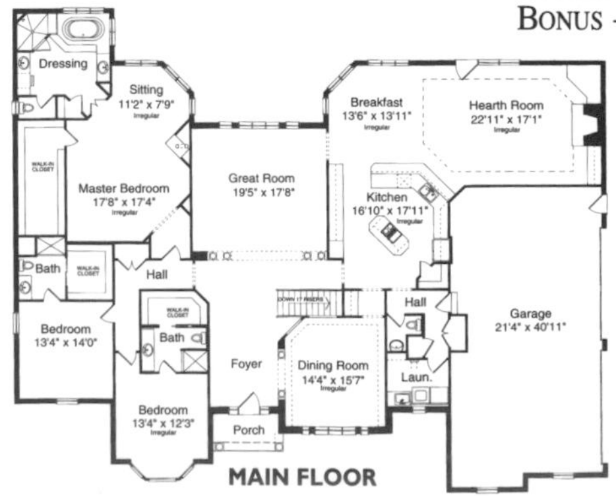

Dressing
Sitting
11'2" x 7'9"
Breakfast
13'6" x 13'11"
Hearth Room
22'11" x 17'1"
Master Bedroom
17'8" x 17'4"
Great Room
19'5" x 17'8"
Kitchen
16'10" x 17'11"
Bath
Hall
Bedroom
13'4" x 14'0"
Bath
Foyer
Dining Room
14'4" x 15'7"
Hall
Garage
21'4" x 40'11"
Laun.
Bedroom
13'4" x 12'3"
Porch

MAIN FLOOR

Ten-Foot Entry

PRICE CODE: B

PLAN NO. 94986

ais plan features:

- hree bedrooms
- wo full baths
- arge volume Great Room highlighted by a fireplace anked by windows
- e-through wetbar enhancing the Breakfast Area d the Dining Room
- ecorative ceiling treatment giving elegance the Dining Room
- ılly equipped Kitchen with a planning desk d a Pantry
- oomy Master Bedroom suite has a volume ceiling d special amenities; a skylighted dressing Bath area, ant shelf, a large walk-in closet, a double vanity and whirlpool tub
- condary Bedrooms with ample closets sharing convenient hall Bath
- ais home is designed with a basement foundation
- ternate foundation options available at an ditional charge. Please call 1-800-235-5700 for ore information.

N FLOOR — 1,604 SQ. FT.
AGE — 466 SQ. FT.

TOTAL LIVING AREA:
1,604 SQ. FT.

MAIN FLOOR

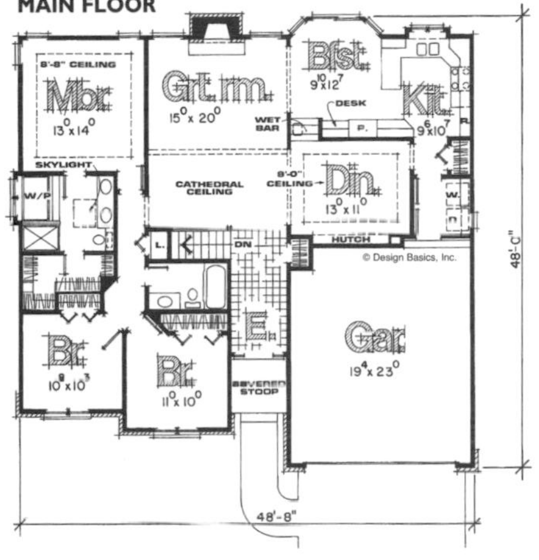
8'-8" CEILING
Mbr.
13⁰x14⁰
Grt.rm.
15⁰x 20⁰
Bfst.
Kit.
DESK
WET BAR
SKYLIGHT
CATHEDRAL CEILING
Din.
13⁰x 11⁰
HUTCH
© Design Basics, Inc.
Gar.
19⁴x 23⁰
Br.
Br.
11⁰x 10⁰
COVERED STOOP
48'-8"
48'-0"

Welcoming Front Porch

PRICE CODE: E

PLAN NO. 99133

ais plan features:

- aree bedrooms
- wo full and one half baths
- ae covered front Porch provides a warm welcome
- ae Great Room has a fireplace with built-in binets to one side
- ter the nook through and arched soffit, e Kitchen is just beyond
- ccess the Screen Porch from the nook
- ae Master Bedroom has a tray ceiling, walk in closet, and a private Bath
- ocated upstairs for privacy are the secondary Bedrooms
- ais home has a three-car Garage
- ais home is designed with a basement foundation

T FLOOR — 1,835 SQ. FT.
OND FLOOR — 573 SQ. FT.
EMENT — 1,835 SQ. FT.

TOTAL LIVING AREA:
2,408 SQ. FT.

SCREEN PORCH
11'4" X 12'8"
KIT.
NK.
12'8" X 16'0"
GRT.RM.
15'8" X 20'0"
MBR.
TRAY CEILING
DIN.
11'8" X 13'8"
3 CAR GAR.
32'0" X 24'0"
BR.#2
13'8" X 13'4"
GRT.RM.
BR.#3
CATHEDRAL CEILING
11'8" X 13'4"

FIRST FLOOR

SECOND FLOOR

PLAN NO. 65251

Peaks and Arches Add Interest

PRICE CODE: B

- This plan features:
- — Three bedrooms
- — One full and one half baths
- This house offers plenty of curb appeal, thanks to its interesting roofline and beautiful windows
- The Living Room offers a circular design, two-story height and angled fireplace shared by the Dining Ro
- The Kitchen has easy access to the Dining Room an the Living Room
- This home is designed with a basement foundation

FIRST FLOOR — 917 SQ. FT.
SECOND FLOOR — 742 SQ. FT.
GARAGE — 300 SQ. FT.

TOTAL LIVING AREA:
1,659 SQ. FT.

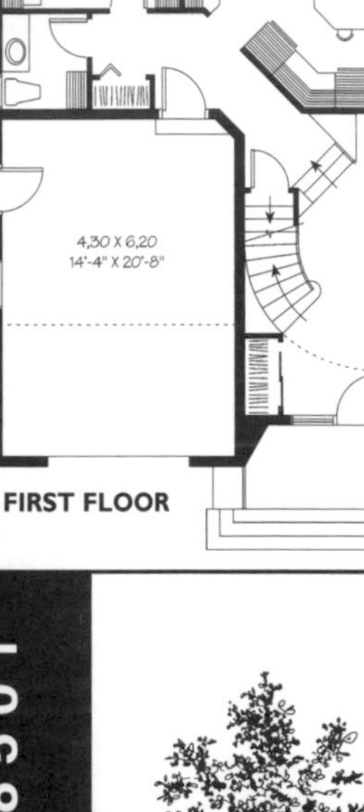

4,30 X 6,20
14'-4" X 20'-8"

FIRST FLOOR

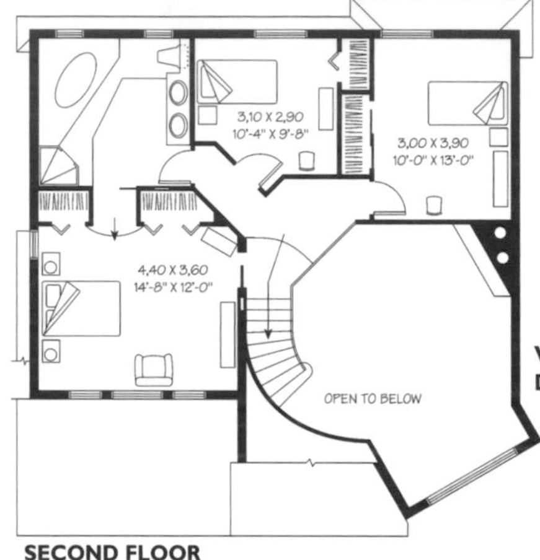

3,10 X 2,90
10'-4" X 9'-8"
3,00 X 3,90
10'-0" X 13'-0"
4,40 X 3,60
14'-8" X 12'-0"
OPEN TO BELOW

SECOND FLOOR

WIDTH 38'-0"
DEPTH 36'-0"

PLAN NO. 98501

Stunning Family Plan

PRICE CODE: D

- This plan features:
- — Four bedrooms
- — Two full and one half baths
- Windows, brick, and columns combine to create an eye-catching elevation
- A pair of columns greets you as you enter the Living Room
- The formal Dining Room is located just steps away from the Kitchen
- Set on a unique angle the Family Room has a rear wall fireplace
- The open Kitchen has a center island, which makes for easy meal prep
- Set away from the active areas the Master Bedroom is a quiet retreat
- Three additional Bedrooms are located in their own wing of the home
- A Patio in the rear and a two-car Garage complete this home plan
- This home is designed with a slab foundation

MAIN FLOOR — 2,194 SQ. FT.
GARAGE — 462 SQ. FT.

TOTAL LIVING AREA:
2,194 SQ. FT.

Patio
FamilyRm.
16x14
Brkfst.
11x9
Bed#4
11x10
Bed#3
11x13
Kit.
MstrBed
15x13
Bed#2
11x11
Gallery
Uti.
FmlDin.
11x12
Ent.
LivRm.
14x12
Gar.
20x22
Por.
57' - 0"

MAIN FLOOR

60' - 0"

PLAN NO. 65252

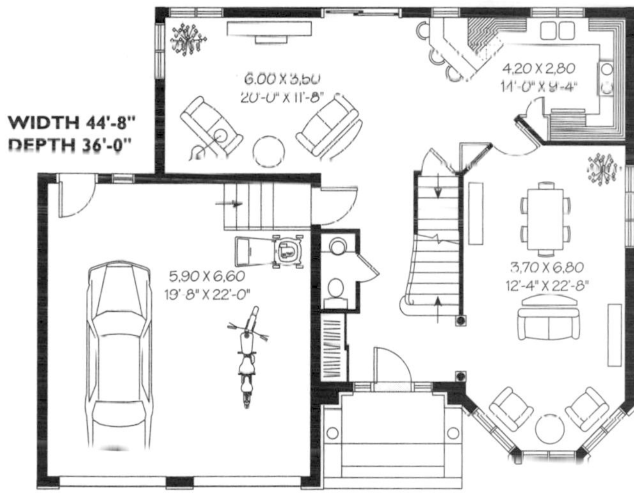

WIDTH 44'-8"
DEPTH 36'-0"
6.00 X 3.60
20'-0" X 11'-8"
4.20 X 2.80
14'-0" X 9'-4"
5.90 X 6.60
19' 8" X 22'-0"
3.70 X 6.80
12'-4" X 22'-8"

FIRST FLOOR

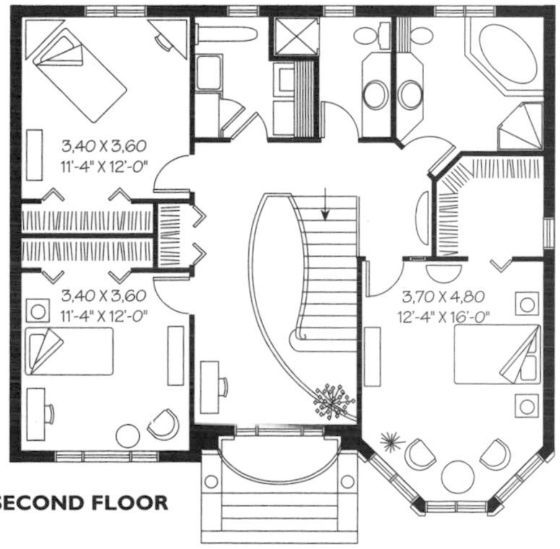

3,40 X 3,60
11'-4" X 12'-0"
3,40 X 3,60
11'-4" X 12'-0"
3,70 X 4,80
12'-4" X 16'-0"

SECOND FLOOR

Two Story-Turret

Price Code: C

- This plan features:
  - — Three bedrooms
  - — Two full and one half bath
- The many windows bring daylight into the house
- The Foyer opens onto the formal Living and Dining Room space
- An informal Family Room is located to the rear of the home and joins the Kitchen
- The well-appointed Kitchen includes a snack bar peninsula
- This home is designed with a basement foundation

FIRST FLOOR — 916 SQ. FT.
SECOND FLOOR — 1,080 SQ. FT.
BASEMENT — 916 SQ. FT.
GARAGE — 436 SQ. FT.

TOTAL LIVING AREA:
1,996 SQ. FT.

PLAN NO.92160

Terrific Open Layout

PRICE CODE: C

- This plan features:
  - — Four Bedrooms
  - — Two full and one half baths
- An impressive entrance leads to an Entry hall that has access to a Powder Room and both the formal and informal areas
- Generous corner Kitchen is open to the bayed Nook bringing in an abundance of natural sunlight
- Family Room including a focal point fireplace enjoyed from the Nook and Kitchen
- Large Master Suite with a luxurious Bath and a walk-in closet
- This home is designed with a crawlspace foundation

FIRST FLOOR — 1,041 SQ. FT.
SECOND FLOOR — 954 SQ. FT.

TOTAL LIVING AREA:
1,995 SQ. FT.

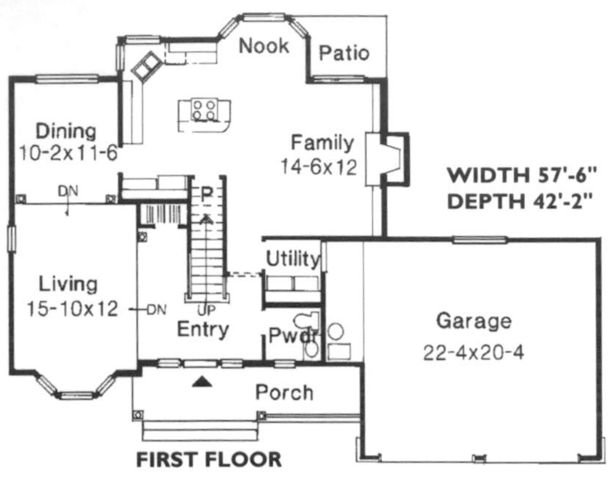
Nook
Patio
Dining
10-2x11-6
Family
14-6x12
DN
Living
15-10x12
DN
Utility
UP
Entry
Pwdr
Porch
Garage
22-4x20-4
WIDTH 57'-6"
DEPTH 42'-2"
FIRST FLOOR

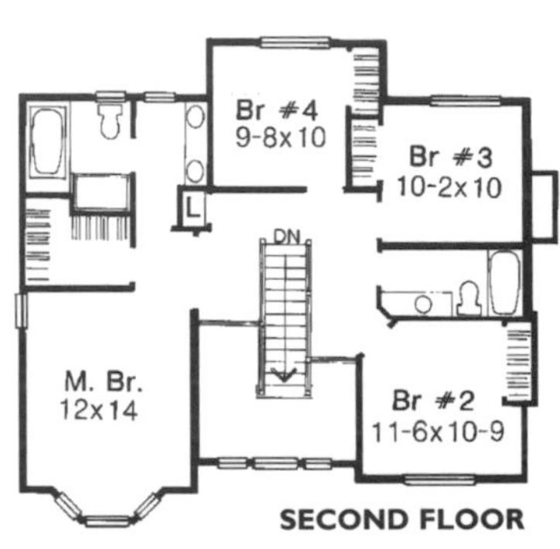
Br #4
9-8x10
Br #3
10-2x10
DN
M. Br.
12x14
Br #2
11-6x10-9
SECOND FLOOR

PLAN NO.81005

Bonus Space

PRICE CODE: G

- This plan features:
  - — Four bedrooms
  - — Two full and one half baths
- A Country covered Porch enhances the front elevatio
- The Kitchen, Nook and Family Room adjoin into a l living space
- The Living Room and Dining Room adjoin with columns accenting the Entry between the rooms
- The bonus area over the Garage offers expansion in the future
- This home is designed with a crawlspace foundation

FIRST FLOOR — 1,618 SQ. FT.
SECOND FLOOR — 1,380 SQ. FT.
BONUS ROOM — 590 SQ. FT.

TOTAL LIVING AREA:
2,998 SQ. FT.

NOOK
DINING
FAMILY
DEN
LIVING
PORCH
FIRST FLOOR
GARAGE
BR. 4
BR. 3
MASTER
BR. 2
SECOND FLOOR
BONUS
WIDTH 53'-0"
DEPTH 77'-0"

Jnique V-Shaped Home

PRICE CODE: I

s plan features:
- o bedrooms
- ree full baths
-)kshelves, interspersed with windows, line the long .way that provides access to the owner's wing
- ır skylights brighten the already sunny Eating Nook he huge Country Kitchen
- valk-in Pantry, range-top work island, built-in becue and a sink add to the amenities of the Kitchen
- vide window bay and an entire wall of windows along ength illuminate the Living Room
- ster Suite with his and her closets, and adjacent ssing Area plus a luxurious private Bath
- uest Suite with a private Sitting Area and full Bath
- s home is designed with a crawlspace foundation

ı FLOOR — 3,417 SQ. FT.
AGE — 795 SQ. FT.

TOTAL LIVING AREA:
3,417 SQ. FT.

PLAN NO. 99721

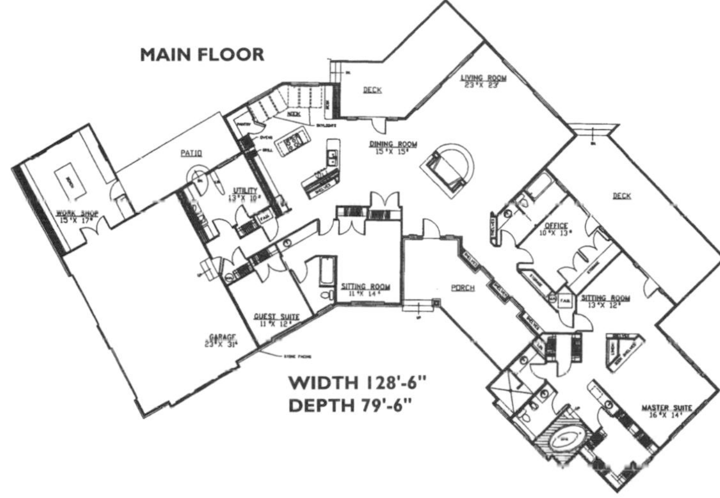
MAIN FLOOR
WIDTH 128'-6"
DEPTH 79'-6"

Arches and Angles

PRICE CODE: D

is plan features:
- ıree bedrooms
- ne full and one half baths
- e Living Room and Dining Room flow together to ke one large living space
- e Kitchen has ample cupboard and countertop space, s a snack bar
- Study offers a quiet place to work away from the nily areas and the Bedrooms
- lumns delineate the Dining Room from the Foyer d Living Room
- e Master Suite is designed for privacy and includes Sitting Area
- is home is designed with a basement foundation

T FLOOR — 1,204 SQ. FT.
)ND FLOOR — 895 SQ. FT.
EMENT — 1,204 SQ. FT.
AGE — 287 SQ. FT.

TOTAL LIVING AREA:
2,089 SQ. FT.

PLAN NO. 65253

WIDTH 43'-0"
DEPTH 40'-0"

FIRST FLOOR

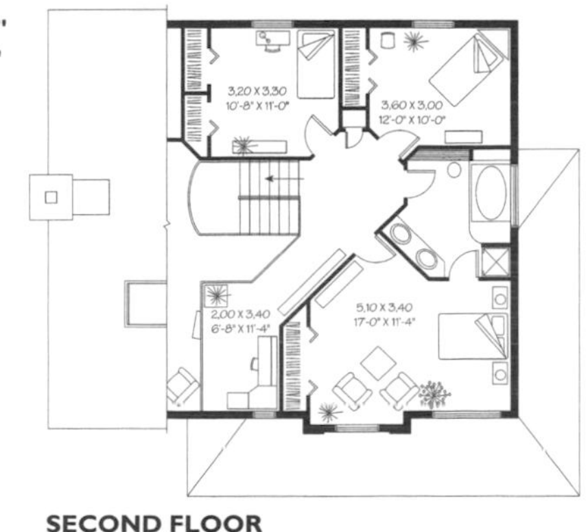

SECOND FLOOR

PLAN NO.65254

Gazebo-Style Interior

Price Code: C

This plan features:

— Three bedrooms

— Two full and one half baths

The octagonal Master Suite tops an octagonal Living Room

The Secondary Bedrooms are connected to a full Bath and a generous walk-in closet

A centralized fireplace offers a warm place for family to gather

The open design of the first floor promotes a sense of community

This home is designed with a basement foundation

FIRST FLOOR — 880 SQ. FT.
SECOND FLOOR — 880 SQ. FT.
BONUS — 31 SQ. FT.
GARAGE — 351 SQ. FT.
PORCH — 193 SQ. FT.

TOTAL LIVING AREA:
1,760 SQ. FT.

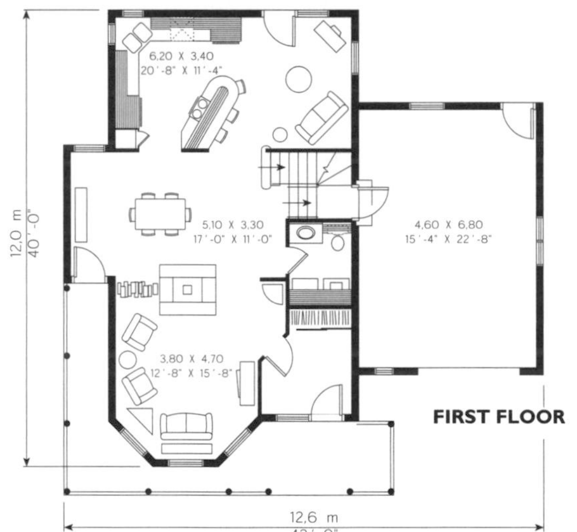
6,20 X 3,40
20'-8" X 11'-4"
5,10 X 3,30
17'-0" X 11'-0"
4,60 X 6,80
15'-4" X 22'-8"
3,80 X 4,70
12'-8" X 15'-8"
12,0 m
40'-0"
12,6 m
42'-0"

FIRST FLOOR

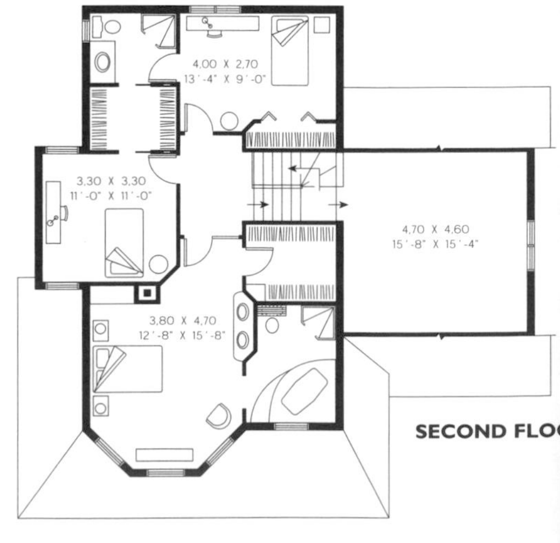
4,00 X 2,70
13'-4" X 9'-0"
3,30 X 3,30
11'-0" X 11'-0"
4,70 X 4,60
15'-8" X 15'-4"
3,80 X 4,70
12'-8" X 15'-8"

SECOND FLO

Cozy and Restful

PRICE CODE: A

PLAN NO.20195

ıis plan features:
- ıree bedrooms
- ıe full and one half baths
- lecorative ceiling in the Master Bedroom with private ɔess to the full hall sky-lit Bath
- ɔonvenient Laundry Center near the Bedrooms
- ı efficient Kitchen with ample counter and cabinet ace and a double sink under a window
- Dining/Living Room combination that makes for easy tertaining
- Family Room with a cozy fireplace and convenient lf Bath
- ıis home is designed with a basement foundation

N FLOOR — 1,139 SQ. FT.
ER FLOOR — 288 SQ. FT.
AGE — 598 SQ. FT.

TOTAL LIVING AREA:
1,427 SQ. FT.

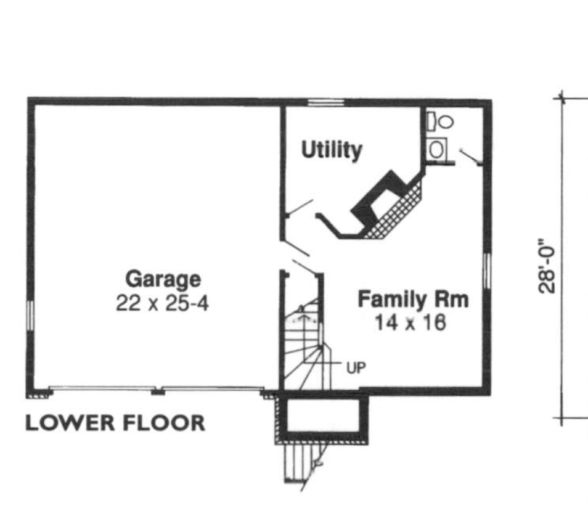

Utility
Garage
22 x 25-4
Family Rm
14 x 16
UP
LOWER FLOOR

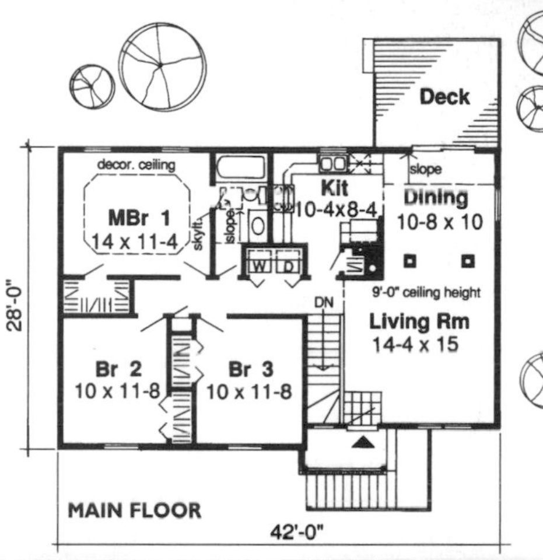

Deck
decor. ceiling
MBr 1
14 x 11-4
skylt
slope
Kit
10-4x8-4
slope
Dining
10-8 x 10
W D
9'-0" ceiling height
DN
Living Rm
14-4 x 15
Br 2
10 x 11-8
Br 3
10 x 11-8
28'-0"
MAIN FLOOR
42'-0"

Victorian Delight

PRICE CODE: D

PLAN NO.65256

ıis plan features:
- hree bedrooms
- ıe full and one half baths
- ıe gingerbread and curved front Porch provide enty of curb appeal
- ıis design features a Study and Sitting Area by e front door, perfect for a Home Office
- ɔlumns delineate the Foyer from the formal Living ıd Dining Rooms
- ıe L-shaped Kitchen has easy access to the ining Room, the Family Room, and a sunny ıting Area
- ıe Laundry Room and half Bath are combined
- ıis home is designed with a sement foundation

T FLOOR — 1,146 SQ. FT.
OND FLOOR — 943 SQ. FT.
AGE — 403 SQ. FT.

TOTAL LIVING AREA:
2,089 SQ. FT.

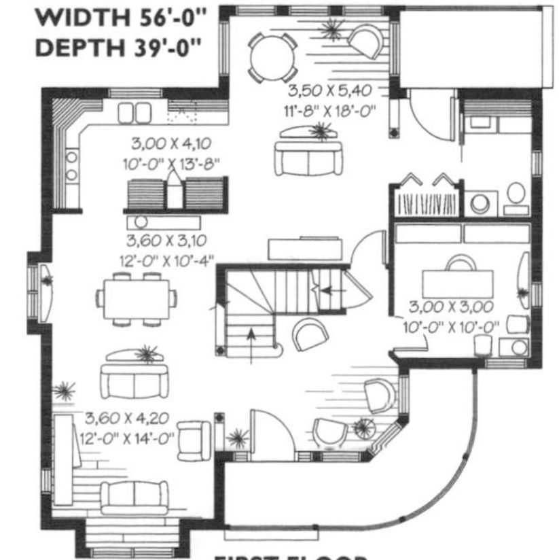

WIDTH 56'-0"
DEPTH 39'-0"
3,50 X 5,40
11'-8" X 18'-0"
3,00 X 4,10
10'-0" X 13'-8"
3,60 X 3,10
12'-0" X 10'-4"
3,00 X 3,00
10'-0" X 10'-0"
3,60 X 4,20
12'-0" X 14'-0"
FIRST FLOOR

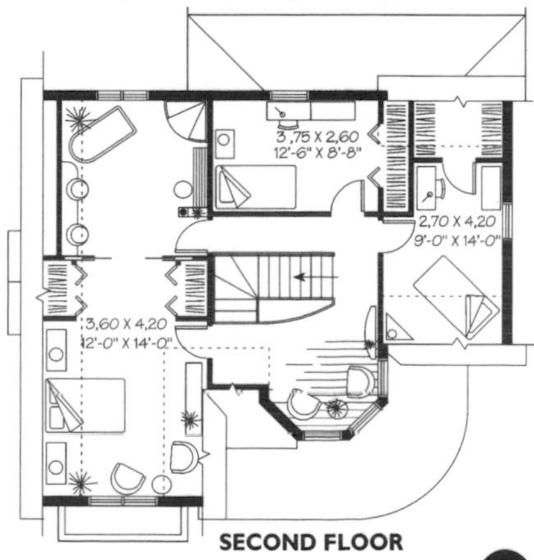

3,75 X 2,60
12'-6" X 8'-8"
2,70 X 4,20
9'-0" X 14'-0"
3,60 X 4,20
12'-0" X 14'-0"
SECOND FLOOR

PLAN NO. 92283

Style and Convenience

PRICE CODE: B

- This plan features:
- — Three bedrooms
- — Two full baths
- A sheltered Porch leads into an easy-care tile Entry
- Spacious Living Room offers a cozy fireplace, triple window and access to Patio
- An efficient Kitchen with a skylight, work island, Dining Area, walk-in Pantry and Utility/Garage Entr
- Secluded Master Bedroom highlighted by a vaulted ceiling, access to Patio and a lavish Bath
- Two additional Bedrooms, one with a cathedral ceili share a full Bath
- This home is designed with a slab foundation

MAIN FLOOR — 1,653 SQ. FT.
GARAGE — 420 SQ. FT.

TOTAL LIVING AREA:
1,653 SQ. FT.

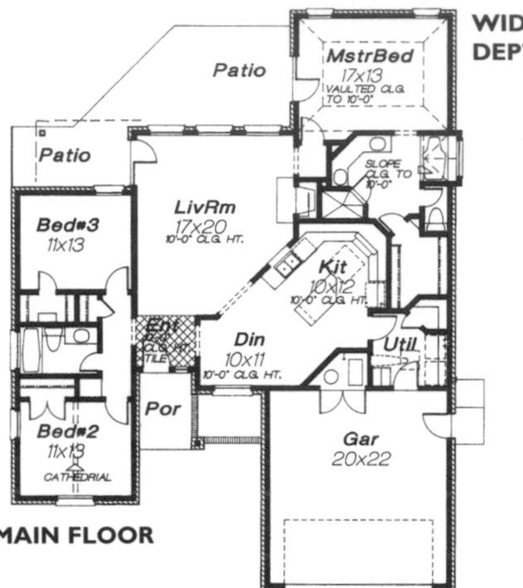

WIDTH 48'-0"
DEPTH 63'-1"
Patio
MstrBed
17x13
VAULTED CLG. TO 10'-0"
Patio
LivRm
17x20
10'-0" CLG. HT.
Bed#3
11x13
Kit
10x12
10'-0" CLG. HT.
Ent
Din
10x11
10'-0" CLG. HT.
Util
Por
Bed#2
11x13
CATHEDRAL
Gar
20x22
MAIN FLOOR

PLAN NO. 97722

Splendor and Hospitality

PRICE CODE: G

- This plan features:
- — Four bedrooms
- — Three full and one half baths
- A Great Room has a fireplace and an 18-foot ceiling height
- The Kitchen, Breakfast Area and Hearth Room arrangement creates an enjoyable family gathering p
- The first floor Master Bedroom Suite has a deluxe B is topped with a raised ceiling treatment
- An open stairway decorated with a rich wood rail lea to the second floor balcony
- This home is designed with a basement foundation

FIRST FLOOR — 2,045 SQ. FT.
SECOND FLOOR — 919 SQ. FT.

TOTAL LIVING AREA:
2,964 SQ. FT.

Screened Porch
FIRST FLOOR
Hearth Room
24'-0" x 14'-0"
Kitchen
14'-8" x 14'-7"
Laun.
Great Room
16'-6" x 20'-3"
Master Bedroom
14'-2" x 16'-8"
Bath
Dining Room
11'-0" x 15'-3"
Foyer
Bath
Dressing
Garage
21'-10" x 24'-10"
Porch
57'-6"
56'-8"

SECOND FLOOR
Bath
Bedroom
12'-0" x 15'-0"
Great Room Below
Bedroom
11'-8" x 14'-6"
Hall
Bath
Bedroom
11'-0" x 15'-7"

PLAN NO. 92681

SECOND FLOOR

Bath

walk-in closet

Bedroom
14' x 11'4"

Hall

wood rail

stairs dn

Bath

linen

Master Bedroom
13'8" x 16'

Foyer
Below

Bedroom
12' x 13'

Sitting Area
13'8" x 7'3"

FIRST FLOOR

Breakfast
11' x 12'4"

Kitchen
17'5" x 13'6"

Great Room
20'6" x 18'2"

Laun.

computer center

Hall

stairs dn

butler's pantry

wood rail

Foyer

Dining Room
12' x 15'4"

Two-car Garage
20' x 35'4"

Library
13'7" x 12'9"

Porch

57'7"

53'4"

Countrified Luxury

Price Code: G

- This plan features:
  - — Three bedrooms
  - — Two full and one half baths
- A Library is located off of the Foyer
- The Dining Room is distinguished by decorative ceiling treatment
- The Great Room and the Kitchen converge at the wetbar
- The dreamy L-shaped Kitchen incorporated a center island into its design
- The upstairs Master Bedroom has a Sitting Area
- An oversized two-car Garage has space for storage or a workshop
- This home is designed with a basement foundation

FIRST FLOOR — 1,625 SQ. FT.
SECOND FLOOR — 1,188 SQ. FT.
BASEMENT — 1,625 SQ. FT.
GARAGE — 592 SQ. FT.

TOTAL LIVING AREA:
2,813 SQ. FT.

PLAN NO. 65304

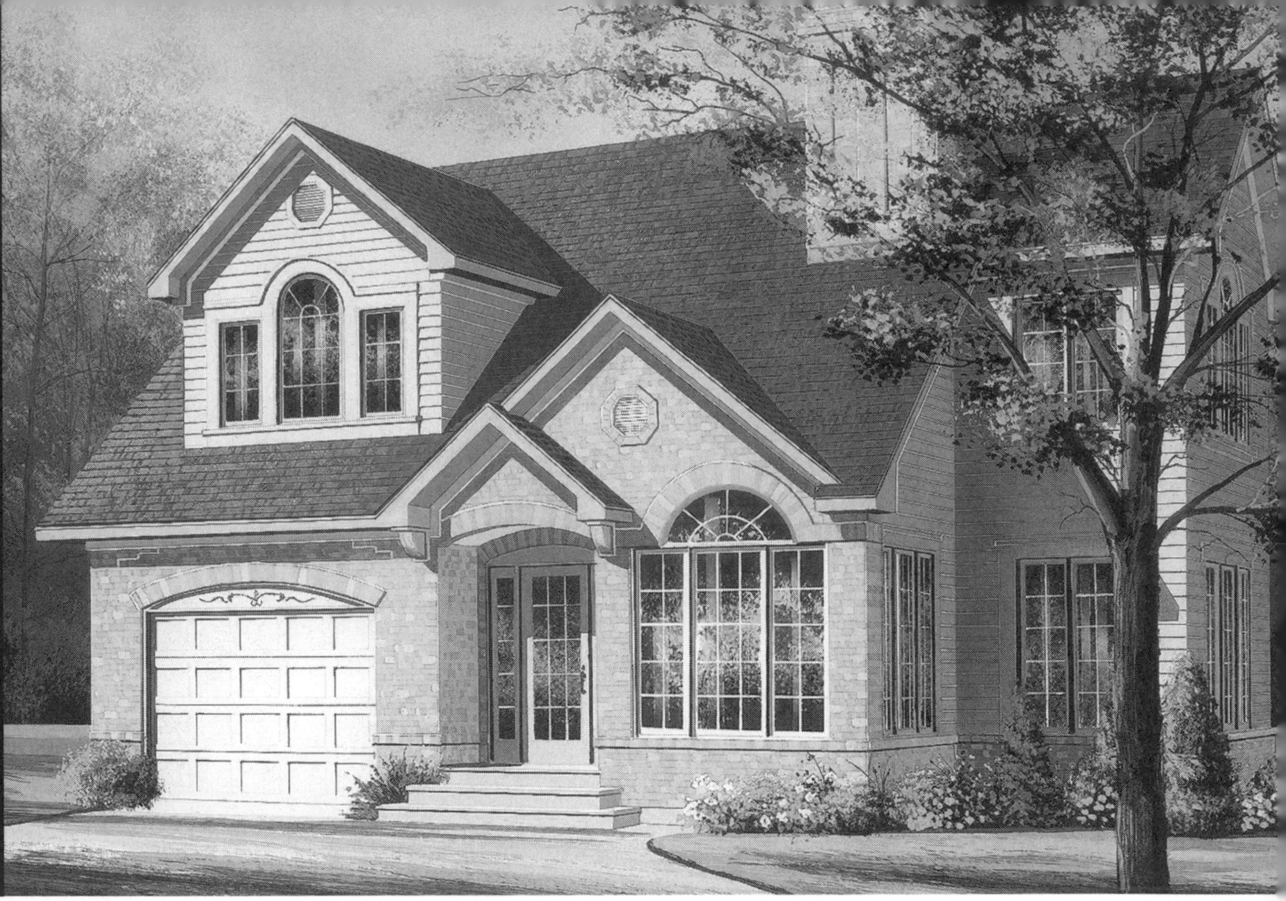

Executive Retreat

Price Code: C

- This plan features:
- — Three bedrooms
- — Three full and one half baths
- The spacious Foyer provides plenty of room to greet guests
- The separate Living Room is ideal for formal or intimate gatherings
- French doors earmark the Master Bedroom Suite, which sweeps across the entire back section of the second floor
- This home is designed with a basement foundation

FIRST FLOOR — 915 SQ. FT.
SECOND FLOOR — 983 SQ. FT.
BASEMENT — 915 SQ. FT.
GARAGE — 271 SQ. FT.

TOTAL LIVING AREA:
1,898 SQ. FT.

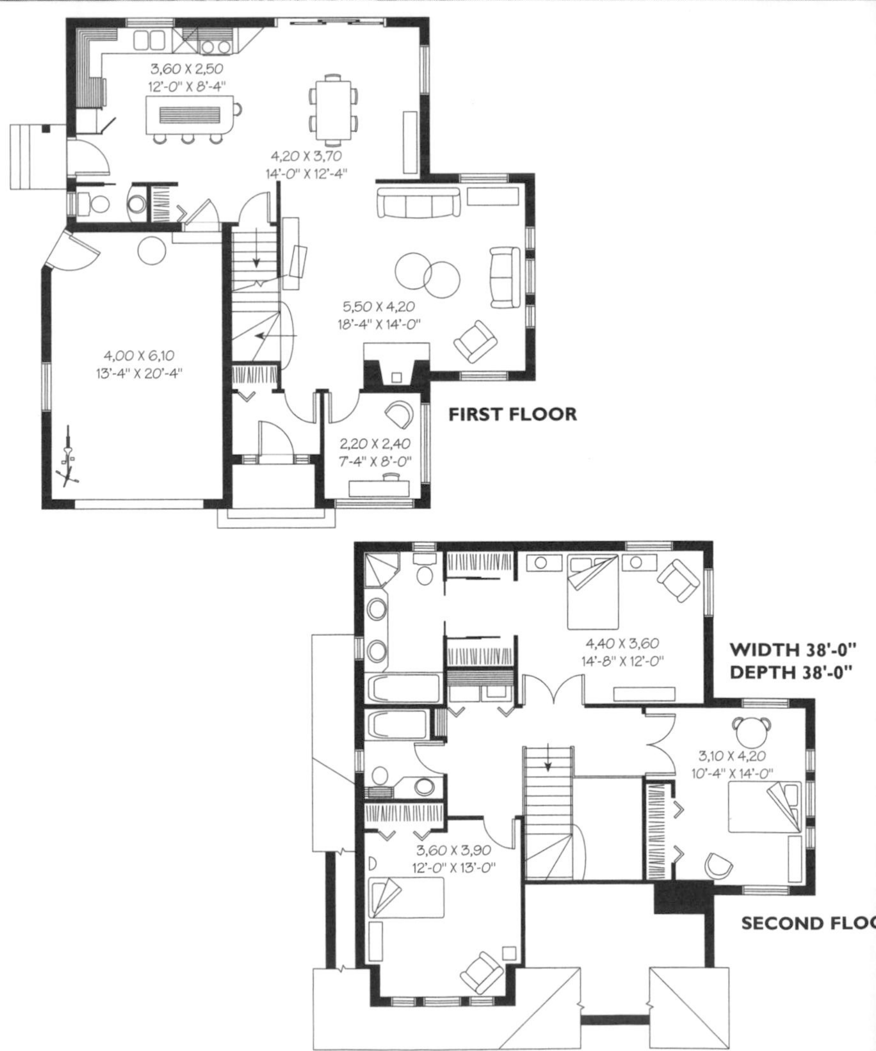

3,60 X 2,50
12'-0" X 8'-4"
4,20 X 3,70
14'-0" X 12'-4"
5,50 X 4,20
18'-4" X 14'-0"
4,00 X 6,10
13'-4" X 20'-4"
2,20 X 2,40
7'-4" X 8'-0"
FIRST FLOOR
4,40 X 3,60
14'-8" X 12'-0"
WIDTH 38'-0"
DEPTH 38'-0"
3,10 X 4,20
10'-4" X 14'-0"
3,60 X 3,90
12'-0" X 13'-0"
SECOND FLOC

ɔntemporary Schoolhouse

PRICE CODE: A

PLAN NO.65365

ıis plan features:
- ne bedroom
- ne full and one half baths
- ıis home turns the clock back with a single-room ulti-functional first floor and spacious Loft Master edroom Suite
- ıe fireplaced Living/Dining Area soars two full stories, hile the Kitchen's triangular center island provides a ntral gathering spot
- ıis home is designed with a basement foundation
- T FLOOR — 726 SQ. FT.
- OND FLOOR — 420 SQ. FT.
- US — 728 SQ. FT.

TOTAL LIVING AREA:
1,148 SQ. FT.

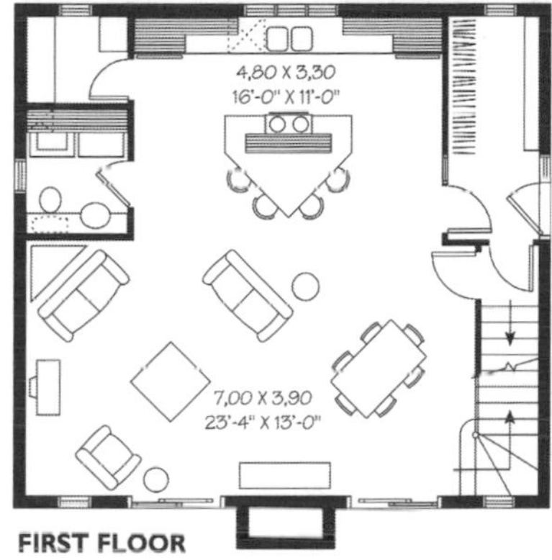
4,80 X 3,30
16'-0" X 11'-0"
7,00 X 3,90
23'-4" X 13'-0"

WIDTH 28'-0"
DEPTH 26'-0"

FIRST FLOOR

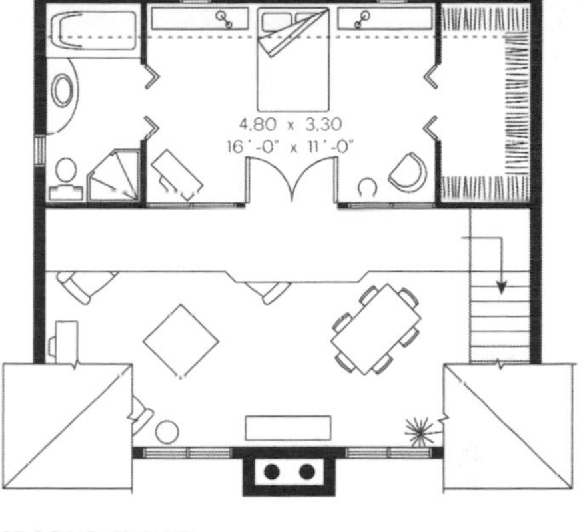
4.80 x 3.30
16'-0" x 11'-0"

SECOND FLOOR

Home on a Hill

PRICE CODE: A

PLAN NO.91026

ıhis plan features:
- 'wo bedrooms
- 'wo full baths
- weeping panels of glass and a wood stove, creating mosphere for the Great Room
- n open plan that draws the Kitchen into the warmth of ıe Great Room's wood stove
- sleeping Loft, complete with a full Bath
- ıhis home is designed with a basement foundation
- T FLOOR — 988 SQ. FT.
- OND FLOOR — 366 SQ. FT.
- EMENT — 742 SQ. FT.
- RAGE — 283 SQ. FT.

TOTAL LIVING AREA:
1,354 SQ. FT.

Rear Elevation

Front Elevation

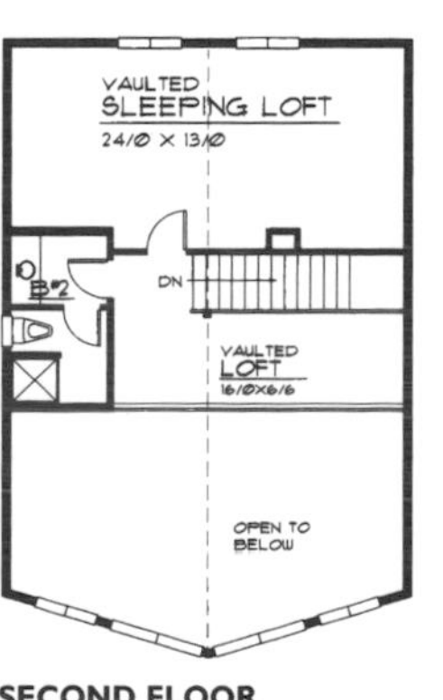
VAULTED
SLEEPING LOFT
24/0 X 13/0
B#2
DN
VAULTED
LOFT
16/0X6/6
OPEN TO
BELOW

SECOND FLOOR

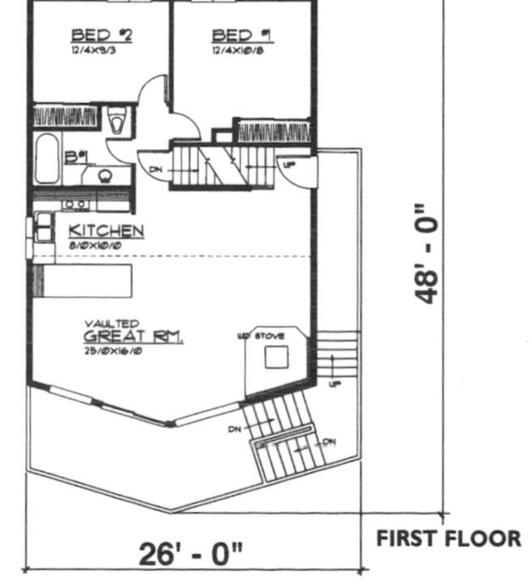
BED #2
12/4X9/3
BED #1
12/4X10/8
B#1
DN
UP
KITCHEN
8/0X10/0
VAULTED
GREAT RM.
25/0X16/0
STOVE
48' - 0"
26' - 0"

FIRST FLOOR

PLAN NO.98406

Easy Living Plan

PRICE CODE: B

- This plan features:
  - Three bedrooms
  - Two full and one half baths
- Kitchen, Breakfast Bay, and Family Room blend into a spacious open Living Area
- Convenient Laundry Center is tucked into the rear of the Kitchen
- Luxurious Master Suite is topped by a tray ceiling wh a vaulted ceiling is in the Bath
- Two roomy secondary Bedrooms share the full Bath in the hall
- This home is designed with basement, slab and crawlspace foundation options

FIRST FLOOR — 828 SQ. FT.
SECOND FLOOR — 772 SQ. FT.
BASEMENT — 828 SQ. FT.
GARAGE — 473 SQ. FT.

TOTAL LIVING AREA:
1,600 SQ. FT

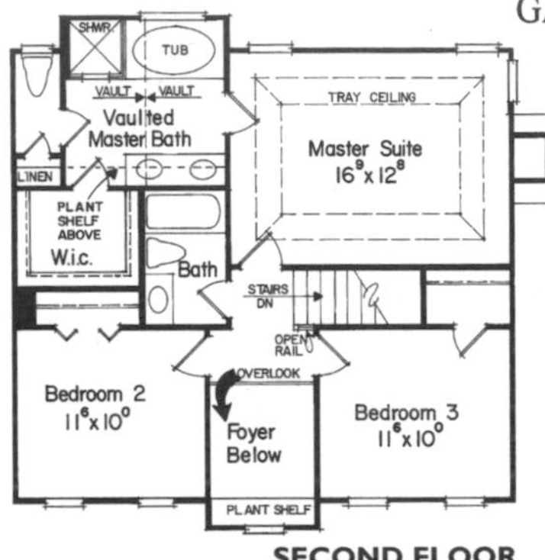

WIDTH 52'-4"
DEPTH 34'-0"

FIRST FLOOR

SECOND FLOOR

PLAN NO.97233

Easy Living

PRICE CODE: B

- This plan features:
  - Three bedrooms
  - Two full baths
- Arched windows, keystones, and shutters highlight the exterior
- The Great Room and the Breakfast Nook feature vaulted ceilings
- There is direct access from the Dining Room to the Kitchen
- The Kitchen has a space-saving Pantry and plenty of counter space
- Both secondary Bedrooms have spectacular front wall windows
- The Master Suite is enormous and features a glass walled Sitting Area
- A walk-in closet, a dual vanity and a whirlpool tub highlight the Master Bath
- This home has a convenient drive-under Garage
- This home is designed with a basement foundation

MAIN FLOOR — 1,743 SQ. FT.
BASEMENT — 998 SQ. FT.
GARAGE — 763 SQ. FT.

TOTAL LIVING AREA:
1,743 SQ. FT.

53'-6"
39'-4"

MAIN FLOOR

PLAN NO. 93163

MBR.
14'4" X 17'0"

KIT.
11'0" X 12'4"

NK.
12'0" X 14'4"

SCREEN PORCH
13'0" X 12'8"

GRT.RM.
10'-1 1/8" CEILING HGT.
15'0" X 26'4"

DIN.
11'4" X 13'0"

2 CAR GAR.
22'0" X 26'0"

WIDTH 61'-0"
DEPTH 52'-8"

FIRST FLOOR

BR.#2
10'4" X 10'4"

BR.#3
10'4" X 16'8"

BR.#4
11'4" X 12'8"

OPEN TO E.

PLANT LEDGE

SECOND FLOOR

Dramatic Two-Story

Price Code: E

- This plan features:
  - Four bedrooms
  - Two full and one half baths
- Unique bay of windows, inviting fireplace and access to Screen Porch accent Great Room
- Spacious Kitchen with a work island, a bright, eating Nook and nearby Laundry/Garage Entry
- Secluded Master Bedroom with an expansive view, a large walk-in closet and an elegant Bath
- Three second floor Bedrooms with double windows and spacious closets
- This home is designed with a basement foundation

FIRST FLOOR — 1,764 SQ. FT.
SECOND FLOOR — 713 SQ. FT.

TOTAL LIVING AREA:
2,477 SQ. FT.

PLAN NO. 65064

Accent Windows Create Quaintness

Price Code: A

This plan features:

— Two bedrooms

— One full bath

A closet in the Entry provides plenty of space for coats and shoes

The Entry opens directly into the Living Room, offering an instant welcome

The open design of the common areas promotes family activity

The Bedrooms are located in the rear for privacy and share a luxurious full Bath

This home is designed with a basement foundation

MAIN FLOOR — 1,191 SQ. FT.
BASEMENT — 1,191 SQ. FT.

TOTAL LIVING AREA:
1,191 SQ. FT.

MAIN FLOOR

2,70 X 3,60
9'-0" X 12'-0"

3,30 X 4,20
11'-0" X 14'-0"

5,10 X 3,00
17'-0" X 10'-0"

3,80 X 4,10
12'-8" X 13'-8"

5,10 X 3,60
17'-0" X 12'-0"

12,0 m

9,5 m
31'-8"

Open Floor Plan

PRICE CODE: D

PLAN NO.81007

'his plan features:
- 'our bedrooms
- Two full and one half baths
- 'he Living Area on the first floor is open
-)pen space, combined with columns and a aulted ceiling in the Living Room, adds plenty f architectural interest
- Den on the second floor is cozy and private, offering a uiet place to relax
- 'his home is designed with a crawlspace foundation

ST FLOOR — 1,072 SQ. FT.
:OND FLOOR — 1,108 SQ. FT.

TOTAL LIVING AREA: 2,180 SQ. FT.

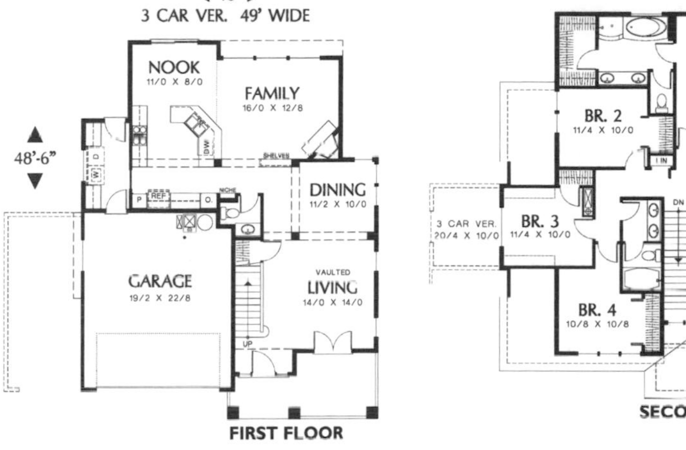

40'
3 CAR VER. 49' WIDE
48'-6"
NOOK
11/0 X 8/0
FAMILY
16/0 X 12/8
DINING
11/2 X 10/0
GARAGE
19/2 X 22/8
VAULTED
LIVING
14/0 X 14/0
MASTER
12/0 X 14/8
BR. 2
11/4 X 10/0
DEN
10/10 X 9/8
3 CAR VER.
20/4 X 10/0
BR. 3
11/4 X 10/0
OPEN TO BELOW
BR. 4
10/8 X 10/8
SECOND FLOOR
FIRST FLOOR

Spectacular Curving Stairway

PRICE CODE: H

PLAN NO.94995

'his plan features:
- Four bedrooms
- Two full, one three-quarter and one half baths
- ;pacious formal Entry with arched transom, is enhanced y a curved staircase
- Great Room is inviting with a cozy fireplace, a wetbar, nd three arched windows
-)pen Kitchen, Breakfast, and Hearth Area combine fficiency and comfort for all
- Aaster Bedroom retreat offers a private back door, a ouble walk-in closet, and a whirlpool Bath
- Generous closets and Baths enhance the three second loor Bedrooms
- 'his home is designed with a basement foundation
- Alternate foundation options available at an dditional charge. Please call 1-800-235-5700 or more information.

ST FLOOR — 2,252 SQ. FT.
:OND FLOOR — 920 SQ. FT.
SEMENT — 2,252 SQ. FT.
RAGE — 646 SQ. FT.

TOTAL LIVING AREA: 3,172 SQ. FT.

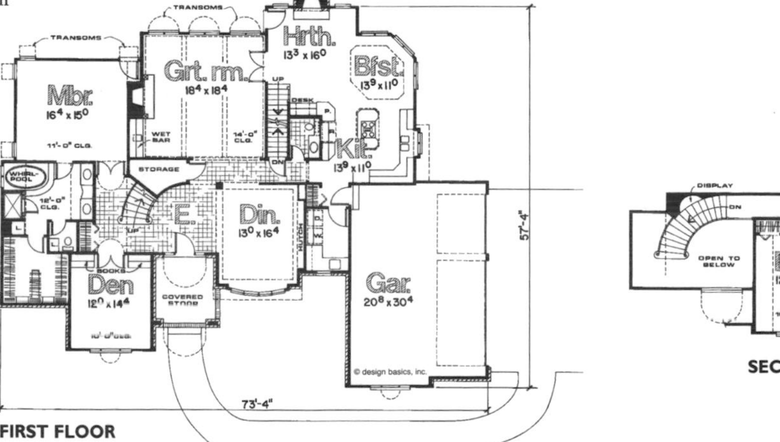

Mbr.
Grt. rm.
18⁴ x 18⁴
Hrth.
Bfst.
Kit.
E.
Din.
Den
Gar.
20⁸ x 30⁴
73'-4"
57'-4"
FIRST FLOOR

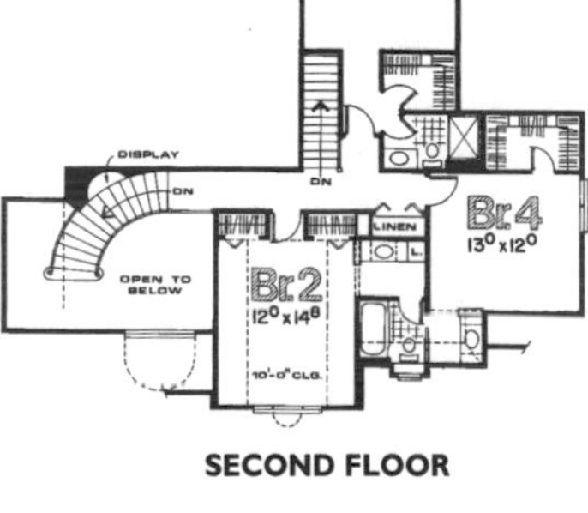

Br.3
Br.4
Br.2
OPEN TO BELOW
SECOND FLOOR

PLAN NO. 20198

Rear Elevatio

Dramatic Ranch

Price Code: C

- This plan features:
- — Three bedrooms
- — Two full baths
- A large Living Room with a stone fireplace and a decorative beamed ceiling
- A Kitchen/Dining Room arrangement which makes the rooms seem more spacious
- A Laundry with a large Pantry located close to the Bedrooms and the Kitchen
- A Master Bedroom with a walk-in closet and a private master Bath
- This home is designed with a basement foundation

MAIN FLOOR — 1,792 SQ. FT.
BASEMENT — 818 SQ. FT.
GARAGE — 857 SQ. FT.

TOTAL LIVING AREA:
1,792 SQ. FT.

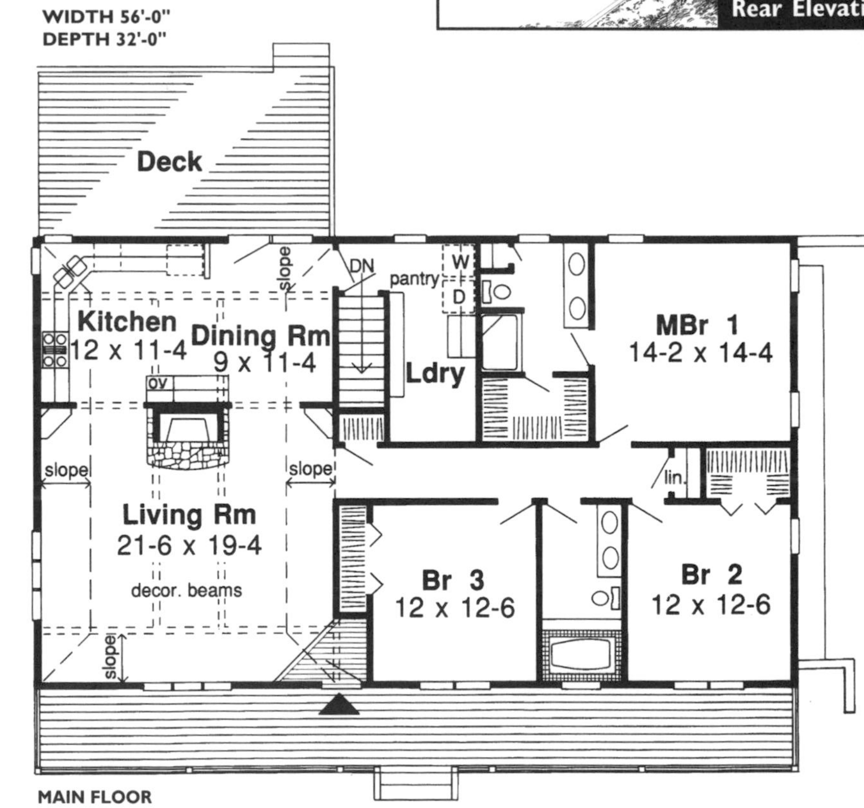
WIDTH 56'-0"
DEPTH 32'-0"
Deck
slope
DN
pantry
W
D
Kitchen
12 x 11-4
Dining Rm
9 x 11-4
OV
Ldry
MBr 1
14-2 x 14-4
slope
slope
lin.
Living Rm
21-6 x 19-4
decor. beams
Br 3
12 x 12-6
Br 2
12 x 12-6
slope
MAIN FLOOR

 To order your Blueprints, call 1-800-235-5700

PLAN NO. 93349

FAM. RM.
VAULTED CLG.
18-0 X 16-0

DINETTE
12-0 X 10-6

WOOD DECK

LND.

KITCHEN
12-0 X 13-6

M. BATH

PDR

FOYER

M.B.R.
TRAY CLG.
14-0 X 16-6

DINING RM.
11-6 X 13-0

GARAGE
24-6 X 26-0

PORCH

WIDTH 63'-0"
DEPTH 47'-0"

FIRST FLOOR

FAM. RM. BELOW

B.R. 3
12-0 X 12-0

BALCONY

BATH 2

STORAGE

FOYER BELOW

B.R. 2
12-0 X 11-0

ROOF

SECOND FLOOR

Conventional and Classic Comfort

Price Code: C

- This plan features:
- — Three bedrooms
- — Two full and one half baths
- Cozy Porch accesses two-story Foyer with decorative window
- Formal Dining Room accented by a recessed window adjoins Kitchen
- Spacious Family Room crowned by a vaulted ceiling over a hearth fireplace
- Efficient Kitchen with an extended counter/eating bar and access to Deck
- First floor Master Bedroom with walk-in closet and Master Bath with double vanity
- This home is designed with a basement foundation

FIRST FLOOR — 1,454 SQ. FT.
SECOND FLOOR — 507 SQ. FT.
BASEMENT — 1,454 SQ. FT.
GARAGE — 624 SQ. FT.

TOTAL LIVING AREA:
1,961 SQ. FT.

PLAN NO. 24400

National Treasure

Price Code: C

This plan features:

— Three bedrooms

— Two full and one half baths

A wraparound covered Porch

Decorative vaulted ceilings in the fireplaced Living Room

A large Kitchen with central island/breakfast bar

A sun-lit Sitting Area

This home is designed with basement, slab and crawlspace foundation options

FIRST FLOOR — 1,034 SQ. FT.
SECOND FLOOR — 944 SQ. FT.
BASEMENT — 984 SQ. FT.
GARAGE — 675 SQ. FT.

TOTAL LIVING AREA:
1,978 SQ. FT.

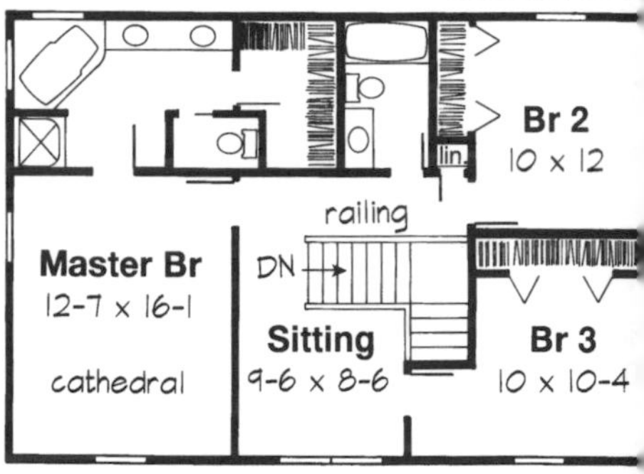

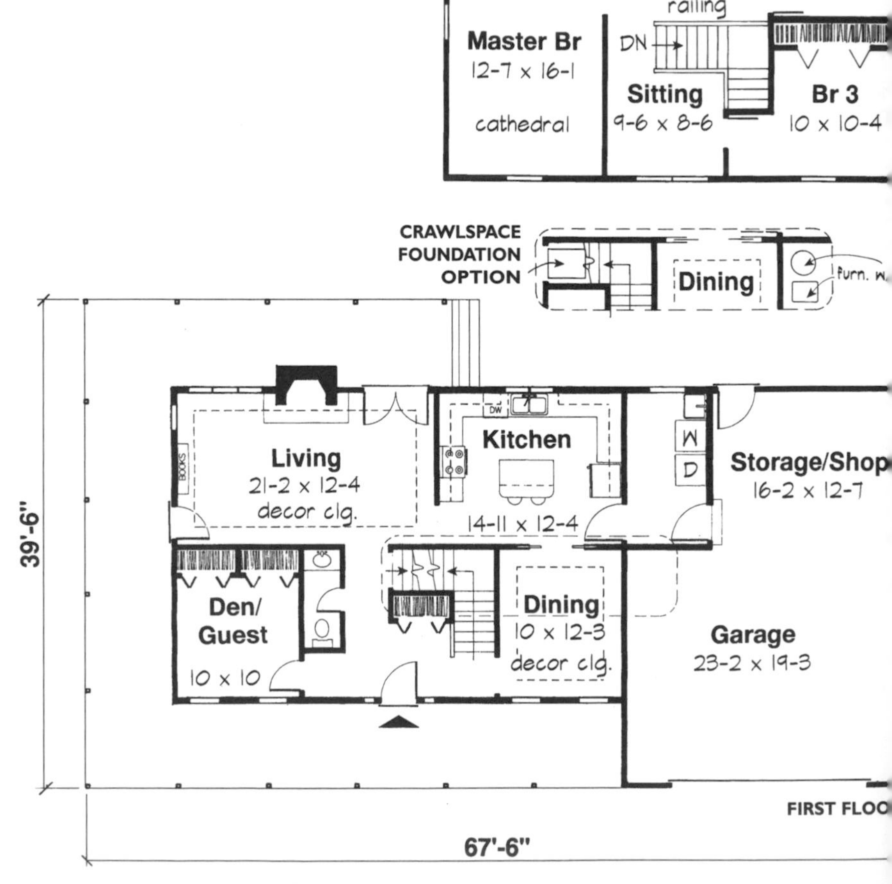

SECOND FLOOR
Br 2
10 x 12
lin.
railing
Master Br
12-7 x 16-1
cathedral
DN
Sitting
9-6 x 8-6
Br 3
10 x 10-4
CRAWLSPACE
FOUNDATION
OPTION
Dining
furn.
Living
21-2 x 12-4
decor clg.
BOOKS
DW
Kitchen
14-11 x 12-4
W
D
Storage/Shop
16-2 x 12-7
Den/
Guest
10 x 10
Dining
10 x 12-3
decor clg.
Garage
23-2 x 19-3
39'-6"
67'-6"
FIRST FLOOR

Traditional Elegance

PRICE CODE: K

PLAN NO.92504

'his plan features:
- Four bedrooms
- Three full and one half baths
- elegant entrance leading into a two-story Foyer with n impressive staircase highlighted by a curved window
- 'loor to ceiling windows in both the formal Living and)ining Rooms
- spacious Den with a hearth fireplace, built-in book- helves, a wetbar and a wall of windows viewing the ackyard
- large, efficient Kitchen, equipped with lots of ounter and storage space, a bright Breakfast Area, nd access to the Dining Room, Utility Room, valk-in Pantry and Garage
- grand Master Suite with decorative ceilings, a private 'orch, an elaborate Bath and two walk-in closets
- 'hree additional Bedrooms on the second floor with valk-in closets, sharing adjoining, full Baths and an deal Children's Den
- 'his home is designed with slab and crawlspace oundation options

ST FLOOR — 2,553 SQ. FT.
:OND FLOOR — 1,260 SQ. FT.
RAGE — 714 SQ. FT.

***TOTAL LIVING AREA:* 3,813 SQ. FT.**

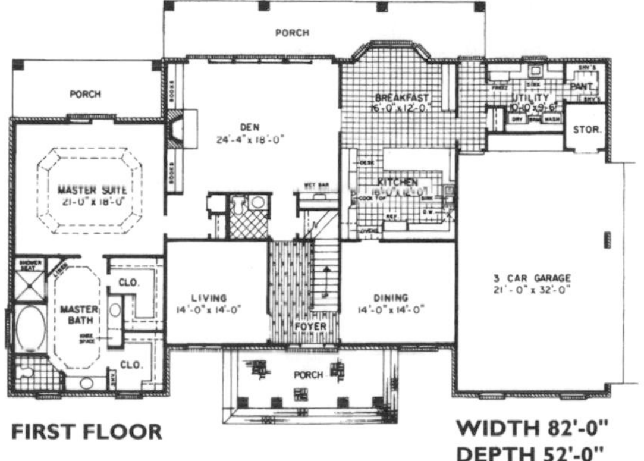
PORCH
PORCH
DEN
24'-4" x 18'-0"
BREAKFAST
KITCHEN
UTILITY
STOR.
MASTER SUITE
21'-0" x 18'-0"
MASTER BATH
CLO.
CLO.
LIVING
14'-0" x 14'-0"
FOYER
DINING
14'-0" x 14'-0"
3 CAR GARAGE
21'-0" x 32'-0"
PORCH
FIRST FLOOR
WIDTH 82'-0"
DEPTH 52'-0"

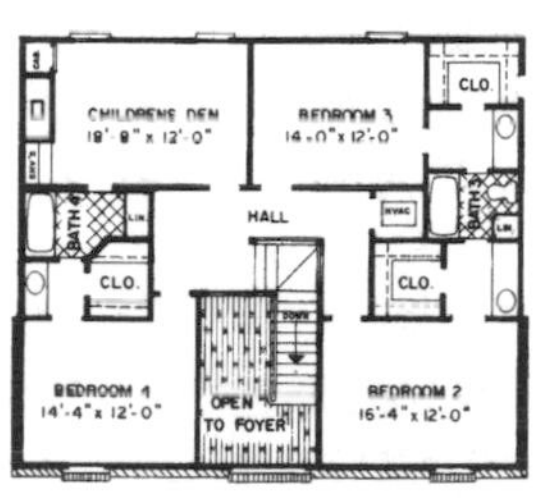
CHILDRENS DEN
18'-8" x 12'-0"
BEDROOM 3
14'-0" x 12'-0"
HALL
CLO.
CLO.
CLO.
BEDROOM 4
14'-4" x 12'-0"
OPEN TO FOYER
BEDROOM 2
16'-4" x 12'-0"

SECOND FLOOR

Elegant Stone Two-Story

PRICE CODE: H

PLAN NO.99149

his plan features:
- 'our bedrooms
- 'wo full and one half baths
- 'he two-story Entry leads into the Great Room
- 'he Kitchen has a center island and is open to the rge Nook
- 'he Master Bedrooms has an access door to the ear Deck
- 'pstairs are two Bedrooms that are serviced y a full Bath
- lso upstairs is a large Game Room for all the kid's toys
- three-season Porch with a cathedral ceiling rounds ut this plan
- his home is designed with a basement foundation

ST FLOOR — 2,039 SQ. FT.
:OND FLOOR — 970 SQ. FT.

***TOTAL LIVING AREA:* 3,009 SQ. FT.**

WIDTH 69'-8"
DEPTH 72'-0"

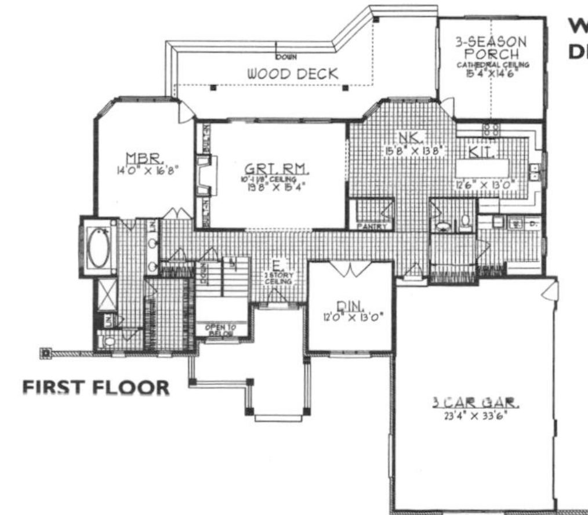
3-SEASON PORCH
WOOD DECK
MBR.
14'0" X 16'8"
GRT. RM.
13'8" X 15'4"
NK.
15'8" X 13'8"
KIT.
12'6" X 13'0"
DIN.
12'0" X 13'0"
3 CAR GAR.
23'4" X 33'6"
FIRST FLOOR

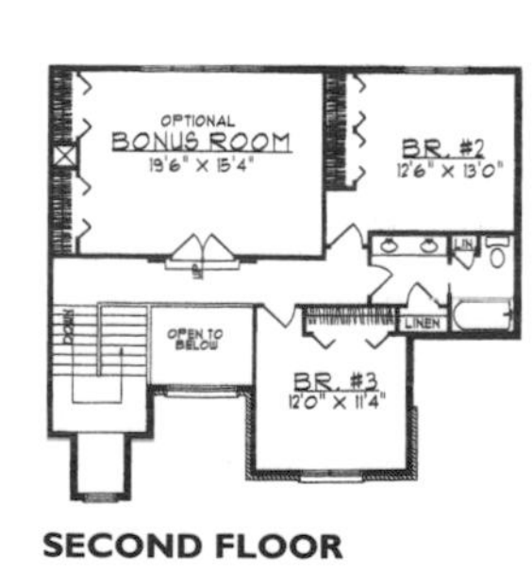
OPTIONAL
BONUS ROOM
19'6" X 15'4"
BR. #2
12'6" X 13'0"
BR. #3
12'0" X 11'4"

SECOND FLOOR

PLAN NO. 99327

Tradition Combined with Contemporary

PRICE CODE: A

- This plan features:
  - — Three bedrooms
  - — Two full baths
- A vaulted ceiling in the Entry
- A formal Living Room with a fireplace and a half-round transom
- A Dining Room with sliders to the Deck and easy access to the Kitchen
- A first floor Master Suite with corner windows, a closet and private Bath access
- Two additional Bedrooms that share a full hall Bath
- This home is designed with a basement foundation

FIRST FLOOR — 858 SQ. FT.
SECOND FLOOR — 431 SQ. FT.
BASEMENT — 858 SQ. FT.
GARAGE — 400 SQ. FT.

TOTAL LIVING AREA:
1,289 SQ. FT.

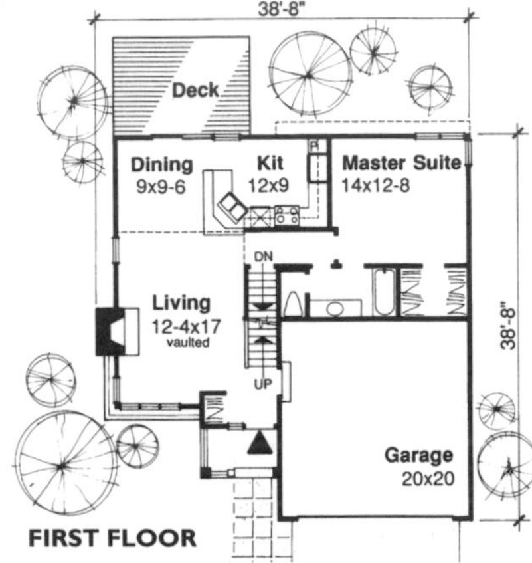
38'-8"
Deck
Dining
9x9-6
Kit
12x9
Master Suite
14x12-8
DN
Living
12-4x17
vaulted
UP
38'-8"
Garage
20x20
FIRST FLOOR

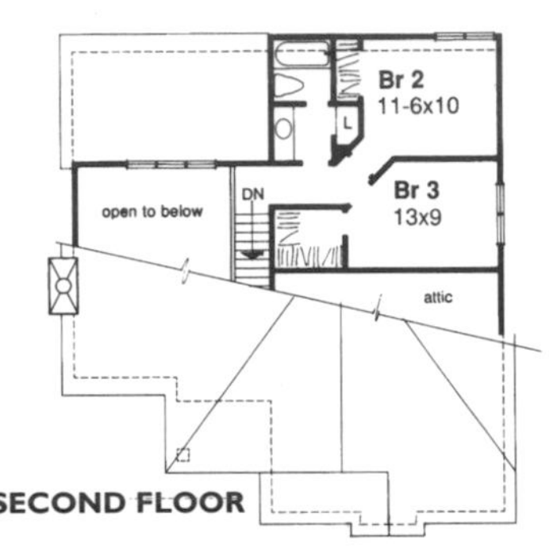
Br 2
11-6x10
open to below
DN
Br 3
13x9
attic
SECOND FLOOR

PLAN NO. 90378

Lots of Space in this Small Package

PRICE CODE: A

- This plan features:
  - — Two or three bedrooms
  - — Two full baths
- A Living Room with dynamic, soaring angles and a fireplace
- A first floor Master Suite with full Bath and walk in-closet
- Walk-in closets in all Bedrooms
- This home is designed with a basement foundation

FIRST FLOOR — 878 SQ. FT.
SECOND FLOOR — 405 SQ. FT.

TOTAL LIVING AREA:
1,283 SQ. FT.

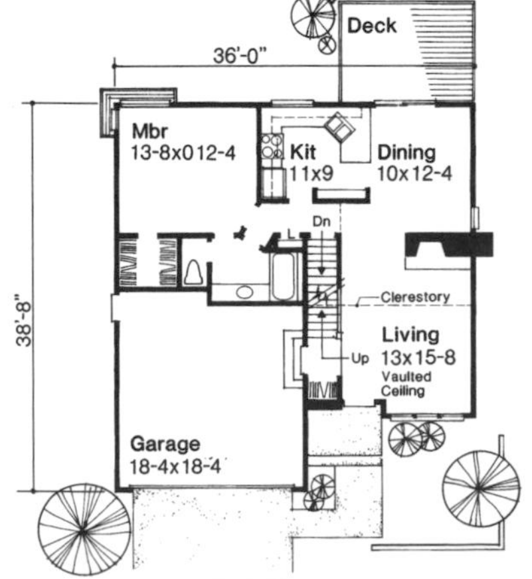
Deck
36'-0"
Mbr
13-8x012-4
Kit
11x9
Dining
10x12-4
Dn
Clerestory
38'-8"
Living
13x15-8
Vaulted
Ceiling
Up
Garage
18-4x18-4
FIRST FLOOR

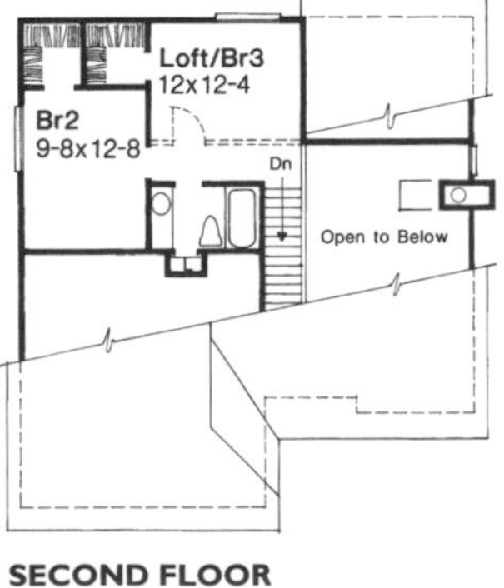
Loft/Br3
12x12-4
Br2
9-8x12-8
Dn
Open to Below
SECOND FLOOR

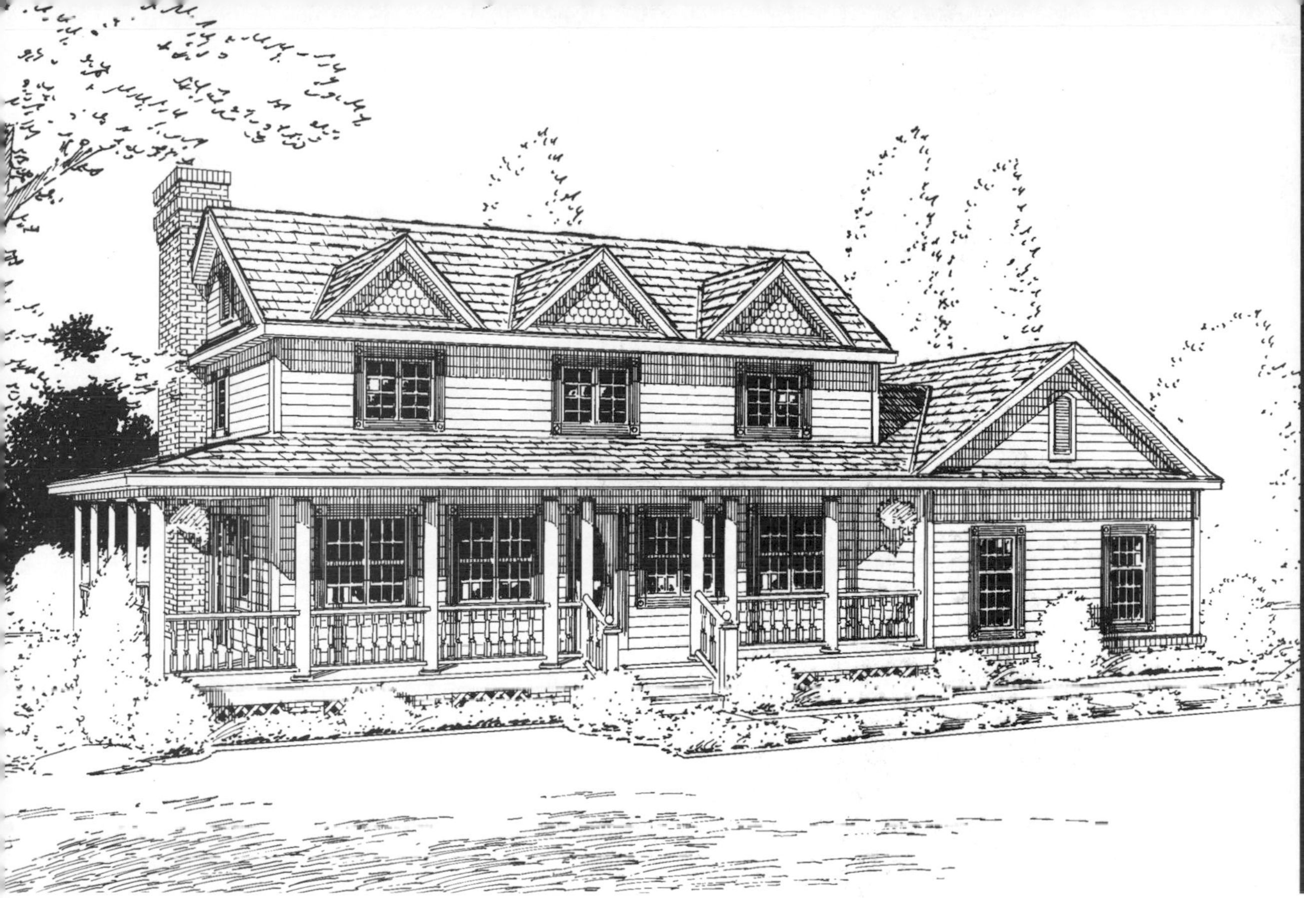

PLAN NO. 24404

Yesteryear Flavor

Price Code: E

- This plan features:
  - — Three or four bedrooms
  - — Two full and one three-quarter baths
- Wraparound Porch invites access into gracious Foyer with landing staircase
- Formal Living Room/Guest Room
- Family Room with a decorative ceiling, cozy fireplace, book shelves and Porch
- Country-sized Kitchen with island snackbar, built-in desk and nearby Dining Room, Laundry/Workshop and Garage access
- Master Bedroom with a walk-in closet and plush Bath with a whirlpool tub
- Two Bedrooms with walk-in closets, share a full Bath and Sitting Area
- This home is designed with basement, slab and crawlspace foundation options

FIRST FLOOR — 1,236 SQ. FT.
SECOND FLOOR — 1,120 SQ. FT.

TOTAL LIVING AREA:
2,356 SQ. FT.

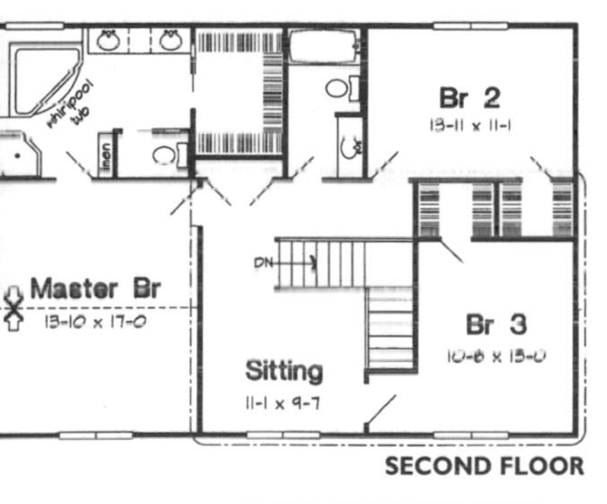
Br 2
13-11 x 11-1
Master Br
13-10 x 17-0
Sitting
11-1 x 9-7
Br 3
10-6 x 13-0
SECOND FLOOR

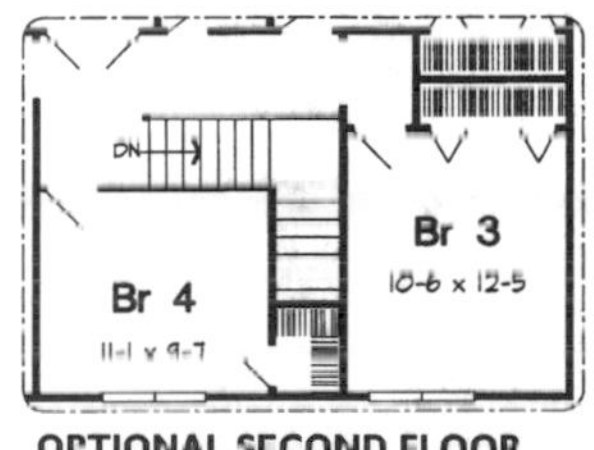
Br 4
11-1 x 9-7
Br 3
10-6 x 12-5
OPTIONAL SECOND FLOOR

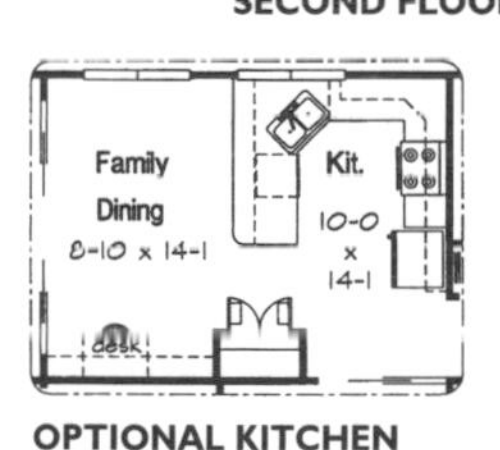
Family
Dining
8-10 x 14-1
Kit.
10-0 x 14-1
OPTIONAL KITCHEN

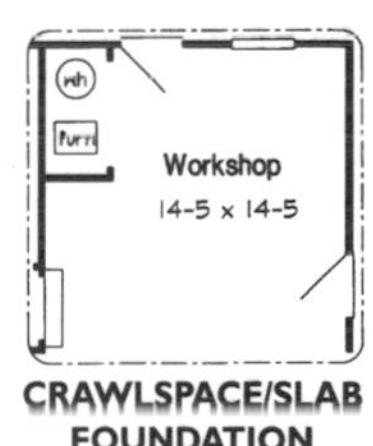
Workshop
14-5 x 14-5
CRAWLSPACE/SLAB FOUNDATION OPTION

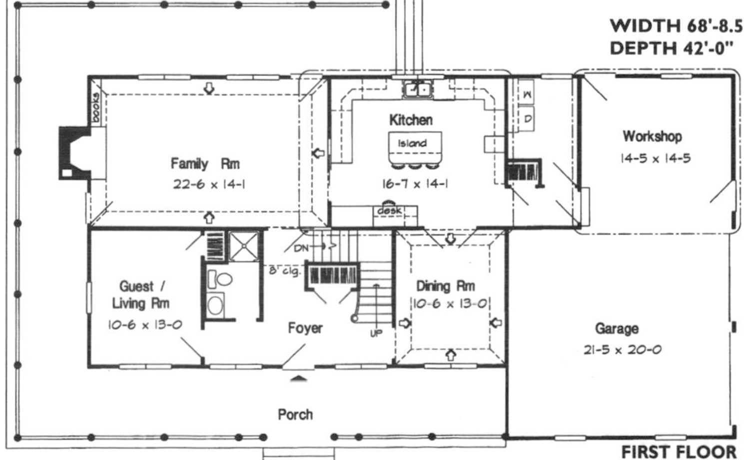
WIDTH 68'-8.5"
DEPTH 42'-0"
Family Rm
22-6 x 14-1
Kitchen
Island
16-7 x 14-1
Workshop
14-5 x 14-5
Guest / Living Rm
10-6 x 13-0
Foyer
Dining Rm
10-6 x 13-0
Garage
21-5 x 20-0
Porch
FIRST FLOOR

PLAN NO. 65150

Family Friendly

Price Code: A

This plan features:

— Three bedrooms

— One full and one half baths

Accent windows and skylights add detail to this home

The open design of the common areas offer a sense of community

On the second floor, the Bedrooms share a full Bath

The Kitchen centers around an eating island and opens up to a Dining Area

This home is designed with a basement foundation

FIRST FLOOR — 702 SQ. FT.
SECOND FLOOR — 715 SQ. FT.
GARAGE — 279 SQ. FT.
PORCH — 32 SQ. FT.

TOTAL LIVING AREA:
1,417 SQ. FT.

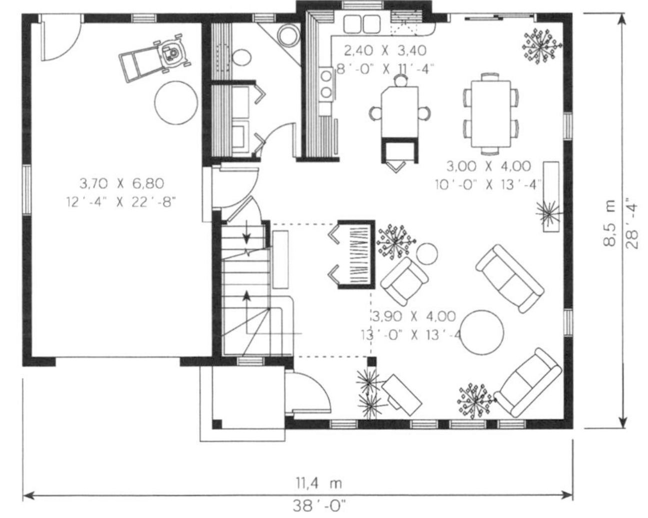
2,40 X 3,40
8'-0" X 11'-4"
3,70 X 6,80
12'-4" X 22'-8"
3,00 X 4,00
10'-0" X 13'-4"
3,90 X 4,00
13'-0" X 13'-4
8,5 m
28'-4"
11,4 m
38'-0"

FIRST FLOOR

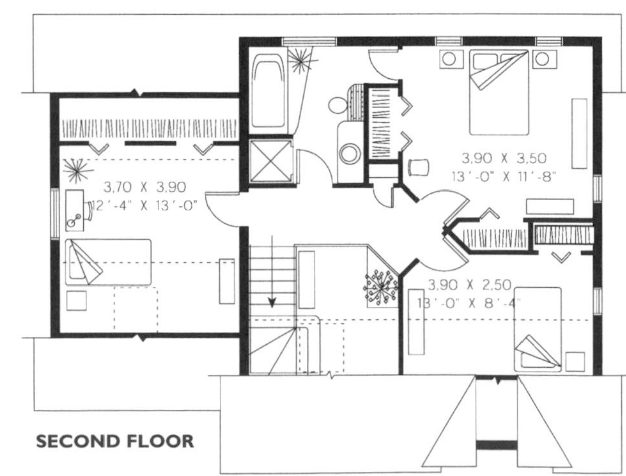
3,70 X 3,90
12'-4" X 13'-0"
3,90 X 3,50
13'-0" X 11'-8"
3,90 X 2,50
13'-0" X 8'-4"

SECOND FLOOR

Brick and Stucco

PRICE CODE: J

This plan features:

- Four bedrooms
- Two full, two three-quarter and one half baths
- The brick, stucco wing walls, and dual chimneys add elegant eye appeal to this home
- A large front Courtyard adds intrigue to front of the home
- The spider-beamed Den with French doors includes arched transom windows
- The formal Dining Room opens to a dramatic high ceiling in the Entry
- The Great Room features a fireplace wall with entertainment center, bookcases and wetbar
- Informal areas include the Gazebo-shaped Dinette, Kitchen with wrapping counters, large island/snack bar, walk-in Pantry, and private stairs accessing the second floor
- The exquisite first floor Master Suite includes a Sitting Room with a built-in bookcase and a fireplace
- This home is designed with a basement foundation
- Alternate foundation options available at an additional charge. Please call 1-800-235-5700 for more information.

RST FLOOR — 2,603 SQ. FT.
COND FLOOR — 1,020 SQ. FT.
SEMENT — 2,603 SQ. FT.
RAGE — 801 SQ. FT.

TOTAL LIVING AREA:
3,623 SQ. FT.

PLAN NO. 94999

WIDTH 76'-8"
DEPTH 68'-0"
Hrth.
15^4 x 15^0
Bfst.
12^0 x 12^0
Grt. rm.
20^4 x 18^6
Kit.
14^0 x 12^4
Mbr.
17^0 x 15^4
Din.
13^0 x 16^0
E.
Sit.
11^0 x 10^8
Den
12^8 x 14^4
Gar.
21^4 x 36^8
COURTYARD
COVERED STOOP
TRANSOMS
SKYLIGHT
WHIRLPOOL
© Design Basics, Inc.
FIRST FLOOR
Br. 2
15^3 x 12^0
Br. 4
12^0 x 14^0
Br. 3
12^0 x 14^6
OPEN TO GREAT ROOM
OPEN TO BELOW
SECOND FLOOR

Three Porches Offer Outdoor Charm

PRICE CODE: A

This plan features:

- Three bedrooms
- Two full baths
- An oversized log burning fireplace in the spacious Living/Dining Area which is two stories high with sliding glass doors
- Three Porches offering the maximum in outdoor living space
- A private Bedroom located on the second floor
- An efficient Kitchen including an eating bar and access to the covered Dining Porch
- This home is designed with a basement foundation

RST FLOOR — 974 SQ. FT.
COND FLOOR — 300 SQ. FT.

TOTAL LIVING AREA:
1,274 SQ. FT.

PLAN NO. 90048

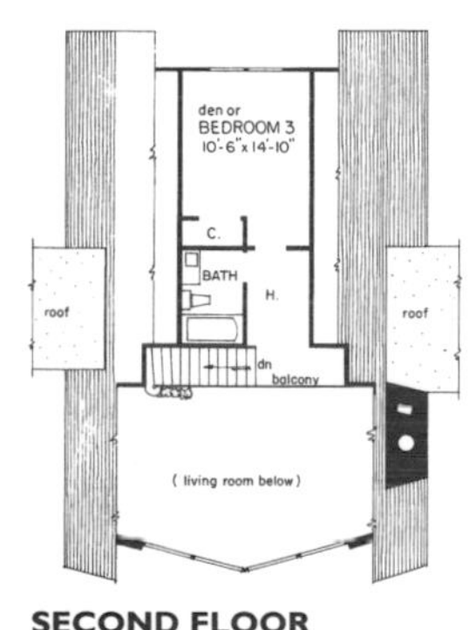

den or BEDROOM 3
10'-6" x 14'-10"
C.
BATH
H.
roof
roof
dn
balcony
(living room below)

SECOND FLOOR

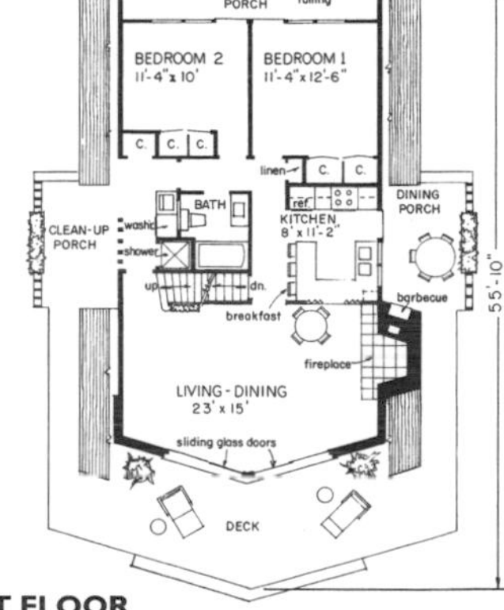

23'-8"
TERRACE
PORCH
railing
BEDROOM 2
11'-4" x 10'
BEDROOM 1
11'-4" x 12'-6"
linen
BATH
CLEAN-UP PORCH
washer
shower
KITCHEN
8' x 11'-2"
DINING PORCH
barbecue
breakfast
fireplace
LIVING - DINING
23' x 15'
sliding glass doors
DECK
55'-10"

FIRST FLOOR

PLAN NO.91002

Lovely Second Home

PRICE CODE: A

- This plan features:
  - — Three bedrooms
  - — One full and one three-quarter baths
- Firedrum fireplace warming both Entry and Living Room
- Dining and Living Rooms opening onto the Deck, whi surrounds the house on three sides
- This home is designed with a crawlspace foundation

FIRST FLOOR — 808 SQ. FT.
SECOND FLOOR — 288 SQ. FT.

***TOTAL LIVING AREA:* 1,096 SQ. FT.**

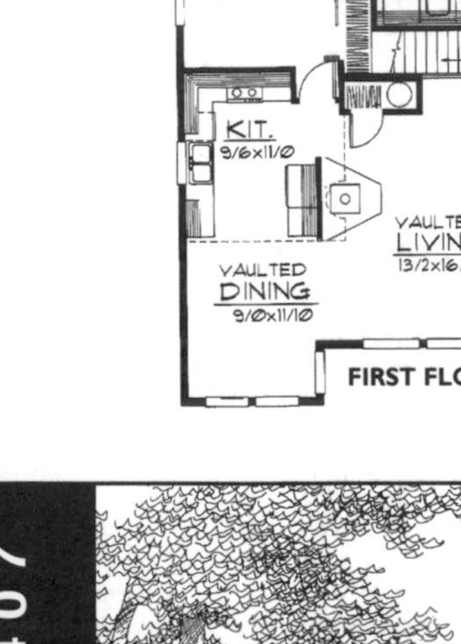
BEDRM-1
10/10x11/10
B-1
UP
KIT.
9/6x11/0
VAULTED
LIVING
13/2x16/0
VAULTED
DINING
9/0x11/10
FIRST FLOOR

VAULTED BDRM-2 9/2x9/6
B-2
DN
PLANT SHELF
VAULTED LOFT 10/10x11/6
OPEN TO BELOW
SECOND FLOOR

WIDTH 24'-0"
DEPTH 32'-0"

PLAN NO.98407

Old Fashioned with Contemporary Interior

PRICE CODE: D

- This plan features:
  - — Four bedrooms
  - — Three full baths
- A two-story Foyer is flanked by the Living Room and the Dining Room
- The Family Room features a fireplace and a French do
- The Pantry and bayed Breakfast Nook are adjacent to the Kitchen
- The Master Suite, with a tray ceiling, has an attached Bath with a vaulted ceiling and radius window
- Upstairs are two additional Bedrooms, a full Bath, a laundry closet and a bonus room
- This home is designed with basement, slab, and crawlspace foundation options

FIRST FLOOR — 1,135 SQ. FT.
SECOND FLOOR — 917 SQ. FT.
BONUS ROOM — 216 SQ. FT.
BASEMENT — 1,135 SQ. FT.
GARAGE — 452 SQ. FT.

***TOTAL LIVING AREA:* 2,052 SQ. FT.**

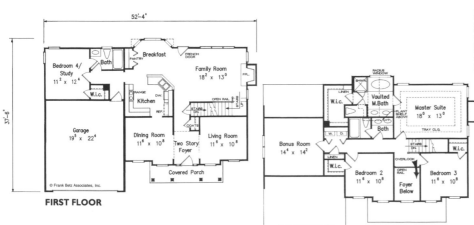

52'-4"
37'-6"
Bedroom 4/ Study 11^{2} x 12^{4}
Bath
W.i.c.
Pantry
Breakfast
French Door
Family Room 18^{2} x 13^{0}
FPL.
Range
DW.
Kitchen
Ref.
Open Rail
Stairs
Garage 19^{5} x 22^{4}
Dining Room 11^{6} x 10^{8}
Two Story Foyer
Coats
Living Room 11^{6} x 10^{8}
Covered Porch
© Frank Betz Associates, Inc.
FIRST FLOOR

Radius Window
W.i.c.
Linen
Vaulted M.Bath
Plant Shelf Above
Master Suite 18^{0} x 13^{0}
Tray Clg.
Bath
W. D.
Stairs
W.i.c.
Bonus Room 14^{4} x 14^{2}
Linen
W.i.c.
Bedroom 2 11^{6} x 10^{8}
Overlook
Open Rail
Foyer Below
Bedroom 3 11^{6} x 10^{8}
SECOND FLOOR

PLAN NO. 65139

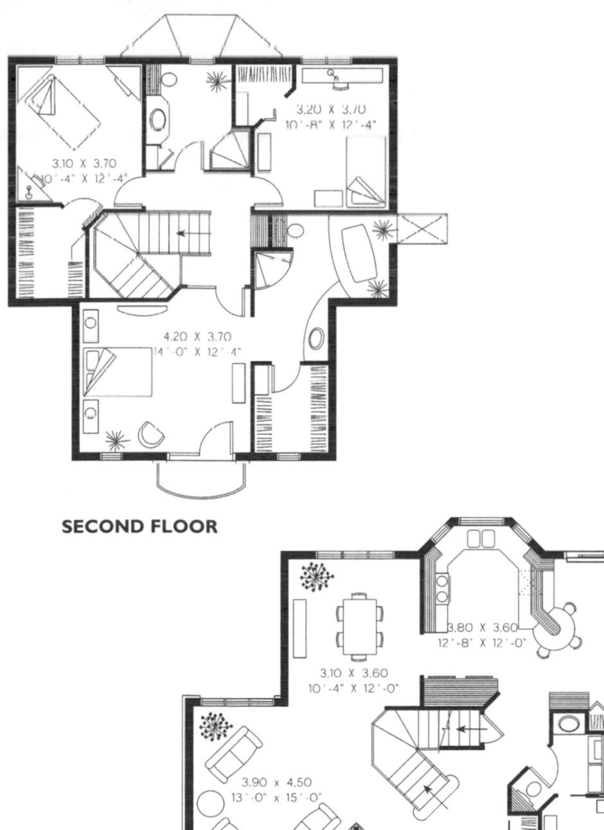
3.20 X 3.70
10'-8" X 12'-4"
3.10 X 3.70
10'-4" X 12'-4"
4.20 X 3.70
14'-0" X 12'-4"
SECOND FLOOR
3.10 X 3.60
10'-4" X 12'-0"
3.90 X 4.50
13'-0" X 15'-0"
FIRST FLOOR
3.00 X 4.50
10'-0" X 15'-0"

WIDTH 54'-0"
DEPTH 44'-0"

3.80 X 3.60
12'-8" X 12'-0"

4.50 X 3.50
15'-0" X 11'-8"

4.10 X 6.00
13'-8" X 20'-0"

3.00 X 6.00
10'-0" X 20'-0"

A Plan with Prestige

Price Code: E

- This plan features:
- — Three bedrooms
- — One full, one three-quarter, and one half bath
- Abundant space and separate Entry for a Home Office in each of the front Turrets
- The U-shaped Kitchen includes a double sink that overlooks the rear yard and a counter top that ends as a circular snack bar
- The Laundry Room and half Bath are combined on the first floor
- The Master Bedroom Suite features a walk-in closet and a Master Bath with garden tub and separate shower
- This home is designed with a basement foundation

FIRST FLOOR — 1,468 SQ. FT.
SECOND FLOOR — 936 SQ. FT.
GARAGE — 276 SQ. FT.

TOTAL LIVING AREA:
2,404 SQ. FT

PLAN NO. 20196

Gorgeous

Price Code: F

■ This plan features:

— Four bedrooms

— Two full and one half baths

- A bay window that enhances the Living Room with natural light
- A Breakfast Room with an incredible shape
- An island Kitchen in close proximity to both the formal Dining Room and the informal Breakfast Room
- A fantastic Master Suite with a decorative ceiling, private Master Bath and a large walk-in closet
- Three additional Bedrooms share a full hall Bath
- This home is designed with a basement foundation

FIRST FLOOR — 1,273 SQ. FT.
SECOND FLOOR — 1,477 SQ. FT.
BASEMENT — 974 SQ. FT.
GARAGE — 852 SQ. FT.

TOTAL LIVING AREA:
2,750 SQ. FT.

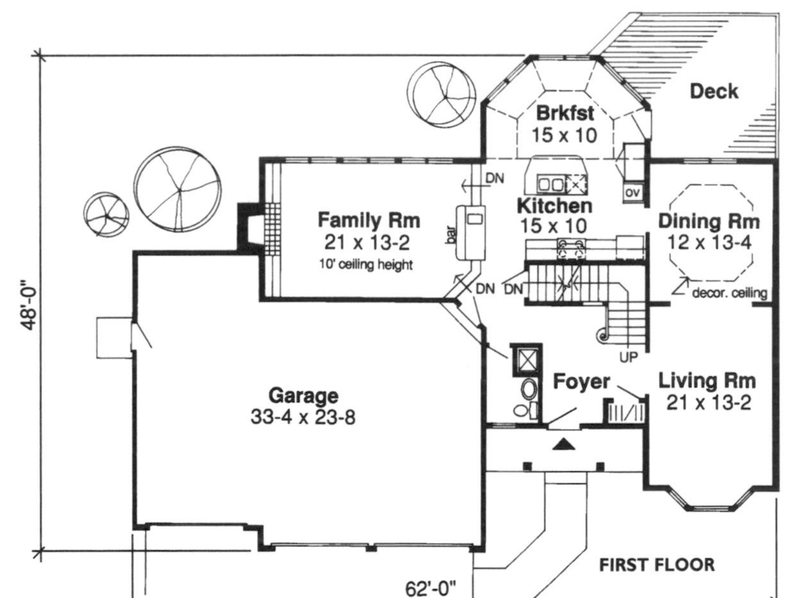
Deck
Brkfst
15 x 10
DN
Family Rm
21 x 13-2
10' ceiling height
bar
Kitchen
15 x 10
ov
Dining Rm
12 x 13-4
decor. ceiling
DN
DN
UP
Foyer
Living Rm
21 x 13-2
Garage
33-4 x 23-8
48'-0"
62'-0"
FIRST FLOOR

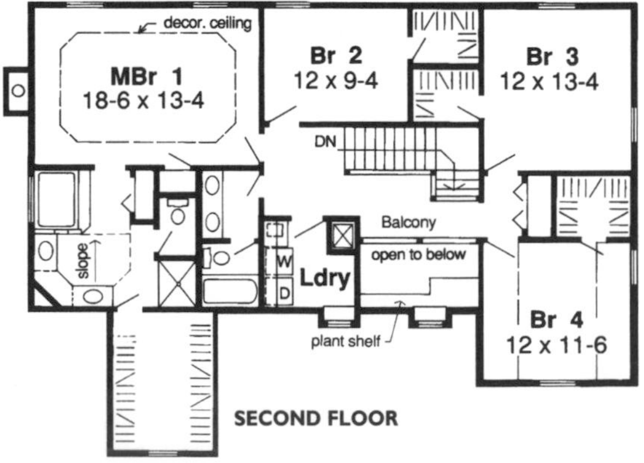
decor. ceiling
MBr 1
18-6 x 13-4
Br 2
12 x 9-4
Br 3
12 x 13-4
DN
slope
Balcony
open to below
W
D
Ldry
plant shelf
Br 4
12 x 11-6
SECOND FLOOR

Easy Living One-Level

PRICE CODE: A

PLAN NO.97724

This plan features:
- Three bedrooms
- Two full baths
- The Great Room, combined with the Dining Area, reates an open spacious effect
- Triple doors lead to a raised Deck creating a favorable ndoor/outdoor relationship
- The Master Bedroom has a large walk-in closet and deluxe Bath
- The rear walk-out basement creates the opportunity f increasing square footage
- This home is designed with a basement foundation
- AIN FLOOR — 1,488 SQ. FT.
- SEMENT — 1,488 SQ. FT.
- RAGE — 417 SQ. FT.

TOTAL LIVING AREA:
1,488 SQ. FT.

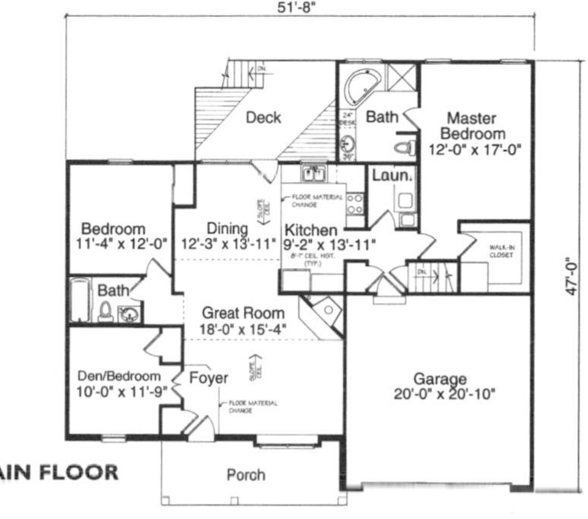
51'-8"
Deck
Bath
Master Bedroom 12'-0" x 17'-0"
Laun.
Bedroom 11'-4" x 12'-0"
Dining 12'-3" x 13'-11"
Kitchen 9'-2" x 13'-11"
Walk-in closet
Bath
Great Room 18'-0" x 15'-4"
47'-0"
Den/Bedroom 10'-0" x 11'-9"
Foyer
Garage 20'-0" x 20'-10"
MAIN FLOOR
Porch

Lap of Luxury

PRICE CODE: E

PLAN NO.98511

This plan features:
- Four bedrooms
- Three full and one half baths
- Entertaining in grand style in the formal Living Room, he Dining Room, or under the covered Patio in the backyard
- A Family Room crowned in a cathedral ceiling, enhanced by a center fireplace, and built-in book shelves
- An efficient Kitchen highlighted by a wall oven, plentiful counter space and a Pantry
- A Master Bedroom with a Sitting Area, huge walk in closet, private Bath, and access to a covered Lanai
- A secondary Bedroom wing containing three additional Bedrooms with ample closet space, and two full Baths
- This home is designed with slab and crawlspace foundation options
- AIN FLOOR — 2,445 SQ. FT.
- RAGE — 630 SQ. FT.

TOTAL LIVING AREA:
2,445 SQ. FT.

WIDTH 65'-0"
DEPTH 68'-8"
FAMILY ROOM 15X17
COVERED
PATIO AREA
BDRM. #4 13X10
BRKFT. 12X11
COVERED LANAI
COVERED
MSTR. BATH
LIVING ROOM 13X13
KIT. 12X13
W-I-CLOS.
SITTING AREA
BDRM. #3 10X12
HALL
GALLERY
HALL
MSTR. BDRM. 14X18
ENT.
FORMAL DINING 11X13
BATH
BDRM. #2 10X13
POR.
THREE CAR GARAGE
MAIN FLOOR

PLAN NO. 97254

Elegant Ceiling Treatments

PRICE CODE: B

- This plan features:
  - — Three bedrooms
  - — Two full baths
- A cozy wrapping front Porch sheltering entrance
- Dining Room defined by columns at the entrances
- Kitchen highlighted by a peninsula counter/serving ba
- Breakfast Room flowing from the Kitchen
- Vaulted ceiling highlighting the Great Room which als includes a fireplace
- Master Suite crowned in a tray ceiling over the Bedroom, a Sitting Room and plush Master Bath
- Two additional Bedrooms are located at the other side of the house
- This home is designed with basement and crawlspace foundation options

MAIN FLOOR — 1,692 SQ. FT.
BONUS ROOM — 358 SQ. FT.
BASEMENT — 1,705 SQ. FT.
GARAGE — 472 SQ. FT.

TOTAL LIVING AREA:
1,692 SQ. FT.

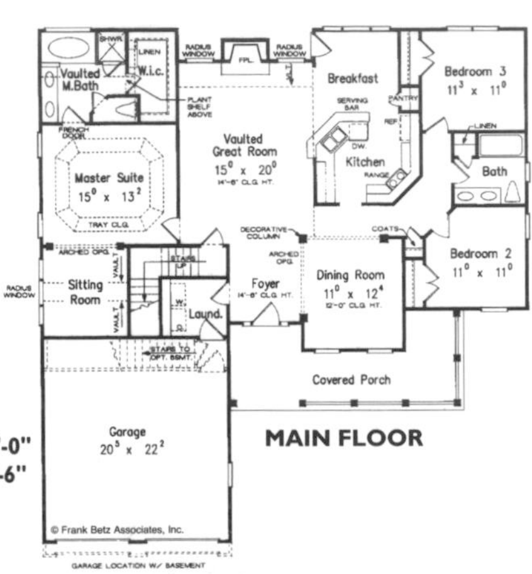

Vaulted M.Bath
W.i.c.
Breakfast
Bedroom 3
Vaulted Great Room
Kitchen
Bath
Master Suite
Sitting Room
Foyer
Dining Room
Bedroom 2
Laund.
Covered Porch
Garage
MAIN FLOOR
© Frank Betz Associates, Inc.

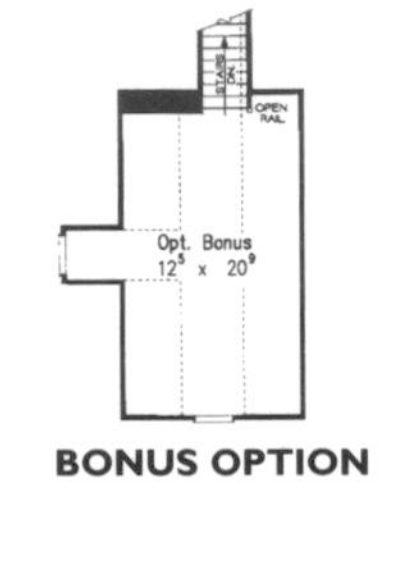

Opt. Bonus
BONUS OPTION

WIDTH 54'-0"
DEPTH 56'-6"

PLAN NO. 96504

Outstanding Family Home

PRICE CODE: D

- This plan features:
  - — Three bedrooms
  - — Two full baths
- Split-bedroom layout, perfect floor plan for a family with older children
- Great Room including a cozy fireplace, access to the r Porch and an open layout with the Nook and Kitchen
- Extended counter in the Kitchen providing a snack ba for meals or snacks
- Formal Dining Room directly accessing the Kitchen
- Bright Nook with a built-in Pantry
- Master Suite includes access to rear Porch and a pampering Bath and walk-in closet
- This home is designed with slab and crawlspace foundation options

MAIN FLOOR — 2,162 SQ. FT.
GARAGE — 498 SQ. FT.

TOTAL LIVING AREA:
2,162 SQ. FT.

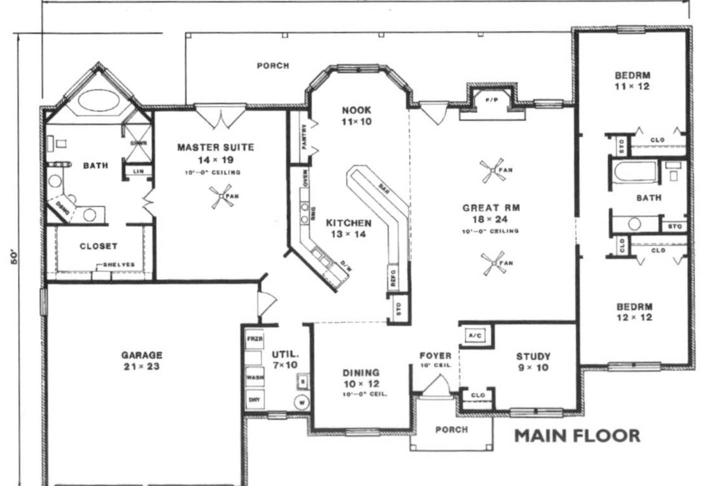

70'
50'
PORCH
NOOK 11×10
BEDRM 11×12
BATH
MASTER SUITE 14×19
KITCHEN 13×14
GREAT RM 18×24
CLOSET
BEDRM 12×12
GARAGE 21×23
UTIL. 7×10
DINING 10×12
FOYER
STUDY 9×10
PORCH
MAIN FLOOR

PLAN NO. 82014

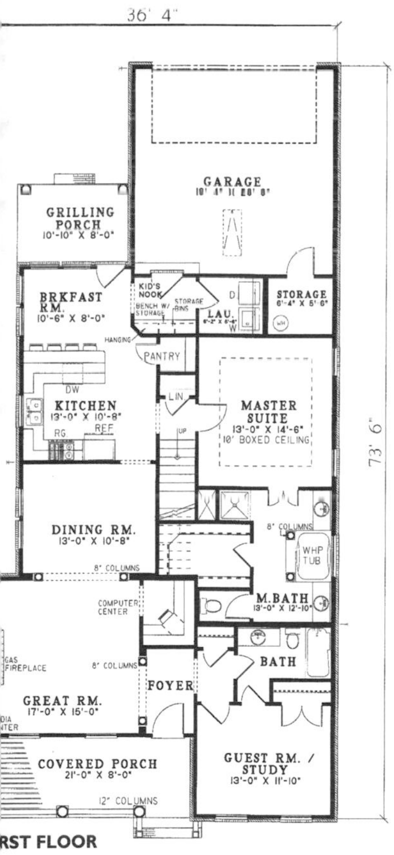

36' 4"
GARAGE
GRILLING PORCH
10'-10" X 8'-0"
BRKFAST RM.
10'-6" X 8'-0"
KID'S NOOK
STORAGE
LAU.
PANTRY
KITCHEN
13'-0" X 10'-8"
LIN.
UP
MASTER SUITE
13'-0" X 14'-6"
10' BOXED CEILING
73' 6"
DINING RM.
13'-0" X 10'-8"
8" COLUMNS
WHP TUB
COMPUTER CENTER
M.BATH
13'-0" X 12'-10"
BATH
FOYER
GREAT RM.
17'-0" X 15'-0"
COVERED PORCH
21'-0" X 8'-0"
12" COLUMNS
GUEST RM. / STUDY
13'-0" X 11'-10"

FIRST FLOOR

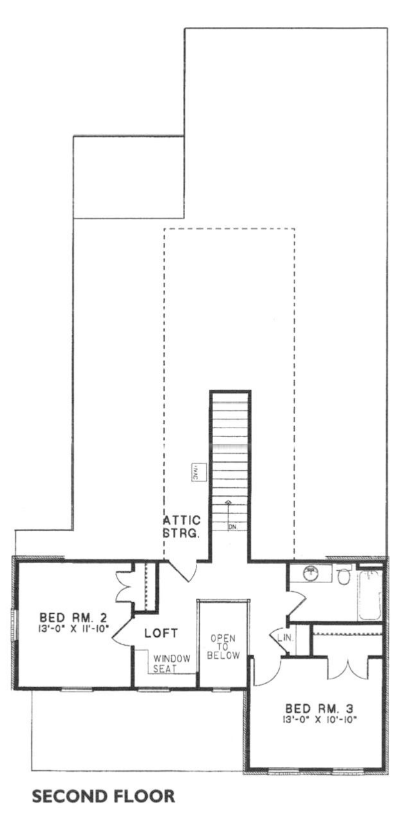

ATTIC STRG.
DN
BED RM. 2
13'-0" X 11'-10"
LOFT
WINDOW SEAT
OPEN TO BELOW
LIN.
BED RM. 3
13'-0" X 10'-10"

SECOND FLOOR

Computer Center

Price Code: C

- This plan features:
  - Four bedrooms
  - Three full baths
- The Great Room includes a gas fireplace and computer center
- The Dining Room has columns accenting its entrance
- The Kitchen/Breakfast Room is efficiently designed and has direct access to the Grilling Porch
- There are two suites located on the first floor: a Master Suite and a Guest Suite
- This home is designed with basement, slab, and crawlspace foundation options

FIRST FLOOR — 1,558 SQ. FT.
SECOND FLOOR — 429 SQ. FT.
GARAGE — 445 SQ. FT.

TOTAL LIVING AREA:
1,987 SQ. FT.

PLAN NO. 91901

Rich Classic Lines

Price Code: D

- This plan features:
- — Four bedrooms
- — Three full and one half baths
- A two-story Foyer flooded by light through a half-round transom
- A vaulted ceiling in the Great Room
- A corner fireplace in the Great Room with French doors to the Breakfast/Kitchen Area
- A center island in the Kitchen with a built-in desk and Pantry
- A tray ceiling in the Dining Room
- A Master Suite with a walk-in closet, a whirlpool tub, and a double sink vanity
- This home is designed with a basement foundation

FIRST FLOOR — 1,496 SQ. FT.
SECOND FLOOR — 716 SQ. FT.
BASEMENT — 1,420 SQ. FT.
GARAGE — 460 SQ. FT.

TOTAL LIVING AREA:
2,212 SQ. FT.

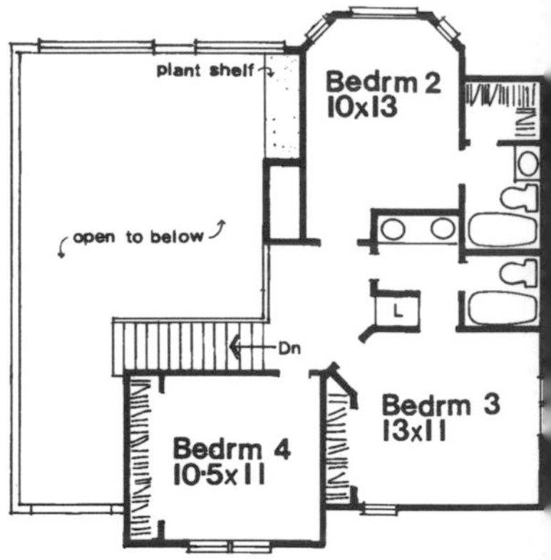

plant shelf
Bedrm 2 10x13
open to below
Dn
Bedrm 3 13x11
Bedrm 4 10-5x11
SECOND FLOOR

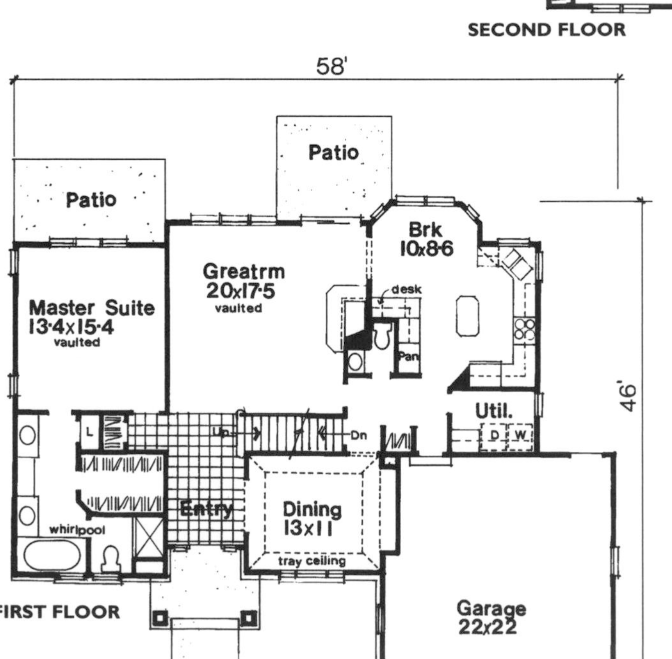
58'
46'
Patio
Patio
Brk
10x8-6
Greatrm
20x17-5
vaulted
desk
Pan
Master Suite
13-4x15-4
vaulted
Util.
Up
Dn
Entry
Dining
13x11
tray ceiling
whirlpool
Garage
22x22
FIRST FLOOR

Fieldstone Facade

PRICE CODE: E

his plan features:

- ʼour bedrooms
- ʼwo full and one half baths
- overed Porch shelters entrance into Gallery and Great oom with a focal point fireplace and Patio access pped by a vaulted ceiling
- ormal Dining Room conveniently located for ıtertaining
- ooktop island, built-in Pantry and a bright Breakfast rea highlight Kitchen
- ecluded Master Bedroom with Patio access, rge walk-in closet and corner Spa tub
- hree additional Bedrooms with ample closets, are a double vanity Bath
- his home is designed with basement ıd slab foundation options

IN FLOOR — 2,261 SQ. FT.

RAGE — 640 SQ. FT.

TOTAL LIVING AREA:
2,261 SQ. FT.

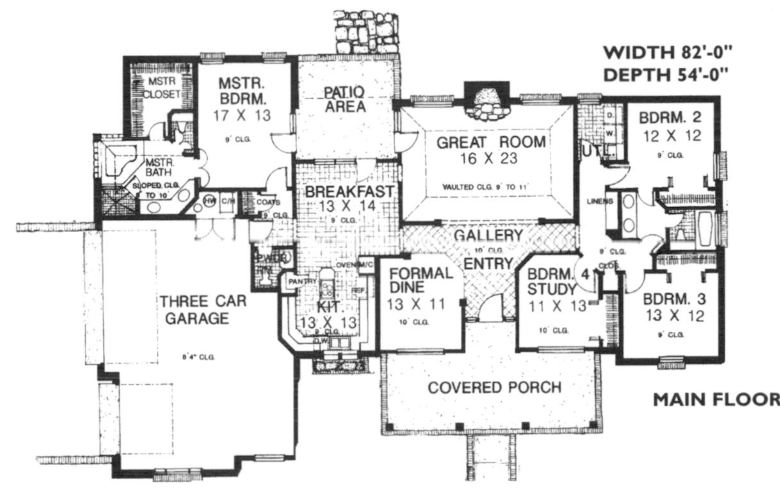

WIDTH 82'-0"
DEPTH 54'-0"
MSTR. CLOSET
MSTR. BDRM. 17 X 13
9' CLG.
PATIO AREA
GREAT ROOM 16 X 23
VAULTED CLG. 9' TO 11'
BDRM. 2 12 X 12
9' CLG.
MSTR. BATH
SLOPED CLG. TO 10
COATS
BREAKFAST 13 X 14
9' CLG.
LINENS
GALLERY
10' CLG.
ENTRY
PWDR.
PANTRY
OVEN/M/C
REF
FORMAL DINE 13 X 11
10' CLG.
BDRM. 4 STUDY 11 X 13
10' CLG.
BDRM. 3 13 X 12
9' CLG.
THREE CAR GARAGE
8'4" CLG.
KIT. 13 X 13
9' CLG.
COVERED PORCH
MAIN FLOOR

Spacious and Bright

PRICE CODE: C

'his plan features:

- Three bedrooms
- Two full and one half baths
- Soaring ceilings in the two-story Family and Dining Rooms and a full-height stone fireplace surrounded by windows creates a spacious, sun-filled interior
- A circular snack bar and separate Dining Area offers informal or formal dining options
- Surrounded by angled balconies, the second floor boasts a private Computer Room and a spacious Bedroom with access to a large Attic
- The home is designed with a basement foundation

RST FLOOR — 1,525 SQ. FT.

COND FLOOR — 470 SQ. FT.

SEMENT — 1,525 SQ. FT.

RAGE — 623 SQ. FT.

TOTAL LIVING AREA:
1,995 SQ. FT.

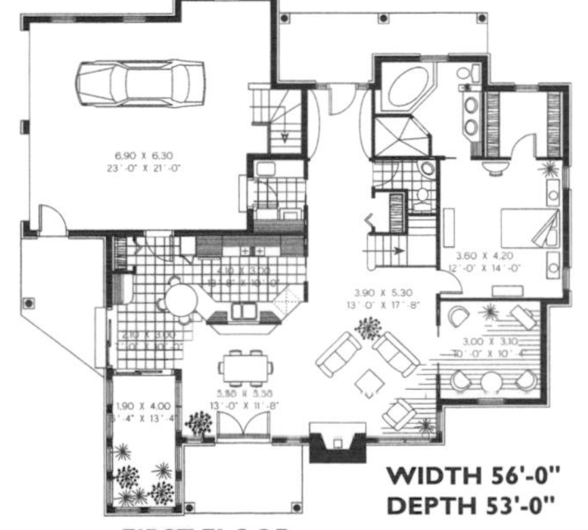

6.90 X 6.30
23'-0" X 21'-0"
3.60 X 4.20
12'-0" X 14'-0"
3.90 X 5.30
13'-0" X 17'-8"
3.00 X 3.10
10'-0" X 10'-4"
3.50 X 3.50
13'-0" X 11'-8"
1.90 X 4.00
WIDTH 56'-0"
DEPTH 53'-0"
FIRST FLOOR

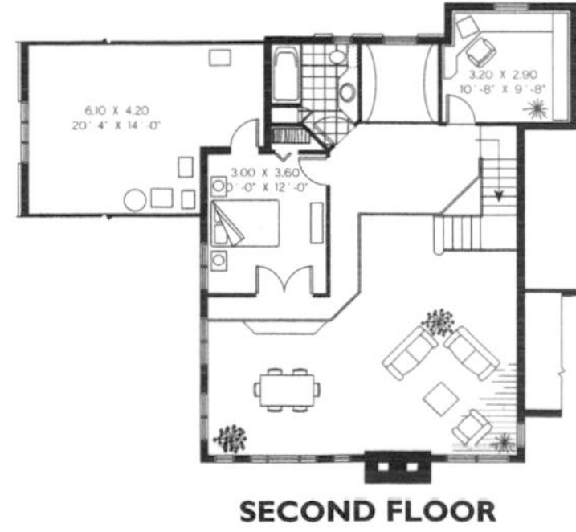

6.10 X 4.20
20'-4" X 14'-0"
3.20 X 2.90
10'-8" X 9'-8"
3.00 X 3.60
10'-0" X 12'-0"
SECOND FLOOR

PLAN NO.20220

Traditional Ranch

PRICE CODE: B

- This plan features:
- — Three bedrooms
- — Two full baths
- A large front arch-top window that gives this home g curb appeal, and allows a view of the front yard from Living Room
- A vaulted ceiling in the Living Room, adding to the architectural interest and the spacious feel of the room
- Sliding glass doors in the Dining Room that lead to a wood Deck
- A built-in Pantry, double sink and breakfast bar in the efficient Kitchen
- A Master Suite that includes a walk-in closet and a private Bath with a double vanity
- Two additional Bedrooms that share a full hall Bath
- This home is designed with basement, slab and crawlspace foundation options

MAIN FLOOR — 1,568 SQ. FT.
GARAGE — 509 SQ. FT.
BASEMENT — 1,568 SQ. FT.

TOTAL LIVING AREA:
1,568 SQ. FT.

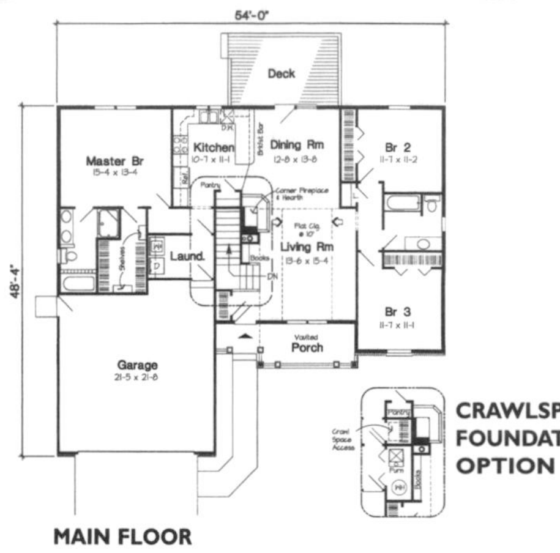
54'-0"
Deck
Master Br
Kitchen
Dining Rm
Br 2
Laund.
Living Rm
Br 3
Garage
Porch
48'-4"
CRAWLSPACE/SLAB
FOUNDATION
OPTION

MAIN FLOOR

PLAN NO.93708

Tailored for a View to the Side

PRICE CODE: F

- This plan features:
- — Three or four bedrooms
- — Three full and one half baths
- A design for a homesite with a view to the side, perfe for entertaining and everyday living
- A sheltered entrance with windows over the door and side light
- A large entry Foyer highlighted by a ceiling dome anc French doors leading to the private Study or Guest Bedroom with a vaulted ceiling
- An elegant formal Dining Room with a high ceiling a a columned and arched entrance
- A sunken Great Room with a tray ceiling, arched and columned openings and a cozy fireplace
- A Breakfast Room, with an optional planning desk, opens to the Kitchen via the eating bar
- An island and walk-in Pantry adding to the Kitchen's efficiency
- A tray ceiling and lavish Bath pamper the owner in th Master Suite
- Two additional Bedrooms that share a split vanity Ba
- This home is designed with crawlspace and slab foundation options

MAIN FLOOR — 2,579 SQ. FT.
GARAGE — 536 SQ. FT.

TOTAL LIVING AREA:
2,579 SQ. FT.

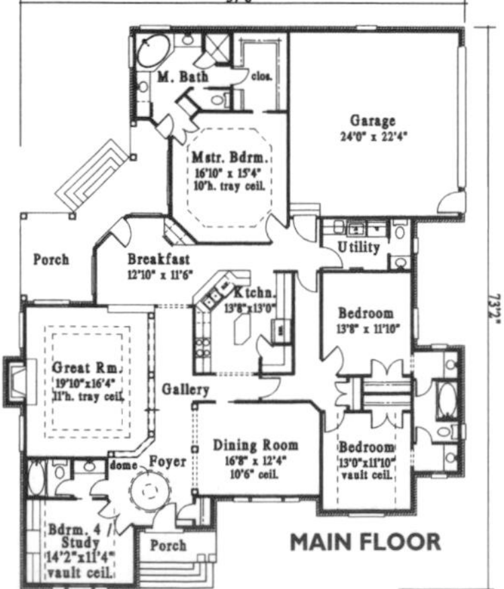
57'6"
M. Bath
clos.
Garage
24'0" x 22'4"
Mstr. Bdrm.
16'10" x 15'4"
10'h. tray ceil.
Porch
Breakfast
12'10" x 11'6"
Utility
Kitchn.
13'8"x13'0"
Bedroom
13'8" x 11'10"
Great Rm.
19'10"x16'4"
11'h. tray ceil.
Gallery
Dining Room
16'8" x 12'4"
10'6" ceil.
Bedroom
13'0"x11'10"
vault ceil.
dome
Foyer
Bdrm. 4 / Study
14'2"x11'4"
vault ceil.
Porch
73'2"

MAIN FLOOR

PLAN NO. 92538

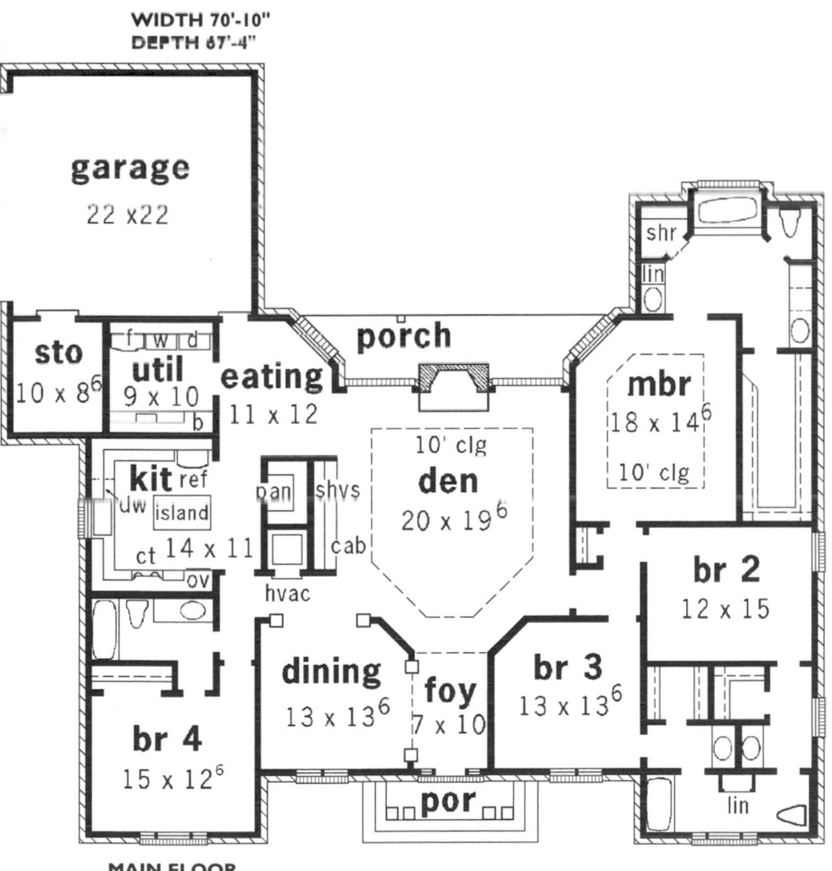

WIDTH 70'-10"
DEPTH 67'-4"
garage
22 x22
sto
10 x 8[6]
util
9 x 10
f w d
b
eating
11 x 12
porch
kit
ref
dw
island
ct
14 x 11
ov
pan
shvs
cab
hvac
10' clg
den
20 x 19[6]
shr
lin
mbr
18 x 14[6]
10' clg
br 2
12 x 15
dining
13 x 13[6]
foy
7 x 10
br 3
13 x 13[6]
br 4
15 x 12[6]
por
lin
MAIN FLOOR

Lavish Accommodations

Price Code: F

- This plan features:
  - — Four bedrooms
  - — Three full baths
- A central Den with a large fireplace, built-in shelves and cabinets and a decorative ceiling
- An island Kitchen that has been well thought out and includes a walk-in Pantry
- An informal Breakfast Room that is directly accessible from either the Kitchen or the Den
- A Master Bedroom enhanced by a decorative ceiling and a walk-in closet as well as a luxurious Master Bath
- This home is designed with crawlspace and slab foundation options

MAIN FLOOR — 2,733 SQ. FT.
GARAGE AND STORAGE — 569 SQ. FT.

TOTAL LIVING AREA:
2,733 SQ. FT.

PLAN NO. 82015

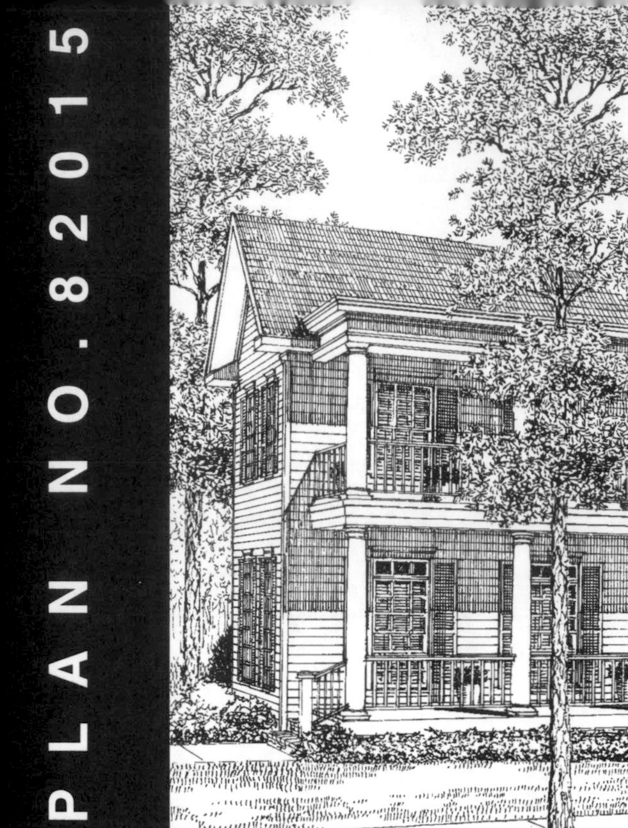

Balcony Porch

Price Code: C

- This plan features:
- — Four bedrooms
- — Two full and one half baths
- The Great Room includes a built-in media center next to the cozy fireplace
- The Dining Room and the Kitchen connect with a breakfast bar
- The Master Bedroom is topped by a boxed ceiling and includes a lavish Bath
- This home is designed with basement, slab, and crawlspace foundation options

First floor — 1,295 sq. ft.
Second floor — 664 sq. ft.
Garage — 498 sq. ft.

Total living area: 1,959 sq. ft.

38' 6"
78' 6"
STORAGE
GARAGE
23'-4" X 20'-4"
MASTER SUITE
16'-0" X 13'-0"
10' BOXED CEILING
GLASS SHWR
WHP TUB
M.BATH
LAU
COMPUTER CENTER
GRILLING PORCH
DINING RM.
15'-4" X 11'-0"
KITCHEN
10'-0" X 11'-0"
REF
DW
FOYER
MEDIA CENTER
GAS FIREPLACE
GREAT RM.
15'-4" X 19'-0"
ENTRY PORCH
8'-0" X 25'-8"
12" COLUMNS
FIRST FLOOR
BED RM. 4
10'-2" X 11'-0"
BED RM. 2
10'-2" X 11'-0"
LIN.
BALCONY PORCH
8'-0" X 25'-8"
12" COLUMNS
BED RM. 3
15'-4" X 10'-8"
SECOND FLOOR

Country-Style Charm

PRICE CODE: C

ıis plan features:
hree bedrooms
wo full baths
ːick accents, front facing gable, and railed
raparound covered Porch
built-in range and oven in a L-shaped Kitchen
Nook with Garage access for convenient unloading
groceries and other supplies
bay window wrapping around the front of the formal
ving Room
Master Suite with French doors opening to the Deck
ıis home is designed with a crawlspace foundation
N FLOOR — 1,857 SQ. FT.
AGE — 681 SQ. FT.

TOTAL LIVING AREA:
1,857 SQ. FT.

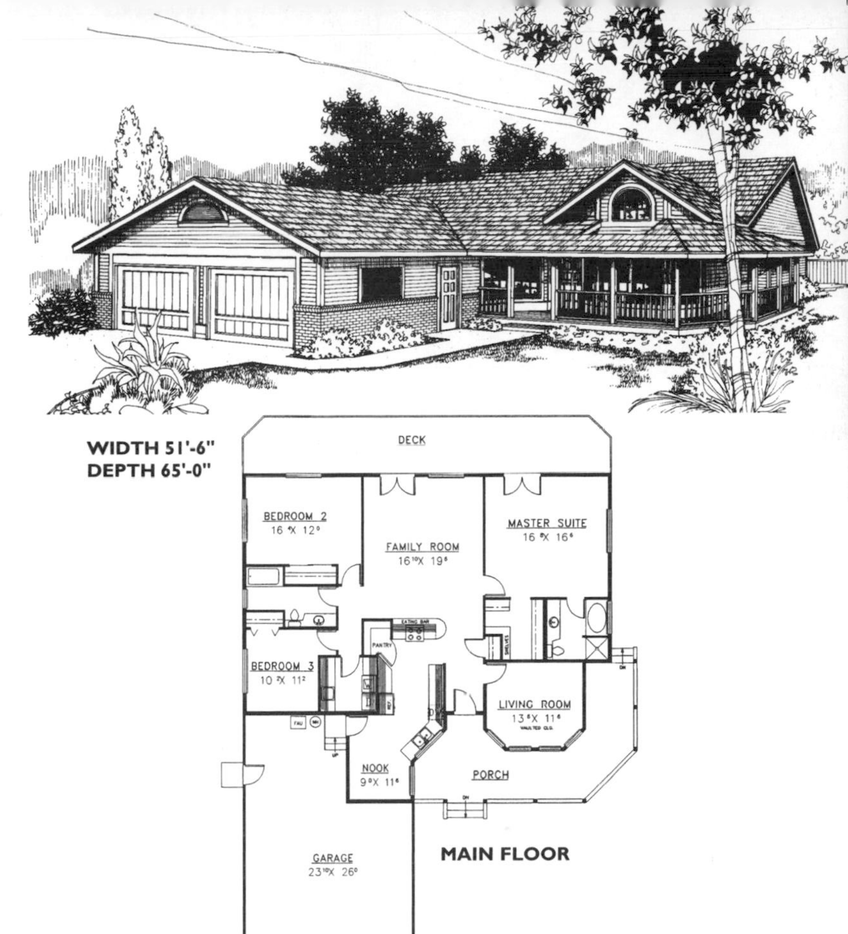

WIDTH 51'-6"
DEPTH 65'-0"
DECK
BEDROOM 2
FAMILY ROOM
MASTER SUITE
PANTRY
BEDROOM 3
LIVING ROOM
NOOK
PORCH
GARAGE
MAIN FLOOR

PLAN NO.91731

Symmetrical and Stately

PRICE CODE: E

'his plan features:
'our bedrooms
Two full and one half baths
)ouble column Porch leads into the open Foyer, the
)ining Room accented by an arched window and pillars,
nd a spacious Den
)ecorative ceiling crowns the Den with a hearth
ireplace, built-in shelves and window access
› the rear Porch
arge, efficient Kitchen with a peninsula serving
ounter, a Breakfast Area, adjoining the Utility
nd the Garage
Master Bedroom Suite with a decorative ceiling,
wo vanities and a large walk-in closet
'hree additional Bedrooms with double closets share
full Bath
'his home is designed with slab and crawlspace
oundation options
IN FLOOR — 2,387 SQ. FT.
RAGE — 505 SQ. FT.

TOTAL LIVING AREA:
2,387 SQ. FT.

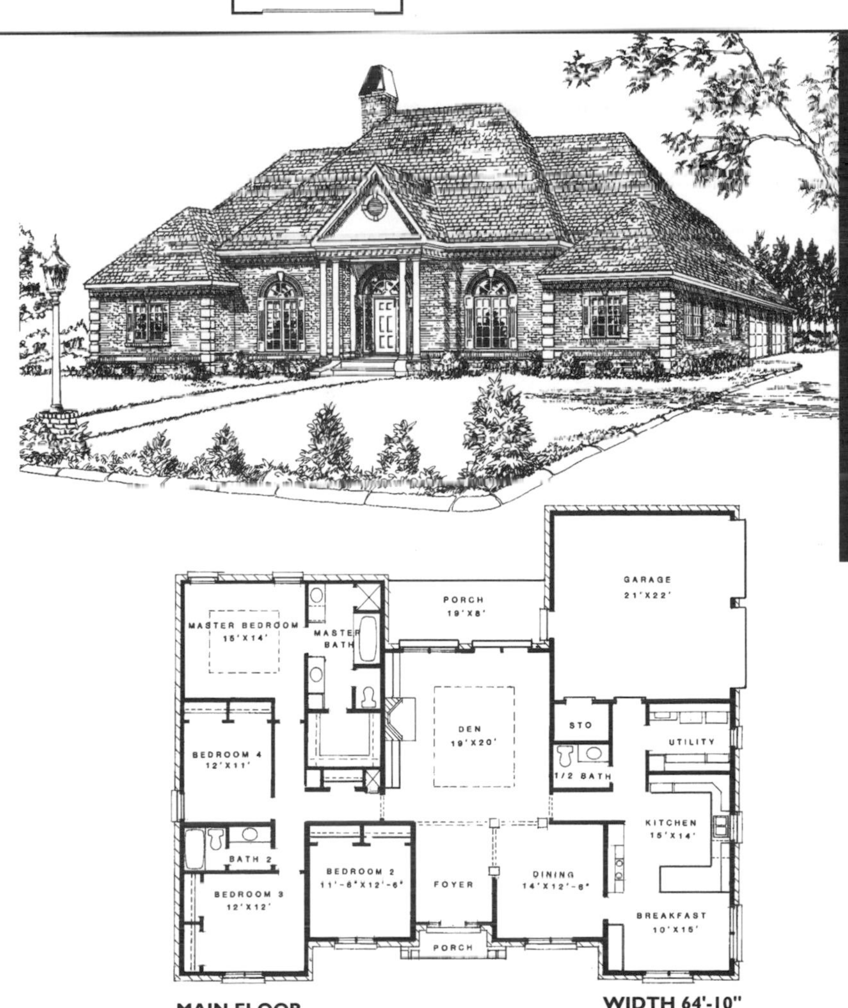

GARAGE
21'X22'
PORCH
19'X8'
MASTER BEDROOM
15'X14'
MASTER BATH
DEN
19'X20'
STO
UTILITY
1/2 BATH
BEDROOM 4
12'X11'
KITCHEN
15'X14'
BATH 2
BEDROOM 2
11'-6"X12'-6"
FOYER
DINING
14'X12'-6"
BEDROOM 3
12'X12'
BREAKFAST
10'X15'
PORCH
MAIN FLOOR
WIDTH 64'-10"
DEPTH 54'-10"

PLAN NO.92546

PLAN NO. 93048

For First Time Buyers

PRICE CODE: A

WIDTH 49-10

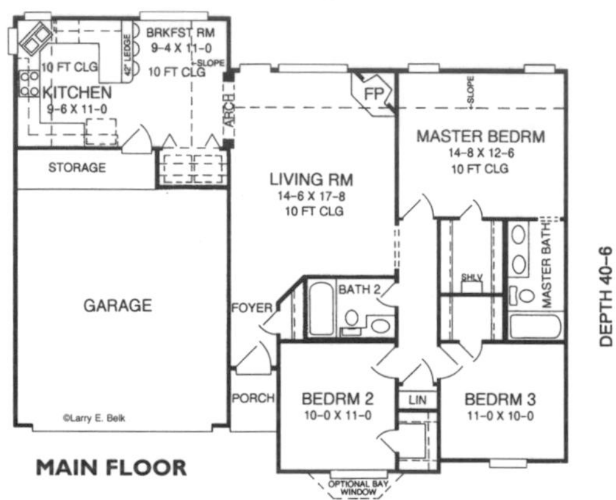

BRKFST RM
9-4 X 11-0
10 FT CLG
10 FT CLG
KITCHEN
9-6 X 11-0
STORAGE
ARCH
FP
SLOPE
LIVING RM
14-6 X 17-8
10 FT CLG
MASTER BEDRM
14-8 X 12-6
10 FT CLG
MASTER BATH
GARAGE
FOYER
BATH 2
DEPTH 40-6
PORCH
BEDRM 2
10-0 X 11-0
LIN
BEDRM 3
11-0 X 10-0
©Larry E. Belk
OPTIONAL BAY WINDOW

MAIN FLOOR

- This plan features:
  - Three bedrooms
  - Two full baths
- An efficiently designed Kitchen with a corner sink, ample counter space and a peninsula counter
- A sunny Breakfast Room with a convenient hide-awa Laundry Center
- An expansive Living Room that includes a corner fireplace and direct access to the Patio
- A private Master Suite with a walk-in closet and a double vanity Bath
- Two additional Bedrooms, both with walk-in closets, that share a full hall Bath
- This home is designed with crawlspace and slab foundation options

MAIN FLOOR — 1,310 SQ. FT.
GARAGE — 449 SQ. FT.

TOTAL LIVING AREA:
1,310 SQ. FT.

PLAN NO. 91418

Carefree Comfort

PRICE CODE: B

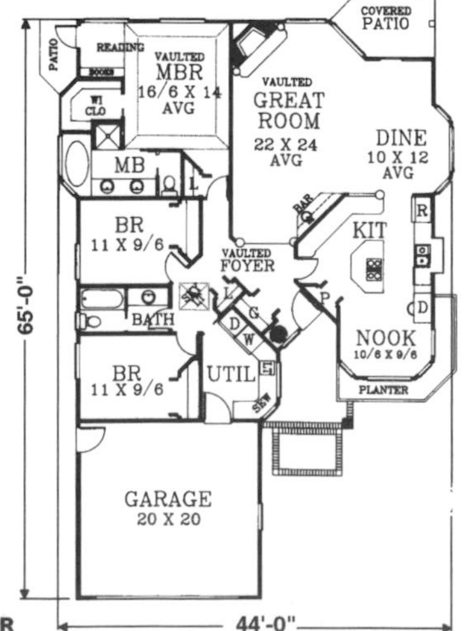

COVERED PATIO
PATIO
READING
VAULTED
MBR
16/6 X 14
AVG
W/I CLO
VAULTED
GREAT ROOM
22 X 24
AVG
DINE
10 X 12
AVG
MB
BR
11 X 9/6
BAR
KIT
VAULTED FOYER
BATH
NOOK
10/6 X 9/6
BR
11 X 9/6
UTIL
PLANTER
GARAGE
20 X 20
65'-0"
44'-0"

MAIN FLOOR

UTIL
D
W

OPTIONAL BASEMENT STAIR LOCATION

- This plan features:
  - Three bedrooms
  - Two full baths
- A dramatic vaulted Foyer
- A range top island Kitchen with a sunny eating Nook surrounded by a built-in planter
- A vaulted ceiling in the Great Room with a built-in b and corner fireplace
- A bayed Dining Room that combines with the Great Room for a spacious feeling
- A Master Bedroom with a private reading Nook, vaul ceiling, walk-in closet, and a well-appointed private I
- Two additional Bedrooms sharing a full hall Bath
- This home is designed with basement, slab and crawlspace foundation options

MAIN FLOOR — 1,665 SQ. FT.

TOTAL LIVING AREA:
1,665 SQ. FT.

Elegant and Efficient

PRICE CODE: C

s plan features:
ree bedrooms
o full baths
vered entrance into the Foyer leads to a spacious ing Room with a decorative ceiling above a hearth place and French doors to the Patio Area
corative window and ceiling highlight the formal ing Room
ge, Country Kitchen with double ovens, ooktop and a peninsula snack bar serving the ght Breakfast Area
ge Master Bedroom Suite with a decorative ceiling, alk-in closet and a plush Bath with a double vanity a whirlpool tub
o additional Bedrooms with walk-in closets share ll Bath
s home is designed with slab and crawlspace ndation options
N FLOOR — 1,959 SQ. FT.
AGE — 512 SQ. FT.

TOTAL LIVING AREA: 1,959 SQ. FT.

PLAN NO. 92515

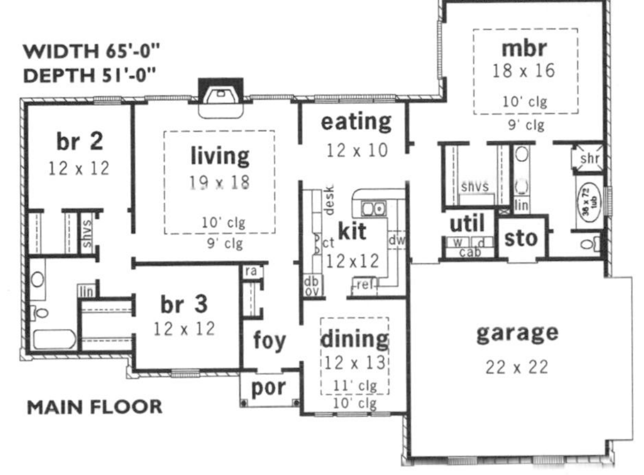
WIDTH 65'-0"
DEPTH 51'-0"
mbr
18 x 16
10' clg
9' clg
br 2
12 x 12
living
19 x 18
10' clg
9' clg
eating
12 x 10
shr
shvs
lin
desk
kit
12x12
util
sto
br 3
12 x 12
foy
dining
12 x 13
11' clg
10' clg
por
garage
22 x 22
MAIN FLOOR

Grace and Style

PRICE CODE: E

is plan features:
hree bedrooms
wo full baths
oyer accented by columns provides Entry into the rmal Dining Room
ngled island Kitchen is open to the Breakfast Bay
eat Room with cathedral ceiling is enhanced a fireplace
cluded Master Suite with a skylit Bath
wo secondary Bedrooms with an alternate Bath design eate a wheel chair accessible option for the disabled
onus Room possibilities include a terrific fourth edroom and Bath
his home is designed with a basement foundation
N FLOOR — 2,283 SQ. FT.
RAGE — 545 SQ. FT.
EMENT — 2,283 SQ. FT.

TOTAL LIVING AREA: 2,283 SQ. FT.

PLAN NO. 97746

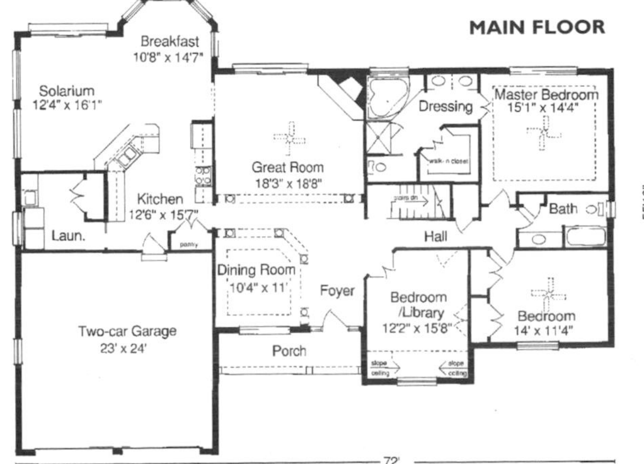
MAIN FLOOR
Breakfast
10'8" x 14'7"
Solarium
12'4" x 16'1"
Great Room
18'3" x 18'8"
Dressing
Master Bedroom
15'1" x 14'4"
Kitchen
12'6" x 15'7"
Laun.
Bath
Hall
Dining Room
10'4" x 11'
Foyer
Bedroom /Library
12'2" x 15'8"
Bedroom
14' x 11'4"
Two-car Garage
23' x 24'
Porch
55'10"
72'

PLAN NO. 98403

Luxurious Yet Cozy

Price Code: I

- This plan features:
- — Four bedrooms
- — Three full and one half baths
- Covered Porch leads into two-story Foyer and Living Room
- Decorative columns define Dining Room and Great Room
- Open and convenient Kitchen with a work island
- Corner Master Suite includes a cozy fireplace
- Three second floor Bedrooms with walk-in closets
- This home is designed with basement, slab and crawlspace foundation options

FIRST FLOOR — 2,467 SQ. FT.
SECOND FLOOR — 928 SQ. FT.
BONUS — 296 SQ. FT.
BASEMENT — 2,467 SQ. FT.
GARAGE — 566 SQ. FT.

TOTAL LIVING AREA:
3,395 SQ. FT.

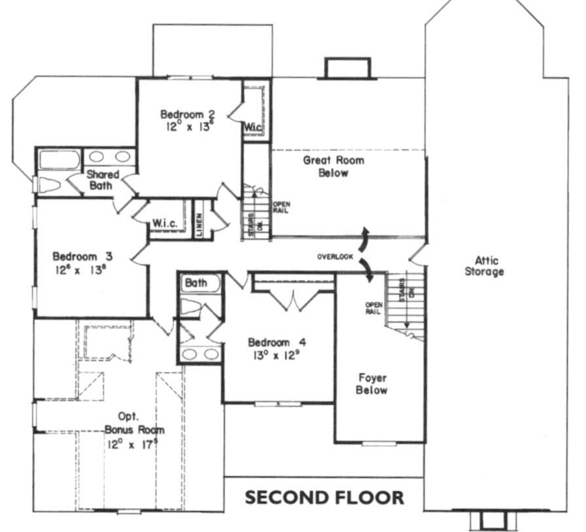

Bedroom 2
W.i.c.
Shared Bath
Great Room Below
Open Rail
W.i.c.
Linen
Bedroom 3
Overlook
Attic Storage
Bath
Bedroom 4
Open Rail
Foyer Below
Opt. Bonus Room
SECOND FLOOR

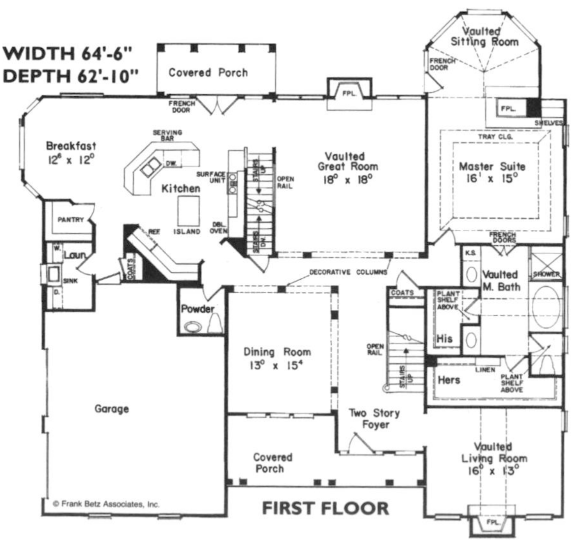

WIDTH 64'-6"
DEPTH 62'-10"
Covered Porch
French Door
FPL.
Vaulted Sitting Room
French Door
Breakfast
Serving Bar
DW
Kitchen
Surface Unit
Island
Dbl. Oven
Ref
Pantry
Laun.
Sink
Coats
Vaulted Great Room
Open Rail
FPL.
Shelves
Tray Clg.
Master Suite
French Doors
Decorative Columns
Vaulted M. Bath
Shower
Coats
Plant Shelf Above
His
Hers
Linen
Plant Shelf Above
Powder
Dining Room
Open Rail
Garage
Two Story Foyer
Covered Porch
Vaulted Living Room
FPL.
© Frank Betz Associates, Inc.
FIRST FLOOR

Attractive Exterior

PRICE CODE: D

PLAN NO.98512

his plan features:
- 'hree bedrooms
- 'wo full baths
- ı the gallery, columns separate space into the Great oom and the Dining Room
- ccess to backyard covered Patio from bayed reakfast Nook
- he large Kitchen is a chef's dream with lots of ›unter space and a Pantry
- he Master Bedroom is removed from traffic areas ıd contains a luxurious Master Bath
- hall connects the two secondary Bedrooms which ıare a full skylit Bath
- his home is designed with a slab foundation

ıN FLOOR — 2,167 SQ. FT.
ʀAGE — 690 SQ. FT.

TOTAL LIVING AREA:
2,167 SQ. FT.

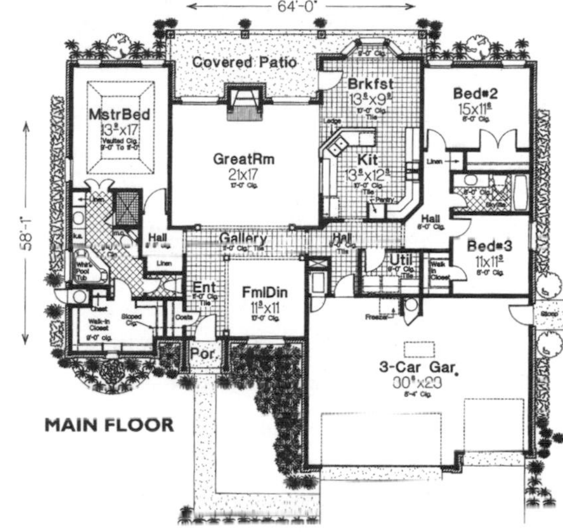

64'-0"
58'-1"
Covered Patio
Brkfst
13⁸x9⁸
MstrBed
13⁸x17
Bed#2
15x11⁸
GreatRm
21x17
Kit
13⁸x12⁸
Gallery
Hall
Bed#3
11x11⁸
Util
Ent
FmlDin
11⁸x11
Por.
3-Car Gar.
30⁸x23
MAIN FLOOR

Demonstrative Detail

PRICE CODE: C

PLAN NO.93410

ıis plan features:
- hree bedrooms
- wo full and one half baths
- ɜystone arched windows, stone and stucco combine ıth shutters and a flower box to create an eye-catching ɜvation
- ıe Foyer accesses the Dining Room, Family Room the Master Suite
- ıe Family Room has a sloped ceiling and is accented a fireplace with windows to either side
- ıe Kitchen/Breakfast Area has easy access to the ıı Porch
- vo roomy Bedrooms on the second floor share the full ll Bath
- ı optional bonus area over the Garage offers ıssibilities for future expansion
- ıis home is designed with a basement foundation

T FLOOR — 1,317 SQ. FT.
ОND FLOOR — 537 SQ. FT.
US — 312 SQ. FT.
EMENT — 1,317 SQ. FT.

TOTAL LIVING AREA:
1,854 SQ. FT.

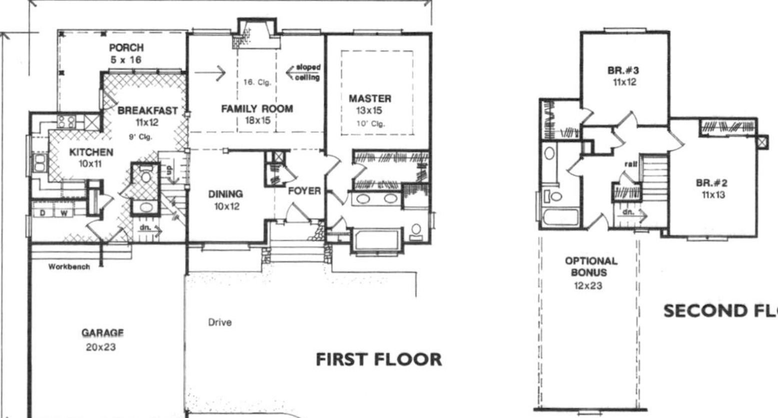

53'
52'
PORCH
5 x 16
BREAKFAST
11x12
KITCHEN
10x11
FAMILY ROOM
18x15
sloped ceiling
MASTER
13x15
DINING
10x12
FOYER
Workbench
GARAGE
20x23
Drive
FIRST FLOOR
BR.#3
11x12
BR.#2
11x13
OPTIONAL BONUS
12x23
SECOND FLOOR

PLAN NO.92561

Classically Appointed

PRICE CODE: C

- This plan features:
  — Three bedrooms
  — Two full baths
- The recessed front Entry leads into a formal Foyer
- The Dining room has a bright front window and dire accesses the Kitchen
- The Kitchen is U-shaped and features a wall oven, and an angled counter eating bar
- There is an Eating Bay that overlooks the back Porcl and is open to the Kitchen
- The Den has a 12-foot raised ceiling and a fireplace
- The Master Suite features a raised ceiling, a full Batl and a walk-in closet
- Two large secondary Bedrooms share a Bath in the h
- This home is designed with slab and crawlspace foundation options

MAIN FLOOR — 1,856 SQ. FT.
GARAGE — 521 SQ. FT.

TOTAL LIVING AREA:
1,856 SQ. FT.

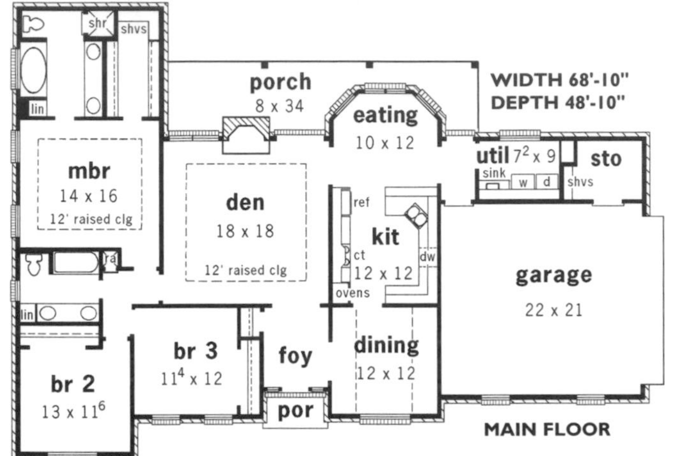
shr
shvs
lin
porch
8 x 34
eating
10 x 12
WIDTH 68'-10"
DEPTH 48'-10"
mbr
14 x 16
12' raised clg
den
18 x 18
12' raised clg
util 7² x 9
sink
w d
sto
shvs
ref
kit
ct
12 x 12
dw
ovens
garage
22 x 21
ra
lin
br 3
11⁴ x 12
foy
dining
12 x 12
br 2
13 x 11⁶
por
MAIN FLOOR

PLAN NO.98408

Covered Porch with Columns

PRICE CODE: C

- This plan features:
  — Three bedrooms
  — Two full baths
- The Foyer with 12-foot ceiling leads past decorative columns into the Family Room with a center fireplac
- The Living Room and Dining Room are linked by th Foyer and have windows overlooking the front Porcl
- The Kitchen has a serving bar and is adjacent to the Breakfast Nook which has a French door that opens to the backyard
- The private Master Suite has a tray ceiling, a vaulted Bath with a double vanity, and a walk-in closet
- The two other Bedrooms share a full Bath
- This home is designed with basement, slab and crawlspace foundation options

MAIN FLOOR — 1,856 SQ. FT.
GARAGE — 429 SQ. FT.

TOTAL LIVING AREA:
1,856 SQ. FT.

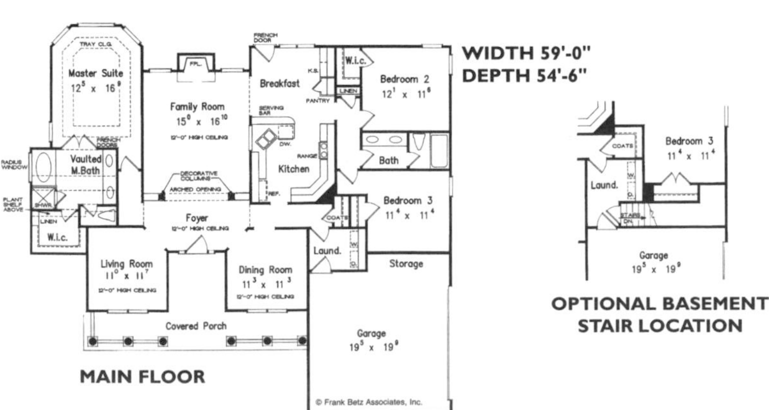
WIDTH 59'-0"
DEPTH 54'-6"
Master Suite
Family Room
Breakfast
Bedroom 2
Vaulted M.Bath
Kitchen
Bath
Bedroom 3
Foyer
W.I.c.
Living Room
Dining Room
Laund.
Storage
Covered Porch
Garage
MAIN FLOOR
© Frank Betz Associates, Inc.
Bedroom 3
Laund.
Garage
OPTIONAL BASEMENT
STAIR LOCATION

PLAN NO. 96516

Country Front Porch

Price Code: A

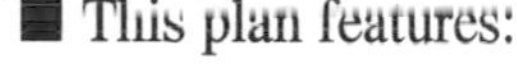

■ This plan features:

— Three bedrooms

— Two full baths

■ A 10-foot high ceiling and a cozy fireplace accent the expansive Great Room

■ The Kitchen and the Dining Room adjoin for a feeling of more space

■ The split-bedroom floor plan is perfect for families with older children

■ The Master Suite is near the Garage entrance for a quick change of clothes after work

■ A rear Porch expands living space to the outside

■ This home is designed with crawlspace and slab foundation options

MAIN FLOOR — 1,458 SQ. FT.
GARAGE — 452 SQ. FT.

TOTAL LIVING AREA:
1,458 SQ. FT.

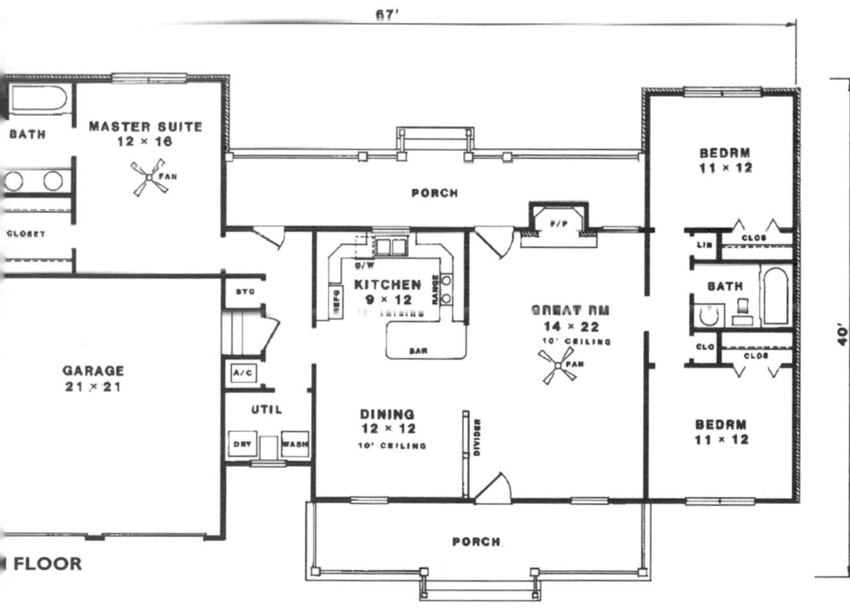

67'
40'
BATH
MASTER SUITE
12 × 16
FAN
CLOSET
PORCH
F/P
BEDRM
11 × 12
LIN
CLOS
BATH
CLO
CLOS
STO
KITCHEN
9 × 12
D/W
REFG
RANGE
BAR
GREAT RM
14 × 22
10' CEILING
FAN
GARAGE
21 × 21
A/C
UTIL
DRY
WASH
DINING
12 × 12
10' CEILING
DIVIDER
BEDRM
11 × 12
PORCH
FLOOR

PLAN NO. 98405

Regal Residence

Price Code: H

- This plan features:
- — Five bedrooms
- — Four full baths
- Keystone, arched windows accent entrance into two-story Foyer
- Kitchen with a cooktop island/serving bar and a walk-in Pantry
- First floor Guest Room/Study adjoins a full Bath
- Master Suite offers a tray ceiling and a vaulted Bath with a radius window
- Three additional Bedrooms have walk-in closets
- This home is designed with basement and crawlspace foundation options

FIRST FLOOR — 1,488 SQ. FT.
SECOND FLOOR — 1,551 SQ. FT.
BASEMENT — 1,488 SQ. FT.
GARAGE — 667 SQ. FT.

TOTAL LIVING AREA:
3,039 SQ. FT.

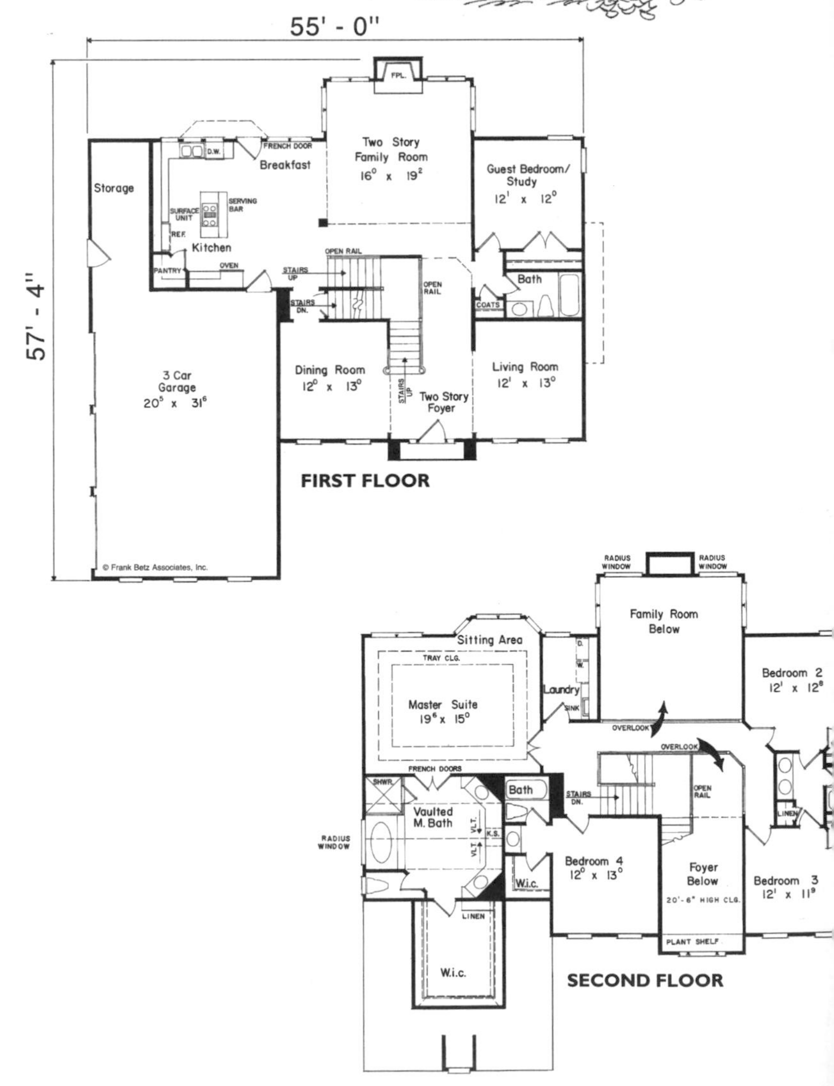

55' - 0"
57' - 4"
FPL.
FRENCH DOOR
D.W.
Breakfast
Two Story Family Room 16^{0} x 19^{2}
Guest Bedroom/ Study 12^{1} x 12^{0}
Storage
SURFACE UNIT
SERVING BAR
REF.
Kitchen
PANTRY
OVEN
OPEN RAIL
STAIRS UP
STAIRS DN.
OPEN RAIL
Bath
COATS
3 Car Garage 20^{5} x 31^{6}
Dining Room 12^{0} x 13^{0}
STAIRS UP
Two Story Foyer
Living Room 12^{1} x 13^{0}
FIRST FLOOR
© Frank Betz Associates, Inc.
RADIUS WINDOW
RADIUS WINDOW
Family Room Below
Sitting Area
TRAY CLG.
Master Suite 19^{6} x 15^{0}
Laundry
SINK
Bedroom 2 12^{1} x 12^{8}
OVERLOOK
OVERLOOK
FRENCH DOORS
SHWR.
Bath
STAIRS DN.
OPEN RAIL
Vaulted M. Bath
VLT.
K.S.
VLT.
RADIUS WINDOW
LINEN
Bedroom 4 12^{0} x 13^{0}
W.i.c.
Foyer Below
20'-6" HIGH CLG.
Bedroom 3 12^{1} x 11^{9}
LINEN
PLANT SHELF
W.i.c.
SECOND FLOOR

Spectacular Traditional

PRICE CODE: A

'his plan features:
- Three bedrooms
- Two full baths
- 'he use of gable roofs and the blend of stucco nd brick to form a spectacular exterior
- high vaulted ceiling and a cozy fireplace, 'ith built-in cabinets in the Den
- n efficient, U-shaped Kitchen with an adjacent ining Area
- Master Bedroom, with a raised ceiling, that includes private Bath and a walk-in closet
- wo family Bedrooms that share a full hall Bath
- his home is designed with slab and crawlspace oundation options

IN FLOOR — 1,237 SQ. FT.
RAGE — 436 SQ. FT.

TOTAL LIVING AREA:
1,237 SQ. FT.

PLAN NO. 92502

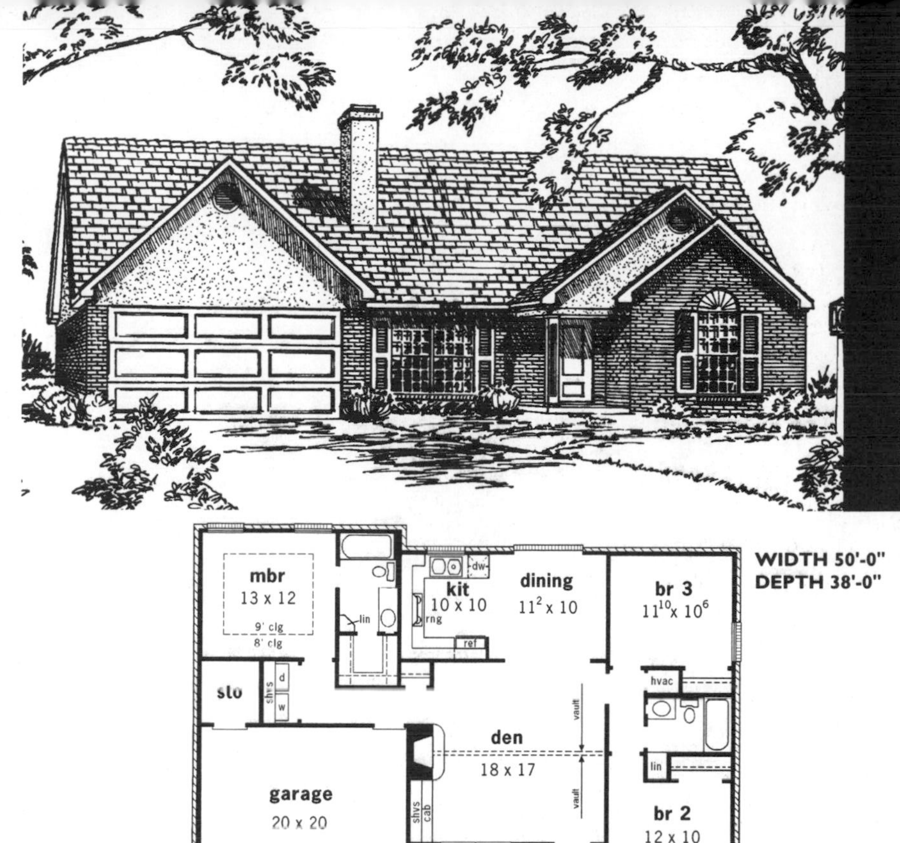

WIDTH 50'-0"
DEPTH 38'-0"

mbr
13 x 12
9' clg
8' clg
lin
kit
10 x 10
dw
rng
ref
dining
11² x 10
br 3
11¹⁰ x 10⁶
hvac
slo
shvs
d
w
den
18 x 17
vault
vault
lin
garage
20 x 20
shvs
cab
br 2
12 x 10
por

MAIN FLOOR

Enhanced by a Columned Porch

PRICE CODE: C

'his plan features:
- Three bedrooms
- Two full baths
- Great Room with a fireplace and decorative ceiling
- large efficient Kitchen with Breakfast Area
- Master Bedroom with a private Master Bath and 'alk-in closet
- formal Dining Room conveniently located near e Kitchen
- 'wo additional Bedrooms with walk-in closets and use f full hall Bath
- 'his home is designed with slab and crawlspace oundation options

IN FLOOR — 1,754 SQ. FT.
RAGE — 552 SQ. FT.

TOTAL LIVING AREA:
1,754 SQ. FT.

PLAN NO. 92531

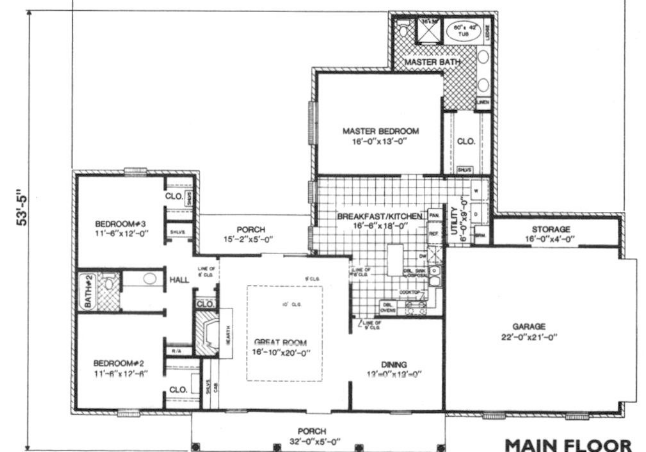

69'-10"
53'-5"
MASTER BATH
MASTER BEDROOM
16'-0"x13'-0"
CLO.
BREAKFAST/KITCHEN
16'-6"x18'-0"
UTILITY
BEDROOM#3
11'-6"x12'-0"
CLO.
PORCH
15'-2"x5'-0"
STORAGE
16'-0"x4'-0"
HALL
BATH#2
GREAT ROOM
16'-10"x20'-0"
GARAGE
22'-0"x21'-0"
BEDROOM#2
11'-6"x12'-6"
CLO.
DINING
13'-0"x13'-0"
PORCH
32'-0"x5'-0"

MAIN FLOOR

PLAN NO. 82016

Family Friendly

Price Code: C

- This plan features:
- — Three bedrooms
- — Two full baths
- The combination Great Room and Dining Room have columns visually separating the rooms
- The Kitchen/Breakfast Nook has easy access to the Grilling Porch
- The Laundry Room is located in proximity to the Kitchen
- The Computer Center is located close to the secondary Bedrooms
- This home is designed with crawlspace and slab foundation options

MAIN FLOOR — 1,934 SQ. FT.
GARAGE — 489 SQ. FT.

TOTAL LIVING AREA:
1,934 SQ. FT.

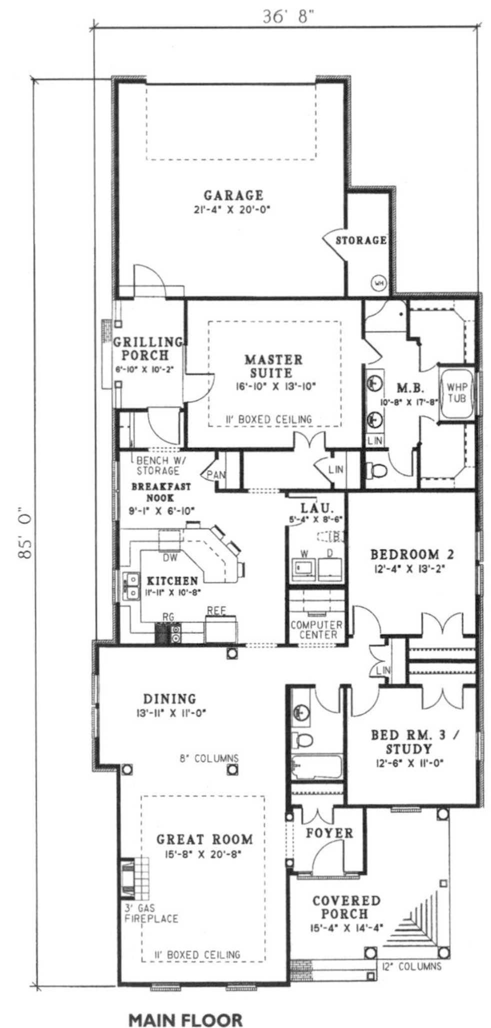

36' 8"
85' 0"
GARAGE
21'-4" X 20'-0"
STORAGE
WH
GRILLING PORCH
6'-10" X 10'-2"
MASTER SUITE
16'-10" X 13'-10"
11' BOXED CEILING
M.B.
10'-8" X 17'-8"
WHP TUB
LIN
BENCH W/ STORAGE
PAN
BREAKFAST NOOK
9'-1" X 6'-10"
LIN
LAU.
5'-4" X 8'-6"
W
D
BEDROOM 2
12'-4" X 13'-2"
DW
KITCHEN
11'-11" X 10'-8"
RG
REF
COMPUTER CENTER
LIN
DINING
13'-11" X 11'-0"
8" COLUMNS
BED RM. 3 / STUDY
12'-6" X 11'-0"
FOYER
GREAT ROOM
15'-8" X 20'-8"
3' GAS FIREPLACE
COVERED PORCH
15'-4" X 14'-4"
11' BOXED CEILING
12" COLUMNS

MAIN FLOOR

PLAN NO. 98410

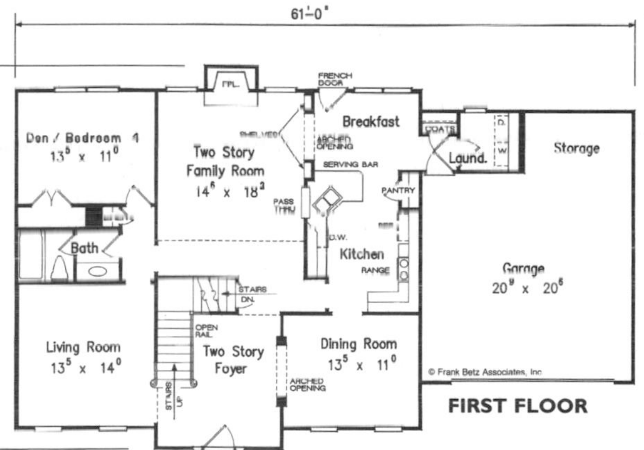

61'-0"
Den / Bedroom 4
13^5 x 11^0
Two Story Family Room
14^6 x 18^3
Breakfast
Laund.
Storage
Bath
Kitchen
Garage
20^9 x 20^5
Living Room
13^5 x 14^0
Two Story Foyer
Dining Room
13^5 x 11^0
FIRST FLOOR

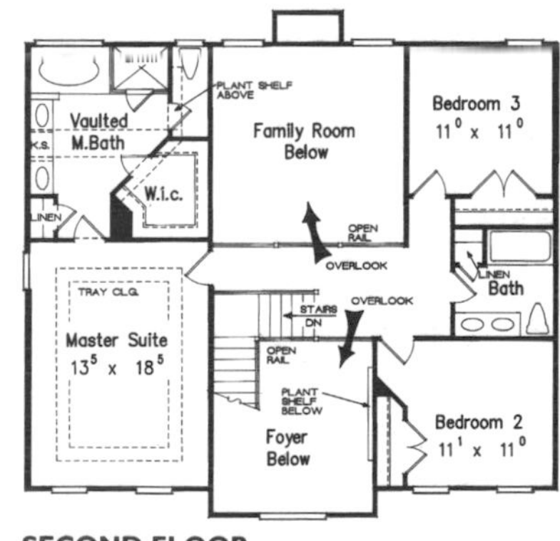

Vaulted M.Bath
W.i.c.
Family Room Below
Bedroom 3
11^0 x 11^0
Master Suite
13^5 x 18^5
Bath
Foyer Below
Bedroom 2
11^1 x 11^0
SECOND FLOOR

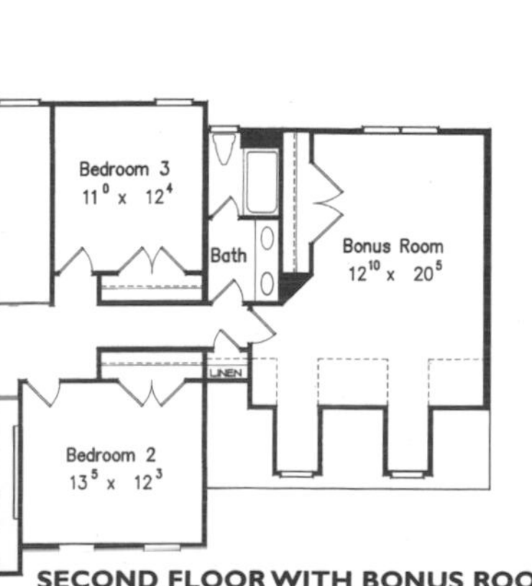

Bedroom 3
11^0 x 12^4
Bath
Bonus Room
12^{10} x 20^5
Bedroom 2
13^5 x 12^3
SECOND FLOOR WITH BONUS ROOM

A Magnificent Manor

Price Code: D

- This plan features:
  - Four bedrooms
  - Three full baths
- The two-story Foyer is dominated by a lovely staircase
- The formal Living Room is located directly off the Foyer
- The Breakfast Area is separated from the Kitchen by an extended counter/serving bar
- The two-story Family Room is highlighted by a fireplace that is framed by windows
- A tray ceiling crowns the Master Bedroom while a vaulted ceiling tops the Master Bath
- This home is designed with basement and crawlspace foundation options

First Floor — 1,428 sq. ft.
Second Floor — 961 sq. ft.
Bonus — 472 sq. ft.
Basement — 1,428 sq. ft.
Garage — 507 sq. ft.

Total Living Area:
2,389 sq. ft.

PLAN NO. 98400

Exquisite Detail

Price Code: I

- This plan features:
- — Four bedrooms
- — Three full and one half baths
- Formal Living Room with access to covered Porch and an arched opening to Family Room
- Spacious and efficient Kitchen with Pantry, cooktop/serving bar, two-story Breakfast Area and a Butler's Pantry
- Expansive Master Bedroom offers a tray ceiling, a cozy Sitting Room, a luxurious Bath and huge walk-in closet
- This home is designed with basement and crawlspace foundation options

FIRST FLOOR — 1,418 SQ. FT.
SECOND FLOOR — 1,844 SQ. FT.
BASEMENT — 1,418 SQ. FT.
GARAGE — 820 SQ. FT.

TOTAL LIVING AREA:
3,262 SQ. FT.

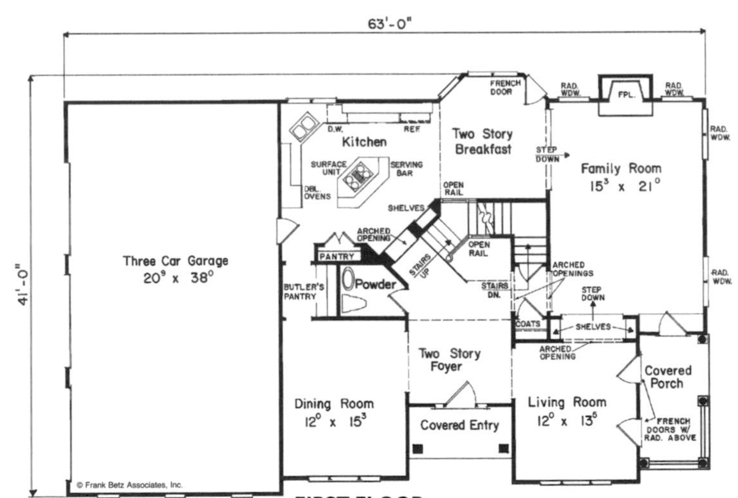

63'-0"
41'-0"
Three Car Garage
20^9 x 38^0
Kitchen
D.W.
REF.
SURFACE UNIT
SERVING BAR
DBL. OVENS
SHELVES
ARCHED OPENING
PANTRY
BUTLER'S PANTRY
Powder
STAIRS UP
Two Story Breakfast
FRENCH DOOR
OPEN RAIL
STEP DOWN
Family Room
15^3 x 21^0
FPL.
RAD. WDW.
ARCHED OPENINGS
STAIRS DN.
STEP DOWN
COATS
SHELVES
Two Story Foyer
Dining Room
12^0 x 15^3
Covered Entry
Living Room
12^0 x 13^6
Covered Porch
FRENCH DOORS W/ RAD. ABOVE
© Frank Betz Associates, Inc.

FIRST FLOOR

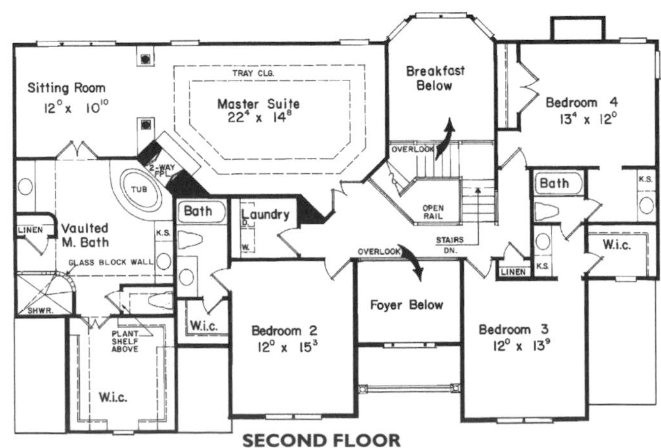

Sitting Room
12^0 x 10^{10}
TRAY CLG.
Master Suite
22^4 x 14^8
Breakfast Below
Bedroom 4
13^4 x 12^0
2-WAY FPL.
TUB
Bath
Laundry
OVERLOOK
OPEN RAIL
STAIRS DN.
Bath
K.S.
LINEN
Vaulted M. Bath
GLASS BLOCK WALL
SHWR.
PLANT SHELF ABOVE
W.i.c.
Bedroom 2
12^0 x 15^3
Foyer Below
Bedroom 3
12^0 x 13^9
W.i.c.

SECOND FLOOR

An Open Concept Home

PRICE CODE: A

PLAN NO.93021

'his plan features:
- Three bedrooms
- Two full baths
- n angled Entry creating the illusion of space
- 'wo square columns that flank the bar and separate the Citchen from the Living Room
- Dining Room that may service both formal and nformal occasions
- Master Bedroom with a large walk-in closet
- large Master Bath with double vanity, linen closet and vhirlpool tub/shower combination
- 'wo additional Bedrooms that share a full Bath
- 'his home is designed with crawlspace and slab oundation options

IN FLOOR — 1,282 SQ. FT.
RAGE — 501 SQ. FT.

TOTAL LIVING AREA:
1,282 SQ. FT.

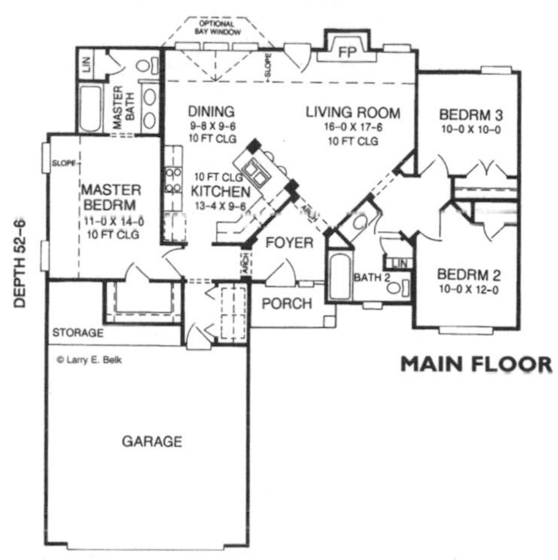

WIDTH 48-10
OPTIONAL BAY WINDOW
FP
LIN
MASTER BATH
DINING
9-8 X 9-6
10 FT CLG
LIVING ROOM
16-0 X 17-6
10 FT CLG
BEDRM 3
10-0 X 10-0
MASTER BEDRM
11-0 X 14-0
10 FT CLG
10 FT CLG
KITCHEN
13-4 X 9-6
FOYER
BATH 2
BEDRM 2
10-0 X 12-0
DEPTH 52-6
PORCH
STORAGE
© Larry E. Belk
MAIN FLOOR
GARAGE

Four Bedroom Favorite

PRICE CODE: J

PLAN NO.97747

'his plan features:
- Four bedrooms
- Two full and one half baths
- The Hearth Room is a warm family retreat
- The open plan between the Kitchen and Breakfast Nook ncourages interaction
- A box bay window and decorative ceiling beautifies the Dining Room
- The split Bedroom plan has the Master Bedroom on the irst floor
- Secondary Bedrooms are located upstairs
- This home is designed with basement foundation

ST FLOOR — 2,543 SQ. FT.
COND FLOOR — 1,072 SQ. FT.
SEMENT — 2,543 SQ. FT.
RAGE — 915 SQ. FT.

TOTAL LIVING AREA:

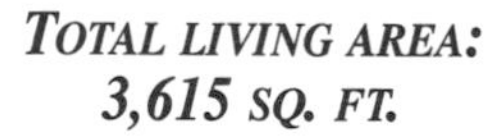
3,615 SQ. FT.

Hearth Room
15'-8" x 18'-9"
Patio
Breakfast
13'-0" x 10'-5"
Laun.
Bath
WIDTH 75'-0"
DEPTH 72'-1"
Bedroom
13' x 14'
Kitchen
17'-0" x 13'-3"
Great Room
19'-7" x 18'-0"
Bedroom
16'8" x 15'1"
Garage
22'-0" x 40'-10"
Master Bedroom
13'-8" x 17'-9"
Balcony
Great Room Below
Dining Room
13'-0" x 13'-4"
Foyer
Bedroom
13' x 13'4"
Master Bath
Porch
Walk in Closet
SECOND FLOOR
FIRST FLOOR

PLAN NO.90433

Cabin in the Country

PRICE CODE: A

- This plan features:
  - — Two bedrooms
  - — One full and one half baths
- A Screened Porch for enjoyment of your outdoor surroundings
- A combination Living and Dining Area with cozy fireplace for added warmth
- An efficiently laid out Kitchen with a built-in Pantry
- Two large Bedrooms located at the rear of the home
- This home is designed with crawlspace and slab found tion options

FIRST FLOOR — 928 SQ. FT.
PORCH — 230 SQ. FT.
STORAGE — 14 SQ. FT.

TOTAL LIVING AREA:
928 SQ. FT.

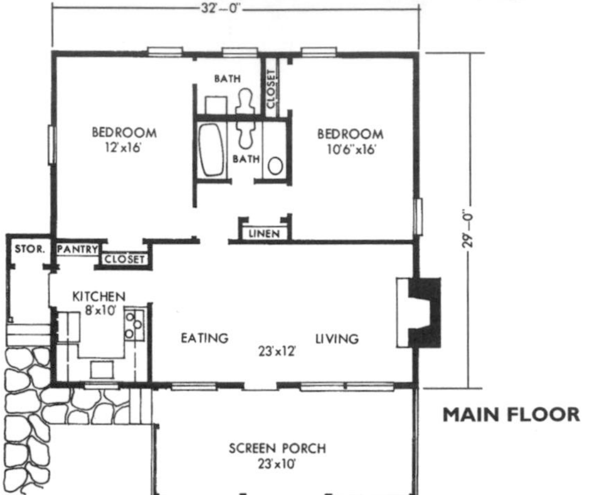

32'–0"
BATH
CLOSET
BEDROOM
12'x16'
BATH
BEDROOM
10'6"x16'
LINEN
29'–0"
STOR.
PANTRY
CLOSET
KITCHEN
8'x10'
EATING
23'x12'
LIVING
SCREEN PORCH
23'x10'

MAIN FLOOR

PLAN NO.96803

Cute and Compact

PRICE CODE: A

- This plan features:
  - — Three bedrooms
  - — One full and one half baths
- Walk in closets are in all of the Bedrooms
- The Master Bedroom has a Sitting Area
- The Living Room has a clean burning gas fireplace
- The Kitchen is arranged in a convenient U-shape
- The Garage has an option for one or two bays
- This home is designed with basement, slab, and crawlspace foundation options

FIRST FLOOR — 732 SQ. FT.
SECOND FLOOR — 667 SQ. FT.
BASEMENT — 732 SQ. FT.
GARAGE — 406 SQ. FT.

TOTAL LIVING AREA:
1,399 SQ. FT.

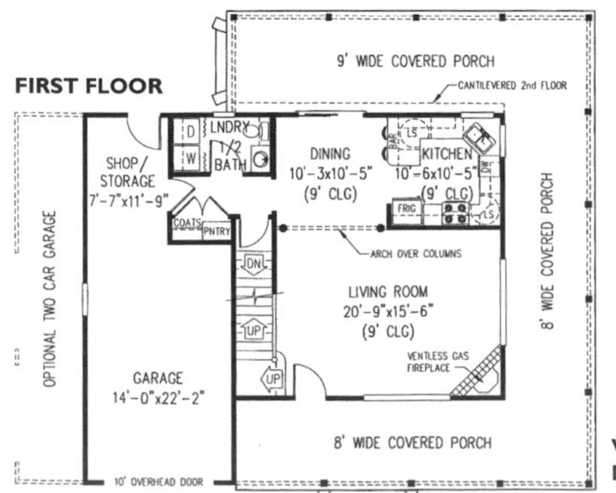

FIRST FLOOR
9' WIDE COVERED PORCH
CANTILEVERED 2nd FLOOR
D
W
LNDRY
1/2 BATH
DINING
10'-3x10'-5"
(9' CLG)
KITCHEN
10'-6x10'-5"
(9' CLG)
FRIG
SHOP/
STORAGE
7'-7"x11'-9"
COATS
PNTRY
ARCH OVER COLUMNS
DN
UP
LIVING ROOM
20'-9"x15'-6"
(9' CLG)
8' WIDE COVERED PORCH
OPTIONAL TWO CAR GARAGE
GARAGE
14'-0"x22'-2"
VENTLESS GAS
FIREPLACE
UP
8' WIDE COVERED PORCH
10' OVERHEAD DOOR

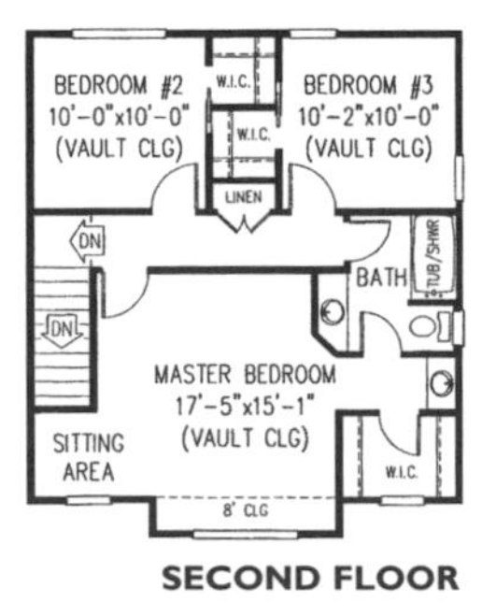

BEDROOM #2
10'-0"x10'-0"
(VAULT CLG)
W.I.C.
W.I.C.
BEDROOM #3
10'-2"x10'-0"
(VAULT CLG)
LINEN
DN
DN
BATH
MASTER BEDROOM
17'-5"x15'-1"
(VAULT CLG)
SITTING
AREA
W.I.C.
8' CLG

SECOND FLOOR

WIDTH 49'-9"
DEPTH 43'-6"

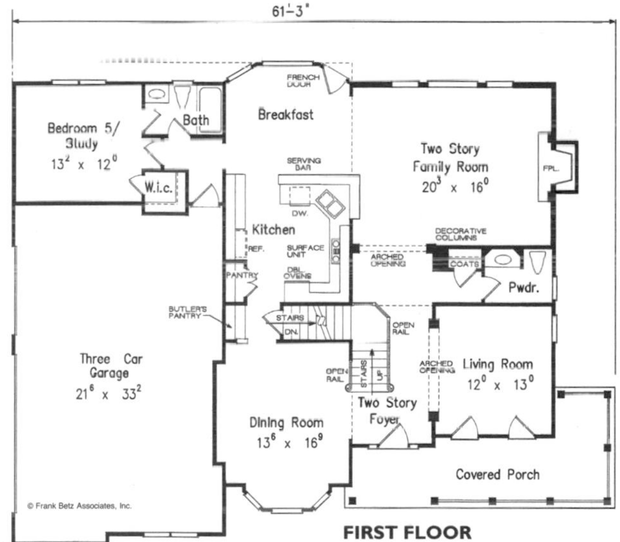
61'-3"
FRENCH DOOR
Bedroom 5/ Study
13[2] x 12[0]
Bath
Breakfast
W.i.c.
SERVING BAR
Two Story Family Room
20[3] x 16[0]
FPL.
DW.
Kitchen
REF.
SURFACE UNIT
DBL. OVENS
PANTRY
DECORATIVE COLUMNS
ARCHED OPENING
COATS
Pwdr.
BUTLER'S PANTRY
STAIRS
DN.
OPEN RAIL
Three Car Garage
21[6] x 33[2]
OPEN RAIL
STAIRS
ARCHED OPENING
Living Room
12[0] x 13[0]
Two Story Foyer
Dining Room
13[6] x 16[9]
Covered Porch
© Frank Betz Associates, Inc.

FIRST FLOOR

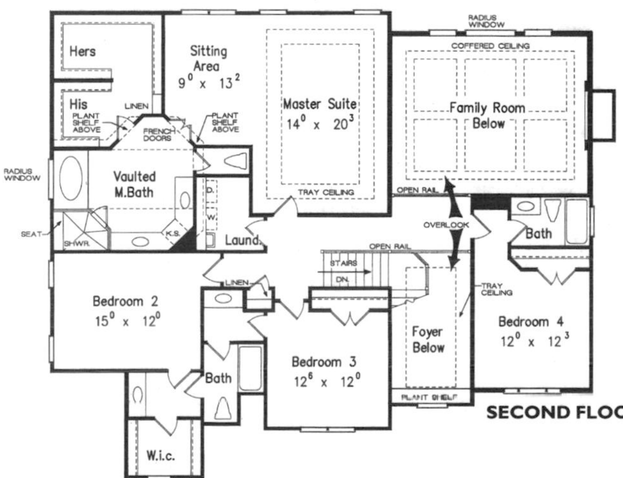
RADIUS WINDOW
Hers
Sitting Area
9[0] x 13[2]
COFFERED CEILING
His
LINEN
PLANT SHELF ABOVE
FRENCH DOORS
PLANT SHELF ABOVE
Master Suite
14[0] x 20[3]
Family Room Below
RADIUS WINDOW
Vaulted M.Bath
TRAY CEILING
OPEN RAIL
SEAT
SHWR.
K.S.
Laund.
OVERLOOK
Bath
OPEN RAIL
STAIRS
DN.
LINEN
TRAY CEILING
Bedroom 2
15[0] x 12[0]
Foyer Below
Bedroom 4
12[0] x 12[3]
Bedroom 3
12[6] x 12[0]
Bath
PLANT SHELF
W.i.c.

SECOND FLOOR

Home Sweet Home

Price Code: I

- This plan features:
  - — Five bedrooms
  - — Four full and one half baths
- An arched opening leads into the Living Room from the two-story Foyer
- The Dining Room has a bay window that overlooks the front yard
- The Breakfast Nook has a French door to the rear yard
- The second floor Master Suite has many special features
- This home is designed with basement and crawlspace foundation options

FIRST FLOOR — 1,615 SQ. FT.
SECOND FLOOR — 1,763 SQ. FT.
BASEMENT — 1,615 SQ. FT.
GARAGE — 747 SQ. FT.

TOTAL LIVING AREA:
3,378 SQ. FT.

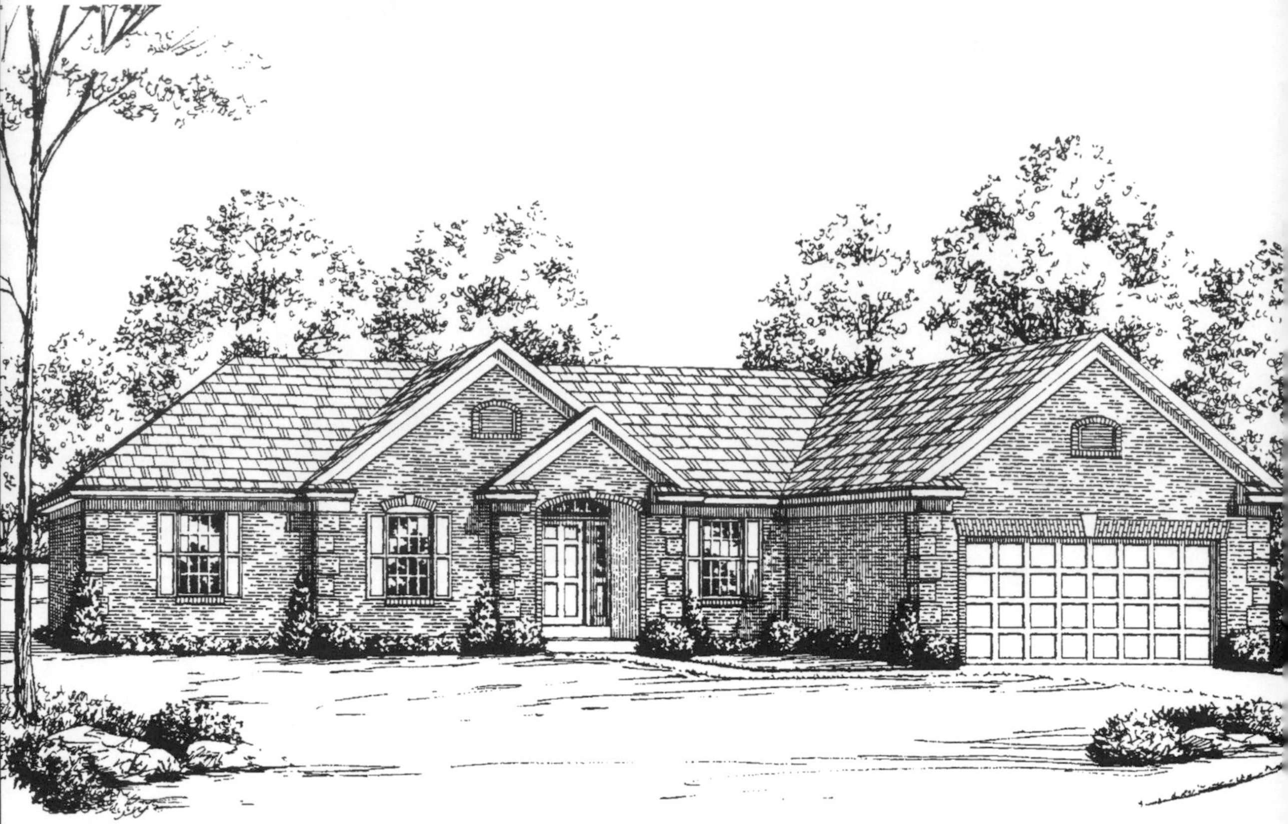

Charming Brick Ranch

Price Code: C

This plan features:

— Three bedrooms

— Two full baths

Sheltered entrance leads into open Foyer and Dining Room defined by columns

Vaulted ceiling spans Foyer, Dining Room, and Great Room with corner fireplace and Atrium door to rear yard

Central Kitchen with separate Laundry and Pantry easily serves Dining Room, Breakfast Area and Screened Porch

Luxurious Master Bedroom offers tray ceiling and French doors to double vanity, walk-in closet and whirlpool tub

This home is designed with a basement foundation

MAIN FLOOR —1,782 SQ. FT.
GARAGE — 407 SQ. FT.
BASEMENT — 1,735 SQ. FT.

TOTAL LIVING AREA:
1,782 SQ. FT.

MAIN FLOOR

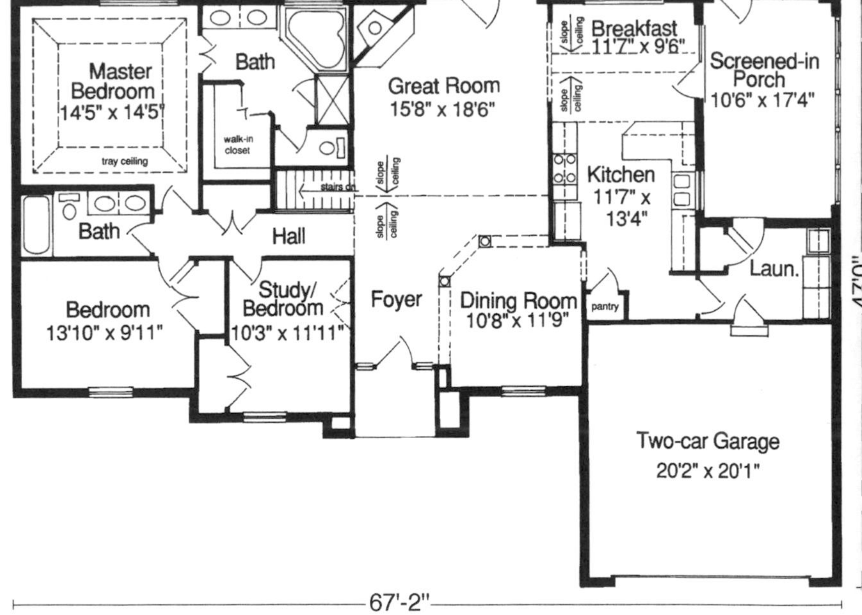
Master Bedroom
14'5" x 14'5"
tray ceiling
Bath
walk-in closet
Great Room
15'8" x 18'6"
Breakfast
11'7" x 9'6"
Screened-in Porch
10'6" x 17'4"
Kitchen
11'7" x 13'4"
stairs dn
slope ceiling
Bath
Hall
Laun.
Bedroom
13'10" x 9'11"
Study/ Bedroom
10'3" x 11'11"
Foyer
Dining Room
10'8" x 11'9"
pantry
Two-car Garage
20'2" x 20'1"
67'-2"

Optional Home Office

PRICE CODE: D

PLAN NO. 65124

This plan features:
- Three bedrooms
- Two full and one half baths
- The Bedrooms are located on the second floor, along with a Study Area
- The U-shape Kitchen features a circular table at the end of an angled snack bar
- One section of the Garage can be finished as a Home Office
- This home is designed with a basement foundation
- ST FLOOR — 955 SQ. FT.
- COND FLOOR — 1,136 SQ. FT.
- SEMENT — 955 SQ. FT.
- RAGE — 484 SQ. FT.

TOTAL LIVING AREA:
2,091 SQ. FT.

4.80 X 2.80
16'-0" X 9'-4"
5.70 X 3.60
19'-0" X 12'-0"
3.70 X 6.90
12'-4" X 23'-0"
3.30 X 5.50
11'-0" X 18'-4"
3.40 X 7.30
11'-4" X 24'-4"
12.0 m
40'-0"
FIRST FLOOR
14.4 m
48'-0"

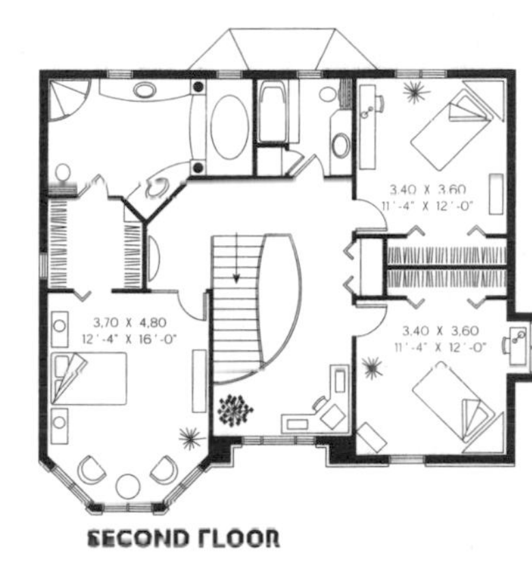

3.40 X 3.60
11'-4" X 12'-0"
3.70 X 4.80
12'-4" X 16'-0"
3.40 X 3.60
11'-4" X 12'-0"
SECOND FLOOR

Your Classic Hideaway

PRICE CODE: C

PLAN NO. 90423

This plan features:
- Three bedrooms
- Two full baths
- A lovely fireplace in the Living Room which is both cozy and a source of heat for the core area
- An efficient Country Kitchen, connecting the large Dining and Living Rooms
- A lavish Master Suite enhanced by a step-up sunken tub, more than ample closet space, and separate shower
- A Screened Porch and Patio Area for outdoor living
- This home is designed with basement, slab and crawl-space foundation options
- AIN FLOOR — 1,773 SQ. FT.
- RCH — 240 SQ. FT.

TOTAL LIVING AREA:
1,773 SQ. FT.

PATIO
16-0x10-0
GARAGE
21-0x21-0
SCR. PORCH
12-0x20-4
DINING
12-0x13-4
KITCHEN
10x13
UTILITY
PANTRY
BEDROOM
11-0x13-4
CLOSET
STEP
M. BATH
SEAT
M. BEDROOM
12-0x18-0
LIVING ROOM
15-6x17-8
DOWN
BEDROOM
12-0x11-4
LINEN
DRESSING
COATS
FOYER
BATH
PORCH
26-0x6-0
MAIN FLOOR
43'-8"
88'-8"

PLAN NO. 98409

Classically Detailed

PRICE CODE: E

- This plan features:
- — Four bedrooms
- — Two full and one half baths
- Keystones and columns accent the front triple arched Porch
- On either side of the two-story Foyer are arched openings to the formal areas
- The Family room has a rear wall fireplace set between a bank of windows
- The Kitchen has a convenient center island and is open to the Nook
- The Master Suite has a tray ceiling and an optional Sitting Room
- Bedroom number two has a window seat in the front of the room
- This home is designed with basement, slab and crawlspace foundation options

FIRST FLOOR — 1,200 SQ. FT.
SECOND FLOOR — 1,168 SQ. FT.
BASEMENT — 1,200 SQ. FT.
GARAGE — 527 SQ. FT.

TOTAL LIVING AREA:
2,368 SQ. FT.

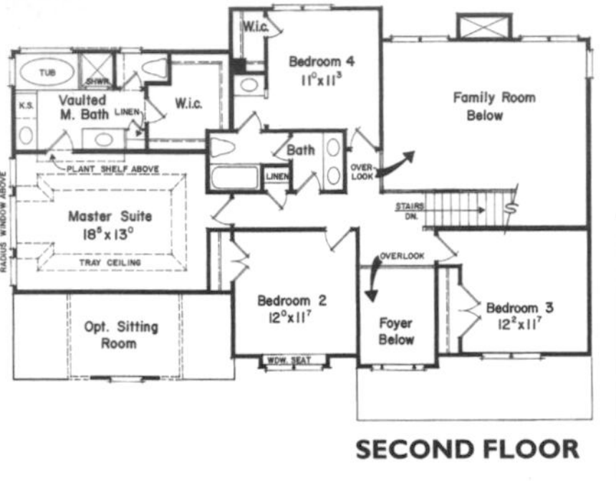
Bedroom 4
Family Room Below
Vaulted M. Bath
W.i.c.
Bath
Master Suite
Bedroom 2
Foyer Below
Bedroom 3
Opt. Sitting Room

SECOND FLOOR

WIDTH 56'-0"
DEPTH 39'-0"

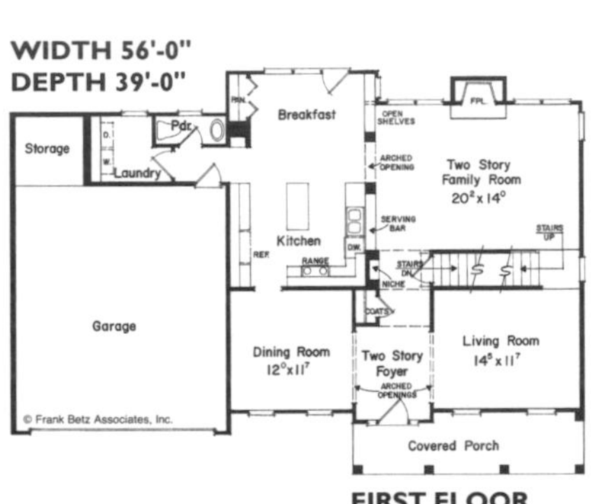
Breakfast
Storage
Laundry
Two Story Family Room
Kitchen
Garage
Dining Room
Two Story Foyer
Living Room
Covered Porch
© Frank Betz Associates, Inc.

FIRST FLOOR

PLAN NO. 90682

Inviting Porch Adorns Affordable Home

PRICE CODE: A

- This plan features:
- — Three bedrooms
- — Two full baths
- A large and spacious Living Room that adjoins the Dining Room for ease in entertaining
- A private Bedroom wing offering a quiet atmosphere
- A Master Bedroom with his and her closets and a private Bath
- An efficient Kitchen with a walk-in Pantry
- This home is designed with basement and slab foundation options

MAIN FLOOR — 1,243 SQ. FT.
BASEMENT — 1,103 SQ. FT.
GARAGE — 490 SQ. FT.

TOTAL LIVING AREA:
1,243 SQ. FT.

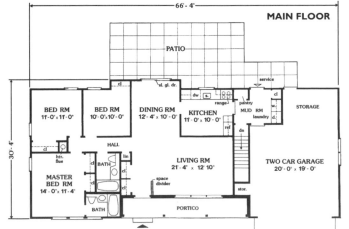

66'- 4"
MAIN FLOOR
PATIO
BED RM 11'-0" x 11'-0"
BED RM 10'-0" x 10'-0"
DINING RM 12'-4" x 10'-0"
KITCHEN 11'-0" x 10'-0"
MUD RM laundry
STORAGE
HALL
LIVING RM 21'-4" x 12' 10"
MASTER BED RM 14'-0" x 11'-4"
BATH
TWO CAR GARAGE 20'-0" x 19'-0"
PORTICO
30'-4"

PLAN NO. 82017

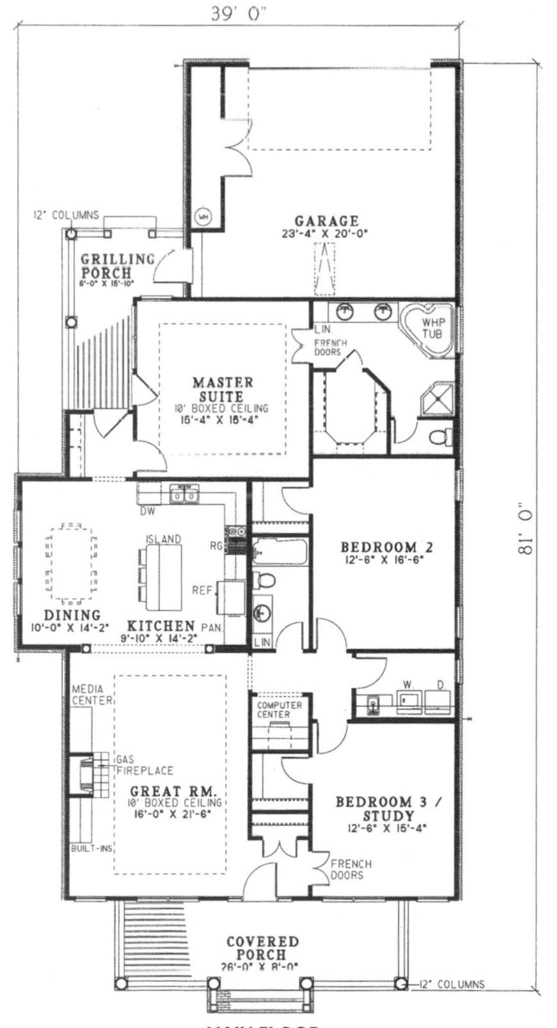

39' 0"
81' 0"
12" COLUMNS
GRILLING PORCH
6'-0" X 15'-10"
GARAGE
23'-4" X 20'-0"
WHP TUB
LIN.
FRENCH DOORS
MASTER SUITE
10' BOXED CEILING
15'-4" X 18'-4"
DW
ISLAND
RG
REF.
PAN.
DINING
10'-0" X 14'-2"
KITCHEN
9'-10" X 14'-2"
BEDROOM 2
12'-6" X 16'-6"
LIN
W
D
MEDIA CENTER
COMPUTER CENTER
GAS FIREPLACE
GREAT RM.
10' BOXED CEILING
16'-0" X 21'-6"
BUILT-INS
BEDROOM 3 / STUDY
12'-6" X 15'-4"
FRENCH DOORS
COVERED PORCH
26'-0" X 8'-0"
12" COLUMNS

MAIN FLOOR

Garage to the Rear

Price Code: C

- This plan features:
  - Three bedrooms
  - Two full baths
- The Great Room includes a box ceiling and built-ins around the gas fireplace
- The Kitchen has a central island and a Dining Area adjoining
- A built-in Computer Center makes efficient use of space
- The front Bedroom could easily become a Study
- This home is designed with crawlspace and slab foundation options

MAIN FLOOR — 1,832 SQ. FT.
GARAGE — 492 SQ. FT.

TOTAL LIVING AREA:
1,832 SQ. FT.

PLAN NO. 93206

Distinctive Brick with Room to Expand

Price Code: F

- This plan features:
- — Four bedrooms
- — Two full and one half baths
- Arched entrance with decorative glass leads into two-story Foyer
- Formal Dining Room with tray ceiling above decorative window
- Kitchen with island cooktop and built-in desk and Pantry
- Master Bedroom wing topped by tray ceiling with French door to Patio, and a lavish Bath
- This home is designed with basement, slab and crawlspace foundation options

FIRST FLOOR — 2,577 SQ. FT.
OPTIONAL SECOND FLOOR — 619 SQ. FT.
BASEMENT — 2,561 SQ. FT.
BRIDGE — 68 SQ. FT.
GARAGE — 560 SQ. FT.

TOTAL LIVING AREA:
2,645 SQ. FT.

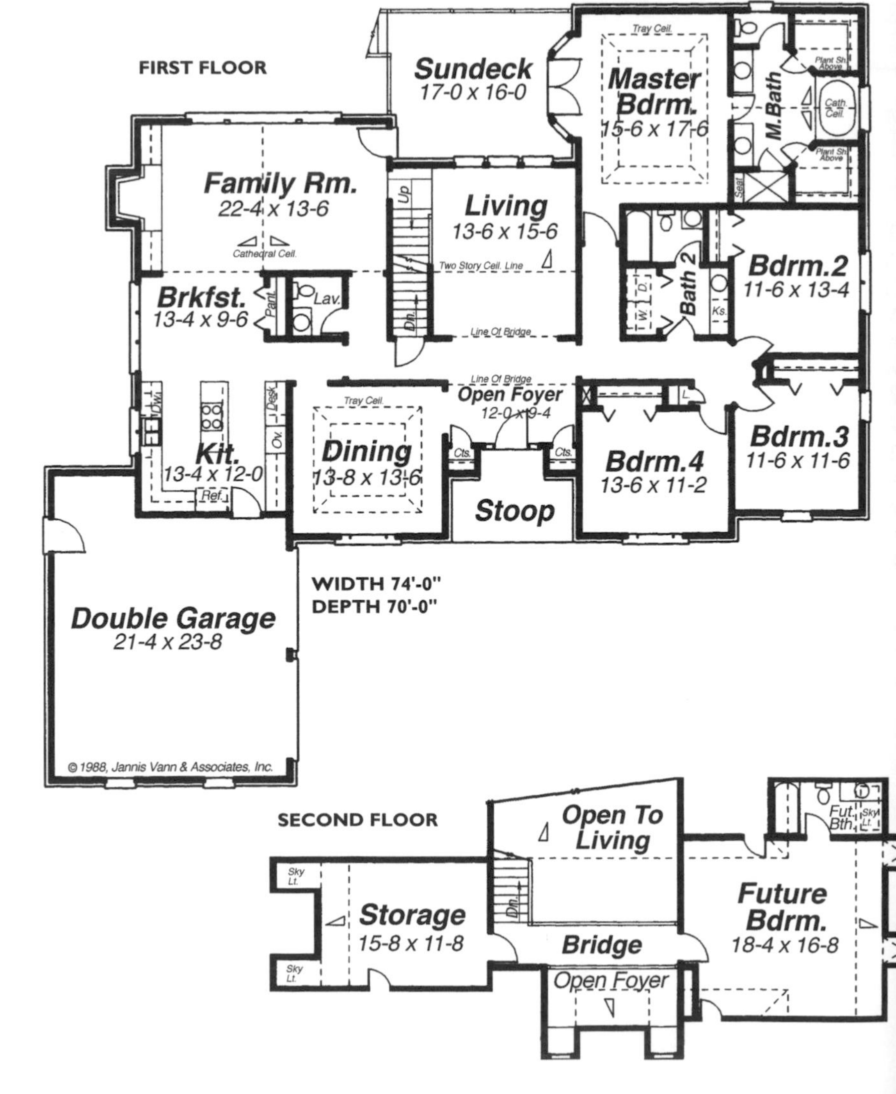
FIRST FLOOR
Sundeck
17-0 x 16-0
Tray Ceil.
Master Bdrm.
15-6 x 17-6
M.Bath
Cath Ceil.
Plant Sh. Above
Seat
Family Rm.
22-4 x 13-6
Cathedral Ceil.
Living
13-6 x 15-6
Two Story Ceil. Line
Up
Dn.
Line Of Bridge
Bdrm.2
11-6 x 13-4
Bath 2
Ks.
Brkfst.
13-4 x 9-6
Pant.
Lav.
Line Of Bridge
Open Foyer
12-0 x 9-4
Tray Ceil.
Dining
13-8 x 13-6
Kit.
13-4 x 12-0
Ov.
Desk
Ref.
Cts.
Stoop
Bdrm.4
13-6 x 11-2
Bdrm.3
11-6 x 11-6
WIDTH 74'-0"
DEPTH 70'-0"
Double Garage
21-4 x 23-8
© 1988, Jannis Vann & Associates, Inc.
SECOND FLOOR
Open To Living
Sky Lt.
Storage
15-8 x 11-8
Dn.
Bridge
Open Foyer
Fut. Bth.
Future Bdrm.
18-4 x 16-8

Tandem Garage

PRICE CODE: C

PLAN NO. 93133

Ihis plan features:
- Three bedrooms
- Two full baths
- Dpen Foyer leads into spacious living highlighted by a wall of windows
- Country-size Kitchen with efficient, U-shaped counter, work island, eating Nook with backyard access, and nearby Laundry/Garage Entry
- French doors open to pampering Master Bedroom with window alcove, walk-in closet and double vanity Bath
- Iwo additional Bedrooms with large closets, share a full Bath
- This home is designed with a basement foundation

AIN FLOOR —1,761 SQ. FT.
RAGE — 658 SQ. FT.
SEMENT — 1,761 SQ. FT.

TOTAL LIVING AREA:
1,761 SQ. FT.

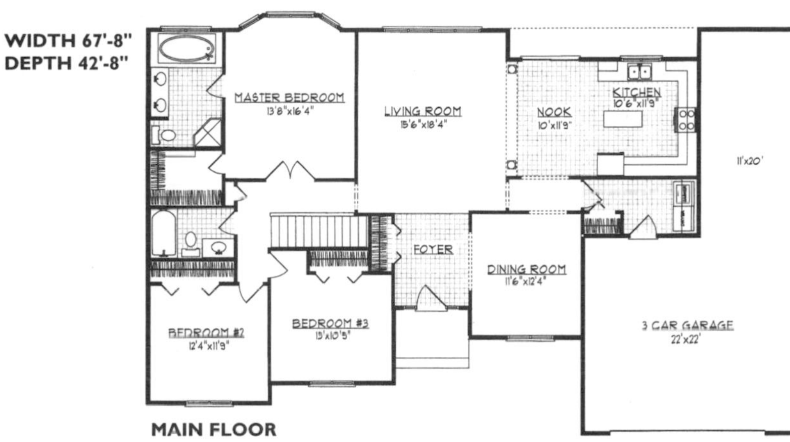

WIDTH 67'-8"
DEPTH 42'-8"
MASTER BEDROOM
13'8"x16'4"
LIVING ROOM
15'6"x18'4"
NOOK
10'x11'9"
KITCHEN
10'6"x11'9"
11'x20'
FOYER
DINING ROOM
11'6"x12'4"
BEDROOM #2
12'4"x11'9"
BEDROOM #3
13'x10'5"
3 CAR GARAGE
22'x22'
MAIN FLOOR

Wide Open and Convenient

PRICE CODE: B

PLAN NO. 20100

This plan features:
- Three bedrooms
- Two full baths
- Vaulted ceilings in the Dining Room and Master Bedroom
- A sloped ceiling in the fireplaced Living Room
- A skylight illuminating the Master Bath
- A large Master Bedroom with a walk-in closet
- This home is designed with basement, slab, and crawlspace foundation options

AIN FLOOR — 1,737 SQ. FT.
ASEMENT — 1,727 SQ. FT.
ARAGE — 484 SQ. FT.

TOTAL LIVING AREA:
1,737 SQ. FT.

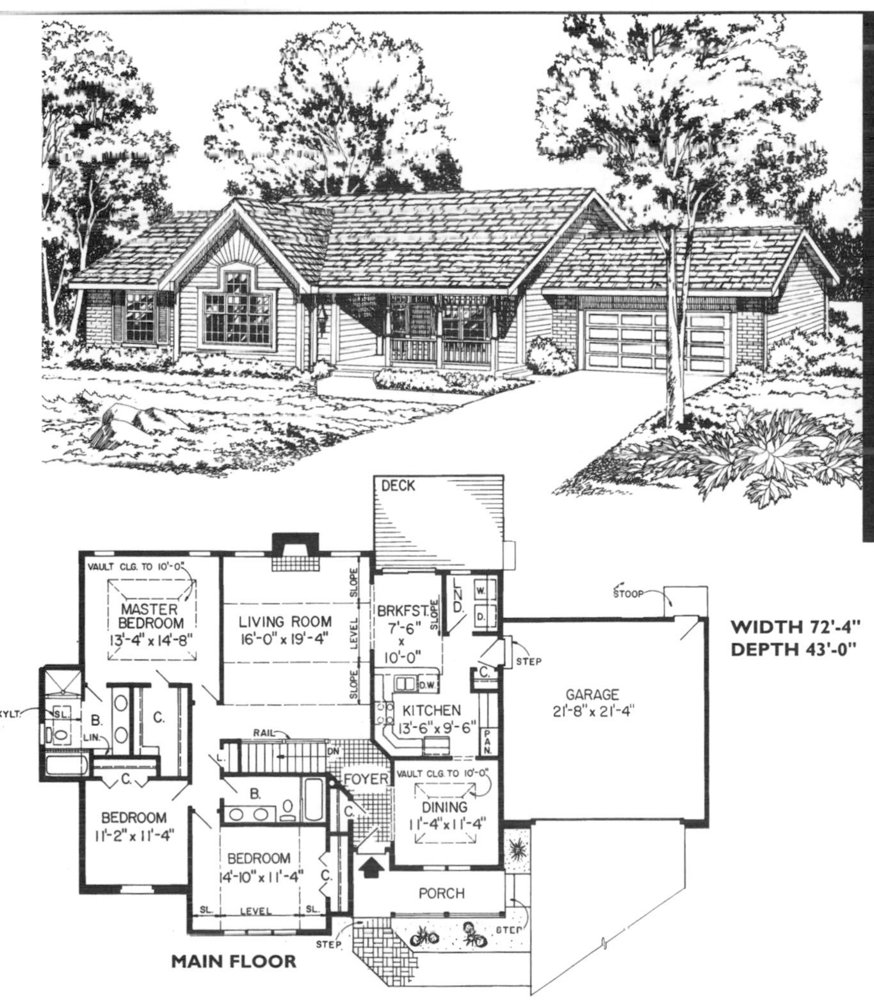

DECK
VAULT CLG. TO 10'-0"
MASTER BEDROOM
13'-4" x 14'-8"
LIVING ROOM
16'-0" x 19'-4"
BRKFST.
7'-6" x 10'-0"
STOOP
STEP
GARAGE
21'-8" x 21'-4"
WIDTH 72'-4"
DEPTH 43'-0"
SKYLT.
KITCHEN
13'-6" x 9'-6"
RAIL
FOYER
VAULT CLG. TO 10'-0"
DINING
11'-4" x 11'-4"
BEDROOM
11'-2" x 11'-4"
BEDROOM
14'-10" x 11'-4"
PORCH
MAIN FLOOR

PLAN NO.93413

Open & Airy

PRICE CODE: C

- This plan features:
  - Three bedrooms
  - Two full and one half baths
- The Foyer is naturally lit by a dormer window above
- Family Room is highlighted by two front windows and a fireplace
- Kitchen includes an angled extended counter/snack bar and an abundance of counter and cabinet space
- Dining Area opens to the Kitchen, for a more spacious feeling
- The roomy Master Suite is located on the first floor and has a private five-piece Bath plus a walk-in closet
- Laundry Room doubles as a Mudroom from the side entrance
- This home is designed with a basement foundation

FIRST FLOOR — 1,271 SQ. FT.
SECOND FLOOR — 537 SQ. FT.
BASEMENT — 1,271 SQ. FT.
GARAGE — 555 SQ. FT.

TOTAL LIVING AREA:
1,808 SQ. FT.

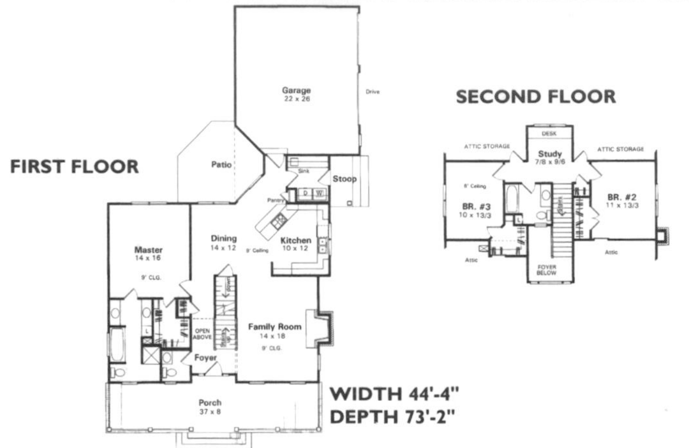
FIRST FLOOR
SECOND FLOOR
Garage
22 x 26
Patio
Stoop
Master
14 x 16
Dining
14 x 12
Kitchen
10 x 12
Family Room
14 x 18
Foyer
Porch
37 x 8
Study
BR. #3
BR. #2
ATTIC STORAGE
WIDTH 44'-4"
DEPTH 73'-2"

PLAN NO.92400

Quaint Starter Home

PRICE CODE: A

- This plan features:
  - Three bedrooms
  - Two full baths
- A vaulted ceiling giving an airy feeling to the Dining and Living Rooms
- A streamlined Kitchen with a comfortable work area, a double sink and ample cabinet space
- A cozy fireplace in the Living Room
- A Master Suite with a large closet, French doors leading to the Patio and a private Bath
- Two additional Bedrooms sharing a full Bath
- This home is designed with basement and slab foundation options

MAIN FLOOR — 1,050 SQ. FT.
GARAGE — 261 SQ. FT.

TOTAL LIVING AREA:
1,050 SQ. FT.

36
MAIN FLOOR
42
PATIO
MASTER BEDROOM 11 X 12
BEDROOM 9 X 12
BEDROOM 9 X 10
W D
KITCHEN 9 X 11
GARAGE 12 x 24
VAULT
VAULT
DINING 9 x 10
LIVING 14 x 14

PLAN NO. 98402

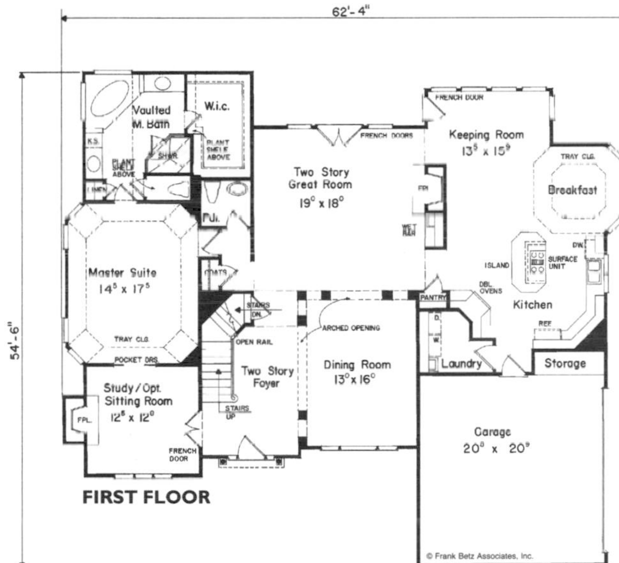

62'- 4"
54'-6"
Vaulted M. Bath
W.i.c.
Two Story Great Room 19° x 18°
FRENCH DOORS
FRENCH DOOR
Keeping Room 13⁵ x 15⁹
TRAY CLG.
Breakfast
Master Suite 14⁵ x 17⁵
TRAY CLG.
POCKET DRS.
Study/Opt. Sitting Room 12⁸ x 12°
FRENCH DOOR
Two Story Foyer
Dining Room 13° x 16°
ARCHED OPENING
OPEN RAIL
STAIRS DN.
STAIRS UP
ISLAND
DBL. OVENS
Kitchen
PANTRY
Laundry
Storage
Garage 20° x 20°
© Frank Betz Associates, Inc.
FIRST FLOOR

RADIUS WINDOWS
Great Room Below
W.i.c.
Bedroom 3 13° x 11²
OVERLOOK
NICHE
STAIRS DN.
OPEN RAIL
Foyer Below
Bedroom 2 13° x 10¹⁰
LINEN
Bath
Bath
W.i.c.
SEAT
Bedroom 4 12⁵ x 14⁹
SECOND FLOOR

Stately Stone and Stucco

Price Code: H

- This plan features:
  - — Four bedrooms
  - — Three full and one half baths
- Two-story Foyer with angled staircase
- Expansive two-story Great Room enhanced by a fireplace
- Convenient Kitchen with a cooktop island
- Open Keeping Room accented by a wall of windows and backyard access
- Master Suite wing offers a tray ceiling, a plush Bath and roomy walk-in closet
- This home is designed with basement, slab and crawlspace foundation options

FIRST FLOOR — 2,130 SQ. FT.
SECOND FLOOR — 897 SQ. FT.
BASEMENT — 2,130 SQ. FT.
GARAGE — 494 SQ. FT.

TOTAL LIVING AREA:
3,027 SQ. FT.

PLAN NO. 65010

Home Artistic Home

Price Code: A

- This plan features:
- — Two bedrooms
- — One full bath
- This home's unique design is of architectural interest
- Windows define the front of the home, flooding natural light into the rooms
- A second floor Bedroom enjoys privacy and access to a Sitting Room
- Both Bedrooms have generous closet space
- The full Bath is centrally located for convenience
- This home is designed with a basement foundation

FIRST FLOOR — 945 SQ. FT.
SECOND FLOOR — 335 SQ. FT.
BASEMENT — 945 SQ. FT.

TOTAL LIVING AREA:
1,280 SQ. FT.

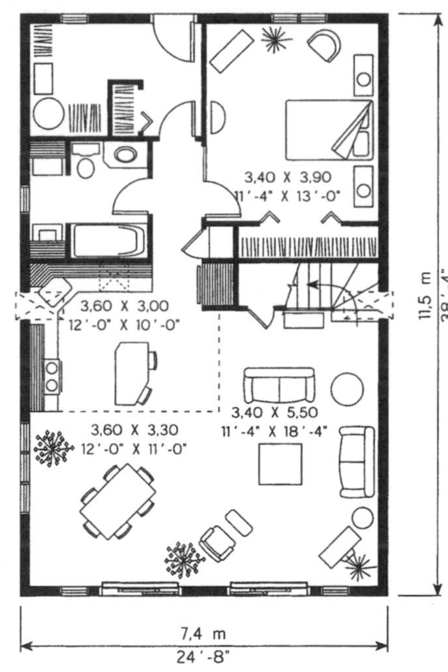

3,40 X 3,90
11'-4" X 13'-0"
3,60 X 3,00
12'-0" X 10'-0"
3,40 X 5,50
11'-4" X 18'-4"
3,60 X 3,30
12'-0" X 11'-0"
11,5 m
38'-4"
7,4 m
24'-8"

FIRST FLOOR

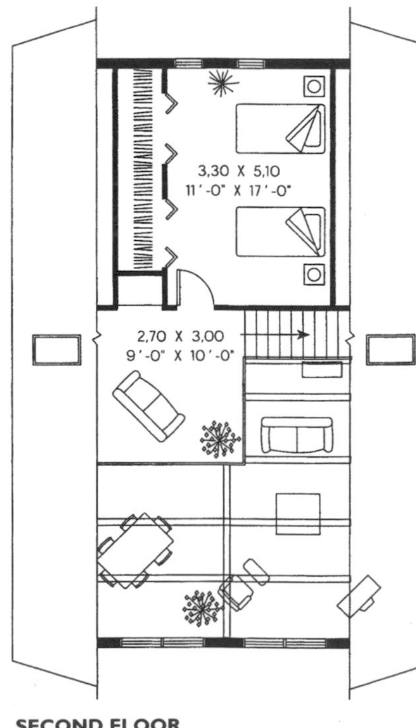

3,30 X 5,10
11'-0" X 17'-0"
2,70 X 3,00
9'-0" X 10'-0"

SECOND FLOOR

Skylight Brightens Master Bedroom

PRICE CODE: B

PLAN NO.34029

This plan features:
- Three bedrooms
- Two full baths
- A covered Porch Entry
- A foyer separating the Dining Room from the Breakfast Area and Kitchen
- A Living Room enhanced by a vaulted beam ceiling and a fireplace
- A Master Bedroom with a decorative ceiling and a skylight in the private Bath
- An optional Deck accessible through sliding doors off the Master Bedroom
- This home is designed with basement, slab and crawlspace foundation options

AIN FLOOR — 1,686 SQ. FT.
SEMENT — 1,676 SQ. FT.
RAGE — 484 SQ. FT.

TOTAL LIVING AREA:
1,686 SQ. FT.

WIDTH 61'-0"
DEPTH 54'-0"

CRAWLSPACE/SLAB FOUNDATION OPTION

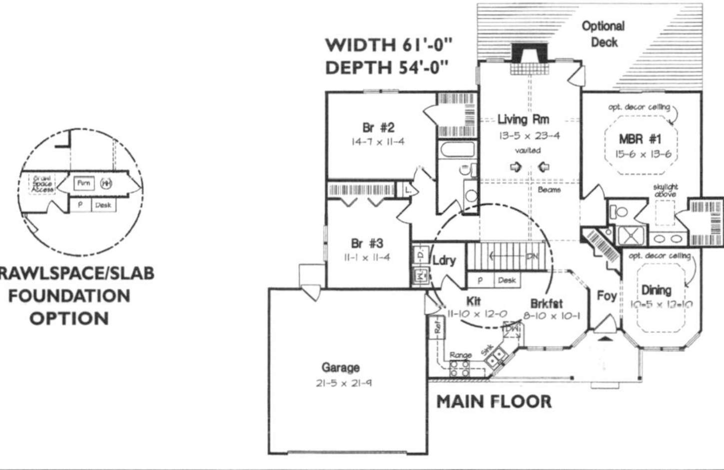

Optional Deck
Br #2
14-7 x 11-4
Living Rm
13-5 x 23-4
vaulted
Beams
opt. decor ceiling
MBR #1
15-6 x 13-6
skylight above
Br #3
11-1 x 11-4
Ldry
Desk
Kit
11-10 x 12-0
Brkfst
8-10 x 10-1
Foy
opt. decor ceiling
Dining
10-5 x 12-10
Range
Garage
21-5 x 21-4
MAIN FLOOR

Rocking Chair Living

PRICE CODE: B

PLAN NO.90409

This plan features:
- Three bedrooms
- Two full baths
- A massive fireplace separating Living and Dining Rooms
- An isolated Master Suite with a walk-in closet and compartmentalized bath
- A galley-type Kitchen between the Breakfast Room and Dining Room
- This home is designed with basement, slab and crawlspace foundation options

AIN FLOOR — 1,670 SQ. FT.
RAGE — 427 SQ. FT.

TOTAL LIVING AREA:
1,670 SQ. FT.

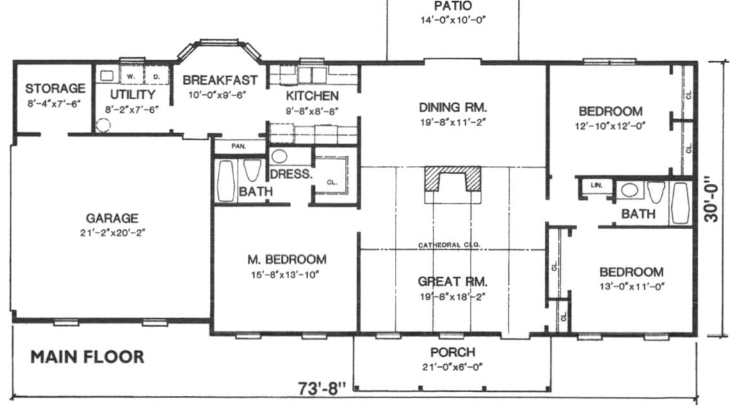

PATIO
14'-0"x10'-0"
STORAGE
8'-4"x7'-6"
UTILITY
8'-2"x7'-6"
BREAKFAST
10'-0"x9'-6"
KITCHEN
9'-8"x8'-8"
DINING RM.
19'-8"x11'-2"
BEDROOM
12'-10"x12'-0"
PAN.
DRESS.
BATH
BATH
GARAGE
21'-2"x20'-2"
CATHEDRAL CLG.
M. BEDROOM
15'-8"x13'-10"
GREAT RM.
19'-8"x18'-2"
BEDROOM
13'-0"x11'-0"
30'-0"
MAIN FLOOR
PORCH
21'-0"x6'-0"
73'-8"

PLAN NO.65125

Stone and Shingle Siding

PRICE CODE: D

- This plan features:
- — Four bedrooms
- — Two full baths
- Informal meals are served at the fan-shaped counter in the Kitchen
- The angled, two-story stone fireplace adds warmth and dramatic appeal to the Living and Dining Rooms
- This home is designed with a basement foundation

FIRST FLOOR — 1,324 SQ. FT.
SECOND FLOOR — 688 SQ. FT.
BASEMENT — 1,324 SQ. FT.
GARAGE — 425 SQ. FT.

TOTAL LIVING AREA: 2,012 SQ. FT.

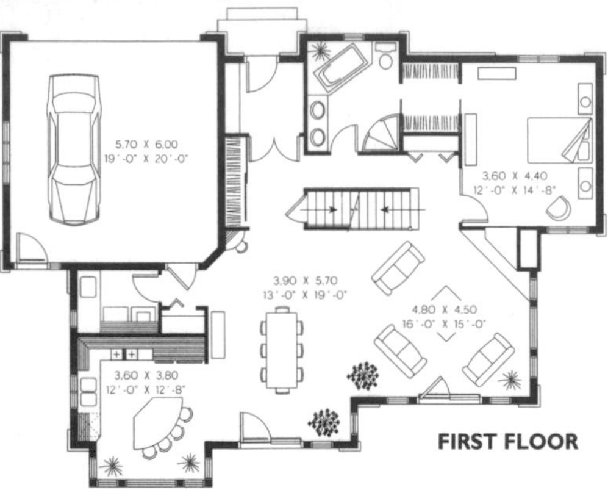
5,70 X 6,00
19'-0" X 20'-0"
3,60 X 4,40
12'-0" X 14'-8"
3,90 X 5,70
13'-0" X 19'-0"
4,80 X 4,50
16'-0" X 15'-0"
3,60 X 3,80
12'-0" X 12'-8"
FIRST FLOOR

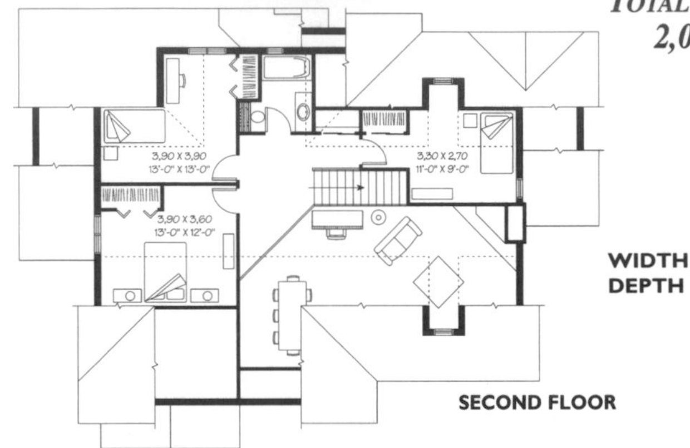
3,90 X 3,90
13'-0" X 13'-0"
3,30 X 2,70
11'-0" X 9'-0"
3,90 X 3,60
13'-0" X 12'-0"
SECOND FLOOR

WIDTH 56'-0"
DEPTH 41'-0"

PLAN NO.98513

French Country Styling

PRICE CODE: I

- This plan features:
- — Four bedrooms
- — Three full and one half baths
- Brick and stone blend masterfully for an impressive French Country exterior
- Separate Master Suite has an expansive Bath and clos
- Study contains a built-in desk and a bookcase
- Angled island Kitchen is highlighted by a walk-in Pan
- Fantastic Family Room includes a brick fireplace and built-in entertainment center
- Three additional Bedrooms have private access to a full Bath
- This home is designed with a slab foundation

MAIN FLOOR — 3,352 SQ. FT.
GARAGE — 672 SQ. FT.

TOTAL LIVING AREA: 3,352 SQ. FT.

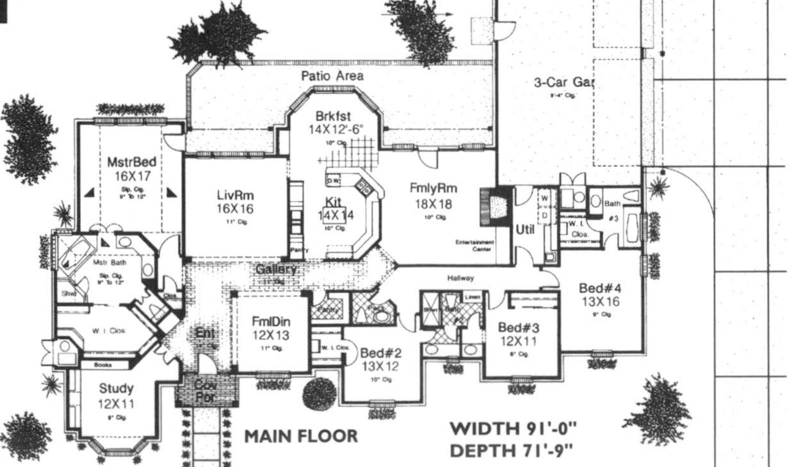
Patio Area
3-Car Gar
Brkfst
14X12'-6"
MstrBed
16X17
LivRm
16X16
Kit
14X14
FmlyRm
18X18
Util
Bath
Mstr Bath
Gallery
Hallway
Bed#4
13X16
W. I. Clos
Ent
FmlDin
12X13
Bed#2
13X12
Bed#3
12X11
Books
Study
12X11
Cov. Por.
MAIN FLOOR

WIDTH 91'-0"
DEPTH 71'-9"

PLAN NO. 82019

39' 0"

72' 0"

WHIP TUB
GLASS SHWR
M. BATH 16'-6" X 13'-0"
GARAGE 19'-4" X 19'-0"
MASTER SUITE 16'-8" X 15'-0"
11' BOXED CEILING
W D
LAU. 7'-0" X 6'-6"
GRILLING PORCH 8'-4" X 8'-11"
KID'S NOOK
PANTRY
REF
BENCH W/ STORAGE
BEDROOM 2 13'-4" X 12'-1"
KITCHEN 13'-2" X 12'-1"
RG
DW
DINING 11'-6" X 11'-9"
8" COLUMNS
LIN
COMPUTER AREA
MEDIA CENTER
GREAT ROOM 17'-8" X 17'-0"
FOYER
3' GAS FIREPLACE
8" COLUMNS
BEDROOM 3 / STUDY 13'-4" X 12'-0"
COVERED PORCH 25'-0" X 8'-0"
12" COLUMNS

MAIN FLOOR

Easy Living

Price Code: C

- This plan features:
  - — Three bedrooms
  - — Two full baths
- This home includes a built-in computer area and a media center in the Great Room
- The Dining Room and the Kitchen are joined by a peninsula counter/snack bar
- A decorative ceiling and a five-piece Bath add to the elegance and convenience of the Master Suite
- This home is designed with crawlspace and slab foundation options

MAIN FLOOR — 1,915 SQ. FT.
GARAGE — 401 SQ. FT.
PORCH — 279 SQ. FT.

TOTAL LIVING AREA:
1,915 SQ. FT.

PLAN NO. 92625

Discriminating Buyers

Price Code: B

- This plan features:
- — Three bedrooms
- — Two full baths
- A sheltered entrance into the Foyer
- A sloped ceiling adding elegance to the formal Dining Room
- A sloped ceiling and a corner fireplace enhancing the Great Room
- A peninsula counter joins the Kitchen and the Breakfast Room in an open layout
- A Master Suite, equipped with a large walk-in closet and a private Bath with an oval corner tub
- This home is designed with a basement foundation

MAIN FLOOR — 1,746 SQ. FT.
BASEMENT — 1,560 SQ. FT.
GARAGE — 455 SQ. FT.

TOTAL LIVING AREA:
1,746 SQ. FT.

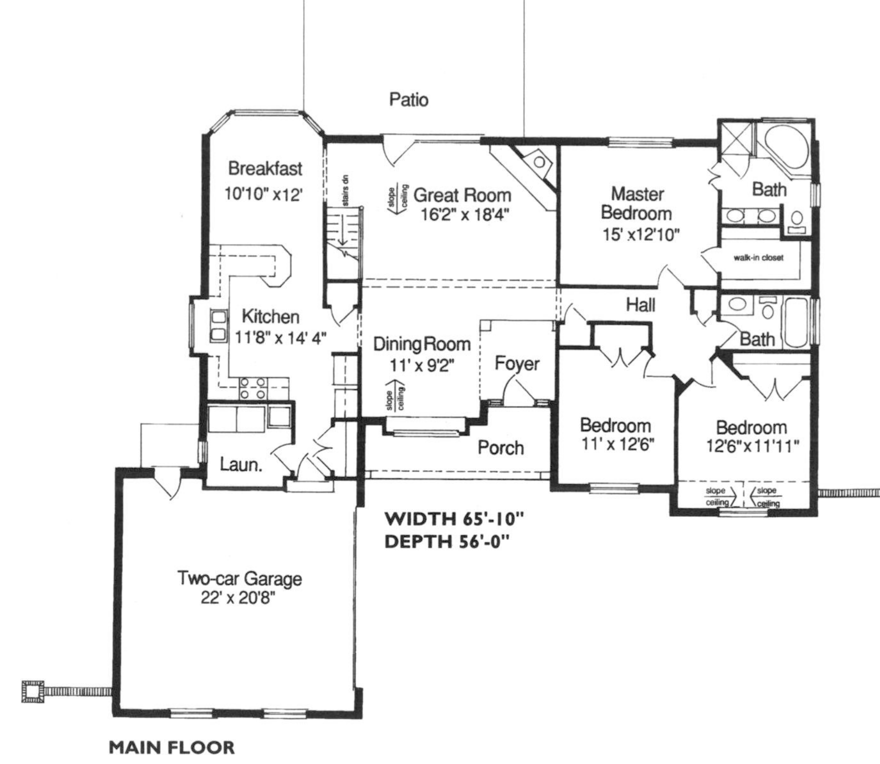
Patio
Breakfast
10'10" x12'
stairs dn
slope ceiling
Great Room
16'2" x 18'4"
Master
Bedroom
15' x12'10"
Bath
walk-in closet
Hall
Kitchen
11'8" x 14' 4"
Dining Room
11' x 9'2"
slope ceiling
Foyer
Bath
Bedroom
11' x 12'6"
Bedroom
12'6"x11'11"
Porch
Laun.
slope ceiling
slope ceiling
WIDTH 65'-10"
DEPTH 56'-0"
Two-car Garage
22' x 20'8"
MAIN FLOOR

Definitely Detailed

PRICE CODE: C

PLAN NO. 97703

'his plan features:
- ;hree bedrooms
- ;wo full baths
- ,n artistically detailed brick exterior adds to the appeal f this home
- 'he Foyer is separated from the Great room by columns
- 'he Great Room has a wall of windows and a warming replace
- 'he Dining Room has a sloped ceiling and is adjacent) the Kitchen
- 'he Kitchen is arranged in a U-shape and features a enter island plus a walk-in Pantry
- 'he Bedrooms are all on one side of the home or privacy
- ,n optional plan for the basement includes a Recreation ,oom, an Exercise Room, and a Bath
- 'his home is designed with a basement foundation

.IN FLOOR — 1,963 SQ. FT.
WER FLOOR — 1,963 SQ. FT.

TOTAL LIVING AREA:
1,963 SQ. FT.

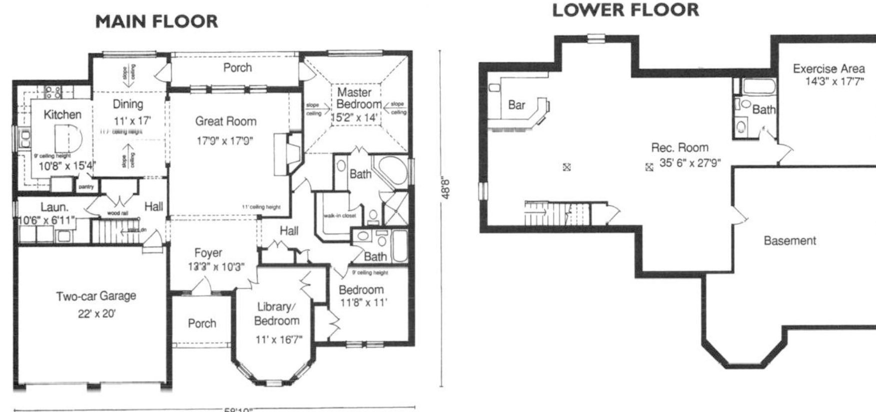
MAIN FLOOR
Porch
Kitchen
Dining
11' x 17'
10'8" x 15'4"
pantry
Great Room
17'9" x 17'9"
Master Bedroom
15'2" x 14'
Bath
Laun.
10'6" x 6'11"
Hall
Foyer
13'3" x 10'3"
Hall
Bath
Bedroom
11'8" x 11'
Two-car Garage
22' x 20'
Porch
Library/ Bedroom
11' x 16'7"
48'8"
58'10"
LOWER FLOOR
Bar
Exercise Area
14'3" x 17'7"
Bath
Rec. Room
35' 6" x 27'9"
Basement

For an Established Neighborhood

PRICE CODE: A

PLAN NO. 93222

'his plan features:
- Three bedrooms
- Two full baths
- ' covered entrance sheltering and welcoming visitors
- 'n expansive Living Room enhanced by natural light treaming in from the large front window
- ' bayed formal Dining Room with direct access to the Sun Deck and the Living Room for entertainment ease
- 'n efficient, galley Kitchen, convenient to both formal nd informal eating areas, and equipped with a double ink and adequate counter and storage space
- 'n informal Breakfast Room with direct access to the Sun Deck
- ' large Master Suite equipped with a walk-in closet and full private Bath
- 'wo additional Bedrooms that share a full hall Bath
- 'his home is designed with a basement foundation

.IN FLOOR — 1,276 SQ. FT.
SEMENT — 392 SQ. FT.
RAGE — 728 SQ. FT.

TOTAL LIVING AREA:
1,292 SQ. FT.

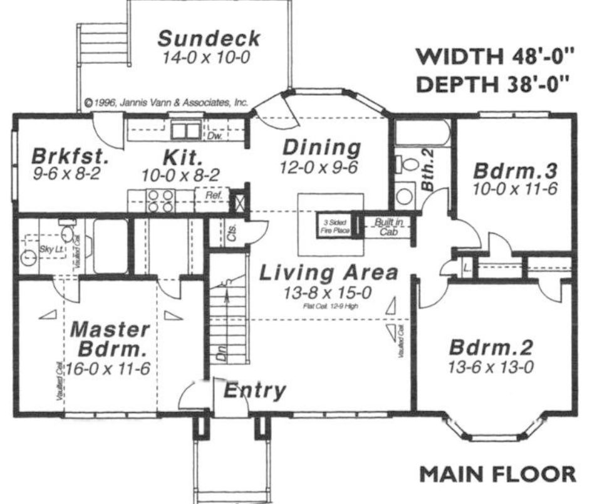
Sundeck
14-0 x 10-0
WIDTH 48'-0"
DEPTH 38'-0"
©1996, Jannis Vann & Associates, Inc.
Brkfst.
9-6 x 8-2
Kit.
10-0 x 8-2
Dining
12-0 x 9-6
Bth.2
Bdrm.3
10-0 x 11-6
Living Area
13-8 x 15-0
Master Bdrm.
16-0 x 11-6
Bdrm.2
13-6 x 13-0
Entry
MAIN FLOOR

PLAN NO.93414

Cute Cottage

PRICE CODE: A

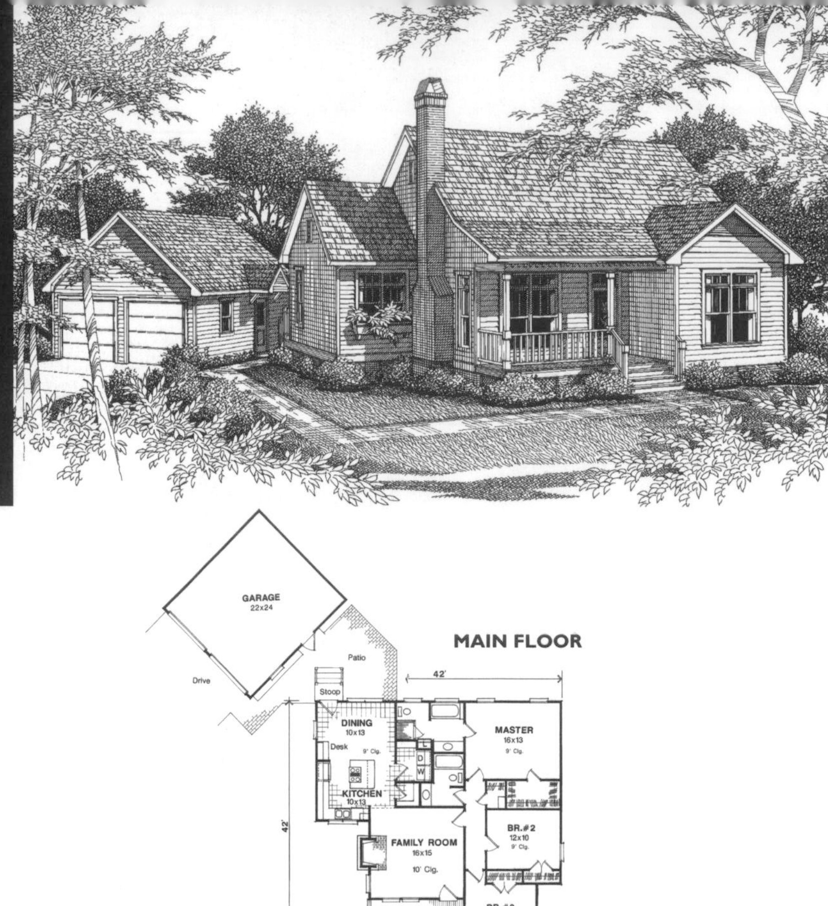

GARAGE
22x24
Patio
Drive
Stoop
MAIN FLOOR
42'
DINING
10x13
Desk
KITCHEN
10x13
MASTER
16x13
FAMILY ROOM
16x15
10' Clg.
BR.#2
12x10
BR.#3
12x10
PORCH
5x16

- This plan features:
  - — Three bedrooms
  - — Two full baths
- A cute covered front Porch adds character to this cottage plan
- The large Family Room has a 10-foot ceiling and a side wall fireplace
- The Kitchen is open to the Dining Room
- The Kitchen is equipped with a center island, a planning desk, and a cooktop
- A convenient Laundry Room is located off of the Kitchen
- The Master Bedroom has a walk in closet and a full B
- Two secondary Bedrooms are identical in size and sh a Bath in the hall
- There is a detached two-car Garage with this plan
- This home is designed with crawlspace and slab foundation options

MAIN FLOOR — 1,393 SQ. FT.
GARAGE — 528 SQ. FT.

TOTAL LIVING AREA:
1,393 SQ. FT.

PLAN NO.96523

Cozy Front and Back Porches

PRICE CODE: B

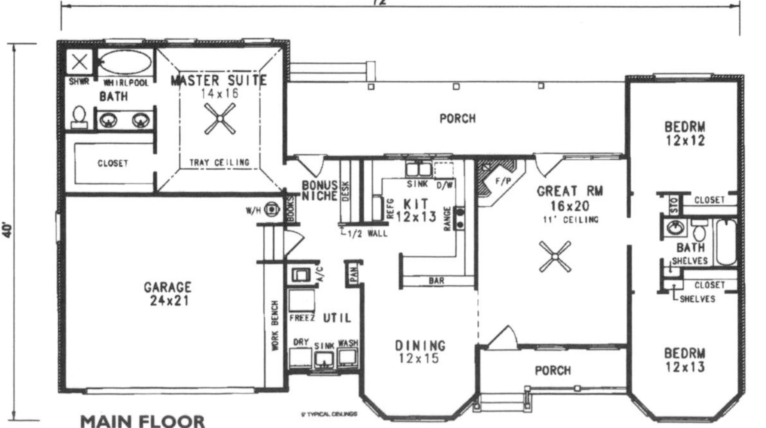

72'
40'
SHWR
WHIRLPOOL
BATH
MASTER SUITE
14x16
CLOSET
TRAY CEILING
PORCH
BONUS NICHE
DESK
SINK
D/W
KIT
12x13
REFG
RANGE
1/2 WALL
F/P
GREAT RM
16x20
11' CEILING
BAR
W/H
GARAGE
24x21
WORK BENCH
FREEZ
UTIL
DRY
SINK
WASH
DINING
12x15
PORCH
BEDRM
12x12
CLOSET
BATH
SHELVES
CLOSET
SHELVES
BEDRM
12x13
MAIN FLOOR

- This plan features:
  - — Three bedrooms
  - — Two full baths
- A spacious Great Room is highlighted by a corner fireplace and access to the rear Porch
- The Dining Area with views of the front yard is separated from the Kitchen by an eating bar
- The private Master Suite is tucked into the rear left corner of the home
- A tray ceiling, a whirlpool tub and a walk-in closet highlight the Master suite
- Two additional Bedrooms are located on the opposite side of the home, a full Bath is between the Bedrooms
- This home is designed with crawlspace and slab foundation options

MAIN FLOOR — 1,652 SQ. FT.
GARAGE — 497 SQ. FT.

TOTAL LIVING AREA:
1,652 SQ. FT.

PLAN NO. 92162

SECOND FLOOR

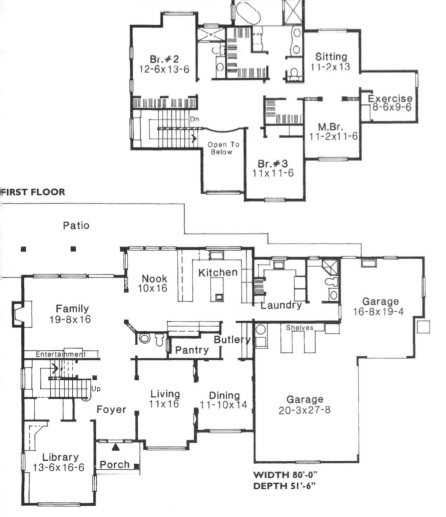

Br.#2
12-6x13-6

Sitting
11-2x13

Exercise
8-6x9-6

Dn

Open To
Below

M.Br.
11-2x11-6

Br.#3
11x11-6

FIRST FLOOR

Patio

Nook
10x16

Kitchen

Laundry

Garage
16-8x19-4

Family
19-8x16

Butlery

Shelves

Pantry

Entertainment

Up

Living
11x16

Dining
11-10x14

Garage
20-3x27-8

Foyer

Library
13-6x16-6

Porch

WIDTH 80'-0"
DEPTH 51'-6"

Rooms for Everything

Price Code: I

- This plan features:
- — Three bedrooms
- — Two full and one half baths
- English Country charm shines through in subtle curves and sharp angles
- A Library, Exercise Room, and Sitting Room offer something for everyone
- Counter space, center island, Pantry, Butlery, and separate Nook, make an impressive Kitchen
- Spanning the entire back of the house, the Patio creates a comfortable, outdoorsy getaway
- This home is designed with a crawlspace foundation

FIRST FLOOR — 2,057 SQ. FT.
SECOND FLOOR — 1,323 SQ. FT.
GARAGE — 886 SQ. FT.

TOTAL LIVING AREA:
3,380 SQ. FT.

PLAN NO.92163

Modern Amenities with a Classic Look

PRICE CODE: L

- This plan features:
  - — Three bedrooms
  - — Two full, one three-quarter, and one half bath
- Easy access to all levels via elevator
- A fireplace exudes coziness into the Master Bedroom its windowed Sitting Area
- A wall of rear windows lines the open design of the f floor for an airy and spacious atmosphere
- A soda fountain creates a magical centerpiece for the Kitchen, Nook, and Family Room
- A Library opens up to the Reading Gallery on the top the tower
- Car aficionados will love the Automobile Gallery wi automobile elevator, two Baths, and adjoining vault
- This home is designed with basement and slab found tion options

FIRST FLOOR — 3,162 SQ. FT.
SECOND FLOOR — 1,595 SQ. FT.
BASEMENT — 2,651 SQ. FT.
GARAGE — 708 SQ. FT.

TOTAL LIVING AREA:* 4,757 *SQ. FT.

WIDTH 110'-2"
DEPTH 68'-11"

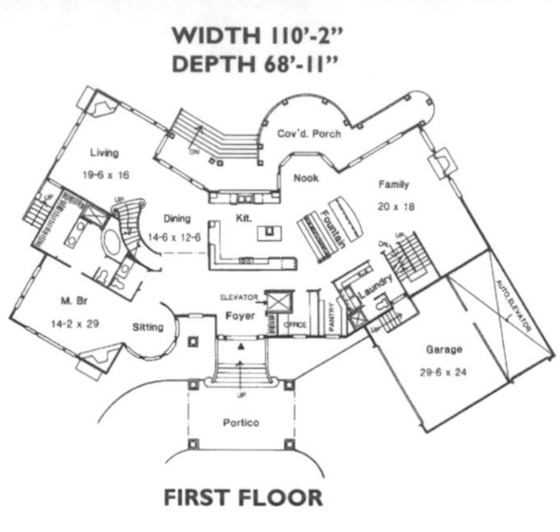
Living
19-6 x 16
Cov'd. Porch
Nook
Family
20 x 18
Dining
14-6 x 12-6
Kit.
Fountain
Laundry
M. Br
14-2 x 29
Sitting
Elevator
Foyer
Office
Pantry
Garage
29-6 x 24
Auto Elevator
Portico

FIRST FLOOR

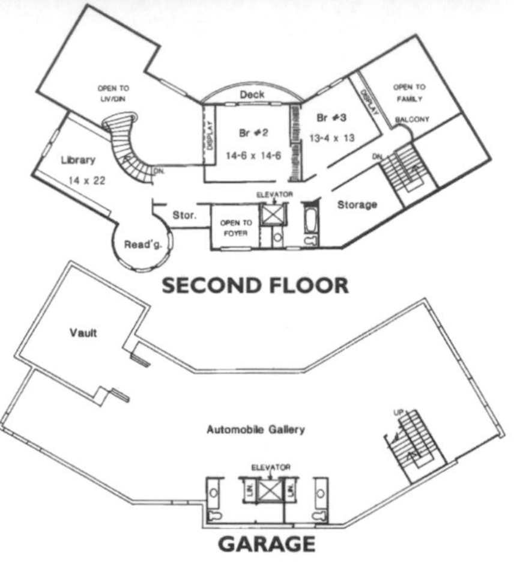
Open to Liv/Din
Deck
Open to Family
Library
14 x 22
Br #2
14-6 x 14-6
Br #3
13-4 x 13
Balcony
Display
Elevator
Storage
Stor.
Open to Foyer
Read'g.
Vault
Automobile Gallery
Elevator

SECOND FLOOR

GARAGE

PLAN NO.51010

A Cook's Dream

PRICE CODE: D

- This plan features:
  - — Four bedrooms
  - — Two full and one half baths
- A Covered Porch, topped with a multiple-window dormer, creates a welcoming appearance
- The two-story vaulted Living Room adds scale to the first floor
- Built-in desk, ample counter space, and octagonal Nc make an impressive Kitchen
- The Bedrooms, each with generous closet space, share the privacy of the second floor
- This home is designed with a basement foundation

FIRST FLOOR — 1,408 SQ. FT.
SECOND FLOOR — 695 SQ. FT.

TOTAL LIVING AREA:* 2,103 *SQ. FT.

WIDTH 50'-0"
DEPTH 47'-8"

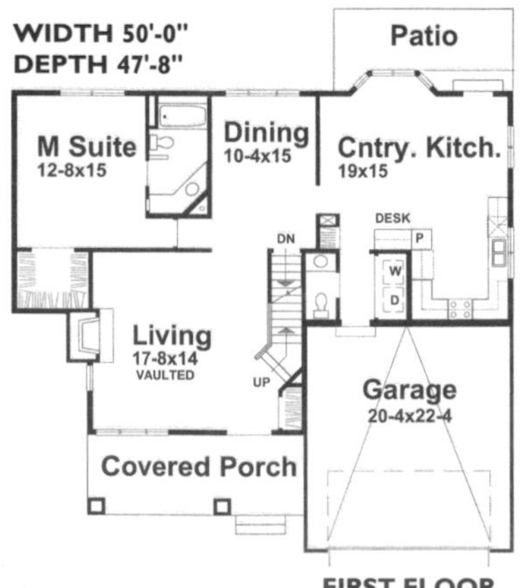
Patio
M Suite
12-8x15
Dining
10-4x15
Cntry. Kitch.
19x15
DESK
DN
P
W
D
Living
17-8x14
VAULTED
UP
Garage
20-4x22-4
Covered Porch

FIRST FLOOR

Br 2
11-8x14-10
Loft/Br 3
12-6x10
Optional Wall
Br 2
11x13-6
DN
OPEN TO BELOW
DORMER OPEN BELOW
L

SECOND FLOOR

Traditional Ranch

PRICE CODE: E

PLAN NO. 92404

his plan features:
- hree bedrooms
- wo full baths
- tray ceiling in the Master Suite that is equipped with s and her walk-in closets and a private Master Bath ith a cathedral ceiling
- formal Living Room with a cathedral ceiling
- decorative tray ceiling in the elegant formal ining Room
- spacious Family Room with a vaulted ceiling d a fireplace
- modern, well-appointed Kitchen with snack bar d bayed Breakfast Area
- wo additional Bedrooms that share a full hall Bath ch having a walk-in closet
- his home is designed with a basement foundation

N FLOOR — 2,275 SQ. FT.
AGE — 512 SQ. FT.
EMENT — 2,207 SQ. FT.

TOTAL LIVING AREA:
2,275 SQ. FT.

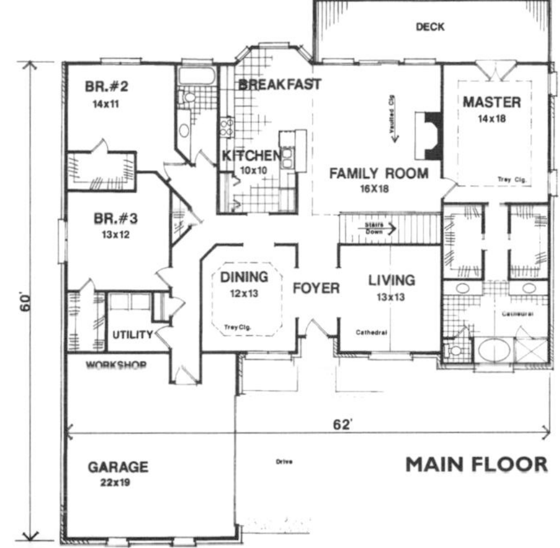

DECK
BR.#2
14x11
BREAKFAST
MASTER
14x18
KITCHEN
10x10
FAMILY ROOM
16X18
BR.#3
13x12
DINING
12x13
FOYER
LIVING
13x13
UTILITY
WORKSHOP
60'
62'
GARAGE
22x19
MAIN FLOOR

This Home Has It All

PRICE CODE: I

PLAN NO. 92164

'his plan features:
- 'our bedrooms
- 'our full and two half baths
- Iome Office, Home Theater, and Kids' Retreat make iis home everything you need in one
- Built-in bookshelves, media center, benches, desks, nd dining table add artistic practicality
- 'ooking island adorns Kitchen and plenty of workspace urrounds the room
-)verlooking the Family Room, Lofts connect the econdary Bedrooms
- 'his home is designed with a basement and crawlspace oundation options

ST FLOOR — 2,120 SQ. FT.
'ONF FLOOR — 1,520 SQ. FT.
NUS ROOM — 183 SQ. FT.
SEMENT — 377 SQ. FT.

TOTAL LIVING AREA:
3,640 SQ. FT.

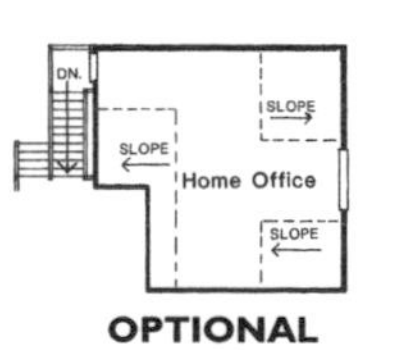

SLOPE
Home Office

OPTIONAL HOME OFFICE

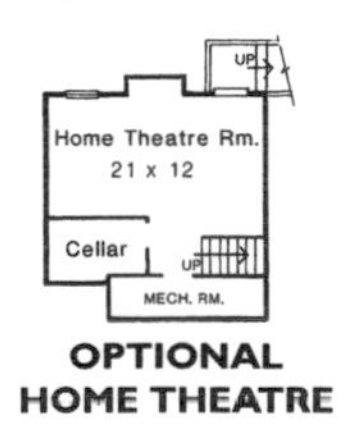

Home Theatre Rm.
21 x 12
Cellar
MECH. RM.

OPTIONAL HOME THEATRE

Kid's
Retreat
12-6 x 13-6

OPTIONAL KIDS RETREAT

SECOND FLOOR

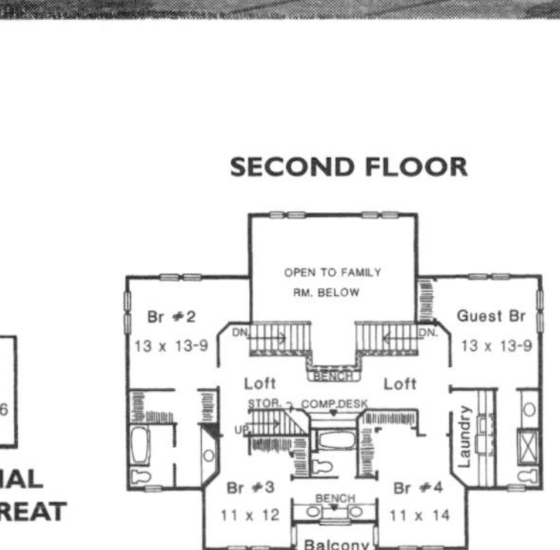

OPEN TO FAMILY
RM. BELOW
Br #2
13 x 13-9
Guest Br
13 x 13-9
Loft
Loft
Laundry
Br #3
11 x 12
Br #4
11 x 14
Balcony

FIRST FLOOR

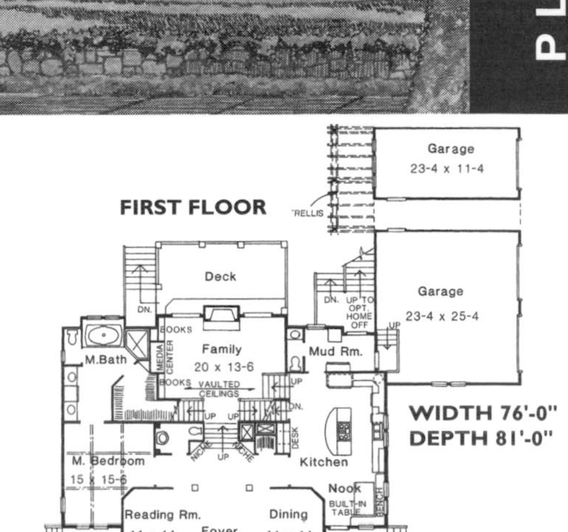

Garage
23-4 x 11-4
Deck
Garage
23-4 x 25-4
M.Bath
Family
20 x 13-6
Mud Rm.
M. Bedroom
15 x 15-6
Kitchen
Nook
Reading Rm.
11 x 14
Foyer
Dining
11 x 14
Cov'd. Porch

WIDTH 76'-0"
DEPTH 81'-0"

PLAN NO. 82018

Romantic Second Floor Porch

Price Code: C

- This plan features:
- — Three bedrooms
- — Two full and one half baths
- The first floor Master Suite is tucked into the rear of the home allowing maximum privacy
- The Great Room includes a gas fireplace for a cozy atmosphere
- The Dining Room is accented by columns at its entrance
- This home is designed with basement, slab, and crawlspace foundation options

FIRST FLOOR — 1,298 SQ. FT.
SECOND FLOOR — 624 SQ. FT.
GARAGE — 431 SQ. FT.
PORCH — 353 SQ. FT.

TOTAL LIVING AREA:
1,922 SQ. FT.

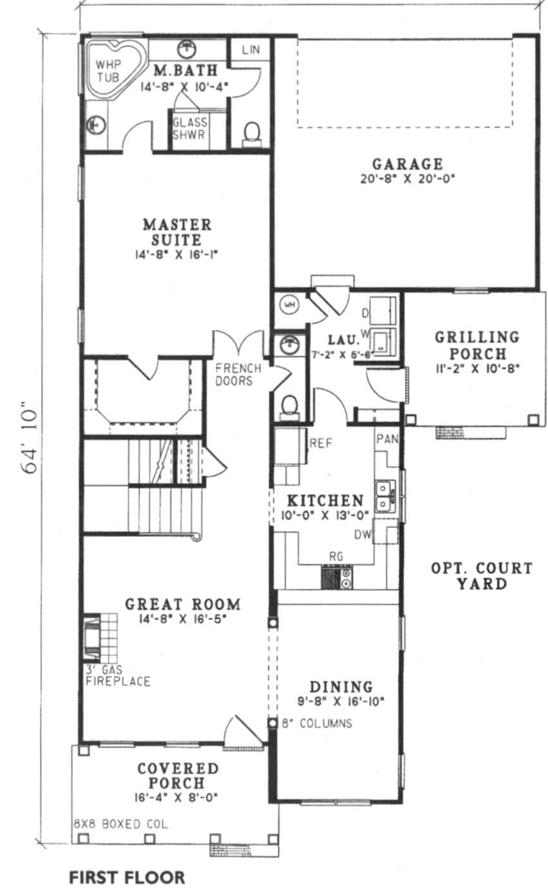

36' 4"
64' 10"
WHP TUB
M.BATH
14'-8" X 10'-4"
LIN
GLASS SHWR
GARAGE
20'-8" X 20'-0"
MASTER SUITE
14'-8" X 16'-1"
WH
LAU.
7'-2" X 5'-6"
D
W
GRILLING PORCH
11'-2" X 10'-8"
FRENCH DOORS
REF
PAN
KITCHEN
10'-0" X 13'-0"
DW
RG
OPT. COURT YARD
GREAT ROOM
14'-8" X 16'-5"
3' GAS FIREPLACE
DINING
9'-8" X 16'-10"
8" COLUMNS
COVERED PORCH
16'-4" X 8'-0"
8X8 BOXED COL.

FIRST FLOOR

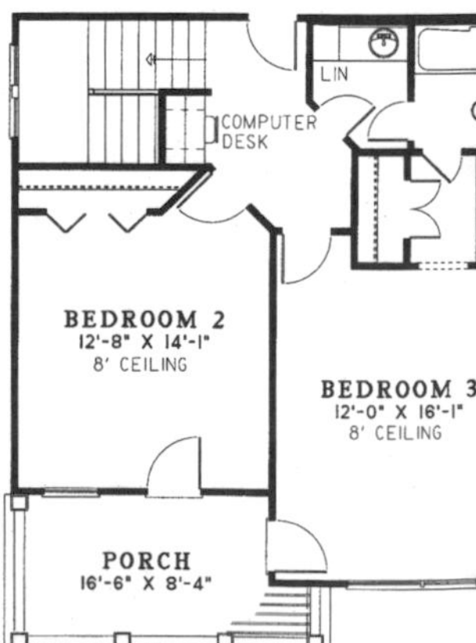

COMPUTER DESK
LIN
BEDROOM 2
12'-8" X 14'-1"
8' CEILING
BEDROOM 3
12'-0" X 16'-1"
8' CEILING
PORCH
16'-6" X 8'-4"

SECOND FLOOR

Rich in Features

PRICE CODE: I

PLAN NO.92165

ıs plan features:
- ree bedrooms
- /o full and one half baths
- ne connoisseurs will love the wine cellar with lt-in racks
- ster Bath features skylight in shower stall
- arport provides protection for automobiles while a arate Garage provides additional protection and space
- e fireplace warms the Family Room and Kitchen ile another heats up the Den and Master Bedroom
- condary Bedrooms share a Bath and the privacy of the ond floor, which overlooks much of the first floor
- is home is designed with a slab foundation

T FLOOR — 2,311 SQ. FT.
ND FLOOR — 904 SQ. FT.
AGE — 528 SQ. FT.

TOTAL LIVING AREA:
3,215 SQ. FT.

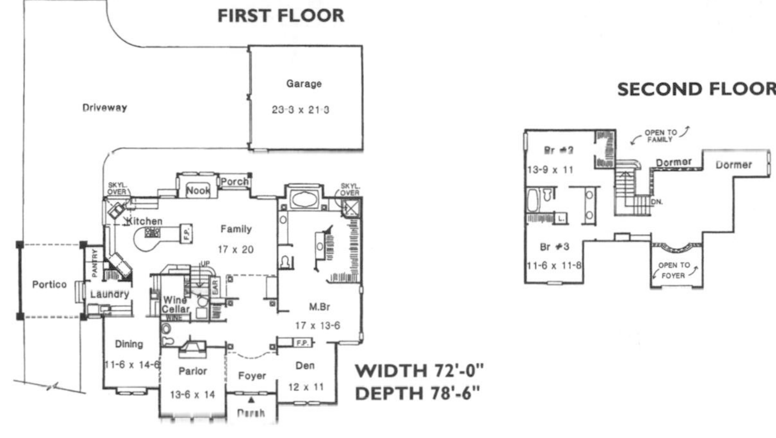
FIRST FLOOR
Driveway
Garage
23-3 x 21-3
Portico
Pantry
Laundry
Kitchen
Nook
Porch
Family
17 x 20
Wine Cellar
M.Br
17 x 13-6
Dining
11-6 x 14-6
Parlor
13-6 x 14
Foyer
Den
12 x 11
WIDTH 72'-0"
DEPTH 78'-6"
SECOND FLOOR
Br #2
13-9 x 11
Br #3
11-6 x 11-8
Dormer
Dormer
OPEN TO FAMILY
OPEN TO FOYER

Columned Entryways

PRICE CODE: F

PLAN NO.51009

ıis plan features:
- our bedrooms
- wo full and one half baths
- ıe open design of the family areas creates a sense community
- ıe Master Suite enjoys the privacy of the left wing, generous walk-in closet, and a luxurious Bath
- ıe second floor Bedrooms share a Loft that opens on th sides
- ght streams through the wall of windows forming the eakfast Nook, which opens up to the rear Deck
- ıis home is designed with a basement foundation

T FLOOR — 1,705 SQ. FT.
OND FLOOR — 804 SQ. FT.
EMENT — 1,705 SQ. FT.
AGE — 484 SQ. FT.

TOTAL LIVING AREA:
2,509 SQ. FT.

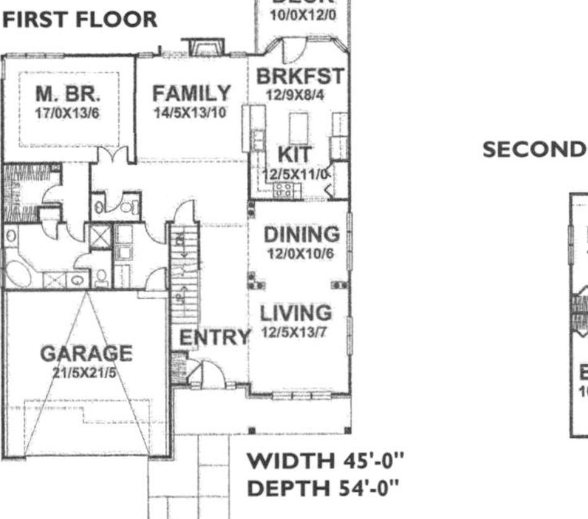
FIRST FLOOR
DECK
10/0X12/0
M. BR.
17/0X13/6
FAMILY
14/5X13/10
BRKFST
12/9X8/4
KIT
12/5X11/0
DINING
12/0X10/6
LIVING
12/5X13/7
ENTRY
GARAGE
21/5X21/5
WIDTH 45'-0"
DEPTH 54'-0"

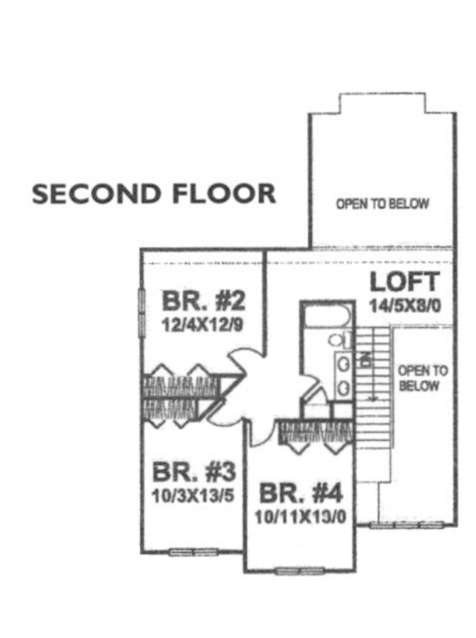
SECOND FLOOR
OPEN TO BELOW
BR. #2
12/4X12/9
LOFT
14/5X8/0
OPEN TO BELOW
BR. #3
10/3X13/5
BR. #4
10/11X13/0

PLAN NO. 96915

For a Golf Course

Price Code: F

- This plan features:
- — Three bedrooms
- — Three full and one half baths
- A combination of exterior textures and a built-in window box gives a warm curb presence to this home
- Great care has been given to enhance the rear views created by living on a golf course by allowing a terrific sight line through many windows
- An second floor Veranda provides a quiet spot and added living space
- This home is designed with a crawlspace foundation

FIRST FLOOR — 1,661 SQ. FT.
SECOND FLOOR — 882 SQ. FT.
GARAGE — 497 SQ. FT.

TOTAL LIVING AREA:
2,543 SQ. FT.

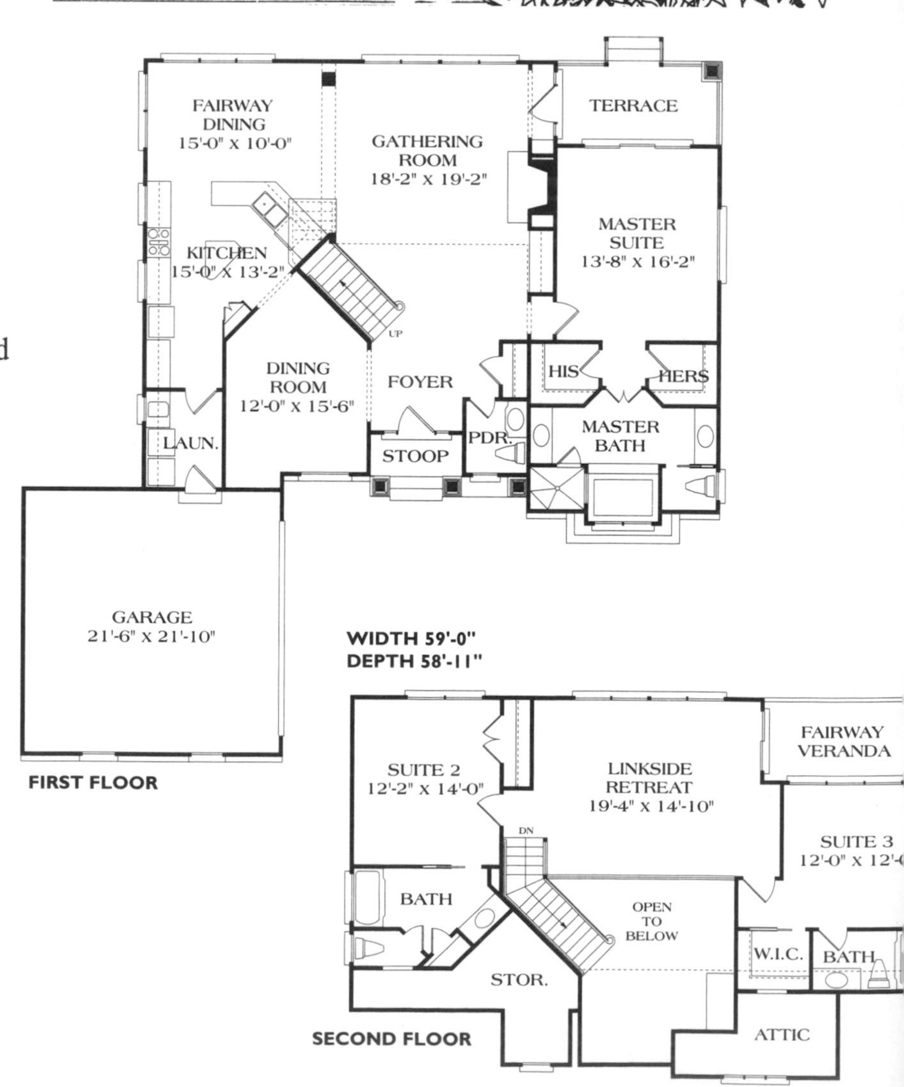

FAIRWAY DINING 15'-0" x 10'-0"
GATHERING ROOM 18'-2" x 19'-2"
TERRACE
KITCHEN 15'-0" x 13'-2"
MASTER SUITE 13'-8" x 16'-2"
UP
DINING ROOM 12'-0" x 15'-6"
FOYER
HIS
HERS
LAUN.
PDR.
STOOP
MASTER BATH
GARAGE 21'-6" x 21'-10"
WIDTH 59'-0"
DEPTH 58'-11"
FIRST FLOOR
SUITE 2 12'-2" x 14'-0"
LINKSIDE RETREAT 19'-4" x 14'-10"
FAIRWAY VERANDA
DN
SUITE 3
BATH
OPEN TO BELOW
W.I.C.
BATH
STOR.
ATTIC
SECOND FLOOR

PLAN NO. 92655

Backyard Views

Price Code: B

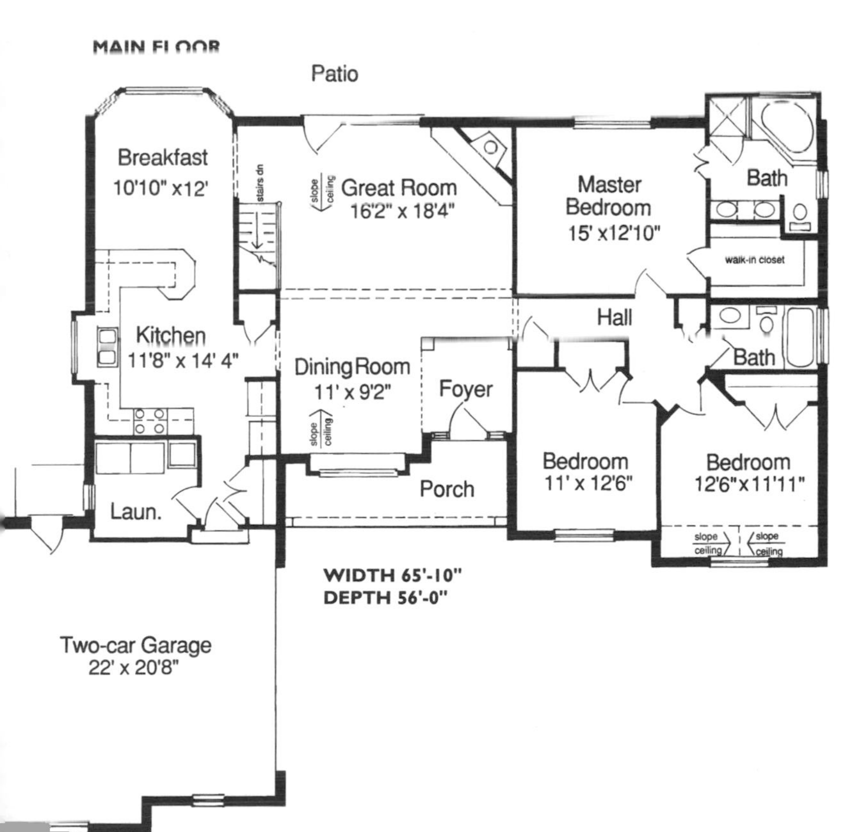

MAIN FLOOR
Patio
Breakfast
10'10" x12'
Great Room
16'2" x 18'4"
slope ceiling
stairs dn
Master
Bedroom
15' x12'10"
Bath
walk-in closet
Hall
Kitchen
11'8" x 14' 4"
Dining Room
11' x 9'2"
Foyer
Bath
Bedroom
11' x 12'6"
Bedroom
12'6"x11'11"
Laun.
Porch
slope ceiling
WIDTH 65'-10"
DEPTH 56'-0"
Two-car Garage
22' x 20'8"

- This plan features:
  - Three bedrooms
  - Two full baths
- Front Porch accesses open Foyer, and spacious Dining Room and Great Room with sloped ceilings
- Corner fireplace, windows and Atrium door to Patio enhance Great Room
- Convenient Kitchen with a Pantry, peninsula serving counter for bright Breakfast Area and nearby Laundry/Garage Entry
- Luxurious Bath, walk-in closet and backyard view offered in Master Bedroom
- This home is designed with a basement foundation

MAIN FLOOR — 1,746 SQ. FT.
BASEMENT — 1,697 SQ. FT.
GARAGE — 480 SQ. FT.

TOTAL LIVING AREA:
1,746 SQ. FT.

PLAN NO.90934

A Nest for Empty-Nester

PRICE CODE: A

- This plan features:
- — Two bedrooms
- — One full bath
- An economical design
- A Covered Sun Deck adding outdoor living space
- A Mudroom/Laundry Area inside the side door, trap dirt before it can enter the house
- An open layout between the Living Room with firep Dining Room, and Kitchen
- This home is designed with a slab foundation

MAIN FLOOR — 884 SQ. FT.

TOTAL LIVING AREA:
884 SQ. FT.

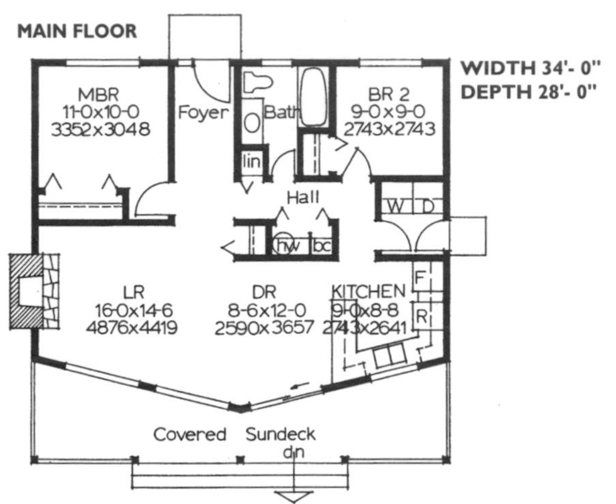

MAIN FLOOR
WIDTH 34'- 0"
DEPTH 28'- 0"
MBR
11-0x10-0
3352x3048
Foyer
Bath
BR 2
9-0x9-0
2743x2743
lin
Hall
W D
hw
bc
LR
16-0x14-6
4876x4419
DR
8-6x12-0
2590x3657
KITCHEN
9-0x8-8
2743x2641
F
R
Covered Sundeck
dn

PLAN NO.98411

Style and Convenience

PRICE CODE: A

- This plan features:
- —Three bedrooms
- —Two full baths
- Large front windows, dormers, and an old-fashioned Porch giving a pleasing style to the home
- A vaulted ceiling topping the Foyer and flowing into Family Room, which is highlighted by a fireplace
- An efficient Kitchen enhanced by a Pantry, a pass-th to the Family Room, and direct access to the Dining Breakfast Rooms
- A decorative tray ceiling, a five-piece private Bath, a walk-in closet in the Master Suite
- Two roomy additional Bedrooms, share the full Bath in the hall
- This home is designed with basement and crawlspac foundation options

MAIN FLOOR — 1,373 SQ. FT.
BASEMENT — 1,386 SQ. FT.

TOTAL LIVING AREA:
1,373 SQ. FT.

WIDTH 50'-4"
DEPTH 45'-0"

Porch
Breakfast
Bedroom 3
11⁶ x 11⁰
W.i.c.
PLANT SHELF ABOVE
Vaulted M. Bath
SHWR
LINEN
PLANT SHELF ABOVE
PANTRY
Vaulted Dining Room
10¹ x 12⁶
Kitchen
DW
RANGE
REF
PASS THRU
Bath
LINEN
W
D
Master Suite
14⁶ x 14⁰
TRAY CLG.
COATS
W/H
OPT. STAIRS TO BSMT.
FPL
Vaulted Family Room
16⁶ x 12⁶
VAULT
Vaulted Foyer
Bedroom 2
11⁰ x 10⁹
Garage
19⁵ x 21⁶
Porch
MAIN FLOOR
© Frank Betz Associates, Inc.
GARAGE LOCATION WITH BASEMENT

Dramatic Dormer

PRICE CODE: B

PLAN NO.51019

is plan features:
- ree bedroooms
- o full and one half baths
- loor-to-ceiling window and dormer give the home lcoming appeal
- between the Living and Dining Rooms, a fireplace rms the hub of family activity
- unter space and a wide-open Eating Area, lined with ndows and bookshelves, define the Country Kitchen
- e Master Suite features a luxurious Bath whose rance is crowned with a plant shelf
- is home is designed with a basement foundation

' FLOOR — 834 SQ. FT.
ND FLOOR — 722 SQ. FT.
MENT — 834 SQ. FT.
AGE — 480 SQ. FT.

TOTAL LIVING AREA:* 1,556 *SQ. FT.

Photography supplied by Bloodgood Plan Services, Inc.

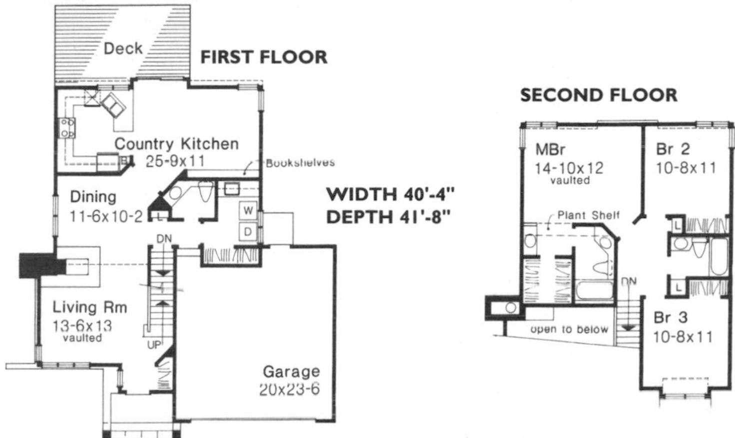
FIRST FLOOR
Deck
Country Kitchen
25-9x11
Bookshelves
Dining
11-6x10-2
W
D
DN
Living Rm
13-6x13
vaulted
UP
Garage
20x23-6
WIDTH 40'-4"
DEPTH 41'-8"
SECOND FLOOR
MBr
14-10x12
vaulted
Br 2
10-8x11
Plant Shelf
DN
open to below
Br 3
10-8x11

All About Windows, Doors, and Ceilings

PRICE CODE: L

PLAN NO.60137

is plan features:
- ve bedrooms
- ur full and one half baths
- e two-story Foyer offers a grand lcome to family and friends
- niche and arch openings in the Dining Room esents a formal atmosphere
- e Master Suite features a tray ceiling, French doors, ulted Bath, room-sized walk-in closet, three-sided eplace, Sitting Area, and private Covered Porch
- Bedrooms have direct access to ull Bath
- second floor Playroom gives kids and adults lace to enjoy themselves away from the center family activity
- is home is designed with basement and wlspace foundation options

T FLOOR — 2,092 SQ. FT.
ND FLOOR — 2,372 SQ. FT.
MENT — 2,092 SQ. FT.
AGE — 674 SQ. FT.

TOTAL LIVING AREA:* 4,464 *SQ. FT.

Photography supplied by Frank Betz Associates, Inc.

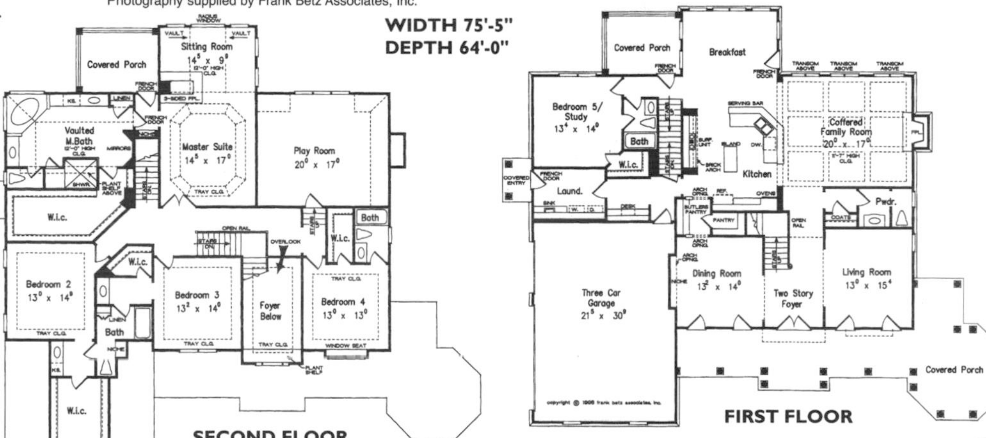
WIDTH 75'-5"
DEPTH 64'-0"
Sitting Room
Covered Porch
Vaulted M.Bath
Master Suite
Play Room
W.i.c.
Bath
Bedroom 2
Bedroom 3
Foyer Below
Bedroom 4
SECOND FLOOR
Covered Porch
Breakfast
Bedroom 5/ Study
Bath
Coffered Family Room
Kitchen
Laund.
Pwdr.
Dining Room
Living Room
Three Car Garage
Two Story Foyer
Covered Porch
FIRST FLOOR

PLAN NO. 98454

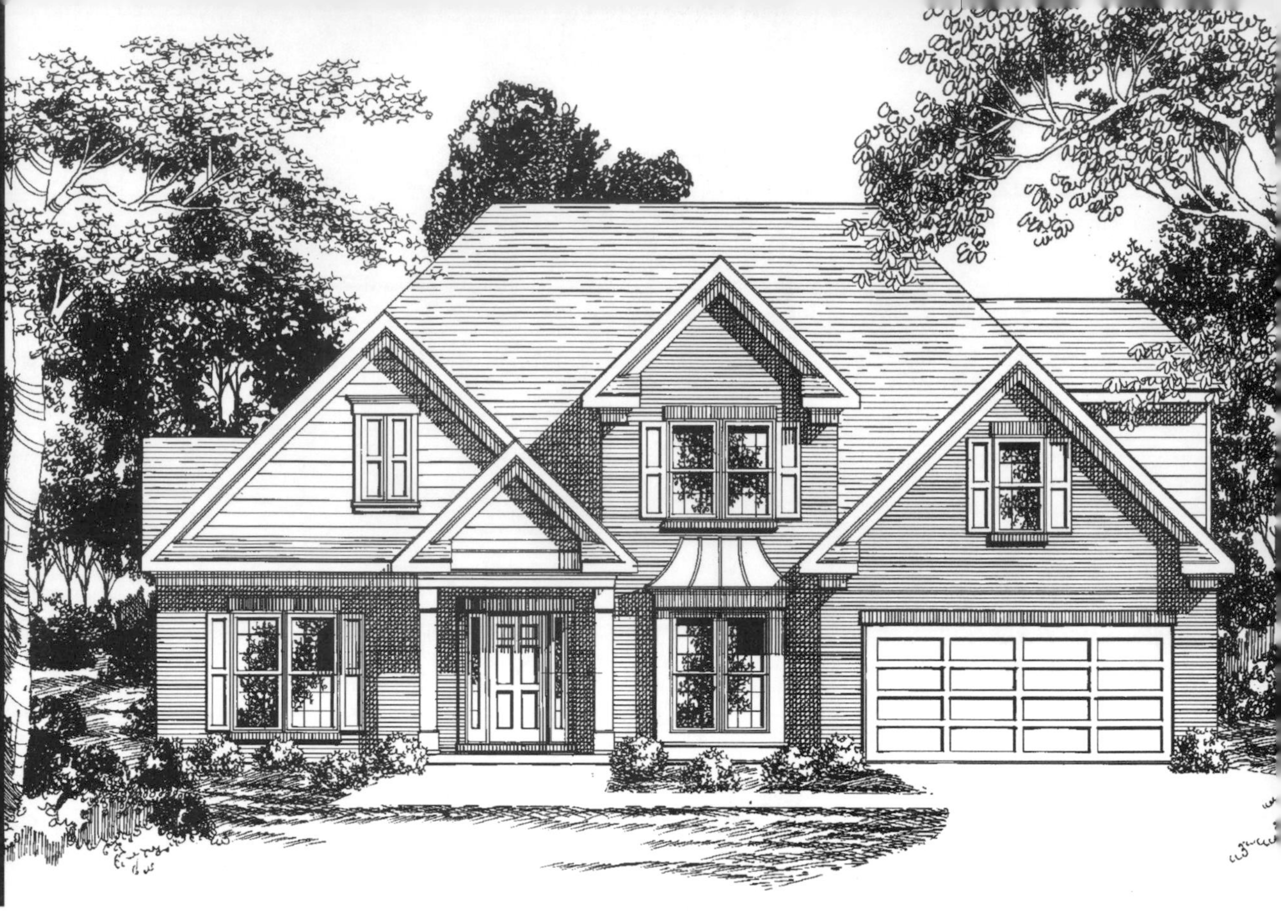

Family-Sized Accommodations

Price Code: C

- This plan features:
- — Four bedrooms
- — Two full and one half baths
- A spacious feeling is created by a vaulted ceiling in Foyer
- A fireplace is nestled by an alcove of windows in Family Room
- An angled Kitchen with a work island and a Pantry easily serves the Breakfast Area and the Dining Room
- The Master Bedroom is accented by a tray ceiling and a lavish Bath
- This home is designed with basement and crawlspace foundation options

FIRST FLOOR — 1,320 SQ. FT.
SECOND FLOOR — 554 SQ. FT.
BONUS ROOM — 155 SQ. FT.
GARAGE — 406 SQ. FT.

TOTAL LIVING AREA:
1,874 SQ. FT.

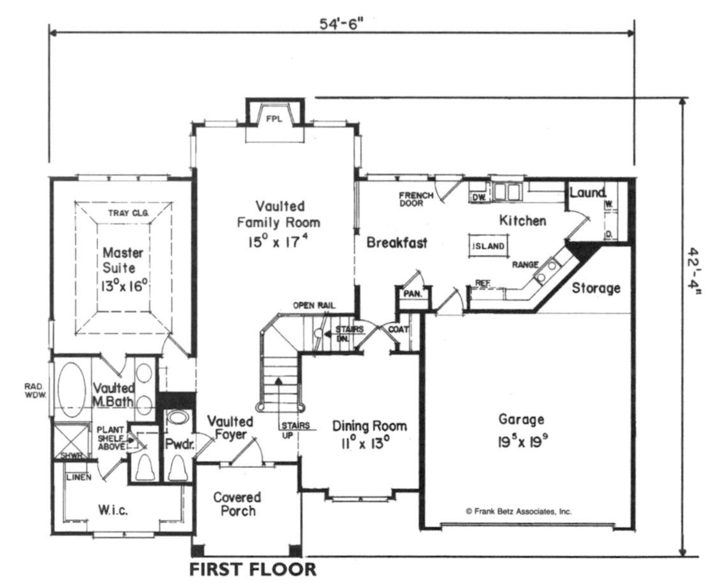

54'-6"
42'-4"
FPL
Vaulted Family Room $15^{0} \times 17^{4}$
TRAY CLG.
Master Suite $13^{0} \times 16^{0}$
FRENCH DOOR
DW.
Kitchen
Laund.
Breakfast
ISLAND
RANGE
REF.
PAN.
Storage
OPEN RAIL
STAIRS DN.
COAT
RAD. WDW.
Vaulted M.Bath
PLANT SHELF ABOVE
SHWR.
Pwdr.
Vaulted Foyer
STAIRS UP
Dining Room $11^{0} \times 13^{0}$
Garage $19^{5} \times 19^{9}$
LINEN
W.i.c.
Covered Porch
© Frank Betz Associates, Inc.

FIRST FLOOR

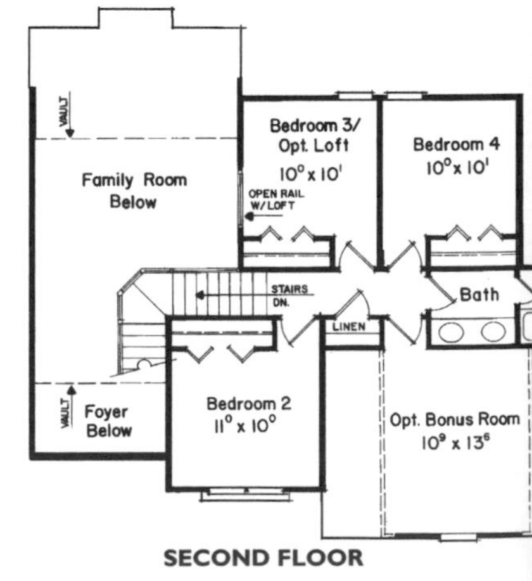

VAULT
Family Room Below
Bedroom 3/ Opt. Loft $10^{0} \times 10^{1}$
OPEN RAIL W/LOFT
Bedroom 4 $10^{0} \times 10^{1}$
STAIRS DN.
Bath
LINEN
Foyer Below
Bedroom 2 $11^{0} \times 10^{0}$
Opt. Bonus Room $10^{9} \times 13^{6}$

SECOND FLOOR

Brick Beauty

PRICE CODE: B

is plan features:
ıree bedrooms
vo full baths
e Great Room includes a 10-foot boxed ceiling
d a fireplace
e Dining Room adjoins with the Kitchen for
nore spacious feel
e Kitchen includes a peninsula counter/breakfast bar
: meals on-the-go
e Dining Room and the Master Bedroom have access
the Courtyard
is home is designed with crawlspace and slab
ındation options

N FLOOR — 1,660 SQ. FT.
AGE — 390 SQ. FT.
CH — 143 SQ. FT.

TOTAL LIVING AREA:
1,660 SQ. FT.

PLAN NO. 82039

WIDTH 33'-10"
DEPTH 69'-6"

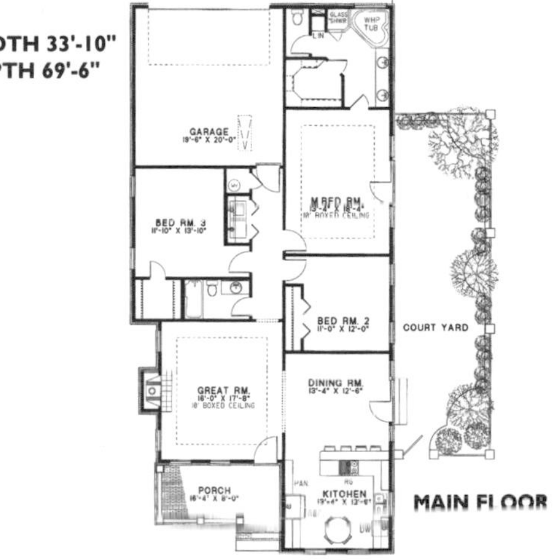
GARAGE
BED RM. 3
M.BED RM.
BED RM. 2
COURT YARD
GREAT RM.
DINING RM.
PORCH
KITCHEN
MAIN FLOOR

ush Master Bedroom Suite

PRICE CODE: C

his plan features:
hree bedrooms
wo full baths
raised, tiled Foyer, with a decorative window, leads
to an expansive Living Room, accented by a tiled fire-
ace and framed by French doors
n efficient Kitchen, with a walk-in Pantry and serving
ır, adjoins the Breakfast and Utility Areas
private Master Bedroom, crowned by a stepped
ɛiling, offering an Atrium door to outside, a huge, walk-
closet, and a luxurious Bath
wo additional Bedrooms, with walk in closets, share a
ll hall Bath
his home is designed with a slab foundation

IN FLOOR — 1,849 SQ. FT.
ɌAGE — 437 SQ. FT.

TOTAL LIVING AREA:
1,849 SQ. FT.

PLAN NO. 92705

WIDTH 60'-0"
DEPTH 57'-4"

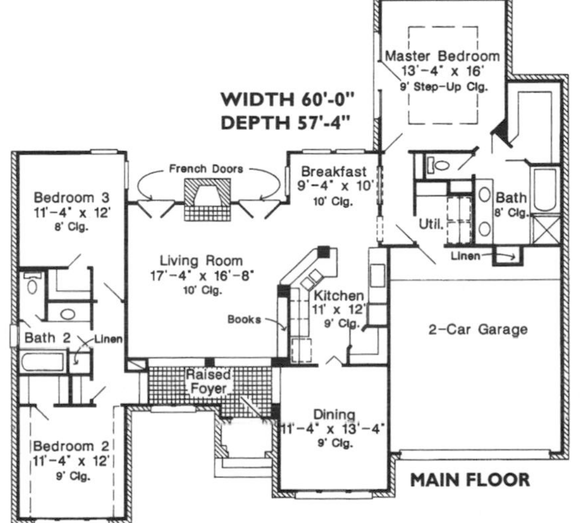
Master Bedroom
13'-4" x 16'
9' Step-Up Clg.
French Doors
Breakfast
9'-4" x 10'
10' Clg.
Bedroom 3
11'-4" x 12'
8' Clg.
Bath
8' Clg.
Util.
Linen
Living Room
17'-4" x 16'-8"
10' Clg.
Kitchen
11' x 12'
9' Clg.
Books
2-Car Garage
Bath 2
Linen
Raised
Foyer
Dining
11'-4" x 13'-4"
9' Clg.
Bedroom 2
11'-4" x 12'
9' Clg.
MAIN FLOOR

PLAN NO.92649

Multiple Gables and a Front Porch

PRICE CODE: B

- This plan features:
  — Three bedrooms
  — Two full and one half baths
- Multiple gables and a cozy front Porch
- A Foyer area that leads to a bright and cheery Great Room capped by a sloped ceiling and highlighted by a fireplace
- The Dining Area includes double hung windows and angles adding light and dimension to the room
- A functional Kitchen providing an abundance of cour space with additional room provided by a Breakfast I
- A rear Porch is accessed from the Dining Area
- A Master Bedroom Suite including a walk-in closet and private Bath
- This home is designed with a basement foundation

MAIN FLOOR — 1,508 SQ. FT.
BASEMENT — 1,439 SQ. FT.
GARAGE — 440 SQ. FT.

TOTAL LIVING AREA:
1,508 SQ. FT.

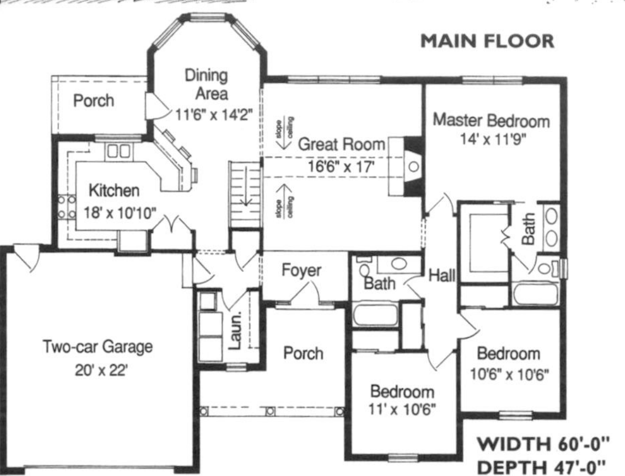
MAIN FLOOR
Porch
Dining Area
11'6" x 14'2"
Master Bedroom
14' x 11'9"
Great Room
16'6" x 17'
Kitchen
18' x 10'10"
Bath
Foyer
Bath
Hall
Laun.
Two-car Garage
20' x 22'
Porch
Bedroom
10'6" x 10'6"
Bedroom
11' x 10'6"
WIDTH 60'-0"
DEPTH 47'-0"

PLAN NO.91592

Cozy Accommodations

PRICE CODE: E

- This plan features:
  — Three bedrooms
  — Two full and one half baths
- A terrific, two-sided fireplace accentuating the Den a Family Room
- This home is designed with a crawlspace foundation

FIRST FLOOR — 1,371 SQ. FT.
SECOND FLOOR — 916 SQ. FT.
GARAGE — 427 SQ. FT.

TOTAL LIVING AREA:
2,287 SQ. FT.

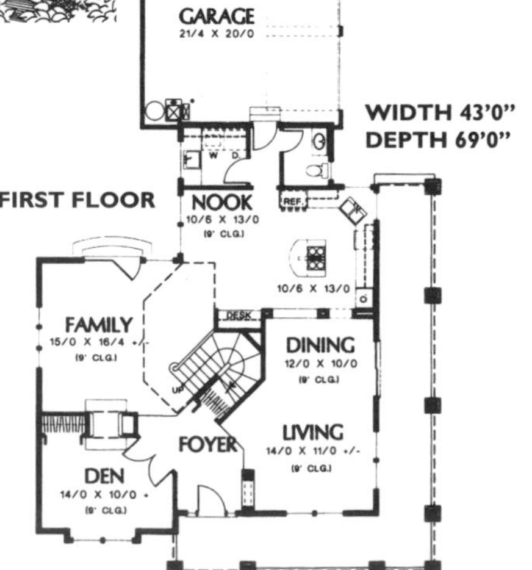
GARAGE
21/4 X 20/0
WIDTH 43'0"
DEPTH 69'0"
FIRST FLOOR
NOOK
10/6 X 13/0
10/6 X 13/0
FAMILY
15/0 X 16/4
DINING
12/0 X 10/0
FOYER
LIVING
14/0 X 11/0
DEN
14/0 X 10/0

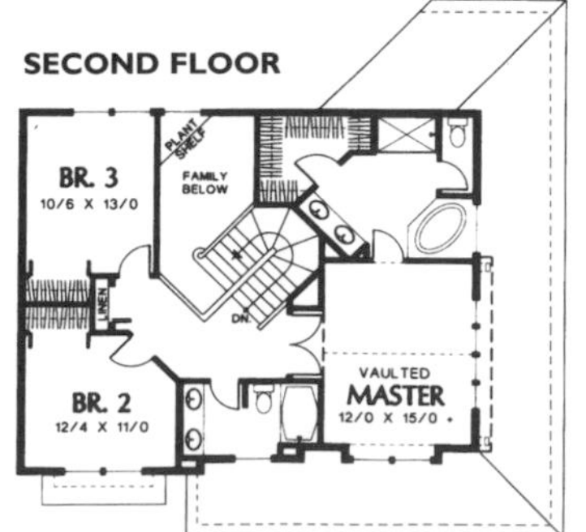
SECOND FLOOR
BR. 3
10/6 X 13/0
FAMILY BELOW
BR. 2
12/4 X 11/0
VAULTED
MASTER
12/0 X 15/0

Outstanding Appeal

PRICE CODE: K

PLAN NO.98437

ıis plan features:
- ve bedrooms
- ›ur full and one half baths
- ıe Formal Dining and Living Rooms are off ȝ two-story Foyer
- Butler's Pantry located between the Kitchen and ɪmal Dining Room for convenience
- ı Island Kitchen with a walk-in Pantry and a peninsula ɯnter/serving bar highlight this room
- ıe Breakfast Room accesses the backyard through a ɛnch door
- ɛ second floor Master Suite is topped by a tray ceiling the Bedroom and by a vaulted ceiling above the ɪting Room and Bath
- ıree additional Bedrooms with private access to full ıths and closet space
- ıis home is designed with basement, crawlspace and ıb foundation options

ɪ FLOOR — 2,002 SQ. FT.
ɔND FLOOR — 1,947 SQ. FT.
ɛMENT — 2,002 SQ. FT.
ʌAGE — 737 SQ. FT.

TOTAL LIVING AREA:
3,949 SQ. FT.

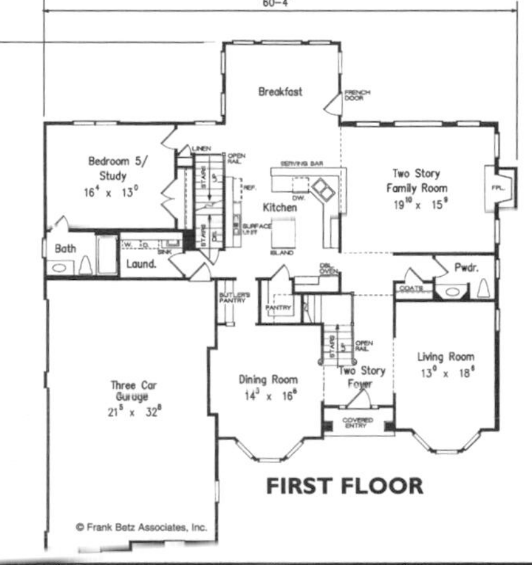

60'-4"
63'-6"
Breakfast
Bedroom 5/ Study
16⁴ x 13⁰
Kitchen
Two Story Family Room
19¹⁰ x 15⁸
Bath
Laund.
Pwdr.
Three Car Garage
21⁵ x 32⁸
Dining Room
14³ x 16⁸
Two Story Foyer
Living Room
13⁰ x 18⁸
FIRST FLOOR
© Frank Betz Associates, Inc.

Vaulted Sitting Room
14⁵ x 10⁰
Vaulted Master Bath
Master Suite
14⁵ x 17⁰
Family Room Below
W.I.c.
Bedroom 4
13⁰ x 13⁰
Bedroom 2
13⁰ x 13⁰
Vaulted Bedroom 3
13³ x 14⁴
Foyer Below
Bath
W.I.c.
SECOND FLOOR

Cozy Bungalow

PRICE CODE: B

PLAN NO.97500

ıis plan features:
- hree bedrooms
- wo full and one half baths
- ıe cover front Porch adds charm
- ıe Master Bedroom includes a private Bath and a alk-in closet
- ıe secondary Bedrooms upstairs share a full Bath
- ıe U-shaped Kitchen has a convenient serving bar
- vo window walls brighten the Breakfast Nook
- ıe Family Room has a warm ɔrner fireplace
- ıis home is designed with a ɛr/post foundation

ɪT FLOOR — 1,050 SQ. FT.
ɔOND FLOOR — 458 SQ. FT.

TOTAL LIVING AREA:
1,508 SQ. FT.

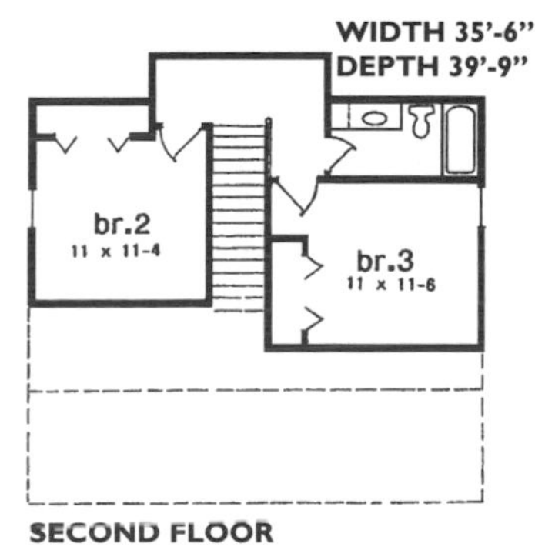

WIDTH 35'-6"
DEPTH 39'-9"
br.2
11 x 11-4
br.3
11 x 11-6
SECOND FLOOR

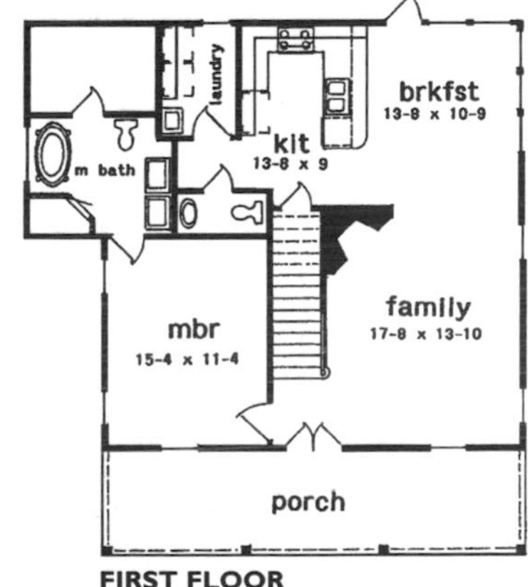

laundry
brkfst
13-8 x 10-9
kit
13-8 x 9
m bath
mbr
15-4 x 11-4
family
17-8 x 13-10
porch
FIRST FLOOR

PLAN NO. 98457

Modern Luxury

Price Code: F

- This plan features:
- — Four bedrooms
- — Three full and one half baths
- A feeling of spaciousness is created by the two-story Foyer and volume ceilings
- Arched openings and decorative windows enhance the Dining and Living Rooms
- The efficient Kitchen has a work island, a Pantry and a Breakfast Area open to the Family Room
- The plush Master Suite features a tray ceiling above and an alcove of windows
- This home is designed with basement and crawlspace foundation options

FIRST FLOOR — 1,883 SQ. FT.
SECOND FLOOR — 803 SQ. FT.
BASEMENT — 1,883 SQ. FT.
GARAGE — 495 SQ. FT.

TOTAL LIVING AREA:
2,686 SQ. FT.

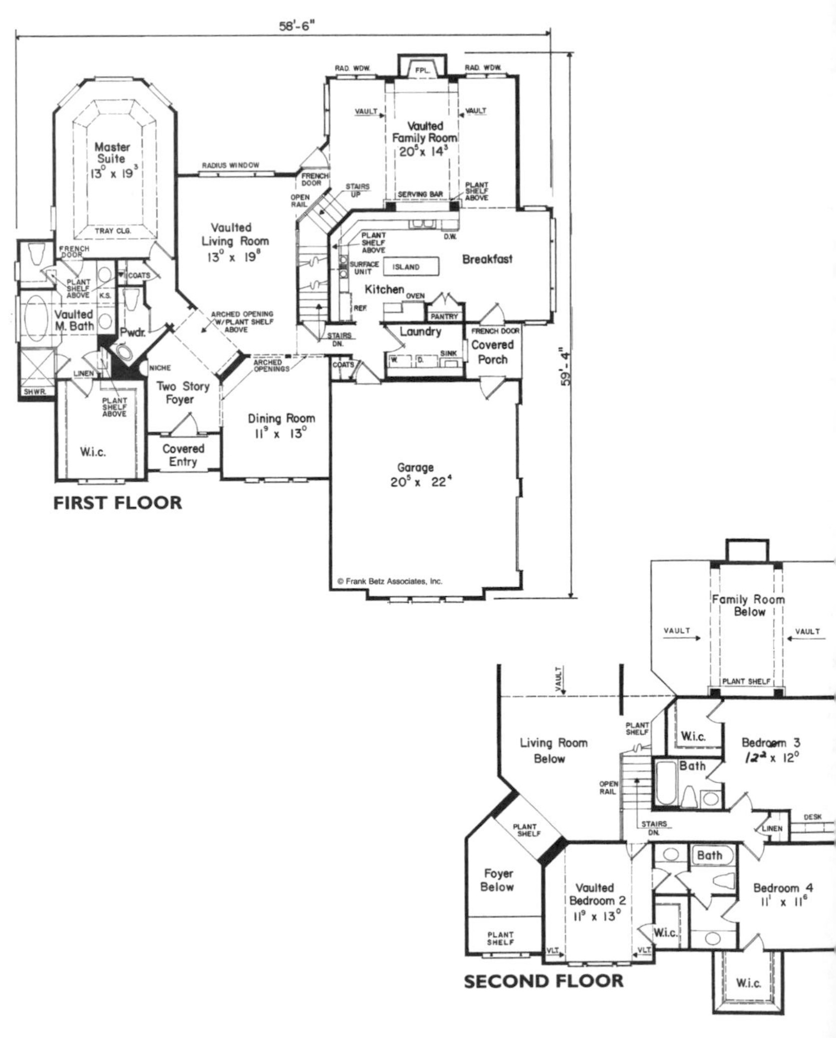
58'-6"
59'-4"
Master Suite 13⁰ x 19³
Vaulted Living Room 13⁰ x 19⁹
Vaulted Family Room 20⁵ x 14³
Breakfast
Kitchen
ISLAND
PANTRY
Laundry
Covered Porch
Vaulted M. Bath
Pwdr.
Two Story Foyer
Dining Room 11⁹ x 13⁰
W.i.c.
Covered Entry
Garage 20⁵ x 22⁴
FIRST FLOOR
© Frank Betz Associates, Inc.
Family Room Below
Living Room Below
Bedroom 3 12³ x 12⁰
Bath
Foyer Below
Vaulted Bedroom 2 11⁹ x 13⁰
Bedroom 4 11¹ x 11⁶
W.i.c.
SECOND FLOOR

Ranch Provides Great Kitchen Area

PRICE CODE: A

PLAN NO.34054

his plan features:
- 'hree bedrooms
- 'wo full baths
- Dining Room with sliding glass doors to the backyard
- ccess to the Garage through the Laundry Room
- Master Bedroom with a private full Bath
- two-car Garage
- his home is designed with basement, slab and rawlspace foundation options

IN FLOOR — 1,400 SQ. FT.
SEMENT — 1,400 SQ. FT.
RAGE — 528 SQ. FT.

TOTAL LIVING AREA:
1,400 SQ. FT.

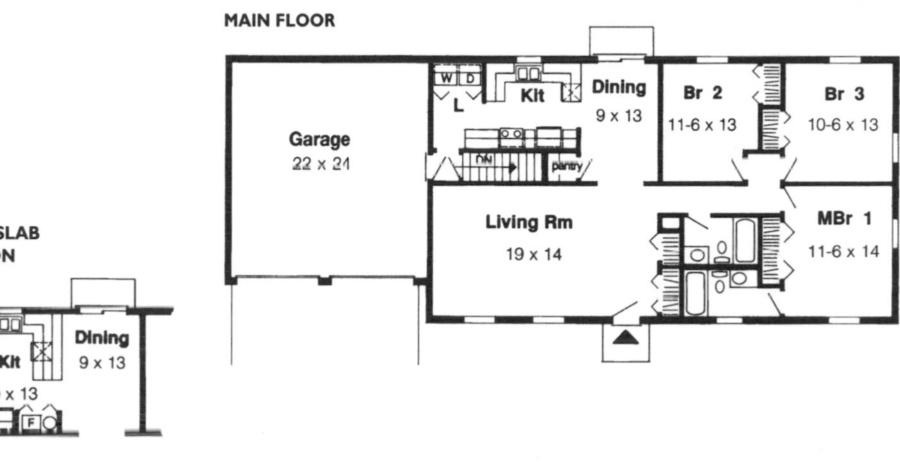

MAIN FLOOR
Garage
22 x 21
W D
L
Kit
Dining
9 x 13
Br 2
11-6 x 13
Br 3
10-6 x 13
DN
pantry
Living Rm
19 x 14
MBr 1
11-6 x 14
CRAWLSPACE/SLAB
FOUNDATION
OPTION
W D
L
Kit
10 x 13
Dining
9 x 13
F

Mind Your Manor

PRICE CODE: I

PLAN NO.98514

his plan features:
- 'ive bedrooms
- Two full, one three-quarter and one half baths
- 'rom the front covered Porch enter into the ntry/Gallery which features a grand spiral staircase
- n the front of the house find the formal Living Room nd Dining Room, each with two palladian windows
- 'he Study has built-in book cases centered etween a window
- 'he large Family Room has a fireplace and a built in tereo cabinet
- 'he bayed Breakfast Nook has a door that leads into the ackyard covered Patio
- 'he first floor Master Bedroom has two walk in closets vith a built-in chest of drawers and a Bath with a athedral ceiling
- 'his home is designed with crawlspace and slab oundation options

ST FLOOR — 2,208 SQ. FT.
OND FLOOR — 1,173 SQ. FT.
NUS — 224 SQ. FT.
RAGE — 520 SQ. FT.

TOTAL LIVING AREA:
3,381 SQ. FT.

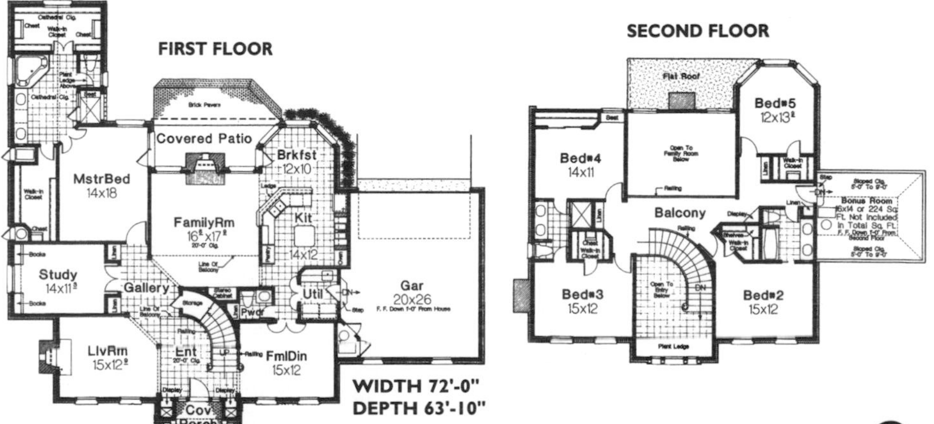

FIRST FLOOR
Covered Patio
Brkfst
12x10
MstrBed
14x18
FamilyRm
16⁸x17⁸
Kit
14x12
Study
14x11⁸
Gallery
Util
Gar
20x26
Pwdr
LivRm
15x12⁸
Ent
FmlDin
15x12
Cov. Porch
WIDTH 72'-0"
DEPTH 63'-10"
SECOND FLOOR
Flat Roof
Bed#5
12x13⁸
Bed#4
14x11
Balcony
Bonus Room
Bed#3
15x12
Bed#2
15x12

PLAN NO. 20156

Family Favorite

PRICE CODE: A

- This plan features:
  - — Three bedrooms
  - — Two full baths
- An open arrangement with the Dining Room that combines with ten-foot ceilings to make the Living Room seem more spacious
- Glass on three sides of the Dining Room which overlooks the Deck
- An efficient, compact Kitchen with a built-in Pantry and peninsula counter
- A Master Suite with a romantic window seat, a compartmentalized private Bath and a walk-in closet
- This home is designed with basement, slab and crawl-space foundation options

MAIN FLOOR — 1,359 SQ. FT.
BASEMENT — 1,359 SQ. FT.
GARAGE — 501 SQ. FT.

TOTAL LIVING AREA:
1,359 SQ. FT.

WIDTH 58'-0"
DEPTH 34'-4"

CRAWLSPACE/SLAB FOUNDATION OPTION

MAIN FLOOR

Deck
Dining 11-0 x 11-2
Br #2 10-10 x 11-10
Den/Br #3 10-0 x 11-10
Optional Door Location
Decor. Ceiling
Kit 10-0 x 11-2
Ldry
Solid Wall w/ Opt. Door Location
Plant Ledge
Living Rm 14-10 x 17-0
10' clg
Decor. Ceiling
MBr #1 11-7 x 13-0
Seat
Garage 20-4 x 21-8

PLAN NO. 90412

No Wasted Space

PRICE CODE: A

- This plan features:
  - — Three bedrooms
  - — Two full baths
- A centrally located Living Room with a cathedral ceil exposed wood beams, and large areas of fixed glass
- The Living and Dining areas separated by a massive stone fireplace
- A secluded Master Suite with a walk-in closet and private Master Bath
- An efficient Kitchen with a convenient Laundry Area
- This home is designed with basement, slab and crawl-space foundation options

MAIN FLOOR — 1,454 SQ. FT.

TOTAL LIVING AREA:
1,454 SQ. FT.

67'-0"
34'-10"

CARPORT 20'-0"x20'-0"
STORAGE
STORAGE
KITCHEN 15'-2"x8'-8"
DINING 15'-0"x12'-0"
BEDROOM 15'-2"x11'-0"
BATH
BATH
M. BEDROOM 15'-2"x13'-6"
CATHEDRAL CEILING
LIVING 15'-0"x21'-10"
BEDROOM 12'-8"x11'-0"
DECK

MAIN FLOOR

PLAN NO. 92666

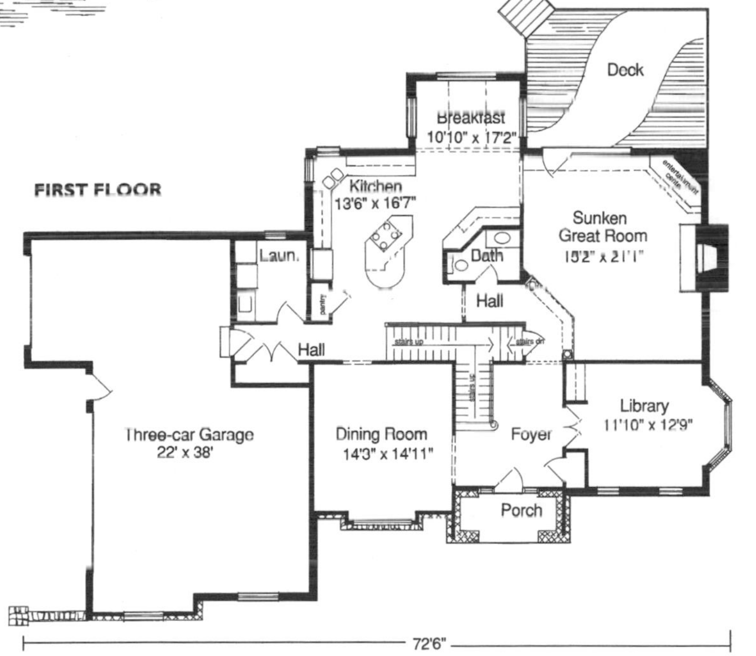
FIRST FLOOR
Deck
Breakfast
10'10" x 17'2"
Kitchen
13'6" x 16'7"
Laun.
Bath
Sunken
Great Room
15'2" x 21'1"
Hall
Hall
Three-car Garage
22' x 38'
Dining Room
14'3" x 14'11"
Foyer
Library
11'10" x 12'9"
Porch
55'8"
72'6"

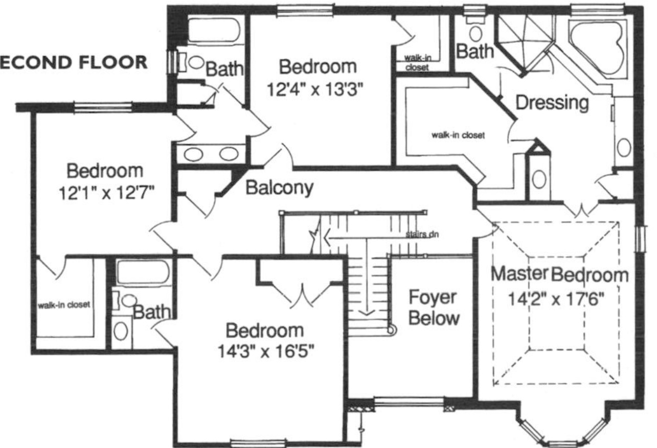
SECOND FLOOR
Bath
Bedroom
12'4" x 13'3"
Bath
Dressing
walk-in closet
Bedroom
12'1" x 12'7"
Balcony
Master Bedroom
14'2" x 17'6"
Foyer
Below
walk-in closet
Bath
Bedroom
14'3" x 16'5"

The Ultimate in Style

Price Code: I

- This plan features:
- — Four bedrooms
- — Three full and one half baths
- A variety of exterior materials combine with a well planned interior for impeccable style
- The Kitchen is open, has ample counter space and features a center island
- Upstairs find the Master Bedroom, which has a walk-in closet and a sumptuous Bath
- Three additional Bedrooms all have access to Baths
- This home is designed with a basement foundation

FIRST FLOOR — 1,678 SQ. FT.
SECOND FLOOR — 1,766 SQ. FT.
BASEMENT — 1,639 SQ. FT.
GARAGE — 761 SQ. FT.

TOTAL LIVING AREA:
3,444 SQ. FT.

PLAN NO.92123

Wraparound Porch

PRICE CODE: E

- This plan features:
  - — Three bedrooms
  - — Two full and one half baths
- The Entry opens directly into the Dining Area and the Den
- A large Utility Room is conveniently located by the stairs and the Garage
- Light cascades through the window-lined, octagonal Nook, into the Kitchen and the Gathering Room
- A Sitting Area, with private Balcony, embellishes the impressive Master Suite
- This home is designed with a crawlspace foundation

FIRST FLOOR — 1,170 SQ. FT.
SECOND FLOOR — 1,091 SQ. FT.
BONUS — 240 SQ. FT.
GARAGE — 707 SQ. FT.

TOTAL LIVING AREA:
2,261 SQ. FT.

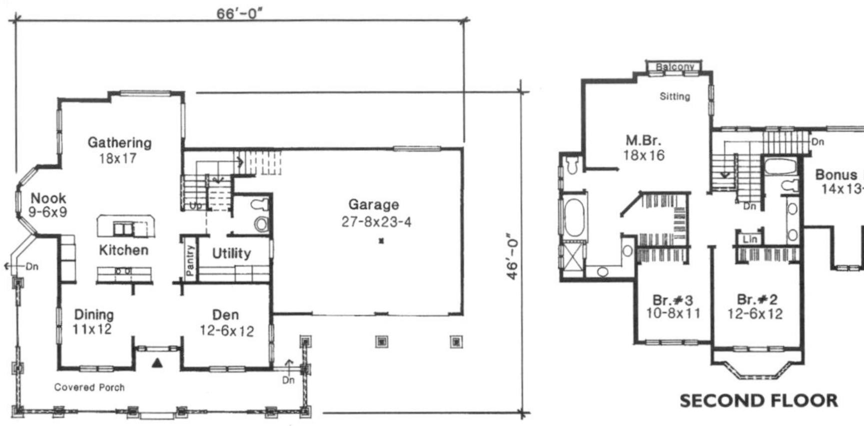

66'-0"
46'-0"
Gathering 18x17
Nook 9-6x9
Kitchen
Pantry
Utility
Garage 27-8x23-4
Dining 11x12
Den 12-6x12
Covered Porch
Dn
Balcony
Sitting
M.Br. 18x16
Bonus Rm. 14x13-6
Lin
Br.#3 10-8x11
Br.#2 12-6x12

SECOND FLOOR

FIRST FLOOR

PLAN NO.51008

Cozy Convenience

PRICE CODE: A

- This plan features:
  - — Three bedrooms
  - — Two full baths
- The Entry leads immediately into the Dining Room or down the Hall to the Family Room
- Counter space defines the Kitchen
- The Bedrooms, each with ample closet space, share the privacy of the second floor
- The Laundry Room is conveniently located at the cor of the Bedrooms
- A focal point fireplace makes the Family Room a war place for family to gather
- This home is designed with a basement foundation

FIRST FLOOR — 748 SQ. FT.
SECOND FLOOR — 738 SQ. FT.
BASEMENT — 748 SQ. FT.
GARAGE — 480 SQ. FT.

TOTAL LIVING AREA:
1,486 SQ. FT.

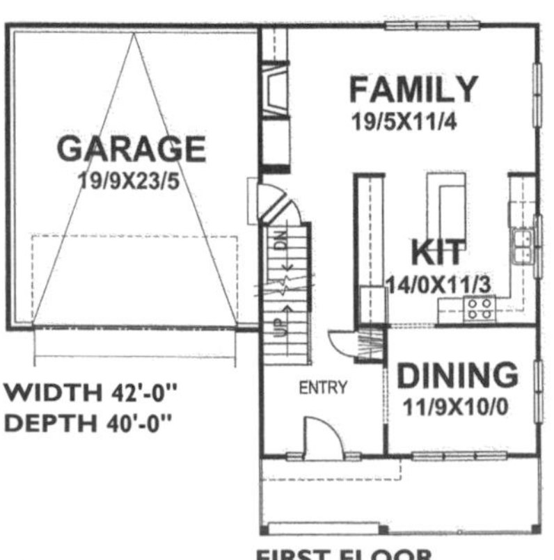

GARAGE 19/9X23/5
FAMILY 19/5X11/4
KIT 14/0X11/3
DINING 11/9X10/0
ENTRY
WIDTH 42'-0"
DEPTH 40'-0"

FIRST FLOOR

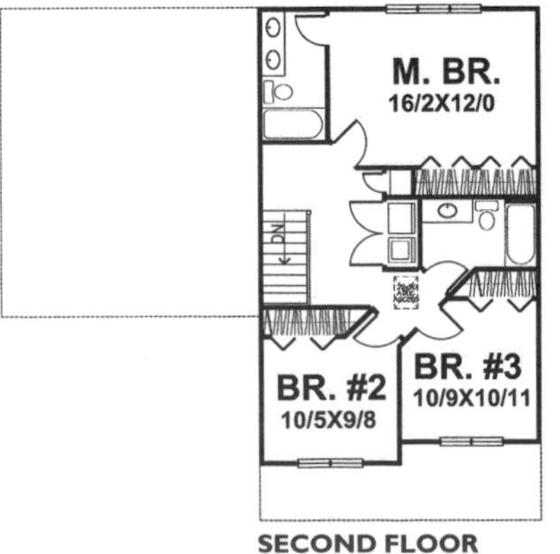

M. BR. 16/2X12/0
BR. #2 10/5X9/8
BR. #3 10/9X10/11

SECOND FLOOR

Impeccable Style

PRICE CODE: D

This plan features:
- Three bedrooms
- Two full and one half baths
- 3rick, stone, and interesting rooflines showcase the mpeccable style of this home
- nside a deluxe staircase highlights the Foyer
- The Dining Room has a bay window at one end and columns at the other
- The U-shaped Kitchen has an island in its center
- The two-story Great Room has a warm fireplace
- The shape of the Master Bedroom adds to its character
- Jpstairs find two Bedrooms and a full Bath
- This home is designed with a basement foundation

ST FLOOR — 1,706 SQ. FT.
COND FLOOR — 492 SQ. FT.
SEMENT — 1,706 SQ. FT.

TOTAL LIVING AREA:
2,198 SQ. FT.

PLAN NO.97710

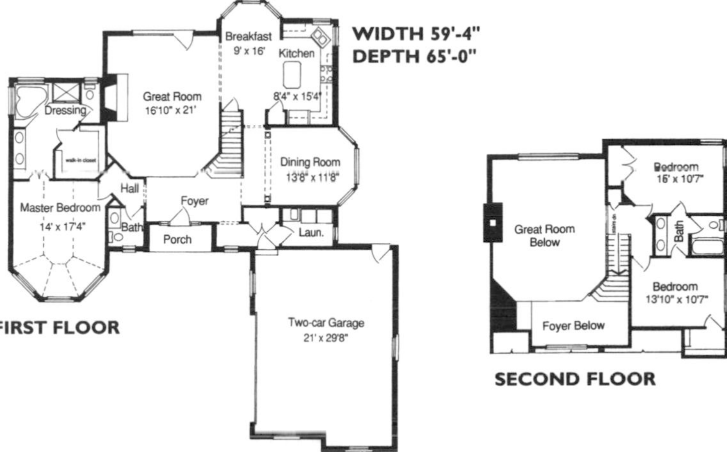
WIDTH 59'-4"
DEPTH 65'-0"
Breakfast
9' x 16'
Kitchen
8'4" x 15'4"
Great Room
16'10" x 21'
Dressing
Dining Room
13'8" x 11'8"
Hall
Foyer
Master Bedroom
14' x 17'4"
Bath
Porch
Laun.
Two-car Garage
21' x 29'8"
FIRST FLOOR
Bedroom
16' x 10'7"
Great Room Below
Bath
Bedroom
13'10" x 10'7"
Foyer Below
SECOND FLOOR

Expansion Ready

PRICE CODE: B

This plan features:
- Three bedrooms
- Two full and one half baths
- Columns accent the entrance into the Dining Room
- The efficient Kitchen includes an island/snack bar and a Nook Area
- Bonus area for future expansion is located next to the secondary Bedrooms
- This home is designed with basement, slab, and crawlspace foundation options

ST FLOOR — 1,155 SQ. FT.
COND FLOOR — 529 SQ. FT.
NUS — 380 SQ. FT.
RAGE — 400 SQ. FT.

TOTAL LIVING AREA:
1,684 SQ. FT.

PLAN NO.82010

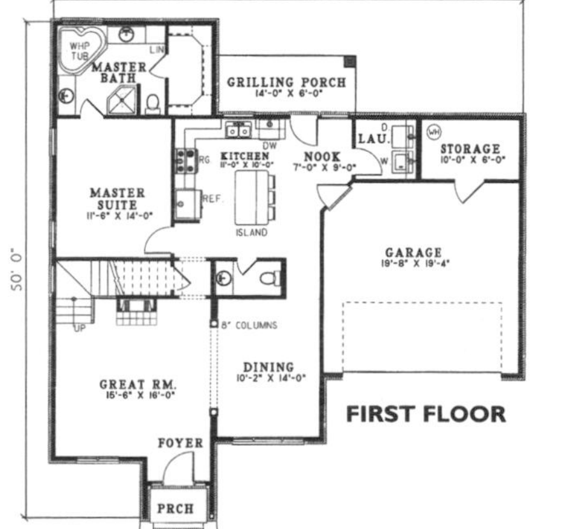
47' 0"
MASTER BATH
GRILLING PORCH
14'-0" X 6'-0"
KITCHEN
NOOK
7'-0" X 9'-0"
LAU.
STORAGE
10'-0" X 6'-0"
MASTER SUITE
11'-6" X 14'-0"
ISLAND
GARAGE
19'-8" X 19'-4"
50' 0"
8" COLUMNS
DINING
10'-2" X 14'-0"
GREAT RM.
15'-6" X 16'-0"
FOYER
PRCH
FIRST FLOOR

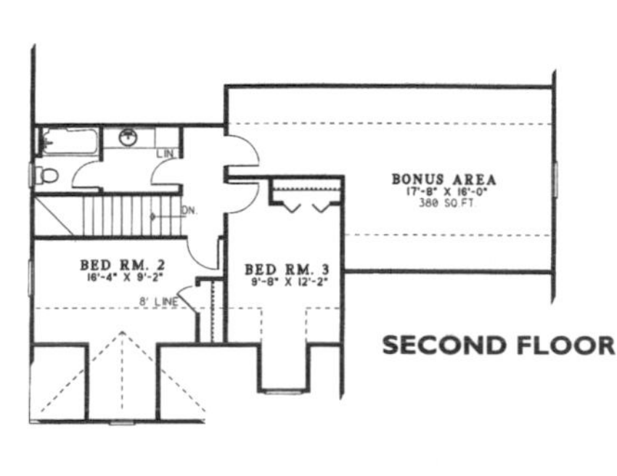
BONUS AREA
17'-8" X 16'-0"
380 SQ FT
BED RM. 2
16'-4" X 9'-2"
BED RM. 3
9'-8" X 12'-2"
SECOND FLOOR

PLAN NO.34003

Delightful, Compact Home

PRICE CODE: A

- This plan features:
  - Three bedrooms
  - Two full baths
- A fireplaced Living Room brightened by a wonderful picture window
- A counter island featuring double sinks separating the Kitchen and Dining Areas
- A Master Bedroom that includes a private Master Bath and double closets
- Two additional Bedrooms with ample closet space that share a full Bath
- This home is designed with basement, slab and crawlspace foundation options

MAIN FLOOR — 1,146 SQ. FT.

TOTAL LIVING AREA:
1,146 SQ. FT.

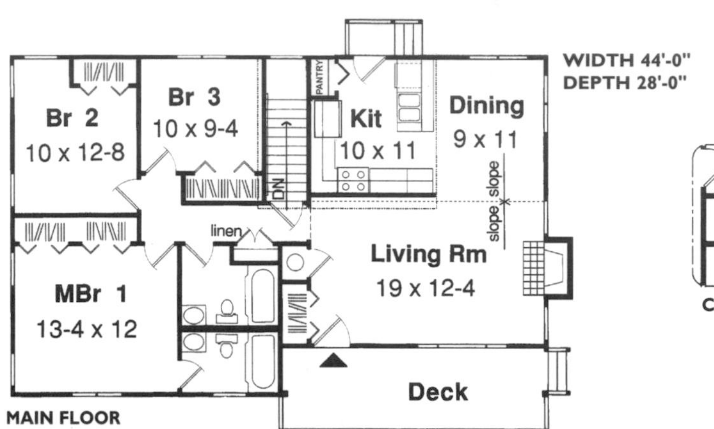

WIDTH 44'-0"
DEPTH 28'-0"
Br 2
10 x 12-8
Br 3
10 x 9-4
PANTRY
Kit
10 x 11
Dining
9 x 11
DN
slope
slope
linen
Living Rm
19 x 12-4
MBr 1
13-4 x 12
Deck
MAIN FLOOR
W
D
CRAWLSPACE/SLAB
FOUNDATION
OPTION

PLAN NO.51000

More Than A Cozy Cottage

PRICE CODE: B

- This plan features:
  - Three bedrooms
  - Two full baths
- The Entry opens directly into the Living Room, presenting an instant welcome
- Centrally located, a Den provides space for more private activities
- Lined with windows, the Dining Room offers a sunlit or moonlit dining experience
- Ample counter space, including casual eating bar, surrounds the Kitchen
- The Master Bath houses features of convenience such as its large walk-in closet and double vanity
- This home is designed with a basement foundation

MAIN FLOOR — 1,548 SQ. FT.
BASEMENT — 1,548 SQ. FT.

TOTAL LIVING AREA:
1,548 SQ. FT.

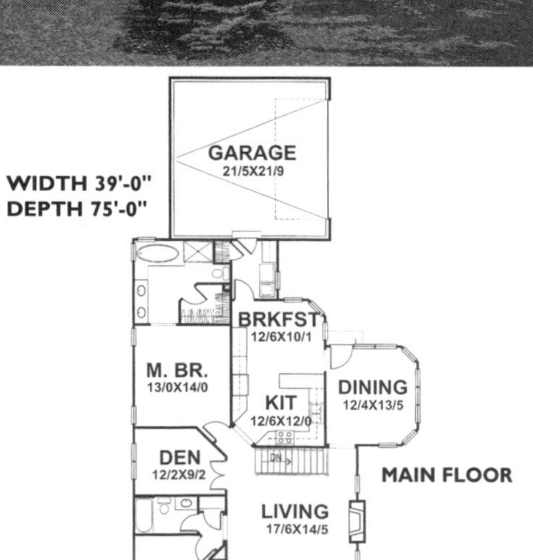

WIDTH 39'-0"
DEPTH 75'-0"
GARAGE
21/5X21/9
BRKFST
12/6X10/1
M. BR.
13/0X14/0
KIT
12/6X12/0
DINING
12/4X13/5
DEN
12/2X9/2
DN
MAIN FLOOR
LIVING
17/6X14/5
BR. #2
10/0X11/6
ENTRY

Terrific Kid's Nook

PRICE CODE: C

PLAN NO. 82021

his plan features:
- 'hree bedrooms
- 'wo full baths
- combination Dining, Kitchen, and Nook living space
- he Great Room includes a fireplace flanked by ıilt-in shelves
- his home is designed with basement, slab, and crawl- ›ace foundation options

IN FLOOR — 1,848 SQ. FT.
ꝶAGE — 429 SQ. FT.
:CHES — 430 SQ. FT.

TOTAL LIVING AREA:
1,848 SQ. FT.

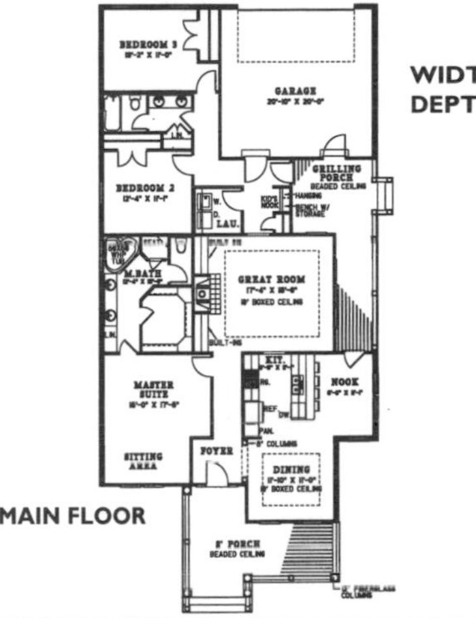

MAIN FLOOR

WIDTH 38'-0"
DEPTH 79'-6"

A Sense of Stature

PRICE CODE: H

PLAN NO. 97400

'his plan features:
- 'our bedrooms
- Three full and one half baths
- bayed Turret and bold double doors add stature › this home
- bay shaped Study is located in the front of the home
- 'he impressive Dining Room features a distinctive front window
- 'he unique Living Room has a fireplace and windows ıat overlook the rear Porch
- 'he Family Room, Breakfast Nook, and Kitchen are rranged in an open manner
- 'he first floor Master Bedroom has a decorative ceiling lus his and her closets
- 'his home is designed with basement and slab oundation options
- lternate foundation options available at an dditional charge. Please call 1-800-235-5700 or more information.

ST FLOOR — 2,112 SQ. FT.
:OND FLOOR — 982 SQ. FT.
SEMENT — 2,112 SQ. FT.
RAGE — 650 SQ. FT.

TOTAL LIVING AREA:
3,094 SQ. FT.

WIDTH 67'-1"
DEPTH 65'-10"

FAMILY ROOM
BREAKFAST
KITCHEN
UTILITY
PORCH
LIVING ROOM
MASTER BEDROOM
HIS CLO.
PWDR
MASTER BATH
ENTRY
DINING ROOM
PORCH
STUDY
HER CLO.
3-CAR GARAGE
FIRST FLOOR

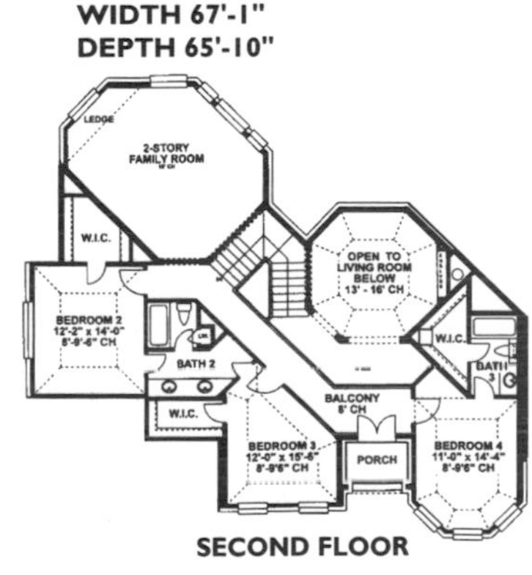

LEDGE
2-STORY FAMILY ROOM
W.I.C.
OPEN TO LIVING ROOM BELOW
BEDROOM 2
BATH 2
W.I.C.
BALCONY
BEDROOM 3
PORCH
BEDROOM 4
SECOND FLOOR

PLAN NO.51001

Window-Lined

PRICE CODE: C

- This plan features:
- — Three bedrooms
- — Two full and one half baths
- Inviting covered Porches, brick, and accent windows give this home a quaint appearance
- The Entry opens to the right wing Living and Dining Rooms and back to the Breakfast Nook and cooking a
- A Sunroom and a Patio offers outdoor living, no matter the weather
- The Bedrooms, all with generous closet space, share the privacy of the second floor
- The Master Suite features a luxurious, private Bath and walk-in closet
- This home is designed with a basement foundation

FIRST FLOOR — 1,232 SQ. FT.
SECOND FLOOR — 975 SQ. FT.
BASEMENT — 1,232 SQ. FT.
GARAGE — 484 SQ. FT.
PORCH — 128 SQ. FT.

TOTAL LIVING AREA:
2,207 SQ. FT.

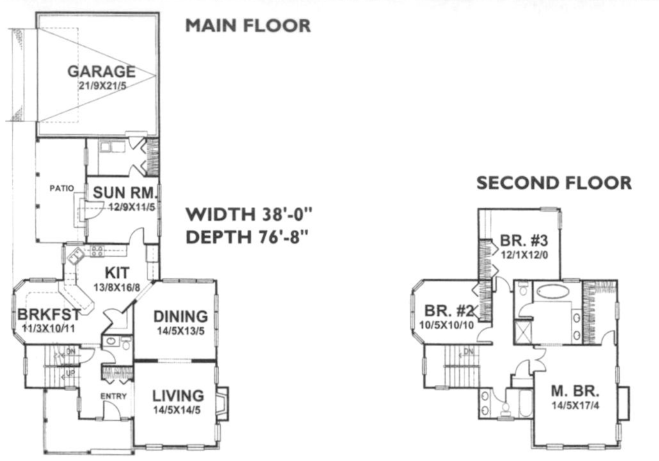
MAIN FLOOR
GARAGE
21/9X21/5
PATIO
SUN RM.
12/9X11/5
WIDTH 38'-0"
DEPTH 76'-8"
KIT
13/8X16/8
BRKFST
11/3X10/11
DINING
14/5X13/5
ENTRY
LIVING
14/5X14/5
SECOND FLOOR
BR. #3
12/1X12/0
BR. #2
10/5X10/10
M. BR.
14/5X17/4

PLAN NO.51006

Spacious Garage

PRICE CODE: B

- This plan features:
- — Four bedrooms
- — Two full baths
- Isolated on the first floor, a fourth Bedroom would make an ideal Den
- The open design of the Living and Dining Rooms allows family to always be nearby
- The Master Suite shares the second floor with two Secondary Bedrooms
- The Kitchen is defined by generous counter space
- This home is designed with a basement foundation

FIRST FLOOR — 835 SQ. FT.
SECOND FLOOR — 803 SQ. FT.
BASEMENT — 835 SQ. FT.
PORCH — 140 SQ. FT.

TOTAL LIVING AREA:
1,638 SQ. FT.

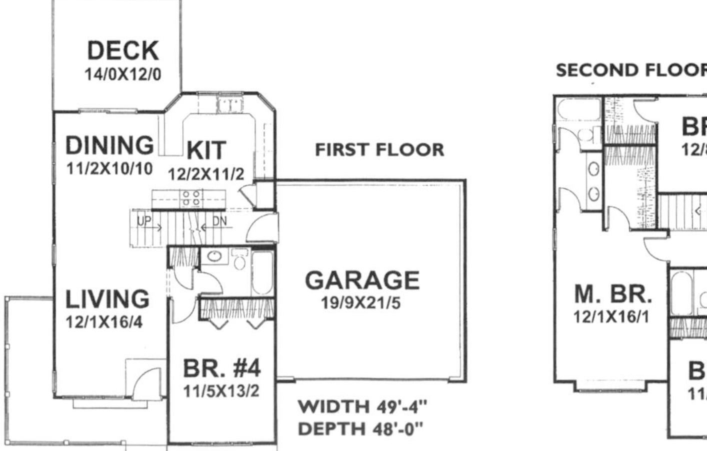
DECK
14/0X12/0
DINING
11/2X10/10
KIT
12/2X11/2
FIRST FLOOR
UP
DN
GARAGE
19/9X21/5
LIVING
12/1X16/4
BR. #4
11/5X13/2
WIDTH 49'-4"
DEPTH 48'-0"
SECOND FLOOR
BR. #3
12/8X10/3
DN
M. BR.
12/1X16/1
BR. #2
11/5X10/4

A Great Idea

PRICE CODE: E

This plan features:
- Three bedrooms
- Two full and one half baths
- French doors lead from the Dining Room to the Porch
- The Kitchen has plenty of counter space
- The Master Suite features a tray ceiling
- A Loft upstairs would make a great play area for the kids
- A Deck in the rear makes for wonderful entertaining
- This home is designed with a crawlspace foundation

RST FLOOR — 1,670 SQ. FT.
ECOND FLOOR — 763 SQ. FT.
ARAGE — 502 SQ. FT.

TOTAL LIVING AREA:
2,433 SQ. FT.

PLAN NO.96921

PATIO / DECK
MASTER SUITE 14'-0" x 14'-8"
BREAKFAST 9'-10" x 13'-2"
GATHERING ROOM 15'-0" x 18'-0"
W.I.C.
MASTER BATH
KITCHEN 13'-0" x 12'-10"
P.
LAUNDRY
DINING ROOM 13'-0" x 12'-2"
GARAGE 23'-8" x 20'-4"
UP
FOYER
PDR.
FRONT PORCH
FIRST FLOOR
WIDTH 53'-0"
DEPTH 54'-0"
SUITE 3 13'-0" x 11'-2"
OPEN TO BELOW
BATH
LOFT 15'-0" x 10'-8"
ATTIC
DN
SUITE 2 13'-0" x 11'-2"
OPEN TO BELOW
PLANT LEDGE
SECOND FLOOR

Two Fireplaces

PRICE CODE: D

This plan features:
- Three bedrooms
- Two full and one half baths
- A facade defined by a covered Porch, dormers, and brick is of artistic interest
- Windows line the home, filtering natural light throughout
- The L-shaped Kitchen with center island overlooks the Breakfast Nook, which features a bay window and a fireplace
- Elegant columns separate the formal Dining Room from the Living Room
- The Master Suite enjoys the privacy of its own wing, a roomy walk-in closet, and a luxurious Bath
- The Secondary Bedrooms share the second floor and a hall Bath with double vanity
- This home is designed with a basement foundation

IRST FLOOR — 1,543 SQ. FT.
ECOND FLOOR — 484 SQ. FT.
ASEMENT — 1,543 SQ. FT.
ARAGE — 400 SQ. FT.
ORCH — 98 SQ. FT.

TOTAL LIVING AREA:
2,027 SQ. FT.

PLAN NO.51002

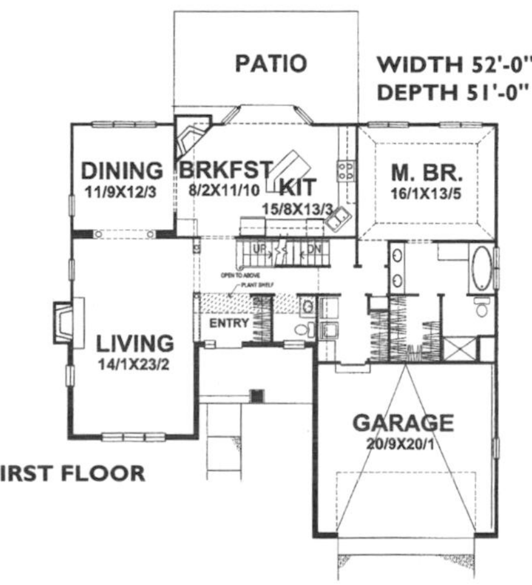
PATIO
WIDTH 52'-0"
DEPTH 51'-0"
DINING 11/9X12/3
BRKFST 8/2X11/10
KIT 15/8X13/3
M. BR. 16/1X13/5
UP
DN
ENTRY
LIVING 14/1X23/2
GARAGE 20/9X20/1
FIRST FLOOR

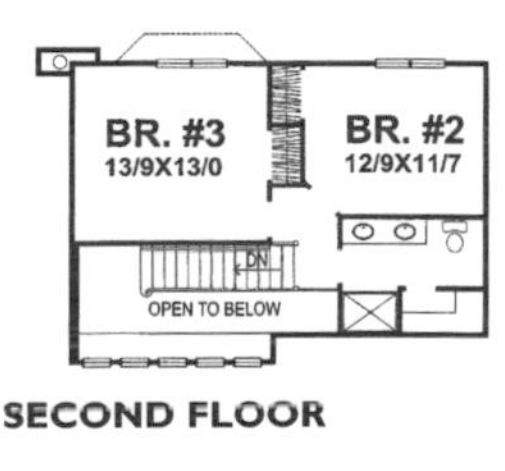
BR. #3 13/9X13/0
BR. #2 12/9X11/7
DN
OPEN TO BELOW
SECOND FLOOR

PLAN NO. 51003

Simple and Sweet

PRICE CODE: A

- This plan features:
  - — Four bedrooms
  - — Two full baths
- The Entry opens directly into the Living Room, presenting an immediate welcome
- The covered Porch and Patio offer places to sit and watch the lazy days of summer go by
- Generous counter space in the Kitchen lends convenience to preparing meals
- Each Bedroom has two windows and ample closet spac
- This home is designed with a basement foundation

FIRST FLOOR — 936 SQ. FT.
SECOND FLOOR — 449 SQ. FT.
BASEMENT — 936 SQ. FT.
PORCH — 120 SQ. FT.

TOTAL LIVING AREA:
1,385 SQ. FT.

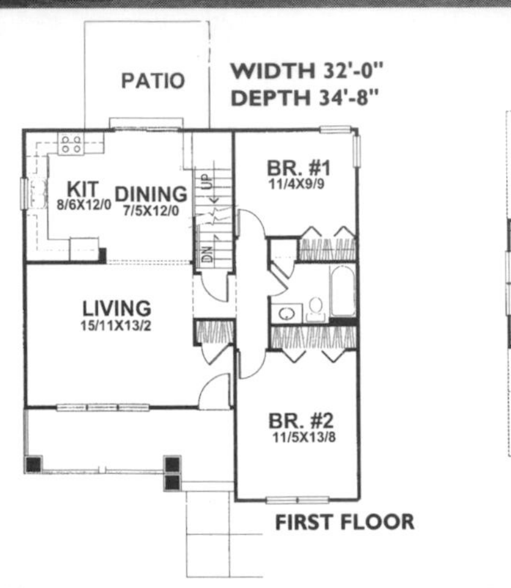

PATIO
WIDTH 32'-0"
DEPTH 34'-8"
KIT
8/6X12/0
DINING
7/5X12/0
BR. #1
11/4X9/9
LIVING
15/11X13/2
BR. #2
11/5X13/8
FIRST FLOOR

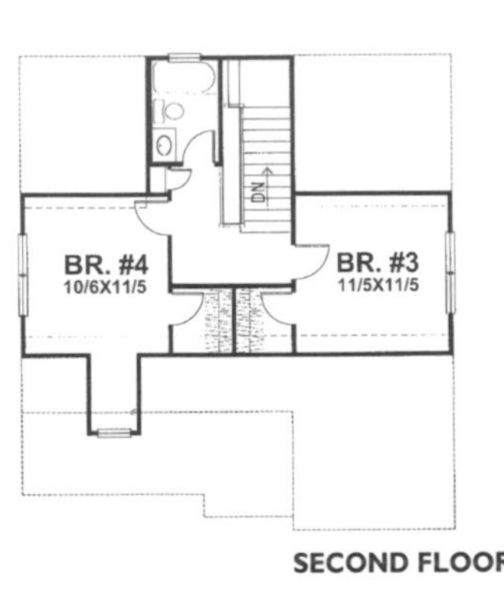

BR. #4
10/6X11/5
BR. #3
11/5X11/5
SECOND FLOOR

PLAN NO. 98518

Elegant Victorian

PRICE CODE: E

- This plan features:
  - — Three bedrooms
  - — Two full and one half baths
- Sit and relax on the front Porch at the end of the day with family and friends
- Serve guests dinner in the bayed Dining Room and ther gather in the Living Room which features a cathedral ceiling
- There is plenty of space for activities in the Family Room which is accented by a fireplace
- The Master Bedroom has a Sitting Area, walk-in closet, and a private Bath
- Two additional Bedrooms share a full Bath, and there is a bonus room upstairs for future expansion
- This plan features a three-car Garage with space for storage
- This home is designed with basement and slab foundation options

FIRST FLOOR — 1,447 SQ. FT.
SECOND FLOOR — 1,008 SQ. FT.
GARAGE — 756 SQ. FT.

TOTAL LIVING AREA:
2,455 SQ. FT.

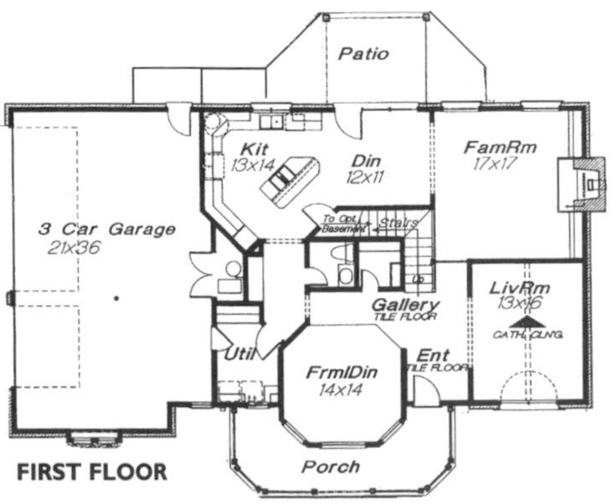

Patio
Kit
13x14
Din
12x11
FamRm
17x17
3 Car Garage
21x36
Gallery
TILE FLOOR
LivRm
13x16
CATH. CLNG.
Util
FrmlDin
14x14
Ent
TILE FLOOR
Porch
FIRST FLOOR

WIDTH 65'-0"
DEPTH 37'-11"

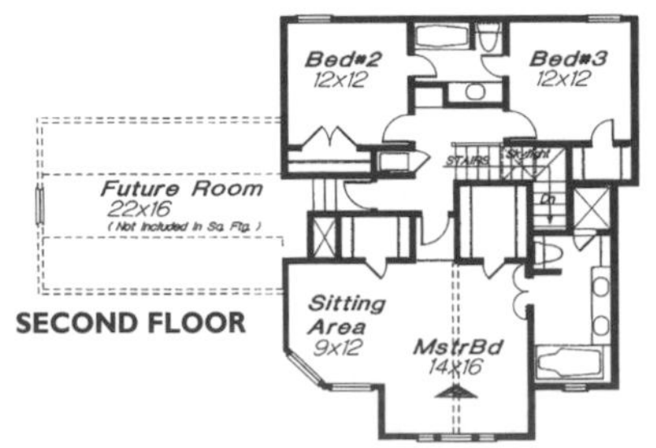

Bed#2
12x12
Bed#3
12x12
Future Room
22x16
(Not Included In Sq. Ftg.)
Sitting
Area
9x12
MstrBd
14x16
SECOND FLOOR

Four Bedrooms

Price Code: B

This plan features:
- Four bedrooms
- Three full baths
- A wraparound Covered Porch adds scale to this home's facade
- The Entry opens directly into the Living Room, instantly welcoming friends and family
- The open design between the Dining and Living Rooms creates a sense of community
- Ample counter space surrounds the Kitchen
- The Master Suite features a roomy walk-in closet and luxurious Bath with double vanity
- A main floor Bedroom would make an ideal Study
- This home is designed with a basement foundation

FIRST FLOOR — 835 SQ. FT.
SECOND FLOOR — 803 SQ. FT.
BASEMENT — 835 SQ. FT.
PORCH — 140 SQ. FT.

TOTAL LIVING AREA:
1,638 SQ. FT.

PLAN NO.51005

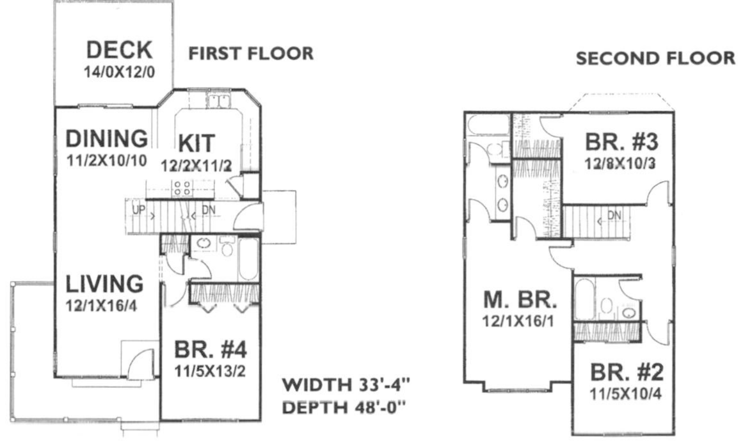

DECK
14/0X12/0
FIRST FLOOR
DINING
11/2X10/10
KIT
12/2X11/2
UP
DN
LIVING
12/1X16/4
BR. #4
11/5X13/2
WIDTH 33'-4"
DEPTH 48'-0"
SECOND FLOOR
BR. #3
12/8X10/3
DN
M. BR.
12/1X16/1
BR. #2
11/5X10/4

Ideal Starter Home

Price Code: A

This plan features:
- Two bedrooms
- One full bath
- Angles, framework, and a column give this home timeless appeal
- The Bedrooms share the left wing of the home, as well as a full Bath
- Counter Space surrounds the Kitchen, which opens to the Dining Area
- A vaulted ceiling adds scale to the Living Room
- This home is designed with a basement foundation

MAIN FLOOR — 936 SQ. FT.
BASEMENT — 936 SQ. FT.

TOTAL LIVING AREA:
936 SQ. FT.

PLAN NO.51004

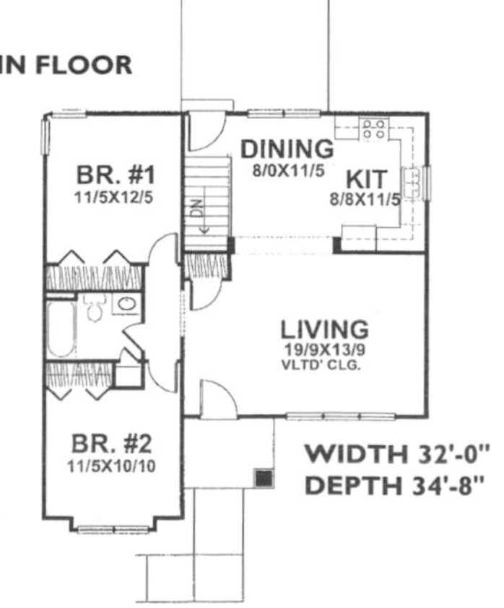

MAIN FLOOR
BR. #1
11/5X12/5
DINING
8/0X11/5
KIT
8/8X11/5
DN
LIVING
19/9X13/9
VLTD' CLG.
BR. #2
11/5X10/10
WIDTH 32'-0"
DEPTH 34'-8"

PLAN NO.92639

Comfortable and Relaxed Environment

Price Code: A

- This plan features:
- — Three bedrooms
- — Two full and one half baths
- An easy flow traffic pattern crating step saving convenience in the interior
- An open stairway adding elegances to the Foyer
- A spacious Great Room and Breakfast Area
- A U-shaped Kitchen with ample counter and storage space
- A Master Suite with a walk-in closet plus a compartmented Bath
- Two additional Bedrooms sharing use of a Bath with skylight
- This home is designed with basement foundation

FIRST FLOOR — 748 SQ. FT.
SECOND FLOOR — 705 SQ. FT.
BASEMENT — 744 SQ. FT.

***TOTAL LIVING AREA:* 1,453 SQ. FT.**

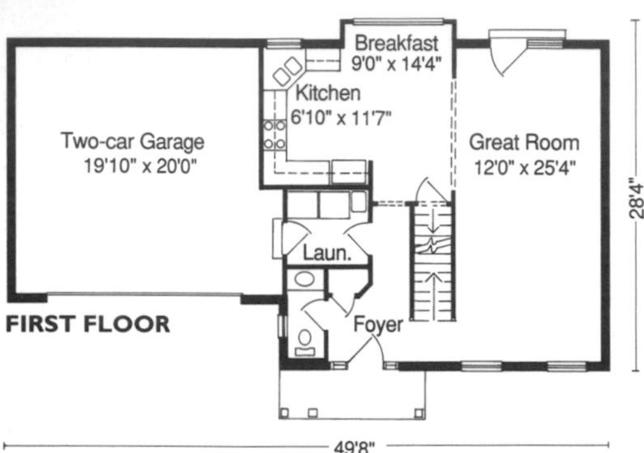

Breakfast
9'0" x 14'4"
Kitchen
6'10" x 11'7"
Two-car Garage
19'10" x 20'0"
Great Room
12'0" x 25'4"
28'4"
Laun.
Foyer
FIRST FLOOR
49'8"

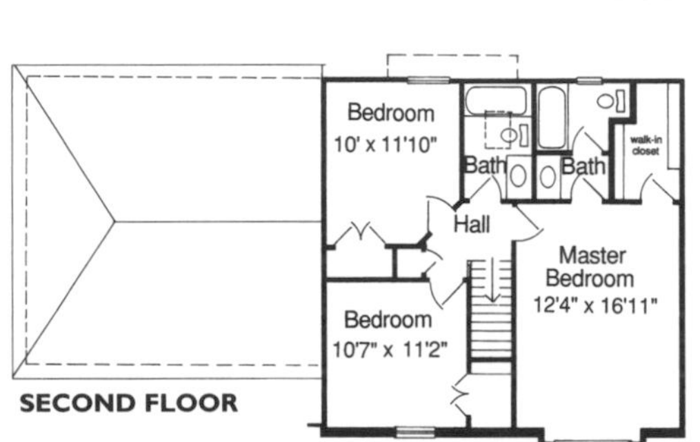

Bedroom
10' x 11'10"
Bath
Bath
walk-in closet
Hall
Master Bedroom
12'4" x 16'11"
Bedroom
10'7" x 11'2"
SECOND FLOOR

PLAN NO.82020

Option to Expand

PRICE CODE: C

- This plan features:
- — Three bedrooms
- — Two full baths
- There is an optional Bonus Room on the second floor to expand the home
- The Great Room has a fireplace and easy access to the formal Dining Room
- The Kitchen has ample cabinet space and a peninsula counter/snack bar
- Columns accent the entrance of the Dining Room
- This home is designed with crawlspace and slab foundation

MAIN FLOOR — 1,845 SQ. FT.
BONUS — 1,191 SQ. FT.
GARAGE — 496 SQ, FT.
PORCH — 465 SQ. FT.

***TOTAL LIVING AREA:* 1,845 SQ. FT.**

WIDTH 41'-4"
DEPTH 83'-8"

BONUS

MAIN FLOOR

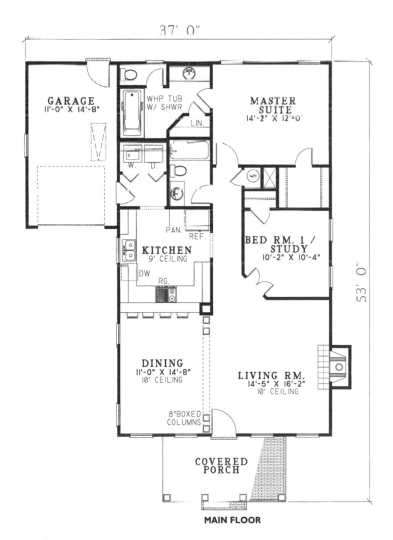

PLAN NO.82040

MAIN FLOOR

Small Yct Stately

Price Code: A

- This plan features:
  - — Two bedrooms
  - — Two full baths
- The Living Room has a 10-foot ceiling and a fireplace
- The Dining Room has a 10-foot ceiling and columns defining it from the Living Room
- The Kitchen include wrapping counters and a Breakfast Bar to the Dining Room
- The Master Suite incorporates a private Bath and a walk-in closet
- This home is designed with crawlspace and slab foundation options

MAIN FLOOR — 1,172 SQ. FT.
GARAGE — 213 SQ. FT.

TOTAL LIVING AREA:
1,172 SQ. FT.

PLAN NO. 92132

Bonus Loft with Balcony

Price Code: C

- This plan features:
- —Three bedrooms
- —Two full and one half baths
- Central Great Room with an inviting fireplace, vaulted, two-story ceiling, entertainment wall, and Deck access
- Open Kitchen efficiently serves bright eating area and Deck with cooktop work island and peninsula counter
- Corner Master Bedroom offers backyard view, large walk-in closet and double vanity Bath with window tub
- This home is designed with a basement and crawlspace foundation options

MAIN FLOOR — 1,941 SQ. FT.
BONUS ROOM — 200 SQ. FT.
BASEMENT — 1,592 SQ. FT.
GARAGE — 720 SQ. FT.

***TOTAL LIVING AREA:* 1,941 SQ. FT.**

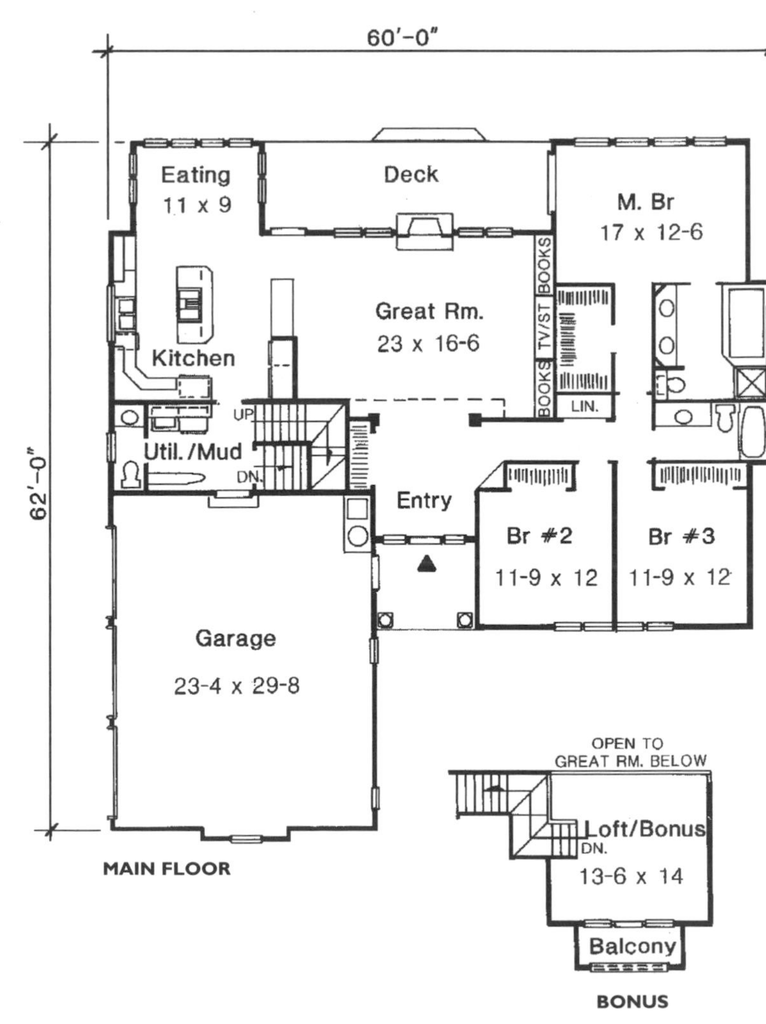

60'-0"
62'-0"
Eating 11 x 9
Deck
M. Br 17 x 12-6
BOOKS
TV/ST
BOOKS
LIN.
Great Rm. 23 x 16-6
Kitchen
UP
Util./Mud
DN.
Entry
Br #2 11-9 x 12
Br #3 11-9 x 12
Garage 23-4 x 29-8
MAIN FLOOR
OPEN TO GREAT RM. BELOW
Loft/Bonus 13-6 x 14
DN.
Balcony
BONUS

"How to obtain a construction cost calculation based on labor rates and building material costs in your Zip Code area!"

ZIP-QUOTE!

HOME COST CALCULATOR

GARLINGHOUSE
ZIP QUOTE
HOME COST CALCULATOR

WHY?

Do you wish you could quickly find out the building cost for your new home without waiting for a contractor to compile hundreds of bids? Would you like to have a benchmark to compare your contractor(s) bids against? ***Well, Now You Can!!,*** with **Zip-Quote** Home Cost Calculator. Zip-Quote is only available for zip code areas within the United States.

HOW?

Our new **Zip-Quote** Home Cost Calculator will enable you to obtain the calculated building cost to construct your new home, based on labor rates and building material costs within your zip code area, without the normal delays or hassles usually associated with the bidding process. Zip-Quote can be purchased in two separate formats, an itemized or a bottom line format.

"How does **Zip-Quote** actually work?" When you call to order, you must choose from the options available, for your specific home, in order for us to process your order. Once we receive your **Zip-Quote** order, we process your specific home plan building materials list through our Home Cost Calculator which contains up-to-date rates for all residential labor trades and building material costs in your zip code area. "The result?" A calculated cost to build your dream home in your zip code area. This calculation will help you (as a consumer or a builder) evaluate your building budget. This is a valuable tool for anyone considering building a new home.

All database information for our calculations is furnished by Marshall & Swift, L.P. For over 60 years, Marshall & Swift L.P. has been a leading provider of cost data to professionals in all aspects of the construction and remodeling industries.

OPTION 1

The **Itemized Zip-Quote** is a detailed building material list. Each building material list line item will separately state the labor cost, material cost and equipment cost (if applicable) for the use of that building material in the construction process. Each category within the building material list will be subtotaled and the entire Itemized cost calculation totaled at the end. This building materials list will be summarized by the individual building categories and will have additional columns where you can enter data from your contractor's estimates for a cost comparison between the different suppliers and contractors who will actually quote you their products and services.

OPTION 2

The **Bottom Line Zip-Quote** is a one line summarized total cost for the home plan of your choice. This cost calculation is also based on the labor cost, material cost and equipment cost (if applicable) within your local zip code area.

COST

The price of your **Itemized Zip-Quote** is based upon the pricing schedule of the plan you have selected, in addition to the price of the materials list. Please refer to the pricing schedule on our order form. The price of your initial **Bottom Line Zip-Quote** is $29.95. Each additional **Bottom Line Zip-Quote** ordered in conjunction with the initial order is only $14.95. **Bottom Line Zip-Quote** may be purchased separately and does NOT have to be purchased in conjunction with a home plan order.

FYI

An **Itemized Zip-Quote** Home Cost Calculation can ONLY be purchased in conjunction with a Home Plan order. The **Itemized Zip-Quote** can not be purchased separately. The **Bottom Line Zip-Quote** can be purchased separately and doesn't have to be purchased in conjunction with a home plan order. Please consult with a sales representative for current availability. If you find within 60 days of your order date that you will be unable to build this home, then you may exchange the plans and the materials list towards the price of a new set of plans (see order info pages for plan exchange policy). The **Itemized Zip-Quote** and the **Bottom Line Zip-Quote** are NOT returnable. The price of the initial **Bottom Line Zip-Quote** order can be credited towards the purchase of an **Itemized Zip-Quote** order only. Additional **Bottom Line Zip-Quote** orders, within the same order can not be credited. Please call our Customer Service Department for more information.

Itemized Zip-Quote is available for plans where you see this symbol. ZIP

Bottom Line Zip-Quote is available for all plans under 4,000 square feet. BL

SOME MORE INFORMATION

Itemized and Bottom Line Zip-Quotes give you approximated costs for constructing the particular house in your area. These costs are not exact and are only intended to be used as a preliminary estimate to help determine the affordability of a new home and/or as a guide to evaluate the general competitiveness of actual price quotes obtained through local suppliers and contractors. However, Zip-Quote cost figures should never be relied upon as the only source of information in either case. **Land, landscaping, sewer systems, site work, contractor overhead and profit and other expenses are not included in our building cost figures. Excluding land and landscaping, you may incur an additional 20% to 40% in costs from the original estimate.** Garlinghouse and Marshall & Swift L.P. can not guarantee any level of data accuracy or correctness in a Zip-Quote and disclaim all liability for loss with respect to the same, in excess of the original purchase price of the Zip-Quote product. All Zip-Quote calculations are based upon the actual blueprints and do not reflect any differences or options that may be shown on the published house renderings, floor plans, or photographs.

Everything You Need...
...to Make Your Dream Come True

You pay only a fraction of the original cost for home designs by respected professionals.

You've Picked Your Dream Home!

You can imagine your new home situated on your lot in the morning sunlight. You can visualize living there, enjoying your family, entertaining friends and celebrating holidays. All that remains are the details. That's where we can help. Whether you plan to build it yourself, act as your own general contractor or hire a professional builder, your Garlinghouse Co. home plans will provide the perfect design and specifications to help make your dream home a reality.

We can offer you an array of additional products and services to help you with your planning needs. We can supply materials lists, construction cost estimates based on your local material and labor costs and modifications to your selected plan if you would like.

For over 90 years, homeowners and builders have relied on us for accurate, complete, professional blueprints. Our plans help you get results fast... and save money, too! These pages will give you all the information you need to order. So get started now... We know you'll love your new Garlinghouse home!

Sincerely,

James D. McNair III

Chief Executive Officer

EXTERIOR ELEVATIONS

Elevations are scaled drawings of the front, rear, left, and right sides of a home. All of the necessary information pertaining to the exterior finish materials, roof pitches, and exterior hei dimensions of your home are defined.

CABINET PLANS

These plans, or in some cases elevations, will detail the layout of the kitchen and bathroom cabinets at a larger scale. This gives you an accurate layout for your cabinets or an ideal star point for a modified custom cabinet design. Available for most plans. You may also show the f plan without a cabinet layout. This will allow you to start from scratch and design your own dream kitchen.

TYPICAL WALL SECTION

This section is provided to help your builder understand the structural components and mater used to construct the exterior walls of your home. This section will address insulation, roof components, and interior and exterior wall finishes. Your plans will be designed with either 2x 2x6 exterior walls, but most professional contractors can easily adapt the plans to the wall thickness you require.

FIREPLACE DETAILS

If the home you have chosen includes a fireplace, the fireplace detail will show typical metho to construct the firebox, hearth and flue chase for masonry units, or a wood frame chase for a zero-clearance unit. Available for most plans.

FOUNDATION PLAN

These plans will accurately dimension the footprint of your home including load bearing point and beam placement if applicable. The foundation style will vary from plan to plan. Your local climatic conditions will dictate whether a basement, slab or crawlspace is best suited for you area. In most cases, if your plan comes with one foundation style, a professional contractor ca easily adapt the foundation plan to an alternate style.

ROOF PLAN

The information necessary to construct the roof will be included with your home plans. Some plans will reference roof trusses, while many others contain schematic framing plans. These framing plans will indicate the lumber sizes necessary for the rafters and ridgeboards based the designated roof loads.

TYPICAL CROSS SECTION

A cut-away cross-section through the entire home shows your building contractor the exact correlation of construction components at all levels of the house. It will help to clarify the loa bearing points from the roof all the way down to the basement. Available for most plans.

DETAILED FLOOR PLANS

The floor plans of your home accurately dimension the positioning of all walls, doors, window stairs and permanent fixtures. They will show you the relationship and dimensions of rooms, closets and traffic patterns. The schematic of the electrical layout may be included in the plan This layout is clearly represented and does not hinder the clarity of other pertinent informatio shown. All these details will help your builder properly construct your new home.

STAIR DETAILS

If stairs are an element of the design you have chosen, the plans will show the necessary info mation to build these, either through a stair cross section, or on the floor plans. Either way, th information provides your builders the essential reference points that they need to build the stairs.

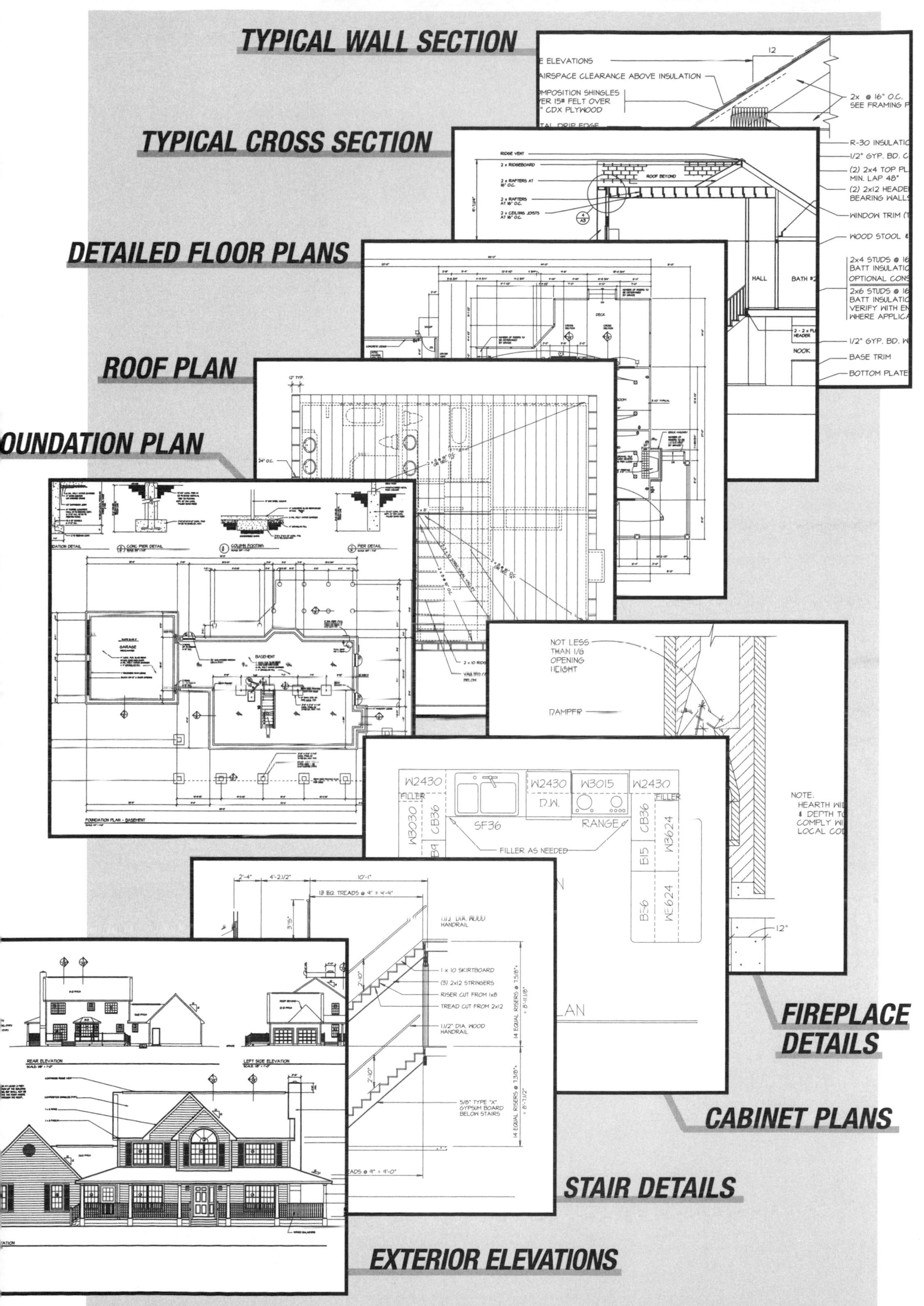

TYPICAL WALL SECTION
TYPICAL CROSS SECTION
DETAILED FLOOR PLANS
ROOF PLAN
OUNDATION PLAN
FIREPLACE DETAILS
CABINET PLANS
STAIR DETAILS
EXTERIOR ELEVATIONS

Garlinghouse Options & Extras ...Make Your Dream A Home

Reversed Plans Can Make Your Dream Home Just Right!

"That's our dream home...if only the garage were on the other side!"

You could have exactly the home you want by flipping it end-for-end. Check it out by holding your dream home page of this book up to a mirror. Then simply order your plans "reversed." We'll send you one full set of mirror-image plans (with the writing backwards) as a master guide for you and your builder.

The remaining sets of your order will come as shown in this book so the dimensions and specifications are easily read on the job site...but most plans in our collection come stamped "REVERSED" so there is no construction confusion.

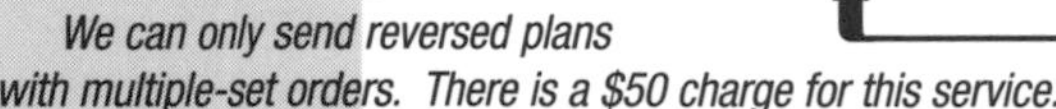
As Shown
Reversed

We can only send reversed plans with multiple-set orders. There is a $50 charge for this service.

Some plans in our collection are available in Right Reading Reverse. Right Reading Reverse plans will show your home in reverse, with the writing on the plan being readable. This easy-to-read format will save you valuable time and money. Please contact our Customer Service Department at (860) 659-5667 to check for Right Reading Reverse availability. (There is a $135 charge for this service.)

Remember To Order Your Materials List

It'll help you save money. Available at a modest additional charge, the Materials List gives the quantity, dimensions, and specifications for the major materials needed to build your home. You will get faster, more accurate bids from your contractors and building suppliers — and avoid paying for unused materials and waste. Materials Lists are available for all home plans except as otherwise indicated, but can only be ordered with a set of home plans. Due to differences in regional requirements and homeowner or builder preferences... electrical, plumbing and heating/air conditioning equipment specifications are not designed specifically for each plan. However, non-plan specific detailed typical prints of residential electrical, plumbing and construction guidelines can be provided. Please see below for additional information.

Specifications & Contract Form

We send this form to you free of charge with your home plan order. The form is designed to be filled in by you or your contractor with the exact materials to use in the construction of your new home. Once signed by you and your contractor it will provide you with peace of mind throughout the construction process.

$19.95 per set
(includes postage)

Detail Plans Provide Valuable Information About Construction Techniques

Because local codes and requirements vary greatly, we recommend that you obtain drawings and bids from licensed contractors to do your mechanical plans. However, if you want to know more about techniques — and deal more confidently with subcontractors — we offer these remarkably useful detail sheets. These detail sheets will aid in your understanding of these technical subjects. **The detail sheets are not specific to any one home plan and should be used only as a general reference guide.**

RESIDENTIAL CONSTRUCTION DETAILS

Ten sheets that cover the essentials of stick-built residential home construction. Details foundation options — poured concrete basement, concrete block, or monolithic concrete slab. Shows all aspects of floor, wall and roof framing. Provides details for roof dormers, overhangs, chimneys and skylights. Conforms to requirements of Uniform Building code or BOCA code. Includes a quick index and a glossary of terms.

RESIDENTIAL PLUMBING DETAILS

Eight sheets packed with information detailing pipe installation methods, fittings, and sized. Details plumbing hook-ups for toilets, sinks, washers, sump pumps, and septic system construction. Conforms to requirements of National Plumbing code. Color coded with a glossary of terms and quick index.

RESIDENTIAL ELECTRICAL DETAILS

Eight sheets that cover all aspects of residential wiring, from simple switch wiring to service entrance connections. Details distribution panel layout with outlet and switch schematics, circuit breaker and wiring installation methods, and ground fault interrupter specifications. Conforms to requirements of National Electrical Code. Color coded with a glossary of terms.

Modifying Your Favorite Design, Made EASY!

PTION #1

odifying Your Garlinghouse Home Plan

Simple modifications to your dream home, including minor non-structural changes and material substitu-s, can be made between you and your builder by marking the changes directly on your blueprints. How-r, if you are considering making significant changes to your chosen design, we recommend that you use services of The Garlinghouse Design Staff. We will help take your ideas and turn them into a reality, just way you want. Here's our procedure!

When you place your Vellum order, you may also request a free Garlinghouse Modification Kit. In this kit, will receive a red marking pencil, furniture cut-out sheet, ruler, a self addressed mailing label and a form specifying any additional notes or drawings that will help us understand your design ideas. Mark your sired changes directly on the Vellum drawings. NOTE: Please use only a **red pencil** to mark your desired nges on the Vellum. Then, return the redlined Vellum set in the original box to us. **IMPORTANT**: Please the Vellums for shipping, **do not fold** the Vellums for shipping.

We also offer modification estimates. We will provide you with an estimate to draft your changes based your specific modifications before you purchase the vellums, for a $50 fee. After you receive your esti-te, if you decide to have us do the changes, the $50 estimate fee will be deducted from the cost of your difications. If, however, you choose to use a different service, the $50 estimate fee is non-refundable. te: Personal checks cannot be accepted for the estimate.)

Within 5 days of receipt of your plans, you will be contacted by the Design Staff with an estimate for the sign services to draw those changes. A 50% deposit is required before we begin making the actual modifi-ions to your plans.

Once the design changes have been completed to your vellum plan, a representative will call to inform that your modified Vellum plan is complete and will be shipped as soon as the final payment has been de. For additional information call us at 1-860-659-5667. Please refer to the Modification Pricing Guide estimated modification costs.

PTION #2

eproducible Vellums for Local Modification Ease

If you decide not to use Garlinghouse for your modifications, we recommend that you follow our same cedure of purchasing our Vellums. You then have the option of using the services of the original designer the plan, a local professional designer, or architect to make the modifications to your plan.

With a Vellum copy of our plans, a design professional can alter the drawings just the way you want, then can print as many copies of the modified plans as you need to build your house. And, since you have eady started with our complete detailed plans, the cost of those expensive professional services will be sig-cantly less than starting from scratch. Refer to the price schedule for Vellum costs.

IMPORTANT RETURN POLICY: Upon receipt of your Vellums, if for some reason you decide you do not want nodified plan, then simply return the Kit and the unopened Vellums. Reproducible Vellum copies of our home ns are copyright protected and only sold under the terms of a license agreement that you will receive with r order. Should you not agree to the terms, then the Vellums may be exchanged, less the shipping and han-g charges, and a 20% exchange fee. For any additional information, please call us at 1-860-659-5667.

MODIFICATION PRICING GUIDE

CATEGORIES	ESTIMATED COST
KITCHEN LAYOUT — PLAN AND ELEVATION	$175.00
BATHROOM LAYOUT — PLAN AND ELEVATION	$175.00
FIREPLACE PLAN AND DETAILS	$200.00
INTERIOR ELEVATION	$125.00
EXTERIOR ELEVATION — MATERIAL CHANGE	$140.00
EXTERIOR ELEVATION — ADD BRICK OR STONE	$400.00
EXTERIOR ELEVATION — STYLE CHANGE	$450.00
NON BEARING WALLS (INTERIOR)	$200.00
BEARING AND/OR EXTERIOR WALLS	$325.00
WALL FRAMING CHANGE — 2X4 TO 2X6 OR 2X6 TO 2X4	$240.00
ADD/REDUCE LIVING SPACE — SQUARE FOOTAGE	QUOTE REQUIRED
NEW MATERIALS LIST	QUOTE REQUIRED
CHANGE TRUSSES TO RAFTERS OR CHANGE ROOF PITCH	$300.00
FRAMING PLAN CHANGES	$325.00
GARAGE CHANGES	$325.00
ADD A FOUNDATION OPTION	$300.00
FOUNDATION CHANGES	$250.00
RIGHT READING PLAN REVERSE	$575.00
ARCHITECTS SEAL	$300.00
ENERGY CERTIFICATE	$150.00
LIGHT AND VENTILATION SCHEDULE	$150.00

Questions?

Call our customer service department at **1-860-659 5667**

IMPORTANT INFORMATION TO READ BEFORE YOU PLACE YOUR ORDER

How Many Sets Of Plans Will You Need?

The Standard 8-Set Construction Package

Our experience shows that you'll speed every step of construction and avoid costly building errors by ordering enough sets to go around. Each tradesperson wants a set — the general contractor and all subcontractors; foundation, electrical, plumbing, heating/air conditioning and framers. Don't forget your lending institution, building department and, of course, a set for yourself.
** Recommended for Construction **

The Minimum 4-Set Construction Package

If you're comfortable with arduous follow-up, this package can save you a few dollars by giving you the option of passing down plan sets as work progresses. You might have enough copies to go around if work goes exactly as scheduled and no plans are lost or damaged by subcontractors. But for only $60 more, the 8-set package eliminates these worries.

The Bidding Set

We offer this set so you can study the blueprints to plan your dream home in detail. They are stamped "study set-not for construction", and you cannot build a home from a them. In pursuant to copyright laws, it is illegal to reproduce any blueprint.

An Important Note About Building Code Requirements:

All plans are drawn to conform to one or more of the industry's major national building standards. However, due to the variety of local building re ulations, your plan may need to be modified to comply with local requirements — snow loads, energy loads, seismic zones, etc. Do check them fu and consult your local building officials.

A few states require that all building plans used be drawn by an archi registered in that state. While having your plans reviewed and stamped by such an architect may be prudent, laws requiring non-conforming plans lik ours to be completely redrawn forces you to unnecessarily pay very large fees. If your state has such a law, we strongly recommend you contact you state representative to protest.

The rendering, floor plans, and technical information contained within publication are not guaranteed to be totally accurate. Consequently, no inf mation from this publication should be used either as a guide to constructi a home or for estimating the cost of building a home. Complete blueprints must be purchased for such purposes.

the
Garlinghouse
company

Order Form

Plan prices guaranteed until 8/12/03—After this date call for updated pricing

Order Code No. **H2BS**

____ set(s) of blueprints for plan #________ $______
____ Vellum & Modification kit for plan #________ $______
____ Additional set(s) @ $50 each for plan #________ $______
____ Mirror Image Reverse @ $50 each $______
____ Right Reading Reverse @ $135 each $______
____ Materials list for plan #________ $______
____ Detail Plans @ $19.95 each
❑ Construction ❑ Plumbing ❑ Electrical $______
____ Bottom line ZIP Quote @ $29.95 for plan #________ $______
____ Additional Bottom Line Zip Quote
@ $14.95 for plan(s) #________
________________________ $______

____ Itemized ZIP Quote for plan(s) #________ $______
Shipping (see charts on opposite page) $______
Subtotal $______
Sales Tax (CT residents add 6% sales tax (Not required for other states) $______
TOTAL AMOUNT ENCLOSED $______

Send your check, money order or credit card information to:
(No C.O.D.'s Please)

Please submit all United States & Other Nations orders to:

Garlinghouse Company
174 Oakwood Drive
Glastonbury, CT. 06033

ADDRESS INFORMATION:

NAME: ________________________

STREET: ________________________

CITY: ________________ **STATE:** ________ **ZIP:** ________

DAYTIME PHONE: ________________ **EMAIL ADDRESS:** ________________

TERMS OF SALE FOR HOME PLANS: *All home plans sold through this publication are copyright protected. Reproduction of these home plans, either in whole or in part, including any direct copying and/or preparation of derivative works thereof, for any reason without the prior written permission of Garlinghouse, Inc., is strictly prohibited. The purchase of a set of home plans in no way transfers any copyright or other ownership interest in it to the buyer except for a limited license to use that set of home plans for the construction of one, and only one, dwelling unit. The purchase of additional sets of that home plan at a reduced price from the original set or as a part of a multiple set package does not entitle the buyer with a license to construct more than one dwelling unit.*

Payment must be made in U.S. funds. Foreign Mail Orders: Certified bank checks in U.S. funds only

Credit Card Information

Charge To: ❑ Visa ❑ Mastercard

Card # | | | | | | | | | | | | | | | |

Signature ________________ Exp. ____/____

BEFORE ORDERING PLEASE READ ALL ORDERING INFORMATION

ORDER TOLL FREE — 1-800-235-5700
Monday-Friday 8:00 a.m. to 8:00 p.m. Eastern Time
or FAX your Credit Card order to 1-860-659-5692
All foreign residents call 1-800-659-5667

Please have ready: 1. Your credit card number 2. The plan number 3. The order code number ⇨ H2BS3

Garlinghouse 2002 Blueprint Price Code Schedule

Additional sets with original order $50

	1 Set	4 Sets	8 Sets	Vellums	ML	Itemized ZIP Quote
A	$345	$385	$435	$525	$60	$50
B	$375	$415	$465	$555	$60	$50
C	$410	$450	$500	$590	$60	$50
D	$450	$490	$540	$630	$60	$50
E	$495	$535	$585	$675	$70	$60
F	$545	$585	$635	$725	$70	$60
G	$595	$635	$685	$775	$70	$60
H	$640	$680	$730	$820	$70	$60
I	$685	$725	$775	$865	$80	$70
J	$725	$765	$815	$905	$80	$70
K	$765	$805	$855	$945	$80	$70
L	$800	$840	$890	$980	$80	$70

BEST PLAN VALUE IN THE INDUSTRY!

hipping — (Plans 1-59999)

	1-3 Sets	4-6 Sets	7+ & Vellums
Standard Delivery (UPS 2-Day)	$25.00	$30.00	$35.00
Overnight Delivery	$35.00	$40.00	$45.00

hipping — (Plans 60000-99999)

	1-3 Sets	4-6 Sets	7+ & Vellums
Ground Delivery (7-10 Days)	$15.00	$20.00	$25.00
Express Delivery (3-5 Days)	$20.00	$25.00	$30.00

International Shipping & Handling

	1-3 Sets	4-6 Sets	7+ & Vellums
Regular Delivery Canada (7-10 Days)	$25.00	$30.00	$35.00
Express Delivery Canada (5-6 Days)	$40.00	$45.00	$50.00
Overseas Delivery Airmail (2-3 Weeks)	$50.00	$60.00	$65.00

ur Reorder and Exchange Policies:

If you find after your initial purchase that you require additional sets of plans you may purchase them from us at special reorder ces (please call for pricing details) provided that you reorder within 6 months of your original order date. There is a $28 reorder pro-ssing fee that is charged on all reorders. For more information on reordering plans please contact our Customer Service Department.

Your plans are custom printed especially for you once you place your order. For that reason we cannot accept any returns.

If for some reason you find that the plan you have purchased from us does not meet your needs, then you may exchange that plan for y other plan in our collection. We allow you sixty days from your original invoice date to make an exchange. At the time of the exchange u will be charged a processing fee of 20% of the total amount of your original order plus the difference in price between the plans (if plicable) plus the cost to ship the new plans to you. Call our Customer Service Department for more information. Please Note: Repro-cible vellums can only be exchanged if they are unopened.

nportant Shipping Information

Please refer to the shipping charts on the order form for service availability for your specific plan number. Our delivery service must ve a street address or Rural Route Box number — never a post office box. (PLEASE NOTE: Supplying a P.O. Box number only will lay the shipping of your order.) Use a work address if no one is home during the day.

Orders being shipped to APO or FPO must go via First Class Mail.

For our International Customers, only Certified bank checks and money orders are accepted and must be payable in U.S. currency. r speed, we ship international orders Air Parcel Post. Please refer to the chart for the correct shipping cost.

Thank you.

INDEXINDEXINDEX

ML *Materials List Available* **ZIP** *Zip Quote Available* **RRR** *Right Reading Reverse* **DUP** *Duplex Pla*

Plan#	Page	Price Code	Sq.Ft.	
9850	206	E	2466	BL/ML/ZIP/RRR
10274	132	C	1783	BL/ML/RRR
10334	339	G	2994	BL/ML
10507	263	D	2194	BL/ML/ZIP
10534	21	I	3440	BL/ML
10686	170	I	3276	BL/ML/ZIP
10690	171	E	2281	BL/ML/ZIP
10698	86	L	4741	ML/ZIP
10839	291	B	1738	BL/ML/ZIP/RRR
19422	19	B	1695	BL/ML/ZIP
20087	297	B	1568	BL/ML/ZIP
20093	314	D	2001	BL/ML
20100	401	B	1737	BL/ML/ZIP/RRR
20144	345	F	2563	BL/ML/ZIP
20156	426	A	1359	BL/ML/ZIP/RRR
20161	302	A	1307	BL/ML/ZIP/RRR
20164	304	A	1456	BL/ML/ZIP/RRR
20195	353	A	1427	BL/ML
20196	372	F	2750	BL/ML
20198	362	C	1792	BL/ML/ZIP
20209	66	E	2387	BL/ML
20220	378	B	1568	BL/ML/ZIP
20230	207	C	1995	BL/ML/ZIP
20507	88	G	2927	BL/ML/ZIP
22004	95	D	2070	BL/ML
24245	1	D	2083	BL/ML/ZIP/RRR
24262	201	E	2411	BL/ML/ZIP
24265	77	F	2672	BL/ML
24268	98	D	2244	BL/ML/ZIP
24302	155	A	988	BL/ML/ZIP
24304	105	A	993	BL/ML
24307	118	A	1038	BL/ML
24319	65	B	1710	BL/ML/ZIP
24400	364	C	1978	BL/ML/ZIP/RRR
24403	64	F	2647	BL/ML/ZIP
24404	367	E	2356	BL/ML/ZIP
24405	96	D	2064	BL/ML/ZIP
24594	22	G	2957	BL/ML/ZIP
24610	35	C	1785	BL/ML/ZIP
24653	42	F	2578	BL/ML/ZIP
24654	57	B	1554	BL/ML/ZIP
24700	114	A	1312	BL/ML/ZIP
24701	135	B	1625	BL/ML/ZIP
24706	324	A	1470	BL/ML/ZIP
24708	138	B	1576	BL/ML/ZIP
24711	159	A	1434	BL/ML/ZIP
24714	144	C	1771	BL/ML/ZIP
24717	143	B	1642	BL/ML/ZIP
24718	146	A	1452	BL/ML/ZIP
24723	259	A	1112	BL/ML/ZIP
24735	50	E	2426	BL/ML/ZIP
24742	16	B	1732	BL
24743	44	C	1990	BL
24746	45	C	2030	BL
24748	54	C	2161	BL
24749	56	D	2219	BL
24750	60	E	2487	BL
24751	62	D	2172	BL/ML
24752	69	H	3150	BL
24753	70	D	2159	BL/ML
24900	73	F	2599	BL
24901	75	E	2332	BL
24951	76	G	2794	BL
24952	81	D	2179	BL
24954	83	E	3028	BL
24955	85	J	3593	BL
24956	87	I	3475	BL
24958	88	E	3026	BL
24960	89	A	1465	BL
24961	90	C	2117	BL
24964	91	D	2240	BL/ML
24965	92	F	2765	BL
24966	93	D	2138	BL
24967	94	D	2228	BL

Plan#	Page	Price Code	Sq.Ft.	
24968	98	G	2877	BL
24969	101	J	3676	BL
24970	103	F	2616	BL/ML
24971	105	H	3084	BL
24972	107	I	3370	BL
24973	108	J	3725	BL
24974	112	J	3717	BL
24975	115	C	1876	BL
24976	116	C	1909	BL
24977	119	E	2305	BL
24978	138	L	4207	
24979	148	E	2296	BL
24980	153	G	3025	BL
24981	155	G	2973	BL
24982	156	D	2078	BL
24984	162	J	3478	BL
24985	163	K	4207	
24986	165	F	2903	BL
24988	173	E	2629	BL/ML
24989	174	F	2592	BL
24990	181	E	2490	BL/ML
26112	266	A	1487	BL/ML/ZIP
32006	47	L	5288	BL/ML/ZIP
32032	280	C	1881	ML/ZIP
32046	63	L	4292	ML/ZIP
32063	28	L	4283	ML/ZIP/RRR
32101	32	G	2764	BL/ML/ZIP
32109	249	D	2038	BL/ML/ZIP
32122	286	A	1112	BL/ML/ZIP
32146	250	K	3895	BL/ML/ZIP
32291	172	C	1852	BL
34003	430	A	1146	BL/ML/ZIP/RRR
34011	274	B	1672	BL/ML/ZIP/RRR
34029	405	B	1686	BL/ML/ZIP/RRR
34031	279	C	1831	BL/ML/ZIP
34043	67	B	1583	BL/ML/ZIP/RRR
34054	425	A	1400	BL/ML/ZIP/RRR
34154	294	A	1486	BL/ML/ZIP/RRR
34601	53	A	1415	BL/ML/ZIP/RRR
34602	323	B	1560	BL/ML/ZIP
34603	314	B	1560	BL/ML/ZIP
34679	311	C	1994	BL/ML/ZIP
34901	225	C	1763	BL/ML/ZIP/RRR
35001	307	B	1609	BL/ML/RRR
35002	293	B	1712	BL/ML/RRR
35003	325	A	1373	BL/ML/RRR
35007	338	A	1027	BL/ML
35009	344	A	1003	BL/ML/RRR
51000	430	B	1548	BL
51001	432	C	2207	BL
51002	433	D	2027	BL
51003	434	A	1385	BL
51004	435	A	936	BL
51005	435	B	1638	BL
51006	432	B	1638	BL
51007	118	F	2682	BL
51008	428	A	1486	BL
51009	415	F	2509	BL
51010	412	D	2103	BL
51019	419	B	1556	BL
60013	229	A	1367	BL
60014	8	A	1382	BL
60017	235	A	1347	BL
60137	419	L	4464	
65000	182	A	1471	BL/ML
65001	194	A	1480	BL/ML
65002	199	B	1460	BL/ML
65003	204	A	976	BL/ML
65004	205	E	2300	BL/ML
65005	209	A	972	BL/ML
65006	221	A	920	BL/ML
65007	224	B	1574	BL/ML
65008	232	H	3072	BL/ML
65009	234	A	947	BL/ML

Plan#	Page	Price Code	Sq.Ft.	
65010	404	A	1280	BL/ML
65011	241	A	996	BL/ML
65012	259	C	1922	BL/ML
65014	261	A	1148	BL/ML
65015	263	A	1360	BL/ML
65019	273	A	920	BL/ML
65022	285	A	1240	BL/ML
65035	288	A	972	BL/ML
65054	299	A	947	BL/ML
65064	360	A	1191	BL/ML
65077	305	B	1504	BL/ML
65078	312	A	1059	BL/ML
65084	315	A	1208	BL/ML
65124	397	D	2091	BL
65125	406	D	2012	BL/ML
65135	318	D	2089	BL
65138	320	D	2257	BL
65139	371	E	2404	BL
65140	321	A	1258	BL
65141	322	B	1550	BL/ML
65145	327	E	2292	BL/ML
65150	368	A	1417	BL/ML
65177	331	C	1938	BL
65210	334	C	1976	BL/ML
65241	336	A	1068	BL/ML
65242	337	A	1152	BL
65244	339	A	1494	BL/ML
65245	219	B	1504	BL/ML
65246	342	J	1659	BL/ML
65248	343	A	1404	BL/ML
65250	346	B	1597	BL/ML
65251	348	B	1659	BL/ML
65252	349	C	1996	BL/ML
65253	351	D	2089	BL/ML
65254	352	C	1760	BL/ML
65255	219	E	2497	BL/ML
65256	353	D	2089	BL/ML
65304	356	C	1898	BL/ML
65365	357	A	1148	BL/ML
65368	377	C	1995	BL/ML
81005	350	G	2998	BL
81006	345	D	2120	BL
81007	361	D	2180	BL/ML
82010	429	B	1684	BL
82014	375	C	1987	BL
82015	380	C	1959	BL
82016	390	C	1934	BL
82017	399	C	1832	BL
82018	414	C	1922	BL
82019	407	C	1915	BL
82020	436	C	1845	BL
82021	431	C	1848	BL
82039	421	B	1660	BL
82040	437	A	1172	BL
82043	66	A	1425	BL
82045	75	A	1289	BL
82046	90	B	1541	BL
82047	86	C	1771	BL
82048	70	B	1595	BL
82049	96	A	1447	BL
82050	126	B	1746	BL
82051	101	C	1921	BL
86012	136	E	2415	BL
86013	152	E	2300	BL
86014	144	B	1582	BL
90007	164	C	1830	BL/ML
90025	169	A	1309	BL/ML
90048	369	A	1274	BL/ML
90356	323	A	1351	BL/ML
90378	366	A	1283	BL/ML
90409	405	B	1670	BL/ML/ZIP
90412	426	A	1454	BL/ML/ZIP
90420	175	E	2473	BL/ML
90423	397	C	1773	BL/ML/ZIP

Plan#	Page	Price Code	Sq.Ft.	
90433	394	A	928	BL/ML/ZIP
90441	189	C	1811	BL/ML/ZIP
90443	39	G	2759	BL/ML/ZIP
90450	254	E	2398	BL/ML/ZIP
90451	179	D	2068	BL/ML
90454	160	D	2218	BL/ML
90458	192	E	2263	BL/ML/ZIP
90467	213	E	2290	BL/ML
90476	67	C	1804	BL/ML/ZIP
90502	220	B	1642	BL/ML
90601	185	B	1613	BL/ML
90630	193	A	1207	BL/ML
90671	123	B	1587	BL/ML
90682	398	A	1243	BL/ML/ZIP
90684	211	B	1590	BL/ML
90689	168	A	1476	BL/ML
90844	330	B	1552	BL/ML
90865	217	A	1313	BL/ML
90870	245	C	1755	BL
90871	230	D	2182	BL
90930	329	B	1702	BL/ML
90934	418	A	884	BL/ML
90986	237	B	1731	BL/ML
90990	72	A	1423	BL/ML
91002	370	A	1096	BL/ML/ZIP
91026	357	A	1354	BL/ML
91033	20	A	1249	BL/ML/ZIP
91053	238	D	2099	BL/ML
91091	226	A	1250	BL/ML
91102	255	B	1701	BL
91109	247	F	2747	BL
91129	252	C	1983	BL
91133	34	G	2786	BL
91149	260	A	1370	BL
91153	267	C	1959	BL
91157	278	C	1862	BL
91160	284	A	1473	BL
91163	257	B	1561	BL
91165	267	B	1589	BL
91323	187	G	1521	BL/ML
91343	23	D	2162	BL/ML
91346	289	D	2185	BL/ML/RRR
91418	382	B	1665	BL/ML
91436	300	F	2591	BL/ML
91514	58	B	1707	BL/ML/RRR
91518	99	F	2550	BL/ML/RRR
91592	422	E	2287	BL/ML
91704	307	C	1837	BL/ML
91731	381	C	1857	BL/ML
91746	310	B	1717	BL/ML
91901	376	D	2212	BL
92048	25	I	3500	BL/ML
92052	82	A	1189	BL/ML
92123	428	E	2261	BL
92132	438	C	1941	BL
92156	334	F	2608	BL/ML
92160	350	C	1995	BL/ML
92162	411	I	3380	BL
92163	412	L	4757	
92164	413	L	3640	
92165	415	I	3215	BL
92166	106	K	3784	BL
92220	344	C	1830	BL/ML/ZIP
92237	6	K	3783	BL/ML/ZIP
92238	191	B	1664	BL/ML/ZIP
92243	337	G	2858	BL
92248	78	K	3921	BL/ZIP
92265	342	K	3818	BL
92277	14	H	3110	BL/ZIP
92283	354	B	1653	BL
92284	377	E	2261	BL
92400	402	A	1050	BL
92404	413	E	2275	BL
92501	188	F	2727	BL/ML

Plan#	Page	Price Code	Sq.Ft.	
92502	389	A	1237	BL/ML
92504	365	K	3813	BL/ML
92515	383	C	1959	BL/ML
92523	76	A	1293	BL/ML
92527	71	B	1680	BL/ML
92531	389	C	1754	BL/ML
92535	52	G	2965	BL/ML
92538	379	F	2733	BL/ML
92546	381	E	2387	BL/ML
92549	15	E	2490	BL/ML
92552	13	C	1873	BL/ML
92557	210	A	1390	BL/ML
92561	386	C	1856	BL/ML
92576	227	G	2858	BL/ML
92609	49	C	1768	BL/ZIP
92613	11	G	2846	BL
92625	408	B	1746	BL/ML/ZIP
92630	396	C	1782	BL/ZIP
92631	27	D	2157	BL/ZIP
92639	436	A	1453	BL
92642	313	D	2082	BL/ZIP
92643	29	D	2209	BL/ZIP
92644	33	C	1897	BL/ML/ZIP
92649	422	B	1508	BL/ML/ZIP
92651	31	E	2403	BL/ZIP
92655	417	B	1746	BL/ML/ZIP
92660	74	C	1964	BL
92666	427	I	3444	BL
92671	3	I	3445	BL
92681	355	G	2813	BL
92692	251	E	2388	BL/ZIP
92697	68	D	2017	BL
92705	421	C	1849	BL
93017	270	A	1142	BL
93018	79	A	1142	BL
93021	393	A	1282	BL
93048	382	A	1310	BL
93075	94	A	1170	BL
93080	87	C	1890	BL
93095	80	E	2409	BL/ML
93098	102	C	1932	BL
93099	109	F	2611	BL
93107	99	C	1868	BL/RRR
93118	127	I	3397	BL/ML/ZIP/
93133	401	C	1761	BL/ML/ZIP/
93143	121	C	1802	BL
93161	100	B	1540	BL/ML/ZIP
93163	359	E	2477	BL
93165	106	A	1472	BL
93171	137	B	1642	BL
93190	124	D	2196	BL/ML/ZIP
93196	122	I	3470	BL
93200	115	L	5730	
93202	135	A	1447	BL/ML
93206	400	F	2645	BL/ML/ZIP
93212	183	D	2091	BL/ML/ZIP
93219	4	B	1668	BL/ML/ZIP
93222	409	A	1292	BL/ML/ZIP/
93241	97	F	2640	BL/ML/ZIP
93254	317	F	2509	BL
93261	150	C	1778	BL/ML/ZIP
93265	306	A	1325	BL/ML/ZIP
93269	146	B	1735	BL/ML
93279	131	A	1388	BL/ML/ZIP
93298	329	B	1683	BL
93333	117	H	3198	BL
93340	159	E	2462	BL
93341	110	E	2457	BL
93342	113	C	1950	BL
93344	162	E	2259	BL
93349	363	C	1961	BL
93410	385	C	1854	BL/ML
93413	402	C	1808	BL
93414	410	A	1393	BL

ML *Materials List Available* **ZIP** *Zip Quote Available* **RRR** *Right Reading Reverse* **DUP** *Duplex Plan*

Ignoring Copyright Laws Can Be
A $100,000 Mistake

*Recent changes in the US copyright laws allow for statutory penalties of up to **$100,000** per incident for copyright infringement involving any of the copyrighted plans found in this publication. The law can be confusing. So, for your own protection, take the time to understand what you can and cannot do when it comes to home plans.*

•••WHAT YOU CANNOT DO•••

You Cannot Duplicate Home Plans

*Purchasing a set of blueprints and making additional sets by reproducing the original is **illegal**. If you need multiple sets of a particular home plan, then you must purchase them.*

You Cannot Copy Any Part of a Home Plan to Create Another

*Creating your own plan by copying even part of a home design found in this publication is called "creating a derivative work" and is **illegal** unless you have permission to do so.*

You Cannot Build a Home Without a License

*You must have specific permission or license to build a home from a copyrighted design, even if the finished home has been changed from the original plan. It is **illegal** to build one of the homes found in this publication without a license.*

What Garlinghouse Offers

Home Plan Blueprint Package

By purchasing a multiple set package of blueprints or a vellum from Garlinghouse, you not only receive the physical blueprint documents necessary for construction, but you are also granted a license to build one, and only one, home. You can also make simple modifications, including minor non-structural changes and material substitutions, to our design, as long as these changes are made directly on the blueprints purchased from Garlinghouse and no additional copies are made.

Home Plan Vellums

By purchasing vellums for one of our home plans, you receive the same construction drawings found in the blueprints, but printed on vellum paper. Vellums can be erased and are perfect for making design changes. They are also semi-transparent making them easy to duplicate. But most importantly, the purchase of home plan vellums comes with a broader license that allows you to make changes to the design (ie, create a hand drawn or CAD derivative work), to make an unlimited number of copies of the plan, and to build one home from the plan.

Deck
Dining
Living Rm
Master Br
Br #2
Garage
MAIN FLOOR

License To Build Additional Homes

With the purchase of a blueprint package or vellums you automatically receive a license to build one home and only one home, respectively. If you want to build more homes than you are licensed to build through your purchase of a plan, then additional licenses may be purchased at reasonable costs from Garlinghouse. Inquire for more information.